THE ENCYCLOPEDIA OF
AIRCRAFT

OVER 3000 MILITARY AND CIVIL AIRCRAFT
FROM THE WRIGHT FLYER TO THE STEALTH BOMBER

THE ENCYCLOPEDIA OF
AIRCRAFT

OVER 3000 MILITARY AND CIVIL AIRCRAFT
FROM THE WRIGHT FLYER TO THE STEALTH BOMBER

GENERAL EDITOR: ROBERT JACKSON

Published in 2004 by Silverdale Books
an imprint of Bookmart Ltd
Registered Number 2372865
Trading as Bookmart Ltd
Blaby Road
Wigston
Leicester LE18 4SE

ISBN 1-85605-887-5

Editorial and design by
Amber Books Ltd
Bradley's Close
74–77 White Lion Street
London N1 9PF
www.amberbooks.co.uk

Authors: Robert Jackson, Martin W. Bowman, Ewan Partridge
Project Editor: James Bennett
Design: Graham Curd
Picture Research: Natasha Jones, Sandra Assersohn

Printed in Singapore

10 9 8 7 6 5 4 3 2 1

CONTENTS

A magnificent air-to-air shot of the X-35 advanced tactical fighter during flight refuelling trials with a KC-135 tanker aircraft. Two versions of the X-35 were proposed, one V/STOL and one conventional.

A Harrier GR.7, the RAF's equivalent of the US Marine Corps' AV-8B, pictured at the point of transition from vertical to horizontal flight.

CONTENTS

The sole Curtiss NC-4, today preserved in the US Naval Air Museum. Glenn Curtiss devoted a great deal of energy to the production of seaplanes, but production was curtailed with the end of World War I.

Known as 'Whistling Death' to the Japanese, the Vought F4U Corsair also performed with distinction in the Korean War.

INTRODUCTION

The dream of flight is as old as the mind of man. Fifty thousand years ago, hunters with flint-tipped spears must occasionally have paused in their quest for food and turned their eyes skywards, looking on with envy as flights of migratory birds winged their way over the African plains to escape the ice creeping from the north. Millennia passed; man kindled fires and tilled the soil; fire kept his families warm and crops filled their bellies, and with the passing of one hunger came another: a thirst for knowledge and discovery, an irresistible urge that prompted man to venture out on the sea in flimsy boats in search of new lands.

And still the birds winged their way southwards, and still man turned his eyes skywards, and wondered.

There were some who were not content to envy. They tried to emulate the birds, leaping from high places and flapping crude wings, only to smash themselves against the earth, without the knowledge that the muscles of their bodies were too puny to defy gravity. Yet as long ago as the fourth century BC, children in ancient China were playing with a little toy whose principle would be used hundreds of years later to bring a whole new dimension to the science of flight: a simple round stick with feathers mounted on top, each feather twisted slightly so that it struck the air at an angle. When the stick was spun, it created enough lift to enable the device to fly up into the air. It was the ancestor of the modern helicopter.

The early pioneers of flight equipped themselves with flimsy planes modelled on the perfection of a bird's wing and groped in darkness towards the achievement of their goal. Yet through the darkness shone brief flashes of light: the thoughts and inspirations of a handful of men who turned their minds from the flight of birds and explored other ways of enabling man to break the chains that bound him to the earth. In the 18th and 19th centuries, a few visionaries shone like beacons on the path towards modern aviation. The Montgolfier brothers, whose hot air balloons gave man the means to fly freely for the first time; Sir George Cayley, the father of modern aeronautics; Stringfellow and Henson; Otto Lilienthal and Clement Ader, to name but a few. All made their contribution to the ultimate achievement, made by the Wright Brothers at Kitty Hawk in 1903, when, with the help of a new invention – the internal combustion engine – the dream of powered flight was translated into reality.

Once that goal had been achieved, there were those who were not slow to appreciate the commercial potential of the aeroplane. At 10am on New Year's Day, 1914, a Benoist XIV flying boat flown by Antony Jannus, an instructor pilot with the Benoist Aircraft Company, took off from St Petersburg, Florida. With him was a solitary passenger, the Mayor of St Petersburg. Twenty-three minutes later, at the end of a 35km (22-mile) flight across Tampa Bay, Jannus alighted, having inaugurated the first scheduled aerial passenger service in the world. The St Petersburg and Tampa Airboat Line, as the service became known, operated for nearly four months, the aircraft making two round trips per day. The fare was $5, provided the passenger weighed no more than 91kg (200lb). Fat people were charged extra. During its short career, the Airboat Line covered some 17,700km (11,000 miles). Only 22 flights were cancelled through bad weather and various other reasons; the total number of passengers carried was 1205.

THE FIRST MILITARY AVIATORS

Meanwhile, the march of aviation had taken a more sinister turn. The aircraft's role as a potential war machine was summarized by an Italian officer, Major Giulio Douhet, in 1909. Douhet wrote: 'At present we are fully conscious of the importance of the sea. In the near future, it will be no less vital to achieve supremacy in the air.' The military potential of the aircraft was demonstrated several times in 1910, the year after Douhet let fall those prophetic words; on 19 January, for example, Lieutenant Paul Beck of the US Army released sandbags representing bombs over Los Angeles from an aeroplane flown by pioneer aviator Louis Paulhan, and on 30 June Glenn H. Curtiss dropped dummy bombs from a height of 50ft (15m) in an area representing the shape of a battleship, marked by buoys on Lake Keuka, New York. The feasibility of discharging firearms from an aircraft was also demonstrated on 20 August 1910, when US Army Lieutenant Jacob Earl Fickel fired a 7.62mm (0.30in) calibre rifle at a ground target at Sheepshead Bay, New York. More significantly in terms of future development, a German named August Euler had filed a patent some weeks earlier for a device enabling a fixed machine gun to be fired from an aircraft.

Widely known by its nickname *Walfisch* (Whale) due to its sleek and streamlined wooden fuselage, the Roland C.II had its heyday in 1916. The C.II was one of the first aircraft flown in combat by legendary ace Manfred von Richtofen on the Eastern Front.

The Ilya Muromets series of heavy bombers was used by the Imperial Russian army during World War I. Bristling with guns, 80 of these aircraft were produced in dozens of different variants including floatplane and ski-equipped versions.

Perhaps fittingly, in the light of Douhet's remarks, it was the Italians who were the first to demonstrate the usefulness of the aircraft in war. On 22 October 1911, following Italy's declaration of war on Turkey over a dispute involving the Italian occupation of Cyrenaica and Tripolitania, Capitano Carlo Piazza, commanding the Italian Expeditionary Force's air flotilla, carried out a reconnaissance of Turkish positions between Tripoli and Azizzia in a Blériot XI. It was the first operational mission by a heavier-than-air craft.

Such were the humble beginnings of military aviation, the first steps on the path that would lead to the stealth bombers, the air superiority fighters and the vertical take-off combat aircraft of today, with all their awesome striking power.

By 1910, the air arms of the world's major air powers were beginning to take shape. When Europe became embroiled in war four years later, the value of the aircraft as an instrument of reconnaissance was soon established, and it was the need to deny this vital element of air reconnaissance to the enemy that led directly to the birth of the fighting aeroplane, armed with one or more machine guns.

THE GREAT WAR

Warfare breeds new technology, and the single most important technological advance in the air war of 1914–18 was the development, in 1915, of the synchronized machine gun, enabling the weapon to fire forwards through the propeller disc. With this new-found ability to use the whole aircraft as an aiming platform came a scientific approach to aerial fighting; experienced pilots began to formulate tactics and combat manoeuvres that formed the principles on which future air combat would be based. Such were the technological strides made during four years of war that the aircraft evolved from flimsy, unreliable machines barely capable of crossing the English Channel into heavy bombers capable of attacking the German capital, Berlin, from bases in eastern England.

Progress followed several diverse paths of air warfare; by 1918 the world's first strategic bombing forces were operational, and the fighting aeroplane had gone to sea on the first aircraft carriers. By the time hostilities ended in November 1918, air power had become a major factor in the military machine of every major nation, and there were few who doubted that it would play a decisive part in the wars of the future.

COMMERCIAL FLIGHT BETWEEN THE WARS

A mere 15 years since the Wright brothers made their historic flight at Kitty Hawk, aviation was no longer in its infancy. The demands of total war had turned the aircraft into a killing machine of awesome potential. On the other hand, apart from limited ventures like the Tampa Airboat Line – which had ceased to operate because it was not economically viable – the aircraft's usefulness as a source of commercial revenue had yet to be explored, and in this context the obstacles seemed almost insurmountable. Commercial aircraft had to have range, speed and adequate capacity; they had to be able to fly in all kinds of climatic conditions; and they had to transport their payloads efficiently and in safety. At the end of World War I, no such aircraft existed. Yet only a decade later, a new generation of airliners was plying the embryo air routes of the world, and new and exciting machines capable of spanning the world's great oceans were on the drawing boards. It was one of mankind's greatest technological triumphs, and one that would not have been possible without the courage and determination of a relatively small band of men; not only the aircrews, but also the managers of the world's pioneer airlines and the financiers who were prepared to stake fortunes on what was then very much an unknown quantity.

Ironically, the first regular commercial air service after World War I was inaugurated in defeated Germany. It began on 5 February 1919, when aircraft of *Deutsche Luft-Reederei* (DLR) started carrying mail, newspapers and passengers between Berlin-Johannisthal and Weimar on a regular daily schedule. DLR, which had been formed in the previous year, had rapidly risen to prominence among the spattering of embryo aviation companies that had come to the surface in Germany after the Armistice, and its expansion was rapid. In March 1919 it inaugurated a second service, between Berlin and Hamburg, and a third route was opened to Warnemunde in April. By mid-1920, the DLR fleet comprised 71 single-engined aircraft, almost all of them ex-military types such as the LVG and AEG, and 13 twin-engined Friedrichshafen FF45 and GIIIA machines, the latter capable of carrying up to six passengers as well as two crew, mail and cargo. In August that year, the airline inaugurated its first international route from Malmö to Amsterdam, via Warnemünde, Hamburg and Bremen, in co-operation with KLM and DDL, the Dutch and Danish airlines.

The organization of Germany's early air services was a world apart from the situation in France, which had been both the cradle and hub of civil aviation before the 1914–18 war. Although the widespread destruction of surface communication led to the rapid establishment of air mail services, with half a dozen different companies all involved, France's attitude towards civil aviation in the years after the war seemed to centre on attempts to recapture former glories. Her aviators and aircraft constructors had led the world in the days before 1914; her air aces had been legends throughout the world before 1918, and the two combined to exercise a strange psychological effect on those responsible for furthering French aviation during the years that followed. Everything, it appeared, was devoted to the creation of more heroes, with huge funds allocated to record-breaking attempts by intrepid young men in stripped-down ex-military machines; there was no attempt at coordinating civil flying, as there was in Germany and elsewhere. Not until the formation of Air France in 1933 would order begin to emerge from the confusion that attended France's post-WWI civil aviation industry, even though in the interim French airmen achieved amazing successes in long-range pioneer flights to Africa, the Far East and Latin America.

One consequence of the lack of a coherent civil aviation programme and a shortage of financial support was that French designers tended to

Known as the 'Empire' boats, Short C-Class flying boats pioneered Britain's long-range mail and passenger routes to the Far East and the Caribbean in the 1930s. This aircraft is *Canopus,* the first of the type to be launched.

concentrate on the development of short- and medium-capacity aircraft; large commercial designs rarely received government backing, although when such aircraft proved successful French governments were not slow to exploit them for propaganda purposes. When the big six-engined flying boat *Lieutenant de Vaisseau Paris* flew the Atlantic via the Azores on 30 August 1938, for example, much was made of the fact; yet no appreciable payload was carried, and in any case, the British, Americans and Germans had already done it.

In these three countries, the impetus behind the development of long-range commercial air transport was the carriage of mail. The British government, in particular, had been quick to recognize the aircraft's potential as a means of communication across the routes of its vast empire. As early as 1925, the decision had been made that the responsibility for the carriage of mail to the Middle East and India should be handed over from the Royal Air Force to the newly established Imperial Airways, but the scheme had been slow to start because of a lack of suitable equipment. The aircraft types which then formed the fleet of Imperial Airways would not stand up to the rigours of continual operation over long distances in tropical climates. What was needed was an entirely new type, specifically designed for long-range operations, and the machine that fulfilled Imperial Airways' needs in this respect was the De Havilland DH.66 Hercules. Other purpose-built commercial designs quickly followed, eventually culminating in the types that symbolized Britain's long-range commercial air operations in the 1930s: the Handley Page HP.42 and the magnificent Short 'C'-class flying boats.

PERFORMANCE PIONEERS

Parallel to this growing commercial success, military aircraft continued to develop. In the two decades following the end of World War I, the major air arms of the world all took part in record-breaking exercises that pushed range, endurance, altitude and speed to the limits of known technology. Such exercises were to have a profound effect on the development of

future aircraft, both military and civil, some of which were directly descended from machines produced specifically for record-breaking purposes. In the early days, the US Navy was at the forefront of range and endurance flying. On 27 May 1919 a Curtiss NC-4 flying boat became the first to make a transatlantic flight, from Newfoundland to Lisbon via the Azores. Just under three weeks later, the honour of making the first non-stop transatlantic crossing fell to two RAF officers, Captain John Alcock and Lieutenant Arthur Whitten Brown, in a converted Vickers Vimy bomber, while on 6 July 1919 the British military rigid airship R34 completed the first east–west non-stop flight. But it was the US Navy which, in 1924, successfully completed the first round-the-world flight, using Douglas DT-2 biplanes which were externally similar to those in service as torpedo-bombers. Apart from bringing well-deserved honour to their crews, this epic voyage brought home a number of lessons which were to make their mark on the design of future aircraft and equipment. One such lesson was that wood and fabric were far from suitable materials for use in hot and humid conditions; another was that the flight would not have been possible without massive support and organization, with US warships carrying spares, fuel and technicians positioned along the route. Logistical support of long-range air operations was something in which the Americans, over the next 20 years, would come to excel.

The key to the whole problem of improving all-round aircraft performance was the aero-engine, and in this respect the record-breaking efforts of the 1920s produced an important spin-off. For much of that decade, it seemed that the French and Americans, whose high-performance aircraft virtually swept the board clear of trophies, had established a commanding lead; but these successes spurred leading British aero-engine manufacturers into reappraisal of their engine design philosophy. From three firms in particular, Rolls-Royce, Bristol and Napier, came a new generation of powerful aero-engines that would change the face of British aviation, both commercial and military. In Germany, aero-engine development would not gain momentum until the early 1930s, when the facade of disarmament was stripped away and massive funds were diverted to the industry.

By the early 1930s, air power was again proving its worth in localized conflicts around the world: particularly in China, the target of Imperial Japan's aggressively expansionist policies. Then came the Spanish Civil War, which saw the biggest use of air power in Europe since 1918 and in which the ideologies that would shape a far greater conflict confronted each other for the first time in battle. In the air, German and Italian airmen whose aircraft bore the markings of fascist Spain fought with opponents from the USSR, France, Britain and America flying aircraft bearing the markings of republican Spain; and it was in Spanish skies that tactics were developed that would dictate the outcome of future air battles.

DEVELOPMENT OF THE JET ENGINE

By the late 1930s, the invention that would revolutionize air travel, the jet engine, was beginning to take shape. Although jet engine technology was pioneered in Britain by Frank Whittle, it was the Germans who made the first successful marriage of a turbojet with an airframe. Developed as a private venture in parallel with the rocket-powered He 176, the Heinkel He 178 was only ever intended as an experimental test-bed, although it made its mark in the history books when, on 27 August 1939, Flugkapitan Erich Warsitz took off in the world's first jet-powered aircraft and circled the Heinkel factory at Rostock-Marienehe before landing safely. However, although the He 178 was demonstrated before leading officials of the Germany Air Ministry in October, little official interest was shown, and there were technical problems associated with the fuselage-mounted turbojet. Development of the He 178 was therefore abandoned in favour of a project with twin wing-mounted jet engines, the Heinkel He 280, which made its first turbojet-powered flight on 2 April 1941 – six weeks before the maiden flight of Britain's first jet aircraft, the Gloster/Whittle E28/39.

WORLD WAR II

At no other time in history did science and technology make faster progress than in the years between 1939 and 1945, with most of the world's nations locked in mortal combat; and in no area was progress swifter and more dramatic than in the design of military aircraft, some of them developed in response to requirements that had scarcely been envisaged in the years prior to World War II. The aircraft which played a key part in the war, from the first early skirmishes to the final air offensives, are all described in this book, together with many projects and prototypes that never saw combat.

On Germany's western frontier, the initial alarms that had followed the outbreak of hostilities gave way to the period known as the 'Phoney War'. Only in the air was there any real activity, as British, French and German fighters met in frequent skirmishes over the threatened borders. During these battles the Messerschmitt 109's performance proved superior to that of the Hawker Hurricane, which equipped four RAF squadrons in France, and the French Morane 406 and Curtiss Hawk fighters. German air superiority was a critical factor in the battle of France in May 1940 when, after the breakthrough at Sedan, the German armoured columns raced across Belgium and northern France with shattering speed, driving for the Channel coast, a path blasted ahead of them by the Junkers Ju 87 Stuka squadrons of VIII *Fliegerkorps*. But at Dunkirk, the Stukas had a foretaste of things to come when, for the first time, they encountered the Supermarine Spitfire.

During the decisive air battle over Britain in the summer of 1940, weaknesses on both sides were quickly exposed. Not the least of these was that the two most widely used German bombers, the Dornier Do 17 and the Heinkel He 111, lacked adequate defensive armament and could not operate by daylight in a hostile fighter environment, with no fighter escort of their own, without suffering punitive losses. That lesson had to be learned and re-learned time and again by the bomber forces of both sides in the course of the war.

The progressive switch of the Luftwaffe to night attacks in the closing weeks of 1940 hastened the development of the dedicated night-fighter, the first of which was the Bristol Beaufighter. Supplemented and then eventually replaced by the night-fighter variants of the de Havilland Mosquito, the aircraft that really defeated the enemy night-bombers, the Beaufighter found a new role as a formidable anti-shipping aircraft, a role also assumed by fighter-bomber Mosquitoes. But it was for its daring low-level attacks on precision targets in occupied Europe that the Mosquito would always be remembered.

In fighter-versus-fighter combat, nowhere was the disparity between combat aircraft more apparent than on the Russian front. Day after day, in the first phase of the invasion, Russian I-153s and I-16s were shot down in their dozens, hopelessly outclassed by the Messerschmitts and by superior tactics. Yet the apparent suicide of the Soviet Air Force was not in vain. During the latter half of 1941 Russian fighter production concentrated on the more modern types that had begun to replace the elderly I-16s and I-153s: the Yakovlev Yak-1, Mikoyan-Gurevich MiG-1 and Lavochkin LaGG-3. By the summer of 1942 the Soviet aircraft industry's output was beginning to pick up, and more new fighter types were making their appearance. The first of these was the La-5, which was developed from the LaGG-3. The other fighter aircraft which made its operational debut in 1942 was the Yak-9, a progressive development of the Yak-1. In the area of ground attack, so vital on the Russian Front, with huge formations of armour constantly in motion, one type in particular shone. Destined to become one of the most famous ground-attack aircraft of all time, the Ilyushin Il-2 played a prominent, and often decisive, part in the campaigns on the Eastern Front. Germany, although it produced a dedicated assault aircraft, the Henschel Hs 129, had nothing to match the Il-2.

The Mk XIV was the first mass-produced Griffon-engined variant of the Supermarine Spitfire. The increased power required a five-bladed propeller.

By the summer of 1943 the air war in the west was taking on a new dimension. The strategic air offensive was gathering momentum, with the RAF's Lancaster and Halifax and the USAAF's B-17 and B-24 heavy bombers pounding Germany by night and day. In the latter half of 1943, however, Germany's air defences were stronger than ever, and Allied bomber losses were severe. Not until 1944, when North American P-51 Mustang long-range escort fighters became available in numbers, would matters improve. Even then other dangers were to emerge, the greatest of which was the operational deployment of the world's first jet-fighter, the Messerschmitt Me 262. The advent of these formidable aircraft in the Battle of Germany might have proved decisive, had they been used in the pure fighter role. Similarly, the Arado Ar 234 jet-bomber might have presented insoluble problems to the Allies, had it been available in sufficient numbers at an earlier time.

Following the Allied landings in Normandy on 6 June 1944, the air war in north-west Europe became one of tactical support. The Germans had learned the value of tactical air support in the Spanish Civil War; the RAF's

Desert Air Force had developed the concept further in North Africa and subsequently in Italy; and now, in the closing months of the war, it was brought to a fine art by aircraft like the Hawker Typhoon and Republic P-47 Thunderbolt, launching merciless attacks on the retreating Germans.

In the Pacific War, range was the keyword. Since 1940, the Imperial Japanese Navy had been fitting long-range fuel tanks to its excellent Mitsubishi A6M Zero fighters so that they could escort bombers on long-range missions into China, and when Japan went to war in the Pacific its pilots were already highly experienced in flying for range and endurance. During the first months of the Pacific war the Zeros carved out an impressive combat record. The Zero retained its superiority throughout 1942, but in 1943 impressive new Allied combat aircraft began to make their appearance. These were the Vought F4U Corsair, the Lockheed P-38 Lightning and the Grumman F6F Hellcat. The carrier-based Hellcat, in particular, was the aircraft that carried the war to the Japanese home islands. In a bid to re-establish at least a measure of air superiority the Japanese produced new combat types, one of which was the Kawanishi N1K Shiden (Violet Lightning). Code-named 'George' by the Allies, the Shiden was unique among World War II's landplane fighters in that it was developed from a floatplane fighter, the N1K1 Kyofu (Mighty Wind). But even aircraft like the Shiden could not stem the bombing storm that overtook Japan in the last desperate months of the war, when the home islands came within range not only of carrier-based fighter-bombers, but also of P-51D Mustang escort fighters, operating from newly captured Iwo Jima.

By July 1945 mastery of the Japanese skies belonged to the Allies, and the Japanese fighters, those that had not been expended in Kamikaze suicide attacks on the Allied fleet, lay immobilized through lack of fuel or pulverized by air attack. When the atomic bombs fell on Hiroshima and Nagasaki, they served merely to underline a victory that had already been won by the relentless application of air and naval might. And the aircraft that dropped the atomic bombs, the mighty Boeing B-29 Superfortress, was the bludgeon that had already destroyed much of Japan's industrial capacity to wage war.

POSTWAR JET AIRLINER DEVELOPMENT

In 1937, when Frank Whittle tested the first turbojet designed specifically to power an aircraft, the reaction engine was still a novelty; less than a decade later it was a practicality, having been blooded in action in World War II in Germany's Me 262 and Britain's Gloster Meteor. In 1952, the British Overseas Airways Corporation inaugurated the world's first jet airliner services, using the De Havilland Comet, a venture tragically curtailed following a series of fatal accidents, the cause of which was eventually established as structural fatigue. Despite this setback, it was a 'stretched' version of the Comet, the Mk 4, that inaugurated the first fare-paying jet service across the Atlantic in October 1957, some three weeks before its American rival, the Boeing 707. The Soviets, meanwhile, had begun their own scheduled jet airliner services in September 1956, with the Tupolev Tu-104, and in 1959 France entered the running with the Sud-Aviation Caravelle. Aero-engine developments generated other success stories in the 1950s. At the forefront was the Vickers Viscount, powered by the revolutionary Rolls-Royce Dart turboprop. The turboprop, economical and efficient, was the engine destined to power future generations of short- and medium-haul 'feeder' airliners operating at medium level, far below the altitudes at which the turbojet engine is at its most effective.

Four Avro Vulcan jet bombers on their Operational Readiness Platform during the Cold War era as their direct ancestor, an Avro Lancaster, flies overhead.

The Embraer EMB-312 Super Tucano is typical of the modern advanced turboprop trainer, being also able to carry out an attack role. It is a 'stretched' version of the earlier Tucano.

MODERN AVIATION TECHNOLOGY

In the years immediately after World War II, the power and the menace of the strategic bomber led to the re-awakening of old concepts. The jet age saw the rebirth of the pure interceptor, aircraft such as America's F-86 Sabre, the Soviet MiG-15 and Britain's Hawker Hunter, high speed gun platforms whose sole purpose, originally, was to climb fast enough and high enough to destroy the strategic bomber. But such a task had to be undertaken by day and night, in all weathers, and this in turn led to the evolution of the 'weapon system', a fully integrated combination of airframe, engine, weapons, fire control systems and avionics. Early examples of the weapon system were the Northrop F-89 Scorpion, the Lockheed F-94 Starfire, and the Gloster Javelin.

In the mid-1950s yet another concept of air warfare came about, partly as a result of the lessons learned during the Korean War, and partly because of the wildly escalating cost of developing new combat types. This reached fruition in such highly successful types as the McDonnell F-4 Phantom and the Dassault Mirage family, whose basic airframe and engine combination was designed from the outset to support long-term development compatible with a wide variety of operational requirements. The high cost of developing new and complex airborne weapon systems also brought about international cooperation on an unprecedented scale, with a highly beneficial pooling of brains, expertise and financial resources which was to result in the production of advanced and versatile military aircraft like the Panavia Tornado and Eurofighter Typhoon.

The list of success stories in the field of military aircraft production since 1945 is a long one. In terms of longevity Britain's Canberra and America's Boeing B-52 are unmatched, both remaining in first-line service more than half a century after their prototypes first flew, while

for sheer proliferation Russia's MiG-15 remains unsurpassed, having been produced in far greater quantities than any other combat type. Then there have been the postwar export successes of France's military aircraft industry, whose products have admirably upheld the French tradition for building machines which combine a high degree of potency with aesthetic appeal.

In the 1960s the turbojet gave way to the powerful and more fuel-efficient turbofan, the engine that today powers jet airliners and combat aircraft of all sizes the world over. The advent of the turbofan, together with new construction materials, made it possible for aircraft designers to take the next step up the technological ladder: the development of the 'wide-body' airliner, with its much increased seating capacity. The first in the field was the Boeing 747, followed by the Lockheed TriStar and the McDonnell Douglas DC-10: all-American in origin, but soon challenged by the European Airbus. In the 1950s and 1960s, considerable thought was given to the development of supersonic transports for long-range airline services. Seen as an irrelevance by many, commercial supersonic flight has not been an economic success. Only two supersonic transports (SSTs) have seen service. The first was Russia's Tu-144, a technological and commercial disaster; and the other the Anglo-French Concorde, a technological success that was beginning to be commercially viable only after a quarter of a century of operation. But the notion of supersonic passenger flight is by no means dead. Advanced SSTs are still being studied, as are hypersonic sub-orbital transports which, skimming the upper reaches of the atmosphere, would be capable of crossing half the globe in 30 minutes. The technology to build such creations, a mixture of aircraft and spacecraft, is here today; they may be a reality tomorrow.

13

ADER *EOLE*

In 1890 Clement Ader's *Eole* became the first aircraft to fly under its own power, although the flight was short and completely uncontrolled. It was powered by a steam engine.

A TALENTED ENGINEER, the Frenchman Clement Ader is assured of a place in aviation history as the man who designed the first aircraft to fly under its own power. Unfortunately his credibility was virtually destroyed by his subsequent claims – quickly disproved – to have made controlled heavier-than-air flights before the Wright brothers.

Born on 4 February 1841 in Muret, France, Clement Ader developed an early love of aviation and in 1892 he began construction of a steam-powered bat-wing monoplane, which he named *Eole* (Aeolus) after the Greek god of the winds. The *Eole* was finished in 1890, and on 9 October that year Ader prepared to make a test flight in the grounds of a friend's estate at Chateau d'Armainvilliers, near Gretz. The steam engine was started, Ader positioned himself in the rudimentary cockpit, and at 4.00pm the *Eole* got under way, taxiing a short distance and then rising into the air to make a short hop of about 50m (164ft).

The brief flight was entirely uncontrolled and could not be sustained by the unsuitable steam engine. Nevertheless, Ader had shown, for the first time, that a heavier-than-air machine was capable of taking off from level ground under its own power. Years later, he claimed that the *Eole* had made further flights, which was untrue.

Crew: 1
Powerplant: one 15kW (20hp) 2-cylinder steam engine
Performance: not known
Dimensions: wingspan 14m (46ft)
Weight: not known

ADER *AVION*

Crew: 1
Powerplant: two 15kW (20hp) 2-cylinder steam engines
Performance: not known
Dimensions: wingspan 16m (52ft 6in)
Weight: not known

WITH THE HELP OF A SUBSIDY from the War Ministry, Ader set about modifying and enlarging the basic *Eole* design, and in 1892 he began constructing a machine which he named *Avion II*. It was never completed, but Ader then embarked on the design of another version, the *Avion III*, which was powered by two 15kW (20hp) steam engines which drove contra-rotating tractor propellers. The machine was tested twice at Satory, on 12 and 14 October 1897, but on neither occasion did it leave the ground. On the first occasion the *Avion* simply trundled along the track that had been laid out for it; on the second occasion it jumped the track and rolled into a nearby field. Further testing was abandoned without the aircraft ever having flown.

In 1906, however, Ader claimed that the *Avion III* had flown for a distance of 300m (984ft), and he wrote an account of the flight which was pure fabrication. Apart from the rather sad nature of what became known as the 'Ader Affair', it was a pity that Ader had persisted in his study of the bat as the model for his flying machine. Had he based his design on the structure of a bird's wing, he might indeed have become the first man to make a controlled heavier-than-air flight; but the *Avion III*, like the earlier *Eole*, was not fitted with an elevator or any other means of flight control. Clement Ader died in Toulouse on 5 March 1926.

Ader's *Avion* was completed with the help of a subsidy from the French War Ministry. It never left the ground, but its name was subsequently applied to all French aircraft.

AEG C.IV

GERMANY: 1916

An AEG C.IV of Flieger-Abteilung (A) 224, Chateau Bellingchamps, France, in the spring of 1917. Some C.IVs were converted to commercial use after the end of World War I.

THE AEG C.II WAS FOLLOWED by the ungainly C.III, which did not enter production; however, in 1916 the company produced its principal type, the C.IV, which remained operational on all fronts until the summer of 1918.

The C.IV first entered service in the early spring of 1916 and was primarily a reconnaissance aircraft, but was occasionally used as a bomber escort. The type was armed with a single Spandau gun offset to starboard in front of the pilot's cockpit, and a Parabellum gun mounted on a Schneider ring for use by the observer. The latter's cockpit could also accommodate up to 90kg (198lb) of bombs.

Around 658 AEG two-seaters of all types were produced, the majority of which were C.IVs, with 170 in use on the Western Front in June 1917. The C.IVN was a specially adapted night-bomber version, with longer span wings, a Benz Bz.III engine and a payload of six 50kg (110lb) bombs.

Some C.IVs were still in service at the end of World War I, and a few examples were converted for commercial work.

Crew: 2
Powerplant: one 119kW (160hp) Mercedes D.III water-cooled in-line engine
Performance: max speed 158km/h (98mph) at sea level; endurance 3 hrs; service ceiling 5000m (16,404ft)
Dimensions: wingspan 13.46m (44ft 2in); length 7.15m (23ft 5in); height 3.35m (11ft)
Weight: 1120kg (2469lb) loaded
Armament: two machine guns; bomb load up to 100kg (220lb)

AEG G.IV

GERMANY: 1916

Crew: 3
Powerplant: two 194kW (260hp) Mercedes D.IVa 6-cylinder liquid-cooled in-line engine
Performance: max speed 165km/h (103mph); endurance 4 hrs 30 mins; service ceiling 4500m (14,760ft)
Dimensions: wingspan 18.4m (60ft 4in); length 9.7m (31ft 10in); height 3.9m (12ft 9in)
Weight: 3630kg (7986lb) loaded
Armament: two machine guns; bomb load up to 400kg (882lb)

THE AEG G.IV WAS BASICALLY similar to the G.III, but was fitted with more reliable direct-drive Mercedes D.IVa engines. It was the most widely used variant of the company's G-series of medium bombers. Entering service in late 1916, and of mixed wood and steel-tubing construction, the G.IV incorporated all the best features of its predecessors and was employed on the Western Front, in Salonika,

The AEG G.IV was the most widely used member of the company's G-series of medium bombers.

Italy, Romania and Macedonia. Because of its limited range and fairly low operational ceiling, the G.IV was used mainly for tactical bombing; however, in 1917 the units equipped with the type deployed to the southern front and began a lengthy series of night-bombing attacks on Italian towns. Fitted with additional fuel tankage in place of a bomb load, the AEG G.IV was also employed for long-range reconnaissance.

AERFER ARIETE

ITALY: 1958

THE AERFER ARIETE (BATTERING RAM) was developed from an earlier jet-fighter prototype, the Sagittario 2, to meet a NATO requirement for a lightweight interceptor. It had a configuration similar to that of its predecessor, except that the rear fuselage was made deeper to house a Rolls-Royce Soar auxiliary turbojet, fitted in addition to the Derwent.

The Ariete flew for the first time on 27 March 1958. It was to be followed by a definitive version, the Leone, powered by either a Bristol Orpheus B.Or.12 or a de Havilland Gyron Junior turbojet, with a de Havilland Spectre rocket

motor replacing the Soar, but the adoption of the Fiat G.91 by the Italian Air Force and NATO brought further work to an end.

Crew: 1
Powerplant: one 1633kg (3600lb) thrust Rolls-Royce Derwent 9 turbojet, plus one 820kg (1810lb) thrust Rolls-Royce Soar auxiliary turbojet
Performance: max speed 1080km/h (670mph); range 1585km (985 miles); service ceiling 13,725m (45,000ft)
Dimensions: wingspan 7.50m (24ft 7in); length 9.60m (31ft 5in); height 3.27m (10ft 9in)
Weight: 3535kg (7794lb)
Armament: two 30mm (1.18in) cannon

The Aerfer Ariete was one of several aircraft designed to meet a NATO requirement for a lightweight fighter in the 1950s.

AERITALIA (ALENIA) G.222

ITALY: 1970

Crew: 3
Powerplant: two 2536kW (3400hp) thrust General Electric T64-GE-P4D turboprops
Performance: max speed 540km/h (336mph) at 4575m (15,000ft); max range 4558km (2832 miles); service ceiling 7620m (25,000ft)
Dimensions: wingspan 40.00m (131ft 3in); length 32.40m (106ft 3in); height 11.65m (38ft 5in)
Weight: 16,000kg (35,270lb) loaded
Armament: none

PRODUCED ORIGINALLY BY FIAT, the G.222 was conceived in a number of versions, including a dedicated anti-submarine patrol aircraft, but most of these were abandoned and it was as a medium transport that the aircraft first flew on 18 July 1970. The first of 50

Seen here is an Italian G.222 equipped for firefighting, a role it took over from the Fairchild C-119.

production aircraft was delivered at the end of 1978, replacing the Fairchild C-119 in the transport squadrons of the Italian Air Force. A prototype ECM version, the 222VS, equipped with extensive electronic installations and with accommodation for 10 systems operators, was also produced in 1978. The transport version had some export success, customers including Argentina (3), Dubai (1), Libya (20), Nigeria (4), Somalia (4), the USA (10) and Venezuela (8). Some G.222s were converted to the radio/radar calibration role and for fire-fighting duties.

AERMACCHI MB.326

ITALY: 1957

DESIGNED BY ERMANNO BAZZOCCHI and first flown on 10 December 1957, the Aermacchi MB.326 light attack and training aircraft was one of the most

effective examples of its type ever built and was produced in many different variants, depending on the customer's requirements. The potential of the basic MB.326 as a

light ground-attack aircraft was first realised in the 326A, which was fitted with underwing hardpoints. The MB.326G variant was fitted with a more powerful

Viper 20 engine. The most important version was the MB.326K single-seater of 1970, which was used in the advanced training and close support roles.

The MB.326 light attack and training aircraft has been a huge success story and has been produced in several variants. The version seen here is an MB.326K.

Crew: 1/2
Powerplant: one 1814kg (4000lb) thrust Rolls-Royce Viper turbojet
Performance: max speed 890km/h (553mph); combat radius 268km (167 miles)
Dimensions: wingspan 10.85m (35ft 7.25in); length: 10.67m (35ft 0.25in); height: 3.72m (12ft 2in)
Weight: 5895kg (13,000lb) loaded
Armament: two 30mm (1.18in) DEFA cannon; external ordnance up to 1814kg (4000lb)

AERMACCHI (SIAI-MARCHETTI) SF.260

ITALY: 1964

Crew: 1-3
Powerplant: one Textron Lycoming
O-540-E4A5 flat-six piston engine rated
at 194kW (260hp)
Performance: max speed 305km/h
(190mph); combat radius 556km (345
miles) on single-seat mission; service
ceiling 4480m (14,700ft)
Dimensions: wingspan 8.35m (27ft
4.75in); length 7.10m (23ft 3.5in); height
2.41m (7ft 11in)
Weight: maximum take-off weight 1300kg
(2866lb)
Payload: three people or maximum
ordnance of 300kg (661lb)

THE SF.260 THREE-SEAT trainer/
aerobatic light aircraft was
originally designed by Aviamilano
as the F.250/F.260, primarily for
civil use. In 1970 a militarized
version was introduced as the

**Originally designed as a fast
trainer and touring aircraft for the
civil market, the SF.260 has also
achieved military success.**

SF.260M, which has been taken up
by a number of customers as a
trainer. This was augmented in
1972 by the SF.260W version
capable of ground-attack work,
with hard points for guns or a
target-towing kit. In 1980 a
turboprop version became

available (as the SF.260TP) with
minimal other changes. More than
650 SF.260s have been produced
and military customers include
Italy, Belgium, Venezuela, Chad
and the Republic of Ireland.
    Specifications given apply to
SF.260W Warrior.

AERMACCHI MB.339

ITALY: 1975

THE AERMACCHI MB.339 HAD its
origin in a study contract issued by
the Italian Air Force for a second-
generation trainer and light attack
aircraft to succeed the MB.326 and
the Fiat G.91T, for service in the
1980s. The company undertook
nine separate design studies, each
with a different powerplant option,
and the Viper-powered version was
selected. A redesigned forward
fuselage provided the instructor in

the rear seat with better all-round
visibility, and the avionics suite
was completely upgraded. The
single-seat version was designated
MB.339K. Customers include
Argentina, Peru, Dubai, Ghana,
Malaysia and Nigeria.

**The prototype Aermacchi
MB.339A two-seat light attack
aircraft is pictured here against
an Alpine background.**

Crew: 1/2
Powerplant: one 1814kg (4000lb) thrust
Rolls-Royce Viper turbojet
Performance: max speed 890km/h
(553mph); combat radius: 371km (230
miles); service ceiling 14,240m (46,700ft)
Dimensions: wingspan 11.22m (36ft
10in); length 11.24m (36ft 11in); height:
3.99m (13ft 1.25in)
Armament: two 30mm (1.18in) DEFA
cannon; external bomb/missile load up to
1814kg (4000lb)

AERMACCHI/AERITALIA/EMBRAER AMX

INTERNATIONAL: 1984

The AMX multi-role combat aircraft was the product of collaboration between the Italian Aermacchi and Aeritalia and the Brazilian EMBRAER.

THE AMX MULTI-ROLE COMBAT aircraft is the product of collaboration between the Italian companies Aeritalia and Aermacchi and the Brazilian EMBRAER concern, and is the result of a joint requirement formulated by both countries for a new lightweight tactical fighter-bomber. The first prototype AMX flew in May 1984. This agile light attack aircraft entered service with the Italian Air Force in 1990, and deliveries to the Brazilian Air Force began a year later. It is capable of reconnaissance, close air support and interdiction missions.

Crew: 1
Powerplant: one 5003kg (11,030lb) thrust Rolls-Royce Spey Mk 807 turbofan
Performance: max speed 1047km/h (651mph); combat radius 556km (345 miles); service ceiling 13,000m (42,650ft)
Dimensions: wingspan 8.87m (29ft 1.2in);
length 13.23m (43ft 5in); height 4.55m (14ft 11in)
Weight: 13,000kg (28,660lb)
Armament: one 20mm (0.79in) M61A1 cannon or two 30mm (1.18in) DEFA cannon (Brazilian aircraft); five external hard points for up to 3800kg (8377lb) of ordnance; wingtip rails for AAMs

AERO A.11/AB.11

CZECHOSLOVAKIA: 1919

ONE OF THE MOST VERSATILE aircraft of the inter-war years, the Aero A.11 general-purpose biplane superseded the earlier Letov-designed aircraft produced shortly after the founding of the Czech aircraft industry in 1918–19. The total of 440 examples built for Czech Army Aviation incorporated 20 different models, including the basic A.11, fitted with photographic equipment and radio for daytime reconnaissance; the A.11N for night reconnaissance; and the Ab 11 and Ab 11N day and night bombers. The reconnaissance variants were powered by the Walter W-IV engine, but the

The Aero A.11 was one of the most versatile general-purpose aircraft of the inter-war years and was a boost to the fledgling Czech aircraft industry.

bomber versions used the Breitfeld Danek Perun II, developing 179kW (240hp). During its career the A.11 established a number of endurance records.

Crew: 2
Powerplant: one 179kW (240hp) thrust Walter W.IV 8-cylinder liquid-cooled engine
Performance: max speed 214km/h (133mph); range 750km (466 miles); service ceiling 7200m (23,600ft)
Dimensions: wingspan 12.77m (41ft 11in); length 8.20m (26ft 11in); height 3.10m (10ft 2in)
Weight: 1480kg (3260lb) empty
Armament: one 7.62mm (0.30in) machine gun

AERO 45 SERIES

CZECHOSLOVAKIA: 1947

THIS EARLY POST-WAR UTILITY light aircraft design proved a great export earner for Czechoslovakia; over 700 were built, of which more than 600 were exported. A good start was made with the Aero 45's first public appearance, when an early model won the Norton-Griffiths Trophy in the National Air Races held at Coventry in 1949.

Underlying the type's popularity and success was the design – the

Aero 45 was an all-metal design, the cockpit had single or dual controls (in versions), and the rear bench carried up to three passengers or could be folded away to stow freight or luggage. The Aero 45 was progressively updated to Super 45 standard; the last version (the 145) had a larger powerplant, but retained the tail wheel. Production ended in 1963. The specifications apply to the Aero Super 45.

Crew: 1/2
Powerplant: two Walter Minor 4-III piston engines each rated at a maximum of 78kW (105hp) for take-off and 60kW (80hp) for cruise
Performance: max speed 270km/h (168mph); range 1600km (994 miles) maximum, or 1400km (870 miles) with

four passengers, full fuel load at normal cruising speed; service ceiling 5050m (16,568ft)
Dimensions: wingspan 12.30m (40ft 4.25in); length 7.54m (24ft 8.75in); height 2.30m (7ft 6.5in)
Weight: 1600kg (3527lb) fully loaded
Payload: up to 5 people

Most Aero 45s were built for export, and this example was the first (Super) 45 imported into the UK in 1959.

AERO L.29 DELFIN

CZECHOSLOVAKIA: 1959

A TWO-SEAT BASIC AND ADVANCED trainer, capable of operating from grass, sand or waterlogged strips, the Aero L-29 Delfin (Dolphin) first flew in April 1959 and in 1961 was selected as standard training equipment for the Soviet Air Force, which took delivery of over 2000 units of the 3600 aircraft built. The type subsequently served with all the Warsaw Pact air forces

and also with many other air arms within the Soviet sphere of influence. The type first entered service in 1963 and remained in production for 11 years. In Soviet service, the L-29 had the NATO reporting name 'Maya'.

First flown in 1959, the Aero L.29 Delfin was selected as standard equipment for the Soviet Air Force.

Crew: 2
Powerplant: one 890kg (1960lb) thrust Motorlet M701 VC-150 turbojet
Performance: max speed 655km/h (407mph); range 640km (397 miles); service ceiling 11,000m (36,100ft)
Dimensions: wingspan 10.29m (33ft 8in); length 10.81m (35ft 5in); height 3.13m (10ft 3in)
Weight: 3280kg (7231lb) loaded
Armament: none

AERITALIA AM 3C
Developed in response to an Italian Army requirement for an L-19 Bird Dog replacement, the Aeritalia AM 3C first flew on 12 May 1967, powered by a 253kW (340hp) Lycoming engine.

AERMACCHI (SIAI-MARCHETTI) S.211
A single-engined two-seat basic military jet trainer, first flown in 1981. Aermacchi acquired rights to the S.211 design in 1997 and 60 examples were built.

AERMACCHI M-290P REDIGO
A single-engined turboprop trainer designed originally by Finland's Valmet as the L-90TP, acquired and renamed by Aermacchi in 1996.

AERMACCHI-LOCKHEED AL.60
Designed by Lockheed, this six-/eight-seat, single-engined high-wing utility transport was subsequently manufactured in Italy because of production costs. First flown in 1959, it was also licence-built by Lockheed-Azcarte in Mexico.

AERO A.12
The Aero A.12 was a Czechoslovakian two-seat reconnaissance and light bomber biplane, 93 being built in 1923. The type was powered by a 179kW (240hp) Maybach engine.

AERO A.14
A Czech version of the Austrian-built Hansa-Brandenburg C.I general-purpose biplane. It was designed by Ernst Heinkel and first flew in 1923.

AERO A.18
The A.18 was a biplane fighter, 20 of which were built for the Czech Army in 1923.

AERO A.21
The Aero A.21 was a two-seat trainer version of the basic Aero A.11 design.

AERO A.24
One of Aero's few unsuccessful designs, the A.24 was a twin-engined biplane bomber of 1924. It did not progress beyond the prototype stage.

AERO A.25
Powered by a 138kW (185hp) Walter engine, this training aircraft first flew in 1925 and served with the Czech Army Aviation from the late 1920s.

AERO COMMANDER SERIES

USA: 1948

THE 520 SERIES FOLLOWED THE L.3805 prototype of this light/executive transport/air taxi series. The 520 was designed by former Douglas engineer Ted R. Smith, also founder of the Aero Design and Engineering Company formed to produce the design. The first of 150 type 520s was delivered in 1952.

The short field, high-visibility and cabin layout qualities of the 520 gave rise to a hugely successful range of derivatives. The 560 series dating from 1954 included a number of improvements, and a version was chosen as a VIP and Presidential transport with the military designation U-4. A lighter, more economical version (the 500) was to follow in 1958, and the company was acquired by Rockwell in 1960 and renamed Aero Commander. Successive design improvements were made to the 500 series throughout the 1960s, and these were rolled up into a 500 series derivative known as the Shrike Commander.

In May 1960 the 680 series was launched, with uprated supercharged engines and a resemblance to the 560; examples of this type were again acquired for a military VIP role, and there a number of

This is a 680-F, which was updated to include fuel-injected engines and an improved landing gear.

further 680 variants/refinements that culminated in the designation Grand Commander. These included the pressurized 720, which sold poorly. The Grand Commander was the basis for a new turboprop-powered version of the 680 – the 680T Turbo Commander/Jetprop, which dates from late 1964. The 680T was further developed in a number of

commercial and military variants, and this pattern continued after the Aero Commander product range became diffused among different ownerships – notably (for the Turbo Commander range) Grumman Aerospace. In the region of 3000 Aero Commanders (of all variants) were built and this popular and ubiquitous type can be seen in service with a variety of operators, including air taxi services throughout the Caribbean.

Specifications apply to the Aero Commander 500U.

Crew: 1
Powerplant: two 216kW (290hp) Avco Lycoming IO-540-E1B5 flat-six piston engines
Performance: max speed 346km/h (215mph) at sea level; max cruising speed at 2745m (9000ft) 326km/h (203mph); range 1735km (1078 miles); service ceiling 5915m (19,400ft)
Dimensions: wingspan 14.95m (49ft 0.5in); length 11.22m (36ft 9.75in); height 4.42m (14ft 6in)
Weight: 3062kg (6750lb) maximum take-off weight
Payload: up to 7 people

AERONCA MODEL 7 CHAMPION/L-16 SERIES

USA: 1945

The Champion was extremely popular with private and club fliers in post-World War II North America. More than 10,000 aircraft were produced in a small range of variants.

IN ANTICIPATION OF A POST-WAR boom in private flying, Aeronca designed a new model – the Model 7 Champion – which was marketed from November 1945

and which sold over 10,000 examples between 1946 and 1951. The Champion was the first new light aeroplane to be certified after World War II. It shared a

similar high-wing monoplane design with its predecessors; however, the Champion was tandem dual-control configuration as standard, a major selling point.

Variants included a 'farm wagon' with the rear seat area converted to carry agricultural supplies, and the military L-16, which was used briefly in the Korean War and by the Civil Air Patrol. The Champion ceased production in 1950, but further examples were produced later by companies that acquired manufacturing rights. Specifications apply to the 7AC Champion.

Crew: 1/2
Power plant: one 48kW (65hp) Continental A-65-8 or A-65-8F flat-four piston engine
Performance: max speed 161km/h (100mph); range 435km (270 miles); service ceiling 3840m (12,600ft)
Dimensions: wingspan 10.72m (35ft 2in); length 6.55m (21ft 6in); height 2.13m (7ft);
Weight: 562kg (1240lb) maximum take-off weight
Payload: 2 people

AÉROSPATIALE (SUD-EST) SE.210 CARAVELLE FRANCE: 1955

The Caravelle was popular with charter operators such as Air Charter International, which operated a fleet of ex-Air France Caravelle IIIs between 1979 and 1987.

Crew: 3
Powerplant: two Pratt and Whitney JT8D-7 turbofan engines each rated at 64.5kN (14,512lb) thrust
Performance: max cruising speed 800km/h (497mph); range 2650km (1646 miles)
Dimensions: wingspan 34.30m (112ft 6in); length 32.00m (105ft); height 8.72m (28ft 7in)
Weight: 56,000kg (123,456lb) maximum take-off weight
Payload: typically around 80 passengers, but the Caravelle 12 was capable of carrying up to 128 passengers in a single-class charter configuration

DESIGNED BY SUD-EST AVIATION in response to a 1951 French Air Ministry requirement for a short- to medium-range turbojet airliner, the Caravelle was France's first jet airliner and the first passenger jet to feature rear fuselage mounted engines. Air France was the launch customer. It became the largest single original customer/operator from the date of its first service on 6 May 1959 and continued to operate the type for over 20 years.

The design was progressively updated. The original turbojet Rolls-Royce Avon engines were replaced with variants of the Pratt and Whitney JT8D turbofans and the airframe underwent two stretches. Including prototypes, 282 Caravelles were built and delivered by the spring of 1973, when production ceased. The Caravelle was operated by a number of major airlines including SAS, SABENA, Iberia, Finnair, Alitalia and United Airlines. It later found favour with a number of charter and secondary operators, but by 2003 there were as few as three operational examples. Specifications apply to the Caravelle 10R.

AERO A.29
The A.29 was a twin-float seaplane derivative of the A.11, nine being produced and used as target tugs by the Czech Army Aviation.

AERO A.32
Developed from the A.11, and first flying in 1926, the Aero A.32 was fitted with a licence-built Bristol Jupiter engine. A total of 31 examples were built and used in the close-support role.

AERO A.100
The winner of a Czech Defence Ministry competition in 1933, the Aero A.100 (of which 44 were built) served in the armed reconnaissance role from 1933.

AERO A.101
The A.101 was a bomber variant of the Aero 100. The last variant of the basic design, the Ab.101, was also to be the last Czech-built biplane bomber.

AERO A.204
A Czechoslovakian twin-engined light transport dating from 1936, the Aero A.204 was designed with national airline CSA in mind. The A.204 was capable of carrying eight passengers. CSA did not buy the A.204, and the one prototype went on to provide a basis for the A.304 bomber.

AERO L-39 ALBATROS
The L-39, which first flew in November 1968, was designed to succeed the Delfin as the standard Warsaw Pact jet trainer. It was produced in two-seat and single-seat versions.

AERO BOREO AB.95/115/180
The first of this series of Argentinian single-piston engine, high-braced wing light aircraft first flew in 1959. More than 600 have been built, some finding work as agricultural sprayers or glider tugs.

AERO SPACELINES B.377 GUPPY 201
The Guppy was a conversion of the Boeing 377 Stratocruiser, with a considerable fuselage area enlargement and replacement of the four piston engines with turboprops. The 201 was the definitive variant, and was first flown in 1970. Four examples were produced for Airbus Industries to transport major airliner components. Progressive retirement came in the second half of the 1990s, when the A300 Beluga conversion replaced the Guppy 201.

Aérospatiale/British Aerospace Concorde

UK/FRANCE: 1969

Crew: 3
Powerplant: four Rolls-Royce/SNECMA Olympus 593 Mk 610 turbojet engines each rated at 169.26kN (38,050lb) thrust with 17 per cent afterburning
Performance: max speed Mach 2.04 (2179km/h / 1354mph) at 15,635m (51,300ft); range 6582km (4090 miles) with maximum fuel reserves and payload of 8845kg (19,500lb); service ceiling 18,290m (60,000ft)
Dimensions: wingspan 25.55m (83ft 10in); wing area 358.22m^2 (3856sq ft); length 62.10m (203ft 9in); height 11.40m (37ft 5in)
Weight: 185,066kg (408,000lb) maximum take-off weight
Payload: 100 passengers normal layout, but provision for up to 128

THE WITHDRAWAL OF CONCORDE from scheduled service in 2003 marks an end to one of the most extraordinary technical achievements of twentieth-century aerospace; however, it should be remembered that the date of Concorde's first flight is now closer to that of the first jet (1939) than today's date.

The major post-war powers – the United States, the Soviet Union, Britain and France – were all engaged in studies and plans in the 1950s to create a supersonic passenger jet in the expectation that this generic type would take over many long- and even medium-haul services. In 1962 the British and French governments (after years of informal cooperation) formally agreed to merge the Bristol 233 and Sud Aviation Super Caravelle projects in order to share the cost and development of what was later named Concorde. A similar agreement was made between Concorde's engine makers, Rolls-Royce and SNECMA.

The technical issues that needed to be surmounted were formidable, particularly in that era prior to computer-aided design tools. First and foremost was the problem of base materials, which would need to be closer to military standards to allow speeds above Mach 2.5, precluding the use of more commonly used non heat-resistant alloys. Ultimately a technical trade-off was achieved by reducing the maximum speed accompanied by the judicious use of titanium and the ingenious use of fuel tanks inside the wings acting as a heatsink to reduce the outside temperature of the wing metal. Another challenge was the variable geometry nose. This was necessary in order to overcome the loss of visibility from the flight deck caused by the need to fly the delta-wing design at 'a high angle of attack' when flying at lower speeds (primarily during landing phase).

Construction work on the prototype began in 1965, which first flew at Toulouse on the 2 March 1969, shortly after the maiden flight of the Boeing 747 and the same year that *Apollo 11* was to make the first moon landing. In the following years there was considerable interest from major airlines around the world and a number of options for delivery were placed. There were also political jitters in the United Kingdom regarding the cost of the project. These and the remaining technical/proving issues were overcome, but when Concorde entered service in 1976 it entered a world economy rocked by the fuel crisis of 1973 and an America that had dropped its own supersonic projects and was now hostile on environmental grounds to the use of Concorde.

The political/environmental issues were surmounted, but Concorde never attracted export orders, due in part to the new economic order, but also to the effect of the sonic boom, which restricted Concorde's market place to long over-sea routes. It consequently suffered uneconomic production numbers. Ultimately only 14 production standard Concorde's were built, seven each for Air France and British

An engineering marvel of the 1970s, Concorde remained in service into the 21st century, despite its economic and environmental shortcomings.

This Air France Concorde was painted to promote Pepsi's new brand livery when it was launched in 1995. It made a round-the-world tour – albeit subsonically due to the special paint job.

Airways, who jointly inaugurated fare-paying services on 21 January 1976 to Rio de Janeiro and Bahrain, respectively. Concorde soon found its niche on trans North Atlantic services, but examples were wet-leased to Singapore Airlines, who extended Bahrain services to Singapore for a period, and Braniff International, who extended Washington DC services to Dallas–Fort Worth.

Into the 1990s the Concorde found extra work as 'add-ons' to luxury holiday packages and cruises, and it was sadly at the beginning of such an excursion that the Air France Paris crash occurred in August 2000. The cause of the accident was the rupture of a fuel tank originating from pressurized debris thrown out by a damaged tyre, which was itself damaged by a foreign object. The Concorde fleet was grounded immediately, and remained so until late 2001 when modification to wing-tank linings and tyres were completed. However, the terrorism of 9/11 and the world economy radically changed the operating environment for airlines, coupled with the soaring costs of supporting 25-year-old Concordes in service. Consequently Air France and British Airways jointly announced cessation of Concorde operations in April 2003. Air France flew its last service in May 2003, with BA continuing services until the end of October 2003 – truly the end of an era.

AÉROSPATIALE SA 360C DAUPHIN/361H/365C DAUPHIN 2 FRANCE: 1972

Accommodation: 10–14
Powerplant: two Turboméca Arriel 1C1 turboshafts each rated at 540kW (724hp) for take-off and 437kW (586hp) for continuous running
Performance: max speed 296km/h (184 mph); combat radius 852km (530 miles); service ceiling 3600m (11,810ft)
Dimensions: main rotor diameter 11.94m (39ft 2in); length 13.88m (45ft 6.5in); height 3.98m (13ft 0.75in)
Weight: 2161kg (4764lb)
Payload: 1420kg (3130lb) internally or 1300kg (2868lb) externally. Ambulance version: four stretchers, a medical attendant and two crew. Mixed-traffic version, six persons plus room for cargo

DEVELOPED AS A REPLACEMENT for the Alouette III, 70 single-engined SA 360/365s had been ordered by 17 operators in 13 countries by early 1978. The 361H was similar but had a more power-ful Astazou XXB turboshaft engine with a Starflex rotor head and was capable of anti-tank operations when armed with 8 HOT missiles, area neutralization using 20mm (0.79in) cannon, 7.62mm (0.30in) machine guns and rockets, and assault missions carrying 8–10 troops. The SA 365C Dauphin 2 is a twin-engined version of the SA 360 powered by 485kW (650hp) Arriel turboshafts. It flew for the first time on 24 January 1975, and deliveries began in 1978. A shipboard version, the much-changed SA 365N, first flew on 31 March 1979 and later entered production in China as the Harbin Z-9 Haitun. The SA 366 was equipped for ASW and armed with torpedoes and MAD. It first flew on 23 July 1980 and the first of 96 HH-65As for the US Coast Guard (designated the HH-65A Dolphin) was received on 1 February 1987.

Specifications apply to the Aérospatiale SA360 Dauphin 2.

Designed initially for the civil market, the Aérospatiale SA 360 was built to accommodate a pilot and up to nine passengers.

AGUSTA A-101G/H

The turbine-powered AGUSTA A-101G medium-sized multi-role helicopter, which first flew on 19 October 1964, was a radical leap forward in design technology, but this was its undoing and only three prototypes were built.

IN 1958 AGUSTA began working on a design to meet an Aeronautica Militare Italiano (AMI) requirement for a medium-sized multi-role helicopter. The AZ-101G differed from its contemporaries in having turbine power in preference to piston engines, being powered by three 559kW (750shp) Turboméca Turmo 3 turboshaft engines, which greatly increased power-to-weight ratio and improved overall performance. In 1959 this specification was changed to three Bristol Siddeley Gnome 746kW (1000shp) engines, and later increased in turn to 932kW (1250shp) H.1200 Gnome turboshafts. The carrying capacity was also increased from 16 to 35 passengers. An A-101G prototype built for the AMI flew on 19 October 1964, but only two more prototypes were constructed; the A-101H civil transport version with three 1305kW (1750shp) Gnome H.1800 turboshaft engines was a project development.

Despite the long development phase, this multi-role helicopter never actually went into production. The knowledge gained of triple-engine configuration did prove useful, however, for future projects.

Crew: 2
Powerplant: three Bristol Siddeley Gnome H.1400 turboshafts 1043kW (1400shp)
Performance: max speed 230km/h (143mph); combat radius 560km (348 miles); service ceiling 2600m (8530ft)
Dimensions: main rotor diameter 19.90m (65ft 3in); length 18.01m (59ft 1in); height 4.94m (16ft 2in)
Weight: 6400kg (14,110lb)
Payload: 35 passengers and 349kg (770lb) of baggage, or the equivalent weight of equipped troops; up to 6500kg (14,330lb) of cargo

AGUSTA A-129 MANGUSTA (MONGOOSE)/A-129 INTERNATIONAL

A HIGHLY AUTOMATED TANDEM two-seat anti-tank and scout/light attack helicopter for the Italian Army, the first A-129 prototype flew on 15 September 1983. Originally, 100 Mangustas were required, but with the ending of the Cold War this was reduced to 60. The first five were accepted in October 1990 and thus became the first dedicated attack helicopter to be designed, built and deployed by a European nation. Production ceased in 1992 after 45 examples had been delivered to the Aviazione Esertcito (AVES). The remaining 15 A-129s on order incorporated many of the improvements developed by the A-129

The Agusta A-129 Mangusta was the first dedicated attack helicopter to be designed, built and deployed by a European nation.

International multi-role/multi-mission version. The prototype A-129 International flew on 9 January 1995. Specifications apply to the Agusta A-129 Mangusta.

Crew: 2
Powerplant: two Piaggio (Rolls-Royce) Gem 2-2 Mk 1004D turboshaft engines each rated at 615kW (825shp)
Performance: max speed 259km/h (161mph); combat radius 100km (62 miles); service ceiling 3750m (12,300ft)
Dimensions: main rotor diameter 11.90m (39ft 0.5in); length 14.29m (46ft 10.5in); height: 3.35m (11ft)
Weight: 2529kg (5575lb)
Armament: maximum weapon load of 1200kg (2646lb)

AGUSTA-BELL AB 212

ITALY: 1961

This is the ASV/ASW version of the AB 212 for the Italian Navy, which received 60 examples beginning in 1976.

THE AGUSTA-BELL AB 212 is a licence-built utility helicopter corresponding with the Bell Model 212 Twin Two-Twelve derivative of the Bell 205. Deliveries of the AB 212 to the Italian Air Force began in late 1971. In its standard form the AB 212 can carry a pilot and up to 14 passengers, although the cabin is easily converted to operate in other roles, notably as an ambulance with space for six stretchers and two medical

attendants, or as a VIP transport. The AB 212 ASV/ASW, a wholly Italian-built modified version of the standard AB 212, was built for the Italian Navy and successfully evaluated in 1973. The first of 60 production examples entered service in 1976 and orders from 14 other countries followed. About 14 EM-3 examples are operational with the Italian Army and 35 AB 212s are operated by the AMI (Italian Air Force).

Crew: 3/4 with provision for up to 7 passengers or 4 litters plus an attendant
Powerplant: one Pratt & Whitney Canada PT6T-6 Turbo Twin Pac coupled turboshaft rated at 1398kW (1875shp)
Performance: max speed 196km/h (122mph); combat radius 667km (414 miles); service ceiling 3200m (10,498ft)
Dimensions: main rotor diameter 14.63m (48ft); length 17.40m (57ft 1in); height 4.53m (14ft 10in)
Weight: 3420kg (7540lb)
Armament: up to 490kg (1080lb)

AICHI D3A 'VAL'

JAPAN: 1938

Crew: 2
Powerplant: one 802kW (1075hp) Mitsubishi Kinsei 44 14-cylinder radial engine
Performance: max speed 389km/h (242mph); service ceiling 10,500m (34,450ft); range 1352km (840 miles)
Dimensions: wingspan 14.37m (47ft 2in); length 10.20m (33ft 5in); height 3.80m (12ft 7in)
Weight: 4000kg (8818lb) loaded
Armament: two 7.7mm (0.303in) machine guns in upper forward fuselage and one in rear cockpit; external bomb load of 370kg (816lb)

The Aichi D3A dive-bomber was the most numerous Japanese aircraft to take part in the Japanese attack on Pearl Harbor in December 1941.

AÉROSPATIALE SA 350 ECUREUIL (SQUIRREL)/ AS 350C ASTAR
Six-seat multi-purpose helicopter intended as a successor to the Alouette, marketed in North America as the AS 350C Astar. It was first flown on 27 June 1974, and by 1 January 1997 Eurocopter (formed by the merger of MBB and Aérospatiale in 1992) had received orders for a total of 2019 Ecureuils.

AÉROSPATIALE (NORD) 262 FREGATE
The Nord 262 succeeded earlier Super Broussard 250 and 260 designs, updated with a pressurized cabin. This 29-seat, two-engined French regional airliner was also produced as the Fregate for military transport use. A combined total of 110 were built, but operational numbers have dwindled to a handful.

AÉROSPATIALE 298 MOHAWK
The Mohawk is a conversion/ upgrade of the Aérospatiale (Nord) 262, including Pratt and Whitney PT6A-45 engines and Avionics upgrades. The nine conversions were carried out by Mohawk Air Services (USA) for Allegheny Airlines. Operational numbers are now below five.

AÉROSPATIALE TB-30 EPSILON
The TB-30 Epsilon was developed in response to a French Air Force requirement for a new basic trainer. It first flew in 1979.

AÉROSPATIALE/ AERITALIA ATR 72
The ATR 72 is a stretched version of the earlier ATR 42 regional airliner, capable of carrying up to 74 passengers. More than 250 have been delivered and this airliner is still in production.

AEROTÉCHNICA AC-12
Two-seat multi-purpose helicopter derived from the experimental AC-11, which, as the MATRA-Cantineau MC 101, first flew in 1952. The first of two prototypes flew on 20 July 1956 and 12 were ordered as the EC-XZ-2 for the Spanish Air Force.

AEROTÉCHNICA AC-14
Five-seat military helicopter powered by a 298kW (400shp) Turboméca Artouste IIB1 turbo-shaft engine, also developed for agricultural and ambulance roles. A pre-production batch of 10 AC-14s (EC-XZ-4s) was built, the first flying on 16 July 1957. Aerotéchnica SA ceased to exist in 1962.

FIRST FLOWN IN JANUARY 1938, the Aichi D3A dive-bomber, later given the Allied code-name 'Val', went into production in December 1939 and saw limited action from land bases in China during the Sino-Japanese war. The D3A1, the world's first all-metal low-wing monoplane dive-bomber, was the most numerous type used in the attack on Pearl Harbor on 7 December 1941, 126 aircraft being launched from the Japanese carrier task force. In 1942 an improved version, the D3A2, made its appearance; this was fitted with a more powerful 969kW (1300hp) Kinsei engine and extra fuel tanks. By 1943 the type was obsolete and many were adapted to the training role as D3A2-K trainers.

Production totalled 478 D3A1s and 816 D3A2s, many survivors being expended in Kamikaze attacks at Leyte and Okinawa. The D3A was fitted with dive brakes similar to those of the German Junkers Ju 87, and these had to be modified at an early development stage to eliminate excessive vibration. Specifications refer to the Aichi D3A-1.

AICHI B7A 'GRACE'   JAPAN: 1942

The Aichi B7A torpedo-bomber, seen here in the markings of the Yokosuka Kokutai (Naval Air Corps), was beset by problems during its development and did not enter service until 1944.

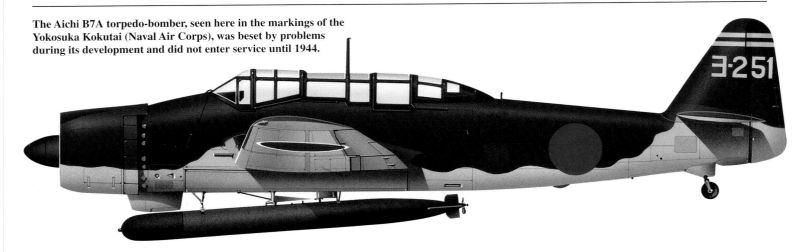

THE B7A RYSEI (SHOOTING STAR) was developed in response to a 1941 Japanese Navy requirement for a new torpedo-bomber, and first flew in 1942. The principal variant, the B7A-2, did not enter service until 1944, relatively late in the war as it turned out. Its production had been delayed by an earthquake and by problems with the Homare engine. By the time the Rysei – code-named 'Grace' by the Allies – became operational the Japanese carrier fleet had been destroyed, and the 114 aircraft built operated from land bases.

Crew: 2
Powerplant: one 1492kW (2000hp) Nakajima NK9C Homare 12 18-cylinder radial engine
Performance: max speed 566km/h (352mph); service ceiling 11,250m (36,910ft); range 3038km (1888 miles)
Dimensions: wingspan 14.40m (47ft 3in); length 11.49m (37ft 8in); height 4.07m (13ft 4in)
Weight: 6500kg (14,330lb) loaded
Armament: two fixed forward-firing 20mm (0.79in) cannon in wing leading edges; one 13mm (0.51in) machine gun in rear cockpit; one 800kg (1764lb) Long Lance torpedo

AIDC CHING-KUO   TAIWAN: 1989

THE CHING-KUO, TAIWAN'S indigenous air defence fighter, was developed with much assistance from a number of US companies, including General Dynamics, and resembles a heavily modified F-16. The prototype flew for the first time on 28 May 1989, but was damaged in a landing accident some months later, and the second prototype crashed in July 1989, killing its pilot. Despite these mishaps, the programme went ahead and the first Ching-Kuo was delivered to the Chinese Nationalist Air Force in 1994, although the lifting of restrictions on the sale of US military aircraft to Taiwan resulted in the original requirement for 250 aircraft being reduced to 130. It is reportedly superior to the Northrop F-5E in all-round performance. Acceleration is better than that of the F-104 Starfighter and its turning radius is smaller than that of the F-5. The aircraft, equipped

Taiwan could not have developed its indigenous Ching-Kuo air defence fighter without much assistance from US aerospace companies.

with four Sidewinder missiles, but no spare fuel tanks, has a combat endurance of three minutes on afterburner and a combat radius of 128–160km (80–100 miles). With a combat radius of 1110km (690 miles) in the armed reconnaissance role, it is capable of conducting pre-emptive raids and strikes on airfields along mainland China's coast.

Crew: 1
Powerplant: two 4291kg (9460lb) thrust ITEC TFE1042-70 turbofans
Performance: max speed 1275km/h (792mph); range classified; service ceiling: 16,760m (55,000ft)
Dimensions: wingspan 9.00m (29ft 6in); length 14.48m (47ft 6in); height 4.65m (15ft 3in)
Weight: 9072kg (20,000lb) loaded
Armament: one 20mm (0.79in) M61A1 Vulcan six-barrel rotary cannon; six external pylons for AAMs, AASMs and various combinations of rockets or gun pods

AIR DEPARTMENT FLYING-BOAT

UK: 1917

DURING WORLD WAR I the British Admiralty maintained a small but thriving Air Department, which had its own team of naval aircraft designers. In 1917 one of the team's designs, the AD Flying-boat, a single-engined biplane, was contracted out to the Supermarine company, which was in the process of being founded. Two prototypes were subsequently built and tested, and a number of flaws were revealed, particularly on take-off

when the aircraft had a tendency to 'porpoise' violently. Nevertheless, a small production run of 27 aircraft was authorized, the first production aircraft passing acceptance trials in September 1917.

In the event, most of the aircraft went into storage, although two were to be used for experimental work at the Isle of Grain naval air station. After the war one AD Flying-boat, N1529, was converted as a civil passenger aircraft.

Crew: 2
Powerplant: one 112kW (150hp) Sunbeam or 149kW (200hp) Hispano-Suiza in-line engine
Performance: max speed 160.9km/h (100mph); endurance 4.5 hrs; ceiling not known
Dimensions: wingspan 15.34m (50ft 4in); length 9.32m (30ft 7in); height 3.98m (13ft 1in)
Weight: 1618kg (3567lb) loaded
Armament: one 7.62mm (0.30in) Lewis machine gun in bow cockpit

AIRBUS A300 SERIES

EUROPEAN CONSORTIUM: 1971

European aerospace companies and their respective governments were exploring the common requirements for a short-/medium-range turbofan-powered airliner in the mid-1960s and collaborative discussions ensued. Initial talks were between British and French companies/governments, but the final line-up was Sud (France) Airbus Gmbh (a specially created German entity), Fokker-VFW (Netherlands) and CASA (Spain). Also included was Britain's Hawker-Siddeley, which entered the consortia without government backing. The British government withdrew, basically due to a lack of enthusiasm for the project, a move that curtailed any likelihood of a Rolls-Royce (ultimately the RB211) engine becoming the aircraft's preferred powerplant.

Nevertheless, the Hawker Siddeley wing design proved

crucial to performance and fuel capacity. The launch customer was Air France, which took delivery of the B2 version on 30 May 1974; however, initial orders were slow to materialize until a breakthrough order from Eastern Airlines (USA) in 1978 – the company ordered the higher weight B4. A further derivative was launched in 1988 in the form of the A300-600R extended-range version.

The A300 went on to sell over 500 examples to national/major airlines in Europe, Asia/Pacific and the Americas. More recently, large numbers have been newly manufactured for freight operator Federal Express, while a number of existing airframes underwent freighter conversion for Federal Express and other cargo airlines at the Airbus plant at Filton (Bristol) in the United Kingdom. The A300 was also chosen as the basis for

Airbus's major component freighter to replace the Aero Spacelines B.377 Guppy, and four examples have been converted to A300ST Beluga standard.

Specifications apply to the Airbus A300-600 series.

Crew: 2
Powerplant: two General Electric CF6-80C2A1 turbofans each rated at 262.45kN (59,000lb)
Performance: max cruising speed 897km/h (557mph); range 6852km (4255 miles) with 266 passengers and baggage; max operating altitude 12,192m (40,000ft)
Dimensions: wingspan 44.84m (147ft 1in); length 54.08m (177ft 5in); height 16.53m (54ft 3in);
Weight: 4309kg (9500lb) maximum take-off weight
Payload: 266-375 passengers depending on layout and seat pitch, or up to 39,885kg (87,931lb) of cargo

Air France was the launch customer for the A300. This A300 B2 series demonstrator was painted in Air France's livery during its spell as a sales vehicle, and was later sold to French operator Air Inter.

AIRBUS A320 SERIES (A318, A319, A320, A321)

Hong Kong-based Dragonair was an early Far East customer for the A320. This, their first aircraft, was delivered in February 1993. Since then the A320 family has achieved creditable sales in the Asian market.

THE AIRBUS A320 PROJECT WAS one which was a long time in gestation. The general concept of a 150-seat, short-/medium-range airliner was an idea considered individually by various European aerospace companies, until Airbus achieved sufficient consensus to launch the A320 in 1982.

The A320 was the first airliner to embody fly-by-wire flight controls. It has an EFIS cockpit and composite materials are used to save weight. Only a small number of 100-series A320s was built before the higher weight 200 series became the definitive model, with more than 1000 sold.

The Airbus A320's British Aerospace (BAe-) designed wing and its fuel capacity have greatly contributed to its superior range and economy over early rival products, and the success with worldwide sales has led to several shortened or stretched versions – the (shortest) A318 which enters service in 2003, the shorter A319 and the larger A321. All these variants share a high level of flight deck and maintenance synergy with the A320.

Specifications apply to the Airbus A320-200.

Crew: 2
Powerplant: two CFM International CFM56-5B4 turbofan engines each rated at 117.88kN (26,523lb), or two IAE V2525-A5 turbofan engines each rated at 111.21kN (25,022lb)
Performance: max cruising speed 903km/h (561mph); range 5463km (3395 miles) with 150 passengers and provision for a 370km (230-mile) diversion; service ceiling 11,887m (39,000ft)
Dimensions: wingspan 33.91m (111ft 3in); length 37.57m (123ft 3in); height 11.80m (38ft 8.5in); maximum take-off weight 64,000kg (141,095lb)
Payload: up to 179 passengers

AIRBUS A330

THE MEDIUM-/LONG-HAUL A330 was developed in parallel with the four-engined A340, consequently the two programmes share a high degree of commonality in terms of wing, hull and systems design, greatly aided by CAD. The 'fly-by-wire' and EFIS cockpit techniques pioneered in the smaller A320 are embodied in both A330 and A340 as well, along with the BAe wing technology. To date the A330 has been launched in two versions: the (smaller) 200 and the 300. The 300 series has sold to mainly major operators, while the 200 series has sold to both major and charter operators, often as a Lockheed TriStar or McDonnell-Douglas DC-10 replacement. Specifications apply to the Airbus A330-300.

The Airbus A330 is a medium-/long-haul version of the type and is produced in two versions, the A330-300 and the smaller A330-200.

Crew: 2
Powerplant: two General Electric CF6-80E1A2 turbofans each rated at 300.25kN (67,500lb) or two Pratt &Whitney PW4164/4168 turbofans each rated at 302.48kN (68,000lb), or two General Electric GE90-75B turbofans or two Rolls-Royce Trent 768/772 turbofan engines each rated at up to 316.27kN (71,100lb)
Performance: max cruising speed 927km/h (576mph); range 8224km (5178 miles) with 335 passengers and reserves for a 370km (230-mile) diversion; service ceiling 12,495m (41,000ft)
Dimensions: wingspan 60.30m (197ft 10in); length 63.65m (208ft 10in); height 16.74m (54ft 11in)
Weight: 212,000kg (467,375lb) maximum take-off weight
Payload: up to 440 passengers

AIRBUS A340 SERIES

THE A340 SERIES WAS developed from 1987 in tandem with the twin-engined A330, and the two types share a high degree of ergonomic and avionic synergy. The A340, however, is aimed at the ultra long-range/thin-traffic market, for airlines that cannot economically or legislatively operate a twin-engined ETOPS compatible airliner due to overall range, or range over water.

This twin-aisle airliner first went into service in 1993 with Lufthansa and Air France in the form of the shorter fuselage and longer range A340-200, the stretched (shorter range) A340-300 entered service with Singapore Airlines in April 1996. Over 300 examples of these initial versions have been delivered to airlines around the world.

In 1997 Airbus launched two ultra long-range variants – the 500

The pictured A340-300 is seen in the colours of Singapore Airlines prior to delivery. Singapore Airlines holds a large stake in Virgin Atlantic, which also operates the A340-300.

and 600 series – with stretched fuselages and more powerful engines. The A340-600 entered service with launch customer Virgin Atlantic in autumn 2002 and has a range of 13,890km (8631 miles), while the A340-500 will be capable of 15,745km (9783 miles). Their advent opens up a new era of non-stop long-range passenger travel. Specifications apply to the Airbus A340-300.

Crew: 2
Powerplant: four CFM International CFM56-5C2 turbofans each rated at 138.78kN (31,200lb) or four CFM-5C3 turbofans each rated at 144.57kN (32,500lb st) or four CFM56-5C4 turbofans each rated at 151.24kN (34,000lb st)
Performance: max cruising speed 915km/h (569mph); range 12,416km (7710 miles) with 295 passengers and reserves for a 370km (230-mile)

diversion; service ceiling 12,495m (41,000 ft)
Dimensions: wingspan 60.30m (197ft 10in); length 63.65m (208ft 10in); height 16.74m (54ft 11in);
Weight: Between 257,000kg and 260,000kg (566,575lb and 573,200lb) maximum take-off weight
Payload: passenger accommodation (in typical mixed class) ranges from 263 (A340-200), 295 (A340-300), 316 (A340-500) and 372 (A340-600)

AIRCO DH.2

UK: 1915

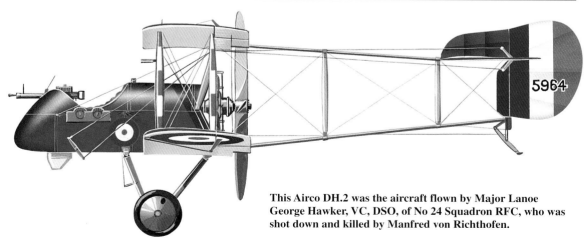

This Airco DH.2 was the aircraft flown by Major Lanoe George Hawker, VC, DSO, of No 24 Squadron RFC, who was shot down and killed by Manfred von Richthofen.

THE PROTOTYPE DH.2, DESIGNED by Geoffrey de Havilland, was sent to France for operational trials in July 1915. The type subsequently equipped No 24 Squadron, which

used it to counter the Fokker Monoplane. The squadron gained its first victory on 2 April 1916 and destroyed its first Fokker on the 25th of that month. From then on

No 24 Squadron's tally rose steadily, its pilots destroying 17 enemy aircraft in June 1916, 15 in August, 15 in September and 10 in November. On 23 November, No

---

24 Squadron's commander, Major L.G. Hawker, was shot down after a lengthy air battle by a German pilot who was destined to become the most famous of all: Manfred von Richthofen. After service on the Western Front, many DH.2s were sent to the Middle East where they saw service in Palestine and Macedonia. At home, 100 DH.2s were issued to training units, but all had been retired by the autumn of 1918. The DH.2 was the RFC's first dedicated fighter aircraft.

Crew: 1
Powerplant: one 75kW (100hp) Gnome Monosoupape piston or 82kW (110hp) Rhone rotary engine
Performace: max speed 150km/h (93mph); endurance 2 hrs 45 mins; service ceiling 1300m (4265ft)
Dimensions: wingspan 8.61m (28ft 3in); length 7.68m (25ft 2in); height 2.91m (9ft 6in)
Weight: 645kg (1421lb) loaded
Armament: one forward-firing 7.62mm (0.30in) Lewis gun on flexible mounting

AIRCO DH.4   UK: 1916

Crew: 2
Powerplant: various, but typically one 187kW (250hp) Rolls-Royce Eagle VI in-line engine
Performance: max speed 230km/h (143mph); endurance 3 hrs 45 mins; service ceiling 6705m (22,000ft);
Dimensions: wingspan 12.92m (42ft 4in); length 9.35m (30ft 8in); height 3.35m (11ft)
Weight: 1575kg (3472lb)
Armament: two fixed forward-firing 7.62mm (0.30in) Vickers machine guns; two 7.62mm (0.30in) Vickers machine guns in rear cockpit; provision for 209kg (460lb) of bombs on external pylons

ONE OF THE MOST OUTSTANDING combat aircraft produced during World War I, the DH.4 day bomber was built in large numbers: 1449 aircraft in Britain and 4846 in the USA, where many were powered by the excellent 298kW (400hp) Liberty 12 engine. The protoype DH.4 flew in August 1916, and pilots were unanimous in their praise of its fine handling qualities, wide speed range and a performance which made it almost immune from interception. The first DH.4s arrived in France with No 55 Squadron in March 1917 and began operations against German targets in April. In addition to its primary bombing role, the aircraft was used for photo-reconnaissance, long-range fighter sweeps and anti-submarine patrols. The DH.4 was widely used by the Royal Naval Air Service (RNAS), and on 15 August 1918 an aircraft from RNAS Great Yarmouth, flown by Major Egbert Cadbury, shot down the Zeppelin L.70. After the war, many DH.4s were used in civilian roles, such as crop-dusting, mail carriage and aerial survey.

The Airco DH.4 was without doubt the best Allied light bomber produced during World War I. It was first deployed to France in March 1917.

AIRCO DH.9/9A   UK: 1917

THE DH.9 ENTERED SERVICE with No 103 Squadron RFC at Old Sarum, Wiltshire, in December 1917, and became operational with No 6 Squadron in France in the following March. Fitted originally with a Beardmore engine, the aircraft proved to be underpowered and its performance was inferior to that of the DH.4, on which its design was based and which it was intended to replace. Engine failures were rife, and fuel consumption above 3050m (10,000ft) was a staggering 15 gallons per hour. Once the DH.9 was re-engined with the Packard Liberty motor, however, it became an entirely different aircraft.

RAF squadrons in France began re-arming with the new variant – designated DH.9A – in August 1918, and the type played an important part in the Allied bombing offensive until the end of World War I. Afterwards, RAF DH.9A squadrons performed a vital policing role in the British-

The Airco DH.9 was intended to supersede the DH.4 in the bombing role, but was underpowered and had a poor performance.

controlled territories in the Middle East and India throughout the 1920s. Many DH.9s were converted for civilian air transport use.

Crew: 2
Powerplant: one 313kW (420hp) Packard Liberty 12 V-type engine
Performance: max speed 198km/h (123mph); endurance 5 hrs 15 mins; service ceiling 5105m (16,750ft)
Dimensions: wingspan 14.01m (45ft 11in); length 9.22m (30ft 3in); height 3.45m (11ft 4in)
Weight: 2107kg (4645lb) loaded
Armament: one fixed forward-firing 7.62mm (0.30in) Vickers machine gun; one or two 7.62mm (0.30in) Lewis machine guns in rear cockpit; external ordnance up to 299kg (660lb)

AIRSPEED AS.5 COURIER

UK: 1933

THE COURIER REPRESENTS TWO important milestones: it was the first Airspeed type to be built in 'production' quantity – there were 16 built – and, while retaining a tail wheel, it was the first British design with a retractable main landing gear. The AS.5 was initially fitted with the less powerful Armstrong Siddeley Lynx IVC engine, but those exported to the Empire (as AS.5A) received the more powerful Cheetah. One

example was loaned to the RAF, but no orders were forthcoming. However, AS.5s did serve with the RAF during World War II, and there was only one post-war survivor. Specifications apply to the Airspeed AS.5B Courier.

The Courier below was the only example produced as an AS5C, principally different in having a Rapier engine driving a four- (as opposed to three-) bladed propeller.

Crew: 1
Powerplant: one Armstrong Siddeley Cheetah V radial piston engine rated at 227kW (305hp)
Performance: max speed 165mph (226km/h); range 1030km (640 miles); service ceiling 5180m (17,000ft)
Dimensions: wingspan 14.33m (47ft); wing area 23.23m² (250.00sq ft); length 8.69m (28ft 6in)
Weight: 1814kg (4000lb) maximum take-off weight
Payload: 5/6 people

AIRSPEED OXFORD

UK: 1937

Crew: 3
Powerplant: two 261kW (350hp)
Armstrong Siddeley Cheetah IX 7-cylinder
radial engines
Performance: max speed 298km/h
(182mph); range 1464km (910 miles);
service ceiling 5852m (19,200ft)
Dimensions: wingspan 16.25m (53ft 4in);
length 10.51m (34ft 6in); height 3.37m
(11ft 1in)
Weight: 3447kg (7600lb) loaded
Armament: none

THE AIRSPEED OXFORD advanced
trainer and air ambulance, known
as the 'Ox-Box' throughout the
RAF, appeared in 1937 and was a
military development of the civil
Envoy airliner. The Oxford was the
RAF's first twin-engined monoplane
trainer, and by the time production

ceased 8751 examples had been
built. The Oxford I was a bombing
and gunner trainer, featuring a
dorsal gun turret, while the Mk II
was used for navigation and radio
training. Widely employed at flying
schools throughout the British
Commonwealth as part of the

Empire Air Training Scheme, the
Oxford was used in the ambulance
role as the Mk III in the Middle
East. The Mk IV was a 'one-off'
used as an engine test-bed, while the
Mk V was used mainly in Rhodesia
and Canada. Specifications apply
to the Airspeed Oxford Mk I.

**This Oxford, a Mk II, belongs to an air navigation
school and carries an identifying number code, rather
than the more usual letters.**

ALBATROS D.III

GERMANY: 1917

THE FIRST OF THE ALBATROS 'V-
strutters', the Albatros D.III was
the most capable of all the Albatros
fighter designs produced during
World War I. The D.III was issued
to the *Jagdstaffeln* from January
1917, and within a few weeks all
37 Jastas on the Western Front
were armed with Albatros fighters
of one kind or another. The D.III

remained in service throughout the
year, 446 being delivered in total.
Albatros D.IIIs also operated
with the German Air Service in
Palestine and Macedonia, and
equipped some squadrons of the
Austro-Hungarian Air Arm. Some
Albatros D.IIIs were also supplied
to the newly established Polish Air
Force in 1919.

Crew: 1
Powerplant: one 131kW (175hp)
Mercedes D.IIIa 6-cylinder liquid-cooled
in-line engine
Performance: max speed 175km/h
(109mph); endurance 2 hrs; service
ceiling 5500m (18,044ft)
Dimensions: wingspan 9.05m (29ft 8in);
length 7.33m (24ft); height 2.98m
(9ft 9in)

Weight: 886kg (1949lb) loaded
Armament: two fixed forward-firing
7.92mm (0.31in) LMG 08/15
machine guns

**The Albatros D.III was the best
Albatros fighter design and saw
widespread service on the Western
Front and in Palestine and
Macedonia during 1917.**

ALBATROS D.VA

An Albatros D.Va being inspected by RAF personnel after the Armistice in 1918. About 3000 D.V/Vas were built, but the type suffered from structural weakness that limited its diving performance.

CHRONOLOGICALLY, THE NEXT aircraft in line after the Albatros D.III was the D.IV. This experienced many problems with its experimental Mercedes D.III engine and never entered production. The D.V was therefore the next production version, entering service in May 1917. It was quickly followed by the D.Va, which differed only in minor detail such as a revised aileron control system. By May 1918, 1512 D.Vs and D.Vas were in service on the Western Front,

but by this time were outclassed by the latest Allied fighter aircraft. Many more served in other theatres; although exact production figures are not known, the total built was probably in the region of 3000. The D.V/D.Va variants were operationally successful because of the numbers used, rather than their performance. For example, the type was subjected to limitations on diving manoeuvres, imposed after a series of crashes caused by failure of the single-spar lower wings.

Crew: 1
Powerplant: one 134kW (180hp) Mercedes D.IIIa 6-cylinder liquid-cooled in-line engine
Performance: max speed 186km/h (116mph); endurance 2 hrs; service ceiling 5700m (18,700ft)
Dimensions: wingspan 9.05m (29ft 8in); length 7.33m (24ft); height 2.70m (8ft 10in)
Weight: 937kg (2066lb) loaded
Armament: two fixed forward-firing 7.92mm (0.31in) LMG 08/15 machine guns

AMIOT 143

FIRST FLOWN IN APRIL 1935, the Amiot 143 was a re-engined version of the Amiot 140, the first of 135 examples being delivered to the Armee de l'Air in mid-1935. On 10 May 1940, when Germany invaded France and the Low Countries, this obsolescent type still equipped four Groupes de Bombardement, which suffered appalling losses in attacks on advancing enemy columns.

The Amiot 143M seen here belonged to the 3rd Escadrille of Groupe de Bombardement GB II/35, which was based at Pontarlier in September 1939.

Crew: 4–6
Powerplant: two 649kW (870hp) Gnome-Rhone Kirs 14-cylinder radial engines
Performance: max speed 310km/h (193mph); range 2000km (1243 miles); service ceiling 7900m (25,920ft)
Dimensions: wingspan 24.53m (80ft 5in);

length 18.26m (59ft 11in); height 5.68m (18ft 7in)
Weight: 6100kg (13,448lb) loaded
Armament: four 7.5mm (0.29in) MAC 1934 machine guns, one each in nose and dorsal turrets and fore and aft in ventral gondola; internal and external bomb load of up to 1600kg (3527lb)

AMIOT 354

DEVELOPED IN PARALLEL WITH the Amiot 351, the Amiot 354 differed principally from the other aircraft in that it featured a single- instead of a twin-fin tail unit, both being interchangeable. Orders totalling

890 examples were placed for both variants, but only about 40 aircraft, mostly Amiot 354s, had been delivered by 10 May 1940. These were used operationally, and only at night, by GB I, 21 and 24.

The graceful Amiot 354 was developed from the Amiot 350 fast mailplane, and was France's finest bomber of World War II.

Crew: 4
Powerplant: two 790kW (1060hp) Gnome-Rhone 14N 14-cylinder radial engines
Performance: max speed 480km/h (298mph); range 3500km (2175 miles); service ceiling 10,000m (32,808ft)
Dimensions: wingspan 22.83m (74ft 10in); length 14.50m (47ft 6in); height 4.08m (13ft 4in)
Weight: 11,300kg (24,916lb) loaded
Armament: one 20mm (0.79in) cannon and two 7.5mm (0.29in) machine guns; internal bomb load of 1200kg (2646lb)

ANF LES MUREAUX

DEVELOPED FROM 1928 ONWARDS, originally under the designation R.2, the Mureaux series of observation aircraft constituted the main equipment of the French Army's Groupes Aeriens d'Observation (GAO) in September 1939. The principal variants were the 115 and 117, built between 1936 and 1939. It was a Mureaux 115 of GAO 553 which, on 8 September 1939, had the dubious distinction of being the first aircraft to be destroyed by the Luftwaffe. During the 'Phoney War' period the Mureaux were progressively replaced by the Potez 63.11, but 110 were still in service

at the time of the German invasion of 10 May 1940. A few were used as makeshift night fighters.

Crew: 2
Powerplant: one 641kW (860hp) Hispano-Suiza 12-cylinder V liquid-cooled engine
Performance: max speed 317km/h (197mph); range 804km (500 miles); service ceiling 8000m (26,246ft)
Dimensions: wingspan 15.40m (50ft 6in); length 10.18m (33ft 4in); height 3.44m (11ft 2in)
Weight: 3450kg (7605lb) loaded
Armament: four or five 7.5mm (0.29in) machine guns; 400kg (882lb) of bombs

The ANF Les Mureaux 115 and 117 observation aircraft were widely used by the French Army in the years leading up to World War II.

ANSALDO A1 BALILLA

DURING WORLD WAR I, Italy's Corpo Aeronautica Militare had relied heavily on French-designed combat aircraft, with the exception

of bombers and naval types. The first Italian-designed fighter, the Ansaldo A1 Balilla (Hunter), did not enter service until 1918, and

only a small number of the 108 aircraft built reached the front-line squadrons. The Balilla was a small, single-bay biplane with equal-chord,

unstaggered wings and a hexagonal cutout in the upper wing trailing edge, providing good forward and upward views. Pilots were enthusiastic about the aircraft's high top speed, but critical of its handling characteristics and manoeuvrability. The majority of Balillas served on home defence duties in mid-1918.

This Ansaldo Balilla fighter was converted as a racing aircraft after World War I and fitted with a 298kW (400hp) Curtiss K-12 engine.

Crew: 1
Powerplant: one 164kW (220hp) SPA 6A water-cooled in-line engine
Performance: max speed 220km/h (137mph); endurance 1 hr 30 min; service ceiling 5000m (16,404ft)
Dimensions: wingspan 7.68m (25ft 2.33in); length 6.84m (22ft 5.25in); height 2.53m (8ft 3.66in)
Weight: 885kg (1951lb) loaded
Armament: two 7.62mm (0.30in) Vickers machine guns

ANTOINETTE MONOPLANES

FRANCE: 1908

INSPIRED BY AIRCRAFT AND engine designer Leon Le Vavasseur, the Antoinette Company created some notable monoplane designs between 1908 and 1912. The company's design approach drew from Le Vavasseur's experience of designing racing motorboats. The Antoinette monoplane aircraft had a large wing area, with a small triangular fuselage.

Early versions met with limited success, but the Antoinette IV first flew in October 1908 and went on to make over 50 flights, including a world distance record of 154.6km (96.06 miles) on the 26 August 1909. In concert with British associate and pilot Hubert Latham, the IV twice made unsuccessful attempts to cross the English channel. Latham and the IV did capture the height record at the

Reims Grande Semain d'Aviation de la Champagne that same year – achieving 155m (509ft).

Later Antoinette Monoplane versions utilized the then more conventional wing-warping techniques to replace the earlier wingtip aileron controls that Le Vavasseur had designed. Around the turn of the decade this successful team turned their

attention to military applications, but government orders were not forthcoming (see Antoinette-Latham Monobloc) and the company ceased to exist.

Specifications apply to the Antoinette IV.

Antoinette monoplanes played a huge part in developing the new science of flight.

Crew: 1
Powerplant: one 37kW (50hp) Antoinette 8-cylinder V-type engine
Performance: max speed 70km/h (43.5mph)
Dimensions: wingspan 12.80m (42ft); length 11.50m (37ft 8.75in)
Weight: not known

ANTONOV AN-2 (AN-3 AND AN-4) 'COLT'

UKRAINE: 1947

Crew: 1/2
Powerplant: one 746kW (1000hp) PZL Kalisz (shvetsov) Asz-621R 9-cylinder single-row radial piston engine
Performance: max speed 258km/h (160mph); range 900km (560 miles) with a 500kg (1102lb) payload; service ceiling 4400m (14,425ft)
Dimensions: wingspan 18.18m (59ft 7.75in); length 12.74m (41ft 9.5in); height 6.10m (20ft) with tail up
Weight: 5500kg (12,125lb) maximum take-off weight
Payload: 12 adults + 2 children, or freight

AFTER WORLD WAR II, Oleg Antonov left the Yakovlev design bureau and started his own. Its first task was to fulfil a requirement from the Soviet Agricultural and Forestry Ministry for a utility light transport – the An-2 metal biplane was the result. Today the An-2 is the world's largest operational biplane. Over 18,000 have been

produced to meet requirements as diverse as Aeroflot scheduled services, crop spraying and covert military operations. Built since 1947, the An-2 remains a current type today, having been built in Poland since 1960. Since 1947 a number of variants have been introduced. Specifications apply to the An-2P passenger model.

This Antonov An-2 is in the markings of DOSAAF, the Soviet paramilitary training organization.

AIRSPEED A.S.65 CONSUL
The Consul was a conversion of the wartime Airspeed Oxford trainer/ light transport. Conversions were carried out between 1946 and 1948, and produced a popular low-cost aircraft carrying six passengers. There were approximately 150 Consul conversions.

AIRSPEED A.S.57 AMBASSADOR
This twin piston-engined airliner entered service with BEA in 1952. BEA were the only 'first line' customer for this 47–60 seat airliner, and only 20 were built. The Elizabethan (as it was also known) went on to serve with other operators until 1971, when Dan Air retired the last example.

AIRTECH/CASA CN-235
The twin-engined CN-235 medium-haul military transport is produced jointly by Indonesia and Spain, and is also offered as a civil feeder-liner. Its first flight was in 1983.

ALBATROS B.II
Designed by Ernst Heinkel, the Albatros B.II of 1914 was the progenitor of a line of fighting aeroplanes whose names were to become legendary.

ALBATROS C.I
The Albatros C.I, which made its appearance in 1915, had excellent flight characteristics and an engine that was more powerful than almost any used by its adversaries.

ALBATROS C.III
Faster and more manoeuvrable than the C.I, the C.III was built in greater numbers than any other C-type Albatros and remained in German first-line service for about a year in 1915–16.

ALBATROS C.V
The Albatros C.V appeared early in 1916. It was slightly larger than the C.III, with a new, more powerful engine, and was almost completely redesigned.

ALBATROS C.VII
The C.VII was produced late in 1916 as an interim reconnaissance and artillery observation aircraft, powed by a 149kW (200hp) Benz Bz.IV engine.

ALBATROS D.I/D.II
The Albatros D.I appeared on the Western Front in September 1916. The D.II was similar, but had N-shaped struts between the fuselage and upper wing, and fuselage-side air intakes.

ANTONOV AN-10 UKRAINA 'CAT'

UKRAINE: 1957

Crew: up to 5
Powerplant: four 2980ekW (3996eshp) Ivchenko AI-20 turboprop engines
Performance: max cruising speed 680 km/h (423mph); range 4075km (2532 miles) service ceiling 12,000m (39,370ft)
Dimensions: wingspan 38.00m (124ft 8in); length 34.00m (111ft 6.5in); height 9.83m (30ft 3in)
Weight: 55,100kg (121,473lb) maximum take-off weight
Payload: 100 passengers

BOTH THE AN-10 AND AN-12 were successor developments to the earlier twin-engined An-8, but at the outset the An-10 was designed for commercial passenger transport. Enlargements and a powerplant change were made during the An-10's design, before delivery to Aeroflot in 1959. Most were delivered as the enlarged AN10A,

The An-10 entered service with Aeroflot, its only operator, in 1959. Note the stabilizing fin mounted on the rear underside of the fuselage to add stability.

but the type suffered serious stability problems resulting in the need to fit distinctive anhedral outer wing panels and vertical ventral fins to most aircraft. The 200-plus An-10s delivered became an important part of Aeroflot's passenger fleet. However, by 1972 investigations into An-10 accidents had revealed structural problems, and the type was quickly withdrawn from use. Specifications apply to An-10A.

ANTONOV AN-12 'CUB'

UKRAINE: 1957

Crew: up to 5
Powerplant: four 3170ekW (4252eshp) ZMDB Progress (Ivchyenko) AI-20M turboprop engines
Performance: max cruising speed 777km/h (482mph); range 3600km (2236 miles) with maximum payload; service ceiling 10,500m (34,450ft)
Dimensions: wingspan 38.00m (124ft 8in); length 33.10m (108ft 7.25in); height 10.53m (34ft 6.5in)
Weight: 61,000kg (134,480lb) maximum take-off weight
Payload: 100 paratroops or 20,000kg (44,092lb) of freight

THE PRINCIPAL DIFFERENCE between the Antonov An-12 and concurrent An-10 airliner was the rear fuselage design. Intended for roll-on/roll-off military and transport operations, the An-12 has a raked rear underside that incorporates a freight door leading to an interior primarily designed for freight carriage.

Initially created for military service, the An-12 was used in a number of roles other than troop/vehicle movement such as: aerial command post, ECM platform, classroom, tanker, VIP transport, and a bomber version realized from India's use of the type in that role in the 1971 war with Pakistan.

Over 1000 examples of the An-12 were built until 1973, and a third of these were produced as commercial freighters for domestic and export customers. Licenced production and derivation continues in China as the Shaanxi Y-8, which first flew in 1974. Today there remain significant numbers of An-12s engaged on freight duties in the CIS, the Middle East and Africa, where they often operate in rough field conditions on a variety of commercial or aid flights.

Specifications apply to the Antonov An-12BK.

Balkan Airlines of Bulgaria has operated a fleet of An-12s on cargo duties for many years, with numbers in the fleet peaking at six. The An-12 was exported to Soviet-influenced countries in appreciable numbers.

ANTONOV AN-24 'COKE'

Crew: 2/3
Powerplant: two 1670ekW (2250eshp) ZMDB Progress (Ivchenko) AI-24A turboprop engines
Performance: max cruising speed 450km/h (279mph); range 640km (397 miles) with maximum payload; service ceiling 8400m (27,560ft)
Dimensions: wingspan 29.20m (95ft 9.5in); wing area 72.46m² (779.98sq ft); length 23.53m (77ft 2.5in); height 8.32m (27ft 3.5in)
Payload: 44–52 passengers or 5700kg (12,566 lb freight)

THE AN-24 WAS DESIGNED to meet a wide utilization criteria, including operation from unpaved runways and extreme variations of airport temperature and altitude. Aeroflot began using the An-24 in 1963, and in the region of 1260 examples were produced in several variants up until 1978, including enhanced performance versions. A number of An-24s remain in service, often used in Africa on freight and aid missions. The An-24 was widely exported in the Eastern Bloc and licence-built as the Xian Y-7 in China.

Specifications apply to the An-24T.

This Antonov An-24 served as a staff transport with the reorganized Czech and Slovak Air Force.

2904

ANTONOV AN-22 ANTEI 'COCK'

WHEN IT FIRST APPEARED the An-22 was the largest and heaviest aircraft in existence. Its purpose was to lift both commercial and military loads of extraordinary weight or size, and it set some major logistical weight/altitude records in 1967. Visually the An-12 differed from its predecessors not just in size; it also had a twin tail unit to add stability, and its engines each have twin rows of propeller blades and some supplementary lifting devices to aid performance. The cockpit and cabin for up to 29 passengers is pressurized. Some versions have been built with the typical Soviet nose but others without. The An-22 has been operated by both Aeroflot and the Soviet/Russian Air Force (the latter from 1969) mostly in civilian colours to enable foreign airport access, but operational numbers have dropped markedly following introduction of the An-124. The numbers quoted as being built vary between 65 and 100, and the numbers still operational are equally contentious. In 2003 a commercial example operated by the Antonov Design Bureau remained extant, often carrying exceptional loads overseas along with Russian Air Force examples.

Specifications apply to the Antonov An-22M.

Crew: 5
Power plant: four 11,185kW (15,000shp) KKBM (Kuznetsov) NK-12MA turboprop engines
Performance: max cruising speed 740km/h (460mph); range 5000km (3106 miles) with maximum payload; service ceiling 7500m (24,605ft)
Dimensions: wingspan 64.40m (211ft 4in); length 57.92m (190ft); height 12.53m (41ft 1.5in);
Weight: 250,000kg (551,146lb) maximum take-off weight
Payload: 80,000kg (176,367lb) of freight

The prototype An-22 is pictured below in June 1965 at the Paris Air Show, where it was first displayed in the West.

ANTONOV AN-124 RUSLAN 'CONDOR'

UKRAINE: 1982

The An-124 illustrated was demonstrated at the 1985 Paris Air Show. The existence of the aircraft came as a shock to the Western world when it was unveiled in 1983.

THE EXISTENCE OF THIS – the world's largest production standard aircraft – shocked the Western world when it appeared in the early 1980s. The An-124 is designed for both commercial and military applications, and the aircraft's hinged nose and rear cargo door enable simultaneous entrance and egress. Historically, the An-124's military application loads include battle tanks. Its main deck possesses a titanium floor. This area is not fully pressurized, but there is also a fully pressurized upper deck capable of holding 88 people.

Although the Aeroflot fleet has declined in post-Soviet years, many of the 60-plus An-124s produced have now found wet-lease roles with companies that specialize in the handling of extraordinary freight loads around the world.

Crew: 6
Powerplant: four ZMKB Progress (Ivchyenko) D-18T turbofan engines each rated at 229.47kN (51,587lb st)
Performance: max cruising speed 865km/h (537mph); range 16,500km (10,250 miles)
Dimensions: wingspan 73.30m (240ft 5.25in); length 69.10m (226ft 8.5in); height 21.08m (69ft 2in)
Weight: 405,000kg (892,857lb) maximum take-off weight
Payload: up to 150,000kg (330,688lb)

ANTONOV AN-225 MRIYA

UKRAINE: 1988

Crew: 6
Powerplant: six 229.47kN (51,587lb st) ZMKB Progress (Lotarev) D-18T turbofan engines
Performance: max cruising speed 850km/h (528mph); range 4500km (2796 miles) with maximum payload.
Dimensions: wingspan 88.40m (290ft); length 84m (275ft 7in); height 18.20m (59ft 8.5in)
Weight: 600,000kg (1,322,275lb) maximum take-off weight
Payload: up to 250,000kg (551,250lb)

THE AN-225 IS THE WORLD'S largest aircraft, with a take-off weight in excess of 453,500kg (1,000,000lb). To date only a single example of the type has been completed. Apart from the increase from four to six engines, the An-225 visibly differs from the An-124 in having a redesigned tail unit featuring twin endplates and no rear ramp door. These features enable the carriage of the Russian space shuttle, *Buran*. Other differences include upper mid-section fixing points for the *Buran* and an increase in wingspan and wing area. The An-225 was placed in storage for the second half of the 1990s and only emerged again in

The Antonov An-225 Mriya – so far only one has been built – is an aircraft of impressive statistics. Its 32.65m (107ft) horizontal tail is wider than the wingspan of a Boeing 737-300.

2001. As well as moving heavy cargoes around the world, the aircraft has performed important humanitarian missions. On 11 December 2002 it left New York, bound for Africa, filled with toys and games for Ugandan children as part of the 'Operation Christmas Child' humanitarian initiative. Like many Russian designs of recent years, the An-225 has not realised its full commercial potential.

ARADO AR 68

GERMANY: 1934

ONE OF THE FIRST SINGLE-SEAT fighters to serve in the still-secret Luftwaffe, the prototype Arado Ar 68V-1 first flew in 1934, powered by a 492kW (660hp) BMW VI engine, and entered production in the same year. The main production models were the Ar 60E with the 455kW (610hp) Junkers Jumo 210B, the Ar 68F with the 503kW (675hp) BMW VI, and the Ar 68G with a 560kW (750hp) BMW VI. The Ar 68H was a one-off experimental version with an enclosed cockpit and a BMW 132 air-cooled radial engine. The Ar 68 was of wood and steel tube construction with fabric covering, and was a single-bay biplane with N-type interplane

The first prototype Arado Ar 68, D-IKIN. The second aircraft, Ar 68b
D-IVUS, was re-engined due to poor performance.

struts and a spatted cantilever
undercarriage. The type entered
service in 1935, but had been
relegated to the fighter training
role by September 1939.
Specifications apply to the Ar 68G.

Crew: 1
Powerplant: one 560kW (750hp) BMW VI
liquid-cooled V-type engine
Performance: max speed 305km/h
(190mph); range 415km (258 miles);
service ceiling 8100m (26,575ft)
Dimensions: wingspan 11m (36ft); length
9.5m (31ft 2in); height 3.28m (10ft 9in)
Weight: 2475kg (5457lb) loaded
Armament: two fixed forward-firing
7.92mm (0.31in) MG 17 machine guns

ARADO AR 95   GERMANY: 1936

Crew: 2
Powerplant: one 656kW (880hp) BMW
132De 9-cylinder radial engine
Performance: max speed 310km/h
(193mph); range 1100km (683 miles);
service ceiling: 7300m (23,945ft)
Dimensions: wingspan 12.5m (41ft);
length 11.1m (36ft 5in); height 3.6m
(11ft 9in)
Weight: 3560kg (7870lb) loaded
Armament: one fixed forward-firing
7.92mm (0.31in) MG 17 machine gun;
one flexible 7.92mm (0.31in) machine
gun in rear cockpit; underfuselage rack for
an 800kg (1764lb) torpedo or 500kg
(1102lb) of bombs

THE ARADO AR 95 WAS designed
as a two-seat torpedo-bomber and
reconnaissance biplane for service
aboard the German Navy's planned
aircraft carriers. The prototype Ar
95V-1 flew for the first time in the
autumn of 1936, fitted with twin

light metal floats. It saw limited
Luftwaffe service, mainly in the
Baltic. The Ar 95A was offered for
export but only Chile showed an
interest, buying three Ar 95A floatplanes and three Ar 95B landplanes.

**A development prototype of the
Arado Ar 95 patrol and light
attack floatplane, D-OHGV, is
pictured taxiing. Tested in the
Spanish Civil War, the Ar 95 was
not ordered for the German forces.**

ARADO AR 96   GERMANY: 1937

Crew: 2
Powerplant: one 336kW (450hp) Argus
As.410 12-cylinder air-cooled V-type
engine
Performance: max speed 340km/h
(211mph); range 990km (615 miles);
service ceiling 7100m (23,295ft)
Dimensions: wingspan 11m (36ft 1in);
length 9.13m (29ft 11in); height 2.6m
(8ft 6in)
Weight: 1695kg (3747lb) loaded
Armament: none

THE ARADO AR 96 WAS BY far the
most important advanced trainer
used by the Luftwaffe. The first of a
small batch of Ar 96A-1 production
aircraft flew in 1937, but the main
production series was the Ar 96B,

ordered in 1940. Very few Ar 96s
were built by Arado; until mid-1941
production was undertaken by the
Ago Flugzeugwerke, but most were

built by the Czechoslovak Avia
Company and Letov of Prague. By
the end of the war no fewer than
11,546 aircraft had been completed.

**A development prototype of the Arado Ar 96 trainer, D-IGME. Most
Ar 96s were built in Czechoslovakia by the Avia company.**

ARADO AR 196

Crew: 1
Powerplant: one 723kW (970hp) BMW 132K 9-cylinder radial engine
Performance: max speed 320km/h (199mph); range 1070km (665 miles); service ceiling 7000m (22,960ft)
Dimensions: wingspan 12.46m (40ft 8in); length 11.00m (36ft 1in); height 4.45m (14ft 7in);
Weight: 3730kg (8223lb) loaded
Armament: two 20mm (0.79in) fixed forward-firing cannon in wing; one 7.92mm (0.31in) machine gun in starboard side of forward fuselage; two 7.92mm (0.31in) machine guns in rear cockpit; external ordnance up to 100kg (220lb)

THE AR 196 RECONNAISSANCE floatplane was designed to replace the Heinkel He 50, a catapult-launched spotter biplane which was carried by major German warships in the 1930s. Arado's prototype Ar 196V-1 flew in the summer of 1938. A pre-production batch of 10 Ar 196A-0 aircraft was followed by 20 production Ar 196A-1s, which operated from Germany's capital ships.

The major production model was the Ar 196A-3, which saw extensive service in all theatres; on 5 May 1940 two examples achieved fame by accepting the surrender of HM submarine *Seal*, forced to the surface with mine damage in the Kattegat. Total production of the Ar 196, all variants, was 536, this total including 69 Ar 196A-5s which were built by Fokker in the Netherlands during 1943–44.

The Ar 196 was heavily armed and manoeuvrable, and could give a good account of itself when confronted by most Allied fighters.

ARADO AR 240

Crew: 4
Powerplant: two 802kW (1075hp) Daimler-Benz DB 601A in-line engines
Performance: max speed 618km/h (384mph); range 2000km (1242 miles); service ceiling 10,500m (34,450ft)
Dimensions: wingspan 13.33m (43ft 9in); length 12.8m (42ft); height 3.95m (12ft 11.5in)
Weight: 9450kg (20,834lb) loaded
Armament: two 20mm (0.79in) MG 151/20 cannon in the nose; two 7.9mm (0.31in) MG 17 machine guns in the wing roots; one 7.9mm MG 81 machine gun in a barbette either side of the fuselage

THE ARADO AR 240 MULTI-PURPOSE aircraft was designed in 1939. The first four prototypes

Seen here is the Ar 240V-3, which first flew in the spring of 1941. The type had poor flight characteristics and was not a success.

were fighters, the next four reconnaissance aircraft, and the final one a night-fighter. The type possessed poor flight characteristics, however, and was not successful. The initial production model, the Ar 240A-0, was a high-altitude reconnaissance aircraft, while the Ar 240B-0 was built in both fighter-bomber and reconnaissance versions. The Ar 240C was a projected multi-role model, while the Ar 240E and F were respectively bomber and fighter developments.

During operational trials, Arado Ar 240A-0s made reconnaissance sorties over both England and Russia. The first prototype flight was in May 1940.

ARADO AR 232

THE AR 232 MILITARY FREIGHTER, which flew early in 1941, was produced in two versions: the Ar 232A with two 1190kW (1595hp) BMW 801A or 801L engines, and the Ar 232B with four 895kW (1200hp) Bramo Fafnir 323 engines. One of the Ar 232's unusual features was its multi-wheel undercarriage, on which the whole aeroplane was lowered for loading or discharging freight. Only 22 examples of this heavy transport aircraft were built, these being issued to Transportgeschwader TG5 and the transport squadron of I/KG200, the Luftwaffe's special duties unit.

Specifications apply to the Arado Ar 232B.

Crew: 4

Powerplant: four 895kW (1200hp) Bramo 323-R Fafnir 9-cylinder radial engines

Performance: max speed 340km/h (211mph); range 1335km (830 miles); service ceiling 6900m (22,640ft)

Dimensions: wingspan 33.50m (109ft 10in); length 23.52m (77ft 2in); height 5.70m (18ft 8.4in)

Weight: 21,160kg (46,649lb) loaded

Armament: one 20mm (0.79in) cannon in dorsal turret; one 13mm (0.50in) machine gun in nose position; one or two 13mm machine guns in rear of fuselage pod

The Arado Ar 232 transport aircraft was used mainly on the Russian Front, where its multi-wheel undercarriage enabled it to operate from unprepared airstrips.

ARADO AR 234

GERMANY: 1943

THE AR 234 BLITZ (LIGHTNING) was the world's first operational jet bomber. The prototype Ar 234V-1, which flew for the first time on 15 June 1943, and the next seven aircraft (Ar 234V-2 to V-8) used a trolley-and-skid landing gear. A second prototype, the Ar 234V-2, was similar in all respects to the first machine, but the Ar 234V-3 was fitted with an ejection seat and rocket-assisted take-off equipment. The trolley-and-skid arrangement was later abandoned and with it the Ar 234A-1, as the initial production version was to have been designated, the aircraft being fitted with a conventional wheeled undercarriage. In this guise it was designated Ar 234B, of which 210 were built. Only two versions were used operationally: the Ar 234B-1 unarmed reconnaissance variant and the Ar 234B-2 bomber. The prototypes for the B series were the V-9 to V-16. One of these, the V-13, had four BMW 003A-1 engines in two paired nacelles, while the BMW-powered V-16 featured swept wing and tail surfaces and had rocket-assisted

take-off gear. It was planned to replace the B series in production with the C series, but only 19 production Ar 234C-3 bombers were completed when the war ended. The proposed initial production models, the Ar 234C-1 and C-2, were basically similar to the B-1 and B-2, with the addition of cabin pressurization and, in the case of the C-1, a pair of rearward-firing MG151/20 cannon. They were abandoned in favour of the multi-role version, the C-3, which appeared in the early part of 1945 and was intended to fulfil both bomber and night-fighter roles. The C-4 was to have been a single-seat reconnaisssance aircraft, while the C-5 and C-6 were two-seat bombers. The C-7 was a projected night-fighter model powered by four Heinkel-Hirth He SO11 engines; these were intended for the D series, but only two Ar 234D-1 reconnaissance aircraft were completed with this powerplant. The projected Ar 234D-2 was a bomber variant.

The first operational Ar 234 sorties were flown by the V-5 and

V-7 prototypes, delivered to I/Versuchsverband.Ob.d.L (Luftwaffe High Command Trials Unit) at Juvincourt, near Reims, in July 1944. Both aircraft were fitted with Walter rocket-assisted take-off units and made their first reconnaissance sorties on 20 July, photographing harbours on the south coast of England from an altitude of 9000m (29,530ft). Several more sorties were made over the United Kingdom before the unit was transferred to Rheine in September. Other reconnaissance trials units received the Ar 234, and in January 1945 these were amalgamated into I/F.100 and I/F.123 at Rheine, and I/F.33 at Stavanger, Norway. The latter unit flew reconnaissance sorties over the British naval base at Scapa Flow in the Orkneys until mid-April 1945. The bomber version of the Ar 234 equipped KG 76 from October 1944, flying its first operational missions during the Ardennes offensive in December. The jet bombers were very active in the early weeks of 1945, one of

An Arado Ar 234B-0 of the Luftwaffe Trials Unit at Rechlin in the summer of 1944.

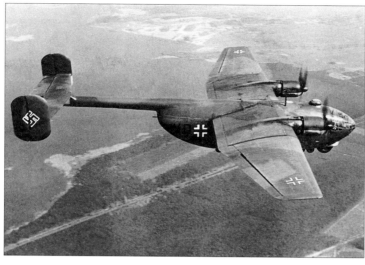

An early Ar 234A prototype leaving its launching trolley. Note the extended landing skid. The trolley-and-skid arrangement was later abandoned and a conventional tricycle undercarriage fitted.

their most notable missions being the 10-day series of attacks on the Ludendorff bridge at Remagen, captured by the Americans in March 1945. Very few Ar 234 sorties were flown after the end of March, although an experimental Ar 234 night-fighter unit, the Kommando Bonow, equipped with two Ar 234s converted to carry upward-firing cannon, continued to operate until the end of the war.

Specifications apply to the Arado Ar 234B-2.

Crew: 1
Powerplant: two 800kg (1764lb) thrust BMW 003A-1 turbojets
Performance: max speed 742km/h (461mph); range 1630km (1013 miles); service ceiling 10,000m (32,810ft)
Dimensions: wingspan 14.11m (46ft 3.5in); length 12.64m (41ft 5.6in); height: 4.30m (14ft 1in)
Weight: 9850kg (21,715lb) loaded
Armament: two fixed rearward-firing 20mm (0.79in) MG 151 cannon in underside of rear fuselage; external bomb load of 1500kg (3307lb)

ARMSTRONG WHITWORTH FK.8

UK: 1916

Crew: 2
Powerplant: one 119kW (160hp) Beardmore water-cooled in-line engine
Performance: max speed 153km/h (95mph); endurance 3 hrs; service ceiling 3690m (12,106ft)
Dimensions: wingspan 13.26m (43ft 6in); length 9.58m (31ft 5in); height 3.33m (10ft 11in)
Weight: 1275kg (2811lb) loaded
Armament: one fixed forward-firing 7.62mm (0.30in) Vickers machine gun; one 7.62mm (0.30in) Lewis machine gun in rear cockpit

DESIGNED BY THE TALENTED Dutchman Frederick Koolhoven, the FK.8 was basically a scaled-up version of the earlier FK.3. Used in

the army cooperation role by the RFC, it entered service with No 35 Squadron, which deployed to France in January 1917. It subsequently served with Nos 2, 8, 10 and 82 Squadrons on the Western Front, and was also issued to Nos 17 and 47 Squadrons in Macedonia and No 142 Squadron in Palestine. The FK.8 was highly regarded by its crews. On 27 March 1918, an FK.8 of No 2 Squadron, flown by 2nd Lt A.A. McLeod with Lt A.W. Hammond as his observer, was attacked by eight Fokker DR.Is and shot four down. McLeod brought down his burning aircraft, despite being badly wounded, and was awarded the Victoria Cross.

Known universally as the 'Big Ack', the Armstrong Whitworth FK.8 was one of the best army cooperation aircraft to see service in World War I.

ARMSTRONG WHITWORTH SISKIN III

UK: 1923

Crew: 1
Powerplant: one 317kW (425hp)
Armstrong Siddeley Jaguar IVS 14-cylinder
radial engine
Performance: max speed 251km/h
(156mph); range 450km (280 miles);
service ceiling 8230m (27,000ft)
Dimensions: wingspan 10.11m (33ft 2in);
length 7.72m (25ft 4in); height 3.10m
(10ft 2in)
Weight: 1366kg (3012lb) loaded
Armament: two 7.62mm (0.30in)
Vickers machine guns in front fuselage;
provision for four 9kg (20lb) bombs under
lower wing

The Siddeley 2R Siskin was the prototype of the Armstrong Whitworth Siskin III which served with the RAF in the 1920s.

THE SISKIN FIGHTER OF THE 1920s
had its origin in the Siddeley 2R,
which flew in 1919 and was named
Siskin. Two civilian Siskin IIs
were built, and one of these, a
single-seater, served as a prototype
fighter. First production version for
the RAF was the Siskin III and was
a complete redesign. An all-metal
biplane with fabric covering, the
aircraft entered service with No 41
Squadron in May 1924. Two
squadrons used the Siskin III (70
built) and nine more the IIIA
(382 built). The Siskin was also used
by the Royal Canadian Air Force.

ARMSTRONG WHITWORTH WHITLEY

UK: 1936

The Armstrong Whitworth Whitley was one of the RAF's standard heavy bomber types at the outbreak of World War II. Its very long range enabled it to fly from England to Czechoslovakia and back.

DESIGNED TO SPECIFICATION
B.3/34, the prototype Whitley
heavy bomber flew on 17 March
1936, first deliveries being made to
No 10 Squadron RAF Bomber
Command in March 1937. Early
marks were powered by Armstrong
Siddeley Tiger radial engines, but
later variants were completed with
Rolls-Royce Merlins. The main
wartime version was the Mk V, of
which 1466 were produced, and
together with the Handley Page
Hampden and Vickers Wellington
the type sustained the RAF's

strategic bombing offensive in the
early part of World War II. The
Whitley VII was a general reconnaissance version for RAF Coastal
Command, equipped with Anti
Surface Vessel (ASV) radar. Bomber
Command's Whitleys carried out
some notable long-range missions,
including the first raid on Italy in
June 1940. The type was also used
for special operations, and after
being withdrawn from first-line
service was used in transport and
glider-tug roles. Whitley production
totalled 1824 aircraft.

Crew: 5
Powerplant: two 802kW (1075hp) Rolls-
Royce Merlin X V-type in-line engines
Performance: max speed 370km/h
(230mph); range 3862km (2400 miles);
service ceiling 7925m (26,000ft)
Dimensions: wingspan 25.60m (84ft);
length 21.49m (70ft 6in); height 4.57m
(15ft)
Weight: 15,195kg (33,500lb) loaded
Armament: one fixed forward-firing
7.62mm (0.30in) Vickers machine gun in
nose; four 7.62mm (0.30in) Browning
machine guns in tail turret; up to 3175kg
(7000lb) of bombs internally

ARMSTRONG WHITWORTH A.W.27 ENSIGN

UK: 1938

THE ENSIGN'S ORIGINS LIE in a
British government directive that
all first-class mail between points
in the Empire should travel by air.

To meet this requirement, Imperial
Airways first issued a specification
in 1934 to which Armstrong
Whitworth responded with the

A.W.27 Ensign design – a passenger
airliner capable of lifting Empire
mail requirements. Development of
this high-wing design was slow

ARADO AR 81
Designed to the same specification
as the Junkers Ju 87 dive-bomber,
by which it was outclassed during
competitive trials, the Arado Ar 81
biplane first flew in 1935.

ARADO AR 195
Intended for operation from
Germany's proposed aircraft
carriers, the Ar 195 floatplane flew
in 1937 but did not go into
production, only three prototypes
being built.

ARADO AR 197
First flown in 1937, the Ar 197
biplane was intended as a carrier-
based interceptor and light bomber.
Three prototypes only were built.

ARADO AR 198
A shoulder-wing monoplane with a
glazed ventral fuselage section, the
Arado Ar 198 was designed as a
short-range reconnaissance aircraft,
but it was unsuccessful in this role.
It flew in 1938.

ARADO AR 199
Flown in 1939, the Ar 199 was a
single-engined floatplane trainer
monoplane. Although a successful
design, it did not enter production.

ARADO AR 231
A small parasol monoplane, the
Ar 231 could be 'collapsed' and
packed into a container for stowage
aboard U-boats. Six prototypes
were completed in 1941.

ARADO AR 233
The Arado Ar 233 was a twin-
engined utility amphibian project
of 1940. It was cancelled in favour
of a more modern design, the
Ar 430, which was also abandoned.

ARADO AR 396
The Ar 396 trainer, designed in
1942 and first flying in 1944, was
intended to replace the Ar 96 in
Luftwaffe service. Post-war, the
Ar 396 was produced by the
French SIPA company.

ARDC RP-440 OMEGA
American flying crane helicopter
which flew for the first time on
26 December 1956.

ARMSTRONG WHITWORTH FK.3
Developed in the late summer of
1915, the Armstrong Whitworth
FK.3 was used as a reconnaissance
bomber by the RFC. Production
totalled 499 aircraft.

Illustrated above is the first Ensign, which was built at Hamble near Southampton and first flew on 24 January 1938. During World War II this aircraft saw service in the Middle East.

due to compounded design changes from Imperial Airways, but there were a number of innovations, such as quick-change cabin configuration and an APU to provide power during technical stops. A total of 14 Ensigns were built, with the last being delivered in 1941. There were early engine reliability problems and these required heavy modification – the last two (military) examples were fitted with Wright Cyclones.

World War II saw the Ensigns pressed into RAF service, in which their capacity proved useful. One captured example was operated by the Vichy French and later by the Luftwaffe. A number of Ensigns survived World War II; however, there was no place for this, the last Empire service airliner, in post-war Britain.

Specifications apply to the Ensign Mk I.

Crew: 5
Powerplant: four 634kW (850hp) Armstrong Siddeley Tiger IXC radial engines
Performance: max speed 330km/h (205mph); range 1384km (860 miles); service ceiling 5485m (18,000ft)
Dimensions: wingspan 37.49m (123ft); length 34.75m (114ft); height 7.01m (23ft); wing area 227.62m² (2450sq ft)
Weight: 22,222kg (49,000lb) maximum take-off weight
Payload: 40 passengers in 'western' layout or 27 passengers in 'eastern' layout

ARMSTRONG WHITWORTH A.W.650 AND A.W.660 ARGOSY   UK: 1959

The Argosy was nicknamed the 'Whistling Wheelbarrow' due to its ungainly shape and noisy turboprop engines. The Series 222 Argosy pictured was delivered to BEA in 1965. After service in Canada and Ireland, in 1973 it was sold to Safe Air in New Zealand and named *Merchant Pioneer*.

ARGOSY WAS THE LAST AIRCRAFT to bear the Armstrong Whitworth name before the company was subsumed into Hawker Siddeley in 1963. The Argosy was a response

to a 1955 Air Ministry requirement for a freighter for civil and military applications. The innovative design that followed offered a rear loading door and ramp by means of a twin

boom and fin arrangement. Surprisingly, the first order (for seven 100 series units) came from Riddle Airlines of the USA in 1961. However, 56 of the 73 examples

produced were ordered by the RAF and were designated A.W.660 or Argosy C.Mk 1. Three further 100 series examples were purchased by British European Airways, but in

44

1965 it traded them in for the more powerful and refined 200 (222) series, of which BEA purchased six examples. The last operational Argosy was retired in 1992.

Specifications apply to the Argosy Series 100.

Crew: 3/4
Powerplant: four 1506kW (2020shp) Rolls-Royce Dart Mk 526 turboprop engines
Performance: cruising speed 451km/h (280mph); range 3219km (2000 miles); service ceiling 6096m (20,000ft)

Dimensions: wingspan 35.05m (115ft); length 26.44m (86ft 9in); height 8.92m (29ft 3in)
Weight: 39,916kg (88,000lb) maximum take-off weight
Payload: up to 12,701kg (28,000lb) of freight or 89 passengers

ATLAS CHEETAH
SOUTH AFRICA: 1986

The Atlas Cheetah was an upgraded version of the Mirage III, produced for the South African Air Force because of an arms embargo that precluded the acquisition of combat aircraft from overseas.

RESEMBLING ISRAEL'S IAI KFIR, the Atlas Cheetah was a direct result of the UN arms embargo imposed on South Africa in 1977. Anxious to upgrade its fleet of ageing Mirage III aircraft, the South African Air Force (SAAF) embarked on a major modification programme that involved the rebuilding of some 50 per cent of the original Mirage airframe, incorporating modifications that

included the addition of intake-mounted canards and dogtooth leading edges. Named Cheetah, the modified aircraft also featured new navigation and weapon systems.

The first aircraft, modified from a Mirage IIID2, was declared operational in July 1987, and 30 aircraft in all were eventually returned to service in their new guise. Both single- and two-seat Mirages were modified.

Crew: 1/2
Powerplant: one 7200kg (15,873lb) thrust SNECMA Atar 9K-50 turbojet
Performance: max speed 2337km (1452mph); combat radius 1200km (745 miles); service ceiling 17,000m (55,775ft)
Dimensions: wingspan 8.22m (26ft 11in); length 15.40m (50ft 6in); height 4.25m (13ft 11in)
Weight: classified
Armament: two 30mm (1.18in) DEFA cannon; external stores

AUSTER AOP.3–AOP.9
UK: 1943–1954

THE AUSTER AOP.3 WAS THE first in a series of air observation posts designed by Auster Aircraft Ltd. It saw wartime service from 1943 and evolved into the AOP.6, of which 296 examples were built for the RAF and the Belgian Air Force, together with 36 of a

slightly modified version for the RCAF. The AOP.7 was a two-seat dual-control trainer version, while the AOP.8 was intended to combine the features of both Mk.6 and Mk.7, but was not furthered. Last in the series was the AOP.9, a tough and versatile monoplane

which first flew on 19 March 1954 and incorporated many lessons learned during the Korean War, in which the AOP.6 was used extensively by the British Army for artillery spotting and other duties. The first AOP.9s were issued to RAF units at the beginning of

1954, and a second order followed in 1959. Austers of various marks were also used by Iraq, Jordan, Rhodesia and South Africa.

Specifications apply to the Auster AOP.9.

Crew: 2/3
Powerplant: one 135kW (180hp) Blackburn Cirrus Bombardier 203 4-cylinder in-line engine
Performance: max speed 204km/h (127mph); range 395km (246 miles);

service ceiling 5640m (18,504ft)
Dimensions: wingspan 11.10m (36ft 5in); length 7.21m (23ft 8in); height 2.56m (8ft 5in)
Weight: 966kg (2130lb) loaded
Armament: none

The Auster AOP.9 was the last of the Auster variants to serve with Britain's Army Air Corps. It remained in service until the 1960s, when it was replaced by rotary-wing types.

AVIA BH.3

CZECHOSLOVAKIA: 1921

THE AVIA COMPANY WAS CREATED in 1919 by the new Czech government in what had been a sugar factory at Cakovice, on the east side of Prague. It brought together a design team led by P. Benes and M. Hajn, hence the letters BH that prefixed the company's early aircraft designations. The first of these was the BH-1 light aircraft, from which Avia went on to develop the BH-3 fighter monoplane in 1921. Fast and highly manoeuvrable, with a 138kW (185hp) BMW IIIa engine that gave it a top speed of 214km/h (133mph), the Avia BH.3 was one of the most advanced warplanes of its day. Five were built with this powerplant, followed by five more fitted with a 164kW (220hp) Walter

W.IV, which raised the maximum speed to 225km/h (140mph). These aircraft were followed by a biplane fighter, the BH.21 of 1924, with a

The Avia BH.3 was a fast fighter monoplane which, in 1921, was one of the most advanced warplanes of its time.

224kW (300hp) Skoda (licence-built Hispano) engine. About 120 were built for the Czech Army Aviation; 50 more were produced under licence by SABCA for the Belgian Air Force. Specifications apply to the BH.1 and BH.21.

Crew: 1
Powerplant: one 224kW (300hp) Skoda in-line engine
Performance: max speed 245km/h (152mph); endurance 2 hrs; service ceiling 5500m (18,045ft)
Dimensions: wingspan 8.90m (29ft 2.5in); length 6.87m (22ft 6.5m); height 2.74m (9ft)
Weight: 1084kg (2390lb) loaded
Armament: two 7.7mm (0.303in) Vickers machine guns

AVIA B.534

CZECHOSLOVAKIA: 1933

Crew: 1
Powerplant: one 634kW (850hp) Hispano-Suiza HS 12Y in-line engine
Performance: max speed 394km/h (245mph); range 580km (360 miles); service ceiling 10,600m (34,777ft)
Dimensions: wingspan 9.40m (30ft 10in); length 8.20m (26ft 10in); height 3.10m (10ft 2in)
Weight: 2120kg (4674lb) loaded
Armament: four fixed forward-firing 7.7mm (0.303in) Model 30 machine guns; underwing racks for up to six 20kg (44lb) bombs

Probably the finest fighter biplane ever built, and one of the last mass-produced biplane fighters, the Avia B.534 first flew in August 1933, and an initial order for 100 machines was placed by the Czech

Pictured above is the first prototype Avia B.534, which flew in 1933. The B.534 was probably the finest biplane fighter ever built. The side view (below) shows the extremely clean lines of the Avia B.534, which became the standard fighter type of the Czech Air Force. It was later used as an advanced trainer by the Germans.

Army Air Force. Early B.534s had an open cockpit, but a sliding hood was introduced on later aircraft. First deliveries were made in the second half of 1935. In 1937 a

B.534 took part in the International Air Meeting at Zurich and outperformed everything except the Messerschmitt Bf 109 – even then it was only 11km/h (7mph) slower than the German fighter. The B.534 was adopted by the Czech Army Air Force as its standard fighter type, and also served in

Bulgaria and with the Luftwaffe, which used it as an advanced trainer. In 1939, after the German occupation of Bohemia and Moravia, large numbers of B.534s were acquired by the Slovak Air Force, which later used them against the Russians. Total B.534 production was 445 aircraft.

AVIAN 2/180 GYROPLANE

CANADA: 1960

Crew: 2/3
Powerplant: one 149kW (200hp) Lycoming 10-360 4-cylinder engine
Performance: max speed 193km/h (120mph); range 644km (400 miles); service ceiling 4265m (14,000ft)
Dimensions: main rotor diameter 11.27m (37ft); length 4.93m (16ft 2in); height 2.92m (9ft 7in)
Weight: 590kg (1300lb)

The innovative Avian Model 2/180 wingless gyroplane. Only two prototypes and three pre-production examples were built.

ARMSTRONG WHITWORTH AW.35 SCIMITAR
The Armstrong Whitworth AW.35 Scimitar was a biplane fighter of 1931, powered by a 477kW (640hp) AS Panther engine. Four were exported to Norway.

ARMSTRONG WHITWORTH ATALANTA
This four-engined high-wing monoplane design first flew in 1932. Eight were produced for Imperial Airways, initially for European services, but later across the Empire.

ARMSTRONG WHITWORTH AW.23
The AW.23 was a prototype bomber, flown in 1935. Only one was built, and used in flight refuelling experiments.

ARMSTRONG WHITWORTH AW.29
The AW.29, flown in 1937, was built in response to a British Air Ministry requirement for a long-range, single-engined day bomber. One prototype only was produced.

ARMSTRONG WHITWORTH ALBEMARLE
Conceived originally as a medium bomber, the Albemarle flew in March 1940 and served from 1943 as a transport and glider tug.

ARMSTRONG WHITWORTH AW.52
An experimental jet-powered flying wing design, the AW.52 flew in 1947 and was the first British aircraft to have an ejection seat.

ARROW AIRCRAFT AND MOTOR CORPORATION SPORT
This American designed single-engined two-seat sports biplane was produced during the late 1920s.

ARROW AIRCRAFT (LEEDS) LTD ACTIVE
A British designed, single-seat sports biplane designed and built in 1931. The first example was accidentally written off in 1935, while the second (Active II) example is still airworthy today.

ARSENAL VG.30 SERIES
The French Arsenal VG.30 series of fighters (VG.33, VG.36 and VG.39) were all tested in prototype form, but development was halted by the German invasion of France.

THE AVIAN 2/180 GYROPLANE was a wingless gyroplane with vertical take-off and landing (VTOL) capability developed by Avian Aircraft Ltd. Two prototypes were built and a flight-testing programme commenced in spring 1960. In January 1962 the first of three pre-production prototype/demonstrators began flight. These differed from the production model in having a shaft drive to the rotor, whereas the production model had compressed air nozzles at the blade tips and no form of mechanical drive. After the rotor was de-clutched from the engine to auto-rotate, twin-shrouded fans or airscrews at the rear of the fuselage provided forward thrust.

AVIAT PITTS S-2 SPECIAL

USA: 1971

Crew: 1/2
Powerplant: one 149kW (200hp) Avco Lycoming IO-360-A1A flat-four piston engine
Performance: max speed 253km/h (157mph); range 552km (343 miles); service ceiling 6125m (20,100ft)
Dimensions: wingspan 6.10m (20ft); length 5.41m (17ft 9in); height 1.94m (6ft 4.5in)
Weight: 1355kg (2987lb) maximum take-off weight
Payload: 2 people and luggage

THE PITTS SPECIAL BIPLANE has enlivened many an air show with stunning aerobatic qualities and inverted flying since its appearance in the 1970s. It has its origins in aerobatic designs by Curtis Pitts

The Rothmans Pitts Special team became a popular feature at British and European air shows during the 1970s.

dating back to 1947. Pitts also made plans available to amateur builders, particularly for the S1. In 1971 the Pitts moved in with an agricultural aircraft facility at Afton Wyoming; the newly designed S2A was produced thereon in certified form. The two-seat S2A could be used in either aerobatic or aerobatic training roles and was a major leap forward for American aerobatic design. Aviat Inc. acquired the facility in 1991 and the S2C version remains available to date. Specifications apply to the Pitts S-2A Special.

AVIATIK B.I–B.III

GERMANY/AUSTRIA: 1914–15

Crew: 2
Powerplant: one 75kW (100hp) Mercedes 6-cylinder liquid-cooled in-line engine
Performance: max speed 100km/h (62mph); endurance 4 hrs; service ceiling not known
Dimensions: wingspan 13.97m (45ft 10in); length 7.97m (26ft 2in); height 3.30m (10ft 10in)
Weight: 1088kg (2400lb) loaded
Armament: none

THE EARLY PRODUCTS OF THE German Automobil und Aviatik AG of Leipzig were copies of French designs, but in 1914 the company built a small, two-seat reconnaissance biplane designated B.I, which was powered by a 75kW (100hp) Mercedes engine and was used in small numbers in the air observation role on the Western Front in the early months of World War I. The type was based on a 1913 design for a racing biplane, the observer being seated in the front cockpit. In 1915 the

company's Austrian subsidiary, the Oesterreichische-Ungarische Flugzeugfabrik Aviatik of Vienna, built a variation of the basic design featuring horn-balanced, overhung ailerons. Designated B.II, the aircraft was fitted with a 89kW (120hp) Austro-Daimler engine and was armed in the sense that the observer carried a rifle and a pair of 10kg (22lb) bombs, which were dropped by hand.

The B.III was an improved version with a 119kW (160hp) Austro-Daimler engine and wings of increased span. The type also

The Aviatik reconnaissance biplanes saw widespread service on all fronts during World War I. Seen here is a B.III.

featured a single communal cockpit, in which the observer – now armed with a Schwarzlose machine gun on a flexible mounting – sat behind the pilot. The B.II saw a good deal of operational service on the Eastern Front, its excellent endurance making it ideal for long reconnaissance flights over the Russian lines. Its main drawback was that it was unstable, particularly in gusty conditions, which made life uncomfortable for the crew. As a consequence, Aviatik produced a second series of B.II airframes, incorporating the 119kW (160hp) Austro-Daimler engine and the machine gun installation of the B.III. Armament was increased to three 20kg (44lb) bombs. In its new form the B.II (known as the Series 34) was much more stable in flight, was faster than the B.III and could climb to twice the altitude of the original B.II.

Specifications apply to the B.I.

AVIATIK C SERIES

GERMANY: 1915

THE C.I RECONNAISSANCE BIPLANE was the first Aviatik aircraft designed from the outset for military use. Developed early in 1915, it was virtually a direct descendant of the B.II, with a similar cockpit arrangement, and although the observer in the front cockpit was armed with a machine gun his field of fire was severely restricted. In the C.Ia the layout was reversed, being similar to that of the B.III. Construction was of wood and fabric, with an aluminium engine bay and tailskid landing gear. Production soon switched to the C.II, with a 149kW (200hp) Benz Bz.IV engine and significantly revised tail surfaces. The most widely used variant was the C.III,

The Austro-Hungarian aero industry produced few world-class warplanes during World War I, but the Aviatik C.I was one of them.

which had reduced-span wings, streamlined nose, an improved exhaust system and a two-gun armament. The type C Aviatik was mainly used during 1916.

Specifications apply to the C.I.

Crew: 2
Powerplant: one 89kW (120hp) Mercedes D.II 6-cylinder in-line engine
Performance: max speed 142km/h (89mph); endurance 3 hrs; service ceiling 3500m (11,483ft)

Dimensions: wingspan 12.50m (41ft); length 7.92m (26ft); height 2.95m (9ft 8in)
Weight: 1340kg (2954lb) loaded
Armament: one 7.92mm (0.31in) Parabellum machine gun on flexible mount

AVIONS FAIREY FOX

BELGIUM: 1933

IN SEPTEMBER 1931 the Fairey Aviation Company of Great Britain set up a daughter enterprise in Belgium, Avions Fairey, to build a private-venture fighter (the Firefly). Firefly production for the Belgian Aeronautique Militaire was followed in 1933 by manufacture of 28 examples of the Fairey Fox II light bomber. Although the aircraft was an outstanding success, the RAF ordered only enough to equip a single squadron, and so Fairey offered the type to Belgium, which

also ordered enough aircraft to equip one squadron. The type then went into production in Belgium, 40 Fox IIs being delivered. A fighter-reconnaissance version was also built, the Fox VI, with an enclosed cockpit. The last version was the Fox VIII, which equipped one squadron in 1938–39. A small number of Foxes saw action during the German invasion of May 1940, but were quickly overwhelmed. The total number of Foxes of all versions built in Belgium was 176.

Crew: 2
Powerplant: one 642kW (860hp) Hispano-Suiza 12 Ydrs 12-cylinder V-type engine
Performance: max speed 360km/h (224mph); endurance 2 hrs 55 mins; service ceiling 10,000m (32,808ft)
Dimensions: wingspan 11.55m (37ft 0.75in); length 9.37m (30ft 9in); height 3.51m (11ft 6.25in)
Weight: 2345kg (5170lb) loaded
Armament: one 7.62mm (0.30in) FN-Browning machine gun on either side of front fuselage, and one in rear cockpit

The Fairey Fox biplane light bomber served with the Belgian Air Force throughout the 1930s. The pilot in the cockpit of this example is Willy Coppens, Belgium's leading air ace of World War I.

AVIONS DE TRANSPORT REGIONAL ATR 42

FRANCE/ITALY: 1984

Crew: 2
Powerplant: two 1491kW (2000shp) Pratt & Whitney Canada PW120 turboprop engines
Performance: max cruising speed 490km/h (305mph); range 1944km (1208 miles); service ceiling 7620m (25,000ft)
Dimensions: wingspan 24.57m (80ft 7.5in); length 22.67m (74ft 0.5in); height 7.59m (24ft 10.75in; 16,700kg (36,817lb) maximum take-off weight
Payload: up to 50 passengers

THE ATR SERIES OF REGIONAL airliners is the result of collaboration between France's Aerospatiale and Italy's Aeritalia (now part of Alenia). Both were engaged in designing for a similar requirement and they subsequently came together to develop the ATR 42. Production was set up at Toulouse, France, where the airframe is built. Aeritalia is responsible for hydraulic, pressurization and air-conditioning systems. During the design phase there were a number of capacity requirement changes, resulting in successive ATR 42 versions being launched with uprated powerplants. Since going into service in 1985, over 350 ATR 42s have been built for freight passenger and combi roles. Specifications apply to the ATR 42-310.

Air Mauritius acquired this ATR 42 in 1986 for inter-island services in the Indian Ocean.

AVRO TYPE D

UK: 1911

THE TYPE D IS NOTABLE in two respects. First, the prototype was at one point fitted with floats to make the first British take-off from water (on 18 November 1911). Secondly, it was a biplane rather than A.V. Roe's previous triplane wing designs. It is believed that six examples of the Type D, with its triangular shape fuselage, were manufactured. They were all different, including one example

The Avro Type D was jointly designed by Briton Alliott Verdon Roe with Australian pioneer John Duigan.

with a 45kW (60hp) engine that was intended to compete in the Daily Mail Air Race, but suffered a prior accident. The Avro Type D was the company's first successful and (semi) production standard design. Avro went on to design the Lancaster bomber.

Crew: 1
Powerplant: one 26kW (35hp) Green in-line piston engine
Performance: max speed 78km/h (48mph) at sea level; range 1030km (640 miles)
Dimensions: wingspan 9.45m (31ft); length 8.53m (28ft); height 2.79m (9ft 2in)
Payload: 2 persons

AVRO 504

UK: 1913

Crew: 2
Powerplant: one 119kW (160hp) Armstrong Siddeley Lynx IV rotary engine
Performance: max speed 130km/h (80mph); range: 402km (250 miles); service ceiling 4450m (14,600ft)
Dimensions: wingspan 10.97m (36ft); length: 8.69m (28ft 6in); height: 3.33m (10ft 11in)
Weight: 1016kg (2240lb) loaded
Armament: none

THE AVRO 504, WHICH first flew at Brooklands in July 1913, was a straightforward development of the Type E, which was already on order for the Royal Flying Corps. In a production life spanning well over a decade, more than 10,000 Avro 504s were built, serving as bomber, reconnaissance, fighter and training aircraft during World War I. It is as a trainer that the

Avro 504 is best remembered; thousands of British and Commonwealth pilots learned to fly in it, and after the war surplus 504s were snapped up for commercial use, being used for joy-riding, 'barnstorming' and for training civilian pilots. The Avro 504N was the peacetime production aircraft, being converted from the standard Avro 504K RAF trainer and having a different engine and undercarriage. Series production totalled 598 examples, the last being completed in 1932. The Avro 504 was then progressively replaced by the Avro Tutor.

Specifications apply to the trainer version of the Avro 504.

Thousands of both British and Commonwealth pilots gained their 'wings' in an Avro 504 cockpit.

AVRO 621 TUTOR

The Avro Tutor was designed to replace the Avro 504 in the RAF's basic flying schools. The type entered service in 1933 and generated limited export orders, also being licence-built in South Africa.

BRAINCHILD OF AVRO designer Roy Chadwick, the Avro Tutor was intended to succeed the Avro 504 and replicate that type's excellent handling characteristics. The prototype was evaluated at the Aircraft and Armament Experimental Establishment, Martlesham Heath, in December 1929 and was selected for production in 1930. Delivery of the first of an eventual 394 aircraft for the RAF's flying schools was made in 1933, with a production total of 795. Export orders to Canada, Eire, Greece, Denmark and China were completed before the line closed in 1936, and a further 57 aircraft were built under licence in South Africa. The Tutor remained in service as the RAF's principal elementary trainer until the late 1930s.

Crew: 2
Powerplant: one 179kW (240hp) Armstrong Siddeley Lynx IVC radial engine
Performance: max speed 196km/h (122mph); range 402km (250 miles); service ceiling 4940m (16,200ft)
Dimensions: wingspan 10.36m (34ft); length 8.08m (26ft 6in); height 2.92m (9ft 7in)
Weight: 1115kg (2458lb) loaded
Armament: none

AVRO ANSON

Crew: 3-5
Powerplant: two 250kW (335hp) Armstrong Siddeley Cheetah IX 7-cylinder radial engines
Performance: max speed 302km/h (188mph); range 1271km (790 miles); service ceiling 5790m (19,000ft)
Dimensions: wingspan 17.22m (56ft 6in); length 12.88m (42ft 3in); height 3.99m (13ft 1in)
Weight: 4218kg (9300lb) loaded
Armament: up to four 7.62mm (0.30in) machine guns on cabin mountings; internal bomb load of 227kg (500lb)

The Avro Anson began its career as a general reconnaissance aircraft, but also served as a crew trainer and as a communications aircraft.

FIRST FLOWN IN MARCH 1935, the Avro Anson went on to enjoy a production run that lasted from 1934 to 1952, and it was built in larger numbers than any other British aircraft except the Hawker Hurricane and Supermarine

Spitfire. Originally intended as a light transport, the Avro Anson was adapted to meet a 1934 requirement for a coastal reconnaissance

aircraft, and the type was ordered into production for RAF Coastal Command as the Anson Mk I with a revised tail unit, a larger cabin

---

AUSTER B.8 AGRICOLA
A one- or three-seat, single-engined, low-wing British-designed agricultural aircraft first flown in 1955. The Auster B.8 Agricola sold poorly and only nine examples of the aircraft were built.

AUSTER J-5Q AND R ALPINE
Developed in two sub-types from the J-5 Autocar, the Q version was a low-powered aircraft and only four were built. The R version was an amalgam of other Autocar variants using the Aiglet Trainer fuselage.

AUSTER J-1U WORKMASTER
Based on the Alpha airframe, the Auster J-1U was configured with a number of design changes to assist operation in inhospitable, hot conditions. In the event only a small number were sold following the first flight in 1958.

AUSTIN GREYHOUND
A fast-climbing two-seat fighter/reconnaissance biplane, the Austin Greyhound was the last military type designed by Austin Motors Ltd in World War I.

AUSTIN WHIPPET
The Austin Whippet is a small British single-seat single-engine civil biplane dating from the end of World War I. Only five were made before production ceased in 1920.

AUSTIN KESTREL
A British 'side-by-side' two-seat, single-engine biplane for civil use, the Austin Kestrel dates from the end of World War I.

AVIA BH.10/11
The BH.10 was a single-seat braced low-wing monoplane trainer, used by the Czech Army Air Force in the 1920s. The BH.11 was a two-seat version.

AVIA BH.21
A Czechoslovakian designed single-seat biplane first flown in 1925 and known as the B.21 in Czech military service.

AVIA BH.25
Dating from 1927, the Avia BH.25 was a commercial transport design capable of accommodating up to five passengers. The aircraft was a biplane, powered by a single Walter Jupiter engine.

AVIA BH.26
The Avia BH.26 was one of a series of Czech training biplanes produced during the 1920s. These aircraft were well designed and very successful.

window area, Cheetah IX radial engines and full military equipment. The Anson entered service in March 1936, and Mk I production eventually ran to a total of 6915 aircraft.

After the aircraft's replacement in the coastal patrol role, it was to find a new career as a crew trainer and communications aircraft, and further orders raised the eventual production total to 8138 Ansons in Britain and a further 2882 in Canada. The last variant of the type to be produced was the Avro Anson C.Mk 19.

AVRO MANCHESTER MK I   UK: 1939

THE PROTOTYPE MANCHESTER flew on 25 July 1939, being followed by a second aircraft on 26 May 1940. The Manchester Mk I, which featured a central tail fin as well as twin fins and rudders, became operational with No 207 Squadron in November 1940, the first 20 aircraft being followed by 200 Manchester IAs with the central fin removed. The bomber was withdrawn from operations in 1942, as its unreliable Vulture engines were prone to catch fire.

Powerplant: two 1313kW (1760hp) Rolls-Royce Vulture 24-cylinder X-type engines
Performance: max speed 426km/h (265mph); range 2623km (1630 miles); service ceiling 5850m (19,200ft)
Dimensions: wingspan 27.46m (90ft 1in); length 21.14m (69ft 4in); height 5.94m (19ft 6in)
Weight: 22,680kg (50,000lb) loaded
Armament: two 7.62mm (0.30in) machine guns in nose turret, two in ventral turret (later replaced by dorsal turret), and four in tail turret; internal bomb load of 4695kg (10,350lb)

An Avro Manchester I of No 207 Squadron, RAF Bomber Command. The Manchester's unreliable engines, which had a tendency to catch fire, caused the squadron to suffer terrible casualties. One Manchester airframe was converted to form the prototype Lancaster.

AVRO LANCASTER   UK: 1941

ONE OF THE MOST FAMOUS bomber aircraft of all time, the Avro Lancaster was developed from the Avro Manchester. While production of the Manchester was in progress, one airframe (BT308) was fitted with four Rolls-Royce Merlin XX engines. This was the prototype Lancaster, which first flew on 9 January 1941 and was delivered to No 44 (Rhodesia) Squadron at Waddington, Lincolnshire, in September that year. The first operational sortie with Lancasters was on 3 March 1942, when four aircraft laid mines in the Heligoland Bight.

The second squadron to be equipped with Lancasters was No 97, and in company with No 44 it carried out a low-level daylight raid on the MAN factory at Augsburg, Bavaria, which was manufacturing U-boat diesel engines. Seven out of the 12 Lancasters involved were lost. Sqn Ldr J.D. Nettleton, one of 44's flight commanders, was awarded the VC for his role in the raid.

As an insurance against possible interruption in supplies of Merlins, it was decided to equip some Lancasters with four 1231kW (1650hp) Bristol Hercules 6 (or 16) radials in place of the Merlin XX, these aircraft becoming the Lancaster Mk II. Several Mks I and II were used for experimental work, particularly as engine testbeds. One of the Mk I experimental aircraft, ED817, had its fuselage underside modified to accommodate development rounds of the special mine used in the famous raid by No 617 Squadron on the Ruhr dams in May 1943.

Little modification was made to the basic Lancaster airframe during its life, a testimony to its sturdiness and reliability, and as a result very little extra work was necessary when the Mk III with Packard-built Merlin engines superseded the Mk 1 on the production lines.

Deployment of the Lancaster Mk III enabled Bomber Command to use first a 3624kg (8000lb) bomb, then the 5436kg (12,000lb) 'Tallboy', and finally the 9966kg (22,000lb) 'Grand Slam', recessed in the doorless bomb bay. The last Lancaster raid of the war was carried out against an SS barracks at Berchtesgaden on 25 April 1945. During the war Lancasters

A Lancaster Mk III of No 463 Squadron, RAAF. This squadron was based at Skellingthorpe, Lincolnshire.

flew 156,192 sorties, dropping 618,380 tonnes (608,612 tons) of bombs. Losses in action were 3431 aircraft, a further 246 being destroyed in operational accidents. At peak strength in August 1944, no fewer than 42 Bomber Command squadrons were armed with the Lancaster. Towards the end of the war in Europe, plans were made for the large-scale use of Lancasters and Lincolns against Japan, the intention being to convert some Lancasters as flight refuelling tankers. Extensive trials were carried out by Flight Refuelling Ltd and a great deal of flight refuelling equipment had already been manufactured when the war ended and the project was abandoned. The much-modified Lancasters Mks IV and V became the Lincoln Mks I and II. The Mk VI, nine of which were converted

from Mks I and III, was equipped for electronic countermeasures.

The last production Lancaster was the Mk VII, 180 of which were built by Austin Motors. The Mks VIII and IX were never built, and the Mk X was a licence-built Mk III, 422 being produced by the Victory Aircraft Co of Canada. Some Lancasters were converted as RAF and later BOAC transports, with faired-over turrets. Lancasters remained in service with RAF Bomber Command for some time after World War II until replaced by the Avro Lincoln, and RAF Coastal Command used the GR.3 maritime patrol version until this was replaced by the Avro Shackleton. Avro refurbished 54 Mk Is and VIIs and converted them to the maritime patrol role for use by France's Aeronavale, and other Mk Is were converted

for photographic survey work as the PR.Mk I. Some Lancasters were converted to the civil air transport role as the Lancastrian. Total Lancaster production, all variants, was 7374 aircraft.

Specification refers to the Lancaster Mk III.

Crew: 7
Powerplant: four 1233kW (1640hp) Rolls-Royce Merlin 28 or 38 12-cylinder V-type engines
Performance: max speed 462km/h (287mph); range 2784km (1730 miles); service ceiling 5790m (19,000ft)
Dimensions: wingspan 31.09m (102ft); length 21.18m (69ft 6in); height 6.25m (20ft 6in)
Weight: 29,484kg (65,000lb) loaded
Armament: two 7.7mm (0.303in) machine guns in nose turret, two in dorsal turret and four in tail turret; maximum internal bomb load 8165kg (18,000lb)

Many Lancasters served as engine and equipment test-beds. This Mk II (LL735) has a Metropolitan-Vickers Beryl turbojet installed in the tail, fed by the single air intake above the rear fuselage.

AVIA BH.33
The Avia BH.33, in service with the Czech Army Air Force from 1927, achieved considerable export success. It was of all-wood construction.

AVIA B.35
The first prototype Avia B.35 low-wing monoplane fighter flew in September 1938.

AVIA B.135
The Avia B.135 prototype, which was derived from the B.35, appeared in mid-1939. Twelve B.135s were delivered to the Bulgarian Air Force in 1940.

AVIATIK D.I
The Aviatik D.I was the first entirely Austrian-built fighter of World War I. It flew at the beginning of 1917, and 700 examples were made in total.

AVIATION TRADERS ATL.90 ACCOUNTANT
This British-designed twin Dart turboprop engine transport dates from 1957. The Aviation Traders ATL.90 Accountant was meant as a DC-3 role successor, but lack of orders curtailed the project with only one example flown.

AVIATION TRADERS ATL.98 CARVAIR
The ATL.98 Carvair was a conversion of the famous Douglas DC-4/C-54 pioneered by Freddie Laker to replace the ageing Bristol Freighter as a car/passenger carrier to the continent. Several of the 21 examples produced are still serviceable.

AVIOMILANO F.14 NIBBIO
Developed from the earlier F8L Falco, this Italian four-seat monoplane design dates from the mid-1950s.

AVIOMILANO P.19 SCRICCIOLO
An Italian two-seat, single-engined, low-wing trainer/light aeroplane design, the Aviomilano P.19 Scricciolo was produced from the 1950s.

AVIONS FAIREY FIREFLY
The Fairey Firefly fighter biplane served with the Belgian Air Force from 1932, having had a lengthy development phase. Production totalled 60 aircraft.

AVRO LINCOLN

UK: 1944

Crew: 7
Powerplant: four Rolls-Royce merlin 85 V-12 in-line engines
Performance: max speed 513km/h (319mph); range 2365km (1470 miles); service ceiling 9300m (30,500ft)
Dimensions: wingspan 36.57m (120ft); length 23.85m (78ft 3in); height 5.25m (17ft 3in)
Weight: 34,020kg (75,000lb) loaded
Armament: twin 12.7mm (0.50in) remotely controlled Browning machine guns in nose turret and two in tail turret; twin 20mm (0.79in) Hispano Mk 4/5 cannon in dorsal turret (later deleted).

DESIGNED AS A LANCASTER replacement to Specification B.14/43, the prototype Avro Lincoln flew for the first time on

9 June 1944, first deliveries being made to No 57 Squadron in the spring of 1945. The Lincoln became operational too late to see active service in World War II, although plans had been made to send several squadrons to the Far East for operations against Japan.

Lincolns were, however, to see action against communist terrorists during the Malayan Emergency of the 1950s. The RAAF took delivery of 73 Lincoln B.30s, all but five being licence-built in Australia, and the Argentine Air Force operated 12 examples.

An Avro Lincoln B.2 of No 57 Squadron, RAF Bomber Command. The squadron operated Lincolns from 1945 to 1951, being based mainly at Waddington, Lincolnshire, during this period – although too late for the aircraft to see action in World War II.

AVRO SHACKLETON

UK: 1949

Avro Shackleton MR.2 of No 228 Squadron, RAF Coastal Command, which was based at RAF St Eval in Cornwall in the 1950s. No 228 eventually became a search and rescue helicopter squadron.

DESIGNED IN 1946 TO MEET A requirement for a new, very long-range maritime patrol aircraft for RAF Coastal Command, the Avro

Type 696 Shackleton (originally designated Lincoln ASR.3) flew for the first time on 9 March 1949. The Avro Shackleton was the first

British aircraft to be fitted with contra-rotating propellers, and the first of 77 production Shackleton MR.1s entered service with No

120 Squadron at Kinloss, Scotland, in April 1951.

The Shackleton MR.2 had a ventral radome, while the MR.3 had a redesigned wing, wingtip tanks and a tricycle undercarriage. The MR.3 was later fitted with Armstrong Siddeley Viper turbojets in the outboard engine nacelles, being designated MR.3 Phase 3. Shackletons were supplied to the South African Air Force, and the type was to serve in the early warning role with No 8 Squadron RAF as the AEW.3.

Specifications apply to the Avro Shackleton MR.3.

Crew: 10–13
Powerplant: four 1831kW (2455hp) Rolls-Royce Griffon 57A V-12 liquid-cooled engines
Performance: max speed 486km/h (302mph); range 6780km (4215 miles); service ceiling 6100m (20,000ft)
Dimensions: wingspan 36.53m (119ft 10in); length 26.62m (87ft 4in); height 7.11m (23ft 4in)
Weight: 45,360kg (100,000lb) loaded
Armament: two 20mm (0.79in) cannon in nose position (later deleted); various internal loads

AVRO 707

UK: 1949

WHILE THE AVRO 698 VULCAN was still on the drawing board, the Avro design team began work on a series of small research aircraft to test the jet bomber's delta-wing planform. The first of these, the

Avro 707, flew on 4 September 1949, but crashed only three weeks later, killing its pilot. A second aircraft, the Avro 707B, flew on 6 September 1950, and subsequently carried out a low-speed research

programme. The third aircraft, the Avro 707A, was intended for high-speed research. It flew on 14 June 1951; with the prototype Vulcan nearing completion it was decided to build a second 707A in order to

accelerate the programme. This flew on 20 February 1953, and was followed by the fifth and last aircraft in the series, the two-seat 707C, which flew on 1 July 1953.

Specifications apply to Avro 707.

Crew: 1
Powerplant: one 1587kg (3500lb) thrust Rolls-Royce Derwent 5 turbojet
Performance: no data published
Dimensions: wingspan 10.41m (34ft 2in); length 12.90m (42ft 4in); height 3.53m (11ft 7in)
Weight: 4303kg (9500lb) loaded
Armament: none

The Avro 707A WD280 was one of the small research aircraft which were designed to investigate the characteristics of the delta wing at various speeds and altitudes. It is now in the RAAF Museum, having been used for research flying in Australia.

AVRO CANADA CF-100

CANADA: 1950

THE CF-100, THE LARGEST fighter in the world at the time of its conception, was designed as a long-range night and all-weather interceptor to counter a Soviet air attack across the Arctic. The prototype Avro Canada CF-100 Mk 1 flew on 19 January 1950, an order for 124 production CF-100 Mk 3s being followed by further orders for 510 Mk 4As and 4Bs, the latter having Orenda 11

engines. Nine RCAF squadrons operated the type, providing round-the-clock air defence coverage. CF-100 squadrons served in Germany as part of Canada's NATO commitment, and 53 examples of the last production version, the Mk 5, were delivered to Belgium.

Avro Canada CF-100 all-weather fighters of No 423 Squadron, Royal Canadian Air Force.

Crew: 2
Powerplant: two 3295kg (7264lb) thrust Avro Orenda turbojets
Performance: max speed 1046km/h (650mph); range 3218km (2000 miles); service ceiling 16,470m (54,000ft)
Dimensions: wingspan 18.54m (60ft 8in); length 16.53m (54ft 2in); height 4.42m (14ft 5in)
Weight: 15,220kg (33,554lb) loaded
Armament: 52 x 75mm (2.95in) HVAR in wingtip pods

AVRO (HAWKER SIDDELEY) VULCAN

UK: 1952

Crew: 5
Powerplant: four 9072kg (20,000lb) thrust Bristol Siddeley Olympus Mk 301 turbojets
Performance: max speed 1038km/h (645mph); range 7403km (4600 miles); service ceiling 19,810m (65,000ft)
Weight: 113,398kg (250,000lb) loaded
Dimensions: wingspan 33.83m (111ft); length 30.45m (99ft 11in); height 8.28m (27ft 2in)
Armament: 21 x 453kg (1000lb) HE bombs; Yellow Sun Mk 2 or WE.177B nuclear weapons; Blue Steel ASM with Red Snow nuclear warhead (Vulcan B.2BS)

THE FIRST BOMBER IN THE world to employ the delta-wing planform, the Avro Type 698 Vulcan prototype (VX770) flew for the first time on 30 August 1952.

The first production Vulcan B.Mk 1 was delivered to No 230 Operational Conversion Unit in July 1956, and No 83 Squadron became the first unit to equip with the new bomber in July 1957. By this time production of the greatly improved Vulcan B.Mk 2 was well under way. The Vulcan B.Mk 2 later received an avionics upgrade, including the fitting of terrain-following radar, and was then designated B.Mk 2A.

In 1969, the RAF's Vulcan force was assigned to NATO and CENTO in the free-fall bombing role. In May 1982, Vulcans were used to carry out attacks on the

The Avro Vulcan was one the trio of 'V-Bombers' – the others being the Vickers Valiant and Handley Page Victor – which maintained Britain's airborne nuclear deterrent from 1956 to 1968.

Falkland Islands in support of British operations to recapture the islands from Argentina.

Total Vulcan production was 136 aircraft, including the two prototypes and 89 B.2s. The last operational Vulcans were six aircraft of No 50 Squadron which had been converted to the flight refuelling role. The type was replaced by the Panavia Tornado fighter-bomber, being finally phased out in 1984.

Specifications apply to the Vulcan B.Mk 2.

AVRO CANADA CF-105 ARROW

CANADA: 1958

Crew: 2
Powerplant: two 10,659kg (23,500lb) thrust Pratt & Whitney J75-P-3 turbojets
Performance: data incomplete: Mach 2.3 recorded during trials
Dimensions: wingspan 15.24m (50ft); length 23.72m (77ft 9.75in); height 6.48m (21ft 3in)
Weight: 25,855kg (57,000lb) loaded
Armament: eight AIM-7 Sparrow air-to-air missiles in internal bay

The Avro Canada CF-105 Arrow had the potential to enter service as one of the most advanced interceptors in the world, but was cancelled in 1959.

THE CF-105 DELTA-WING all-weather interceptor first flew on 25 March 1958, powered by two Pratt & Whitney J75 turbojets. Four more aircraft were built, designated CF-105 Mk 1; four more – designated Mk 2, with Orenda PS-13 engines – were almost complete when the project was abruptly cancelled in February 1959. The CF-105 was one of the most advanced interceptors in the world, but escalating costs and an offer by the US government to equip three RCAF air defence squadrons with the F-101B Voodoo brought about its demise. During its brief career, however, it had made a significant contribution to aviation technology.

AVRO/BAE 146 SERIES AND AVRO RJ70, RJ85 AND RJ100

UK: 1981

The RJ100 demonstrator, launched in 1992. British Airways is among the operators of the 146.

ORIGINATING IN A HAWKER SIDDELEY design of 1973 for a STOL-capable regional jet, the 146 took some years to come to market after Hawker Siddeley was absorbed in British Aerospace (BAe) in 1977. Produced in three marques, the largest 300 series carries up to 128 passengers. A total of 221 were built until 1994, when the design was re-engineered and renamed Avro and included more powerful Allied Signal LF 507 engines (the series designations RJ70, RJ85 and RJ100 replaced previous Bae 146-100, 200 and 300, respectively). A total of 166 Avro-liner examples were produced until 2001. Specifications apply to the BAe 146 series 100.

Crew: 2
Powerplant: four 31.00kN (6975lb) thrust Avco Lycoming ALF502R-3 or -5 turbofans
Performance: max speed 767km/h (477mph); range 1631km (1013 miles) with maximum payload
Dimensions: wingspan 26.21m (86ft); length 26.20m (85ft 11in); height 8.61m (28ft 3in)
Weight: 38,102kg (84,000lb) maximum take-off weight
Payload: typical load, 70 passengers

AVRO 561 ANDOVER
Originally designed as a mail carrier for the RAF, the Avro 561 Andover first flew in 1921 and actually saw service as an air ambulance. Only three examples of the aircraft were built.

AVRO 581 AVIAN
The Avro 581 Avian single-engined biplane design dates from 1925, and it was a successively enhanced prototype that led to later 594, 605 and 616 production standard variants of the Avian light aircraft.

AVRO 618
A licence-built version of the Fokker F.VIIB, 14 examples of this tri-motor design were produced from 1929.

AVRO TYPE 689 TUDOR
The four-piston-engine-powered Tudor was produced in post-war Britain, initially for BOAC, to carry up to 32 passengers primarily on trans-Atlantic services. The Tudor suffered development and in-service difficulties. In total 33 Tudors were produced.

AVRO ASHTON
Developed from the Avro Tudor airliner and powered by four Rolls-Royce Nene turbojets, the Avro Ashton was used for research in the 1950s, with a total of six examples being built.

AVRO CANADA C-102
The Avro Canada C-102 was designed as a medium-range jetliner with four wing-mounted engines (the powerplant was later reduced to two larger capacity engines), and a pressurized 50-seat cabin. It first flew in 1949, but lack of orders led to abandonment.

AVRO 730
The Avro 730 was a projected reconnaissance bomber with an estimated speed of Mach 2.5 at high altitude. The prototype was under construction in 1957 when the project was cancelled.

AYRES LM200 LOADMASTER
Designed as a single turboprop engine high-wing utility transport, the Ayres LM200 Loadmaster first flew in 1999 and has attracted freight line customers, receiving an initial order for 50 from the company Federal Express.

BAC (British Aircraft Corporation) One-Eleven

UK: 1963

THE FIRST VERSION OF THE BAC One-Eleven airliner, the Series 200, first flew on 20 August 1963, the type entering service with British United Airways in 1965. The One-Eleven, a major export success story, was produced in several different variants, including the Series 400 for the American market. The Series 500, first flown on 30 June 1967, had a considerably lengthened fuselage, a redesigned wing, increased capacity and more powerful engines. The final version was the versatile Series 475, which combined the 400's fuselage with the 500's extended wings. The Series 475 could be used on Class 2 airfields in 'hot and high' conditions, making it suitable for operations in mountainous regions. Specifications apply to the Series 500.

Crew: 2/3
Powerplant: two 5692kg (12,550lb) thrust Rolls-Royce Spey turbofan engines
Performance: max speed 871km/h (541mph); range 2735km (1700 miles); service ceiling 10,668m (35,000ft)
Dimensions: span 28.5m (93ft 6in); length 32.61m (107ft); height 7.47m (24ft 6in)
Weight: 47,400kg (104,500lb) loaded
Payload: 84–119 passengers

The BAC One-Eleven was a major success for Britain's aircraft industry in the 1960s. It was produced in several versions, each tailored to meet particular customer requirements.

BAC TSR-2

UK: 1964

Crew: 2
Powerplant: two 13,884kg (30,610lb) thrust Bristol Siddeley Olympus 320 turbojet engines
Performance: max speed 2390km/h (1485mph); range 1287km (800 miles); service ceiling 16,459m (54,000ft)
Dimensions: wingspan 11.28m (37ft); length 27.13m (89ft); height 7.32m (24ft)
Weight: 43,545kg (96,000lb) loaded
Armament: up to 2722kg (6000lb) of weapons internally; four underwing pylons for up to 1814kg (4000lb) of ordnance

ORIGINALLY DESIGNED BY ENGLISH ELECTRIC to Operational Requirement 339, and developed jointly with Vickers-Armstrong, the TSR-2 was intended as a replacement for the English Electric Canberra in the low-level tactical strike and reconnaissance role. A remarkable aircraft at the very cutting edge of aviation technology, the TSR-2 had the most advanced nav/attack system in the world and would have been able to deliver its weapons with

pinpoint accuracy. A contract was placed for nine development TSR-2s in October 1960. The prototype flew on 27 September 1964, by

which time four more aircraft were in various stages of construction. On 6 April 1965, however, the whole programme was cancelled.

Intended as a replacement for the English Electric Canberra, the BAC TSR-2 was axed in 1965 on grounds of economy.

BAC (VICKERS) VC-10

UK: 1964

Crew: 4
Powerplant: four 9905kg (21,800lb) thrust Rolls-Royce Conway 301 turbofan engines
Performance: max speed 935km/h (580mph); range 7600km (4725 miles); service ceiling 11,600m (38,057ft)
Dimensions: wingspan 44.55m (146ft 3in); length 52.32m (171ft 9in); height 12.04m (39ft 6in)
Weight: 152,000kg (335,160lb) loaded
Payload: 139 passengers

DEVELOPED BY VICKERS AS a four-jet long-haul airliner, the VC-10 was not a commercial success, being used only by BOAC and East African Airways. Designated VC-10 C.Mk 1, 14 examples were delivered to No 10 Squadron RAF Air Support Command, between 1966 and 1968.

Four standard VC-10s and five Super VC-10s (simply a stretched version of the VC-10, with various modifications) were later converted as flight refuelling tankers and delivered to the RAF in 1984 and 1985 as VC-10 K.Mk 2s and VC-10 K.Mk 3s. A final batch of five ex-British Airways Super VC-10s, converted in the early 1990s, received the designation VC-10 K.Mk 4. In all, 54 VC-10s and Super VC-10s were built.

Specifications apply to the BAC VC-10 C.Mk 1.

One of the finest jet airliners ever designed, the BAC VC-10 was nevertheless not a commercial success, being used only by BOAC – in the livery of which it is seen here – and East African Airways.

BACHEM BA 349 NATTER

GERMANY: 1945

ONE OF THE MOST EXTRAORDINARY aircraft ever built, the Bachem Ba 349 Natter (Viper) was conceived as a rocket-powered target-defence interceptor. It was conceived as a possible counter to Allied daylight bombing raids towards the end of World War II. Basically a piloted rocket armed with a battery of 73mm (2.87in) unguided rockets in the forward fuselage, the Natter was launched from a vertical ramp with the aid of four jettisonable solid-fuel rocket boosters and climbed to altitude under the control of an autopilot, the human pilot only taking control during the attack phase. After firing his salvo

Crew: 1
Powerplant: one 1995kg (4400lb) thrust Walter HWK 509C-1 bi-fuel rocket motor
Performance: max speed 997km/h (620mph); range 58km (36.25 miles); absolute ceiling 13,996m (45,920ft)
Dimensions: wingspan 3.60m (11ft 9.5in); length 6.10m (20ft); height 2.24m (7ft 4.5in)
Weight: 2230kg (4920lb) loaded
Armament: 24 x 73mm (2.87in) rockets

of rockets into a formation of bombers, the pilot was supposed to bail out. Several unpowered gliding test flights were made before the first and only manned vertical launch took place in February 1945. Unfortunately, the Natter crashed, killing its pilot.

Designed as a target-defence interceptor, the Natter proved easy to fly during air-launched gliding trials, but a death-trap when rocket-launched.

BARLING XNBL-1

One of the ugliest aircraft ever built, the Barling Bomber was an attempt to provide the US Army Air Service with an indigenous design for its planned strategic bomber fleet.

Crew: 9
Powerplant: six 313kW (420hp) Liberty in-line engines
Performance: max speed 154km/h (96mph); range 274km (170 miles); service ceiling 2355m (7725ft)

Dimensions: wingspan 36.58m (120ft); length 19.81m (65ft); height 8.23m (27ft)
Weight: 19,309kg (42,569lb) loaded
Armament: seven 7.5mm (0.29in) machine guns on flexible mountings, plus up to 2268kg (5000lb) of bombs

THE BARLING XNBL-1 WAS a huge and curiously designed aircraft conceived by Walter Barling of the US Army Air Service's Engineering Division. It was produced in response to a requirement for a strategic bomber issued by the US Chiefs of Staff. The sole prototype was built by the Witteman-Lewis Aircraft Corporation of Newark, New Jersey, but was popularly known as the 'Barling Bomber'. Designated XNBL-1 (Experimental Night Bomber Long-Range), the aircraft had triplane wings, six engines with 10 propellers, a 10-wheel main landing gear and positions for seven machine guns around the fuselage. At the time of its maiden flight in August 1923, it was the largest aircraft in the world and also the most cumbersome. Flight testing soon showed that it was seriously underpowered, and further development was abandoned in 1925. An improved XNBL-2 had been planned, but funding for this was not forthcoming.

BEAGLE 206 (BASSETT)

Crew: 1/2
Powerplant: two 254kW (340hp) Rolls-Royce Continental GTSIO-520-C flat-six engines
Performance: max speed 415km/h (258mph); range 2575km (1600 miles); service ceiling 8260m (27,100ft)
Dimensions: wingspan 13.96m (45ft 9.5in); length 10.26m (33ft 8in); height 3.45m (11ft 4in)
Weight: 3401kg (7499lb) maximum take-off weight
Payload: eight people

THE BEAGLE 206 WAS Beagle's first wholly original design – an all metal construction light transport/executive type with a retractable undercarriage. Sadly the Bassett failed to live up to its commercial promise, in part due to early vacillation over capacity and powerplant.

The RAF was the first customer (20 examples), and the type was designated Bassett CC.Mk1 for use as a communications aircraft and V bomber crew ferry. Although well thought of only 85 Beagle 206s were built until 1969, when production ended.

Specifications apply to the B.206 Series 2.

The Beagle 206 pictured above is the second prototype – designated a 206Y. The Beagle 206 was a British attempt to break into the twin-engined executive aircraft market, but the type failed to live up to its expectations.

BEARDMORE INFLEXIBLE

UK: 1928

UNTIL THE APPEARANCE OF the Bristol Brabazon in the late 1940s, the Inflexible was the largest landplane ever built in the UK. Designed by Dr Adolf Rohrbach at the invitation of the British Air Ministry, it was intended to investigate the feasibility of very large all-metal aircraft. The aircraft's components were so massive that the Beardmore company had to

ship them from the Clyde by sea to Felixstowe prior to assembly at Martlesham Heath. The first flight was made by Squadron Leader J. Noakes on 5 March 1928. To his surprise the aircraft became airborne very quickly and proved almost viceless in flight, being very stable. But the Inflexible was badly underpowered, and after extensive flight trials it was placed in storage.

Crew: 2
Powerplant: three 485kW (650hp) Rolls-Royce Condor engines
Performance: max speed 175km/h (109mph); range not known; service ceiling not known
Dimensions: wingspan 48.00m (157ft 6in); length 23.00m (75ft 6in); height 6.40m (21ft 2in)
Weight: 16,761kg (37,000lb) loaded
Armament: none

The huge Beardmore Inflexible appeared on the air display circuit in 1929 before being placed in storage.

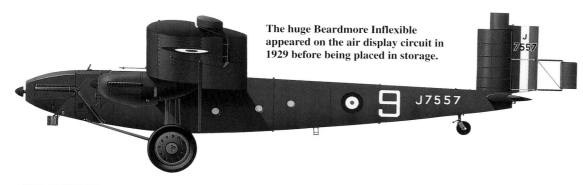

BEECH C-45 EXPEDITER

USA: 1937

THE BEECH 18 WAS A small, twin-engined monoplane that originated in 1937 as a civil transport and feeder-liner. Several developed versions saw military service during World War II as the C-45 Expediter. Transport and general-purpose versions were produced in large numbers for the USAAF (C-45 Expediter and UC-45) and the US Navy (JRB). The AT-7 and AT-11 were respectively navigation and

bombing/gunnery trainer versions. The type was continually updated as an executive aircraft in civilian use. Two of its most attractive features, to both civil and military users, were its low operating costs and excellent serviceability. Taking requisitioned civil aircraft into account, some 1400 C-45s served with the US armed forces from 1941, when the Air Corps placed an order for 11 militarized Beech 18s.

Crew: 2
Powerplant: two 336kW (450hp) Pratt & Whitney R-985 AN-1 9-cylinder radial engines
Performance: max speed 345km/h (215mph); range 1130km (700 miles); service ceiling 6100m (20,000ft)
Dimensions: wingspan 14.53m (47ft 8in); length 10.44m (34ft 3in); height: 2.95m (9ft 8in)
Weight: 3960kg (8727lb) loaded
Payload: 5–8 passengers

The Beech C-45 Expediter's most attractive features were its reliability and low operating costs. It was widely used by the US armed forces during World War II.

BAUMGARTL HELIOFLY
The Heliofly was really little more than a strap-on autogyro glider for sporting use. It was produced in 1941 by Austrian engineer Paul Baumgartl. In 1942 the Heliofly III-57 appeared, powered by an 6kW (8hp) Argus As-8 engine. In 1943 this was redesigned as the Heliofly III-59 to be powered by a single 12kW (16hp) engine.

BEAGLE A.61 TERRIER
The Terrier was a civilianized rebuild of the military Auster design (mostly using AOP.6 airframes). It was essentially a re-working of surplus military airframes for the private ownership civil market.

BEAGLE A.109 AIREDALE
Of this single-engined, high-wing touring or sporting light aircraft first flown in 1961, only 43 examples were produced in a highly competitive market.

BEAGLE B.121 PUP
A single engined two/three seat low-wing fixed undercarriage light aircraft dating from the mid-1960s. Commercial production ceased in 1970 with Beagle's insolvency but military derivative work was transferred to Scottish Aviation who produced the Bulldog trainer.

BEAGLE (BEAGLE-MILES) M.218X AND B.242X
A British experimental low-wing monoplane, twin-engined light aircraft design first flown in 1962. The M.218 was later rebuilt as the B.242X with a number of design changes. However, the project was eventually abandoned.

BEARDMORE WB.III
Based on the Sopwith Pup, the Beardmore WB.III was a shipborne aircraft with folding wings and retractable undercarriage. It was built as a prototype only and first flew in 1917.

BEECH MODEL 35 BONANZA

USA: 1945

This Bonanza features the classic V-tail design that sold very well in the North American private flying market despite its radical appearance.

OVER 10,400 VARIANTS of this type were built from 1945 to 1982. The accommodation level, low-wing design and retractable undercarriage were extremely popular with postwar American private flyers. The stretched, V-tailfinned V35 became the classic version and was progressively uprated in terms of power and weight. In 1967 the Beech 33 Debonair was renamed as part of the Bonanza family. Specifications apply to the Beech V35 Bonanza.

Crew: 1
Powerplant: one 138kW (185hp) Continental E-185-1 flat-six rated piston engine
Performance: max speed 394km/h (245mph); range 1553km (965 miles); service ceiling 7620m (25,000ft)

Dimensions: wingspan 10.20m (33ft 6in); length 8.10m (26ft 7in); height 2.30m (7ft 6in)
Weight: 1746kg (3850lb) maximum take-off weight
Payload: five/six people and 122.47kg (270lb) of baggage

BEECH T-34 MENTOR

USA: 1948

The Beech T-34 Mentor military trainer was a development of the civilian Bonanza. It saw widespread service with the US armed forces and those of other nations within the US sphere of influence.

Crew: 2
Powerplant: one 298kW (400hp) Pratt & Whitney PT6A-25 turboprop
Performance: max speed 464km/h (288mph); range 1205km (748 miles); service ceiling 9145m (30,000ft);
Dimensions: wingspan 10.16m (33ft 3in); length 8.75m (28ft 8in); height 3.02m (9ft 7in)
Weight: 1978kg (4360lb) loaded
Armament: none

FIRST FLOWN IN DECEMBER 1948, the Beechcraft T-34 Mentor was developed from the civilian Beechcraft Bonanza and was built in large numbers, serving with the US services and many countries within the US sphere of influence. Variants were the T-34A for the USAF (450 built), T-34B for the US Navy and T-34C, which had a PTRA turboprop in place of the earlier Continental piston engine. Export T-34C-1s could be equipped to carry out light attack missions.

BEECH MODEL 50/ L-23 (A TO E) SEMINOLE

USA: 1949

Crew: 1
Powerplant: two 254kW (340hp) Avco Lycoming O-480-1 flat-six engines.
Performance: max speed 375km/h (233mph); range 2181km (1355 miles); service ceiling 8015m (26,300ft)
Dimensions: wingspan 13.80m (45ft 3.5in); length 9.61m (31ft 6.5in); height 3.45m (11ft 4in)
Weight: 3175kg (7000lb) maximum take-off weight
Payload: six/seven persons

SIMILARLY TO THE MODEL 35 Bonanza, the Model 50 was advanced for its day, but the Model 50 was a twin-engined design, with a conventional tail and excellent range and altitude performance. It shared the Model 35's all-metal construction and retractable under-carriage. Sales of this larger type would clearly be lower than the

The Model 50 interested the US military for use in a light transport role. It was first designated YL-23 when it entered service in 1952.

Bonanza, therefore Beech aimed the design at both civil and military applications. The economics of taking up a type already in civilian

service were attractive to the US Army, which designated it the L-23 (later U-8). Specifications apply to the Beech L-23D Seminole.

BEECH KING AIR AND SUPER KING AIR

USA: 1964

THE MODEL 90 (developed from the Model 65) was another Beech designed for commercial or military applications. The first customer was the US Army which designated it U-21 for light transport work, but later produced electronic recon-naissance versions. Civil models have been progressively updated. Production exceeds 1400 and the Model F90 Super King Air now includes a T tail arrangement. The Beech 100 dates from 1969 and is a stretch of the Model 90. This too was taken up by the military and

The model depicted is a C90B, the most recent of the 90/100 series, identified by their conventional rather than T-form tailplane.

progressively improved and uprated, but production ceased in 1983; the type has been superseded by the Model 200, 300 and 350 Super King Air range that dates from 1972, easily discerned by their T tail and produced in high numbers for civil/executive and military customers. Specifications apply to the Beech Model B100.

Crew: 2
Powerplant: two Garrett TPE331-6-252B turboprop engines each rated at 533kW (715shp)
Performance: max cruising speed 495km/h (307mph); range 2456km (1525 miles); service ceiling 8575m (28,140ft)
Dimensions: wingspan 14.00m (45ft 11in); length 12.17m (39ft 11in); height 4.70m (15ft 5in)
Weight: 5352kg (11,800lb) maximum take-off weight
Payload: up to 13 passengers or equivalent freight

BEECH MODEL 1900C AND 1900D

USA: 1982

THE BEECH 1900 WAS LAUNCHED as a higher capacity successor to the Beech 99, and is one of the few commuter airliners of its class/capacity still in production. The 1900C first saw service in 1984 and went on to be produced in executive form and in specialized military format, notably in the USA as the C-12J mission support aircraft. The 1900D succeeded the C version in 1991. Over 330 Beech 1900s have been delivered. Specifications apply to the 1900D.

Crew: 1/2
Powerplant: two 954kW (1279shp) Pratt & Whitney PT6A-67D flat-rated turboprop engines
Performance: max cruising speed 533km/h (331mph); range 2778km (1726 miles) with 10 passengers; service ceiling 10,060m (33,000ft)
Dimensions: wingspan 17.67m (58ft) over winglets; length 17.63m (57ft 10in); height 4.72m (15ft 6in)
Weight: 7688kg (16,950lb) maximum take-off weight
Payload: up to 19 passengers or equivalent freight

This model 1900D was delivered to Mesa Airlines in 1991. The 1900D is most readily discerned from the 1900C by its taller cabin and the stabilization devices on the tailplane and rear underside of the fuselage.

BEECH MODEL 2000 STARSHIP

USA: 1986

Crew: 2
Powerplant: two 895kw (1200shp) flat-rated Pratt & Whitney PT6A-67A turboprop engines
Performance: max speed 620km/h (385mph) at 7620m (25,000ft); range 2804km (1742 miles); service ceiling 10,910m (35,800ft)
Dimensions: wingspan 16.60m (54ft 4.75in); length 14.05m (46ft 1in); height 3.94m (12ft 11in)
Weight: 6758kg (14,900lb) maximum take-off weight
Payload: up to six passengers

The Starship 2000 was a radical small-business aircraft design, drawing on the experience of Burt Rutan and his concurrent Voyager project. The main wings of the Starship 2000 are rear mounted, and forward of the cockpit area are mounted variable geometry canards. The Starship 2000 also extensively utilizes composite materials. The pusher-mode engines

The Beech Model 2000 Starship, a very advanced design, proved too radical in concept and did not appeal to conservative elements in the commercial aircraft market.

(with five-bladed propellers) are mounted on the upper wing surface for noise reduction.

Sales of the aircraft were poor, the Starship 2000 proving a victim of conservatism in the market, and only 53 examples were built until 1995 when production ceased. By 2003 Beech was acquiring examples for destruction in order to delete the type from service and eradicate the associated in-service support costs.

Specifications apply to the Beech Model 2000A Starship 1.

BELL P-39 AIRACOBRA

USA: 1939

A P-39D Airacobra flown by Aleksandr Pokryshkin, who scored most of his 59 'kills' while flying the type.

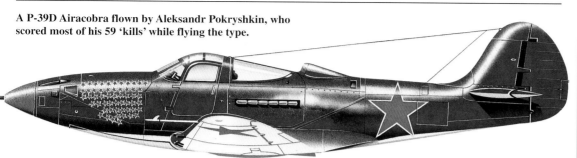

Crew: 1
Powerplant: one 895kW (1200hp) Allison V-1710-85 12-cylinder V-type engine
Performance: max speed 642km/h (399mph); range 1207km (750 miles); service ceiling 11,735m (38,500ft)
Dimensions: wingspan 10.36m (34ft); length 9.19m (30ft 2in); height 3.78m (12ft 5in)
Weight: 3720kg (8200lb) loaded
Armament: one hub-firing 37mm (1.46in) gun; two 12.7mm (0.50in) machine guns in upper forward fuselage; four 7.62mm (0.30in) machine guns in the wings; provision for one 227kg (500lb) bomb under the fuselage

THE DESIGN OF THE BELL P-39 Airacobra was unusual in that its Allison in-line engine was installed below and behind the pilot's seat, driving the propeller via an extension shaft coupled to a gearbox in the nose of the aircraft. The XP-39 prototype flew in April 1939 and, although no orders were immediately forthcoming from the US military, France placed an order for 100 aircraft. Some of these were taken over by the RAF in 1941, but the type fell far short of British expectations and only one squadron (No 601) was issued with it and then only for a short time. The RAF's conviction that the P-39 would fare badly in the European theatre was borne out in 1942, when the USAAF's 31st Fighter Group brought its P-39s to England. In a sweep over Europe it lost six out of 12 aircraft, and hurriedly rearmed with Spitfires.

The first model to serve with the USAAF was the P-39C, which was followed by the P-39D with self-sealing fuel tanks. The Airacobra went into action with the 8th Pursuit Group in northern Australia early in 1942, which subsequently deployed its aircraft to forward airstrips in New Guinea. Shortly afterwards the unit's designation was changed to the 8th Fighter Group and it was joined by the 35th Fighter Group, also equipped with P-39s. The fighters were a mixture of P-39Ds and Airacobra Mk 1s, drawn from the cancelled British order. The Airacobra pilots soon found themselves fighting a desperate battle against superior forces with excellent equipment in the form of the Mitsubishi A6M Zero, an aircraft that could outperform the P-39 on almost every count. The Americans were forced to develop new tactics when attacking enemy bomber formations, in order to avoid engaging in a dogfight with the Zeros; P-39 pilots would try to make one high-speed pass at the enemy, preferably from a higher

P-39 Airacobras of the USAAF Training Command Central Instructors' School. Many P-39s were assigned to training schools.

altitude, then escape at full throttle. If they hit anything with their 37mm (1.46in) cannon during this single pass, destruction of enemy aircraft was virtually assured, as Japanese aircraft were unarmoured.

P-39s were also used by the 347th Fighter Group in New Caledonia, with detachments being deployed to Guadalcanal for air defence. There, primitive airstrips added to the problems faced by Airacobra pilots and ground crews, who had

to cope with the vagaries of the P-39s' Allison engines, which began to overheat almost as soon as the fighter started to taxi. It became common practice to tow the fighters to the end of the runway, so that the engine coolant would not overheat in the high tropical temperatures. Other P-39 variants were the P-39F, -J, -K, -L, -M, -N and -Q, all with progressively uprated engines. As well as the Pacific, P-39s saw action in Tunisia

and during the invasion of southern France, where they were used by Free French squadrons. After the armistice with Italy in September 1943, some fighter-bomber units of the Italian Co-Belligerent Air Force, fighting on the side of the Allies, were also armed with P-39s.

The biggest operator, however, was the Soviet Union, which was supplied with 4773 under Lend-Lease and used them to very good effect. One of the principal

exponents of the P-39 in the Soviet Air Force was Colonel Aleksandr Pokryshkin, who gained most of his 59 victories while flying the type with the 9th Guards Air Regiment. Pokryshkin used much the same tactics as the Americans employed in the Pacific, attacking the enemy from a higher altitude and at high speed. Total P-39 production was 9558 aircraft.

Specifications apply to the Bell P-39N Airacobra.

BELL P-59 AIRACOMET

USA: 1942

AMERICA'S FIRST JET FIGHTER was the Bell P-59 Airacomet, the protoype of which first flew on 1 October 1942 under the power of

two General Electric I-A turbojets, derived from the Whittle W.2B engine. A higher-powered engine, the 635kg (1400lb) thrust I-16, was

The Bell P-59 Airacomet was America's first jet fighter, flying for the first time in October 1942. It did not see operational service.

installed in the 13 trials aircraft which followed.

The Airacomet proved to be underpowered and its performance fell far below expectations, so the original order for 100 aircraft was reduced. Twenty P-59As were built with J31-GE-3 engines, and 30 P-59Bs with J31-GE-5s. The Airacomet did not see operational service in World War II.

Crew: 1
Powerplant: two General Electric J31-GE-3 turbojets
Performance: max speed 664km/h (413mph); range 837km (520 miles); service ceiling 14,080m (46,200ft)
Dimensions: wingspan 13.87m (45ft 6in); length 11.62m (38ft 1in); height 3.66m (12ft)
Weight: 6214kg (13,700lb) loaded
Armament: one 37mm (1.46in) gun and three 12.7mm (0.50in) machine guns in the nose; external bomb or rocket load of 907kg (2000lb)

BELL MODEL 47

USA: 1945

DEVELOPED FROM THE experimental Model 30 in the summer of 1945, the Model 47 broke many helicopter records throughout its long life, remaining in production until the end of 1973. Power was provided by a vertically mounted 131kW (175hp) Franklin. The prototype first flew on 8 December 1945 and on 8 March 1946 received the first full certification for a civil helicopter anywhere in the world. The first commercial deliveries began on 31 December 1946, and 28 Model 47As were delivered to the USAF for evaluation as the YH-13-BE in 1947. In the Korean War H-13Ds were used on medevac duties and evacuated 17,700 casualties. As the OH-13 Sioux, the helicopter was used on observation duties in the war in Vietnam. On 11 December

1957 Bell completed the 2000th Model 47. In Italy, Agusta produced well over 1000 47G/J variants. During 1964, 50 47G-3B-1s were delivered to the British Army (as

Firmly establishing Bell as a leading name in the field of rotary-wing design, the Bell Model 47 earned its reputation during the Korean War (1950–53).

the Sioux AH Mk.1), which also received most of the 253 Model 47G-3B-1s built by Westland. In Japan, Kawasaki built the Model 47 under licence until 1975 as the KH-4 and KHR-1. In all more than 40 overseas countries' air forces or naval air arms operated the Model 47. Specifications apply to the Bell 47G-5.

Crew: 2/3
Powerplant: one Avco Lycoming VO-435-B1A flat-six rated at 198kW (265hp)
Performance: max speed 196km/h (105mph) at sea level; combat radius 412km (256 miles); service ceiling 3200m (10,500ft)
Dimensions: main rotor diameter 11.32m (37ft 1.5in); length 13.17m (43ft 2.5in); height 2.82m (9ft 3in)
Weight: 786kg (1733lb)

BELL X-1

USA: 1947

Captain Charles 'Chuck' Yeager in the cockpit of the Bell X-1, in which he became the first man to exceed the speed of sound on 14 October 1947.

THE FIRST OF THE SO-CALLED X-craft, funded for research purposes by the US Air Force and Navy under the supervision of NACA (later NASA), the Bell X-1 was the first rocket-powered American aircraft. The initial three X-1 prototypes became the first aircraft in the world to achieve supersonic flight on 14 August 1947, being launched from a B-29 Superfortress at 9000m (29,500ft). Piloted by Captain Charles Yeager, the aircraft reached a speed of 1078km/h (670mph) or Mach 1.015 in level flight. On 8 August 1949, Major Frank Everest flew the X-1 to a record 21,925m (71,881ft). Another three improved aircraft were built (the X-1A, X-1B and X-1D), and in the first of these Yeager reached a speed of 2655km/h (1650mph) or Mach 2.435 on 12 December 1953. On 4 June 1954, another pilot, Arthur Murray, reached 27,435m (over 90,000ft). The last of the series was the X-1E, converted from the second X-1 to test a new high-speed wing. In all, X-1 series aircraft made 231 flights. Specifications apply to the basic X-1.

Crew: 1
Powerplant: one 2721kg (6000lb) thrust Reaction Motors Model 6000 C4 rocket motor
Performance: max speed 1609km/h (1000mph); range n/a; ceiling 27,435m (90,000ft)
Dimensions: wingspan 8.53m (28ft); length 9.45m (31ft); height 3.3m (10ft 10in)
Weight: 6078kg (13,400lb) loaded
Armament: none

BELL X-5

USA: 1951

FIRST FLOWN ON 20 JUNE 1951, the Bell X-5 was the world's first variable-geometry aircraft, its wing sweep able to be altered in flight at angles between 20 and 60 degrees. To achieve this, the wing was supported on rollers which moved along tracks located on the inboard

The Bell X-5 was the world's first variable-geometry design and owed much to the German Messerschmitt P.1101.

ends of the wing panels, and sweep from 20 to 60 degrees required only 30 seconds to complete.

Two X-5s were built, both being extensively flight-tested by the USAF and NACA (later NASA). One crashed in October 1953, but the other went on to serve as a chase plane until it was eventually retired in October 1955.

Crew: 1
Powerplant: one 2222kg (4900lb) thrust Allison J35-A-17A turbojet
Performance: max speed 1135km/h (705mph); service ceiling 12,800m (42,000ft); range 1207km (750 miles)
Dimensions: wingspan 9.98m (32ft 9in); length 9.85m (32ft 4in); height 3.65m (12ft)
Weight: 4536kg (10,000lb) loaded
Armament: none

BELL MODEL 204 H-40 AND UH-1A-C, E-F, K-M, P IROQUOIS   USA: 1956

Crew: 1
Powerplant: (HU-1A) 642kW (860hp) Lycoming T53-L-1A engine derated to 574kW (770shp)
Performance: max speed 227km/h (141mph); combat radius 325km (202 miles); service ceiling 4400m (14,400ft)
Dimensions: main rotor diameter 13.41m (44ft); length 16.15m (53ft); height 3.36m (11ft)
Weight: 2631kg (5800lb)
Armament/Payload: (HU-1B) two 7.62mm (0.30in) machine guns and packs of 24 70mm (2.75in) air-to-surface rockets. Seven passengers or three litters or 1361kg (3000lb) of freight

THE KOREAN WAR PROVED the helicopter in combat, and in February 1955 the US Army sought a new, more powerful utility helicopter with greater payload. Bell responded with the Model 204 powered by a 522kW (700shp) Lycoming XT-53-L free turbine (turboshaft) which made the H-40 the first turbine-powered aircraft, either fixed-wing or rotary, ordered

by the US Army. The first of three XH-40 prototypes flew on 20 October 1956 and was followed by six YH-40 service test models and nine HU-1 pre-production models. Delivery of 173 HU-1A Iroquois began in June 1959. Soon 'Huey', which derived from the HU prefix, became the helicopter's accepted name and remained so even when in 1962 the service designation changed to UH-1. During 1961–1965 1010 improved HU-1B-BF (UH-1B-BF) examples were delivered, followed by a number of main types with 749 UH-1C, 192 UH-1E and 119 UH-1F examples being built.

Hueys were among the first helicopters sent to Vietnam, where their reputation as superb gunships and medevac aircraft was gained. In Italy, Agusta built 238 AB 204B models equivalent to the US Army's UH-1B for military and civil use with seating for a pilot and 10 passengers. The first AB 204B flew in May 1961, and production

In 1962 Hueys were among the first helicopters sent to Vietnam. They subsequently became the most important helicopters in Southeast Asia.

models appeared in four main sub-variants. When production ended in 1974 some 238 Italian Hueys had been produced. In Japan Fuji-Bell built 90 UH-1Bs for the JGSDF and 34 Model 204Bs for

commercial operators. As well as operating with the US Army, USAF, USN and USMC, Hueys were operated by the air arms of 18 overseas nations. Specifications apply to the Bell UH-1A.

BELL MODEL 205 UH-1D/H/N/U/V/X IROQUOIS   USA: 1961

Crew: 1
Powerplant: one Textron Lycoming T53-L-13 turboshaft engine rated at 1044kW (1400shp)
Performance: max speed 204km/h (127mph); combat radius 511km (318 miles); service ceiling 3840m (12,600ft)
Dimensions: main rotor diameter 14.63m (48ft); length 17.62m (57ft 9in); height 4.41m (14ft 5.5in)
Weight: 2363kg (5210lb)
Armament/Payload: up to 14 passengers or six litters and one medical attendant; or 1814kg (4000lb) of freight

ALTHOUGH OVERALL THE HUEY performed well in Vietnam, in the hot regions and at high elevations especially, it lacked sufficient lifting capacity. A redesign of the Model 204 led to a slightly longer fuselage, increased cabin space to accommodate a pilot and up to 12 troops or six stretchers and a medical attendant, or 1814kg (4000lb) of freight, and the installation of a more powerful 820kW (1100shp) Lycoming T53-l-11

Initially the UH-1N was delivered to the USAF in 1970 and the USN, USMC and CAF in 1971.

turboshaft engine. Larger cargo doors, twin cabin windows on each side and a larger transmission housing with twin louvres made the Model 205 outwardly distinguishable from the Model 204. The first YUH-1D flew on 16 August

1961, and delivery of 2008 UH-1D-BFs began in May 1963. Some 3573 more powerful UH-1H versions were delivered to the US Army and 1317 were built for export. The Model 204A-1 was produced under licence by Agusta,

which built 490 AB-205s by early 1988 when production ended. Fuji-Bell built 107 HU-1H models. No fewer than 48 nations have used the Model 205.

Specifications apply to the Bell UH-1H Iroquois.

BELL MODEL 206 JET RANGER (OH-58/ TH-57)　　　USA: 1962

An OH-58 Kiowa firing its port-mounted 7.62mm (0.30in) Minigun over Vietnam on 2 December 1969.

PRODUCED ORIGINALLY AS THE Model D-250, this four-seat helicopter was designed to meet a 1960 US Army requirement for a lightweight observation helicopter (LOH). The first YHO-4A-BF flew on 8 December 1962, but the Hughes Model 369 (YHO-6A-HU) was declared the winner in May 1965. A commercial derivative of the OH-4A emerged as the Model 206A (JetRanger) with a completely new fuselage and was powered by a 236kW (317shp) Allison 250-C18A turboshaft engine. The prototype flew in December 1965 and deliveries began on 13 January 1967. By December 1968 some 361 commercial examples had been built in the USA.

In 1967 rising production costs of the OH-6A saw the US Army re-open the LOH competition. On 8 March 1968 the Bell Model 206A was declared the winner and an initial order for 2200 OH-58A Kiowas (the militarized version of the 206A) followed. In January 1968 the USN ordered 40 TH-57A SeaRangers and later acquired 51 TH-57B and 89 TH-57C models. In the 1970s improved Model 206B JetRanger II and III versions appeared while Beech Aircraft produced airframes for both the commercial and military variants of the Model 206A. In 1983 the Model L-3 LongRanger III appeared and was followed in 1992 by the LongRanger IV. By the late 1990s over 1650 LongRangers had been built, and in total Bell and its licensees had produced over 7700 Model 206s, 4400 of which were 206Bs and 2200 military variants.

Manufactured in Italy since the end of 1967, the Agusta AB 206 JetRanger is virtually identical. A small number of the thousand or so Italian-built JetRangers were purchased by civil operators, but the majority were acquired for the Italian Army and by other nations for military use.

Specifications apply to the Bell 206B-3 JetRanger III.

Crew: 1
Powerplant: 313kW (420shp) Allison 250-C20B turboshaft engine flat-rated to 236kW (317shp)
Performance: max speed 214km/h (133mph); combat radius 732km (455 miles); service ceiling 3900m (12,800ft)
Dimensions: main rotor diameter 10.16m (33ft 4in); length 11.82m (38ft 9.5in); height 3.17m (10ft 4.25in)
Weight: 760kg (1677lb)
Payload: up to four passengers or 635kg (1400lb) of freight carried internally or 680kg (1500lb) of freight carried externally

BELL MODEL 209 (AH-1G HUEYCOBRA)　　　USA: 1965

Crew: 2
Powerplant: 1342kW (1800shp) AlliedSignal (originally Textron Lycoming) T53-L-703 turboshaft engine transmission limited to 962kW (1290shp)
Performance: max speed 227km/h (141mph); combat radius 507km (315 miles); service ceiling 3720m (12,200ft)
Dimensions: main rotor diameter 13.41m (44ft); length 16.18m (53ft 1in); height 4.09m (13ft 5in)
Weight: 2993kg (6598lb)
Armament/Payload: one 20mm (0.79in) M197 three-barrel cannon; up to 998kg (2200lb) of disposable stores

IN MARCH 1965 BELL began work at its own expense on the Model 209 'Cobra'. This highly innovative combat helicopter design owed its origins to the Design D-255 Iroquois Warrior project of 1962 and the scaled-down and heavily armed and armoured D-262, which

in 1964 lost out to Lockheed's AH-56A Cheyenne in the Advanced Aerial Fire Support System (AAFSS) competition. Bell then

The United States Marine Corps AH-1W SuperCobra was originally conceived to meet an Iranian requirement.

BELL MODEL 61 (HSL-1)
The Model 61 (HSL-1) was a large tandem-rotor four-seat ASW helicopter which won a US Navy design competition in June 1950. It was powered by a single 1790kW (2400hp) P&W R-2800-50 engine in the centre fuselage. The XHSL-1 prototype first flew on 4 March 1953, and in total 50 HSL-1 examples were built.

BELL X-2
Two X-2 research aircraft were built, using stainless-steel wings and tails. They established speed (3370km/h / 2093mph) and altitude (38,405m / 126,000ft) records, and first flew in 1954.

BELL X-14
The X-14 was a research aircraft, built in 1956 to investigate jet-deflection systems. First transition from the hover to forward flight was made on 24 May 1958.

BELL MODEL 200 (XV-3)
The Bell Model 200 resulted from an August 1950 design competition for the development of a US Army 'convertiplane', where flight is a compromise between a helicopter's VTOL capabilities and the level flight characteristics of the aeroplane. Two test aircraft with two wing-mounted sets of rotors were built, and the first full conversion flight took place on 18 December 1958. Ultimately the project was unsuccessful.

BELL D-188A
The D-188A was a projected Mach 2 V/STOL strike-fighter for the US Navy. A mock-up of the design was built in 1959.

BELL MODEL 533
The Model 533 was a highly modified YH-40-BF which was used as a research test-bed in 1959–69 to test a range of rotor systems and methods of drag reduction for helicopters.

put forward the Model 209 in competition with other proposals from Kaman, Boeing-Vertol, Piasecki and Sikorsky for an interim gunship to meet immediate combat needs in Southeast Asia. The Model 209 flew on 7 September 1965 and

on 11 March 1966 beat the three remaining competing helicopters. A production contract for 110 AH-1Gs followed. Deliveries began in June 1967 and deployment to Vietnam late that year. By 1971 orders were increased to 1126 and

the last Cobra was delivered in February 1973. The USMC also operated 38 AH-1Gs (1969–April 1971) and 69 twin-engined AH-1J SeaCobras, the last being produced in February 1975. Iran received 202 AH-1Js and a number of overseas

customers operated both the AH-1G and -1H. Some 57 AH-1T Improved SeaCobras with the TOW system were also built for the USMC; the first was delivered in October 1977.

Specifications apply to the Bell AH-1F HueyCobra.

BELLANCA MODEL P AIRBUS AND AIRCRUISER

USA: 1930

THE AIRBUS SINGLE-ENGINE D transport aircraft was developed from an earlier high-wing design – the Model K – and the type took Bellanca's wing bracing concept to a new level by creating a partial lower wing with an undercarriage which was enclosed below the main bracing point.

Although the onset of the Great Depression impacted sales, an order was received from the USAAC for 14 examples initially, the first four deliveries designated Y1C-27 and the later 10 with an uprated engine.The Airbus was further developed and renamed as the Aircruiser; however, regulation changes in the USA during the mid-1930s made operation of

single-engined aircraft for transport services difficult. Remaining sales of the Aircruiser were therefore concentrated in

This Aircruiser was donated to the Tillabrook Air Museum in Oregon, USA, where it remains the sole airworthy example.

Canada, where float conversion was popular because of the many lakes and isolated settlements. There were 23 examples of all types built.

Specifications apply to the

Crew: 1/2
Powerplant: one 485kW (650hp) Pratt & Whitney Hornet S3D1G radial engine
Performance: max speed 259km/h (161mph); range 1046km (650 miles); service ceiling 4875m (16,000ft)
Dimensions: wingspan 19.81m (65ft); length 13.03m (42ft 9in); height 3.52m (11ft 6.5in)
Weight: 4613kg (10,170lb) maximum take-off weight
Payload: up to 12 passengers or 1499kg (3305lb) of freight

BELLANCA MODEL 28 FLASH

USA: 1933

Crew: 2
Powerplant: one 729kW (1050hp) Pratt & Whitney R-1830-S3C3G Twin Wasp radial engine
Performance: max speed 467km/h (290mph); range 1287km (800 miles); service ceiling 10,670m (35,000ft)
Dimensions: wingspan 14.65m (46ft 1.75in); length 7.90m (25ft 11in); height 2.64m (8ft 8in)
Weight: 3835kg (8454lb) maximum take-off weight
Armament: four 7.62mm (0.30in) Browning fixed forward-firing machine-guns and one 7.62mm (0.30in) Browning trainable rearward-firing machine gun; up to 726kg (1600lb) of bombs carried under the wing

THE MODEL 28 TOOK two forms, the first being the Model 28-70 built as a two-seat racing aircraft, slightly less powerful than the rebuilt Model

28-90. The Model 28-70 was designed to compete in the 1934 MacRobertson Air Race from Britain to Australia, but following

The Bellanca Flash pictured here was first built as the sole Model 28-70. Rebuilt it was designated 28-90.

a rebuild as the 28-90 it made a record transatlantic crossing in 1936, piloted by James Mollison. Military development of the 28-90 (also known as Flash) proceeded with France ordering 10 as communications types. These were earmarked for the Republican side in the Spanish Civil War and delivery was stopped. The Model 28-110 was ordered by the Chinese Government in 1937. Specifications apply to the Model 28-110.

BELL/BOEING MODEL 901 (V-22 OSPREY)

USA: 1989

THE MODEL 901 WAS DEVELOPED to meet a December 1981 DoD requirement for a Joint Services Vertical Lift Aircraft (JVX) fitted with the tilt-rotor configuration derived from the XV-15. In April 1982, the Bell/Boeing Tilt-Rotor Team began preliminary design, Bell being responsible for the wing, nacelles, transmissions, rotor, hub assemblies and the integration of the engines, Boeing-Vertol for the tail unit, overwing fairings,

fuselage and avionics integration. Originally, the project was Army-led but in January 1983 the US Navy took over. After experiments with different scale models, a Full-Scale Development (FSD) proposal programme was accepted and this began in June 1985.

The first of six FSD (YV-22A) aircraft flew on 19 March 1989 and the first conversion from helicopter to aeroplane mode was made on 14 September. During

tests the four FSD aircraft flew at altitudes up to 4572m (15,000ft) and achieved a 457km/h (284mph) airspeed in level flight. The fifth FSD was badly damaged on its first flight and on 21 July 1992 the fourth FSD crashed, killing all seven people on board. Attempts were already under way to cancel the programme and by now only the USMC still saw a need for the Osprey. Flight-testing resumed in June 1993. In August it was obvious

that only a tilt-rotor type, and not competing helicopters, could meet the USMC's pressing demands for speed and range. It was estimated that 425 Ospreys would be needed to replace the CH-53 and CH-46 helicopters. In September 1994 production of the V-22 was finally authorized, with the MV-22A scheduled for delivery to the USMC, 50 CV-22As to the USAF from 2003 and 48 HV-22As to the USN from 2010. Following two fatal crashes in 2000 the grounded aircraft had to be redesigned.

Specifications apply to the Bell Boeing MV-22A Osprey.

Crew: 3/4
Powerplant: two Allison T406-AD-400 turboshaft engines each rated at 4586kW (6150shp)
Performance: max speed 185km/h (115mph) at sea level; combat radius 935km (581 miles); service ceiling 7925m (26,000ft)
Dimensions: width overall 25.55m (83ft 10in); length 17.47m (57ft 4in); height 6.63m (21ft 9in)
Weight: 15,032kg (33,140lb)
Payload: up to 24 troops or 12 litters plus medical attendants; or 9072kg (20,000lb) of freight carried internally

When it enters service the V-22 Osprey will be capable of lifting payloads of 24 troops or 9072kg (20,000lb) of internal freight.

BENSEN GYRO-COPTERS

USA: 1955

A POWERED AUTOGYRO conversion of the Gyro-Glider designed for home construction from kits or plans. Models B-8M, B-8V, Super Bug and the B-8MW twin-float Hydro-Copter utilized various engines, the Super-Bug being powered by a twin-engine to spin up the rotor prior to take-off.

The B-8HD of 1979 was based on the Super Bug design and used a hydraulic drive to feed about 3kW (4hp) from the engine to the rotor, instead of having a separate engine for pre-rotation. The B-8MJ had a power head fitted to enable the aircraft to take off vertically without ground roll. The B-8MH Hover-Gyro, which appeared in 1976, was a 'Hovering Gryo-Copter' powered by a 52–82kW (70–110hp) modified water-cooled outboard engine driving the lower of the two rotors; the upper rotor autorotated.

Specifications apply to the Bensen Model B-8M Gyro-Copter.

Crew: 1/2
Powerplant: one McCulloch Model 4318GX or AX flat-four engine rated at 67kW (90shp) or 54kW (72hp) respectively
Performance: max speed 137km/h (85mph) at sea level; range 161km (100 miles); service ceiling 3810m (12,500ft)
Dimensions: main rotor diameter 6.10m (20ft); length 3.45m (11ft 4in); height 3.45m (11ft 4in)
Weight: 112kg (247lb)

The Bensen Gyro-Copter has been produced in several variants, including one with twin floats known as the Hydro-Copter. Climbing at 366m/min (1200fpm), Bensens have been known to reach 4572m (15,000 ft) or more.

**BELL MODEL 208
TWIN DELTA**
The Model 208 Twin Delta was a twin-engined configuration giving the UH-1 more power by using two Continental T72-T-2 Model 217 turboshafts. It flew for the first time on 29 April 1965.

**BELL MODEL 214
HUEY PLUS AND 214ST
SUPER TRANSPORT**
This was a more powerful 1970s variant of the UH-1, powered by a 1417kW (1900shp) Lycoming T53-L-702. Orders for 287 machines for Iran were received in December 1972. Some 70 Model 214B commercial derivative models and over 200 214ST 'Stretched Twin'/Super Transport variants followed worldwide.

**BELL MODEL 309
KINGCOBRA**
Essentially a scaled-up AH-1G Cobra armed with TOW missiles. Two prototypes were built, one with a single 2126kW (2850shp) Avco-Lycoming T55-L-7C turboshaft engine, the other with the 1343kW (1800shp) P&W T400-CP-400 turboshaft TwinPac.

BELL MODEL 409 (YAH-63)
One of two designs selected by the US Army in June 1973 for the Advanced Attack Helicopter (AAH) competition ultimately won by the Hughes Model 77 (YAH-64) on 10 December 1976.

BELL MODEL 222
A twin-turbine 10-seat helicopter, the first of five prototypes flying on 13 August 1976. Over 156 Model 222Bs and 72 222UTs (Utility Twin) were delivered, mainly to the civil market, before production ceased in the late 1980s.

BELL MODEL 301 (XV-15)
The first of two tilt-rotor XV-15s flew on 3 May 1977. The second prototype successfully went from vertical to horizontal flight in July 1979, paving the way for future tilt-rotor projects.

BEREZNIAK-ISAYEV BI-1

Crew: 1
Powerplant: one 300kg (662lb) thrust Dushkin D-1A rocket motor
Performance: max speed 600km/h (370mph); endurance 8 minutes; ceiling 9000m (29,520ft)
Dimensions: wingspan 7.20m (23ft 7.5in); length 7.00m (22ft); height 2.10m (6ft 10.74in)
Weight: 1650kg (3638lb) loaded
Armament: two 20mm (0.79in) ShVAK cannon in fuselage nose

THE BEREZNIAK-ISAYEV BI-1 was the first Russian attempt to produce a short-range, rocket-propelled target-defence interceptor, designed to have a rate of climb of 180m/sec (35,400ft/min). It was to be powered by a Dushkin D-1 rocket motor, which was successfully tested in a glider that had been towed to altitude. Of mixed construction, the BI-1, a small low-wing monoplane, was built in only 40 days and was flown as a glider for the first time on 10 September 1941. The first powered test flight of the aircraft was made on 15 May 1942 and was successful, but shortly afterwards the prototype was destroyed when it crashed during a maximum-power run at

The Berezniak-Isayev BI-1 was designed as a short-range, rocket-propelled target-defence interceptor. Seven pre-series aircraft were built, but the project was abandoned.

low level. Despite this setback, seven pre-series aircraft were built and the programme went ahead. Subsequent flight trials, however, were to reveal unforeseen aerody-

namic problems with the monoplane. These difficulties, together with the fact that Dushkin's work on a multi-chamber rocket motor encountered innumer-

able snags, and that the BI-1's powered endurance of just eight minutes was considered insufficient for operational purposes, were to bring an end to the project.

BERIEV MBR-2 'MOTE'

The MBR-2 was the first flying boat produced by the Beriev Design Bureau, and saw widespread service with the Soviet Navy during and after World War II.

THE BERIEV MBR-2 was Georgi Beriev's first flying-boat design and one that went on to achieve great success. Deliveries of the aircraft to the Soviet Navy began

in 1934, and the definitive version was the MBR-2AM-34, which had a fully enclosed cockpit, glazed mid-ship gunner's position, and a redesigned fin and rudder. Around

1300 examples were built and saw considerable service in World War II with all four Soviet fleets from the winter of 1939–40 to the last actions in 1945.

Following the war, the Beriev MBR-2 was to serve on fishery protection duties for nearly a decade, hence the NATO reporting name 'Mote' which was allocated to it. The MBR-2 could be fitted with a ski undercarriage for use on Arctic operations if necessary.

Crew: 4/5
Powerplant: one 507kW (680hp) M-17 12-cylinder in-line engine
Performance: max speed 200km/h (124mph); range 650km (404 miles); service ceiling 4400m (14,435ft)
Dimensions: wingspan 19.00m (62ft 4in); length 13.50m (44ft 3in); height 5.00m (16ft 5in)
Weight: 4100kg (9039lb)
Armament: one 7.62mm (0.30in) ShKAS machine gun on ring mount in bow position and one in mid-ship position; up to 500kg (1102lb) of bombs on underwing racks

BERIEV BE-6 'MADGE'

USSR: 1945

DESIGNED IN 1945, the Be-6 flying boat's flight-testing was completed in 1947. The first production aircraft for the Soviet Navy flew early in 1949, and it formed the mainstay of the Morskaya Aviatsiya's maritime patrol squadrons during the 1950s.

Crew: 7
Powerplant: two 1716kW (2300hp) Shvetsov ASh-73TKs 18-cylinder radial engines
Performance: max speed 415km/h (258mph); range 4900km (3045 miles); **service ceiling** 6100m (20,000ft)

Dimensions: span 33.00m (108ft 4in); length 23.55m (77ft 3in); height 7.48m (24ft 7in)
Weight: 28,112kg (61,976lb) loaded
Armament: five 23mm (0.91in) cannon; 4000kg (8820lb) of bombs or depth charges

When it first flew in 1945 the Beriev Be-6 was the USSR's most advanced flying boat. Given the NATO code-name 'Madge', it was the mainstay of the Soviet Navy's maritime patrol force in the 1950s.

BERIEV BE-12 'MAIL'

USSR: 1960

Crew: 5/6
Powerplant: two 2984kW (4000hp) Ivchenko AI-20D turboprop engines
Performance: max speed 610km/h (379mph); range 4000km (2485 miles); service ceiling 12,185m (40,000ft)
Dimensions: span 32.91m (108ft); length 29.18m (95ft 9in); height 6.68m (21ft 11in)
Weight: 29,500kg (65,035lb) loaded
Armament: up to 10,092kg (22,252lb) of bombs and depth charges; no defensive armament

FIRST SEEN PUBLICLY IN 1961, the turboprop-powered Beriev Be-12 amphibian was the type selected to replace the Be-6 as the Soviet Navy's principal maritime patrol flying-boat. The prototype flew in 1960 and service deployment was rapid; by 1965 it was identified in widespread service with the Soviet Northern and Black Sea Fleets. The Be-12 featured a sharply cranked, high-set wing similar to the Be-6's, a configuration dictated by the need to raise the engines well clear of the water. The single-step hull had a high length-to-beam ratio and was fitted with two long strakes to keep spray away from the engines on take-off. There was a glazed observation position in the nose, surmounted by a long

thimble-type radome, and a 'stinger' tail-housed Magnetic Anomaly Detection (MAD) equipment. During its service career, the Be-12 established numerous records for turboprop-powered amphibians. Allocated the NATO reporting name 'Mail', it was most frequently encountered over the Mediterranean,

The turboprop-powered Be-12 'Mail' was designed to replace the Be-6 in the Soviet Navy's maritime patrol squadrons.

where it deployed to bases in Egypt and Syria, and in the Far East, where it operated from bases in the Vladivostok area.

BERIEV BE R-1

USSR: 1952

Crew: 5
Powerplant: two 2700kg (5953lb) thrust WK-1 turbojet engines
Performance: 760km/h (470mph); range 2000km (1242 miles); ceiling 11,500m (37,720ft)
Dimensions: span 21.40m (70ft 2.5in); length 19.43m (63ft 9in); height n/a
Weight: 17,000kg (37,485lb)
Armament: Two NR-23 cannon in nose and two in tail barbette

THE EXPERIMENTAL BE R-1 flying boat was built in 1951, first flew on 30 May 1952, and had a relatively high performance, although the Soviet naval authorities were not impressed and did not order a production run. Beriev went on to develop a more advanced jet-powered flying boat, the Be-10, first seen publicly in 1961, when four aircraft appeared in formation at the Tushino Air Display. The

Be-10 was evaluated by the Soviet Navy and made a number of record-breaking flights, but did not enter series production; further develop-

ment of jet-powered flying boats was abandoned. It is not known how many aircraft were produced, other than the four seen at Tushino.

A twin-jet, high-wing flying boat, the Be R-1 flew in 1949, powered by two Klimov VK-1 engines. Flight-testing continued until 1951.

BERLINER HELICOPTERS

EMILE AND HENRY BERLINER (father and son) became the most prolific helicopter pioneers in the USA during the early 1920s. They built a series of rotorcraft powered mostly by Le Rhône engines driving rotors mounted side by side above the wings. These designs

were characterized by rigid wooden lifting rotors and fixed wings (sometimes biplane or even triplane wings) and the tail surfaces of a conventional aircraft. Control was achieved using moveable vanes mounted vertically under the rotors. When lowered into a horizontal

position, the vanes caught the slipstream from the rotors, which caused the wing on which they were mounted to drop, which the pilot could use to turn the machine, albeit erratically. The first Berliner helicopter, piloted by Henry, made a brief lurch into the air on 16 June

1922. Later Berliners achieved flights of 91m (300ft) lasting up to a minute and a half, but the control system employed was never really effective. When superior European designs were developed and introduced, the two men soon abandoned their work on helicopters.

BLACKBURN KANGAROO

UK: 1916

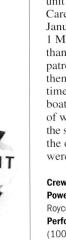

THE BLACKBURN KANGAROO WAS originally designed as a naval reconnaissance and bomber seaplane, but was later converted to

a landplane. Twenty-four Kangaroos were built, the first example flying in July 1916, and 10 of these were issued to No 246 Squadron (the only

The Blackburn Kangaroo was one of the last heavy bombers to be built in Britain before the end of World War I.

unit to operate the type) at Seaton Carew, on the Durham coast, from January 1918. Operations began on 1 May, the Kangaroos flying more than 600 hours on anti-submarine patrols over the North Sea between then and 11 November. During that time they were credited with 12 U-boat sightings and 11 attacks, one of which, on 28 August, resulted in the shared destruction of UC 70 with the destroyer HMS *Ouse*. They were withdrawn in May 1919.

Crew: 4
Powerplant: two 190kW (255hp) Rolls-Royce Falcon II 12-cylinder in-line engines
Performance: max speed 161km/h (100mph); endurance 8 hours; service ceiling 3200m (10,500ft)
Dimensions: wingspan 22.82m (74ft 10in); length 14.02m (46ft); height 5.13m (16ft 10in)
Weight: 3636kg (8017lb) loaded
Armament: two 7.62mm (0.30in) machine guns; up to 453kg (1000lb) of bombs

BLACKBURN RIPON

UK: 1926

Crew: 2
Powerplant: one 425kW (570hp) Napier Lion 12-cylinder liquid-cooled V-type engine
Performance: max speed 203km/h (126mph); range 1310km (815 miles); service ceiling 3050m (10,000ft)
Dimensions: wingspan 13.66m (44ft 10in); length 10.97m (36ft); height 4.06m (13ft 4in)
Weight: 3359kg (7405lb) loaded
Armament: one forward-firing 7.62mm (0.30in) Vickers machine gun; one 7.7mm (0.303in) Lewis gun in rear cockpit; one Mk VIII or Mk X torpedo, or up to 750kg (1653lb) of other ordnance

THE BLACKBURN RIPON torpedo-bomber, the prototype of which flew on 17 April 1926, was a more powerful development of the Blackburn Dart, which it actually replaced in Fleet Air Arm service from 1929. The type was produced in three principal variants, the Mk II, Mk IIA, and Mk IIC, the latter having an all-metal wing structure. Production of the Ripon continued until 1933, with 91 aircraft being built for British military service. The Ripon was a very versatile

A versatile aircraft, the Blackburn Ripon was widely used by the Royal Navy in the 1930s. Its primary role was torpedo-bomber, but it was also used for long-range reconnaissance, fitted with extra fuel tanks.

aircraft and not restricted to the role of a torpedo-bomber; indeed, in the long-range reconnaissance role, with the guns removed and auxiliary fuel tanks fitted, it had an endurance of up to 10 hours. A Pegasus-engined version was built under licence in Finland.

Specifications apply to the Blackburn Ripon Mk II.

BLACKBURN BAFFIN

UK: 1932

THE BAFFIN TWO-SEAT TORPEDO bomber was developed by Blackburn as a private venture, the company marrying what was already a well-proven airframe design to a Bristol Pegasus radial engine. The two Baffin prototypes appeared in 1932 and 1933, and production began in September of the latter year. Only 29 Baffins were built, but 60 Blackburn Ripons were also re-engined with

The Blackburn Baffin torpedo-bomber was basically a Ripon fitted with a Bristol Pegasus engine. The type served with the Royal Navy until 1937.

the Pegasus and converted into Baffins. The aircraft served on three aircraft carriers until 1937, when they were replaced by the Fairey Swordfish. Some of the ex-RN Baffins were shipped to New Zealand in 1938, equipping three squadrons of the RNZAF.

Crew: 2
Powerplant: one 421kW (565hp) Bristol Pegasus 1.M3 radial engine
Performance: max speed 219km/h (136mph); range 869km (540 miles); service ceiling 4570m (15,000ft)
Dimensions: wingspan 13.88m (45ft 6in); length 11.68m (38ft 3in); height 3.91m (12ft 10in)
Weight: 3452kg (7610lb) loaded
Armament: one fixed forward-firing 7.7mm (0.303in) Vickers machine gun; one 7.7mm (0.303in) gun on flexible mounting in rear cockpit; under-fuselage rack for one torpedo or up to 907kg (2000lb) of bombs

BELLANCA MODEL 14
A single-engined, low-wing light aircraft first flown in 1937, the Bellanca Model 14 went through numerous variants and updates until 1980, by which point some 1600 plus had been built.

BELLANCA 260
A tricycle undercarriage version of the Bellanca Model 14, the Bellanca 260 was powered with a 194kW (259hp) engine.

BELLANCA 28-110
The Bellanca 28-110 was a low-wing monoplane fighter-bomber, a few of which were supplied to China in 1938.

BELLANCA 14-19 CRUISEMASTER
A development from the single-enginedCruisair 14 series of Bellanca light aircraft, the Cruisemaster rights were sold to Northern Aircraft Inc. (later Downer) in 1959, and more than 100 examples were built.

BELLANCA SKYROCKET AND SKYROCKET II
This Giuseppe Bellanca design has been offered in a number of variants by successor companies since 1975. The Skyrocket is a single-engined low-wing cabin monoplane with up to six seats.

BENNETT AVIATION P.L.11 AIRTRUK
A single-engined agricultural monoplane, the Bennett Aviation P.L.11 Airtruk was designed in New Zealand and is similar to the Kingsford Smith P.L.7 (both of which were designed by Luigi Pellarini), first flown in 1960.

BENOIST XIV
On 1 January 1914, a two-seat Benoist XIV flying boat inaugurated the world's first daily scheduled commercial service, flying between St Petersburg (Florida) and Tampa. The flight time was just 22 minutes.

BLACKBURN SHARK

UK: 1933

Crew: 2/3
Powerplant: one 567kW (760hp) Armstrong Siddeley Tiger VI 14-cylinder radial engine
Performance: max speed 245km/h (152mph); range 1005km (625 miles); service ceiling 5000m (16,400ft)
Dimensions: wingspan 14.02m (46ft); length 10.72m (35ft 2in); height 3.68m (12ft 1in)
Weight: 3651kg (8050lb) loaded
Armament: one forward-firing 7.7mm (0.303in) Vickers machine gun; one Lewis gun in rear cockpit; one Mk VIII or Mk X torpedo, or up to 715kg (1576lb) of other ordnance

The Blackburn Shark succeeded the Baffin as the Royal Navy's primary torpedo-bomber and reconnaissance aircraft. It was replaced by the Fairey Swordfish from 1938.

THE BAFFIN'S SUCCESSOR on the Royal Navy's aircraft carriers in the torpedo-bomber and reconnaissance roles was the Blackburn Shark. It first flew on 24 August 1933. A contract was signed covering an initial batch of 16 aircraft, the first Shark Mk I entering service in May 1935. A month later a new contract was signed for three aircraft of the second series (Mk II), and further orders in 1935 and 1936 brought the eventual total built to 126. The final version was the Shark Mk III, which had a glazed cockpit canopy. The Shark was progressively replaced by the Fairey Swordfish from 1938. A seaplane variant was used for reconnaissance and gunnery spotting on board the battleship *Warspite* and battlecruiser *Repulse*. Seventeen Mk IIIs were built under licence in Canada for the RCAF, while six Shark IIAs were exported to Portugal. Specifications apply to the Shark Mk II.

BLACKBURN SKUA/ROC

UK: 1937

THE BLACKBURN SKUA two-seat naval dive-bomber was designed to meet the requirements of Specification O.27/34, and the prototype flew in 1937. The Skua was the first monoplane to be adopted by the Royal Navy, and it saw more action as a fighter than it did in its intended role. Skuas shot down the first German aircraft to fall victim to British fighters in World War II. It happened on 25 September 1939, when a Dornier 18 maritime reconnaissance seaplane was brought down by Skuas of No 803 Squadron Fleet Air Arm from the aircraft carrier HMS Ark Royal.

In operations off Norway in April–May 1940, Skuas dive-bombed and sank the steamer *Bahrenfels* and the light cruiser *Konigsberg*. The bombing was highly accurate, particularly in the case of the *Konigsberg*, which exploded and sank after suffering three direct hits and a dozen near misses. She was the first major warship to be sunk by air attack in war. The success of this operation reinforced the belief that emphasis should be laid on the Skua's dive-bombing role, but at this stage in the war the Royal Navy was desperately short of modern fighters for fleet protection, and this was the role increasingly performed by the Blackburn aircraft. The fact that the type was not especially suited to the task was underlined in July 1940, when Skuas were detailed to escort Fairey Swordfish torpedo-bombers attacking French warships in Oran harbour. The Skuas were engaged by French Curtiss Hawk 75A fighters, and suffered two losses.

Skuas operated in the North Sea, Atlantic and Mediterranean, and in the later theatre they saw considerable action during the early naval battles between British and Italian forces. On 27 November 1940, for example, Skuas from the *Ark Royal* proved effective in breaking up formations of Italian bombers that were attempting to attack a small convoy heading from Gibraltar for Malta and Alexandria. On several occasions Skuas were used to lead

The Blackburn Skua was an excellent dive-bomber, but the Fleet Air Arm's lack of modern fleet defence fighters led to its use in this role.

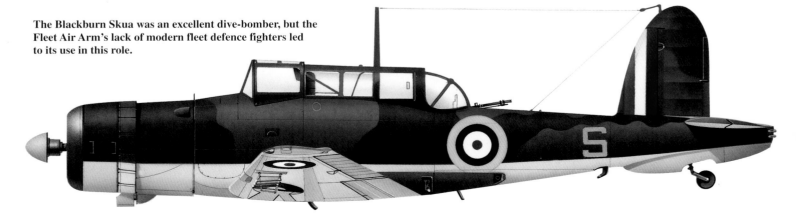

formations of RAF fighters, launched from aircraft carriers, to the besieged island of Malta.

The Skuas were replaced by Fairey Fulmars and Hawker Sea Hurricanes in 1941. After being withdrawn from first-line service, Skuas continued to serve for some years as target tugs and training aircraft. In all, the Skua served with 27 Fleet Air Arm squadrons, four of which were first-line units. The Fleet Air Arm Museum at RNAS Yeovilton, Somerset, UK, has the forward cockpit section of a Skua that crash-landed in Norway in 1940. Restoration and reconstruction was undertaken by the FAA Museum in conjunction with the Norsk Luftfartsmuseum, Bodo, Norway.

The Blackburn Roc was a fighter variant with a dorsal power-operated turret mounting four 7.62mm (0.30in) Browning machine guns, and was developed to meet Specification O.30/35. The installation of the turret resulted in a fuselage that was slightly wider than the Skua's, and increased wing dihedral replaced the upturned wingtips that had been a

The Skua served with 27 Fleet Air Arm squadrons before and during World War II. It was the first British fighter to destroy a German aircraft in 1939.

recognition feature of the earlier aircraft. The Roc flew for the first time on 23 December 1938, one of the three prototypes being converted to floatplane configuration. The Blackburn Roc was not a success, however, serving with only two land-based squadrons before being relegated to second-line duties. Production totalled 192 Skuas and 136 Rocs, the latter all being built by Boulton Paul.

Specifications apply to Skua II.

Crew: 2
Powerplant: one 664kW (890hp) Bristol Perseus XII 9-cylinder radial engine
Performance: max speed 363km/h (225mph); range 1220km (761 miles); service ceiling 5820m (19,100ft)
Dimensions: wingspan 14.07m (46ft 2in); length 10.85m (35ft 7in); height 3.81m (12ft 6in)
Weight: 3727kg (8228lb)
Armament: five forward-firing 7.62mm (0.30in) Browning machine guns; 335kg (740lb) of bombs

BLACKBURN FIREBRAND

UK: 1942

The Blackburn Firebrand was developed as a torpedo-bomber, but was too late to see service in World War II.

Crew: 1
Powerplant: one 1865kW (2500hp) Bristol Centaurus IX 18-cylinder radial engine
Performance: max speed 563km/h (350mph); range 1200km (746 miles); service ceiling 8690m (28,510ft)
Dimensions: wingspan 15.62m (51ft 3in); length 11.86m (38ft 11in); height 4.55m (14ft 11in)
Weight: 7938kg (17,500lb) loaded
Armament: four 20mm (0.79in) Hispano cannon; one 839kg (1850lb) torpedo or two 435kg (1000lb) bombs

THE FIREBRAND WAS DESIGNED as a short-range, heavily armed naval interceptor, the first of three prototypes flying on 27 February 1942. Nine pre-series aircraft were ordered, designated Firebrand F.Mk 1, and following carrier evaluation it was decided to re-develop the aircraft as a torpedo-fighter, designated Firebrand TF.Mk 2. Because of a shortage of Sabre engines, it was then decided to re-engine the aircraft with a Bristol Centaurus

radial, the new model emerging as the Firebrand TF.Mk 3. With further modifications the aircraft became the TF.Mk 4 and entered service with No 813 Squadron in September 1945, too late to see action in World War II. Only Nos 813 and 827 Squadrons were armed with the Firebrand, 225 of which were built. The last variant of the type was the TF.Mk 5A, with powered ailerons.

Specifications apply to the Blackburn Firebrand TF. Mk 5.

BLACKBURN BEVERLEY

The Blackburn Beverley heavy-lift transport performed sterling work for RAF Transport Command until it was replaced by the Lockheed Hercules in the mid-1960s. It entered service in April 1956.

THE BEVERLEY C.1 MILITARY transport entered service with RAF Transport Command in April 1956, an initial order for 20 aircraft having been placed in 1952. The first squadron to receive the type, in March 1955, was No 47. It was also used by Nos 30, 34, 53 and 84 Squadrons until replaced by the Lockheed Hercules a decade later. It could carry 94 passengers in the freight bay and 32 more in the tail boom. In all, 47 aircraft were built before production ceased in 1958.

Crew: 4
Powerplant: four 2126kW (2850hp) Bristol Centaurus 273 18-cylinder radial engines
Performance: max speed 383km/h (238mph); range 2090km (1300 miles); service ceiling 4880m (16,000ft)
Dimensions: wingspan 49.38m (162ft); length 30.30m (99ft 5in); height 11.81m (38ft 9in)
Weight: 4865kg (143,000lb) loaded
Payload: 20,142kg (45,000lb) of freight or 126 passengers

BLACKBURN (BRITISH AEROSPACE) BUCCANEER

Crew: 2
Powerplant: two 5105kg (11,255lb) thrust Rolls-Royce Spey Mk 101 turbofans
Performance: max speed 1040km/h (646mph); range 3700km (2297 miles); service ceiling 12,190m (40,000ft)
Dimensions: wingspan 13.42m (44ft); length 19.33m (63ft 5in); height 4.97m (16ft 3in)
Weight: 28,123kg (62,000lb) loaded
Armament: four 454kg (1000lb) bombs on inside of rotary bomb door; up to 5443kg (12,000lb) of bombs or missiles on underwing pylons

THE BLACKBURN B.103 Buccaneer, which flew for the first time on 30 April 1958, was designed in 1954 to meet a Royal Navy requirement for a high-speed strike aircraft capable of operating from existing carriers and having sufficient

The Blackburn Buccaneer's immensely strong airframe made it ideal for low-level operations with the RAF.

firepower to destroy major enemy surface vessels. Forty production Buccaneer S.Mk 1 aircraft, with Bristol Siddeley Gyron Junior turbojets, were delivered from 1962. They were followed by 84 more powerful S.Mk 2s with Rolls-Royce Spey turbofans. Sixteen S.2s were also supplied to the South African Air Force, these being fitted with an auxiliary rocket motor to assist 'hot and high' take-off.

In 1969 the Royal Navy began transferring its surviving S.2s to the RAF, which had been left without a low-level strike replacement for the Canberra following the cancellation of TSR-2. The ex-RN Buccaneers were designated S.2A, a further 43 new aircraft being equipped to carry the Martel anti-radar missile and designated S.2B. Specifications apply to the S.Mk 2.

BLERIOT V TO X TYPES
FRANCE: 1907

Crew: 1
Powerplant: one Antoinette 37.5kW (50hp) 8-cylinder water-cooled piston engine
Performance: cruising speed 80.5km/h (50mph)
Dimensions: wingspan 11.00m (36ft); length 8.00m (26ft 3in); height 2.75m (9ft)
Payload: one person

PRIOR TO THE SUCCESSFUL English Channel crossing in the Bleriot XI, Louis Bleriot designed and built a number of predecessors. Bleriot V was the first to achieve sustained flight, but the VII may be viewed as the forerunner of later tractor-propelled monoplanes. It had a covered fuselage and engine, and used tailplane elevons as a control surface. Bleriot VII made six flights in 1907, but was lost in an accident in December of that year. Bleriot IX was a variation on the VII and utilized tandem horizontal tail surfaces. Before moving on to the renowned XI, Bleriot experimented with Bleriot X, of a similar configuration to Wright brothers' designs. Specifications apply to VII.

Bleriot's first monoplane, the VII, being prepared for a flight in 1907. The monoplane configuration is a clear forefather of the later monoplanes.

BLERIOT XI
FRANCE: 1909

Crew: 1-3
Powerplant: one 37kW (50hp), 52kW (70hp) or 104kW (140hp) Gnome rotary engine
Performance: max speed 106km/h (66mph); endurance 3 hrs 30 mins; service ceiling 1000m (3280ft)
Dimensions: wingspan 10.33m (33ft 11in); length 8.48m (27ft 10in); height 2.65m (8ft 5in)
Weight: 834kg (1838lb) loaded
Armament: none

IN DECEMBER 1908, Louis Bleriot, who had begun building experimental aircraft that year, exhibited three of his designs at the Salon de l'Automobile et de l'Aéronautique, Paris. Of these, the Bleriot IX was a monoplane with a 75kW (100hp) Antoinette engine, which succeeded in making only a few brief hops, while the Bleriot X, a pusher biplane, was never completed. It was the third machine, the Bleriot XI, that was destined to make Bleriot's reputation and his fortune. Another tractor monoplane type, the Bleriot XI, flew for the first time at Issy on 23 January 1909, powered by a 22kW (30hp) REP engine fitted with a crude four-bladed metal propeller. When the aircraft was modified in April, the REP was replaced by a 19kW (25hp) Anzani engine with a more refined propeller. The aircraft used a wing-warping technique for lateral control, and was the first European aircraft to employ this system effectively.

After making several excellent flights in the spring and summer of 1909, including one of 50 minutes, Bleriot took off in the Type XI from Le Baraques, near Calais, and landed in a field near Dover Castle about half an hour later, so winning the prize of £1000 offered by Lord Northcliffe, proprietor of the London *Daily*

This Bleriot XI is part of the Shuttleworth Collection based at Old Warden, Biggleswade, England. It is in flying condition, but needs a calm day.

Mail, to the first aviator to fly across the English Channel from coast to coast in either direction. The exploit provided an enormous boost for the Type XI, which was soon in production for the French Aviation Militaire and other air arms. On 23 October 1911, Captain Carlo Piazza of the Italian Army Air Service made the first ever war flight by an aircraft, carrying out a reconnaissance of Turkish positions between Tripoli and Azizzia in a Bleriot XI.

During the first year of World War I the Bleriot XI was among the most widely used of Allied observation aircraft. The type served with at least eight escadrilles of the French Aviation Militaire and with six squadrons of the Royal Flying Corps in France. When Italy entered the war in 1915 her air arm had six squadrons equipped with the Bleriot XI.

The type also served with the Belgian Aviation Militaire. As well as performing the all-important reconnaissance role, some Bleriots were used as nuisance bombers, carrying small hand-dropped bombs or flechettes (metal darts) in racks along the fuselage sides under the cockpit coaming. Rifles or pistols were the only other form of armament carried by the crew. In a notable mission which took place on 14 August 1914, Lieutenant Cesari and Corporal Prudhommeaux of the Aviation Militaire, flying a Bleriot XI, bombed the German airship sheds at Metz-Frescaty, and during another similar mission on 18 August French aviators claimed to have destroyed three enemy aircraft and an airship on the ground, although this was unconfirmed. It was also in a Bleriot XI that Captain Joubert de la Ferte of No 3 Squadron made the RFC's first reconnaissance sortie of World War I, flying from Maueuge, Belgium, on 19 August 1914.

The Bleriot XI was produced in five basic variants, 132 aircraft being built in total. The XI Militaire and the XI Artillerie were single-seaters with 37kW (50hp) Gnome rotary engines, the XI-2 Artillerie and XI-2 Genie were two-seaters with 52kW (70hp) Gnome engines, while the XI-3 was a three-seater with a 104kW (140hp) Gnome. A parasol-wing version of the design was designated XI-BG, and was used by the French Aviation Militaire, the RFC and the RNAS. Once their days of first-line service were over, many Bleriots found their way into training units.

A variant of the Bleriot XI seen at Brooklands, Surrey, date unknown. The Bleriot XI was produced in five basic variants, and a parasol-winged version was used by the French Military Air Service.

BLOCH MB.200

FRANCE: 1934

Crew: 4/5
Powerplant: two 649kW (870hp) Gnome-Rhone 14Kirs 14-cylinder radial engines
Performance: max speed 283km/h (176mph); range 1000km (621 miles); service ceiling 8000m (26,245ft)
Dimensions: wingspan 22.45m (73ft 7in); length 15.80m (51ft 10in); height 3.92m (12ft 10in)
Weight: 7480kg (16,490lb) loaded
Armament: one 7.5mm (0.29in) machine gun each in nose and dorsal turrets and ventral gondola; external bomb load of 1200kg (2646lb)

DEVELOPED TO A SPECIFICATION issued in 1932, the French Bloch MB.200 medium-sized twin-engined bomber first flew in 1934, and 12 Escadres de Bombardement were equipped with the type by the end of 1935. At the outbreak of World War II in September 1939, 92 Bloch 200s were still in first-line service in France, and the type was operational on the Lorraine front during the first weeks of the conflict. On 9 September of that year, an aircraft of GB II/31 was

shot down by flak near Saarbrücken, and another MB.200 was forced down on a German airfield and subsequently captured. The aircraft was retired from first-line service in the winter of 1939–40, most being allocated to navigation schools. In March 1940, several aircraft were destroyed by a tornado which devastated the Rhone Valley. Additionally, some captured MB.200s were operated by the Luftwaffe in the training role between 1942 and 1944.

The cumbersome Bloch MB.200 was still in first-line service at the outbreak of World War II, but it was soon retired and the surviving examples assigned to training establishments.

BLOCH MB.151/152

FRANCE: 1938

FIRST FLOWN IN AUGUST 1938, the Bloch MB.151 fighter was a redesign of an earlier unsuccessful prototype, the MB.140. The French Air Force took delivery of 140 examples, but in the meantime production had switched to the MB.152, which had the same airframe but a more powerful engine. It flew for the first time in December 1938, and 482 were delivered to the French Air Force

146 kills and 34 probables during the Battle of France, losing 86 of their own number.

Specifications apply to the Bloch MB.152.

During the Battle of France, Bloch MB.152 pilots claimed the destruction of 146 enemy aircraft. The top-scorer with 7 kills was Sous-Lt Thollon of GC I/8, whose aircraft is pictured below.

Crew: 1
Powerplant: one 806kW (1080hp) Gnome-Rhone 14N-25 14-cylinder radial engine
Performance: max speed 509km/h (316mph); range 540km (335 miles); service ceiling 10,000m (32,808ft)
Dimensions: wingspan 10.54m (34ft 7in); length 9.10m (29ft 10in); height 3.03m (9ft 11in)
Weight: 2800kg (6173lb) loaded
Armament: four 7.5mm (0.29in) fixed forward-firing machine guns, or two 20mm (0.79in) cannon and two 7.5mm (0.30in) machine guns

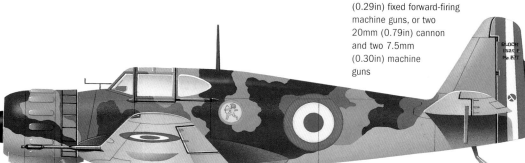

BLOCH MB.174/5

Crew: 3
Powerplant: two 850kW (1140hp) Gnome-Rhone 14N 14-cylinder radial engines
Performance: max speed 530km/h (329mph); range 1285km (798 miles); service ceiling 11,000m (36,090ft)
Dimensions: wingspan 17.90m (58ft 8in); length 12.25m (40ft 2in); height 3.55m (11ft 7in)
Weight: 7160kg (15,784lb) loaded
Armament: three to seven MAC 1934 7.5mm (0.29in) machine guns; internal bomb load of up to 500kg (1,102lb)

THE BLOCH MB.174 reconnaissance bomber was developed from the MB.170, which flew in prototype form only in 1938. Two variants of the type were operated by the French Air Force, the MB.174A3 reconnaissance aircraft and the MB.174B-3 light bomber.

The MB.174's first operational mission was carried out on 29 March 1940 by an aircraft of GR.II/33, flown by Capitaine Antoine de Saint-Exupery, the famous author and philosopher. About 49 Bloch MB.174s (both variants) were used on operations.

The MB.175 was a postwar torpedo-bomber development, with an increased bomb load to that of the MB.174. Eighty examples were produced for service with land-based units of the French Navy. Specifications apply to the Bloch MB.174B-3.

The Bloch MB.174 was an excellent reconnaissance bomber, but it was developed too late to make an impact against the Luftwaffe.

BLOHM UND VOSS BV 138

THE BV 138 RECONNAISSANCE flying boat was designed in 1936–37 and three prototypes of the aircraft flew in 1938. These were fitted with 448kW (600hp) Junkers Jumo engines. These engines were also to have powered the Bv 138A production version; however, extensive modifications to the airframe made some changes necessary. The circular tail booms were replaced by booms of rectangular section, and the rear section of the hull and the vertical tail surfaces were also redesigned. With these modifications and the addition of 522kW (700hp) Jumo 205D engines, the aircraft entered service in 1940 as the Bv 138A-1. The definitive version was the Bv 138C-1, of which 227 were built, bringing the overall total produced to 272. The Bv 138 saw widespread service in the North Atlantic and Arctic waters.

Specifications apply to the Blohm und Voss Bv 138C-1.

Crew: 5
Powerplant: three 746kW (1000hp) Junkers Jumo 205D 12-cylinder diesel engines
Performance: max speed 285km/h (177mph); range 4300km (2672 miles); service ceiling 5000m (16,405ft)
Dimensions: wingspan 26.94m (88ft 4in); length 19.85m (65ft 1in); height 5.90m (19ft 4in)
Weight: 17,650kg (38,912lb) loaded
Armament: one 20mm (0.79in) trainable cannon in bow turret and one in rear hull turret; one 13mm (0.51in) trainable rearward-firing machine gun behind central engine nacelle; one trainable 7.92mm (0.31in) lateral-firing machine gun in starboard hull position; bomb load of 300kg (661lb)

This Bv 138C-1/U1 of 1(F)SAgr 130 was based at Trondheim, Norway, in April 1944.

BLOHM UND VOSS BV 141

GERMANY: 1938

Crew: 3
Powerplant: one 1164kW (1560hp) BMW 801A 14-cylinder radial engine
Performance: max speed 438km/h (272mph); range 1900km (1181 miles); service ceiling 10,000m (32,810ft)
Dimensions: span 17.46m (57ft 3in); length 13.95m (45ft 9in); height 3.60m (11ft 9in)
Weight: 6100kg (13,448lb) loaded
Armament: two 7.92mm (0.31in) machine guns; external bomb load of 200kg (441lb)

THE BV 141 WAS DESIGNED as a tactical reconnaissance aircraft. It had a very unusual asymmetric configuration, with the fully glazed crew nacelle offset to starboard of the centreline and a boom, which carried the engine at the front and the tail unit at the rear, offset to port. The first of three prototypes flew in February 1938. Following flight trials, the airframe was

Although production aircraft had a tailplane offset to port, the first prototype Bv 141A-0 did not have this unusual feature.

strengthened and the tail unit redesigned, the aircraft then being designated Bv 141B. The type was not a success and only a dozen or so examples were built, some being

delivered to Aufklarungsschule 1 at Grossenhain, Saxony for evaluation. Plans were made to equip a Bv 141 unit on the Eastern Front, but these were abandoned.

BLOHM UND VOSS BV 222

GERMANY: 1940

Crew: 11
Powerplant: six 746kW (1000hp) Junkers 207C 12-cylinder radial engines
Performance: max speed 390km/h (242mph); range 6100km (3790 miles); service ceiling 7300m (23,850ft)
Dimensions: wingspan 46.00m (150ft 11in); length 37.00m (121ft 4in); height 10.90m (35ft 9in)
Weight: 49,000kg (108,025lb) loaded
Armament: one 20mm (0.79in) trainable cannon in the dorsal turret and each of the two power-operated wing turrets; 13mm (0.51in) machine guns in the bow position and each of the four lateral hull positions

ORIGINATING IN A DESIGN for a large four-engined commercial flying boat to fly between Berlin and New York, the Bv 222 Wiking (Viking) was reconfigured as a long-range maritime patrol aircraft. The prototype Bv 222V-1 flew on 7 September 1940, and was followed by seven more. Thirteen Bv 222s were completed in total, and these aircraft were pressed into Luftwaffe service as long-range transports or maritime reconnaissance aircraft. Only three survived the war, four additional aircraft

being left uncompleted when further work on the type was halted in 1944. The Bv 222 was the largest flying boat to see operational service in World War II.

The fifth Blohm und Voss Bv 222, seen here, was delivered to Lufttransportstaffel (See) 222 at Petsamo, Finland, in 1943 for transport duties over the northern sector of the Eastern Front. Note the over-wing gun turret.

BOEING FB-1 TO FB-5

USA: 1925

Crew: 1
Powerplant: one 388kW (520hp) Packard 2A-1500 12-cylinder V-type engine
Performance: max speed 256km/h (159mph); range 628km (390 miles); service ceiling 5770m (18,925ft)

Dimensions: wingspan 9.75m (32ft); length 7.14m (23ft 5in); height 2.49m (8ft 2in)
Weight: 1286kg (2835lb) loaded
Armament: one 12.7mm (0.50in) and one 7.62mm (0.30in) fixed forward-firing machine guns

EARLY IN 1925, THE US Navy placed an order for 16 examples of the Boeing PW-9 fighter, which were delivered later that year under the designation FB-1. These aircraft were not adapted for carrier use and were deployed to

US Marine Corps units operating in China. With the installation of arrester gear on two more aircraft for carrier trials on the USS *Langley*, the aircraft's designation was changed to FB-2; the FB-3 and FB-4 were modifications leading to the major production version, the Boeing FB-5. The 27 examples built operated from the carrier USS *Lexington*.

Specifications apply to the Boeing FB-5.

This photograph shows to good advantage the bulky engine and radiator installation on the Boeing FB-3, which caused a massive amount of drag.

BOEING F3B-1   USA: 1928

IN FEBRUARY 1928, the prototype of a new fighter, developed jointly by the US Navy and Boeing in the course of the preceding year, was to make its appearance. This was the F3B-1, 74 of which were delivered from 1929 for service on board the USS *Langley*, *Lexington* and *Saratoga*. The type was based on the F2B-1, but was much more refined – it could be fitted with a single central duralumin float and two wingtip floats, specially designed for launching from standard US Navy catapults.

The F3B-1 showed much cleaner lines than previous Navy fighters. Seventy-four examples saw service on the aircraft carriers *Langley*, *Lexington* and *Saratoga*.

Crew: 1
Powerplant: one 310kW (415hp) Pratt & Whitney Wasp 9-cylinder radial engine
Performance: max speed 253km/h (157mph); range 547km (340 miles); service ceiling 6550m (21,500ft)
Dimensions: wingspan 10.06m (33ft); length 7.57m (24ft 10in); height 2.79m (9ft 2in)
Weight: 1336kg (2945lb) loaded
Armament: one 12.7mm (0.50in) and one 7.62mm (0.30in) fixed forward-firing machine guns

BOEING B-9   USA: 1931

IN JANUARY 1930, as a private venture, designer John Sanders began work on an aerodynamically clean low-wing bomber project, using the Boeing Monomail fast mail-carrier design as his basis. The result was a twin-engined

aircraft bearing the company designation Model 215. The Air Corps encouraged the project, although no funds were made available, and the aircraft was to fly for the first time on 29 April 1929 with the military designation

YB-9. Testing did reveal some shortcomings, including excessive engine vibration and a tendency for the long fuselage to twist in flight. After various improvements, however, the aircraft was adopted for service, undergoing trials as the

Y1B-9A. During these, it was found to be faster than any contemporary bomber, and indeed faster than most of the fighter aircraft of the time.

Disappointingly for Boeing, the Air Corps was to order only

six production B-9s, plus the prototype. The big contract went to the Glenn L. Martin Company's B-10 bomber, which was to be the backbone of the Air Corps' bomber arm for a decade to come.

Crew: 4
Powerplant: two 448kW (600hp) Pratt & Whitney R-1831-13 radial engines
Performance: max speed 299km/h (186mph); range 593km (368 miles); service ceiling 6862m (22,500ft)
Dimensions: wingspan 23.40m (76ft 10in); length 15.70m (51ft 6in); height 3.66m (12ft)
Weight: not known
Armament: one flexible 7.62mm (0.30in) machine gun in nose and one in upper rear fuselage position; up to 996kg (2200lb) of bombs internally and on underwing racks

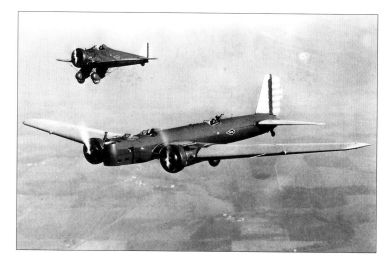

The Boeing B-9 was the first step along the road that led to the evolution of the B-17. Here, a B-9 is seen in company with a P-26.

BOEING P-26

USA: 1932

THE USA WAS TO TAKE its first step on the road to all-metal monoplane fighters with the Boeing P-26, which first flew in March 1932. Deliveries of production P-26As to the US Army Air Corps began at the end of 1933. Its pilots soon bestowed the affectionate nickname of 'Peashooter' on the little fighter. The P-26 became standard pursuit equipment in Hawaii and the Panama Canal area, and in 1940 surplus American P-26s were used

to form the Philippine Army Air Force. Production for the USAAC totalled 111 P-26As and 25 P-26Bs, the latter with a more powerful engine. A further 11 P-26s (P-26Bs) were supplied to China, and these aircraft saw action against the Japanese in Manchuria in 1937. Specifications apply to the P-26A.

P-26 aircraft of the US Army Air Corps. The P-26 was the Air Corp's first all-metal monoplane fighter.

Crew: 1
Powerplant: one 448kW (600hp) Pratt & Whitney Wasp 9-cylinder radial engine
Performance: max speed 377km/h (234mph); range 1000km (621 miles); service ceiling 8300m (27,230ft)
Dimensions: wingspan 8.52m (27ft 11in); length 7.18m (23ft 7in); height 3.05m (10ft)
Weight: 1340kg (2955lb) loaded
Armament: two 12.7mm (0.50in) or 7.62mm (0.30in) fixed forward-firing machine guns

BOEING MODEL 247

A United Air Lines Boeing 247. United ordered 59 examples of the 247 before the prototype had flown, as replacements for its Ford Trimotor fleet.

THE MODEL 247 IS PERHAPS the design that defines the beginning of Boeing's unique lineage of airliners. It had an enclosed cockpit, a retractable undercarriage (but retained a tail wheel), de-icing gear, could operate adequately with one engine out and was considerably faster than the older tri-motors it was designed to replace. The relatively low number produced (75) is partly due to a United Air Lines requirement to have all its launch order delivered before other orders were fulfilled, and the challenge from the Douglas DC-2 and later DC-3.

One example was specially customized for the 1934 MacRobertson air race (Britain to Australia), and many of the improvements were incorporated in the Model 247D variant, while existing aircraft were retrofitted to that standard. Other customers included Deutsche Luft Hansa and the USAAF, which impressed examples of the type during World War II as the C-73. Specifications apply to the Model 247D.

Crew: 3
Powerplant: two Pratt & Whitney S1H1C Wasp radial engines each rated at 410kW (550hp)
Performance: max speed 322km/h (200mph); range 1199km (745 miles); service ceiling 7740m (25,400ft)
Dimensions: wingspan 22.56m (74ft); length 15.72m (51ft 7in); height 3.60m (12ft 1.75in)
Weight: 6192kg (13,650lb) max take-off weight
Payload: up to 10 passengers and 181kg (400lb) of mail.

BOEING B-17 FLYING FORTRESS

THE B-17 FLYING FORTRESS was designed in response to a US Army Air Corps requirement, issued in 1934, for a long-range, high-altitude daylight bomber. The prototype, bearing the company designation Boeing Model 299, flew for the first time on 28 July 1935.

Although the prototype was later destroyed in an accident, the cause was attributed to human error and the project went ahead. Thirteen Y1B-17s and one Y1B-17A were ordered for evaluation, and after the trials period these versions were designated B-17 and B-17A

Boeing B-17G Fortresses setting out on a daylight mission into Germany. The B-17G was fitted with a chin turret as a defence against head-on attacks by heavily-armed German fighters.

A Boeing B-17E Fortress. This variant was the first to feature the distinctive 'Fortress tail' with its long fairing and rear gun turret. It was the first B-17 version to see combat with the USAAF in Europe.

respectively. The first production batch of 39 B-17Bs were all delivered by the end of March 1940; meanwhile a further order had been placed for 38 B-17Cs, which were powered by four Wright 895kW (1200hp) Cyclone engines and featured some minor changes. Twenty of these were supplied to the RAF as the Fortress I in 1941, but after sustaining several losses on bombing operations the remainder were diverted to Coastal Command or the Middle East. By the time the Pacific War began, the B-17D, 42 of which had been ordered in 1940, was in service. This was generally similar to the C model, and the Cs which were in service were subsequently modified to D standard.

A new tail design, the main recognition feature of all subsequent Flying Fortresses, was introduced with the B-17E, together with improved armament which for the first time included a tail gun position. The B-17E was the first version of the Flying Fortress to see combat in the European theatre of operations. The RAF received 42 B-17Es in 1942 under the designation Fortress IIA. A total of 512 B-17Es was produced, this

variant being followed into service by the further refined B-17F, which entered production in April 1942. Total production of the B-17F was 3400, including 61 examples converted to the long-range reconnaissance role as the F-9. Another 19 were delivered to RAF Coastal Command as the Fortress II. The last 86 B-17Fs were fitted with a chin-mounted power-operated Bendix turret mounting a pair of 12.7mm (0.50in) guns, which proved invaluable as the Luftwaffe increasingly adopted frontal fighter attacks. This became standard on the B-17G, the major production model.

The RAF was to receive 85 B-17Gs as the Fortress III, some of these being used for electronic countermeasures. Ten B-17Gs were converted for reconnaissance as the F-9C, while the US Navy and Coast Guard employed 24 PB-1Ws and 16 PB-1Gs for maritime surveillance and aerial survey. About 130 were modified for air–sea rescue duties as the B-17H or TB-17H, with a lifeboat carried under the fuselage and other rescue equipment.

Production of the Fortress, from the B-17F onwards, was shared

between Boeing, Douglas and Lockheed-Vega, which between them produced 8680 B-17Gs. The Free French Air Force used a small number of B-17Fs in Indo-China during the closing stages of the war against Japan, and also used modified B-17Gs in transport and survey roles. Thirteen B-17Gs in all were acquired between 1947 and 1955, all from surplus USAAF or US Government sources, and one of the B-17Fs already in French Air Force service was retained for spares.

Specifications apply to the Boeing B-17G Flying Fortress.

Crew: 10
Powerplant: four 895kW (1200hp) Wright Cyclone R-1820-97 radial engines
Performance: max speed 462km/h (287mph); range 3220km (2000 miles); service ceiling 10,850m (35,000ft)
Dimensions: wingspan 31.62m (103ft 9in); length 22.78m (74ft 9in); height 5.82m (19ft 1in)
Weight: 32,660kg (72,000lb) loaded
Armament: twin 12.7mm (0.50in) machine guns under nose, aft of cockpit, under centre fuselage and in tail, and single-gun mountings in sides of nose, in radio operator's hatch and waist positions; maximum bomb load 7983kg (17,600lb)

BOEING MODEL 307 STRATOLINER

USA: 1938

Crew: 5
Powerplant: four 671kW (900hp) Wright GR-1820 Cyclone radial engines
Performance: max speed 396km/h (246mph); range 3846km (2390 miles); service ceiling 7985m (26,200ft)
Dimensions: wingspan 32.61m (107ft); length 22.66m (74ft 4in); height 6.34m (20ft 9in)
Weight: 19,050kg (42,000lb) maximum take-off weight
Payload: up to 33 passengers.

THE MODEL 307 ORIGINATED IN earlier projects that utilized B-17 commonality, but the Model 307 adopted a rounded, spacious fuselage and was the first operational pressurized airliner, offering service above lower level turbulence on long-distance flights. Only 10 were

Depicted here is one of the five TWA Boeing 307s designated C-75 during World War II.

built – four Model S-307s, five Model SA-307s for TWA (with two-speed engine superchargers) and one for Howard Hughes's personal use. The five TWA examples were pressed into USAAF wartime service as the C-75 and performed several thousand trans-atlantic crossings. Afterwards the Model 307 served with TWA until 1951, but varied examples saw second-line service until 1968.

One Model 307 survived and was recently (in 2003) restored to flying condition by the Boeing trust in Seattle.
Specifications apply to the Model SA-307B.

BOEING MODEL 314 CLIPPER

USA: 1939

Crew: 10
Powerplant: four 1118kW (1500hp) Wright R-2600 Double Cyclone radial engines
Performance: max speed 311km/h (193 mph); range 5633km (3500 miles); service ceiling 4085m (13,400ft)
Dimensions: wingspan 46.33m (152ft); length 32.31m (106ft); height 8.41m (27ft 7in); wing area 266.34m² (2867sq ft)
Weight: 37,422kg (82,500lb) max take-off weight
Payload: up to 74 passengers

THE MODEL 314 CLIPPER was designed specifically to meet a Pan American Airways (PAA) require-ment to start transatlantic services, these requiring a high passenger capacity amphibious flying boat. Initially six basic models were ordered and built.
Prior to completion the design switched from Pratt & Whitney Twin Wasp engines to Wright Cyclones and several tail-unit configurations were tried before the triple fin arrangement solved stability problems. Subsequently

the Clipper entered service as the largest airliner of its day.
PAA ordered six more improved Model 314As, but three of these

were sold to BOAC and most early versions were converted to 314A standard. The 314 saw extensive wartime service (designated C-98

by the US Navy) crewed by airline staff. The main operators retired the type in 1946 and second-line activity ended around 1951.

An early photograph of the prototype Model 314, with the original single-piece tail fin. Following trials this and all versions were finally fitted with a triple tail-fin arrangement to enhance stability.

BOEING B-29 SUPERFORTRESS

USA: 1942

FAMOUS AS THE HEAVY bomber that brought strategic air warfare to the Japanese home islands during the last year of the Pacific war, and above all as the aircraft that carried out the nuclear attacks

on Hiroshima and Nagasaki, the Boeing B-29 Superfortress was the outcome of design studies that started in 1937. The definitive design, to meet a US Army Air Corps requirement for a

'Hemisphere Defense Weapon', an aircraft capable of carrying 907kg (2000lb) of bombs for 8582km (5333 miles) at 644km/h (400 mph), was prepared in 1940. Three prototypes were ordered in that

year, the first XB-29 flying on 21 September 1942. By that time orders for 1500 aircraft had already been placed, the B-29 programme having been given maximum priority following the Japanese attack on Pearl Harbor. The first YB-29 evaluation aircraft were delivered to the 58th Bombardment Wing in July 1943, B-29-BW production aircraft following three months later. The other main versions of the B-29 that made their appearance during the war were the B-29A-BN with a four-gun forward upper turret and increased wing span, and the B-29B-BA with a reduced gun armament and increased bomb load. A reconnaissance version was designated F-13A (later RB-29).

The B-29 had many technical innovations, including the installation of remotely controlled gun turrets, periscopically sighted by gunners seated within the fuselage. At the end of 1943 the decision was taken to use the B-29 exclusively in the Pacific theatre. Two bombardment wings, the 58th and 73rd, were assigned to XX Bomber Command. The first units to be equipped with the B-29 were deployed to bases in India and southwest China in the spring of 1944, the first combat mission being flown on 5 June against Bangkok in Japanese-held Thailand before attacks on the Japanese mainland were initiated 10 days later. The establishment of five operational bases in the Marianas in March 1944 brought the B-29s much closer to Japan, and four bombardment wings, the 73rd, 313th, 314th and 315th, were quickly redeployed there from their bases in India and China, being followed a little later by the 58th BW. All the B-29 wings were now under the control of XXI

Long before the atomic bombing of Hiroshima and Nagasaki, conventional bombing by B-29s had brought Japan to its knees.

The B-29 was used for a variety of experimental tasks. This aircraft is about to air-launch a Bell X-1 for supersonic research.

Bomber Command, with its HQ on Guam. The move was followed by a complete revision of tactics, the B-29s now carrying out large-scale night incendiary area attacks on Japan's principal cities, with devastating results.

The B-29s that dropped the atomic bombs on Hiroshima and Nagasaki on 6 and 9 August 1945 – 'Enola Gay' and 'Bock's Car' – belonged to the 509th Bombardment Wing (Provisional), which was to become the principal US nuclear weapons trials unit. The B-29 continued to be the mainstay of the USAF Strategic Air Command for several years after 1945, and saw almost continual action during the three years of the Korean War. Production of the B-29 ended in May 1946, after 3970 aircraft had been built, but the basic design subsequently underwent several modifications. These included the SB-29 (search and rescue), TB-29 (trainer), WB-29 (weather reconnaissance) and KB-29 (tanker).

Although two planned production variants, the B-29C and B-29D, were cancelled at the end of World War II, the design of the B-29 Superfortress still underwent substantial changes and became the B-50. This version of the aircraft began to replace the B-29 in Strategic Air Command's first-line units in 1947.

Specifications apply to the Boeing B-29-BW Superfortress.

Crew: 10
Powerplant: four 1641kW (2200hp) Wright R-3350-57 radial engines
Performance: max speed 576km/h (358mph); range 6598km (4100 miles); service ceiling 9695m (31,800ft)
Dimensions: wingspan 43.36m (142ft 3in); length 30.18m (99ft); height 9.01m (29ft 7in)
Weight: 64,003kg (141,100lb) loaded
Armament: four-gun turret over nose, two-gun turrets under nose, over and under rear fuselage, all with guns of 12.7mm (0.50in) calibre, and one 20mm (0.79in) and two 12.7mm (0.50in) guns in tail; up to 9072kg (20,000lb) of bombs

BLOCH MB.135
Flown in 1938, the Bloch 135 was a four-engined medium bomber with exceptionally clean lines. It did not enter production.

BLOCH MB.210
The MB.210 first flew in 1934 and was numerically the most important bomber in French service at the outbreak of World War II. It was a low-wing, retractable-undercarriage development of the MB.200.

BLOCH MB.220
The Bloch 220 was a sound, capacious twin-engined commercial transport operated on Air France's European routes. The prototype flew in 1935, and five were still in service in 1949, re-engined and designated Bloch 221.

BLOCH MB.162
The MB.162 four-engined bomber, roughly in the same class as the Boeing B-17, was virtually a scaled-up MB.135. The sole prototype flew early in 1940.

BLOCH MB.700
The MB.700 was a single-seat fighter of wooden construction, first flown on 19 April 1940. The aircraft was burned when the Germans occupied its test airfield at Buc in June.

BLOHM UND VOSS HA 137
A German low-wing single-engined monoplane, first flown in 1936, the Blohm und Voss Ha 137 dive-bomber competed without success against the Junkers Ju 87. Five prototypes were built.

BLOHM UND VOSS HA 139
Three Ha 139 floatplanes were built and were used by Deutsche Luft Hansa for commercial operations over the Atlantic from 1937. The aircraft served with the Luftwaffe in World War II.

BOEING B-47 STRATOJET

USA: 1947

IN SEPTEMBER 1945, THE Boeing aircraft company commenced design of a strategic jet-bomber project designated Model 450. The aircraft, which was a radical departure from conventional design, featured a thin, flexible wing based on wartime research data with 35 degrees of sweep and carrying six turbojets in underwing pods, the main undercarriage being housed in the fuselage. Basic design studies were completed in June 1946, and the first of two XB-47 Stratojet prototypes flew on 17 December 1947, powered by six Allison J35 turbojets. The first production model was the B-47B, which was powered by J47-GE23 engines and featured a number of structural modifications, including a strengthened wing. The most numerous version of the Stratojet

Pictured moments after take-off, this B-47E is trailing a plume of smoke from its rocket-assisted take-off (RATOG) bottles.

was the B-47E, which first flew on 30 January 1953; 1359 were built. Variants included the RB-47E, RB-47H and RB-47K reconnaissance aircraft. About 1800 B-47s of all variants were built between 1946 and 1957. Specifications apply to the Boeing B-47E Stratojet.

Crew: 3
Powerplant: four 2721kg (6000lb) thrust General Electric J47-GE25 turbojet engines
Performance: max speed 975km/h (606mph); range 6435km (4000 miles); service ceiling 12,345m (40,500ft)
Dimensions: wingspan 35.35m (116ft); length 33.47m (109ft 10in); height 8.50m (27ft 11in)
Weight: 93,759kg (206,700lb) loaded
Armament: two 20mm (0.79in) cannon in tail position; 9072kg (20,000lb) of conventional bombs; Mk 15/39 or Mk 28 nuclear stores

BOEING MODEL 377 STRATOCRUISER

USA: 1947

Crew: 5
Powerplant: four Pratt & Whitney R-4360 Wasp Major radial engines each rated at 2610kW (3500hp)
Performance: max speed 604km/h (375mph); range 6759km (4200 miles); service ceiling exceeding 9755m (32,000ft)
Dimensions: wingspan 43.05m (141ft 3in); length 33.63m (110ft 4in); height 11.66m (38ft 3in)
Weight: 66,134kg (145,800lb) maximum take-off weight
Payload: up to 112 passengers

THE MODEL 377 STRATOCRUISER was a development of contemporary military Model 367 and KC-97 designs, and was offered in a variety of cabin configurations varying between 55 and 112 passengers, with some configurations offering sleeping berths and cocktail bars by means of including a lower deck in the design.

Only 55 Model 377s were built, 10 of which were equipped with extra fuel capacity and General Electric CH-10 turbochargers for

transatlantic operation and were known as Super Stratocruisers. The small number built is a reflection of the competition the Stratocruiser faced from the Douglas DC-7 and Lockheed Constellation. Although the latter two aircraft were more utilitarian, they had superior operational efficiency to the Model 377.

Customers for the Stratocruiser included Pan Am, BOAC and Northwest, all of whom operated the type for significant periods.

Although there are no operational Stratocruiser examples (since 1963), a number of C97/KC-97s found their way into civil freight operation, and isolated examples still find work as fire bombers in Alaska to date.

Specifications apply to the Boeing Model 377 Stratocruiser.

A pressurized fuselage and the ability to cruise above the weather meant that the 377 offered new standards of comfort.

BOEING C-97 AND KC-97

USA: 1951

Crew: 5
Powerplant: four 2611kW (3500hp) Pratt & Whitney R-4360 Wasp Major 28-cylinder radial engines
Performance: cruising speed 550km/h (340mph); range 6760km (4200 miles); service ceiling 9755m (32,000ft)
Dimensions: wingspan 43.00m (141ft); length 33.60m (110ft); height 11.65m (38ft)
Weight: 79379kg (175,000lb)
Payload: 96 passengers

THE BOEING C-97 was a military freighter version of the Model 377 Stratocruiser and was the mainstay of the USAF's military transport squadrons during the 1950s. The KC-97 was, in turn, developed from the C-97 freighter to support Strategic Air Command's B-47 strategic bomber force, with 20 tankers assigned to every SAC bomber wing. Normal interior equipment provided for 96 equipped troops or 69 stretcher cases, without the need to remove transfer tanks and the boom operator's station. The major production version was the KC-97G, accounting for 592 aircraft out of the total of 888 C/KC-97s.

The Boeing KC-97G-120BO serial 52-2632, seen here, was one of 592 aircraft of the basic G series.

BOEING B-52

USA: 1952

Crew: 6
Powerplant: eight 4536kg (10,000lb) thrust Pratt & Whitney J57-P-29WA turbojet engines
Performance: max speed 1014km/h (630mph); range 13,680km (8500 miles); service ceiling 16,765m (55,000ft)
Dimensions: wingspan 56.40m (185ft); length 48.00m (157ft 7in); height 14.75m (48ft 3in)
Weight: 204,120kg (450,000lb) loaded
Armament: remotely controlled tail barbette with four 12.7mm (0.50in) machine guns; up to 12,247kg (27,000lb) of conventional bombs; Mk 28 or Mk 43 nuclear free-falling weapons; two North American AGM-28B Hound Dog strategic stand-off missiles on underwing pylons

THE B-52 WAS THE PRODUCT of a USAAF requirement, issued in April 1946, for a new jet heavy bomber to replace the Convair B-36 in Strategic Air Command. Two prototypes were ordered in September 1949, the YB-52 flying for the first time on 15 April 1952 powered by eight Pratt & Whitney J57-P-3 turbojets. On 2 October 1952 the XB-52 also made its first flight, both aircraft having the same powerplant. The two B-52 prototypes were followed by three B-52As, the first of which flew on 5 August 1954. These aircraft featured a number of modifications and were used for extensive trials, which were still in progress when the first production B-52B was accepted by SAC's 93rd Bomb Wing at Castle AFB, California. Fifty examples were produced for SAC (including 10 of the 13 B-52As originally ordered, which were converted to B-52B standard). It was followed on the production line by the B-52C, 35 of which were built.

The focus of B-52 production then shifted to Wichita with the appearance of the B-52D, first

For many years during the Cold War era, the B-52 provided the manned bomber component of the American strategic deterrent.

A B-52G pictured in flight over Washington State. The B-52G was developed to carry the GAM-77 Hound Dog long-range stand-off air-to-surface missile.

flying on 14 May 1956; 170 were eventually built. Following the B-52E (100 built) and the B-52F (89) came the major production variant, the B-52G. The B-52G was the first aircraft to be armed with a long-range stand-off air-to-surface missile, the North American GAM-77 Hound Dog. At the missile's peak in 1962 there were 592 Hound Dogs on SAC's inventory, and it is a measure of the system's effectiveness that it remained in operational service until 1976. B-52G production totalled 193 examples, 173 of

these being converted in the 1980s to carry 12 Boeing AGM-86B Air Launched Cruise Missiles. The last version was the B-52H, which had been intended to carry the cancelled Skybolt air-launched IRBM, but was modified to carry four Hound Dogs instead. The B-52 was also armed with the Short-Range Attack Missile (SRAM), the first being delivered to the 42nd Bomb Wing at Loring AFB, Maine, on 4 March 1972. The B-52 was capable of carrying 20 SRAMs, 12 in three-round underwing clusters and eight in the aft bomb bay,

together with up to four Mk 28 thermonuclear weapons.

The B-52 was the mainstay of the West's airborne nuclear deterrent forces for three decades, but it was in a conventional role that it went to war, first over Vietnam, then in the Gulf War of 1991, and more latterly in support of operations in the former Yugoslavia, Afghanistan and Iraq. In all, 729 B-52 sorties were flown during the Linebacker II bombing offensive in Vietnam, and more than 15,000 tons of bombs dropped out of a total of 20,370

tons. Fifteen B-52s were lost to the SAM defences, and nine damaged. Thirty-four targets had been hit, and some 1500 civilians killed. Of the 92 crew members aboard the shot-down bombers, 26 were recovered by rescue teams, 29 were listed as missing, and 33 baled out over North Vietnam to be taken prisoner and later repatriated. The later variants of the Boeing B-52 were extensively rebuilt and upgraded during the bomber's long career.

Specification refers to the Boeing B-52D.

BOEING 707 USA: 1954

THE OVERALL IMPORTANCE of the Boeing 707 has to some extent been overshadowed by the later and larger Boeing 747. However, the introduction of the still larger Airbus A380 may serve to put the 707s contribution to intercontinental commercial travel into full historical perspective.

The 707 has its origins in a 1952 Boeing project for a turbojet-powered transport that could be adapted for commercial airline or US military use (to replace piston-powered military tankers/transports with a high-speed jet).

This Boeing 707 served as Air Force One from 1972 to 2001, and has now been donated to the Reagan Library.

The resulting design was designated internally as the Model 367-80, which first flew on 15 July 1954. The 367-80 drew upon aerodynamic experience gained from the B-47 bomber project, but was designed with a low wing, and the four wing-mounted engines were separately podded to increase the aircraft's overall reliability and safety.

The potential of the 367-80 resulted in a large long-running line of military versions which is separately dealt with, but the US military did sanction the concurrent development of the type for commercial purposes, and Pan American were the first of several US airlines to place orders for the subsequent Boeing 707-100 series. These initial Boeing 707 versions were powered by Pratt & Whitney JT3C-8 turbojet engines, and the first aircraft flew on 20 December 1957, followed by Pan American's introduction of the type to service on 26 October 1958 on a New York–London service. This was a statement of national pride – BOAC's de Havilland Comet 4 inaugurated jet services on the route a few weeks earlier. However, these early 707s were designed primarily for domestic operation, although later engine improvements allowed them to operate to South America.

The Boeing 707-300B and C were the predominant versions of this airliner, powered by the more advanced JT3D turbofan engines.

Boeing would rapidly need to introduce a fully practical inter-continental version of the 707 to compete with the Comet 4 and Douglas's DC-8, which was not far behind the 707's development. Boeing's response came in the form of the 707-320 series, which was offered with more powerful Pratt & Whitney JT4-11 turbojet engines, increased fuel/range, and a carrying capacity of 121 transatlantic passengers in a two-class cabin. Again this version was purchased by several American and overseas operators; however, another group of customers led by BOAC ordered the first turbofan powered version – the 707-420 series, which first flew in 1959 powered by four Rolls-Royce Conway 508 engines.

The 707-420 was not built in large numbers, but British CAA requirements necessitated a taller fin and changes to the rudder controls. These modifications stayed with the 707 when Boeing first offered the Pratt & Whitney JT3D series of turbofan engines that powered the classic version of the 707 – the Boeing 707-320B and C, which first flew on 31 January 1962 – and Pan American was once again the aircraft's launch customer.

A total of 856 Boeing 707s was built for commercial and military customers until 1982. The 707 outsold the rival DC-8 and its sales also far outstripped other competitors; the 320C series alone

was sold to more than 45 civil operators in a number of versions, offering greater weights, pure cargo or combi configurations, while military applications included executive transport and specialist electronics roles.

Early turbojet-powered 707s passed on to charter operators as the turbofan 707 versions and a new generation of 'Jumbo' jets succeeded them in the early 1970s. Yet some turbofan 707-320B/C series examples were still in service with a few small flag carriers at the beginning of the 1990s. By the new millennium operational numbers of 707 dropped below the 100 mark, nearly all of which are commercial freighters operating in Africa, the Middle East or South America.

Specifications apply to the Boeing 707-300C intercontinental.

Crew: 3
Powerplant: four Pratt & Whitney JT3D-7 turbofan engines each rated at 84.52kN (19,000lb)
Performance: max speed 1009km/h (627mph) at optimum altitude; cruising speed 974km/h (605mph) at 7620m (25,000ft); range 9262km (5755 miles); service ceiling 11,890m (39,000ft)
Dimensions: wingspan 44.42m (145ft 9in); length 46.61m (152ft 11in); height 12.93m (42ft 5in); wing area 285.35m² (3050sq ft)
Weight: 151,318kg (333,600lb) maximum take-off weight
Payload: up to 215 passengers or 42,229kg (93,093lb) of freight

BOEING 727

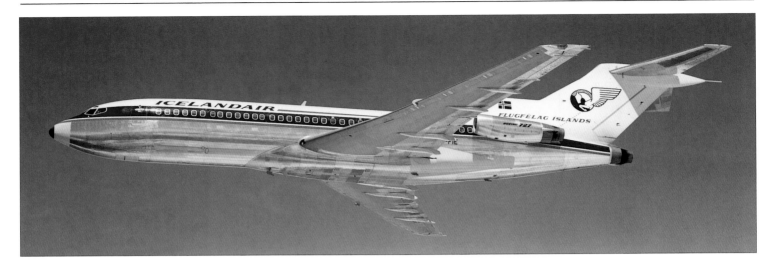

The Boeing 727-100 pictured was the first of several operated by Icelandair. This aircraft was delivered to the airline in June 1967 and served with that operator until 1984.

FOR THE USA THE 727 became the symbol of the short-/medium-haul trunk route and shuttle air travel that opened the country up and dominated that business for two decades or more. In total 1832 727s were built.

The 727 borrowed a degree of experience and commonality from the 707/720, but this tri-jet was designed for good hot and high performance and thrust reversal for shorter fields, noise reduction at city airports, and cruising speed at

lower altitude. Its airframe and component design kept in mind the demands of a high utilization/rotation rate, along with the needs of independent operation at smaller airports.

Sales of the 100 series were initially slow, although 570 were sold; however, the classic stretched 200 series (from 1967) sold 1260 examples which have been operated by nearly all major American airlines, as well as achieving major export success.

While the events of 9/11, in combination with higher operating costs compared to newer designs, have hastened the retirement of the 200 series from most major United States carriers, significant numbers of 100 and 200 series examples have found new roles as freighters or executive jets. This has often been achieved by incorporating engine noise reduction 'hush kits' into existing aircraft.

Specifications apply to the Boeing 727-200.

Crew: 2
Powerplant: three 64.50kN (14,500lb) Pratt & Whitney JT8D-9A turbofan engines.
Performance: max cruising speed 999km/h (621mph); range 4002km (2487 miles) with maximum payload; service ceiling 10,060m (33,000ft)
Dimensions: wingspan 32.92m (108ft); length 46.69m (153ft 2in); height 10.36m (34ft)
Weight: 86,638kg (191,000lb) maximum take-off weight
Payload: up to 189 passengers or 18,598kg (41,000lb) of freight

BOEING 737 SERIES 100 TO 900

Crew: 2
Powerplant: two 68.95kN (15,500lb) Pratt & Whitney JT8D-15 turbofan engines
Performance: max cruising speed 943km/h (586mph); range 4262km (2648 miles) with maximum payload; service ceiling 10,670m (35,000ft)
Dimensions: wingspan 28.35m (93ft); length 30.53m (100ft 2in); height 11.28m (37ft)
Weight: 53,071kg (117,000lb) maximum take-off weight
Payload: up to 129 passengers

THE 737 WAS LATE ONTO the market when compared to its early competitors in the 89- to 130-seat short-haul passenger group. It shared a commonality of design and appearance with the Boeing 727, but its twin jets were wing mounted. Although the launch (and only) customer for the 100 series was Lufthansa, the classic 200 series sold 1114 examples of the

The Boeing 737-300 series in particular was the aircraft of choice for many of the new wave of budget airlines, including EasyJet, pictured here.

4200-plus 737s built or ordered to date, serving with many major airlines worldwide. The low capacity combined with good

runway performance and service ubiquity attracted many customers, and the 200 series was built until 1988. The updated and enlarged

(147-seat) 300 series became from 1990 the talisman of a new wave of low-cost operators (Southwest, Easyjet and Go), while the further enlarged 400 and 500 (a 200 equivalent) series also sold and exported well. Further economic and technological advancement of the range, however, was required to compete with the Airbus A320 family. Therefore deliveries of these three marques ended in 2000. They were succeeded by a range of 'new generation' 737s: the shortest 100+ seat 600, the 700 (300 series replacement), 800 (400 series replacement) and the 900 which is an Airbus A321 competitor with a 177+ seating capacity. The new generation of 737s has newer technology engines, greater wing surfaces, EFIS flight deck and greater crew rating commonality.

Specifications apply to the Boeing 737-200.

BOEING 747

USA: 1969

Crew: 3 (2 on series 300 and 400)
Powerplant: four General Electric CF6-50E2 turbofan engines each rated at 233.53kN (52,500lb st), or Pratt & Whitney JT9D-7R4G2 turbofan engines each rated at 243.54kN (54,750lb st), or Rolls-Royce RB.211-524D4 turbofan engines each rated at 236.24kN (53,110lb st)
Performance: max speed 969km/h (602mph) at 9145m (30,000ft); range 11,397km (7082 miles); service ceiling 13,715m (45,000ft)
Dimensions: wingspan 59.64m (195ft 8in); length 70.66m (231ft 10in); height 19.33m (63ft 5in)
Weight: 377,849 kg (833,000lb) maximum take-off weight
Payload: up to 516 passengers

Only 44 Boeing 747SP (Special Performance) series were built, for airlines such as Qantas which operate long range/thin traffic services.

THE 747 IN SUCCESSIVE marques will have held the mantle of the largest passenger airliner for at least 37 years when the Airbus A380 is scheduled to surpass it in 2006. It is an astonishing record. The original 747 was a response to a 1966 Pan American requirement under the visionary leadership of Juan Trippe, and the airline initially ordered 25 examples. Beyond all expectations more than 1300 had been built by 2003.

In service the earlier Boeing 747-100 and 200 revolutionized the economics of air travel and made long-distance travel accessible to many millions of people. The 747 introduced the twin-aisle cabin configuration and some early examples utilized the upper deck as a bar area. By the mid-1970s most of the world's major airlines had acquired 747s.

Special variants were produced for short-haul high-volume requirements, notably for Japanese airlines, and there was a freighter version with a forward-opening nose. Many other 100 and 200 series passenger examples were later converted to freighters. There was also the 747SP, a shortened version for 'long thin' route requirements – 44 examples of this aircraft were built.

Introduction of the 300 and 400 series brought another revolution: they increased both capacity and range, and the 400 series incorporated an EFIS flight deck, winglets and aerodynamic improvements. The series 400, similarly to early marques, was taken up by most major airlines after its introduction in 1989. Further developments have been considered, but shelved, although the 747-400ER (extended range) has recently gone into service with Qantas.

Specifications apply to the Boeing Model 747-200B.

The Boeing 747-400 has largely superseded 'classic' 100 and 200 series examples in the fleets of most major international carriers such as British Airways and Virgin Atlantic, pictured.

BOEING (MCDONNELL DOUGLAS/HUGHES) AH-64A APACHE

USA: 1975

The Apache can carry a mix of up to 16 Hellfire missiles or 76 Hydra unguided rockets and 1200 rounds of ammunition for its M230 cannon.

WHEN, ON 9 AUGUST 1972, the US Army finally terminated the Lockheed Cheyenne, the US Army revised its requirement in the new AAH (Advanced Attack Helicopter) programme. The Hughes tandem, two-seat Model 77 design was declared the winning contender on 10 December, and this became the AH-64 Apache. On 26 March 1982 Hughes received an order for 11 Apaches and deliveries began in January 1984, just as Hughes became a division of McDonnell Douglas, which in 1997 was merged into Boeing. Some 603 AH-64As and 224 up-engined examples have been built. Specifications apply to the Boeing (McDonnell Douglas/ Hughes) AH-64A Apache.

Crew: 2
Powerplant: originally two 1145kW (1536shp) GE T700-GE-700C turboshafts derated for normal operations, later two 1342kW (1800shp) GE T700-GE-701C engines
Performance: max speed 293km/h (182mph); combat radius 1899km (1180 miles); service ceiling 6400m (21,000ft)
Dimensions: main rotor diameter 14.63m (48ft); length 17.76m (58ft 3in); height 4.66m (15ft 3.5in)
Weight: 5165kg (11,387lb)
Armament: one 30mm (1.18in) M230 Chain Gun cannon in trainable under-fuselage mounting; up to 771kg (1700lb) of disposable stores, normally 16 AGM-114A Hellfire long-range, laser-guided anti-tank missiles

BOEING MODEL 767 SERIES 200, 300 AND 400

USA: 1981

The Boeing 767-200 illustrated was the first 767 delivered to American Airlines in November 1982. American Airlines operate both the 200 and 300 series on domestic and international services, including transatlantic operations which are performed by variants with an ER suffix designating 'extended range'.

Crew: 2/3
Powerplant: two General Electric CF6-80A or Pratt & Whitney JT8D-7R4D turbofan engines each rated at 213.51kN (48,000lb st) or CF6-80A2, JT9D-7R4E, JT9D-7R4E4 or PW4050 turbofan engines each rated at 222.41kN (50,000lb st), or PW4052 turbofan engines each rated at 231.31kN (52,000lb st), or CF6-80C2B4 turbofan engines each rated at 233.53kN (52,500lb st)
Performance: max speed 914km/h (568mph); range between 5852km and 7129km (3636 and 4430 miles) depending on power plant and version; service ceiling between 11,795m and 12,100m (38,700ft and 39,700ft)
Dimensions: wingspan 47.57m (156ft 1in); length 48.51m (159ft 2in); height 15.85m (52ft)
Weight: 136,080 or 142,884kg (300,000 or 315,000lb) maximum take-off weight depending on powerplant and version
Payload: up to 290 passengers

THE MEDIUM-RANGE 767 design has a wide-body twin aisle, while retaining a good deal of flight-deck synergy with the narrow-body 757. The launch customer was United Airlines, which initially ordered 30 units. An extended range 767-200ER introduced in 1984 proved popular with export customers. The 767 underwent a stretch in 1986, taking mixed-class operation up to 269 passengers. This version was later enhanced in 1988 as the 767-300ER,

with a range up to 11,223km (6974 miles). Again popular, it introduced Rolls-Royce RB.211 engines onto the 767 when British Airways made its purchase. Another stretched version – the 767-400ER – was introduced in 1999, incorporating a further stretch, a 'new generation' EFIS flight deck, and a number of other improvements available from the Boeing 777 programme. Specifications apply to the Boeing 767-200.

BOEING MODEL 757 SERIES 200 AND 300 USA: 1982

THE BOEING 757 IS THE SMALLEST of the three twin-engined jet designs that Boeing initiated at the end of the 1970s. Although the 757 is essentially a successor to the 727, it shares a great deal of technological compatibility with the wide-body 767. Aimed at the short- and medium-haul markets, with economy and efficiency of operation in mind, the 757 received launch orders from British Airways and Eastern Air Lines in 1978, both of which chose the RB.211-engine option, in part due to their pre-existing RB.211 powered Tristar fleets. In more recent years the 757 has been stretched as the

The Boeing 757-200 proved enormously popular with charter operators such as My Travel; however, competition from budget operators is rendering the type too large.

300 series, a version which sold in more limited numbers.

Nearly a thousand Model 757s of all marques have been built to date, and these aircraft have proved popular with scheduled and charter airlines alike. A number of older examples of the type are undergoing freighter conversion.

Specifications apply to the Boeing Model 757-200.

Crew: 2
Powerplant: two Rolls-Royce RB.211-535C or -535E4 turbofan engines each rated at 166.36 or 178.37kN (37,400 or 40,100lb st), or two Pratt & Whitney PW2037 or PW2040 turbofan engines each rated at 169.92 or 186.16kN (38,200 or 41,886lb st)
Performance: max speed 951km/h (591mph); range 3662 miles (5893 km) with maximum payload; service ceiling 11,580m (38,000ft)
Dimensions: wingspan 38.05m (124ft 10in); length 47.32m (155ft 3in); height 13.56m (44ft 6in)
Weight: 108,864kg (240,000lb) maximum take-off weight
Payload: up to 239 passengers

BOEING MODEL 777-200 AND 300 SERIES USA: 1994

THE BOEING MODEL 777 was to arrive in the aviation marketplace considerably later than its 757 and 767 forebears. The timing and

market were focused on airlines operating ageing first-generation 747 (100/200 series), DC-10 and MD-11s or Lockheed TriStars on

medium- to long-range, but thinner or high-frequency, routes.

The Boeing 777 is in fact the first airliner designed totally by the

Many major long-haul airlines such as British Airways have now replaced their Boeing 747-100/200 or tri-jet DC-10s and TriStars with the more economical Boeing 777-200.

use of CAD tools. It was Boeing's first 'fly by wire' design, with a high-tech glass cockpit.

The appeal of this type and its competitors is the economics of the twin engines over the three- and four-engined predecessors, combined with a high-occupation wide-body layout. Since the aircraft entered service with United Airlines in 1995, Boeing has received orders for more than 450 777s of all variants, including the extended range (ER) version of the 777-200 which has a range of up to 11,168km (6939 miles). This was followed by the 777-300 with a stretched fuselage and further up-rating. This version was aimed particularly at the Asia/Pacific markets, and it was briefly the world's longest airliner.

Specifications apply to the Boeing 777-200.

Crew: 2/3
Powerplant: two Pratt & Whitney PW4074 turbofan engines each rated at 329.1kN (74,000lb), or two PW4077 turbofan engines each rated at 342.5kN (77,000lb), or two General Electric GE90-75B turbofan engines each rated at 333.3kN (75,000lb), or two General Electric GE90-76B turbofan engines each rated at 338.0kN (76,000lb), or two Rolls-Royce Trent 875 turbofan engines each rated at 333.6kN (75,000lb), or two Rolls-Royce Trent 877 turbofan

engines each rated at 342.5kN (77,000lb)
Performance: max speed 946km/h (588mph); range 7785km (4840 miles) with 363 passengers; service ceiling between 11,795m and 13,135m (38,697 and 43,100ft)
Dimensions: wingspan 60.93m (199ft 11in); length 63.73m (209ft 1in); height 18.51m (60ft 9in)
Weight: 233,604kg (515,000lb) maximum take-off weight
Payload: up to 440 passengers

BOEING-STEARMAN PT-17 KAYDET

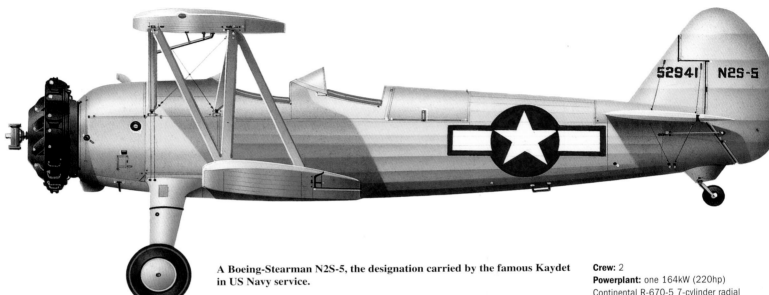

A Boeing-Stearman N2S-5, the designation carried by the famous Kaydet in US Navy service.

ONE OF THE MOST WIDELY used basic trainers of World War II, the Boeing-Stearman Kaydet was produced in several versions, differing in powerplant and equipment. The PT-13 Kaydet of 1935 had a Lycoming engine, while the PT-17 of 1940 and the PT-18 had Continental and Jacobs engines respectively. The PT-27, with different instrumentation and an enclosed cockpit, was built for Canada. In US Navy service the Kaydet was designated as the N2S.

Production total of the type reached 10,346 aircraft, and many PT-17 Kaydets are still in the hands of private owners. These machines are greatly prized by enthusiasts for their ruggedness and excellent flying qualities.

Crew: 2
Powerplant: one 164kW (220hp) Continental R-670-5 7-cylinder radial engine
Performance: max speed 199km/h (124mph); range 812km (505 miles); service ceiling 3415m (11,200ft)
Dimensions: wingspan 9.80m (32ft 2in); length 7.63m (25ft); height 2.79m (9ft 2in)
Weight: 1232kg (2712lb) loaded
Armament: none

BOEING-VERTOL CH-46 SEA KNIGHT

Crew: 2/3
Powerplant: two 783kW (1050shp) GE T58-GE-8B turboshaft engines each rated at 932kW (1250shp)
Performance: max speed 249km/h (155mph) at sea level; combat radius 426km (265 miles); service ceiling 4265m (14,000ft)
Dimensions: rotor diameter 15.24m (50ft); length 25.40m (83ft 4in); height 5.09m (16ft 8.5in)
Weight: 5627kg (12,406lb)
Armament/Payload: up to 25 troops or 1814 kg (4000lb) of freight carried internally or 2871kg (6330lb) of freight externally

THE CH-46 SEA KNIGHT is a USMC medium assault transport version of the Vertol Model 107-II. In July 1958 the US Army ordered 10 slightly modified YHC-1A aircraft, the first flying on 27 August 1959. Yet with interest in the larger and more powerful Model 114 Chinook, the original order was reduced to three. The prototype was modified as the

In Vietnam, the Sea Knight's ability to carry up to 17 combat-equipped troops made it the USMC's primary assault transport.

Model 107M (HRB-1) and the first of 160 CH-46As entered production in November 1964, although the type did not enter service until early 1965. Deliveries of the first of 14 UH-46A Sea Knights (similar to the CH-46A) for the US Navy were made in 1964 and were followed

by 10 UH-46D examples. Some 266 CH-46D examples with more powerful engines and 174 CH-46F models with additional avionics were delivered to the USMC, which subsequently updated 273 of its older Sea Knights to CH-46E standard with 1394kW (1870shp)

T58-GE-16 turboshaft engines and other improvements. The USMC continues to use the Sea Knight for troop transport, while the USN mainly uses it in the vertical replenishment role.

Specification applies to the Boeing-Vertol CH-46 Sea Knight.

BOEING-VERTOL MODEL 114, 234 & 414 (H-47 CHINOOK)   USA: 1961

IN 1959 THE BOEING Vertol Model 114 was declared the winning design in the Weapon System SS471L competition. Five manufacturers contested the competition to develop a new all-weather battle-field mobility helicopter capable of carrying 40 fully equipped troops. The Chinook was an outgrowth of the Boeing Vertol 107 tandem-rotor, turbine-engined helicopter family. Five YHC-1B service test Chinooks were ordered in June 1959 and in 1960 the US Army ordered five HC-1Bs. On 21 September 1961 the second aircraft of the test batch was the first to fly, and by the end of 1961 Chinook orders had risen to 47 examples.

In mid-1962, under the new service designating system, the HC-1 Chinook became the CH-47A for the US Army and the first deliveries were made in December that same year. Orders for 108 CH-4B aircraft with more powerful engines and 270 improved CH-47C (Model 234) versions followed. The first CH-47C flew on 14 October 1967 and

Britain was to become the first international Chinook customer, upgrading its fleet of HC.Mk.1 Chinooks to CH-47D configuration.

deliveries of the helicopter began in early 1968. Nine not dissimilar versions were built for the CAF under the designation CH-147. The CH-47D prototype flew on 26 February 1982 powered by the more forceful 3356kW (4500shp) T55-L-712 turboshaft engines and fitted with updated avionics. All older examples of the Chinook were remanufactured to this standard.

In Britain the Ministry of Defence at first ordered 33 (later increased to 41) Chinook Mk 1s for the RAF to a standard based on the CH-147. These machines were subsequently upgraded to HC.Mk 1A standard, and 32 examples were later modernized to HC.Mk 2 (basically CH-47D) standard. Furthermore, eight HC.Mk 2 standard Chinooks and nine HC.Mk 3 standard (similar to the MH-47E) were ordered, the Mk 3 for special operations missions. In

1970 Elicotteri Meridionali in Italy began co-production for European and Middle Eastern countries. In Japan licence-production of the CH-47J was undertaken by Kawasaki, while new military Chinooks manufactured in the USA were limited to the Model 414 (CH-47D) International Chinook. In addition to the UK, Canada and Japan, Chinooks have been sold to 14 overseas nations.

Specifications apply to the Boeing-Vertol CH-47C Chinook.

Crew: 2/3
Powerplant: two Avco Lycoming T55-L-11A turboshaft engines each rated at 2796kW (3750shp)
Performance: max speed 286km/h (178mph); combat radius 185km (115 miles); service ceiling 3290m (10,800ft)
Dimensions: rotor diameter 18.29m (60ft); length 30.18m (99ft); height 5.68m (18ft 11in)
Weight: 9736kg (21,464lb)
Armament/Payload: up to 55 troops, or 24 litters; or 3175kg (7000lb) of freight carried internally or externally

BOMBARDIER (DE HAVILLAND CANADA) DHC-7 (DASH 7)

THE DASH 7 UTILIZED de Havilland Canada's considerable experience with previous designs to create a larger capacity regional airliner. In part this was in anticipation of STOL city airports such as London City being built in large numbers. The STOL airport trend failed to fully materialize, as did the short-term growth in volumes of commuter traffic, and only 113 examples were sold until 1988 to both civil and military customers. However, the Dash 7 proved to be an important progression towards the Dash 8, which was (and is) well positioned in this market.

Specifications apply to the Series 100 Dash 7.

Crew: 2
Powerplant: four 835kW (1120shp) flat-rated Pratt & Whitney PT6A-50 turboprop engines
Performance: max cruising speed 428km/h (266mph); range 1279km (795 miles) with 50 passengers; service ceiling 6400m (21,000ft)
Dimensions: wingspan 28.35m (93ft); length 24.58m (80ft 7in); height 7.98m (26ft 2in)
Weight: 19,954kg (44,000lb) maximum take-off weight
Payload: up to 50 passengers

Brymon Airways was a high-profile operator of the DHC-7, pioneering passenger flights into London City Airport.

BOMBARDIER (CANADAIR) CL-215/CL-415

THE CL-215 DESIGN ORIGINATES in a requirement for a firefighting amphibious flying boat to detect and suppress forest fires. The aircraft is built for reliability and longevity, with use of corrosion-resistant materials. Water loads are drawn in and can be mixed internally with fire retardants; speed is essential and missions can take as little as 10 minutes. The CL-215 has also been used in a paramilitary SAR role. A conversion programme involving improved powerplant and controls takes retrofits to CL-215T standard. The CL-415 (from 1993) offers a new powerplant, stabilizing features and avionics, thus offering greater payload and speed.

Specifications apply to CL-415.

Firefighting is the prime role of the CL-215. It performs this service reliably for several operators in North America and southern Europe.

Crew: 2-6
Powerplant: two 1775kW (2380hp) Pratt & Whitney Canada PW123AF turboprop engines
Performance: max cruising speed 376km/h (234mph); range 2426km (1507 miles) with a 499kg (1100lb) payload
Dimensions: wingspan 28.63m (93ft 11in); length 19.82m (65ft 0.5in); height 8.98m (29ft 5.5in)
Weight: 17,168kg (37,850lb) maximum take-off weight from water
Payload: 6123kg (13,500lb) of water in the firefighting role

BOMBARDIER (CANADAIR) CL-600 CHALLENGER SERIES CANADA: 1978

CANADAIR ENTERED THE business jet market in 1976 when it procured the rights to Bill Lear's (of LearJet fame) LearStar 600 series. The Canadair company would subsequently develop the design, but the aircraft's principal attraction was its wide-body 'stand-up' interior. This made it an attractive proposition for business customers looking for performance and comfort. The first delivery was made in December 1980, and the CL-601 became the first production

The relatively 'wide-body' cabin offered by the Bombardier (Canadair) CL-600 Challenger was a milestone development in the business jet market.

standard. It was progressively updated with more powerful engines, a 'glass' cockpit and range/capacity increases. To date more than 550 examples have been built for business, commuter and military customers. Specifications apply to the Challenger 601-3R.

Crew: 2
Powerplant: two 41kN (9220lb st) General Electric CF34-3A1 turbofans
Performance: max cruising speed 882km/h (548mph); range 6639km (4124 miles) with five passengers; service ceiling 12,495m (41,000ft)
Dimensions: wingspan 19.61m (64ft 4in); length 20.85m (68ft 5in); height 6.30m (20ft 8in)
Weight: 20,457kg (45,100lb) maximum take-off weight
Payload: up to 19 passengers with a 2377kg (5240lb) payload

BOMBARDIER (DE HAVILLAND CANADA) DHC-8 (DASH 8) CANADA: 1983

Crew: 2
Powerplant: two Pratt & Whitney Canada PW123A turboprop engines rated at 1775kW (2380shp)
Performance: max cruising speed 531km/h (330mph); range 1626km (1010 miles) with 50 passengers; service ceiling 7620m (25,000ft)
Dimensions: wingspan 27.43m (90ft); length 25.68m (84ft 3in); height 7.49m (24ft 7in); wing area 56.20m² (605sq ft)
Weight: 15,649kg (34,500lb) maximum take-off weight
Payload: up to 56 passengers

IN THE EARLY 1980S, de Havilland Canada perceived the growing need for a new generation of more efficient turboprop commuter airliners, with a reasonable – but not full – STOL performance. The

In production for more than 20 years, the Dash 8 has sold well in Europe as well as in North and Central America.

initial 100 series, featuring a retractable undercarriage and a T tail arrangement, and the slightly larger uprated 200 series sold well and led to the launch of the stretched 300 series. The Dash 8 has remained in production since 1983, during which

time many competitor products have ceased manufacture, partly due to the rise of the regional jet and their perceived popularity with customers.

Bombardier launched the larger Q400 series, which first flew in

1998. At the same time it offered noise and vibration reduction, signified by the 'Q', on new builds of preceding models. The Q400 is capable of carrying 78 passengers while offering the advantage of turboprop economics to compete

with the regional jets. In the new 'low cost' era this option is being considered by a number of operators. More than 600 Dash 8s have been sold.

Specifications apply to the Series 300A.

BOMBARDIER (CANADAIR) CRJ100, CRJ200, CRJ700 AND CRJ900 SERIES CANADA: 1991

SUCCESS WITH THE CHALLENGER business jet led Canadair to develop a regional jet airliner, which became feasible due to technological advances that translate into lower operating costs. The launch customer was Lufthansa Cityline, which began operations in 1992. Since then CRJ100s and CRJ200s have been ordered by airlines around the world, with up to 600 built. The larger 68-seat CRJ700 flew in 1999 and has entered service in numbers, and the CRJ900 90-seat regional airliner entered service in 2003 with America West Airlines.

Specifications apply to CRJ100.

Crew: 2
Powerplant: two 41kN (9220lb) thrust GE CFE34-3A1 turbofan engines
Performance: max cruising speed 851km/h (529mph); range 1818km (1128 miles); service ceiling 12,500m (41,000ft)
Dimensions: wingspan 21.21m (69ft 7in); length 26.77m (87ft 10in); height 6.22m (20ft 5in)
Weight: 21,523kg (47,450lb) maximum take-off weight
Payload: up to 52 passengers

Customer preference for travel in jet aircraft rather than propeller-driven models in the 1990s led to a boom in orders for regional jets from US carriers such as American Eagle – pictured here is a CRJ700.

BOMBARDIER BD-700 GLOBAL EXPRESS CANADA: 1996

EXTERNALLY SIMILAR TO THE CRJ-700 airliner, the Global BD-700 Express was specifically designed to create a new level of speed, range and comfort in the business jet class. The Global Express is capable of non-stop operation from New York to Tokyo, cruising at Mach 0.8 as high as 15,545m (51,000ft) altitude, with sufficient crew to effect an in-flight changeover. In order to achieve this requirement the Global Express was subject to computer-aided design (CAD)

Bombardier has drawn on its experience with the Challenger business jet and CRJ regional jet, and developed new technologies to design and produce the BD-700 Global Express.

techniques and extensive use of composite materials in the finished aircraft. Deliveries of the Global Express to date exceed 70.

Specifications apply to the Global Express BD-700.

Crew: 3/4
Powerplant: two BMW Rolls-Royce BR710-A2-20 turbofan engines each rated at 66kN (14,850lb)
Performance: max cruising speed 1091km/h (678mph); range 12,046km (7485 miles) with eight passengers; service ceiling 15,545m (51,000ft)
Dimensions: wingspan 28.65m (94ft); length 30.30m (99ft 5in); height 7.57m (24ft 10in)
Weight: 42,525kg (93,750lb) maximum take-off weight
Payload: up to 19 passengers within the context of a 3266kg (7200lb) payload

BOULTON PAUL P.64/P.71A MAIL-CARRIER

UK: 1933

This is the sole P.64 model. It first flew in 1933, but was written off during a test flight the same year. The cause of the accident remains uncertain.

THE MAIL-CARRIER'S SEMINAL importance is due to its high speed for the time, but only three examples were built. The P.64 Mail-Carrier was an all-metal frame, fabric-covered design, built in response to an Imperial Airways requirement of 1928. It proved too expensive and the single example was lost in an unsolved accident in

October 1933. Undeterred Boulton Paul developed the P.71A version, which had more powerful engines, a modified tail unit and was slimmer and longer. Two were built in 1935, and they served as VIP transports. Both were lost in accidents within 20 months.

Specifications apply to the Boulton Paul P.71A.

Crew: 2
Powerplant: two 365kW (490hp) Armstrong Siddeley Jaguar VIA radial engines
Performance: maximum speed 314km/h (195mph); range 950km (600 miles); service ceiling 1370m (4500ft)
Dimensions: wingspan 16.50m (54ft 1.5in); length 13.46m (44ft 2in); height 4.62m (15ft 2in)
Weight: 4309kg (9500lb) maximum take-off weight
Payload: seven to 13 passengers and/or mail load

BOULTON PAUL OVERSTRAND

UK: 1933

FIRST FLOWN IN 1933, THE Overstrand was the first RAF bomber to feature a power-operated gun turret when it entered service in the following year. The Overstrand prototype was developed on the production line from the airframe of the eighth production Sidestrand medium bomber. The first three conversions were designated Sidestrand Mk V,

Pictured here is a Boulton Paul Overstrand bomber of No 101 Squadron RAF. The only other unit to use the Overstrand was the No 144 Squadron.

but the name Overstrand was adopted in March 1934. No 101 Squadron, based at RAF Bicester, received the first of 27 production Overstrands in January 1935.

Crew: 5
Powerplant: two 433kW (580hp) Bristol Pegasus 11M.3 radial engines
Performance: max speed 246km/h (153mph); range 877km (545 miles); service ceiling 6860m (22,500ft)
Dimensions: wingspan 21.95m (72ft); length 14.02m (46ft); height 4.72m (15ft 6in)
Weight: 5443kg (12,000lb) loaded
Armament: one 7.7mm (0.303in) Lewis gun in nose turret; one 7.7mm (0.303in) Lewis gun in each of the dorsal ventral positions; up to 726kg (1600lb) of bombs internally

BOULTON PAUL DEFIANT

UK: 1937

THE BOULTON PAUL DEFIANT was the RAF's third fighter monoplane and was very different in concept from its contemporaries, the

Hurricane and the Spitfire. The aircraft was designed to Air Ministry Specification F.9/35, calling for a two-seat fighter in which the entire

armament was concentrated in a power-operated, centrally mounted turret permitting a 360-degree field of fire in the hemisphere above the aircraft. The prototype Defiant flew on 11 August 1937, and some 400 had been ordered by the outbreak of World War II, although a protracted trials programme meant that only three had been delivered. The first Defiant squadron, No 264, began to rearm with the type at Martlesham Heath on 8 December 1939. As a day fighter the Defiant was a disaster, suffering heavy losses in combat, but it went on to enjoy considerable success in the night-fighter/intruder role.

Crew: 2
Powerplant: one 768kW (1030hp) Rolls-Royce Merlin III 12-cylinder V-type engine
Performance: max speed 489km/h (304mph); range 748km (465 miles); service ceiling 9250m (30,350ft)
Dimensions: wingspan 11.99m (39ft 4in); length 10.77m (35ft 4in); height 4.39m (14ft 5in)
Armament: four 7.7mm (0.303in) machine guns in dorsal turret

A Boulton Paul Defiant of No 264 Squadron. After some initial success over Dunkirk the Defiant suffered heavily during the Battle of Britain, and assumed the night-fighter role.

BRANTLY MODEL B.2

USA: 1953

IN 1943 N.O. BRANTLY began designing the Model B-1 using a co-axial twin-rotor configuration, which was distinctive in having coincident flapping and lag hinges at approximately 40 per cent of the blade length. The B-1 first flew in 1946, but it was too heavy and too complex to appeal to the private pilot. The B-2 was a two-seat light utility helicopter with a single main rotor and an anti-torque tail rotor. The B.2 prototype first flew on 21 February 1953, while a second prototype incorporating several refinements flew on 14 August 1956.

The Brantly B-2 finally entered production in 1959; by 1970 about 400 machines had been constructed. Although intended primarily as an executive or private owner type, it could be equipped for agricultural purposes, and the US Army evaluated five B-2s under the designation YHO-3BR.

Brantly-Hynes was formed in 1975 and the B.2B, which differs from the earlier B.2A principally in having a fuel-injection system, was put back into production.

Specifications apply to the Brantly-Hynes Model B.2B.

Crew: 2
Powerplant: Avco Lycoming IVO-360-A1A flat-four engine rated at 134kW (180hp)
Performance: max speed 161km/h (100mph); radius 402km (250 miles); service ceiling 3290m (10,800ft)
Dimensions: main rotor diameter 7.24m (23ft 9in) length 8.53m (28ft); height 2.06m (6ft 9in)
Weight: 463kg (1020lb)

The Brantly-Hynes Model B.2B helicopter offered side-by-side two-seat accommodation with dual controls as standard.

BRATUKHIN HELICOPTERS

SOVIET UNION: 1942

The early Omega had an in-line engine at the end of each outrigger, but when the G2 appeared in 1944 it was powered by two radial engines.

IN SPRING 1940, IVAN PAVLOVICH Bratukhin became chief of the rotary-wing design bureau at the Moscow Aviation Institute (TsAGI). Greatly influenced by the Focke-Achgelis Fa 61 in Germany, he began work on an experimental helicopter of similar configuration based on a side-by-side pair of counter-rotating rotors carried on long outrigger arms. Bratukhin designated his prototype the Omega, or the 2MG (twin-engined helicopter), and powered it with two 164kW (220hp) MV-6 in-line engines. Early hovering tests begun in August 1940 revealed inherent weaknesses before the German advance in Russia halted work for six months. It was not until mid-1942 that the Omega flew again. In September 1944 the G-2 (Helicopter No 2) flew for the first time. Other variants followed which included the B-5 five-seater passenger version and the B-9 air ambulance. Bratukhin's final twin-rotor designs were the B-10 flying observation post, which flew in 1947, and the B-11 transport helicopter. Specifications apply to the Bratukhin B-11.

Crew: 3
Powerplant: two Ivchyenko AI-26GRF radial engines each rated at 429kW (575shp)
Performance: max speed 155km/h (96mph); combat radius 328km (204 miles); service ceiling 2550m (8365ft)
Dimensions: main rotor diameter 10.00m (32ft 10in); length 9.76m (32ft 0.75in)
Weight: 3398kg (7491lb)

BREDA BA.65

ITALY: 1935

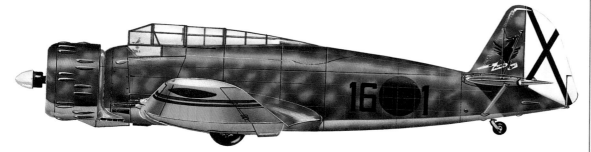

A LOW-WING MONOPLANE with a fully enclosed glazed cockpit, the Breda Ba.65 was derived from the Ba.64 army cooperation aircraft, which was produced in the early 1930s as a ground-attack aircraft – something Italy's Regia Aeronautica lacked at the time. The Ba.65 made its operational debut in the Spanish Civil War on the Nationalist side, where it met with some success against minimal opposition. About

A Breda Ba.65 in the colours of the Italian Expeditionary Force, which fought in Spain on the side of the Nationalists.

150 were still in first-line service when Italy entered World War II in June 1940; most were deployed in North Africa and suffered heavily at the hands of British fighters. Many of the Ba.65 units operated two-seat versions.

Crew: 1
Powerplant: one 768kW (1030hp) Fiat A.80 RC.41 18-cylinder radial engine
Performance: max speed 430km/h (267mph); range 550km (342 miles); service ceiling 8300m (27,230ft)
Dimensions: wingspan 12.10m (39ft 8in); length 9.60m (31ft 6in); height 3.20m (10ft 6in)
Weight: 3490kg (7695lb) loaded
Armament: four 7.62mm (0.30in) machine guns; 1000kg (2200lb) of bombs

BREGUET BR.XIV

FRANCE: 1916

Crew: 2
Powerplant: one 224kW (300hp) Renault 12F in-line engine
Performance: max speed 184km/h (114mph); endurance 2 hrs 45 mins; service ceiling 6000m (19,690ft)
Dimensions: wingspan 14.36m (47ft 1in); length 8.87m (29ft 1in); height 3.30m (10ft 10in)
Weight: 1565kg (3450lb) loaded
Armament: one fixed forward-firing 7.9mm (0.31in) machine gun; twin 7.7mm (0.303in) machine guns on mounting in rear cockpit; up to 40kg (88lb) of bombs on underwing racks

LOUIS BREGUET'S MOST EFFECTIVE product of World War I was without doubt the Br.XIV. The design of this two-seat reconnaissance/ bomber aircraft was started in the late summer of 1916 by Breguet's chief engineer, Louis Vullierme, the prototype making its first flight on 21 November that year. In the spring of 1917, the first Br.XIVA-2 production aircraft entered service with the Aéronautique Militaire, and the aircraft quickly established a reputation for both toughness and reliability. The Br.XIVB-2 was the principal variant to serve with the French strategic day bombing force,

which was completely transformed by the introduction of the new type. In January 1918 the bomber force was organized into two fighting groups, each with the same structure. The first, known as the Groupement Menard, comprised Escadre de Combat 1 and Escadre de Bombardement 2, the former consisting of four Escadrilles, each with 18 fighters for escort duty, and the latter of three bomber groups, each with three Escadrilles of Breguets.

The other fighting group, the Groupement Fequant, comprised Escadre de Combat 2, with three fighter groups, and Escadre de Bombardement 13 with two

bomber groups. By May 1918, both fighting groups had a collective total of 50 Breguet XIV day bombers and 130 fighters. In that month, both fighting groups were united under the newly created 1st Air Division, whose Breguet XIVs now undertook night bombing operations against industrial objectives in the Saar during the summer months of 1918. In the main, however, the Breguets remained committed to the support role, attacking communications to a depth of about 32km (20 miles) behind the front line. In all, Breguet XIVs served with 71 French Escadrilles on the Western Front, and also

The Breguet Br.XIV, seen here in the colours of the United States Air Service, was an excellent light bomber with a good range.

A Breguet Br XIXA2 of the French Aviation Militaire, Western Front, 1918. Breguet XIVs carried out many attacks on targets in Western Germany, operating with a strong fighter escort.

equipped five Escadrilles in Serbia, three in Greece, six in Morocco and eight in Macedonia. Two Belgian Escadrilles and several squadrons of the American Expeditionary Force also flew Breguet XIVs.

By the end of World War I, orders for the Breguet XIV had reached 5500 aircraft, a figure that would rise to 8000 by the time the production lines shut down in 1926. Variants included the unsuccessful BR.XIVH floatplane and the Br.XIVS air ambulance, which was used in small numbers during 1918, and then on a fairly large scale during the 1920s. The Br.16Bn-2 was an enlarged night-bomber version, produced in some numbers, while the Br.17C2 was a two-seat escort version with a 298kW (400hp) Renault 12K engine and twin forward-firing Vickers machine guns. It came too late to see war service.

Postwar, the Breguet XIV was used extensively by the French military and also by the civil authorities pioneering air routes throughout France's colonial empire. In doing so the aircraft established many records, including the first double crossing of the Mediterranean in 1919.

Specifications apply to the Br.XIVB-2.

BREGUET BR.521 BIZERTE

FRANCE: 1933

Crew: 8
Powerplant: three 672kW (900hp) Gnome-Rhone 14Kirs 14-cylinder radial engines
Performance: max speed 243km/h (151mph); range 2100km (1305 miles); service ceiling 6000m (19,685ft)
Dimensions: wingspan 35.18m (15ft 5in); length 20.48m (67ft 2in); height 7.50m (24ft 6in)
Weight: 16,600kg (36,597lb) loaded
Armament: five 7.5mm (0.29in) machine guns; 300kg (660lb) of bombs

THE BREGUET BR.521 BIZERTE was a long-range maritime reconnaissance flying boat, the prototype of which flew in September 1933, and was developed from Britain's Short Calcutta commercial flying-boat. Three pre-production aircraft were built, the second with minor modifications that became standard on the production version. Thirty production Bizertes followed, the first examples being delivered in 1935, and the type ultimately served with five squadrons of the French Naval Air Arm from 1935 until their disbandment in June 1940. Two of the five squadrons were reformed under Vichy French control and continued to operate

from bases on the Mediterranean coast until the latter were seized by the Germans in November 1942, following the Allied landings in North Africa. Some Bizertes were taken over by the Germans and used for air–sea rescue work, operating from the Biscay coast.

A French version of Britain's Short Calcutta flying boat. Some Bizertes were used by the Germans for air–sea rescue work in North Africa.

BREGUET BR.691/693

FRANCE:1938

Crew: 2
Powerplant: two 615kW (825hp) Pratt &
Whitney R-1830-SB4G Twin Wasp 14-
cylinder radial engines
Performance: max speed 560kmh
(348mph); range 1500km (932 miles);
service ceiling 9000m (29,530ft)
Dimensions: wingspan 15.36m (50ft 3in);
length 9.67m (31ft 8.75in); height 3.19m
(10ft 5.75in)
Weight: 5400kg (11,905lb) loaded
Armament: one forward-firing 20mm
(0.79in) cannon and two 7.5mm (0.29in)
machine guns; four rearward-firing 7.5mm
(0.29in) machine guns; internal bomb
load of 400kg (882lb)

**The Breguet 693, the full production version of the Br 691 seen here, was
an excellent assault aircraft which saw service in the Battle of France.**

THE BREGUET 693 SERIES of
combat aircraft stemmed from a
1934 specification for a three-seat
heavy fighter. In June 1938 Breguet
received an order for 100 production
Br.691s, but only 78 were delivered.
One of these became the prototype

Br.693, which first flew on 25
October 1939. French Air Force
units were just beginning to equip
with the type on 10 May 1940, when
the Germans invaded. In all, the two
fully equipped Br.693 groups flew
some 500 sorties, losing 47 aircraft

of the 106 delivered. Total
production was 224. The final
version was the Br.695, which had
Pratt & Whitney Twin Wasp Junior
engines; 50 were built and 33
delivered before France's collapse.
Specifications apply to the Br.693.

BREGUET BR.1050 ALIZÉ

FRANCE: 1956

IN 1954, TWO YEARS AFTER the
first flight of the second prototype
Br.960 Vultur strike aircraft, the
French Navy's requirement altered
dramatically, and it was decided
that this aircraft would serve as the
prototype of a new shipboard anti-
submarine aircraft. It flew in this
form on 26 March 1955 with the
designation Br.965 and was
followed by three prototypes of the
new anti-submarine aircraft, the
Breguet Br.1050 Alizé (Tradewind).

**The Alizé was the backbone of the
French Navy's carrier-borne anti-
submarine squadrons during much
of the Cold War.**

The first of these flew on 6
October 1956 and the type was
ordered into production, 75 aircraft
eventually being delivered for
service on France's aircraft carriers
and at shore establishments.
Twelve aircraft were also supplied
to the Indian Navy.

Crew: 3
Powerplant: one 1566kW (2100hp) Rolls-
Royce Dart RDa21 turboprop engine
Performance: max speed 458kmh
(285mph); range 2872km (1785 miles);
service ceiling 6100m (20,000ft)
Dimensions: wingspan 15.60m (51ft 2in);
length 13.87m (45ft 6in); height 4.76m
(15ft 7in)
Weight: 8199kg (18,100lb) loaded
Armament: three depth charges or one
torpedo internally; two depth charges and
six RPs or two ASMs underwing

BREGUET BR.1001 TAON

Crew: 1
Powerplant: one 2199kg (4850lb) thrust
Bristol Orpheus B.Or.3 turbojet engine
Performance: max speed 1126km/h
(700mph); combat radius 322km
(200 miles); service ceiling 13,725m
(45,000ft)
Dimensions: wingspan 6.93m (22ft 9in);
length 11.72m (38ft 4in); height 3.73m
(12ft 3.5in)
Weight: 5662kg (12,500lb) loaded
Armament: four 12.7mm (0.50in) Colt-
Browning machine guns; external load of
bombs, napalm tanks or missile pods

A PROMISING FRENCH DESIGN,
the Breguet 1100 Taon (Horsefly)
was designed to meet a NATO
requirement for a lightweight
fighter. The prototype flew on
26 July 1957, powered by a Bristol
Orpheus turbojet. Preliminary flight
trials of the aircraft proved very
satisfactory, with the Taon meeting
every aspect of the NATO requirement. Meanwhile, the prototype of
a twin-engined version, the
Br.1100, had also flown, but its test
programme was halted when the

French Air Force requirement for a
twin-engined strike-fighter (which
was eventually met by the
SEPECAT Jaguar) was withdrawn.

Development of the Taon (whose
name was an anagram of NATO)
was abandoned when the Fiat G.91
was chosen.

**Developed for NATO but ultimately
overshadowed by the Fiat G.91,
the Taon project was eventually
abandoned.**

BREGUET ATLANTIC

**The Atlantic was an excellent
anti-submarine aircraft. This
photo shows the prototype shortly
after its maiden flight in 1961.**

THE BREGUET BR.1150 ATLANTIC
was an early example of international collaboration, with the
development costs and work being

shared by the USA, France, West
Germany, the Netherlands, Belgium
and Britain, the latter contributing
the Rolls-Royce Tyne engines.

The aircraft was developed in
response to a NATO requirement
for a Lockheed P-2 Neptune
replacement. The prototype
Breguet Atlantic flew on 21
October 1961, and first deliveries
were made to the French Navy in
December 1965. France ordered
40 aircraft, Germany 20, Italy 18
and the Netherlands 6.

A much modified and upgraded
version, the Dassault-Breguet
Atlantic Nouvelle Generation
(ALT-2), was developed for the
French Navy, with the first of 42
planned aircraft entering service
in October 1989.

Crew: 12
Powerplant: two 4548kW (6105hp)
Rolls-Royce Tyne RTy.20 Mk 21 turboprop
engines
Performance: max speed 658km/h
(409mph); range 9000km (5590 miles);
service ceiling 10,000m (32,800ft)
Dimensions: wingspan 36.30m (119ft
1in); length 31.75m (104ft 2in); height
11.33m (37ft 2in)
Weight: 43,500kg (95,917lb) loaded
Armament: Mk 43 Brush or LK4 homing
torpedoes; standard NATO bombs, High-
Velocity Aircraft Rockets (HVAR), underwing
ASMs or depth charges

BREWSTER BUFFALO

USA: 1938

A US Army Air Corps Brewster Buffalo assigned to the defence of Northern Australia in early 1942.

THE PROTOTYPE BREWSTER MODEL 139, or XF2A-1, flew for the first time in 1938, and as the F2A-1 single-seat carrier fighter entered service with the US Navy the following year. Underpowered, it was soon declared surplus to requirements, with 44 being sold to Finland in 1940. The F2A-2 (Model 339) and F2A-3 (Model 439) saw limited service with the US Navy, 21 fighters of the latter type forming the bulk of Midway Island's air defence when the Japanese attacked

it in June 1942. Meanwhile, the British Purchasing Commission placed a contract for 170 Model 339 fighters, the type being named Buffalo by the RAF, which also took over an additional 38 aircraft which had been ordered by Belgium. The Netherlands ordered 72 Model 339s and 439s for service in the East Indies. While the RAF rejected the Buffalo for operational service in Europe, it did deem it suitable for service in the Far East. Specifications apply to Model 339.

Crew: 1
Powerplant: one 895kW (1200hp) Wright R-1820-40 Cyclone 9-cylinder radial engine
Performance: max speed 517km/h (321mph); range 1553km (965 miles); service ceiling 10,120m (33,200ft)
Dimensions: wingspan 10.67m (35ft); length 8.03m (26ft 4in); height 3.68m (12ft 1in)
Weight: 3247kg (7159lb) loaded
Armament: four 12.7mm (0.50in) machine guns, two in upper forward fuselage and two in wing

BRISTOL M1C BULLET

UK: 1916

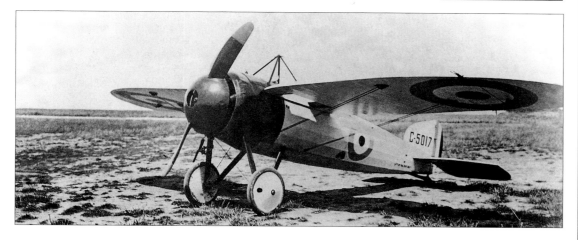

Crew: 1
Powerplant: one 82kW (110hp) Le Rhone 91 rotary engine
Performance: max speed 209km/h (130mph); endurance 1 hr 45 mins; service ceiling 6069m (19,911ft)
Dimensions: wingspan 9.37m (30ft 9in); length 6.24m (20ft 5in); height 2.37m (7ft 9in)
Weight: 611kg (1348lb) loaded
Armament: one fixed forward-firing 7.7mm (0.303in) Vickers machine gun

POTENTIALLY A SUPERB FIGHTER, the Bristol M1C Bullet was rejected for large-scale production ostensibly on the grounds that its landing speed was too high for the small French airfields from which it would be operating. The real reason that the aircraft was rejected, however, was that the Bullet was a monoplane, a configuration against which there was much prejudice in the RFC, an attitude that rightly or

A Bristol M1C Bullet of the RAF in Mesopotamia (Iraq) in 1918. An excellent fighter design, the Bullet suffered from the prejudice against monoplanes that prevailed throughout World War I.

wrongly prevailed during the Great War. The result was that only 125 Bullets were built, some being issued to squadrons in the Middle East and the Balkans in 1917.

BRISTOL F.2B FIGHTER

UK: 1916

Crew: 2
Powerplant: one 205kW (275hp) Rolls-
Royce Falcon III in-line engine
Performance: max speed 198km/h
(123mph); endurance 3 hrs; service
ceiling 5485m (18,000ft)
Dimensions: wingspan 11.96m (39ft 3in);
length 7.87m (25ft 10in); height 2.97m
(9ft 9in)
Weight: 1474kg (3250lb) loaded
Armament: one forward-firing Vickers
7.7mm (0.303in) machine gun;
two 7.7mm (0.303in) Lewis guns
in rear cockpit

After a poor start in air combat over the Western Front, the Bristol F2B fighter, with the help of revised tactics, became a superb fighting machine. This example is preserved in flying condition by the Shuttleworth Collection.

FIRST FLOWN ON 19 SEPTEMBER 1916, the Bristol F.2A two-seat fighter made its operational debut during the Allied spring offensive of 1917. Fifty F.2As were built, powered by 142kW (190hp) Rolls-Royce Falcon engines.

The first F.2As arrived in France with No 48 Squadron RFC in March 1917 and were rushed into action before their crews were able to develop proper tactics. At first they were flown in the same manner as earlier two-seaters, orientated around the observer's gun as the primary weapon, and consequently losses were heavy. Yet when flown offensively, in the same way as a single-seat fighter, the Bristol Fighter proved to be a superb weapon, and the type went on to log a formidable record of success in action. The Bristol F.2A was succeeded by the F.2B, with

an uprated Falcon engine, wide-span tailplane, modified lower-wing centre section and an improved view from the front cockpit.

The F.2B equipped six RFC squadrons on the Western Front, four in the UK and one in Italy. Indeed, the RAF did not retire the

last of its F.2Bs until 1932. Total production was 5308 aircraft, and the type also saw service with 10 overseas air forces.

BRISTOL BULLDOG

UK: 1927

This Bristol Bulldog II, originally sold to Latvia, was flown by foreign volunteer pilots for the Republican forces during the Spanish Civil War, supporting Basque troops.

as the Bulldog Mk II, and 25 production aircraft were ordered to equip Nos 3 and 17 Squadrons. The Bulldog eventually equipped 10 RAF home defence squadrons, the main version being the Mk IIA. It also served in small numbers with the air forces of Denmark, Estonia, Finland, Latvia, Siam and Sweden, 456 being built in total.

Crew: 1
Powerplant: one 298kW (400hp) Bristol
Jupiter VIIF radial engine
Performance: max speed 280km/h
(174mph); range 482km (300 miles);
service ceiling 8940m (29,300ft)
Dimensions: wingspan 10.30m (33ft
10in); length 7.70m (25ft 3in); height
2.70m (8ft 9in)
Weight: 1583kg (3490lb) loaded
Armament: two fixed forward-firing 7.7mm
(0.303in) Vickers machine guns; up to four

IN SEPTEMBER 1926, the British Air Ministry issued a requirement for a new single-seat day and night fighter to be armed with two

machine guns and powered by a radial air-cooled engine. The tender submitted by the Bristol Aeroplane Company was successful, and its

prototype fighter, the Bulldog I, flew for the first time on 17 May 1927. After some necessary structural modifications the type re-emerged

BRISTOL BOMBAY

UK: 1935

Crew: 3
Powerplant: two 752kW (1010hp) Bristol Pegasus XXII 9-cylinder radial engines
Performance: max speed 309km/h (192mph); range 3589km (2230 miles); service ceiling 7620m (25,000ft)
Dimensions: wingspan 29.18m (95ft 9in); length 21.11m (69ft 3in); height 5.94m (19ft 6in)
Weight: 9072kg (20,000lb) loaded
Armament: one 7.7mm (0.303in) machine gun in nose and one in tail turret; two more optionally in beam positions; up to 907kg (2000lb) of bombs internally

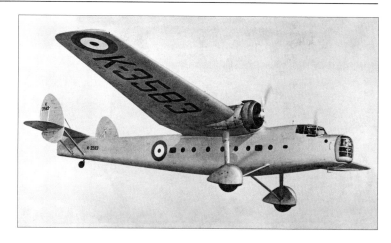

Although obsolete by the start of World War II, the Bristol Bombay gave invaluable service as a troop carrier and casualty evacuation aircraft.

THE BRISTOL BOMBAY STEMMED from a 1931 requirement for a bomber/transport optimized for service in Africa, the Middle East and India, where it was intended to replace the elderly Vickers Valentia. The primary requirement was for the aircraft to be able to carry 25 fully equipped troops, with bombing as a secondary role. The first of 50 production aircraft entered service in March 1939, by which time the type was already practically obsolete. Nevertheless, the Bombay rendered invaluable service as a transport and casualty evacuation aircraft in the UK and North Africa for much of World War II, and also carried out bombing missions against Benghazi. The type was retired in 1944.

BRISTOL BLENHEIM

UK: 1935

Bristol Blenheim I of No 108 Squadron RAF, which used the type from June 1938 to April 1940.

Crew: 3
Powerplant: two 742kW (995hp) Bristol Mercury XV radial engines
Performance: max speed 428km/h (266mph); range 2340km (1460 miles); service ceiling 6705m (22,000ft)
Dimensions: wingspan 17.70m (56ft 6in); length 12.98m (42ft 7in); height 2.99m (9ft 10in)
Weight: 6537kg (14,400lb) loaded
Armament: one 7.7mm (0.303in) Browning machine gun in leading edge of port wing, two in dorsal turret, and two in rearward-firing blister position under nose; max internal bomb load of 454kg (1000lb)

THE BRISTOL BLENHEIM WAS developed from the Bristol Type 142, an eight-passenger civil airliner funded by Lord Rothermere, owner of the *Daily Mail* newspaper. The aircraft, named 'Britain First', was evaluated by the RAF as a potential medium bomber. It performed impressively, and in August 1935 the Air Ministry issued Specification B28/35, covering the conversion of the aircraft to the bomber role under the designation Type 142M. In September 1935 the Air Ministry placed an initial order for 150 aircraft under the service designation Blenheim Mk I, to be powered by 627kW (840hp) Mercury VIII radial engines. When the test programme ended in December 1936 the RAF ordered full-scale production of the Blenheim Mk I and awarded Bristol a contract for another 434 aircraft.

The first Blenheims were delivered to No 114 Squadron in March 1937; 1280 Mk Is were built in total, and of these 1007 were on RAF charge at the outbreak of World War II in September 1939. These included 147 completed as Mk IF fighters, fitted with a ventral gun pack containing four Browning machine guns; some of these were later equipped with Airborne Interception (AI) radar and served as interim night-fighters in the autumn of 1940. By the time war broke out, however, most of the Mk I bombers were serving in the Middle and Far East, the home-based squadrons having rearmed with the improved Blenheim Mk IV. Twelve Blenheims were supplied to Finland (which built an additional 55 between 1941 and 1944), 13 to Romania and 22 to Yugoslavia, where a further 48 were built under licence by Ikarus.

The Blenheim Mk IV was basically a Mk I airframe with

extra fuel tankage, a much redesigned, lengthened nose and two 742kW (995hp) Mercury XV radials driving de Havilland three-blade variable pitch propellers. By 3 September 1939 the RAF had 197 Blenheim IVs on strength, and on the second day of the war aircraft of Nos 107 and 110 Squadrons from Marham, Norfolk, carried out the RAF's first offensive operation when they attacked units of the German Navy in the Elbe Estuary. The attack was unsuccessful, many of the bombs failing to explode, and five of the 10 Blenheims involved were shot down. The total inadequacy of the Blenheim's defensive armament became apparent in the battles of Norway and France, when the UK-based Blenheim squadrons engaged in anti-shipping operations in the North Sea and those deployed to France suffered appalling losses. The armament was subsequently increased to five machine guns.

In 1941 most of the RAF's home-based Blenheim IVs were under the control of No 2 Group, based in East Anglia, from where they carried out ongoing anti-shipping patrols (Operation Channel Stop) and attacks on targets in

The Blenheim Mk IV was an improvement on the Mk I, but it proved a vulnerable target for German fighters and suffered serious losses in the Battle of France and over the English Channel.

France and the Low Countries. Channel Stop cost the Blenheim squadrons dearly; about 25 per cent of all aircraft despatched failed to return. Nevertheless, the Blenheims carried out some spectacular low-level missions, notably an attack

on enemy power stations near Cologne. They were eventually replaced in No 2 Group by the Douglas Boston and the de Havilland Mosquito. In all, 1930 Mk IVs were built. One final version of the Blenheim, the Mk V,

was built in Britain to Specification B.6/40. In Canada, Fairchild built 676 Blenheims for the RCAF, by whom they were designated Bolingbroke Mks I to IV.

Specification refers to the Blenheim Mk IV.

BRISTOL BEAUFORT

UK: 1938

The Bristol Beaufort was a very effective torpedo-bomber and took part in some notable actions. Operating from Malta, it inflicted huge losses on Axis supply convoys to North Africa.

Crew: 4
Powerplant: two 843kW (1130hp) Bristol Taurus VI 14-cylinder radial engines
Performance: max speed 426km/h (265mph); range 2575km (1600 miles); service ceiling 5050m (16,500ft)
Dimensions: wingspan 17.62m (57ft 10in); length 13.59m (44ft 7in); height 3.79m (12ft 5in)
Weight: 9630kg (21,228lb) loaded
Armament: four 7.62mm (0.30in) machine guns; up to 453kg (1000lb) of bombs internally and 227kg (500lb) externally, or one 728kg (1605lb) torpedo semi-recessed

THE BEAUFORT MK I torpedo-bomber first flew on 15 October 1938. It went into service in 1939 and took part in an attack on the German battlecruiser *Gneisenau* in Brest harbour on 6 April 1941, resulting in serious damage to the warship and the posthumous award of the VC to Flying Officer Kenneth Campbell of No 22 Squadron. The type operated mainly in the North Sea and Atlantic areas, but some were deployed to Malta in 1942. Seven hundred Beauforts (Mks V–VIII) were built in Australia.

BRISTOL BEAUFIGHTER

UK: 1939

Crew: 2
Powerplant: two 1220kW (1636hp) Bristol Hercules VI 14-cylinder radial engines
Performance: max speed 536km/h (333mph); range 2382km (1480 miles); service ceiling 8075m (26,500ft)
Dimensions: wingspan 17.63m (57ft 10in); length 12.70m (41ft 8in); height 4.82m (15ft 10in)
Weight: 9798kg (21,600lb) loaded
Armament: four Hispano 20mm (0.79in) fixed forward-firing cannon in underside of forward fuselage; six 7.7mm (0.303in) machine guns in leading edges of wing

A Bristol Beaufighter Mk X of a Coastal Command Strike Wing pictured on a muddy airfield in northern Scotland in 1944.

IN OCTOBER 1938, THE Bristol Aeroplane Company submitted a proposal to the RAF Air Staff for a twin-engined night-fighter, heavily armed with a mixture of cannon and machine guns and equipped with AI radar. The proposal was based on the design of the Beaufort torpedo-bomber, which had just made its first flight, and was initially called the Beaufort Fighter. The first of four Beaufighter prototypes flew on 17 July 1939, deliveries of production aircraft beginning in September

1940. Fourteen Beaufighter squadrons were assigned to the night defence of Great Britain in 1941–42. Total Mk I production was 914 aircraft, while 450 Merlin-engined Mk IIs were built. The Mk VI was also a night-fighter. The Beaufighter TF Mk X

was a torpedo-bomber, and the Mk XIC was an anti-shipping strike variant. The Beaufighter TF Mk X was also built in Australia as the TF Mk 21 (364 examples). British production of the Beaufighter (all variants) was 5562.

Specification refers to the Mk VI.

BRISTOL TYPE 173, 191 AND 192 BELVEDERE

UK: 1952

BRITAIN'S FIRST TANDEM-ROTOR helicopter first flew on 3 January 1952. It had tandem rotors and was capable of carrying 10 passengers. This prototype was subsequently evaluated by the Royal Navy, in tests carried out from the aircraft carrier HMS *Eagle*. The sea trials were successful and in 1956 an order was placed for 68 Bristol 191 ASW models. Meanwhile, the RAF ordered 26 examples for use as heavy transport helicopters. In 1957, however, the Navy order was

cancelled as part of defence cuts and the RAF version only entered service in 1961 as the Belvedere. The all-purpose helicopter was withdrawn from service in 1969.

Bristol's proposal for a 23-seat passenger version (192C) for BEA was never to progress beyond the project stage. The airline selected proven Westland-built versions of American helicopters in preference to the British design.

Specifications apply to the Bristol Belvedere HC-Mk 1.

Crew: 2/3
Powerplant: two Napier-Gazelle NGa.2 Mk 100 turboshaft engines each rated at 1092kW (1465shp)
Performance: max speed 222km/h (138mph) at optimum altitude; combat radius 740km (460 miles); service ceiling 5273m (17,300ft)
Dimensions: rotor diameter 14.91m (48ft 11in); length 27.36m (89ft 9in); height 5.26m (17ft 3in)
Weight: 5277kg (11,634lb)
Armament/payload: up to 18 fully armed troops or 2722kg (6000lb) of freight

The first twin-engined twin-rotor helicopter to enter RAF service, Belvederes served in Transport Command, Aden and the Far East.

BRISTOL TYPE 175 BRITANNIA

UK: 1952

Flying in formation are the first and second prototypes of the Britannia. G-ALRX, seen in the foreground, was later lost in a non-fatal crash caused by an engine fire.

THE BRITANNIA WAS BRISTOL'S winning response to a postwar (1947) BOAC requirement for a medium-range civil passenger transport which was capable of use across the Empire.

However, the Britannia suffered development problems, notably recurring flameout of the Centaurus engine. The great potential of this design for major orders was thus overtaken by pure jet designs – the stretched series 300 was not available until 1956. Consequently, only 85 examples of the Britannia were built, including 23 dash 200 series, built for the RAF. Examples of the type remained in freight service for many years, with the last retiring in the late 1990s.

Specifications apply to the Bristol Britannia Series 310.

Crew: 3
Powerplant: four Bristol Proteus 755 turboprop engines each rated at 3072ekW (4120ehp)
Performance: max speed 639km/h (397mph); range 6869km (4268 miles) with maximum payload; service ceiling 7315m (24,000ft)
Dimensions: wingspan 43.00m (142ft 3in); length 37.00m (118ft 4in); height 11.43m (37ft 6in)
Weight: 83,915kg (185,000lb) maximum take-off weight
Payload: up to 133 passengers

BRITISH AEROSPACE (ENGLISH ELECTRIC) CANBERRA

UK: 1949

ORIGINALLY DESIGNED AS A replacement for the de Havilland Mosquito, the English Electric Canberra was the greatest success story of Britain's postwar aviation industry and is still in service in the 21st century, more than 50 years after the prototype was rolled out. Four prototypes of the Canberra B.Mk 1 were produced, and the first of these flew on 13 May 1949, powered by Rolls-Royce Avon turbojets. Problems with the radar

bomb-aiming equipment, however, led to the redesign of the nose with a visual bomb-aiming position, and with this modification the fifth aircraft became the Canberra B.2, the type entering service with No 101 Squadron RAF Bomber Command in May 1951. By this time a photo-reconnaissance version, the Canberra PR.3, had also flown; this was basically a B.2 with a battery of seven cameras for high-level photo-reconnaissance,

and entered service with No 540 Squadron in 1953.

The next variant was the T.4 dual-control trainer, which entered service in 1954. This was followed by the B.5, a converted PR.3 intended for target marking, but only a few examples of the B.5 were produced before it was superseded by the B.6, a version with more powerful Avon 109 engines The B(I)Mk 6 was an interim night interdictor version, while the PR.7

was a photo-reconnaissance variant. The Canberra B(I).8, which entered service in 1956, featured some radical modifications, the most notable being an entirely redesigned fuselage nose and an offset fighter-type cockpit, the navigator being 'buried' in the starboard fuselage.

In October 1955, Peru ordered eight B(I).8s and a similar number, together with two T.4s, was ordered by Venezuela in January

Canberra B.2 WD995, seen here while serving with No 617 Squadron, crashed after colliding with a Gloster Javelin during a practice interception near Akrotiri, Cyprus, in October 1961.

A trio of PR.7 Canberras. The photo-reconnaissance versions of the Canberra made some highly secret flights during the Cold War, and the latest – the PR.9 – was still operational in 2003.

1957. The Canberra PR.9 high-altitude photo-reconnaissance variant also had an offset cockpit and an increased wing span, as well as RR Avon 206 engines.

In January 1957 the Indian Air Force became a major Canberra customer, ordering 54 B(I).58s and eight PR.57s, with further aircraft acquired at a later date. The Canberra B.15/16 was a modified B.6 with underwing points for bombs or rocket packs. Other Canberra variants included the unmanned U.Mk 10 target aircraft,

the T.17 ECM trainer, the E.15 electronic reconnaissance variant, the T.18 target tug, the T.19 target facilities aircraft, and the T.22 trainer for the Royal Navy. The Canberra was built under licence in the USA as the Martin B-57, and in Australia it was built as the B.20 and T.21.

During their lengthy career, Canberras saw action in many parts of the world. RAF aircraft operated against communist terrorists in Malaya in the 1950s and bombed Egyptian airfields during the Suez crisis of 1956, and Indian Air Force aircraft fought in the Indo-Pakistan conflicts of 1965 and 1971. Refurbished Canberras were sold to Argentina (two being lost in the 1982 Falklands war), Chile, Ecuador, France, Peru,

Rhodesia (Zimbabwe), South Africa, Sweden, Venezuela and West Germany.

Specification refers to the English Electric Canberra B. Mk 6.

Crew: 3
Powerplant: two 3397kg (7500lb) thrust Rolls Royce Avon Mk 109 turbojet engines
Performance: max speed 917km/h (570mph); range 4274km (2656 miles); service ceiling 14,630m (48,000ft)
Dimensions: wingspan 19.49m (63ft 11in); length 19.96m (65ft 6in); height 4.78m (15ft 8in)
Weight: 24,925kg (54,950lb) loaded
Armament: up to 2727kg (6000lb) of bombs internally, with provision for 907kg (2000lb) of external stores on underwing pylons; B.15/16 armed with 'Red Beard' 15-kiloton 792kg (1750lb) nuclear bomb; B(I)8 with US Mk 7/43

BREWSTER SBA/SBN
The Brewster SBA/SBN was a two-seat scout-bomber, first flown in 1936. Thirty examples were built by the Naval Aircraft Factory as SBN-1s.

BREWSTER SB2A BUCCANEER
The Brewster SB2A Buccaneer was designed as a shipboard reconnaissance aircraft and dive-bomber. It first flew in 1941, but only a few examples were to reach the US Navy before production was abandoned.

BREWSTER BERMUDA
The RAF received 450 examples of the Brewster SB2A. Named Bermuda in RAF service, it was found unsatisfactory and was used for training and target towing.

BREWSTER XA-32
The Brewster XA-32 was a naval torpedo and dive-bomber project. Only two prototypes were built, the first flying in 1942.

BRISTOL SCOUT
One of Britain's first military aeroplanes, the Bristol Scout deployed to France with the RFC in 1914. It was built in four versions, totalling 373 aircraft.

BRISTOL TYPE 26 PULLMAN
Dating from 1918, the Pullman was an attempt to create a 14-passenger airliner derivative of the Type 24 Braemar triplane bomber. This four-engined aircraft was not sold and a subsequent Type 37 was similarly abandoned.

BRISTOL BRAEMAR
First flown in July 1918, the Bristol Braemar was a four-engined triplane designed to bomb German targets from British bases. Two prototypes were built.

BRITISH AEROSPACE (ENGLISH ELECTRIC) LIGHTNING

UK: 1957

THE ENGLISH ELECTRIC LIGHTNING was based on the P.1A research aircraft, which first flew on 4 August 1954 powered by two Bristol Siddeley Sapphires. Three operational protoypes, designated P.1B, were also built. The first of these flew on 4 April 1957, powered by two Rolls-Royce Avons, and exceeded Mach 1.0 on its first flight. On 25 November 1958 it became the first British aircraft to reach Mach 2.0, which it did in level flight. The first production Lightning F.Mk 1 flew on 29 October 1959, and fully combat-equipped Lightnings began entering RAF service in July 1960. The Lightning, which had a phenomenal initial climb rate of 15,240m (50,000ft) per minute, was constantly improved during its career, evolving via the F.2 and F.3 into the F.6 version.

Specification refers to the Lightning F.Mk 3.

Crew: 1
Powerplant: two 7112kg (15,680lb) thrust Rolls-Royce Avon 211R turbojet engines
Performance: max speed 2415km/h (1500mph); range 1287km (800 miles); service ceiling 18,920m (60,000ft) plus
Dimensions: wingspan 10.61m (34ft 10in) wing area 35.31m² (380sq ft); length 16.84m (55ft 3in); height 5.97m (19ft 7in)
Weight: 22,680kg (50,000lb) loaded
Armament: two nose-mounted 30mm (1.18in) Aden guns; two Firestreak or Red Top AAMs

In this picture, a Lightning T.4 is flanked by F.6s of No 5 (top) and 11 Squadrons. They were among the last UK-based Lightning squadrons, the former at Binbrook, Lincolnshire, and the latter at Leuchars, Scotland.

BRITISH AEROSPACE (HAWKER SIDDELEY) HARRIER

UK: 1960

A KEY ELEMENT IN MODERN offensive battlefield support is the short take-off, vertical-landing (STOVL) aircraft, epitomized by the British Aerospace/McDonnell Douglas Harrier. One of the most important and certainly the most revolutionary combat aircraft to emerge during the postwar years, the Harrier V/STOL (Vertical/Short Take-Off and Landing) tactical fighter-bomber began its career as a private venture in 1957 following discussions between Hawker Aircraft Ltd and Bristol Aero-engines Ltd, designers of the BS53 Pegasus turbofan engine. The development of this powerplant, which featured two pairs of

The Hawker P.1127, which went on to become the Harrier.

connected rotating nozzles, one pair to provide jet lift, was partly financed with American funds, and in 1959–60 the Ministry of Aviation ordered two prototypes and four development aircraft under the designation P.1127. The first prototype made a tethered hovering flight on 21 October 1960 and began conventional flight trials on 13 March 1961. In 1962 Britain, the USA and West Germany announced a joint order for nine Kestrels, as the aircraft was now known, for evaluation by a tripartite handling squadron at RAF West Raynham in 1965. Six of these aircraft were subsequently shipped to the USA for further trials. In its single-seat close-support and tactical-reconnaissance version, the aircraft was ordered into production for the RAF as the Harrier GR.Mk 1, the first of an initial order of 77 machines flying on 28 December 1967. On 1 April 1969, the Harrier entered service with the Harrier OCU at RAF Wittering, and the type subsequently equipped No 1 Squadron at Wittering and Nos 3, 4 and 20 Squadrons in Germany.

The Harrier GR.3 was a development of the Harrier GR.1,

being fitted with improved attack sensors, electronic countermeasures and a more powerful engine. The simplicity and flexibility inherent in the Harrier design proved their worth in service in Germany. In time of war the Harrier was to be deployed away from established airfields, which were vulnerable to attack. Instead it was to be operated from short, rough strips of ground and hidden in camouflaged 'hides' from which it would attack the enemy's approaching armoured formations. The Harrier force was withdrawn from Germany in 1999.

During the 1982 Falklands War, RAF Harriers were deployed to the Royal Navy aircraft carrier HMS *Hermes* as part of the Task Force sent to recapture the Falkland Islands. The Harrier GR.3 performed attack sorties from the aircraft carrier, and later from basic landing strips on the islands, often in conditions that would have grounded conventional aircraft. In addition to operations with RAF Germany, the Harrier GR.3 has also seen service with the Royal Air Force in Norway and Belize.

Latest versions of the Harrier to serve with the RAF are the GR.5

and GR.7, the latter with a night attack capability. These Harrier II variants are fitted with leading-edge root extensions (LERX) to enhance the Harrier's air-combat agility by improving the turn rate, while longitudinal fences (LIDS, or Lift Improvement Devices) are incorporated beneath the fuselage and on the gun pods to capture ground-reflected jets in vertical take-off and landing, give a much bigger ground cushion and reduce hot gas recirculation.

Specification refers to the Harrier GR.5.

Crew: 1
Powerplant: one 10,796kg (23,800lb) thrust Rolls-Royce F402-RR-408 vectored thrust turbofan engine
Performance: max speed 1065km/h (661mph); combat radius 277km (172 miles); service ceiling 15,240m (50,000ft)
Dimensions: wingspan 9.25m (30ft 4in); length 14.12m (46ft 4in); height 3.55m (11ft 7in)
Weight: 14,061kg (31,000lb) loaded
Armament: one 25mm (0.98in) GAU-12U cannon; six external hardpoints with provision for up to 7711kg (17,003lb) or 3175kg (7000lb) of stores/ordnance (short and vertical take-off respectively)

The Harrier GR.7 is the RAF's equivalent of the US Marine Corps' AV-8B Harrier II. Throughout the Harrier's career, there has been the closest possible collaboration between the two Services.

BRITISH AEROSPACE (HAWKER SIDDELEY/DE HAVILLAND) 125

UK: 1962

Crew: 2
Powerplant: two 13.88kN (3120lb st) Rolls-Royce (Bristol Siddeley) Viper Mk 301 turbojet engines
Performance: max speed 805km/h (500mph); range 2153km (1338 miles); service ceiling 12,190m (40,000ft)
Dimensions: wingspan 14.33m (47ft); length 14.45m (47ft 5in); height 5.03m (16ft 6in); wing area 32.79m² (353sq ft)
Weight: 9616kg (21,200lb) maximum take-off weight
Payload: up to eight passengers, or laid out for three pupils and one instructor

THE 125 ORIGINATED WITH the de Havilland Jet Dragon design as a first-generation 6–8 seat business jet/military role trainer powered by two rear fuselage mounted turbojet engines. De Havilland built early examples, before being incorporated into Hawker Siddeley (in turn this became part of BAe), which developed greater weight, range and payload derivatives, culminating in the 700 series which featured Garrett TFE731-3-1H turbofan engines. Specification applies to the Dominie T.Mk 1.

Designated the Dominie in military service, the 125 provided RAF navigators and air electronics officers with jet training experience.

BRITISH AEROSPACE (HAWKER SIDDELEY) NIMROD

UK: 1967

From 1979 the Nimrod fleet was substantially upgraded to MR.2 standard, with improved avionics and weapon systems. A further upgrade, involving new wings and undercarriage and BMW/Rolls-Royce fuel-efficient engines, has resulted in the Nimrod MRA.4.

Specifications apply to the MR. Mk 2.

Crew: 13
Powerplant: four 5507kg (12,140lb) thrust Rolls-Royce Spey Mk 250 turbofan engines
Performance: max speed 925km/h (575mph)· range 9262km (5755 miles); service ceiling 12,800m (42,000ft)
Dimensions: wingspan 35.00m (114ft 10in); length 39.34m (129ft 1in); height 9.08m (29ft 9in)
Weight: 87,090kg (192,000lb)
Armament: up to 6123kg (13,500lb) of stores internally, including nine torpedoes and/or depth charges; underwing pylons for anti-ship missiles or Sidewinder AAMs

This British Aerospace Nimrod MR.2 is armed with Sidewinder air-to-air missiles for self-defence. This modification was carried out during the 1982 Falklands War, when Nimrods patrolled the South Atlantic.

DEVELOPED FROM THE de Havilland Comet 4C airliner, the Nimrod, which first flew on 23 May 1967, was intended to replace the Shackleton as the RAF's

standard long-range maritime patrol aircraft. Deliveries of production Nimrod MR.Mk 1 aircraft began in October 1969. The Nimrod equipped five

squadrons and No 236 Operational Conversion Unit, 46 aircraft being delivered. Three more served in the electronic intelligence role as Nimrod R.1s.

BRITISH AEROSPACE (HAWKER SIDDELEY) HAWK

UK: 1974

Crew: 2
Powerplant: one 2359kg (5200lb) thrust Rolls Royce/Turbomeca Adour Mk 151 turbofan engine
Performance: max speed 1038km/h (645mph); endurance 4 hrs; service ceiling 15,240m (50,000ft)
Dimensions: wingspan 9.39m (30ft 9in); wing area 16.69m² (179.64sq ft); length 11.17m (36ft 7in); height 3.99m (13ft 1in)
Weight: 7750kg (17,085lb) loaded
Armament: under-fuselage/wing hardpoints for up to 2567kg (5660lb) of stores

The Hawk LIFT (Lead-In Fighter Trainer) is an updated version of the Hawk 100, developed for the Royal Australian Air Force.

THE HAWKER SIDDELEY HAWK was designed as a replacement for the Gnat and Hunter in the advanced training and strike roles. The prototype flew in August 1974, and the first two operational Hawk T.Mk 1s (out of an eventual total of 175) were handed over in November 1976. The Hawk T.Mk 1A is a tactical weapons trainer.

The Hawk Series 60 and Series 100 are two-seat export versions, while the Hawk 200 is a single-seat dedicated ground-attack variant which was designed from the outset to be a cost-effective, multi-role combat aircraft. Hawks have been exported to some 20 countries, Australia, Canada, Indonesia, South Korea, Saudi Arabia and Zimbabwe among them, and a modified variant serves with the US Navy as the T-45A Goshawk. Specifications apply to the Hawk T.Mk 1A.

BRITISH AEROSPACE SEA HARRIER

UK: 1979

British Aerospace Sea Harrier FRS.1s of No 899 naval Air Squadron, one of the three Sea Harrier squadrons that flew combat missions during the Falklands War of 1982.

Crew: 1
Powerplant: one 9752kg (13,100lb) thrust Rolls-Royce Pegasus Mk 106 vectored thrust turbofan engine
Performance: max speed 1185km/h (736mph); combat radius 185km (115 miles); service ceiling 15,545m (51,000ft)
Dimensions: wingspan 7.70m (25ft 3in); wing area 18.68m² (201.1sq ft); length 14.17m (46ft 6in); height 3.71m (12ft 2in)
Weight: 11,884kg (26,200lb) loaded
Armament: two 25mm (0.98in) Aden cannon; five external pylons with provision for AIM-9 Sidewinder, AIM-120 AMRAAM, and two Harpoon or Sea Eagle anti-ship missiles, up to a total of 3629kg (8000lb)

THE SEA HARRIER FRS.1 was developed from the basic Harrier airframe and was ordered to equip the Royal Navy's three Invincible class aircraft carriers. The nose was lengthened to accommodate the Blue Fox AI radar, and the cockpit was raised to permit the installation of a more substantial avionics suite and to provide the pilot with a better all-round view. An initial production batch of 24 aircraft, plus three development aircraft, were ordered to expedite testing and clearance, and, while the first Sea Harrier neared completion in the summer of 1978, the testing of its entire range of operational equipment was under way in two specially modified Hawker Hunter T.8 aircraft. The first Sea Harrier FRS.1 took off for its maiden flight from Dunsfold on 20 August 1978; this aircraft, XZ450, was not in fact a prototype, but the first aircraft of a production order that had now risen from 24 to 31. On 13 November it became the first Sea Harrier to land on an aircraft carrier, HMS *Hermes*.

The second production Sea Harrier, XZ451, flew on 25 May 1979 and became the first example to be taken on charge by the Royal Navy on 18 June 1979. No 800A Naval Air Squadron was commissioned at Royal Naval Air Station, Yeovilton, Somerset, on 26 June 1979 as the Sea Harrier Intensive Flying Trials Unit (IFTU), and on 31 March 1980 this unit was disbanded and reformed as No 899 Headquarters and Training Squadron. A second Sea Harrier squadron, No 800, was commissioned on 23 April 1980, and was followed by No 801 Squadron on 26 February 1981.

The planned peacetime establishment of each squadron was five Sea Harriers; No 800 was to embark on HMS *Hermes*, while No 801 was to go to HMS *Invincible*. Meanwhile, an additional

This Sea Harrier FRS.Mk I is in the colours of No. 801 Squadron, based at RNAS Yeovilton, knowun to the Royal Navy as HMS *Heron*. The code '000' shows that it is the aircraft assigned to the squadron commander.

batch of 10 Sea Harriers had been ordered from British Aerospace; the first of these flew on 15 September 1981 and was delivered to No 899 Squadron.

Armed with Sidewinder AAMs, the Sea Harrier FRS.1 was to distinguish itself in the 1982 Falklands War. At the height of the campaign, on 21 May 1982, Sea Harriers were being launched on combat air patrols at the rate of one pair every 20 minutes.

The Sea Harrier force was later upgraded to FA.2 standard, the forward fuselage being redesigned to accommodate the Ferranti Blue Vixen pulse-Doppler radar. The avionics suite was wholly upgraded and the aircraft armed with the AIM-120 AMRAAM medium-range air-to-air missile, enabling it to engage multiple targets beyond visual range. Deliveries of the 38 converted aircraft began in 1992, followed by 28 new-build machines; all were scheduled to be withdrawn from use from 2004. The Royal Navy's strike task will then be undertaken by the RAF's Harrier GR.7s/9s until the anticipated deployment of a new generation of aircraft carriers and V/STOL aircraft.

Specification refers to the Sea Harrier FA.2

BRITISH AEROSPACE/MCDONNELL DOUGLAS T-45 GOSHAWK

USA: 1988

Crew: 2
Powerplant: one 2507kg (5527lb) thrust Rolls-Royce F405-RR-401 turbofan engine
Performance: max speed 1038km/h (645mph); range 1288km (800 miles); service ceiling 12,962m (42,500ft)
Dimensions: wingspan 9.39m (30ft 10in); length 11.98m (39ft 4in); height 4.11m (13ft 6in)
Weight: 6075kg (13,400lb) loaded
Armament: none

THE T-45A GOSHAWK, the US Navy version of the British Aerospace Hawk, first flew in April 1988 and is used for intermediate and advanced portions of the Navy/Marine Corps pilot training programme for jet carrier aviation and tactical strike missions. The T-45A replaced the T-2 Buckeye and TA-4 Skyhawk trainers with an integrated training system that includes operations and instrument fighter simulators, academics, and training integration systems. The T-45A, operational in 1991, contains an analogue design cockpit, while the new T-45C, the first delivered in December 1997, is built around a new digital 'glass cockpit' design. It is equipped with two monochrome 12.7cm (5in) multifunction displays providing navigation, weapon delivery, aircraft performance and communications data. Martin Baker Mk 14 NACES ejection seats are fitted.

The T-45A Goshawk is the US Navy's version of the British Aerospace Hawk. The primary contractor in the USA is Boeing. It became operational in 1991 and is a component part of a fully integrated training system.

BRITISH ARMY AEROPLANE NO 1

UK: 1908

BUILT BY EXPATRIATE AMERICAN Samuel Franklin Cody, then kiting instructor to the Royal Engineers at the Balloon Factory, Farnborough, British Army Aeroplane No 1 made its first fully authenticated take-off on 29 September 1908, when it made a 'hop' of 71.3m (234ft). On 16 October, at Farnborough, it made what is recognised officially as the first sustained powered flight in Great Britain by a heavier-than-air machine, covering 423.7m (1390ft) before crash-landing.

On 8 September 1909, after undergoing many modifications, the aircraft made a sustained flight of more than an hour around Laffan's Plain (Farnborough), travelling about 64km (40 miles).

Crew: 1
Powerplant: one 37.3kW (50hp) Antoinette 8-cylinder water-cooled V-type engine
Performance: max speed 64km/h (50mph); no further details
Dimensions: wingspan 15.85m (52ft); length 13.41m (44ft); height 3.96m (13ft)
Weight: 1152kg (2540lb) loaded
Armament: none

Built by pioneer aviator Samuel Franklin Cody, the British Army Aeroplane No 1 made the first sustained powered flight by an aeroplane in Britain at Laffan's Plain (Farnborough) in October 1908.

BRITTEN-NORMAN BN-2 ISLANDER

UK: 1965

Crew: 1
Powerplant: two 194kW (260hp) Avco Lycoming O-540-E4C5 horizontally opposed piston engines
Performance: max cruising speed 257km/h (160mph) at 2135m (7000ft); range 1400km (870 miles); service ceiling 4010m (12,832ft)
Dimensions: wingspan 14.94m (49ft); length 10.86m (35ft 7.75in); height 4.18m (13ft 8.75in)
Weight: 4536kg (10,000lb) maximum take-off weight
Payload: up to nine passengers

THE ISLANDER'S DESIGNERS, John Britten and Desmond Norman, perceived the worldwide need for a small feeder passenger transport with good hot and high capabilities in the early 1960s. Development work on the aircraft was begun at

The Islander has been utilized in many roles, including that of lifting parachutists – as is the case with this example based in Kent, UK.

BRISTOL TYPE 167 BRABAZON
Specified as a 100–180-seat airliner, requiring eight piston engines in coupled pairs, the prototype Type 167 flew in 1949. Serious structural problems in the engine area contributed to the cancellation of the project.

BRISTOL TYPE 188
The Type 188 was Bristol's first (twin) turbojet design, produced in response to a military high-speed research aircraft requirement. It first flew in 1962. Only three Type 188s were built and excessive fuel consumption curtailed the project.

BRITISH AEROSPACE (SCOTTISH AVIATION) BULLDOG
Originally produced by Scottish Aviation, the BAe Bulldog primary trainer was a military version of the Beagle Pup, and first flew on 19 May 1969. It was adopted by the RAF and the air forces of Sweden, Kenya and Malaysia.

BRITISH AEROSPACE JETSTREAM 31 AND 32 (HANDLEY PAGE HP.137)
This is a twin-turbo-engined, 19-seat airliner developed from the original Handley Page version of 1969. A total of 381 aircraft were produced in addition to the original 67 Handley Page builds. Many examples remain in service.

BRITISH AEROSPACE ATP
This twin-turbo-powered commuter liner was based upon the successful Avro 748, but stretched for higher capacity. First flown in 1986, its sales were slow and totalled only 61. Production has ceased.

BRITISH AEROSPACE JETSTREAM 41
A stretched and uprated successor to the earlier Jetstream 31/32, the J41 dates from 1991 and does away with spar intrusion into the cabin. Capable of carrying 29 passengers, over 100 examples were produced.

BRITISH AIRCRAFT CORPORATION DRONE
Derived from a glider design, the parasol-wing drone was fitted with a Douglas motorbike engine. It dates from 1933 and was built for private flyers.

Bembridge on the Isle of Wight in 1964 and, after a period of nearly 40 years, successive ownerships (Fairey and Pilatus), bankruptcies and many different versions, the Britten-Norman BN-2 Islander remains in production today.

The original high-wing design has been refined aerodynamically, ergonomically and in terms of range and payload. The turbine version BN-2T with Allison 250 turboprops was introduced in 1980 and remains available today, as does the armed military Defender version. The Islander has proved immensely popular for feeder and bush commuter services, particularly in hot, high or STOL environments, although it is not often sold in large batches.

In recent years production has been at lower levels and builds are often to meet a specific role requirement. The Islander is also licence-built in Romania.

Specifications apply to Britten-Norman BN-2B Islander II.

BÜCKER BÜ 131 JUNGMANN
GERMANY: 1934

Crew: 1/2
Powerplant: one Hirth HM-504A-2 inverted in-line engine rated at 78kW (105hp)
Performance: max speed 183km/h (114mph) at sea level; range 650km (404 miles); service ceiling 3000m (9845ft)
Dimensions: wingspan 7.40m (24ft 3.33in); length 6.60m (21ft 8in); height 2.25m (7ft 4.5in)
Weight: 680kg (1499lb) maximum take-off weight
Armament/Payload: two people; unarmed provision was made for racks and manually delivered bombs

DESIGNED BY SWEDE ANDERS ANDERSSEN, the Bü 131 was Bücker's first product – the type's development dates from 1932. Initially designed for flying schools, it was also built in large numbers for the Luftwaffe as a trainer in an era when Germany intended to rebuild its international position. This successful primary trainer was also licence-built in Switzerland and Japan. The Japanese built more than a thousand

The Jungmann remains highly prized and desirable in more modern times – as is the case with this example, which was privately owned in the UK for many years.

under several designations (initially Ki-86a) with a Hitachi engine. The Jungmann (Youth) saw service throughout World War II, sometimes in a nocturnal ground-attack role. Afterwards Aero in Czechoslovakia built it as the C4. Many examples survived hostilities and indeed some of those still remain airworthy today.

Specifications apply to the Bü 131B Jungmann.

BÜCKER BÜ 133 JUNGMEISTER
GERMANY: 1935

Crew: 1
Powerplant: one Siemens Sh 14A-4 119kW (160hp) radial piston engine
Performance: max speed 220km/h (137mph); range 500km (311 miles); service ceiling 4500m (14,765ft)
Dimensions: wingspan 6.60m (21ft 7.75in); length 6.00m (19ft 9in); height 2.20m (7ft 2.5in)
Weight: 585kg (1290lb) maximum take-off weight
Payload: single seat

BASED UPON THE BÜ 131 Jungmann, but with a single seat, the Jungmeister was an advanced trainer with aerobatic qualities, ideal for training fighter pilots. It was the aircraft that most German World War II fighter pilots learned

This Jungmeister is painted in pre-war Luftwaffe livery; however, it is in fact a privately owned example based in the UK.

their trade on in thinly disguised paramilitary associations.

The prototype flew with a Hirth engine, but this was subsequently upgraded to the Siemens type. The Jungmeister went on to win many pre-World War II aerobatic competitions, and is still considered by many to be the greatest aerobatic trainer ever – surviving examples are still prized today. Large numbers were utilized by the Luftwaffe, and a further 50 were produced by Dornier-Werke in Switzerland for the Swiss Air Force. CASA produced a modest quantity for the Spanish Air Force. Specifications apply to Bü 133C Jungmeister.

BÜCKER BÜ 181 BESTMANN
GERMANY: 1939

THE BÜ 181 BESTMANN was a more successful follow-on to the earlier Bü 180 Student – Bucker's first monoplane trainer. By 1939 the requirement was for military use, and although designated a trainer the Bestmann was often used by squadrons for communications duties, collections and deliveries. This was in part due to competition from the Me-108, which served in a similar role. Still, the Bestmann was utilized by most Axis powers, as well as being licence-built as a trainer in Czechoslovakia, Holland, Sweden and Egypt. Specifications apply to Bu 181 Bestmann.

Bestmanns were licence-built in a number of countries, including Egypt, as seen here. Production continued after World War II.

Crew: 2
Powerplant: one 78kW (105hp) Hirth HM 504A inverted in-line engine
Performance: max speed 215km/h (134mph); range 800km (497 miles)
Dimensions: wingspan 10.60m (34ft 9.25in); length 7.85m (25ft 9in); height 2.05m (6ft 8.25in)
Weight: 750kg (1653lb) maximum take-off weight
Payload: two-seat trainer

BURNELLI CB-16
USA: 1928

Crew: 2
Powerplant: two 371kW (500hp) Curtiss Conqueror piston engines
Performance: max cruising speed 185km/h (115mph); range 1287km (800 miles)
Dimensions: wingspan 27.40m (90ft); length 14.00m (46ft)
Payload: up to 20 passengers in a luxury configuration

THE CB-16 MONOPLANE WAS built as an executive transport for banker Paul W. Chapman and was designed by Vincent Burnelli. The design of Burnelli's first monoplane embodied his 'lifting body' techniques, which involved a more extensive blending of the fuselage with the wing to provide greater lift – and accident survival. The high-wing, open-cockpit CB-16 is also notable for being the first multi-engined aircraft capable of single-engined operation, and possesses a retractable landing gear and an all-stressed metal design.

Despite its promising nature and Burnelli's ideas, the CB-16 was lost due to a maintenance error. But it was Burnelli's problematic political connections which really lost him the opportunity to redefine the shape of aviation.

Specifications apply to CB-16.

Burnelli's lifting-body designs were ahead of their time and are one of the great 'might have been' inventions of the 20th century.

CAB GY.20 MINICAB

THE GY.20 WAS AN EARLY postwar light aircraft design by Yves Gardan. It was a remarkably modern-looking low-wing, single-engined cabin monoplane. CAB built the Minicab in small numbers in France before ceasing operations. The GY.20 design data was then purchased by A.W.J.G. Ord-Hume. The GY.20 was licence-built or home-built in the UK, Canada, Australia and New Zealand.

Crew: 1
Powerplant: one 67kW (90hp) Continental C-90 engine
Performance: max speed 180km/h (112mph); range 740km (460 miles); service ceiling 6000m (19,700ft)

Dimensions: wingspan 7.62m (25ft); length 5.18m (17ft)
Payload: two people
Weight: 485kg (1069lb) maximum take-off weight

CANADAIR CL-28 ARGUS

Based on the Bristol Britannia civil airliner, the great range of the Canadair CL-28 Argus enabled it to perform a valuable maritime patrol task in NATO's northern waters.

IN APRIL 1954 CANADAIR was awarded a development contract for a long-range maritime patrol aircraft design based on the Bristol Britannia airliner, the new aircraft retaining the Britannia's wings, tail assembly, landing gear and flying controls. The aircraft's fuselage was completely redesigned, provision being made for a weapons bay and new internal installations, and the Britannia's turbo-prop engines were replaced by Wright Cyclone turbo-compound units. The prototype CL-28 Argus flew on 28 March 1957 and the first fully operational Argus Mk 1 was delivered to No 405 Squadron RCAF in May 1958, followed by No 404 Squadron in May 1959. Other units to equip with the Argus were Nos 407 and 415 Squadrons, No 449 Maritime Training Squadron, and the RCAF Maritime Proving and Evaluation Unit. In all but No 415 Squadron the Argus replaced the Lockheed Neptune, which had been purchased as an interim patrol aircraft. Argus production totalled 33 aircraft , of which 13 were Mk 1s and 20 Mk 2s, the two differing in the size of the chin radome, which was much larger on the earlier mark. Specifications apply to the Canadair CL-28 Mk 2.

Crew: 15
Powerplant: four 2536kW (3400hp) Wright Cyclone R-3350-EA1 turbo-compound engines
Performance: max speed 464km/h (288mph); range 6436km (4000 miles); service ceiling 7838m (25,700ft)
Dimensions: wingspan 43.38m (142ft 3in); length 38.26m (125ft 5in); height 11.20m (36ft 8in)
Weight: 71,121kg (157,000lb) loaded
Armament: up to 3642kg (8000lb) of offensive maritime stores

CANADAIR CL-44

Crew: 4/5
Powerplant: four 4273ekW (5730ehp) Rolls-Royce Tyne RTy.12 MK 515/10 turboprop engines
Performance: cruising speed 621km/h (386mph); range 4627km (2875 miles) with maximum payload; service ceiling 9145m (30,000ft)
Dimensions: wingspan 43.37m (142ft 3.5in); length 41.73m (136ft 10.75in); height 11.79m (38ft 8in)
Weight: 95,254kg (210,000lb) maximum take-off weight
Payload: up to 28725kg (63,272lb) freight

THE CL-44 WAS DERIVED from the Bristol Britannia airframe, the result of a 1954 licence-build agreement. The fuselage was stretched and engines changed along with other less overt alterations. Initial orders came from the Royal Canadian Air Force, which purchased a version designated CC-

American cargo operator Flying Tiger Line was one of the largest customers for the CL-44, operating 12 examples between 1961 and 1972. Flying Tigers went on to replace the CL-44 with the DC-8.

106 Yukon. However, the definitive freighter version came in the form of a radical new development – a swing tail for freight loading embodied in the CL-44D4 series.

Icelandic budget operator Loftleider ordered a 178-seat version, which was later stretched to accommodate 214 passengers as the CL-44J. One example of the 39 built was converted to CL-44-O Conroy Guppy for transport of extraordinary-size loads, and remains operational in 2003.

Specifications apply to CL-44D4.

CANT Z.501

ITALY: 1934

The CANT Z.501 pictured here is in the markings of the Spanish Nationalist Air Force.

DESIGNED BY THE ENGINEER Filippo Zappata and first flown in 1934, the CANT (Cantieri Riuniti dell'Adriatico) Z.501 Gabbiano (Seagull) was the standard equipment of Italy's maritime reconnaissance squadrons at the outbreak of World War II, and 202 were in service in 15 squadrons when Italy entered the conflict on 10 June 1940. The type was still in service at the time of the Italian armistice of September 1943. On

19 May 1934, the Z.501 prototype established a world seaplane distance record of 4130km (2566 miles), flying from Monfalcone to Massawa, Eritrea, in 26 hours 35 minutes. It lost the record to a French aircraft shortly afterwards, but recaptured it in July 1935 with a 4957km (3080-mile) flight from the same point of departure to Berbera in Somaliland. The Z.501 was of wooden construction, with fabric-covered wings and tail.

Crew: 5
Powerplant: one 671kW (900hp) Isotta-Fraschini XI R2C 15-cylinder radial engine
Performance: max speed 275km/h (171mph); range 2400km (1491 miles); service ceiling 7000m (22,965ft)
Dimensions: wingspan 22.50m (73ft 9in); length 14.30m (46ft 11in); height 4.40m (14ft 6in)
Weight: 7050kg (15,542lb) loaded
Armament: three 7.7mm (0.303in) machine guns; external bomb load of 640kg (1411lb)

CANT Z.506B

ITALY: 1937

Crew: 5
Powerplant: three 556kW (750hp) Alfa Romeo 126 RC.34 nine-cylinder radial engines
Performance: max speed 350km/h (217mph); range 2745km (1705 miles); service ceiling 8000m (26,245ft)
Dimensions: wingspan 26.50m (86ft 11in); length 19.24m (63ft 1in); height 7.45m (24ft 5in)
Weight: 12,705kg (28,008lb) loaded
Armament: one 12.7mm (0.50in) and three 7.7mm machine guns; internal bomb load of 1200kg (2646lb)

The Z.506B was widely used in the Mediterranean theatre during World War II, mainly as a maritime reconnaissance and anti-submarine aircraft.

THE CANT Z.506B Airone (Heron) was derived from the civilian Z.506A, which was responsible for establishing a number of international seaplane records in the 1930s. The military Z.506B entered production as a reconnaissance bomber for the Regia Aeronautica in 1938, and differed mainly from the civil version in having a long ventral gondola and a dorsal gun turret.

Production of the Z.506 totalled 324 aircraft, 94 being operational at the time of Italy's entry into World War II. The production total included 30 examples ordered by Poland, but only one of these had been delivered before the German invasion, and the remainder were requisitioned by the Italian Navy.

The type was initially used in the bomber role, but was later fitted with heavier defensive armament and operated as a maritime reconnaissance, convoy escort and anti-submarine aircraft. Some aircraft were converted to the air–sea rescue role as the Z.506S, remaining in service until 1959.

CALDERARA SEAPLANE
Following on from powered flight experiments resulting from collaboration with the Wright brothers, Italian Mario Calderara designed and flew a seaplane – the largest aircraft of its day – that carried three passengers in 1912.

CAMPBELL CRICKET
A British single-seat light autogyro from Campbell Aircraft Ltd, which previously manufactured Bensen Gyro-Gliders and Gyro-Copters under licence, the Cricket flew in July 1969. Its maximum speed was 129km/h (80mph). The Campbell Curlew is a two-seat light autogyro.

CAMS 33
The CAMS 33 was a twin-engined biplane maritime reconnaissance flying boat, first flown in 1923. The French Navy operated 12, and some were sold to Yugoslavia.

CAMS 37
A biplane flying boat, the CAMS 37 was powered by a 336kW (450hp) Lorraine pusher engine. Carrying a three-man crew, it was used for coastal patrol by the French Navy in the late 1920s.

CAMS 55
Four prototype CAMS 55 twin-engined flying boats were built in 1928. Over 60 CAM 55s were then built for use by the French Navy.

CAMS 53/1
A French flying-boat design first flown in 1929, the CAMS 53/1 had two engines and good range and payload characteristics. It was built in a number of marques.

CANADAIR C-4 ARGONAUT
The C-4 Argonaut was a licence-built version of the Douglas DC-4 powered by Rolls Royce Merlin engines. Seventy-one examples were produced between 1946 and 1950, notably for TCA and BOAC.

CANADAIR CL-41
First flown in January 1960, the Canadair CL-41 was produced both as a basic jet trainer and a counter-insurgency trainer, the latter version being used by the Royal Malaysian Air Force.

CANADAIR CL-84
A twin propeller turbine research convertiplane, the CL-84's wing and powerplants could be tilted hydraulically through 100 degrees to the vertical from a normal flight angle to those for STOL and VTOL characteristics. The first flights in hover and conventional modes took place in 1965.

CANT Z.1007

The CANT Z.1007 played a prominent part in the Italian air attacks on Malta, which began as soon as Italy entered the war in June 1940. Seen here is a Z.1007bis, one of the main production versions.

THE CANT Z.1007 ALCIONE (Kingfisher) first flew in 1937 and entered service with the Regia Aeronautica late in 1938. The type was produced in three versions: the Z.1007 (35 built), the Z.1007bis and the Z.1007ter (526 built). The last sub-variant featured a larger airframe, better defensive armament and uprated engines. Widely used by the Italians throughout the Balkans and the Mediterranean, it featured prominently in the Axis bombing campaign against Malta.

Crew: 5
Powerplant: three 746kW (1000hp) Piaggio P.XI R2C.40 14-cylinder radial engines
Performance: max speed 466km/h (290mph); range 1750km (1087 miles); service ceiling 8200m (26,900ft)

Dimensions: wingspan 24.80m (81ft 4in); length 18.35m (60ft 2in); height 5.22m (17ft 5in)
Weight: 13,621kg (30,029lb) loaded
Armament: two 12.7mm (0.50in) and two 7.7mm (0.303in) machine guns; internal bomb load of 1200kg (2646lb)

CAPRONI CA.1

The Caproni Ca.1 was one of the world's first heavy bombers. This is a Ca.1 of France's Aéronautique Militaire, based on the Plateau de Malzéville in 1916.

Crew: 4
Powerplant: three 75kW (100hp) Fiat A.10 6-cylinder engines
Performance: max speed 116km/h (72mph); range 550km (340 miles); service ceiling not known;
Dimensions: wingspan 22.20m (72ft 10in); length 10.90m (35ft 9in); height 3.70m (12ft 2in)
Weight: 3302kg (7280lb) loaded
Armament: one or two 7.7mm (0.303in) machine guns; up to 850kg (1874lb) of bombs

ALTHOUGH THERE IS STILL a widespread belief that Britain and Germany were the first nations to produce heavy bombers – Handley Pages on the one hand and Gothas on the other – both Italy and Russia had developed aircraft suitable for long-range bombing operations by the outbreak of World War I. In Italy, the pioneering constructor in this field was the Societa de Aviazione Ing Caproni, which designed and flew its first heavy bomber type in 1913. A derivative, the Ca.31, flew late in 1914, two of its three Fiat engines mounted on the front of the tail booms and the third at the rear of the crew nacelle. This heavy bomber biplane design went into production as the Ca.1, 162 aircraft being produced.

CAPRONI CA.101

Crew: 3
Powerplant: three 179kW (240hp) Alfa Romeo D.2 9-cylinder radial engines
Performance: max speed 165km/h (103mph); range 2000km (1243 miles); service ceiling 6100m (20,015ft)

Dimensions: wingspan 19.68m (64ft 6.75in); length 14.37m (47ft 1.75in); height 3.89m (12ft 9.25in)
Weight: 4975kg (10,968lb) loaded
Armament: up to five 7.7mm (0.303in) machine guns; bomb load of 500kg (1102lb)

THE CAPRONI CA.101 high-wing medium bomber monoplane entered service with the Regia Aeronautica in the mid-1930s, and was used mainly in Italy's African colonies. The Ca.101 was to see widespread use during the Italian invasion of Abyssinia (Ethiopia) in 1935, when it was used as a troop transport and air ambulance, as well as in the roles of bombing and reconnaissance.

CAPRONI CA.133 | ITALY: 1934

AN IMPROVED VERSION OF the Ca.101, the Ca.133 introduced a number of drag-reducing features, including long-chord engine cowlings, faired undercarriage legs and spatted wheels. The design of the tail unit was also improved. On 6 March 1936, a Ca.133 made the first photo-reconnaissance sortie over the Ethiopian capital, Addis Ababa, in support of Italian operations. Out of 419 Ca.133s produced for the Regia Aeronautica,

One of the most widely used Italian aircraft of World War II, the Caproni Ca.133 was used in a great many roles, including reconnaissance, transport and casualty evacuation.

329 were Ca.133T transports and 21 Ca.133S ambulance aircraft. During World War II, Ca.133s operated in all theatres of war where Italian forces were engaged, including the USSR.

Crew: 3
Powerplant: three 343kW (460hp) Piaggio Stella P.VII C.16 7-cylinder radial engines
Performance: max speed 265km/h (165mph); range 1350km (838 miles); service ceiling 5500m (18,045ft)
Dimensions: wingspan 21.24m (69ft 8in); length 15.36m (50ft 4.75in); height 4.00m (13ft 1in)
Weight: 6700kg (14,771lb) loaded
Armament: four 7.7mm (0.303in) machine guns; external bomb load of 1200kg (2646lb)

CAPRONI CA.309–310 | ITALY: 1936

This Caproni Ca.310 is pictured in the markings of the Royal Norwegian Air Force. The light general-purpose aircraft was immensely popular with its crews.

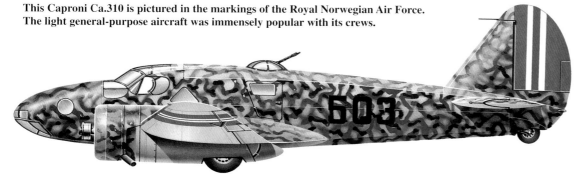

THE MOST PROLIFIC general-purpose light twin-engined aircraft family ever produced by the Italian aircraft industry was the Caproni Ca.309–314 family. The two principal versions of the type were the Ca.309 Ghibli (Desert Wind) and the Ca.310 Libeccio (South-West Wind). The Ca.310, which appeared in 1937, was a refined version of the Ca.309, with a

retractable undercarriage and modernized airframe.
    The Ca.310 was widely used by reconnaissance units of Italy's Regia Aeronautica, despite the aircraft's somewhat disappointing performance. The Ca.310 was also to see service in Hungary, Norway, Peru and Yugoslavia.
    Specifications apply to the Caproni Ca.310.

Crew: 3
Powerplant: two 351kW (470hp) Piaggio P.VII C.35 7-cylinder radial engines
Performance: max speed 365km/h (227mph); range 1200km (746 miles); service ceiling 7000m (22,965ft)
Dimensions: wingspan 16.20m (53ft 1in); length 12.20m (40ft); height 3.52m (11ft 6in)
Weight: 4650kg (10,251lb)
Armament: three 7.7mm (0.303in) machine guns; internal bomb load of 400kg (882lb)

CANADIAN CAR AND FOUNDRY COMPANY/ CANCARGO CBY-3 LOADMASTER
A 'lifting body' design, the CBY-3 Loadmaster was a Burnelli design with twin engines, capable of carrying 22 passengers or 19.82m³ (700cu ft) of freight. Only one example was built, in 1945.

CANT Z.511
First flown in 1940, the CANT Z.511 was a large, long-range four-engined seaplane intended for commerical operations to South America. Only one was built.

CAO 200
First flown early in 1940, the French CAO 200 fighter was a development of the experimental Loire-Nieuport LN.161. About 40 had been built at the time of France's collapse in June 1940.

CAO 700
The CAO 700 was a French four-engined heavy bomber prototype, completed in 1940 and based on the LN-10 twin-engined floatplane.

CAPELIS XC-12
The single XC-12 example was created as a promotional aeroplane in California, dating from 1933. This twin-engined, low-wing transport aircraft had a biplane tail arrangement.

CAPRONI CA.30
The Ca.30, which flew in 1913, was Caproni's first heavy bomber design, featuring a central crew nacelle and two slender booms supporting the tail unit.

CAPRONI CA.2
The Caproni Ca.2 (Ca.32) carried out the first Italian bombing raids of World War I against Austria-Hungary on 25 August 1915 and was also the first major production version, with 164 being built.

CAPRONI CA.3
The Caproni Ca.3 (Ca.33), which entered service with the Italian Air Corps in 1917, was the most successful Allied bomber of World War I. More than 80 were licence-built in France.

CAPRONI CA.42
The Ca.42 was Caproni's last production triplane bomber; 23 were built, six being supplied to the Royal Naval Air Service.

CAPRONI CA.311–314

APPEARING IN 1939, the Caproni Ca.311 featured a modified and glazed forward fuselage designed to provide maximum visibility for the observer. It was followed by the Ca.313 of 1940, which was fitted

with two Isotta-Fraschini Delta in-line engines instead of the Ca.311's Piaggio radials. Next came the Ca.314, which was further refined and provided with increased power. Specifications apply to the Ca.311.

Crew: 3
Powerplant: two Piaggio P.VII RC.35 7-cylinder radial engines
Performance: max speed 365km/h (226mph); range 1600km (990 miles); service ceiling 7400m (24,280ft)

Dimensions: wingspan 16.20m (53ft 1in); length 11.74m (38ft 6in); height 3.69m (12ft 1in)
Weight: 4822kg (10,645lb) loaded
Armament: three 7.7mm (0.303in) machine guns; 400kg (880lb) of bombs

CAPRONI-CAMPINI N.1

Crew: 2
Powerplant: one 750kg (1654lb) thrust Campini ducted fan, driven by a 671kW (900hp) V-12 Isotta-Fraschini L.121 MC40 Asso piston engine
Performance: max speed 360km/h (223mph); range not established; service ceiling 4000m (13,123ft)
Dimensions: wingspan 14.63m (48ft); length 12.10m (39ft 8in); height 4.70m (15ft 5in)
Weight: 4217kg (9300lb) loaded
Armament: none

ALTHOUGH IT COULD NEVER BE described as successful, the Caproni-Campini N.1 (often erroneously referred to as the CC.2) deserves its place in history as the first Italian aircraft powered by a form of jet engine. Designed by Secondo Campini as a two-seat all-metal research aircraft with a low-mounted elliptical wing, it was flown for the first time on 28 August 1940 at Taliedo airfield near Milan, with test pilot Mario De Bernardi at the controls. Its power unit was a 671kW (900hp) Isotta-Fraschini piston engine mounted in the main fuselage section and driving a variable-pitch, three-stage ducted fan compressor. A ring of fuel injectors (a primitive form of after-burner) heated the compressed air, developing a thrust of 750kg

The Caproni-Campini N.1 pictured at Taliedo airfield near Milan after its first test flight in August 1940, together with a group of Regia Aeronautica officers. Flight trials were not satisfactory.

(1654lb). The jet flow through the exhaust orifice could be varied by an adjustable 'bullet'.

This system of jet propulsion was only partially successful, but

The N.1's powerplant was a ducted fan, driven by a piston engine mounted in the main fuselage section.

a number of test flights were completed. On 30 November 1941, De Bernardi flew the N.1 from Milan to Rome carrying a consignment of mailbags; the aircraft landed at Pisa to refuel and finished the 270km (168-mile) flight at an average speed of 209km/h (130mph). It was then handed over to the Regia Aeronautica at the

Guidonia Research Establishment; however, the unsatisfactory results of further flight trials led to the programme being abandoned in September 1942.

CASA C-101 AVIOJET

THE C-101 ADVANCED FLYING and weapons trainer was developed by the Spanish CASA company as a replacement for the Hispano

HA.200 jet trainer. The type made its first flight in June 1977, and deliveries of the 92 production aircraft on order for the Spanish

Air Force began in 1980. The CASA C-101's weapons system was upgraded in the 1990s, and the improved aircraft was the subject

of limited export orders to Chile (where the type was assembled under licence by ENAER and known as the A/T-36 Halcon),

The CASA C-101 Aviojet was developed as a replacement for the HA.200 jet trainer. Its weapons system was upgraded in the 1990s, leading to a limited number of export orders.

Halcon), Honduras and Jordan. The C-101 Aviojet is very similar to the Argentine IA-63 Pampa – the main visual cue to discerning the difference between the two is by the Aviojet's low-mounted wing.

Crew: 2
Powerplant: one 1588kg (3500lb) thrust Garrett AiResearch TFE731 turbofan engine
Performance: max speed 806km/h (501mph); endurance 7 hrs; service ceiling 12,800m (42,000ft)

Dimensions: wingspan 10.60m (34ft 9in); length 12.50m (41ft); height 4.25m (13ft 11in)
Weight: 4850kg (10,692lb) loaded
Armament: one 30mm (1.18in) DEFA cannon; up to 2000kg (4410lb) of external stores on six hardpoints

CAUDRON G.4

FRANCE: 1915

Crew: 2
Powerplant: two Le Rhone 9C rotary engines each rated at 60kW (80hp)
Performance: max speed 132km/h (82mph); endurance 3 hrs 30 mins; service ceiling 4300m (14,110ft)
Dimensions: wingspan 16.89m (55ft 4.75in); length 7.19m (23ft 7in); height 2.55m (8ft 4.5in)
Weight: 1232kg (2716lb) maximum take-off weight
Armament: one or two 0.303in (7.7mm) trainable machine guns plus, in the G.4B.2 model, up to 100kg (220lb) of bombs carried externally

The G.4 had a forward cockpit for a gunner or observer, although the field of view was limited by the engines.

DESPITE BEING STRUCTURALLY SIMILAR to the earlier G.3, the G.4 biplane was specifically developed to lift an effective bomb load while being able to defend itself. The Caudron G.4 was the first Allied bomber to become available in large squadron formation.

There were two versions of the G.4, the first being the Cau 4B.2

day bomber, which had a relatively short front-line service career – due to its high loss rate it was withdrawn during 1916. The second version was the Cau 4A.2, which was used for artillery observation and reconnaissance duties from November 1915.

Production of both types totalled 1358. A small number were licence-built in Britain, and the type served with French, British, Italian and Russian forces. Post-World War I, the G.4 made some pioneering flights and found favour with flying clubs.

CAUDRON C.440 GOELAND SERIES

Crew: 2
Powerplant: two 164kW (220hp) Renault 6Q-00/01 or 6Q-08/09 Bengali 6 inverted in-line engines.
Performance: max speed 300km/h (186mph); range 1000km (621 miles); service ceiling 7000m (22,965ft)
Dimensions: wingspan 17.59m (57ft 8.5in); length 13.68m (44ft 10.5in); height 3.40m (11ft 1.75in)
Weight: 3500kg (7716lb) maximum take-off weight
Payload: up to six passengers

DEVELOPED IN THE EARLY 1930s as a fast, economical small transport, this low, wooden-wing design was operated by (among others) Air France and Yugoslavia's Aeroput, most often as the C.445 version, as well as serving with the French Armée de l'Air as the

C.445M. Following the World War II German occupation of France, a number of Goelands were put into service with Lufthansa, some being rebuilt to German military requirements as the C.449 for utility purposes – training, ambulance or communications.

This Goeland was pressed into service with the Free French forces after the Battle of France in 1940.

Postwar commercial production continued as the AA.1, and a total of 1702 were built.
   Specifications apply to the C.445M Goeland.

CAUDRON C.714 CYCLONE

Crew: 1
Powerplant: one 373kW (500hp) Renault 12R-03 12-cylinder inverted-V engine
Performance: max speed 460km/h (286mph); range 900km (559 miles); service ceiling 9100m (29,855ft)
Dimensions: wingspan 8.97m (29ft 5.13in); length 8.63m (28ft 3.88in); height 2.87m (9ft 5in)
Armament: three 7.5mm (0.29in) machine guns

A Caudron C.714 Cyclone in the markings of Groupe de Chasse GC I/145, which was manned by Polish pilots during the Battle of France.

THE CAUDRON C.714 WAS developed from the C.710 light-weight fighter, which first flew in July 1936. The type was in direct competition with the Morane 406,

which was selected for major production, but smaller orders were placed for the Caudron fighter. On 10 May 1940 the Armée de l'Air had 46 C.714s on

charge, most serving with GC I/145, manned by Polish pilots. The Caudron C.714's operational career was brief, lasting only from 2–13 June 1940. During this time

GC I/145's pilots destroyed 12 enemy aircraft for the loss of 13 Caudrons. Six were also supplied to Finland during the 'Winter War' of 1939–40.

CAYLEY AERONAUTICAL DESIGNS

'ABOUT 100 YEARS AGO AN Englishman, Sir George Cayley, carried the science of flying to a point which it had never reached before and which it scarcely reached again during the last century.' That tribute was paid in 1909 by no less a person than Wilbur Wright, to the work of an English baronet, Sir George Cayley, who was one of the most talented and versatile pioneers in the history of aviation. Cayley, who lived at Brompton Hall near Scarborough, Yorkshire, was the first to define the

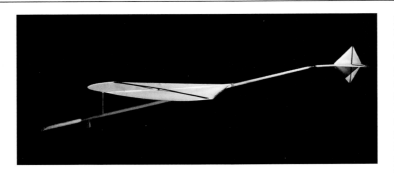

Sir George Cayley's model glider of 1804 is considered to be the first rigid aircraft design in history, featuring a fixed wing set and a cruciform tail.

principles of mechanical flight, the relationship between weight, lift, drag and thrust. In 1804, after experimenting with various model glider designs, he built what is considered to be the first rigid aircraft in history, a glider about 1.5m (5ft) long, with a fixed wing set at an angle of six degrees and a cruciform tailplane attached to the fuselage by universal joints. Five years later he built a larger glider flown successfully with ballast, and sometimes for a few yards with a man or boy clinging to it.

After building several more models, and producing an ingenious design for a convertiplane (a helicopter-cum-aircraft) in 1843, Cayley built a triplane glider in 1849, first of all carrying out trials with ballast, then with the 10-year-old son of one of his servants. The manned flights of the so-called 'Boy Carrier' are likely to have been hops of only a few yards.

In 1853 Cayley completed his Glider No 3, which was almost certainly a triplane similar to the previous one, and some time after June of that year this aircraft made a famous brief flight with Cayley's coachman on board. Despite the fact that the coachman has been referred to by the name of John Appleby, the truth is that his actual identity remains a mystery to this day. The glider, complete with its terrified occupant, is said to have flown a distance of about 457m (1500ft) across a small valley behind Brompton Hall before crashing to the ground. There is no doubt that this flight took place. It may fairly be described as the first manned (but not piloted) glider flight in history. The coachman, incidentally (or, according to one account, the butler), is said to have suffered a broken leg in the crash and resigned on the spot.

Apart from practical experiments such as these, Cayley's scientific papers were to have a profound influence on the expanding world of aeronautics. Perhaps his most important work, entitled 'On Aerial Navigation', discussed the principles of aerodynamics and their practical application, and appeared in 1909–10 in a scientific publication called *Nicholson's Journal of Natural Philosophy, Chemistry and the Arts*. It was a long time, however – some 20 years after his death – before Cayley's writings reached a wider audience, his papers being published in England in 1876 and in France in 1877.

In one passage, Cayley stated

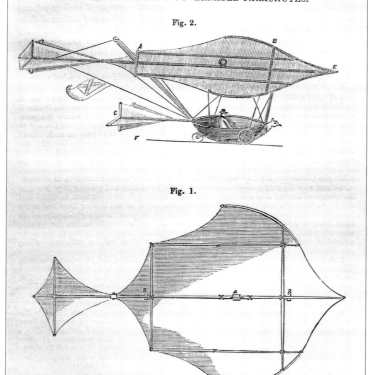

Mechanics' Magazine,

MUSEUM, REGISTER, JOURNAL, AND GAZETTE.

No. 1520.] SATURDAY, SEPTEMBER 25, 1852. [Price 3*d.*, Stamped 4*d.*

Edited by J. C. Robertson, 166, Fleet-street.

SIR GEORGE CAYLEY'S GOVERNABLE PARACHUTES.

Fig. 2.

Fig. 1.

One of Cayley's glider designs of the mid-19th century, described as a 'Governable [i.e. steerable] Parachute'.

that he was 'totally convinced that this noble art will soon be within man's competence and that we will eventually be able to travel with our families and baggage more safely than by sea … All that is needed is an engine which can produce more power per minute than can the human muscle system.'

That, in essence, is the tragedy of Sir George Cayley: his designs were adequate enough to become airborne, but lacked the power to sustain them in the air. Had a suitable power source – such as the internal combustion engine – been available, it is virtually certain that powered flight would have been achieved in the Yorkshire dales a good half-century before the Wright Brothers launched into the pages of history at Kitty Hawk.

CEA (JODEL) DR.100–DR.1051 FRANCE: 1965

Crew: 1
Powerplant: one 80kW (100hp) Continental O-200-A engine
Performance: max speed 193km/h (120mph); range 1046km (650 miles)
Dimensions: wingspan 8.71m (28ft 7.5in); length 6.50m (21ft 4in)
Payload: three seats

THIS SERIES HAS ITS ORIGINS in the DR.100 series of light aircraft which were designed by Jean Delemontez of Jodel, who was later to combine with Pierre Robin at CEA. The DR.100 is a three-seat development of the Jodel D.11 series, and the type was widely licence-built in France. The CEA (Jodel) DR.100–1050 series marks the period of transition from the single-engined, low-wing touring monoplanes of Jodel to the designs of Robin.

Specifications apply to the DR.1050-M Ambassadeur.

CASA 201 ALCOTAN
CASA's first transport aircraft, the 201 Alcotan, first flew in 1949. It was a twin-engined design with a low wing and tail wheel, carrying 10 passengers. More than 100 examples saw service with the Spanish Air Force.

CASA 202 HALCON
Designed as an enlarged tricycle undercarriage version of the 201, but for commercial use, the 20 CASA 202 examples produced found service only in the Spanish Air Force.

CASA 207 AZOR
The CASA 207 of 1955 is another enlarged tricycle undercarriage derivative from the original 201, capable of carrying 37 passengers. All deliveries went to the Spanish Air Force, which operated the type until the early 1980s.

CASA C.212 AVIOCAR
First flown on 26 March 1971, the C-212 transport was intended to replace the Junkers Ju 52 in Spanish Air Force service. The type has had huge export success.

CASA/IPTN CN.235
Jointly developed by CASA and Indonesia's IPTN, the CN.235 first flew in 1983. This twin turboprop airliner can carry 45 passengers. Military sales account for all but 30 of the 230 built.

CAUDRON R.11
A French twin-engined biplane escort fighter operational in small but increasing numbers during the last year of the Great War. A total of 370 were built.

CAUDRON C.60
Designed as an intermediate trainer, the C.60 was similar to the C.59, but with a lower-powered engine. It was not favoured for French military use, but found work at civilian flying schools and for export.

CAUDRON C.460
A single-engined retractable undercarriage racing design dating from 1932, four of this type with differing powerplants were built, including one which was the winner of the 1934 Greve Trophy.

CAUDRON C.635 SIMOUN
This aircraft was a development of the C.630 Simoun fitted with a more powerful Renault engine, 46 C.635s were manufactured, and a number of C.630s were converted to C.635 standard.

CESSNA L-19 BIRD DOG

USA: 1950

The Cessna L-19 Bird Dog was one of the most widely used observation and liaison aircraft of the post-World War II years.

THE CESSNA L-19 OBSERVATION and liaison aircraft, developed from the commercial Cessna 170, was one of the USAF's most widely used light aircraft. The initial production aircraft, the L-19A, was mass-produced to the extent of 2500 aircraft ordered by October 1954. Those built under the earlier contracts saw extensive service in the Korean War. During the conflict, L-19s were to play a prominent part as observation aircraft. Up to the beginning of 1951 they often penetrated several miles into enemy territory in search of worthwhile targets for UN artillery and fighter-bombers, but as enemy ground fire intensified they were forced to restrict their operations to areas in the immediate vicinity of the front line. For direct communication with ground forces, the L-19 was equipped with an SCR-300 'walkie-talkie' type infantry radio. One L-19 was also used in Korea by No 1913 Light Liaison Flight RAF, whose pilots pronounced the American aircraft to be superior to the Auster AOP.6 observation aircraft which formed its primary equipment. The TL-19D, ordered in 1956, was a trainer (310 built), while the last version was the L-19E of 1957 (376 built).

Specifications apply to L-19A.

Crew: 2
Powerplant: one 159kW (213hp) Continental C-470 4-cylinder horizontally opposed air-cooled engine
Performance: max speed 243km/h (151mph); range 850km (530 miles); service ceiling 5640m (18,500ft)
Dimensions: wingspan 10.97m (36ft); length 7.85m (25ft 9in); height 2.21m (7ft 3in)
Weight: 1088kg (2400lb)
Armament: none

CESSNA MODEL 310 AND U-3

USA: 1953

Crew: 1/2
Powerplant: two Continental IO-520-MB flat-six piston engines each rated at 213kW (285hp)
Performance: max speed 383km/h (238mph); range 2840km (1765 miles); service ceiling 6020m (19,750ft)
Dimensions: wingspan 11.25m (31ft 11.5in); length 9.74m (36ft 11.5in); height 3.25m (10ft 8in)
Weight: 2495kg (5500lb) maximum take-off weight
Payload: five/six people

THE MODEL 310 WAS Cessna's first twin-engined design. Aimed at the executive market's lower end, it differed from contemporary Cessna designs in having a low wing and a tricycle undercarriage. The Model 310 was notable for its wingtip fuel tanks and application

of military derived engines. Sales were initially slow, but the qualities of this design overcame initial conservatism and over 5400 were sold to domestic and export markets, including the U-3 military communications and light freight derivative and the derivative Model 320 Skynight. Specifications apply to Cessna Model 310R.

Although the Cessna Model 310 sold widely around the world, operational examples are not common today. The wingtip fuel tanks remain distinctive.

CESSNA T-37 AND A-37 DRAGONFLY

USA: 1954

Crew: 1
Powerplant: two 1293kg (2850lb) General Electric J85-GE-17A turbojet engines
Performance: max speed 816km/h (507mph); range 740km (460 miles) with 1860kg (4100lb) load; service ceiling 12,730m (41,765ft)
Dimensions: wingspan 10.93m (35ft 10in); length 8.62m (28ft 3in); height 2.70m (8ft 10in)
Weight: 6350kg (14,000lb)
Armament: one 7.62mm (0.30in) GAU-2 Minigun six-barrel machine gun; eight underwing hardpoints for 2268kg (5000lb) of stores

THE CESSNA A-37B light attack aircraft was developed from the T-37, the USAF's first purpose-built jet trainer, which appeared in 1954. The war in Vietnam produced a requirement for attack aircraft, and 39 T-37s were converted as A-37As in 1966, being fitted with eight underwing hardpoints, wingtip fuel tanks and more powerful engines. The A-37B version had a reinforced structure, increased fuel capacity and provision for in-flight refuelling.

The Cessna T-37 Dragonfly was the USAF's first purpose-built jet trainer, and was later adapted to the light attack role as the A-37A. The A-37B was an upgraded version.

CESSNA MODEL 172 AND T-41

USA: 1955

Crew: 1/2
Powerplant: one 108kW (145hp) Continental O-300-C flat-six engine
Performance: max speed 224km/h (139mph); range 1030km (640 miles); service ceiling 3995m (13,100ft)
Dimensions: wingspan 10.86m (35ft 7.5in); length 8.20m (26ft 11in); height 2.68m (8ft 9in)
Weight: 1043kg (2300lb) maximum take-off weight
Payload: four people

THE MODEL 172 WAS a tricycle undercarriage equipped successor to the earlier Model 170 touring light aircraft, and it was built in a number of successive marques that included improvements to cabin and performance. The total number of model 172s built over 30 years amounts to an astonishing 40,000.

These numbers include the T-41, which itself was built in several different versions for domestic and export consumption as a military trainer. Specifications apply to the Cessna Model T-41A.

The hugely popular Cessna Model 172 was also licence-built in France by Reims Aviation as the Reims Rocket (designated FR172E), an example of which is shown here.

CESSNA MODEL 150 AND 152

USA: 1957

Crew: 1/2
Powerplant: one Lycoming O-235-L2C flat-four engine rated at 82kW (110hp)
Performance: max speed 204km/h (127mph); range 1278km (794 miles); service ceiling 4480m (14,700ft)

Dimensions: wingspan 9.97m (32ft 8.5in); length 7.34m (24ft 1in); height 2.59m (8ft 6in)
Weight: 757kg (1670lb) maximum take-off weight
Payload: two people

LIGHT UTILITY MODELS FOR touring, sporting or training, both the Cessna Model 150 and Model 152 became the two-seat light aeroplanes of their day. In its initial form, the 150 immediately differed

---

CAUDRON C.690
A single-seat trainer for fighter pilots first flown in 1936, the C.690 was ordered by the French Air Force as the unarmed C.690M.

CAUDRON C.670 TYPHON
Developed from the twin-engined C.640 mailplane design, the Caudron C.670 was produced in 1937 only in prototype form, for a high-speed bombing role.

CESSNA AT-17
Based on the prewar T-50 commercial cabin monoplane, the AT-17 twin-engined trainer entered service in 1942, 450 being built.

CESSNA MODEL 120 AND 140
These two-seat, single-engined, high-wing, tail-wheel light aircraft designs date from 1945. The Model 140 was effectively a deluxe version of the 120, and 7604 examples of both were produced until 1950.

CESSNA 170
A single-engined, high-wing, tail-wheel light aircraft seating four persons dating from 1947.

CESSNA 195
Very similar to the Cessna 190, the 195 had a more powerful radial engine. This high-wing early post-World War II design light aircraft was produced in high numbers, totalling 860 in all.

CESSNA 180/185 SKYWAGON
Derived from the earlier Model 170, this six-seat, single-engined light aircraft was produced and used in great variety for civil and military purposes and had a strengthened airframe. More than 10,000 were made.

CESSNA 320 SKYKNIGHT
The Model 320 is a larger variant of the Cessna 310 series, featuring six seats and one more window.

CESSNA CH-1
Cessna Helicopter Division was formed on 1 March 1952. The CH-1 two-seat light helicopter first flew in July 1954 powered by a 194kW (260hp) Continental FSO-470 engine giving a maximum speed of 196km/h (122mph) at sea level. No orders were forthcoming.

CESSNA 175 SKYLARK
A derivative of the Cessna 172. Changes included an uprated engine and redesigned cowlings. More than 2000 Skylarks have been manufactured.

Cessna 150s have also seen service with armed forces in training/communications roles – this one served with Ecuador's Air Arm.

from its predecessors in having a tricycle undercarriage and only a single bracing strut on each side of the high wing. While early marques, including the Model 150E, retained an unswept tail fin, thereafter (and more familiarly) the fin was swept.

Successive versions of the Model 150 were developed right up to the Model 150M, which was discontinued in favour of the Model 152 in late 1977, when more than 21,000 of all marques had been built, including the A150 aerobatic version. The Cessna 152 was essentially a 150M with a new more powerful engine, and was available in dual control and aerobatic options. More than 7500 examples were produced until discontinued in the mid-1980s.

Specifications apply to Cessna Model 152.

CESSNA MODEL 336 SKYMASTER AND MODEL 337 SUPER SKYMASTER
USA: 1961

THE SKYMASTER WAS A RADICAL departure from previous Cessna light aircraft designs. While the six-seat cabin had a familial resemblance to single-engine Cessnas, the Skymaster had a second pusher engine fitted at the cabin's rear, with a twin-boom tail arrangement. The principal advantage of this was the easy maintenance of trim in the event of single-engined operation. The initial Model 336 sold modestly at 195 examples, but the improved Model 337, which had retractable landing gear and later a pressurized cabin, sold nearly 2800 models. Specifications apply to the Model 337 Super Skymaster.

Cessna 337s served with the US military in observation and forward air control roles (as well as others) in the Vietnam War.

Crew: 1/2
Powerplant: two 157kW (210hp) Continental IO-360-GB flat-six piston engines
Performance: max speed 336km/h (206mph); range 2288km (1422 miles); service ceiling 5485m (18,000ft)
Dimensions: wingspan 11.63m (38ft 2in); length 9.07m (29ft 9in); height 2.79m (9ft 2in)
Weight: 2100kg (4630lb) maximum take-off weight
Payload: six people

CESSNA MODEL 421 GOLDEN EAGLE
USA: 1965

DEVELOPMENT OF THE twin-engined Model 421 was aimed at the small business/executive market. The Model 421B became production standard, and two derivatives were pursued, the Golden Eagle and the Executive Commuter version, which had quick passenger/freight changeover and up to 10 seats. The Model 421C superseded the 421B in 1976, replacing the 421B's wing-tip fuel tanks with internal wing tanks, plus greater power and capacity.

The Cessna 421 was one of several Cessna designs aimed at the air taxi/executive market following the success of the Model 310.

Over 2000 Model 421s were built until production ceased in the mid-1980s. Specifications apply to Model 421C Golden Eagle.

Crew: 1/2
Powerplant: two 280kW (375hp) Continental GTSIO-520-N flat-six piston engines
Performance: max speed 478km/h (297mph); range 2752km (1710 miles); service ceiling 9205m (30,200ft)
Dimensions: wingspan 12.53m (41ft 1.5in); length 11.09m (36ft 4in); height 3.49m (11ft 5in)
Weight: 3379kg (7450lb) maximum take-off weight
Payload: seven people

CESSNA CITATION SERIES

USA: 1969

Crew: 1/2
Powerplant: two 13.55kN (3045lb st) Pratt & Whitney Canada JT15D-5D turbofan engines
Performance: max cruising speed 796km/h (495mph) at 10,670m (35,000ft); range 3630km (2255 miles); certificated ceiling 13,715m (45,000ft)
Dimensions: wingspan 15.91m (52ft 2.5in); length 14.90m (48ft 10.75in); height 3.49m (11ft 5in)
Weight: 7393kg (16,300lb) maximum take-off weight
Payload: up to eight passengers

CESSNA'S FIRST FORAY INTO the business jet market took into account the need for quietness and economy that turbofan engines offered. Nevertheless, the Citations bear visual resemblance to their predecessors, and the unswept wings are also characteristic. Nearly 700 examples of the Model 501 have been delivered to civil and military customers. The slightly larger Model 550 series dates from 1977 and nearly 900 have been produced (including the T-47A for the USN). The later 560 series dates from 1987. Larger again, it incorporates an EFIS cockpit with extra range and performance. Sales number more than 550, including a number of specific military variants.

Specifications apply to the Model 560 Citation V.

The Cessna 560 or Citation V was the last of Cessna's straight-winged designs. It differs from earlier models in having a stretched cabin.

CHANCE VOUGHT F6U PIRATE

USA: 1946

ONE OF THE EARLIEST American shipboard jet fighters, the first of three prototype XF6U-1 Pirates flew on 2 October 1946. A production batch of 30 aircraft was ordered under the designation F6U-1, the first of these flying in July 1949. The F6U-1 differed from the XF6U-1 in several respects: small auxiliary fins were mounted near the tailplane tips and a large dorsal fillet was fitted, large fillets were attached to the wing trailing edges at approximately quarter-span, and an armament of four 20mm (0.79in) cannon was installed in the fuselage. The F6U-1 made considerable use of Metalite skinning in its structure. After evaluation, the Pirate was withdrawn from service.

The Chance Vought F6U Pirate was one of the US Navy's first carrier-based jet fighters, flying for the first time in 1946.

Crew: 1
Powerplant: one 1902kg (4200lb) thrust Westinghouse WE-30A turbojet engine
Performance: max speed 894km/h (555mph); range 1206km (750 miles); service ceiling 12,505m (41,000ft)
Dimensions: wingspan 9.98m (32ft 10in); length 11.43m (37ft 7in); height 3.90m (12ft 11in)
Weight: 5119kg (11,300lb) loaded
Armament: four 20mm (0.79in) cannon

CESSNA 182 SKYLANE
A development of the Model 180, principally different in having a tricycle undercarriage, and later a retractable landing gear. Over 21,000 have been delivered.

CESSNA 210 CENTURION
Another single-piston engined design, the Model 210 Centurion is notable for being the first of the series to feature a retractable tricycle undercarriage. Produced from 1959, more than 9000 have been delivered.

CESSNA 205 SKYWAGON AND 206 SUPER SKYWAGON/ STATIONAIR
Essentially the 205/206 is a fixed undercarriage version of the Model 210. The Model 206 differs from the 205 in having an uprated engine and a double cargo door.

CESSNA 335/340
Dating from 1969 this six position, twin engined, light aircraft was sold in two versions: the low-cost 335 and the pressurised 340, which has sold more than 1200 examples.

CESSNA 401/402
Designed as a lower cost version of the Cessna 411 twin-engined business transport, the Cessna 401/402 first flew in 1965. The 402 variant was the predominant of the two very similar designs and production continued into the 1980s.

CESSNA M-DEL 188 AGWAGON
This agricultural design dates from 1965, and has a low gull-wing single-engined profile similar to contemporaneous designs.

CESSNA 177 CARDINAL
Designed as a replacement for the Model 172, the piston-powered 177 first flew in 1966, and more than 4000 have been produced.

CESSNA 207 SKYWAGON/STATIONAIR
A stretched version of the Model 205/206, the Skywagon variant has seven seats and the Stationair eight. Production ceased in 1985.

CESSNA 411
This twin-piston engined light aircraft dates from 1962. More than 400 were produced and customers included the French Air Force.

CESSNA 414
Another twin engined, air taxi/ executive design from Cessna – known as the Chancellor it first flew in 1968 – the 414 was built in several versions. Production numbers in the thousands.

CHANCE VOUGHT XF5U-1

USA: 1946

Crew: 1
Powerplant: two 1007kW (1350hp) Pratt & Whitney R-2000 radial engines
Performance (estimated): max speed 684km/h (425 mph); range 1143km (710 miles); service ceiling 10,515m (34,500ft)
Dimensions: wingspan 9.91m (32ft 6in); length 8.56m (28ft 1in); height 5.08m (16ft 8in)
Weight: 7585kg (16,722lb) loaded
Armament: six 12.7mm (0.50in) machine guns or four 20mm (0.79in) cannon; two 454kg (1000lb) bombs

BASED ON THE DESIGN OF its low-powered predecessor, the V-173, the highly unconventional XF5U-1 prototype naval strike-fighter had a roughly circular wing planform and was powered by two 1007kW

The V-173, seen here in flight, was a flying test-bed for the proposed XF5U-1 circular-wing naval fighter, which was built but which never flew.

(1350hp) Pratt & Whitney R-2000 Twin Wasp engines buried in the wing and driving large four-bladed propellers via extension shafts. The blades were specially articulated, like those of a helicopter, so that at high angles of attack they would move forward at constant pitch and flatten out to enable the machine to hover. The very low aspect ratio wing also housed the fuel tanks and armament, the pilot's cockpit being situated in the extreme nose. It was claimed that the aircraft possessed a speed range of between 64 and 725km/h (40 and 450mph). The prototype was rolled out in July 1946 amid much publicity, but it never flew and was eventually scrapped.

CHILTON DW.1

UK: 1937

The example of this light private/sports aircraft pictured is a DW.1a – the letter 'a' signifies the use of a French-built Train 4T 33kW (44hp) piston engine.

A LOW-WING, FIXED undercarriage wooden light aircraft, the DW.1 was built in small numbers. It won the 1939 Lympne–Folkestone air race. For many, this type epitomizes the golden era of pre-World War II British light aircraft design. As a consequence examples survive today and others are being newly built from plans by enthusiasts.

Crew: 1
Powerplant: one Carden Ford piston engine rated at 23kW (30hp)
Performance: max speed 180km/h (112mph); range 160km (100 miles)

Dimensions: wingspan 7.30m (24ft); length 5.49m (18ft); height 1.30m (4ft 10in)
Payload: one person

CHRISLEA CH.3 ACE, SUPER ACE AND SKYJEEP

UK: 1946

This photograph shows an example of the Super Ace, which did not feature the Ace's controversial control system. This particular aircraft was unfortunately written off in an accident in the mid-1950s.

HAVING HAD EARLIER DESIGNS interrupted by World War II, Chrislea launched new light aircraft designs shortly afterwards, featuring a high wing, a tricycle undercarriage and a dual tail fin. In addition, a new design of control system (a wheel and universal joint) replaced the general standard aircraft control column. The controversial control system was replaced on the later Super Ace version due to its unpopularity, but only 21 examples were produced. The last version, the Series 4 Skyjeep, had a tail wheel and a more powerful engine. Several examples were produced and exported before the company ceased trading in 1952.

Specifications apply to the CH.3 Series 2 Super Ace.

Crew: 2
Powerplant: one 108kW (145hp) de Havilland Gipsy Major 10 inverted in-line piston engine
Performance: max speed 203km/h (126mph); range 644km (400 miles)
Dimensions: wingspan 14.10m (46ft 4in); length 8.50m (27ft 9in); height 2.50m (8ft 2in)
Weight: 1066kg (2350lb) maximum take-off weight
Payload: four people

CIERVA AUTOGYROS

SPAIN: 1921–1936

IN 1919 IN SPAIN, 24-year-old Juan de la Cierva y Cordonia witnessed the crash of a new three-engined biplane bomber which lost speed, stalled and spun while trying to land at Getafe Airfield near Madrid. Cierva was determined to design an aircraft that could fly slowly without a sudden loss of lift resulting in a stall. His experiments with models revealed that a rotor, turning freely as it was pulled along through the air, could be used to produce sufficient lift to get an aircraft off the ground and sustain it in forward flight if thrust were provided by an engine driving a conventional propeller. If the engine failed, the windmilling rotor would continue to produce enough lift to lower the aircraft safely.

In 1921–22, using converted Deperdussin monoplanes, Cierva built three autogyros, all of which had non-flexible rotors, to test his

The C.6A was built using the fuselage of an Avro 504K, Bristol Fighter ailerons on outriggers and horn-balanced elevators.

theories in flight. Unfortunately, as soon as the C.1, 2 and 3 designs left the ground they showed a tendency to roll uncontrollably.

This was because the rotor blades produced unbalanced lift. Cierva solved the problem by reverting to the design principles used on one

This Cierva C-30A Rota I was one of 12 delivered to the RAF during 1934–35, and operated by No. 529 Squadron in 1943–44, mostly on coastal radar calibration work.

of his early models, and he built the C.4 using flexible blades attached to the hub by hinges to allow them to flap up and down as they rotated. The C.4 successfully flew on 9 January 1923 powered by a 82kW (110hp) Le Rhône rotary engine. By the end of the month it had flown a 4.02km (2.5-mile) closed circuit in four minutes at a height of 30m (100ft).

Cierva's next machine, the C.5, flew in July 1923 and was fitted with a three-bladed rotor. With financial help from the Spanish government, Cierva produced the C.6A which first flew in May 1924. Cierva used the fuselage of an Avro 504K fitted with a four-bladed articulated rotor, Bristol Fighter ailerons on outriggers and horn-balanced elevators. In October 1925 Cierva shipped his

machine to Britain and it was successfully demonstrated at Farnborough. A.V. Roe & Co (Avro) were asked to build two identical aircraft (C.6C and the two-seat C.6D) for evaluation and experimentation work. During the 1920s and 1930s Avro and six other British companies built Cierva autogyros under licence.

Meanwhile, in 1926 the Cierva Autogiro Company was formed – its founder, Mr (later Cdr) James Weir, later formed a breakaway company – and its first autogyro was completed in June 1933. A Cierva C.6D became the first two-seat autogyro in the world and on 30 July 1927 Cierva himself became the first passenger to fly in a rotating-wing aircraft. On 18 September 1928, a Cierva autogyro became the first rotorcraft to fly the English Channel when the Spaniard and his passenger, Mademoiselle Helène Boucher, flew in a Cierva C.8L Mk II from London to St

Inglevert in 1 hr 6 mins at an altitude of 4265m (4000ft). After this Cierva completed a three-week tour of Europe, flying the C.8L back to London on 13 October after covering a distance of almost 2897km (1800 miles).

By the 1930s 500 autogyros had been built throughout the world. In America the US Navy placed a contract with Pitcairn, which, like the Kellett Autogiro Corporation formed in 1929, manufactured the Cierva under licence. In Russia the KaSkr-I was a virtual copy of the Cierva C.8 Autogiro. During 1934–35, Avro delivered 12 104.3kW (140hp) Siddeley Genet Major-engined C.30A autogyros to the RAF as Rota Is, which operated initially at the Army Co-Operation school at Old Sarum. In 1933 Cierva produced an autogyro (C.30) which could take off vertically without a forward run, and the first public demonstrations of a vertical take-off by an autogyro took place in July 1936

on Hounslow Heath. As a result, the RAF ordered five more advanced C.40 versions (Rota Mk II) with two side-by-side seats and a 131kW (175hp) Salmson engine. On 9 December 1936, Cierva was travelling as a passenger in a fixed-wing aircraft when it stalled and hit the ground, killing everyone on board. It was a final, tragic irony that Cierva had become a victim of the very hazard he had spent his lifetime trying to eradicate.

Specifications apply to the Cierva C.30A.

Crew: 1
Powerplant: one Armstrong Siddeley Genet Major 1A radial piston engine rated at 104kW (140hp)
Performance: max speed 177km/h (110mph); radius 459km (285 miles); service ceiling 2440m (8000ft)
Dimensions: rotor diameter 11.28m (37ft); length 6.01m (19ft 8.5in); height 3.38m (11ft 1in)
Weight: 553kg (1220lb)

COANDA BIPLANE   ROMANIA: 1910

THE TALENTED YOUNG AIRCRAFT designer Henri Coanda was born in Bucharest, Romania, in 1886. In December 1907, at an exhibition in the Berlin Sporthalle, he exhibited a model aircraft designed to fly by reaction propulsion. While studying at the Ecole Superieur Aéronautique in Paris, he constructed a full-size reaction-propelled aircraft, which

was exhibited at the second Salon de l'Aéronautique in October 1910. Through a series of multiple gears, the aircraft's piston engine drove a centrifugal compressor installed in the forward part of the fuselage. Despite reports to the contrary, it is almost certain that the little biplane never flew; the thrust provided by the compressor

(220kg/485lb) would have been too weak to sustain flight. Still, the Coanda biplane deserves its place in the history of flight not only because it was the world's first jet aircraft design, but also for its elegance. For the first time, struts and bracing wires were reduced to a minimum, while the airframe was of plywood-covered steel tube.

Crew: 1
Powerplant: one 37kW (50hp) Clerget 4-cylinder water-cooled in-line engine, driving a centrifugal air compressor
Performance: not flown
Dimensions: wingspan 10.08m (33ft 1.5in); length 12.70m (40ft 6in); height 2.74m (9ft 0.25in)
Weight: 420kg (926lb)
Armament: none

CODY MICHELIN CUP   UK: 1910

AFTER CARRYING OUT MORE than a year of test flights in his British Army Aeroplane No 1, in which he made the first powered heavier-

than-air flight in Great Britain on 16 October 1908, the American expatriate Samuel Franklin Cody built another biplane to compete

for the first Michelin Cup. This aircraft, named simply the Cody Michelin Cup Biplane, resembled his first machine, but had improved

controls and used ailerons instead of the wing-warping technique.

In this second biplane, Cody established British records for endurance and distance, flying 152.08km (94.5 miles) in 2 hours 45 minutes. On 31 December 1910, he won the Michelin Cup and broke his own records, covering a distance of 298.47km (185.46 miles) in a time of 4 hours 47 minutes.

Crew: 1
Powerplant: one 45kW (60hp) E.N.V. F 8-cylinder water-cooled V-type in-line engine
Performance: max speed 105km/h (65mph)
Dimensions: wingspan 14.02m (46ft); length 11.73m (38ft 6in); height 3.96m (13ft)
Weight: 1138kg (2509lb) loaded
Armament: none

Designed by Samuel Franklin Cody to compete in the Michelin Cup air race of 1910, the aircraft was based on Cody's model of 1908.

COMMONWEALTH WIRRAWAY

AUSTRALIA: 1939

The Commonwealth Wirraway saw service as a ground-attack aircraft in New Guinea in 1942, its manoeuvrability proving an asset.

IN 1939 THE COMMONWEALTH Aircraft Corporation, set up three years earlier by the Australian government to create a national aircraft industry, produced the CA-1 Wirraway advanced armament trainer, a licence-built version of the North American NA-33. The first of two CA-1 prototypes flew in March 1939, and these were followed by 755 production aircraft, the first of which entered service in June 1939. Good performance and excellent manoeuvrability saw the type pressed into operational service in New Guinea in 1942.

Crew: 2
Powerplant: one 448kW (600hp) Pratt & Whitney R-1340-S1H1-G Wasp 9-cylinder radial engine
Performance: max speed 354km/h (220mph); range 1159km (720 miles); service ceiling 7010m (23,000ft)
Dimensions: wingspan 13.11m (43ft); length 8.48m (27ft 10in); height 2.66m (8ft 8.75in)
Weight: 2991kg (6595lb) loaded
Armament: three 7.7mm (0.303in) machine guns; external bomb load of 454kg (1000lb)

COMMONWEALTH CA-12 BOOMERANG

AUSTRALIA: 1942

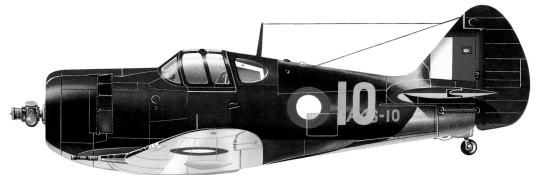

IN 1941, AS INSURANCE against being cut off from overseas help by a Japanese offensive in the Pacific, Australia accelerated its weapons manufacturing capability. One result was the Commonwealth CA-12 'emergency' fighter, much of which was assembled from

The Commonwealth Boomerang was developed as an insurance against Australia becoming cut off from outside aid in the event of further Japanese offensives in the Pacific during World War II.

components already in production for the CA-3 Wirraway. The aircraft, named Boomerang, first flew in May 1942, only 14 weeks after the design had been approved, and 105 production Boomerang Mk Is were followed by 95 Mk IIs. The type

performed well in the support role in New Guinea, where its excellent manoeuvrability proved a major asset in mountainous jungle terrain. Production ran to 250 aircraft. Specifications apply to the Boomerang Mk II.

Crew: 1
Powerplant: one 895kW (1200hp) Pratt & Whitney R-1830-S3C4G Twin Wasp 14-cylinder radial engine
Performance: max speed 491km/h (305mph); range 2575km (1600 miles); service ceiling 10,365m (34,000ft)

Dimensions: wingspan 10.97m (36ft); length 7.77m (25ft 6in); height 2.92m (9ft 7in)
Weight: 3742kg (8249lb) loaded
Armament: two 20mm (0.79in) cannon and four 7.7mm (0.303in) machine guns; external bomb load of 227kg (500lb)

COMPER CLA.7 SWIFT
UK: 1930

Crew: 1
Powerplant: one Pobjoy R radial piston engine rated at 56kW (75hp)
Performance: max speed 225km/h (140mph); range 611km (380 miles); service ceiling 6705m (22,000ft)
Dimensions: wingspan 7.32m (24ft); length 5.40m (17ft 8.5in); height 1.61m (5ft 3.5in)
Weight: 447kg (985lb) maximum take-off weight
Payload: single-seat sports type

THE SWIFT LIGHT SPORTS aircraft was designed by Lt Nicholas Comper. Formerly of the RAF and Airco, Comper had previously designed amateur builds with the Cranwell Light Aeroplane Club. Of wooden construction with a plywood and fabric covering, the Swift's wing was mounted directly atop the fuselage, ahead of the cockpit, and braced. Initially an A.B.C. Scorpion 30kW (40hp) engine was fitted. That type, however, was superseded by a 37kW (50hp) Salmson AD9 radial type, before the specified Pobjoy engine was fitted or retrofitted to

This Swift was built in 1932. It survived World War II because it was stored for the duration, but it had to be rebuilt by its new owner afterwards and it did not fly again until 1956.

most of the 41 examples built. Edward VIII, then Prince of Wales, counted himself among the Swift's owners, and his machine competed

in the 1932 (as well as the 1933/4) Kings Cup Race – coming second – powered by a Gipsy Major engine. The Swift participated in many

contests and held a number of records in its heyday. Several examples of this exclusive but much loved type remain airworthy today.

CONSOLIDATED MODEL 16 COMMODORE (XPY-1)
USA: 1929

THE COMMODORE TWIN-ENGINE D flying boat failed to gain military orders in the form of XPY-1. A total of 14, however, were ordered

for commercial use. This was fortuitous, as the Commodore design is recognized as the basis for the important and famous

PBY-5 Catalina. The Commodores were ordered by a US-owned South American-based airline called NYRBA which challenged

Pan American's regional dominance and was later leveraged to sell its assets to Pan Am (circa 1930). Subsequently Pan Am went on to operate Commodores up to and through World War II, and some machines had short careers with successor operators.

Specifications apply to the Model 16-1 Commodore.

Crew: 3
Powerplant: two 429kW (575hp) Pratt & Whitney R-1860 Hornet radial piston engines
Performance: max speed 206km/h (128mph); range 1609km (1000 miles); service ceiling 3430m (11,250ft)
Dimensions: wingspan 30.48m (100ft); length 18.80m (61ft 8in); height 4.76m (15ft 8in)
Weight: 7983kg (17,600lb) maximum take-off weight
Payload: up to 22 passengers

NYRBA (New York Rio Buenos Aires Line) was the primary operator of the Commodore.

CONSOLIDATED PBY CATALINA

USA: 1935

Crew: 7/9
Powerplant: two 896kW (1200hp) Pratt & Whitney R-1830-92 Twin Wasp 14-cylinder radial engines
Performance: max speed 288km/h (179mph); range 4095km (2545 miles); service ceiling 4480m (14,700ft)
Dimensions: wingspan 31.70m (104ft); length 19.45m (63ft 10in); height 6.15m (20ft 2in)
Weight: 16,067kg (35,420lb) loaded
Armament: two 12.7mm (0.50in) machine guns in bow turret and one in each beam blister; one 7.62mm (0.30in) machine gun in ventral tunnel; up to 1814kg (4000lb) of bombs, mines or depth charges, or two torpedoes

The PBY-3 Catalina, seen here, was also licence-built in the Soviet Union, where it was powered by M87 engines and known as the GST.

ON 28 FEBRUARY 1928, the US Navy issued a contract for a prototype flying boat, the XPY-1, to the Consolidated Aircraft Corporation. This aircraft, which was designed for an alternative installation of two or three engines, was the first large monoplane flying boat to be procured by the US Navy. It was also the initial configuration which eventually evolved into the most outstanding parasol monoplane flying boat of all time, the PBY Catalina. A contract for construction of the prototype PBY, then known as the XP3Y-1, was issued to Consolidated on 28 October 1933. The aircraft flew for the first time on 21 March 1935, with operational deliveries being made to Patrol Squadron VP-11F in October 1936.

The initial version, the PBY-1, demonstrated its long-range capability when 12 aircraft of Patrol Squadron VP-3 flew from San Diego to Coco Solo in the Panama Canal Zone, a distance of 5297km (3292 miles), in 27 hours and 58 minutes. The PBY-1 was followed into service in 1937 by 50 PBY-2s. Three examples of the next variant, the PBY-3, were delivered to the USSR in 1938, along with a manufacturing licence. The Soviet version, designated GST and powered by Russian-built 709kW (950hp) M87 engines, was used in the transport role. The PBY-4, which appeared in 1938, featured the large midships 'blister' observation and gun

positions that were to become well-known characteristics of the PBY. In April 1939 an amphibious version was ordered by the US Navy, and this became the prototype for the PBY-5A, which was to be widely used in World War II. In July 1939 the RAF received a PBY for evaluation, and this resulted in an order for 50 aircraft similar to the US Navy's PBY-5. The RAF named them Catalina Mk I, and the name Catalina was subsequently adopted by the US Navy. The RAF doubled its original order during 1940, and orders also began to flow in from other countries; Australia ordered 18, Canada 50, France 30 and the Netherlands East Indies 36. Total

From the PBY-4 onwards, the Catalina featured the large midships observation and gun blisters. In RAF service, the Catalina had an impressive record of hunting and sinking U-boats.

CNNA HL-6
A tandem two-seat, single-engined low-wing trainer designed in Brazil and dating from 1943, the HL-6 was the last product from CNNA.

COMMONWEALTH CA-6 WACKETT
The CA-6 Wackett trainer was named after the RAAF officer who designed it, Wng Cdr L.J. Wackett.. The prototype flew in October 1939, and 200 were built.

COMMONWEALTH CA-11 WOOMERA
Powered by two Pratt & Whitney radial engines, the CA-11 Woomera light bomber was intended to fulfil a variety of roles, but only two examples were built.

COMMONWEALTH CA-15
Strongly influencd by the P-51 Mustang, the CA-15 fighter flew in March 1946 powered by a Rolls-Royce Griffon engine. Only one prototype was built.

COMMONWEALTH CA-28 CERES
An agricultural light aeroplane design first flown in Australia circa 1958. A total of 21 were built between then and 1963.

COMPER (FANE) F.1/40
Originally designed as a sporting aircraft by Nick Comper, the F.1/40 was further developed as an air observation post by Capt Gerard Fane after Comper's death. The sole example flew early in 1941.

CONAL W-151
This single-engined high-wing cabin monoplane was designed in Brazil and dates from 1964. The five-seat W-151 did not go into production.

CONSOLIDATED PT SERIES
Consolidated's PT series of trainers, beginning with the PT-1 (225 built) of 1925, were designed to replace the famous Curtiss JN-4 Jenny. The Consolidated trainers remained in service until 1939.

CONSOLIDATED PY-1
The Consolidated PY-1, flown in 1928, was a three-engined parasol-wing flying boat. Aircraft of similar design were also built by Glenn L. Martin.

CONSOLIDATED MODEL 17, 18 AND 20 FLEETSTER
A single radial-engined high parasol-wing monoplane dating from 1930, the Fleetster was designed for carrying mail or up to nine passengers to Central and South American destinations. It also saw military service as the C11A.

production of the PBY-5 was 750, followed by 794 PBY-5As, 56 of which went to the USAF as OA-10s. On 21 September 1939 the US Navy's Patrol Squadron 21, with 14 PBYs, deployed to the Philippines, becoming the first patrol unit in the Asiatic Fleet since 1932. A few weeks later, in the spring of 1941, the first Catalina

Mk I aircraft became operational with RAF Coastal Command, and in May they played a key part in the hunting down of the German battleship *Bismarck*.

In 1942 the RAF and US Navy's Catalina squadrons combined to destroy several U-boats. In June 1942, on the other side of the world, it was reconnaissance by

Catalinas that detected the whereabouts of a Japanese carrier task force approaching Midway Island, enabling the Japanese aircraft carriers to be destroyed by strike aircraft, and Catalinas subsequently carried out offensive operations against Japanese forces in the Aleutian Islands. Lend-Lease supplies to Britain included

225 PBY-5Bs (Catalina IA) and 97 Catalina IVAs, the latter fitted with ASV radar. Production of the Catalina, which ended in April 1945, included 2398 by Consolidated and 892 by other manufacturers, plus an unknown number built in the USSR.

Specifications apply to the Consolidated PBY-5 Catalina.

CONSOLIDATED B-24 LIBERATOR

USA: 1939

A Consolidated Liberator Mk VI (B-24H) of No 356 Squadron RAF. This unit, based in India, made many bombing sorties across the Bay of Bengal into Japanese-occupied Burma.

Crew: 8/10
Powerplant: four 895kW (1200hp) Pratt & Whitney R-1830-65 radial engines
Performance: max speed 467km/h (290mph); range 3218km (2000 miles); service ceiling 8535m (28,000ft)
Dimensions: wingspan 33.53m (110ft); length 20.47m (67ft 2in); height 5.49m (18ft)
Weight: 29,484kg (65,000lb) loaded
Armament: two-gun turrets in nose, tail, upper fuselage, aft of cockpit and under centre fuselage, and single manual guns in waist (beam) positions, totalling ten 12.7mm (0.50in) machine guns; a normal bomb load of 3992kg (8800lb)

THE CONSOLIDATED B-24 Liberator long-range bomber was built in larger numbers than any other US warplane of World War II – 18,431 in total – and was delivered in greater quantities than any other bomber in aviation history. The aircraft had its origin in US Army Air Corps Specification C-212, issued in 1935 and calling for a new four-engined heavy bomber with a top speed of 483km/h (300mph), a range of 4830km (3000 miles), a service ceiling of 10,675m (35,000ft) and a maximum bomb load of 3624kg (8000lb). A contract for one prototype, designated XB-24, was approved on 30 March 1939, and this aircraft (39-556) took off on its maiden flight from Lindberg Field, California, on 29 December 1939. It was followed by seven

YB-24 service evaluation aircraft.

The first Liberators to come off Consolidated's San Diego production line were six LB-30As, part of an order placed by the French government in September 1939. With France overrun, the aircraft were diverted to the RAF, which found them unacceptable for combat over Europe (for one

thing, they lacked self-sealing fuel tanks). The aircraft were taken on RAF charge in November 1940 and relegated to ferry duties. The production model for the USAAC was the B-24A, the first of nine being delivered in May 1941. A further development batch of nine B-24Cs was also delivered, leading to the first major production

models, the B-24D, B-24E and B-24G with a power-operated nose turret. Further Liberator developments were the B-24H; the B-24J; an improved B-24H with an autopilot and other operational upgrades, including a more effective bomb sight; the B-24L with two manually operated tail guns rather than a turret; and the

A B-24 Liberator over Alaska. The Liberator's very long range made it an ideal maritime patrol aircraft, and it went a long way to closing the 'mid-Atlantic gap' where U-boats preyed on Allied convoys.

B-24M, which was an improved version of the B-24J.

The six unarmed LB-30 transport Liberators initially used by the RAF were soon followed by armed variants, beginning with 20 Liberator Mk I aircraft that were equivalents of the B-24A. Some of these were used for maritime reconnaissance, equipped with ASV radar and a ventral gun tray. These were in turn followed, from August 1941, by 139 Liberator Mk II and 260 Liberator Mk III aircraft, also for the maritime reconnaissance role, and 112 B-24Gs for service as Liberator B Mk V bombers and GR Mk V

maritime reconnaissance aircraft. The numbers of later Liberator variants delivered to the RAF and Commonwealth air forces were 1302 B-24J, 437 B-24L and 47 B-24M aircraft. The B-24J machines served as Liberator B Mk VI bombers with a ball turret or as Liberator GR Mk VI long-range maritime reconnaissance aircraft with ASV radar replacing the ball turret, while the equivalent marks based on the B-24L and B-24M were the Liberator B Mk VIII and the Liberator GR Mk VIII.

The Liberator bombers served mainly in Southeast Asia, where they equipped 14 squadrons, while

their maritime reconnaissance counterparts succeeded in closing the 'mid-Atlantic gap' where air cover for the vital Allied Atlantic convoys had hitherto been absent. The B-24 made its operational debut in June 1942 with long-range raids from Egypt against the Romanian oilfields. In the Pacific during World War II, although it was Boeing B-29 which was to prosecute the strategic air offensive against the Japanese home islands, it was the Liberator that remained the principal strategic bomber elsewhere in the theatre.

Specification refers to the Consolidated B-24J Liberator.

CONSOLIDATED P-30 (PB-2A)
With the exception of some biplane trainers, the PB-2A monoplane fighter and attack aircraft of the early 1930s was the last production landplane built by Consolidated before the Liberator bomber.

CONSOLIDATED P2Y
The Consolidated P2Y flying-boat of 1932 was derived from the 1928 PY-1 Admiral. A total of 46 P2Ys were built, with deliveries of the aircraft beginning in 1933.

CONSOLIDATED PB2Y CORONADO
Developed in 1935 to succeed the Catalina, the Consolidated Coronado never managed to equal the PBY's exceptional operational qualities. The XPB2Y-1 prototype flew on 17 September 1937.

CONSOLIDATED XP4Y-1 CORREGIDOR
The XP4Y-1 Corregidor was a twin-engined long-range flying-boat, which flew in 1939. The sole prototype was used for experimental purposes, a contract for 200 aircraft having been cancelled.

CONSOLIDATED (VOUGHT) TBY-2 SEAWOLF
Originally designed by Vought, Consolidated were awarded the production order for this single-engined torpedo-bomber, first flown in 1941. Only 180 were built before order cancellation and none were used operationally.

CONSOLIDATED B-32 DOMINATOR
Conceived as an insurance against the failure of the B-29, the B-32 entered production in January 1944, and 15 aircraft were deployed to the Pacific in April 1945. Production of the B-32 was cancelled at the war's end.

CONSOLIDATED VULTEE R2Y-1
The R2Y-1 was a long-range transport with an enlarged fuselage mated with B-32 wings. Only one prototype was built, flying in 1943.

CONSOLIDATED (CONVAIR MODEL 104) MODEL 39 LIBERATOR LINER
Based upon the Model 32 (B-24 Liberator), the Model 39 first flew in 1944 and was designed with the postwar civil transport market in mind. There was initial interest in a military derivative, but the glut of cheap ex-military transports curtailed orders and only two examples were built.

CONSOLIDATED PB4Y-2 PRIVATEER

USA: 1943

Crew: 11
Powerplant: four 1007kW (1350hp) Pratt & Whitney R-1830-94 Twin Wasp 14-cylinder radial engines
Performance: max speed 462km/h (287mph); range 4500km (2800 miles); service ceiling 6300m (20,700ft)
Dimensions: wingspan 33.53m (110ft); length 22.73m (74ft 7in); height 9.17m (30ft 1in)
Weight: 29,485kg (65,000lb) loaded
Armament: 12 12.7mm (0.50in) machine guns; up to 5800kg (12,800lb) of bombs

DEVELOPED FROM THE US Navy's PB4Y-1 anti-submarine version of the B-24, the Consolidated PB4Y Privateer fulfilled a pressing need for a very long range strategic reconnaissance aircraft. The first of three prototypes flew on 20 September 1943, and the aircraft entered production as the PB4Y-2, 1370 being ordered in two separate batches. In the event, only 736 Privateers were delivered before the end of the war. The type was not widely used, but saw service as an electronic intelligence aircraft

(one was shot down by Soviet fighters over the Baltic in October 1950) and as a maritime patrol aircraft during the Korean War.

This photo shows a Consolidated PB4Y-2 Privateer of the US Navy on a reconnaissance mission over the Pacific in 1945.

CONVAIR B-36

USA: 1946

THE FIRST BOMBER WITH a truly global strategic capability to serve with any air force, the Convair B-36 was to fly for the first time on 8 August 1946. An initial production batch of 22 B-36As was built, with the first of the aircraft being delivered to Strategic Air Command in the summer of

The B-36 gave the USAF SAC the ability to undertake operations on a global scale, and to attack the Soviet Union from any direction.

1947. The second production model, the Convair B-36B, was powered by six Pratt & Whitney R-4630-41 engines with water injection, and was fully combat equipped. The most important production version, however, was the B-36D, which had four J47 turbojets as well as its six radial engines; 22 aircraft were built in total and 64 earlier models were brought up to B-36D standard. This version was followed by the B-36F (of which 28 were built), the B-36H (81 built) and the B-36J (33 built). Reconnaissance variants were the RB-36D, RB-36E and RB-36H.

Specifications are for the Convair B-36D.

Crew: 15
Powerplant: six 2835kW (3800hp) Pratt & Whitney R-4360-53 Wasp Major 28-cylinder radial engines, plus four 2358kg (5200lb) thrust General Electric J47-GE-19 turbojet engines
Performance: max speed 661km/h (411mph); range 10,940km (6,800 miles); service ceiling 12,160m (39,900ft)
Dimensions: wingspan 70.10m (230ft); length 49.40m (162ft 1in); height 14.22m (46ft 8in)
Weight: 185,976kg (410,000lb) loaded
Armament: one 4530kg (10,000lb) Mk 7 nuclear store; up to 38,052kg (84,000lb) of conventional bombs; 12.20mm (0.79in) cannon in six retractable turrets, plus two 20mm (0.79in) cannon in the nose and two in the tail

CONVAIR CV-240, CV-340, CV-440 (C-131, R4Y AND T-29)   USA: (1947)

Over 500 Convair 240/340s were built as T-29s, C-131s or R4Ys for the US military. Many of these were sold for commercial use in the 1970s.

THE CV-240 WAS A RESPONSE to the need for a postwar DC-3 replacement with the added benefit of a pressurized cabin. It sold in large numbers to the military (364 of the 540 built were military T-29s), many of which later became commercial freighters. The larger and more powerful CV-340 sold 207 commercial examples and the performance-improved CV-440 sold 177 examples. A further 152 military C-131/R4Y hospital ships/trainers/transports were produced. Both civil and military types were exported to a number of customers.

Specifications apply to the Convair CV-440.

Crew: 2/3
Powerplant: two 1864kW (2500hp) Pratt & Whitney R-2800-CB16 or CB17 Double Wasp radial piston engines
Performance: max speed 542km/h (337mph); range 756km (470 miles) with maximum payload; service ceiling 7590m (24,900ft)
Dimensions: wingspan 32.11m (105ft 4in); length with weather radar 24.84m (81ft 6in) height 8.59m (28ft 2in)
Weight: 22,226kg (49,000lb) maximum take-off weight
Payload: up to 52 passengers

CONVAIR XB-46   USA: 1947

Crew: 3
Powerplant: four 1812kg (4000lb) thrust Allison J35A-A-3 turbojet engines
Performance: max speed 877km/h (545mph); range 4618km (2870 miles); service ceiling 13,115m (43,000ft)
Dimensions: wingspan 34.46m (113ft); length 32.25m (105ft 9in); height 8.50m (27ft 11in)
Weight: 43,307kg (95,600lb) loaded
Armament (proposed): two 12.7mm (0.50in) machine guns in tail position; up to 9966kg (22,000lb) of bombs

Designed in competition with the Boeing B-47, the highly stream-lined Convair XB-46 flew for the first time on 2 April 1947.

THE CONVAIR XB-46 was developed in response to a USAAF requirement for a jet-powered bomber capable of 800km/h (497mph), with a 1600km (1000-mile) combat radius and a service ceiling in excess of 12,192m (40,000ft). Three prototypes were ordered in early 1945, but the USAAF decided to purchase the North American B-45 before the XB-46 was completed. This effectively killed the XB-46 programme, but a single aircraft was completed and test-flown. The XB-46 first flew on 2 April 1947 and continued in a test programme into the 1950s. The aircraft was scrapped in early 1952.

CONVAIR XF2Y-1 SEA DART   USA: 1953

A transonic, delta-wing seaplane fighter, the XF2Y-1 (originally Y2-2) Sea Dart flew for the first time on 9 April 1953. The project was abandoned after the loss of one of the prototypes, which broke up in mid air.

Crew: 1
Powerplant: two 1540kg (3400lb) thrust Westinghouse J34-WE-32 turbojet engines
Performance: max speed 1116km/h (694mph); range 825km (513 miles); service ceiling 15,311m (50,200ft)
Dimensions: wingspan 10.26m (33ft 8in); length 15.58m (51ft 1.5in); height 5.18m (16ft 6in)
Weight: 9979kg (22,000lb) loaded
Armament: none

ORIGINALLY DESIGNATED Y2-2, the Convair XF2Y-1 Sea Dart was a small, transonic delta-wing seaplane fighter fitted with retractable hydro-skis. After protracted taxiing trials, the Sea Dart made its first true flight on 9 April 1953, having already made a short hop during a taxi run on 14 January. Three YF2Y-1 evaluation aircraft were built, the first of these breaking up over San Diego Bay on 4 November 1954 when the pilot inadvertently exceeded the airframe limitations. Testing continued with the two remaining YF2Y-1s and the XF2Y-1 prototype, but difficulties persisted with the hydro-skis, which set up excessive vibration during high-speed runs on the water. This led to the Sea Dart programme being abandoned in 1956.

CONVAIR F-102 DELTA DAGGER   USA: 1953

Crew: 1
Powerplant: one 7802kg (17,200lb) thrust Pratt & Whitney J57-P-23 turbojet
Performance: max speed 1328km/h (825mph); range 2172km (1350 miles); service ceiling 16,460m (54,000ft)
Dimensions: wingspan 11.62m (38ft 1in); length 20.84m (68ft 4in); height 6.46m (21ft 2in)
Weight: 14,288kg (31,500lb) loaded
Armament: up to six AAMs; 12 folding-fin aircraft rockets

The Convair F-102 Delta Dagger was once flown by US President George W. Bush when he was an Air National Guard pilot.

IN 1950, THE USAF formulated a requirement for a night and all-weather interceptor incorporating the latest fire-control system. This eventually emerged as the Convair F-102, the design of which was based on experience gained during flight-testing of the XF-92 delta-wing research aircraft. Two prototype YF-102s were built. The first flew on 24 October 1953, but was damaged beyond repair only a week later. Testing resumed with the second machine in January 1954. Eight more YF-102s were built for evaluation, but performance fell short of expectations. Substantial airframe redesign saw it re-emerge in December 1954 as the YF-102A, and the type was ordered into full production. The first F-102A Delta Dagger was handed over to Air Defense Command in June 1955.

CONVAIR CV-540, 580, 600, 640 AND 5800

USA: 1955

THE CONVAIR 240/340/440 airframe proved robust enough to merit a turboprop conversion programme. Excluding 10 examples built from new by Canadair, over 200 conversions were undertaken. During the 1990s, Kelowna undertook a stretch and modernization programme designated CV5800. Specifications apply to the Convair CV-580.

Crew: 2
Powerplant: two 2796kW (3750hp) Allison 501-D13H turboprop engines
Performance: cruising speed 550km/h (342mph); range 3651km (2268 miles) with a 2268kg (5000lb) payload; service ceiling 7590m (24,900ft)
Dimensions: wingspan 32.11m (105ft 4in); length 24.84m (81ft 6in); height 8.89m (29ft 2in)
Weight: 26,372kg (58,140lb) maximum take-off weight
Payload: up to 52 passengers

The Convair 640 pictured here was an early production Convair 340 built in 1952. The aircraft was converted to a Convair 640 in 1965 for Caribair.

CONVAIR F-106 DELTA DART

USA: 1956

THE F-102B WAS AN advanced fighter design featuring an electronic weapons-control system. It first flew on 26 December 1956 and only entered service two and a half years later as the F-106 Delta Dart, after a protracted development history. The first production F-106 was delivered to the 539th Fighter Interceptor Squadron in June 1959. Production ended in 1962 after 257 examples had been built, equipping 13 fighter interceptor squadrons. In the early 1960s the F-106A was the most important type on the inventory

A Convair F-106 Delta Dart of the 49th Fighter Interceptor Squadron, Griffiss AFB.

of Air Defense Command, which it served exclusively. It also equipped several Air National Guard units.

Crew: 1
Powerplant: one 11,113kg (24,500lb) thrust Pratt & Whitney J75-P-17 turbojet
Performance: max speed 2553km/h (1587mph); range 925km (575 miles); service ceiling 16,765m (55,005ft)
Dimensions: wingspan 11.66m (38ft 3.5in); length 21.58m (70ft 9in); height 6.18m (20ft 3in)
Weight: 15,876kg (35,000lb) loaded
Armament: four AAMs

CONVAIR B-58 HUSTLER

USA: 1956

The Convair B-58 Hustler was designed to make a supersonic dash over the target area and had a high accident rate.

THE FIRST SUPERSONIC bomber to enter service with the USAF, the Convair B-58 prototype flew on 11 November 1956. It was anticipated that the type would replace the B-47, but only two Bomb Wings, the 43rd and 305th, were equipped with it. A bold departure from conventional design, the B058 had a delta wing with conical-cambered leading edge, an area-ruled fuselage, four podded turbojets and tandem cockpits. The B-58 was the first aircraft in the world in which the crew had

individual escape capsules for use at supersonic speed. Weapons and extra fuel were carried in a large, jettisonable under-fuselage pod.

Crew: 3
Powerplant: four 7075kg (15,600lb) thrust General Electric J79-GE-5 turbojet engines
Performance: max speed 2228km/h (1385mph); range 8248km (5125 miles); service ceiling 19,507m (64,000ft)
Dimensions: wingspan 17.32m (56ft 10in); length 29.49m (96ft 9in); height 9.58m (31ft 5in)
Weight: 72,576kg (160,000lb) loaded
Armament: one 20mm (0.79in) Vulcan six-barrel cannon; 8820kg (19,450lb) of nuclear or conventional stores

CONVAIR MODEL 22 CV-880

USA: 1959

Crew: 4/5
Powerplant: four 49.8kN (11,200lb) General Electric CJ-805-3A turbojet engines
Performance: max cruising speed 983km/h (610mph); range 5150km (3200 miles); service ceiling 12,497m (41,000ft)
Dimensions: wingspan 36.58m (120ft) length 39.42m (129ft 4in); height 11.07m (36ft 4in)
Weight: 87,544kg (193,000lb) maximum take-off weight
Payload: up to 110 passengers.

THE CV-880 WAS A smaller, lighter and faster competitor to the Boeing 707/720 and Douglas DC-8, although of generally similar configuration to both. However, only 65 examples were produced. This was due to the combination of

Convair's wrong reading of the market – the CV-880's size versus operating costs were unattractive – and Howard Hughes' (of Convair and TWA) manipulation of the early delivery slots.

Delta Air Lines acquired a fleet of 17 Convair CV-880s from new and operated the type between 1961 and 1974. Only 65 examples of the type were built in part as a result of high operating costs.

CONVAIR MODEL 30 CV-990 CORONADO

USA: 1961

The CV-990 pictured first saw service with American Airlines in 1963. Spantax acquired it in 1969 and retained it until the mid-1980s.

FACED WITH POOR SALES of the CV-880, Convair opted to produce an effective competitor by stretching the design and adding both speed and payload. The result was the first-generation turbofan-powered CV-990, later named Coronado by Swissair. But the design suffered aerodynamic problems and did not meet its specified performance. This meant an expensive retrofit programme for all 37 examples produced. Like its predecessor, the CV-990 suffered in terms of cabin layout and economics of operation. Specifications apply to CV-990A.

Crew: 4/5
Powerplant: four 73.40kN (16,500lb st) General Electric CJ805-23B turbofan engines
Performance: max cruising speed 1006km/h (625mph); range 6116km (3800 miles) with maximum payload;

service ceiling 12,495m (41,000ft)
Dimensions: wingspan 36.58m (120ft); length 42.49m (139ft 5in); height 12.04m (39ft 6in)
Weight: 115,668kg (255,000lb) maximum take-off weight
Payload: up to 149 passengers

CORNU HELICOPTERS

FRANCE: 1906–1907

IN 1906 PAUL CORNU BUILT and flew a scale model powered by a 1.4kW (2hp) engine. He then set to work building his 'flying bicycle', a tandem rotor design powered by an 18kW (24hp) Antoinette engine mounted in an open V-shaped framework, together with fuel tanks and the pilot's seat. The machine was fitted with paddle-shaped and

Near Lisieux on 13 November 1907 Cornu's 'flying bicycle' became the first machine to take off vertically with a pilot and make a free flight.

CTA (IPD) BF-1 BEIJA-FLOR ('HUMMING BIRD')

A two-seat light helicopter which owed its design origins to Prof. Heinrich Focke and was built by the Centro Technico de Aeronautica (CTA). It became the first helicopter to be designed, built, and flown in Brazil in 1959.

CUNLIFFE-OWEN CONCORDIA

The Cunliffe-Owen Concordia was a 10-seat, twin-piston engined, medium-range airliner designed in the UK in 1946. Two examples of the aircraft were built before lack of orders curtailed further work on the project.

CURTISS GOLDEN FLYER

The Golden Flyer, also called the Gold Bug, was the first aircraft built by US aviation pioneer Glenn H. Curtiss. Built in 1909, it was flown to victory by Curtiss to win the Scientific American prize by making a non-stop flight of 40km (25 miles) in July that year.

CURTISS A.1

In 1911, Glenn Curtiss demonstrated one of his early seaplanes, an amphibian, to the US Navy, who ordered a similar model under the designation A.1 (US Navy Airplane No.1).

CURTISS MODEL D

The Curtiss Model D, sometimes called the Triad, was a development of the Golden Flyer of 1909. It was the second aircraft to be delivered to the US Signal Corps.

CURTISS MODEL F

The Model F of 1912 was the first Curtiss hull-type flying-boat, and was the first aircraft to be fitted with the newly invented Sperry gyroscopic automatic pilot.

CURTISS HS-2L

More than 1000 HS-2L single-engined anti-submarine and escort flying-boats were built in 1917–18, and 40 were still in US Navy service in 1925.

CURTISS CR-1

The CR-1 racing biplane was built to compete for the 1921 Pulitzer Trophy, which it won at an average speed of 284.44km/h (176.75mph), piloted by Bert Acosta.

CURTISS CS SERIES

The Curtiss CS-1 torpedo-bomber appeared in 1923, and about 80 examples were delivered to the US Navy, mostly under the revised designation SC-1 and SC-2.

fabric-covered rotors mounted on large bicycle-type wheels, which were turned horizontally by a belt drive from the engine. On 13

November 1907, at Coquainvilliers near Lisieux, Cornu's flying bicycle became the first machine to take off vertically with a pilot and make

a free flight. It hovered for 20 seconds at a height of 0.3m (1ft). Cornu increased this to just over 1.82m (6ft) on subsequent flights.

Lack of funds and serious technical problems, not least with the transmission system, forced Cornu to abandon further development.

COUZINET ARC-EN-CIEL
FRANCE: 1929

Crew: 4
Powerplant: three 485kW (650hp) Hispano-Suiza 12Nb 12-cylinder V-type liquid-cooled engines
Performance: max speed 236km/h (147mph); range 6800km (4225 miles); service ceiling unknown
Dimensions: wingspan 30m (98ft 5.25in); length 16.15m (53ft); height 3.99m (13ft 1in)
Weight: 16,790kg (37,015lb)
Payload: 600kg (1322lb)

THE COUZINET 70 Arc-en-Ciel (Rainbow) was a three-engined commercial monoplane designed for the South Atlantic sector of the

France–South America route. First flown in 1929, the Arc-en-Ciel was modified in January 1933 and, as the Model 71, began a regular mail run to South America on 28 May 1934. From 24 July that year there was a regular monthly crossing. The Model 70 was derived from an earlier design, the Couzinet 10-01, which was also named Arc-en-Ciel. The Model 70 made a number of record-breaking pioneer flights.

The Couzinet Arc-en-Ciel made headlines through its pioneering transatlantic flights, which began in May 1934.

CURTISS JN-4
USA: 1916

The Curtiss JN-4 'Jenny' was built in the thousands during World War I, and many found their way into civil hands after the war.

THE FAMOUS CURTISS JN-4 'Jenny' was the result of a 1914 US Army specification calling for a biplane trainer with a tractor engine. By

the end of World War I, 7471 examples had been built, including 2041 of the basic JN-4, 781 JN-4As, 2765 JN-4Ds, 929 JN-4Hs and

1035 JN-6Hs. By the time production ceased, engine power had virtually doubled. The JN-4 saw operational service in 1916, supporting the US Expeditionary Force against the revolutionary army of Pancho Villa in Mexico. Specifications apply to the JN-4.

Crew: 2
Powerplant: one 67kW (90hp) Curtiss OX-5 8-cylinder V-type engine
Performance: max speed 121km/h (75mph); endurance 2 hrs 15 mins; service ceiling: 3353m (11,000ft)
Dimensions: wingspan 13.28m (43ft 7in); length 8.33m (27ft 4in); height 3.00m (9ft 10in)
Weight: 966kg (2130lb) loaded

CURTISS H.16
USA: 1917

Crew: 4
Powerplant: two 298kW (400hp) Liberty 12-cylinder V-type engines
Performance: max speed 153km/h (95mph); range 608km (378 miles);
Service ceiling: 3033m (9950ft)
Dimensions: wingspan 28.98m (95ft); length 14.06m (46ft 1in); height 5.40m (17ft 8in)
Weight: 4944kg (10,900lb)
Armament: 5–6 7.7mm (0.303in) machine guns; up to 417kg (920lb) of bombs

THE CURTISS H.16, the prototype of which appeared at the end of 1917, was the largest and most

effective American maritime reconnaissance flying boat of World War I. Heavily armed, and with a useful bomb load, the Curtiss H.16 was produced in substantial numbers; 150 were built by the Naval Aircraft Factory at Philadelphia, 77 of them for the US Navy with 298kW (400hp) Liberty 12 engines. A further 125 H.16s were ordered for the RNAS, but 50 were cancelled and another 50 placed in storage in the UK. The remaining 25, delivered from March 1918, saw service from British coastal bases during the closing months of the war.

The Curtiss H-16. was the largest, heaviest and certainly the most effective American reconnaissance flying boat produced during World War I.

CURTISS NC SERIES

USA: 1918

Crew: 4
Powerplant: four 298kW (400hp) Liberty 12A in-line engines
Performance: max speed 137km/h (85mph); endurance 14 hrs 45 mins; service ceiling 7600m (24,928ft)
Dimensions: span 38.40m (126ft); length 20.80m (68ft 3in); height 7.44m (24ft 5in)
Weight: 12,701kg (28,000lb)
Armament: none

IN 1917, GLENN H. CURTISS worked closely with the US Navy Board of Construction and Repair to produce an aircraft capable of carrying out extended Atlantic patrols to provide cover for American shipping against German U-boats. The first of the NC Types, the Curtiss NC-1, was a biplane with three tractor engines and a biplane tail mounted on twin booms; successive aircraft were numbered NC-2 to NC-4, these machines having four engines, but only the NC-1 was delivered before the end of World War I.

The NC-1 flew for the first time on 4 October 1918, and the NC-4 on 30 April 1919. In May 1919,

the NC-4 made the first crossing of the North Atlantic via the Azores, and is today preserved in the Smithsonian Institution.

Specifications apply to the NC-4.

The Curtiss NC-4 made the first aerial crossing of the Atlantic in May 1919, flying from Halifax, Nova Scotia, via the Azores to Lisbon, Portugal.

CURTISS PW-8

USA: 1922

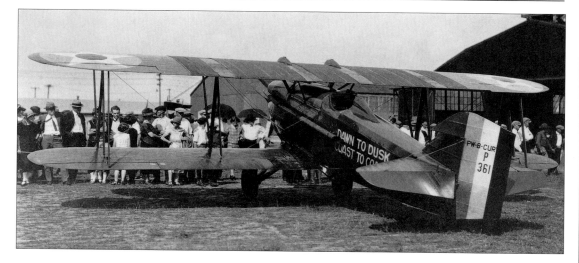

Crew: 1
Powerplant: one 325kW (435hp) Curtiss D-12 engine
Performance: max speed 275km/h (171mph); range 875km (544 miles); service ceiling 6206m (20,350ft)
Dimensions: wingspan 9.60m (31ft 6in); length 7.06m (23ft 2in); height 2.72m (8ft 11in)
Weight: 1429kg (3155lb) loaded
Armament: two 7.62mm (0.30in) machine guns

THE FIRST FIGHTER BASED on the new 325kW (435hp) Curtiss D-12 engine originated in 1922 as a private venture by Curtiss. The design was given the company designation of Model 33. Three prototypes were ordered by the US Army Air Service on 27 April 1923 under the designation PW-8. The first Curtiss PW-8 prototype was delivered to the US Army Air Service on 14 May 1923.

In June 1924, a Curtiss PW-8 made the first dawn-to-dusk crossing of the continental United States, flown by Lt Russell Maughan. It is pictured here in front of an admiring crowd.

On 23 June 1924, Lt Russell Maughan of the US Army Air Service completed a dawn-to-dusk transcontinental flight across the USA in one of these machines.

CURTISS MODEL 40 CARRIER PIGEON
A single-engined, single-seat biplane designed as a mail carrier, the Model 40 dates from 1925 and 10 were procured for operation by the US Post Office.

CURTISS R3C-1
On 12 October 1925, the Curtiss R3C-1 crushed all opposition in the Pulitzer Trophy race, winning with an average speed of 400.68km/h (248.957mph). The R3C-2 floatplane version set up a world seaplane record.

CURTISS O-1
The Curtiss O-1 was the winner of a US Army compeition of 1925 for a light observation aircraft. In total, 127 were delivered to the USAAC.

CURTISS F7C
First flown in February 1927, the Curtiss F7C was a single-seat carrier-based fighter. Seventeen production aircraft were ordered, deliveries beginning in 1928.

CURTISS F9C SPARROWHAWK
Originally intended for carrier-based operations, the Curtiss F9C of 1931 was modified as a parasite fighter to be launched and retrieved in flight by the airships USS AKRON and MACON.

CURTISS A-12 SHRIKE
A clumsy, low-wing monoplane and a contemporary of the Boeing P-26 fighter, the Curtiss A-12 Shrike was a typical USAAC assault aircraft of the 1930s and was designed to replace the Curtiss Falcon biplane. The prototype A-12 flew in 1931.

CURTISS FLEDGELING
A two-seat biplane trainer of 1932, the Curtiss Fledgeling was delivered to the US Navy as the N2C-1/2 (51 examples) and was operational throughout most of the 1930s.

CURTISS CONDOR I (MODEL 18) AND T32 (CONDOR II)
Essentially the Model 18 was a modified version of the twin-engined B-2 bomber/ biplane. The later T32 (and variants) was a complete redesign, although still a generally similar biplane. It was first flown in 1933 and carried up to 15 passengers; 45 were built.

CURTISS SOC-1 SEAGULL
First flown in 1934, the dependable Seagull floatplane observation aircraft served on every US capital ship and outlasted the SO3C-1 Seamew built to replace it.

CURTISS P-1/P-6 HAWK

USA: 1926

This Curtiss P-6E Hawk is on display in the USAF Museum. The P-6 was a modified version of the P-1, which in turn was developed from the Curtiss PW-8 fighter.

THE CURTISS P-1 STEMMED from the PW-8. Fifteen P-1s were ordered initially, their design being based on the XPW-8B, which had tapered upper and lower wings. The P-1 was the first of the famous Curtiss Hawk series of fighters, the USAAC acquiring 25 P-1As, 25 P-1Bs and 33 P-1Cs from 1924. In 1928, two Curtiss P-1 aircraft were modified and, designated XP-6 and XP-6A, took part in the National Air Races, the winner registering 323km/h (201mph). This achievement led the US Army to order 18 examples of a fighter

variant (nine YP-6s and nine P-6As). Successive modifications produced the P-6D and the final Hawk variant, the P-6E, 46 of which were delivered in 1932. The F6C was the naval version of the P-6, 75 being purchased by the US Navy.
Specifications apply to the P-6E.

Crew: 1
Powerplant: one 448kW (600hp) Curtiss V-1570-23 Conqueror in-line engine
Performance: max speed 319km/h (198mph); range 917km (570 miles); service ceiling 7530m (24,700ft)
Dimensions: wingspan 9.60m (31ft 6in); length 7.06m (23ft 2in); height 2.72m (8ft 11in)
Weight: 1539kg (3392lb) loaded
Armament: two fixed forward-firing 7.62mm (0.30in) machine guns

The Curtiss P-6E's success was attributable mainly to its prowess in the US National Air races, which the XP-6 won comfortably in 1928 with a speed of 323km/h (201mph).

CURTISS F8C

USA: 1928

Crew: 2
Powerplant: one 336kW (450hp) Pratt & Whitney R-1340-4 Wasp 9-cylinder radial engine
Performance: max speed 235km/h (146mph); range 1159km (720 miles); service ceiling 4953m (16,250ft)
Dimensions: wingspan 9.75m (32ft); length 7.82m (25ft 7.75in); height 3.12m (10ft 3in)
Weight: 1823kg (4020lb) loaded
Armament: three 7.62mm (0.30in) machine guns, one in rear cockpit; one 227kg (500lb) or two 53kg (116lb) bombs under fuselage

The Curtiss F8C was the result of a USMC requirement for a general-purpose aircraft.

IN 1927, THE US Marine Corps issued a requirement for a new fighter/attack/observation aircraft to replace the DH.4. Two prototypes were completed in 1928 as XF8C-1s, followed by four F8C-1 and 21 F8C-3 aircraft. In USMC service, they were later redesignated OC-1 and OC-2. Two other prototypes, the XF8C-2 and XF8C-4, appeared in 1929 as dive-bomber variants, and 27 of the latter were built for Navy and Marine Corps service. The last two F8C-4s were converted to F8C-5s by substituting a different model Wasp engine, and a further 61 F8C-5s (later O2C-1s) were delivered from 1931. Specifications apply to the Curtiss F8C-3.

CURTISS F11C-2 GOSHAWK

USA: 1932

THE CURTISS F11C-2 Goshawk flew for the first time on 25 March 1932, the first of 27 aircraft being delivered to the US Navy in the following year for service on the carrier USS *Saratoga*. The F11C-3 with a retractable undercarriage

followed. The US Navy received 28 examples of the F113-C in 1934, when the designations of both variants were changed to BFC-2 and BF2C-1 respectively, indicating a bombing capability. Specifications apply to the F11C-3.

Crew: 1
Powerplant: one 522kW (700hp) Wright R-1820-78 Cyclone 9-cylinder radial engine
Performance: max speed 319km/h (198mph); range 901km (560 miles); service ceiling 7407m (24,300ft)

Dimensions: wingspan 9.60m (31ft 6in); length 7.62m (25ft); height 3.23m (10ft 7in)
Weight: 2104kg (4638lb) loaded
Armament: two 7.62mm (0.30in) machine guns

CURTISS SBC HELLDIVER

USA: 1933

The second US Navy type to bear the name, the SBC Helldiver was the last fighting biplane produced in the United States.

THE CURTISS SBC was the second US naval aircraft to bear the name Helldiver; the first being the F8C dive-bomber of 1928. The SBC began as a high-wing monoplane design of 1933, the XF12C-1, and ended by becoming the last combat biplane to be built in the USA. A second prototype was built in biplane configuration; this was flown on 9 December 1935. Orders for 83 SBC-3s and 174 SBC-4s followed, and 50 of 90 aircraft produced to meet a French requirement were actually on their way to Europe when France was overrun, being abandoned at Martinique. Specifications apply to the SBC-4.

Crew: 2
Powerplant: one 709kW (950hp) Wright R-1820-34 Cyclone 9-cylinder radial engine
Performance: max speed 381km/h (273mph); range 950km (590 miles); service ceiling 8320m (27,300ft)

Dimensions: wingspan 10.36m (34ft); length 8.63m (28ft 4in); height 3.83m (12ft 7in)
Weight: 3462kg (7632lb) loaded
Armament: two 7.62mm (0.30in) machine guns; 454kg (1000lb) of bombs

CURTISS P-36

USA: 1935

ALTHOUGH NOT PARTICULARLY a success story, the Curtiss P-36 did have the distinction of being the USAAC's first 'modern' monoplane fighter. Designed as a private venture, the prototype flew in May 1935. Three YP-36 aircraft were ordered for evaluation, these being followed by 178 P-36A fighters, which entered service in 1938, and 31 P-36C fighters with two additional wing-mounted 7.62mm (0.30in) machine guns.

The type was exported as the Curtiss Hawk 75. The Hawk 75A featured a retractable undercarriage and other improvements; this version was ordered by France, which placed orders totalling 730, but deliveries were still incomplete when France was invaded in May 1940, and the remaining aircraft were diverted to the RAF, in the service of which the aircraft was known as the Mohawk.

Specifications apply to P-36C.

Crew: 1
Powerplant: one 895kW (1200hp) Pratt & Whitney R-1830-17 14-cylinder radial engine
Performance: max speed 500km/h (311mph); range 1320km (820 miles); service ceiling 10,270m (33,700ft)
Dimensions: wingspan 11.37m (37ft 3in); length 8.79m (28ft 10in); height 2.82m (9ft 3in)
Weight: 2726kg (6010lb)
Armament: one 12.7mm (0.50in) and three 7.62mm (0.30in) machine guns

These Curtiss P-36 fighters are pictured in pre-World War II USAAC camouflage. Pilots found the P-36 a pleasant and 'sporty' aircraft to fly, but as a combat aircraft it was soon outclassed by other contemporary types.

CURTISS P-40

THE CURTISS P-40 originated as a development of the radial-engined Curtiss P-36A Hawk. The prototype XP-40, which flew for the first time in October 1938, proved to be some 48km/h (30mph) faster than the P-36A, and although it lacked some of the latter aircraft's manoeuvrability the XP-40's handling characteristics were praised by the USAAC test pilots who flew it. On 27 April 1939, the USAAC awarded Curtiss-Wright a contract for 524 production P-40s, the largest order ever placed for an American fighter up to that time; this was subsequently scaled down to 200, all of which were delivered to the Air Corps by September 1940. France placed an order for 140 P-40s, but before these could be delivered France fell; the full order was taken over by the British Purchasing Commission on behalf of the RAF. Although considered unsuitable for operational use by Fighter Command, the P-40s were fitted with four wing-mounted Browning 7.7mm (0.303in) machine guns and allocated to Army Co-operation Command as the Tomahawk I.

Deliveries of P-40s to the USAAC resumed in February 1941, the armament now having

With an interested onlooker in the form of his pet monkey, a crewman paints a Japanese 'kill' marking on his pilot's P-40. The photograph was probably taken in Burma in 1942.

been brought up to the standard of the batch intended for France by the addition of four 7.7mm (0.303in) machine guns in the wings. An armoured windscreen and armour plating for the pilot

were also fitted. The modified aircraft was designated P-40B and 130 were delivered to the USAAC, together with 110 identical aircraft which went to the RAF as the Tomahawk IIA. The next P-40

variant was the P-40C, which was fitted with larger, self-sealing fuel tanks and two more wing guns. Of this variant, 193 went to the USAAF (as the USAAC had now become) and 930 to the RAF as

A Curtiss P-40F in flight. The F model was fitted with the Packard-Merlin engine, which was far superior to the original Allison powerplant.

the Tomahawk IIB, although 146 of these were diverted to the Soviet Union following the German invasion of June 1941 and another 100 went to the American Volunteer Group (AVG) operating in China. In all, 2430 P-40s were allocated to the Soviet Union in World War II, of which 2097 were actually delivered; many of the aircraft were lost in transit.

The RAF's Tomahawk IIBs performed sterling work in the tactical support role in the Western Desert. USAAF P-40Cs saw action with the 15th Pursuit Group, flying in defence of the Hawaiian Islands; the 24th Pursuit Group, operating first from the Philippines and later from northern Australia and New Guinea; and with the American Volunteer Group, the 'Flying Tigers', which began operations in December 1941.

The P-40D was substantially redesigned, its four wing guns being upgraded to 12.7mm (0.50in) calibre and the nose armament removed. Provision was also made for the carriage of bombs under the wings or fuselage. Only 22 P-40Ds went to the USAAF as the Hawk 87A Warhawk, but 560 were allocated to the RAF, which gave them the new name Kittyhawk I.

The USAAF preferred the P-40E, with six wing guns; it ordered 820 of this model, and another 1500 examples became Kittyhawk IAs. Installation of the much superior Packard-Merlin engine produced the Curtiss P-40F, of which 1311 were built, some being supplied to the Soviet Union and others to the Free French Air Force.

The RAF received 21 P-40Ks, 600 P-40Ms (Kittyhawk III) and 586 P-40Ns (Kittyhawk IV). US

production ended in December 1944, after 13,738 aircraft had been built. This total included 1300 P-40Ks (with increased fin area), 700 P-40Ls (with only four guns), and 4219 P-40Ns. The latter version had a 1015kW (1360hp) V-1710-81 engine.

Specifications apply to the Curtiss P-40N.

Crew: 1
Powerplant: one 1015kW (1360hp) Allison V-1710-81 V-12 engine
Performance: max speed 609km/h (378mph); range 386km (240 miles); service ceiling 11,580m (38,000ft)
Dimensions: wingspan 11.38m (37ft 4in); length 10.16m (33ft 4in); height 3.76m (12ft 4in)
Weight: 5171kg (11,400lb) loaded
Armament: six 12.7mm (0.50in) machine guns in the wings; bomb load of up to three 227kg (500lb) bombs

CURTISS SB2C HELLDIVER

USA: 1942

A Curtiss Helldiver preparing for launch from a US carrier in the Pacific. The Helldiver proved to be of immense value in the Pacific theatre, sinking a huge tonnage of Japanese shipping.

Crew: 2
Powerplant: one 1268kW (1700hp) Wright R-2600-8 Cyclone 14-cylinder radial engine
Performance: max speed 452km/h (281mph); range 2213km (1375 miles); service ceiling 7375m (24,200ft)
Dimensions: wingspan 15.15m (49ft 8in);

length 11.18m (36ft 8in); height 4.00m (13ft 1in)
Weight: 7626kg (16,812lb) loaded
Armament: four wing-mounted 12.7mm (0.50in) machine guns; two 7.62mm (0.30in) machine guns in rear cockpit; bomb load of up to 907kg (2000lb), or one torpedo in the lower fuselage weapons bay

THE SB2C HELLDIVER WAS designed as a replacement for the SBD Dauntless, a type that achieved fame in the Battle of Midway in June 1942. The first production Helldiver flew in the same month, entering service with the US Navy in December 1942 and making its operational debut on 11 November 1943 in an attack on the Japanese-held island of Rabaul. The SB2C-1 was followed in production by the SB2C-3,

featuring an uprated engine (the SB2C-2 was an abandoned floatplane version), and the SB2C-4, which had underwing bomb or rocket attachments and perforated

landing flaps. The SB2C-5 had extra fuel tankage, while the USAAF took delivery of 900 examples of a ground-attack version, the A-25A. The Helldiver was of such great

value in the Pacific theatre that the US Navy absorbed almost the entire production of more than 7000 aircraft. Specifications apply to the Curtiss SB2C-3 Helldiver.

CURTISS-WRIGHT CW-21 DEMON

USA: 1939

Crew: 1
Powerplant: one 746kW (1000hp) Wright R-1820-G5 9-cylinder radial engine
Performance: max speed 505km/h (314mph); range 1014km (630 miles); service ceiling 10,455m (34,300ft)
Dimensions: wingspan 10.67m (35ft); length 8.28m (27ft 2in); height 2.72m (8ft 11in)
Weight: 2041kg (4500lb) loaded
Armament: two 12.5mm (0.50in) and two 7.62mm (0.30in) machine guns in upper front fuselage

BASED ON AN EARLIER DESIGN, the CW-19R, the Curtiss-Wright CW-21 was developed in 1938 as a lightweight interceptor intended

mainly for export. The prototype flew in January 1939, and three production CW-21Bs were ordered for evaluation by the Chinese Air Force, but all three crashed due to faulty fuel on the final stage of their delivery flight and no further order was forthcoming. The Netherlands, however, were to take delivery of 25 aircraft for service in the East Indies, and these saw action against the invading Japanese in February 1942.

This photograph shows a Curtiss-Wright CW-21 Demon in the insignia of the Netherlands East Indies Air Arm.

CURTISS-WRIGHT XP-87 NIGHTHAWK

USA: 1948

DEVELOPED FROM AN EARLIER wartime project, the XA-43 attack aircraft, the XP-87 was the first multi-seat jet combat aircraft designed specifically for the radar intercept role at night. Provision was made for the proposed armament of four 20mm (0.79in) cannon to be installed in a remotely controlled nose turret, so that the angle of fire could be

varied, but this was never fitted. The XP-87 prototype flew for the first time on 5 March 1948, and work began on a second aircraft, which was intended to have two jet engines. The first aircraft was known as the Nighthawk, and the second as the Blackhawk. However, the project was cancelled in favour of the Northrop F-89 Scorpion. This had devastating

consequences for Curtiss-Wright, which was forced to shut down its Aeroplane Division. The XP-87 was its last design.

The Curtiss XP-67 Nighthawk was the first jet aircraft designed specifically to undertake the radar interception role at night. The XP-67 was the last design of the Curtiss Aircraft Corporation.

Crew: 2
Powerplant: four 1359kg (3000lb) thrust Westinghouse XJ34-WE-7 turbojet engines
Performance: max speed 941km/h (585mph); range 1609km (1000 miles); service ceiling 12,200m (40,025ft)
Dimensions: wingspan 18.30m (60ft); length 18.91m (62ft); height 6.10m (20ft)
Weight: 22,604kg (49,900lb) loaded
Armament (proposed): four 20mm (0.79in) cannon

DASSAULT OURAGAN

The Dassault Ouragan was France's first home-designed combat jet to see operational service. It was exported to India and Israel, in whose hands it proved very useful in the ground-attack role.

FOR THE FIRST FEW YEARS of its post-World War II existence, the French Air Force had to rely on foreign jet aircraft for its first-line equipment. Then, on 28 February 1949, Avions Marcel Dassault flew the prototype of a straightforward, no-frills jet fighter begun as a private venture in November 1947. Powered by a Rolls-Royce turbojet and built under licence by Hispano-Suiza, the Dassault MD.450 Ouragan (Hurricane) became the

first jet fighter of French design to be ordered in quantity, some 350 production aircraft being delivered to the French Air Force from 1952. It was exported to India, where it was known as the Toofani (Whirlwind), and to Israel, which received 75 examples. In the Middle East the Ouragan was inferior to the MiG-15, the principal jet-fighter type equipping the Egyptian Air Force at that time, but it performed well in the ground-attack role.

Crew: 1
Powerplant: one 2300kg (5070lb) thrust Hispano-Suiza Nene 104B turbojet
Performance: max speed 940km/h (584mph); range 1000km (620 miles); service ceiling 15,000m (49,210ft)
Dimensions: wingspan 13.20m (43ft 2in); length 10.74m (35ft 3in); height 4.15m (13ft 7in)
Weight: 7600kg (16,755lb) loaded
Armament: four 20mm (0.79in) cannon; up to 907kg (2000lb) of underwing ordnance

DASSAULT MYSTERE IIC

Crew: 1
Powerplant: one 3000kg (6613lb) thrust SNECMA Atar 101D3 turbojet
Performance: max speed 1060km/h (658mph); range 1200km (745 miles); service ceiling 13,000m (42,650ft)
Dimensons: wingspan 13.10m (42ft 9in); length 11.70m (38ft 6in); height 4.25m (13ft 11in)
Weight: 5250kg (11,574lb) loaded
Armament: two 30mm (1.18in) Hispano 603 cannon

THE DASSAULT MD 452 Mystere IIC first flew on 23 February 1951, and was a straightforward swept-wing development of Dassault's Ouragan. The French Air Force took delivery of 150 aircaft, and Israel had plans to purchase some in 1954–55; however, in view of the type's poor accident record – several of the earlier machines were lost through structural failure – the decision was made to

The Dassault Mystere IIC was a straightforward swept-wing development of the Ouragan. It was not particularly successful and had a poor accident record, several breaking up in mid-air.

buy the far more promising Mystere IV instead. In fact, even by the time the last IIC was being delivered to the French Air Force, it had been moved to a training role.

DASSAULT MYSTERE IV

THE DASSAULT MYSTERE IV was unquestionably one of the finest combat aircraft of its era. The prototype Mystere IVA flew for the first time on 28 September 1952, and early trials proved so promising that the French government placed an order for 325 production aircraft seven months later in April 1953. The fighter was also delivered to India, and Israel acquired the first of 60 in April 1956, the type replacing the Gloster Meteor F.8 in Israeli Air Force service.

Production of the Mystere IVA was completed in 1958, totalling 421 aircraft. The type was to see extensive action in the Arab–Israeli Six-Day war of 1967, and also in the Indo-Pakistan conflict of 1965.

Crew: 1
Powerplant: one 2850kg (6280lb) thrust Hispano-Suiza Tay/Verdon 250A turbojet
Performance: max speed 1120km/h (696mph); range 1320km (820 miles); service ceiling 13,716m (45,000ft)
Dimensions: wingspan 11.10m (36ft 5in); length 12.90m (42ft 2in); height 4.40m (14ft 5in)
Weight: 9500kg (20,950lb) loaded
Armament: two 30mm (1.18in) DEFA 551 cannon; up to 907kg (2000lb) of ordnance

The Dassault Mystere IV, seen here in prototype form, was a very successful jet fighter design.

DASSAULT MIRAGE III

Crew: 1
Powerplant: one 6200kg (13,668lb) thrust SNECMA Atar 9C turbojet engine
Performance: max speed 1390km/h (863mph); combat radius 1200km (745 miles); service ceiling 17,000m (55,755ft)

Dimensions: wingspan 8.22m (26ft 11in); length 16.50m (56ft); height 4.50m (14ft 9in)
Weight: 13,500kg (29,760lb) loaded
Armament: two 30mm (1.18in) DEFA cannon; provision for up to 3000kg (6612lb) of external ordnance, including special (i.e. nuclear) weapons

DEVELOPED FROM THE Mirage I of 1954, the Mirage III made its first flight on 17 November 1956 and exceeded Mach 1.5 in level flight on 30 January 1957. The French government instructed Dassault to proceed with a multi-mission

version, the Mirage IIIA, the prototype (Mirage IIIA-01) flying on 12 May 1958. In a test flight on 24 October 1958, this aircraft exceeded Mach 2 in level flight at 12,500m (41,010ft). A pre-series batch of 10 aircraft was built, powered by the SNECMA Atar 09B turbojet. The last six aircraft were equipped to production standard with the CSF Cyrano Ibis air-to-air radar. The Mirage IIIB was a two-seat version of the IIIA, with tandem seating under a one-piece canopy; the radar was deleted, but radio beacon equipment was fitted. Although intended primarily as a trainer, the IIIB could also be configured for strike sorties, and carried the same air-to-air armament as its predecessor. The prototype flew for the first time on 20 October 1959, followed by the first production model on 19 July 1962.

The Mirage IIIC, which flew on

9 October 1960, was identical to the IIIA, with an Atar 09B3 turbojet and a SEPR 841 or 844 auxiliary rocket motor. One hundred Mirage IIICs were ordered by the Armée de l'Air, equipping the 2e and 13e Escadres de Chasse. A further 72 similar aircraft, without rocket motors or missiles, were supplied to the Israeli Air Force, first deliveries being made to No 101 Squadron in 1963. These aircraft were designated Mirage IIICJ and saw considerable action during the subsequent Arab–Israeli wars. Sixteen more aircraft of the IIIC series were supplied to South Africa as Mirage IIICZs, deliveries beginning in December 1962 and the aircraft entering service with No 2 'Cheetah' Squadron at Waterkloof in April 1963. Over the next decade, these were supplemented by deliveries of Mirage IIIEZs, IIIDZs, IIID2Zs and IIIRZs.

The SAAF also took delivery of three Mirage IIIBZ two-seaters, which carried the same armament as the IIIC. During the mid-1970s, the SAAF's Mirage IIIs were gradually replaced by Mirage F1s; some of the later-model Mirage IIIs were rebuilt as the Atlas Cheetah.

The Mirage IIID was a two-seat version of the Mirage IIIO, which was manufactured under licence in Australia. The first of 16 ordered for the Mirage Operational Conversion Unit was assembled in Australia and delivered in November 1966. The Mirage IIIE was a long-range tactical strike variant, 453 examples being produced for the Armée de l'Air and further aircraft for export. The first of three prototypes flew on 5 April 1961, and the first production example was delivered in January 1964.

A Dassault Mirage IIICJ of No 101 Squadron, Israeli Air Force. Israel's Mirages gave a superb account of themselves in the Six-Day War of June 1967.

A Dassault Mirage IIIEZ of the South African Air Force. A re-engined version became the Atlas Cheetah.

A version of the IIIE, the IIIO, was manufactured under licence in Australia. The Royal Australian Air Force received 50 Mirage IIIO(F) interceptors, 50 Mirage IIIO(A) ground-attack aircraft and the 16 Mirage IIID two-seat trainers. All remaining Mirage IIIO(F)s were converted to IIIO(A) standard in 1976–70. The Mirage IIIEE (the second E denoting 'Espagne') came on to the Spanish Air Force's inventory in 1970, while the Mirage IIIP version for Pakistan saw action in 1971 against India. Another version of the Mirage IIIE was the IIIS, delivered to the Swiss Air Force. These remained in service for 35 years, eventually being replaced by the F-18 Hornet.

The Mirage IIIR was the reconnaissance version of the IIIE, equipped with a battery of five OMERA Type 31 cameras in place of the nose radar. In Argentine service, Mirages saw combat against the British Task Force in the Falklands War in 1982.

Specifications apply to the Mirage IIIE.

DASSAULT ETENDARD/SUPER ETENDARD

FRANCE: 1958

Crew: 1
Powerplant: one 5000kg (11,023lb) thrust SNECMA Atar 8K-50 turbojet
Performance: max speed 1180km/h (733mph); combat radius 850km (528 miles); service ceiling 13,700m (44,950ft)
Dimensions: wingspan 9.60m (31ft 6in); length 14.31m (46ft 11in); height 3.86m (12ft 8in)
Weight: 12,000kg (26,455lb) loaded
Armament: two 30mm (1.18in) DEFA cannon; provision for up to 2100kg (4630lb) of external ordnance; two Exocet ASMs; MATRA Magic AAMs

THE DASSAULT ETENDARD (standard) was originally designed to meet the requirements of a mid-1950s tactical strike-fighter contest, which it lost to the Fiat G.91. It showed such outstanding qualities that a development contract was awarded on behalf of the French Navy, which at that time was looking for a strike aircraft capable of high-altitude interception. The navalized prototype Etendard IVM-01 flew on 21 May 1958, powered by a SNECMA Atar 8B turbojet, and began service trials the following October. The first of 69 production Etendard IVMs was delivered to the Aéronavale on 18 January 1962, being followed into service

by the Etendard IVP, an unarmed reconnaissance/tanker variant.

The Dassault Super Etendard, which flew for the first time on 3 October 1975, was intended for the low-level attack role, primarily against shipping. Fourteen Super Etendards were supplied to Argentina from 1981, and the five that had been delivered at the time of the Falklands War of May–June 1982 were to prove highly effective against British vessels when armed with the Exocet ASM.

Specifications apply to the Dassault Super Etendard.

The Super Etendard, seen here in the colours of France's Aéronavale, was developed following the decision to abandon the naval version of the Jaguar.

DASSAULT BALZAC
The Balzac was an experimental VTOL aircraft with eight lift engines and a ninth for forward propulsion. It made its first tethered flight on 18 October 1962.

DASSAULT MD 320 HIRONDELLE
First flown in 1968, the Dassault MD 320 Hirondelle was a twin piston-engined light executive/ transport type only built in prototype form. It provided the design basis for the Falcon 10 small business jet.

DASSAULT MIRAGE 5
First flown in May 1967, the Dassault Mirage 5 was a ground-attack version of the Mirage IIIE, intended primarily for export.

DASSAULT MERCURE
This French short-haul 120- to 162-seat jet airliner first flew in 1971. The Mercure's weakness was its inferior range compared to competitors. Only 12 were built (including prototypes), 10 being delivered to Air Inter, which retired all examples by 1996.

DASSUALT MYSTERE/FALCON 10/100
Smallest of the twin-engined business jet family, first flown in 1971 and updated to include EFIS. Over 200 were sold.

DASSAULT MIRAGE G8
Two prototypes of a small, twin-engined variable-geometry aircraft, the Dassault Mirage G8, were ordered by the French government; the first flew on 8 May 1971 and reached Mach 2.03 four days later, but the type was not adopted.

DASSAULT MIRAGE 50
Also intended for export, the Dassault Mirage 50 was an improved version of the Mirage 5, powered by a SNECMA Atar 9K-50 turbojet giving a 16 per cent thrust increase.

DASSAULT MIRAGE 4000
First flown in 1979, the Dassault Mirage 4000 was a scaled-up version of the Mirage 2000, and it was originally known as the Delta Super Mirage. The project was abandoned.

DASSAULT MIRAGE IV

A Mirage IVP armed with an ASMP (Air-Sol Moyenne Portée) nuclear missile. The aircraft is using rocket-assisted take-off equipment.

IN 1956, THE FRENCH AIR MINISTRY issued a draft specification for a new supersonic bomber to carry France's first atomic bomb. Avions Marcel Dassault's scaled-up version of the Mirage III was accepted.

Designated Mirage IVA in its definitive form, the prototype Mirage IV-01 flew for the first time in June 1959; the first production aircraft entered service in 1964. It was withdrawn in the 1990s.

Crew: 2
Powerplant: two 7000kg (15,432lb) thrust SNECMA Atar 9K turbojets
Performance: max speed 2340km/h (1454mph); range 1240km (770 miles); service ceiling 20,000m (65,000ft)

Dimensions: wingspan 11.84m (38ft 10in); length 23.41m (76ft 10in); height 5.46m (17ft 8in)
Weight: 31,600kg (69,995lb)
Armament: up to 7257kg (16,000lb) of conventional or nuclear ordnance

DASSAULT FALCON/MYSTERE 20/200

Crew: 2
Powerplant: two 23.13kN (5200lb st) AlliedSignal (Garrett) ATF3-6A-4C turbofan engines
Performance: max cruising speed 870km/h (540mph); range 4650km (2889 miles) with eight passengers and maximum fuel; service ceiling 13,715m (45,000ft)
Dimensions: wingspan 16.32m (53ft 6.5in); length 17.15m (56ft 3in); height 5.32m (17ft 5in)
Weight: 14,515kg (32,000lb) maximum take-off weight
Payload: up to 14 passengers

DEVELOPED IN COOPERATION with Sud Aviation in the 1950s, the original title of this business jet was the Mystere 20, and it was

The Falcon 20/200 has been designated as the HU-25 by the US military and it is used in a number of roles, including search and rescue, coastal tracking/surveillance, target towing and electronic countermeasures.

aimed at the higher end of the market. In 1983 the design was updated to 200 series standard. Changes included the powerplant and extra fuel/range capability.

The Dassault Falcon 20/200 has also found a number of specialist military applications, notably as the HU-25A Guardian with the US Coastguard – other derivatives of

the type include the Interceptor and Guardian 2, among the total of nearly 700 aircraft sold.

Specifications apply to the Falcon/Mystere 200.

DASSAULT MIRAGE F.1 FRANCE: 1966

THE MIRAGE F.1 SINGLE-SEAT strike-fighter was developed as a private venture, the prototype flying for the first time on 23 December 1966. The first production aircraft entered service with the 30e Escadre of the French Air Force at Reims early in 1974. Variants produced included the F.1A ground-attack aircraft, the F.1C interceptor and the F.1B two-seat trainer. Its service was not, however, limited to France. Over

The Mirage F.1 was another French success story of the Cold War era, being used in both the interception and ground-attack roles. It was exported to a number of overseas air forces.

700 aircraft were sold to more than 11 countries. Export Mirage F.1s were distinguished by a suffix letter – for example the F.1CK for Kuwait. The Mirage F.1AZ was a version produced for South Africa.

Crew: 1
Powerplant: one 7200kg (15,873lb) thrust SNECMA Atar 9K-50 turbojet
Performance: max speed 2350km/h (1460mph); range 900km (560 miles); service ceiling 20,000m (65,615ft)
Dimensions: wingspan 8.40m (27ft 6in); length 15.00m (49ft 2in); height 4.50m (14ft 9in)
Weight: 15,200kg (33,510lb) loaded
Armament: two 30mm (1.18in) 553 DEFA cannon; up to 6300kg (13,889lb) of external stores

DASSAULT/DORNIER ALPHA JET FRANCE/GERMANY: 1973

Crew: 1
Powerplant: two 1350kg (2976lb) Turbomeca Larzac 04 turbofan engines
Performance: max speed 927km/h (576mph); range 583km (363 miles); service ceiling 14,000m (45,930ft)
Dimensions: wingspan 9.11m (29ft 10in); length 13.23m (43ft 5in); height 4.19m (13ft 9in)
Weight: 8000kg (17,637lb) loaded
Armament: one 27mm (1.06in) IWKA Mauser cannon; five hardpoints with provision for up to 2500kg (5511lb) of stores

THE FRANCO-GERMAN Alpha Jet was produced in two major versions, the Alpha Jet A (A for Appui, or Support) and the Alpha Jet E (E for Ecole, or School). It proved effective in both its strike and training roles. In February 1972 two prototypes each were ordered by France and Germany, and the type (the French-built

version) flew for the first time on 26 October 1973. The French Air Force was to take delivery of 176 aircraft between 1978 and 1985, while deliveries of the A model to the Luftwaffe began in 1979. Export customers for the Alpha Jet included Belgium, Cameroon, Cote d'Ivoire, Egypt, Morocco, Portugal, Qatar, Thailand and Togo.

This Dassault-Dornier Alpha Jet E carries the national markings of Togo, one of the many countries to have acquired this versatile aircraft.

5V·MBA

DASSAULT FALCON/MYSTERE 50, 900 AND 2000 SERIES

THE FALCON 50 WAS THE first of this long-range, tri-jet family, initially intended for trans-North-American operations. Over 300 examples have been sold. The 900 series dates from 1984 and has a larger cabin and uprated engines, widening its appeal with military derivatives, while the 900EX has transatlantic capability. The 900 series approaches 300 deliveries. The latest version – the Falcon 2000 – has reverted to the original two-engine format of the Falcon 20. It dates from 1993, and retains the cabin format of the 900 series whilst sacrificing range. Over 150 have been delivered. Specifications apply to Falcon/Mystere 900B.

Crew: 2/3
Powerplant: three 21.13kN (4750lb st) AlliedSignal (Garrett) TFE731-5BR-1C turbofan engines
Performance: max cruising speed 927km/h (575mph); range 7408km (4603 miles) with eight passengers; certificated ceiling 15,550m (51,000ft)
Dimensions: wingspan 19.33m (66ft 5in); length 20.21m (66ft 3.75in); height 7.55m (24ft 9in)
Weight: 20,640kg (45,503lb) maximum take-off weight
Payload: up to 19 passengers

The Falcon 900 pictured here is a little larger than the earlier 50 series. It has the same capacity, but a far greater range.

DASSAULT MIRAGE 2000

Crew: 1
Powerplant: one 9700kg (21,384lb) thrust SNECMA M53-P2 turbofan engine
Performance: max speed 2338km/h (1453mph); range 1480km (920 miles); service ceiling 18,000m (59,055ft)
Dimensions: wingspan 9.13m (29ft 11in); length 14.36m (47ft 1in); height 5.20m (17ft)
Weight: 17,000kg (37,480lb) loaded
Armament: two 30mm (1.18in) DEFA 554 cannon; provision for up to 6300kg (13,885lb) of external stores

THE MIRAGE 2000, THE first of the Mirage family to take advantage of 'fly-by-wire' technology, was designed as an interceptor to replace the Mirage F.1. A single-seater flew for the first time at Istres on 10 March 1978, while the two-seat version, the Mirage 2000B (the fifth prototype) first flew on 11 October 1980.

The first production Mirage 2000C-1 made its inaugural flight on schedule on 20 November

The potent Dassault Mirage 2000 was the first of the Mirage family to use fly-by-wire technology. The Mirage 2000 carries a formidable war load and saw combat in Iraq.

1982, and the first production two-seat Mirage 2000B flew on 7 October 1983. The Mirage 2000N, first flown on 2 February 1983, was developed as a replacement for the Mirage IIIE and is armed with the ASMP medium-range

nuclear missile. Seventy-five production aircraft were delivered from 1987. Like its predecessors, the Mirage 2000 has been the subject of substantial export orders from countries such as Abu Dhabi, Egypt, Greece, India and Peru. In its service with the Indian Air Force the aircraft, designated the Mirage 2000H, is known as the Vajra (Thunderstreak).

Specification refers to the Mirage 2000C.

DASSAULT RAFALE

FRANCE: 1986

The Dassault Rafale is the result of France's decision to 'go it alone' in producing an advanced multi-role aircraft for the French armed forces.

Crew: 1
Powerplant: two 7450kg (16,424lb) SNECMA M88-2 turbofan engines
Performance: max speed 2130km/h (1324mph); combat radius 1854km (1151 miles); service ceiling classified
Dimensions: wingspan 10.90m (35ft 9in); length 15.30m (50ft 2in); height 5.34m (17ft 6in)
Weight: 19,500kg (42,990lb) loaded
Armament: one 30mm (1.18in) DEFA 791B cannon; up to 6000kg (13,228lb) of external stores

THE DASSAULT RAFALE (Squall) is produced in three versions, the Rafale-C single-seat multi-role aircraft for the French Air Force, the two-seat Rafale-B, and the navalized Rafale-M. Employing the latest technological innovation, including cutting-edge electronics systems and the use of composite materials to reduce radar profile, the type possesses a great plus in its agility. In the strike role, the

Rafale can carry one Aérospatiale ASMP stand-off nuclear bomb. France, which plans to have 140 Rafales in air force service by 2015 (in 2002 orders stood at 60 aircraft for the Air Force; and 24 Rafale M for the Navy), sees the aircraft as vital to the defence of her territory. There was no Rafale prototype as such, but a technology demonstrator, known as Rafale-A, flew for the first time on 4 July 1986.

DE HAVILLAND DH.60 MOTH

UK: 1925

Crew: 1
Powerplant: one de Havilland Gipsy I in-line piston engine rated at 75kW (100hp)
Performance: max speed 164km/h (102mph) at sea level; range 515km (320 miles); service ceiling 4420m (14,500ft)
Dimensions: wingspan 9.14m (30ft); length 7.29m (23ft 11in); height 2.68m (8ft 9.5in)
Weight: 748kg (1650lb) maximum take-off weight
Payload: One passenger

THE MOTH SERIES PERHAPS best characterizes the golden era of private and club flying that occurred in Britain during the interwar years. The success of the initial DH.60 Moth, powered by the Cirrus I engine, led to unprecedented orders, exports and overseas licence builds of the type, which was also of interest to the RAF and its sponsored flying clubs. Only obsolescence of the

original engine was an issue. This was solved by the original designer developing a new one for de Havilland, called the Gipsy. Consequently the aeroplane was named Gipsy Moth, which went on to win the 1928 King's Cup Air Race. Other examples achieved distance records, including Amy Johnson's 1930 Croydon–Darwin flight. Specifications apply to the DH.60G Gipsy Moth.

The Gipsy Moth pictured is a DH.60M, which differed from earlier marques in having a welded steel tube airframe (rather than the earlier wood) and it remained airworthy until 1996, when it was retired to static display.

DE HAVILLAND DH.15 GAZELLE

The DH.15 Gazelle was basically a DH.9 airframe modified as an engine test-bed. It underwent extensive trials of the 373kW (500hp) Galloway Atlantic engine in 1919–20.

DE HAVILLAND DH.16

An early post-World War I design based on the DH.9A, the de Havilland DH.16 was capable of carrying four passengers. Nine examples were built.

DE HAVILLAND (AIRCO) DH.18

The de Havilland DH.18 was the first of its lineage designed for commercial use and was a single-engined biplane, capable of carrying eight passengers. The aircraft was first flown in 1920.

DE HAVILLAND DH.34

This single-engined biplane dating from 1921 could carry up to nine passengers. The DH.34 was also more powerful and economic than its predecessors.

DE HAVILLAND DH.29 DONCASTER

The DH.29 Doncaster was a long-range research aircraft built on behalf of the Air Ministry Research Department and was first flown in July 1921. Only two examples were built.

DE HAVILLAND DH.37

The DH.37 two-seat biplane was the first de Havilland product aimed at the private ownership market, and first flew in 1922. Two examples were produced, one of which was converted to a racer.

DE HAVILLAND DH.27 DERBY

A long-range heavy day-bomber, the single-engined de Havilland Derby was the first military aircraft designed by the new de Havilland Company. Two prototypes were built, the first flying in 1922, but no production was undertaken.

DE HAVILLAND DH.52

This high-wing, single-seat glider dates from 1922. Only two aircraft of this type were built.

DE HAVILLAND DH.66 HERCULES

Crew: 2
Powerplant: three Bristol Jupiter VI radial piston engines each rated at 313kW (420hp)
Performance: max speed 206km/h (128mph) at optimum altitude; range 845km (525 miles); cruising speed 177km/h (110mph) at optimum altitude; initial climb rate 233m (765ft) per minute; service ceiling 3960m (13,000ft)
Dimensions: wingspan 24.23m (79ft 6in); length 16.92m (55ft 6in); height 5.56m (18ft 3in)
Weight: 7076kg (15,600lb) maximum take-off weight
Payload: seven passengers and mail, rising to 14 passengers and very little mail

DESIGNED TO AN Imperial Airways requirement initially to take over Middle East and Indian sub-continent mail/passenger services from the Royal Air Force, the DH.66 Hercules entered service in 1926, featuring three engines and a triple fin arrangement. Early models had an open cockpit, but this was later enclosed on most builds.

The Hercules was to become an important feature of Empire communications, serving as postal

The DH.66 pictured is one of seven delivered to Imperial Airways starting in 1927. These differed from those built for Western Australian Airways in having a tail wheel rather than a tail skid.

and freight transport, and indeed four examples of the 11 built were delivered to West Australia Airways as extended versions

capable of carrying 14 passengers. These aircraft had a tail wheel instead of a skid. Imperial Airways' purchases included some

replacements due to fleet attrition, but the Hercules continued in scheduled operation until 1935 and thereafter until mid-World War II.

DE HAVILLAND TIGER MOTH

rather than fabric and stringers, and provision for an instrument training hood over the rear cockpit. By the end of World War II, 7290 Tiger Moths had been produced in Britain, and large numbers of aircraft were sold on the civil market as war-surplus stock.

This classic aircraft was also licence-built in Canada, New Zealand, Australia, Portugal, Norway and Sweden, bringing total production to 8700. Tiger Moths continued to serve as basic trainers in the RAF until being replaced by the Percival Prentice and de Havilland Chipmunk in the late 1940s, and the aircraft continues to inspire devotees today.

Crew: 2
Powerplant: one 97kW (130hp) de Havilland Gipsy Major in-line engine
Performance: max speed 167km/h (104mph); range 483km (300 miles); service ceiling 4145m (13,600ft)
Dimensions: wingspan 8.94m (29ft 4in); length 7.29m (23ft 11in); height 2.69m (8ft 10in)
Weight: 828kg (1825lb) loaded
Armament: none

PROBABLY THE MOST FAMOUS, and certainly one of the most attractive, basic training aircraft of all time, the DH.82A Tiger Moth was to fly for the first time on 26 October 1931, and it went into large-scale

production almost immediately, mostly for the Royal Air Force. The majority of Tiger Moths were built to Air Ministry Specification T.26/33 as Tiger Moth Mk IIs, with a rear fuselage decking in plywood

The aircraft in which thousands of RAF and Commonwealth pilots learnt to fly, the de Havilland Tiger Moth is one of the most famous basic trainers of all time – and certainly one of the most attractive.

DE HAVILLAND DH.86

USA: 1934

Crew: 2
Powerplant: four 149kW (200hp) de Havilland Gipsy Six inverted in-line piston engines
Performance: max speed 267km/h (166mph); range 1287km (800 miles); service ceiling 5305m (17,400ft)
Dimensions: wingspan 19.66m (64ft 6in); length 14.05m (46ft 1in); height 3.96m (13ft)
Weight: 4649kg (10,250lb) maximum take-off weight
Payload: up to 10 passengers

THIS FIRST FOUR-ENGINED de Havilland airliner was designed to meet Qantas's need for an airliner to ply the Australia–Singapore route network. The DH.86 was an enclosed cabin biplane taken up by a number of other British and empire airlines in two differing

cockpit/crew configurations – a two-pilot version and a single-pilot with navigator/wireless operator. Only 32 examples were built. Specifications apply to the DH.86B.

Pictured is one of the six Qantas Imperial Airways DH.86s, which were used on the airline's routes to empire destinations such as Singapore.

DE HAVILLAND DH.89 DRAGON RAPIDE AND DOMINIE

UK: 1934

Crew: 1/2
Powerplant: two de Havilland Gipsy Queen inverted in-line piston engines each rated at 149kW (200hp)
Performance: max speed 241km/h (150mph) at optimum altitude; range 837km (520 miles); service ceiling 4875m (16,000ft)
Dimensions: wingspan 14.63m (48ft); length 10.52m (34ft 6in); height 3.12m (10ft 3in)
Weight: 2722kg (6000lb) maximum take-off weight
Payload: up to eight passengers

THE DE HAVILLAND DRAGON RAPIDE is the definitive model of this series based on the company's earlier DH.84, but the larger part of the 730 built were DH.89Bs for British and Empire military use. Initially (in the mid- to late 1930s), however, the Dragon Rapide was much sought after by short-haul airlines because of its enclosed cabin, reliability and economy.

During World War II the duties of the Dominie, the other model of the series, included reconnaissance (for which it was lightly armed) and wireless training, and small numbers went to overseas military customers. After World War II, however, large numbers became available for commercial use. British European Airways retired its last example from Scilly Isles services in 1960. Nevertheless, small numbers of the aircraft remain airworthy to date in private and commercial ownership.

Specifications apply to the DH.89A Dragon Rapide Mk 4.

British European Airways was a post-war operator of the Rapide. It was popular with a wide variety of scheduled, charter and air taxi/club operators, particularly as the 450-plus built for the RAF became available.

DE HAVILLAND DH.91 ALBATROSS

UK: 1937

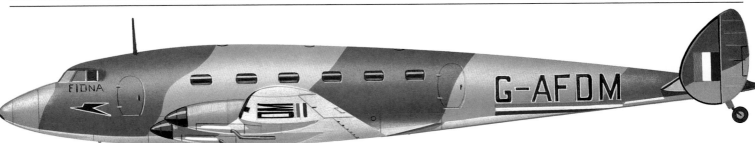

Crew: 4
Powerplant: four 391kW (525hp) de Havilland Gipsy Twelve 1 inverted-V piston engines
Performance: max speed 362km/h (225mph); range 1674km (1040miles); cruising speed 338km/h (210mph); service ceiling 5455m (17,900ft)
Dimensions: wingspan 32.00m (105ft); length 21.79m (71ft 6in); height 6.78m (22ft 3in)
Weight: 13,381kg (29,500lb) maximum take-off weight
Payload: up to 22 passengers

ONLY SEVEN EXAMPLES OF this all-wooden frame pre-World War II airliner were produced. The Albatross was originally designed to an Air Ministry specification for a transatlantic mail plane. Imperial Airways, however, also procured five for European services where the Albatross broke several service speed records. But this clean design

Two DH.91s were taken over by the RAF to provide services to Iceland, but both were damaged beyond repair on landing.

was less popular with passengers, who disliked the vibration and (comparative) lack of legroom.

The Albatross represents what the British industry might have

gone on to achieve without World War II's intervention; however, it also provided the design/proving basis for the important wartime Mosquito fighter-bomber. All seven Albatrosses were either written off or retired (some after military use) by 1943. Specifications apply to the DH.91 Albatross (passenger version).

DE HAVILLAND DH.95 FLAMINGO

UK: 1938

Crew: 3
Powerplant: two 694kW (930hp) Bristol Perseus XVI radial piston engines
Performance: max speed 385km/h (239mph); range 1947km (1210 miles); service ceiling 6370m (20,900ft)
Dimensions: wingspan 21.34m (70ft); length 15.72m (51ft 7in); height 4.65m (15ft 3in)
Weight: 7983kg (17,600lb) maximum take-off weight
Payload: up to 20 passengers

THIS SHORT-HAUL AIRLINER was de Havilland's first with an all-metal stressed skin, but World War II interfered with orders and develop-ment, and only 16 were built. Production of the Hertfordshire troop-carrying variant was cancelled.

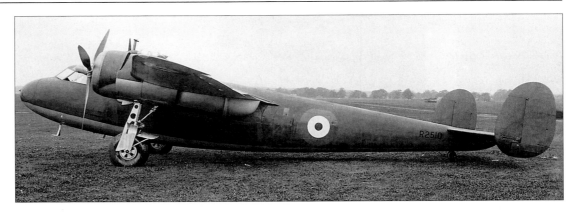

During wartime the Flamingo saw service with both BOAC and the British military – an example was assigned to the King's Flight for

the eventuality of the Royal Family's evacuation. One Flamingo survived World War II and saw commercial service until 1954.

A number of DH.95s were put into wartime RAF service, including two that had been operated by Guernsey and Jersey Airlines.

DE HAVILLAND DH.98 MOSQUITO

UK: 1940

THE ALL-WOOD DE HAVILLAND DH.98 Mosquito was, without doubt, one of the most versatile and successful aircraft of World War II. Offical interest in the Mosquito was slow to awaken, but in March 1940 the Air Ministry issued Spec-ification B.1/40, covering the building of three prototypes – one fighter, one light bomber and one photo-reconnaissance (PR) – and an initial production batch of 50 aircraft. The first prototype flew on 25 November 1940.

The PR Mosquito was the first into service, being issued to No 1 Photographic Reconnaissance Unit at RAF Benson, Oxfordshire, in September 1941. The first operational sortie was flown on 20 September. Mosquito B.IV bombers went to No 105 Squadron at Marham, Norfolk, in May 1942, and began their operational sorties on the 31st. Five aircraft were sent to Cologne to photograph the damage caused by the previous night's 1000-bomber raid and to

drop a few bombs of their own. One Mosquito was hit by flak and crashed in the North Sea. Total production of the B.IV, which eventually equipped 12 squadrons, was 273 aircraft.

The Mosquito NF.Mk II night-fighter prototype was completed with Airborne Interception (AI) Mk IV radar in a 'solid' nose and a powerful armament of four 20mm (0.79in) cannon and four machine guns. The first Mosquito night-fighter squadron, No 157, was

formed at Debden in Essex on 13 December 1941. Ninety-seven Mk II night-fighters were later converted to NF.Mk XII standard, followed by 270 NF.Mk XIIIs, the production counterpart of the Mk.XII. These and subsequent night-fighter Mosquitoes retained only the 20mm (0.79in) cannon armament. Other specialist night-fighter Mosquitoes were the Mks XV and XVII, 100 of which were converted from Mk IIs and the NF.Mk XIX. The latter aircraft,

Without doubt one of the most famous combat aircraft ever, the Mosquito – de Havilland's 'wooden wonder' – saw action in every combat role during World War II and remained in service for several years afterwards.

and the Mk XVII, were equipped with the US-made AI.Mk X.

The major Mosquito production version, the FB.MkVI, flew for the first time in February 1943. The standard NF.II gun armament was retained, and the aircraft could carry two 113 or 227kg (250 or 500lb) bombs in the rear of the bomb bay, with two additional bombs or auxiliary fuel tanks beneath the outer wing sections.

In the late spring of 1943, trials were carried out on Mk VI HJ719 equipped with rocket projectiles (RPs). These were to prove very successful, and RAF Coastal Command began equipping some of its strike wings with Mk VI Mosquitoes armed with eight 27kg (60lb) rocket projectiles under each wing. The Mosquito Mk VI entered service with No 418 Squadron in the spring of 1943 and subsequently armed several squadrons of No 2 Group, replacing such aircraft as the Lockheed Ventura. These squadrons carried

out some daring low-level precision attacks during the last year of World War II, including the raid on Amiens prison in February 1944 and attacks on Gestapo headquarters buildings in Norway and the Low Countries.

The Mosquito FB.Mk XVIII (27 built) carried eight rockets and two 227kg (500lb) bombs, and was armed with a single 57mm (2.24in) gun in the nose. Known as the Mosquito 'Tsetse', this variant was used by only two squadrons, Nos 248 and 254. The first high-altitude bomber version was the B.IX (54 built), and this was followed by 387 examples of the B.XVI, fitted with a pressurized cabin. Its successor was the B.35, which did not become operational before the end of the war. The photo-reconnaissance equivalents were the PR.IX, XVI and 34.

The last night-fighter variant was the NF.30, which was similar to the Mk XIX, but with improved Merlins. Canadian Mosquito

production ran to 1134 aircraft. Specification refers to the de Havilland Mosquito FB.Mk VI.

Crew: 2
Powerplant: two 1104kW (1480hp) Rolls-Royce Merlin 21 or 23 12-cylinder V-type engines
Performance: max speed 595km/h (370mph); range 2744km (1705 miles); service ceiling 10,515m (34,500ft)
Dimensions: wingspan 16.51m (54ft 2in); length 13.08m (42ft 11in); height 5.31m (17ft 5in)
Weight: 9072kg (20,000lb)
Armament: four 20mm (0.79in) fixed forward-firing cannon and four 7.7mm (0.303in) fixed forward-firing machine guns in the nose; an internal and external load of bombs, rockets or drop tanks up to 907kg (2000lb)

A de Havilland Mosquito B.IV of No 105 Squadron, RAF Marham, in 1942.

DE HAVILLAND DH.71
Two examples of this single-engined, low-wing monoplane, high-speed research light aircraft were built and flown in 1927 and went on to be involved in probing both speed and height records.

DE HAVILLAND DH.61 GIANT MOTH
Another of de Havilland's series of single-engined biplanes, the DH.61 Giant Moth first flew in 1927. Up to eight passengers could be carried and nine examples were built, one of which served as a flying office for the *Daily Mail* newspaper.

DE HAVILLAND DH.75 HAWK MOTH
A high-wing monoplane design with accommodation for four persons, the single-engined de Havilland DH.75 Hawk Moth first flew in 1928.

DE HAVILLAND DH.67 (GLOSTER AS.31)
The de Havilland DH.67 was a twin-engined biplane designed for photographic and survey work. Two DH.67s were built by Gloster as the AS.31, and the first was flown in 1929.

DE HAVILLAND DH.77
A single-engined, low-wing monoplane fighter with a single seat, the de Havilland DH.77 was produced in prototype form only and first flown in 1929.

DE HAVILLAND DH.80 PUSS MOTH
A high-wing cabin monoplane, the DH.80 Puss Moth first flew in September 1929. Although the aircraft's early career was marred by a series of accidents, it went on to set many records.

DE HAVILLAND DH.83 FOX MOTH
Designed as a low-cost transport aircraft, the de Havilland DH.83 Fox Moth had a high degree of commonality with the famous Tiger Moth. This single-engined biplane carried three passengers in an enclosed cabin. Ninety-eight examples were built in the UK, and over 50 more were built in Canada following the end of World War II.

DE HAVILLAND DH.100 VAMPIRE

UK: 1943

This illustration shows a Vampire FB.5 of No 112 Squadron, 2nd Allied Tactical Air Force, Germany.

Crew: 1
Powerplant: one 1420kg (3100lb) thrust de Havilland Goblin 2 turbojet engine
Performance: max speed 882km/h (548mph); range 1960km (1220 miles); service ceiling 13,410m (44,000ft)
Dimensions: wingspan 11.58m (38ft); length 9.37m (30ft 9in); height 2.69m (8ft 10in)
Weight: 5600kg (12,345lb) loaded
Armament: four 20mm (0.79in) British Hispano cannon; up to 907kg (2000lb) of bombs or rockets

THE VAMPIRE PROTOTYPE first flew on 20 September 1943; deliveries of production Vampire F.1s began in 1946. The Vampire Mk 2 was a Mk 1 airframe fitted with a Rolls-Royce Nene turbojet and did not enter service, only three being built. It was followed by the Vampire F.3, a long-range version with extra internal fuel, underwing tanks and a de Havilland Goblin 2 turbojet. The first Vampire variant specifically developed for ground attack was the FB.5. The Vampire FB.9 was a tropicalized version of the FB.5, while the NF.10 was a night-fighter. Navalized versions of the Mk1 were produced as the Sea Vampire F.20 and F.21. The T.11 was a two-seat trainer. The Vampire was widely exported and licence-built abroad; one of the biggest overseas users was France, which produced the Nene-engined Vampire Mk 53 as the Mistral.

Specification refers to the de Havilland Vampire FB.5.

DE HAVILLAND (CANADA) CHIPMUNK

CANADA: 1946

Crew: 2
Powerplant: one de Havilland Gipsy Major 8 4-cylinder in-line engine
Performance: max speed 222km/h (138mph); range 480km (300 miles); service ceiling 4880m (16,000ft)
Dimensions: wingspan 10.46m (34ft 4in); length 7.82m (25ft 8in); height 2.16m (7.1ft)
Weight: 907kg (2000lb) loaded

ORIGINALLY DESIGNED BY de Havilland (Canada), the Chipmunk T.10 was developed by the parent company to meet RAF basic

The Chipmunk T.10 assumed the RAF's basic training role in the late 1940s and served for many years until it was replaced by the Bulldog.

training requirements, which the aicraft fulfilled until the Chipmunk was replaced by the Scottish Aviation Bulldog in the 1970s.

Canadian production came to 218 examples, and a further 1014 aircraft were built in the UK, the UK aircraft comprising military T.10s and civilian Mk 21s. Sixty were built under licence in Portugal and large numbers of ex-RAF machines were subsequently civilianised as Mks 22 or 22A. Canadian-built Chipmunks carried the designation T.30.

DE HAVILLAND (CANADA) DHC-2 BEAVER AND TURBO BEAVER

CANADA: 1947

THE RUGGED HIGH-WING Beaver was designed in 1946 and it became the ultimate STOL bush aeroplane design of its day. The design criteria were influenced by the requirements of Canadian government agencies, but ultimately the US military purchased 980 of the 1600 plus built, and designated it the U-6 (formerly L-20A).

The Beaver was also adapted as a float plane, amphibious float plane, ski plane, as well as the standard tail-wheel mode. A few later examples were built with Pratt & Whitney Canada PT6A turboprop engines; others have since been converted. Production ended in the mid-1960s, but many former US and British military

A Beaver is seen in a role well suited to its rugged construction – serving businesses and communities in the frontier areas of Canada and Alaska.

examples have joined existing civil Beavers in North America, where large numbers are used to service remote areas. Specifications apply to the DHC-2 Beaver I.

Crew: 1
Powerplant: one Pratt & Whitney R-985-AN-14B/-16B Wasp Junior radial piston engine rated at 336kW (450hp)
Performance: max speed 262km/h (163mph) at 1525m (5000ft); range 1278km (794 miles); service ceiling 5485m (18,000ft)
Dimensions: wingspan 14.63m (48ft); length 9.22m (30ft 3in); height 2.74m (9ft)
Weight: 2313kg (5100lb) maximum take-off weight
Payload: up to eight people or 680kg (1500lb) of freight

DE HAVILLAND DH.112 VENOM

UK: 1949

The de Havilland Venom night fighter filled a gap in the UK's night defences until the deployment of more advanced aircraft such as the Gloster Javelin. It appeared in two versions, the NF2 and NF3 (seen here).

THE PROTOTYPE DE HAVILLAND Venom, developed from the twin-boom Vampire, first flew on 2 September 1949. Series production began with the FB.1, of which 373 were built. The definitive version, the FB.4, flew in December 1953; 150 were supplied to the RAF, 250 were licence-built in Switzerland and others were exported to Iraq and Venezuela. The NF.2 and NF.3, night-fighter variants, appeared in 1950 and 1953, respectively. Sweden acquired 62 NF.51s between 1952 and 1957, these being designated J.33 in Swedish Air Force service. The type was produced for the Royal Navy as the Sea Venom FAW 20, FAW 21 and FAW 22, 256 being built. Sea Venoms were also built under licence in France as the Aquilon (North Wind). RAF and Royal Navy Venoms and Sea Venoms saw action during the Suez campaign of 1956.

Specifications apply to the FB.4.

Crew: 1
Powerplant: one 2336kg (5150lb) de Havilland Ghost 105 turbojet
Performance: max speed 1030km/h (640mph); range 1730km (1075 miles); service ceiling 14,630m (48,000ft)
Dimensions: wingspan 12.70m (41ft 8in); length 9.71m (31ft 10in); height 1.88m (6ft 2in)
Weights: 6945kg (15,310lb) loaded
Armament: four 20mm (0.79in) British Hispano cannon; two 454kg (1000lb) bombs or eight 27.2kg (60lb) rockets

DE HAVILLAND DH.72
A night-bomber design, the DH.72 was built in prototype form only and first flown in 1931.

DE HAVILLAND DH.84 DRAGON
First of the Dragon series of biplanes, and first flown in 1932, the two-engined DH.84 was a short-haul airliner carrying up to eight passengers. A total of 202 were built in the UK and Australia for civil and military use.

DE HAVILLAND DH.85 LEOPARD MOTH
A similar-looking successor to the DH.80 Puss Moth, but with a wooden rather than steel tube frame, the DH.85 Leopard Moth first flew in 1933 and won the King's Cup air race that same year. In all, 132 examples were built.

DE HAVILLAND DH.87 HORNET MOTH
A single-engined touring biplane with an enclosed cabin first flown in 1934. It was aimed at the comfort end of the touring market, and 165 examples were produced.

DE HAVILLAND DH.88 COMET
This twin-engined, low-wing monoplane was designed to compete in the 1934 Victorian Centenary air race (Mildenhall to Melbourne) and two of the three examples entered achieved distinctions. A further two examples were built.

DE HAVILLAND DH.82B QUEEN BEE
The DH.82B Queen Bee, first flown in January 1935, was a radio-controlled target aircraft externally similar to a Tiger Moth. It was designed to be catapulted from a vessel.

DE HAVILLAND DH.90 DRAGONFLY
Visually similar to the DH.89 Dragon Rapide, the Dragonfly was substantially different in terms of base materials and process of manufacture. The Dragonfly offered superior range, but inferior performance to the Dragon Rapide.

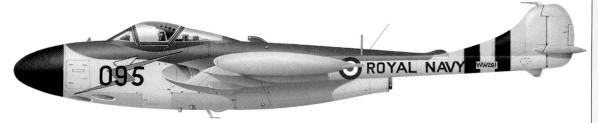

The de Havilland Sea Venom was an important addition to the Royal Navy's striking power during the 1950s, and saw action during the Anglo-French operations at Suez in 1956.

DE HAVILLAND DH.106 COMET

Middle East Airlines operated a fleet of four Comet 4Cs, three of which were destroyed on the ground at Beirut by an Israeli commando raid in 1968.

THE NEED FOR A jet-powered mail plane/airliner was identified by the famous Brabazon Committee that sat during wartime, tasked with identifying post–World War II British commercial aviation requirements. This produced Specification IV, to which de Havilland initially responded in 1944.

With the end of the war in 1945, de Havilland was able to turn its full attention to the design of the Comet 1 passenger airliner, which first flew on 27 July 1949 piloted by John Cunningham. During the intervening period the emphasis had shifted from mail carriage to passenger airliner. At this stage the Comet was three to five years ahead of alternative American and Russian designs, embodying some leading-edge technology, including an all-metal stressed skin (bonded using the redux metal-to-metal bonding method pioneered on earlier de Havilland designs), a much greater level of cabin pressurization, high-pressure refuelling and hydraulic-powered flight controls.

The Comet 1 was powered by four de Havilland Ghost MK50-1 turbojet engines built and blended into the wing root in pairs either side of the fuselage.

After an extensive flight test programme by prototypes, the first production standard Comet 1 was delivered to BOAC in January 1951. Early examples were used on freight services to conduct trials and route proving until 2 May 1952, when BOAC operated

The RAF operated Comet 2s and Comet C.4s (a derivative of the commercial 4C). Here a Comet 2 is pictured in front of a trio of C.4s.

the world's first fare-paying jet airliner service from London to Johannesburg (with stops).

Export orders were received for the Comet 1 (1A) from UTA, Air France, Canadian Pacific and the Royal Canadian Air Force, with potentially many more to follow. On 2 May 1953, however, a BOAC Comet 1 was the first of several to suffer a catastrophic failure when it crashed shortly after take-off from Calcutta. As a result of subsequent seemingly inexplicable losses, the Comet was grounded. The Air Ministry along with de Havilland then undertook a vast, expensive and exhaustive investigation, which included the use of pressurized Comet airframes on soak test. This eventually resulted in the total failure of one airframe due to stress cracking around the cornering of a rectangular cabin window.

These investigations were of immense use to the entire aircraft industry, which was now able to counter stress cracking/cornering on pressurized jet transports by designing out rectangular apertures and surfaces. Yet the loss of prestige, resource and confidence effectively eradicated Britain's lead in passenger aviation and

wiped out the incipient Comet 2's commercial prospects – most of the 16 built were used for research or by the RAF as unpressurized transports.

Despite this, de Havilland proceeded to launch the stretched Comet 4, with a revised airframe design and powered by four Rolls-Royce Avon engines. It first flew on 27 April 1958, shortly ahead of the Boeing 707. The launch customer was BOAC, which ordered 19, and two more variants were introduced – the further stretched/clipped-wing Comet 4B for shorter/European sectors and the Comet 4C which retained the 4B's stretch while reverting to the original Comet 4's wing with its distinctive fuel tanks.

Both BEA and Olympic Airways were customers for the Comet 4B, while the Comet 4 and 4C were exported in modest numbers to airlines such as Aerolineas Argentinas, Sudan Airways, Malaysian Airways and Kuwait Airways. Seventy-six Comet 4 series airframes were built out of a total of 114 Comets of all marques.

The Comet 4 was no match for larger versions of the Boeing 707 and DC-8. Consequently it was

retired relatively early by frontline operators, but it found a second career with charter operators BEA Airtours and Dan Air from the mid-1960s. Dan Air purchased a total of 48 second-hand Comet 4s of all variants and became the last regular operator when it acquired the RAF Transport Command's five Comet 4Cs in 1975. Dan Air ceased Comet operations in 1980, but one example remained operational as a testbed with the RAE until 1997.

Specifications apply to the DH.106 Comet 4.

Crew: 3

Powerplant: four Rolls-Royce Avon 524 turbojet engines each rated at 46.71kN (10,500lb)

Performance: cruising speed 809km/h (503mph) at 7620m (25,000ft); range 5190km (3225 miles) with maximum payload; service ceiling 12,800m (42,000ft)

Dimensions: wingspan 35.00m (114ft 10in); length 33.99m (111ft 6in); height 8.99m (29ft 6in); wing area 197.04m² (2,121.00sq ft)

Weight: 73,482kg (162,000lb) maximum take-off weight

Payload: up to 84 people in a mixed passenger class, or 119 five abreast in single-class charter layout

---

DE HAVILLAND DH.110 SEA VIXEN   UK: 1957

THE DE HAVILLAND SEA VIXEN originated in the DH.110, which had been in competition with the Gloster Javelin for an RAF all-weather fighter requirement, but suffered a catastrophic breakup at

the 1952 Farnborough air display. In 1956, the surviving DH.110 prototype underwent carrier trials, and the first fully navalized machine, with folding wings, flew on 20 March 1957. Known initially

A de Havilland Sea Vixen FAW.2 of No 899 Squadron, Fleet Air Arm, launching a salvo of 50mm (2in) unguided air-to-air rockets. The Sea Vixen could carry 124 of these missiles in underwing pods.

DE HAVILLAND DH.93 DON
Designed as a multi-role trainer for liaison and gunnery activities, this single-engined cabin monoplane (circa 1937) suffered design and weight problems and was not fully utilized. Thirty examples of the DH.93 Don were fully deployed on communications duties.

DE HAVILLAND DH.94 MOTH MINOR
This single-engined monoplane was designed as a light touring aircraft and first flown in 1937. Seventy-one examples were produced in the UK prior to World War II, and further examples were built in Australia for the RAAF.

DE HAVILLAND DH.103 HORNET/SEA HORNET
First flown in July 1944, the de Havilland Hornet fighter-bomber was the fastest twin-piston-engined aircraft to serve with any air arm. It equipped several RAF squadrons post-war. The Sea Hornet was the navalized version.

DE HAVILLAND DH.104 DOVE
Produced from the requirement for a post-war feeder-liner, this twin-piston-engined monoplane first flew in 1945. Over 540 variants of this 11-seat design were produced up until 1967.

DE HAVILLAND DH.108
The de Havilland DH.108 was claimed as the first turbojet-powered aircraft in the world to exceed Mach 1. It was designed for research into swept-wing behaviour and three aircraft were built, the first flying on 15 May 1946. Two examples were destroyed in accidents.

DE HAVILLAND (AUSTRALIA) DHA-3 DROVER
The triple-piston-engined DHA-3 Drover was designed with the Australian Flying Doctor Service in mind and first flew in 1948. Twenty Drovers were manufactured up until 1953. Other customers included Australia's international carrier Qantas. The Royal Flying Doctor Service retired its last example in 1970.

by the designation FAW.20, the aircraft was later named Sea Vixen and re-designated FAW.Mk 1. In 1961, two FAW.Mk 1s received extra fuel tanks in forward extensions of the tail booms, and these served as the prototype FAW.Mk 2, which was issued to squadrons in 1965. Total Sea Vixen production was 120 Mk 1s and 30 Mk 2s, with 67 Mk 1s being brought up to Mk 2 standard.

Crew: 2
Powerplant: two 5094kg (11,230lb) thrust Rolls-Royce Avon 208 turbojets
Performance: max speed 1110km/h (690mph); range 965km (600 miles); service ceiling 14,630m (48,000ft)

Dimensions: wingspan 15.54m (51ft); length 17.02m (55ft 7in); height 3.28m (10ft 9in)
Weight: 18,858kg (41,575lb) loaded
Armament: four Firestreak or Red Top AAMs; Bullpup ASMs on underwing pylons

DE HAVILLAND CANADA DHC-4 CARIBOU

CANADA: 1958

Crew: 2
Powerplant: two 1081kW (1450hp) Pratt & Whitney R-2000-7M2 piston engines
Performance: max cruising speed 348km/h (216mph); range 389km (242 miles) with maximum payload; service ceiling 7560m (24,800ft)
Dimensions: wingspan 29.15m (95ft 7.5in); length 22.12m (72ft 8in); height 9.68m (31ft 9in)
Weight: 12,927kg (28,500lb) maximum take-off weight
Payload: up to 32 troops or 3964kg (8740lb) of freight

DESIGNED AS A TRANSPORT of DC-3 volume and ruggedness, with an STOL capability, the de Havilland Caribou was taken up by both the Canadian and the United States militaries. Production of the type continued until 1973, with 307 examples of the aircraft seeing service in a number of conflicts and emergencies. Many examples were later acquired by other governments/militaries, aid/relief agencies and cargo operators, where the advantages of the type's rear cargo door and STOL capabilities continue to be exploited.

Specifications apply to the DHC-4A Caribou.

The STOL qualities of the Caribou, along with its ability to operate from unprepared airstrips, made it popular with many armed forces the world over. This is a Swedish example.

DE HAVILLAND CANADA DHC-6 TWIN OTTER

CANADA: 1965

The Twin Otter has been used in large numbers in North America in landplane, float and ski derivatives, often serving communities subject to extreme weather or those in remote or water-bound locations.

Crew: 3
Powerplant: two 429kW (575hp) Pratt & Whitney R-1860 Hornet radial piston engines
Performance: max speed 206km/h (128mph); range 1609km (1000 miles); service ceiling 3430m (11,250ft)
Dimensions: wingspan 30.48m (100ft); length 18.80m (61ft 8in); height 4.76m (15ft 8in)
Weight: 7983kg (17,600lb) maximum take-off weight
Payload: up to 22 passengers

THE STOL AND UNPAVED runway capabilities of this high-wing commuter airliner have made the DHC-6 Twin Otter popular with airlines and operators which face restrictive environments, to the extent that it has been exported to more than 75 countries worldwide, working in conditions ranging from ice to desert. The Twin Otter was produced for more than 20 years until 1988, by which time 844 had been built for civil and military customers. Its military customers include the Canadian Air Force (designation CC-138) and the US military (designation V-18 and UV-18). Specifications apply to the de Havilland (Canada) DHC-6 Series 300 Twin Otter.

DEWOITINE D.27   FRANCE: 1929

Crew: 1
Powerplant: one 373kW (500hp) Hispano-Suiza 12Mc 12-cylinder liquid-cooled Vee-type engine
Performance: max speed 312km/h (194mph); range 600km (373 miles); service ceiling 9200m (30,185ft)
Dimensions: wingspan 9.80m (32ft 2in); length 6.50m (21ft 4in); height 2.79m (9ft)
Weight: 1382kg (3046lb)
Armament: two 7.62mm (0.30in) machine guns

THE DEWOITINE D.27 WAS one of a long series of fighter monoplanes which stemmed from the Dewoitine D.21. Although not adopted by the French Air Force, the aircraft was to serve as the standard single-seat fighter type with the Swiss Fliegertruppe, which ordered 60 licence-built examples in 1929. In 1932, with a new Gnome-Rhone Mistral radial engine as its

A restored and privately owned Dewoitine D.27 in Swiss markings seen at the Wycombe Air Park in Buckinghamshire, England.

powerplant, the basic design was redesignated D.37, and as the D.371 it was produced for the French and Lithuanian Air Forces.

The D.372 had a more powerful engine, and the D.373 was a shipboard version which served aboard the carrier *Bearn* in 1937.

DEWOITINE D.500/510   FRANCE: 1932

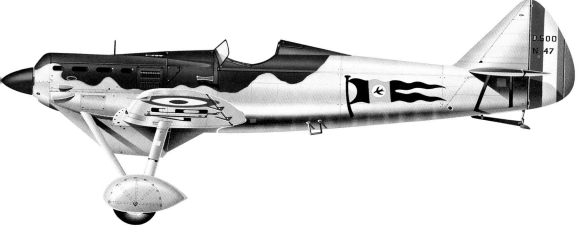

FRANCE'S FIRST CANTILEVER low-wing monoplanes were those of the graceful all-metal Dewoitine D.500 series, the prototype of which first flew on 18 June 1932. Development progressed to the D.510, which flew in August 1934 and which went on to achieve considerable success. In addition to serving with the Armée de l'Air, the type was widely exported, and Chinese D.510s saw action against the Japanese in the summer of

A Dewoitine D.500 of the 2eme Escadrille de Chasse, Armée de l'Air, 1938.

1938. France received 99 D.500s, 143 D.501s (which differed only in having no propeller spinner) and 88 D.510s. The D.510 was an upgraded version with a more powerful engine and a cannon firing through the propeller shaft.

Specifications apply to the Dewoitine D.510.

Crew: 1
Powerplant: one 514kW (690hp) Hispano-Suiza 12Kbrs 12-cylinder liquid-cooled Vee-type engine
Performance: max speed 359km/h (223mph); range 860km (535 miles); service ceiling 10,200m (33,465ft)
Dimensions: wingspan 12.00m (39ft 4in); length 7.74m (25ft 5in); height 2.38m (7ft 10in)
Weight: 1710kg (3770lb) loaded
Armament: two 7.5mm (0.29in) machine guns; one 20mm (0.79in) cannon

DE HAVILLAND DH.114 HERON
A stretched, four-engined feeder liner derived from the DH.104 Dove. the de Havilland DH.114 Heron could carry up to 17 passengers. Fewer than 150 were manufactured. Production of the type ended in 1963.

DE HAVILLAND DHC-3 OTTER
Following the success of the DHC-2 Beaver, de Havilland Canada launched the larger DHC-3 Otter, which seats up to 14 passengers. The Otter first flew in 1951 and 460 were built for civil and military customers with wheels or floats.

DE HAVILLAND (HAWKER SIDDELEY) DOMINIE
The RAF's Dominie navigational crew trainer was developed from the DH.125 executive jet, which first flew in 1962.

DE HAVILLAND (CANADA) DHC-5 BUFFALO
A successor development of the earlier DHC-4 Caribou STOL military transport aircraft, the de Havilland (Canada) DHC-5 Buffalo dates from 1964 and is powered by turboprop engines.

DE MARCAY C-1
The de Marcay C-1 was a French biplane fighter prototype, flown in 1919. The design used a SPAD XIII fuselage married to new sesquiplane wings.

DE PISCHOF NO 1
Constructed of wood and bamboo with a fabric covering, the de Pischof tractor biplane No 1 of 1907 was powered by an Anzano three-cylinder radial engine. It proved a failure.

DE SCHELDE S.21
The de Schelde S.21 was a twin-boom 'pusher' fighter which was under construction in Holland when the Germans invaded in May 1940, during World War II. It was never completed.

Dewoitine D.520

FRANCE: 1938

Crew: 1
Powerplant: one 694kW (930hp) Hispano-Suiza 12Y-45 12-cylinder Vee-type engine
Performance: max speed 540km/h (336mph); range 1540km (957 miles); service ceiling 11,000m (36,090ft)
Dimensions: wingspan 10.20m (33ft 5in); length 8.76m (28ft 8in); height 2.56m (8ft 5in)
Weight: 2790kg (6151lb) loaded
Armament: one HS 404 20mm (0.79in) fixed forward-firing cannon in the nose; four 7.5mm (0.29in) machine guns in wing leading edges

THE DEWOITINE D.520 WAS without doubt the best of France's home-produced fighters at the time of the German invasion in May 1940. It originated as a private venture, design work starting in 1936, and the first prototype flew on 2 October 1938. An initial order for 200 was placed in April 1939, and the eventual total on order up to April 1940 was 2200 for the Armée de l'Air and 120 for the Aéronavale. When the Germans struck in the west on 10 May 1940

only 36 D.520s had been delivered, and these were operational with GC I/3. Four more groupes de chasse and three naval escadrilles rearmed with the type before

France's surrender, but only GC I/3, II/7, II/6 and the naval AC 1 saw any action. The D.520 groupes claimed 114 victories and 39 probables; 85 D.520s were lost.

The Dewoitine D.520 was the best fighter available to the French in May 1940, but comparatively few were issued to the Armée de l'Air before the armistice.

DFS 230

GERMANY: 1937

THE DFS (DEUTSCHES FORSCHUNGSINSTITUT FUR SEGELFLUG) 240 was Germany's principal troop-carrying assault glider for a substantial part of World War II. It carried out some notable operations, particularly the assault on the Belgian fortress of Eben Emael on 10 May 1940, when a glider-borne party of combat engineers landed on its roof. DFS 230s also played a prominent part in the assault on Crete in May 1941. Perhaps the most daring operation involved the rescue of Italian dictator Benito Mussolini by German special forces, who landed in 12 gliders – each fitted with braking rockets in the nose – on a plateau near the hotel where he was being held prisoner. He was flown out by Fieseler Storch.

Crew: 1 pilot plus 8 troops
Performance: max diving speed 290km/h (180mph); max towing speed 210km/h (130mph)
Dimensions: wingspan 20.87m (68ft 5.5in); length 11.24m (36ft 10.5in); height 2.74m (9ft)
Weight: 2100kg (4630lb) loaded

The DFS 230 assault glider played a prominent part in the invasion of Belgium in May 1940, and in the airborne assault on Crete two years later. It could be fitted with braking rockets in the nose.

DFS 346

GERMANY/FORMER USSR: 1946

Crew: 1
Powerplant: two 2000kg (4408lb) thrust Walter HWK 109-409B rocket motors
Performance: max speed 2125km/h (1320mph); absolute ceiling 35,000m (114,828ft)
Dimensions: wingspan 8.9m (29ft 2in); length 11.65m (38ft 3.5in); height 3.5m (11ft 6in)
Weight: unknown
Armament: none

THE DFS 346 WAS THE culmination of various DFS projects relating to high-altitude rocket-powered aircraft. Work on the DFS 346 was started in November 1944 by the Siebel company, but little progress had been made before the end of the war. The project was completed by the Russians, and in 1946 the DFS 346, flown by former Siebel test pilot Wolfgang Ziese, was carried to altitude under the wing of a B-29 Superfortress (one of several that had force-landed in the USSR) and released. Under rocket power, the aircraft is said to have reached 1100km/h (683mph). Two other improved examples were built by the Russians, one of which is claimed to have exceeded Mach One before breaking up.

DOBLHOFF/WNF-342

AUSTRIA: 1943

LATE IN 1939 FRIEDRICH VON DOBLHOFF, an engineer working in the German-controlled Wiener Neustadt Flugzeugwerke in Vienna, made several rough designs for a helicopter using jet drive at the rotor tips. The German Air Ministry was sufficiently interested in the project to build a test rig for a demonstration of the proposed rotor-drive principle. The whole assembly lifted several feet until it crashed, but the officials were impressed and Doblhoff was awarded more funds and facilities. With the German Navy in mind, the prototype WNF-342V-1 was tailored for submarines or surface vessels. Preliminary flight-testing began in 1943 until Allied bombing began to take its toll and a second prototype was built near Vienna. The third prototype revealed vibration problems, which literally shook the machine to pieces on the ground, while prototype No 4 differed in having two seats fitted with side-by-side open cockpits. The V-4 was accepted by the advancing Americans and later Doblhoff joined McDonnell Aircraft, where his considerable experience was used in the development of the XV-1 convertiplane. His two principal colleagues also joined foreign companies: Theodor Laufer joined SNCA du Sud-Ouest in France, and A. Stephan went to work for Fairey Aviation in Britain.
Specifications apply to Doblhoff/WNF 342 V4.

Crew: 1
Powerplant: one 104kW (140hp) BMW-Bramo Sh.14A radial piston engine
Performance: max speed 48km/h (30mph)
Dimensions: rotor diameter 10.00m (32ft 9.75in)
Weight: 430kg (948lb)

DORNIER DO X

SWITZERLAND: 1929

THE ALL-METAL CONSTRUCTION Do X was designed to combine the level of comfort and service of a cruise liner with the speed of a flying boat. The largest aircraft of its day, it required 12 engines mounted in six tractor/pusher pairs mounted atop the wing. The cabin had three decks, complete with sleeper cabins and kitchens. The first aircraft carried 169 people on one occasion; however, its one transatlantic flight in 1930 was dogged by problems and delays, after which it became a research aircraft. Two other Do X examples were acquired by the Italian Air Force, which equipped them with Fiat engines and operated them experimentally. Specifications apply to the Do X.

The prototype Do X was destroyed in Berlin during a World War II air raid, having been placed on display in a museum there.

Crew: 5
Powerplant: 12 477kW (640hp) Curtiss V-1570 Conqueror Vee piston engines
Performance: max cruising speed 210km/h (130mph); range 2200km (1367 miles). service ceiling 1250m (4100ft)
Dimensions: wingspan 48.00m (157ft 5.75in); length 40.00m (131ft 4in); height 10.10m (33ft 1.5in)
Weight: 56,000kg (123,459lb) maximum take-off weight
Payload: up to 100 passengers

DELANNE 20T
Flown in 1937, the Delanne 20T was a tandem-wing two-seat research prototype. Building of a fighter derivative, the Arsenal-Delanne 10C-2, had just begun when France was overrun by the Germans in 1940.

DEL MAR DH-2 WHIRLYMITE/DH-2A WHIRLYMITE SCOUT
An ultra-light helicopter trainer which first flew in California on 15 June 1960, this type was powered by a 42kW (56hp) Kiekhaefer Mercury piston engine. The DH-2A first flew in May 1963.

DEL MAR DH2-C TARGET DRONE
A low-cost destructible target for use in the development of anti-helicopter missiles and for training, the Del Mar DHs-C Target Drone was cancelled in 1969.

DEPERDUSSIN MONOCOQUE
The Deperdussin Monocoque was a three-float seaplane and the only French aircraft to gain the Schneider Trophy, winning the inaugural race in 1912.

DEPERDUSSIN TT
A frail monoplane, the Deperdussin TT equipped two escadrilles of France's Aviation Militaire at the outbreak of World War I. Its operational life was short.

DEWOITINE D.1 AND D.9
A parasol-wing monoplane fighter, the Dewoitine D.1 first flew in November 1922. Its main customer was Italy, where 126 examples were built. The French Navy used 30 modified as carrier aircraft. The Dewoitine D.9, with a redesigned tail, was also used by the Italians.

DEWOITINE D.332
The Dewoitine D.332 commercial transport flew in 1933 and was followed by the Dewoitine D.333, which had its first flight in 1935. Both of these aircraft were used in limited numbers by Air France, and two of the total of three D.333s produced were flown in Spain.

DORNIER DO J, DO R, DO 15 WAL AND SUPER WAL

Crew: 2

Powerplant: two BMW VI Vee piston engines each rated at 559kW (750hp)

Performance: max speed 220km/h (137mph) at sea level; range 2200km (1367 miles); service ceiling 3000m (9845ft)

Dimensions: wingspan 23.20m (76ft 1.5in); length 18.30m (60ft 0.5in); height 5.35m (17ft 6.6in)

Weight: 8000kg (17,637lb) maximum take-off weight

Armament/Payload: one 7.92mm (0.31in) MG 15 trainable forward-firing machine gun in the bow; one 7.92mm (0.31in) MG 15 trainable rearward-firing machine gun in each of the two staggered side-by-side dorsal positions; up to 200kg (440lb) of bombs carried in hard points under the wing; four seats on the commercial passenger version

THE DORNIER WAL (WHALE) SERIES encompasses a wide range of two-engined flying-boats built to German design, but often abroad under licence (due to Versailles treaty limitations) from 1922 to 1935, and applied to civil and military roles. The originating Do J was itself a development from World War I types, but the later enclosed cabin versions of 1934 (Do R) were capable of carrying 21 passengers and mail on transatlantic services. Numerous engine types were utilized. Exploits of the

type included a round-the-world flight in 1932 and two examples supported Roald Amundsen's 1926 North Pole expedition. Re-supply for transatlantic operations – such as to South America – was provided

The Wal was produced in a number of countries to overcome the restrictions of the treaty of Versailles, including Italy, Spain, Netherlands, Japan and later Germany itself – amounting to a total of around 300.

from specialist depot ships. The Wal's success can be judged by the fact that over 300 were built and it was responsible for opening up air services to many new destinations, such as the Canary Islands. It also

saw service with Spanish Nationalist and German armed forces (as the Militar Wal 33). The Wal was re-designated Do 15 in the mid-1930s. Specifications apply to the Do 15 Wal (military-Wal 33).

DORNIER DO 17

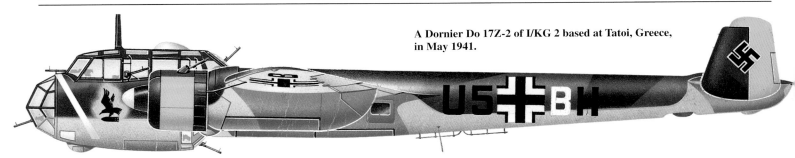

A Dornier Do 17Z-2 of I/KG 2 based at Tatoi, Greece, in May 1941.

POPULARLY KNOWN AS THE 'Flying Pencil' because of its long, slim fuselage, the Dornier Do 17 was widely used in both bomber and reconnaissance roles in the early part of World War II. It was originally intended as a fast mail plane for Deutsche Lufthansa, but was never used in that capacity. The first of 12 prototypes flew in 1934 and the first military examples, the Do 17E-1 and Do 17F-1, entered service in 1939.

These were intended for the high-speed bomber and long-range reconnaissance roles respectively, the latter having extra fuel tankage and two Rb 50/30 or Rb 75/30 bomb-bay cameras. The aircraft were powered by two BMW VI 12-cylinder V-type engines and were evaluated in combat during the Spanish Civil War. Development of the Do 17E/F led to the Do 17M/P medium bomber/reconnaissance types with Bramo 323 radial

engines. These were followed by 18 Do 17S/U pre-production types, which preceded the introduction of the definitive radial-engined variant, the Do 17Z, more than 500 of which were built.

The type was to play a very important part in the German invasion of Poland, which began with an attack on the Dirschau railway bridge by a squadron of Do 17Zs from III/KG 3 on 1 September 1939. Although faster

than most contemporary fighters when it entered service, the Do 17 quickly became obsolete and suffered heavy losses in the battles of France and Britain. The Do 17's defensive armament was poor, and was upgraded as a result of losses suffered in these campaigns, particularly in the Battle of Britain. The Do 17K was an export version for Yugoslavia, where the type was built under licence; some were later handed over to the

Croatian Air Force. The Do 215 was another export version, 100 examples of which were taken over by the Luftwaffe early in World War II. Some of these aircraft were modified for photographic reconnaissance, and in May–June 1941 mapped large areas of the western Soviet Union prior to the German invasion.

The Do 17's glazed nose area was subjected to several changes during the aircraft's career, the Dornier Do 17Z bomber series

having the most extensive glazing. An inflatable life raft was carried in the housing between the cockpit and the gun position. Concentrating all the crew members in a relatively small area simplified escape procedures. The original civil version of the Do 17 featured a single fin and rudder. Three aircraft were to be built with this configuration before twin fins were adopted for the military variant.

Specification applies to the Dornier Do 17P.

Crew: 4/5
Powerplant: two 746kW (1000hp) BMW Bramo 323P Fafnir 9-cylinder radial engines
Performance: max speed 410km/h (255mph); range 1500km (932 miles); service ceiling 8200m (26,905ft)
Dimensions: wingspan 18.00m (59ft); length 15.80m (51ft 10in); height 4.60m (15ft 1in)
Weight: 8590kg (18,937lb) loaded
Armament: one or two 7.92mm (0.31in) trainable machine guns in the windscreen, nose, dorsal and ventral positions; internal bomb load of 1000kg (2205lb)

This Dornier Do 17E-1 is painted in 'enemy' markings for the Luftwaffe war games that took place in 1938. This picture gives a good indication of why the type was nicknamed the 'Flying Pencil'.

DORNIER DO 18

GERMANY: 1935

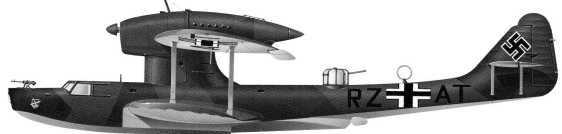

Crew: 4
Powerplant: two 656kW (880hp) Junkers Jumo 205D 6-cylinder diesel engines
Performance: max speed 267km/h (166mph); range 3500km (2175 miles); service ceiling 4200m (13,780ft)
Dimensions: wingspan 23.70m (77ft 9.25in); length 19.37m (63ft 7in); height 5.32m (17ft 5.5in)
Weight: 10,800kg (23,809lb) loaded
Armament: one 20mm (0.79in) cannon in dorsal turret; one 13mm (0.51in) machine gun in bow; external bomb load of 100kg (220lb)

This Do 18 belongs to 6 Seenotstaffel and features the midships upper gun turret of the later variants.

THE DORNIER DO 18 WAS designed to fulfil the dual roles of medium-range maritime reconnaissance aircraft and flying-boat mail plane.

The first of four prototypes flew in March 1935. Only six civil flying boats were completed, the majority of the 148 production aircraft being earmarked for military service by the Germans from 1938. Principal military variants were the Do 18D, the Do 18G (with improved armament and provision for rocket-assisted take-off units) and the Do 18H trainer. Many Do 18Gs were converted to Do 18N air–sea rescue aircraft. The Do 18 was often seen flying over the North Sea and English Channel, especially during the Battle of Britain.

DORNIER DO 24 GERMANY: 1937

Crew: variable
Powerplant: three 746kW (1000hp) Bramo BMW-Bramo Fafnir radial engines
Performance: max speed 295km/h (183mph); range 2900km (1801 miles); service ceiling 5900m (19,325ft)
Dimensions: wingspan 27.00m (88ft 7in); length 22.00m (72ft 2in); height 5.75m (18ft 10in)
Weight: 17,800kg (39,249lb) loaded
Armament: one 20mm (0.79in) Mauser MG151 cannon in dorsal turret

THE LARGE, THREE-ENGINED Do 24 flying boat was designed in 1935 to fulfil a requirement of the Royal Netherlands Naval Air service. The first of three prototypes flew on 3 July 1937, the Netherlands Navy subsequently receiving 11 Do 24Ks built in Germany, and a further 24 built under licence in Holland. In 1940,

the Germans impressed some of the Dutch-built Do 24s for air–sea rescue duty. Fifty aircraft were also built for the Germans as Do 24Ts by the French CAMS concern. In 1944, Spain purchased 12 Do 24T-3s for its air–sea rescue service, the surviving aircraft operating until 1970. Specifications apply to the Dornier Do 24T.

Dornier Do 24s served for many years after World War II in the air–sea rescue role with the Spanish Air Force. One of these aircraft, a Do 24T-3, is seen taking off.

DORNIER DO 217 GERMANY: 1938

Crew: 4
Powerplant: two 1179kW (1580hp) BMW 801ML 14-cylinder radial engines
Performance: max speed 515km/h (320mph); range 2800km (1740 miles); service ceiling 9000m (29,530ft)
Dimensions: span 19.00m (62ft 4in); length 18.20m (59ft 8.5in); height 5.03m (16ft 6in)
Weight: 16,465kg (36,299lb) loaded
Armament: one 15mm (0.59in) cannon; two 13mm (0.51in) and three 7.92mm (0.31in) machine guns; bomb load of 4000kg (8818lb); two Hs 293 or Fritz-X anti-ship missiles

DEVELOPED IN RESPONSE to a 1937 requirement for a long-range heavy bomber which, in keeping with German policy at the time, was also to be stressed for dive-bombing, the Do 217 prototype first flew in August 1938; the first operational model was the Do 217E, 800 aircraft being produced as sub-variants from Do 217E-0 to E-4

The Dornier Do 217 was fast and difficult for the RAF's night fighters to catch. One version was a very effective anti-shipping aircraft, armed with Henschel Hs 293 air-to-surface missiles.

with BMW 801 radial engines. These were followed by 950 examples of the Do 217K night bomber and finally the Do 217M development of the Do 217K with DB 603 engines. Prototype and pre-production variants were the Do 217C bomber, Do 217P high-altitude reconnaissance, and Do 217R missile-launching aircraft. There were also Do 217E and Do 217K sub-variants armed with the Henschel Hs 293 anti-ship missiles and Fritz-X guided bombs. Specifications apply to Do 217E.

DORNIER DO 335 PFEIL GERMANY: 1943

THE DORNIER DO 335 PFEIL (Arrow) heavy fighter was one of the more unconventional designs to emerge from World War II and was in production when the war ended. It was powered by two DB 603 engines mounted in tandem, one forward and one aft with the cockpit in between. Fast and heavily armed, it would have presented the Allies with a formidable challenge had it been available in quantity some months earlier. The prototype Do 335 flew in September 1943, and the first Do 335A-1 production aircraft

DORNIER DO 27

were delivered for operational evaluation early in 1945. The type was fitted with an ejection seat.

Crew: 1
Powerplant: one 1305kW (1750hp) DB 603A-2 in-line engine in the nose and one in the tail
Performance: max speed 763km/h (474mph); range 1380km (858 miles); service ceiling 11,400m (37,400ft)
Dimensions: wingspan 13.80m (45ft 3in); length 13.85m (45ft 5in); height 5.00m (16ft 4in)
Weight: 9610kg (21,186lb) loaded
Armament: one 30mm (1.18in) and two 15mm (0.59in) cannon; provision for one 500kg (1102lb) bomb in internal bay

The Dornier Do 335 was on the point of entering operational service at the end of World War II. It would have been a formidable opponent.

DORNIER DO 27

WEST GERMANY/SPAIN: 1955

Crew: 1
Powerplant: one 201kW (270hp) Lycoming GO-480-B1A6 flat-six piston engine
Performance: max speed 227km/h (141mph); range 1100km (684 miles); service ceiling 3300m (10,825ft)
Dimensions: wingspan 12.00m (39ft 4.5in); length 9.60m (31ft 6in); height 2.80m (9ft 2.25in)
Weight: 1850kg (4079lb) maximum take-off weight
Payload: five people

THE DO 27 WAS WEST GERMANY'S first post-World War II production aircraft. It was designed in collaboration with CASA, who also licence-built some versions – the type was in fact first designed to a Spanish Military STOL requirement. The STOL capabilities of the tail-wheel undercarriage, along with excellent all-round vision were the Do 27's selling points. It was often used in military applications for training, photographic,

ambulance, agricultural and glider-towing purposes. Of the 620 built up until 1965, 432 were for West German military/paramilitary or civil consumption, whilst the remainder were widely exported. Specifications apply to the Do 27A.

The Do 27 was originally designed to a Spanish military requirement and was also produced under licence in Spain. This is a German-built Do 27.

DFW B.I
The DFW (Deutsche Flugzeug Werke) B.I made its appearance in 1914 and was used for observation work on both Eastern and Western Fronts during the early months of World War I.

DFW C.V
The DFW C.V, which was preceded into service in 1916 by the C.IV, was one of the finest German two-seaters to see operational use in World War I. About 600 C.Vs were still in service when the war ended.

DINFIA IA.58 GUARANI
The Dinfia IA.58 Guarani was a twin-engine low-wing 10-seat light transport developed in Argentina in the early 1960s and operated by the Argentine government/military until the late 1980s.

DOMAN LZ-1A
An experimental version of the Sikorsky R-6, the Doman LZ-1A has a hingeless rotor unit (the blades are dynamically flexible but otherwise unarticulated) and a hydraulic rotor control system.

DOMAN LZ-2A PELICAN
This helicopter was designed by Doman for Curtiss-Wright under the designation CW.40 and flew for the first time on 7 November 1950. The LZ-2A Pelican which followed was built for agricultural use and other roles.

DORAND AR.1
First flown in 1916, the Dorand AR.1 reconnaissance aircraft equipped 18 observation squadrons of the Aviation Militaire on the Western and Italian Fronts during World War I.

DORNIER RS-1
The Dornier RS-1 was a three-engined flying boat built in 1914. Its designer, Claudius Dornier, took the extremely bold step for the time of using all-metal construction. In fact, Dornier was to improve the design of flying boats in general with several successive types.

DORNIER DO 28, DO 28D SKYSERVANT AND 128 TURBO-SKYSERVANT　　WEST GERMANY: 1966

Crew: 2
Powerplant: two 283kW (380hp)
Lycoming IGSO-540-A1E flat-six piston
engines
Performance: max speed 325km/h
(202mph); range 642km (399 miles) with
maximum payload; service ceiling 7680m
(25,195ft)
Dimensions: wingspan 15.55m (51ft
0.25in); length 11.41m (37ft 5.25in);
height 3.90m (12ft 10in)
Weight: 3842kg (8470lb) maximum
take-off weight
Payload: up to 10 passengers or freight

FOLLOWING ON FROM success with
the Do 27, Dornier decided to
pursue design of a twin-engined
STOL aircraft, resulting in the Do
28A and B dating from 1959. These
versions were essentially similar
volume derivatives of the Do 27;
they sold in reasonable numbers to
mainly military customers. The
early version pioneered the
unusual engine/undercarriage array
mounted on a lateral boom each

side of the cockpit, while retaining
a tail wheel, and this arrangement
was taken forward into the larger
Do 28D Skyservant design, which
attracted more than 340 civil and
military orders and was later up-

rated with turboprop engines. The
Do 28 flies in a variety of military
roles including coastal patrol. A
few commercial examples remain
active. Specifications apply to the
Do 128-2 Skyservant.

**The Spanish Air Force were
among the many military
customers for this practical twin-
engined STOL transport. Sales of
Do 28s to the military outstripped
civilian orders.**

DOUGLAS WORLD CRUISER　　USA: 1923

THE DOUGLAS WORLD CRUISER
(DWC) was developed from the
DT torpedo-bomber specifically
for carrying out a round-the-world

flight. The prototype was completed
in the late summer of 1923 and,
once official approval had been
gained, four more were delivered

by March 1924. On 24 April 1924
these four aircraft set out on the
round-the-world attempt. Two of
the World Cruisers were lost en

route, luckily without injury to
their crews; however, the surviving
aircraft were able to complete the
flight and did so on 28 September,
having covered a distance of
46,582km (28,945 miles).

**One of the four Douglas World
Cruisers that set out to fly around
the world in April 1924. Two
aircraft were lost en route, but the
survivors completed the flight on
28 September.**

Crew: 2
Powerplant: one 313kW (420hp) Liberty
V-12 in-line engine
Performance: max speed 166km/h
(103mph); range 3541km (2200 miles);
service ceiling 3050m (10,000ft)
Dimensions: wingspan 13.56m (44ft 6in);
length 8.81m (28ft 11in); height 3.07m
(10ft 1in)
Weight: 3137kg (6915lb) loaded

DOUGLAS A-17/DB-8　　USA: 1934

Crew: 3
Powerplant: one 615kW (825hp) Pratt &
Whitney R-1535-13 engine
Performance: max speed 331km/h
(206mph); range 1287km (800 miles);
service ceiling 6313m (20,700ft)
Dimensions: wingspan 14.56m (47ft 9in);

length 9.65m (31ft 8in); height 3.66m
(12ft)
Weight: 3425kg (7550lb) loaded
Armament: four wing-mounted 7.62mm
(0.30in) machine guns and one in rear
cockpit; bomb load of up to 544kg
(1200lb)

THE DOUGLAS A-17 ORIGINATED
in the Northrop YA-13 attack
bomber of 1934. With modifications, the YA-13 became the YA-16
and ultimately the YA-17; 110
production A-17s for the USAAC
were followed by 129 A-17As,

which featured a retractable main
undercarriage and other refinements.
In August 1937 the Northrop
Corporation became the El
Segundo Division of the Douglas
company. This meant that,
although the A-17 and A-17A

attack aircraft used by the US Army retained the Northrop name, the export version of the aircraft was designated Douglas DB-8A. The fixed-undercarriage DB-8A-1 was built under licence in Sweden; the similar DB-8A-2 was supplied to Argentina; and the DB-8A-3, with a retractable undercarriage, was supplied to the Netherlands Army Air Corps. Most were destroyed during the German invasion of May 1941. DB-8A variants were also supplied to Iraq, Norway and Peru, while 61 A-17As were supplied to the RAF, which passed them on to South Africa. France received 32 examples before she was overrun.

Specifications apply to the Douglas A-17A.

Douglas TBD Devastator

USA: 1935

Crew: 3
Powerplant: one 671kW (900hp) Pratt & Whitney R-1830-64 Twin Wasp 14-cylinder radial engine
Performance: max speed 332km/h (206mph); range 1150km (716 miles); service ceiling 6005m (19,700ft)
Dimensions: wingspan 15.24m (50ft); length 10.67m (35ft); height 4.60m (15ft 1in)
Weight: 4951kg (10,914lb) loaded
Armament: one 7.62mm (0.30in) in upper front fuselage and one in rear cockpit; one 533mm (21in) torpedo or one 454kg (1000lb) bomb

FIRST FLOWN ON 15 APRIL 1935, the Douglas TBD Devastator suffered from inadequate defensive firepower throughout its first-line service, suffering terrible losses to Japanese fighters. At the time of the bombing of Pearl Harbor there were 100 TBD-1 Devastators in US Navy service, 69 of which were first-line aircraft.

During the first six months of the Pacific war they were flown intensively against Japanese

The Douglas TBD Devastator suffered terrible losses during the Battle of Midway in 1942, pressing home torpedo attacks on Japanese carriers.

shipping and land targets, reaching a pinnacle of success in the Battle of the Coral Sea in May 1942. A month later, during the Battle for Midway, 41 TBDs were launched against the Japanese task force and 35 were destroyed. One squadron, VT-8, was to lose all 15 aircraft. After this disaster, the Devastator was quickly relegated to second-line duties and replaced by the Grumman Avenger.

Douglas SBD Dauntless

USA: 1935

The SBD Dauntless, one of the most successful World War II dive-bombers, sunk a greater tonnage of Japanese shipping than any other type.

THE EVOLUTION OF THE Douglas SBD Dauntless began in November 1934, when a Northrop design team based a proposal for a new navy dive-bomber on the Northrop A-17. A protoype was ordered and flew in July 1935 with the designation XBT-1.

In February 1936 an order was placed for 54 production BT-1s with 615kW (825hp) Wright R-1535-94 engines. The last aircraft of this batch was fitted with a 746kW (1000hp) R-1820-32 engine and completed as the XBT-2. Further modifications were carried out, mainly to the landing gear and vertical tail surfaces, and when the Northrop Corporation became a division of Douglas on 31 August 1937 the aircraft was redesignated XSBD-1.

Delivery of 57 SBD-1s to the US Marine Corps began in mid-1940, the aircraft now having been

DORNIER DO L1, L2, L3 DELPHIN
A single-engined high-wing flying boat series starting with the L1 (circa 1921), the Delphin series had an enclosed cabin with the engine mounted atop. The L2 first flew in 1924 and could accommodate up to six passengers.

DORNIER KOMET
This high-wing single-engined monoplane was developed from the Delphin flying boat and could carry four passengers.

DORNIER MERKUR
A more powerful and enlarged development of the Komet, the Merkur was produced in a number of variants. The Merkur could carry six passengers and more than 70 were built from 1925 onward.

DORNIER DO C, D AND T
The Dornier Do C was a single-engined parasol-wing trainer of 1925. The Do D was a twin-float variant, and was built as a torpedo-bomber for the Yugoslav Navy in 1927, while the Do T was an ambulance version.

DORNIER DO 11
First flown in May 1932 as the Do F transport, the twin-engined Dornier Do 11 was developed in secret as the Luftwaffe's first bomber. A developed version, the Do 13, flew in 1933.

DORNIER DO 13
The Do 13 was a development from the Do 11 bomber. It first flew in 1933 and was a four-engined monoplane bomber. Initial instability problems were alleviated to some extent, and the type was consequently re-designated Do 23.

DORNIER DO 23
The Dornier Do 23, which appeared in 1934, was an improved version of the Do 13. The main production model was the Do 23G, which equipped many Luftwaffe bomber units until being replaced in 1937–38.

DORNIER DO 19
The Do 19 was a prototype four-engined heavy bomber which flew in October 1936. It was not adopted, and the Luftwaffe was to pay dearly for lack of such an aircraft in World War II.

The Douglas Dauntless served from the beginning to the end of the Pacific war. It was also used by the Royal New Zealand Air Force and by the French Navy.

fitted with the large, perforated dive flaps that were a distinctive feature of the Dauntless. At the same time, the US Navy ordered 87 SBD-2s with extra fuel tankage, protective armour and autopilots. Delivery of the SBD-2 began in November 1940, the aircraft being followed into service by the SBD-3.

Delivery of the first 174 SBD-3s began in March 1941, the US Navy subsequently receiving a further 410. The Dauntless formed the attack element of the Navy's carrier air groups at the time of the Japanese strike on Pearl Harbor, and in the early months of 1942 the SBDs, operating from the carriers *Lexington* and *Yorktown*, carried out a number of offensive operations against enemy shore installations and shipping. In May 1942, during the Battle of the Coral Sea, SBDs joined with TBD

Devastator torpedo aircraft to sink the Japanese light carrier *Shoho* and damage the fleet carrier *Shokaku*, forcing the Japanese to abandon plans to occupy Port Moresby, New Guinea. In June 1942, during the Battle of Midway, the two aircraft types again joined forces to make coordinated dive-bombing and torpedo attacks on units of the Japanese fleet, and it was the SBDs from the carriers *Enterprise*, *Hornet* and *Yorktown* that scored the major successes, sinking the Japanese carriers *Akagi*, *Kaga* and *Soryu*, and damaging the *Hiryu* so badly that she had to be sunk by her own forces.

In October 1942 a new version, the SBD-4, made its appearance; 780 were delivered, fitted with radar and radio-navigation equipment. They were followed by the major production variant, the SBD-5,

which had a more powerful 895kW (1200hp) engine. The US Navy took delivery of 2965 SBD-5s, while 65 SBD-5As, originally built to a Navy contract, were delivered to the US Marine Corps instead. One SBD-5, fitted with a 1007kW (1350hp) R-1820-66 engine, was used as the prototype for 450 SBD-6 aircraft, with which Douglas ended its Dauntless production in July 1944. Overall production of the Dauntless was 5936 aircraft, a total that included 178 aircraft for the USAAC, delivered from June 1941 as the A-24, a further 170 as the A-24A, and 615 as the A-24B. Eighteen SBD-3s were issued to the Royal New Zealand Air Force, followed by 27 SBD-4s and 23 SBD-5s. Thirty-two SBD-5s were supplied to the French Navy, along with about 40 A-24Bs to the Armée de l'Air, in 1944, but they were all

employed in training and other second-line duties. Nine SBD-5s were also delivered to the Royal Navy, but never used operationally.

Specifications apply to the Douglas SBD-5 Dauntless.

Crew: 2
Powerplant: one 895kW (1200hp) Wright R-1820-60 Cyclone 9-cylinder radial engine
Performance: max speed 410km/h (255mph); range 2519km (1565 miles); service ceiling 7780m (25,530ft)
Dimensions: wingspan 12.66m (41ft 6in); length 10.09m (33ft 1in); height 4.14m (13ft 7in)
Weight: 4853kg (10,700lb) loaded
Armament: two 12.7mm (0.50in) fixed forward-firing machine guns in the upper part of the forward fuselage; two trainable 7.7mm (0.303in) machine guns in rear cockpit; external bomb or depth-charge load of 1021kg (2250lb)

DOUGLAS DC-3 AND C-47 SKYTRAIN/DAKOTA

USA: 1935

The Douglas DC-3 has had a unique postwar career with major airlines, charter/air taxi and freight firms. Here an Air BVI (British Virgin Islands) DC-3 is seen on an inter-island service.

ORIGINALLY DESIGNED TO ONE particular airline's specification, the DC-3 was to become the most important transport aircraft of World

War II and the means by which normal communications, supplies and stability were restored to many areas of the world at the war's end.

It then provided the backbone for early post-war civilian passenger and freight services, roles in which hundreds of examples still continue.

In 1934 American Airlines asked Douglas to enlarge and improve the DC-2 airliner in order to provide an overnight/sleeper airliner for its domestic trans-continental services. This resulted in the DST (Douglas Sleeper Transport) design with 14 berths, first flown on 17 December 1935. The DST design was itself varied as the daytime DC-3, a 21–28-seat airliner which American Airlines used when it entered service on 25 June 1936. The early production DSTs were powered by Wright Cyclone piston engines, but later DSTs utilized the specified Twin Wasps. This was similarly the case with early DC-3s (the DC-3A and most DC3B day/night cabin convertible models used the Twin Wasp).

The DC-3 low-wing, tail-wheeled, all-metal construction monoplane raised the reliability, standards and economics of commercial air travel to new levels. Its ubiquity contributed to a growth in airline networks – over 430 had been delivered to airlines worldwide by late 1941. The United States's entry into World War II brought with it the need for a utility transport aircraft capable of operating in any theatre. The DC-3 fitted the bill and it was available off-the-shelf. Many existing DC-3s were impressed into military service, but they were joined by over 10,000 examples built for the military and designated C-47 Skytrain (or Dakota in Britain) – in the region of 9000 being powered by the Twin Wasp engine. Additionally, a further 2000 examples were built in the Soviet Union under the designation Lisunov Li-2. Hundreds more derivatives were built by Japan under the auspices of Mitsui.

The C-47 flew in every theatre of operations. Roles included dropping paratroopers, glider towing, air supply and cargo lifts, often conducted in the most inhospitable combat, geographic and climatic conditions. Many thousands of the rugged DC-3s survived these experiences and were the obvious choice to undergo rapid conversion programmes in order to plug the gap in availability of commercial transports when hostilities ended in 1945.

Although major airlines moved on to newer airliners within a few years, the DC-3 became extremely popular with independent airlines operating short-haul passenger services, and remained so well into the 1970s. The C-47 was no less popular with post-war militaries including the US, which operated an extraordinary range of sub-types including the AC-47 gunship conversion used in the Vietnam War.

Hundreds of DC-3s remain in service today, mostly with civilian operators as freighters or pollution/bug sprayers. Passenger/combi versions remain operable in South America and there are a number engaged on passenger work associated with nostalgia/leisure trips in the northern hemisphere, sometimes run by preservation or enthusiast groups.

Specifications apply to DC-3A.

Crew: 2
Powerplant: two 895kW (1200hp) Pratt & Whitney R-1830 Twin Wasp radial piston engines
Performance: max speed 370km/h (230mph) at 2590m (8500ft); range 3420km (2125 miles); service ceiling 7070m (23,200ft)
Dimensions: wingspan 28.96m (95ft); wing area 91.69m^2 (987sq ft) length 19.65m (64ft 5.5in); height 5.16m (16ft 11in)
Weight: 8419kg (18,560lb) maximum take-off weight
Payload: up to 28 passengers in a pre-war 'day' configuration; up to 36 passengers in a post-WWII single-class layout

DOUGLAS B-18

USA: 1936

Crew: 5
Powerplant: two 746kW (1000hp) Wright R-1820-53 Cyclone 9-cylinder radial engines
Performance: max speed 346km/h (215mph); range 1931km (1200 miles); service ceiling 7285m (23,900ft)
Dimensions: span 27.28m (89ft 6in); length 17.63m (57ft 10in); height 4.62m (15ft 2in)
Weight: 12,552kg (27,673lb) loaded
Armament: one 7.62mm (0.30in) machine in nose, dorsal and ventral positions; up to 2948kg (6500lb) of bombs

THE DOUGLAS B-18 (DB-1) was a medium–heavy bomber evolved from the DC-3 commercial transport and winner of the 1936 USAAC bomber competition. An initial order was placed for 177 machines, but only 133 were delivered, the remainder of the order being transferred to the

improved B-18A, 217 examples of which were produced. Twenty aircraft were transferred to the Royal Canadian Air Force, in whose service the type was known as the Digby I. In 1939–40, 122 B-18As were converted to B-18B standard by the installation of specialist radio equipment for maritime patrol duties, two aircraft being transferred to the Brazilian Air Force. The B-18 ended its career as a paratroop trainer.

The Douglas B-18 was rapidly outclassed by more modern bomber types and was relegated to paratroop training duties.

DOUGLAS DC-4E, DC-4/C-54 SKYMASTER

USA: 1938

The vast majority of the type were built as C-54 variants for the US military, as was the case with this C-54D, which was based in West Germany.

WHEN DOUGLAS'S INITIAL DESIGN of a 52-seat pressurized airliner with a triple tailfin arrangement (later designated DC-4E) failed to attract orders, it decided to design a smaller, simpler unpressurized airliner – the result was the DC-4/C-54. The onset of World War II necessitated production for the military, and over 1200 were built to military C-54 requirements. After the war, 79 civilian DC-4-1009s were built, but many more were converted from C-54 standard. Along with the Canadair C-4 Argonaut these became the backbone of many early post-war airlines' long-haul fleets.

The C-54 served with the US military in many marques and roles, including VIP transport, but it is most readily associated with the 1948–9 Berlin airlift. A few examples survive in service to date.

Specifications apply to the Douglas DC-4-1009.

Crew: 4
Powerplant: four 1081kW (1450hp) Pratt & Whitney R-2000-2SD13G Twin Wasp radial piston engines

Performance: max speed 451km/h (280mph); range 4023km (2500 miles) with a 5189kg (11,440lb) payload; service ceiling 6800m (22,300ft)
Dimensions: wingspan 35.81m (117ft 6in); length 28.60m (93ft 10in); height 8.38m (27ft 6in)
Weight: 33,112kg (73,000lb) maximum take-off weight
Payload: up to 86 passengers

DOUGLAS BOSTON

USA: 1939

Crew: 3
Powerplant: two 1268kW (1700hp) Wright R-2600-13 14-cylinder radial engines
Performance: max speed 546km/h (339mph); range 3380km (2100 miles); service ceiling 7225m (23,700ft)
Dimensions: wingspan 18.69m (61ft 4in); length 14.63m (47ft 11in); height 5.36m (17ft 7in)
Weight: 12,338kg (27,200lb) loaded
Armament (Boston III Intruder): six 12.7mm (0.50in) machine guns in the nose, two in dorsal position, and one in ventral position; bomb load of 1814kg (4000lb)

THE DOUGLAS BOSTON WAS the Royal Air Force's name for the DB-7 attack bomber, part of a French consignment of 100 aircraft taken over by the RAF after France was overrun in 1940. Designated Boston I and Boston II, these aircraft were respectively used for crew conversion and intruder

One of the batch of Douglas Boston IIIs earmarked for delivery to the RAF. The Boston gave excellent service with the squadrons of No 2 Group RAF, being eventually replaced by the Mosquito.

operations. A total of 1100 examples had been ordered by France in February 1940 and 186, designated A-20 and A-20A, by the USAAC three months later. These, with the manufacturer's designation DB-7, had a narrower and deeper fuselage than the original model. The French order was subsequently increased to 270 DB-7s and 100 DB-7As, the latter having 1194kW

(1600hp) Wright Cyclone engines. The RAF also received 781 improved DB-7As, named Boston III, and 202 Boston IIIAs. A total of 808 similar aircraft were produced for the USAAC/USAAF as the A-20C. The next major variant was the A-20G, 2850 being built with the 'solid' nose of the fighter variants and an increased bomb-carrying capacity. Later variants

were the A-20J (450 built) and A-20K (413), which had a moulded plastic one-piece transparent nose; these were designated Boston IV and V in RAF service. Total production of the DB-7 series, including the fighter variants, was 7385, almost half of this output going to the Soviet Union.

Specifications apply to the Douglas Boston A-20G.

DOUGLAS A-26 INVADER

USA: 1942

Crew: 3
Powerplant: two 1492kW (2000hp) Pratt & Whitney R-2800-27 18-cylinder radial engines
Performance: max speed 571km/h (355mph); range 2092km (1300 miles) service ceiling 6735m (22,100ft)
Dimensions: wingspan 21.34m (70ft); length 15.42m (50ft 7in); height 5.64m (18ft 6in)
Weight: 12,893kg (28,423lb)
Armament: six 12.7mm (0.50in) machine guns in nose and two in dorsal barbette; bomb load of 2722kg (6000lb)

THE DOUGLAS A-26 INVADER first flew in July 1962 and was ordered for the USAAF in three variants: the A-26 light attack bomber, the A-26A two-seat night-fighter and the A-26B heavy assault aircraft. The A-26B, of which 1355 were

The A-26 Invader (re-designated B-26) saw service as a night intruder during the Korean War, attacking North Korean supply convoys at night.

built, was the fastest US bomber of World War II and entered service in 1944. The other production variant was the A-26C, of which

1091 were delivered. The Invader, re-designated B-26B and B-26C, saw extensive service in the Korean War. Specifications apply to A-26B.

DOUGLAS AD SKYRAIDER

USA: 1945

The Skyraider played a prominent part in the Korean War, carrying out many precision attacks on bridges, road junctions and other targets.

DESIGNED IN 1944 and intended as a potent carrier-borne attack aircraft for use in the projected invasion of Japan, the prototype Skyraider flew for the first time on 18 March 1945.

An order was placed for 548 AD-1 production aircraft, this being reduced to 277 after VJ-Day. The Skyraider was produced in many variants, including the AD-3W

early warning aircraft. Forty AD-4W early warning aircraft were supplied to the Royal Navy as the Skyraider AEW.1. A further variant of the basic AD-4 was the AD-4B, which had four wing-mounted 20mm (0.79in) cannon and could carry nuclear weapons. The Skyraider played a prominent part in the Korean War, going into action for the first time on 3 July 1950 from the USS *Valley Forge*.

Specifications apply to A3D-2.

Crew: 1
Powerplant: one 2014kW (2700hp) Wright R-3350-26W Cyclone 18-cylinder radial engine
Performance: max speed 518km/h (322mph); range 1840km (1143 miles); service ceiling 8690m (28,500ft)
Dimensions: wingspan 15.24m (50ft); length 11.83m (38ft 10in); height 4.77m (15ft 8in)
Weight: 11,340kg (25,000lb) loaded
Armament: four wing-mounted 20mm (0.79in) cannon; 3628kg (8000lb) of bombs

DORNIER DO 31E
An experimental VTOL/STOL jet design dating from 1967, with two main wing-mounted Rolls-Royce Pegasus engines and two pairs of four wing-tip pod-mounted VTOL assisting engines.

DORNIER DO 228
Successor to the earlier Do 27/28 designs, this high-wing, twin-turboprop commuter airliner first flew in 1981. Over 240 have been produced. The Do 228 is now licence-built by HAL in India.

DORNIER (FAIRCHILD) DO 328TP
The 33-seat Do 328 first flew in 1991 and over 100 have been produced. Opportunities in the regional jet market have led to the launch of a turbofan jet version.

DOUGLAS DT SERIES
The Douglas DT-1 and DT-2 were two-seat torpedo-bomber floatplanes built for the US Navy in the early 1920s and also exported to Norway and Peru.

DOUGLAS C-1
The Douglas C-1 was a transport biplane of 1924, powered by a Liberty engine. The USAAC took delivery of 27 examples.

DOUGLAS O-2
The Douglas O-2 and its derivatives were two-seat armed observation aircraft that served with the USAAC from the late 1920s until the outbreak of World War II.

DOUGLAS M-2
A single-engined biplane designed primarily for use as a mail carrier, derived from the M-1 and dating from 1926.

DOUGLAS M-4
Last in the M series of Douglas single-engined biplanes designed for mail carriage, the M-4 had an improved payload achieved by stretching the wings. The aircraft dates from 1926.

DOUGLAS O-31
First flown in 1930, the O-31 was the progenitor of a series of braced high-wing or parasol-wing observation monoplanes that ended with the O-46A, the last observation aircraft built by Douglas.

DOUGLAS DC-6 (C-118 AND R6D)

USA: 1946

THE DC-6 WAS DESIGNED as an enlarged, pressurized version of the DC-4/C-54 transport aircraft, with possible wartime military applications in mind. However, cessation of hostilities changed Douglas's emphasis towards a post-war long-haul airliner. Larger than the DC-4/C-54, the DC-6 introduced some innovations such as thermal de-icing systems, weather radar, pre-containerized cargo receptacles and reversible propellers. The DC-6 went into service with American Airlines in 1947 and over 700 were built, including C-118s and R6Ds for the USAF. Specifications apply to DC-6B.

Crew: 4
Powerplant: four 1864kW (2500hp) Pratt & Whitney R-2800-CB17 Double Wasp radial piston engines
Performance: cruising speed 507km/h (315mph); range 7596km (4720 miles) with maximum payload; service ceiling 7620m (25,000ft)
Dimensions: wingspan 35.81m (117ft 6in); length 32.18m (105ft 7in; height 8.74m (28ft 8in)
Weight: 48,534kg (107,000lb) maximum take-off weight
Payload: up to 102 passengers

The DC-6B pictured has been internally converted to carry fuel to outlying communities in Alaska.

DOUGLAS F3D SKYKNIGHT

USA: 1948

Crew: 2
Powerplant: two 1542kg (3400lb) thrust Westinghouse J34-WE-36 turbojet engines
Performance: max speed 965km/h (600mph); range 1930km (1200 miles); service ceiling 12,192m (40,000ft)
Dimensions: wingspan 15.24m (50ft); length 13.86m (45ft 6in); height 4.87m (16ft)
Weight: 12,179kg (26,850lb) loaded
Armament: four 20mm (0.79in) cannon

The F3D Skyknight was developed in response to a 1946 US Navy specification calling for an all-weather jet fighter. The prototype flew for the first time on 28 March 1948; after evaluation 28 examples were ordered of the first production series, the F3D-1. The improved F3D-2 appeared in February 1951, and this variant accounted for 237 aircraft out of a total of 268 built. Specifications apply to F3D-2.

In addition to its night-intruder role in Korea, the Douglas F3D Skyknight was brought out of retirement to act as an electronic warfare aircraft during the Vietnam war, under the designation EF-10.

DOUGLAS XA2D-1 SKYSHARK

USA: 1950

Crew: 1
Powerplant: one 3805kW (5100hp) Allison XT40-A-2 twin turboprop engine
Performance: max speed 792km/h (492mph); range 3539km (2200 miles); service ceiling 14,670m (48,100ft)
Dimensions: wingspan 15.25m (50ft); length 12.5m (41ft); height 5.18m (17ft)
Weight: 7349kg (16,224lb) loaded
Armament: bombs and underwing ordnance up to 2728kg (6000lb)

NOT LONG AFTER THE AD Skyraider entered service, Douglas embarked on the design of a turboprop-powered successor, the

Designed as a successor to the Skyraider, the XA2D-1 Skyshark was powered by an Allison turboprop driving contra-rotating propellers.

XA2D-1 Skyshark, which was intended to make use of as many existing Skyraider components as possible. Powered by an Allison XT40-A-2 turboprop, consisting of twin Allison T38 engines mounted side-by-side and mounting co-axial propellers, the prototype Skyshark flew for the first time on 26 May 1950, and during trials reached a speed of 792km/h (492mph) at 8235m (27,000ft). Constant trouble with the engine resulted in a US Navy production order being cut back to 10 aircraft, and these were used for a variety of engine trials.

DOUGLAS F4D SKYRAY

THE DESIGN OF THE Douglas F4D Skyray, which first flew on 23 January 1951, owed much to the wartime work of Dr Alexander Lippisch, whose delta-wing designs had made an impression on the US Navy's Bureau of Aeronautics. When the first production F4D-1 exceeded Mach One in level flight on 5 June 1954, it seemed probable that the aircraft would soon enter service, but serious problems – including a dangerous high-speed stall at altitude – had to be overcome

The Douglas Skyray was a radical departure fom traditional US Navy jet fighter design, its delta wing owing much to the ideas of German designer Dr Alexander Lippisch.

before the aircraft could be deployed operationally in 1956. Production of the Skyray ended in 1958 with the 419th aircraft, but the type remained in first-line service until well into the 1960s. During its operational career the Skyray established five new time-to-height records.

Crew: 1
Powerplant: one 4626kg (10,200lb) thrust Pratt & Whitney J57-P-8A turbojet engine
Performance: max speed 1162km/h (722mph); range 1931km (1200 miles); service ceiling 16,764m (55,000ft)
Dimensions: wingspan 10.21m (33ft 6in); length 13.93m (45ft 8in); height 3.96m (13ft)
Weight: 11,340kg (25,000lb)
Armament: four 20mm (0.79in) cannon; up to 1814kg (4000lb) of ordnance, including Sidewinder AAMs, on six underwing hardpoints

DOUGLAS XB-7
The Douglas XB-7 twin-engined light bomber was developed in 1931 from the YO-36 observation aircraft. It was evaluated as the Y1B-7, seven examples being built.

DOUGLAS DC-1/DC-2
Predecessor and foundation to the more famous and powerful DC-3, only one DC-1 was produced. Effectively the DC-2 became the production version, with 198 being manufactured in total. The DC-1 first flew in 1933.

DOUGLAS DOLPHIN
A twin-engined amphibian design with a characteristic high wing, the Dolphin dates from 1934 and served with Pan American Airways and other operators.

DOUGLAS DF-151
The DF-151 was an amphibious two-engined flying-boat design dating from 1936. Four examples were built with Pan American in mind, but were not taken up. Two were subsequently sold to Japan Air Lines and the other two to Aeroflot (re-designated as DF-195).

DOUGLAS B-23 DRAGON
The Douglas B-23 Dragon medium bomber was first projected in November 1938 to supersede the B-22, which in effect was to have been an uprated B-18A. The B-23 was the first American bomber to carry a tail gunner. There was no prototype, and the first of 38 production B-23 Dragons flew on 27 July 1939.

DOUGLAS DB-7
The origins of the DB-7 attack bomber series began with the Model 7A, submitted in response to a USAAC requirement of 1938. The first prototype, which was designated Model 7B and featured a tricycle undercarriage, flew on 26 October 1939.

DOUGLAS HAVOC
In 1940, the RAF converted many Boston IIs as night-fighters and intruders, the aircraft being renamed Havoc. Some were fitted with a Turbinlite searchlight for target illumination.

Douglas A3D Skywarrior

USA: 1952

Crew: 3
Powerplant: two 5635kg (12,400lb) Pratt
& Whitney J57-P-10 turbojets
Performance: max speed 982km/h
(610mph); range 3220km (2000 miles);
service ceiling 13,110m (43,000ft)
Dimensions: span 22.10m (72ft 6in);
length 23.30m (76ft 4in); height 7.16m
(23ft 6in)
Weight: 37,195kg (82,000lb) loaded
Armament: two remotely controlled 20mm
(0.79in) cannon in tail turret; provision for
5443kg (12,000lb) of conventional or
nuclear weapons in internal bomb bay

FIRST FLOWN ON 28 OCTOBER
1952, the Douglas A3D (later A-3)
Skywarrior was the first carrier-
borne bomber designed for
strategic nuclear strike, and was
intended to operate from the US
Navy's Forrestal-class carriers.
Deliveries of production A3D-1s
began in the latter half of 1954,
this version being replaced by the
structurally strengthened A3D-2,
which entered service with the
US Pacific Fleet early in 1957.
Variants were the A3D-2P photo-
reconnaissance aircraft, the
A3D-2Q ELINT aircraft, and the
A3D-2T trainer. The Skywarrior –
its variants redesignated A-3A,
A-3B, RA-3B, EA-3B and TA-3B
in 1962 – remained in first-line
service until the late 1960s. The
Skywarrior was the world's largest
and heaviest shipboard aircraft,
and it brought a new strategic
dimension to sea power, enabling
the US Navy to strike at targets
in the heart of hostile territory.
Specifications apply to the A3D-2.

**The Douglas A3D Skywarrior
was the first naval aircraft
designed specifically for the
nuclear attack role.**

Douglas DC-7

USA: 1953

**The DC-7 was the last of Douglas's long-range piston-powered airliners. The DC-7B pictured entered service with
National Airlines in 1957, but was sold on to a secondary operator as early as 1964 – the jet age had arrived.**

Crew: 4
Powerplant: four 2535kW (3400hp)
Wright R-3350-18EA1 Turbo-Compound
radial piston engines
Performance: max speed 653km/h
(406mph); range 7411km (4605 miles)
with maximum payload; service ceiling
6615m (21,700ft)
Dimensions: wingspan 38.86m (127ft
6in); length 34.21m (112ft 3in); height
9.70m (31ft 10in)
Weight: 64,864kg (143,000lb) maximum
take-off weight
Payload: up to 105 passengers

THE DC-7 WAS THE LAST OF
Douglas's piston-engined airliners
and the DC-7C perhaps defines the
beginning of the era of non-stop
transatlantic passenger aircraft.
    The DC-7 was derived from the
preceding DC-6 and appeared very
similar, although stretched (the later
DC-7C version had a lengthened
wing) and offering new range and
route capabilities to its operators.
A total of 338 DC-7s were built

for major airlines, but they had short service lives with the majors due to the introduction of the Boeing 707-300 jet airliner.

Some examples passed to charter operators while others were converted to freighters (including swing-tail conversions).

By 2000 there were only two or three remaining examples capable of operation. Specifications apply to the Douglas DC-7C.

DOUGLAS B-66

USA: 1954

IN 1953, DOUGLAS RECEIVED an order from the USAF to modify the A3D as a land-based reconnaissance and bomber aircraft, and five RB-66As were produced for service evaluation in 1954. These were followed by the first production version, the B-66B (72 built), which began to replace the Martin B-57 Canberra in the USAF's tactical bomber wings from March 1956. It was preceded slightly by

the RB-66B reconnaissance aircraft, of which 145 examples were built; this was followed by the RB-66C and the WB-66D (77 built of both sub-types), the latter a specialized weather reconnaissance version. The RB-66C equipped two tactical reconnaissance wings. Many B-66/RB-66 aircraft were modified for the electronic warfare role as EB-66s and saw action in the Vietnam War. Specifications apply to the RB-66B.

Crew: 3
Powerplant: two 4627kg (10,200lb) thrust Allison J71-A-11 turbojet engines
Performance: max speed 1015km/h (631mph); range 3220km (2000 miles); service ceiling 11,855m (38,900ft)
Dimensions: wingspan 22.10m (72ft 6in); length 22.90m (75ft 2in); height 7.19m (23ft 7in)
Weight: 37,648kg (83,000lb)
Armament: two remotely controlled 20mm (0.79in) cannon in tail barbette

The Douglas RB-66 performed well in the tactical reconnaissance role and was followed by the B-66B, a dedicated bomber variant. The type served in the electronic warfare role as the EB-66.

DOUGLAS A-4 SKYHAWK

USA: 1954

IN 1950, HAVING ABANDONED the XA2D Skyshark as a potential replacement for the Skyraider, the Douglas Aircraft Company began design studies for a turbojet-powered shipboard attack aircraft capable of delivering nuclear weapons and performing a wide variety of conventional attack missions. The result was the XA4D-1 Skyhawk, the prototype of which flew on 22 June 1954.

The prototype was, in fact, one of four pre-production aircraft which were ordered by the US Navy for evaluation, the normal practice of ordering two experimental aircraft and a static test machine having been waived in this case. The first of 165 production A4D-1 Skyhawks were delivered to Attack Squadron VA-27 on 27 September 1956 and were replaced on the production line by the A4D-2, production of

which ran to 542 examples. Plans had been made to re-engine the Skyhawk with the Pratt & Whitney J52-P-2 turbojet as the A4D-3, but this variant was cancelled, and the next Skyhawk to appear was the A4D-2N, which had a lengthened nose to accommodate terrain-clearance radar. The variant also featured a rocket-boosted low-level ejection seat. Deliveries to the US Navy were to begin in 1959 and ended in 1962, after a total of 638 aircraft had been built.

The 1000th production Skyhawk was delivered in February 1961, and in July that year another variant, the A4D-5 (which was later redesignated A-4E), made its appearance, with an uprated engine, greater offensive load and a 27 per cent range increase. Cockpit refinements included a Douglas Escapac zero-height zero-speed rocket-powered ejection seat. Five hundred were built. The next variant, the A-4F, was an attack bomber with a J52-P-8A turbojet, heavily armoured cockpit and updated avionics housed in a 'hump' aft of the cockpit. Production was completed in 1968 after 146 machines had been built.

The TA-4F was a tandem two-seat trainer, and the A-4G and TA-4G were similar aircraft supplied to the Royal Australian Navy. The A-4H was a variant supplied to Israel, the TA-4J was a simplified version of the TA-4F for the US Naval Air Advanced Training Command, with most of the weapons delivery systems deleted. Deliveries to the US Navy began in June 1969. The A-4K was a variant for the Royal New Zealand Air Force, which took delivery of ten aircraft in 1970, and the A-4M was developed for the USMC. The Marine Corps received an initial batch of 50 A4Ms, which were similar to the A4F but with an uprated engine. The A4L was a

modified A4C (A4D-2N), also with an uprated engine and avionics 'hump'.

During the 1960s the Skyhawk equipped some 40 USN and USMC squadrons, and saw extensive action during the Vietnam War. About 40 per cent of Israel's Skyhawks were lost during the Yom Kippur War of 1973, but this attrition was made good by the delivery of A-4N Skyhawk IIs, a light attack version. The A-4Y was an updated A-4M for the USMC. The 2900th Skyhawk was delivered in 1977, and 2960 were built in total. Skyhawks were supplied to Singapore and Argentina, the latter using them during the Falklands War of 1982. Skyhawks were also delivered to the Royal Australian Navy, which took delivery of 16 A-4E/Fs and four TA-4s. In RAN service the aircraft were designated A-4G and were modified to suit Australian requirements.

Specifications apply to the Douglas A-4E Skyhawk.

Crew: 1
Powerplant: one 3855kg (8500lb) thrust Pratt & Whitney J52-P-6 turbojet engine
Performance: max speed 1102km/h (685mph); range 1480km (920 miles); service ceiling 14,935m (49,000ft)
Dimensions: wingspan 8.38m (27ft 6in); length 12.21m (40ft 1in); height 4.62m (15ft 2in)
Weight: 11,113kg (24,500lb) loaded
Armament: two 20mm (0.79in) cannon; 3719kg (8200lb) of external ordnance

Dramatic shot of a Royal New Zealand Air Force A-4K Skyhawk. The RNZAF took delivery of 10 A-4Ks in 1970. and the type was withdrawn from service in the 1990s.

The Royal Australian Navy took delivery of 16 A-4E/F Skyhawks and four TA-4s, these being designated A-4G and TA-4G in Australian service.

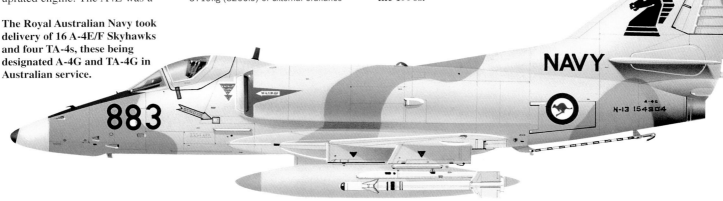

DOUGLAS DC-8

USA: 1958

LAUNCHED IN 1955, THE DC-8 was Douglas's counter to the Boeing 707, which it ultimately trailed into service by just under a year – although it was offered as an over-water version from the outset.

The DC-8 retained its original dimensional size from the 10 series

through to the 50 series, differences being mainly in powerplant, range and payload. In 1967 the Super Sixty series was introduced for customers with greater/differing payload requirements. The 61 series offered a stretched fuselage, while the 62 retained similar length to its

predecessor but ultra long range. The later 63 series retained the length of the 61 and added some of the 62's range characteristics.

The 60 series models amounted to half the total sales. These later three marques were re-engineered with new-generation engines from

1981 to form the 70 series. Of the 556 DC-8s built nearly half remain operable (largely as freighters), in part due to the 70 series conversion, but also because of the titanium strengtheners placed at key riveting points. Specifications apply to the DC-8 Series 63.

Many DC-8s have enjoyed long and varied service lives. This example was built as a DC-8-63 for Viasa of Venezuela. From 1984 it saw service with several French charters, and it was converted to use as a freighter in 1994.

Crew: 3
Powerplant: four 84.52kN (19,000lb) Pratt & Whitney JT3D-7 turbofan engines
Performance: max cruising speed 966km/h (600mph); range 7242km (4500 miles) with maximum payload

Dimensions: wingspan 45.24m (148ft 3in); length 57.12m (187ft 5in); height 12.93m (42ft 5in)
Weight: 158,757kg (350,000lb) maximum take-off weight
Payload: up to 269 passengers

DRUINE (ROLLASON) D.31 TURBULENT · FRANCE: 1950

Crew: 1
Powerplant: one 33.5kW (45hp) 1500cc (91 cu in) Ardem Mk IV modified Volkswagen automobile piston engine
Performance: cruising speed 150km/h (93mph); service ceiling 2740m (9000ft)
Dimensions: wingspan 6.5m (21ft 5in); length 5.23m (17ft 4.5in)
Weight: 281kg (620lb) maximum take-off weight
Payload: single-seat light aeroplane

THE D.31 WAS ROGER DRUINE'S second post-war design following the Aigle and was intended for both production and home-build markets. Production build rights for the low-wing monoplane were acquired by Rollason Aircraft and Engine in the UK and Stark Flugzeugbau in

Germany, and both companies produced modest quantities to add to those home-built versions. Many examples remain extant.
Specifications apply to the D.31.

The example pictured was built under the auspices of Druine rather than Rollason. It is powered by a 1500cc (91 cu in) Ardem 4C02 Mk.2 engine.

DRUINE (ROLLASON) D.62 CONDOR · FRANCE: 1954

A LATER AND LARGER SUCCESSOR to the D.31 Turbulent of 1951, the D.62 Condor was similarly a low-wing, wooden-framed monoplane

This Rollason-built 1964 Condor was operated by the British Women Pilots Association for a number of years.

available as a licence built product or as a home build from plans. The D.62 was, like the D.31, built under licence by Rollason in the UK from 1961. Variants include versions converted for glider towing. Specifications apply to the D.62.

Crew: 1
Powerplant: one 55kW (75hp) Continental A 75 piston engine
Performance: cruising speed 160km/h (100mph); range 627km (390 miles)
Dimensions: wingspan 8.72m (28ft 7in); length 6.95m (22ft 10in); height 1.75m (5ft 9in); maximum take-off weight 669kg (1475lb)
Payload: two-seat light aeroplane

DOUGLAS C-124 GLOBEMASTER II
The Douglas C-124 first flew in November 1949 and was an extensively modified version of the earlier C-74 Globemaster I, 14 of which were delivered to the USAF. The C-124 was the largest heavy cargo and troop transport produced in the early 1950s; 445 were built.

DOUGLAS X-3
First flown in October 1952, the primary purpose of the stiletto-like Douglas X-3 was to test the aerodynamics used in the design of a radical new interceptor, the F-104 Starfighter.

DOUGLAS F5D SKYLANCER
The Douglas F5D Skylancer was a proposed supersonic Skyray successor. It never went into production, although four examples were evaluated. The prototype flew in April 1956.

DOUGLAS C-133 CARGOMASTER
First flown on 23 April 1956, the giant C-133 entered service with the USAF Military Air Transport Service in 1957 and subsequently equipped the 1st and 84th Air Transport Squadrons.

DOUGLAS-NORTHROP BT-1
The Douglas-Northrop BT-1 was a US Navy dive-bomber of 1935. One example was experimentally fitted with a tricycle undercarriage, and became the first aircraft to land on a carrier with this configuration.

DU TEMPLE MONOPLANE
In 1874 a French naval officer, Felix du Temple, built a steam-powered monoplane which made an uncontrolled 'hop' from a sloping ramp. It was not a true flight.

DUFAUX NO 4
Switzerland's first pilot, Armand Dufaux, built this biplane in 1910. On 28 August of that year he flew it across Lake Geneva.

DUNNE D.5
Built by Short Brothers and designed by John William Dunne, the D.5 was the world's first 'flying wing'. It featured swept-back biplane wings and first flew on 11 March 1910. Test flights, which showed it to be extremely stable, continued throughout 1911. It was destroyed in an accident, but later rebuilt as the D.8.

EH INDUSTRIES EH-101 MERLIN

ITALY/UK: 1987

An ASW Merlin of the Italian Navy hovering close to the *Giuseppe Garibaldi*. The Italian Merlin version is powered by three 1278kW (1,714shp) GE turboshaft engines assembled in Italy.

THE EH-101 MERLIN EVOLVED from the WG.34 design of late 1978, which was intended as a replacement for the Sea King. The WG.34 was cancelled before a prototype was built, but Agusta and Westland established European

Helicopter Industries Ltd in February 1984 to produce a revised design for both the Royal Navy and Italian Navy. The EH-101 is a three-engined helicopter with a single main rotor carrying five blades of composite construction

with Westland/RAE British Experimental Rotor Programme (BERP) derived high-speed tips. Nine prototype aircraft were ordered, the first Westland-built model flying on 9 October 1987 and the first Agusta-built prototype on 26 April

1989. The RTM 322 engines were first flown in the fourth prototype in July 1993. The Italian version has the alternative powerplant of three 1278kW (1714shp) GE T700-GE-T6A turboshaft engines assembled in Italy. The RN order is for 44 HH Mk 1 anti-ship Merlins and the RAF initially ordered 22 HC Mk 3 medium-lift versions.

Specifications apply to the EH-101 (naval variant).

Crew: 2
Powerplant: HH.Mk.I/III: three Rolls-Royce/Turboméca RTM 322-01 turboshaft engines each rated at 1724kW (2312shp)
Italian ASW version: Alfa Romeo Avio/Fiat assembled GE T700-GE-401A turboshaft engines, each maximum continuous rated at 1072kW (1437shp)
Performance: max speed 296km/h (184mph); combat radius 5 hr endurance; service ceiling not known
Dimensions: main rotor diameter 18.59m (61ft); length 22.81m (74ft 10in); height 6.65m (21ft 10in)
Weight: 13,530kg (29,828lb)
Armament/Payload: four torpedoes (including Marconi Sting Ray), anti-ship missiles and/or other weapons according to mission; for military airlift, 35 equipped troops or up to 5443kg (12,000lb) of freight carried internally or as a slung load

ELLEHAMMER AEROPLANE NO IV

DENMARK: 1908

ALTHOUGH THE DESIGNS OF the Danish constructor Jacob Christian Hansen Ellehammer made only a limited contribution to development of the aeroplane, the remarkable aspect was that he worked entirely alone, without recourse to the ideas

of any contemporary pioneers. His most promising design was the Ellehammer IV of 1908; this was a tractor biplane which was test-flown in Germany. It remained airborne for 11 seconds, winning a prize of 5000 marks for its designer.

Ellehammer built his first aircraft in 1905; fitted with a 7kW (9hp) engine, it made a 'hop' of 42m (138ft) on 12 September 1906. There are some who believe that it was Ellehammer who made the first successful flight in Europe.

Crew: 1
Powerplant: one 26kW (35hp) Ellehammer air-cooled 5-cylinder radial engine
Performance: max speed 67.5km/h (42mph)
Dimensions: wingspan 12m (39ft 4.5in)
Weight: 130kg (287lb)

ELLEHAMMER HELICOPTERS

DENMARK: 1912–1916

IN 1903 DANISH ENGINEER Jacob Christian Ellehammer, notable pioneer in the rotary-wing field during the early part of the 20th century, constructed what was perhaps the first radial engine in the world. By 1910 he was developing rotary-wing machines as a lifting medium and built a model helicopter in 1911. In 1912 he built a full-size machine powered by a 27kW (36hp) engine of his own design. The engine drove both the main rotor system and a tractor propeller. The lifting rotor consisted of two contra-rotating rings mounted on the same axis, the lower ring

being fabric-covered to increase lift. Spaced around the rings were six vanes, 1.52m (5ft) long by 0.61m (2ft) wide. The angle of attack of these vanes could be altered in flight and were an early form of cyclic pitch control. After a number of tethered flights indoors, Ellehammer's machine made a free vertical take-off in late 1912.

Ellehammer made several short duration flights in his helicopter, pictured, until September 1916, when after take-off the rotor blades hit the ground and the machine disintegrated.

EMBRAER EMB-110 BANDEIRANTE & EMB-111   BRAZIL: 1972

Crew: 2
Powerplant: two 559kW (750shp) Pratt & Whitney Canada PT6A-34 turboprop engines
Performance: max cruising speed 417km/h (259mph); range 1964km (1220 miles); service ceiling 6858m (22,500ft)
Dimensions: wingspan 15.32m (50ft 3in); length 15.10m (49ft 6.5in); height 4.92m (16ft 2in)
Weight: 7000kg (15,432lb) maximum take-off weight
Armament/payload: commercial versions: up to 19 passengers; military version: (EMB-111 Patrulha) 1000kg (2205lb) of disposable stores carried on underwing hardpoints, generally comprising unguided rockets

THE BANDEIRANTE (the name itself meaning 'pioneer') marks Embraer's arrival on the scene as a significant manufacturer of regional airliners. The design of this light transport/commuter airliner was to a Brazilian Air Ministry requirement, with French designer Max Holste providing consultancy. Early customers for this unpressurised light transport were the Brazilian Air Force and Brazilian airlines; however, exports to the United States and Europe followed, and something in the region of 500 examples of the Bandeirante sold until 1992, when production of the type ended.

The design of the Bandeirante originates from a Brazilian Air Force requirement for the type's use in a number of specialist and general roles.

Military versions of the aircraft include armed maritime patrol and reconnaissance versions, such as the EMB-111 Patrulha (which means 'patrol' in Portuguese). These aircraft include specialized radar and electronics, as well as wingtip tanks for increased range and weapons pylons, and there is also a derivative SAR version.
Specifications apply to the Embraer EMB-110P1.

EMBRAER ERJ-135, ERJ-140, ERJ-145 & LEGACY   BRAZIL: 1995

Crew: 2
Powerplant: two 31.32kN (7040lb st) Rolls-Royce Allison AE3007-A1 turbofan engines
Performance: cruising speed 823km/h (511mph); range 1569km (975 miles); with maximum payload; service ceiling 11,280m (37,000ft)
Dimensions: wingspan 20.04m (65ft 9in); length 29.87m (98ft); height 6.75m (22ft 1.75in)
Weight: 19,200kg (42,328lb) maximum take-off weight
Payload: up to 50 passengers

EMBRAER UNDERTOOK IN 1989 to develop a 50-seat regional jet airliner to cater for that burgeoning market and customers' desire to fly

Embraer has also developed specialist military versions of the ERJ-135 such as this R-99A AEW surveillance aircraft of the Brazilian Air Force.

EAGLE AIRCRAFT
EAGLE XT-S 150
An Australian-designed, single-engined two-seat light aircraft first flown in 1988. The Eagle features forward-mounted wide-span canards in addition to a high-mounted main wing and a conventional tailplane.

EDGAR PERCIVAL EP.9 (LATER LANCASHIRE PROSPECTOR)
A single-engine, high-wing utility light aeroplane first flown in 1955, the Edgar Percival EP.9 achieved sales to both commercial and military customers.

EDGLEY OPTICA
A radical design for slow-speed observation work, dating from the early 1980s, the Optica features a bubble cockpit with a rearward-mounted engine and twin-boom tailplane arrangement.

EDO XOSE-1
The Edo XOSE-1 floatplane was designed for catapult operation from warships. The first of two prototypes flew in 1946, but the type did not enter production.

EDWARDS RHOMBOIDAL
A freakish design, this aircraft took its name from the fact that its biplane wings were rhomboid-shaped. Hardly surprisingly, the Edwards Rhomboidal proved a total failure when tested in 1911.

EKW C-35
The C-35 two-seat general-purpose biplane was developed by the Eidgenossische Kriegstechnische Werkstatten (EKW) in Switzerland. Fifty examples of the aircraft were built during 1932–36.

EKW C-3603-4
First flown in 1941, the EKW C-3603 fighter-bomber, which looked rather like a single-engined Messerschmitt 110, entered service with the Swiss Air Force in the following year. One hundred and sixty were produced. The heavier-armed C-3604 of 1944 was intended to replace it, but only 13 examples were built.

EL GALIVAN SA
GALIVAN 358
A recent Colombian venture into the burgeoning single-engined utility transport market, the 358 is a high-wing design with a turbo-charged piston engine. It is capable of carrying eight passengers or the equivalent weight in freight.

by jet. The result was the ERJ-145 with rear fuselage-mounted jet engines, while the cabin retained a degree of resemblance and commonality with the preceding Brasilia turboprop. More than 600 had been sold by 2003, and a military surveillance version was under development. Embraer added the shortened 37-seat ERJ-135, which flew in 1998 (entering service with Continental Express and American Eagle in 1999), and later the equidistant ERJ-140. These jets have proved enormously popular with major airlines and their commuter subsidiaries/partners in the USA and Europe – builds and orders exceed 500. There are also business jet (the Legacy) and mission-specific military electronic versions.

Specifications apply to the Embraer ERJ-145ER.

EMBRAER ERJ-170, ERJ-175, ERJ-190 AND ERJ-195 — BRAZIL: 2002

THE SUCCESS OF THE ERJ-145 range and the collapse of rival Fokker led Embraer to launch a range of larger regional jets with a wider body and a new level of sophistication and comfort, including a 2+2 seat/cabin configuration. The earliest and smallest of this series, the ERJ-170, entered service with Alitalia in 2003.

Vindication of the type's ground-breaking comfort and capability recently came in the form of large orders from the USA for the 90 plus seat ERJ-190 from low-cost carrier JetBlue. The ERJ-170 series may well become the aviation success story in the first decade of the 21st century.

Specifications apply to the Embraer ERJ-170.

Crew: 2
Powerplant: two 62.3kN (14,000lb) thrust GE CFE34-8 turbofan engines
Performance: max speed 851km/h (529mph); range 3333km (2071 miles) with maximum payload
Dimensions: wingspan 26.00m (85ft 4in); length 29.90m (98ft 1in); height 9.70m (31ft 9in);
Weight: 34,000kg (74,957lb) maximum take-off weight
Payload: up to 70

The Embraer 170 series has suffered some development programme delays – as did the earlier ERJ-145 range – will it go on to achieve similar sales success?

ENSTROM MODEL F-28F FALCON/F-28F-P SENTINEL/480 EAGLE/TH-28 — USA: 1960

Crew: 3
Powerplant: one Lycoming H10-360-F1AD flat-four position engine rated at 168kW (225hp)
Performance: max speed 180km/h (112mph); combat radius 423km (263 miles); service ceiling 3660m (12,000ft)
Dimensions: main rotor diameter 9.75m (32ft); length 8.92m (29ft 3in); height 2.79m (9ft 2in)
Weight: 712kg (1570lb)

THE F-28F FALCON IS A basic utility helicopter first delivered from October 1986, with the F-28F-P Sentinel being a dedicated police patrol version. In 1989, 15 Model 280FX examples were acquired by the Chilean Army for primary

This photograph shows an F-28F prior to delivery to the *Ejército Peruano* (Peruvian Army).

training. To date the Peruvian Army and Colombia have also bought F-28F examples. The Model 280FX served as the basis for the four- to five-seat Model 480 Eagle, which in turn became the TH-28 entrant for the US Army's NTH (New Training Helicopter) competition. The 480, powered by an Allison 250-C20B turboshaft engine and first flown in 1988, lost out to the Bell TH-67. Specifications apply to the F-28F.

ENTWICKLUNGSRING-SUD VJ 101 GERMANY: 1963

The VJ101C was to have been the first step along the road leading to a supersonic German V/STOL interceptor, but plans to produce an operational version were never implemented.

THE SUPERSONIC VJ 101, built by German consortium Messerschmitt, Heinkel and Bölkow, employed a lift plus lift/cruise propulsion concept, powered by six Rolls-Royce/MTU RB.145 turbojet engines. Two of these engines were mounted in tandem aft of the cockpit; the other four engines were in pairs in swivelling wingtip nacelles. The first VJ 101C hovering flight occurred on 10 April 1963, and the first horizontal take-off was accomplished on 31 August

1963. The VJ 101 X1 became the world's first supersonic V/STOL aircraft in July 1964 when it broke the sound barrier in a shallow dive. This aircraft was lost in an accident on 14 September 1964.

Following a second accident, the rotating nacelle design was abandoned, and the proposed follow-on, the VJ 101D, dispensed with the wingtip-mounted engines but retained the lift plus lift/cruise propulsion concept. Its use of five RB.162 lift engines and two aft

fuselage RB.153 lift/cruise engines (with internal thrust deflectors) was very complex and the VJ 101D was cancelled after engine testing had begun.

Crew: 1
Powerplant: six 1247kg (2749lb) thrust Rolls-Royce/MAN RB.145 turbojet engines
Performance: max speed Mach 1.08
Dimensions: wingspan 6.61m (21ft 7in); length 15.70m (51ft 5in); height 4.13m (13ft 5in)
Weight: 6000kg (13,230lb) loaded

ERCO ERCOUPE, FORNEY FORNAIR & ALON AIRCOUPE USA: 1937

Crew: 1
Powerplant: one 63kW (85hp) Continental C85-12 flat-four piston engine
Performance: max speed 196km/h (122mph); cruising speed 177km/h (110mph); range 724km (450 miles); service ceiling 3660m (12,000ft)
Dimensions: wingspan 9.14m (30ft); length 6.32m (20ft 9in); height 1.80m (5ft 11in)
Weight: 635kg (1400lb) maximum take-off weight
Payload: two-seat light aircraft

THE ORIGINS OF THE Ercoupe date back to 1930 and a company called the Engineering and Research Corporation. The importance of this monoplane was its ergonomic

The classic configuration of the Ercoupe is the twin end-plated 'H' tail-fin design, although later derivatives have a conventional tail-fin arrangement.

simplification of flight control systems, with no separate rudder controls (unless specified by the customer). Early models had a fixed undercarriage, but were mostly metal construction airframes. This simple design proved popular and many thousands were sold, particularly shortly after World War II. The Ercoupe was then often marketed as Aircoupe or Forney Fornair. In 1963 Erco ceased trading, Alon took over the assets and launched an improved version designated Alon Model A-2 Ercoupe, which remained available until 1967 when Mooney acquired the company.

Specifications apply to the Erco Model 415-E Ercoupe.

EUROCOPTER EC 665 TIGRE AND TIGER

FRANCE/GERMANY: 1991

Crew: 2
Powerplant: two MTU/Turboméca/Rolls-Royce MTR 390 turboshaft engines each rated at 958kW (1285shp) for take-off
Performance: max speed 269km/h (167mph); combat radius 800km (497 miles); service ceiling 3200m (10,500ft)
Dimensions: main rotor diameter 13.00m (42ft 7.75in); length 15.80m (51ft 10in); height 5.20m (17ft 0.75in)
Weight: 3300kg (7275lb)
Armament/Payload: one 30mm (1.18in) GIAT M30/781B cannon; two multiple launchers each carrying either 22 or 12 68mm (2.68in) air-to-surface rockets; eight AAMs (Mistral, Stinger or Trigat)

A Tigre HAP combat support/escort version with underwing MATRA Mistral AAMs and multiple ASR launchers, with a SFIM/TRT STRIX gyro-stabilized roof-mounted sight in place of the mast-mounted sight of the HAC variant.

DEVELOPED IN THE MID-1980s to meet West German and French helicopter requirements, the Eurocopter EC 665 evolved into a common French and German anti-tank helicopter and a French Gerfaut (Gyrfalcon) escort variant (from 1993, known as Tigre HAP – Hélicoptère d'Appui et de Protection). Contracts for five Tiger aerodynamic prototypes were received in November 1989, three of which were to be unarmed, and two armed. The first example flew on 29 April 1991. The French Army had a requirement for 100 Tigre HACs (Hélicoptère Anti-Char, or anti-tank helicopter) and 115 Tigre HAP models. Originally ordering the Tiger designated as the PAH-2 (Panzerabwehr-hubschrauber-2, or anti-tank helicopter no 2), Germany has a requirement for 212 Tiger support helicopters, redesignated UHU and later UHT (Unterstützungs-hubschrauber Tiger).

Specifications apply to the Eurocopter UHT.

EUROFIGHTER TYPHOON

INTERNATIONAL: 1994

IN OCTOBER 1981, THE Royal Air Force Operational Requirements Branch began planning for a next-generation fighter to replace the F-4 Phantom in the air defence role and the Jaguar in the offensive support role. The need crystallized in Air Staff Requirement (Air) 414, which specified a short-range, highly agile air defence/offensive support aircraft. The European Fighter Aircraft (EFA) programme was the project that met this requirement. An outline staff target for a common European fighter aircraft was issued in December 1983 by the air chiefs of staff of France, Germany, Italy, Spain and the UK; the initial feasibility study was completed in July 1984, but France withdrew from the project a year

A development Eurofighter Typhoon pictured on a test flight from Boscombe Down in Wiltshire.

Eurofighter shows its paces. The Typhoon is a highly agile aircraft, and delays in development have enabled the manufacturers to incorporate some very advanced equipment into the basic design.

later. A definitive European Staff Requirement (Development), giving operational requirements in greater detail, was issued in September 1987; the main engine and weapon system development contracts were signed in November 1988. To prove the necessary technology for EFA, a contract was awarded in May 1983 to British Aerospace for development of an agile demonstrator aircraft – not a prototype – under the heading Experimental Aircraft Programme, or EAP. The cost was to be shared between the partner companies of the EFA consortium and the UK Ministry of Defence (MoD). The EAP demonstrator flew for the first time on 8 August 1986, only three years after the programme was conceived. The task of Eurofighter, as EFA ultimately became known, is to fight effectively throughout the combat spectrum, from engagements beyond visual range down to close-in combat. The technologies that enable it to do this are so advanced, and in some cases so unique, that the role of the EAP aircraft was vital to the Eurofighter project as a whole.

The Cold War's end led, in 1992, to a reappraisal of the programme.

Germany in particular demanded substantial cost reductions. Several low-cost configurations were examined, but only two were cheaper than the original EFA, and both were inferior to the MiG-29 and Su-27. Finally, in December 1992, the project was re-launched as Eurofighter 2000, the planned in-service entry having now been delayed by three years.

To engage targets, particularly in the vital beyond-visual-range battle, the aircraft is equipped with the Euroradar ECR90 multimode pulse-Doppler radar. The ECR90 is designed to minimize pilot workload: radar tracks are presented constantly, analysed, allocated priority or deleted by track-management software. A third-generation coherent radar, the ECR90 benefits from a considerable increase in processing power and has all-aspect detection capability in look-up and look-down modes; it also has covert features to reduce the risk of detection by enemy radar-warning receivers.

The first two Eurofighter prototypes flew in 1994, followed by several more. The original customer requirement was 250 each for the UK and Germany,

165 for Italy and 100 for Spain. Spain announced a firm requirement for 87 in January 1994, while Germany and Italy revised their respective needs to 180 and 121, the German order to include at least 40 examples of the fighter-bomber version. The UK's order was 232, with options on a further 65 aircraft. Deliveries to the air forces of all four countries were scheduled to begin in 2001, but not for the first time the schedule slipped. The RAF received its first aircraft on 30 June 2003. Eurofighter has broken into the export market with an Austrian order for 35 aircraft.

Crew: 1/2
Powerplant: two 9185kg (20,250lb) Eurojet EJ.200 turbofan engines
Performance: max speed 2125km/h (1321mph); combat radius 1389km (862 miles); service ceiling 18,288m (60,000ft)
Dimensions: wingspan 10.50m (34ft 5in); length 14.50m (47ft 4in); height 4.00m (13ft 1in)
Weight: 21,000kg (46,297lb) loaded
Armament: one 23mm (0.91in) Mauser cannon; 13 fuselage hardpoints for a wide variety of ordnance including AMRAAM, ASRAAM, ASMs, ARMs, guided and unguided bombs

ENSTROM 280 SHARK/ MODEL 280L HAWK
A 1973 advanced version of the basic F-28A, the Model 280C is available with a 153kW (205hp) Lycoming HIO-360-E1AD engine with Rajay 301 E-10-2 turbo-supercharger. The Model 280L Hawk four-seat version first flew on 27 December 1978, and deliveries began in 1979.

ESNAULT-PETRIE REP-1
Robert Esnault-Petrie's first design, the REP-1 monoplane, was tested in France in 1907–8 and managed to make five short flights under the power of its 22kW (30hp) engine, but it was not a success.

ETRICH TAUBE
Designed in 1910 by the Austrian Igo Etrich, the Taube (Dove) monoplane became enormously successful. Etrich gave up his rights to the design, which ultimately was built by about 10 different firms.

EUROCOPTER DEUTSCHLAND EC 135
The EC 135, originally named the BO 108, first flew on 5 June 1991. The three main models are the EC 135P1 and the EC 135T1 with different powerplants and the EC 135 ACT/FHS (Active Control Technology/Flying Helicopter Simulator) built to develop 'fly-by-wire' technology.

EUROCOPTER EC 120B COLIBRI
The EC 120B Colibri is a five-seat light helicopter produced as a collaborative venture between Eurocopter France, the China National Aero-Technology Import and Export Corporation (CATIC), and Singapore Aerospace Technologies (ST Aero). Prototype assembly began in 1995; the first deliveries started in January 1998.

EUROCOPTER FRANCE AS 355 ECUREUIL (SQUIRREL) 2 AND AS 555 FENNEC (DESERT FOX)
The Ecureuil was originally intended mainly for the civil market until the creation of Eurocopter, when it became the militarized AS555 Fennec. The Helibras HB 355F-2 Esquilo is the Brazilian licence-built model.

EXTRA 400
This single-engined, high-wing six-seat light aircraft was designed in Germany in collaboration with Delft University. It dates from 1996 and a small number have been sold.

FAIRCHILD ARGUS

The Fairchild Argus proved to be a very useful light transport aircraft during World War II, many civilian-owned examples being impressed into military service. Most of the early models were used by the RAF.

IN 1933 FAIRCHILD PRODUCED the Model 24 three-seat touring aircraft. One variant, the 24W-41, was developed for service with the USAAC as the UC-61 Forwarder. Of 163 built, only two were retained. The rest were supplied to the UK under Lend-Lease and were known as the Argus I. The type was the Air Transport Auxiliary's standard transport for the carriage of ferry pilots. A further 512 UC-61As were built to a USAAC order, with 364 of these going to the UK as Argus IIs. A number of civil models were also impressed into Army Air Corp service in 1942, designated UC-61B to UC-61J.

Crew: 4
Powerplant: one 123kW (165hp) Warner R-500 Super Scarab radial engine
Performance: max speed 212km/h (132mph); range 1030km (640 miles); service ceiling 4785m (15,700ft)
Dimensions: wingspan 11.07m (36ft 4in); length 7.24m (23ft 9in); height 2.32m (7ft 7.5in)
Weight: 1162kg (2562lb) loaded

FAIRCHILD C-119 BOXCAR

Crew: 4 (plus 40 paratroops)
Powerplant: two 2611kW (3500hp) Wright R-3350-89 Cyclone 18-cylinder radial engines
Performance: max speed 350km/h (218mph); range 2850km (1770 miles); service ceiling 7285m (23,900ft)
Dimensions: wingspan 33.32m (109ft 4in); length 26.36m (86ft 6in); height 8.00m (26ft 3in)
Weight: 38,556kg (85,000lb) loaded

THE FAIRCHILD CORPORATION'S first post World War II operational transport design, the C-82 Packet, soon gave way to a much modified version, the C-119 Boxcar, which first flew in November 1947. By the time production of the aircraft ceased in 1955, 1150 had been built. The C-119 saw widespread service with the USAF, the US Navy (as the R4Q) and the air forces of Belgium, Brazil, Canada, Nationalist China, France, India, Italy, Morocco and Norway. Some USAF C-119s were specially modified for reconnaissance satellite recovery. The C-119 was very active in the Korean War, dropping both airborne forces and supplies, and was used by the French in Indo-China.

The C-119 experienced a new lease of life in the Vietnam War, this time in the ground-support role as the AC-119G 'Shadow' and the AC-119K 'Stinger' gunships mounting side-firing weapons capable of unleashing up to 6000 rounds per minute per gun. When acting as a transport, the C-119 was capable of carrying up to 62 fully equipped troops or a 13,608kg (30,000lb) cargo load.

The Fairchild C-119, widely used for transport and paratrooping missions in the 1950s, found a change of role in the Vietnam War, when it was turned into a highly effective gunship.

196

FAIRCHILD C-123 PROVIDER

USA: 1949

THE C-123 WAS DEVELOPED from the experimental Chase XG-20 transport glider, two examples of which were built in 1948. One was fitted with Pratt & Whitney R-2800 engines and became the XC-123 Avitruc; the other was fitted with four J47 turbojets and became the sole C-123A. The aircraft entered production as the C-123B, and 302 were built between 1954 and 1958.

The Fairchild C-123 Provider was widely used by a number of air forces in the 1950s and 1960s and saw extensive service in Vietnam.

Of these, six went to Saudi Arabia, 18 to Venezuela, and others to Thailand and South Vietnam. Fifty or so C-123Bs were used by 315th Air Command Group in Vietnam, mostly in defoliation programmes.

Crew: 2 (plus 61 passengers)
Powerplant: four 1716kW (2300hp) Pratt & Whitney R2800-99W Double Wasp 8-cylinder radial engines
Performance: max speed 330km/h (205mph); range 2365km (1470 miles); service ceiling 8840m (29,000ft)
Dimensions: wingspan 33.53m (110ft); length 23.08m (75ft 9in); height 10.38m (34ft 1in)
Weight: 27,000kg (60,000lb) loaded

FAIRCHILD REPUBLIC A-10 THUNDERBOLT II

USA: 1972

Crew: 1
Powerplant: two 4112kg (9065lb) thrust General Electric TF34-GE-100 turbofan engines
Performance: max speed 706km/h (438mph); combat radius 463km (287 miles); service ceiling 7625m (25,000ft)
Dimensions: wingspan 17.53m (57ft 6in); length 16.26m (53ft 4in); height 4.47m (14ft 8in)
Weight: 22,680kg (50,000lb)
Armament: one 30mm (1.18in) GAU-8/A rotary cannon with 1350 rounds; 11 hardpoints for up to 7528kg (16,000lb) of ordnance, including Rockeye cluster bombs, Maverick ASMs and SUU-23 20mm (0.79in) cannon pods

IN DECEMBER 1970, Fairchild Republic and Northrop were each selected to build a prototype of a new close-support aircraft for evaluation under the USAF's A-X programme, and in January 1973 it was announced that Fairchild Republic's contender, the YA-10, had been chosen. The aircraft had

A-10 Thunderbolt IIs armed with AGM-65 Maverick television-guided ground-attack missiles on the inboard wing pylons.

made its first flight on 10 May 1972. Fairchild met the armour requirement by seating the pilot in what virtually amounted to a

titanium 'bathtub', resistant to most firepower except a direct hit from a heavy-calibre shell, and added to this a so-called redundant

FABRE HYDRAVION
On 28 March 1910, the first-ever powered take-off from water was made by a fragile canard monoplane named the Hydravion, designed by Henri Fabre. The aircraft flew for 2km (1.24 miles) near Marseilles and landed safely.

FAIRCHILD FC-2W
A derivative of the FC-1 and FC-2 photographic aircraft designs (also used as mail planes), the FC-2Ws single engine was more powerful and it had a greater wingspan. A further derivative FC-2W2 had a stretched fuselage to accommodate up to six passengers.

FAIRCHILD AT-21
The twin-engined Fairchild AT-21 was ordered into production in 1942 as a gunnery trainer. The aircraft was a five-seater, and 175 examples were built.

FAIRCHILD SUPER 71
First flown in 1934, the Fairchild 71 was designed for operations in the Arctic regions of Canada. A single-engined high-wing monoplane, it could be fitted with wheels, floats or skis.

FAIRCHILD MODEL 91 BABY CLIPPER
An amphibious monoplane flying boat with a single piston engine mounted in a tall housing atop the fuselage, the Baby Clipper dates from 1934 and seven were built, seeing civil and military service, domestic and overseas.

FAIRCHILD MODEL 82
A single-engined, high-wing nine-seat monoplane available in tail-wheel undercarriage, float or ski configuration, the Model 82 first flew in 1935. Twenty-three examples were built, plus another variant with a different powerplant (Model 34-42 Niska).

FAIRCHILD F-11 HUSKY
A single radial-engined high-wing utility transport first flown in 1946, the Husky was produced in small numbers (12) before dissolution of the company, and later converted to F-11-2 standard by the Husky Aircraft Company of Vancouver.

FAIRCHILD-DORNIER 328JET
Developed from the similarly sized 328 Turboprop, the turbofan jet-powered Fairchild-Dornier 328JET first flew in 1998. It has a capacity of up to 34 passengers and more than 70 have been delivered.

The A-10 was designed to operate from short, unprepared airstrips close to the battle area, so that aircraft could be summoned to carry out strikes at short notice by commanders on the ground.

structure policy whereby the pilot could retain control even if the aircraft lost large portions of its airframe, including one of the two rear-mounted engines. The core of the A-10's built-in firepower was its massive GAU-8/A seven-barrel 30mm (1.18in) rotary cannon, which was mounted on the centreline under the forward fuselage. The aircraft also had eight underwing and three underfuselage attachments for up to 7257kg (16,000lb) of bombs, missiles, gun pods and jammer pods, and carried the Pave Penny laser

system pod for target designation. It was fitted with very advanced avionics including a central air data computer, an inertial navigation system and a head-up display.

The A-10 was designed to operate from short, unprepared strips less than 457m (1500ft) long. Deliveries began in March 1977 to the 354th Tactical Fighter Wing at Myrtle Beach, South Carolina; in all, the USAF took delivery of 727 aircraft for service with its tactical fighter wings, the emphasis being on European

operations. The operational tactics developed for the aircraft involved two A-10s giving one another mutual support, covering a swathe of ground two or three miles wide, so that an attack could be quickly mounted by the second aircraft once the first pilot had made his firing pass on the target. The 30mm (1.18in) ammunition drum carried enough rounds to make 10 to 15 firing passes. In order to survive in a hostile environment dominated by radar-controlled anti-aircraft artillery, A-10 pilots

trained to fly at around 30m (100ft) or lower, never remaining straight and level for more than four seconds. One of the aircraft's big advantages in approaching the combat zone was that its twin General Electric TF34-GE-100 turbofan engines were very quiet, so that it was able to achieve total surprise as it popped up over a contour of the land for weapons release. Attacks on targets covered by anti-aircraft artillery involved close cooperation between the two A-10s; while one engaged the target the other stood off and engaged anti-aircraft installations with its TV-guided Maverick missiles, six of which were normally carried. The A-10 also had a considerable air-to-air capability, the tactic being for the pilot to turn towards an attacking fighter and use coarse rudder to spray it with 30mm (1.18in) shells.

In general, operations by the A-10s envisaged cooperation with US Army helicopters; the latter would hit the mobile surface-to-air missile and anti-aircraft artillery systems accompanying a Soviet armoured thrust. With the enemy's defences at least temporarily stunned or degraded, the A-10s would be free to concentrate their fire on the tanks. Twelve years later, these tactics were used to deadly effect in the 1991 Gulf War.

FAIRCHILD-DORNIER (SWEARINGEN) METRO USA: 1969

Crew: 2
Powerplant: two 701kW (939shp) Garrett AiResearch turboprop engines
Performance: max cruising speed 472km/h (293mph); range with 19 passengers 346km (226 miles); service ceiling 7620m (25,000 ft)
Dimensions: wingspan 14.10m (46ft 3in); length 18.10m (59ft 5in); height 5.10m (16ft 8in)
Weight: 7257kg (16,000lb) maximum take-off weight
Payload: up to 19 passengers or 2268kg (5000lb) freight

THE METRO COMMUTER AIRLINER was a fundamentally new design based on experience gained from the smaller Merlin light transport, which itself was derived from the Beech Queen Air. In 1971 the Swearingen Company was acquired by Fairchild. Thereon the Metro continued to be produced in progressively improved variants until 1999, when production ceased with 1053 examples built.

Versions include the C-26A and B variants operated on a variety of missions for the Air National Guard. Meanwhile the Metro remains in

service with many commuter and light freight operators, particularly in North/Central America.

Specifications apply to Metro II.

More than 1000 Metros were sold to a wide range of commercial, military and corporate customers over a period of 30 years.

FAIRCHILD-HILLER FH-1100 (OH-5A)

USA: 1963

THE FH-1100 WAS A REFINED development of the five-seat YOH-5A. In May 1965 the YOH-5A lost out to the Hughes CH-6A in the US Army LOH (Light Observation Helicopter) competition and was subsequently developed as the FH-1100, a four- to five-seat civil utility/executive helicopter. The first FH-1100 was completed on 3

Illustration shows an FH-1100 of the Fuerza Aerea Panama (Panama Air Force).

June 1966 and production ended in 1974 when 246 examples had been produced. Several military versions were operated by South American nations. Specifications apply to the Hiller FH-1100A Pegasus.

Crew/accommodation: 5
Powerplant: one 313kW (420shp) Allison 250-C20B turboshaft engine
Performance: max speed 196km/h (122mph); range 692km (430 miles); service ceiling 6550m (21,500ft)
Dimensions: main rotor diameter 10.80m (35ft 5in); length 9.08m (29ft 9.5in); height 2.83m (9ft 3.5in)
Weight: 680kg (1500lb)

FAIREY CAMPANIA

UK: 1917

Crew: 2
Powerplant: one 257kW (345hp) Rolls-Royce Eagle VIII 12-cylinder Vee-type engine
Performance: max speed 129km/h (80mph); endurance 3 hrs; service ceiling 1676m (5500ft)
Dimensions: wingspan 18.78m (61ft 7in); length 13.12m (43ft); height 4.60m (15ft 1in)
Weight: 2566kg (5657lb)
Armament: one 7.7mm (0.303in) Lewis machine gun in rear cockpit; light bomb load

THE FAIREY CAMPANIA general-purpose seaplane was the first-ever aeroplane to be designed for operation from an aircraft carrier. The prototype flew for the first time on 16 February 1917 and the aircraft appeared in two main variants, the F.17 and F.22. At the end of World War I there were 42 Campanias on RAF charge, 26 of them with Rolls-Royce Eagle engines. They remained on active

The first aircraft to be designed from the outset for operation from carriers, the Fairey Campania did not enter service until the closing months of WWI.

duty for some time after the end of hostilities, carrying out mine detection patrols in British coastal waters. Campanias served on the

seaplane carriers *Campania*, *Nairana* and *Pegasus*.
Specifications apply to the Fairey Campania F.22.

FAIREY III SERIES

UK: 1917

Crew: 3
Powerplant: one 336kW (450hp) Napier Lion IIB 12-cylinder Vee-type engine
Performance: max speed 171km/h (105mph); range 885km (550 miles); service ceiling 5180m (17,000ft);
Dimensions: wingspan 14.05m (46.1ft);

length 11.28m (37ft); height 3.45m (11ft 4in)
Weight: 2231kg (4918lb)
Armament: one 7.7mm (0.303in) Vickers machine gun in front fuselage and one 7.7mm (0.303in) Lewis gun in rear cockpit; provision for small bombs under lower wing

THE PROGENITOR OF THE Fairey III series was a twin-float seaplane, built to Admiralty requirements in 1917. The prototype was converted to landplane configuration to become the Fairey IIIA, 50 production examples of which were built for the RNAS/RAF. The

FAIREY FAWN
The Fairey Fawn biplane light bomber, which first appeared in 1923, had a performance inferior to the DH.9A, which it was intended to replace. Production of the type totalled 50 Fawn Mk II aircraft and 20 Mk IIIs.

FAIREY FOX
The Fairey Fox light bomber prototype flew on 3 January 1925 and was a good 48km/h (30mph) faster than any contemporary RAF fighter, but only one RAF squadron was equipped with it.

FAIREY LONG-RANGE MONOPLANE
Two Fairey Long-Range Monoplanes were built, specifically so that the RAF could undertake long-range proving flights. The first aircraft flew non-stop from the UK to India in 1929, and the second aircraft made the first non-stop flight from the UK to South Africa in 1933.

FAIREY GORDON
The Fairey Gordon bomber/general-purpose aircraft was a development of the Fairey IIIF. The prototype, which flew in 1930, was a converted IIIF Mk IVM.

FAIREY HENDON
The Hendon night bomber was built in 1930 to meet Specification B.19/27, and it was the first low-wing bomber monoplane to be built in Britain. Fifteen aircraft were issued to No 38 Squadron RAF.

FAIREY FANTOME
The Fairey Fantome of 1935 was one of the most beautiful biplanes ever built, but was outmoded when it appeared. Three were built in Belgium, and two of these fought in the Spanish Civil War.

FAIREY SEAFOX
The Fairey Seafox, one of the most widely used British aircraft during the early part of World War II, was designed to be catapult-launched from the Royal Navy's capital ships. The prototype of this little biplane flew on 27 May 1936.

FAIREY ALBACORE
Resulting from a 1936 requirement, the Fairey Albacore was in effect a modernized and technically improved development of the Fairey Swordfish, with an enclosed cockpit. The prototype Albacore flew in December 1938, and 798 examples were built.

IIIA was followed by the IIIB naval bomber with an increased span and the same 260 Sunbeam Maori II engine as the IIIA; of the 30 ordered, the last six were completed to IIIC standard with the Rolls-Royce Eagle VIII engine, as were 30 further aircraft. The second most numerous variant was the Fairey IIID, the prototype (first flight August 1920) being followed by 207 production aircraft. In March/ April 1926, four RAF Fairey IIIDs carried out a spectacular long-distance formation flight from Northolt to Cape Town, returning to Lee-on-Solent via Greece, Italy and France in June. The final and most numerous variant of this versatile aircraft was the IIIF, of which 597 aircraft were built. Specifications apply to IIID.

The Fairey III series was notable for its long-range endurance flights, which helped to pioneer the British Empire mail routes in the years between the world wars.

FAIREY FLYCATCHER

UK: 1923

A nimble and popular fleet fighter, the Flycatcher served the Fleet Air Arm for more than a decade. It saw service aboard five British aircraft carriers in home and foreign waters.

Crew: 1
Powerplant: one 30kW (40hp) Armstrong Siddeley Jaguar III 14-cylinder radial engine
Performance: max speed 215km/h (134mph); range 420km (260 miles); service ceiling 6200m (20,341ft)
Dimensions: wingspan 8.84m (29ft); length 7.01m (23ft); height 3.65m (12ft)
Weight: 1373kg (3028lb) loaded
Armament: two 7.7mm (0.303in) machine guns; 36kg (80lb) of bombs

THE ROYAL NAVY'S FIRST post-World War I fighter was the Gloster Nightjar, one of a series of aircraft derived from the Nighthawk. Twenty-two were built, and were replaced in 1923 by the Fairey Flycatcher, a highly popular little aircraft that was to remain in service for 11 years. Although the initial production order was for only nine aircraft, subsequent contracts brought the final number produced to 193. Flycatchers were delivered to eight fighter flights.

FAIREY SWORDFISH

UK: 1934

THE FAIREY SWORDFISH PROTOTYPE was to fly for the first time on 17 April 1934. A contract for 86 production Swordfish Mk I aircraft was placed in April 1935, the aircraft entering service with No 825 Squadron of the Fleet Air Arm

in July 1936. Early war roles for the Fairey Swordfish included fleet escort and convoy protection, with the first offensive missions being flown during the Norwegian campaign, April–June 1940. In the Mediterranean, Swordfish inflicted

considerable damage on Italian shipping, culminating in the spectacular night attack on the Italian fleet at Taranto on 11 November 1940. Other notable Swordfish actions included the Battle of Cape Matapan in March 1941, the

crippling of the German battleship *Bismarck* in May, and the gallant action against the *Scharnhorst*, *Gneisenau* and *Prinz Eugen* during the famous 'Channel Dash' of February 1942, when all six Swordfish of No 825 Squadron involved were shot down and their commander, Lt Cdr Eugene Esmonde, was awarded a posthumous Victoria Cross.

The Swordfish Mk II, which appeared in 1943, had metal-covered lower wings, enabling it to carry rocket projectiles. Later Mk II Swordfish were fitted with the 612kW (820hp) Pegasus XXX engine, and this also powered the Swordfish Mk III, which carried ASV radar in a housing between the main landing gear legs. Swordfish production ended on 18 August 1944, by which time 2391 aircraft had been built.

Specifications apply to the Fairey Swordfish Mk II.

Although seemingly obsolescent, the Fairey Swordfish torpedo-bomber became legendary due to its exploits, including the crippling of the Italian fleet at Taranto in November 1940.

Crew: 3
Powerplant: one 612kW (820hp) Bristol Pegasus XXX radial engine
Performance: max speed 222km/h (138mph); range 879km (546 miles); service ceiling 5867m (19,250ft)
Dimensions: wingspan 12.97m (42ft 6in); length 10.87m (35ft 8in); height 3.76m (12ft 4in)
Weight: 3406kg (7510lb) loaded
Armament: two 7.7mm (0.303in) machine guns; one 457mm (18in) torpedo or eight 27.2kg (60lb) rocket projectiles

FAIREY BATTLE

UK: 1936

Crew: 3
Powerplant: one Rolls-Royce Merlin II 12-cylinder Vee-type engine
Performance: max speed 406km/h (252mph); range 1931km (1200 miles); service ceiling 7925m (26,000ft)
Dimensions: wingspan 16.45m (54ft); length 12.93m (42ft 5in); height 4.57m (15ft)
Weight: 5307kg (11,700lb) loaded
Armament: one 7.7mm (0.303in) machine gun in leading edge of starboard wing and one in rear cockpit; internal and external bomb load of 680kg (1500lb)

Fairey Battle of No 12 Squadron RAF. Five aircraft of this squadron carried out an attack on the bridges at Maastricht on 12 May 1940. All were lost.

THE FAIREY BATTLE single-engined light bomber, one of the types chosen for large-scale production, first flew in March 1936, and first deliveries of the aircraft were made to No 63 Squadron in May 1937. On 2 September 1939, 10 Battle squadrons of the Advanced Air Striking Force deployed to France, and in May 1940 they suffered appalling losses during attempts to bomb enemy columns and bridges over the River Meuse. As a result, the Fairey Battle was soon assigned to second-line duties.

FAIREY FIREFLY

As can be seen in this photograph, the Fairey Firefly's pilot had a good all-round view from the elevated cockpit.

THE PROTOTYPE FAIREY FIREFLY two-seat naval fighter first flew on 22 December 1941, production getting under way towards the end of the following year. It became operational in October 1943 on board the carrier HMS *Indefatigable*. Fireflies provided fighter cover during the series of Fleet Air Arm attacks on the battleship *Tirpitz* in the summer of 1944; in January 1945, while deploying to the Pacific, they took part in the destruction of Japanese-held oil refineries in Sumatra. The first major postwar variant was the Firefly Mk IV, which in turn was replaced by the Mk V. Operating from light carriers, Fireflies carried out many strikes during the Korean War. The Firefly AS.6 was an anti-submarine variant. Specifications apply to the Mk I.

Crew: 2
Powerplant: one 1291kW (1730hp) Rolls-Royce Griffon IIB 12-cylinder Vee-type engine
Performance: max speed 508km/h (316mph); range 2100km (1300 miles); service ceiling 8500m (28,000ft)
Dimensions: wingspan 13.56m (44ft 6in); length 11.46m (37ft 7in); height 4.14m (13ft 7in)
Weight: 6350kg (14,020lb) loaded
Armament: four 20mm (0.79in) Hispano cannon

FAIREY GANNET

THE FAIREY GANNET PROTOTYPE first flew on 19 September 1949, and the aircraft was ordered into production as the Gannet AS.1, its first operational squadron, No 826, forming in January 1945.

The 170th production AS.1 received a more powerful Double Mamba 101 engine and became the Gannet AS.4, this variant equipping the Royal Navy's ASW squadrons until 1960, when it began to be replaced by ASW helicopters. The Gannet was also supplied to the Federal German Navy and to Indonesia. The Mks T2 and T4 were trainers. The last version of the Gannet was the AEW.3 early warning aircraft, which equipped four flights of No 849 Squadron.

Specifications apply to the Fairey Gannet AS.4.

Crew: 3
Powerplant: one 2264kW (3035hp) Armstrong Siddeley Double Mamba 101 coupled turboprop
Performance: max speed 481km/h (299mph); range 1510km (943 miles); service ceiling 7629m (25,000ft)
Dimensions: wingspan 16.56m (54ft 4in); length 13.10m (43ft); height 4.16m (13ft 8in)
Weight: 10,208kg (22,506lb) loaded
Armament: 907kg (2000lb) of torpedoes, mines, depth charges etc.

The Fairey Gannet, although far from pretty to look at, combined twin-engined reliability with single-engined performance, and proved very effective in its intended role of submarine-hunter. This is a trainer version.

FAIREY FD.2

UK: 1954

The Fairey Delta 2, flown by Lt Cdr Peter Twiss, became the first aircraft to set a world air speed record of more than 1600km/h (1000mph) in March 1956. Two aircraft were built.

THE FAIREY FD.2 (Fairey Delta 2) research aircraft was assured of its place in aviation history when, on 10 March 1956, it became the first aircraft to set a world speed record of more than 1600km/h (1000mph). On that date, test pilot Peter Twiss flew the aircraft to a new record speed of 1821km/h (1132mph).

The first of two FD.2 prototypes flew on 6 October 1954. From the beginning it showed itself to be an aircraft of enormous potential. The second FD.2 flew on 15 February 1956, and the two aircraft had made well over 100 flights by the time Peter Twiss captured the speed record. They made an enormous contribution to high-speed flight research, the first later being fitted with a model of the ogival wing planform used later on Concorde.

Crew: 1
Powerplant: one 4590kg (10,250lb) thrust Rolls-Royce Avon RA.28 turbojet engine
Performance: max speed Mach 1.7; range 1335km (830 miles); service ceiling 12,192m (40,000ft)
Dimensions: wingspan 8.18m (26ft 10in); length 15.74m (51ft 7.5in); height 3.35m (11ft)
Weight: 6298kg (13,884lb)

FARMAN MF.11 SHORTHORN

FRANCE: 1914

Crew: 2
Powerplant: one 75kW (100hp) Renault 8-cylinder air-cooled Vee-type in-line engine
Performance: max speed 106km/h (66mph); endurance 3 hrs 45 mins; service ceiling 3800m (12,467ft)
Dimensions: wingspan 16.16m (53ft); length 9.45m (31ft); height 3.18m (10ft 5in)
Weight: 928kg (2045lb) loaded
Armament: one machine gun; 130kg (288lb) of bombs

DESIGNED IN 1914, the Farman MF.11 served in considerable numbers, equipping 37 French escadrilles, six squadrons of the RFC on the Western Front and other RFC/RNAS units in Mesopotamia, the Dardanelles and the Aegean. It was the first Farman design to be armed, being employed on bombing and reconnaissance duties. A Farman MF.11 of the

Many Allied airmen had their first taste of flight in the draughty cockpit of a Farman Shorthorn during World War I.

Royal Naval Air Service made the first night bombing raid of World War I, attacking German gun emplacements near Ostend on 21 December 1914. Following their frontline service, the MF.11 and its predecessor, the MF.7, were widely used for training.

FARMAN F.60 GOLIATH SERIES

FRANCE: 1919

Crew: 2
Powerplant: two Salmson CM.9 radial piston engines each rated at 194kW (260hp)
Performance: max speed 140km/h (87mph); service ceiling 4000m (13,125ft); range 400km (249 miles).
Dimensions: wingspan 26.50m (86ft 11.25in); length 14.33m (47ft 0.25in); height 4.91m (16ft 1.25in)
Weight: 4770kg (10,516lb) maximum take-off weight
Payload: up to 12 passengers in two cabin areas

THE GOLIATH SERIES ORIGINATES from a two-engined biplane bomber design planned to enter service in 1919. After cessation of World War I hostilities, two prototypes were converted for use in civil transports, thus forming the basis of a series that would be one of the most plentiful types of the 1920s. More than 350 were built, ending with the 160 series of 1929, which was itself re-developed for military bomber use. In August 1919 an F.60 set a world record by travelling 2050km (1274

A clumsy design, the Farman Goliath series nevertheless proved successful as both commercial aircraft and bombers. Several different variants were produced in the 1920s.

miles) nonstop to Casablanca in 18 hours 23 minutes, with a crew of eight. Scheduled F.60 services began with a Le Bourget to Croydon service and the type went on to be sold or licence-built for airlines and air forces in a number of countries. The F.60 was produced in civil and military versions, with a variety of nose configuration and engine changes. The French Navy operated a floated version. The last commercial variant was withdrawn from service in 1933. Specifications apply to the F.60.

FARMAN F.160 TO F.168

FRANCE: 1929

Crew: 4
Powerplant: two 373kW (500hp) Gnome-Rhone Jupiter radial engines
Performance: max speed 174km/h (108mph); range 1000km (621 miles); service ceiling 4503m (14,764ft)

Dimensions: wingspan 26.76m (87ft 7.2in); length 14.88m (48ft 9in); height 5.33m (17ft 5in)
Weight: 6841kg (15,102lb)
Armament: four 7.62mm (0.30in) machine guns; 2000kg (4409lb) of bombs

THE SUCCESS OF THE commercial Farman F.60 Goliath, which also gave rise to the F.62/F.63 series of bombers, persuaded Farman to modernize the basic design. This resulted in the F.160, F.161 and

F.165 landplane night bombers, and the F.162, F.166, F.167 and F.168 naval torpedo-bomber/reconnaissance aircraft capable of operating on either wheel or float undercarriages. Specifications apply to F.168.

FARMAN F.222/223

FRANCE: 1938

The angular Farman F.222 four-engined heavy bomber, pictured here, was still in first-line service at the outbreak of World War II and carried out several night bombing attacks on German targets.

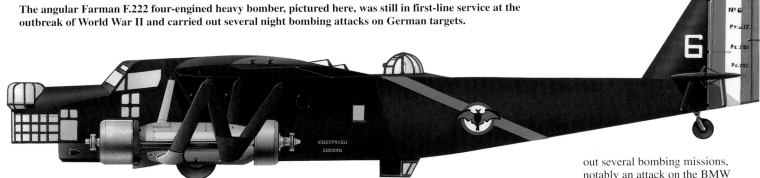

Crew: 5
Powerplant: four 724kW (970hp) Gnome-Rhone 14N-11/15 radial engines
Performance: max speed 320km/h (199mph); range 2000km (1243 miles); service ceiling 8000m (26,245ft)

Dimensions: wingspan 36.00m (118ft 1.33in); length 21.45m (70ft 4.5in); height 5.19m (17ft 0.33in)
Weight: 18,700kg (41,226lb)
Armament: three 7.5mm (0.30in) machine guns; internal bomb load of 4200kg (9259lb)

THE FARMAN F.222 heavy bomber was a progressive development of the F.220/221 series with a retractable undercarriage and other refinements; 24 were in service at the outbreak of World War II. In May and June 1940 they carried

out several bombing missions, notably an attack on the BMW factory in Munich. The Farman F.223, about eight of which were built, had still more aerodynamic refinements. One of these, operated by the Aéronavale, became the first Allied aircraft to bomb Berlin, on the night of 7/8 June 1940.

Specifications apply to the F.222.

FELIXSTOWE F.2A

UK: 1917

Crew: 4
Powerplant: two 257kW (345hp) Rolls-Royce Eagle VIII Vee-type engines
Performance: max speed 135km/h (84mph); endurance 6 hrs; service ceiling 2930m (9600ft)
Dimensions: wingspan 29.15m (95ft 7in); length 14.10m (46ft 3in); height 5.33m (17ft 6in))
Weight: 4980kg (10,978lb)
Armament: four-seven 7.7mm (0.303in) machine guns; 208kg (460lb) of bombs

DERIVED FROM THE Curtiss H-12 maritime patrol flying boat, the Felixstowe F.2A set the pattern for all British maritime aircraft up to the 1920s. The F.2A was a first-class aircraft, and was used with great success on long North Sea patrols. In October 1918 there

The Felixstowe F.2A flying boat carried out both anti-ship and anti-Zeppelin patrols during World War I.

were 53 F.2As on RAF charge, together with 96 examples of a larger variant, the F.3. This served in the Mediterranean and the North

Sea. The last variant was the F.5, which remained the standard RAF flying boat until 1925.
Specifications apply to the F.2A.

FFA P-16

SWITZERLAND: 1955

The FFA P-16 was intended to be the Swiss Air Force's standard jet ground-attack type, but it was cancelled after the loss of two prototypes.

THE FFA P-16 WAS designed to meet the needs of the postwar Swiss forces. The aircraft was to be a single-seater, able to fly in and out of short strips in narrow, high mountain valleys. Two prototypes were ordered in 1952, the first flying in April 1955. A third prototype and four pre-series aircraft were ordered, but the project was cancelled after two of the prototypes crashed.

Crew: 1
Powerplant: one 4990kg (11,000lb) thrust Armstrong Siddeley Sapphire 200 turbojet engine
Performance: max speed 1100km/h (685mph); range 1000km (620 miles); service ceiling 14,000m (46,000ft)
Dimensions: wingspan 11.15m (36ft 7in); length 14.24m (46ft 9in); height 4.10m (13ft 5in)
Weight: 11,700kg (25,795lb) loaded
Armament: two 20mm cannon; 2000kg (4400lb) of bombs

FFVS J.22

SWEDEN: 1942

Crew: 1
Powerplant: one 794kW (1065hp) Pratt & Whitney Twin Wasp 14-cylinder radial engine
Performance: max speed 576km/h (358mph); range 1250km (776 miles); service ceiling 9300m (30,511ft)
Dimensions: wingspan 10.00m (32ft 10in); length 7.80m (25ft 7in); height 2.79m (9ft 2in)
Weight: 2850kg (6300lb) loaded
Armament: four 7.7mm (0.303in) machine guns

THE J.22 SINGLE-SEAT fighter project was initiated in the autumn of 1940. Around 350 fighters had been ordered from the USA, but unfortunately only 60 had been delivered, and aircraft purchased from Italy did not measure up to requirements. It was decided that the only solution was to produce a fighter of national design, and the task was assigned to the Swedish Air Board's works at Bromma. The

prototype flew in September 1942, followed by the first production aircraft in September 1943. Delivery of production machines, 198 in all, began two months later. The J.22 was constructed of wood and steel, and its Pratt & Whitney Twin Wasp engine was manufactured in Sweden without a licence, such was the urgency. The fighter was somewhat underpowered, but despite this its performance was good.

FARMAN F.301
A high-wing monoplane tri-motor design capable of carrying eight passengers, the F.301 was first flown in 1930.

FARMAN MONITOR
An early postWorld War II monoplane design powered by a single engined, the initial Monitor I was developed in series II, III and IV. The IV was taken up by Stampe et Renard.

FFA AS-202 BRAVO
A primary trainer design with aerobatic capability and two/three seats, the Bravo has sold in a number of variants since first flying in 1969. This single-engine Swiss/Italian collaboration was produced for mostly military export customers.

FIAT R.2
Designed by Celestino Rosatelli, the R.2 reconnaissance aircraft of 1918 was one of the first machines to carry the Fiat name. Only 129 were built, some remaining in service until 1925.

FIAT CR.20
Celestino Rosatelli followed up the CR.1 with the CR.20, which flew in June 1926 and had improved reliability, manoeuvrability and structural strength. It had a lengthy career, with more than 670 aircraft being produced.

FIAT CR.30
The CR.20's successor was the Fiat CR.30, which first flew on 5 March 1932 and which was designed in response to a requirement issued by the Italian Air Minister, Italo Balbo, for a 'super fighter'. The first of 121 CR.30s was delivered in the spring of 1934.

FIAT G.19
A very advanced aircraft for its day, the Fiat G.18 twin-engined monoplane airliner was in the same category as the Douglas DC-3.

FIAT RS.14
Conceived in 1938 as a land-based bomber and later adapted, the Fiat RS.14 maritime reconnaissance seaplane had a troubled development phase, and did not enter service until 1942. The RS.14 was the last Italian floatplane torpedo-bomber.

FIAT G.12T
The Fiat G.12T was one of a number of three-engined transports used by the Regia Aeronautica during World War II. Developed from the commercial G.12C of 1937, the type was militarized in 1941.

FIAT CR.1

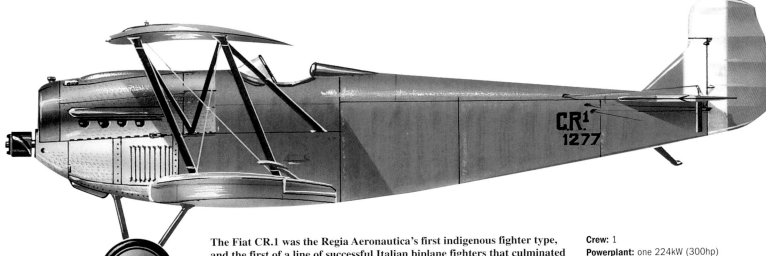

TWO PROTOTYPES OF THE Fiat CR.1 biplane fighter, designed by Celestino Rosatelli (hence the CR prefix), were flown in 1923, and the type was selected for large-

The Fiat CR.1 was the Regia Aeronautica's first indigenous fighter type, and the first of a line of successful Italian biplane fighters that culminated in the CR.42. It saw service from 1925.

scale production for the newly formed Regia Aeronautica. First deliveries of an eventual 240 production aircraft, designated CR.1, began in 1925.

During the 1930s many Italian CR.1s were given more powerful Isotta Fraschini engines, and these

were to continue in service until 1937. Nine aircraft were exported to Latvia. The Fiat CR.2, CR.5 and CR.10 were variants of the basic aircraft fitted with different engines, usually on an experimental basis. Specifications apply to the Fiat CR.1.

Crew: 1
Powerplant: one 224kW (300hp) Hispano-Suiza 42 8-cylinder radial engine
Performance: max speed 272km/h (169mph); endurance 2 hrs 35 mins; service ceiling 7450m (24,440ft)
Dimensions: wingspan 8.95m (29ft 4in); length 6.16m (20ft 2in); height 2.40m (7ft 10in)
Weight: 1154kg (2544lb) loaded
Armament: two Vickers 7.7mm (0.303in) machine guns

FIAT CR.32

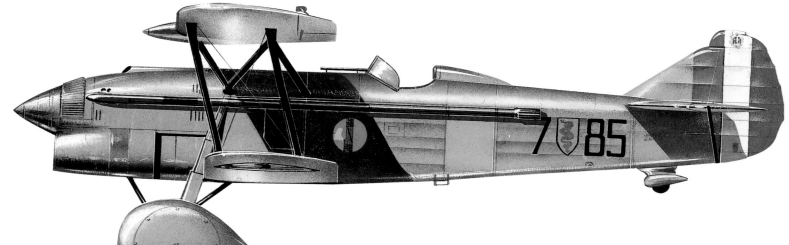

THE FIAT CR.30 WAS soon superseded by the more refined CR.32, which made its appearance in 1933. It was considerably faster than the CR.30 and much more manoeuvrable. Delivery of the first series (383 aircraft) began in 1935, this being followed by 328 examples of the improved CR.32bis. Two

more variants, the CR.32ter (100 aircraft) and CR.32quater (401) were produced, these differing in armament and airframe detail. Total production of the CR.32 consequently amounted to 1212 aircraft, making it numerically the most important biplane of its era. It was used extensively in the

The Fiat CR.32 saw action in the Spanish Civil War, where it was flown by leading pilots. Among them was the top-scoring Spanish Nationalist air ace, Captain Joaquin Garcia Morato.

Spanish Civil War and in the early months of World War II in Greece and East Africa. Specifications apply to the Fiat CR.32.

Crew: 1
Powerplant: one 448kW (600hp) Fiat A.30 RAbis 12-cylinder Vee-type engine
Performance: max speed 375km/h (233mph); range 680km (422 miles); service ceiling 8800m (28,870ft)
Dimensions: wing span 9.50m (31ft 2in); length 7.45m (24ft 5in); height 2.63m (8ft 7in)
Weight: 1850kg (4079lb) loaded
Armament: two fixed forward-firing 7.7mm (0.303in) Breda-SAFAT machine guns

FIAT BR.20 CICOGNA

ITALY: 1936

Crew: 5
Powerplant: two 768kW (1030hp) Fiat
A.80 RC.41 14-cylinder radial engines
Performance: max speed 430km/h
(267mph); range 1240km (770 miles);
service ceiling 7200m (23,620ft)
Dimensions: wingspan 21.56m (70ft 8in);
length 16.17m (53ft); height 4.30m
(14ft 1in)
Weight: 10,340kg (22,795lb) loaded
Armament: four 7.7mm (0.303in)
machine guns; internal bomb load of
1600kg (3527lb)

ALTHOUGH THE FIAT BR.20
bomber was modern and technically
advanced when the prototype flew
in February 1936, it was already
obsolete by the time Italy entered
World War II in 1940. Nevertheless,
500 examples were built before
production ceased in 1942. Eighty-
five of these were delivered to Japan,
which used the aircraft as interim

**The original version of the Fiat BR.20 remained in production until 1940,
by which time it was obsolete. 233 of this type were completed.**

bombers during its operations in
Manchuria during the Sino-Japanese
war of 1938–40. About half the total
production involved the BR.20M,
an improved version with better
streamlining, heavier defensive

armament and more armour. The
BR.20 saw service on all fronts in
World War II, taking part in night
attacks on the British Isles in
October and November 1940.
Specifications apply to the BR.20.

**The Fiat BR.20 first saw action in Manchuria, where it was found to be
under-armed and vulnerable to attack.**

FIAT G.50 FRECCIA

ITALY: 1937

THE FIAT G.50 FRECCIA (Arrow)
was Italy's first monoplane fighter.
The prototype flew for the first time
on 26 February 1937. Comparative
trials with the Macchi MC.200
showed the latter to be superior,
but the G.50 was considered good
enough to go into production, and
783 examples were built. Although
basically sound, it suffered from
being underpowered.

Crew: 1
Powerplant: one 627kW (840hp) Fiat
A.74 RC38 14-cylinder radial engine
Performance: max speed 473km/h
(294mph); range 675km (420 miles);
service ceiling 10,700m (35,200ft)
Dimensions: wingspan 10.98m (36ft);
length 7.80m (25ft 7in); height 2.95m
(9ft 8in)
Weight: 2395kg (5280lb) loaded
Armament: two 12.7mm (0.50in) Breda-
SAFAT machine guns

**The Fiat G.50 was Italy's first monoplane fighter design and was popular
with pilots who preferred an open cockpit to an enclosed one. It saw
service in North Africa in 1940–41.**

FIAT CR.42 FALCO

ITALY: 1938

Crew: 1
Powerplant: one 627kW (840hp) Fiat
A.74 R1C 14-cylinder radial engine
Performance: max speed 472km/h
(293mph); range 670km (416 miles);
service ceiling 9835m (32,265ft)
Dimensions: wingspan 10.96m (35ft
11in); length 7.79m (25ft 6in); height
2.96m (9ft 8in)
Weight: 2415kg (5324lb) loaded
Armament: two 12.7mm (0.50in) Breda-
SAFAT fixed forward-firing machine guns in
upper forward fuselage

DESPITE THE FACT THAT the age of
the monoplane had dawned, Fiat's
Celestino Rosatelli persisted with
the open-cockpit, fabric-covered
fighter biplane concept and
developed the Fiat CR.41, a variant

**The Fiat CR.42 Falco gave a good account of itself in encounters with its
British equivalent, the Gloster Gladiator.**

of the CR.32 with a radial engine
and modified tail surfaces. This
was further developed into the
CR.42 Falco (Falcon), the last of
Italy's fighting biplanes.

The Fiat CR.42 has been called
a contemporary of the Gloster
Gladiator, but in fact there was a
four-year gap between the first
flights of their respective prototypes,
the first Gladiator flying in
September 1934 and the CR.42 in
May 1938. Like the Gladiator, the
CR.42 was the subject of substantial
export orders, serving with the air
arms of Hungary, Belgium and
Sweden.. Some 300 were in
service at the time of Italy's entry
into the war in June 1940, and
production totalled 1781 aircraft.

FIAT G.91

ITALY: 1956

THE FIAT G.91 LIGHTWEIGHT
ground-attack fighter was designed
in response to a NATO requirement
issued in 1954. Fiat was awarded a
contract for three prototypes and
27 pre-production aircraft. The
first prototype flew on 9 August
1956. Total procurement of all
G.91 variants from 1956 to 1977
was 756 examples.

The initial version, the G.91R,
was built in four sub-series for the
Italian Air Force and the Federal
German Luftwaffe. The second
basic version of the type was the
G.91T two-seat trainer. Forty-two
ex-Luftwaffe G.91R-3/4s, and
eight G.91Ts were also operated
by the Portuguese Air Force. The
last G.91 variant produced was the

twin-engined G.91Y, which was
produced for the Italian Air Force
and was substantially redesigned.
Specifications apply to the
Fiat G.91R.

Crew: 1
Powerplant: one 2268kg (5000lb) thrust
Fiat-built Bristol Siddeley Orpheus 803
turbojet engine

Performance: max speed 1086km/h
(675mph); combat radius 320km (200
miles); service ceiling 13,100m (42,978ft)
Dimensions: wingspan 8.56m (28ft 1in);
length 10.30m (33ft 9in); height 4.00m
(13ft 1in)
Weight: 5500kg (12,125lb)
Armament: two 30mm (1.18in) DEFA
cannon; four underwing pylons for various
ordnance

A Fiat G.91T trainer of the Italian Air Force. The Fiat G.91 was the winner of a 1950s NATO competition to find a lightweight strike fighter.

FIESELER FI 156 STORCH

GERMANY: 1937

The Fieseler Fi 156 Storch was a remarkable short take-off and landing aircraft, and carried out some remarkable missions during World War II, including the rescue of the Italian dictator Benito Mussolini.

A REMARKABLE AIRCRAFT, the Fieseler Fi 156 Storch (Stork) was fitted with powerful high-lift devices that permitted it to take off in only 65m (213ft), land in 18m (59ft) and virtually hover in a 40km/h (25mph) headwind without any loss of control. The result of a 1935 requirement for an army cooperation, casualty evacuation and liaison aircraft, the Fi 156 first flew in the spring of

1937 and entered service later that year. About 2900 examples were built, the main variants being the unarmed Fi 156A model, the Fi 156C armed model in four sub-variants, and the Fi 156D air ambulance model in two sub-variants. The Storch was widely used on all fronts. Other countries using the Fi 156 included Sweden, Finland, Switzerland and Italy. Specifications apply to the Fi 156A.

Crew: 3
Powerplant: one 179kW (240hp) Argus As 10C-3 8-cylinder inverted-Vee-type engine
Performance: max speed 175km/h (109mph); range 1015km (631 miles); service ceiling 5200m (17,060ft)
Dimensions: wingspan 14.25m (46ft 9in); length 9.90m (32ft 5in); height 3.05m (10ft)
Weight: 1320kg (2910lb) loaded
Armament: one 7.92mm (0.31in) machine gun in rear of cockpit

FIESELER FI 167

GERMANY: 1938

Crew: 2
Powerplant: one 821kW (1100hp) Daimler-Benz DB 601B 12-cylinder inverted-Vee-type engine
Performance: max speed 325km/h (202mph); range 1500km (932 miles); service ceiling 8200m (26,905ft)
Dimensions: wingspan 13.50m (44ft 3in); length 11.40m (37ft 4in); height 4.80m (15ft 9in)
Weight: 4850kg (10,692lb) loaded
Armament: two 7.92mm (0.31in) machine guns; bomb or torpedo load of 1000kg (2205lb)

FIRST FLOWN IN 1938, the Fieseler Fi 167 biplane was intended to form the torpedo-bomber/reconnaissance element in the air group assigned to the *Graf Zeppelin*, Germany's proposed aircraft carrier. The aircraft handled well and had several innovations, including full-span automatic slots on the leading edges of both wings that gave the aircraft exceptional low-speed characteristics and permitted near-vertical descents.

The Fieseler Fi 167 ably fulfilled the requirements for a carrier-based attack aircraft, but no German carrier was completed.

Twelve pre-production Fi 167As were ordered and were ready for evaluation by the summer of 1940, but work on the *Graf Zeppelin* was halted and the aircraft were withdrawn, all but three being sold to Romania for Black Sea coastal patrol work.

FIESELER FI 103

Thousands of V-1s were launched against London and other cities during World War II. This captured example is about to be test-launched in the USA.

THE MISSILE THAT WAS to be best known as the V-1 – the V denoting Vergeltungswaffe, or 'revenge weapon' – was also known as the Flakzielgerat 76 (FGZ 76) and Kirschkern (Cherry Stone). The former, which means flak target device, was a cover name, while the latter was the weapon's official code name. To the British, the V-1 – which in effect was the world's first cruise missile – would become enshrined in history as the 'Doodlebug', or 'Buzz Bomb'.

The Fieseler Fi 103, to give the missile its correct designation, was conceived in 1942 as an expendable pilotless aircraft using as its power source the Argus As 014 impulse duct, or pulsating athodyd, a simple form of jet engine first developed by the fluid dynamicist Paul Schmidt in the 1920s.

The first prototypes arrived at the Peenemünde research station in December 1942, and to determine the Fi 103's aerodynamic qualities a missile was launched on an unpowered test flight from a Focke-Wulf Fw 200, the first ramp launch being made on 24

December. Numerous test missiles were fired over the Baltic from the test sites, some even reaching Sweden's southern coast.

The flying-bomb assault on Britain was given the code name Operation Rumpelkammer (lumber room), and such was the success achieved during the initial test phase with the Fi 103 that the date for the start of the operation was set for 15 December 1943. This date proved to be over optimistic, however, for by October 1943 only one battery of Flakregiment 155W, the unit which was trained to operate the Fi 103, had reached the launching sites that were being built in the Pas de Calais, France. Few fully trained personnel were available, and in any case the sites themselves were by then coming under heavy Allied air attack. By March 1944, of the original 96 launching sites only 14 had escaped damage.

It was not until the night of 12/13 June 1944 that Operation Rumpelkammer began, and from that date until 31 August 1944, when the majority of the sites had

been overrun by British forces, 8564 V-1s were launched against London and 53 against Southampton, with the latter being air-launched by Heinkel 111s. The total number of hits recorded on London was 2419. The main problem for the fighter pilots engaged in air defence against the V-1, apart from the fact that the missiles presented very small targets, was that their small margin of speed over the flying bombs, coupled with the short time available to make an interception, demanded that they should be quickly and accurately directed on to the V-1's course before the missile reached the gun and balloon belts.

Meanwhile, new launch sites had been prepared in the Eifel for V-1 attacks on Brussels, Antwerp and Liege. In all, 8696 missiles were launched against the vital port of Antwerp and 151 against Brussels between 1 September 1944 and 30 March 1945. Final V-1 operations against the British Isles were carried out by the Heinkel 111s of KG3 and KG53,

the last air-launched missile falling on London on 29 March 1945.

The Fi 103 was a simple mid-wing cantilever monoplane, its fuselage being divided into six compartments containing the magnetic compass, warhead, fuel tank, compressed air containers, autopilot and height and range-setting controls, and the servo-mechanisms controlling the rudder and elevators. The cantilever wing was built around a single tubular spar which passed through the centre of the fuel compartment. The Argus As 014 pulse-jet was mounted above the rear portion of the body, supported at its forward end by a crutch and aft by the vertical fin.

Powerplant: one 350kg (772lb) thrust Argus As 014 pulse jet
Performance: max speed 772km/h (480mph); launch velocity 105m/sec (345ft/sec); range 320km (200 miles)
Dimensions: wingspan 5.30m (17ft 4.5in); length 7.90m (25ft 3in); body diameter 0.838m (2ft 9in)
Weight: 2180kg (4796lb)
Warhead: 850kg (1870lb)

FIESELER FI 103R REICHENBERG IV

GERMANY: 1944

The Fi 103R was a desperate last-ditch measure to combat Allied shipping.

THE PILOTED VERSION OF the V-1 was developed under the code name Reichenberg when difficulties and delays beset the development of the Messerschmitt Me 328, which had been selected to equip a Luftwaffe suicide group. Four versions of the piloted V-1 were produced by the Henschel factory. The Reichenberg I was a single-seat training glider; while the Reichenberg II was a two-seat training version complete with power unit, and the Reichenberg III was a test version with a dummy 850kg (1870lb) warhead. The definitive operational version was the Reichenberg IV anti-ship aircraft, which was designed to be air-launched from a Heinkel He 111. The cockpit was equipped with an aiming device that enabled the pilot to compute the depth of the target vessel below the surface and indicate how far from the ship the missile would need to impact with the water in order for its warhead

to pass beneath the vessel's keel, where it would explode by means of a time fuse. Plans were made for the piloted missiles to be used against Allied shipping when the anticipated invasion of Europe came, but the invasion happened before the Fi 103R could be made operational, and the project was abandoned.

Crew: 1
Powerplant: one 350kg (770lb) thrust Argus 109-014 pulse jet
Performance: max speed 649km/h (403mph); endurance 20 mins
Dimensions: wingspan 5.72m (18ft 9.25in); length 8.00m (26ft 3in)
Weight: 2180kg (4806lb)
Warhead: 850kg (1874lb)

This view of the Reichenberg clearly shows the very basic design of the pulse-jet motor.

FLETTNER FL 282 KOLIBRI (HUMMING BIRD)

GERMANY: 1942

Crew: 1/2
Powerplant: one Bramo Sh.14A radial piston engine rated at 119kW (160hp)
Performance: max speed 150km/h (93mph); combat radius 170km (106 miles); service ceiling 300m (985ft)
Dimensions: rotor diameter 11.96m (39ft 0.75in); length 6.56m (21ft 6.25in); height 2.20m (7ft 2.5in)
Weight: 760kg (1676lb)

IN 1940 ANTON FLETTNER received instructions to gear up for full production of the Fl 265, but work was by then well advanced on a new two-seat Fl 282 version. Work began in the summer of 1940 on 30 prototypes and 15 production aircraft with flight testing starting in early 1941. Further testing was so successful that by early 1944 the

German Air Ministry had placed an order for 1000 production Fl 282s. By the end of the war only 24 Fl 282s had been delivered. Specifications apply to FL 282 V21.

This illustration shows Fl 282 V21 (Fl 282B) while under evaluation in 1943.

FLETTNER FL 184
In 1930 Anton Flettner designed a helicopter having a single, torqueless rotor. Applying the drive directly to the rotor eliminated torque, two 22kW (30hp) Anzani engines driving small airscrews attached to the rotor blades. Flettner's next design was the Fl 184 two-seat autogyro with a fully enclosed fuselage and tail surfaces. The 12m (39ft 4.5in) diameter rotors employed cyclic pitch control. Power was supplied by a 104kW (140hp) Siemens-Halske Sh 14 radial engine driving a two-bladed wooden propeller. In 1936, however, before trials with the German Navy to prove the Fl 184's suitability for reconnaissance and anti-submarine duties could begin, the only prototype caught fire in flight and it was destroyed.

FLETTNER FL 185
This experimental prototype was designed to act as a helicopter when the three-bladed main rotor was powered or an autogyro when the rotor auto-rotated in forward flight. Power was supplied by a 104kW (140hp) Siemens-Halske Sh 14 radial engine, and two anti-torque/forward-thrust airscrews were mounted on outriggers.

FLETTNER FL 265
In 1937 Anton Flettner designed a helicopter which incorporated the revolutionary counter-rotating, inter-meshing twin rotors, and it was used in his Fl 265-V1 prototype which flew for the first time in May 1939. It was powered by a 112kW (150hp) Bramo Sh 14A air-cooled engine giving a top speed of 159km/h (99mph). In 1938 the German Navy ordered six of these machines for experimental purposes. Operating from the decks of U-boats throughout 1940, they offered a huge advantage over naval fixed-wing aircraft, which required catapult launching and special recovery procedures.

FLETTNER FL 285
The Fl 285 was a reconnaissance and fleet spotter helicopter, a more advanced version of the Fl 282 with an endurance of 2 hrs at 129km/h (80mph). It was under development at the end of World War II, and was to have carried two SC-50 bombs and been powered by an Argus As-10C engine.

FMA IAE 58 PUCARA

ARGENTINA: 1969

THE HEAVILY ARMED Pucara presented a serious threat to British forces engaged in re-occupying the Falkland Islands in 1982, and a daring raid was launched to destroy the aircraft deployed there. Originally known as the Delfin, the type first flew on 20 August 1969, powered by two AirResearch TPW331 turboprop engines. It was designed primarily for counter-insurgency operations, and entered service with the Argentine Air Force's 11th Escuadron de Exploration y Ataque in June 1978. A

single-seat version was built with increased internal armament and fuel, but the programme was suspended. The Pucara has been exported in small numbers to Uruguay, Sri Lanka and Colombia.

Crew: 2
Powerplant: two 762kW (1022hp) Turboméca Astazou XVIG turboprop engines
Performance: max speed 500km/h (310mph); range 3042km (1890 miles); service ceiling 10,000m (32,808ft)
Dimensions: wingspan 14.50m (47ft 6in); length 14.25m (46ft 7in); height 5.36m (17ft 6in)
Weight: 3600kg (7936lb) loaded
Armament: two 20mm (0.79in) cannon and four 7.62mm (0.30in) machine guns; up to 1620kg (3571lb) of external stores

The heavily armed Pucara posed a serious threat to British ground forces sent to recapture the Falklands from Argentina in 1982.

FOCKE-ACHGELIS FA 61 (FW 61)

GERMANY: 1936

IN 1932, PROFESSOR HEINRICH Karl Focke began building Cierva autogyros under licence. His first indigenous helicopter showed all the signs of having been influenced by the Cierva C.19 Autogyro, although it did have twin rotors mounted side by side driven by a nose-mounted 119kW (160hp) Bramo Sh 14A radial engine. The Fa 61 first flew on 26 June 1936 and on 25 June 1937 set an altitude record of 2439m (8000ft) and an endurance record of 1 hr 20 mins. Further records followed. On 25 October 1937, Hanna Reitsch broke the straight-line record when she flew the Fa 61 108.9km (67.6 miles) between Bremen and Berlin. She also flew the helicopter indoors in the Deutschlandhalle in

Berlin in February 1938. Although the Fa 61 did not enter production, by 1938 it did lead to greater interest from Deutsche Lufthansa in a passenger-carrying development, which subsequently became the Fa 266 (Fa 223). By this time a new company, Focke-Aschgelis & Co GmbH had been formed and the Fw 61 was redesignated Fa 61.

Crew: 1
Powerplant: one 119kW (160hp) Bramo Sh.14A 7-cylinder radial piston engine
Performance: max speed 112km/h (70mph); combat radius 230km (143 miles); service ceiling 2620m (8600ft);
Dimensions: rotor diameter 7.00m (22ft 11.5in); length 7.30m (23ft 11.5in); height 2.65m (8ft 8.25in)
Weight: 800kg (1764lb)

The Fa 61 fuselage was that of an Fw 44 Stieglitz biplane. The two three-bladed rotors turned in opposite directions.

FOCKE-ACHGELIS FA 266 HORNISSE (HORNET)/FA 223 DRACHE (KITE)

GERMANY: 1940

After WWII two examples were built in Czechoslovakia (VR-1) and one in France (SE 3000) by SNCA du Sud-Est, using spare and salvaged parts.

Crew: 2
Powerplant: one 746kW (1000hp) BMW 301R 9-cyclinder radial piston engine
Performance: max speed 175km/h (109mph); range 700km (435 miles); service ceiling 2010m (6595ft)
Dimensions: rotor diameter 12.00m (39ft 4.5in); length 12.25m (40ft 2.25in); height 4.35m (14ft 3.25in)
Weight: 3175kg (7000lb)
Armament: one 7.92mm (0.31in) MG 15 machine gun and 250kg (551lb) bombs

THE FA 266 WAS AN enlarged version of the Fa 61 designed for Deutsche Lufthansa as a six-seat civil transport, the world's first

genuine transport helicopter. The prototype was completed in late 1939, but with the onset of war it was decided to develop the machine for military use. In August 1940 the Fa 266, which by this time had been redesignated Fa 223 Drache, carried out its first free flight, and 30 pre-production Fa 223s were ordered to be used in evaluation tests in a variety of roles. Trials finally began in July 1942 after disruption from bombing. The Fa 223 was successful (100 were ordered), but in the end only 10 or 11 were test flown. Specifications apply to the Fa 223.

FOCKE-WULF A 16, A 17, A 29 AND A 38 MOWE

GERMANY: 1924

Crew: 1
Powerplant: one Siemens 56kW (75hp) Sh.11 7-cylinder radial piston engine
Performance: max speed 135km/h (84mph); range 550km (342 miles); service ceiling 2500m (8200ft)
Dimensions: wingspan 13.90m (45ft 7.25in); length 8.50m (27ft 10.75in); height 2.30m (7ft 6.5in)
Weight: 970kg (2138lb) maximum take-off weight
Payload: four passengers

A total of 23 A 16s (pictured) were built in five marques, all of which served with German operators.

THE A 16 WAS A single-engined all-wooden frame commercial design, with a high wing, accommodating up to four passengers and first flown in 1924. It was Focke-Wulf's first commercial transport product. More than 20 A 16s were built with differing capacity engines, including examples for Deutsche Lufthansa. The larger A 17, or Mowe (Gull), followed in 1928, but this had a tubular steel rather than wooden frame and accommodated eight passengers and two crew. Twelve were produced for domestic customers. In 1929, the A 17 was fitted with a more powerful 485kW (650hp) engine and redesignated A 29, of which five were built. The final version of this series was the A 38 of 1931, which had a 298kW (400hp) engine and a revised fuselage capable of carrying 10 passengers and a radio operator. The Mowe airliner family was extensively utilized by Lufthansa until 1933, when superseded by the Junkers Ju 52 trimotor.

Specifications apply to the Focke-Wulf A 16.

FOCKE-WULF FW 56 STÖSSER

GERMANY: 1933

Crew: 2
Powerplant: one 179kW (240hp) Argus AS 10C 8-cylinder inverted-Vee air-cooled engine
Performance: max speed 278km/h (173mph); range 400km (250 miles); service ceiling 6200m (20,336ft)
Dimensions: wingspan 10.50m (34ft 5in); length 7.60m (25ft 3in); height 3.52m (11ft 7in)
Weight: 996kg (2196lb) loaded
Armament: none

THE FOCKE-WULF FW 56 Stösser (Falcon Hawk) advanced trainer first flew in 1933, and was the first Focke-Wulf aircraft with which designer Kurt Tank was fully involved. It was built in large numbers for the civil flying clubs, for export (to the Austrian and Hungarian Air Forces) and for the Luftwaffe. The aircraft possessed excellent high-speed diving characteristics, and was used by Ernst Udet to demonstrate dive-bombing techniques to the German General Staff, leading to the type's official adoption. Total production of the Fw 56 Stösser was in the region of 1000 aircraft.

The Fw 56 was a clean, attractive design that proved superior to other contemporary German aircraft in its class, and served the Luftwaffe well as a fighter trainer.

FOCKE-WULF FW 187 FALKE

Crew: 2
Powerplant: two 522kW (700hp) Junkers
Jumo 210Ga 12-cylinder inverted-Vee
engines
Performance: max speed 529km/h
(329mph); range not known; service
ceiling 10,000m (32,810ft)
Dimensions: wingspan 15.30m (50ft 2in);
length 11.10m (36ft 5in); height 3.85m
(12ft 7in)
Weight: 5000kg (11,023lb) loaded
Armament: two 20mm (0.79in) cannon;
four 7.92in (0.31in) machine guns

DESIGNED AS A high-performance,
twin-engined, long-range escort
fighter, the heavily armed Focke-
Wulf Fw 187 Falke (Falcon) first
flew in the summer of 1937. It was
considerably underpowered, but
the prototype attained a maximum
speed of 525km/h (326mph), and
its handling characteristics were
superb, its turn radius being superior
to that of many contemporary
single-engined fighters.

Orders for seven pre-production
Fw 187A-0 aircraft were placed;
however, despite being superior to
the Bf 110 in most respects the

type was not adopted. The Fw
187A-0s were assigned to the
defence of the Focke-Wulf aircraft
factory at Bremen.

**The Fw 187 was a better design
than the Messerschmitt Bf 110, but
internal politics decreed that the
latter aircraft should succeed.**

FOCKE-WULF FW 200 CONDOR

**In the early months of 1941 the
Fw 200 was responsible for sinking
a greater tonnage of British
shipping than enemy submarines.**

than submarines to Allied shipping
in the Atlantic and North Sea in
1940–41. The final operational
version of the Condor was the
Fw 200C-6, developed to carry a
Henschel Hs 293B air-to-surface
missile under each outer engine
nacelle. The total number of
Condors produced during the war
years was 252 aircraft. Many were
relegated to transport duties in
1942, nine being lost in attempts
to resupply the German garrison at
Stalingrad. Specifications apply to
the Focke-Wulf Fw 200C.

Crew: 6
Powerplant: four 895kW (1200hp)
BMW-Bramo 323R-2 Fafnir nine-cylinder
radial engines
Performance: max speed 360km/h
(224mph); range 4440km (2759 miles);
service ceiling 6000m (19,685ft)
Dimensions: wingspan 32.84m (107ft
8in); length 23.85m (76ft 3in); height
6.30m (20ft 8in)
Weight: 22,700kg (50,044lb) loaded
Armament: two 7.92mm (0.31in) and
three 13mm (0.51in) machine guns; one
20mm (0.79in) cannon, plus a maximum
bomb load of 2100kg (4630lb)

THE FOCKE-WULF Fw 200 Condor
was designed in 1936 as a 26-
passenger commercial airliner, the
prototype flying on 27 July 1937.
The bomber version was the Fw

200C, which had a strengthened
structure. By the time the first Fw
200C had been completed World
War II had begun, and conversion
of the Condor was taken over by

the Luftwaffe, the aircraft being
ordered into production for the
maritime reconnaissance role.
Operated by KG40, Condors
presented a far more serious threat

FOCKE-WULF FW 189

GERMANY: 1938

Crew: 3
Powerplant: two 347kW (465hp) Argus As 410A-1 12-cylinder engines
Performance: max speed 350km/h (217mph); range 670km (416 miles); service ceiling 7300m (23,950ft)
Dimensions: wingspan 18.40m (60ft 4in); length 12.03m (39ft 5in); height 3.10m (10ft 2in)
Weight: 4170kg (9193lb) loaded
Armament: four 7.92mm (0.31in) machine guns; bomb load of 200kg (441lb)

The Fw 189 proved very successful as a short-range reconnaissance aircraft, operating on the dangerous Eastern Front.

THE FOCKE-WULF Fw 189 Uhu (Owl) short-range reconnaissance aircraft first flew in July 1938 and entered service in 1940. It was of unorthodox design, featuring two tail booms, each bearing an engined, on either side of a heavily glazed central nacelle. Sixteen prototypes and pre-production aircraft were built, followed by 848 production aircraft. Sub-variants included the Fw 189A-2, with heavier defensive armament, the Fw 189A-3 dual-control trainer, and the Fw 189A-4 tactical support version with ventral armour and 20mm (0.79in) cannon. The type proved extremely successful on the Eastern Front, where it was nicknamed 'Das Fliegende Auge' (The Flying Eye). Specifications apply to Fw 189A.

FOCKE-WULF FW 190

GERMANY: 1939

A Focke-Wulf Fw 190A-3 of 8 Staffel Jagdgeschwader 2, showing the unit's eagle emblem on the fuselage sides.

THE FOCKE-WULF Fw 190 stemmed from a suggestion by the German Air Ministry in 1937 that the company should develop an interceptor fighter to complement the Bf 109. Instead of opting for the Daimler Benz DB601 in-line engine, already in production for the Bf 109, Kurt Tank (Focke-Wulf's technical director) chose the BMW type 139 18-cylinder radial, which was still in the development stage. Three prototypes were built, the first of which flew on 1 June 1939. Apart from some engine over-heating problems the flight tests went very well, and construction of the other prototypes was acceler-ated. The fifth Fw 190 was re-engined with the new 1238kW (1660hp) BMW 14-cylinder 801C-0 engine, and this met all the Luftwaffe requirements. Its success led to the construction of 30 pre-production aircraft designated Fw 190A-0, these being followed by the Fw 190A-1, which went into service with JG26 at Le Bourget, Paris, in August 1941.

The Fw 190A-1 was followed into production by the A-2 (426 built), with a longer span and heavier armament, and 509 A-3 fighter-bombers. The next variant, the Fw 190A-4, of which 494 were built, had a methanol-water power-boost system. The A-5 was a development of the A-4, with the engine relocated 0.15m (5.9in) farther forward, which restored the centre of gravity to the position it had occupied before it was moved by the addition of extra equipment in the rear fuselage; 723 aircraft were delivered, and undertook a variety of roles including assault, night-fighting, torpedo-bomber and bomber destroyer. Some A-5s were modified as two-seat Fw 190S-5 trainers, the S denoting *Schulflugzeug* (training aircraft). The Fw 190A-6, of which 569 were built, was a version of the Fw 190A-5/U10 fighter with a lightened wing structure and fixed armament of four 20mm (0.79in) cannon. There was a number of A-6 sub-variants, one being a fighter-bomber with provision for 1000kg (2205lb) of bombs, and others being bomber destroyers, with 30mm (1.18in) cannon and extra armour to protect the pilot in head-on attacks. The Fw 190A-7, which entered production in December 1943, had a revised armament of two 20mm (0.79in) cannon in the wing roots and two 12.7mm (0.50in) machine guns in the forward fuselage. Only 80 aircraft were built before it was supplanted by the Fw 190A-8, the last new-build variant

This Focke-Wulf Fw 190 features an armoured engine cowling ring. Extra engine armour was fitted as German fighter pilots adopted new tactics that involved head-on attacks on American daylight bombers.

lengthened rear fuselage. The first major production model was the Fw 190D-9 interceptor, which entered service with JG3 in 1943. The Fw 190G was a long-range attack variant which was followed, out of sequence, by the Fw 190F fighter-bomber, which was basically an Fw 190A-5 airframe with strengthened landing gear, more armour protection, and a combination of one ETC 501 bomb rack under the fuselage and four ETC 50 bomb racks under the wings. Specifications apply to the Focke-Wulf Fw 190A-8.

Crew: 1
Powerplant: one 1575kW (2100hp) BMW 801D-2 radial engine with water-methanol boost
Performance: max speed 654km/h (406mph); range 1470km (915 miles); service ceiling 11,400m (37,402ft)
Dimensions: wingspan 10.50m (34ft 5in); length 8.84m (29ft); height 3.96m (13ft)
Weight: 4900kg (10,802lb) loaded
Armament: two 7.92mm (0.31in) machine guns in nose and up to four 20mm (0.79in) cannon in wings; provision for wide range of under-fuselage and under-wing bombs and RPs

of the Fw 190A series. Total production was 1334 aircraft. The A-8 was fitted with a nitrous-oxide power-boost system and an extra fuel tank in the rear fuselage. Some were converted to the training role with the designation Fw 190S-8.

The next major production version, the Fw 190D, had a lengthened nose accommodating a 1325kW (1776hp) Junkers Jumo 213A-1 engine, a liquid-cooled unit fitted with an annular radiator duct that gave it a radial-engined appearance. The aircraft also had a

FOCKE-WULF TA 183 HUCKEBEIN

GERMANY: 1945

THE FOCKE-WULF Ta 183 Huckebein (a raven which in German folklore made trouble) was a jet-fighter design which originated in 1942. The aircraft was characterized by its stubby fuselage, mid-mounted wings swept at an angle of 40 degrees and a long, slender fin swept back 60 degrees with a dihedral tailplane mounted on top.

The Ta 183 Huckebein was ordered into mass production in March 1945, two versions being contemplated, but the factories were overrun by the Allies before a prototype could be completed. Unconfirmed stories persist that Ta 183 technical data, captured by the Russians, played a part in the design of the MiG-15 jet-fighter.

Crew: 1
Powerplant: one 1300kg (2866lb) thrust Heinkel-Hirth 109-011A turbojet engine
Performance: max speed 955km/h (593mph); range not known; service ceiling 14,000m (45,920ft)
Dimensions: wingspan 10.00m (32ft 9.75in); length 9.40m (30ft 10in)
Weight: 4300kg (9481lb) loaded
Armament: two 30mm (1.18in) Mk 108 cannon

The Focke-Wulf Ta 183 was ordered into mass production in March 1945, but like other advanced German jet-fighter projects it came far too late for any such plan to be implemented.

FOKKER E.I–E.III

GERMANY: 1915

Crew: 1
Powerplant: one 75kW (100hp) Oberursel U.1 9-cylinder rotary engine
Performance: max speed 134km/h (83mph); endurance 2 hrs 45 mins; service ceiling 3500m (11,500ft)
Dimensions: wingspan 9.52m (31ft 3in); length 7.30m (23ft 11in); height 2.89m (9ft 6in)
Weight: 635kg (1400lb) loaded

THE FOKKER E.I WAS the military designation of the Fokker M5K monoplane, fitted with a simple engine-driven system that enabled a Parabellum machine gun to be fired through the aircraft's propeller arc. The Fokker Eindecker (Monoplane) consequently became the first German aircraft dedicated to the pursuit and destruction of enemy machines.

The 'Fokker Scourge', as it became known, began on 1 July 1915, when Lieutenant Kurt Wintgens of Feldflieger Abteilung 6b, flying the M5K, shot down a French Morane monoplane. The production Fokker E.I had begun to reach the frontline units in June, and the small number of machines available, in the hands of pilots whose names would soon become legendary, began to make their presence felt.

The E.I was superseded by a refined and strengthened version, the E.II. The definitive version of the Fokker Monoplane was the E.III, some of which were armed with twin Spandau machine guns. The Fokker Monoplane was the first dedicated fighter aircraft to see operational service, and for months it ruled the sky over the Western Front.

Specifications apply to the E.III.

The Fokker E.III Monoplane, mounted with a machine gun that was synchronized to fire through the propeller blades, caused havoc among Allied aircraft in 1915.

FOKKER DR.I

GERMANY: 1917

Crew: 1
Powerplant: one 82kW (110hp) Oberursel Ur11 9-cylinder rotary engine
Performance: max speed 185km/h (115mph); endurance 1 hr 30 mins; service ceiling 6100m (20,000ft)
Dimensions: wingspan 7.19m (23ft 7in); length 5.77m (18ft 11in); height 2.95m (9ft 8in)
Weight: 586kg (1291lb) loaded
Armament: two 7.92mm (0.31in) machine guns

MADE FAMOUS AS THE red-painted mount of Baron Manfred von Richthofen and his Flying Circus at the time of his greatest success – and his death – the Fokker Dr.I (the 'Dr' denoting Dreidecker, or

FOCKE-WULF FW 58 WEIHE
The Focke-Wulf Fw 58 Weihe (Kite) general-purpose twin-engined monoplane, which appeared in 1935, was built in very large numbers and fulfilled many different roles.

FOCKE-WULF FW 159
The Focke-Wulf Fw 159 parasol-wing fighter of 1935 was designed to replace the He 51 and Ar 68 fighter biplanes. It did not enter production.

FOCKE-WULF FW 57
Designed as a high-speed bomber, the Fw 57 flew in 1937 and was Focke-Wulf's first all-metal aircraft. It was seriously overweight, and was scrapped.

FOCKE-WULF FW 186
This was a 1938 German jump-start autogyro based on the Cierva C.30.

FOCKE-WULF FW 191
First flown in 1942, the Focke-Wulf Fw 191 was an extremely clean medium bomber design which made much use of electrical systems. Three prototypes only were built.

FOCKE-WULF TA 154
The Focke-Wulf Ta 154 was an all-wood night-fighter design, the prototype flying in 1943. Nine production aircraft were completed, but the type was not a success.

FOCKE-WULF TA 400
The Focke-Wulf Ta 400 was a six-engined long-range bomber design initiated in 1943. Several versions were proposed, but no prototype was built.

FOCKE-WULF TA 152
The Focke-Wulf Ta 152 was a long-span development of the Fw 190D with increased armament and a boosted Jumo 213E/B engine. The production version was the Ta 152H.

FOCKE-WULF PROJEKT VII FLITZER
Designed in 1944, the Flitzer was a single-engined jet fighter that bore a close resemblance to the de Havilland Vampire, with its central nacelle and twin tail booms. A mock-up only was completed.

FOCKE-WULF TRIEBFLÜGEL
Designed in September 1944, the Triebflügel was a revolutionary fighter that was to take off vertically from a tail-sitting position and derived its lift and thrust from three wings rotating round the fuselage. It was never built.

triplane) was introduced into service in October 1917. Although the aircraft was extremely manoeuvrable, the Dr.I was already outclassed by a new generation of fighter biplanes, and it was consequently never used in large numbers. Indeed, the fact that the Dr.I achieved success in air combat was due more to the skill of the experienced pilots who flew it, rather than the design itself.

The Fokker DR.I triplane became famous as the mount of Rittmeister Freiherr Manfred von Richthofen, the 'Red Baron'.

FOKKER D.VII   GERMANY: 1917

THE FOKKER D.VII WAS the first of a series of new German fighter types which, had they been available in numbers a few weeks earlier, might have wrested air superiority from the Allies during the German spring offensives of 1918. The D.VII had its origins late in 1917, at a time when the German Air Corps was beginning to lose the ascendancy and technical superiority it had enjoyed for nearly three years. The German High Command considered the situation to be so serious that it ordered German aircraft manufacturers to give top priority to the development of new fighter types; these would be subjected to a

The Fokker D.VII was one of the best fighter aircraft to see service on any side in World War II and found its way into many air arms after the conflict was over.

competitive fly-off, and the winning design would be awarded large production contracts.

The fly-off, which took place at Johannistal in late January and early February 1918, involved some 30 aircraft, six of them alternative Fokker designs. By the fourth day there was no longer any doubt that the aircraft designed by Fokker's Reinhold Platz, and then known as the V.11, was by far the best all-round design, superior to the other competitors on every count except, perhaps, rate of climb. The Fokker company received an immediate contract for the production of 400 aircraft, which would receive the military designation D.VI; however, it took some time to set up the necessary machinery and it was not until the last days of April that the first examples were delivered to Jagdgeschwader 1.

The D.VII, which underwent some modifications to improve its stability in a dive, proved easy to fly, but its main advantage over earlier German fighters was its ability to maintain performance at high altitude. Its qualities were further enhanced in the late summer of 1918 with the appearance of the Fokker D.VIIF, which had a 138kW (185hp)

BMW D.IIIa engine in place of the 119kW (160hp) Mercedes engine, the powerplant which had been specified for all the contending aircraft at Johannistal. This gave the aircraft greater reserves of power above 5000m (16,400ft), which height it could reach in 14 minutes compared with the 38 minutes of the original Mercedes-powered D.VII.

By the beginning of September 1918, more than 800 D.VIIs were in service with 48 Jagdstaffeln. Of these, 366 had been delivered by Fokker, and the remainder by other sub-contractors, such as Albatros. At the end of the war, Article IV of the Armistice Agreement singled out the Fokker D.VII for special mention among the items of German military equipment to be handed over, such was the respect it had earned. Anthony Fokker circumvented this by smuggling 400 engines and the components of 120 aircraft, most of them D.VIIs, out of Germany into Holland, where he set up a

production line. Post war, the D.VII saw service in the Dutch East Indies, Poland, the USA, Switzerland, Belgium, Sweden, Romania, Russia, Denmark, Finland and Italy. Some of these aircraft were re-engined with 187kW (250hp) BMW or 172kW (230hp) Siddeley motors. Russia was one of the most important customers, acquiring 92 D.VIIs, many of which were used to train German pilots in secret at the Lipetsk flying school, pilots who would form the nucleus of the future Luftwaffe.

Many Fokker D.VIIs passed into civilian hands in the 1920s and were greatly prized by the film industry, particularly Hollywood, where they featured prominently in the making of such films as the classic *Hell's Angels*.

Crew: 1
Powerplant: one 138kW (185hp) BMW III 6-cylinder in-line engine
Performance: max speed 200km/h (124mph); endurance 1 hr 30 mins; service ceiling 7000m (22,965ft)
Dimensions: wingspan 8.90m (29ft 2in); length 6.95m (22ft 9in); height 2.75m (9ft)
Weight: 880kg (1940lb) loaded
Armament: two 7.92mm (0.31in) Spandau machine guns

This D.VII replica is seen bearing the markings of an aircraft flown by Germany's second top-scoring air ace, Ernst Udet, who later flew D.VIIs in several film roles in the United States.

FOCKE-WULF FW 1000X1000X1000
The Fw 1000x1000x1000 was a twin-engined jet bomber project of 1944, its designation stemming from the fact that it was intended to carry a bomb load of 1000kg (2205lb) over a radius of 1000km (621 miles) at 1000km/h (621mph).

FOKKER SPIN
The Fokker Spin monoplane was the first aircraft designed by the Dutch constructor Anthony Fokker. It flew in 1910, and several examples were built.

FOKKER D.VIII
The Fokker D.VIII was a promising parasol monoplane design that appeared on the Western Front in 1918. Only about 90 had been delivered before the end of World War I.

FOKKER F.II
Developed from an earlier fighter, this high-wing, single-engined monoplane first flew in 1919. About 30 examples were built, accommodating five passengers.

FOKKER C.I
The Fokker C.I was a two-seat reconnaissance development of the D.VII. A total of 250 were built from 1921, many serving with the Red Air Force.

FOKKER S SERIES
The Fokker S series of two-seat trainers began with the S.I parasol-wing monoplane of 1920 and evolved via a series of biplanes to the S.IX of 1937. They were not produced in large numbers.

FOKKER F.IV
The Fokker F.IV of 1921, powered by a 313kW (420hp) Liberty engine, was designed as an airliner, but no orders were forthcoming. The two examples built were sold to the US Army Air Service, which used them as transports with the designation T.2.

FOKKER T.II
The Fokker T.II, which appeared in 1921, was a three-seat, low-wing monoplane floatplane, designed for bombing and torpedo-dropping. Only one was built, this being purchased by the US Navy.

FOKKER F.III
A development of the F.II, the single-engined F.III could carry five passengers. More than 70 were built in Holland and Germany, first being flown in 1921.

FOKKER C.II 'AMERICA'

NETHERLANDS: 1920

The Fokker C.II was the first of Anthony Fokker's civil designs. It was based on the smaller Fokker C.I.

DERIVED FROM THE Fokker C.I reconnaissance and training aircraft, the C.II biplane was Anthony Fokker's first venture into the field of commercial aviation and was named 'America' in expectation of US sales. Modified to carry two passengers, the C.II was intended for use as an air taxi.

The converted aircraft was first flown in 1920, and examples of the C.II were sold in Holland, the USA, South America and Canada, where the normal wheeled undercarriage was replaced by skis to allow it to fly into remote areas.

Crew: 1
Powerplant: one 138kW (185hp) BMW in-line engine
Performance: max speed 150km/h (93mph); range not known; ceiling not known
Dimensions: wingspan 10.61m (34ft 10in); length 7.44m; (24ft 5in) height 2.86m (9ft 4in)
Weight: 1170kg (2575lb) loaded
Payload: two passengers

A 172kW (230hp) Siddeley Puma engine was sometimes fitted to the aircraft as an alternative powerplant to the BMW.

FOKKER F.VII AND F.VII-3M

NETHERLANDS: 1924

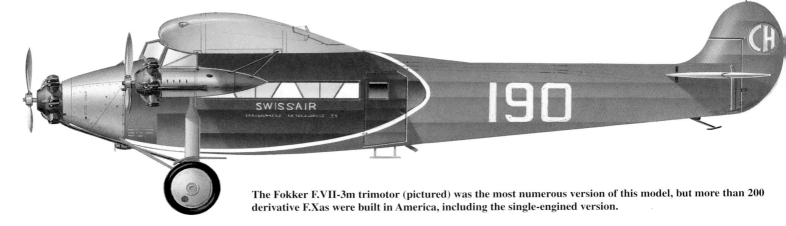

The Fokker F.VII-3m trimotor (pictured) was the most numerous version of this model, but more than 200 derivative F.Xas were built in America, including the single-engined version.

THE ORIGINAL SINGLE-ENGINED Fokker VII was designed to service KLM's long-range (often Far East) routes, but the early version (of which five were built) proved slow. Consequently, the version VIIa was developed in 1925 utilizing a single Bristol Jupiter 358kW (480hp) engine, and subsequently built or licence-built for a number of overseas operators using a variety of engine types.

The tri-motor version F.VIIa-3m was developed in 1924 to a KLM specification to carry 10 passengers with one of its three engines shut down. The prototype went on to win the Ford reliability tour of the USA in 1925, and was modified to support Commander

In 1928 this FVIIb-3m, named 'Southern Cross', made the first trans-Pacific flight from the United States to Australia, piloted by the pioneering Australian aviator Captain Charles Kingsford Smith.

R.E. Bird's Arctic expedition in 1926. This F.VIIa-3m version was built for both civil and military applications, and it was produced by Fokker and its many foreign licensees in appreciable numbers – total Fokker VII production exceeded 190 examples, and the F.VII-3m was produced in the highest numbers. Specifications apply to the Fokker F.VIIb-3m/M.

Crew: 3
Powerplant: three Wright R-975 Whirlwind J-6 radial piston engines each rated at 242kW (325hp)
Performance: max cruising speed 207km/h (129mph); range 850km (528 miles); service ceiling 3100m (10,170ft)
Dimensions: wingspan 21.71m (71ft 2.5in); length 14.55m (47ft 8.75in); height 3.90m (12ft 9.5in)
Weight: 5190kg (11,422 lb) maximum take-off weight
Armament/payload: one trainable rearward-firing 7.7mm (0.303in) Lewis machine gun in the ventral position and one 7.7mm (0.303in) Lewis machine gun in the dorsal position; up to 1000kg (2205lb) of disposable stores carried on hardpoints under the fuselage, generally comprising free fall bombs or one torpedo; up to 10 passengers or six litters

FOKKER F.XI UNIVERSAL/SUPER UNIVERSAL   USA/NETHERLANDS:1925

THE UNIVERSAL WAS designed by Robert Noorduyn, and developed and initially built by Fokker subsidiary the Atlantic Aircraft Company of New Jersey. Initially a four-seat, high-wing airliner with an open cockpit, a total of 45 examples were built to this standard, and a further three were built in Holland to a hybrid Universal/Super Universal standard. However, the larger, enclosed-cockpit Super Universal dating from 1927 was

built in larger numbers still – 94 in the USA and another 29 licence-built in Japan. The quantity built and their widespread use made this type an important contributor to the growth of air travel during the interwar years. Specifications apply to the Super Universal.

The Fokker Universal Special (pictured) was larger and heavier than the initial version. It also featured an enclosed cockpit.

Crew: 2
Powerplant: one 317kW (425hp) Pratt & Whitney Wasp radial piston engine
Performance: max cruising speed 190km/h (118mph) at optimum altitude; range 1086km (674 miles)
Dimensions: wingspan 15.44m (50ft 8in); length 11.15m (36ft 7in); height 2.77m (9ft 1in)
Weight: 2390kg (5269lb) maximum take-off weight
Payload: up to six passengers

FOKKER F.VIII   NETHERLANDS: 1927

Crew: 2
Powerplant: two 358kW (480hp) Gnome-Rhone (Bristol) Jupiter VI radial piston engines
Performance: max speed 200km/h (124mph); cruising speed 170km/h (106mph); range 1045km (649 miles); service ceiling 5500m (18,045ft)
Dimensions: wingspan 25.00m (80ft 5.5in); length 23.00m (73ft 6in); height 4.20m (13ft 9.25in)
Weight: 5700kg (12,566lb) maximum take-off weight
Payload: up to 15 passengers

KLM REQUIRED AN aircraft with a greater payload than the successful Fokker VII, and Fokker responded with the twin-engined VIII. This had an enlarged cabin, and the vacant nose area was utilized as a baggage compartment. Fokker only built eight examples of this airliner – seven for KLM and one for Hungary's Malert. Another two were licence-built in Hungary. The KLM examples were all later re-engined with Wright Cyclone or Pratt &

Whitney Wasp engines, one example later seeing wartime service with the Finnish Air Force. Specifications apply to the Fokker F.VIII.

The last example of the six Fokker F.VIIIs built for KLM and delivered in 1928 was destroyed during the German invasion of 1940.

FOKKER F.XVIII AND FOKKER F.XX

NETHERLANDS: 1932

THE MODEL XVIII AND its one-off successor the F.XX proved to be the last of Fokker's tri-motor series. The XVIII shared construction methods and appearance with its predecessors – wooden high wing and fixed undercarriage. Five XVIIIs were built for KLM's Far East services. Incorporating a sleeper compartment, the XVIII also made a record flight on that service – 73 hours 34 minutes. The XVIII was withdrawn from Far East services in 1935, but continued work on some transatlantic and other services. Some examples were operational until 1946. The similar F.XX had a retractable undercarriage, but was unable to compete with new American designs; only one was built in 1933. Specifications apply to the F.XVIII.

Crew: 2-4
Powerplant: three 313kW (420hp) Pratt & Whitney Wasp C radial piston engines
Performance: max speed 240km/h (149mph); range 1820km (1131 miles); service ceiling 4800m (15,750ft)
Dimensions: wingspan 24.50m (80ft 4.5in); length 18.50m (60ft 8.25in); height 4.80m (15ft 9in)
Weight: 7850kg (17,306lb) maximum take-off weight
Payload: up to 13 passengers

One of KLM's five Fokker F.XVIIIs is seen here undergoing maintenance. This picture offers a good view of the three Pratt & Whitney Wasp C nine-cylinder radial engines.

FOKKER D.XXI

NETHERLANDS: 1936

Crew: 1
Powerplant: one 619kW (830hp) Bristol Mercury VIII 9-cylinder radial engine
Performance: max speed 460km/h (286mph); range 930km (578 miles); service ceiling 11,000m (36,090ft)

Dimensions: wingspan 11.00m (36ft 1in); length 8.20m (26ft 10in); height 2.95m (9ft 8in)
Weight: 2050kg (4519lb) loaded
Armament: four 7.92mm (0.31in) machine guns

This Fokker D.XXI formed part of the Dutch force attempting to repel the advancing Germans during the invasion of the Netherlands in 1940.

FIRST FLOWN IN 1936, the Fokker D.XXI was a radial-engine monoplane fighter with a fixed, spatted under-carriage. Although it was originally intended for service with the Royal Netherlands East Indies Army Air Service, it was decided to equip the latter with American fighter types, and so 36 D.XXIs were ordered for the home air force. Seven D.XXIs were supplied to Finland, which subsequently built 93 more under licence. The Dutch aircraft fought against hopeless odds during the German invasion of 1940, while the Finnish D.XXIs were to see much action in the 'Winter War' against the USSR in 1939–40, where they performed well.

FOKKER T.VIII

NETHERLANDS: 1938

The Fokker T.VIII was outclassed by the time the Germans invaded Holland in May 1940 – a few which escaped were used for coastal patrols.

THE FOKKER T.VIII, which first flew in 1938, was designed in response to a Dutch naval Air Service requirement for a modern torpedo-bomber and reconnaissance floatplane suitable for service at home and in the Dutch East Indies. About 30 aircraft had been delivered, or were about to be so, when the Germans invaded Holland in May 1940. Nine aircraft escaped to the UK and were operated by No 320 (Dutch) Squadron until they were grounded for lack of spares. The T.VIIIs seized by the Germans were used for patrol work in the Mediterranean. The T.VIII-L was the sole prototype of a landplane version intended for inland.

Crew: 3
Powerplant: two 336kW (450hp) Wright R-975-E3 Whirlwind 9-cylinder radial engines
Performance: max speed 285km/h (177mph); range 2750km (1709 miles); service ceiling 6800m (22,310ft)
Dimensions: wingspan 18.00m (59ft); length 13.00m (42ft 7in); height 5.00m (16ft 4in)
Weight: 5000kg (11,023lb)
Armament: two 7.92mm (0.31in) machine guns; internal bomb or torpedo load of 600kg (1323lb)

FOKKER S.14 MACHTRAINER

NETHERLANDS: 1951

Crew: 2
Powerplant: one 1574kg (3470lb) Rolls-Royce Derwent turbojet engine
Performance: max speed 716km/h (445mph); range 900km (560 miles); service ceiling 11,125m (36,500ft)
Dimensions: wingspan 11.89m (39ft); length 13.30m (43ft 8in); height 4.67m (15ft 4in)
Weight: 5532kg (12,196lb) loaded
Armament: none

THE FOKKER S.14 MACHTRAINER was the first jet aircraft in the world to be designed specifically for the training role, and was also the first jet aircraft designed and built in Holland. The prototype flew for the first time on 20 May 1951. Production ceased in 1955,

by which time 20 S.14s had been delivered to the Royal Netherlands Air Force. A further five were assembled in Brazil, while 45 more were built there under licence.

The Fokker S.14 Machtrainer was the first jet aircraft ever to be designed for the training role, and was also the first jet type to be designed and built in Holland.

FOKKER F27 FRIENDSHIP

NETHERLANDS: 1955

THE DOUGLAS DC-3 had a lasting and significant effect upon the development of short-haul air services in late wartime and early post World War II Europe. It is therefore understandable that a number of European designers and manufacturers sought to create a DC-3 replacement.

Fokker was one of the companies involved with this quest, and the F27 Friendship, which originates from the study project designation P.275 of 1950, was the most successful of the contenders. The F27 that emerged from the design office embodied a number of attractive features such as an all-metal rounded and pressurized cabin and tricycle undercarriage. Fokker, similarly to contemporary rivals, chose the Rolls-Royce Dart engine to power the F27. Other design features included good short-field performance and the high-wing design favoured by many smaller operators which were using smaller and lower specification airfields.

During these early stages Fokker entered an agreement with the Fairchild Engine and Aeroplane Company, later Fairchild-Hiller, in the USA, whereby Fairchild would market and manufacture the design in the USA. While the prototype of the F27 had first flown in the Netherlands on 24 November 1955, it was a Fairchild-built

FOKKER C.VI
The Fokker C.VI was a C.V-D re-engined with a 336kW (450hp) Hispano-Suiza engine. Twenty-six examples of this light, two-seater observation sesquiplane were built.

FOKKER C.VII-W
The Fokker C.VII-W of 1928 was a light reconnaissance and advanced training floatplane. Thirty examples of this two-seat biplane were built.

FOKKER C.VIII
First flown in 1928, the Fokker C.VIII was a three-seat, long-range reconnaissance, parasol-wing monoplane. The C.VIII-W was a twin-float version which was produced for the Dutch Navy.

FOKKER D.XVI
First flown in 1929, the Fokker D.XVI sesquiplane fighter was light and manoeuvrable. Ten were acquired by the Dutch Army Air Corps, four by Hungary and one each by Italy and China.

FOKKER F.IX
The F.IX was Fokker's largest tri-motor design. Initially flown in 1929, this 17-seat airliner was only produced in small numbers. Avia produced derivatives as the F.39 and the F.IXM bomber.

FOKKER F.XIV
The Fokker F.XIV, which flew in 1929, was designed purely as a freight carrier. It might have succeeded had it not been for the worldwide depression, which discouraged potential buyers. Only one example was built.

FOKKER F.XXXII
Designed and built in the USA as a 32-seat airliner, this Fokker product was powered by four engines mounted in tandem pairs. First flying in 1929, only 10 were built.

FOKKER F.XXXVI
Although KLM ordered six of this four-engined high-wing design, only one was built. Effectively superseded by Douglas designs, the single example of this airliner had a short service life with KLM.

FOKKER D.XVII
A sleek, attractive fighter biplane powered by a Rolls-Royce Kestrel engined, the Fokker D.XVII flew in 1931. Twelve were built, remaining in Dutch service until 1940.

FOKKER F.XII
This triple-engine, high-wing monoplane was designed for KLM and could carry 16 passengers. It first flew in 1931.

This Fairchild-produced F27 was delivered to Bonanza Airlines in 1959 and later served with its successor Hughes Airwest. Built as an F27A (100 series) it was converted to F27B (200 series) early in its career.

example that was to be the first to enter operational service with West Coast Airlines (USA) in November 1958, shortly before the first Dutch-built example flew for Ireland's Aer Lingus in December of that year. Fairchild was also instrumental in improving capacity to 40 seats, increasing fuel capacity and adding a nose-coned weather radar scanner.

The capacity of the early Dutch F27-100 and Fairchild F27 was for 40–52 passengers depending on cabin density/layout, and this was succeeded by the F27-200 (Fairchild F27A) which offered increased gross weight, and the F27-300 (F27B) which offered a large cargo door.

Fairchild F27 production was to have ceased in 1968; however, Fairchild had proceeded to develop the stretched FH227 version (stretched by 1.83m/6ft) which first flew on 27 January 1966 and was capable of accommodating up to 56 passengers. Production of the Fokker FH227 ended in 1968 after production of 78 aircraft.

Fokker first flew its (slightly smaller) stretched version, the F27-500, in 1967. The F27-500 could accommodate up to 60 passengers, and also embodied a number of cockpit and cabin improvements and enhancements, such as enclosed overhead luggage bins. This version, along with the F27-200, remained in production until 1986, when production ended and the F27 Friendship was superseded by the F50.

Fokker also offered military versions of the F27 in various marques for general transport or specialist maritime patrol/search-and-rescue roles – some of these were produced under licence in France, Belgium and Germany.

The final version F27 was the F27-600, which offered the large freight door of the 300/400 series (which was aimed at combi and freight operators) married with the unreinforced cabin floor of the earlier 200 series.

A total of 579 F27s of all marques was built by Fokker and Fairchild produced a further 207 F27/FH227s. The F27 flew with a wide range of major airlines and niche operators across the world and more than 200 examples of the type remain in service today, predominantly in freight roles, although passenger versions also remain in service.

The F27 significantly outsold its main competitors (the Handley Page Herald, Hawker Siddeley 748 and NAMC YS-11) and created a postwar standard for commuter airliners. The type's longevity also owes much to Fokker's used-aircraft policy, which involved refurbishment and equipment standardization made available to secondary operators, increasing the aircraft's desirability.

Specifications apply to the Friendship F27 Mk 200.

Crew: 2
Powerplant: two Rolls-Royce Dart Rda.7 Mk 532-7R turboprop engines each rated at 1596ekW (2140eshp) plus 2.36kN (525lbst) for take-off
Performance: cruising speed 480km/h (298mph) at 6095m (20,000ft); range 1926km (1197 miles) with 44 passengers; initial climb rate 451m (1480ft) per minute; service ceiling 8990m (29,500ft)
Weight: 20,410kg (44,996lb) maximum take-off weight
Dimensions: wingspan 29.00m (95ft 1.75in); wing area 70.00m² (753.50sq ft); length 23.56m (77ft 3.5in); height 8.50m (27ft 10.5in)
Payload: up to 52 passengers within the context of a 4690kg (10,340lb) maximum payload

The F27 was popular on the second-hand market for use by second line or freight operators. This F.27-200 was first operated by Ansett Airlines of Australia in 1964 and was acquired by Comair of South Africa in 1986.

FOKKER F28 FELLOWSHIP

NETHERLANDS: 1967

Crew: 2
Powerplant: two 44.04kN (9900lb st) Rolls-Royce RB.183-2 MK.555-15P Spey turbofan engines
Performance: max cruising speed 843km/h (524mph); range 2743km (1704 miles) with 65 passengers; max cruising altitude 10,670m (35,005ft)
Dimensions: wingspan 25.07m (82ft 3in); length 27.40m (89ft 10.75in); height 8.47m (27ft 9.5in)
Weight: 33,110kg (72,995lb) maximum take-off weight
Payload: up to 65 passengers

BASED ON THE SUCCESS of the F27 turboprop regional airliner, Fokker decided to develop an airliner with over 50 seats and greater performance – a decision which required that jet engines be employed.

Fokker settled on a similar design configuration to some other contemporary small jets: a low wing, T tail and rear fuselage mounted engines.

Subsequently Fokker stretched the fuselage to accommodate 79 passengers in the MK 2000 and later offered improved variants of the two early versions in the MK 3000 and 4000. Sales of the aircraft totalled 241 built up until 1987, when production ceased.

A significant number of F28s remain in service. Although they are fast being superseded by regional jets, the F28 Fellowship may still be regarded as the first successful application of that generic type.

Specifications apply to the Fellowship F28-3000.

The smaller capacity (compared to rivals) of the F28 attracted sales from a number of smaller nations and their operators. The F28 MK 4000 pictured was first operated by the Benin Government.

FOKKER F100

NETHERLANDS: 1986

THE F100 WAS DEVELOPED as an enlarged, modernized successor to the Fokker F28 incorporating new engines, an EFIS cockpit and use of composite materials. It was launched into the competitive 100-seat airliner market in early 1988; Swissair was the launch customer. Fokker went on to produce 283 examples of the type. Specifications apply to the F100.

Crew: 2
Powerplant: two 61.61kN (13,850lb st) Rolls-Royce Tay MK 620 turbofan engines
Performance: cruising speed 856km/h (532mph); range between 2389 and 3111km (1484 and 1933 miles); max operating altitude 10,670m (35,000ft)
Dimensions: wingspan 28.08m (92ft 1.5in); length 35.53m (116ft 6.75in); height 8.51m (27ft 10.5in)
Weight: 41,500kg (91,500lb) maximum take-off weight
Payload: up to 107 passengers

KLM have operated the F100 since 1989. The aircraft has also been popular with a number of the new low-cost airlines in Europe.

FOLLAND (HAWKER SIDDELEY) GNAT

UK: 1955

The Gnat T.MkI was renowned for its sparkling performances in the hands of the Royal Air Force aerobatic team, the Red Arrows.

THE FOLLAND GNAT, which flew for the first time on 18 July 1955, was derived from the Folland Midge lightweight fighter project.

Sixteen Gnat fighters were subsequently sold to Finland and two to Yugoslavia, and the type was built under licence by Hindustan Aero-

nautics in India. Despite the promise shown by the Gnat fighter, which had a phenomenal performance, the RAF was not interested, but ordered a two-seat advanced trainer version instead. The Gnat T.Mk I remained in service with the RAF's advanced flying schools until 1978, when it was replaced by the BAe Hawk. A Mk II version of the single-seat Gnat fighter, the Ajeet (Invincible), was produced for the Indian Air Force. In RAF service, the Gnat became famous as the first mount of the RAF aerobatic team, the Red Arrows. Specifications apply to the Gnat T.Mk I.

Crew: 2
Powerplant: one 1919kg (4230lb) thrust Bristol Siddeley Orpheus turbojet engine
Performance: max speed 1024km/h (636mph); range 1852km (1151 miles); service ceiling 14,630m (48,000ft)
Dimensions: wingspan 7.32m (24ft); length 9.68m (31ft 9in); height 2.93m (9ft 7.5in)
Weight: 3915kg (8630lb) loaded
Armament: none

FORD TRI-MOTOR

USA: 1926

Crew: 1/2
Powerplant: three 313kW (420hp) Pratt & Whitney R-1340-C1 or SC1 Wasp radial piston engines
Performance: max speed 241km/h (150mph) at optimum altitude; range 885km (550 miles); service ceiling 5640m (18,500ft)
Dimensions: wingspan 23.72m (77ft 10in); wing area 77.57m² (835sq ft); length 15.32m (50ft 3in); height 3.86m (12ft 8in)
Weight: 6123kg (13,500lb) maximum take-off weight
Payload: up to 17 passengers carried in an enclosed cabin within the confines of a 1698kg (3743lb) payload

THE TRI-MOTOR WAS the classic American landplane of the pre-DC-3 era, and it played a substantial role in the growth of air transport and mail carriage across the USA. Nearly 200 Tri-Motors were built, but unlike their equivalents in Europe the Tri-Motor did not suffer the full depredations of climate or

Grand Canyon Airlines owns and occasionally operates this 5-AT series Tri-Motor, often from the Grand Canyon Airport.

war. Consequently, a few (semi) operational examples have survived, and are able to demonstrate the realities of pre-DC-3 air travel to new generations. The Ford Tri-Motor originates not with the Ford

Motor Company, but the Stout Metal Airplane Company, run by designer William B. Stout.

Prior to acquisition of that company by Ford in 1925, two single-engined aircraft designated

the 1-AS Air Sedan and 2-AT Pullman had been developed. Ford's purchase of the company facilitated the further development of a three-engined version of the Pullman designated 3-AT, while continuing

production of the single-engined 2-AT. Under Ford ownership the first Tri-Motor was designed and built as the Model 3-AT, retaining the Pullman's high wing, corrugated metal skin and tailskid. However, the nose cabin/engine section was a rather inelegant arrangement and the design did not perform well – Ford ordered its redesign. At some point during this period Stout left the company in uncertain circumstances.

The Tri-Motor 5-AT was the most plentiful model of the Tri-Motor with 117 examples built, of which 41 were 5-AT-B variants.

The Model 4-AT was the result of the 3-AT's re-design and can be viewed as the first successful implementation of the Ford Tri-Motor series. Overall configuration was still similar to the Pullman, but the nose area was redesigned in a more conventional manner. Early

models of the 4-AT were powered by three Wright Whirlwind 149kW (200hp) radial piston engines, one of which was nose-mounted and the other two mounted in a strut arrangement below each wing. Later versions of the 4-AT were subject to engine upgrades. The 4-AT first flew on 11 June 1926 and subsequent versions were capable of carrying up to 15 passengers. Specifications apply to the 5-AT-D Tri-Motor.

FOUGA MAGISTER

FRANCE: 1952

Crew: 2
Powerplant: two 400kg (880lb) thrust Turbomeca Marbore II turbojet engines
Performance: max speed 659km/h (410mph); range 1250km (775 miles); service ceiling 13,500m (43,200ft)
Dimensions: wingspan 12.20m (39ft 10in); length 10.10m (33ft); height 2.90m (9ft 2in)
Weight: 3200kg (7055lb)
Armament: two 7.5mm (0.29in) or 7.62mm (0.30in) machine guns; rocket projectiles, bombs or guided weapons under wings

FAMOUS AS THE EQUIPMENT of the French Patrouille de France and the Belgian Diables Rouges aerobatic teams, the Fouga CM.170 Magister was one of the most successful jet trainers ever built, seeing widespread service with the French and several other air forces. The first of three prototypes flew for the first time on 23 July 1952 and the type, easily recognizable by its 'butterfly' tail-unit, became the first jet trainer to enter service anywhere in the world. In the light

ground-attack role, the Magister distinguished itself in the Arab-Israeli war of 1967, carrying out devastating rocket attacks against Egyptian armour in Sinai. Over 900 Magisters were built, of which 400 went to the French Air Force and 250 to the Federal German Luftwaffe. The CM.175 Zephyr, fitted with an arrester hook, was a version for the French Navy, 45 being delivered. In French, Belgian and German service, the Magister was replaced by the Alpha Jet.

The Fouga Magister was the aircraft chosen for the French and Belgian aerobatic teams. It was equally as effective in the ground-attack role during the Arab–Israeli Six-Day War of 1967.

FOKKER 70
A shortened, 79-seat version of the Fokker 100, first flown in 1993. Production ceased in 1997 (due to Fokker's ceasing trading) with fewer than 50 examples sold.

FOLKERTS SK-3 JUPITER
A single-engined, single-seat, low-wing racing/aerobatic design by Clayton Folkerts. It won the 1937 Cleveland Air Races – another signal that the biplane era was coming to a close.

FOUND MODEL 100 CENTENNIAL
A Canadian single-engine light aeroplane first flown in 1967, the Model 100 was a more powerful successor to the earlier FBA-1 and FBA-2 models. Insolvency (in 1968) precluded transition to production standard.

FOURNIER RF-01
Dating from 1960 this was the first of a series of ultra-light designs from Rene Fournier. The RF-01 was based upon a single-seat sailplane design with a 19kW (25hp) Volkswagen engine added.

FOURNIER RF-6 SERIES
Originating in a 1970 design for a single-engined, tandem two-seat light sports aircraft, the RF-6B first flew in 1974. The RF-6 was also the basis for the Sportavia RS 180 Sportsman design, but Fournier went on to further develop the RF-6 design with different powerplants and innovations. These proved the basis for Slingsby in the UK to licence build and develop the type further under the designation T67.

FUJI T-1A
The Fuji T-1A, which entered service with the Japanese Air Self-Defence Force in 1958, was a swept-wing jet advanced trainer based on the F-86 Sabre. The T-1A replaced the T-6 Texan, with 60 examples being produced.

FUJI KM-2
A two-seat (side by side), single-engined trainer of Japanese design, first flown in 1962. A later version saw the two-seat T-34 trainer's cockpit substituted, making the KM-2B (1974) with a turboprop powerplant replacement (1982).

FUJI FA-200 AERO SUBARU
Japan's first post-World War II light aircraft, and first flown in 1965, the single engined FA-200 Aero Subaru has space for three passengers. A little fewer than 300 examples were produced.

FOURNIER/ALPAVIA/SPORTAVIA RF-3, RF-4 AND RF-5 FRANCE/GERMANY: 1963

Crew: 1
Powerplant: Rectimo 4AR-1200 rated at 29kW (39hp)
Performance: max speed 210km/h (130mph)
Dimensions: wingspan 11.30m (37ft); length 6.00m (19ft 7in)
Weight: 390kg (859lb) maximum take-off weight
Payload: one person

FOLLOWING THE SUCCESSES of the prototype and pre-production RF-01 and RF-2, themselves based upon sail planes powered by Volkswagen engines, Rene Fournier was granted government aid and went into partnership with Alpavia. Consequently, production of the RF-3 began and over 90 examples of this ultra-light sports aircraft, which included a retractable under-

carriage, were produced. In 1966, the Sportavia-Putzer company was created in Germany. This occurred at a similar time to the development of the RF-4 improved design and over 160 RF-4s were built by Sportavia, including one RF-4D flown by Miro Slovak that crossed the North Atlantic in 175 hrs 42 mins. The RF-4 was followed by the stretched two-seat RF-5 which was built in similar numbers. Specifications apply to the RF-3.

This photograph shows a two-seater RF-5 (foreground) flying alongside a single-seat RF-3. The aircraft are German and French-registered respectively, representing the two nations in which this series of designs was produced.

FRIEDRICHSHAFEN G.III GERMANY: 1916

Crew: 3
Powerplant: two 194kW (260hp) Mercedes D.IVa 6-cylinder liquid-cooled in-line engines
Performance: max speed 135km/h (84mph); endurance 5 hrs; service ceiling 4500m (14,765ft)
Dimensions: wingspan 23.70m (77ft 9in); length 12.80m (42ft); height 3.66m (12ft)
Weight: 3930kg (8664lb) loaded
Armament: two 7.9mm (0.31in) machine guns; up to 1500kg (3307lb) of bombs

ENTERING SERVICE IN February 1917, the Friedrichshafen G.III twin-engined night-bomber was developed from the G.I and G.II, the last of which went into limited production. The G.III, which was a larger and more powerful

aircraft than its predecessors, partnered the G.V in constituting the main German bombing strength up to the end of World War I, operating mainly against targets in France and Macedonia, but occasionally taking part in attacks on south-eastern England. One bomber group, Kagohl 1, undertook a series of heavy night attacks against British forces in the Dunkirk area in the summer of 1917, causing very heavy damage. Later versions were the G.IV and G.V, both of which were short-nosed variants without a front gun position and with tractor instead of pusher propellers. The G.IIIa was a modified version, with a biplane tail and other structural

The Friedrichshafen G.III was one of the most effective bombers to serve on either side in World War I. It carried out many attacks on targets in France, and against some in England.

modifications. The total number of G.IIIs produced reached 338.

Specifications apply to the Friedrichshafen G.III.

FUJI FA-300 AND ROCKWELL COMMANDER 700 AND 710 USA/JAPAN: 1975

The FA-300/Rockwell Commander offered standard accommodation for a pilot and co-pilot plus four passengers.

THE COMMANDER 700 series/Fuji FA-300 light/executive transport was the result of a formal collaboration between Fuji and Rockwell. The prototype first flew in Japan in 1975, and the uprated 710 model was developed in parallel. Full rights were passed to Fuji when the Rockwell General Aviation division was divested to the Gulfstream American Corporation. Further efforts came to nothing and production of the 700 and 710 ceased. Specifications apply to Rockwell Commander 700.

Crew: 1/2
Powerplant: two 254kW (340hp) Lycoming TIO-549-R2AD flat-six piston engines
Performance: max speed 409km/h (254mph); range 2227km (1384 miles); service ceiling 8350m (27,400ft)
Dimensions: wingspan 12.94m (42ft 5.5in); length 12.03m (39ft 5.5in); height 4.05m (13ft 3.5in)
Weight: 3151kg (6947lb) maximum take-off weight
Payload: up to six persons

GALAXY AEROSPACE (IAI) ASTRA & GALAXY

ISRAEL/USA: 1984

FOLLOWING THE SUCCESS of the earlier IAI 1121–1124 designs, IAI moved on to design the IAI 1125 Astra with low swept-wing, which extensively utilized composite materials. Later, the Astra SP and SPX included an EFIS cockpit, and the SPX featured winglets plus avionics and engine upgrades. In 1997, IAI joined with US backers and moved to Texas, where the IAI 1126 Galaxy was launched.

The Galaxy differs from its predecessors in having a 'wide

The Astra (pictured) and Galaxy differ substantially from the earlier IAI Westwind models, most overtly in having a low swept wing, rather than the former's high unswept configuration.

body' and transatlantic range of 6708km (4169 miles), and is powered by two Pratt & Whitney PW306A turbofan engines. It is aimed at the medium (seven-passenger) market. Specifications apply to the IAI 1125 Astra.

Crew: 2
Powerplant: two 16.24kN (3654lb st) Garrett TFE731-3A-200G turbofan engines
Performance: max cruising speed 862km/h (535mph); range 5763km (3581 miles); certificated ceiling 13,715m (45,000ft)
Dimensions: wingspan 16.05m (52ft 8in); wing area 29.40m² (316.60sq ft); length 16.94m (55ft 7in); height 5.54m (18ft 2in)
Weight: 10,659kg (23,500lb) maximum take-off weight
Payload: up to six passengers

GENERAL DYNAMICS F-111

USA: 1964

Crew: 2
Powerplant: two 11,385kg (25,100lb) Pratt & Whitney TF-30-P100 turbofan engines
Performance: max speed 2655km/h (1650mph); range 4707km (2925 miles); service ceiling 17,985m (59,000ft)
Dimensions: wingspan 19.20m (63ft) unswept, 9.74m (32ft 11in) swept; length 22.40m (73ft 6in); height 5.22m (17ft 1in)
Weight: 45,359kg (100,000lb) loaded
Armament: one 20mm (0.79in) M61A-1 multi-barrelled cannon; one 340kg (750lb) B43 nuclear store, or two B43s in internal bay; provision for up to 14,290kg (31,000lb) of ordnance on eight underwing hardpoints

THE PROTOTYPE F-111A variable-geometry interdictor/strike aircraft first flew on 21 December 1964. The initial variant was followed into service by the F-111E, which featured modified air intakes to improve performance above Mach 2.2. Re-equipment of the 20th TFW at Upper Heyford in the UK was completed in 1971, and the unit was assigned the war role of interdicting targets deep inside

After experiencing serious technical problems in its early development career, the F-111 went on to bring a new dimension to air warfare.

hostile territory as part of NATO's 2nd Allied Tactical Air Force. The other UK-based F-111 TFW was the 48th based at Lakenheath, Suffolk. It was assigned to 4 ATAF in its war role and could interdict targets as far away as the Adriatic.

The 48th TFW was armed with the F-111F, a fighter-bomber variant combining the best of the F-111E and FB-111A, and fitted with more powerful engines. The F-111C was a strike version for the RAAF. Specifications apply to F-111F.

GENERAL DYNAMICS (LOCKHEED MARTIN) F-16 FIGHTING FALCON

USA: 1974

programme provides core computer and colour cockpit modifications. The second phase, begun in September 2002, involves fitting the advanced interrogator/responder and Lockheed Martin Sniper XR advanced FLIR (Forward-Looking Infra-Red) targeting pod; while the third phase, starting in July 2003,

Crew: 1
Powerplant: either one 10,800kg (23,770lb) Pratt & Whitney F100-PW-200 or one 13,150kg (28,984lb) thrust General Electric F110-GE-100 turbofan engine
Performance: max speed 2142km/h (1320mph); combat radius 925km (578 miles); service ceiling 15,240m (50,000ft)
Dimensions: wingspan 9.45m (31ft); length 15.09m (49ft 6in); height 5.09m (16ft 8in)
Weight: 16,057kg (35,400lb) loaded
Armament: one 20mm (0.79in) General Electric M61A1 multi-barrelled cannon; seven external hardpoints for up to 9276kg (20,450lb) of ordnance

THE F-16, DESIGNED AND BUILT by General Dynamics, had its origin in a USAF requirement of 1972 for a lightweight fighter and first flew on 2 February 1974. It carries an advanced GEC-Marconi HUDWACS (Head-Up Display and Weapon Aiming Computer System) in which target designation cues are shown on the head-up display as well as flight symbols. The HUDWAC computer is used to direct the weapons to the target, as designated on the HUD. The F-16 HUDWAC shows horizontal and vertical speed, altitude, heading, climb and roll bars and range-to-go information for flight reference. There are five ground-attack modes and four air-combat modes. In air combat, the 'snapshoot' mode lets the pilot aim at crossing targets by drawing a continuously computed impact line (CCIL) on the HUD. The F-16's underwing hardpoints are stressed for manoeuvres up to 9g, enabling the aircraft to dogfight while still carrying weaponry. The F-16B and F16-D are two-seat versions, while the F-16C, delivered from 1988, featured numerous improvements in avionics and was available with a choice of engine.

F-16s have seen action in the Lebanon (with the Israeli Air Force), in the Gulf Wars and in the Balkans. A typical stores load might include two wingtip-mounted Sidewinders, with four

The F-16 Fighting Falcon has proved hugely successful, equipping US-aligned air forces around the world.

more on the outer underwing stations; a podded GPU-5/A 30mm (1.18in) cannon on the centreline; drop tanks on the inboard underwing and fuselage stations; a Pave Penny laser spot tracker pod along the starboard side of the nacelle; and bombs, ASMs and flare pods on the four inner underwing stations. The aircraft can carry advanced beyond-visual-range missiles, Maverick ASMs, HARM and Shrike anti-radar missiles, and a weapons dispenser carrying various types of sub-munition including runway denial bombs, shaped-charge bomblets, anti-tank and area-denial mines.

The F-16 Fighting Falcon has been constantly upgraded to extend its life well into the twenty-first century. Its latest upgrade involves 650 Block 40/50 USAF F-16s, which are being updated under the Common Configuration Implementation Program (CCIP). The first aircraft was completed in January 2002, and the first phase

An F-16 approaches a USAF tanker aircraft to take on fuel. Flight refuelling is an essential component of modern air warfare.

adds Link 16 datalink, the Joint Helmet-Mounted Cueing System and an electronic horizontal situation indicator.

The export version of the Sniper XR pod, the Pantera, has been selected by the Royal Norwegian Air Force. The Sniper XR (Extended Range) incorporates a high-resolution mid-wave FLIR, dual-mode laser, CCD TV, laser spot tracker and laser marker, combined with advanced image-processing algorithms.

The F-16 Fighting Falcon, now produced by Lockheed Martin, is the world's most prolific combat aircraft, with more than 2000 in service with the United States Air Force and a further 2000 in service with 19 other air forces around the world. Current orders (in 2002) include Bahrain (10), Greece (50), Egypt (24), New Zealand (28), United Arab Emirates (80), Singapore (20), South Korea (20), Oman (12) and Chile (10). Israel, with the world's largest F-16 fleet

outside the United States, plans to procure 110 F-16I aircraft; deliveries began in 2003. These aircraft will be fitted with Pratt & Whitney F100-PW-229 engines, Elbit avionics, Elisra electronic-warfare systems and Rafael weapons and sensors, including Litening II laser target-designating pods. Italy is to lease 34 aircraft until Eurofighter Typhoon is deployed, and Hungary is to acquire 24 ex-USAF aircraft.

Specifications apply to F-16C.

GLOSTER GREBE

UK: 1923

Gloster Grebe Mk II J7407 served with Nos 56, 25 and 19 Squadrons RAF in the 1920s.

THE FIRST POST WORLD WAR I all-British fighter design, the Gloster Grebe was the brainchild of Harry Folland, Chief Designer of the Gloucestershire Aircraft Company. The Grebe prototype was originally ordered as a Nighthawk. The aircraft made its first public appearance at the RAF Air Pageant, Hendon, in June 1923 and entered RAF service with No 111 Squadron in October that year, subsequently equipping five more RAF fighter squadrons.

One of them, No 25 Squadron, subsequently became famous for its spectacular aerobatic displays in the mid-1920s.

Crew: 1
Powerplant: one 298kW (400hp) Armstrong Siddeley Jaguar IV 14-cylinder radial engine
Performance: max speed 243km/h (151mph); endurance 2 hrs 45 mins; service ceiling 7010m (23,000ft)
Dimensions: wingspan 8.94m (29ft 4in); length 6.17m (20ft 3in); height 2.82m (9ft 3in)
Weight: 1189kg (2622lb) loaded
Armament: two fixed forward-firing 7.7mm (0.303in) Vickers machine guns

GLOSTER GAMECOCK

UK: 1925

THE GLOSTER GAMECOCK prototype, the last wooden biplane fighter designed for the RAF, flew for the first time in February 1925, and the type equipped five RAF squadrons from May 1926. The Gamecock's service life was relatively short-lived. This was partly because of an abnormally high accident rate – of the 90 Gamecocks built, 22 were lost in spinning or landing accidents.

Although assigned to No 22 Squadron, Gloster Gamecock Mk II J8804 spent its entire career as a test aircraft.

Despite this, the Gamecock was very popular with its pilots, as it was extremely light and responsive on the controls and was a superb aerobatic aircraft. The Gamecock I's shortcomings were to some extent cured in the Gamecock II, which had a longer span top wing, a revised vertical tail unit and other improvements. Fifteen examples were built under licence in Finland as the Kukko.

Crew: 1
Powerplant: one 317kW (425hp) Bristol Jupiter VI 9-cylinder radial engine
Performance: max speed 250km/h (155mph); range 587km (365 miles); service ceiling 6700m (22,000ft)
Dimensions: wingspan 9.08m (29ft 9in); length 7.67m (25ft 2in); height 2.99m (9ft 10in)
Weight: 1589kg (3505lb)
Armament: two fixed forward-firing 7.7mm (0.303in) Vickers machine guns

GLOSTER IV RACING SEAPLANES

UK: 1927

IN 1926 GLOSTER embarked on the design of a new racing seaplane, the Gloster IV, to take part in the 1927 Schneider Trophy contest in Venice. Three aircraft, designated Gloster IV, IVA and IVB, were built, each with a slightly different configuration. The Gloster IVB was selected to take part in the 1927 race, but was withdrawn because of technical trouble. The Gloster IV racers were also made available for subsequent contests, but it was Supermarine's S.5 and S.6 designs that secured the trophy for Britain. Specifications apply to Gloster IV.

Crew: 1
Powerplant: one 671kW (900hp) Napier Lion VIIA 12-cylinder liquid-cooled engine
Performance: max speed 426km/h (265mph); endurance 1 hr 6 mins; service ceiling n/a
Dimensions: wingspan 6.90m (22ft 7.5in); length 8.02m (26ft 4in); height 2.79m (9ft 2in)
Weight: 1419kg (3130lb) loaded

The Gloster IV series of racing seaplanes were powerful contenders in the 1927 Schneider Trophy contest, but a run of technical misfortune caused them to be withdrawn.

GLOSTER GAUNTLET

UK: 1928

This is the original Gloster Gauntlet, J9125, which underwent many modifications during its development career.

THE BRISTOL BULLDOG was replaced in RAF service by the Gloster Gauntlet. This was to be the last of the RAF's open-cockpit fighter biplanes. The aircraft was developed as a private venture, fitted with a 477kW (640hp) Bristol Mercury engine, which gave it a top speed of 370km/h (230mph), well in excess of the Bulldog's. A production order for 24 aircraft was placed, and the Gauntlet Mk I entered service with No 19 Squadron in May 1935. The Gauntlet Mk II, with an uprated Mercury engine, began to enter service a year later, and at the peak of its service in the spring of 1937 it equipped 14 home-based fighter squadrons. Gauntlet Mk II production was 204 aircraft.

Specifications apply to the Gloster Gauntlet Mk I.

Crew: 1
Powerplant: one 477kW (640hp) Bristol Mercury VI 9-cylinder radial engine
Performance: max speed 370km/h (230mph); range 740km (460 miles); service ceiling 10,120m (33,500ft)
Dimensions: wingspan 9.99m (32ft 9in); length 8.05m (26ft 5in); height 3.12m (10ft 3in)
Weight: 1801kg (3970lb) loaded
Armament: two 7.7mm (0.303in) Vickers machine guns

GLOSTER GLADIATOR

UK: 1934

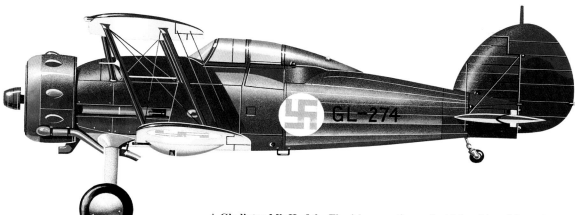

DESIGNATED SS.37 AND designed as a more advanced successor to the open-cockpit Gauntlet fighter, the prototype Gladiator was flown in September 1934 and evaluated by the Air Ministry in the following year. The trials resulted in a production order for 23 machines, followed by two further orders for 100 and 28 aircraft. First deliveries were made to No 27 Squadron at Tangmere in February 1937, and the type went on to equip eight squadrons of Fighter Command. The Gladiator II was

A Gladiator Mk II of the Finnish Air Force. Thirty ex-RAF aircraft were supplied to Finland in December 1939–January 1940 and took part in the defence of Helsinki.

developed to fulfil foreign orders, 147 being produced for this purpose, and 252 were also built for the RAF. The RAF's Gladiators fought in Norway, France, North Africa, the Middle East and the Balkans. Foreign air forces operating the Gladiator were those of Belgium, China, Eire, Greece, Latvia, Lithuania, Norway, Portugal and Sweden. The naval equivalent was the Sea Gladiator,

three of which achieved fame for their defence of the island of Malta in 1940.

Specifications apply to Gladiator II.

Crew: 1
Powerplant: one 619kW (830hp) Bristol Mercury VIIIA 9-cylinder radial engine
Performance: max speed 414km/h (257mph); range 708km (440 miles); service ceiling 10,120m (33,500ft)
Dimensions: wingspan 9.83m (32ft 3in); length 8.36m (27ft 5in); height 3.53m (11ft 7in)
Weight: 2206kg (4864lb) loaded
Armament: four 7.7mm (0.303in) machine guns

GLOSTER METEOR

UK: 1943

Crew: 1
Powerplant: two 906kg (2000lb) thrust Rolls-Royce Derwent 1 turbojet engines
Performance: max speed 675km/h (415mph); range 1580km (988 miles); service ceiling 13,106m (43,000ft)
Dimensions: wingspan 13.10m (43ft); length 12.50m (41ft 3in); height 3.96m (13ft)
Weight: 6314kg (13,920lb) loaded
Armament: four 20mm (0.79in) Hispano cannon

APART FROM THE FACT that it was jet-powered, the Gloster Meteor was entirely conventional in design. It served the Royal Air Force and other air forces until more advanced equipment came along in the 1950s. The Gloster Meteor was the Allies' first operational jet-fighter, and was Gloster's answer to Air Ministry specification F.9/40, calling for a single-seat interceptor powered by gas turbine engines. The low thrust output of the engines available at the time dictated a twin-engined configura-

The Gloster Meteor F.Mk.8 had an excellent rate of climb, but few other attributes when compared with first-generation swept-wing jet-fighters.

tion. Twelve prototypes were ordered and eight were completed, the first flying on 5 March 1943.

The aircraft was powered by two 680kg (1500lb) thrust Halford H.1 turbojets, but the first 20

production aircraft were fitted with the 771kg (1700lb) Rolls-Royce Welland. Twelve of these were issued to No 616 Squadron, which began operational patrols against V-1 flying bombs in July 1944.

One of the F.9/40 Meteor Mk 1 prototypes, DG205/G. Directional stability was a major problem encountered during development test flying – modifications to cure it included an enlarged fin and rudder.

The squadron flew Meteors until August 1945, when it disbanded. Re-formed in 1947, it operated Mosquitoes and then Meteor Mks 3, 4 and 8 before disbanding for the last time in 1957. The second variant to enter squadron service, the Meteor F.Mk 3, was a much better proposition than the F.Mk 1, as it used the 906kg (2000lb) thrust Rolls-Royce Derwent I engine; however, deliveries to No 616 Squadron did not begin until December 1944. The Mk 3 version, which eventually equipped 15 squadrons of RAF Fighter Command in the immediate post-war years, and which had been operationally tested in a ground-attack role in Belgium with Nos 616

and 504 Squadrons in the closing weeks of the war, was followed into service by the Meteor F.Mk 4. Powered by two Rolls-Royce Derwent Vs, the F.Mk 4 first flew in April 1945 and subsequently, in November, set up a new world air speed record of 975km/h (606mph).

The Meteor Mk 5 was a photo-reconnaissance version of the Mk 4; only a few were built. The Mk 6 was a swept-wing Meteor project that never left the drawing board, while the T.Mk 7 was a two-seat trainer variant, of which 640 were built. To improve the range and performance of the F.4, Gloster designed a new high-speed tail unit, lengthened the forward fuselage, installed an extra internal fuel tank

and introduced a one-piece sliding cockpit canopy over a Martin Baker ejection seat, the modified aircraft emerging as the Meteor F.Mk 8 in October 1948. The F.8 was the most prolific of the Meteor variants and formed the mainstay of RAF Fighter Command in the early 1950s, equipping 32 regular and 11 R.Aux.AF squadrons. The Meteor F.8, which was supplied to both Egypt and Israel, saw considerable action during the Arab–Israeli war of 1956; it was also used by No 77 Squadron RAAF in Korea, where it proved greatly inferior to the MiG-15 but excelled in the ground-attack role.

The Meteors FR.9 and Fr.10 were reconnaissance variants,

while the 'long-nose' Meteor NF.11, NF.12, NF.13 and NF.14 were ASI-equipped night-fighters. The NF.4, the last of the Meteor fighters, had a new clear-vision cockpit canopy, and deliveries to the RAF were completed in 1955. In October 1955, Flight Refuelling Ltd began the conversion of a number of ex-RAF Meteor F.8s as target aircraft, 233 being converted between 1956 and 1969 with the designation U.Mk 15 and U.Mk 16. A further batch was converted for use by the RAAF with the designation U.Mk 21. The Meteor TT.20, converted from the NF.11, was a target tug.

Specifications apply to the Gloster Meteor F.Mk 3.

GLOSTER E.1/44

UK: 1948

IN 1944, GLOSTER embarked on the construction of a single-seat day jet-fighter prototype to meet Specification E.1/44, which called for the smallest efficient airframe that could be built around a Rolls-Royce Nene RN2 turbojet. In all, three prototypes were built. The first was wrecked in transit to Boscombe Down by road in July 1947, and it was March 1948 before the second aircraft flew. A third prototype also flew, but a fourth was uncompleted. The three flying prototypes were used at the Royal Aircraft Establishment for some years.

Crew: 1
Powerplant: one 2268kg (5000lb) thrust Rolls-Royce Nene RN.2 turbojet engine
Performance: max speed 997km/h (620mph); endurance 1 hour; service ceiling 14,691m (48,000ft)
Dimensions: wingspan 10.70m (36ft); length 11.50m (38ft); height 3.50m (11ft 8in)
Weight: 5203kg (11,470lb) loaded
Armament: four 20mm (0.79in) cannon

The second prototype Gloster E.1/44, TX148. This aircraft was used for experimental work and was still flying at the Royal Aircraft Establishment, Farnborough, in 1951.

GLOSTER JAVELIN

UK: 1951

Crew: 2
Powerplant: two 4988kg (11,000lb) thrust Armstrong Siddeley Sapphire Sa.7R turbojet engines
Performance: max speed 1130km/h (700mph); range 1931km (1200 miles); service ceiling 15,849m (52,000ft)
Dimensions: wingspan 15.80m (52ft); length 17.10m (56ft 3in); height 4.80m (16ft) Weight: 19,282kg (42,510lb) loaded
Armament: two fixed 30mm (1.18in) Aden cannon in outer mainplanes; provision for four Firestreak AAMs

DEVELOPED AS A REPLACEMENT for the night-fighter versions of the Meteor, Vampire and Venom, the Gloster GA.5 Javelin prototype – the world's first twin-jet delta and an extremely radical design for its day – flew for the first time on 26 November 1951. The first production Javelin FAW.1 flew on 22 July 1954 and deliveries began to No 46 Squadron at RAF Odiham in February 1956.

The Gloster Javelin FAW.2 was basically similar to the FAW.1

with the exception of its radar, which was the American-designed AI22 (APQ43). Next on the production line was the FAW.4, the prototype of which was the 41st FAW.1 with an all-moving tailplane. The last production model was the FAW.8, while the FAW.9 was an FAW.7 with reheat. The T.3 was a trainer version. The Javelin was withdrawn from service in 1967.

Specifications apply to the Gloster Javelin FAW.9.

The heavy, delta-wing Gloster Javelin gave RAF Fighter Command a powerful all-weather fighter capability. The early model FAW.1 had a vicious stall characteristic, making modification of the wing necessary.

GLOSTER-WHITTLE E.28/39

UK: 1941

Crew: 1
Powerplant: one 390kg (860lb) thrust Power Jets W.1 turbojet engine
Performance: max speed 749km/h (466mph); service ceiling 9756m (32,000ft)
Dimensions: wingspan 8.80m (29ft); length 7.60m (24ft 3.25in); height 2.70m (8ft 6in)
Weight: 1699kg (3748lb) loaded
Armament: none

THE GLOSTER-WHITTLE E.28/39 was Britain's first jet-propelled aircraft. The engine initially installed in the aircraft was a Power Jets W.1X turbojet, developed by Frank Whittle; this was used only for taxi tests, being considered below standard for flight. Fitted with the fully operational W.1 engine, the type made its first flight from Cranwell, Lincolnshire, on 15 May 1941. Two E.28/39s were built, but

the second aircraft was destroyed on 30 July 1943 when its ailerons jammed and it entered an inverted spin. The pilot, Squadron Leader Douglas Davie, baled out at

10,065m (33,000ft), the first pilot to do so from a jet aircraft. The first prototype E.28/39, W4041, is today on display in the Science Museum, Kensington, London.

The first Gloster-Whittle E.28/39 outside its hangar. The aircraft was placed on permanent display in London's Science Museum on 28 April 1946.

GLOSTER GNATSNAPPER
The Gloster Gnatsnapper of 1928 was designed as a single-seat carrier fighter to Specification N.21/26. It was not selected for production.

GLOSTER AS.31
The Gloster AS.31, flown in 1929, was a two/three-seat, twin-engined photographic air survey biplane. Two aircraft were built.

GLOSTER TC.33
The Gloster TC.33 bomber transport, first flown in February 1932, was Gloster's only four-engined aircraft, and the biggest. Flight-test results were not encouraging, however, and the type was abandoned.

GLOSTER TSR.38
The Gloster TSR.38 was a three-seat torpedo/spotter/reconnaissance biplane, the sole prototype of which flew in April 1932. The Fairey Swordfish was selected to fill the Royal Navy's requirement.

GLOSTER F.5/34
First flown in December 1937, the Gloster F.5/34 was a single-seat day-fighter monoplane, designed to the specification that produced the Spitfire and Hurricane. Two aircraft were built.

GLOSTER F.9/37
A twin-engine single-seat day and night fighter, the F.9/37 was the last of Gloster's pre-war piston-engined designs, and was heavily armed. Two prototypes of the F.9/37 were built.

GLOSTER F.153D
The Gloster F.153D was a design for a transonic 'Super Javelin' with a new, thin wing and a heavy air-to-air missile armament. It was cancelled in 1957.

GOTHA TAUBE LE-3
In 1914, one of the principal German/Austrian military aircraft was the Taube (Dove) originally designed by Igor Etrich. The design was adopted by several firms, including Gotha.

GOTHA G.I–G.V

Crew: 3
Powerplant: two 194kW (260hp)
Mercedes D.IVa water-cooled in-line
engines
Performance: max speed 140km/h
(87mph); range 500km (310 miles);
service ceiling 6500m (21,325ft)
Dimensions: wingspan 23.70m (77ft 9in);
length 11.86m (38ft 11in); height 4.30m
(14ft 1in)
Weight: 3975kg (8763lb) loaded
Armament: four 7.92mm (0.31in)
machine guns; 500kg (1102lb) of bombs

THE GOTHA G.I BOMBER, which
first flew in January 1915, was
designed by Oskar Ursinus and
Major Friedel of the German
Army. A few examples were used
for ground-attack and general
tactical duties. The Gotha G.II,
which flew for the first time in
April 1916, suffered repeated
crankshaft failures and was soon
replaced by the G.III. The first
major production model was the

Gotha G.IV, built specifically to
carry out raids on Britain. From
August 1917 this version was
gradually replaced by the new

Gotha G.V, which carried a heavy
defensive armament.
Specifications apply to the
Gotha G.V.

**A Gotha G.III bomber of Kagohl 6
(Kampfgeschwader der Obersten
Heeresleitung/Army High
Command Bomber Wing 6).**

GOTHA GO 242

THE GO 242 TRANSPORT glider was
the only Gotha design to see large-
scale operational service during
World War II. A twin-boom aircraft
with shoulder-mounted wings, the
prototype flew in 1941. The first
production variant, the Go 242A-1,
was intended as a freight carrier, but
the Go 242A-2 was an assault
glider with provision for 21 troops.
The Heinkel He 111H was the most
usual towing aircraft, and
sometimes the He 111Z five-

**The Gotha 242 heavy glider was
used in some numbers in North
Africa and on the Eastern Front.
Total production was 1528.**

engined tug was employed. A
variety of rocket-assisted take-off
equipment could also be used to
help get a heavily laden glider off
the ground. The Go 242 was first
used operationally in the Middle
East in 1942. The Go 242C-1 was
capable of alighting on water. Specifications apply to the Go 242A-2.

Crew: 2
Performance: max towing speed 240km/h
(149mph)
Dimensions: wingspan 24.50m (80ft 4in);
length 15.80m (51ft 10in); height 4.40m
(14ft 4.25in)
Weight: 7100kg (15,656lb) loaded
Payload: 21 troops

GRIGOROVICH I-5 SERIES

IN 1930 THE RUSSIAN DESIGNER
Dmitri Grigorovich, with fellow
designer N.N. Polikarpov, produced
the I-5 single-seat biplane, a very
light, manoeuvrable fighter with a
maximum speed of 322km/h
(200mph). It was very successful,
with about 800 being built. He then
produced a two-seat biplane fighter,
the DI-3, characterized by its twin
fins and rudders; it was fitted with
a 447kW (600hp) M-17 engine and
three 7.62mm (0.30in) machine
guns. The I-7, which appeared

shortly afterwards, was a landplane
version of a proposed floatplane
fighter for Soviet Naval Aviation,
which in fact was not built. The
years 1930–33 saw three more
fighter designs which never left the
drawing board. These were the
twin-engined I-9, to have been
fitted with two 358kW (480hp) M-

**The stubby little Grigorovich I-5
biplane was an instant success and
set the pattern for other Soviet
biplane fighter designs of the 1930s.**

22 engines, giving it an estimated top speed of 215km/h (130mph); and the I-10 single-seat gull-wing monoplane with a 466kW (625hp) M-25 radial engine.

Specifications apply to the I-5.

Crew: 1
Powerplant: one 358kW (480hp) M-22 radial engine
Performance: max speed 272km/h (170mph); range 790km (490 miles); service ceiling 6300m (20,669ft)

Dimensions: wingspan 11.80m (38ft 9in); length 7.80m (25ft 7in)
Weight: 2020kg (4080lb) loaded
Armament: two fixed forward-firing 7.62mm (0.30in) machine guns

GROB GF 200   GERMANY: 1991

Crew: 2
Powerplant: one 233kW (310hp) Teledyne Continental TSIOL550 turbocharged and fuel-injected flat-six piston engine
Performance: max cruising speed 370km/h (230mph); range 1850km (1149 miles);

service ceiling 7625m (25,000ft)
Dimensions: wingspan 11.00m (36ft 1in); length 8.70m (28ft 6in); height 3.42m (11ft 3in)
Weight: 1600kg (3528lb) maximum take-off weight
Payload: four people

THE GF 200 differs greatly from other Grob designs in having its single pusher engine mounted in the rear of the fuselage, serving to reduce noise. Other features include winglets, a T tail and a retractable undercarriage.

The GF 200 is radically different from other Grob designs, but it does share a similarity with other Grob models in terms of cockpit glazing, with good crew and passenger vision offered by the large window sections.

GRUMMAN FF-1 SERIES   USA: 1931

Crew: 1
Powerplant: one 709kW (950hp) Wright R-1820-22 Cyclone 9-cylinder radial engine
Performance: max speed 418km/h (260mph); range 1819km (1130 miles); service ceiling 9845m (32,300ft)
Dimensions: wingspan 9.75m (32ft); length 7.01m (23ft); height 2.84m (9ft 4in)
Weight: 2155kg (4750lb) loaded
Armament: one 12.7mm (0.50in) and one 7.62mm (0.30in) machine gun in upper forward fuselage; external bomb load of 105kg (232lb)

This photograph shows a preserved US Navy FF-1. About 40 examples of the FF-1 fought on the Republican side in the Spanish Civil War.

ON 2 APRIL 1931, the US Navy signed its first contract with Grumman Aircraft for the building of 27 fighter and 33 reconnaissance versions of the Grumman FF-1, the first military aircraft to be fitted with a retractable undercarriage, all for service on the USS *Lexington*. The prototype XFF-1 flew towards

the end of 1931 and entered service in June 1933, followed in March 1934 by the SF-1. The success of the FF-1, which was a two-seater, encouraged the US Navy to order a

single-seat version, the XF2F-1, first flown on 18 October 1933. The final variant was the F3F-3, 27 of which were produced. Specification refers to the F3F-3.

GOTHA WD.22
Powered by four engines in a tractor/pusher arrangement, the Gotha WD.22 was a twin-float torpedo-bomber built towards the end of World War I.

GOTHA GO 145
The Gotha Go 145 biplane trainer was the first aircraft produced by the re-established Gotha company. The design was so successful that several other firms became involved in its construction.

GOTHA GO 147
The Gotha Go 147, flown in 1935, was a prototype short-range observation and gunnery-training monoplane. A 'flying wing' design, it had poor flight characteristics.

GOTHA GO 244
The Gotha Go 244 was a powered version of the Go 242, fitted with two Gnome/Rhone radial engines. One unit only operated the type, on the Russian front.

GOUPY NO 2
The Goupy No 2 was a biplane, built in France at the Bleriot factory and flown in 1909. One famous pilot who was to fly the Goupy was Jules Vedrines, the pioneer aviator.

GOURDOU-LESEURRE GL810 HY
The Gourdou-Leseurre 810 HY (Hydravion) was an armed reconnaissance and attack seaplane of 1927. The French Navy took delivery of 86 for operation from its warships.

GOURDOU-LESEURRE GL823 HY
The Gourdou-Leseurre GL832 was a single-engined twin-float seaplane which first flew in 1932. About 30 were built, and these were still serving with the French Navy in World War II.

GRUMMAN G-21 GOOSE (JRF, OA-9 AND OA-13)

USA: 1937

This model G-21A is operated by Aero Float, one of 30 built before World War II for commercial use. Although based in Virginia, it crosses the Atlantic occasionally to attend air shows and seaplane rallies in Europe.

THE GOOSE WAS DEVELOPED prior to World War II with civil executive/light transport roles in mind, but the high-wing amphibian's potential for armed coastal protection duties was realised. Early deliveries were commercial, but the Portuguese and then US military placed orders and the Goose was designated JRF or OA-13 (in various marques) by the US Navy and OA-9 by the US Army. Some versions were pure amphibian, with the retractable landing gear removed. At the end of World War II there were many surplus examples in the US and UK. Some were sold on for overseas military use and others converted for civil work, often with specialized airline/air-taxi operators – for example in the Florida Keys. A US company, McKinnon Enterprises, was a specialist in Goose conversions and refurbishments, and even made modifications to features such as powerplants. Conversions were available until 1980 in several forms, including retractable floats or turboprop engines (G-21G). Specifications apply to McKinnon (Grumman) G-21G Turbo-Goose.

Crew: 2
Powerplant: two 507kW (680shp) Pratt & Whitney PT6A-27 turboprop engines
Performance: max speed 391km/h (243mph); range 2575km (1600 miles); service ceiling 6095m (20,000ft)
Dimensions: wingspan 15.49m (50ft 10in); length 12.06m (39ft 7in)
Weight: 5670kg (12,500lb) maximum take-off weight
Payload: variable – passengers or freight

GRUMMAN F4F WILDCAT

USA: 1939

IN MARCH 1936, THE Grumman Aircraft Corporation was awarded a development contract to build an all-metal biplane fighter, the XF4F-1, for the US Navy. However, the biplane configuration was quickly shelved in favour of a monoplane design, the XF4F-2. This flew on 2 September 1937, powered by a 782kW (1050hp) Pratt & Whitney R-1830-66 Twin Wasp radial engine. The US Navy

The Wildcat held the line in the Pacific war for a critical period until more modern US naval fighters could be deployed.

decided to develop the aircraft still further by installing a super-charged XR-1830-76 engine in a much redesigned airframe. The revamped machine, which was designated XF4F-3, flew for the first time on 12 February 1939. In August, the Navy issued its first production contract for 53 Grumman F4F-3 Wildcats, as the fighter had been named. The first production aircraft flew in February 1940; however, deliveries of the type were slow and by the end of 1940 only 22 Wildcats had been handed over.

In 1939, meanwhile, France – which had one aircraft carrier in commission and two more under construction – had expressed an interest in acquiring 100 Wildcats under the export designation G-36A. As the Twin Wasp engine was in short supply, the French machines were to be powered by the 895kW (1200hp) R-1820-G205A Cyclone. The order was later reduced to 81, and flight testing of the first of these aircraft was still in progress when France was overrun by the Germans.

The order was taken over by the British, with the first aircraft being delivered on 27 July 1940, a month in fact before the US Navy was to receive its first Wildcat. In April 1941, 30 G-36As ordered by Greece were also diverted to Britain as Martlet IIIs, these aircraft having been offloaded at

Gibraltar when the Germans invaded the Balkans.

Neither the F4F-3 nor the Martlet I had folding wings, but these were incorporated in all but 10 of an order for 100 Martlet IIs (G-36As) placed by Britain in 1940. The total number of Martlets of all marks supplied to Britain eventually reached 1191, including 220 Martlet IVs, 311 Martlet Vs and 370 Wildcat VIs, the American name having by then been adopted by the Fleet Air Arm.

In American service, the Wildcat with folding wings received the designation F4F-4, the first example flying on 14 April 1941. As 1941 drew to a close the Wildcat was rapidly replacing all other US carrier-borne fighters. At the time of the Japanese attack on Pearl Harbor, Wildcats belonging to Marine fighter squadron VMF-211 were divided between Oahu, where nine were destroyed or damaged on the ground during the attack, and Wake Island, where seven of eight aircraft on the ground suffered a similar fate as their Oahu counterparts. The four surviving aircraft were used to put up a desperate and heroic defence before they too were overwhelmed. The first encounters between the Wildcat and the Zero showed that the F4F was inferior to the Japanese fighter on almost every count. Nevertheless, a number of US Navy pilots scored noteworthy

A Grumman Martlet of the Fleet Air Arm taxiing on the deck of a Royal Navy escort carrier.

victories while flying the Wildcat. On 20 February 1942, for example, Lieutenant Edward H. O'Hare destroyed five Japanese bombers over Rabaul, while Lieutenant J.G. McCuskey destroyed five during the Coral Sea battle. Another notable Wildcat pilot was Captain Joe Foss, a Marine officer who went on to shoot down 26 enemy aircraft. In US Marine Corps hands, the Wildcat will forever be remembered for its defence of Guadalcanal in the latter half of 1942. The total number of Grumman Wildcats built, including 21 examples of an unarmed reconnaissance version of the aircraft, the F4F-7, was 7885.

Specifications apply to the Grumman F4F-3.

Crew: 1

Powerplant: one 895kW (1200hp) Pratt & Whitney R-1830-66 radial engine

Performance: max speed 512km/h (318mph); range 1239km (770 miles); service ceiling 10,638m (34,900ft)

Dimensions: wingspan 11.58m (38ft); length 8.76m (28ft 9in); height 3.61m (11ft 10in)

Weight: 3607kg (7952lb) loaded

Armament: six 12.7mm (0.50in) machine guns in wings; external bomb load of 91kg (200lb)

GRUMMAN TBF AVENGER

Crew: 3
Powerplant: one 1268kW (1700hp)
Wright R-2600-8 Cyclone 14-cylinder
radial engine
Performance: max speed 414km/h
(257mph); range 1780km (1105 miles);
service ceiling 6525m (21,400ft)
Dimensions: wingspan 16.51m (54ft 2in);
length 12.19m (40ft); height 5.00m
(16ft 5in)
Weight: 7876kg (17,364lb) loaded
Armament: three 12.7mm (0.50in) and
two 7.62mm (0.30in) machine guns;
torpedo, bomb and rocket load up to
1134kg (2500lb)

DESPITE A DISASTROUS start to its
operational career at the Battle of
Midway in June 1942, when five
out of six aircraft were shot down
in an attack on the Japanese task
force, the Grumman TBF Avenger
went on to become one of World
War II's best shipborne torpedo-
bombers. The XTBF-1 prototype
was first flown on 1 August 1941,
with an order for 286 aircraft already
in place. The first production TBF-1
aircraft were delivered to torpedo
squadron VT-8 in May 1942; it was
this unit that suffered severe losses
at Midway. Sub-variants included
the TBF-1C, with two wing-
mounted 20mm (0.79in) cannon;
the TBF-1B, supplied to the Royal
Navy; the TBF-1D and TBF-1E
with ASV radar; and the TBF-1L
with a searchlight in the bomb bay.
Specifications apply to the TBF-1.

Grumman Avenger Mk Is of No 846 Squadron, Royal Navy, pictured in December 1943. The squadron was then based at Machrihanish in western Scotland, and about to deploy on the escort carrier HMS *Ravager*.

GRUMMAN F6F HELLCAT

THE GRUMMAN HELLCAT flew for
the first time on 26 June 1942, its
design having benefited from
combat lessons learned by its
predecessor, the Wildcat. First
deliveries of the Grumman F6F-3
Hellcat were made on 16 January
1943, and the aircraft saw its first
combat over Marcus, one of the
Caroline Islands, on 31 August.
Britain received 252 F6F-3s under
the terms of Lend-Lease. In the
Pacific, the Hellcat played a
prominent role in all US naval
operations, in particular the Battle
of the Philippine Sea (19/20 June
1944). In what became known as
the 'Marianas Turkey Shoot',
American combat air patrols and
anti-aircraft fire destroyed 325
enemy aircraft. Night-fighter
variants of the F6F-3 were the
F6F-3E and F6F-3N. In April 1944

The Hellcat incorporated many of the lessons learned in combat by F4F Wildcat pilots, and established US air superiority in the Pacific.

manufacture switched to the
improved F6F-5, with a Pratt &
Whitney R-2800-10W engine. The
Royal Navy took delivery of 930
F6F-5s as Hellcat IIs. In all,
12,272 Hellcats were built.
Specifications apply to the F6F-5.

Crew: 1
Powerplant: one 1492kW (2000hp) Pratt
& Whitney R-2800-10W radial engine
Performance: max speed 612km/h
(380mph); range 1521km (945 miles);
service ceiling 11,369m (37,300ft)
Dimensions: wingspan 13.05m (42ft
10in); length 10.24m (33ft 7in); height
3.99m (13ft 1in)
Weight: 7025kg (15,487lb)
Armament: six 12.7mm (0.50in) machine
guns in wings, or two 20mm (0.79in)
cannon and four 12.7mm (0.50in)
machine guns; provision for two 453kg
(1000lb) bombs or six 12.7cm (5in) RPs

GRUMMAN F7F TIGERCAT

USA: 1943

ALTHOUGH IT APPEARED too late to see operational service in World War II, the Grumman F7F Tigercat was significant in that it was the first twin-engined carrier-borne aircraft with a tricycle undercarriage to enter series production.

The prototype XF7F-1 flew on 3 November 1943 and 34 series aircraft were produced with the designation F7F-1D, these being intended for long-range escort and

tactical support. The F7F-2N (64 built) was a night-fighter version, while the F7F-3 was the major production version, 189 being built. During the Korean War, Tigercats operated as night intruders, with limited success. Specifications apply to the F7F-3.

This photograph shows one of six surviving F7F Tigercats, a two-seat version adapted for air racing.

Crew: 2
Powerplant: two 1567kW (2100hp) Pratt & Whitney R-2800-34W Double Wasp 18-cylinder radial engines
Performance: max speed 700km/h (435mph); range 1930km (1200 miles); service ceiling 12,405m (40,700ft)
Dimensions: wingspan 15.69m (51ft 6in); length 14.27m (46ft 10in); height 5.05m (16ft 7in)
Weight: 11,690kg (25775lb) loaded
Armament: four 20mm (0.79in) cannon

GRUMMAN F8F BEARCAT

USA: 1944

Crew: 1
Powerplant: one 1567kW (2100hp) Pratt &Whitney R-2800-34W 18-cylinder Double Wasp radial engine
Performance: max speed 677km/h (421mph); range 1780km (1105 miles); service ceiling 11,800m (38,713ft)
Dimensions: wingspan 10.92m (35ft 10in); length 8.61m (28ft 3in); height 4.21m (13ft 10in)
Weight: 5872kg (12,947lb) loaded
Armament: four 20mm (0.79in) cannon

DESIGNED TO REPLACE the F6F Hellcat, the F8F was the last of Grumman's piston-engined 'cats'. The prototype flew on 21 August 1944 and the first of 765 F8F-1s was delivered to the US Navy in

The Grumman F8F Bearcat saw service in the attack role in French Indo-China and, in recent years, has been adapted as a racer.

May 1945, followed in 1946 by 100 F8F-1Bs and 36 F8F-1F night-fighters. In 1948 the more powerful F8F-2 appeared; production of this variant totalled 305, of which 12 were F8F-2N night-fighters and 30

F8F-2P photo-reconnaissance aircraft. France was supplied with 100 Bearcats and used them in Indo-China; about 100 were also delivered to the Royal Thai Air Force. Specifications apply to F8F-2.

GRUMMAN SA-16 ALBATROSS

USA: 1947

The Grumman Albatross saved countless lives in its air–sea rescue role, serving at US shore bases around the world from the United Kingdom to Japan.

FIRST FLOWN IN OCTOBER 1947, the SA-16 Albatross air–sea rescue and utility transport amphibian entered US military service in 1949. Over 500 were built, including the HU-16A/B for USAF air–sea

rescue duties, the HU-16C for the US Navy and Coast Guard, and the HU-16D for the utility transport role with the USN.

Specifications apply to the Grumman HU-16A/B Albatross.

Crew: 5/6
Powerplant: two 1100kW (1475hp) Wright R-1820-76A Cyclone 8-cylinder radial engines
Performance: max speed 379km/h (236mph); range 5148km (3200 miles);

service ceiling 7625m (25,000ft)
Dimensions: wingspan 29.58m (96ft 8in); length 18.60m (61ft 3in); height 7.93m (25ft 10in)
Weight: 14,400kg (32,000lb) loaded
Armament: none

GRUMMAN F9F PANTHER

USA: 1947

Crew: 1
Powerplant: one 2270kg (5000lb) thrust Pratt & Whitney J-42-P-6 turbojet engine
Performance: max speed 846km/h (526mph); range 2180km (1353 miles); service ceiling 13,600m (44,600ft)
Dimensions: wingspan 11.58m (38ft); length 11.35m (37ft 3in); height 3.45m (11ft 4in)
Weight: 8842kg (19,452lb) loaded
Armament: four 20mm (0.79in) cannon; 907kg (2000lb) of ordnance

TWO XF9F-2 PROTOTYPES were ordered, the first of which flew on 24 November 1947 with a Rolls-Royce Nene turbojet. The second aircraft, designated XF9F-3, flew in August 1948 and was equipped

The Grumman F9F Panther served with the US Navy and US Marines in the Korean War, carrying out thousands of ground-attack and fighter missions.

with an Allison J33A-8 engine. The first production batch of F9F-2 Panthers (47 aircraft) featured the Pratt & Whitney J42-P-6 turbojet, the licence-built Nene. It entered service with VF-51 in May 1949, replacing the FJ-1 Fury, and went into action for the first time when aircraft of this unit, operating from the USS *Valley Forge*, flew top cover for strikes on enemy airfields and supply lines near Pyongyang. During this mission, two VF-51 pilots shot down two Yak-9s, the US Navy's first kills in Korea. Total production of the F9F-2 and its successor, the uprated F9F-3, was 437 aircraft. The next variant was the F9F-4; 73 examples were built. This was followed by 655 F9F-5s and 23 examples of a photo-reconnaissance variant, the F9F-5P.

Specifications apply to the Grumman F9F-2 Panther.

GRUMMAN S-2 TRACKER

USA: 1952

The Grumman Tracker was developed in response to a US Navy requirement for a hunter-killer aircraft that would be an effective counter to the Soviet Union's growing fleet of ocean-going submarines.

ONE OF THE MOST important carrier-borne aircraft of the post-war years, the Grumman XS2F-1 Tracker prototype flew for the first time on 4 December 1952.

The initial series production S2F-1 (later designated S-2A) was powered by two 1138kW (1525hp) Wright R-1820-82 engines; 755 examples were built, with the first deliveries to the US Navy being made in February 1954. It was also supplied to Argentina, Japan, Italy, Brazil, Taiwan, Thailand, Uruguay and the Netherlands. Variants of the aircraft were the S-2C, S-2D and S-2E.

Specifications apply to the Grumman S-2A Tracker.

Crew: 4
Powerplant: two 1138kW (1525hp) Wright R-1820-82WA Cyclone 9-cylinder radial engines
Performance: max speed 461km/h (287mph); range 1450km (900 miles); service ceiling 7010m (23,000ft)
Dimensions: wingspan 21.23m (69ft 8in); length 12.87m (42ft 3in); height 4.95m (16ft 3in)
Weight: 11,930kg (26,300lb) loaded
Armament: two homing torpedoes, two Mk 101 depth bombs or four depth charges internally; six 113kg (250lb) bombs, 11.25cm (5in) HVARS or Zuni rockets on external pylons

GRUMMAN F11F TIGER

USA: 1954

Crew: 1
Powerplant: one 3488kg (7700lb) thrust Wright J65-W-18 turbojet engine
Performance: max speed 1432km/h (890mph); combat radius 611km (380 miles); service ceiling 16,775m (55,000ft)
Dimensions: wingspan 9.66m (31ft 7in); length 13.57m (44ft 6in); height 3.90m (12ft 8in)
Weight: 9592kg (21,174lb) loaded
Armament: four 20mm (0.79in) Mk 12 cannon

The F11F Tiger gave the US Navy a true supersonic capability. It filled an important gap in fleet defence until the deployment of the F-4 Phantom.

TO REPLACE THE PANTHER and its swept-wing version, the F9F-8 Cougar, Grumman conceived the F11F Tiger supersonic fighter, Its design featured area ruling and other aerodynamic refinements which were then novel. The Tiger entered service with Navy Squadron VA-156 in March 1957. Only 201 examples were built, but the type made its mark on aviation history. On 18 April 1958, an F11F-1F, a variant powered by an afterburning J79-GE-1 engine, broke the world altitude record for the second time in three days, reaching a height of 23,466.4m (76,939ft).

Specifications apply to the F11F.

GRUMMAN A-6 INTRUDER

USA: 1960

Crew: 2
Powerplant: two 4218kg (9300lb) Pratt & Whitney J52-P-8A turbojet engines
Performance: max speed 1043km/h (648mph); range 1627km (1011 miles); service ceiling 14,480m (47,500ft)
Dimensions: wingspan 16.15m (53ft); length 16.64m (54ft 7in); height 4.93m (16ft 2in)
Weight: 27,397kg (60,400lb) loaded
Armament: five external hardpoints for up to 8165kg (18,000lb) of ordnance

THE A-6 INTRUDER WAS designed specifically as a carrier-based low-level attack bomber with the ability to deliver both nuclear and conventional warloads with pinpoint accuracy in all weathers. It was one of 11 competitors in a US Navy design contest of 1957, and was selected as the winner in December that year. The A-6A prototype flew on 19 April 1960 and the first operational aircraft entered service with Attack Squadron VA-42 on 1 February 1963. The last delivery took place in December 1969, by which time 488 had been built. The A-6A saw extensive action over Vietnam. The next variant was the EA-6A electronic-warfare aircraft, 27 of which were produced for the

The Grumman A-6E Intruder was the last basic attack variant of the type. It entered service in the 1970s and saw action in the Gulf War of 1991, where it delivered weapons with great precision.

US Marine Corps; this was followed by the EA-6B Prowler, with advanced avionics and a longer nose section to accommodate two extra

ECM specialists. The last basic attack variant was the A-6E, which first flew in February 1970. Other conversions of the basic A-6A were

the A-6C, with enhanced night-attack capability, and the KA-6D flight refuelling tanker. Specifications apply to the A-6E.

GRUMMAN E-2 HAWKEYE

USA: 1960

THE GRUMMAN E-2 HAWKEYE was the US Navy's principal electronic-surveillance aircraft in the Gulf War, and the mainstay of the US

Navy's early-warning capability for many years. The prototype of the aircraft first flew on 20 October 1960. The first 20 E-2As were

The highly effective Grumman E-2 Hawkeye is seen here in the markings of the Japanese Air Self-Defence Force.

used for service evaluation and carrier trials, and the type was formally accepted into US Navy service in January 1964.

The E-2B, which flew in February 1969, had a number of refinements, including an L-304 micro-electronic computer, and all operational E-2A Hawkeyes were subsequently updated to E-2B standard. An advanced search radar, the APS-120, was installed in a new model, the E-2C. Two derivatives of the E-2C were the TE-2C trainer and the C-2A Greyhound carrier on-board delivery transport.

Crew: 5
Powerplant: two 3021kW (4050hp) Allison T56-A-8A turboprop engines
Performance: max speed 595km/h (370mph); range 3060km (1900 miles); service ceiling 9660m (31,700ft)
Dimensions: wingspan 24.56m (80ft 7in); length 17.17m (56ft 4in); height 4.88m (15ft 7in)
Weight: 22,453kg (49,500lb)
Armament: none

GRUMMAN F-14 TOMCAT

USA: 1970

Crew: 2

Powerplant: two 9480kg (20,900lb) thrust Pratt & Whitney TF30-P-412A turbofan engines

Performance: max speed 2517km/h (1564mph); range 1994km (1239 miles); service ceiling 17,070m (56,000ft)

Dimensions: wingspan 19.55m (64ft 1in) unswept, 11.65m (38ft 2in) swept; length 19.10m (62ft 8in); height: 4.88m (16ft)

Weight: 33,724kg (74,349lb) loaded

Armament: one 20mm (0.79in) M61A1 Vulcan rotary cannon, plus a combination of AIM-7 Sparrow medium-range AAMs, AIM-9 short-range AAMs, and AIM-54 Phoenix long-range AAMs

More than 30 years after the prototype first flew, the Tomcat remains a potent long-range interceptor in US Navy service.

ALTHOUGH ITS DEVELOPMENT history was beset by problems, the variable-geometry F-14 Tomcat emerged from them all to become one of the most formidable interceptors of all time, designed from the outset to establish complete air superiority in the vicinity of a carrier task force and also to attack tactical objectives as a secondary role. Selected in January 1969 to replace the US Navy's Phantom, the prototype F-14A first flew on 21 December 1970. The variable-geometry fighter completed carrier trials in the summer of 1972 and deliveries to the US Navy began in October that year.

At the heart of the Tomcat's offensive capability is the Hughes AN/AWG-9 weapons control system, enabling the two-man crew to detect airborne targets at ranges of up to 315km (170nm) depending on their size, and cruise missiles at

120km (65nm). A task force's Tomcats are normally required to fly three kinds of mission: Barrier Combat Air Patrol (CAP), Task Force CAP and Target CAP. Barrier CAP involves putting up a defensive screen at a considerable distance from the task force under the direction of a command-and-control aircraft. As fighters flying Barrier CAP are likely to encounter the greatest number of incoming enemy aircraft, Tomcats usually carry their full armament of six Phoenix AAMs. These weapons are highly suitable for long-range interception of aircraft flying at all levels and also sea-skimming missiles. If targets still show signs of breaking through, the Tomcats can continue the engagement with their Vulcan cannon at close range.

In total, 478 F-14As were supplied to the US Navy, and 80

more F-14As were exported to Iran in the later 1970s. The proposed F-14B, with Pratt & Whitney F401-P-400 turbofans, was cancelled, but 32 F-14As were fitted with the General Electric F110-GE-400 and redesignated F-14B. The F-14D is an improved version with more powerful radar, enhanced avionics, a redesigned cockpit and a tactical jamming system; 37 aircraft were built from new and 18 converted from F-14As.

During the 1991 Gulf War, the type shared the air combat patrol task with the McDonnell Douglas F-15 Eagle. Since then the type has seen active service in the Balkans and Afghanistan, and was involved in the second war with Iraq in 2003, although it is now being gradually replaced by the Boeing F/A-18 Super Hornet. Specifications apply to the F-14A.

The F-14 Tomcat is combat-proven, having seen action against Libyan combat aircraft over the Gulf of Sirte in the 1980s and in two Gulf wars, when it was employed in the interceptor and ground-attack roles.

HAL HF-24 MARUT

A bold attempt to produce an indigenous jet fighter-bomber, the Hindustan Aeronautics Ltd (HAL) HF-24 Marut took years to develop and the project was costly. It was not particularly successful.

DESIGNED BY A TEAM under the leadership of Dr Kurt Tank, architect of Germany's wartime Focke-Wulf fighters, the Hindustan Aeronautics Ltd (HAL) HF-24 Marut (Wind Spirit) underwent a protracted development history, with more than a decade elapsing between design work starting in 1956 and the first fully operational examples being delivered. The first series production Marut flew in November 1967 and the type eventually equipped three Indian Air Force squadrons, seeing combat in the ground-attack role during the 1971 Indo-Pakistan war. Including a pre-production batch, 100 single-seat Marut Mk Is and 18 two-seat Mk IT trainers were delivered. Despite the Marut's impressive-looking swept-wing design, the aircraft was lacking when it came to engine power.

Crew: 1
Powerplant: two 2200kg (4850lb) thrust Rolls-Royce Orpheus 703 turbojet engines
Performance: max speed 1112km/h (691mph); range 1000km (620 miles); service ceiling 12,200m (40,000ft)
Dimensions: wingspan 9.00m (29ft 6in); length 15.87m (52ft 1in); height 3.60m (11ft 10in)
Weight: 10,908kg (24,048lb) loaded
Armament: four 30mm (1.18in) cannon; 1815kg (4000lb) of bombs

HALBERSTADT CL.II

Crew: 2
Powerplant: one 119kW (160hp) Mercedes D.III water-cooled in-line engine
Performance: max speed 165km/h (102.5mph); endurance 3 hrs; service ceiling 5100m (16,732ft)
Dimensions: wingspan 10.77m (35ft 4in); length 7.30m (23ft 11in); height 2.75m (9ft 0.25in)
Weight: 1133kg (2498lb) loaded
Armament: three 7.92mm (0.31in) machine guns; five 10kg (22lb) bombs

The Halberstadt CL.II proved an excellent ground-attack aircraft when used in World War I.

THE HALBERSTADT CL category of fighting aircraft, introduced in 1917, was intended for escort duty and ground attack. The first of the type was the CL.II, a neat, compact biplane with the crew seated in tandem in a long, communal cockpit. It entered service in mid-1917, and in September proved its worth when 24 aircraft launched a devastating attack on Allied troops crossing the river Somme. The Halberstadt CL.II formed the main equipment of the German Air Service's newly formed *Schlachtstaffeln*, each of which had six aircraft.

HANDLEY PAGE O/100

THE HANDLEY PAGE O/100 originated in a British requirement, issued in December 1914, for a 'bloody paralyser of an aeroplane' for the bombing of Germany. The O/100 adequately met, and in some cases exceeded, the tasks it was intended to perform. It first flew in December 1915 and entered service with No 3 Wing of the Royal Naval Air Service in November 1916. From the spring of 1917 its two squadrons, Nos 14 and 16, mounted regular night attacks on major German installations such as U-boat bases, railway yards and industrial complexes, operating from forward airfields on the Western Front. Fifty-six O/100s were delivered to the RNAS.

Crew: 3
Powerplant: two 187kW (250hp) Rolls-Royce Eagle II V-12 engines
Performance: max speed 122km/h (76mph); range 724km (450 miles); service ceiling 2590m (8500ft)
Dimensions: wingspan 30.48m (100ft); length 19.16m (62ft 10in); height 6.70m (22ft)
Weight: 6350kg (14,000lb) loaded
Armament: four 7.7mm (0.303in) machine guns; eight 113kg (250lb) or 16 x 51kg (112lb) bombs

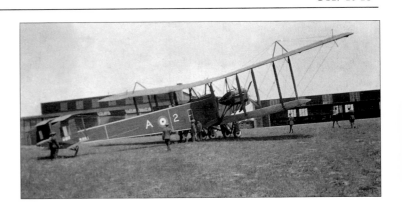

The Handley Page O/100 was one of the world's first strategic bombers, being developed specifically to attack targets in Germany.

HANDLEY PAGE O/400

UK: 1916

Crew: 3
Powerplant: two 269kW (360hp) Rolls-Royce Eagle VIII V-12 engines
Performance: max speed 156.9km/h (97.5mph); endurance 8 hrs; service ceiling 2591m (8500ft)
Dimensions: wingspan 30.48m (100ft); length 19.16m (62ft 10in); height 6.71m (22ft)
Weight: 6060kg (13,360ft)
Armament: four 7.7mm (0.303in) machine guns; eight 113kg (250lb) or 16 x 51kg (112lb) bombs

THE HANDLEY PAGE O/400 was a development of the O/100 with more powerful Eagle engines. Among other improvements, it was fitted with a new bomb sight, the Drift Sight Mk 1A, which computed the aircraft's height above the target, airspeed, wind

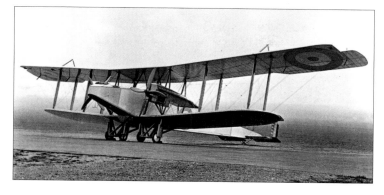

The Handley Page O/400 was a development of the O/100, with more powerful engines and other refinements.

velocity and drift. In the summer of 1918 the O/400 was the backbone of the RAF's strategic bombing force, and it ultimately equipped 11 squadrons at home and overseas. Total production was 657, including 107 assembled from components built in the United States.

HANDLEY PAGE V/1500

UK: 1918

The Handley Page V/1500 was the RAF's first four-engined heavy bomber and had sufficient range to reach Berlin from bases in East Anglia. It carried out some notable long-range flights in the postwar years.

Crew: 4
Powerplant: four 280kW (375hp) Rolls-Royce Eagle VIII 12-cylinder Vee-type engines
Performance: max speed 156km/h (97mph); endurance 6 hrs; service ceiling 3048m (10,000ft)

Dimensions: wingspan 38.41m (126ft); length 18.90m (62ft); height 7.01m (23ft)
Weight: 11,204kg (24,700lb)
Armament: six 7.7mm (0.303in) machine guns (including 2 x twin mountings); 3402kg (7500lb) of bombs

THE HANDLEY PAGE V/1500 was the first heavy bomber designed specifically to strike at targets in Germany from airfields in eastern England. Orders for 225 were placed, but only 35 were completed before the Armistice intervened.

HAFNER GYROPLANE AR.III
Austrian-born engineer Raoul Hafner began designing helicopters in 1929 and his first rotary-wing craft, the R.I, was test flown at Vienna's Aspem Airport in 1930. The R.11 followed a year later and shortly afterwards Hafner emigrated to England where he designed a 'jump-start' autogyro known as the AR.III.

HAFNER ROTACHUTE
From 1940 Raoul Hafner headed a design team in the United Kingdom whose first task was to develop a rotor-borne infiltration system for covert operations. The Rotachute resulted, a small single-seat rotary-wing glider. Despite protracted trials the project was terminated in late 1943.

HAFNER (ML AVIATION) ROTABUGGY/ROTABANK
The Rotabuggy was an ordinary jeep and the Rotabank a Valentine tank, both fitted with detachable rotors and tail units. The Rotabuggy, when towed behind a supercharged 4.5-litre Bentley, became airborne on 16 November 1943. Although it was later airtowed behind a Whitley aircraft, the Rotabuggy never made a free flight. Both vehicles were rendered obsolete by troop- and vehicle-carrying gliders.

HAL HUL-26 PUSHPAK
A single-engined, high-wing lightweight trainer or sporting type, this Indian aircraft dates from 1958 and about 160 were built.

HAL LAS (LOGISTIC SUPPORT AIRCRAFT)
This Indian single piston-engined high-wing 8- to 10-seat transport design dates from 1960. The engine proved to be underpowered and the LAS project was abandoned due to the redesign cost of switching to a turboprop engine.

HAL HJT-16 KIRAN
The Hindustan HJT-16 Kiran Mk I, which flew for the first time on 4 September 1964, was designed as a basic and advanced jet trainer. The Mk II was a light attack version.

HAL HA-31
This Indian-designed, single-seat, single-engined agricultural aircraft dates from 1969. The type did not go into production.

HALBERSTADT D.II
The Halberstadt D.II was the second of the 'D' series of fighters which replaced the Fokker E.III. They were soon replaced by the much superior Albatros types.

HANDLEY PAGE W.8 (HP.18 AND HP.26), W.9 (HP.27) AND W.10 (HP.30)

UK: 1919

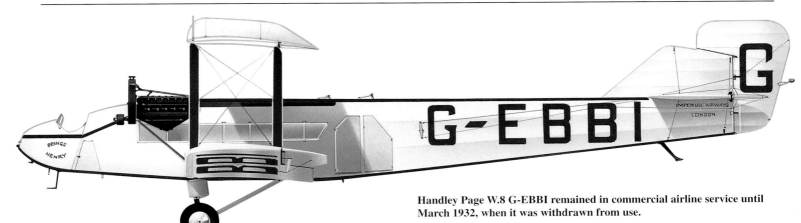

Handley Page W.8 G-EBBI remained in commercial airline service until March 1932, when it was withdrawn from use.

Crew: 2
Powerplant: three 287kW (385hp) Armstrong Siddeley Jaguar IV radial piston engines, later replaced by three 336kW (450hp) Bristol Jupiter VI radial piston engines
Performance: max speed 183km/h (114mph); range 644km (400 miles);

service ceiling 4115m (13,500ft)
Dimensions: wingspan 24.08m (79ft); length 18.39m (60ft 4in)
Weight: 6577kg (14,500lb) maximum take-off weight
Payload: up to 16 passengers in an enclosed cabin

A DEVELOPMENT OF THE O/400 World War I bomber with extensive structural improvements, the W.8 went on to serve with airlines in a number of variants with different twin or triple (Bristol) engines, plus other structural and interior changes. The later one-off W.9 had

three more powerful engines and capacity for 14 passengers, and the W.10 reverted to a twin (Lion) engine configuration – both served with Imperial Airways, the latter until 1933. A total of 25 W series airliners were built. Specifications apply to W.9a (HP.27) Hampstead.

HANDLEY PAGE HP.42 AND HP.45

UK: 1930

HP.42E G-AAGX Hannibal was the prototype of the series and made the first proving flight from London to Paris on 9 June 1931. It subsequently operated from Cairo.

Crew: 3
Powerplant: four 414kW (555hp) Bristol Jupiter XFBM radial piston engines
Performance: max speed 204km/h (127mph); range 805km (500 miles)
Dimensions: wingspan 39.62m (130ft); length 28.09m (92ft 2in); height 8.23m (27ft)
Weight: 12,701kg (28,000lb) maximum take-off weight
Payload: up to 38 passengers (HP.42E – 24 passengers)

THE HP.42 WAS Handley Page's successful response to an Imperial Airways requirement for a long-range airliner to service empire routes. Eight HP.42s were built – four HP.42Es (Eastern) and four HP.42Ws (Western) in the same unequal biplane configuration with two engines mounted on each wing. The Western was capable of lifting a higher maximum weight due to being fitted with a more powerful version of the Jupiter engine, and is believed to have been internally designated as HP.45 by Handley Page. The HP.42 was the classic British airliner of this late empire period. Its reliability, safety and comfort were valued up until the outbreak of World War I. Some were impressed into RAF service, but none survived the hostilities. Specifications apply to HP.42W.

HANDLEY PAGE HAMPDEN

UK: 1937

THE HANDLEY PAGE HAMPDEN was one of the RAF's most important medium bombers at the outbreak of World War II. The prototype flew for the first time in June 1937, and the first of 1430 Hampdens was delivered to the RAF in September 1938. The Hampden was highly manoeuvrable, but badly underarmed to begin with, the defensive armament being increased from two to six machine guns following heavy losses in the

A Hampden of No 455 Squadron, RAAF. Formed in June 1941 as part of No 5 Group, RAF Bomber Command.

first months of the war. Hampdens carried out some notable attacks, including the breaching of the Dortmund-Ems Canal in August 1940. About 140 Hampdens were converted to the torpedo-bomber role, some being supplied to the Soviet Naval Air Arm.

Crew: 4
Powerplant: two 746kW (1000hp) Bristol Pegasus XVIII 9-cylinder radial engines
Performance: max speed 426km/h (265mph); range 3034km (1885 miles); service ceiling 6920m (22,700ft)
Dimensions: wingspan 21.08m (69ft 2in); length 16.33m (53ft 7in); height 4.55m (14ft 11in)
Weight: 5343kg (11,780lb) loaded
Armament: four/six 7.7mm (0.303in) machine guns; up to 1814kg (4000lb) of bombs

HANDLEY PAGE HALIFAX

UK: 1939

Handley Page Halifax B.VI of No 346 (Guyenne) Free French Squadron. This unit began operations from RAF Elvington, near York, in June 1944.

DESTINED TO BECOME one of the most famous bomber aircraft of all time, the prototype HP.57 Halifax flew for the first time on 25 October 1939, followed by a second aircraft in August 1940. In November 1940, the prototype was borrowed from the Ministry of Aircraft Production and flown to RAF Leeming in Yorkshire to be used for training by No 35 Squadron, which was forming as the first Halifax Mk I squadron in Bomber Command. In December the squadron moved to Linton-on-Ouse, near York, and it was from

there, on the night of 10/11 March 1941, that six of its Halifaxes made the type's first operational sortie.

Early production aircraft became known as the Halifax Mk I Series I, which was followed by the Mk I Series II, with a higher gross weight, and the Series III, with increased fuel tankage. The first major modification appeared in the Mk II Series I, which had a two-gun dorsal turret and uprated 1037kW (1390hp) Merlin XX engines. The Mk II Series I (Special) had a fairing in place of the nose turret, and the engine exhaust muffs were

Crew: 7
Powerplant: four 1205kW (1615hp) Bristol Hercules VI or XVI 14-cylinder two-row radial engines
Performance: max speed 454km/h (282mph); range 3194km (1985 miles); service ceiling 7315m (24,000ft)
Dimensions: wingspan 30.07m (98ft 8in); length 21.82m (71ft 7in); height 6.32m (20ft 9in)
Weight: 30,845kg (68,000lb) loaded
Armament: one 7.7mm (0.303in) machine gun in nose position, four 7.7mm (0.303in) machine guns each in dorsal and tail turrets; internal bomb load of 6577kg (14,500lb)

HALBERSTADT CL.IV
The Halberstadt CL.IV, which appeared early in 1918, was a modified version of the CL.II with a greater degree of manoeuvrability.

HALBERSTADT C.V.
The Halberstadt C.V, which appeared on the Western Front in 1918, was widely used for reconnaissance during the final months of World War I.

HALL PH-2 AND PH3
Based on the earlier PH-1 (which was itself based on the British Felixstowe F.5 hull), the PH-2 was a twin-engined biplane flying boat operated by the US Coast Guard during World War II along with a later version, the PH-3.

HAMC (HARBIN) Y-11
This smaller, 10-seat predecessor to the Y-12, which dates from 1975, was designed as a twin-turboprop replacement for Chinese-built An-2s.

HAMC Y-12
Derived from the earlier 10-seat Y-11, the Y-12 is a 17-seat, twin-engined utility transport which first flew in 1982 and is utilized internationally by both civil and military organizations. More than 100 have been produced.

HANDLEY PAGE HINAIDI
First flown in 1927, the HP Hinaidi biplane bomber entered service with the RAF in 1929, Handley Page delivering 12 Hinaidi Is and 33 metal-structured Hinaidi IIs.

HANDLEY PAGE HEYFORD
The Handley Page Heyford was the last of the RAF's biplane bombers and was of unusual configuration in that the upper wing was attached to the fuselage. The prototype flew in 1930, 38 Mks I/IA being followed by 16 Mk IIs and 71 Mk IIIs.

HANDLEY PAGE CLIVE
A troop transport version of the Hinaidi bomber, the Handley Page HP.35 Clive coould carry up to 23 passengers. Production aircraft entered RAF service in 1931.

HANDLEY PAGE HP.43
The Handley Page HP.43 was a military bomber-transport developed from the HP.42 airliner. The sole prototype flew in mid-1932.

HANDLEY PAGE HARROW
The Handley Page Harrow monoplane heavy bomber, which first flew in 1936, was a development of the HP.51. The Harrow fulfilled an important transport role in World War II.

omitted, while the Mk II Series IA was the first variant to introduce the drag-reducing moulded perspex nose that was a feature of all subsequent Halifaxes, a four-gun dorsal turret, and Merlin 22 engines. The Mk II Series IA also had large, rectangular vertical tail surfaces, as serious control difficulties had been experienced with the original tail configuration.

As more modifications crept into the basic airframe, the aircraft gradually became heavier and consequently underpowered, and in 1943 the Merlin engines were replaced by four 1205kW (1615hp) Bristol Hercules XVI radial engines in the Halifax Mk III. Merlin-engined Halifaxes were, however, retained by the RAF's special duties squadrons, which used them to drop agents and supplies to resistance groups throughout occupied Europe, as these aircraft had a longer range than the Mk III. The Halifax Mk IV was a project

An early development Halifax B.Mk I 'somewhere over England' in 1941. Note the difference between this aircraft and the B.VI on the previous page.

only. The next operational variants were the ultimate bomber versions, the Mks VI and VII, and were built in relatively small numbers. Some Halifax IIIs, Vs and VIIs were converted to paratroop dropping and glider towing. The Halifax Mk VIII, which entered service just before the end of the war, was a transport version with faired-over

gun positions and a detachable 3624kg (8000lb) freight panner under the fuselage, and the final version, produced after the war, was another transport, the Mk IX.

Various marks of Halifax also served with some squadrons of RAF Coastal Command as a long-range maritime patrol aircraft, supplementing very long-range (VLR) aircraft such as the Liberator and Fortress. Although overshadowed by the Lancaster, the Halifax proved to be a far more versatile aircraft in that it could be adapted to many different roles, including electronic counter-measures. Total Halifax production of 6176 aircraft included 2050 Mks I and II, 2060 Mk III, 916 Mk V, 480 Mk VI, 395 Mk VII, 100 Mk VIII and the rest Mk IX. During World War II, Halifaxes flew a total of 75,532 sorties, dropping 231,263 tonnes (227,610 tons) of bombs. Specifications apply to the Halifax III.

HANDLEY PAGE VICTOR

UK: 1952

LAST IN A LONG LINE of Handley Page bombers, the prototype HP80 Victor flew from Boscombe Down on 24 December 1952. The first Victor B.Mk I squadron, No 10, became operational in April 1958. The B.Mk II was a more powerful

version with a larger span; two squadrons were armed with the Avro Blue Steel stand-off missile. Victor B.(PR Mk I and B.(PR).Mk II were photo-reconnaissance variants. Specifications refer to the Victor B.Mk II (Blue Steel).

Crew: 5
Powerplant: four 9344kg (20,600lb) thrust Rolls-Royce Conway Mk. 201 turbofan engines
Performance: max speed 1040km/h (640mph); range 7400km (4600 miles); service ceiling 14,335m (47,000ft)

Dimensions: wingspan 36.58m (120ft); length 35.05m (114ft 11in); height 9.20m (30ft 1in)
Weight: 105,687kg (233,000lb) loaded
Armament: one HS Blue Steel ASM (Red Snow warhead)

After its days as a strategic nuclear bomber were over, the Handley Page Victor gave sterling service as a flight refuelling tanker.

HANDLEY PAGE HP.R.3/HP.R.7 HERALD/DART HERALD   UK: 1955

Air Manila of the Philippines were one of the few overseas customers that purchased Dart Heralds, operating a fleet of two. One was wrecked when a hangar collapsed on it in 1970.

THE ORIGINAL HP.R.3 Herald design utilized four Alvis Leonides radial piston engines; consequently it bore a general resemblance to its predecessor, the Marathon. The Herald was one of several designs launched as a DC-3 replacement in the mid-1950s, aimed at local or regional airline services.

Availability of the Rolls-Royce Dart turboprop engine and its successful application on the Vickers Viscount, and forthcoming use on the rival Fokker F27,

caused Handley Page to delay and redesign the Herald using two Dart engines. The Herald only achieved orders for 50 aircraft; early orders were from BEA followed by a series of small, mostly civil orders. The Herald continued in service with second-line operators into the late 1990s (notably as a freighter with Channel Express), but major component obsolescence hastened its retirement.

Specifications apply to the Dart Herald Series 200.

Crew: 2
Powerplant: two 1570kW (2105ehp) Rolls-Royce Dart Mk 527 turboprop engines
Performance: max cruising speed 441km/h (274mph); range 1786km (1110 miles); service ceiling 8505m (27,900ft)
Dimensions: wingspan 28.88m (94ft 9in); length 23.01m (75ft 6in); height 7.34m (24ft 1in)
Weight: 19,504kg (43,000lb) maximum take-off weight
Payload: up to 56 passengers

HANNOVER CL.IIIA   GERMANY: 1917

Crew: 2
Powerplant: one 134kW (180hp) Argus As III 9-cylinder liquid-cooled radial engine
Performance: max speed 165km/h (103mph); endurance 3 hrs; service ceiling 7500m (24,600ft)
Dimensions: wingspan 11.70m (38ft 5in); length 7.58m (24ft 10in); height 2.80m (9ft 2in)
Weight: 1081kg (2378lb) loaded
Armament: three 7.92mm (0.31in) machine guns

The Hannover CL.IIIa, easily identified by its biplane tail, served in a variety of roles on the Western Front.

THE HANNOVER CL.IIIA, which was deployed on the Western Front early in 1918, was what would later be termed a multi-role aircraft, being used for reconnaissance, escort and close support. Like its predecessors, the CL.II and CL.III, it had a biplane tail, designed to eliminate any blind spots for the observer. One of the greatest assets of the CL.IIIa, 537 of which were

built, was its excellent ceiling, which gave it a huge advantage in the photo-reconnaissance role.

Its immediate predecessor, the CL.III, had a Mercedes engine;

this powerplant was needed for fighter manufacture and only 80 were produced with this engine before production switched to the Argus-engined CL.IIIa.

HANRIOT HD.1

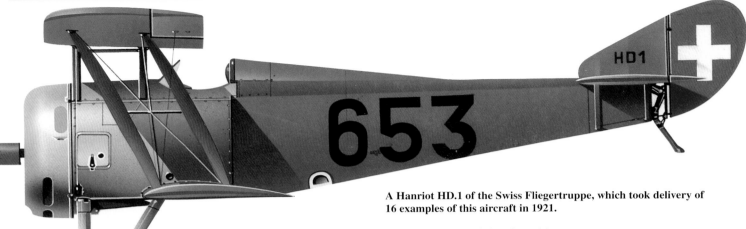

A Hanriot HD.1 of the Swiss Fliegertruppe, which took delivery of 16 examples of this aircraft in 1921.

DESIGNED BY PIERRE DUPONT in 1916, the Hanriot HD.1 was a small, light and manoeuvrable scout which, although rejected for service by the French Aviation Militaire, was used with great success by the Belgians and Italians. The HD.1 entered service on the Italian front in the summer of 1917 and ultimately equipped 16 of the 18 operational Italian fighter squadrons, the initial batch of 100 aircraft being followed by a further 831, licence-built by Macchi, before the war ended. In one memorable engagement, on 26 December 1917, Hanriots of Grupo 6 shot down 11 German reconnaissance aircraft for no loss. In Belgium, the HD.1 entered service in August 1917, and remained first-line equipment until 1926. The Hanriot HD.1 was the type flown by Willy Coppens, the Belgian ace who shot down 37 enemy aircraft before being badly wounded by an incendiary bullet in October 1918. His Hanriot was painted cobalt blue.

Crew: 1
Powerplant: one 90kW (120hp) Le Rhone 9JB 9-cylinder air-cooled rotary engine
Performance: max speed 184km/h (115mph); endurance 2 hrs 30 mins; service ceiling 6000m (19,685ft)
Dimensions: wingspan 8.70m (28ft 6in); length 5.85m (19ft 2in); height 2.94m (9ft 7in)
Weight: 605kg (1334lb) loaded
Armament: one 7.7mm (0.303in) machine gun

HANSA-BRANDENBURG W.29

THE HANSA-BRANDENBURG W.29 was one of the last German seaplane fighters and considered the best of Ernst Heinkel's naval warplane designs. It was a monoplane, and consequently its performance was greatly superior to that of Heinkel's earlier floatplane designs. The 78 W.29s produced for the Imperial German Naval Air Service operated from bases on Germany's North Sea coast from April 1918.

Crew: 2
Powerplant: one 112kW (150hp) Benz Bz III 6-cylinder liquid-cooled in-line engine
Performance: max speed 175km/h (108mph); endurance 4 hrs

Dimensions: wingspan 13.50m (44ft 4in); length 9.38m (30ft 8in); height 3.00m (9ft 11in)
Weight: 1494kg (3285lb) loaded
Armament: two or three 7.92mm (0.31in) machine guns

Designed by Ernst Heinkel, the Hansa-Brandenburg W.29 was a very effective fighter floatplane and was a constant threat to the Royal Navy's airships.

HANSA-BRANDENBURG W.33 — GERMANY: 1918

A Hansa-Brandenburg W.33 of No 1 Detached Maritime Flying Squadron, Finnish Air Force, Viipuri, in the late 1920s.

THE HANSA-BRANDENBURG W.33 was a scaled-up version of the W.29, produced in the summer and autumn of 1918. Although wartime production of the aircraft totalled only 26, after the war the type was built in Finland by the IVL state factory near Helsinki as the A.22

until the late 1920s. The aircraft could be fitted with skis for winter operations. Some surviving examples of the German-built W.33s were taken over by Denmark, and about 300 aircraft of the W.29/W.33 series were built in Japan by Aichi and Nakajima.

Crew: 2
Powerplant: one 183kW (245hp) Maybach Mb.IV in-line engine
Performance: max speed 175km/h (109mph); endurance 5 hrs; service ceiling 5000m (16,404ft)
Dimensions: wingspan 15.85m (52ft); length 11.10m (36ft 4in); height 3.39m (11ft 1in)
Weight: 2045kg (4510lb) loaded
Armament: two or three 7.92mm (0.31in) machine guns

HAWKER HART — UK: 1928

A Hawker Hart of No 23 Squadron RAF, which used the type as a two-seat fighter from 1931 to 1938.

THE HAWKER HART, designed by Sydney Camm, was the most widely used RAF light bomber of the 1930s. The prototype flew in June 1938, and deliveries to the RAF began in 1930. A trainer version of the Hart was produced, also the Hart C general-purpose aircraft, the Hart Special and the Hart India, the last two being tropicalized versions. Eight Harts were exported to Estonia and four to Sweden, the

latter building a further 24 under licence which were powered by Pegasus radial engines.

The Hart, which was faster than any contemporary RAF fighter, was to see widespread service in trouble spots such as the turbulent northwest frontier of India.

Crew: 2
Powerplant: one 392kW (525hp) Rolls-Royce Kestrel IB 12-cylinder Vee-type engine
Performance: max speed 298km/h (184mph); range 756km (470 miles); service ceiling 6500m (21,320ft)
Dimensions: wingspan 11.35m (37ft 3in); length 8.94m (29ft 4in); height 3.17m (10ft 5in)
Weight: 2066kg (4554lb)
Armament: two 7.7mm (0.303in) machine guns; up to 236kg (520lb) of bombs

HAWKER FURY — UK: 1929

Crew: 1
Powerplant: one 522kW (700hp) Rolls-Royce Kestrel VI 12-cylinder V-type engine
Performance: max speed 359km/h (223mph); range 435km (270 miles); service ceiling 8990m (29,500ft)

Dimensions: wingspan 9.14m (30ft); length 8.13m (26ft 8in); height 3.10m (10ft 2in)
Weight 1637kg (3609lb) loaded
Armament: two 7.7mm (0.303in) machine guns

THE HAWKER FURY was the epitome of British fighter biplane design and one of the most beautiful aircraft ever built. The first of 118 Fury Mk Is entered service with No 43 Squadron at

HANNOVER CL.V
The Hannover CL.V was built with either a biplane or a single tail unit, and about 50 were produced in 1918. The CL.V was powered by a BMW engine.

HANRIOT H.230
The Hanriot H.230, which appeared in 1937, was a twin-engined monoplane advanced trainer. About 50 examples of the production version, the H.232, were built.

HANRIOT NC.600
The Hanriot NC.600 was a long-range, twin-engined escort fighter, the prototype of which flew in 1937. Although an outstanding aircraft, the NC.600 was not ordered into production.

HANRIOT H.530
The Hanriot H.530, which flew in 1937, was a twin-engined army co-operation aircraft, developed via the earlier H.510 and H.511. Prototypes only were completed.

HANSA-BRANDENBURG CC
The Hansa-Brandenburg CC was designed by Ernst Heinkel and first flown in 1916. The 135 examples built under licence by Austrian firm Phønix were used for the defence of the Adriatic ports.

HANSA-BRANDENBURG C.I
Although designed in Germany by Ernst Heinkel, the Hansa-Brandenburg C.1 of 1916 was licence-built in Austria by the Phønix and Ufag firms. It was widely used for reconnaissance and light bombing.

HANSA-BRANDENBURG D.I
Like other Hansa-Brandenburg aircraft, the D.I scout was designed by Ernst Heinkel in Germany and built in Austria. Despite problems that earned it the nickname of 'The Coffin', the Austrians used it well into 1917.

HANSA-BRANDENBURG KDW
The Hansa-Brandenburg KDW (Kampf Doppeldecker, Wasser – Fighting Biplane, Water) was used for the defence of the Adriatic coast. About 60 examples were built in 1916.

HANSA-BRANDENBURG W.12
The Hansa-Brandenburg W.12 floatplane fighter prototype flew in 1917 and was followed by 146 production aircraft, one of which shot down the British airship C.27.

RAF Tangmere in May 1931, and the type also served with Nos 1 and 25 Squadrons.

Further development of a version known as the High Speed Fury led to a production order for 23 Fury Mk IIs, followed by another 75, and the first of these entered service with No 25 Squadron in December 1936, also serving with four other squadrons of what was, by then, RAF Fighter Command. The Fury II was exported to Persia, Spain and Portugal.

Specifications apply to the Mk I.

A Hawker Fury I biplane fighter in flight. The Fury was without doubt the most elegant biplane ever to serve with the RAF, and it was dearly loved by all who flew it.

HAWKER HIND   UK: 1934

THE HAWKER HIND, which first flew on 12 September 1934, began to replace the Hart as the RAF's standard light bomber late in 1935. The aircraft was essentially an improved Hart with a more powerful engine and refined aerodynamics.

The decision to build it came as part of an RAF expansion scheme put in place in the light of the perceived threat from Nazi Germany. The Hind, 527 examples of which were produced, equipped no fewer than 47 RAF bomber squadrons.

Crew: 2
Powerplant: one 477kW (640hp) Rolls-Royce Kestrel V 12-cylinder Vee-type engine
Performance: max speed 298km/h (184mph); range 692km (430 miles); service ceiling 8045m (26,400ft)

Dimensions: wingspan 11.35m (37ft 3in); length 9.02m (29ft 7in); height 3.23m (10ft 7in)
Weight: 2403kg (5298lb) loaded
Armament: two 7.7mm (0.303in) machine guns; two 113kg (250lb) bombs

Hawker Hind K5414 in the markings of No XV Squadron RAF. This aircraft is part of the Shuttleworth Collection at Old Warden in the United Kingdom.

HAWKER HURRICANE

UK: 1935

Crew: 1
Powerplant: one 1089kW (1460hp) Rolls-Royce Merlin XX 12-cylinder Vee-type engine
Performance: max speed: 518km/h (322mph); range 1448km (900 miles); service ceiling 9785m (32,100ft)
Dimensions: wingspan 12.19m (40ft); length 9.81m (32ft 2in); height 3.98m (13ft 1in);
Weight: 3674kg (8100lb) loaded
Armament: two 40mm (1.57in) Vickers 'S' guns under each wing; two Browning 7.7mm (0.303in) machine guns in each wing

Hawker Hurricane IIC PZ865 'The Last of the Many', the last Hurricane ever built, now forms part of the Battle of Britain Memorial Flight.

THE HAWKER HURRICANE was the first of Britain's new monoplane fighters, powered by the Rolls-Royce Merlin engine and given an armament of eight 7.7mm (0.303in) Colt-Browning machine guns. Developed from the Hawker Fury biplane (it was originally known as the Fury Monoplane), under the design leadership of Sydney Camm to meet Air Ministry Specification F.36/34, the prototype flew on 6 November 1935. An order for 600 machines eventually materialized in June 1936, and the first of these flew on 12 October 1937, an initial batch being delivered to No 111 Squadron at Northolt in November. At a later date the Merlin II was replaced by the Merlin III, driving a three-blade Rotol or de Havilland propeller. In 1938 the first deliveries were made to foreign customers (Portugal, Yugoslavia, Persia and Belgium); Hurricanes were also exported to Romania and Turkey. Eventual production of the Hurricane Mk I, shared between the Hawker and Gloster factories in the United Kingdom and the Canadian Car and Foundry Co of Montreal, amounted to 3954.

On 11 June 1940, Hurricane P3269 flew with a 884kW (1185hp) supercharged Merlin XX engine, serving as prototype for the Hurricane Mk II. As more Mk IIs reached the squadrons, many Mk Is

were sent to the Middle East. Early Mk IIs, which retained the eight-gun armament, were designated Mk IIAs; with 12 machine guns the designation became Mk IIB, while the Mk IIC had a wing armament of four 20mm (0.79in) Hispano cannon. The Mk IID was a special anti-tank version, armed with two underwing 40mm (1.57in) Vickers 'S' guns and two 7.7mm (0.303in) Brownings in the wings. Both IIBs and IICs were fitted with cameras and used for reconnaissance as the Mks PR.IIB and PR.IIC. In 1942, Hurricane Is and IIAs operated in Singapore, the Netherlands East Indies, Ceylon and Burma. It was during the Burma Campaign that the aircraft really came into its own as a tactical support aircraft when armed with a pair of 227kg (500lb) bombs. The only other British production model, the Mk IV, was also a ground-attack type, armed principally with eight 27kg (60lb) rocket projectiles and fitted with a 1208kW (1620hp) Merlin 24 or 27 engine. Alternative payloads included two 113kg (250lb) or 227kg (500lb) bombs, or two Vickers 'S' guns. The Hurricane Mk V was designed to take the

higher powered Merlin 27 or 32 engine, but only two were built.

In 1941 the Hurricane was adopted by the Royal Navy for fleet protection duties, the first Sea Hurricane Mk IAs being deployed on escort carriers in 1941. One major Hurricane user was the Soviet Union, the first batch to be delivered comprising 24 Mk IIBs turned over to the Soviet Navy's 72nd Fighter Air Regiment by No 141 Wing RAF, which operated in North Russia in the late summer of 1941. One variant shipped to Russia during 1943 was the Mk IID, with the 40mm (1.57in) cannon. Sixty were delivered from RAF stocks in the Middle East and were followed by 30 Hurricane IVs with similar armament. Tank-busting Hurricanes were used to good effect in the battles of Kuban and Kursk in 1943. Altogether, 2952 Hurricanes were delivered to the USSR. Overall Hurricane production in the United Kingdom was 13,080 by Hawker, Gloster and Austin Motors; another 1451 Mks X, XI, XII and XIIA were produced by the Canadian Car and Foundry Co.

Specification refers to the Hurricane Mk IID.

Hawker Hurricane Mk II Z2961 was part of the fifth production batch of 1000 aircraft built by Hawker Aircraft Ltd at Kingson, Langley and Brooklands in 1940–41.

HAVERTZ HZ-5
This West German single-seat light helicopter was developed from two earlier designs, the HZ-3 of 1953 and the HZ-4 of 1966.

HAWKER WOODCOCK
The true successor to the Sopwith Snipe was the Hawker Woodcock of 1923. The Woodcock equipped only one other RAF squadron, No 17, but a version of it known as the Dankok served with the Danish Army and Naval Air Services until 1937.

HAWKER HORSLEY
The Hawker Horsley was designed to be used either as a day-bomber or a torpedo-bomber. The prototype flew in 1925 and was followed by 128 production aircraft.

HAWKER TOMTIT
First flown in 1928, the Hawker Tomtit biplane primary trainer served with the RAF in small numbers during the 1930s, others going to Canada and New Zealand.

HAWKER AUDAX
The Hawker Audax army co-operation aircraft, which entered RAF service in 1932, was a highly successful design and was still in service in India a decade later.

HAWKER OSPREY
The Hawker Osprey was the naval version of the RAF's Hart light bomber. First flown in 1931, it was produced in several versions.

HAWKER DEMON
The Hawker Demon, first produced in 1931, was a two-seat fighter variant of the Hawker Hart light bomber. In all, 304 Demons were built, including 64 for the RAAF.

HAWKER NIMROD
The Hawker Nimrod, which replaced the Fairey Flycatcher in Fleet Air Arm service, was a naval member of Sydney Camm's extensive Hart and Fury family. The prototype first flew on 2 September 1931.

HAWKER DANTORP
The Hawker Dantorp was a version of the Horsley for the Danish Naval Air Service, fitted with a Leopard III 14-cylinder radial engine. Two were delivered in 1932.

HAWKER HARDY
The Hawker Hardy general-purpose biplane, produced in 1934, was a tropicalized version of the Hart intended primarily for policing operations in Iraq. Forty-seven were built.

HAWKER TYPHOON

THE FIRST OF TWO Typhoon prototypes initially flew on 24 February 1940, but it was not until September 1941 that the type was issued to the RAF, with many snags still remaining. During the summer months of 1942, still suffering from technical problems, the first Typhoon squadrons were engaged in air-defence duties. By the end of 1943, with technical problems cured and the growing number of Typhoon squadrons striking hard at enemy communications, shipping and airfields, the Typhoon was heading for its place in history as the most potent Allied fighter-bomber of all. After the Allied landings in Normandy, the rocket-armed Typhoon's name became

The Hawker Typhoon was used to deadly effect against German armour in the Normandy campaign of 1944.

synonymous with the breakup of an enemy armoured counterattack at Mortain and the destruction of the retreating German army at Falaise. Each aircraft carried a pair of 227kg (500lb) bombs or eight underwing rocket projectiles in addition to the built-in cannon armament. In all, 3330 Typhoons were produced. Specifications apply to the Mk IB.

Crew: 1
Powerplant: one 1566kW (2100hp) Napier Sabre 24-cylinder in-line engine
Performance: max speed 663km/h (412mph); range 1577km (980 miles); service ceiling 10,730m (35,200ft)
Dimensions: wingspan 12.67m (41ft 7in); length 9.73m (31ft 11in); height 4.67m (15ft 4in)
Weight: 5171kg (11,400lb) loaded
Armament: four 20mm (0.79in) cannon in wing; external bomb load up to 907kg (2000lb) or eight 27kg (60lb) RPs

HAWKER TEMPEST V

Crew: 1
Powerplant: one 1686kW (2260hp) Napier Sabre IIA, IIB or IIC 24-cylinder H-type engine
Performance: max speed 700km/h (435mph); range 2092km (1300 miles); service ceiling 10,975m (36,000ft)

Dimensions: wingspan 12.50m (41ft); length 10.26m (33ft 8in); height 4.90m (16ft 1in)
Weight: 6187kg (13,640lb) loaded
Armament: four 20mm (0.79in) Hispano Mk V cannon; external stores up to 907kg (2000lb)

FIRST FLOWN IN 1943, the Hawker Tempest V was the fastest and most powerful fighter in the world when it entered RAF service in April 1944. Two months later the Tempest squadrons were assigned to the air defence of Great Britain,

operating against the V-1 flying bombs which were being launched against London. The Tempest's high speed made it the ideal interceptor in this new role. The Tempest squadrons subsequently moved to the continent with 2nd TAF.

Hawker Tempest EJ743, flown by Hawker test pilot Bill Humble. This particular aircraft was one of the early production models.

HAWKER SEA FURY

UK: 1946

THE SEA FURY CAME too late to see action in World War II, the prototype making its first flight on 21 February 1945. The first production Sea Fury F.Mk X flew in September 1946 and deliveries to the Fleet Air Arm began in July 1947. The type performed very effectively in the Korean War. Total production was 565 aircraft.

Crew: 1
Powerplant: one 1850kW (2480hp) Bristol Centaurus 18 18-cylinder radial engine
Performance: max speed 740km/h (460mph); service ceiling 10,970m (36,000ft); range 1130km (700 miles)

Dimensions: wingspan 11.71m (38ft 5in); length 10.56m (34ft 8in); height 4.82m (15ft 10in)
Weight: 5670kg (12,500lb) loaded
Armament: four 20mm (0.79in) Hispano cannon; 907kg (2000lb) of bombs or RPs

Hawker Sea Fury FB.Mk.II of No 805 Squadron, Royal Australian Navy, RNAS Eglinton.

HAWKER SEA HAWK

UK: 1947

Crew: 1
Powerplant: one 2449kg (5400lb) thrust Rolls-Royce Nene 103 turbojet engine
Performance: max speed 969km/h (602mph); range 1287km (800 miles) service ceiling 13,565m (44,500ft)
Dimensions: wingspan 11.89m (39ft); length 12.09m (39ft 8in); height 2.64m (8ft 8in)
Weight: 7348kg (16,200lb) loaded
Armament: four 20mm (0.79in) Hispano cannon; provision for four 227kg (500lb) bombs, or four 227kg (500lb) bombs and 10 20cm (8in) or 16 12.7cm (5in) rocket RPs

THE HAWKER SEA HAWK started life as the P.1040, a prototype single-seat land-based interceptor. The first prototype Sea Hawk flew on 2 September 1947, and the aircraft entered production as the Sea Hawk F.Mk I. Later Sea Hawk variants, culminating in the FGA.VI, possessed a strengthened wing to accommodate bombs, rockets or drop tanks.

Sea Hawks were issued to Fleet Air Arm squadrons in 1953, and three years later the type was to see action with six squadrons

during the Suez crisis, carrying out many ground-attack operations. Sea Hawks also served with the Royal Netherlands Navy, the Federal German Naval Air Arm, and the Indian Navy.

Specifications apply to the Sea Hawk FGA.VI.

Hawker Sea Hawks, wings folded, ranged on the deck of a Royal Navy aircraft carrier in the 1950s. Astern are the light fleet carriers HMS *Ocean* and HMS *Albion* and the cruiser HMS *Gambia*.

HAWKER HUNTER

Hawker Hunter Mk 58 J-4058 of the Swiss Air Force. At the height of its service, the Hunter equipped nine Swiss squadrons and proved readily adaptable to operating conditions in Switzerland.

EARLY IN 1946, both Hawker and Supermarine were studying schemes for swept-wing jet fighters. Two specifications were issued by the Ministry of Supply, both calling for experimental aircraft fitted with swept flying surfaces. Both companies submitted proposals in March 1947, the Hawker design being designated P.1052. This aircraft flew in November 1948, and its performance was such that at one point the air staff seriously considered ordering the type into full production to replace the Gloster Meteor. Instead, the design was developed further under Air Ministry Specification F.3/48, the operational requirement calling for a fighter whose primary role would be the interception of high-altitude, high-speed bombers. The fighter was given the designation P.1067.

The outbreak of the Korean War, together with fears that it might escalate into wider conflict, led to the acceleration of combat aircraft re-equipment programmes in both east and west. In Britain, the two

new swept-wing fighter types, the Hawker P.1067 – soon to be named the Hunter – and Supermarine's design, the Type 541 Swift, flew in prototype form on 20 July and 1 August 1951, respectively, and both types were ordered into 'super-priority' production for RAF Fighter Command. The Hunter F.Mk 1, which entered service early in 1954, suffered from engine surge problems during high-altitude gun-firing trials, resulting in some modifications to its Rolls-Royce Avon turbojet. This measure, together with increased fuel capacity and provision for underwing tanks, led to the Hunter F.4, which gradually replaced the Canadair-built F-86E Sabre (which had been supplied to the RAF as an interim fighter) in the German-based squadrons of the 2nd Tactical Air Force.

The Hunter Mks 2 and 5 were variants powered by the Armstrong Siddeley Sapphire engine. In 1953 Hawker equipped the Hunter with the large 4535kg (10,000lb) thrust

Avon 203 engine, and this variant, designated Hunter F.Mk 6, flew for the first time in January 1954. Deliveries began in 1956 and the F.6 subsequently equipped 15 squadrons of RAF Fighter Command. The Hunter FGA.9 was a development of the F6 optimized for ground attack, as its designation implies. The Hunter Mks 7, 8, 12, T52, T62, T66, T67 and T69 were all two-seat trainer variants; the FR.10 was a fighter-reconnaissance version, converted from the F.6. The GA.11 was an operational trainer for the Royal Navy.

In a career spanning a quarter of a century, the Hunter equipped 30 RAF fighter squadrons in addition to numerous units of foreign air forces. The aircraft was licence built in Holland and Belgium. Principal customers for the British-built aircraft were India,

Switzerland and Sweden. Indian Hunters saw considerable action in the 1965 and 1971 conflicts with Pakistan, 10 Hunters being lost in the three-week air war of 1965 and 22 in the 1971 battle, some of these being destroyed on the ground. The grand total of Hunter production, including two-seat trainers, was 1972 aircraft, and more than 500 were subsequently rebuilt for sale overseas.

In August 1953 the prototype Hawker P.1067 was fitted with a Rolls-Royce RA.7R afterburning engine, in effect a 'racing' Avon, for an attack on the World Absolute Air Speed Record. Fitted with a sharply pointed nose cone fairing, the aircraft was flown to Tangmere, Sussex, at the end of August for practice runs. On 7 September, Hawker's Chief Test Pilot, Neville Duke, broke the record with an average speed of 1171km/h (727.63mph). Twelve days later, the aircraft also established a 100km (62-mile) closed circuit world record at an average speed of 1141km/h (709.2mph). The aircraft, subsequently referred to as the Hunter Mk 3, is now part of the RAF Museum collection.

Specifications apply to the Hawker Hunter F.Mk 6.

Crew: 1
Powerplant: one 4535kg (10,000lb) thrust Rolls-Royce Avon 203 turbojet
Performance: max speed 1117km/h (694mph); range 689km (429 miles); service ceiling 14,325m (47,000ft)
Dimensions: wingspan 10.26m (33ft 8in); length 13.98m (45ft 10in); height 4.02m (13ft 2in)
Weight: 7802kg (17,200lb) loaded
Armament: four 30mm (1.18in) Aden cannon; underwing pylons with provision for two 453kg (1000lb) bombs and 24 76mm (3in) rockets

A Hunter Mk.51 of No 724 Squadron, Royal Danish Air Force. Denmark took delivery of 30 Hunters, which served from 1956 to 1974, when the squadron disbanded.

HAWKER SIDDELEY (BAe/AVRO) 748 AND ANDOVER

UK: 1960

FOLLOWING DEFENCE expenditure cuts in 1956, Avro decided to diversify into the civil transport market and produced the 748 as a DC-3 successor. Included were 31 of the modified C.1 (Andover) version for the RAF, easily identified by their longer, raked rear fuselage, which incorporated a loading ramp. A total of 381 748s were built until 1988. The launch customer was Skyways Air Coach, who began operations with the 748 in April 1962, and the 748 went on to be produced in a number of

British Airways (pictured) operated a pair of 748s in Scotland between 1975 and 1991 to serve on some 'highlands and islands' routes.

versions, including 89 licence-built by HAL in India. The series 2C with a large freight door was a popular option with original and secondary operators such as the United Kingdom's Emerald Airways, which continue to operate a number of examples. Specifications apply to the Andover C.Mk 1.

Crew: 2/3
Powerplant: two 1719kW (2305ehp) Rolls-Royce Dart RDA.12 Mk 201C turboprop engines
Performance: max cruising speed 415km/h (258mph); range 1891km (1175 miles); service ceiling 7315m (24,000ft)
Dimensions: wingspan 29.87m (98ft); length 23.75m (77ft 11in); height 8.92m (29ft 3in)
Weight: 22,680kg (50,000lb) maximum take-off weight
Payload: 6691kg (14,750lb) maximum payload; civil versions maximum 58 passengers

HAWKER SIDDELEY HS.121 TRIDENT

UK: 1962

Crew: 3
Powerplant: three Rolls-Royce Spey RB.163-25 MK 512-5W turbofan engines each rated at 53.20kN (11,960lb st)
Performance: cruising speed 974km/h (605mph) at 7620m (25,000ft); range 3965km (2464 miles) with typical payload; service ceiling 10,058m (33,000ft)
Dimensions: wingspan 29.87m (98ft); length 34.98m (114ft 9in); height 8.23m (27ft)
Weight: 65,318kg (144,000lb) maximum take-off weight
Payload: up to 132 passengers within the context of a 12,156kg (26,800lb) payload

The Trident 2 (pictured) was larger than the Trident 1, but it arrived on the market too late to compete with Boeing's 727.

ORIGINATING IN A de Havilland design (prior to its incorporation into Hawker Siddeley), the Trident was developed in response to a BEA requirement for a short-/medium-range airliner with up to

140 seats. However, meddling by BEA in the Trident 1's final configuration resulted in a smaller powerplant for the three engines and a smaller cabin, which temporarily satisfied BEA, but

limited the Trident's general appeal. The consequent disadvantage and delay handed the market for this generic type of airliner to Boeing's rival Model 727. BEA later decided that it required a larger Trident version, which came in the form of the Trident 2E and which also sold in modest export numbers. The final version was the further stretched Trident 3, with BEA again the launch customer.

The Trident 3 had a capacity for 180 passengers and required a fourth (RB.162) turbojet booster engine mounted adjacent to the No.2 engine in the fin. Although the Trident 1 had a relatively short

career with BEA, most BEA Trident's were fitted with the important Smiths Autoland system for all-weather operation, which provided a major operational advantage in northern Europe.

Economics and poor airfield performance dictated that all Trident operations had ceased by the early 1990s.
Specifications apply to the Trident 2E.

HEINKEL HE 59 — GERMANY: 1931

THE HEINKEL HE 59 was designed in 1930 as a large twin-engined attack and reconnaissance biplane, the prototype flying in September 1931. The production version was the He 59B twin-float seaplane, 140 examples of which were

produced. Ten of these were sent for evaluation in Spain and flew a number of night-bombing operations. By September 1939, the He 59 had been largely relegated to air–sea rescue duties. Specifications apply to the He 59B.

Crew: 4
Powerplant: two BMW VI 12-cylinder Vee-type engines each rated at 492kW (660hp)
Performance: max speed 220km/h (137mph); range 1750km (1087 miles); service ceiling 3500m (11,480ft)

Dimensions: wingspan 23.70m (77ft 9in); length 17.40m (57ft 1in); height 7.10m (23ft 3.5in)
Weight: 9000kg (19,845lb) loaded
Armament: three 7.9mm (0.31in) machine guns; up to 1000kg (2205lb) of bombs or a torpedo

HEINKEL HE 51 — GERMANY: 1933

Crew: 1
Powerplant: one 560kW (750hp) BMW VI 12-cylinder Vee-type engine
Performance: max speed 330km/h (205mph); range 570km (354 miles); service ceiling 7700m (25,260ft)
Dimensions: wingspan 11.00m (36ft 1in); length 8.40m (27ft 7in); height 3.20m (10ft 6in)
Weight: 1895kg (4178lb) loaded
Armament: two 7.92mm (0.31in) machine guns

THE HEINKEL HE 51, the prototype of which flew in 1933, evolved through a series of small, stream-lined fighter prototypes, the He 37, He 38, He 49 and He 49A. It was the fourth He 49A, with modifications, that became the prototype He 51. The aircraft was quickly put

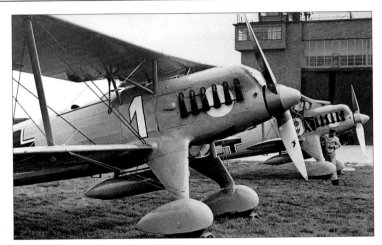

The Heinkel He 51 was the Luftwaffe's first fighter and saw service in the Spanish Civil War, where it was used mainly for ground attack.

into production as part of the new Luftwaffe's equipment programme; first deliveries of the He 51A were made to JG 132 in April 1935, and the type was also issued to JG 131 and JG 134. In all, 700 He 51 production aircraft were built. Variants were the He 51B, which replaced the He 51A on the production line; the He 51B-2 floatplane, which was fitted with catapult spools for operations at sea; and the C-1 and C-2 ground-attack fighters, which saw action in Spain alongside the Condor Legion's He 51A-1s. Many of Germany's leading fighter aces of World War II sharpened their skills while flying He 51s in the Spanish Civil War. Specifications apply to the He 51A.

HEINKEL HE 111 — GERMANY: 1935

THE HEINKEL HE 111 was designed early in 1934 as a high-speed transport and as a bomber for the still-secret Luftwaffe. The

first prototype, the He 111A (later redesignated He 111 V1), flew for the first time on 24 February 1935, and was followed by the V2, which

was to make its maiden flight on 12 March 1935.
This aircraft, D-ALIX, was a transport version with a reduced

This He 111B served with the Kondor Legion in Spain and was subsequently handed over to the Nationalist Air Force.

A CASA-built Heinkel He 111 (C2111) with Rolls-Royce Merlin engines. The first Spanish-built Heinkel did not fly until 1945, by which time the supply of German aero-engines had dried up.

span and a straight trailing edge; it was delivered to Luft Hansa and named Rostock, and was later used for clandestine reconnaissance missions. The He 111 V3, D-ALES, was a bomber with a further reduced wingspan, and was the forerunner of the He 111A production model. Following the success of the He 111 V3, Heinkel was ordered to proceed with the construction of a pre-production batch of 10 He 111A-0s. Two aircraft were sent to Rechlin for trials; however, they were found to be unsuitable for operational use because their handling characteristics were badly affected by the extra weight of military equipment. All 10 examples were shipped to China for use against the Japanese.

Meanwhile, development of the civil transport series continued with the He 111 V4 D-AHAO, which was capable of carrying 10 passengers. It was delivered to Luft Hansa in January 1936 and was followed by six production Heinkel He 111C-0s, all named after German cities.

In the meantime, Heinkel had been working on a replacement for the He 111B, which possessed two 746kW (1000hp) Daimler-Benz DB 600A engines. The prototype was the He 111 V5 D-APYS. The aircraft was ordered into production

for the Luftwaffe as the He 111B-1, with the first examples being delivered to I/KG 154 'Boelcke' at Hannover-Langenhagen late in 1936. In 1937 the He 111B-1 was tested under combat conditions with the Kondor Legion in Spain and proved very successful, its speed alone enabling it to evade fighter interception.

The 300 He 111Bs were followed by the He 111D, only a few of which were completed before production was switched to the He 111E bomber with Junkers Jumo engines and a small number of He 111Fs similarly powered, the latter being the first to feature a wing with a straight leading edge. These variants also saw service in Spain, and after the civil war they were taken over by the Spanish Air Force. The He 111G was another transport version, five examples being delivered to Luft Hansa and four to Turkey.

About 1000 examples of all these He 111s variants had been produced by mid-1939, by which time a new model had made its appearance. This was the He 111P, which was powered by two 858kW (1150hp) Daimler-Benz DB 601Aa engines and which incorporated a fully glazed asymmetric nose, with its offset ball turret, in place of the stepped-up cockpits of the earlier variants. Relatively few He 111Ps were

completed before production switched to the He 111H, powered by two 821kW (1100hp) Junkers Jumo 211 engines.

Subvariants of this series were to form the backbone of the Luftwaffe's bomber force between 1940 and 1943, with about 6150 being built before production ended in 1944. The first version of the type to carry torpedoes was the He 111H-6, followed by the He 111H-15. The He 111 scored some notable successes against the wartime Arctic convoys to Russia, notably against the ill-fated PQ17 in July 1942, when the convoy was virtually destroyed.

Specifications refer to the Heinkel He 111H-16.

Crew: 5
Powerplant: two 1007kW (1350hp) Junkers Jumo 211F inverted V12 engines
Performance: max speed 436km/h (271mph); range 1950km (1212 miles); service ceiling 6700m (21,980ft)
Dimensions: wingspan 22.60m (74ft 1in); length 16.40m (53ft 9in); height 4m (13ft 1in)
Weight: 14,000kg (30,865lb) loaded
Armament: one 20mm (0.79in) MG FF cannon in nose, one 13mm (0.51in) MG 131 gun in dorsal position, two 7.92mm (0.31in) MG 15 guns in rear of ventral gondola and two 7.92mm (0.31in) MG 81 guns in each of two beam positions; up to 2000kg (4409lb) of bombs internally and a similar load externally

HEINKEL HE 24
The Heinkel He 24, which appeared in 1930, was a two-seat seaplane training aircraft powered by a BMW IV engine.

HEINKEL HE 25
The Heinkel He 25 of 1930 was a large two-seat reconnaissance biplane designed to a Japanese Navy requirement for catapult operations from ships.

HEINKEL HE 26
The Heinkel He 26 reconnaissance seaplane was also built for the Imperial Japanese Navy for shipboard operation.

HEINKEL HE 28
The Heinkel He 28, designed in 1930, was a three-seat twin-float seaplane powered by a 485kW (650hp) Lorraine engine.

HEINKEL HE 29
The Heinkel He 29 of 1930 was a two-seat biplane basic trainer powered by a 75kW (100hp) Siemens engine.

HEINKEL HE 30
The Heinkel He 30 was a two-seat biplane, developed from the He 19. It was powered by a 336kW (450hp) Bristol Jupiter VI engine.

HEINKEL HE 32
Similar to the He 21 and He 29, the Heinkel He 32 was a biplane basic trainer with an interchangeable undercarriage.

HEINKEL HE 36
The Heinkel He 36 of 1930 was a two-seat biplane basic trainer powered by a 119kW (160hp) Mercedes D.III engine. It was not a success.

HEINKEL HE 42
First flown in March 1931, the Heinkel He 42 was a two-seat twin-float biplane reconnaissance and training aircraft. Large numbers were built, some remaining operational as trainers until 1944.

HEINKEL HE 45
Production of the Heinkel He 45 general-purpose biplane for the clandestine Luftwaffe began in 1932, the prototype having flown in the previous year. More than 500 examples were built.

HEINKEL HE 46
The Heinkel He 46, first flown in 1931, was a parasol-wing army cooperation and reconnaissance monoplane. Production totalled 478 aircraft, some being exported to Bulgaria, Hungary and Spain.

HEINKEL HE 112

A Heinkel He 112B-0 of Grupo 5-G-5 of the Spanish Nationalist Air Force. After the Spanish Civil War, the 15 surviving He 112s were transferred to Grupo 27 in Spanish Morocco.

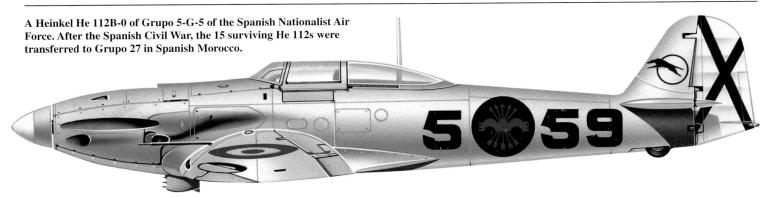

Crew: 1
Powerplant: one 507kW (680hp) Junkers Jumo 210Ea 12-cylinder inverted-Vee engine
Performance: max speed 510km/h (317mph); range 1100km (683 miles); service ceiling 8500m (27,890ft)

Dimensions: wingspan 9.10m (29ft 10in); length 9.30m (30ft 6in); height 3.85m (12ft 7.5in)
Weight: 2250kg (4960lb) loaded
Armament: two 20mm (0.79in) cannon and two 7.92mm (0.31in) machine guns

THE HEINKEL HE 112, first flown in 1935, was the unsuccessful rival for the lucrative contract for the Luftwaffe's first monoplane fighter, won by the Messerschmitt Bf 109.

A small number of aircraft were produced, however, and these saw service in the Spanish Civil War, and on the Eastern Front.

Specifications apply to the He 112B-0.

HEINKEL HE 114

Crew: 2
Powerplant: one 716kW (960hp) BMW 132N radial engine
Performance: max speed 335km/h (208mph); range 1050km (652 miles); service ceiling 4800m (15,744ft)
Dimensions: wingspan 13.60m (44ft 7.5in); length 11.09m (36ft 4.25in); height 5.15m (16ft 10.75in)
Weight: 3400kg (7497lb) loaded
Armament: two 7.92mm (0.31in) machine guns; two 50kg (110lb) bombs

THE HEINKEL HE 114 floatplane, which first flew in 1936, was designed to succeed the He 60 in the shipboard reconnaissance role.

Although somewhat outdated, it saw operational service for much of World War II, operating from coastal bases and also from German commerce raiders. Its principal operating bases were Greece and Crete. The main version was the He 114A-2, of which 14 were exported to Sweden; 18 He 114s were also exported to Romania, bearing the designation He 114B. Specifications apply to He 114A-2.

During World War II, the Heinkel He 114 was utilized by both the Germans and Romanians over the Black Sea.

HEINKEL HE 115

THE HEINKEL 115 HAD its origin in a 1935 requirement for an advanced torpedo-bomber floatplane, with reconnaissance and minelaying as its secondary roles. The first of four prototypes flew for the first time in August 1937, and the type was ordered into production in 1938, 10 He 115A-0 pre-production aircraft being followed by 137 production He 115As and He 115Bs, the latter having undergone some structural strengthening. The He 115 was extremely active in the North Sea area during the early

The He 115 was used in intensive minelaying operations in British waters in the early months of World War II.

months of World War II, particularly in its minelaying role. Variants of the basic design were the He 115C-1, which had a heavy 15mm (0.59in) machine gun installed in

the nose position; the He 115C-2, which had strengthened floats; the He 115C-3 minelayer; and He 115C-4, equipped for Arctic operations. The final variant was

the He 115E-1. Some He 115s, originally supplied to Norway, were captured and brought to Britain for use in clandestine operations. Specifications apply to He 115C-1.

Crew: 3
Powerplant: two 716kW (960hp) BMW 132K 9-cylinder radial engines
Performance: max speed 510km/h (317mph); range 2600km (1616 miles); service ceiling 5200m (17,060ft)
Dimensions: wingspan 22.28m (73ft 1in); length 17.30m (56ft 9in); height 6.59m (21ft 7in)
Weight: 10,680kg (23,545lb) loaded
Armament: one 15mm (0.59in) and four 7.92mm (0.31in) machine guns; torpedo, bomb and mine load up to 920kg (2028lb)

HEINKEL HE 100

Crew: 1
Powerplant: one 877kW (1175hp) Daimler-Benz DB 601M 12-cylinder inverted-Vee engine
Performance: max speed 670km/h (416mph); range 1010km (627 miles); service ceiling 11,000m (36,090ft)
Dimensions: wingspan 9.40m (30ft 10in); length 8.20m (26ft 10in); height 3.60m (11ft 9in)
Weight: 2500kg (5511lb) loaded
Armament: one 20mm (0.79in) cannon; two 7.92mm (0.31in) machine guns

ORIGINALLY DESIGNATED He 113, the Heinkel He 100 monoplane fighter was developed as a potential successor to the Messerschmitt Bf 109. The prototype first flew in January 1938 and proved to be very fast. Despite the fact that subsequent prototypes established a number of speed records, the type was not selected for production, the six prototypes and three pre-production aircraft being sold respectively to the USSR and Japan.

Twelve production He 100D-1s were in fact built and exploited by the German propaganda machine, being adorned with false markings to imply that the fighter was in large-scale service. Specifications apply to the He 100D-1.

The 12 pre-production He 100s were painted in a variety of spurious squadron markings to give the false impression of widespread service.

HEINKEL HE 176

ALTHOUGH THE HEINKEL He 176 was not the first aircraft to fly under rocket power, it was the first to fly solely with a liquid-fuel rocket motor fitted. The first full rocket-powered flight occurred on 30 June 1939 at Usedom island in the Baltic, when pilot Erich Warsitz made a safe landing after

remaining airborne for 50 seconds. Several more flights were made, but the He 176 was heavy for its size, resulting in a high wing loading and underpowering, and its performance never matched expectations. The aircraft was destroyed at the Berlin Air Museum during a bombing raid in 1943.

Crew: 1
Powerplant: one 600kg (1323lb) thrust Walter R.1 rocket motor
Performance: max speed 700km/h (435mph); endurance 50 secs
Dimensions: wingspan 5.00m (16ft 5in); length 5.20m (17ft 1in); height 1.50m (4ft 11in)
Weight: 2000kg (4409lb) loaded

HEINKEL HE 178

Crew: 1
Powerplant: one 454kg (1000lb) thrust Heinkel HeS 3b turbojet engine
Performance: max speed (est) 700km/h (435mph)
Dimensions: wingspan 7.20m (23ft 7.5in); length 7.48m (24ft 6.5in); height 2.10m (6ft 10.5in)
Weight: 1998kg (4396lb) loaded

THE HEINKEL He 178 was the first aircraft in the world to fly powered solely by a turbojet. The engine, a Heinkel HeS 3 using an axial-flow impeller and a centrifugal

compressor, was flight tested beneath a Heinkel He 118 while the He 178 airframe was being completed. The latter was a simple design, emerging as a shoulder-wing monoplane with the pilot's cockpit situated well forward of the leading edge. On 24 August 1939, with Erich Warsitz at the controls, the He 178 made a short 'hop' along the runway at

The Heinkel He 178 was the first aircraft in the world to fly under turbojet power, in August 1939.

Marienehe. The first true flight was made three days later. In November 1939 the aircraft was demonstrated before a group of senior German Air Ministry officials, but the concept was shortsightedly greeted with little enthusiasm. Development of the He 178 was abandoned in favour of the He 280, which had wing-mounted turbojets.

HEINKEL HE 177 GREIF

Crew: 6
Powerplant: four 2313kW (3100hp) DB 610A 24-cylinder engines in coupled pairs
Performance: max speed 488km/h (303mph); service ceiling 8000m (26,245ft); range 5500km (3418 miles)
Dimensions: wingspan 31.44m (103ft 1in); length 22m (72ft 2in); height 6.39m (20ft 11in)
Weight: 31,000kg (68,343lb) loaded
Armament: two 20mm (0.79in) cannon; three 7.92mm (0.31in) and two 13mm (0.50in) machine guns; 6000kg (13,228lb) of bombs

THE HEINKEL HE 177 GREIF (Griffon) heavy bomber was to be plagued by engine trouble throughout its career. In an effort to reduce drag and enhance the type's performance, the bomber's four engines were arranged in coupled pairs, giving it a twin-

A captured Heinkel He 177 in British markings and identification stripes. The He 177, potentially a fine bomber, was plagued by constant engine trouble during its career.

engined appearance. The He 177V-1 prototype first flew on 17 November 1939, but it was not until July 1942 that the first He 177A-1s were delivered to I/KG 40 for operational trials. In all, 130 He 177A-1s and 170 He 177A-3 production aircraft were built, some of the latter being modified to carry three Henschel Hs 293 anti-ship missiles. Specifications apply to the He 177A-1.

HEINKEL HE 280

Crew: 1
Powerplant: two 600kg (1323lb) thrust Heinkel HeS 8A turbojet engines
Performance: max speed 800km/h (497mph); range 650km (404 miles); service ceiling (est) 11,500m (37,720ft)
Dimensions: wingspan 12.00m (39ft 4in); length 10.40m (34ft 1in); height 3.06m (10ft 0.5in)
Weight 4340kg (9550lb) loaded
Armament: various trial installations

IN THE WINTER OF 1939–40, Heinkel abandoned work on the He 178, with its fuselage-mounted turbojet, and concentrated on

The Heinkel He 280 was the world's first true jet fighter, several of the prototypes being armed with cannon, but never entered production.

developing the twin-jet He 280. Because of problems with the turbojets, the inaugural flight on 22 September 1940 was made without these installed, the aircraft being towed to height by an He 111 and released. It was not until April 1941 that the aircraft flew under turbojet power. Nine prototypes were built and flown, some being armed experimentally with cannon, but the aircraft's performance was poor and it did not enter production. The prototypes carried out much trials work, mostly in connection with jet-engine development.

HEINKEL HE 219 UHU

IN THE FIRST HALF OF 1943 General Kammhuber, commanding Germany's night-fighter defences, pressed strongly for the production of new twin-engined types designed specifically for night fighting. At the forefront of these was the Heinkel He 219 Uhu

(Owl), the prototype of which had flown in November 1942 after months of delay caused by a lack of interest on the part of the German Air Ministry. By April 1943, 300 examples had been ordered; Kammhuber wanted 2000, but in the event only 294 were built

before the end of the war. Formidably armed with six 20mm (0.79in) cannon and equipped with the latest AI radar, the He 219 would certainly have torn great gaps in the ranks of the RAF's night bombers had it been available in quantity. It also had a perfor-

mance comparable to that of the Mosquito, which other German night-fighters did not, and could therefore have fought the RAF's night intruders on equal terms. Admittedly, the He 219 suffered from a series of technical troubles in its early development career, but

The Heinkel He 219 was a formidable night-fighter and one of the first aircraft to be fitted with ejection seats.

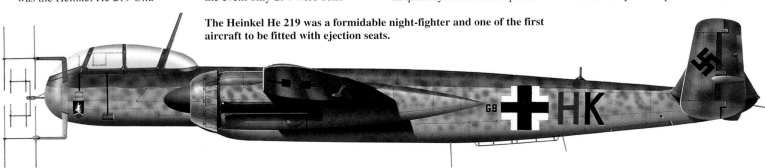

what it might have achieved in action was ably demonstrated on the night of 11/12 June 1943 by Major Werner Streib of I/NJG 1. Flying a pre-production He 219 on operational trials from Venlo, he infiltrated an RAF bomber stream heading for Berlin and shot down five Lancasters in half an hour. The only sour note for Streib sounded when the flaps of the He 219 failed to function and the aircraft overran the runway on landing, breaking into three pieces. Streib and his observer escaped without injury.

The He 219 was conceived as a private venture in the summer of 1940, the intention being to produce a multi-role combat aircraft. The problems experienced by Ernst Heinkel AG in bringing the design to operational fruition were compounded when, in March 1942, over three-quarters of the drawings were destroyed in a night attack by the RAF on the Heinkel works at Rostock. As well as the night-fighter variant, Heinkel intended to produce the He 219A-1 reconnaissance bomber, the He 219A-3 high-speed bomber, and the He 219A-4 high-altitude reconnaissance aircraft with long-span wooden wings, but these projects were abandoned and production concentrated on the He 219A-2 night-fighter. In May 1944, however, General Field Marshal Milch, in charge of aircraft production, persuaded the German Air Ministry to abandon the He 219 in favour of two new night-fighters, the Junkers Ju 388J, which in the event never went into operational service, and the Focke-Wulf Ta

Seen here is the He 219A-7's airborne interception radar aerial array. The He 219 was fitted with Lichtenstein SN-2 or FuG 220 AI radar equipment.

154, an all-wooden design which was prone to structural failure. As a consequence of this disastrous decision, the He 219, which was readily available and had already proven itself a lethal weapon, saw service only in limited numbers.

The He 219 was universally popular with both air and ground crews, and introduced several new features. It was the first operational German aircraft to feature a tricycle undercarriage, and the fact that the armament was concentrated behind the pilot in the wing roots and in a ventral tray, prevented him from being temporarily blinded when the weapons were fired. It was also the first aircraft in the world to be fitted with ejection seats. Various armament installations were tested in the He

219 sub-variants; the He 219A-7/R1, for example, had no fewer than eight cannon, two MK 108s in the wing roots, two MK 103s and two MG 151/20s in the ventral tray, and two MK 108s in a Shräge Musik installation aft of the cockpit, firing obliquely upwards.

Specifications apply to the Heinkel He 219A-2.

Crew: 2
Powerplant: two 1417kW (1900hp) DB 603G 12-cylinder inverted-Vee engines
Performance: max speed 670km/h (416mph); range 2000km (1243 miles); service ceiling 12,700m (41,665ft)
Dimensions: wingspan 18.50m (60ft 8in); length 15.54m (50ft 11in); height 4.10m (13ft 5in)
Weight: 15,300kg (33,730lb) loaded
Armament: six 20mm (0.79in) cannon

HEINKEL HE 162 SALAMANDER

GERMANY: 1944

Crew: 1
Powerplant: one 790kg (1741lb) thrust BMW 109 003E turbojet engine
Performance: max speed 905km/h (562mph); range 975km (606 miles); service ceiling 12,000m (39,370ft)
Dimensions: wingspan 7.20m (23ft 7in); length 9.05m (29ft 8in); height 2.60m (8ft 6in)
Weight: 2605kg (5742lb) loaded
Armament: two 20mm (0.79in) cannon

DEVELOPED AS A LAST-DITCH air fighter in the closing stages of World War II, the Heinkel He 162 Salamander, also known as the Volksjäger (People's Fighter), progressed from drawing board to first flight on 6 December 1944 in only 10 weeks. Built mainly of wood

The Heinkel He 162 Salamander was almost fully operational with Jagdgeschwader 1 at Leck, in Schleswig-Holstein, when the airfield was captured by the rapidly advancing British forces in May 1945.

due to a shortage of strategic metals, 31 prototypes and 275 production aircraft were built. A few contacts were made with Allied aircraft, with one He 162 possibly shot down by an RAF Tempest on 19 April 1945.

HEINKEL HE 343
The Heinkel He 343 was a four-jet, multi-role aircraft, several prototypes of which were initiated but not completed. The Ilyushin Il-22 prototype jet bomber, tested in the USSR in 1947, was almost certainly based on it.

HEINKEL P.1077 JULIA
The Heinkel He 1077 Julia was a rocket-powered target-defence interceptor, similar in concept to the Bachem Ba 349 Natter. It remained a project only.

HEINKEL P.1078
The Heinkel He 1078 was a tailless jet-fighter project, with its wing swept at an angle of 40 degrees. It was to have been armed with two 30mm (1.18in) cannon.

HELIO COURIER
A four-seat STOL transport dating from 1954, and superseded by later more powerful and larger Super Courier versions, the Helio Courier was to see USAF military service as the U-10.

HELIO H-550 STALLION (AU-24)
Following from the Courier design, the Stallion was a larger turbo-powered version first flown in 1964. The Helio H-550 Stallion proved too expensive in the civil market; however, the USAF secured 15 units as the AU-24, and the aircraft was used for armed reconnaissance and clandestine missions, largely in Southeast Asia.

HENSCHEL HS 124
The Henschel Hs 124, which flew in 1935, was a twin-engined multi-role aircraft built to the same requirement as the Junkers Ju 88, to which the production contract was awarded.

HENSCHEL HS 128
A twin-engined monoplane flown in 1939, the Henschel Hs 128 was a high-altitude research aircraft, used to test pressurization systems and other equipment associated with flight at extreme altitudes.

HENSCHEL HS 130
The Henschel Hs 130 high-altitude bomber/reconnaissance aircraft which was first flown in 1942 and was developed from the Hs 128. Several prototypes and production aircraft were built before the project was abandoned.

HENSCHEL HS 123

Crew: 1
Powerplant: one 656kW (880hp) BMW
132Dc radial engine
Performance: max speed 340km/h
(211mph); range 855km (531 miles);
service ceiling 9000m (29,530ft)
Dimensions: wingspan 10.50m (34ft 5in);
length 8.33m (27ft 4in); height 3.20m
(10ft 6in)
Weight: 2215kg (4883lb) loaded
Armament: two 7.92mm (0.31in)
MG 17 machine guns; up to 450kg
(992lb) of bombs

THE FIRST PROTOTYPE Hs 123V-1
flew for the first time in May 1935.
The test programme was hit by
early tragedy, with two of the
prototypes shedding their wings
during dives. Investigations
revealed that the wing had torn
away from the centre-section
struts, and so the fourth aircraft
was substantially strengthened.
The type was ordered into
production, five Hs 123As being
sent to Spain for operational

**The Henschel Hs 123V-2, which
was fitted with a modified engine
cowling that was a feature of all
subsequent production aircraft.**

evaluation with the Kondor Legion
in 1936. This resulted in the
improved Hs 123B, which was
dedicated to ground attack (rather
than dive-bombing) and saw
combat during the German
invasions of Poland, France and
the USSR. Although the Hs 123

carried comparatively light
armament, its BMW radial engine
was very noisy, especially in a
dive, and this was used as a device
to spread panic among horses and
men alike. Despite the Hs 123
being obsolescent, one unit,
II/SG 2, continued to use it on the
Russian Front until 1944. The Hs
123C was a variant armed with
20mm (0.79in) cannon.
Specifications apply to the
Henschel Hs 123B.

HENSCHEL HS 126

Crew: 2
Powerplant: one 634kW (850hp) BMW
Bramo 323A-1 9-cylinder radial engine
Performance: max speed 356km/h
(221mph); range 720km (447 miles);
service ceiling 8229m (27,000ft)
Dimensions: wingspan 14.50m (47ft 7in);
length 10.85m (35ft 7in); height 3.75m
(12ft 3in)
Weight: 3270kg (7209lb) loaded
Armament: two 7.9mm (0.31in) machine
guns

THE HENSCHEL HS 126, which first
flew in the autumn of 1936, was
probably the best medium-range
observation aircraft to see service

**The Henschel Hs 126 was an excellent army cooperation aircraft, working
closely with Stuka dive-bombers to ensure precision attacks on targets.**

in the early part of World War II. A
large, parasol-wing monoplane, it
entered Luftwaffe service in 1938,
having been evaluated in Spain, and
large numbers were subsequently
built to replace the obsolete Heinkel
He 45 and He 46. The main
production version was the Hs
126B-1, which entered service in
1939 and saw widespread use from
the outbreak of World War II. Over
600 Hs 126s were built, including
six for the Spanish Air Force and
16 for the Greek Air Force. The Hs
126 was progressively withdrawn
from first-line service during 1942.
Specifications apply to Hs 126B-1.

HENSCHEL HS 129

GERMANY: 1939

Crew: 1
Powerplant: two 522kW (700hp) Gnome-Rhone 14M-4/5 14-cylinder radial engines
Performance: max speed 1112km/h (691mph); range 690km (429 miles); service ceiling 12,200m (40,000ft)
Dimensions: wingspan 14.20m (46ft 7in); length 9.75m (31ft 11in); height 3.25m (10ft 8in)
Weight: 4020kg (8862lb) loaded
Armament: two 20mm (0.79in) and two 13mm (0.51in) cannon; up to 450kg (992lb) of bombs

DESIGNED AS A HEAVILY armed close-support aircraft, the Henschel Hs 129 prototype flew in 1939, but technical problems delayed the deployment of operational aircraft until April 1942. The aircraft went into action on the Eastern Front, 843 Hs 129Bs being delivered. The Hs 129B-1 was followed by the more heavily armed B-2, introduced in 1943. The final variant was the Hs 129B-3, armed with a 75mm (2.95in) gun, but only 25 were

built. The Hs 129 saw action in North Africa, and in France after the D-Day landings, but it is best remembered for the Battle of Kursk in July 1943, when it destroyed hundreds of enemy tanks. Specifications apply to Hs 129B-1.

After many delays, the Henschel Hs 129 made its operational debut in Tunisia and on the Russian Front, where it proved highly effective in the anti-armour role.

HENSON AERIAL STEAM CARRIAGE

UK: 1842

Crew: 1
Powerplant: one19–22kW (25–30hp) steam engine driving two pusher propellers
Dimensions: wingspan 45.72m (150ft); wing area 418m2 (4500 sq ft)

IN 1842, AN ENGINEER of Somerset, England, William Samuel Henson, designed and patented a flying machine that was to have enormous influence on subsequent development of heavier-than-air craft. His design, the Aerial Steam Carriage, was inspired by Sir George Cayley's technical writings and was the first ever concept of a fixed-wing aircraft along modern lines, comprising a boatlike fuselage surmounted by a conventional wing and with a tail unit attached. Such was Henson's enthusiasm for the project that he tried to set up an air freight business, the Aerial Steam Transit Company, in partnership with John Stringfellow. In the event the Aerial Steam carriage was never built, Henson losing interest after tests with a scale model failed.

W.S. Henson's flying machine never flew, but if it had, and if it had flown as far as Egypt's pyramids, this is how it might have looked...

HENSCHEL HS 132
The Henschel Hs 132 was a turbojet-powered dive-bomber, the engine being mounted on top of the fuselage. Three prototypes were nearing completion when World War II ended.

HESTON PHOENIX
This was a single-engined, five-seat, high-wing monoplane design, with a retractable undercarriage. The Heston Phoenix dates from 1935, after Heston took over the assets of Comper.

HESTON (NAPIER) TYPE 5 RACER
The Type 5 racing aeroplane was fitted with a Napier Sabre 1716kW (2300hp) engine, and was designed with the intention of breaking the world speed record. The aircraft made only a single flight in June 1940, suffering a cooling problem and sustaining damage on an improvised landing.

HESTON A.2/45
The Heston A.2/45 (JC.6) was a twin-boom, two-seat light observation aircraft, powered by a Gipsy Queen 33 pusher engine. The sole prototype flew in 1947.

HILLER XH-44
Hiller was established in 1942 to develop and produce co-axial rotor helicopters. Its first design, the single-seat XH-44, was powered by a 93kW (125hp) engine and first flew in August 1944, the first US helicopter to use co-axial twin rotors successfully.

HILLER MODEL 1099
The Hiller Model 1099 was a six-seat utility helicopter.

HILLER X-18
The Hiller X-18 was an experimental twin-engined tilt-wing convertiplane contracted in February 1957 by the USAF. It used a Chase YC-122 (Fairchild C-123 Provider) as the basis for the airframe and a wing that could be pivoted through 90° for take-off.

HILLER XROE-1 ROTORCYCLE
The Rotorcycle prototype was built to a 1954 US Navy contract for a one-man portable utility helicopter and first flown on 10 January 1957. Only a small number of pre-production YROE-1s were built, and Saunders-Roe Ltd built a few under licence in Britain, but no production contract resulted.

HILLER MODEL 360, UH-12 AND OH-23 RAVEN

USA: 1942

THE UH-4 COMMUTER began flight testing in June 1946 and this was followed the same year by the J-5. The new 'Rota-Matic' control system was installed on a tail-rotor helicopter and resulted in the Model 360 prototype, claimed to be the first American helicopter using jet torque conversion. This light utility helicopter was later known as the UH-12/Model 12 and the H-23 Raven was the military version, being produced under several designations for the US forces (OH-23A–D with the US Army and UH-12A/HTE-1–HTE-2 with the US Navy). In January 1973, Fairchild-Hiller put the UH-12E back into production. Essentially a

The UH-12/Model 12 light utility helicopter, which originated from the Model 360 prototype, is easily distinguishable by the tail rotor driveshaft running from the main gearbox to the low-slung tailboom.

three-seat dual-control version of the OH-23D, the UH-12E was built also as the military OH-23G. The four-seat civil UH-12E4 was produced as the military OH-23F

and later civil versions with uprated engines followed. Altogether, over 2300 aircraft of the entire series were produced. Specifications apply to the Hiller OH-23D Raven.

Crew: 3
Powerplant: one 241kW (323hp) Avco Lycoming VO-540-A1B flat-six piston engine
Performance: max speed 153km/h (95mph); combat radius 330km (205 miles); service ceiling 4025m (13,200ft)
Dimensions: main rotor diameter 10.82m (35ft 6in); length 8.53m (28ft); height 2.97m (9ft 9in)
Weight: 824kg (1816lb)

HILLER HJ-1 (YH-32) HORNET

USA: 1950

Crew: 2
Powerplant: two Hiller-designed ramjet units developing 14kg (31lb) net thrust
Performance: max speed 128km/h (80mph); range 80km (50 miles); service ceiling 3660m (12,000ft)
Dimensions: rotor diameter 7.00m (23ft); length 3.86m (12ft 8in); height 2.13m (7ft)
Weight: 161.6kg (356lb)

DESIGNED ORIGINALLY FOR commercial use, this two-seat helicopter was quite small because of the absence of a conventional powerplant and lengthy tail boom. The power was supplied by two Hiller-designed ramjet units, each

developing 14kg (31lb) thrust, one being mounted at the tip of each rotor blade. With no rotor-induced torque to worry about, the small tail rotor that was included was purely for directional control. The civil prototype first flew in 1950 and the US Army ordered 14 pre-production YH-32 examples for evaluation, but no further civil or military versions were produced.

YH-32, one of 14 pre-production examples which were evaluated by the US Army in the early 1950s. None was subsequently ordered for the military or for civil use.

HISPANO HA-200 SAETA

SPAIN: 1955

The Hispano HA-200 Saeta was not a particularly successful design and certainly not in the same class as other contemporary trainer/strike aircraft. Only Egypt used it in any numbers.

Crew: 2
Powerplant: two 400kg (880lb) thrust Turbomeca Marbore IIA turbojet engines
Performance: max speed 700km/h (435mph); range 1700km (1056 miles); service ceiling 12,000m (40,000ft)
Dimensions: wingspan 10.42m (34ft 2in); length 8.88m (29ft 2in); height 3.26m (10ft 8in)
Weight: 3173kg (6995lb) loaded
Armament: two 12.7mm (0.50in) machine guns

THE HA-200 SAETA (Arrow) advanced jet trainer was the first jet aircraft to be produced by the Spanish aviation industry, and was designed by a team under the leadership of Professor Willi Messerschmitt. The prototype first flew on 12 August 1955 and was followed by 35 production HA-200As. The HA-200D and E models were upgraded for tactical support and counterinsurgency roles. The aircraft was also built under licence in Egypt as the Al Kahira (Cairo), 90 examples being produced. The Al Kahira in America's National Air and Space Museum collection was a gift from the Egyptian government. Initially, the museum had requested either a MiG 15 or MiG 17 from Egypt, but since none was available the Al Kahira was offered instead. It was flown in an Egyptian Air Force C-130 to Washington International Airport on 9 April 1984, at which time it was accepted for permanent display by the museum. Specifications apply to the HA-200A.

HISPANO HA-300   SPAIN/EGYPT: 1964

ORIGINALLY DESIGNED IN Spain in the late 1950s by a Spanish-German team led by Willi Messerschmitt, the HA-300 delta-wing fighter project was transferred to the Helwan Aircraft factory in Egypt in 1961. Four prototypes were completed, the first flying at Helwan on 7 March 1964, powered by a Bristol Siddeley Orpheus 703 turbojet. A second prototype, which joined the test programme on 22 July 1965, had supersonic intakes and a power control for the rudder. With the Orpheus 703-S-10 turbojet, the HA-300 attained Mach 1.13. The third prototype began taxi trials in November 1969, but the programme was cancelled before it flew.

Crew: 1
Powerplant: one 2200kg (4851lb) thrust Bristol Siddeley Orpheus 703 turbojet engine

Performance: max speed 2124km/h (1320mph); combat radius 643km (400 miles); service ceiling 12,000m (39,360ft)
Dimensions: wingspan 5.84m (19ft 2in); length 12.40m (40ft 7in); height 3.15m (10ft 3in)
Weight: 5443kg (12,000lb) loaded
Armament: two 30mm (1.18in) Hispano or four 23mm (0.91in) Nudelmann-Suranov NS-23 cannon; two to four infra-red (IR) homing air-to-air missiles

HORTEN HO I–HO VIII   GERMANY: 1934

Crew: 1
Powerplant: two 60kW (80hp) Hirth HM 60R four-cylinder in-line air-cooled pusher engines
Performance: max speed 215km/h (134mph)
Dimensions: wingspan 16m (52ft 6in)
Weight: 1100kg (2426lb) loaded

THE STORY OF THE 'flying wings' designed by the brothers Reimar and Walter Horten began with a series of models, followed by the Horten Ho I sailplane of 1934, in which the pilot occupied a prone position in the wing centre section. As with all Horten aircraft, the Ho I had no vertical flying surfaces, elevons being used for pitch and roll control, and yaw control being effected by brake flaps above and below the leading edges near the wingtips. Although quite a successful design, the Ho 1 did not satisfy the Hortens, who destroyed it and replaced it with the Ho II.

The main feature of the new aircraft was that it had sweepback on the wing trailing edges, as well as the leading edges. Four Ho IIs were built, one of which was fitted with a 60kW (80hp) Hirth engine in 1935. This was tested in 1938 by Hanna Reitsch and attracted the attention of Ernst Udet, Director of the Technical Department of the German Air Ministry, who made funds available for further development. In 1938, with this official backing, the Hortens set up a facility at Berlin's Tempelhof Airport, where they constructed the Ho III sailplane. This was in effect a scaled-up Ho II, and was fitted with a retractable tandem-wheel undercarriage. Four Ho IIIs were built, one of which was fitted with an engine, the propeller blades folding in flight to reduce drag.

The next Horten flying wing design, the Ho IV, was built primarily to investigate the effects of high aspect ratio. Two Ho IVs were built, one of which crashed after entering a spin. The Ho V, constructed between 1936 and 1938, was a two-seater sailplane, but in 1942 it was converted to single-seat configuration. A second Ho V made much use of plastic in its construction. From the outset,

The Horten Ho IIID was the only one of Horten's early gliders to be fitted with an engine. The propeller blades folded during gliding flight to reduce drag.

the Ho V was designed as a powered research aircraft. Its wing had pronounced sweepback on the outer panels, but the centre section had greatly reduced sweep on the leading edge and a straight, unswept trailing edge. The centre section had a welded steel tube structure to support two 60kW (80hp) Hirth engines, driving pusher propellers through extension shafts. In a bid to acquire more funds, the Hortens proposed a glider-tug version of the Ho V, but this was not taken up.

The Horten Ho VI, only one prototype of which was built, had a wing with the very high aspect ratio of 32.4 to 1, which proved to be structurally weak and too flexible for practical ground handling. The next design, the Ho VII, was similar to the Ho V, but was fitted with more powerful 179kW (240hp) Argus As 10C engines. The sole Ho VII is thought to have been tested at Oranienburg, where it was located in March 1945.

The Ho VIII was by far the largest of the Horten flying wings, and was designed as a commercial aircraft with accommodation for about 60 passengers. Originally to have had a span of 80m (262.5ft), it was to have been powered by six 448kW (600hp) BMW pusher engines; range was estimated to be 6000km (3725 miles) at a cruising speed of between 300 and 350km/h (186 and 217mph). A prototype was expected to fly in November

1945, but the defeat of Germany prevented its development. The concept was resurrected after the war by Reimar Horten, who went to Argentina and incorporated the idea in the unsuccessful I.A.38 tailless cargo aircraft, which flew in prototype form in 1958.

Specifications apply to the Horten Ho VIII.

The Horten Ho IIL. Four aircraft in the Ho II series were built, one being tested at Darmstadt in 1938 by the famous woman test pilot Hanna Reitsch.

HORTEN HO IX   GERMANY: 1944

THE HORTEN HO IX was the Horten brothers' only combat-aircraft design. It was intended to power the prototype with two BMW 003A-1 turbojets, but as these were not available the first

Ho IXV-1 was later completed as a glider and tested at Oranienburg in 1944. The second prototype was completed with two Junkers Jumo 004B turbojets and first flew in January 1945. The initial success

of the flight tests resulted in the placing of an order for 30 aircraft with the Gothaer Waggonfabrik. The production model was to have been designated Gotha Go 229, but the production prototype, the Go

229V-3, had not been completed when development ceased. The second aircraft, the Ho IXV-2, was destroyed on the ground after two hours of flight testing. Specifications apply to the Go 229.

The Horten Ho IXV-2 seen at Oranienburg in 1944. The aircraft was destroyed in a forced landing after logging only a few hours of flying time. It reached speeds of up to 800km/h (500mph).

Crew: 1
Powerplant: two 900kg (1984lb) thrust BMW 004B turbojet engines
Performance (est): max speed 1000km/h (621mph); range 1500km (932miles); service ceiling 15,000m (49,280ft)
Dimensions: wingspan 16.78m (55ft); length 7.47m (24ft 6in)
Weight: 8500kg (18,743lb) loaded
Armament (proposed): four 30mm (1.18in) MK 108 cannon

HUFF-DALAND DUSTER

USA: 1925

THE HUFF-DALAND DUSTER biplane of 1925 was a derivative of a Huff-Daland military/commercial design, called the Petrel 5, which was used by the US Navy in both landplane and seaplane versions. It was a fabric-covered, cantilever-winged biplane structurally designed so that it had none of the wing brace wires that were common to the biplane designs of that era. The fuselage and tail surfaces were made of welded steel tubing and the wings were single-piece units made of spruce and mahogany. The dust hopper carried 363kg (800lb) of calcium arsenate. The Huff-Daland Duster was the first aircraft used by the forerunner of the company that was to become Delta Air Lines.

Crew: 1
Powerplant: one 149kW (200hp) Wright J-W air-cooled nine-cylinder radial engine
Performance: max speed 128km/h (80mph); endurance 2 hrs; service ceiling n/a
Dimensions: wingspan 10.10m (33ft 3in); length 7.00m (23ft 1in); height 2.50m (8ft 4in)
Weight: 643kg (1420lb) empty

HUGHES XR-11

USA: 1946

DESIGNED SPECIFICALLY FOR long-range photographic reconnaissance, the Hughes XR-11 (formerly XF-11) twin-engined, twin-boom monoplane flew for the first time on 7 July 1946 but lost a propeller, the flight ending in a crash that nearly cost pilot Howard Hughes his life. A second aircraft flew on 5 April 1947 and subsequently went to Eglin Field, Florida (now Eglin Air Force Base), to be tested, but the US Air Force cancelled the programme in favour of utilizing the much more economical Boeing RB-50 to meet the long-range photo-reconnaissance requirement.

Crew: 1
Powerplant: two Pratt & Whitney 2611kW (3500hp) 28-cylinder R-4360 radial engines
Performance: data never released
Dimensions: wingspan 30.90m (101ft 4in); length 19.97m (65ft 5in); height not known
Weight: 26,416kg (58,315lb) loaded

Pioneer aviator, aircraft manufacturer and millionaire Howard Hughes almost lost his life when the XR-11 reconnaissance aircraft prototype shed a propeller during a test flight and crashed.

HUGHES H-4 HERCULES

USA: 1947

Crew: 5
Powerplant: eight Pratt & Whitney R-4360 Wasp Major 28-cylinder radial engines
Performance: cruising speed (est) 281km/h (175mph); range (est) 5633km (3500 miles)
Dimensions: wingspan 97.54m (320ft); length 66.75m (219ft); height 24.15m (79ft 3in)
Weight: 181,436kg (400,000lb) loaded (est)
Payload: 500–700 passengers

THE TRULY MASSIVE HUGHES H-4 Hercules flying boat was conceived by reclusive millionaire entrepreneur Howard Hughes in 1942 as a means of delivering massive quantities of men and materiel to various war zones, hence avoiding the submarine menace that presented a constant threat to merchant ships.

On 2 November 1947, the Hercules – nicknamed the 'Spruce Goose' because of its wooden construction, although the wood was mainly birch, not spruce – made a short flight of about a mile over Los Angeles roadstead in front of an excited crowd estimated at 50,000 people, rising 21m (70ft) off the water and reaching a speed of 129km/h (80mph). Yet by 1947 the aircraft no longer had any strategic value, and it never flew again. Today, it is on permanent display at the Evergreen Air Venture Museum, McMinnville, Portland, Oregon. It is still the largest aircraft in the world.

Nicknamed the 'Spruce Goose', Howard Hughes' massive Hercules flying boat made only one brief flight over Los Angeles roadstead in November 1947 before ending its days as a museum piece.

HUGHES XV-9A
Research helicopter built under US Army contract to prove a concept known as 'hot-cycle' propulsion, first flying in November 1964. Two GE YT64-GE-6 turbojets used as gas generators provided power. The hot efflux was ducted to nozzles at the blade tips of the 16.76m (55ft) diameter rotor, thus eliminating the complicated and heavy gear associated with normal shaft-engined helicopters. The rotor blades also incorporated cooling ducts in their leading and trailing edges.

HUGHES MODEL 269/200/300 AND TH-55A
The first of two prototypes of this two-/three-seat light helicopter flew in October 1956. Production of the Model 269A for civil use began in October 1961 and 792 TH-55A Osage light helicopter primary trainers for the US Army followed. The Model 300 was a three-seat version of the Model 269B, and Models 300C (1000 built) and 300CQ (with quiet tail rotor) were further development versions.

HUGHES MODEL 369 (OH-6A CAYUSE)
The Model 369 (YHO-6A-HU) first flew on 7 March 1963. It later won a US Army Light Observation Helicopter (LOH) competition in May 1965 and was widely used in Vietnam, with 658 lost in action and 297 destroyed in accidents. Only 1434 OH-6As from the 4000 requirement were completed when in 1967 falling production and rising costs resulted in the Cayuse contract being terminated.

HUMPHREYS WATERPLANE
Designed by Jack Humphreys in 1909, the Waterplane was a sesquiplane with twin pusher propellers driven by a 26kW (35hp) JAP engine. It sank under test on the River Colne, Essex.

HUNTING (PERCIVAL) P.50 PRINCE/PRESIDENT
A high-wing twin piston-engined light transport, the Prince first flew in 1948, and was successfully taken up by military customers as the Pembroke and Sea Prince. It was hoped to gain commercial orders as the President 10-seat airliner, but no orders materialized.

HUNTING H.126
First flown in 1963, the Hunting H.126 was a research aircraft, built to test the high-lift qualities of blown flaps. Sixty per cent of the jet exhaust was ducted on to the wing trailing edge.

HUGHES (McDonnell Douglas) Model 500, MD Helicopters 520N–600 USA: 1963

THIS LARGELY COMMERCIAL version of the Hughes Model 369 entered production in 1968 and found an extensive worldwide civil and military market, with licence production in Argentina, Japan and Italy adding to US sales and many sub-variants.

Specifications apply to the McDonnell Douglas MD 500.

A McDonnell Douglas 530F Lifter with a mast-mounted sight to enable the crew to locate enemy targets while hidden.

Crew: 1
Powerplant: one 236kW (317shp) Rolls-Royce Allison 250-C18A turboshaft derated to 207kW (278shp) for take-off and 181kW (243shp) for continuous running
Performance: max speed 244km/h (152mph); service ceiling 4390m (14,400ft)
Dimensions: main rotor diameter 8.03m (26ft 4in); length 9.24m (30ft 3.75in); height 2.48m (8ft 1.5in)
Weight: 493kg (1088lb)
Payload: up to six passengers or two litters plus one medical attendant, or freight carried in the cabin

HUNTING PROVOST UK: 1950

Crew: 2
Powerplant: one 410kW (550hp) Alvis Leonides 126 air-cooled 9-cylinder radial engine
Performance: max speed 322km/h (200mph); range 1040km (650 miles); service ceiling 7,620m (25,000ft)
Dimensions: wingspan 10.71m (35ft); length 8.73m (28ft 6in); height 3.70m (12ft)
Weight: 1995kg (4399lb)

FIRST FLOWN IN February 1950, the Hunting Percival Provost began to replace the Percival Prentice in RAF Flying Training Command from 1953. The piston-engined type took a student pilot through his basic training to the point where he could begin his advanced

training on de Havilland Vampire T.11 jet aircraft. The 461 Provosts built up to 1956 continued in service until the early 1960s. As the

T.53, the type was also supplied to Burma, Iraq and the Sudan, while the T.51 and T.52 were used by Eire and Rhodesia/Zimbabwe.

This Provost T.Mk 1 was refurbished by Hunting for Malaysian service. Malaysia received twelve refurbished aircraft in total.

HUNTING (BAC) JET PROVOST UK: 1954

Crew: 2
Powerplant: one 794kg (1750lb) thrust Armstrong Siddeley Viper ASV.8 turbojet engine
Performance: max speed 530km/h (330mph); range 793km (493 miles); service ceiling 9450m (31,000ft)
Dimensions: wingspan 10.72m (35ft 2in); length 9.73m (31ft 11in); height 3.86m (12ft 8in)
Weight: 2654kg (5850lb) loaded

THE JET PROVOST WAS designed as an ab initio jet trainer in 1953, replacing the piston-engined Provost from which it was developed. Nine aircraft were ordered under the designation T.1,

the first flying on 26 June 1954, and the type served with the RAF in three versions, the Mks 3, 4 and 5, the latter having a redesigned nose and pressurized cockpit. The BAC Strikemaster was a ground-

attack version of the T.5, with provision for various underwing loads, and enjoyed considerable export success. The first Jet Provost T.3 flew in June 1958 and production continued until 1965.

A Hunting (BAC) Jet Provost T.Mk.5 in the colours of No 1 Flying Training School, RAF Linton-on-Ouse, near York.

IAI KFIR

ISRAEL: 1971

THE ISRAELI AIRCRAFT INDUSTRIES (IAI) Kfir (Lion Cub) was developed as an expedient after France imposed an embargo on the sale of combat aircraft to Israel, and was basically a Dassault Mirage III airframe married with a General Electric J79 turbojet. IAI produced 27 Kfir C.1s, which equipped two squadrons of the Israeli Air Force; after replacement by the improved C.2, all but two were leased to the US Navy for aggressor training, bearing the designation F-21A.

The IAI Kfir was produced after France imposed an embargo on the sale of Mirage 5 aircraft to Israel.

The Kfir C.2, which appeared in 1976, was the major production version, with 185 being delivered. Most C.2s were upgraded to C.7 standard between 1983 and 1985. The Kfir saw a great deal of action in Lebanon's Bekaa Valley in the 1980s, and the Kfir was exported to Colombia and Sri Lanka. Specifications apply to Kfir C.2.

Crew: 1
Powerplant: one 8119kg (17,902lb) thrust General Electric J79-J1E turbojet engine
Performance: max speed 2445km/h (1520mph); combat radius 346km (215 miles); service ceiling 17,680m (58,000ft)
Dimensions: wingspan 8.22m (26ft 11in); length 15.65m (51ft 4in); height 4.55m (14ft 11in)
Weight: 16,200kg (35,715lb) loaded
Armament: one 30mm (1.18in) cannon; up to 5775kg (12,732lb) of external ordnance

IAR-80

ROMANIA: 1938

Crew: 1
Powerplant: one IAR-built 701kW (940hp) Gnome-Rhone 14K 14-cylinder radial engine
Performance: max speed 510km/h (317mph); range 950km (590 miles); service ceiling 10,500m (34,500ft)
Dimensions: wingspan 10.00m (32ft 10in); length 8.16m (26ft 9in); height 3.60m (11ft 10in)
Weight: 2286kg (5040lb) loaded
Armament: two 20mm (0.79in) cannon and four 7.7mm (0.303in) machine guns

BEARING A NUMBER of design features copied from the PZL P.24 fighter, which Industria Aeronautica Romana (IAR) had built under licence in the 1930s, the IAR-80 was the only fighter of Romanian origin to be built in quantity during World War II. It flew in 1938 and became operational early in 1942. About 125 were built, being used mainly in the defence of the Romanian oilfields. The IAR-81 was a fighter-bomber development,

Despite not being as advanced as types such as the Focke-Wulf Fw 190, the IAR-80 performed well in its primary role of defence.

only a few being produced, and the IAR-80 DC was a two-seat training version.. The IAR-80 had a very powerful armament and remained in first-line service until 1944. The aircraft reportedly had excellent handling characteristics and was highly manoeuvrable.

IAI ARAVA 101/201
This Israeli twin-turboprop engine, twin-boom, fixed undercarriage, general-purpose STOL aircraft first flew in 1969 and was IAI's first fielded aircraft design. More than a hundred examples were built up until the mid-1980s.

IAI WESTWIND
Originating from an Aero Commander design, this twin-engined, medium/long-range business jet design was sold to IAI following the former's acquisition by Rockwell. First flown in 1970, and later improved by IAI, over 440 Westwinds were delivered.

IAR-23
The IAR-23, which appeared in 1934, was a small, two-seat, low-wing monoplane of exceptionally fine design. The aircraft excelled in endurance competitions.

IAR-37, 38 AND 39
The IAR-37, 38 and 39 were single-engined bomber-reconnaissance biplanes which entered service with the Romanian Air Force from 1938.

IKARUS IK-2
The Ikarus IK-2, which flew in 1936, was a high-wing fighter monoplane. Only 12 aircraft were built in total, some of which saw action with the Yugoslav Air Force in 1941.

IKARUS TYPE 451
The Ikarus Type 451, which flew in 1951, was a twin-engined prone pilot research monoplane based on the B.5 Pionir, a pre–World War II design.

IKARUS TYPE 452-M
Powered by two Turbomeca Palas turbojets, the Ikarus Type 452-M was a single-seat swept-wing aircraft with twin tail booms supporting a swept tailplane. It flew in 1953.

IKARUS S-49

THE FIRST POSTWAR fighter to be designed in Yugoslavia, the Ikarus S-49 was a development of the pre-war Ikarus IK-3, production of which had been halted by the German invasion after only a few evaluation aircraft had been completed. The prototype flew in 1948, and the first examples entered service as the S-49A in 1951. The last variant produced was the S-49C. About 100 aircraft were built in all, being replaced in first-line service by the Republic F-84G Thunderjet.

Specifications apply to S-49C.

Crew: 1
Powerplant: one 1119kW (1500hp) Hispano-Suiza 12Z-11Y in-line engine
Performance: max speed 640km/h (398mph); range 799km (497 miles); service ceiling 10,000m (32,810ft)
Dimensions: wingspan 10.29m (33ft 9in); length 9.10m (29ft 10in); height 2.90m (9ft 6in)
Weight: 3463kg (7634lb) loaded
Armament: one 20mm (0.79in) Mauser MG151 cannon and two 12.7mm (0.50in) machine guns; four 82mm (3.23in) or 110mm (4.33in) RPs; four 24.9kg (55lb) or 50kg (110lb) bombs on underwing racks

ILYUSHIN IL-4 (DB-3)

Crew: 4
Powerplant: two 821kW (1100hp) Tumanskii M-88B 14-cylinder radial engines
Performance: max speed 420km/h (261mph); range 2600km (1616 miles); service ceiling 9400m (30,840ft)
Dimensions: wingspan 21.44m (70ft 4in); length 14.80m (48ft 7in); height 4.10m (13ft 5in)
Weight: 10,300kg (22,707lb) loaded
Armament: three 7.62mm (0.30in) machine guns; up to 2700kg (5952lb) of bombs or torpedoes

THE MOST WIDELY USED Soviet bomber of World War II, the Ilyushin Il-4 was designed in 1936 as the TsKB-26 and given the military designation DB-3, the letters denoting Dalnii Bombardirovchtchik ('long-range bomber'). The main production version was the DB-3F (Forsirovanni, or 'boosted') with Tumanskii M-88B radial engines.

The Il-4 was used extensively by both the Soviet Air Force and Soviet Navy; on the night of 8/9 August 1941 it carried out the first Soviet attack on Berlin, and continued to carry out similar attacks at intervals for the duration of the war. It also operated during the Soviet–Finnish Winter War of 1939–40, where it suffered heavy losses because of its inadequate defensive firepower.

The Ilyushin Il-4 was the first Soviet bomber to attack Berlin. Aircraft of this type were also used to attack the German battleship *Tirpitz* while it was sheltering in a Norwegian fjord.

ILYUSHIN IL-2

IN THE AUTUMN OF 1938 – a time of great international tension – the Soviet Air Force General Staff, influenced by the air combat lessons of the Spanish Civil War, issued a requirement for a new close-support aircraft capable of destroying the latest tanks and armoured vehicles of the types then being mass-produced in Nazi Germany. Two designers, Sergei Ilyushin and Pavel Sukhoi, were ordered to proceed with the design of such an aircraft.

The Ilyushin design was accepted and materialized in the BSh-2 (or TsKB-55) prototype, which flew for the first time on 30 December 1939. BSh was an abbreviation of Bronyirovanni Shturmovik, or 'Armoured Assaulter', and it was as the Shturmovik that the definitive aircraft would be known throughout its operational career.

On successfully completing its State Acceptance Trials in March 1941, the TsKB-55 was ordered into full production as the Il-2,

with 249 being produced before the German invasion of June 1941. The lack of a rear gun position proved a serious drawback, and losses in action were heavy. A modified single-seat Il-2M, with boosted engine and new armament, began to reach front-line units in the autumn of 1942 and was used in considerable numbers during the battle for Stalingrad that winter. Meanwhile, further modifications were under way. The armoured forward section was extended

rearwards to accommodate a rear gunner's cockpit. The new two-seater variant, the Il-2m3, entered service in August 1943, and thereafter played a prominent, and often decisive, part in the campaigns

For winter operations, Ilyushin Il-2s were quickly painted with a soluble white paint scheme over their normal camouflage. This aircraft served at Stalingrad in February 1943.

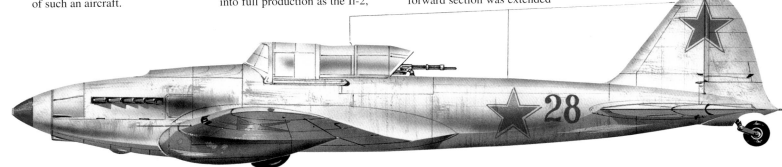

on the Eastern Front. By the winter of 1943–44 vast numbers of Il-2m3s were in service (some sources put the total as high as 12,000), equipping units of the Soviet Naval Air Arm as well as the Soviet Air Force. Naval Il-2s were used extensively for attacks on shipping in the Baltic and Black Sea, usually with bombs and rocket projectiles, but sometimes with torpedoes. During the summer months of 1943, anti-tank grenades were added to the warload that could be carried by the Il-2, as many as 200 of these small hollow-charge weapons being carried in launchers beneath the wings. If the aircraft came under attack, the launchers could be jettisoned and lowered to the ground by parachute to friendly forces.

It is for its part in the battle of Kursk that the Il-2 is probably best

remembered. Following a series of experiments, Il-2s were fitted with two long-barrelled anti-tank cannon, and these were used with devastating effect at Kursk on the latest German Tiger and Panther tanks. During 20 minutes of concentrated attacks on the 9th Panzer Division, Il-2 pilots claimed to have destroyed 70 tanks. During the course of the battle, the 3rd Panzer Division, with a strength of 300 tanks and 180 men per infantry company, was claimed to have been reduced to 30 tanks and 40 men per infantry company, largely as a result of Il-2 attacks.

The Il-2's main drawback was that it had a limited endurance, which sometimes meant that the aircraft had difficulty in keeping up with Soviet armour as the latter made increasingly rapid thrusts

into enemy territory during the closing months of World War II.

The number of Ilyushin Il-2s built reached the staggering total of 36,183, more than any other type of aircraft in history.

Crew: 2
Powerplant: one 1320kW (1770hp) Mikulin AM-38F liquid-cooled in-line engine
Performance: max speed 404km/h (251mph); range 800km (497 miles); service ceiling 6000m (19,685ft)
Dimensions: wingspan 14.60m (47ft 10in); length 11.60m (38ft); height 3.40m (11ft 1in)
Weight: 6360kg (14,021lb) loaded
Armament: (typical) wing-mounted armament of two 37mm (1.46in) and two 7.62mm (0.30in) guns; one 12.7mm (0.50in) machine gun in the rear cockpit; 200 PTAB hollow-charge anti-tank bombs, or eight RS-82 or RS-132 rocket projectiles

Once its defensive armament had been increased, the Shturmovik proved to be a formidable and effective ground-attack aircraft. It played a major part in the Soviet victory at Kursk.

ILYUSHIN IL-12 'COACH'

FORMER USSR: 1946

DURING WORLD WAR II, the Soviet Union had turned to building the DC-3 (as the Lisunov Li-2) to support the logistics of its vast war effort. The Soviets also realized that air transport would have a much greater role in the postwar world in both civil and military applications. A requirement was therefore issued in 1943 for Ilyushin to design a Li-2 replacement. This actually made it the Ilyushin design bureau's first passenger type, a not insubstantial requirement given the variation of geographic and climatic conditions that occur in the Soviet

Union and grass or unpaved airstrips being commonly used, often in semi-icebound conditions.

The continuing war effort took priority over the building of prototypes; however, during this period the use of a diesel-fuelled powerplant was examined, but ultimately dropped. The prototype Il-12 first flew in January 1946 and was publicly displayed the same year. The fuselage had a general resemblance to the Li-2, while the fin had similarity with earlier Ilyushin bombers. The Il-12 had two engines mounted on a low wing,

but with four-bladed propellers, and a tricycle undercarriage was introduced after early consideration of a tail wheel arrangement similar to the Li-2. Initially two basic versions were developed: civil and military. The Il-12D was a military transport/assault type, fitted with larger double cargo doors and machine-gun points.

Delivery of production standard aircraft began in 1947, and these were initially used for military and domestic civilian Aeroflot service, but in 1948 international Aeroflot services were initiated. During

Estimates of how many Il-12s were produced differ considerably, but the numbers built for commercial application are believed to be around 250.

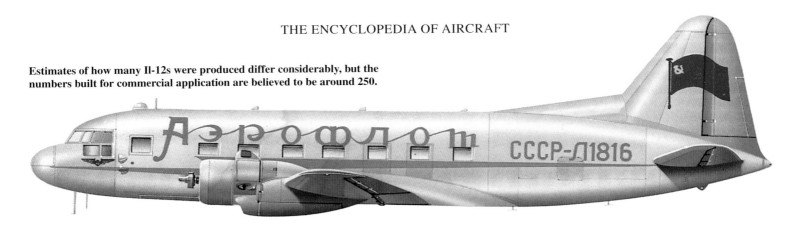

these early postwar years the Il-12 became the backbone of Aeroflot's domestic medium- and long-haul operations, and operated demanding services such as Moscow to Vladivostok, a 33-hour journey including a number of technical stops. There were, however, some in-service problems that resulted in retrospective modification, These included the fitting of a dorsal fin

fillet to improve stability, improvement of the nose wheel gear and the fitting of de-icing equipment. Airframes modified to this standard were designated Il-12B and unmodified versions were reassigned as Il-12A. It was poor performance in the event of a single engine failure, particularly during take-off, which was the most serious problem that beset the

Il-12, and the subsequent thorough and hazardous investigation led Aeroflot to reduce the maximum take-off weight to a less than economically viable load, often reducing the carriage of passengers to fewer than 19 persons.

There remains considerable uncertainty regarding the number of Il-12s actually built, partly due

to the fact that the Soviet military were the largest customer. At least 660 were produced until the late 1940s or early 1950s, when the similar but improved Il-14 superseded the Il-12 in production.

Although the preponderance of Ilyushin Il-12s produced were military transports, the Il-12 was also exported for use by other Eastern Bloc airlines. These included LOT of Poland, which used the Il-12 internationally from 1949, CSA of Czechoslovakia and China's CAAC. An operational example was reported in China as

Crew: 4
Powerplant: two 1365kW (1830hp) Shvetsov Ash-82FNV radial piston engines
Performance: max speed 407km/h (253mph) at 2500m (8200ft); range 2000km (1243 miles); service ceiling 6700m (21,980ft)
Dimensions: wingspan 31.70m (104ft); wing area 100.00m² (1076 sq ft); length 21.31m (69ft 11in); height 8.00m (26ft 3in)
Weight: 18,000kg (39,690lb) maximum take-off weight
Payload: 27-32 passengers

Trials were undertaken with an Il-12 to evaluate the effect of losing an engine during take off. These proved extremely hazardous, and the crew involved were fortunate to survive the programme.

ILYUSHIN IL-28 'BEAGLE' 〔FORMER USSR: 1948〕

Powerplant: two 2700kg (5952lb) thrust Klimov VK-1 turbojet engines
Performance: max speed 902km/h (560mph); range 2180km (1355 miles); service ceiling 12,300m (40,355ft)
Dimensions: wingspan 21.45m (70ft 4in); length 17.65m (57ft 10in); height 6.70m (22ft)
Weight: 21,200kg (46,738lb) loaded
Armament: four 23mm (0.91in) NR-23 cannon; up to 3000kg (6614lb) of bombs; two 400mm (15.75in) light torpedoes

DESIGNED AS A TACTICAL light bomber to replace the piston-engined Tupolev Tu-2, Ilyushin's Il-28 formed the mainstay of the Soviet Bloc's tactical striking forces during the 1950s and was

widely exported to countries within the Soviet sphere of influence. The first VK-1-powered Il-28 flew on 20 September 1948, and deliveries to Soviet tactical squadrons began in the following year. Around 10,000 Il-28s were produced, variants including the Soviet

Navy's Il-28T torpedo bomber and the Il-28U two-seat trainer (NATO code name Mascot). Some 500 Il-28s were supplied to China, where the type was also built under licence as the Harbin H-5. Egypt acquired 60, of which 20 were destroyed at Luxor by French F-

84F Thunderstreaks during the 1956 Suez crisis. Il-28s were part of the package of combat aircraft and missiles delivered to Cuba in 1962, provoking the so-called 'missile crisis'.

Ilyushin Il-28 Beagle of the Polish Air Force. The Il-28 was an excellent light bomber and was widely used by the Soviet satellite air forces.

ILYUSHIN IL-14 'CRATE'

FORMER USSR: 1950

ALTHOUGH VISUALLY SIMILAR to the Il-12, the Il-14 embodied a number of structural, aerodynamic and ergonomic improvements, as well as more powerful engines. Like most Soviet transports, the Il-14 was used for Aeroflot airline and military applications – passenger and freight work. However, not all the legacy of operational and safety issues from the Il-12 were eradicated. Single-engined operation with a full load was marginal, therefore passenger numbers were often restricted to 30. In the region of 3500 Il-14s were produced, including 80 by VEB in East Germany and about 80 by the Czechoslovakian company Avia (known as the Avia 14). A number were exported. Isolated operational examples still ply a trade today.

The aircraft photographed is an Avia 14FG aerial survey variant easily identified by an extended and glazed nose section – for use by the Czech government.

Crew: 2/3
Powerplant: two 1417kW (1900hp) Shvetsov Ash-82T radial piston engines
Performance: max speed 417km/h (259mph); range 1305km (811 miles) with full payload; service ceiling 7400m (24,280ft)
Dimensions: wingspan 31.70m (104ft); wing area 99.70m² (1,073 sq ft); length 22.30m (73ft 2in); height 7.90m (25ft 11in)
Weight: 18,000kg (39,683lb) maximum take-off weight
Payload: 30–36 passengers

ILYUSHIN IL-18 'COOT'

FORMER USSR: 1957

Crew: 5
Powerplant: four 3169ekW (14,250ehp) ZMDB Progress (Ivchyenko) AI-20M turboprop engines
Performance: max cruising speed 675km/h (419mph); range 3700km (2299 miles) with maximum payload; service ceiling 10,000m (32,810ft)
Dimensions: wingspan 37.42m (122ft 9.25in); length 35.90m (117ft 9in); height 10.17m (33ft 4in)
Weight: 64,000kg (141,093lb) maximum take-off weight
Payload: up to 122 passengers

Operable Il-18s are now used mainly in Africa and the Middle East. The example here is climbing out of Sharjah, UAE, carrying a freight load.

THE IL-18 WAS DESIGNED in the 1950s to meet a requirement for a 100-seat short- to medium-haul airliner. The improved Il-18E became the workhorse of Aeroflot's short-haul operation, and over 700 Il-18s were produced until 1968. Appreciable numbers were exported to the Eastern Bloc and to other aligned nations. The Soviet military operated Elint-role derivatives designated Il-20, Il-22 and Il-24. Today significant numbers of Il-18s undertake combi/freight work.

ILYUSHIN IL-38
The Ilyushin Il-38 (NATO reporting name 'May'), which became operational in 1973, is a long-range maritime patrol development of the Il-18 civil airliner.

ILYUSHIN IL-114
Originating in the requirement for an An-24 replacement, this twin-engined, turboprop, 60-plus seat regional airliner/freighter design dates from 1986. The dissolution of the Soviet Union, and funding and development problems contributed to delays.

ILYUSHIN IL-103
A recent departure from airliner designs by Ilyushin, the IL-103 is a multirole/trainer light aircraft design with a single engine, two seats and a fixed landing gear.

IMAM (MERIDIONALI) RO.37
Although it made its first appearance in 1934, the Ro.37 reconnaissance biplane was still widely used during World War II in Africa and the Mediterranean, appearing in two production versions with different engines.

IMAM (MERIDIONALI) RO.43
The Imam Ro.43 floatplane was the naval equivalent of the Ro 47, designed for use on the Italian Navy's capital ships. The aircraft took part in all the major naval encounters in the Mediterranean.

IMAM (MERIDIONALI) RO.44
The Ro.44 of 1936 was a single-seat fighter version of the Ro.37. Its performance was greatly inferior to that of contemporary Allied fighters, and only a few examples were built.

IMAM (MERIDIONALI) RO.51
The IMAM Ro.51, first flown in 1938, was a single-seat interceptor monoplane. The Macchi C.200 and Fiat G.50 were selected for production in preference to it.

ILYUSHIN IL-62 'CLASSIC'

The US embargo of Cuba has meant that the Il-62 has played a prominent, long-range role for Cuba's national carrier, Cubana.

THE IL-62 WAS DEVELOPED for Aeroflot's long-range routes, and was also the first intercontinental jet transport built in the Soviet Union. Designed with a T tail and four engines mounted in pairs on the rear fuselage, the Il-62 initially flew with Lyul'ka AL-7 turbojet engines, but these were replaced by Kuznetsov NK-8-4 turbofans in production. The Il-62 spent a long period in development before becoming operational in 1967 with Aeroflot. About 250 Il-62s were manufactured up until 1995. Improved engine Il-62M and MK variants were exported widely to the Eastern Bloc, China and Cuba. Despite the Il-62's banishment from scheduled services into the EU, around 100 Il-62 examples remain operable in the CIS, Middle East, Africa and Cuba.

Specifications apply to Il-62M.

Crew: 5
Powerplant: four PNPP 'Aviadvigatel' (Soloviev) D-30KU turbofan engines each rated at 107.87kN (24,250lb st)
Performance: max cruising speed 900km/h (560mph) at between 10,000 and 12,000m (32,810 and 39,370ft); range 7800km (4848 miles) with a 5100kg (11,243lb) payload
Dimensions: wingspan 43.20m (141ft 9in); length 53.12m (174ft 3.5in); height 12.35m (40ft 6.25in)
Weight: 165,000kg (363,757lb) maximum take-off weight
Payload: up to 186 passengers within the context of a 23,000kg (50,705lb) payload

ILYUSHIN IL-76 'CANDID'

Crew: 5
Powerplant: four 12,000kg (26,455lb) thrust Soloviev D-30KP turbofan engines
Performance: max speed 850km/h (528mph); range 5000km (3100 miles); service ceiling 15,500m (50,850ft)
Dimensions: wingspan 50.50m (165ft 8in); length 46.59m (152ft 11in); height 14.76m (48ft 5in)
Weight: 170,000kg (374,785lb) loaded
Armament: none

THE ILYUSHIN IL-76 WAS designed to meet an important requirement of both civil operator Aeroflot and the Soviet military air transport service V-TA for a replacement for the Antonov An-12BP, the most numerous heavy cargo transport. The Il-76 first flew on 25 March 1971. A three-point hose-and-drogue tanker variant, the Il-78 (NATO reporting name Midas) became operational in 1987 to replace the Soviet Air Force's ageing Mya-4 Bison tankers, and the type was also converted to the airborne early-warning role. The military Il-76M also serves with the Indian Air Force. Another overseas customer was Iraq. Specifications apply to Il-76M.

The Ilyushin Il-76 heavy transport, seen here in the colours of the Indian Air Force, has proved a great success.

ILYUSHIN IL-86

Crew: 5
Powerplant: four 127.5kN (28,660lb) Kuznetsov NK-86 turbofan engines
Performance: max cruising speed 950km/h (590mph); range 3600km (2235 miles) with maximum payload; service ceiling 12,497m (41,000ft)
Dimensions: wingspan 48.00m (157ft 8in) length 59.40m (194ft 11in); height 15.80m (51ft 10in)
Weight: 208,000kg (458,554lb) maximum take-off weight
Payload: up to 350 passengers in a single-class layout

THE IL-86 WAS DESIGNED with the intention of producing a wide-body successor to the Il-62 airliner for Aeroflot's longer routes, but failed to live up to its range expectations due to a higher than expected fuel consumption. An interesting feature of the type is the facility to carry on luggage for stowage on a lower deck. A total of 103 Il-86s were produced in a single main version, mostly for Aeroflot – the only exports were to China.

Specifications apply to Il-86.

Aeroflot was the only original customer for the Il-86. More recently, the type has served with a number of other/successor CIS operators.

ILYUSHIN IL-96

IN TERMS OF ITS BASIC hull appearance, the Ilyushin Il-96 is little changed from the Il-86, but there are many other changes, including a redesigned wing, the use of composite materials internally and externally, a glass cockpit, modern turbofan engines and a redesigned wingletted wing. The Il-96-300 entered service in 1993; however, the aircraft has attracted little export interest and sales of the type have been slow, despite its being positioned as a competitor to the Airbus A330, MD-11 and Boeing 777. As a

The Il-96 has thus far only been utilized by Russian operators – principally Aeroflot – despite versions having been offered with Western engines and avionics.

consequence of this, Ilyushin launched the stretched Il-96M and later Il-96T programmes, which include Western avionic systems and options for Pratt & Whitney PW2337 engines. Despite this, to date orders have only been taken from Aeroflot for use on its long, thin routes. Specifications apply to the Il-96-300.

Crew: 3-5
Powerplant: four 156.90kN (35,273lb st) Aviadvigatel (Soloviev) PS-90A turbofan engines
Performance: cruising speed between 850km/h (528mph) and 900km/h (559mph) at between 10,100m (33,135ft) and 12,100m (39,700ft); range 7500km (4660 miles) with a maximum payload
Dimensions: wingspan 60.11m (197ft 2.5in) length 55.35m (181ft 7.25in); height 17.55m (57ft 7in)
Weight: 216,000kg (476,190lb) maximum take-off weight
Payload: up to 300 passengers

INTERSTATE TDR-1

Crew: 1 (for test flights only)
Powerplant: two 164kW (220hp) Lycoming O-435-2 piston engines
Performance: max speed 225km/h (140mph); range 685km (425 miles)
Dimensions: wingspan 14.60m (48ft)
Weight: 2700kg (5900lb)
Armament: one 900kg (2000lb) general-purpose bomb or torpedo

THE TDR-1 WAS A TV-guided drone powered by two Lycoming O-435-2 piston engines. It had a very simple cockpit which was manned by a backup pilot for test flights, the pilot only taking over the controls when the remote-control TV equipment failed or when the aircraft was landed. In unmanned operational missions,

The Interstate TDR-1, developed as a stand-off weapon, was not a success. This is the XBQ-4 prototype, the cockpit being for manned test flights.

the cockpit canopy was replaced by a flush fairing, and the landing gear was dropped after take-off. A TDR-1 unit was deployed to the

Pacific in 1944, the drones being guided to their targets by TBM Avengers. Of 46 TDR-1s launched, only 18 hit their targets.

JUNKERS J.1

THE JUNKERS J.1, which flew for the first time early in 1917 and became operational at the beginning of 1918, was an all-metal biplane designed for close support and tactical reconnaissance. Its crew, whose main task was to fly at low level over enemy lines and report troop and vehicle movements via a radio link, was protected by a considerable weight of armour. This made the J.1 heavy, earning it the nickname *Møbelwagen* (Furniture Van). Manufacture was shared between the Junkers and Fokker factories, which produced a total of 227 aircraft between them. Instead of radio equipment, early J.1s carried two downward-firing Parabellum machine guns, but these were deleted because of problems with accurate aim.

The Junkers J.1 was the 'Stuka' of World War I, being designed for the close support of ground forces. It was heavily armoured.

Crew: 2
Powerplant: one 149kW (200hp) Benz Bz.IV water-cooled in-line engine
Performance: max speed 155km/h (96.3mph); range 310km (193 miles); service ceiling 6000m (19,685ft)
Dimensions: wingspan 16.00m (52ft 6in); length 9.10m (29ft 10.25in); height 3.40m (11ft 2in)
Armament: three 7.62mm (0.30in) machine guns

JUNKERS F13

Crew: 2
Powerplant: variable – for example, one BMW III 6-cylinder in-line piston engine rated at 198kW (265hp)
Performance: max speed 177km/h (110mph); range 648km (402.5 miles); cruising speed 140km/h (87mph)
Dimensions: wingspan 17.75m (58ft 3in); length 9.60m (31ft 6in); height 3.61m (11ft 10in)
Weight: 2703kg (5959lb) maximum take-off weight
Payload: four passengers

THE JUNKERS F13 was a post-World War I design, purpose-built for commercial purposes, and also

Brazilian airline Varig, itself started with German backing and finance, purchased this F13 in 1932 and it remained in active service until 1949.

the first all-metal airliner. Unusually for its era, it was a monoplane. Over 320 examples of this historic aircraft were built over 20 years up until 1932, with Deutsche Luft Hansa a significant purchaser (of 72 examples). Some variants were equipped with skis or floats, and F13s were still in service up until World War I – in all more than 70 variants were fielded. This rugged, heavily braced aircraft with its trademark Junkers corrugated metal skin helped to develop air transport services in many parts of Europe and beyond, including South America. Specifications apply to F13a.

JUNKERS G23 AND G24

THE G23 WAS ANOTHER first for Junkers – the world's first all-metal three-engined passenger/transport aircraft. Only nine were built before the G24, with more powerful engines, was introduced in 1925. It was intended for new long-range Deutsche Luft Hansa services. Eleven of the 56 examples built were converted for single-engined operation, their wing-mounted engine units removed. These were redesignated F24 (circa 1928).

Specifications apply to the Junkers G24 – standard.

Crew: 3
Powerplant: three Junkers L.5 in-line piston engines each rated at 231kW (310hp)
Performance: max speed 200km/h (124mph); range 1300km (808 miles)
Dimensions: wingspan 27.76m (91ft 1in); length 15.70m (51ft 6in)
Weight: 6500kg (14,330lb) maximum take-off weight
Payload: up to nine passengers

Some Luft Hansa–owned G24 aircraft (pictured) were subject to conversion to single-engined operations and redesignated F24.

JUNKERS W33 AND W34

GERMANY: 1926

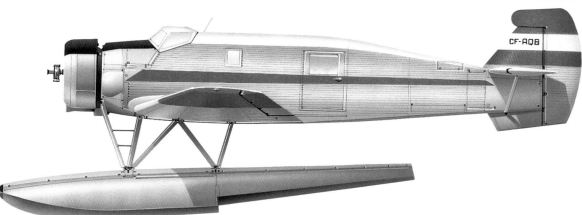

THESE LIGHT TRANSPORTS were derived from the earlier F13. Indeed the prototype was a converted F13 with a lengthened fuselage and more powerful engine, but with the fixed undercarriage retained. The W33 and W34 came in ski and float versions and copious other variants. There were nearly 200 W33s built, but the W34 totalled nearly 1800 examples, which were

Several Junkers W34 floatplanes were operated in Canada for many years, one as late as 1962.

extensively used by civil operators. A total of 900 saw service with the Luftwaffe as trainers and transports during World War II. A W33 made the first east–west Atlantic crossing in 1928 from Dublin to Labrador. Specifications apply to the W34h.

Crew: 2
Powerplant: one BMW 132 radial piston engine rated at 492kW (660hp)
Performance: max speed 265km/h (165mph); range 900km (560 miles); service ceiling 6300m (20,670ft)
Dimensions: wingspan 17.75m (58ft 2.75in); length 10.27m (33ft 8.5in); height 3.53m (11ft 7in)
Weight: 3200kg (7055lb) maximum take-off weight
Payload: six passengers or equivalent freight

JUNKERS JU 60/160

GERMANY: 1932

Crew: 2
Powerplant: one 448kW (600hp) BMW Hornet radial engine
Performance: max speed 340km/h (211mph); endurance 3 hrs 12 mins; service ceiling 5200m (17,060ft)
Dimensions: wingspan 14.32m (46ft 11.75in); length 12.00m (39ft 4.5in); height 3.92m (12ft 10in)
Weight: 3450kg (7606lb) loaded
Payload: six passengers

THE JUNKERS JU 60, which first flew in 1932, was a single-engined, low-wing monoplane in the same class as the Lockheed Orion high-speed airliner. Only two Ju 60s were built, but in 1934 an improved version, the Ju 160, made its appearance. Forty-eight Ju 160s were built, entering service with Lufthansa during 1935–36. As well as operating on domestic

One of the Junkers Ju 160A-0s, D-UQOR 'Löwe' (Lion) which saw service on several of Lufthansa's internal routes.

routes, the Ju 160s also flew on the Breslau–Prague–Munich route. Most were commandeered by the Luftwaffe on the outbreak of World War II and were widely used for communications and training.

JUNKERS JU 52/3M

GERMANY: 1934

Crew: 2/3
Powerplant: three 545kW (730hp) BMW 132T-2 9-cylinder radial engines
Performance: max speed 286km/h (178mph); range 1305km (811 miles); service ceiling 5900m (19,360ft)

Dimensions: wingspan 29.20m (95ft 10in); length 18.90m (62ft); height 4.52m (14ft 10in)
Weight: 11,030kg (24,317lb) loaded
Armament/Payload: four 7.92mm (0.31in) machine guns; 18 troops or 12 stretcher cases

IN 1934, A MILITARY version of the civil Junkers Ju 52/3m airliner was produced for use by the still-secret Luftwaffe. Designated Ju 52/3mg3e, the aircraft was designed as a heavy bomber, but became most famous as a transport. From 1934–35, no

---

JODEL D.9 BEBE
This single-seat French monoplane light aircraft was designed shortly after World War II. Today, successor companies continue to offer this wood/fabric design in kit form.

JODEL D.140 MOUSQUETAIRE
A French light, single-engined touring and club aeroplane also produced by a number of other companies under licence and dating from the 1940s.

JODEL D.11 SERIES
A two-seat development of the single-seat D.9 light aircraft, with a Salmson engine, the D.11 proved equally popular with private flyers and clubs.

JONA J-6/S
The Jona J-6/S, which appeared in 1935, was an Italian two-seat sesquiplane trainer. The aircraft was powered by a 179kW (240hp) Alfa D2C30 engine.

JOVAIR SEDAN 4E
The Sedan 4E was a four-seat tandem rotor helicopter of the early 1960s designed by D.K. Jovanovich as a refinement of the JOV-3 of 1948 and the McCulloch MC-4 of 1951, both tandem two-seaters. In 1953 a further two-seat version, the MC-4C, was evaluated by the USAF as the YH-300, and the prototype Sedan 4E was actually an MC-4C airframe.

JUNKERS CL.I
An angular, low-wing all-metal monoplane that first flew in March 1918, the Junkers CL.I was the best assault aircraft produced by Germany in World War I; however, only 47 examples were delivered before the Armistice.

JUNKERS RO2
Developed from the Junkers A20 mailplane of 1923, the Junkers RO2 low-wing monoplane reconnaissance aircraft was built for the Red Air Force, with which it served in the late 1920s.

fewer than 450 Ju 52/3ms were delivered to the Luftwaffe. The type featured prominently in the Spanish Civil War, flying 5400 sorties for the loss of eight aircraft. In April 1940, the Ju 52 was at the forefront of the German invasions of Denmark and Norway. About 475 Ju 52s were available for the invasion of the Netherlands, while 493 took part in the invasion of Crete in May 1941. By the end of the year, around 300 Ju 52s were operating in the Mediterranean theatre. On the Russian front, five Ju 52 Gruppen took part in the Stalingrad airlift. Total production of the Ju 52/3m between 1939 and 1944, including civil models, was 4845 aircraft.

The venerable 'Tante Ju' (Auntie Ju) saw widespread service as an airliner and a military transport, as well as being adapted for special roles. Seen here is an aircraft of Swissair.

JUNKERS JU 86   GERMANY: 1934

THE JUNKERS JU 86 was designed in 1934 to the same specification as the Heinkel He 111, the requirement being for an aircraft capable of filling the dual roles of bomber and commercial transport. The first two production variants, the Ju 86D and Ju 86E, entered service in the first half of 1936. The aircraft was further developed as a civil transport (Ju 86B, Ju 86F and Ju 86Z), bomber trainer (Ju 86G) and export bomber (Ju 86K), the latter being sold to Sweden, Chile, Portugal and Hungary. The Ju 86P and Ju 86R were high-altitude photo-reconnaissance versions.

A civilian Junkers Ju 86 is pictured here. The South African Air Force used the Ju 86 in the bombing role during East African operations in 1941.

Thirteen civilian Ju 86s were converted to bombers by the South African Air Force in 1939.
Specifications apply to Ju 86K.

Crew: 4
Powerplant: two 448kW (600hp) Junkers Jumo 205C-4 diesel engines
Performance: max speed 325km/h (202mph); range 1140km (708 miles); service ceiling 5900m (19,360ft)
Dimensions: wingspan 22.50m (73ft 9in); length 17.57m (58ft 7in); height 5.06m (16ft 7in)
Weight: 8200kg (18,078lb) loaded
Armament: three 7.92mm (0.31in) machine guns; 1000kg (2205lb) internal bomb load

JUNKERS JU 87 STUKA   GERMANY: 1935

Crew: 2
Powerplant: one 1044kW (1400hp) Junkers Jumo 211J inverted-Vee engine
Performance: max speed 410km/h (255mph); range 1535km (954 miles); service ceiling 7300m (23,950ft)
Dimensions: wingspan 13.80m (45ft 3.33in); length 11.50m (37ft 8in); height 3.88m (12ft 9in)
Weight: 6600kg (14,550lb) loaded
Armament: three 7.92mm (0.31in) machine guns; external bomb load of up to 1800kg (3968lb)

THE WORD 'Stuka' was applied to all German bomber aircraft with a dive-bombing capability during World War II, but it will forever be associated with the Junkers Ju 87. The first prototype Ju 87V1 flew in the late spring of 1935, powered by a 477kW (640hp) Rolls-Royce Kestrel engine. In December 1937, three production Ju 87A-1s were sent to Spain for operational trials with the Kondor Legion, flying in support of the Spanish Nationalists. The Ju 87A-2 subseries, the next to appear, was succeeded on the production line in 1938 by an extensively modified version, the Ju 87B. An anti-shipping version of the Ju 87B-2 was known as the Ju 87R. The next production model was the Ju 87D. The Ju 87E and F were proposals only, and the last Stuka variant was the Ju 87G, a standard Ju 87D-5 converted to carry two BK37 cannon (37mm/1.46in Flak 18 guns) under the wing. Specifications apply to the Ju 87D.

A Junkers Ju 87D-3 of the 6th Dive Bomber Group, 1st Romanian Air Corps, in 1943. Originally Germany's ally, Romania changed sides in 1944 and turned its surviving Stukas against German targets.

JUNKERS JU 88

GERMANY: 1936

A Junkers Ju 88A-4 of KG.30. This unit specialized in anti-shipping attacks, and this particular aircraft's tally of Allied vessels sunk is recorded on its tail fin.

ONE OF THE MOST versatile and effective combat aircraft ever produced, the Junkers Ju 88 remained of vital importance to the Luftwaffe throughout World War II, serving as a bomber, dive-bomber, night-fighter, close-support aircraft, long-range heavy fighter, reconnaissance aircraft and torpedo-bomber. The prototype Ju 88 (D-AQEN) flew for the first time on 21 December 1936, powered by two 746kW (1000hp) DB 600A in-line engines. A pre-series batch of Ju 88A-0s was completed during the summer of 1939, with the first production Ju 88A-1s being delivered to a test unit, Erprobungskommando 88. In August 1939, this unit was redesignated I/KG 25, and soon afterwards it became I/KG 30, carrying out its first operational mission – an attack on British warships in the Firth of Forth – in September. The same target was attacked on 16 October, when two Ju 88s were shot down by Spitfires. The Ju 88A was built in 17 different variants up to the Ju 88A-17, with progressively uprated engines, enhanced defensive armament and improved defensive capability. The most widely used variant was the Ju 88A-4, which served in both Europe and North Africa. Twenty Ju 88A-4s were supplied to Finland, and some were supplied to Italy, Romania and Hungary. Some 7000 examples of the Ju 88A series were delivered. The Ju 88As saw considerable action in the Balkans and the Mediterranean, and on the Eastern Front. They operated intensively during the German invasion of Crete, and were the principal threat to the island of Malta and its supply convoys. Some of their most outstanding service, however, was in the Arctic, where aircraft of KG 26 and KG 30, based in northern Norway, carried out devastating attacks on Allied convoys to Russia.

The Ju 88B was the subject of a separate development programme, and eventually evolved into the Ju 188, which made its operational debut later in the war. Chronologically, the next major production model was the Ju 88C heavy fighter, which entered service with NJG.1 in the late summer of 1940 and was used for intruder operations over the British Isles. It was followed by a relatively small number of Ju 88C-4s, using the same extended-span wing of the Ju 88A-4, and the C-5. The Ju 88C-6, and the last variant in this series, the C-7, were used as both day and night fighters. In the day fighter role, the principal area of operations was the Bay of Biscay, where the Ju 88s provided cover for U-boats transiting to and from their patrol areas in the Atlantic. The last fighter variant of the Ju 88, which made its appearance in the spring of 1944, was the Ju 88G. This version, which used the angular tail unit of the Ju 188 and carried improved Lichtenstein AI radar, was a highly effective night-fighter. Two more

subvariants, the Ju 88H-2 and the Ju 88R, brought the fighter Ju 88 line to an end. A specialist version of the Ju 88, the Ju 88P, also made its appearance during World War II. This was designed for ground-attack and anti-tank work, mainly on the Russian Front, and was armed with either a 75mm (2.95in) gun (Ju 88P-1) or two 37mm (1.46in) cannon (Ju 88P-2). Total Junkers 88 production was 14,676 aircraft, of which about 3900 were fighter or ground-attack variants.

Specifications apply to the Junkers Ju 88A-4.

Crew: 4
Powerplant: two 1000kW (1340hp) Junkers Jumo 211J inverted V-12 engines
Performance: max speed 450km/h (280mph); range 2730km (1696 miles); service ceiling 8200m (26,900ft)
Dimensions: wingspan 20.00m (65ft 7in); length 14.40m (47ft 3in); height 4.85m (15ft 11in)
Weight: 14,000kg (30,865lb) loaded
Armament: up to seven 7.92mm (0.31in) MG15 or MG81 machine guns; maximum internal and external bomb load of 3600kg (7935lb)

Junkers 88 crews are seen here being briefed by their flight commander before taking off on a sortie during World War II.

JUNKERS G31
A larger triple-engined successor to the G23 and G24, the G31 had capacity for 15 passengers and first flew in 1926. Thirteen examples of the G.31 were built, and some were used in a freight role until 1942.

JUNKERS R42
First flown in 1927, the Junkers R42 monoplane medium bomber was built in the USSR, Sweden and Turkey. It was designated G1 in Russian service

JUNKERS G38
Another all-metal Junkers design with four engines. First flying in 1929, only two G38 examples were built, but it could carry a remarkable 34 passengers. Another six were produced in Japan as the Mitsubishi Ki.20 for military use.

JUNKERS JU 46
A development of the Junkers W.34, the Ju 46 of 1932 was a single-engined floatplane, designed to be catapulted from fast mail vessels on the transatlantic routes.

JUNKERS EF 61
The Junkers EF 61, flown in 1936, was a high-altitude research aircraft. It provided valuable data for the programmes which resulted in the Ju 86P and Ju 86R reconnaissance aircraft.

JUNKERS JU 89
The Junkers Ju 89 was a four-engined heavy bomber, first flown in December 1936. A second prototype was also built before the programme was abandoned.

JUNKERS JU 187
The Junkers Ju 187 was a planned replacement for the Ju 87 Stuka, with an extended wing, improved engine and fully retractable undercarriage. It was not adopted.

JUNKERS JU 90

THE JUNKERS JU 90 used the same wings, tail assembly and undercarriage of the abandoned Ju 89 bomber, the two types having been developed in parallel. The 40-passenger Ju 90 commercial transport began trials in August 1937 and subsequently made several record flights, but suffered many teething troubles and was lost on a test flight when a wing failed. The Ju 90 did not see airline service, but 13 development aircraft were built, and seven of these were impressed by the Luftwaffe for transport duties in 1943 as Ju 90B-1s.

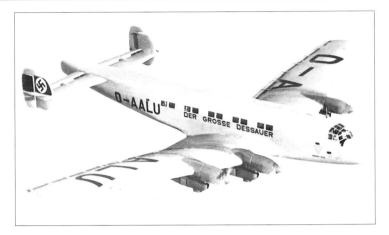

The Junkers Ju 90V-1 D-AALU, which was adapted from the Ju 89V-3 and crashed during flutter trials on 6 February 1938.

Crew: 4/5
Powerplant: four 1119kW (1550hp) BMW 139 radial engines
Performance: max speed 350km/h (217mph); range 2092km (1300 miles); service ceiling 5500m (18,044ft)
Dimensions: wingspan 35.02m (114ft 10in); length 26.30m (86ft 3in); height 6.10m (20ft)
Weight: 23,000kg (50,706lb) loaded
Armament: one 7.9mm (0.31in) machine gun

JUNKERS JU 188/388

CHARACTRERIZED BY ITS large, bulbous 'glasshouse' nose and an extended wing with pointed tips, the Junkers Ju 188 first flew in the latter half of 1940, the production Ju 188E-1 becoming operational in 1942. Several variants followed. The Ju 388 was a progressive development of the Ju 188. Specifications apply to the Ju 188E-1.

The Junkers Ju 388V-3 pictured in 1944. The V-3 was the prototype for the Ju 388K bomber.

Crew: 4
Powerplant: two 1194kW (1600hp) BMW 801ML radial engines
Performance: max speed 500km/h (310mph); range 2480km (1541 miles); service ceiling 9300m (30,513ft)
Dimensions: wingspan 22.00m (72ft 2in); length 15.06m (49ft 5in); height 4.46m (14ft 7in)
Weight: 14,570kg (32,121lb) loaded
Armament: one 20mm (0.79in) cannon; two 13mm (0.51in) and one 7.92mm (0.31in) machine guns; 3000kg (6614lb) of bombs

JUNKERS JU 290

Crew: 7-9
Powerplant: four 1194kW (1600hp) BMW 810L 14-cylinder radial engines
Performance: max speed 439km/h (273mph); range 6150km (3820 miles); service ceiling 6000m (19,685ft)
Dimensions: wingspan 42.00m (137ft 9in); length 28.63m (93ft 11in); height 6.83m (22ft 5in)
Weight: 40,970kg (90,323lb) loaded
Armament: six 20mm (0.79in) cannon and one 13mm (0.51in) machine gun

THE JUNKERS JU 290 was a progressive development of the Ju 90. The prototype, which flew in 1941, was the re-engined Ju 90V-7. The first two production Ju 90A-1s were transports, but in 1943 the design was adapted to the maritime reconnaissance role. The aircraft was given an anti-ship capability, being able to carry a pair of Hs 293 or Fritz-X missiles. In the transport role, the Ju 290 was capable of carrying 40 troops. Fifty Ju 290s were delivered to the Luftwaffe.

Early in 1939, the Junkers Ju 90V-5 Württemberg, seen here, was withdrawn from service and completely rebuilt as the first development aircraft in the Ju 90S (later Ju 290) programme.

JUNKERS JU 390

GERMANY: 1943

Early in 1944, a six-engined Ju 390 flew from its base in Mont-de-Marsan, France, to within 20km (12 miles) of New York.

Crew: 10
Powerplant: six 1268kW (1700hp) BMW 801D radial engines
Performance: max speed 505km/h (314mph); range 9700km (6027 miles); service ceiling 6100m (20,000ft)
Dimensions: wingspan 50.30m (165ft 1in); length 34.00m (112ft 2.5in); height 6.90m (22ft 7.75in)
Weight: 75,500kg (146,477lb)
Armament: five 20mm (0.79in) cannon; three 13mm (0.51in) machine guns

IN DECEMBER 1941, following the entry of the United States into the war, the German Air Ministry began to reconsider several proposals already made by various aircraft manufacturers for a bomber with sufficient range to attack New York from bases in Europe. One such proposal was the Junkers Ju 390, which made use of a large number of existing Ju 290 components. The Ju 390 was a larger aircraft, a substantial increase in wingspan allowing the installation of two additional engines. The prototype Ju 390V-1 flew in August 1943 and the Ju 390V-2 in October. The latter aircraft was delivered FAGr 5 (Long-Range Reconnaissance Group 5) at Mont-de-Marsan, France, in January 1944. A third prototype, the Ju 390V-3, was begun, but never completed.

JUNKERS JU 287

GERMANY: 1944

ONE OF THE MORE unorthodox aircraft to emerge from World War II, the Junkers Ju 287 jet bomber featured swept-forward wings, two of its four turbojets being wing-mounted and the others mounted on either side of the forward fuselage. The fuselage itself was adapted from that of a Heinkel He 177A bomber. The Ju 287V-1 made its first flight on 16 August 1944, the heavy machine being assisted by a rocket unit on take-off.

Crew: 4
Powerplant: four 900kg (1980lb) Junkers Jumo 109-004B-1 turbojet engines
Performance: max speed 865km/h (537mph); range 2125km (1320mph); service ceiling 12,000m (39,360ft)
Dimensions: wingspan 20.11m (65ft 11.75in); length 18.6m (61ft); height not known
Weight: 21,520kg (47,450lb) loaded
Armament: (planned) bomb load of 4000kg (8820lb)

This view clearly shows the unorthodox configuration of the Ju 287V-1, with its swept-forward wings.

JUNKERS JU 252
The all-metal Junkers Ju 252, which first flew in 1941, was designed as a successor to the Ju 52. Only 15 aircraft were built before production switched to the Ju 352.

JUNKERS JU 288/488
The Junkers Ju 288 was an elegant twin-engined bomber with twin fins. The first Ju 288 flew in the spring of 1941 and several prototypes were built, some being issued for service use. The Ju 488 was a four-engined bomber prototype, which was built, but did not fly.

JUNKERS JU 322 MAMMUT
The Junkers Ju 322 Mammut (Mammoth) was a massive transport glider with a wingspan of 62m (203ft 5in). It was flight tested in 1941, but abandoned.

JUNKERS JU 352 HERKULES
First flown in 1943, the Junkers Ju 352 Herkules three-engined transport was of mixed wood and steel construction with fabric covering. In all, 33 production Ju 352A-1s were delivered, being used mainly for special operations.

JUNKERS EF 126 ELLI
The Junkers EF 126 Elli, designed for ground attack, was similar in layout to the Fi 103 flying bomb. It never flew in Germany, but the Russians built an unpowered prototype which crashed on landing, killing its pilot.

JUNKERS EF 128
The Junkers EF 128 was a tailless jet-fighter project and was designed to be armed with two 30mm (1.18in) cannon. It was never built.

JUNKERS EF 130
The Junkers EF 130 was an all-wing four-jet bomber project, the engines being grouped side by side above the wing centre section. It was not built.

KAMAN MODEL 600 (H-43A/B/HH-43F HUSKIE)

USA: 1947

Crew: 2 (total accommodation for 11 people)
Powerplant: one 615kW (825shp) Lycoming T53-L-11A turboshaft engine
Performance: max speed 193km/h (120mph); combat radius 810km (500 miles); service ceiling 7010m (23,000ft)
Dimensions: rotor diameter 14.33m (47ft); length 7.67m (25ft 2in); height 4.73m (15ft 6.5in)
Weight: 2095kg (4619lb)
Armament: one 7.62mm (0.30in) flexible mount machine gun

CHARLES H. KAMAN established the Kaman Aircraft Corporation in December 1945 to manufacture a new rotor and control system. Late in 1946, his basic intermeshing rotor system and its servo flap control appeared in the experiential K-125A, which flew on 15 January 1947. In 1948 the improved K-190 appeared, while in 1950 the three-

An H-43A at Kaman's Bloomfield facility in 1963. Some 18 H-43A Huskies were ordered by the USAF.

seat K-225 appeared. That same year the US Navy acquired two examples for evaluation purposes, and a contract for 29 HTK-1 trainers (from 1962, TH-43E) models followed. On 10 December

1951, meanwhile, one of the original K-225s powered by a 130kW (175shp) Boeing YT50 gas turbine engine was the first helicopter in the world to have its rotors powered by a turbine

engine. The K-600 was ordered by the USMC and USN as the HOK-1 and HUK-1 (redesignated UH-43C and OH-43D in 1962) respectively. Some 18 H-43A Huskies, similar to the USMC HUK-1 were ordered by the USAF and were followed by 193 examples of the more powerful and slightly larger H-43B (later HH-43B) first flown on 13 December 1958. Some 31 of these were supplied under the US Military Assistance Program to Burma, Colombia, Morocco, Pakistan and Thailand. Final production version was the HH-43F, 40 of which were built for the USAF and 17 for Iran.

Specifications apply to the Kaman HH-43F Huskie.

KAMAN UH-2 SEASPRITE AND SUPER SEASPRITE

USA: 1959

THE UH-2 WAS WINNER of a 1956 US Navy design competition for a high-performance, all-weather, long-range search-and-rescue, liaison and utility helicopter. The award led to a contract in late 1957 for four single-engined prototypes and 12 production HU2K-1 helicopters (later UH-2A Seasprite). The

prototype flew on 2 July 1959 and 84 HU2K-1 (from 1962 UH-2A) production models with single GE T58-GE-8 turboshafts followed. Next came 190 UH-2B examples. From 1967 all surviving UH-2A/B Seasprites were progressively converted to UH-2C standard with two 932kW (1250shp) GE T58-

GE-8B turboshafts in place of the former single T58. Further modification to SH-2D standard followed under the US Navy's LAMPS (Light Airborne Multi-Purpose System) programme to provide helicopters for ASW (anti-submarine warfare) and ASMD (anti-ship missile defence)

operations. The Seasprite was first used in the ASW role in October 1970. In May 1973, deliveries of the definitive SH-2F LAMPS I began. Some 88 machines were converted from earlier variants and 16 surviving SH-2D examples were also brought up to the same standard, which introduced an improved main rotor, strengthened landing gear, a tail wheel located almost 1.83m (6ft) further forward and 1007kW (1350shp) T58-GE-8F engines. In 1981 production of the Seasprite was resumed with the first of 60 new-build SH-2Fs. These subsequently received upgrades and modifications with the addition of chaff/flare dispensers to allow them to operate in the 1991 Gulf War. Specifications apply to the SH-2G Super Seasprite.

Crew: 3
Powerplant: two GE T700-GE-401/401C turboshaft engines each rated at 1285kW (1723shp)
Performance: max speed 256km/h (159mph); combat radius 885km (500 miles); service ceiling 7285m (23,900ft)
Dimensions: main rotor diameter 13.51m (44ft 4in); length 16.08m (52ft 9in); height 4.58m (15ft 0.5in)
Weight: 3483kg (7680lb)
Armament/payload: (with sonobuoy removed) up to four passengers, or two litters or freight carried in the cabin, or 1814kg (4000lb) of freight carried as a slung load

This photograph shows an SH-2D of the US Navy's HSL-31 from the USS *Harold E. Holt*.

KAMOV KA-20 'HARP'/KA-25 'HORMONE'   FORMER USSR: 1960

Ka-25 'Hormones' aboard the anti-submarine cruiser *Moskva*. The 'Hormone-B' (Ka-25K) is able to acquire targets for ship-launched missiles. The Hormone-C (Ka-25PS) is a dedicated SAR and transport version.

Crew: 2
Powerplant: (early versions) two OMKB 'Mars' (Glushenkov) GTD-3F turboshaft engines each rated at 671kW (898shp)
Performance: max speed 209km/h (130mph); combat radius 400km (249 miles); service ceiling 3350m (10,990ft)
Dimensions: rotor diameter 15.74m (52ft 7.75in); length 9.75m (32ft)
Weight: 4765kg (10,505lb)
Armament: two ASW torpedoes, conventional or nuclear depth charges and other stores up to a maximum of 1900kg (4190lb)

FIRST SEEN BY WESTERN observers at the 1961 Soviet Aviation Day, the Ka-20 was later regarded as the prototype of the Ka-25 (NATO reporting name 'Hormone'). Although larger and with twin-turbine powerplant, it was obviously derived from the Ka-15 and Ka-18. Three versions of the Hormone totalling about 460 examples were built from 1966–75. Some 260 'Hormone-A' ASW basic ship-based helicopters were produced. The 'Hormone-B' (Ka-25K), externally

identifiable by its bulbous instead of flat-bottomed undernose radome and small datalink radome under the rear fuselage, is a target-seeking electronics variant. The 'Hormone-C' (Ka-25PS) is a dedicated SAR and transport version able to carry up to 12 passengers or a practical load of freight. About 190 Ka-25K and –25PS versions were built and the latter has been largely replaced by SAR versions of the Ka-27 'Helix'. Specifications apply to Ka-25BSh 'Hormone-A'.

KAMOV KA-27/32 'HELIX'   FORMER USSR: 1974

Crew: 3
Powerplant: two Klimov (Isotev) TV3-117V turboshaft engines each rated at 1633kW (2190shp)
Performance: max speed 250km/h (155mph) combat radius 800km (497 miles); service ceiling 5000m (16,404ft)
Dimensions: rotor diameter 15.90m (52ft 2in); length 11.27m (36ft 11.75in); height

5.45m (17ft 10.5in)
Weight: 6100kg (13,448lb)
Armament/Payload: up to 2000kg (4410lb) of disposable stores in a lower fuselage weapons bay, comprising (typically) four APR-2E homing torpedoes or four groups of S3V guided anti-submarine bombs; up to 5000kg (11,023lb) of freight

The Ka-27PL ('Helix-A') basic anti-submarine warfare version, a replacement for the Ka 25BSh.

SIMILAR IN APPEARANCE to the Ka-25 'Hormone' which it was designed to replace, the Ka-27 'Helix' offered more than twice the power and the ability to operate with sonar at night and in all weathers. The prototype of the Ka-27PL ('Helix-A') basic ASW version flew in December 1974 and service delivery began in 1982 in the hunter-killer role. The principal SAR and planeguard variant is the radar-equipped Ka-27PS 'Helix-D', and the Ka-28 'Helix-A' is the export version of the Ka-27PL for China, India, Vietnam and Yugoslavia. Ka-32 'Helix-C' is the multi-role development of the Ka-27 for military and civil use. A number of Ka-32 subversions are used for utility, transport, fire-fighting and marine duties.

Specifications apply to the Ka-27PL 'Helix A'.

KAMOV KA-50 AND KA-52 'HOKUM' FORMER USSR: 1982

A SINGLE-SEAT BATTLEFIELD air-combat and close-air support helicopter, the Ka-50 has a super-imposed pair of contra-rotating co-axial rotors in combination with an aircraft-type fuselage. The first prototype flew on 17 June 1982, and the Ka-50 was adopted late in 1986. The Ka-50N nocturnal version first flew in mid-1997. The Ka-52 Alligator ('Hokum-B') is a two-seat conversion trainer and day/night combat derivative of the Ka-50. Specifications apply to the Ka-50 Chernaya Akula 'Hokum-A'.

Crew: 1
Powerplant: two Klimov TV3-117VK turboshaft engines each rated at 1635kW (2193shp)
Performance: max speed 300km/h (186mph); combat radius 540km (279 miles); service ceiling 5500m (18,040ft)
Dimensions: rotor diameter 14.50m (47ft 7in); length 16.00m (52ft 6in); height 4.93m (16ft 2in)
Weight: 7800kg (17,196lb)
Armament: one 30mm (1.18in) 2A42 cannon plus up to 3000kg (6614lb) of disposable stores carried on four underwing hardpoints

The Ka-50's nose sensors reduce the pilot's workload and include provision for third-party target acquisition. In an emergency, the pilot's ejection sequence begins with automatic explosive separation of the two rotor's six blades and the doors before egress.

KAWANISHI H6K 'MAVIS' JAPAN: 1936

THE KAWANISHI H6K, known to the Allies by the code name 'Mavis', was designed to meet an Imperial Japanese Navy requirement for a high-performance long-range reconnaissance flying boat. The prototype flew on 14 July 1936, and the first 10 aircraft entered service as the H6K-2. The H6K-4, which appeared in 1940, was the major production model, 127 examples being produced. In 1941 production switched to an updated version, the H6K-5, of which 36 were built. The H6K proved extremely vulnerable to fighter attack, mainly because it lacked armour protection for the crew and its fuel tanks were not self-sealing. From 1943, it was gradually assigned to the transport role. Specifications apply to the H6K-4.

Crew: 9
Powerplant: two 969kW (1300hp) Mitsubishi Kinsei 51/53 14-cylinder radial engines
Performance: max speed 385km/h (239mph); range 6772km (4208 miles); service ceiling 9560m (31,365ft)
Dimensions: wingspan 40.00m (131ft 2in); length 25.63m (84ft); height 6.27m (20ft 6in)
Weight: 23,000kg (50,706lb) loaded
Armament: one 20mm (0.79in) cannon and four 7.7mm (0.303in) machine guns; torpedo and bomb load of 1600kg (3527lb)

The Kawanishi H6K 'Mavis' had an excellent long-range performance, but lacked some essentials, including self-sealing fuel tanks, which made it easy prey for Allied fighters.

KAWANISHI H8K 'EMILY'   JAPAN: 1941

Crew: 10
Powerplant: four 1380kW (1850hp)
Mitsubishi Kasei 22 14-cylinder radial
engines
Performance: max speed 467km/h
(290mph); range 7180km (4460 miles);
service ceiling 8760m (28,740m)
Dimensions: wingspan 38.00m
(124ft 6in); length 28.13m (92ft 3in);
height 9.15m (30ft)
Weight: 32,500kg (71,650lb) loaded
Armament: five 20mm (0.79in) cannon
and four 7.7mm (0.303in) machine guns;
up to 2000kg (4409lb) of bombs or two
800kg (1764lb) torpedoes

CONSIDERED BY MANY to be one
of the finest flying boats ever
produced, the Kawanishi H8K,
known to the Allies as 'Emily',
was designed to replace the H6K.
The prototype flew in January
1941, and the first production
model, the H8K-1, entered service
with the Imperial Japanese Navy
early in 1942. Only 14 H8K-1s
were built before production
switched to the H8K-2, with 148
examples of this version being
delivered. These included a batch

This photograph of a Kawanishi H8K flying boat on take-off shows the aircraft's hull shape to good advantage.

of 36 H8K-2L transports. The Emily
carried a very heavy defensive
armament and was by no means an
easy opponent for Allied fighters.

Indeed, this defensive armament
was one of its best features.
   Specifications apply to the
Kawanishi H8K-2.

KAWANISHI N1K1-J SHIDEN 'GEORGE'   JAPAN: 1943

Production of the Kawanishi N1K1-J Shiden was seriously disrupted by American strategic bombing offensives.

KNOWN BY THE Allied code name
'George', the Shiden (Violet
Lightning) was a land-based
fighter which rather unusually was
developed from the Kyofu fighter
floatplane. Production started in

August 1943, and the Shiden proved
to be one of the finest fighter
aircraft to see action in the Pacific
Theatre. It was produced in two
models, the N1K1-J and the
N1K2-J model 21, the latter having

a redesigned airframe that had its
wing lowered from the mid-fuselage
point to the lower fuselage and
featured modified tail surfaces. Both
operational models were prominent
in the Philippines, around Formosa
and in the defence of the Japanese
home islands. Production totalled
1098 N1K1-Js and 415 N1K2-Js.
In the hands of a skilled pilot the
Shiden was a formidable weapon;
in February 1945, for example, the
Japanese ace Kaneyoshi Muto
engaged 12 US Navy Hellcats
single-handed and destroyed four
of them, forcing the others to break
off combat. Specifications apply to
the N1K2-J Shiden.

Crew: 1
Powerplant: one 1485kW (1990hp)
Nakajima NK9H Homare 21 18-cylinder
radial engine
Performance: max speed 581km/h
(361mph); range 2544km (1581 miles);
service ceiling 12,500m (41,010ft)
Dimensions: wingspan 12.00m (39ft 4in);
length 8.88m (29ft 1in); height 4.06m
(13ft 3in)
Weight: 4000kg (8818lb) loaded
Armament: four 20mm (0.79in) cannon
and two 7.7mm (0.303in) machine guns

KAWANISHI H3K2
Designed by Short Brothers, the
Kawanishi H3K2 was a biplane
flying boat used for reconnaissance
and training by the Imperial
Japanese Navy between 1932 and
1936.

KAWANISHI E15K-1 SHIUN
Code-named 'Norm' by the Allies,
the Kawanishi E15K-1 Shiun
(Violet Cloud) was a fast three-seat
reconnaissance floatplane. It first
flew in December 1941.

KAWANISHI N1K KYOFU
The Kawanishi N1K Kyofu
(Mighty Wind) fighter floatplane,
which appeared in 1942, had an
excellent performance. Only 89
were built, the decision having
been taken to convert the type to a
landplane fighter configuration.

KAWASAKI KI-32
The Kawasaki Ki-32 monoplane
bomber made its appearance in
1937 and was ordered into
production for the Japanese Army
as the Type 98. The 846 examples
built were used mainly in China.

KAWASAKI KI-48
The Kawasaki Ki-48 was a twin-
engined light bomber monoplane.
It first flew in July 1939 and
entered production as the Type 99.
Its Allied code-name was 'Lily'.

KAWASAKI KI-56
The Kawasaki Ki-56 twin-engined
transport, first flown in 1940, was
an improved version of the
Lockheed 14. Code-named 'Thalia'
by the Allies, the type was used in
airborne operations.

KAWASAKI KI-66
The Kawasaki Ki-66 was a twin-
engined dive-bomber. Six
prototypes were built between
October 1942 and April 1943, but
development work was suspended.

KAWASAKI KI-78
The Kawasaki Ki-78 was a single-
engined high-speed research
aircraft, first flown in 1942. It
made 32 flights, reaching a
maximum speed of 699.6km/h
(434.9mph).

KAWASAKI KI-91
Initiated in 1943, the Kawasaki
Ki-91 was a four-engined heavy
bomber project. It was suspended
in February 1945 when tooling was
destroyed in a B-29 raid.

KAWASAKI KI-3

Crew: 2
Powerplant: one 492kW (660hp) BMW
VIII liquid-cooled in-line engine
Performance: max speed 259km/h
(161mph); endurance 3 hrs; service
ceiling 7005m (22,982ft)
Dimensions: wingspan 13.00m (42ft 8in);
length 10.00m (32ft 8in); height 3.00m
(9ft 10in)
Weight: 3097kg (6827lb) loaded
Armament: two 7.7mm (0.303in) machine
guns; up to 500kg (1104lb) of bombs

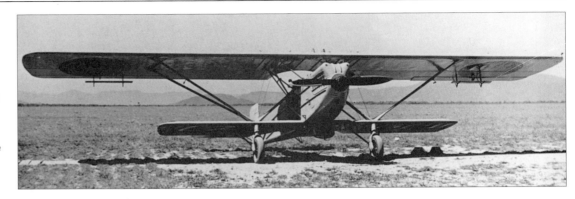

Like other Japanese types of the interwar years, the Kawasaki Ki-3 was designed with foreign – in this case,
German – help. It was not an outstanding aircraft.

DEVELOPED FROM THE KDA-6
private venture reconnaissance
prototype, the Kawasaki Ki-3 was
designed by German engineer
Richard Vogt, who later became
chief designer for Blohm und Voss.
The first Ki-3 flew in March 1933
and featured an unusual annular
cowling with a nose radiator, but

production aircraft had a more
normal chin radiator. It entered
Japanese Army service as the Type
93, 203 being built by Kawasaki

and a further 40 by Tachikawa. It
was a rugged aircraft, but the Ki-3's
liquid-cooled engine was a constant
source of trouble. The Ki-3 first

saw service with the 6th Composite
Air Regiment in Korea. The type,
which was Japan's last biplane
bomber, saw action in China.

KAWASAKI KI-45 TORYU 'NICK'

The Ki-45 Toryu –Allied code name 'Nick' – was one of the most effective Japanese home defence night-fighters.

EARLY IN 1937, THE Imperial
Japanese Army ordered Kawasaki
to initiate design and development
of a twin-engined heavy fighter
suitable for long-range operations
over the Pacific. The result was the
Kawasaki Ki-45 Toryu (Dragon
Slayer), the prototype of which
flew in January 1939. The type did

not enter service until autumn 1942
as the Ki-45 Kai-a fighter and the
Ki-45 Kai-b ground-attack and
anti-shipping strike aircraft. The
Ki-45 Kai-c was a night-fighter
version, while the Kai-d was an
improved ground-attack/anti-
shipping variant. Specifications
apply to the Ki-45 Kai-c.

Crew: 2
Powerplant: two 806kW (1080hp)
Mitsubishi Ha-102 14-cylinder radial
engines
Performance: max speed 540km/h
(336mph); range 2000km (1243
miles); service ceiling 10,000m
(32,810ft)
Dimensions: wingspan 15.02m (49ft 3in);

length 11.00m (36ft 1in); height 3.70m
(12ft 1in)
Weight: 5500kg (12,125lb) loaded
Armament: one 37mm (1.45in) fixed
forward-firing cannon in underside of
forward fuselage; two obliquely mounted
20mm (0.79in) cannon in upper central
fuselage; one 7.92mm (0.31in) machine
gun in rear cockpit

KAWASAKI KI-61 HIEN 'TONY'

JAPAN: 1941

The Kawasaki Ki-61 Hien was fitted with a licence-built Daimler-Benz DB.601 in-line engine, which led Allied pilots to believe erroneously that they were encountering Japanese-built Messerschmitt 109s.

CODE-NAMED 'TONY' by the Allies, the Kawasaki Ki-61 Hien (Swallow) was designed to replace the Nakajima Ki-43 Hayabusa in Japanese Army service. Delivered to frontline air units from August 1942, it was the only operational Japanese fighter to feature an inverted-Vee engine (a licence-built Daimler-Benz DB.601). Until Allied pilots became familiar with its appearance it gave rise to erroneous reports that the Japanese

were using Messerschmitt 109s. By the end of the Pacific war, 3028 Ki-61s had been built, serving in all areas. Principal versions were the Ki-61-I (1380 aircraft built in two subvariants, differentiated by their armament); the Ki-61 Kai, with a lengthened fuselage and different armament fits (1274 built); and the Ki-61-II, optimized for high-altitude operation with a Kawasaki Ha.140 engine (374 built). Specifications apply to the Ki-61-I.

Crew: 1
Powerplant: one 877kW (1175hp) Kawasaki Ha.40 12-cylinder inverted-Vee engine
Performance: max speed 592km/h (368mph); range 1100km (684 miles); service ceiling 11,600m (37,730ft)
Dimensions: wingspan 12.00m (39ft 4in); length 8.75m (28ft 8in); height 3.70m (12ft 1in)
Weight: 2950kg (6504lb) loaded
Armament: four 12.7mm (0.50in) machine guns

KAWASAKI KI-100

JAPAN: 1945

Crew: 1
Powerplant: one 1119kW (1500hp) Mitsubishi Ha.112-II 14-cylinder radial engine
Performance: max speed 580km/h (360mph); range 2000km (1242 miles); service ceiling 11,000m (36,090ft)
Dimensions: wingspan 12.00m (39ft 4in); length 8.82m (28ft 11in); height 3.75m (12ft 3in)
Weight: 3495kg (7705lb) loaded
Armament: two 20mm (0.79in) cannon and two 12.7mm (0.50in) machine guns

THE KAWASAKI KI-100, never allocated an Allied code name, was a marriage of convenience between the Ki-61 Hien airframe and the 1119kW (1500hp) Mitsubishi Ha.112-II radial engine, the licence-built DB.601 being in short supply

(these had proved to be unreliable in any case). The 'new' aircraft flew for the first time on 1 February 1945 and conversion of 275 Ki-61-II airframes began immediately. The Ki-100 showed itself to be a very effective high-altitude interceptor.

The Kawasaki Ki-100 was the last single-engined fighter type to enter service with the Imperial Japanese Army Air Force.

KEYSTONE B-4A

THE MOST WIDELY USED USAAC bombers of the late 1920s and early 1930s were those built by the Keystone Aircraft Corporation, beginning with the LB-5 of 1927. The LB-5 fixed the basic configuration of the Keystone bombers, subsequent aircraft (250 being produced in total) differing only in minor structural alterations and engine detail. The last production models were the B-4A and B-6A, both appearing in 1932.

Crew: 5
Powerplant: two 429kW (575hp) Pratt & Whitney Hornet 9-cylinder radial engines
Performance: max speed 195km/h (121mph); range 1376km (855 miles); service ceiling 4300m (14,000ft)
Dimensions: wingspan 22.78m (74ft 9in); length 14.88m (48ft 10in); height 4.80m (15ft 9in)
Weight: 6000kg (13,200lb) loaded
Armament: three 7.62mm (0.30in) Browning machine guns; up to 1130kg (2500lb) of bombs

A Keystone B-4 bomber pictured in flight over Luzon in the Philippines. The design was still in first-line service in 1936, even though it was hopelessly obsolete by that time.

KLEMM KL 107 (MBB BO 207)

The three-seat Kl-107C (pictured) was the last version of this type before it was absorbed into the MBB consortium as the Bo 207.

THE KL 107 LOW-WING, wooden-framed monoplane trainer was designed in Germany during World War II. Early versions were powered by the Hirth HM 500 74.5kW (100hp) engine, and only a small number were completed before the factory was erased by Allied bombing. In 1956 it was decided to reintroduce the Kl-107 as a civil training/touring type, initially as the Kl-107B, but then as the three-seat Kl-107C. Rights to the design were acquired by what became the MBB consortium, and the final version became the Bo 207. Specifications apply to the Kl 107C.

Crew: 1/2
Powerplant: one Continental O-320 112kW (150hp) piston engine
Performance: max speed 234km/h (146mph); range 820km (510 miles)
Dimensions: wingspan 10.80m (35ft 6.75in); length 8.30m (27ft 2.75in)
Weight: not available
Payload: three seats

KOOLHOVEN FK.55

Crew: 1
Powerplant: one 895kW (1200hp) Lorraine-Sterna Vee-type in-line engine
Performance: max speed 520km/h (317mph); range 850km (528 miles); service ceiling 10,106m (33,137ft)
Dimensions: wingspan 9.60m (31ft 6in); length 9.25m (30ft 5in); height 2.60m (8ft 6in)
Weight: 2280kg (5026lb) loaded
Armament: one 20mm (0.79in) cannon and four 7.7mm (0.303in) machine guns

THE KOOLHOVEN FK.55 single-seat fighter monoplane of 1936 was of extremely advanced conception, but was perhaps too radical an idea for its time. The sole prototype built was powered by a special version of the Lorraine-Sterna 12-cylinder water-cooled engine driving two-blade metal controllable-pitch contra-rotating propellers via an extension shaft and Duplex reduction gear.

The FK.55's engine was mounted immediately aft of the cockpit, above the centre of gravity, the extension shaft passing under the pilot's seat. The pilot was seated right over the nose and had an unobstructed view in all directions except vertically downwards, and the plane featured an enclosed cockpit and single-strut landing gear. Early testing, however, revealed insurmountable problems

of ground stability and engine cooling, and the FK.55 project was abandoned after only one example had been built. Despite its ultimate lack of success, the FK.55 did leave a valuable legacy. The FK.55 was the first aircraft to feature an engine 'buried' in the fuselage (ie behind the pilot). Three years later, this concept was revived in the United States by the Bell Company in the design of its P-39 Airacobra.

KOOLHOVEN FK.58

NETHERLANDS: 1938

Crew: 1
Powerplant: one 806kW (1080hp) Gnome-Rhone 14-N9-39 radial engine
Performance: max speed 475km/h (295mph); range 750km (466 miles); service ceiling 10,000m (32,800ft)
Dimensions: wingspan 10.97m (36ft); length 8.68m (28ft 6.5in); height 2.99m (9ft 10in)
Weight: 2750kg (6063lb) loaded
Armament: four 7.5mm (0.29in) machine guns

THE KOOLHOVEN FK.58 was a single-seat monoplane fighter, the prototype flying on 22 September 1938. Fifty examples were ordered by the French Air Force, but supply of the Gnome-Rhone radial engines which were to be installed was subject to serious delays, and only 13 FK.58s became operational. An order placed by the Netherlands Army Air Corps was never fulfilled.

The Koolhoven FK.58's prospects of large-scale production were destroyed when the Germans overran Holland in May 1940.

KYUSHU J7W1 SHINDEN

JAPAN: 1945

THE KYUSHU J7W1 SHINDEN (Magnificent Lightning) was the only aircraft of canard configuration to be ordered into quantity production anywhere in the world during World War II. It was designed in response to a desperate need by the Imperial Japanese Navy for a high-performance, heavily armed interceptor. To test the aircraft's handling qualities three glider models, designated MXY6, were built, and these began trials in the autumn of 1943.

Work on the J7W1 Shinden began in earnest in June 1944, the first prototype being completed within 10 months. The engine, with its 'pusher' propeller, was installed behind the cockpit. The wings were swept, each carrying a fin and rudder assembly at mid-point, while the elevators were mounted close to the extreme nose, which housed four 30mm (1.18in) Mk 5 cannon.

The first prototype J7W1 finally took to the air on 3 August 1945, three days before the Allied atomic bombing of Hiroshima. Two other short flights before Japan's surrender brought the total flight time of the J7W1 Shinden to just 45 minutes. Today, the aircraft resides in the National Air and Space Museum, Washington DC.

Crew: 1
Powerplant: one 1589kW (2130hp) Mitsubishi MK9D 18-cylinder radial engine
Performance: max speed 750km/h (466mph); range 850km (529 miles); service ceiling 12,000m (39,370ft)
Dimensions: wingspan 11.14m (36ft 5in); length 9.66m (31ft 8in); height 3.92m (12ft 10.5in)
Weight: 5228kg (11,526lb) loaded
Armament: four 30mm (1.18in) cannon

The Kyushu J7W1 Shinden seen at Wright Field, Ohio, following the end of World War II. This view clearly shows the aircraft's unorthodox layout. Its armament had not yet been fitted.

Seppo Kokkola's single-seat gyroglider crashed on its first flight in spring 1959. Fitted with a 20kW (28hp) Poinsard engine it was redesignated Ko-2 and first flown in February 1960, but again crashed. As the modified Ko-3 Nousukas, the gyroplane flew successfully on 9 February 1961. The KO-4 two-seat light autogyro first flew on 12 December 1968.

KOKUSAI KI.59
First flown in June 1938, the Kokusai Ki.59 twin-engined light transport went into production as the Army Type 1 Transport. It was known to the Allies as 'Theresa'.

KOKUSAI KI.76
The Kokusai Ki.76 Army Type 3 was an artillery spotter and liaison aircraft closely resembling the Fieseler Storch, except that it was powered by a radial engine. First flight was in May 1941.

KOKUSAI KU-8
The Kokusai Ku-8 was the only Japanese glider to be used in combat, and was basically a Ki.59 light transport with the engines removed. It flew in December 1941.

KOKUSAI KU-7 MANAZURU
The largest glider built in Japan, the Kokusai Ku-7 Manazuru (Crane) first flew in August 1944. It remained experimental.

KOKUSAI KI.105 OHTORI
The Kokusai Ki.105 Ohtori (Phoenix) was a powered version of the Ku.7 glider, designed to ship fuel to Japan. Nine prototypes were tested from April 1945.

KOOLHOVEN FK.50
The Koolhoven FK.50 was a twin-engined eight-passenger monoplane, three of which wre built for a Swiss airline in 1935–38. The FK.50B was a projected bomber version, not developed.

KOOLHOVEN FK.56
The Koolhoven FK.56 of 1937 was a cantilever low-wing monoplane training and reconnaissance aircraft, powered by a Wright Whirlwind radial engine.

KRESS SEAPLANE
A complicated machine designed by Austrian engineer William Kress, and powered by a single engine driving two pusher propellers, the Kress Seaplane was the first floatplane in history. In 1901 it was launched on Lake Tullenbach, near Vienna. Unfortunately, it sank.

KYUSHU K11W SHIRAGIKU

JAPAN: 1942

THE KYUSHU K11W Shiragiku (White Chrysanthemum) was an important aircraft in the Imperial Japanese Navy's inventory, as it was used to train an entire bomber crew. A single-engined, mid-wing monoplane, the prototype K11W flew for the first time in November 1942, and the flight trials programme for the aircraft was completed quickly, with no major problems being encountered.

A Kyushu K11W1 Shiragiku, with surrender markings, seen at Shanghai in late 1945. The aircraft in the background are USAAF Curtiss C-46 transports.

The cockpit arrangement for the crew of five was interesting. The pilot and radio operator/gunner were seated above the wing under a transparent canopy, while the instructor, navigator and

bombardier were accommodated in a cabin below the wing.

The K11W2 was a utility transport and anti-submarine development, produced in small numbers. Late in World War II, an attempt was made to produce a specialized anti-submarine version, which was known as the Q3W1 Nankai (South Sea); however, the prototype was wrecked in a landing accident in January 1945.

Crew: 5
Powerplant: one 358kW (480hp) Hitachi GK2B Amakaze 21 9-cylinder radial engine
Performance: max speed 230km/h (143mph); service ceiling 5620m (18,440ft); range 1758km (1093 miles)
Dimensions: wingspan 14.98m (49ft 1.75in); length 10.24m (33ft 7in); height 3.93m (12ft 11in)
Weight: 2800kg (6173lb) loaded
Armament: one 7.7mm (0.303in) machine gun

KYUSHU Q1W TOKAI

JAPAN: 1943

Crew: 3/4
Powerplant: two 455kW (610hp) Hitachi GK2C 9-cylinder radial engines
Performance: max speed 322km/h (200mph); range 1342km (834 miles); service ceiling 4490m (14,730ft)
Dimensions: wingspan 16.00m (52ft 6in); length 12.00m (39ft 7in); height 4.10m (13ft 6in)
Weight: 4800kg (10,582lb) loaded
Armament: one or two 20mm (0.79in) cannon and one 7.7mm (0.303in) machine gun; two 250kg (551lb) bombs or depth charges

FIRST FLOWN IN September 1943, the Kyushu Q1W Tokai (Eastern Sea) was Japan's first specialized anti-submarine patrol aircraft. It was developed in response to a requirement issued by the Imperial Japanese Navy late in 1942, at a time when US submarines were beginning to take an increasing toll on Japanese shipping. The Q1W1

prototype had pleasant handling characteristics, and the Japanese Navy eventually took delivery of about 150 aircraft. The Q1W

(Allied code name 'Lorna') had a defensive armament of only a single machine gun, which made it vulnerable to fighter attack.

The Kyushu Q1W1 Tokai was designed to make dive-bombing attacks, most of its weapon stations being under the fuselage.

LAKE LA-4 BUCCANEER/RENEGADE/SEAFURY/SEAWOLF   USA: 1959

THE LA-4 SERIES originated in the earlier Colonial C-1 Skimmer of 1948, which was further improved until the Lake Aircraft Company acquired the production facilities and launched the LA-4-200 Buccaneer in 1959. Since then, this single pusher-engine amphibian has been progressively updated with versions such as the six-seat LA-250 Renegade and the LA-270 Renegade with uprated engine, as well as the LA-250 Seawolf armed

Although designed specifically for operations from water, the appropriately named Lake series is capable of using conventional landing strips as required.

military derivative and the LA-270 Seafury with improved salt-water corrosion resistance. Total production is more than 1200 examples of all versions.
Specifications apply to the Lake LA-4-200 Buccaneer.

Crew: 1
Powerplant: one 149kW (200hp) Avco Lycoming IO-360-BIA engine
Performance: max cruising speed 241km/h (150mph); range 1328km (825 miles) with maximum payload; service ceiling 4480m (14,700ft)
Dimensions: wingspan 11.58m (38ft); length 7.59m (24ft 11in); height 2.84m (9ft 4in)
Weight: 1220kg (2690lb) maximum take-off weight
Payload: four persons

LANGLEY AERODROME   USA: 1903

SAMUEL PIERPONT LANGLEY was a leading figure in US 19th-century scientific research. His investigations into heavier-than-air flight began in the 1880s, and he designed a succession of model flying machines, all named the Aerodrome. After several failures with designs too fragile and under-powered to sustain themselves, Langley had his first genuine success on 6 May 1896, when his Aerodrome No 5 made the first

successful flight of an unpiloted, engine-driven, heavier-than-air craft of substantial size. It was launched from a spring-actuated catapult mounted on top of a houseboat on the Potomac River near Quantico, Virginia. Two flights were made that afternoon, one of 1005m (3300ft) and another of 700m (2300ft), at a speed of approximately 40km/h (25mph). On 28 November, a similar model, the Aerodrome No 6, flew a distance

Samuel Pierpont Langley abandoned his efforts to be the first to make a sustained powered flight after the Wright brothers made their historic flight in 1903.

Crew: unpiloted
Powerplant: one 39kW (52.4hp) Balzer water-cooled radial engine
Dimensions: wingspan 14.80m (48ft 5in); length 16.00m (52ft 5in); height 3.5m (11ft 4in)
Weight: 340kg (750lb)

LAIRD LC-DW-300
The Laird LC-DW-300 was an American racing biplane of the early 1930s, which achieved success in the hands of notable pilots such as Jimmy Doolittle. It was the only biplane ever to win the Thomson Trophy.

LAIRD-TURNER LRT METEOR
The Laird-Turner LRT Meteor was an American racing monoplane. It was used by the celebrated aviator Roscoe Turner to win the coveted Thompson Trophy in 1938 and 1939.

LANCAIR LC-40 COLUMBIA
The Lancair LC-40 Columbia made its first flight in 1996 and entered service in 2000. It is a four-seat, single-engined light aeroplane with a fixed tricycle undercarriage.

LATÉCOÈRE 28
The Latécoère 28, which appeared in 1929, was produced in both landplane and seaplane versions, and established several speed, endurance and distance records.

LATÉCOÈRE 28/9
The Latécoère 28/9 was a single-seat, three-engined, high-wing monoplane bomber, three being operated by the Venezuelan Air Force in the early 1930s.

LATÉCOÈRE 521
Named 'Lieutenant de Vaisseau Paris', the Laté 521 stemmed from the Laté 520 commercial flying-boat project of 1930. Rebuilt after being wrecked in a typhoon in 1936, it flew many Atlantic patrols with the French Navy.

LATÉCOÈRE 300 'CROIX DU SUD'

Crew: 4
Powerplant: four 485kW (650hp)
Hispano-Suiza 12Nbr 12-cylinder liquid-
cooled Vee-type engines
Performance: max speed 160km/h
(99.4mph); range 4800km (2982 miles);
service ceiling 4600m (15,090ft)
Dimensions: wingspan 44.20m (145ft);
length 26.20m (85ft 11.5m); height
6.39m (20ft 11in)
Weight: 23,000kg (50,706lb) loaded
Payload: 1000kg (2204lb) of freight

THE LATÉCOÈRE 300 was one of
the most famous flying boats of its
day. It was developed in 1931 in
response to a French government
requirement calling for an aircraft

**The prototype Latécoère 300 'Croix du Sud' with record-breaking aviator
Jean Mermoz standing by the cockpit.**

capable of carrying a tonne of mail
over the South Atlantic route. The
prototype, named 'Croix du Sud'
('Southern Cross') entered service
on 31 December 1933 and established a world record on its
inaugural flight, flying 3679km
(2285 miles) from Marseille to St
Louis, Senegal, in just under 24
hours. The Croix du Sud completed
15 Atlantic crossings between
Dakar and Natal, Brazil, before
being lost at sea on 7 December
1936 with pilot Jean Mermoz and
his crew. Six other Laté 300s were
built, three for Air France and three
for the French Navy, the latter
being designated Laté 302.

LATÉCOÈRE 298

THE LATÉ 298 floatplane, first flown
in 1936, was without doubt one of
the most versatile Allied combat
aircraft to take part in the Battle of
France, serving in the surveillance,
reconnaissance, bomber and attack
roles. Eighty aircraft were delivered
to the Aéronavale before the
armistice; they were never used in
their primary role of torpedo-
bomber during the campaign, being
mainly employed on ground-attack
work in support of the French Army.
Thanks to the aircraft's rugged
construction and high degree of
manoeuvrability, combat losses
were relatively light. There were
four main variants, all of which
were almost identical externally.

The main differences were whether
the wings folded (they did on the
Laté 298B, but not the A and D
models) and whether dual controls

**The Latécoère 298 performed well
during the Battle of France, its
agility enabling it to survive
without suffering excessive losses.**

were fitted (Laté 298 B and F).
Some Laté 298s escaped to French
bases in North Africa, and the type
remained in service until 1946.

Crew: 2/3
Powerplant: one 656kW (880hp)
Hispano-Suiza 12Ycrs-1 12-cylinder Vee-
type engine
Performance: max speed 290km/h
(180mph); range 2200km (1367 miles);
service ceiling 6500m (21,325ft)
Dimensions: wingspan 15.50m (50ft
10in); length 12.56m (41ft 2in); height
5.23m (17ft 1in)
Weight: 4800kg (10,582lb) loaded
Armament: three 7.5mm (0.30in)
machine guns; bomb or torpedo load of
670kg (1477lb)

LAVOCHKIN LaGG-1/LaGG-3

IT WAS NOT UNTIL 1939–40 that
the prototypes of three Soviet
fighters that could really be classed
as modern made their appearance.
The first was the LaGG-1 (I-22). It
was a remarkable little aircraft,
built entirely of wood and bearing
a strong resemblance to France's
Dewoitine D.520. The LaGG-1
flew for the first time in March
1940 and was superseded by an

improved variant, the LaGG-3,
after 100 examples had been built.
Production ended in 1942 after
6427 had been built. Specifications
apply to the LaGG-3.

**This LaGG-3 carries the word
'Moscow' under the cockpit, being
used for the air defence of the
Soviet capital in 1941.**

Crew: 1
Powerplant: one 940kW (1260hp) Klimov
VK-105PF-1 12-cylinder Vee-type engine
Performance: max speed 575km/h
(357mph); range 1000km (621 miles);
service ceiling 9700m (31,825ft)

Dimensions: wingspan 9.80m (32ft 1in);
length 8.81m (28ft 11in); height 2.54m
(8ft 4in)
Weight: 3190kg (7032lb) loaded
Armament: one 20mm (0.79in) cannon,
two 7.62mm (0.30in) machine guns and
one 12.7mm (0.50in) machine gun

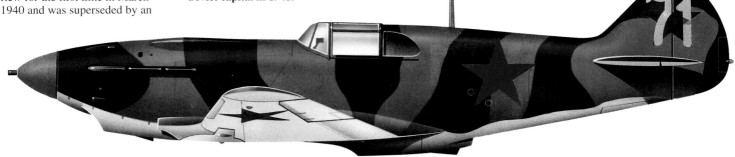

LAVOCHKIN LA-5/LA-7

FORMER USSR: 1942

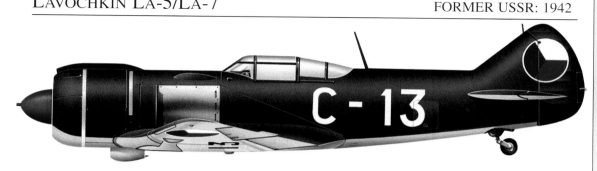

A Lavochkin La-5 of the Czech Air Force. The Czechs manned an La-5 fighter regiment on the Eastern Front in World War II and subsequently retained their aircraft.

Crew: 1
Powerplant: one 1231kW (1650hp) Ash-82FN radial engine
Performance: max speed 647km/h (402mph); range 765km (475 miles); service ceiling 11,000m (36,090ft)
Dimensions: wingspan 9.80m (32ft 1in); length 8.67m (28ft 6in); height 2.54m (8ft 4in)
Weight: 3402kg (7500lb) loaded
Armament: two 20mm (0.79in) or 23mm (0.91in) cannon; provision for four 8.2cm (3.23in) RS-82 rockets or 150kg (330lb) of bombs or anti-tank mines

THE LAVOCHKIN LA-5 was developed from the earlier LaGG-3 in response to a desperate requirement from the Soviet Air Force, which had suffered appalling casualties at the hands of the Luftwaffe in the second half of 1941, for a modern fighter that could hold its own with the Messerschmitt 109. Semyon Lavochkin retained the basic LaGG-3 airframe, which was lightweight, of wooden construction and easy to assemble, and married it with a 992kW (1330hp) Shvetsov M-82F radial engine. Other modifications included a cut-down rear fuselage, providing much improved pilot visibility, and a heavier armament. The prototype La-5 completed its State Acceptance Trials in May 1942 and entered production two months later. The first combat

formation to equip with the new fighter was the 287th Fighter Air Division, commanded by Colonel S.P. Danilin, which was assigned to the 8th Air Army on the Volga Front, in the defence of Stalingrad. The division went into action on 21 August 1942, and in the next month its pilots took part in 299 air combats, claiming the destruction of 97 enemy aircraft. By the end of the year, 1182 La-5s had been issued to frontline units, a remarkable achievement by any standard.

Early combats showed that the La-5 was a better all-round performer than the Messerschmitt 109G, although its rate of climb was inferior. Lavochkin therefore undertook some redesign work to reduce the fighter's weight, and re-engined it with the 1126kW (1510hp) M-82FN direct-injection engine. This endowed the La-5 with better climbing characteristics and manoeuvrability than either the Bf 109G or the Focke-Wulf FW 190A-4. The modified aircraft, designated La-5FN, made its appearance at the front in March 1943, and soon began to make its presence felt in the hands of some very competent Soviet fighter pilots. Among them was Ivan Kozhedub, who made his combat debut just before the battle of Kursk in the summer of 1943 and went on to score 62 kills while

flying Lavochkin fighters, making him the top-scoring Allied air ace. In addition to Soviet Air Force units, the La-5FN also equipped the 1st Czech Fighter Regiment.

The advent of the La-5FN, with its clear superiority over opposing German fighters, enabled the Soviet Air Force to develop new tactics in readiness for the planned offensives of 1943. Soviet fighters now operated at full regiment strength, flying in stepped-up battle formation. Usually they were employed in escorting assault and light bomber aircraft (Ilyushin Il-2s and Petlyakov Pe-2s), and the ratio of fighters to bombers on these missions depended on the number of bombers engaged. For example, four bombers would be escorted by 10 fighters, 16–24 bombers by 20 fighters. A variant of the La-5, the La-7, had a similar engine and differed only in minor design detail. A two-seat trainer version, the La-5UTI, was also produced, bringing total production of the La-5/La-7 series to 21,975 examples by the end of the war. The primary role of the La-5/La-7 series was that of low- and medium-level fighter, but it was occasionally assigned ground-attack missions. For these the aircraft could carry a variety of rocket and bomb loads on underwing pylons. Specifications apply to the La-5FN.

Lavochkin La-7 flown by top-scoring Allied air ace Ivan Kozhedub when he scored the last of his 62 'kills' on 19 April 1945. Kozhedub was three times created a Hero of the Soviet Union.

LAVOCHKIN LA-9/LA-11

THE LA-9 AND LA-11 were the last of the Lavochkin piston-engined fighter line. Design work on the La-9 began in 1944, and development continued during the last months of World War II, although it entered service too late to see action. It was slightly larger than the La-5/La-7, and differed from its predecessors in having all-metal construction, a redesigned cockpit canopy and square-cut wingtips. The La-11 had a slightly smaller

The Lavochkin La-11 was widely used by the Soviet satellite air forces in the years immediately following World War II.

wing area than the La-9 and carried a reduced armament. Both types were supplied to Soviet satellite air forces, including China and North Korea, and saw action in the Korean War. Specifications apply to La-9.

Crew: 1
Powerplant: one 1395kW (1870hp) Ash-82 radial engine
Performance: max speed 692km/h (430mph); range 1744km (1084 miles); service ceiling 10,850m (35,600ft)
Dimensions: wingspan 10.59m (34ft 9in); length 9.2m (30ft 2in); height 2.54m (8ft 4in)
Weight: 3624kg (8000lb) loaded
Armament: four 20mm (0.79in) cannon

LAVOCHKIN LA-15 'FANTAIL'

Crew: 1
Powerplant: one 1590kg (3500lb) thrust RD-500 (Rolls-Royce Derwent V) turbojet engine
Performance: max speed 1026km/h (637mph); range 1170km (727 miles); service ceiling 13,716m (45,000ft)
Dimensions: wingspan 8.38m (29ft); length 9.00m (29ft 6in); height 3.90m (13ft)
Weight: 3850kg (8488lb) loaded
Armament: two 23mm (0.91in) NR-23 cannon

ORIGINALLY DESIGNATED La-174, the Lavochkin La-15 tactical fighter was a refined version of the La-168 experimental interceptor and flew for the first time early in 1948,

The Lavochkin La-15 was designed to meet the same requirement as the MiG-15, but the latter proved the better aircraft.

undergoing acceptance trials in August and September that year. The type was ordered into production, but its performance was found to be inadequate for the interceptor role and only a few tactical fighter units were equipped with it, the MiG-15 becoming the Soviet Air Force's standard jet fighter. It was known to NATO by the code name Fantail.

The La-15UTI was a two-seat trainer version. The La-15 was well liked by its pilots and remained in first-line service until 1954.

LAVOCHKIN LA-200A/B

THE LAVOCHKIN LA-200A, which flew in 1949, was designed around a Soviet Air Force requirement for an all-weather fighter. In 1951 Lavochkin set about modifying the La-200A to carry a new radar scanner in a lengthened fuselage nose. The result was the La-200B, one of the ugliest aircraft ever flown. The aircraft was very heavy, and trials showed it to be greatly inferior to the other main contender, the Yakovlev Yak-25, which was selected in preference. The race to develop an effective night and all-weather fighter was given high

The Lavochkin La-200B was hurriedly developed as a night-fighter in the early 1950s, but proved greatly inferior to the Yakovlev Yak-25.

priority, to counter incursions by American and British reconnaissance aircraft into Soviet air space. Specifications apply to La-200B.

Crew: 2
Powerplant: two 2700kg (5950lb) thrust Klimov VK-1 turbojet engines
Performance: max speed 1030km/h (640mph); range 960km (596 miles); service ceiling 14,135m (46,363ft)
Dimensions: wingspan 12.96m (42ft 6in); length 15.90m (52ft 2in); height not known
Weight: 11,050kg (24,354lb)
Armament: three 37mm (1.46in) cannon

LEARJET MODELS 23, 24, 25, 28 AND 29

USA: 1963

THE LEARJET 23 WAS the initial version of this famous series of business jets. Origins are to be found in the Swiss government's (cancelled) FFA P-16 fighter project, which was taken up by Bill Lear and re-engineered into a business jet. Learjet was acquired by Gates Rubber Co. in 1967, shortly after the launch of the classic 1960s/1970s status symbol business jet – the Learjet 24.

The Learjet 25 series featured a stretched, eight-seat cabin, and later 25 series variants offered greater range and payload. The Learjet 28 series featured a new wing with winglets replacing the distinctive wingtip tanks, and the Learjet 29 Longhorn is a long-range version. A total of 738 series 20 Learjets was produced until 1979.

Specifications apply to the Learjet 24B.

Crew: 2
Powerplant: two 13.12kN (2950lb st) General Electric CJ610-6 turbojet engines
Performance: max speed 877km/h (545mph); range 3278km (2037 miles); certificated ceiling 13,715m (45,000ft)
Dimensions: wingspan 10.84m (35ft 7in); length 13.18m (43ft 3in); height 3.84m (12ft 7in)
Weight: 6124kg (13,500lb) maximum take-off weight
Payload: up to six passengers

The combination of the Learjet's clean lines derived from a fighter design and its cabin comfort made it a market leader and a status symbol (Learjet 25 pictured).

LEDUC 021/022

FRANCE: 1953

RENÉ LEDUC'S EXPERIMENTS with ramjet-powered aircraft dated back to 1937. A small research ramjet designated Leduc 010 eventually took to the air in November 1946, mounted on the back of a Bloch 161 transport and making its first gliding flight on 21 October 1947. On 21 April 1949, after a series of gliding trials, it took to the air for the first time with ramjet lit, and on 31 May that year it reached a speed of 905km/h (562mph) at 7625m (25,000ft). Subsequent testing was not trouble-free; on 27 November 1951 it was badly damaged in a crash-landing, its pilot being seriously injured, and on 25 July 1952, after repair, it

struck its Languedoc launch aircraft on release and the pilot was forced to make a belly landing.

Meanwhile, Leduc had been building a larger and more powerful ramjet research vehicle, the Leduc 021. Air tests began on 16 May 1953, with the aircraft mounted above a Languedoc, and several gliding trials were made before the first powered flight on 7 August 1953. Subsequent flight trials were carried out throughout the flight envelope up to a limiting Mach number of 0.85, and among other spectacular performance figures the 021 showed an initial climb rate of 200m/sec (39,370ft/min) and a ceiling of

20,000m (65,600ft). A second Leduc 021 was built, and this flew under its own power for the first time on 1 March 1954. The 021's pilot was accommodatred semi-reclined in a bullet-like nose fairing that protruded from the main engine tube; it could be jettisoned in an emergency, a parachute system being located immediately aft of the pilot. Aft of the cabin, the central body contained the Turboméca Artouste I turbine which drove the fuel pumps and generators, together with fuel tanks, batteries and radio. Aft of this central core were 21 burners arranged in seven banks through which fuel was

LAZAROV LAZ-1OH
The Lazarov LAZ-1OH was a 1960s Bulgarian two-seat light helicopter with tip-mounted pulse jets.

LEARJET 35/36
The Learjet 35 and Learjet 36 are larger turbofan-engined successors to the Learjet 24 business jet series. The Learjet 36 is the longer-range version.

LEARJET 55/60
Dating from 1977, the 55 series made its first flight in 1979. The salient feature of this twin engined business jet was the larger 'stand up' cabin. The Learjet 55 was superseded by the stretched Learjet 60 version in 1993. A combined total of over 350 have been sold.

LEARJET 31
This business jet is essentially a hybrid of the Learjet Model 35/36 fuselage, married with the modern wing of the Learjet 55 series.

LEBED 12
The Lebed 12 was a two-seat Russian reconnaissance biplane, first flown in December 1916. Over 200 were built.

LE BRIS GLIDERS
A French naval officer, Jean-Marie Le Bris, built and tested two gliders between 1856 and 1868. He flew the first himself, breaking both legs on landing. The second (unmanned) became the first flying machine ever to be photographed.

LEDUC 016
The Leduc 016 ramjet-powered research aircraft first flew in May 1951, mounted on the back of a Bloch 161 transport. It made several flights before being retired in 1954.

The Leduc 022 was to have been the prototype of a Mach 2 plus French ramjet interceptor. Although the aircraft's performance was phenomenal, its endurance was very poor, and the project was abandoned.

sprayed. Each bank could be lit separately, depending on the amount of power required.

The Leduc 021 was designed to be the research vehicle for an operational interceptor, and as the next step towards this goal a more advanced prototype, the Leduc 022, was designed and built. The 022 was larger than its predecessors and had swept flying surfaces; it was equipped with an Atar 101D-3 turbojet, installed inside the ramjet duct, that enabled the aircraft to take off under its own power and accelerate to the point where the ramjet could take over. The aircraft was to fly for the first time on 26 December 1956 and quickly showed enormous performance potential, including an ability to climb to 25,010m (82,000ft) in four minutes. With flight testing of the 022-01 well under way, construction of a second prototype was started. However, the 022's limiting factor was endurance; at

an estimated maximum combat speed of Mach 2.4 (it actually achieved Mach 1.5 during its trials), the aircraft was capable of carrying sufficient fuel for only 10 minutes' flying.

Besides, French Air Ministry requirements were now turning more towards the concept of multi-role combat aircraft, a policy dictated by wildly escalating research and development costs. The day of the pure interceptor was over, and the Leduc 022, one of the most radical aircraft designed anywhere during the post–World War II years of experiment, was abandoned.

Specifications apply to the 021.

Crew: 1
Powerplant: one 6500kg (14,326lb) thrust Leduc ramjet engine
Performance: max speed 900km/h (600mph); service ceiling 20,000m (65,616ft); initial climb rate 200m/sec (39,370ft/min)
Dimensions: wingspan 11.60m (38ft); length 12.50m (41ft); height not known
Weight: 6000kg (13,227lb) loaded

LET (CZAL/MRAZ) M-1 SOKOL, L-20 AND L-40 METASOKOL   CZECHOSLOVAKIA: 1954

MRAZ DEVELOPED THE M-1 three-seat, wooden construction trainer in the late 1940s. By 1954 the M-1 was developed into the L-20 three-seat touring/training light aircraft and swiftly the four-seat L-40, which had a particularly high tail fin and a reverse tricycle undercarriage. Only small numbers of the L-20 were produced, but overall some 200 MetaSokols were built until 1961, with a number being exported within the Eastern Bloc and to the West. Specifications apply to L-40.

Crew: 1
Powerplant: one flat-rated 85kW (115hp) Walter M332 in-line inverted 'four' piston engine
Performance: max speed 237km/h (147mph); range 850km (528 miles); service ceiling 4500m (14,765ft)

Dimensions: wingspan (without tip tanks) 10.00m (32ft 10in); length 8.70m (28ft 9in); height 2.47m (8ft 1in)
Weight: 935kg (2062lb) maximum take-off weight
Payload: five seats

LET L-200 MORAVA   CZECHOSLOVAKIA: 1957

THE L-200 MORAVA WAS a postwar light aircraft notable for its wingtip fuel tanks and twin fin. Production was undertaken in Czechoslovakia and later in the former Yugoslavia. The L-200 incorporated a tricycle undercarriage, and later versions had a three-bladed constant propeller. Over 1000 L-200s were produced up until 1968. Specifications apply to the L-200D Morava.

Crew: 1
Powerplant: two Walter M337 157kW (210hp) in-line piston engines
Performance: max cruising speed 285km/h (177mph); range 1800km (1118 miles); service ceiling 6200m (20,340ft)
Dimensions: wingspan 12.30m (40ft 4.25in); length 8.60m (28ft 2.5in); height 2.25m (7ft 4.5in)
Weight: 2000kg (4409lb) maximum take-off weight
Payload: five people and/or freight

The L-200 Morava has been used extensively for air taxi services in several countries, including a number used by Aeroflot. A turboprop-powered version designated L-300 was designed, but never entered production.

LET L-410

CZECHOSLOVAKIA: 1969

Crew: 2
Powerplant: two 544kW (210eshp) Walter M601B turboprop engines
Performance: max cruising speed 365km/h (227mph); range with maximum payload and reserves 390km (242 miles); operating altitude 6000m (19,685ft)
Dimensions: wingspan 19.48m (63ft 10.75in); length 14.47m (47ft 5.75in); height 5.83m (19ft 1.5in)
Weight: 5800kg (12,787lb) maximum take-off weight
Payload: up to 15 passengers

THE L-410 WAS DESIGNED to meet the challenging environment of local 'bus-stop' and feeder services in Eastern Europe, often involving

The L-410 has become popular with parachute clubs throughout Europe – this example operates at Headcorn, Kent.

unpaved airstrips, with reliability and maintainability major criteria. The initial L-410A utilized Pratt & Whitney Canada PT6A-27 engines, but subsequent L-410M versions include the Walter engine and the MA variant embodied a number of

improvements specified for Aeroflot use. The definitive L-410UVP embodied further structural/stability and format improvements required by Aeroflot, and the UVP-E version has a 19-passenger cabin. Specifications apply to L-410UVP.

LEVASSEUR PL-8 OISEAU BLANC

FRANCE: 1927

Crew: 2
Powerplant: one Lorraine-Dietrich 12-cylinder water-cooled Vee-type piston engine rated at 333kW (450hp)
Performance: max speed 193km/h (120mph); cruising speed 160km/h (100mph); range 6000km (3725 miles)
Dimensions: wingspan 14.63m (48ft); length 9.75m (32ft); height 3.96m (13ft)
Weight: not available
Payload: two seats

THE PL-8 OISEAU BLANC was derived from the military PL-7 and PL-8 used by the French Navy, but it was specially adapted to include, among other things, a 4028-litre (886-gallon) fuel capacity so that French World War I fighter ace Charles Nungessor and his co-pilot Francois Coli could attempt to cross the Atlantic from east to west. The Oiseau Blanc departed Le Bourget

(Paris) on 10 May 1927, leaving behind its special jettisonable undercarriage (a weight-saving measure). The weather was poorer than forecast, however, and strong headwinds became prevalent. The Oiseau Blanc carrying the French nation's hopes and expectations was last seen off Ireland. The headwinds would have decimated the Oiseau Blanc's fuel stock.

LILIENTHAL GLIDERS

GERMANY: 1891–1896

OTTO LILIENTHAL (1848–96) was a German engineer and inventor who became the first man in history to take off and make a controlled flight. He became interested in the mechanics of flight while still a boy and at the age of 14 experimented with two rudimentary gliders. In the late 1860s he began serious research into aeronautics with his brother Gustave, investigating the mechanics and aerodynamics of bird flight.

Between 1891 and 1896, he put his research into practice in the form of a series of highly successful full-size glider trials. During this period Lilienthal

Otto Lilienthal pictured on a test flight in one of his gliders in October 1895. He died of injuries sustained in a crash in August 1896.

made close to 2000 brief flights in 16 different glider designs based on his aerodynamic investigations. Lilienthal built at least eight gliders of this type. He did most of his gliding from a man-made hill he had constructed near his home at Gross-Lichterfelde, and from the hills surrounding the small village of Rhinow, about 80km (50 miles)

from Berlin. His best efforts with these gliders covered more than 300m (985ft) and were 12–15 seconds in duration.

Lilienthal's experiments came to an abrupt and tragic end in the summer of 1896. On 9 August, while soaring in one of his standard monoplane gliders, a strong gust of wind caused the craft to nose up sharply, stall, and

crash from an altitude of 15m (50ft). Lilienthal suffered a broken spine and died the following day in a Berlin hospital.

Remarkably, six of Lilienthal's original gliders are still in existence, one of them in the National Air and Space Museum in Washington DC.

Specifications apply to Lilienthal's 1894 glider.

Crew: 1
Powerplant: none (glider)
Dimensions (1894 glider): wingspan 7.93m (26ft); length 4.19m (13ft 0.75in); height 1.53m (5ft)
Weight: not available

LIORÉ ET OLIVIER LEO 25 FRANCE: 1928

Rugged and reliable, the LeO 25 saw widespread service between the two world wars – some were still in operational use at the outbreak of World War II.

THE PROTOTYPE OF THE LeO 25 series of bomber/reconnaissance aircraft flew for the first time in May 1928. This aircraft was later fitted with twin floats and tested by the French Navy in 1931 as the LeO 252-01. The LeO 25 No 2

was a landplane bomber, purchased by Romania, and the LeO 253 was also a landplane, three being purchased by Brazil. The remaining aircraft in the series were all seaplanes, designations ranging from LeO H-254 to H-258.

They saw widespread service, carrying out neutrality patrols during the Spanish Civil War among other duties. Some aircraft, their floats exchanged for land undercarriages, equipped Groupe de Bombardment GB II/25 in North Africa. The LeO 25 series was still in limited operational service at the outbreak of World War II. A few saw action during the German invasion of May 1940, and suffered heavy losses.

Crew: 4
Powerplant: two 429kW (575hp) Hispano-Suiza Mbr liquid-cooled engines
Performance: max speed 249km/h (155mph); range 2000km (1243 miles); service ceiling 8005m (26,247ft)
Dimensions: wingspan 25.54m (83ft 8in); length 17.61m (57ft 7in); height 6.80m (22ft 4in)
Weight: 9368kg (20,679lb) loaded
Armament: four 7.62mm (0.30in) machine guns; one 655kg (1447lb) torpedo or 600kg (1323lb) of bombs

LIORÉ ET OLIVIER LEO 451 FRANCE: 1937

THE FIRST FLIGHT OF the prototype LeO 45-01 on 16 January 1937 was followed by an initial order for 20 production LeO 451 medium bombers. In the following two years total orders reached 749, of which 449 were built before the armistice. The first unit to receive the new bomber was GB I/31. By 10 May 1940, 110 LeO 451s were on Armée de l'Air charge, 59 of them operational. Seven groupes were equipped or partially equipped with the type during the Battle of France in May–June 1940, in which about 130 LeO 451s were lost from all causes. At the armistice 183 LeO 451s remained in southern France and about 100 in North Africa. Some were used

against Allied forces during the Syrian campaign in the summer of 1941, and other examples were used as transports and navigational trainers by the Luftwaffe.

Crew: 4
Powerplant: two 850kW (1140hp) Gnome-Rhone 14N-48/49 14-cylinder radial engines
Performance: max speed 495km/h (307mph); range 2300km (1429 miles); service ceiling 9000m (29,530ft)
Dimensions: wingspan 22.52m (73ft 10in); length 17.17m (56ft 4in); height 5.24m (17ft 2in)
Weight: 7815kg (17,229lb) loaded
Armament: one 20mm (0.79in) cannon and two 7.5mm (0.30in) machine guns; internal bomb load of 2000kg (4409lb)

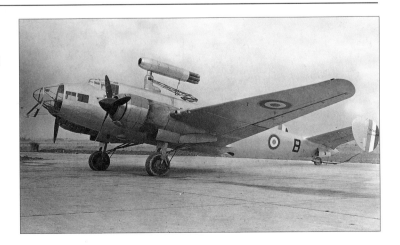

The LeO 451 was the best bomber in service with the French Air Force at the time of the Battle of France in 1940.

LIPPISCH P.10 TO P.15

GERMANY: 1944–5

Crew: 1
Powerplant: one solid-fuel ramjet, plus
a booster rocket for take-off
Performance (est): 1650km/h
(1025mph); endurance 45 mins
Dimensions: wingspan 5.92m (19ft 5in);
length 6.70m (21ft 11.75in); height
3.18m (10ft 5.25in)
Weight: not available

THE LIPPISCH P.10 fighter-bomber
was the last of Dr Alexander
Lippisch's piston-engined projects
and was generally similar to the
Messerschmitt Me 329. His next
project, the delta-wing P.11, was to
have been powered by two Junkers
Jumo 004 turbojets, while the P.12
was to have had a built-in ramjet
unit. This was abandoned in favour
of the P.13a, which reached the
most advanced development stage,
but no prototype was completed.
The ramjet was to use solid fuel,
which would burn and combine
with oxygen passing through the
ramjet duct. Initial acceleration
was to be provided by a booster
rocket. The P.14 was another
ramjet design, while the P.15 was a
projected development of the Me
163 powered by a turbojet.
Specifications apply to the P-13a.

**The piston-engined Delta 1 of 1931 was the first of Dr Alexander
Lippisch's all-wing designs.**

LLOYD C TYPES

AUSTRIA-HUNGARY: 1914

Crew: 2
Powerplant: one 108kW (145hp) Hiero
water-cooled in-line engine
Performance: max speed 128km/h
(79mph); endurance 2 hrs; service ceiling
3000m (9843ft)
Dimensions: wingspan 14.00m (45ft
11in); length 9.00m (29ft 6in); height
3.40m (11ft 2in)
Weight: 1350kg (2976lb) loaded
Armament: one 7.5mm (0.30in)
machine gun

DESPITE THE FACT that about 500
aircraft were built, the Lloyd C
series of two-seat reconnaissance
aircraft produced by the Ungarische
Lloyd Flugzeug und Motorenfabrik
were among the lesser known
types of World War I. The series
began with the C.I of 1914, an
example of which set up a record
by reaching an altitude of 6170m
(20,243ft) that summer, and
progressed to the C.V. The Lloyd

**The Lloyd C.V was the last of the
little-known Austrian two-seat
reconnaissance Lloyd C types.**

C.II of 1915 was followed by the
C.III of 1916, these being used
extensively on the Italian and
Romanian fronts. The service
status of the C.IV is unknown, and
the C.V, the last in the series, was
withdrawn in 1917. Specifications
apply to the Lloyd C.II.

LETOV S-20
The Letov S-20 was a Czech
fighter biplane, first flown in 1925.
Around 140 aircraft of the S-20
series were built, some of which
were used by Lithuania.

LETOV S-228
First flown in 1932, the Czech-built
Letov S-228 was a general-purpose
single-engined biplane, used by the
Estonian Air Force.

LETOV S-328
The Letov S-328 general-purpose
biplane, which appeared in 1934,
was the workhorse of the Czech
Army Aviation for several years.
Three S-328s saw action with
Slovak insurgents during WWII,
flying against occupying German
forces in 1944.

LETOV S-50
The Letov S-50 was a twin-
engined, three-seat reconnaissance
monoplane, first flown in 1938.
The prototype was seized by the
Germans and displayed in the
Berlin Air Museum.

LEVASSEUR PL 2
An early torpedo-bomber, the PL 2
biplane dates from 1922.

LEVASSEUR PL-15
A single-engined, twin-float
biplane first flown in 1932, the PL-
15 could operate from a seaplane
carrier and was armed with bombs
or torpedoes. A PL-15 was the first
French seaplane to sink a German
submarine.

LE VIER COSMIC WIND
Designed and built by Lockheed
engineers, the Cosmic Wind was a
single-engined, all-metal
monoplane racing type, powered by
a Continental C85 engine and
dating from 1947. Only three
examples were built.

LOCKHEED 1, 2 AND 5 VEGA

USA: 1927

The Vega photographed (registered NC-965-Y) was one of those owned by pioneering aviatrix Amelia Earhart. This particular aircraft was involved in a number of record-breaking exploits, including the 1935 flight between Oahu (Hawaii) and Oakland (California).

THE VEGA WAS Lockheed's first type of note. Its fuselage was made of plywood formed in two halves in a concrete pressure mould. A total of 128 examples of this high-wing clean-lined aircraft were sold, many to passenger and mail operators. They were also used for pioneering record attempts, including the first transarctic flight and the first flight over Antarctica. Specifications apply to the 5C Landplane.

Crew: 1
Powerplant: one 336kW (450hp) Pratt & Whitney Wasp SC-1 radial piston engine
Performance: max speed 298km/h (185mph); range 885km (550 miles); service ceiling 5485m (18,000ft)

Dimensions: wingspan 12.50m (41ft); wing area 25.55m² (275.00 sq ft); length 8.38m (27ft 6in); height 2.59m (8ft 6in)
Weight: 2155kg (4750lb) maximum take-off weight.
Payload: six passengers

LOCKHEED 9 ORION

USA: 1931

A number of current American airlines have their origins in mail service operators. Varney Speed Lanes Air Service (who operated this Orion) were an early incarnation and component of today's Continental Airlines.

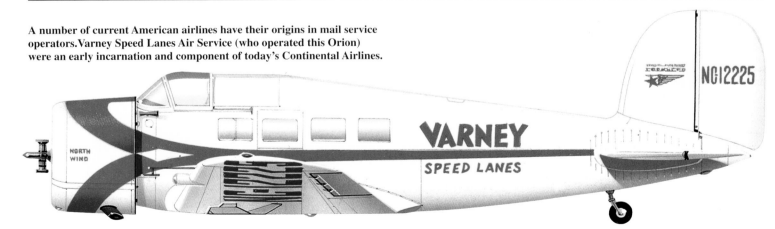

THE ORION WAS an important advance in Lockheed's range of single-engined high-performance passenger/mail aircraft, combining the fuselage of the high-wing Vega with the wing and retractable undercarriage of the low wing Altair. In all, 35 aircraft were built, including examples for Swissair and Northwest Airlines, and 13 were flown in the Spanish Civil War. Specifications apply to Orion 9D.

Crew: 1
Powerplant: one 410kW (550hp) Pratt & Whitney Wasp S1D1 radial piston engine
Performance: cruising speed 330km/h (205mph); range 1159km (720 miles); service ceiling 6705m (22,000ft)

Dimensions: wingspan 13.04m (42ft 9.25in); length 8.64m (28ft 4in); height 2.95m (9ft 8in)
Weight: 2359kg (5200lb) maximum take-off weight
Payload: six passengers

LOCKHEED MODELS 10 (ELECTRA) AND 12 (ELECTRA JUNIOR) USA: 1934

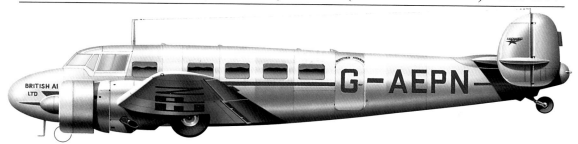

A larger L.10 Electra, which served with British Airways in the late 1930s on Scandinavian routes before the merger with Imperial Airways.

THE ELECTRA, WHICH sold 148 examples to domestic and overseas airlines, marks Lockheed's entry into the manufacture of major transport aircraft. With an all-metal construction, low wing, a retractable main landing gear and twin fin, the Electra was a distinctive aircraft. It was aimed at airlines requiring a

smaller capacity than the Douglas DC-2 offered. The shortened Electra Junior was first flown in 1936 in response to the needs of air taxi operators; however, this type also proved popular with US military as the C-40, and 130 were built. Specifications apply to the 12-A Electra Junior.

Crew: 2
Powerplant: two 336kW (450hp) Pratt & Whitney Wasp Junior SB radial piston engines
Performance: max speed 362km/h (225mph); range 1287km (800 miles); service ceiling 6980m (22,900ft)
Dimensions: wingspan 15.09m (49ft 6in); length 10.97m (36ft); height 2.97m (9ft 9in)
Weight: 3810kg (8400lb) fully loaded
Payload: up to six passengers; Electra Model 10, 10 passengers

LOCKHEED HUDSON USA: 1938

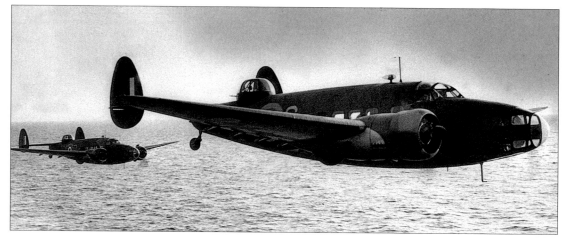

Crew: 6
Powerplant: two 821kW (1100hp) Wright GR-1820-G102A Cyclone radial engines
Performance: max speed 357km/h (222mph); range 3154km (1960 miles); service ceiling 6400m (21,000ft)
Dimensions: wingspan 19.96m (65ft 6in); length 13.50m (44ft 3in); height 3.32m (10ft 10in)
Weight: 8845kg (19,500lb) loaded
Armament: seven 7.7mm (0.303in) machine guns; internal bomb load of 612kg (1350lb)

THE LOCKHEED HUDSON was a military version of the Lockheed Model 14 twin-engined commercial airliner, one of the success stories of the late 1930s. It was developed at short notice in 1938 to meet a

British requirement for a maritime reconnaissance aircraft to replace the Avro Anson in the squadrons of RAF Coastal Command. The RAF placed an initial order for 200 aircraft, the first of which were delivered to No 224 Squadron at Leuchars, Scotland, in May 1939. Lockheed supplied 350 Hudson Is and 20 Hudson IIs (the same as the Mk I except for different propellers) before introducing the improved Mk III. In the Far East, RAAF Hudsons fought in the Malayan campaign. In the North Atlantic, one of the Hudson's most famous actions occurred on 27 August 1941, when the German submarine U-570 was attacked and damaged by an aircraft of No 269 Squadron

Lockheed Hudson maritime patrol bombers of RAF Coastal Command on patrol over the North Sea in early World War II.

and forced to surrender. The Hudson also served in USAAC/ USAAF colours as the A-28 and A-29. The USAAC took delivery of 82 A-28s and 418 A-29s in 1941–42, 20 A-28s subsequently being transferred to the US Navy as the PBO-1. On 1 March 1942, a PBO-1 Hudson of VP-82 attacked and sank the submarine U-656 south-west of Newfoundland; this was the first German U-boat sunk by US forces during World War II.

Specifications apply to the Hudson Mk I.

LOCKHEED MODELS 14 (SUPER ELECTRA) AND 18 (LODESTAR)

Crew: 3
Powerplant: two Pratt & Whitney Hornet S1E2-G radial piston engines each rated at 652kW (875hp)
Performance: max speed 351km/h (218mph); range 2897km (1800 miles); service ceiling 6220m (20,400ft)
Dimensions: wingspan 19.96m (65ft 6in); length 15.19m (49ft 10in); height 3.61m (11ft 10in)
Weight: 8709kg (19,200lb) maximum take-off weight
Payload: up to 26 passengers

THE SUPER ELECTRA first flew in 1937 and had a similar low-wing, twin-fin configuration to the preceding models 10 and 12, but with a markedly deeper fuselage. Primarily the Model 14 airliner

An L.14 of Dutch national carrier KLMs Antilles (Dutch Caribbean) division, reported as being involved in an accident in Jamaica in 1943.

was offered as a direct competitor to the Douglas DC-2 and DC-3, but its smaller (12–14 passenger) capacity proved a disadvantage. However, it did prove to be the basis for the extremely important Hudson patrol aircraft of World War II. The Lodestar was closely derived from the preceding Super Electra. Although 625 aircraft were built, fewer than 150 were first supplied to civil customers. The remainder were ordered by the US and British militaries for wartime transport/paratroop roles as the Lodestar I, C-56, C-57, C-59 and C-60. A number of these were converted as postwar commercial transports. Specifications apply to the Model 18 Lodestar.

LOCKHEED P-38 LIGHTNING

Crew: 1
Powerplant: two 1063kW (1425hp) Allison V-1710-91 12-cylinder Vee-type engines
Performance: max speed 666km/h (414mph); range 3600km (2260 miles); service ceiling 13,400m (44,000ft)
Dimensions: wingspan 15.85m (52ft); length 11.53m (37ft 10in); height 2.99m (9ft 10in)
Weight: 9798kg (21,600lb) loaded
Armament: one 20mm (0.79in) cannon and four 12.7mm (0.50in) machine guns; external bomb and rocket load of 1814kg (4000lb)

A Lockheed P-36F Lightning on a test flight. The F series Lightnings could carry bombs or fuel tanks under the outer wing panels.

ALTHOUGH IT TENDED to be over-shadowed by the Republic P-47 Thunderbolt and the North American P-51 Mustang, the Lockheed P-38 Lightning played a vital part in winning air superiority for the Allies, particularly in the Pacific theatre. The P-38 was designed to meet the exacting requirements of a 1937 USAAC specification, calling for a high-altitude interceptor capable of 580km/h (360mph) at 6100m (20,000ft) and 467km/h (290mph)

at sea level. The sole XP-38 prototype flew on 27 January 1939 and was followed by 13 YP-38 evaluation aircraft. An initial production batch of 30 P-38s was built, these being delivered from the summer of 1941; the next

A P-37 Lightning of the 401st Fighter Squadron, 370th Fighter Group, USAAF, which became operational at Andover, Hampshire, in May 1944.

production model was the P-38D, 36 of which were produced.

The Lockheed P-38 Lightning had supercharged engines. In the early part of the war, the RAF wanted to buy substantial numbers of P-38s (in fact, it was the British

who bestowed the name Lightning on the type), but orders were cancelled when the Americans refused to fit the superchargers, which were deemed to be secret. In November 1941 the P-38E appeared, with a more powerful armament; however, the P-38F, appearing early in 1943, was the first variant to be used in large numbers, operating in Europe from the summer of 1942 and in North Africa from November; 527 were built. This was followed by the P-38G (1082) and P-38H (601), these variants featuring either armament or engine changes. The next variant, the P-38J Lightning, had deepened air intakes under the propeller spinners and enlarged Prestone radiators on the tail booms.

The largest production quantity was achieved with the P-38L (3923 built), which like the J was equipped with a glazed nose and

used as a bomber. The last version was the P-38M, a two-seat variant designed as a night-fighter and equipped with radar. Total Lightning production was 9923, of which more than 1000 examples were converted into photo-reconnaissance aircraft as F-4s and F-5s. From the raised cockpit of the P-38 the pilot had an excellent view forward, unobstructed by a propeller. The canopy hinged backwards and had downward-winding side windows. The

Lightning's twin tail booms were the distinctive recognition feature, and led the Germans to nickname it the 'Gabelschwanzteufel', or 'Fork-tailed Devil'.

One of the most famous of all operations carried out by the Lightning took place on 18 April 1943, when P-38s of the 339th Fighter Squadron, USAAF, shot down a Japanese bomber carrying Admiral Isoroku Yamamoto, the Japanese Navy Commander-in-Chief. To carry out the job, the

Lightnings made a 1770km (1100-mile) round trip from Guadalcanal to intercept Yamamoto's aircraft over Kahili Atoll. The two top-scoring pilots of the Pacific war, Major Richard I. Bong and Major Tommy McGuire, both flew P-38s; Bong ended the war with a score of 40 enemy machines destroyed, while McGuire shot down 38 before his death in action over the Philippines in January 1945.

Specifications apply to the P-38J Lightning.

LOCKHEED C-69, L-049, L-649 AND L-749 CONSTELLATION   USA: 1943

THE LOCKHEED CONSTELLATION was the classic early postwar airliner, with a distinctive triple fin tail and a humped back. It began its life as a response to a TWA civil transport requirement in 1939. However, World War II intervened and the project was sequestered by the USAAF – 22 military examples were produced before the end of hostilities. At this point military interest in the Constellation was withdrawn and remaining work in progress was converted to airliner standard as the L-049 for airlines such as TWA and BOAC. Lockheed then turned its efforts to

producing the L-649 airliner, which included more powerful engines, increased weights and onboard systems for commercial use. The Lockheed L-749, with structural improvements and consequently greater maximum weights, became the definitive version – there was also a military transport derivative, designated the C-121. A total of 233 examples of all versions were built, mostly for major airlines; however, the Constellation was gradually superseded by the greater weight L-1049 Super Constellation. Specifications apply to the L-749.

The first of four L-749As delivered to South African Airways in 1950. This example ended its days in England working as a freighter.

Crew: 4
Powerplant: four 1864kW (2500hp) Wright R-3350-C18-BA1 Cyclone radial piston engines
Performance: cruising speed 480km/h (298mph); range 4185km (2600 miles)
Dimensions: wingspan 37.49m (123ft); length 29.67m (97ft 4in); height 7.21m (23ft 8in)
Weight: 48,535kg (107,000lb) maximum take-off weight
Payload: up to 81 passengers

LOCKHEED F-80 SHOOTING STAR

USA: 1944

Lockheed F-80C Shooting Stars in echelon formation. Although outclassed as an interceptor by 1950, the F-80 proved to be well adapted to the ground-attack role.

AMERICA'S FIRST FULLY operational jet fighter was the Lockheed P-80 Shooting Star, which like its British counterparts was of extremely conventional design and which was to become the workhorse of the American tactical fighter-bomber and fighter-interceptor squadrons for five years after World War II. The prototype XP-80 was designed around a de Havilland H-1 turbojet supplied to the United States in July 1943, and the aircraft was finished in just 143 days, making its first flight on 9 January 1944.

In April 1945, two YP-80s were sent to England, where they were attached to the Eighth Air Force, and two more went to Italy, but none experienced any operational flying in Europe before the war's end. Early production P-80As entered USAAF service late in 1945 with the 412th Fighter Group, which became the 1st Fighter Group in July 1946 and

comprised the 27th, 71st and 94th Fighter Squadrons. On 12 July 1948, as part of a reinforcement plan following the Russian blockade of Berlin, 16 Lockheed F-80A Shooting Stars of the 56th Fighter Wing (Lt Col David Schilling), a unit then assigned to Strategic Air Command, left Selfridge Field, Michigan, and flew via Dow AFB, Maine, Goose

Bay in Labrador, Bluie West One in Greenland and Reykjavik in Iceland to make its UK landfall at Stornoway after a total transatlantic flight time of five hours 15 minutes. On 21 July the fighters flew on to Odiham, Hampshire. After their Odiham visit, the F-80s flew on to Fürstenfeldbruck, where they spent six weeks on exercises, including fighter affiliation with B-29s, before returning to the United States. Early in August, 72 F-80s of the 36th Fighter Wing were shipped to Glasgow in the aircraft carrier USS *Sicily* and the US Army transport vessel *Kirschbaum*, and after being offloaded and overhauled they departed for Fürstenfeldbruck between 13 and 20 August.

The P-80A was followed by the P-80B, but the major production version was the F-80C (the P for 'pursuit' prefix having changed to the much more logical F for 'fighter' in the meantime). The F-80C was the fighter-bomber workhorse of the Korean War, flying 15,000 sorties in the first four months alone. While pilots found the aircraft ideal for strafing, the F-80 was rarely able to outmanoeuvre North Korea's piston-engined Yakovlev and Lavochkin fighters, nor were the American jets initially equipped to carry bombs or rockets for effective ground-attack work. In spite of these deficiencies, F-80s managed to claim a number of North Korean aircraft, the first on the third day of the war, 28 June 1950, when the 35th Fighter Squadron, nicknamed the

The F-80C Shooting Star was the ground-attack workhorse of the Korean War, until it began to be replaced by the F-84 Thunderjet in 1952.

'Panthers' and operating out of Itazuke in Japan, became the first American jet squadron to destroy an enemy aircraft. The engagement took place while the F-80s were protecting a flight of North American Twin Mustangs. Captain Raymond E. Schillereff led four aircraft into the Seoul area and caught a quartet of Ilyushin Il-10s which were attempting to interfere with US transport aircraft embarking civilians at Seoul's Kimpo airfield; all four Il-10s were shot down.

The Shooting Star was assured of its place in history when 1st Lt Russell Brown of the 51st Fighter Wing shot down a MiG-15 jet fighter on 8 November 1950 during history's first jet-versus-jet battle. Other sporadic attacks, against which the Shooting Stars were the main USAF defence, were to follow during the early part of the war, until the arrival of the more capable F-86A Sabre in December 1950.

Specifications apply to F-80C.

Crew: 1
Powerplant: one 2449kg (5400lb) thrust Allison J33-A-35 turbojet engine
Performance: max speed 966km/h (594mph); range 1328km (825 miles); service ceiling 14,265m (46,800ft)
Dimensions: wingspan 11.81m (38ft 9in); wing area 22.07m² (237.6 sq ft); length 10.49m (34ft 5in); height 3.43m (11ft 3in)
Weight: 7646kg (16,856lb) loaded
Armament: six 12.7mm (0.50in) machine guns; two 454kg (1000lb) bombs and eight rockets

---

LOCKHEED P2V NEPTUNE

USA: 1945

A Lockheed P2V-7 Neptune of the Royal Australian Navy. The aircraft's long tail boom housed magnetic anomaly detection (MAD) submarine detection equipment.

THE FIRST LAND-BASED aircraft designed specifically for the long-range maritime reconnaissance role, the Lockheed Neptune was destined to be one of the longest-serving military aircraft ever built. The first of two XP2V-1 prototypes flew on 17 May 1945, orders already having been placed for 15 pre-production and 151 production P2V-1s. Deliveries to the US Navy began in March 1947, by which time another variant, the P2V-2, had also flown. Next was the P2V-3 and another engine change produced the

P2V-4, with underwing fuel tanks. The P2V-5 Neptune was the first variant supplied to foreign air arms, 36 P2V-5Fs being supplied to the RAF as Neptune MR 1s. The P2V-5F was fitted with two Westinghouse J34-WE-36 turbojets in underwing pods outboard of the main engine nacelles. The P2V-6 (P2F) Neptune had a minelaying capability in addition to its ASW role; 83 were delivered to the US Navy and 12 to France's Aéronavale. The last production version was the P2V-7. Specifications apply to P2V-7.

Crew: 10
Powerplant: two 2611kW (3500hp) R-3350-32W piston engines and two 1542kg (3400lb) thrust Westinghouse K34-WE-36 auxiliary turbojet engines
Performance: max speed 555km/h (345mph); range 3540km (2200 miles); service ceiling 6700m (22,000ft)
Dimensions: wingspan 31.65m (103ft 10in); length 27.83m (91ft 4in); height 8.94m (29ft 4in)
Weight: 34,246kg (75,000lb) loaded
Armament: full range of maritime offensive stores internally; provision for air-to-surface missiles on underwing racks

---

LOCKHEED T-33

USA: 1948

The Lockheed T-33 jet trainer, affectionately known as the 'T-Bird', trained thousands of jet pilots all over the world.

THE MOST WIDELY used advanced trainer in the world, the Lockheed T-33 first flew in 1948 and was developed from the F-80C Shooting Star airframe. It is estimated that

some 90 per cent of the West's military jet pilots, and also friendly foreign pilots from other nations, trained on the T-33 during the 1950s and 1960s. T-33 production totalled

5691 in the United States alone; many others were built under licence in Canada and Japan. A version adapted to carry underwing offensive stores was offered to small air arms in the counterinsurgency role.

Crew: 2
Powerplant: one 2449kg (5400lb) thrust Allison J33-A-35 turbojet engine
Performance: max speed 879km/h (546mph); endurance 3 hrs 7 mins; service ceiling 14,630m (48,000ft)
Dimensions: wingspan 11.85m (38ft 10in); length 11.51m (37ft 10in); height 3.56m (11ft 8in)
Weight: 6551kg (14,442lb) loaded
Armament: two 12.7mm (0.50in) machine guns

LOCKHEED F-94 STARFIRE

USA: 1949

Crew: 2
Powerplant: one 2742kg (6000lb) thrust Allison J33-A-33 turbojet engine
Performance: max speed 933km/h (580mph); range 1850km (1150 miles); service ceiling 14,630m (48,000ft)
Dimensions: wingspan 11.85m (38ft 10in) not including tip tanks; length 12.20m (40ft 1in); height 3.99m (13ft 1in)
Weight: 7125kg (15,710lb)
Armament: four 12.7mm (0.50in) machine guns or 24 unguided folding-fin aircraft rockets

THE LOCKHEED F-94 Starfire all-weather fighter was developed from the T-33A trainer, two production T-33 airframes being converted as YF-94s. The first of these flew on 16 April 1949. The F-94A went into production in 1949; 200 were built, the first

The Lockheed F-94 Starfire saw action in the Korean War, where it was used to intercept North Korean intruders – a task for which it was unsuited because it was too fast.

entering service in June 1950 with the 319th All-Weather Fighter Squadron. The next variant, the F-94B, was followed by the F-94C, which differed so extensively from its predecessors that it was originally known as the YF-97A. Total production of the F-94C

came to 387 aircraft before the series was completed in 1954.
Specifications apply to F-94C.

LOCKHEED L-1049 SUPER CONSTELLATION AND L-1649A STARLINER

USA: 1950

FOLLOWING ON FROM the success of the Constellation series, Lockheed launched the L-1049 Super Constellation. It featured a fuselage lengthened by 5.59m

(18ft 4in) and an uprated powerplant, consequently offering greater range and payload. The Super Constellation was purchased in a number of marques by many

major operators including TWA, Eastern, Qantas, Air France and KLM. A total of 265 commercial versions were sold, as well as 320 military C-121 versions for roles

such as AEW, ASW, ECM and reconnaissance. The last version of the Constellation series was the L-1649 Starliner, which featured a redesigned wing and further uprated engines, making it superior in range to competitors. However, only 43 examples were ordered by the likes of TWA, Air France and Lufthansa before the Boeing 707 jet rendered the Connie and its direct competitors obsolete. Specifications apply to L-1649A.

Crew: 4
Powerplant: four 2535kW (3400hp) Wright 988TC-18EA-2 turbo-compound radial piston engines
Performance: max speed 606km/h (377mph); range 7950km (4940 miles) with maximum payload; service ceiling 7225m (23,700ft)
Dimensions: wingspan 45.72m (150ft); length 35.41m (116ft 2in); height 7.54m (24ft 9in)
Weight: 72,575kg (160,000lb) maximum take-off weight
Payload: up to 92 passengers

This airframe was built as the prototype L-049 and delivered to the USAF in 1943. Interestingly, the aircraft was reacquired by Lockheed in 1950 and converted into the prototype L-1049 Super Constellation.

LOCKHEED F-104 STARFIGHTER

USA: 1954

DEVELOPMENT OF THE F-104 was begun in 1951, when the lessons of the Korean air war were starting to bring about profound changes in combat aircraft design. A contract for two XF-104 prototypes was placed in 1953, and the first of

these flew on 7 February 1954, only 11 months later. The two XF-104s were followed by 15 YF-104s for USAF evaluation, most of these, like the prototypes, being powered by the Wright J65-W-6 turbojet. The aircraft was ordered

into production as the F-104A, with deliveries to the USAF Air Defense Command beginning in January 1958. As a result of its lack of all-weather capability, the F-104A saw only limited service with Air Defense Command,

equipping just two fighter squadrons. F104As were also supplied to Nationalist China and Pakistan, and saw combat during the Indo-Pakistan conflict of 1969. The F104B was a two-seat version, and the F-104C was a tactical fighter-bomber, the first of 77 examples being delivered to the 479th Tactical Fighter Wing (the only unit to use it) in October 1958. Two more two-seat Starfighters, the F-104D and F-104F, were followed by the F-104G, which was numerically the most important variant.

A single-seat multi-mission aircraft based on the F-104C, the F-104G had a strengthened structure and many equipment changes, including an upwards-ejecting Lockheed C-2 seat (earlier variants had a downward-ejecting seat). The first F-104G flew on 5 October 1960 and 1266 examples were produced up to February 1966, 977 by the European Starfighter Consortium and the remainder by Lockheed. Of these, the Luftwaffe received 750, the Italian Air Force 154, the Royal Netherlands Air Force 120 and the Belgian Air Force 99. The basically similar CF-104 was a strike-reconnaissance aircraft, 200 of which were built by Canadair for the RCAF. Canadair also built 110 more F-104Gs for delivery to the air forces of Norway, Nationalist China, Spain,

Denmark, Greece and Turkey. Also similar to the F-104G was the F-104J for the Japan Air Self-Defence Force; the first one flew on 30 June 1961, and 207 were produced by Mitsubishi. The F-104S was an interceptor development of the F-104G, with provision for external stores, and was capable of Mach 2.4; 165 were licence-built in Italy.

Pilots were generally fond of the F-104. The cockpit was well designed and roomy, having all the instruments and switches conveniently located and affording an excellent view. Nosewheel steering made for easy ground manoeuvring, and was used up to 185km/h (115mph) during the take-off roll. In the air the Starfighter was remarkably stable, but the stick forces were heavy. Aerobatics in the rolling plane were quite conventional, but a great deal of sky was used up in the looping plane. A loop with maximum dry power was started from 926km/h (575mph) indicated airspeed and required about 3050m (10,000ft) of air space. Approach and landing presented

no special problems. Constant speed approaches were flown, speed over the threshold being 324–380km/h (201–236mph) depending on fuel weight. The wheel brakes were very effective, brake protection being provided by an electrical generating device in each wheel, and the 5.5m (18ft) brake parachute could be used at speed of up to 380km/h (236mph). An arrester hook was installed for emergency use.

Specification refers to the F-104G.

Crew: 1
Powerplant: one 7076kg (15,600lb) thrust General Electric J79-GE-11A turbojet engine
Performance: max speed 1845km/h (1146mph); range 1740km (1081 miles); service ceiling 15,240m (50,000ft)
Dimensions: wingspan 6.36m (20ft 10in); length 16.66m (54ft 8in); height 4.09m (13ft 5in)
Weight: 13,170kg (29,035lb) loaded
Armament: one 20mm (0.79in) General Electric M61A1 cannon; Sidewinder air-to-air missiles on wing or fuselage stations; up to 1814kg (4000lb) of ordnance, including Bullpup air-to-surface missiles

Two-seat F-104DJ Starfighters of the Japanese Self-Defence Forces Air Force (JSDAF). The Japanese used over 200 Starfighters, most of which were licence-built by Mitsubishi.

LOCKHEED C-130 HERCULES

The Lockheed C-130 Hercules first flew in 1954, and since then the type has been supplied to more than 60 air forces worldwide.

Crew: 4
Powerplant: four 3021kW (4050hp) Allison T56-A-7 turboprop engines
Performance: max speed 547km/h (340mph); range 6145km (3820 miles); service ceiling 10,060m (33,000ft)
Dimensions: wingspan 40.41m (132ft 7in); length 29.79m (97ft 9in); height 11.68m (38ft 4in)
Weight: 70,308kg (155,000lb) loaded
Payload: 19,051kg (42,000lb)

WITHOUT DOUBT THE most versatile tactical transport aircraft ever built, the Lockheed C-130 Hercules flew for the first time on 23 August 1954, and many different variants were produced over the next half-century. The initial production versions were the C-130A and C-130B, of which 461 were built, and these were followed by the major production variant, the Lockheed C-130E, 510 examples of which were produced. Other versions include the AC-130E gunship, the WC-130E weather reconnaissance aircraft, the KC-130F assault transport for the US Marine Corps, the HC-130H for aerospace rescue and recovery, the C-130K for the RAF, and the LC-130R, which has wheel/ski landing gear. Total production of the Hercules, including all variants, was some 2000 aircraft. As well as the US forces and the RAF, the Hercules was supplied to no fewer than 61 air forces around the world. The RAF is the second-largest Hercules user, operating 80 aircraft (C.1s, C.3s, C.4s and C.5s).

Specifications apply to the Lockheed C-130E Hercules.

LOCKHEED U-2

Powerplant: one 7711kg (17,000lb) thrust Pratt & Whitney J75 P-13B turbojet engine
Performance: max speed 796km/h (495mph); range 4183km (2600 miles); service ceiling 27,430m (90,000ft)
Dimensions: wingspan 31.39m (103ft); length 19.13m (62ft 9in); height 4.88m (16ft)
Weight: 18,733kg (41,300lb) loaded
Armament: none

ONE OF THE MOST controversial and politically explosive aircraft of all time, the Lockheed U-2 high-altitude reconnaissance aircraft made its first flight in August 1955, an order for 52 production aircraft following quickly. Overflights of the Soviet Union and Warsaw Pact territories began in 1956, and continued until 1 May 1960, when a Central Intelligence Agency

pilot, Francis G. Powers, was shot down near Sverdlovsk by a Soviet SA-2 missile battery. U-2s were used to overfly Cuba during the missile crisis of 1962, one being shot down; the type was also used by the Chinese Nationalists to overfly mainland China, all four aircraft being subsequently lost. U-2s also operated over North Vietnam in 1965–66. The last U-2 variant was the U-2R, but in 1978 the production line was reopened for the building of 29 TR-1A battlefield surveillance aircraft, developed from the U-2R. All TR-1As were redesignated U-2R in the 1990s. Specifications apply to the Lockheed U-2R.

Lockheed's famous 'Black Lady', the U-2, has been the subject of much controversy and publicity. This is a U-2R.

LOCKHEED L-188 ELECTRA

USA: 1957

Crew: 3

Powerplant: four Allison 501D-13 or 501D-13A turboprop engines each rated at 2796kW (3750shp) or 501D-13A turboprop engines each rated at 3020kW (4050shp)

Performance: max cruising speed 652km/h (405mph); range 3541km (2200 miles); service ceiling 8655m (28,400ft)

Dimensions: wingspan 30.18m (99ft); length 31.85m (104ft 6in); height 10.01m (32ft 10in)

Weight: 51,256kg (113,000lb) maximum take-off weight

Payload: up to 98 passengers (in a high density layout)

WORK ON THE L-188 Electra – the United States' only indigenous turboprop airliner design of the era – began in 1954, and attracted significant orders from American Airlines and Eastern Airlines. There were fatal accidents early in the Electra's service life, however, caused at root by an engine vibration problem. Investigation and redesign, coupled with the arrival of pure jet airliners, limited

the Electra's potential, and only 170 examples were built up until 1961. However, the military Orion P-3 derivative met with great success. The L-188 Electra found a second wind as a freight liner. Today the highest concentration of the type is to be found operating in the United Kingdom with Channel Express and Atlantic Airlines.

Specifications apply to L-188A.

Fred Olsen Flyveselskap operated a fleet of second-hand Electras for many years – the example depicted was manufactured in 1961 and purchased by Olsen in 1973.

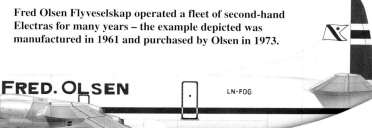

LOCKHEED P-3 ORION

USA: 1958

A DEVELOPMENT OF the Lockheed Electra airliner, the P-3 (formerly P3V-1) Orion was Lockheed's winning submission in a 1958 US Navy contest for a new off-the-shelf ASW aircraft which could be

brought into service very rapidly by modifying an existing type. The first of two YP3V-1 prototypes flew on 19 August 1958 and deliveries of production P-3As began in August 1962. The WP-3A was a

weather reconnaissance version, the next patrol variant being the P-3A. Total P-3A/B production ran to 286 aircraft for the US Navy, plus five for the RNZAF, 10 for the RAAF and five for Norway. The

The Lockheed P-3 Orion replaced the P2V Neptune in service with the Royal Australian Air Force. Pictured is one of 10 aircraft supplied for service with No 10 Squadron.

LOCKHEED XFV-1
Designed to the same specification as the Convair XFY-1, the Lockheed XFV-1 was an experimental VTOL fighter intended to take off in an upright position from a vessel. It began flight trials in March 1954, and was abandoned in 1956.

LOCKHEED L.1329 JETSTAR
This four-engined business jet/corporate transport jet was initially designed for the USAF as the C-140, but from 1961 it entered the civil market with a capacity for 10 passengers. More than 200 examples were built.

LOCKHEED MODEL 186 (XH-51A)
Two experimental rigid-rotor helicopter prototypes for the US Army and US Navy, the first flying on 2 November 1962. One was subsequently converted to the XH-51A compound helicopter with a PW J60-P-2 turbojet mounted on the left side of the fuselage and stub-wings added to off-load the rotor.

LOCKHEED XV-4A HUMMINGBIRD
The XV-4A Hummingbird, which was first flown in July 1962, was an experimental VTOL aircraft, designed to investigate thrust augmentation systems. Two prototypes of the aircraft were built, one of which crashed.

LOCKHEED YO-3A
The Lockheed YO-3A was a 1968 development of the earlier Q-Star quiet reconnaissance aircraft, based on the Schweizer SGS 2-32 sailplane and fitted with a Continental engine.

definitive P-3C variant appeared in 1969; in addition to the 132 P-3Cs delivered to the US Navy, 10 aircraft were ordered by the RAAF. Further variants of the Orion include the EP-3A electronic intelligence

aircraft, the P-3F (six of which were delivered to the Imperial Iranian Air Force in 1975), and the CP-140 Aurora for the Canadian Armed Forces.

Specifications apply to P-3C.

Crew: 10
Powerplant: four 3663kW (4910hp) Allison T56-A-14 turboprop engines
Performance: max speed 761km/h (473mph); range 3835km (2383 miles); service ceiling 8625m (28,300ft)

Dimensions: wingspan 30.37m (99ft 8in); length 35.61m (116ft 10in); height 10.29m (33ft 8in)
Weight: 61,235kg (135,000lb) loaded
Armament: up to 8735kg (19,250lb) of ASW stores

LOCKHEED C-141 STARLIFTER
USA: 1963

For many years, the Lockheed C-141 StarLifter provided the USAF with a global transport system that was second to none, enabling US troops to deploy to overseas trouble spots within hours.

FIRST FLOWN ON 17 December 1963, the C-141A StarLifter heavy-lift strategic transport was designed to provide the USAF Military Air Transport Service with a high-speed global airlift and strategic deployment capability. Deliveries to the USAF began in April 1965, and the aircraft ultimately equipped 13 squadrons of Military Airlift Command, 277 being built in total. Starting in 1976, all surviving C-141A aircraft were upgraded to C-141B standard, with the fuselage being stretched by 7.11m (23ft 4in).

Crew: 4
Powerplant: four 9526kg (21,000lb) thrust Pratt & Whitney TF33-7 turbofan engines
Performance: max speed 912km/h (567mph); range 10,370km (6445 miles); service ceiling 12,800m (42,000ft)
Dimensions: wingspan 48.74m (159ft 11in); length 51.29m (168ft 3in); height 11.96m (39ft 3in)
Weight: 155,582kg (343,000lb)
Payload: 32,161kg (70,848lb)

LOCKHEED A-12/SR-71A
USA: 1964

THE AIRCRAFT THAT BECAME known as the SR-71 was actually designated RS (Reconnaissance System) 71 to begin with, but it was erroneously referred to as the SR-71 by US President Lyndon B. Johnson when the secret programme was first unveiled, and an official decided that it was easier to rename the aircraft than inform Johnson that he had made a mistake.

Work on the SR-71 system began in 1959, when a team led by Clarence L. Johnson, Lockheed's

Vice President for Advanced Development Projects, embarked on the design of a radical new aircraft to supersede the Lockheed U-2 in the strategic reconnaissance role. Designated A-12, the new machine took shape in conditions of the utmost secrecy in the highly restricted section of the Lockheed Burbank plant, the so-called 'Skunk Works', and seven aircraft had been produced by the summer of 1964, when the project's existence was revealed. By that

time, the A-12 had already been extensively tested at Edwards Air Force Base, reaching speeds of more than 3219km/h (2000mph) at heights of over 21,336m (70,000ft). Early flight tests were aimed at assessing the A-12's suitability as a long-range interceptor, and the experimental interceptor version was shown to the public at Edwards in September 1964, bearing the designation YF-12A.

Two YF-12As were built, but the interceptor project was abandoned.

However, work on the strategic reconnaissance variant went ahead, and the prototype SR-71A flew for the first time on 22 December 1964. The first aircraft to be assigned to Strategic Air Command, an SR-71B two-seat trainer (61-7957), was delivered to the 4200th SRW at Beale Air Force Base, California, on 7 January 1966. The 4200th SRW had been activated a year earlier, and by the time the first SR-71 was delivered selected crews had already undergone a

The prototype Lockheed YF-12 strategic fighter, 60-6934. When the fighter programme was cancelled, this aircraft was converted to two-seat SR-71C configuration.

The Lockheed SR-71 made an enormous contribution to the West's intelligence-gathering operations during the height of the Cold War. Its speed enabled it to outrun hostile surface-to-air missiles.

comprehensive training programme on Northrop T-38s, eight of which were delivered to Beale from July 1965. On 25 June 1966, with deliveries of the SR-71 continuing, the 4200th SRW was redesignated 9th SRW, its component squadrons becoming the 1st and 99th SRS. In the spring of 1968, because of the growing vulnerability of the U-2 in a surface-to-air missile environment, it was decided to deploy four SR-71s to Kadena Air Base, Okinawa, for operations over South-East Asia. This deployment, known as Giant Reach, was on a 70-day TDY basis, with crews rotating between Beale and Kadena. The aircraft remained in situ and formed the nucleus of Detachment One of the 9th SRW. The first SR-71 mission over Vietnam was

flown in April 1968, with up to three missions per week being flown thereafter.

SR-71 operations from the United Kingdom began on 20 April 1976, when 64-17972 arrived at RAF Mildenhall on a 10-day TDY. In the years that followed, SR-71 deployments of RAF Mildenhall became a regular feature, the UK-based aircraft operating as Detachment Four, 9th SRW. (Detachment Four was originally a U-2 detachment, but the U-2s moved to RAF Alconbury in the early 1980s.) Two SR-71s were stationed in the United Kingdom at any one time, the aircraft flying stand-off surveillance missions over the Soviet Arctic, the Baltic and the Mediterranean. On 15 and 16 April 1986, two SR-71As

of Detachment Four (64-17960 and 64-17980) carried out post-strike reconnaissance following the attacks on Libya (Operation Eldorado Canyon) by UK-based F-111s and US Navy aircraft; both SR-71s were used on each occasion.

Crew: 2
Powerplant: two 14,742kg (32,500lb) thrust Pratt & Whitney JT11D-20B turbojet engines
Performance: max speed 3220km/h (2000mph) at 24,385m (80,000ft); range 4800km (2983 miles); service ceiling 24,385m (80,000ft)
Dimensions: wingspan 16.94m (55ft 7in); wing area 149.10m² (1605 sq ft); length 32.74m (107ft 5in); height 5.64m (18ft 6in)
Weight: 78,017kg (172,000lb) loaded
Armament: none

LOCKHEED C-5 GALAXY

USA: 1968

THE LARGEST TRANSPORT aircraft in the world at the time of its appearance, the Lockheed C-5 Galaxy was first flown on 30 June 1968; the first production aircraft was delivered to Military Airlift Command in December 1969. Although the Galaxy has provision

The Lockheed C-5 Galaxy brought a massive boost to USAF Military Airlift Command's strategic airlift capabilities in the 1970s.

for 270 troops on the lower deck and 75 on the upper, the lower deck is intended for freight and can accommodate complete tactical missile systems or M1 Abrams main battle tanks. Despite its size,

the Galaxy can operate from rough airstrips. The C-5B is an improved version, with uprated engines, better avionics and an extended-life wing. Specifications apply to the C-5A Galaxy.

Crew: 5
Powerplant: four 18,642kg (41,000lb) General Electric TF39 turbofan engines
Performance: max speed 919km/h (571mph); range 6033km (3749 miles); service ceiling 10,360m (34,000ft)

Dimensions: wingspan 68.88m (226ft); length 75.54m (247ft 10in); height 19.85m (65ft 1in)
Weight: 348,810kg (769,000lb)
Payload: up to 345 passengers

LOCKHEED L-1011 TRISTAR

USA: 1970

Crew: 3/4
Powerplant: three 222.41kN (50,000lb st) Rolls-Royce RB.211-524B or RB.211-524B4 turbofan engines
Performance: max cruising speed 974km/h (605mph); range 9905km (6155 miles) with maximum payload; service ceiling 12,800m (42,000ft)
Dimensions: wingspan 47.35m (155ft 4in); length 50.05m (164ft 2.5in); height 16.87m (55ft 4in)
Weight: 224,982kg (496,000lb) maximum take-off weight
Payload: up to 330 passengers

PSA ordered five Lockheed L-1011 TriStars. Two were placed into service in August 1974 between Los Angeles and San Francisco, but withdrawn in March 1975 because of their high fuel consumption and unprofitability.

THE L-1011-1 and its direct competitor the DC-10 were originally designed to meet US airline industry requirements for a transcontinental wide-body airliner. Both manufacturers settled on a tri-jet design. Lockheed's TriStar was the more technologically advanced design, embodying a number of new manufacturing and avionic features.

The Rolls-Royce RB.211 was selected as the sole choice of engine, but financial crises at both Rolls-Royce and Lockheed contributed to delays, lost orders and the delayed launch of the longer range

200 and 500 series. Consequently, only 250 examples were sold, but they served with distinction in many major carriers' fleets. TriStar was Lockheed's last airliner design – its (then) technologically

advanced aspects and maintenance requirements have been less popular with second-line or freight operators, and operational numbers are fast diminishing. Specifications apply to the L-1011-500.

LOCKHEED S-3A VIKING

USA: 1972

Crew: 4
Powerplant: two 4207kg (9275lb) General Electric TF34-GE-2 turbofan engines
Performance: max speed 814km/h (506mph); range 3705km (2302 miles); service ceiling 10,670m (35,000ft)
Dimensions: wingspan 20.93m (68ft 8in); length 16.26m (53ft 4in); height 6.93m (22ft 9in)
Weight: 19,278kg (42,500lb) loaded
Armament: up to 907kg (2000lb) of ASW stores; two underwing pylons for bombs, rockets, missiles etc.

THE S-3A VIKING was designed in response to a 1969 US Navy requirement for a carrier-borne ASW system built around a Univac digital computer. The prototype flew for the first time on 21 January 1972, and deliveries to VS-41, an operational training unit, began in March 1974. The last of 187 Vikings was delivered to the US Navy in 1978. The Viking fleet was substantially updated to S-3B standard in the early 1990s, some aircraft being converted to the electronic warfare role as ES-3As. Specifications apply to S-3A.

The Lockheed S-3 Viking gave the US Navy an impressive anti-submarine warfare capability in the later years of the Cold War, at a time when a new generation of Soviet nuclear submarines was entering service.

LOCKHEED F-117A NIGHT HAWK

USA: 1981

THE AMAZING F-117A 'Stealth' aircraft began life in 1973 as a project called 'Have Blue', launched to study the feasibility of producing a combat aircraft with little or no radar and infrared signature. Two Experimental Stealth Tactical (XST) 'Have Blue' research aircraft were built and flown in 1977 at Groom Lake, Nevada (Area 51). One was destroyed in an accident, but the other went on to complete the test programme successfully in 1979. The Have Blue prototypes validated the faceting concept of the stealth aircraft, and the basic aircraft shape. A key difference between these aircraft and the production F-117 was the inward canting of the fins, which were mounted on the outside of the main fuselage body and much further forward than on production aircraft. The leading edge was set at a very sharp 72.5 degrees. Have Blue utilized many off-the-shelf systems from other aircraft, including the fly-by-wire system of the F-16. The aircraft also had the F-16's sidestick controller, while the undercarriage came from the Northrop F-5. The two engines came from a Rockwell T-2 Buckeye. Flight-control systems were served by three static pressure sensors on the forward fuselage, and three total pressure probes, one on the nose and two on the cockpit windscreen post. Have Blue 1001 also had the instrumentation boom which correlated data from the primary systems. The exhaust slot for the Have Blue had a greater extension on its lower lip than was featured on the F-117, with its two exhaust slots meeting at a common point on the centreline.

The evaluation of the two Have Blue aircraft led to an order for 65 production F-117As. The type made its first flight in June 1981

The F-117 possesses the ability to approach a heavily defended target undetected, then destroy it with Paveway laser-guided bombs.

One of the most remarkable aircraft ever designed, the Lockheed F-117 was the end product of many years of research into 'stealth' technology.

and entered service in October 1983. The F-117A is a single-seat, subsonic aircraft powered by two non-afterburning GE F404 turbofans with shielded slot exhausts to dissipate heat emissions (aided also by heat-shielding tiles), thus minimizing the infrared signature. The use of faceting (angled flat surfaces) scatters incoming radar energy; radar-absorbent materials and transparencies treated with conductive coating reduce the radar signature still further. The aircraft has highly swept wing leading edges, a W-shaped trailing edge, and a V-shaped tail unit. Armament is carried on swing-down trapezes in two internal bays. The F-117A has quadruple redundant fly-by-wire controls, steerable turrets for FLIR and laser designator, head-up and head-down displays, laser communications and nav/attack system integrated with a digital avionics suite.

F-117As played a prominent part in the Gulf Wars of 1991 and 2003, making first strikes on high-

priority targets; they were also used in the Balkans and Afghanistan. The last of 59 F-117As was delivered in July 1990. Along with the Northrop Grumman B-2 Spirit 'stealth bomber', the Night Hawk is the US Air Force's primary attack weapon, the F-117 force being able to exert an influence on an air campaign that far outweighs its size.

Crew: 1
Powerplant: two 4899kg (10,800lb) thrust General Electric F404-GE-F1D2 turbofan engines
Performance: max speed Mach 0.92; range classified; service ceiling classified;
Dimensions: wingspan 13.20m (43ft 4in); length 20.08m (65ft 11in); height 3.78m (12ft 5in)
Weight: 23,814kg (52,500lb) loaded
Armament: provision for 2268kg (5000lb) of stores on rotary dispenser in weapons bay, including the AGM-88 HARM anti-radiation missile, AGM-65 Maverick ASM, GBU-19 and GBU-27 optronically guided bomb, BLU-109 laser-guided bombs, and B61 free-fall nuclear bomb

LOIRE 46
The Loire 46 was a French gull-winged monoplane fighter, first flown in 1934. Sixty were built for the Armée de l'Air, some being tested operationally during the Spanish Civil War.

LOIRE 70 AND 130
The Loire 70 and 130 were three-engined and single-engined French reconnaissance flying-boats of the mid-1930s.

LOIRE 210
The Loire 210 was a low-wing fighter seaplane, the prototype flying in March 1935. The first of 20 production aircraft entered service with the French Navy in 1938.

LOIRE-GOURDOU-LESEURRE 32C-1
The Loire-Gourdou-Leseurre 32C-1 parasol-wing fighter of 1925 was built in substantial numbers, about 460 being produced for France (395), Romania (50), Turkey (12) and Japan (1).

LOIRE-NIEUPORT LN-161 FRANCE
The Loire-Nieuport LN-161 monoplane fighter of 1935 was a clean design and showed some promise, three prototypes being built. However, in the end the Morane-Saulnier MS.405 was selected for production.

LOIRE-NIEUPORT LN-10
The Loire-Nieuport LN-10 was a French torpedo-bomber/reconnaissance seaplane. The sole prototype of the aircraft flew in July 1939, and it was destroyed in June 1940 to prevent its capture by the Germans.

LOCKHEED MARTIN F-22 RAPTOR

USA: 1990

Crew: 1
Powerplant: two 15,872kg (35,000lb) thrust Pratt & Whitney F119-P-100 turbofan engines
Performance: max speed 2335km/h (1450mph); combat radius 1285km (800 miles); service ceiling 19,812m (65,000ft)
Dimensions: wingspan 13.10m (43ft); length 19.55m (64ft 2in); height 5.39m (17ft 8in)
Weight: 27,216kg (60,000lb)
Armament: AIM-9X and AMRAAM air-to-air missiles; GBU-32 Joint Direct Attack Munition and other advanced weapons

WITHOUT DOUBT, THE most exciting combat aircraft of the early twenty-first century is the Lockheed Martin F-22 Raptor. In the late 1970s, the US Air Force identified a requirement for 750 examples of an Advanced Tactical Fighter (ATF) to replace the F-15 Eagle. Flown by a single pilot, it must be able to survive in an environment filled with people, both in the air and on the ground, whose sole purpose is to destroy it. To test the concepts that would eventually be combined in the ATF, the USAF initiated a series of parallel research programmes. The first was the YF-16 control-configured vehicle (CCV) which flew in 1976–77 and demonstrated the decoupled control of aircraft flight path and attitude; in other words, the machine could skid sideways, turn without banking, climb or descend without changing its attitude, and point its nose left or right, or up or down, without changing its flight path. Other test vehicles involved in the ATF programme included the Grumman X-29, which flew for the first time in December 1984 and which was designed to investigate forward-sweep technology, and an F-111 fitted with a mission adaptive wing (MAW) – in other words, a wing capable of reconfiguring itself automatically to mission requirements.

Flight testing of all these experimental aircraft came under the umbrella of the USAF's Advanced Fighter Technology Integration (AFTI) programme. In September 1983, while the AFTI programme was well under way, the USAF awarded ATF concept definition study contracts to six American aerospace companies and, of these, two – Lockheed and Northrop – were selected to build

The Lockheed Martin F-22 Raptor is the end product of one of the most costly research and development programmes in the history of aviation.

demonstrator prototypes of their respective proposals. Each company produced two prototypes, the Lockheed YF-22 and the Northrop YF-23, and all four aircraft flew in 1990. Two different powerplants, the Pratt & Whitney YF119 and the General Electric YF120, were evaluated, and in April 1991 it was announced that the F-22 and F119 were the winning combination. The F119

advanced technology engine, two of which power the F-22, develops 155kN (35,000lb st) and is fitted with two-dimensional convergent/divergent exhaust nozzles with thrust vectoring for enhanced performance and manoeuvrability. The first definitive F-22 prototype was rolled out at the Lockheed Martin plant at Marietta, Georgia, on 9 April 1997. There were numerous problems with this

aircraft, including software troubles and fuel leaks, and the first flight was delayed to 7 September 1997. The second prototype first flew on 29 June 1998. By late 2001, there were eight F-22s flying.

The F-22 combines many stealth features. Its air-to-air weapons, for example, are stored internally; three internal bays house advanced short-range, medium-range and beyond-visual-range air-to-air missiles. Following an assessment of the aircraft's combat role in 1993, it was decided to add a ground-attack capability, and the internal weapons bay is also capable of accommodating 454kg (1000lb) GBU-32 precision-guided missiles.

The F-22 is designed for a high sortie rate, with a turnaround time of less than 20 minutes, and its avionics are highly integrated to provide rapid reaction in air combat, much of its survivability depending on the pilot's ability to locate a target very early and take it out with a first shot. The F-22 was designed to meet a specific threat, which at that time was presented by large numbers of highly agile Soviet combat aircraft, its task being to engage them in their own airspace with beyond-visual-range weaponry. It will be a key component in the Global Strike Task Force, formed in 2001 to counter any threat worldwide. The USAF requirement is for 438 aircraft.

Although a highly complex aircraft, the F-22 is designed for a high sortie rate, with a turnaround time of less than 20 minutes. It will form a key component of the Global Strike Task Force.

LOCKHEED MARTIN X-35

USA: 2000

Far from attractive to look at, the Lockheed Martin X-35B combines all the knowledge of previous V/STOL strike aircraft with the latest advances in aviation technology.

Crew: 1
Powerplant: one 19,026kg (42,000lb) thrust Pratt & Whitney F119-PW-611S turbofan engine and one 8154kg (18,000lb) thrust Rolls-Royce lift fan (X-35B only)
Performance: max speed Mach 1.4+ at altitude; combat radius 1000km (621 miles); service ceiling 15,240+m (50,000+ft)
Dimensions: wingspan 10.05m (33ft); length 15.52m (50ft 11in); height not known
Weight: 22,680kg (50,000lb) loaded
Armament: six AIM-120C AMRAAM or two AIM-120C AMRAAM and two 907kg (2000lb) JDAM in internal fuseleage bay; provision for one 20mm (0.79in) M61A2 rotary cannon with 400 rounds in starboard wing root (USAF CTOL variant); provision for four underwing pylons with 2268kg (5000lb) of stores each

THE X-35 JOINT STRIKE FIGHTER project originated in a 1980s requirement by the US Marine Corps and the Royal Navy that a replacement for the Sea Harrier and AV-8B would be needed early in the twenty-first century. Various research studies were undertaken on both sides of the Atlantic into advanced short take-off and vertical landing (STOVL) concepts, the most promising of which appeared to involve the use of a dedicated lift-fan located behind the cockpit. In 1989, DARPA (Defense Advanced Research Projects Agency) took over leadership of the advanced STOVL project and focused the on-going effort into a phased development programme leading to a flying demonstrator aircraft using the powerful new engines

developed for the YF-22 and YF-23 Advanced Tactical Fighter.

As the studies progressed, it was realized that a STOVL aircraft with the lift-fan removed and replaced by a large fuel tank would result in a fighter with excellent long-range capability. Such a fighter would fulfil the needs of the US Air Force, which was looking for a longer-ranged fighter capability in the light of Gulf War operations. So was born the Common Affordable Lightweight Fighter (CALF) project, aimed at producing a single aircraft design with both STOVL and conventional take-off and landing (CTOL) variants. In March 1993, study contracts were issued to Lockheed and McDonnell Douglas under the CALF project. In addition, Boeing

LOIRE-NIEUPORT CAO-200
The Loire-Nieuport CAO-200 was a progressive development of the LN-161 fighter prototype, and was in production for the Armée de l'Air at the time of France's defeat in 1940.

LOIRE-NIEUPORT CAO-700
The CAO-700 four-engined heavy bomber of 1940 was based on the design of the LN-10 twin-float seaplane. It was completed and test flown by the SNCA de l'Ouest.

LOMBARDI & CIE LM-7
An Italian single-engined light aeroplane design dating from 1949 that achieved only prototype standard.

LORING R1 TO R3
The Loring R1, R2 and R3 were two-seat reconnaissance biplanes, about 30 being delivered to the Spanish Army in the late 1920s.

LTV XC-142A
First flown in September 1964, the Ling-Temco-Vought (LTV) XC-142A was an experimental tilt-wing V/STOL military transport. Despite its promise and versatility, the project was abandoned.

LUALDI L.55 AND L.57
The Lualdi L.55 and L.57 were Italian two-seat light general-purpose helicopters which were developed from the ES.53 of 1953 and which incorporated the Hiller 'Rotor-Matic' rotor system and a gyroscopic system developed by Lualdi. The Lualdi L.59 was a four-seat version.

The operational F-35 is intended for operations from both land and aircraft carrier bases. A competitor aircraft, the X-32, was built by Boeing.

and Northrop Grumman initiated private venture design studies.

In 1995, CALF was absorbed into the Joint Advanced Strike Technology (JAST) programme, which was originally intended to focus on technology studies and demonstration of various equipment for next-generation strike aircraft. In fact, JAST soon evolved into a firm requirement for an advanced single-seat, single-engined lightweight multi-role fighter

which could be operated by the USAF, US Navy and US Marine Corps in closely similar variants. In 1996, JAST was renamed JSF (Joint Strike Fighter), and in November that year Boeing and Lockheed Martin were awarded contracts to build two Concept Demonstrator Aircraft (CDA) – one CTOL version and one STOVL version – each. The aircraft were not intended to be fighter prototypes, but rather to prove that

the selected design concepts would work, hence the use of X-series designations. The Boeing design received the designation X-32, while the Lockheed Martin design was given the designation X-35. For the two Concept Demonstrator Aircraft, the designation X-35A was allocated to the CTOL version and X-35B to the STOVL version.

Unlike Boeing, Lockheed Martin introduced a third version, the X-35C, to undertake simulated

aircraft carrier (CV/CTOL) testing. This aircraft was produced by converting the existing X-35A after it had completed its planned flight trials. The Lockheed Martin X-35A and X-35B possess very similar airframes, including the aft cockpit bulge and associated doors for the lift-fan, which is only fitted to the X-35B.

The Lockheed Martin X-35A made its first flight on 24 October 2000 from Palmdale, California.

LOIRE-NIEUPORT LN-40

FRANCE: 1938

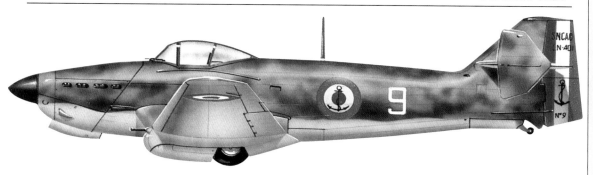

THE LOIRE-NIEUPORT LN-40, which first flew in 1938, was a carrier-borne dive-bomber with an inverted gull wing, similar to that of the Ju 87 Stuka. The designation was later altered to LN-401, and the Armée de l'Air ordered 40 examples of a de-navalized version without folding wings and arrester hook under the designation LN-411. The 23 examples delivered before the German invasion in World War II were handed over to

The small number of Loire-Nieuport LN-40 aircraft delivered to the French Navy were to suffer terrible losses in May 1940.

the French Navy in May 1940, and these aircraft equipped Escadrilles AB 2 and AB 4; however, they were to suffer disastrous losses. On 19 May 1940, in a mission against German armoured columns, 10 out of the 20 aircraft dispatched for the mission were shot down.

Crew: 1
Powerplant: one Hispano-Suiza 12 Xcrs Vee-type engine
Performance: max speed 380km/h (236mph); range 1200km (746 miles); service ceiling 9500m (31,170ft);
Dimensions: wingspan 14.00m (45ft 11.25in); length 9.75m (31ft 11.75in); height 3.50m (11ft 5.75in)
Weight: 2823kg (6224lb) loaded
Armament: one 20mm (0.79in) cannon and two 7.5mm (0.30in) machine guns; external bomb load of 225kg (496lb)

LUSCOMBE MODEL 8 SILVAIRE

USA: 1938

Crew: 1
Powerplant: one 63kW (85hp) Continental C-85 flat-four piston engine
Performance: max speed 196km/h (122mph); range 821km (510 miles); service ceiling 4875m (16,000ft)
Dimensions: wingspan 10.67m (35ft); length 6.10m (20ft); wing area 13.01m² (140.00 sq ft); height 1.91m (6ft 3in)
Weight: 635kg (1400lb) maximum take-off weight
Payload: two seats

FOLLOWING A SERIES OF LESS successful designs of similar configuration came the lighter, highly regarded and commercially successful Luscombe Model 8, which proved popular in both private and flying school markets.

Donald A. Luscombe founded the Luscombe Aeroplane Company five years before the Model 8 first flew, having moved the company from Kansas to New Jersey. Luscombe himself was eased out of the company in 1939, just as early versions of the Model 8 were being rolled out.

The Model 8 Silvaire was the Luscombe company's most notable design – neither predecessor or successor designs achieved anywhere near the same level of sales and popularity.

The Model 8 was a high-wing, tail-wheel monoplane, with an all-metal fuselage and fabric covered wings. In 1949, the company was sold to Temco, and then to the

Silvaire Aircraft Company. When production ceased in 1961, an estimated 6000 Model 8s had been produced. Specifications apply to the Model 8-E.

LUSCOMBE 185 11E SPARTAN
A new Luscombe company has produced a modernized successor to the Luscombe Sedan four-seat, single-engined light aeroplane dating from the 1950s. The Spartan is today fitted with modern avionics and a Teledyne Continental IO 360-ES 138kW (185hp) engine.

LUTON BUZZARD I &11
The initial Luton Buzzard (wood-based) was an ultra-light, single-seat, high-wing design with the 26kW (35hp) engine mounted aft of the cockpit. Only one example was built and it suffered accident damage. This aircraft was later rebuilt as the Buzzard II with an enclosed cockpit.

LWD JUNAK
A Polish-designed, two-seat basic trainer dating from 1948 and powered by a Polish engine, the Junak was first built with a tail wheel but later versions feature a tricycle undercarriage.

LWD MIS
The LWD Mis was a prototype twin-engined feederliner, built in 1949 by the Aircraft Experimental Workshops, Lodz. It did not enter production.

LWS 4
The LWS 4 was a twin-engined monoplane bomber, first flown in 1936. The Polish Air Force ordered 16 and Romania 24, but the latter order was cancelled when the prototype broke up in mid-air. The type was strengthened, fitted with a twin-tail assembly and re-designated LWS 6.

LVG C.II

DURING THE EARLY months of World War I, German manufacturer Luft-Verkehrs Gesellschaft produced a small series of unarmed B-type two-seat observation aircraft; these formed the basis for the C-type armed reconnaissance aircraft, introduced in the spring of 1915. The C.I was followed by the C.II, built in substantial numbers and used for light bombing as well as visual and photographic reconnaissance.

On 28 November 1916, an LVG C.II (sometimes identified as a C.IV) crewed by Deck Officer Paul Brandt and captained by Lieutenant Walther Ilges made a daring daylight attack on London.

One aircraft carried out a daylight bombing attack on London on 28 November 1916, dropping six 10kg (22lb) bombs on Victoria railway station (the actual target was the Admiralty). It suffered engine failure on the way home and was forced to land near Boulogne; the crew was captured. An enlarged version of the C.II, the C.IV, appeared in 1916, with a 164kW (220hp) Mercedes D.IV engine.

Crew: 2
Powerplant: one 119kW (160hp) Mercedes D.III 6-cylinder liquid-cooled in-line engine
Performance: max speed 130km/h (81mph); endurance 4 hrs; service ceiling 5000m (16,405ft)
Dimensions: wingspan 12.85m (42ft 2in); length 8.10m (26ft 7in); height 2.93m (9ft 7.25in)
Weight: 1405kg (3091lb) loaded
Armament: one or two 7.5mm (0.30in) machine guns

LVG C.V AND C.VI

Crew: 2
Powerplant: one 149kW (200hp) Benz Bz.IV water-cooled in-line engine
Performance: max speed 170km/h (105.6mph); endurance 3 hrs 30 mins; service ceiling 6500m (21,325ft)
Dimensions: wingspan 13.00m (42ft 7.75in); length 7.45m (24ft 5.33in); height 2.80m (9ft 2.25in)
Weight: 1310kg (2888lb) loaded
Armament: two 7.7mm (0.30in) machine guns; up to 115kg (254lb) of bombs

IN 1917 THE LVG C.V made its appearance on the Western Front, and was in widespead use by the autumn of that year, also serving in Palestine. An excellent all-round aircraft, it was well able to defend itself. In 1918 it was joined by the C.VI, about 1000 examples of which were produced. This type had a number of modifications and improved visibility for the crew. The final variant was the C.VIII, only one of which was built. Specifications apply to LVG C.V.

The LVG C.V was one of the best German designs of World War I, and saw widespread service on the Western Front in 1917–18, together with the improved C.VI.

LWS RWD-14

THE LWS RWD-14 Czapla (Heron) was a two-seat parasol-wing army cooperation aircraft. The prototype flew for the first time in 1935 and the type entered service in 1938. By the time of the German invasion of September 1939, the Polish Air Force had 65 RWD-14s in its strength. Quite a number of these successfully escaped to Romania after Poland was overrun by German and Russian forces on 17 September.

Crew: 2
Powerplant: one 313kW (420hp) PZL G1620B Mors II radial engine
Performance: max speed 247km/h (153mph); range 675km (419 miles); service ceiling 5100m (16,728ft)

Dimensions: wingspan 11.90m (39ft); length 9.00m (29ft 6in); height 3.00m (9ft 10in)
Weight: 1700kg (3746lb) loaded
Armament: two 7.7mm (0.303in) machine guns

MACCHI M.5   ITALY: 1918

Crew: 1
Powerplant: one 187kW (250hp) Isotta-Fraschini V6B liquid-cooled in-line engine
Performance: max speed 209km/h (130mph); endurance 3 hrs 40 mins; service ceiling 5000m (16,405ft)
Dimensions: wingspan 9.95m (32ft 7in); length 8.10m (26ft 7in); height 2.95m (9ft 8in)
Weight: 1080kg (2381lb) loaded
Armament: two 7.7mm (0.303in) fixed forward-firing machine guns

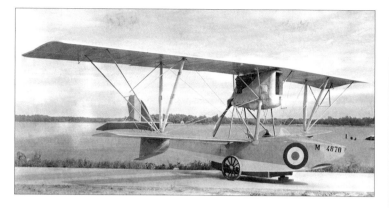

A neat little design, the Macchi M.5 was widely used over the Adriatic during the closing months of World War I.

THE MACCHI M.5 was Italy's first flying-boat fighter and was a single-seater, previous designs having been two-seaters. Some 240 M.5s were built, these equipping five Italian maritime patrol squadrons from early 1918 until after the Armistice. The M.5mod had a more powerful 187kW (250hp) engine. The M.5 was extremely manoeuvrable and proved invaluable for escort duty over the Adriatic, as it possessed a substantial endurance. It had an excellent rate of climb, being able to reach 4000m (13,123ft) in 20 minutes. Specifications apply to the Macchi M.5mod.

MACCHI MC.200 SAETTA   ITALY: 1937

THE MC.200 SAETTA (Lightning), the second of Italy's monoplane fighters, was designed by Mario Castoldi. He had been responsible for some highly successful seaplane racers between the wars and drew on experience gained with the M.39, winner of the 1926 Schneider Trophy, and the MC.72, holder of the world air-speed record in its class. Powered by a Fiat A74 radial engine, the bulk of which tended to spoil the aircraft's otherwise neat contours, the MC.200 first flew on 24 December 1937, deliveries to the Regia Aeronautica beginning in October 1939. About 150 aircraft were in service by June 1940. Production C.200s were C.200A-1 and A-2, the latter having a strengthened wing for carriage of two small bombs. Early production C.200s had a fully enclosed cockpit, but this was later altered to an open and then a semi-enclosed type. About 1000 MC.200s were built.

Crew: 1
Powerplant: one 649kW (870hp) Fiat A.74 RC.38 14-cylinder radial engine
Performance: max speed 503km/h (312mph); range 870km (541 miles); service ceiling 8900m (29,200ft)
Dimensions: wingspan 10.58m (34ft 8in); length 8.19m (26ft 10in); height 3.51m (11ft 5in)
Weight: 2208kg (4874lb) loaded
Armament: two 12.7mm (0.50in) machine guns; external bomb load of 320kg (705lb)

The fully enclosed cockpit of this Macchi MC. 200 Saetta betrays the fact that it is an early production model. The type was outclassed by contemporary Allied monoplane fighters.

MACCHI MC.202 FOLGORE

ITALY: 1940

Crew: 1
Powerplant: one 802kW (1075hp) Alfa Romeo RA 1000 RC.411 12-cylinder inverted Vee-type engine
Performance: max speed 600km/h (373mph); range 610km (379 miles); service ceiling 11,500m (37,730ft)
Dimensions: wingspan 10.58m (34ft 8in); length 8.85m (29ft); height 3.50m (11ft 6in)
Weight: 3010kg (6636lb) loaded
Armament: two 12.7mm (0.50in) Breda-SAFAT and two 7.7mm (0.303in) machine guns; late production aircraft, two 20mm (0.79in) cannon in wings

RAF pilots who encountered the Macchi MC.202 Folgore over Malta during World War II found it a formidable opponent.

EFFORTS TO IMPROVE the MC.200's performance began in 1938, but it was not until early in 1940 that a suitable engine became available in the shape of the Daimler-Benz DB 601A-1 liquid-cooled in-line engine. This was installed in a standard Saetta airframe and flown on 10 August 1940. Subsequent flight tests produced excellent results, and the aircraft, designated MC.202 Folgore (Thunderbolt), was ordered into production fitted with the licence-built DB 601, the engine being produced by Alfa Romeo as the RA.1000 RC.411. The type entered service with the 1st Stormo at Udine in the summer of 1941, moving to Sicily to take part in operations over Malta in November. It stayed in production until the Italian armistice of September 1943, but the rate of production was always influenced by the availability of engines. Macchi built 392 MC.202s; around 1100 more were produced by other companies.

MACCHI MC.205 VELTRO

ITALY: 1943

Crew: 1
Powerplant: one 1100kW (1475hp) Daimler-Benz DB605A 12-cylinder Vee-type engine
Performance: max speed 650km/h (403mph); range 1040km (646 miles); service ceiling 11,350m (37,200ft)
Dimensions: wingspan 10.59m (34ft 8in); length 8.85m (29ft 1in); height 3.05m (10ft)
Weight: 3224kg (7120lb) loaded
Armament: two 20mm (0.79in) cannon and two 12.7mm (0.50in) machine guns

THE ULTIMATE FIGHTER of the MC.200 series was the MC.205 Veltro (Greyhound), which went into operational service in April 1943. When the Italians concluded a separate armistice with the Allies on 8 September 1943, some 40 aircraft re-mustered with the Italian Co-Belligerent Air Force, which fought on the Allied side and saw active service until the end of the war. About 30 more escaped to join the Aviazione della RSI, which continued to fight on the German side, and which acquired 112 more Veltros built up to May 1944.

The Macchi MC.205 Veltro was the best Italian fighter to see service in World War II and fought on both sides. However, visibility from the cockpit was poor, both on the ground and in the air.

MAKHONINE MAK-123

FRANCE: 1947

THE MAKHONINE MAK-123 came from a remarkable concept for an aircraft with telescopic wings devised by Ivan Makhonine, a Russian refugee living in France. His idea was to telescope the wing outer sections into the inner sections to reduce wing area after take-off. The first flying prototype flew in August 1931 and testing continued throughout the 1930s, with varying success. The aircraft was deliberately wrecked to prevent its capture by the Germans in World War II, and was later completely destroyed in an air raid. After the war Makhonine built a second prototype, which he tested in 1947. This aicraft was a four-seater. On its second flight from Toussous-le Noble, Makhonine climbed to 3965m (13,000ft), extended the outer wing sections and succeeded in gliding for more than an hour. Testing continued for some time before this, the world's first variable-geometry aircraft, was abandoned.

Crew: 4
Powerplant: one 1343kW (1800hp) BMW radial engine
Performance: max speed 300km/h (186mph); range not established; service ceiling 5500m (18,040ft)
Dimensions: wing area variable between 20m² and 36.5m² (215sq ft and 393sq ft)
Weight: 10,000kg (22,046lb)

MARTIN MB-1/MB-2

Crew: 4
Powerplant: two 313kW (420hp) V-1650 Liberty 12A 12-cylinder Vee-type engines
Performance: max speed 159km/h (99mph); range 898km (558 miles); service ceiling 2591m (8500ft)
Dimensions: wingspan 22.61m (74ft 2in); length 13.00m (42ft 8in); height 4.47m (14ft 8in)
Weight: 5472kg (12,064lb) loaded
Armament: five 7.5mm (0.29in) machine guns; up to 907kg (2000lb) of bombs

THE MARTIN MB-1 and MB-2 bombers were designed to succeed the Handley Page O/400, which was built under licence in the United States at the end of World War I. They were the first twin-engined bombers to be produced in the United States. The MB-1 flew for the first time in August 1918. The MB-2 was a developed version intended for night bombing, and it was this type which made history

The Martin MB-1 and MB-2 remained the standard bomber type with the US Army Air Service for several years. An MB-2 is seen here over Washington DC.

when it became the first aircraft to sink a capital ship by bombing the old German battleship *Ostfriesland* on 21 July 1921.

Specifications apply to the Martin MB-2.

MARTIN B-10

Crew: 4
Powerplant: two 578kW (775hp) Wright R-1820 G-102 Cyclone 9-cylinder radial engines
Performance: max speed 322km/h (200mph); range 950km (590 miles); service ceiling 7680m (25,200ft)
Dimensions: wingspan 21.60m (70ft 10in); length 13.46m (44ft 2in); height 3.53m (11ft 7in)
Weight: 7210kg (15,894lb) loaded
Armament: one 7.62mm (0.30in) machine gun in nose, dorsal and ventral positions; up to 1025kg (2260lb) of bombs

ALTHOUGH OBSOLETE by the outbreak of World War II, the Martin B-10 was a very advanced aircraft when it first appeared in 1932. It was the first American bomber of all-metal construction to enter large-scale production, the first US warplane to feature gun turrets, and the US Army Air Corps' first cantilever low-wing

monoplane. The USAAC took delivery of 151 B-10s and a slightly improved version, the B-12. Although the type was retired from first-line US service by the time World War II began, the production line remained open to fulfil orders from Argentina (35), China (9), Thailand (26), Turkey (20) and the Netherlands East Indies (120).

A Martin B-10B bomber of the 28th Bombardment Squadron, US Army Air Corps, based at Luzon in the Philippines from 1937 to 1941.

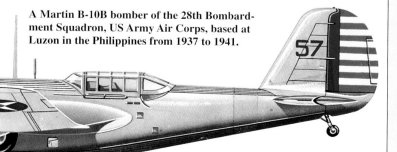

MACCHI M.16
A single-seat floatplane powered by a single engine, the M.16 dates from the mid-1930s. During this period several examples were acquired by the US Navy for experimental purposes.

MACCHI C.94
Built and flown in 1936, the Macchi C.94 was a twin-engined light transport monoplane with a capacity for 12 passengers. Twelve were produced.

MACCHI C.100
The Macchi C.100 was a transport trimotor, powered by three Alfa Romeo engines. The prototype flew in 1939 and three aircraft were built, all being pressed into military service.

MACCHI MB.308
A postwar design dating from 1946, this high-wing monoplane light aircraft design was both popular and successful! in several seating configurations, and as a seaplane.

MACCHI MB.320
First flown in 1949, the Macchi MB.320 was a light twin-engined feederliner in the same class as the de Havilland Dove. Only six were built, these being used by East African Airways.

MACCHI-CASTOLDI MC.72
Although it came too late to compete for the Schneider Trophy, which was won permanently by Britain in 1931, the Macchi-Castoldi MC.72 racing floatplane did set a new world speed record of 709.209km/h (440.7mph) in June 1933.

MARTIN 130 CHINA CLIPPER

USA: 1934

PAN AMERICAN AIRWAYS ambitions included the implementation of trans-Pacific services, but the geo-political climate of the mid-1930s dictated that a long-range amphibious flying boat was the only means of achieving the goal. The 130 was Martin's response to the requirement and three 'China Clippers' were built. The inaugural service was from San Francisco to the Philippines in 1935, taking around 60 hours. All three examples were lost in accidents, one before World War II, and the other two while on impressed military service during the war.

Crew: 4
Powerplant: four 619kW (830hp) Pratt & Whitney R-1830-S1A4G Twin Wasp 14-cylinder radial piston engines
Performance: max speed 290km/h (180mph); cruising speed 253km/h (157mph); range 6437km (4000 miles)
Dimensions: wingspan 39.62m (130ft); length 27.61m (90ft 7in); height 7.49m (24ft 7in)
Weight: 23,587kg (52,000lb) maximum take-off weight
Payload: up to 48 day passengers or 18 night-berth passengers

One China Clipper was lost near Manila in a storm, another flew into a Californian mountain returning from Pearl Harbor in fog and the third was inexplicably torn asunder landing at Port of Spain, Trinidad, in early 1945.

MARTIN 167 MARYLAND AND MARTIN BALTIMORE

USA: 1938

THE MARTIN 167 WAS developed in 1938 to meet a USAAC medium-bomber competition which, in the event, was won by the Douglas DB-7. Although the Martin design bore the Air Corps designation A-22, it never entered US service. In 1939 the French government placed an order for 215 aircraft, which carried the export designation 167F. When Germany invaded France in May 1940 the two groupes operational with the type in France flew 363 sorties against the Germans and 55 against the Italians. All surviving aircraft were evacuated to North Africa. Seventy-six aircraft from the French order were diverted to the RAF, where they were known as the Maryland Mk I; the RAF received a further 150 aircraft as Maryland Mk IIs. These performed a useful reconnaissance role in the early part of World War II.

The Martin Baltimore was an improved version of the Maryland. The type served exclusively in the Mediterranean theatre with the RAF and Allied air forces under RAF command. Specification refers to the Martin 167 Maryland.

The Martin 167 Maryland, seen here, served the RAF well during World War II in the reconnaissance role both at home and overseas.

Crew: 4
Powerplant: two 783kW (1050hp) Pratt & Whitney R-1830-S1C3-G radial engines
Performance: max speed 489km/h (304mph); range 2092km (1300 miles); service ceiling 8992m (29,500ft)
Dimensions: wingspan 18.69m (61ft 4in); length 14.22m (46ft 8in); height 3.07m (10ft 1in)
Weight: 6939kg (15,297lb) loaded
Armament: six 12.7mm (0.50in) machine guns; up to 567kg (1250lb) of bombs

MARTIN PBM MARINER

USA: 1939

Crew: 9
Powerplant: two 1417kW (1900hp) Wright
R-2600-22 Cyclone 14-cylinder radial
engines
Performance: max speed 319km/h
(198mph); range 3440km (2137 miles);
service ceiling 5150m (16,900ft)
Dimensions: wingspan 35.97m (118ft);
length 24.33m (79ft 10in); height 8.38m
(27ft 6in)
Weight: 26,308kg (58,000lb) loaded
Armament: eight 12.7mm (0.50in)
Browning machine guns; up to 3628kg
(8000lb) of bombs or depth charges

AN IMPORTANT WEAPON in the
Allied anti-submarine arsenal
during World War II, the Martin
PBM Mariner was a powerful
adjunct to the PBY Catalina,
although it never quite achieved
the same popularity. The prototype
flew on 18 February 1939, and the
PBM-1 entered service in 1941. The
principal version was the PBM-3,
a few of which were to see service
with the RAF as the Mariner GR.I,
and the final wartime version was
the PBM-5, which had more

**An early model Martin PBM Mariner is seen here. The Mariner was a
useful addition to the US Navy's maritime patrol forces, seeing service
during World War II and in the Korean War.**

powerful engines and armament
and improved radar equipment.
The PBM-5A, which was produced
after the war, saw service during

the Korean conflict. Total Mariner
production was 1289 aircraft.
Specifications apply to the
Martin PBM-3 Mariner.

MARTIN B-26 MARAUDER

USA: 1940

**A Martin B-26G-1-MA Marauder of the 456th Bomb Squadron, 323rd
Bombardment Group, Ninth US Army Air Force. The 323rd BG was
based at Laon, France, in 1945.**

Crew: 7
Powerplant: two 1492kW (2000hp) Pratt
& Whitney R-2800-41 radial engines
Performance: max speed 510km/h
(317mph); range 1850km (1150 miles);
service ceiling 7165m (23,500ft)
Dimensions: wingspan 19.81m (65ft);
length 17.75m (58ft 3in); height 6.04m
(19ft 10in)
Weight: 15,513kg (34,200lb) loaded
Armament: two 7.7mm (0.303in) machine
guns (one each in nose and ventral
positions), or two 12.7mm (0.50in)
machine guns in beam positions instead
of ventral gun; two 12.7mm (0.50in)
machine guns in dorsal and two in tail
turrets; maximum bomb load of 2359kg
(5200lb)

ONE OF THE MOST controversial
Allied medium bombers of World
War II, at least in the early stages
of its career, the Glenn L. Martin
179 was entered in a US Army light
and medium bomber competition
of 1939. Its designer, Peyton M.
Magruder, placed the emphasis on
high speed, producing an aircraft
with a torpedo-like fuselage, two
massive radial engines, tricycle
undercarriage and stubby wings.
The advanced nature of the aircraft's
design proved so impressive that
an immediate order was placed for
201 examples off the drawing
board, without a prototype. It was
a configuration that was to result in

an exceptionally high accident rate,
created in the main by inexperienced
pilots handling a fast, unfamiliar
and unusually heavy aeroplane,
with its dangerously high wing
loading and rather vicious single-
engine flying characteristics.
The first B-26 flew on 25
November 1940, powered by two
Pratt & Whitney R-2800-5 engines;
by this time, orders for 1131 B-26A
and B-26B bombers had been
received. The first unit to rearm
with a mixture of B-26s and B-26As
was the 22nd Bombardment Group
at Langley Field in February 1941.
The 22nd BG was still the only
B-26 unit when war broke out in

MAEDA KU-1
The Maeda Ku-1 (Type 2 Transport
Glider) first flew in 1941 and was
produced in small numbers for the
Japanese Army. It was capable of
carrying eight troops.

**MANFRED WEISS (WM)
WM 21 SOLYOM**
This was a Hungarian-designed
reconnaissance/fighter biplane of
the World War II period, powered
by a single engine and capable of a
top speed of 320km/h (198mph).

MANSYU Ki 71
The Ki 71 was an experimental
tactical reconnaissance version of
the Mitsubishi Ki 51 Army Type 99
assault aircraft. Flown in 1941, the
Ki 71 received the Allied code
name Edna.

MANSYU Ki 79
In 1942, Mansyu redesigned the
Nakajima Ki 27 fighter, which it
was manufacturing under licence,
as a two-seat advanced trainer. The
type was built in four versions.

MANSYU Ki 98
The Mansyu Ki 98 was a twin-
boom, single-seat ground-attack
aircraft with a pusher engine.
The prototype was still under
construction when Japan
surrendered at the end of World
War II.

MANZOLINI LIBELLULA
The original Libellula single-seat
light co-axial helicopter designed
by Count Manzolini flew on 7
January 1952, leading to the
improved Libellula II powered by a
75kW (100hp) Walter Minor four-
cylinder engine. The Libellula III
differed in having a 104kW
(140hp) M 332 engine and slightly
larger dimensions.

the Pacific, and in December 1941–January 1942 it moved to Muroc, California, to carry out anti-submarine patrols off the west coast of the United States. It then moved to Australia, where it became part of the US Fifth Air Force, attacking enemy shipping, airfields and installations in New Guinea and New Britain. It carried out its first attack, a raid on Rabaul, on 5 April 1942. During the Battle of Midway, four B-26As of the 22nd and 38th BG attacked units of the Japanese fleet with torpedoes. The

22nd BG used B-26s exclusively until October 1943, when some B-25s were added. In February 1944 it became a heavy bombardment group, equipped with B-24s.

The B-26B variant had uprated engines and increased armament. Of the 1883 built, all but the first 641 aircraft featured a new extended-span wing and taller tail fin. The B-26B made its debut in the European Theatre in March 1943, when the 322nd Bombardment Group deployed to Great Saling, Essex, and began

training for low-level attack missions. The group flew its first combat mission, an attack on a power station near Ijmuiden, Holland, on 14 May 1943.The B-26C, of which 1210 were built, was essentially similar to the later B-26B models. These were succeeded by the B-26F (300 built), in which the angle of incidence (i.e. the angle at which the wing is married to the fuselage) was increased in order to improve take-off performance and reduce the accident rate, which was still

unacceptably high. The final model was the B-26G, which differed from the F model in only minor detail; 950 were built. Only two RAF squadrons, Nos 14 and 39, used the Marauder, but the type was used extensively by the Free French Air Force and the South African Air Force. Many Marauders were converted as AT-23 or TB-26 trainers for the USAAF and JM-1s for the US Navy, some being used as target tugs. Total production was 4708 aircraft.

Specifications apply to B-26B.

MARTIN P4M MERCATOR

USA: 1946

The Martin P4M Mercator played an important electronic intelligence role during the Cold War. One was shot down by Chinese fighters in August 1956.

THE MARTIN P4M MERCATOR was designed to meet a US Navy requirement issued in July 1944 for a long-range maritime reconnaissance bomber. The first of two XP4M-1 prototypes flew on 20 September 1946, and a contract was subsequently placed for 19

production P4M-1s, the first entering service with patrol squadron VP-21 in June 1950. A second Mercator squadron, VQ-1, was formed in June 1955; this was equipped with P4M-1Q aircraft and was in fact the US Navy's first electronic countermeasures squadron.

Crew: 10-13
Powerplant: two 1865kW (2500hp) Pratt & Whitney R-4360-20 Wasp Major radial engines and two 2083kg (4600lb) thrust Allison J33 auxiliary turbojet engines
Performance: max speed 609km/h (379mph); range 4570km (2840 miles); service ceiling 10,553m (34,600ft)

Dimensions: wingspan 34.77m (114ft); length 25.62m (84ft); height 9.07m (29ft 9in)
Weight: 36,903kg (81,463lb) loaded
Armament: twin 20mm (0.79in) cannon and two 12.7mm (0.50in) machine guns; various ASW stores internally, including two torpedoes

MARTIN 2-0-2 AND 4-0-4

USA: 1946

Eastern Air Lines ordered 40 Martin 4-0-4s and the first example (pictured) entered service in October 1951 – it served with the airline for over ten years and continued in service with successive operators until the late 1980s.

Crew: 2/3
Powerplant: two 1790kW (2400hp) Pratt & Whitney R-2800-CB16 radial piston engines
Performance: max speed 502km/h (312mph); range 1738km (1080 miles) with maximum payload; service ceiling 8840m (29,000ft)
Dimensions: wingspan 28.42m (93ft 3in); length 22.73m (74ft 7in); height 8.66m (28ft 5in)
Weight: 20,366kg (44,900lb) maximum take-off weight
Payload: 40 passengers

THE MARTIN 2-0-2, like its direct rival the Convair CV-240, was aimed at the requirement for a postwar DC-3 replacement for short-/medium-haul services. It was also Martin's first low-wing twin-engine type; however, unlike the Convair, it was not pressurized. Early orders from TWA, Northwest and others were promising, but the loss of a Northwest example due to structural failure in 1948 made necessary modification of all existing examples and curtailment

of 2-0-2 production. Remedial action, pressurization and other design changes were channelled into the slightly larger Martin Model 4-0-4, which superseded the planned 3-0-3 and gained 101 orders from TWA and Eastern. A total of 148 of all types were built until 1952, and examples served well into the 1980s with commuter airlines. Operational numbers are now in the single figures.

Specifications apply to the Martin 4-0-4.

MARTIN XB-48

USA: 1947

The Martin XB-48 experimental jet bomber was powered by six GE J35-A-5 turbojets mounted in three-cell underwing pods.

THE MARTIN XB-48, known by the company designation Model 223, was designed to meet the same medium bomber requirement as the

Boeing B-47. The prototype flew for the first time on 22 June 1947. The XB-48 was of conventional design and carried a three-man crew; like the Convair XB-46, it was designed to carry a 3624kg (8000lb) bomb load, but its range was less. Evaluation of the two XB-48 prototypes soon revealed the type's operational shortcomings, and no production order was placed.

Crew: 3
Powerplant: six 2083kg (4600lb) thrust General Electric J35-A-5 turbojet engines
Performance: max speed 796km/h (495mph); range 4022km (2500 miles); service ceiling 13,115m (43,000ft)
Weight: 46,206kg (102,000lb) loaded
Armament: one 20mm (0.79in) cannon; normal bomb load of 3624kg (8000lb)

MARTIN P5M MARLIN

DEVELOPED FROM THE Martin PBM Mariner, the prototype XP5M-1 flew for the first time on 30 April 1948. The P5M-1 had a conventional tail unit, with the tailplane set at the base of the fin; however, the P5M-2 had a T tail. The P5M-2 entered service with both the US Navy and US Coast Guard in 1954, and 80 P5M-1s were subsequently brought up to P5M-2 standard. In addition, 10 P5M-2s were supplied to France's Aéronavale. Total production of the Marlin was 239 aircraft.

Specifications apply to P5M-2.

A Martin P5M-2 of US Navy Patrol Squadron VP-47. The Marlin was a very effective long-range maritime patrol aircraft.

Crew: 11
Powerplant: two 2574kW (3450hp) Wright R-3350-32WA Cyclone 18-cylinder radial engines
Performance: max speed 404km/h (251mph); range 3300km (2050 miles); service ceiling 7315m (24,000ft)
Dimensions: wingspan 36.01m (118ft 2in); length 30.65m (100ft 7in); height 9.96m (31ft 8in)
Weight: 38,556kg (85,000lb) loaded
Armament: two 20mm (0.79in) cannon; up to 7257kg (16,000lb) of ASW stores

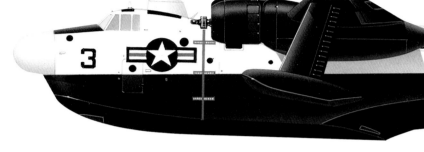

MARTIN XB-51

A RADICAL LIGHT jet-bomber design, the Martin XB-51 had a thin variable-incidence wing swept at 35 degrees and was powered by three turbojets, two mounted in pods under the forward fuselage and a third in the tail. Two prototypes were built, the first flying on 28 October 1949. The XB-51 was fast and would have been heavily armed, but further development was abandoned when the Martin B-57 Canberra was found far more suited to Tactical Air Command's requirements.

Crew: 2
Powerplant: three 2356kg (5200lb) thrust General Electric J47-GE-13 turbojet engines
Performance: max speed 1038km/h (645mph); range 1730km (1075 miles); service ceiling 12,352m (40,500ft)

Dimensions: wingspan 16.19m (53ft 1in); length 25.95m (85ft 1in); height 5.27m (17ft 4in)
Weight: 28,293kg (62,457lb) loaded
Armament: eight 20mm (0.79in) cannon; maximum bomb load of 4716kg (10,400lb)

Originally designated XA-45, the Martin XB-51 was designed to replace the B-26 Invader in the high-speed tactical bombing role.

MARTIN B-57 CANBERRA

USA: 1953

Crew: 2
Powerplant: two 3226kg (7200lb) thrust Wright J65-W5 turbojet engines
Performance: max speed 937km/h (582mph); range 3710km (2300 miles); service ceiling 14,630m (48,000ft)
Dimensions: wingspan 19.51m (64ft); length 19.96m (65ft 6in); height 4.75m (15ft 7in)
Weight: 24,950kg (55,000lb) loaded
Armament: eight 12.7mm (0.50in) machine guns or four 20mm (0.79in) cannon; 16 rocket projectiles on underwing rails and up to 2722kg (6000lb) of bombs in internal bomb bay

IN 1953, THE Glenn L. Martin company began licence production of the English Electric Canberra B2 under the USAF designation B-57. The first production model was the B-57A, but only eight were built before production switched to the RB-57A reconnaissance variant, the first of 67 aircraft being delivered in March 1954. The next US Canberra variant, the B-57B, incorporated much redesign, including a tandem two-seat cockpit under a one-piece canopy, a pre-loaded revolving bomb bay which rotated through 180 degrees, a wing-mounted armament of cannon and machine guns, and underwing points for rockets or napalm tanks; 202 examples were delivered. The B-57C (38) was similar, but had dual controls for conversion training. Twenty-six B-57B/C aircraft were supplied to Pakistan, and saw combat during

A Martin B-57A Canberra. Only eight of this model were built before production switched to the RB-57A and the B-57B.

that country's conflicts with India in 1965 and 1971. The B-57E (68 produced) was a target-towing version, while the RB-57D (20 built) was a reconnaissance variant with an entirely new long-span wing, uprated engines and a redesigned fuselage housing specialist equipment. The ultimate reconnaissance variant was the RB-57F, converted by General Dynamics; its span was extended to 37.21m (122ft), and power was supplied by two Pratt & Whitney TF-33 turbofans and two J-60 auxiliary turbojets. Only 21 were delivered. The last US Canberra variant was the B-57G, developed for night interdiction during the Vietnam War. Also used in Vietnam was the EB-57, an electronic-warfare variant of the basic B-57.

Specifications apply to the Martin B-57B.

MARTIN XP6M-1 SEAMASTER

USA: 1955

Crew: 4
Powerplant: four 7940kg (17,500lb) thrust Pratt & Whitney J57-P-2 turbojet engines
Performance: max speed 1010km/h (630mph); range 3200km (1987 miles); service ceiling 12,192m (40,000ft)
Dimensions: wingspan 31.37m (102ft 11in); length 40.84m (134ft); height 9.88m (32ft 5in)
Weight: 80,000kg (176,400lb) loaded
Armament: up to 13,600kg (30,000lb) of bombs, mines or torpedoes

THE MARTIN MODEL 275 SeaMaster was developed in response to a US Navy requirement for a jet-powered bomber/reconnaissance flying boat. The XP6M-1 prototype flew on 14 July 1955, but crashed on 7 December following a control malfunction. The second prototype

The XP6M-1 programme was abandoned due to a combination of escalating costs, ongoing technical problems and strategic policy changes.

flew on 18 May 1956, but this also crashed, on 9 November, following a hydraulic system failure. After necessary modifications, the YP6M-1 evaluation aircraft flew in January 1958. It was to be followed by five more YP6M-1s and an initial production batch of 24 P6M-2s. As well as the two prototypes, six YP6M-1s and four P6M-2s were completed before the programme was abandoned.

MARTIN-BAKER MB.5

CONSIDERED BY SOME to be the best piston-engined fighter produced in Britain during World War II, the Martin-Baker MB.5 was a much-developed version of the earlier MB.3. The sole prototype flew for the first time on 23 May 1944, and it was praised for its exceptional performance, agility, handling and engineering qualities. The MB.5 was fitted with a Rolls-Royce Griffon 83 engine driving contra-rotating propellers. By the time it appeared the Air Ministry was beginning to concentrate on jet aircraft development, and no production was undertaken.

Crew: 1
Powerplant: one 1746kW (2340hp) Rolls-Royce Griffon 83 engine
Performance: max speed 740km/h (460mph); range 1770km (1100 miles); service ceiling 12,192m (40,000ft)
Dimensions: wingspan 10.67m (35ft); length 11.30m (37ft); height 4.37m (14ft 4in)
Weight: 4994kg (11,000lb) loaded
Armament: four 20mm (0.79in) cannon

The Martin-Baker MB.5 was the best British piston-engined fighter and was much praised for its superb performance, but it was overtaken by the end of World War II and the advent of jet aircraft.

MARTINSYDE F.4 BUZZARD

AN OUTSTANDING FIGHTER aircraft, the Martinsyde F.4 Buzzard was designed by George Handasyde and first flown in 1917. Orders were placed for 1500, but only 52 had been delivered at the time of the Armistice. The aircraft was originally intended to have the Rolls-Royce Falcon engine, but as Falcon production was earmarked for the Bristol Fighter a 224kW (300hp) Hispano engine was installed instead.

Crew: 1
Powerplant: one 224kW (300hp) Hispano-Suiza 8-cylinder Vee-type engine
Performance: max speed 233km/h (145mph); endurance 2 hrs 30 mins; service ceiling 7620m (25,000ft)
Dimensions: wingspan 10.00m (32ft 9in); length 7.77m (25ft 6in); height 3.15m (10ft 4in)
Weight: 1038kg (2289lb) loaded
Armament: two 7.7mm (0.303in) Vickers machine guns

The Martinsyde F.4 Buzzard would probably have gone down in history as the best British fighter of World War I, but it had no chance to prove itself before the Armistice of November 1918.

MAULE M-4 TO M-7 ROCKET/COMET/ORION

USA: 1961

Crew: 2
Powerplant: one 175kW (235hp) Avco Lycoming 0-540-0 J1A5D flat-six piston engine
Performance: max speed 277km/h (172mph); range 885km (550 miles); service ceiling 6096m (20,000ft)
Dimensions: wingspan 9.40m (30ft 10in); length 7.16m (23ft 6in); height 1.89m (6ft 2.5in)
Weight: 1043kg (2300lb) maximum take-off weight
Payload: five persons

The M-4 was initially designed with kit building in mind, but by 1960 when the first M-4 flew, a production version was offered and became prevalent.

THE DESIGN OF this series of rugged, STOL high-wing light aircraft dates back to 1956, when Belford Maule began work on the M-4. Between then and 1984 (when the company ceased trading), over 1100 aircraft of all marques were produced. The M-5, dating from 1968, further improved STOL performance; the M-6 increased the MTOW. Later versions were also available in tricycle undercarriage or floated configuration. After the 1984 bankruptcy, a new company was formed. The M-6 was developed into the M-7, in production to date, with over 500 examples produced. Specifications apply to the Maule 5-235C Lunar Rocket.

MAX HOLSTE MH.152 BROUSSARD

FRANCE: 1951

This beautifully restored Max Holste Broussard is on the British civil register as G-BWGG. It is seen in the typical colour scheme of the French Army Aviation of the 1950s.

Crew: 1
Powerplant: one 336kW (450hp) Pratt & Whitney R-985-AN-1 radial piston engine
Performance: max speed 222km/h (138mph); range 1260km (782 miles); service ceiling 4757m (15,600ft)
Dimensions: wingspan 13.75m (45ft 1.25in), length 8.65m (28ft 4.5in); height 3.65m (12ft)
Weight: 2500kg (5512lb) loaded
Payload: five passengers

A BRACED HIGH-WING monoplane, the Max Holste MH.152 was designed to meet a French Army requirement for a lightweight liaison/observation aircraft. The first prototype, which flew in June 1951, was originally powered by a 164kW (220hp) Salmson Argus engine; however, the company then decided to develop a slightly larger and considerably more powerful version, ideally for ambulance and photographic work. Named the Broussard (Bushman), the modified aircraft flew for the first time on 17 November 1952. The first civil production aircraft was flown on 16 June 1954, followed eight days later by the first specially equipped military aircraft. The type was built in considerable numbers for both civil and military users.

MBB Bo 209 Monsun

WEST GERMANY: 1967

Crew: 1/2
Powerplant: one 112kW (150hp)
Lycoming O-360-E2C piston engine
Performance: cruising speed 254km/h
(158mph); range 1046km (650 miles)
Dimensions: wingspan 8.40m (27ft 7in);
length 6.40m (21ft)
Weight: 820kg (1807lb) maximum take-
off weight
Payload: two seats

FOLLOWING THE SUCCESS of the
Klemm Kl-107-derived Bo 207,
Messerschmitt-Bolkow launched a
new two-seat touring/training light
aircraft to complement the single-
seat Bo 208 Junior, and this was
later named the Monsun (designated
Bo 209). The Monsun has a 'side
by side' seat configuration, a
tricycle undercarriage, folding
wings for easy storage and the
nose wheel is retractable in later
versions. About 100 of the type
were produced (and more than
270 orders were in place) until
1972, when production of this light
aircraft ended. Specifications apply
to the MBB Bo 209C.

The example of an MBB Bo 209 photographed here is a late production version built in 1972 – it remains on the
British register to date, although it is inactive.

McDonnell FH-1 Phantom

USA: 1945

THE FIRST JET AIRCRAFT designed
to operate from carriers, the FH-1
originated in 1943. Initially known
as the XFD-1, it flew for the first
time on 25 January 1945. After
carrier trials, an order was placed
for 100 production aircraft, but this
was cut to 60. On 5 May 1948
Fighter Squadron 17-A became the
US Navy's first carrier-qualified jet
squadron. The type remained in
first-line service until July 1950.

Crew: 1
Powerplant: two 726kg (1600lb) thrust
Westinghouse J30-WE-20 turbojet engines
Performance: max speed 771km/h
(479mph); range 1118km (695 miles);
service ceiling 12,525m (41,000ft)

Dimensions: wingspan 12.42m (40ft 9in);
length 11.35m (37ft 3in); height 4.32m
(14ft 2in)
Weight: 5459kg (12,035lb) loaded
Armament: four 12.7mm (0.50in)
machine guns

McDonnell F2H Banshee

USA: 1947

THE FH-1'S SUCCESSOR, the F2H
Banshee, stemmed from a 1945
contract for a jet fighter-bomber.
The prototype, designated XF2D-1,
first flew on 11 January 1947,
powered by two Westinghouse J34
turbojets, and the first series
production F2H-1s were delivered
to Navy Fighter Squadron VF-171
in March 1949. The Banshee went
into combat in Korea for the first
time on 23 August 1951, when
F2H-2s of VF-172 struck at targets

in north-west Korea. The F2H-2P
was a photo-reconnaissance
variant, 89 of which were built.
The F2H-3 (redesignated F2-C in
1962) was a long-range limited all-
weather development; 250 were
built, and the type equipped two
squadrons of the Royal Canadian
Navy, operating from the carrier
HMCS *Bonaventure*. The F2H-4
(F2-D) was a variant equipped for
flight refuelling. Specifications
apply to the F2H-2.

Crew: 1
Powerplant: one 1474kg (3250lb) thrust
Westinghouse J34-E-34 turbojet engine
Performance: max speed 933km/h
(580mph); range 1883km (1170 miles);
service ceiling 14,205m (46,600ft)
Dimensions: wingspan 12.73m (41ft 9in);

length 14.68m (48ft 2in); height 4.42m
(14ft 6in)
Weight: 11,437kg (25,214lb) loaded
Armament: four 20mm (0.79in) cannon;
underwing racks with provision for
two 227kg (500lb) or four
113kg (250lb) bombs

A McDonnell F2H-2P Banshee of Marine Reconnaissance Squadron VMJ-1, which carried out
surveillance work over Korea from 1950 to 1953.

McDONNELL XF-85 GOBLIN

USA: 1948

6523

THE XF-85 PARASITE aircraft was developed to protect B-36 bombers flying beyond the range of conventional escort fighters. The idea was that a B-36 penetrating enemy territory would carry its protecting fighter in the bomb bay. If attacked by enemy aircraft, the bomber would lower the Goblin on a trapeze and release it to combat the attackers. After the enemy had been driven away, the parasite fighter would return to the bomber, hook onto the trapeze, fold its wings and be lifted back into the bomb bay. Although the XF-85 was successfully launched and flown from an EB-29B on several test flights, the aircraft was never successfully recovered in flight or flown from a B-36. The test programme was cancelled in late 1949 when midair refuelling of fighter aircraft for range extension began to show greater promise. Two Goblins were built, the first flight being made on 23 August 1948.

The McDonnell XF-85 Goblin was a radical attempt to provide fighter protection for Strategic Air Command's long-range B-36 bombers in the face of ever-strengthening Soviet air defences.

Crew: 1
Powerplant: one 1361kg (3000lb) thrust Westinghouse XJ-34 turbojet engine
Performance: max speed 1046km/h (650mph); endurance 1 hr 20 mins; service ceiling 14,249m (46,750ft)
Dimensions: wingspan 6.43m (21ft 1in); length 4.30m (14ft 1in); height 2.51m (8ft 3in)
Weight: 2063kg (4550lb) loaded
Armament: four 12.7mm (0.50in) machine guns

McDONNELL F-101 VOODOO

USA: 1954

IN 1951, THE US AIR FORCE briefly resurrected its long-range escort fighter requirement as a result of combat losses suffered in Korea by SAC's B-29s. McDonnell used the XF-88 design as the basis for a totally new aircraft, lengthening the fuselage to accommodate two Pratt & Whitney J57-P-13 engines, giving it a top speed of over 1600km/h (1000mph) a ceiling of 15,860m (52,000 feet), and increased fuel tankage. In its new guise, it became the F-101A Voodoo, an aircraft that was to serve the USAF well for many years in the tactical support and reconnaissance role. The type went into production as the F-101A; the 75 examples built equipped three squadrons of Tactical Air Command. The next Voodoo variant, the two-seat F-101B, equipped 16 squadrons of Air Defense Command, and production ran to 359 aircraft. The F-101C was a single-seat fighter-bomber version for TAC. Specification refers to F-101B.

Crew: 2
Powerplant: two 7672kg (16,900lb) thrust Pratt & Whitney J57-P-55 turbojet engines
Performance: max speed 1965km/h (1221mph); range 2494km (1550 miles); service ceiling 16,705m (54,800ft)
Dimensions: wingspan 12.09m (39ft 8in); length 20.54m (67ft 4in); height 5.49m (18ft)
Weight: 23,768kg (52,400lb) loaded
Armament: two Mb-2 Genie nuclear-tipped air-to-air missiles and four AIM-4C, -4D or -4G Falcon missiles, or six Falcons

80270
03
U.S. AIR FORCE

A two-seat McDonnell F-101B Voodoo of USAF Air Defense Command. The Voodoo was the first US Interceptor to be armed with the Genie nuclear-tipped air-to-air missile.

MCDONNELL XH-20
The XH-20 was an experimental ramjet-powered helicopter tested by the US Air Force in 1950.

MCDONNELL F3H DEMON
The McDonnell F3H Demon carrier fighter flew for the first time on 7 August 1951, the aircraft becoming operational with VF-14 in March 1956. Production of the Demon ended in 1959, 119 aircraft being built.

MCDONNELL XV-1
The XV-1 was the first American convertiplane, featuring a three-bladed rotor with pressure jets at the rotor tips and a pusher propeller in the rear fuselage. It was built primarily as a research vehicle for the US Army and US Air Force. The first of two prototypes made free flight on 14 July 1954 and the first conversion from vertical to horizontal flight was made on 29 April 1965.

MCDONNELL MODEL 120
The McDonnell Model 120 was an experimental flying crane developed as a private venture, with tip-mounted pressure jets and the ability to carry a payload up to 1.5 times its own weight. The first of two prototypes flew on 13 November 1957, but further development was abandoned.

MCDONNELL DOUGLAS KC-10 EXTENDER
The McDonnell Douglas KC-10 flight refuelling tanker was based on the DC-10 Series 30CF convertible freighter. The KC-10 first flew on 30 October 1980.

MCDONNELL DOUGLAS MD-11
The MD-11 is derived from the DC-10, but it features a significant stretch, avionics and engine updates. In the region of 200 of this 410-seat airliner were produced before Boeing's acquisition of the company curtailed the programme.

McDonnell F-4 Phantom

An air-to-air view of four F-4 Phantom II aircraft from the 51st Tactical Fighter Wing. The top two are armed with AIM-9 Sidewinder air-to-air missiles.

Crew: 2
Powerplant: two 8119kg (17,900lb) thrust General Electric J79-GE-17 turbojet engines
Performance: max speed 2390km/h (1485mph); range 2817km (1750 miles); service ceiling 17,907m (58,750ft)
Dimensions: wingspan 11.70m (38ft 5in); length 17.76m (58ft 3in); height 4.96m (16ft 3in)
Weight: 26,308kg (58,000lb) loaded
Armament: one 20mm (0.79in) M61A1 Vulcan cannon; four AIM-7 Sparrow air-to-air missiles recessed under fuselage; up to 5888kg (12,980lb) of ordnance and stores on underwing pylons

ONE OF THE MOST potent and versatile combat aircraft ever built, the McDonnell (later McDonnell Douglas) F-4 Phantom II stemmed from a 1954 project for an advanced naval fighter. The XF4H-1 prototype flew for the first time on 27 May 1958. Twenty-three development aircraft were procured, followed by 45 production machines for the US Navy. These were originally designated F4H-1F, but this was later changed to F-4A. The F-4B was a slightly improved version with J79-GE-8 engines, and between them the F-4A and F-4B captured many world records over a four-year period.

Carrier trials were carried out in 1960, and in December that year the first Phantoms were delivered to training squadron VF-121. The first fully operational Phantom squadron was VF-114. It was commissioned with F-4Bs in October 1961, and in June 1962 the first US Marine Corps deliveries were made to VMF(AW)-314. Total F-4B production was 649 aircraft. Twenty-nine F-4Bs were loaned to the US Air Force for evaluation in 1962 and proved superior to any Air Force fighter-bomber. A production order was quickly placed for a USAF variant; this version was originally

designated F-110A, but later changed to F-4C. Deliveries to the USAF began in 1963, with 583 aircraft being built. The RF-4B and RF-4C were unarmed reconnaissance variants for the USMC and USAF, while the F-4D was basically an F-4C with improved systems and redesigned radome. The major production version was the F-4E, 913 of which were delivered to the USAF between October 1967 and December 1976. F-4E export orders totalled 558. The RF-4E was the tactical reconnaissance version. The F-4F (175 built) was a version for the Luftwaffe,

intended primarily for the air superiority role, but retaining multi-role capability, while the F-4G Wild Weasel was the F4E modified for the suppression of enemy defence systems. The successor to the F-4B in US Navy/USMC service was the F-4J, which possessed greater ground-attack capability; the first of 522 production aircraft was delivered in June 1976.

The first foreign nation to order the Phantom was Great Britain, the British aircraft being powered by Rolls-Royce RB168-25R Spey 201 engines. Versions for the Royal Navy and the Royal Air Force were designated F-4K and F-4M, respectively. Fifty-two F-4Ks were delivered to the RN in 1968–69, and these were progressively handed over to the RAF with the run-down of the Royal Navy's fixed-wing units, becoming the Phantom FG.1 in RAF service and used in the air defence role. The RAF's own version, the F-4M Phantom FGR.2, equipped 13 air defence, strike and reconnaissance squadrons. By 1978 all the RAF's F-4M Phantoms, of which 118 examples were delivered, were assigned to air defence, replacing the Lightning in this role.

An F-4J Phantom of the Japanese Self-Defence Air Force (JSDAF). Japan was a major customer for Phantoms, mostly licence-built.

Other foreign customers for the Phantom included the Imperial Iranian Air Force, which received some 200 F-4Es and 29 RF-4Es; the surviving aircraft, under new management, saw combat during the long-running war between Iran and Iraq in the 1980s. Israel also received over 200 F-4Es between 1969 and 1976, these aircraft seeing considerable action during the Yom Kippur War of 1973. F-4D Phantoms were delivered to the Republic of Korea Air Force as a temporary measure, pending the arrival of Northrop F-5As. The Japanese Self-Defence Air Force equipped five squadrons with 140 Phantom F-4EJs, most of which were licence-built, and in 1970 the Royal Australian Air Force leased 24 F-4Es. Phantoms were delivered to Spain, Greece and Turkey, so that by the mid-1970s several key NATO air forces were standardized on the type. Specification refers to F-4E Phantom II.

McDonnell Douglas DC-9 USA: 1965

Crew: 2
Powerplant: two Pratt & Whitney JT8D-17 turbofan engines each rated at 71.15kN (16,008lb st)
Performance: max cruising speed 898km/h (558mph); max range with 97 passengers 3327km (2067 miles)
Dimensions: wingspan 28.47m (93ft 5in); length 40.72m (133ft 7.25in); height 8.53m (28ft)
Weight: 54,885kg (121,000lb) maximum take-off weight
Payload: up to 139 passengers

The DC-9-30 series (pictured) was operated by a number of North American and European airlines well into the 1990s.

THE DC-9 ENTERED the competitive short-haul airliner market in the 1960s, similarly configured to BAC's 1.11 preceding design in having a T tail and twin rear fuselage mounted engines. Douglas benefited from BAC's early tribulations associated with investigating and curing the stall speed characteristics associated with these early T tail jet designs. Although initial DC-9 orders were both modest and slow in coming, the type would eventually far outsell the BAC 1.11 and become a commercial success, with 976 DC-9s delivered until it was superseded by the MD-80 series in the late 1970s. Early short-fuselage 14 and 15 series DC-9s were superseded by stretched and uprated versions up to the (last) 50 series. The DC-9 sold worldwide over a period of 15 years to both scheduled and charter operators, as well as to the US military as the C-9 transport. Specifications apply to the Series 50.

McDonnell Douglas DC-10 USA: 1970

Northwest Airlines is the last major airline operator of the DC-10 in a passenger role – it is being replaced with the Airbus A330.

LIKE ITS RIVAL THE Lockheed TriStar, the DC-10 was a response to a US operators' requirement for a wide-body airliner, primarily for 'coast to coast' domestic journeys. For McDonnell Douglas this resulted in the early tri-jet design DC-10-10 model. The company rapidly launched the 30 series in 1972, the appeal of which lay in its transatlantic (and other) long-haul reach, particularly on routes with thinner traffic (not economic for a Boeing 747), and this attracted domestic and export customers such as KLM, Lufthansa and SAS.

The DC-10 sold 446 examples including 60 KC-10A Extender tankers for the USAF. Today the DC-10 remains in limited airline service, but its simple rugged design and ease of maintenance has made it a popular freighter conversion. Specifications apply to the Series 30.

Crew: 3
Powerplant: three General Electric CF6-50C turbofan engines each rated at 226.80kN (51,000lb st) thrust
Performance: max cruising speed 908km/h (564mph) at 9145m (30,000ft); range with maximum payload 7411km (4605 miles); service ceiling at average cruise weight 10,180m (33,400ft)
Dimensions: wingspan 50.41m (165ft 4.5in); length 55.50m (182ft 1in); height 17.70m (58ft 1in)
Weight: 263,084kg (580,000lb) maximum take-off weight
Payload: up to 380 passengers in an all-economy configuration

McDonnell Douglas F-15 Eagle

USA: 1972

A McDonnell Douglas F-15 Eagle of Alaskan Air Command pulls up in a vertical climb, with majestic Mount McKinley in the background. The F-15's engines have a thrust-to-weight ratio better than 1:1.

operations in the 1991 Gulf War, while the F-15C established and maintained air superiority.

The F-15E was supplied to Israel as the F-15I and to Saudi Arabia as the F-15S. In all, the USAF took delivery of 1286 F-15s (all versions), Japan 171, Saudi Arabia 98 and Israel 56. F-15s saw much action in the 1991 Gulf War, and Israeli aircraft were in combat with the Syrian Air Force over the Bekaa Valley in the 1980s.

To increase the F-15 Eagle's survivability, redundancy is incorporated in its structure; for example, one vertical fin or one of three wing spars can be severed without causing the loss of the aircraft. Redundancy is also inherent in the F-15's twin engines, and its fuel system incorporates self-sealing features and foam to inhibit fires and explosions. Primary armament of the F-15 is the AIM-7F Sparrow radar-guided air-to-air missile, with a range of up to 56km (35 miles). The Eagle carries four of these, backed up by four AIM-9L Sidewinders for shorter range interceptions and a General Electric 20mm (0.79in) M61 rotating-barrel cannon for close-in combat. The gun is mounted in the starboard wing root and is fed by a fuselage-mounted drum containing 940 rounds. The aircraft's Hughes AN/APG-70 pulse-Doppler air-to-air radar provides a good look-down capability and can be used in a variety of modes; it is capable of picking up targets at around 180km (100nm) range and, in the raid assessment mode, can resolve close formations into individual targets, giving the F-15 pilot an important tactical advantage.

Specifications apply to the F-15E Strike Eagle.

THE UNITED STATES AIR FORCE and various aircraft companies in the United States began discussions on the feasibility of an aircraft and associated systems to replace the F-4 Phantom in 1965. Four years later it was announced that McDonnell Douglas had been selected as prime airframe contractor for the new aircraft, then designated FX. As the F-15A Eagle it flew for the first time on 27 July 1972, and first deliveries of operational aircraft were made to the USAF in 1975. Urgent impetus was given to the programme

following the appearance of Russia's MiG-25 Foxbat interceptor, an aircraft that was itself developed to meet a potential threat from a new generation of US strategic bombers such as the North American XB-70 Valkyrie, a project which was subsequently cancelled.

The tandem-seat F-15B was developed alongside the F-15A, and the main production version was the F-15C. The latter was built under licence in Japan as the F-15J. The F-15E Strike Eagle is a dedicated strike/attack variant and is the F-15's latest incarnation. It

was originally developed as a private venture and the prototype first flew in 1982. The Strike Eagle carries a two-man crew – the pilot up front and a weapons and defensive systems operator in the back seat. The avionics suite is substantial, and to accommodate it one of the fuselage tanks has been reduced. More powerful engines have been fitted without the need for extensive airframe modifications. Strengthened airframe and landing gear allow a greater weapons load. The F-15E Strike Eagle was at the forefront of precision bombing

Crew: 2
Powerplant: two 10,885kg (23,810lb) thrust Pratt & Whitney F100-PW-220 turbofan engines
Performance: max speed 2655km/h (1650mph); range 5745km (3570 miles) with conformal fuel tanks; service ceiling 30,500m (100,000ft)
Dimensions: wingspan 13.05m (42ft 9in); length 19.43m (63ft 9in); height 5.63m (18ft 5in)
Weight: 36,741kg (81,000lb) loaded
Armament: one 20mm (0.79in) M61A1 cannon; four AIM-7 or AIM-120 and four AIM-9 air-to-air missiles; many combinations of underwing ordnance

MCDONNELL DOUGLAS F/A-18 HORNET

USA: 1978

Crew: 1
Powerplant: two 7264kg (16,000lb)
thrust General Electric F404-GE-400
turbofan engines
Performance: max speed 1912km/h
(1183mph); combat radius 1065km
(662 miles); service ceiling 15,240m
(50,000ft)
Dimensions: wingspan 11.43m (37ft 6in);
length 17.07m (56ft); height 4.66m
(15ft 3in)
Weight: 25,401kg (56,000lb) loaded
Armament: one 20mm (0.79in) M61A1
Vulcan cannon; external hardpoints with
provision for up to 7711kg (17,000lb)
of stores

WHILE THE F-14 REPLACED the
Phantom in the naval air-superiority
role, the aircraft that replaced it in
the tactical role (with both the US
Navy and US Marine Corps) was
the McDonnell Douglas F-18
Hornet. First flown on 18 November
1978, the prototype Hornet was
followed by 11 development aircraft.
The first production versions were
the fighter/attack F/A-18A and the
two-seat F/A-18B operational
trainer; subsequent variants are the
F/A-18C and F/A-18D, which have
provision for AIM-120 air-to-air
missiles and Maverick infrared

**The F/A-18E/F Super Hornet
pictured on its first flight from St
Louis Lambert International
Airport on 29 November 1995.**

missiles, as well as an airborne
self-protection jamming system.
The aircraft also serves with the
Canadian Armed Forces as the
CF-188 (138 aircraft). Other
customers are Australia (75),
Finland (64), Kuwait (40), Spain
(72) and Switzerland (34). Total
US deliveries, all variants, were
1150 aircraft. Specifications apply
to the F/A-18A.

MCDONNELL DOUGLAS/BRITISH AEROSPACE HARRIER II

USA/UK: 1978

ALTHOUGH IT WAS the British who
were responsible for the early
development of this remarkable
aircraft, it was the US Marine Corps
which identified the need to upgrade
its original version, the AV-8A.
The Harrier used 1950s technology
in airframe design and construction
and in its systems, and by the 1970s,
despite systems updates, this was
restricting the further improvement
of the aircraft's potential. In
developing the USMC's new Harrier
variant the basic design concept
was retained, but new technologies
and avionics were fully exploited.
One of the major improvements
was a new wing, with a carbon-
fibre composite structure, a
super-critical aerofoil and a greater
area and span. The wing has large
slotted flaps linked with nozzle

**It took American funding and technology to develop the Harrier into a
really outstanding weapons platform in the shape of the AV-8B Harrier II.**

deflection at short take-off unstick
to improve control precision and
increase lift. Leading-edge root
extensions (LERX) are fitted to

enhance the aircraft's air combat
agility by improving the turn rate,
while longitudinal fences (LIDS,
or Lift Improvement Devices) are

The AV-8B Harrier is combat-proven, having seen action in Iraq and in the Balkans. It can be called in to support ground forces in a matter of minutes.

incorporated beneath the fuselage and on the gun pods to capture ground-reflected jets in vertical take-off and landing, giving a much bigger ground cushion and reducing hot gas recirculation.

A prototype YAV-8B Harrier II first flew in November 1978, followed by the first development aircraft in November 1981, and production deliveries to the USMC began in 1983. The first production AV-8B was handed over to Training Squadron VMAT-203 at Cherry Point, North Carolina, on 16 January 1984, the aircraft making its acceptance check flight four days

later. Operational Harrier pilots were assigned to Marine Air Group (MAG) 32, the first tactical squadron (VMA 331) reaching initial operational capability (IOC) with the first batch of 12 aircraft early in 1985. The squadron's strength had reached the full complement of 20 by March 1987. The second AV-8B tactical squadron, VMA-231, achieved IOC in July 1986 with 15 aircraft, and a third squadron, VMA-457, also achieved IOC at the end of 1986. The fourth squadron to equip was the first of the West Coast units, VMA-513, which had stood

down as the last of the USMC's AV-8A squadrons in August 1986.

Delivery of the RAF's equivalent, the Harrier GR5, began in 1987; production GR5s were converted to GR7 standard. This version, similar to the USMC's night-attack AV-8B, has FLIR, a digital moving map display, night-vision goggles for the pilot and modified head-up display. The Spanish Navy also operated the AV-8B, delivered from October 1987. In 1994 the Italian Navy took delivery of an initial batch of eight AV-8Bs and one TAV-8B two-seater. Specifications apply to the AV-8B Harrier II.

Crew: 1
Powerplant: one 10,796kg (23,800lb) thrust Rolls-Royce 402-RR-408 vectored-thrust turbofan engine
Performance: max speed 1065km/h (661mph); combat radius 277km (172 miles) with 2722kg (6000lb) payload; service ceiling 15,240m (50,000ft)
Dimensions: wingspan 9.25m (30ft 4in); length 14.12m (46ft 4in); height 3.55m (11ft 7in)
Weight: 14,061kg (31,000lb) loaded
Armament: one 25mm (0.98in) GAU-12U cannon; six external hardpoints with provision for up to 7711kg (17,000lb) or 3175kg (7000lb) of stores (short and vertical take-off respectively)

McDonnell Douglas MD-80 and MD-90 series

USA: 1979

Crew: 2
Powerplant: two 82.29kN (18,500lb st) Pratt & Whitney JT8D-209 turbofan engines
Performance: cruising speed 924km/h (574mph); range 2896km (1800 miles) with 155 passengers
Dimensions: wingspan 32.87m (107ft 10in); length 45.06m (147ft 10in); height 9.04m (29ft 8in)
Weight: 63,503kg (140,000lb) maximum take-off weight
Payload: up to 172 passengers

THE MD-80 SERIES started as a development of the successful DC-9, and it was originally known as DC-90-80. Changes initially focused on use of newer versions of the JT8D engine, which allowed

The MD-80 proved a popular choice of airlines across the world – Spain's Iberia operated a fleet of MD-83s (pictured).

higher weights and a stretched fuselage, leading to the MD-81, MD-82 and MD-83 versions. These were followed by the truncated MD-87, essentially a successor to the DC-9-30 series and the MD-88, which is similar to the MD-82 but with an updated flight deck. The MD-90 first flew in 1993, the largest of the series powered by IAR V2500 series new-generation turbofan engines, and this was followed by the shortened MD-95, which became the Boeing 717 following the acquisition of McDonnell Douglas by Boeing. The MD-90 was then discontinued. Specifications apply to the MD-81.

MCDONNELL DOUGLAS C-17 GLOBEMASTER III
USA: 1991

Crew: 4
Powerplant: four 18,915kg (41,700lb) thrust Pratt & Whitney F-117-P-100 turbofan engines
Performance: max speed 829km/h (515mph); range 5190km (3225 miles); service ceiling 13,715m (45,000ft)
Dimensions: wingspan 50.29m (165ft); length 53.04m (174ft); height 16.79m (55ft 1in)
Weight: 263,083kg (580,000lb) loaded
Payload: 76,664kg (168,967lb) of cargo; 102 troops

SELECTED IN 1981 as the US Air Force's CX long-range transport designed to replace the C-141 StarLifter, McDonnell Douglas's C-17 Globemaster III made its first flight in September 1991 and entered service in 1994. While the C-17 is similar in size to the C-141, it carries twice the payload – the aircraft has the fuselage diameter of the C-5 Galaxy, which enables it to carry the M-1 Abrams tank and other outsize cargo over strategic

The Globemaster III has twice the payload capacity of its predecessor, the C-141 StarLifter, even though the two aircraft are roughly the same size. It can operate from unprepared strips.

distances to land on unprepared strips. The 120th and last C-17 was due to be handed over in 2004.
Four C-17s are used by the Royal Air Force, which operates the type under lease.

MCDONNELL DOUGLAS MD 900 AND MH-90
USA: 1992

DELIVERIES OF THIS eight-seat general-purpose helicopter began in December 1994. The Combat Explorer military derivative was launched in June 1995, and the MD 902 Enhanced Explorer flew on 7 September 1997. Armed

MH-90 Explorers and Enhanced Explorers proved successful in trials with the US Coast Guard from 1999, and the organization has identified a need for up to 12 of these helicopters. Specifications apply to the MD Explorer.

Easily configured for utility, medevac or combat, this Combat Explorer has a seven-tube 70mm rocket pod, a .50 calibre machine gun pod, a chin-mounted FLIR night pilotage system and roof-mounted Nighthawk surveillance and targeting system.

Crew: 8
Powerplant: two P&W Canada PW206B or PW206E turboshaft engines each rated at 469kW (629shp)
Performance: max speed 259km/h (161mph); combat radius 584km (363 miles); service ceiling 5490m (18,000ft)
Dimensions: rotor diameter 10.31m (33ft 10in); length 11.83m (38ft 10in); height 3.66m (12ft)
Weight: 1543kg (3402lb)
Payload: up to 1292kg (2848lb) of freight carried internally or 1361kg (3000lb) of freight carried in a slung load

MESSERSCHMITT BF 109

Messerschmitt Bf 109G FM+BB seen after restoration in the summer of 1986. The 109 had just about reached the limit of its design with the G variant, which fought on until the end of World War II.

Crew: 1
Powerplant: one 1100kW (1474hp) Daimler-Benz DB 605AM 12-cylinder inverted-Vee engine
Performance: max speed 621km/h (386mph); range 1000km (620 miles); service ceiling 11,550m (37,890ft)
Dimensions: wingspan 9.92m (32ft 6in); length 8.85m (29ft); height 2.50m (8ft 2in)
Weight: 3400kg (7496lb) loaded
Armament: one 20mm (0.79in) or 30mm (1.18in) cannon and two 12.7mm (0.50in) machine guns; external bomb load of 250kg (551lb)

THE DEVELOPMENT OF Willi Messerschmitt's famous Bf 109 fighter began in 1933, when the Reichsluftministerium (RLM) issued a requirement for a new monoplane fighter. (The prefix 'Bf', incidentally, is a company designation denoting Bayerische Flugzeugwerke, the Bavarian Aircraft Factory where the type was first manufactured.) The prototype Bf 109V-1 flew for the first time in September 1935 powered by a 518kW (695hp) Rolls-Royce Kestrel engine, as the 455kW (610hp) Junkers Jumo 210A which was intended for it was not yet available – it was installed in the second prototype, which flew in January 1936. The third aircraft, the Bf 109V-3, was intended to be the prototype for the initial production model, the Bf 109A; however, its armament of only two MG 17 machine guns was rightly considered to be inadequate and was increased in subsequent aircraft. The Bf 109V-7, armed with two machine guns and a single MG FF (20mm/0.79in Oerlikon cannon), consequently became the prototype for the first

series production model, the Bf 109B, which was powered by a 455kW (610hp) Jumo 210 engine.

One innovation, the Bf 109's narrow-track undercarriage, was designed so that the fuselage rather than the wings bore the weight of the aircraft on the ground; however, five per cent of all 109s built, some 1750 aircraft, were destroyed in landing accidents. Three of the Bf 109 prototypes were evaluated in Spain in February and March 1937, and were followed by 24 Bf 109B-2s, which immediately proved superior to any other fighter engaged in the civil war.

It was the use of the Bf 109 in Spain that helped the Luftwaffe to develop the fighter tactics that would wreak havoc among its opponents in the early years of World War II. By the time that

conflict began in September 1939, 1060 Bf 109s of various subspecies were in service with the Luftwaffe's fighter units. These included the Bf 109C and Bf 109D, which were already being replaced by the Bf 109E series; this model was to be the mainstay of the Luftwaffe's fighter units throughout 1940. Ten Bf 109Es were converted for operations from Germany's planned aircraft carrier, the *Graf Zeppelin*, under the designation Bf 109T. Nineteen Bf 109E-3s were exported to Bulgaria, 40 to Hungary, two to Japan, 69 to Romania, 16 to Slovakia, 80 to Switzerland, five to the USSR and 73 to Yugoslavia. The best of all Bf 109 variants, the Bf 109F, began to reach Luftwaffe units in France in May 1941 and was superior in most respects to the principal RAF fighter of the time, the Spitfire Mk V. The Bf 109F differed from the Bf 109E in having a generally cleaned-up airframe with redesigned engine cowling, wing, radiators and tail assembly. The Bf 109F was succeeded by the Bf 109G, which appeared late in 1942. The last operational versions of the Bf 109 were the K-4 and K-6, which both had DB 605D engines with MW 50 power boost. The last variant was the Bf 109K-14, with a DB-605L engine, but only two examples saw service with JG 52. The Bf 109G was built in both Spain (as the Hispano Ha-1109) and Czechoslovakia (as the Avia S-199). The Spanish aircraft, some re-engined with Rolls-Royce Merlins, served for many years after World War II and some of the Czech-built aircraft were acquired by Israel in 1948, equipping No 101 Squadron. In all, Bf 109 production reached a total of approximately 35,000 aircraft.

Specifications apply to the Bf 109G-6.

A Messerschmitt Bf 109E-3 in Swiss markings. The Swiss Air Force took delivery of 80 Messerschmitt 109s and also repaired some examples that crash-landed on Swiss territory.

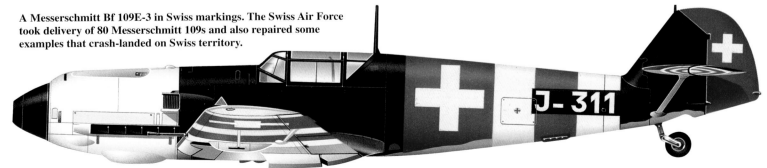

MESSERSCHMITT BF 110

GERMANY: 1936

A Messerschmitt Bf 110 in Iraqi markings. The Germans sent a few Bf 110s to Iraq in 1941.

THE MESSERSCHMITT BF 110 was designed in response to a 1934 Reichsluftministerium (RLM) specification for a long-range escort fighter. Three prototypes were completed with DB600 engines, the first of these flying on 12 May 1936. First deliveries of production Bf 110C-1s were made in 1938. The Bf 110C-2 differed from the C-1 in its radio equipment, and the C-2 and C-3 had modified 20mm (0.79in) cannon. A fighter-bomber version, the Bf 110C-4B, carried two 250kg (550lb) bombs under the centre section, and the C-5 was a special reconnaissance version. Numerous other variants appeared, including the Bf 110C-7 specialized bomber. The Bf 110D and E could be used in either fighter or bomber roles. The Bf 110F-1 (bomber), F-2 (heavy fighter), F-3 (long-range reconnaissance aircraft) and F-4 (night-fighter) had 970kW (1300hp) DB 601F engines, but the most numerous production aircraft, the Bf 110G, adopted the 1007kW (1350hp) DB 605 engine. It was as a night-fighter, equipped with Lichtenstein AI radar, that the Bf 110 truly excelled. Specifications apply to the Bf 110G.

Crew: 2/3
Powerplant: two 1007kW (1350hp) Daimler-Benz DB 605B-1 12-cylinder inverted-Vee type engines
Performance: max speed 550km/h (342mph); range 1300km (808 miles); service ceiling 8000m (26,245ft)
Dimensions: wingspan 16.25m (53ft 3in); length 13.05m (42ft 9in) including SN-2 radar antenna; height 4.18m (13ft 8in)
Weight: 9888kg (21,799lb) loaded
Armament: two 30mm (1.18in) cannon in the nose, two 20mm (0.79in) cannon in ventral tray, and one twin-barrel machine gun in the rear cockpit position; alternatively, two upward-firing 20mm (0.79in) cannon in rear fuselage dorsal position

Messerschmitt Bf 110s were early arrivals in the North African theatre, where they provided air support for the German Afrika Korps in 1941.

MESSERSCHMITT ME 209

GERMANY: 1938

Crew: 1
Powerplant: one 1716kW (2300hp) (max) Daimler-Benz DB 601 ARJ 12-cylinder inverted-Vee liquid-cooled engine
Performance: max speed (normal) 600km/h (373mph); service ceiling 11,000m (36,080ft)
Dimensions: wingspan 10.04m (32ft 11.25in); length 7.24m (23ft 9in)
Weight: 2800kg (6174lb)

THE MESSERSCHMITT ME 209 was designed specifically to capture the World Air Speed Record, which it did by logging a speed of 755.138km/h (469.22mph) on 26 April 1939. This record for a piston-engined type was to stand for more than 30 years, until it was beaten by a Grumman F8F Bearcat in August 1969. An ugly little machine, and one described by its pilots as a brute to fly for even the most experienced, the Me 209V-2 flew for the first time on 1 August 1938. Four Me 209s were built, the second being destroyed in a crash, and plans were made to modify the fourth aircraft as a fighter, but these came to nothing. The Me 209 was called the Me 109R by the German propaganda machine, to foster the impression that it was a variant of the Bf 109 fighter.

Known as the 'Me 109R' for propaganda purposes, the record-breaking Messerschmitt Me 209 was a dangerous aircraft to fly.

MIKOYAN-GUREVICH I-270
In 1946, Mikoyan built and tested a rocket-powered target defence interceptor, the I-270, based on the German Me 263 rocket fighter project. It was capable of reaching 15,000m (49,215ft) in just over three minutes.

MIKOYAN-GUREVICH MIG-8 UTKA
An experimental 'tail first' three-seat light monoplane design first revealed to Western eyes in 1946.

MIL MI-1 'HARE' AND MI-2 'HOPLITE'
Mikhail Mil's GM-1 (later Mi-1) was the first conventional helicopter to enter series production in the Soviet Union. The Mi-2, which first flew in September 1961, differed in having two small turbine engines in place of the two 336kW (450hp) Isotov turboshafts.

MIL MI-4 'HOUND'
An assault and troop transport design, the MI-4 'Hound' flew for the first time in May 1952. Able to carry up to 14 troops, the type has clam shell rear doors and military versions are distinguishable by their ventral gondola, originally designed for a navigator/observer, but which can also house avionics equipment. When production ended in 1964, about 3200 examples had been built.

MIL MI-8 'HIP' AND MI-17 'HIP-H'
The 'Hip-A' single-engined prototype flew in June 1961 and the 'Hip-B' second prototype, fitted with two 1044kW (1400shp) Isotov TV2-117 turboshafts, flew in August 1962. A host of military and civil Mi-8 sub-versions followed and finally, the Mi-17 (military designation Mi-8MT) appeared with a more powerful engine for improved performance.

MESSERSCHMITT ME 210

Crew: 2
Powerplant: two 1100kW (1475hp) Daimler-Benz 12-cylinder inverted-Vee engines
Performance: max speed 620km/h (385mph); range 2400km (1491 miles); service ceiling 7000m (22,967ft)
Dimensions: wingspan 16.40m (53ft 9.75in); length 11.20m (36ft 8.25in); height 4.30m (14ft 0.5in)
Weight: 8100kg (17,857lb) loaded
Armament: two 20mm (0.79in) cannon and two 7.9mm (0.31in) machine guns; two 1000kg (2205lb) bombs

DESIGNED AS A MULTI-PURPOSE combat aircraft to replace the Bf 110, the Me 210V-1 prototype first flew on 2 September 1939 and was originally fitted with twin fins, but serious instability problems were encountered and subsequent aircraft featured a single fin and rudder assembly. The Me 210 was produced as a destroyer (Me 210A-1), and fighter-bomber (A-2). The Me 210B-1 was a photo-reconnaissance version, only four examples being built. Total number of Me 210s built was 325. Specifications apply to the Me 210A-2.

The Messerschmitt Me 210 was to have been the successor to the Bf 110, but it was plagued with troubles and it had unpleasantly vicious handling characteristics and a high accident rate, so its operational use was limited.

MESSERSCHMITT ME 163 KOMET

THE ME 163 KOMET was based on the experimental DFS 194, designed in 1938 by Professor Alexander Lippisch. It was transferred, together with its design staff, to the Messerschmitt company for further development. The first two Me 163 prototypes were flown in the spring of 1941 as unpowered gliders, the Me 163V-1 being transferred to Peenemunde later in the year to be fitted with its 750kg (1653lb) thrust Walter HWK R.II rocket motor. The fuel used was a highly volatile mixture of T-Stoff (80 per cent hydrogen peroxide and 20 per cent water) and C-Stoff (hydrazine hydrate, methyl alcohol, and water). The first rocket-powered flight was made in August 1941, and during subsequent trials the Me 163 broke all existing world air speed records, reaching speeds of up to 1000km/h (620mph). In May 1944 an operational Komet unit, JG 400, began forming at Wittmundhaven and Venlo. Many Me 163s were lost in landing accidents. About 300 Komets were built, but JG 400 remained the only operational unit and the rocket fighter recorded only nine kills during its brief career.

Crew: 1
Powerplant: one 1700kg (3748lb) thrust Walter 109-509A-2 rocket motor
Performance: max speed 955km/h (593mph); range 36km (22 miles); service ceiling 12,000m (39,370ft)
Dimensions: wingspan 9.33m (30ft 7in); length 5.85m (19ft 2in); height 2.76m (9ft)
Weight: 4310kg (9502lb) loaded
Armament: two 30mm (1.18in) Mk 108 cannon in wing roots

A Messerschmitt Me 163 Komet on its transporter trolley. Although not difficult to fly, the Me 163's volatile rocket fuels made it a dangerous aircraft, and many pilots were killed in landing accidents.

MESSERSCHMITT ME 262

Crew: 1
Powerplant: two 900kg (1984lb) thrust Junkers Jumo 109-004B turbojet engines
Performance: max speed 870km/h (541mph); range 1050km (652 miles); service ceiling 11,450m (37,565ft)
Dimensions: wingspan 12.51m (41ft); length 10.60m (34ft 9in); height 3.83m (12ft 6in)
Weight: 7130kg (15,720lb) loaded
Armament: four 30mm (1.18in) MK108 cannon in nose; 24 R4M unguided air-to-air missiles on underwing racks

Quite a number of Me 262s survived the war and ended their days as museum pieces. Flying replicas have also been built in the United States.

DESIGN WORK ON the Me 262, the world's first operational jet fighter, began in September 1939, a month after the successful flight of the world's first jet aircraft, the Heinkel He 178. However, because of delays in the development of satisfactory engines, plus the massive damage caused by Allied air attacks and Hitler's later obsession with using the aircraft as a bomber rather than a fighter, six years elapsed between the 262 taking shape on Messerschmitt's drawing board and its entry into Luftwaffe service. The lack of jet engines meant that the prototype Me 262V-1 flew on 18 April 1941 under the power of a Jumo 210G piston engine; it was not until 18 July 1942 that the Me 262V-3 made a flight under turbojet power. December 1943 saw the first flight of the Me 262V-8, the first of the type to carry a full armament of four 30mm (1.18in) MK 108 cannon.

By the end of 1944, 730 Me 262s had been completed and a further 564 were built in the early months of 1945, making a total of 1294 aircraft. The Me 262 initially went into production as a pure fighter, entering service with a trials unit

known as Erprobungskommando 262 (EK262) at Lechfeld, near Augsburg, in August 1944. It was originally commanded by Captain Tierfelder, who was killed when his aircraft crashed in flames during one of the unit's first operational missions. Tierfelder's successor was Major Walter Nowotny, who, at the age of 23, was one of the Luftwaffe's top fighter pilots with a score of 258 kills, 255 of them achieved on the Eastern Front. By the end of October the Kommando Nowotny, as the unit had come to be known, had reached full operational status and was deployed to the airfields of Achmer and Hesepe near Osnabruck, astride the main US daylight bomber approach route. A shortage of adequately trained pilots and technical problems meant that the Kommando Nowotny was usually able to fly only three

or four sorties a day against enemy formations, yet in November 1944 the 262s destroyed 22 aircraft. By the end of the month, however, the unit had only 13 serviceable aircraft out of an established total of 30, a rate of attrition that was accounted for mainly by accidents, rather than enemy action. The Me 262 presented a serious threat to Allied air superiority during the closing weeks of 1944.

Two versions were now being developed in parallel: the Me 262A-2a Sturmvogel (Stormbird) bomber variant and the Me 262A-1a fighter. The Sturmvogel was issued to Kampfgeschwader 51 'Edelweiss' in September 1944; other bomber units that armed with the type at a later date were KG 6, 27 and 54. Problems encountered during operational training delayed the aircraft's combat debut, but in the autumn of 1944 the 262s began to

MIL MI-10 'HARKE'
A specialized flying-crane version of the Mi-6 'Hook' which first flew in prototype form in 1960. It is powered by two 4847kW (6495hp) turboshaft engines and has a maximum payload of 14,000kg (30,864lb).

MIL MI-12 (V-12) 'HOMER'
Only two of these massive twin counter-rotating rotor helicopters were built in prototype (V-12) form, first flying on 10 July 1968. On 6 August 1969 the V-12 set a world record which remains unbroken when it lifted a payload of 40,204.5kg (88,636lb) to a height of 2255m (7398ft).

MIL MI-14 'HAZE'
A new version of the Mi-8, designed to replace the Mi-4 'Hound' in service with the AV-MF, with a boat-like hull, flotation gear and other refinements. Development began in 1968 and the prototype (V-14) flew in 1973. Production versions include the Mi-14PL 'Haze-A' dedicated ASW platform, Mi-14PLM and Mi-14BT 'Haze-B' dedicated minesweeper. The Mi-14PS 'Haze-C' is a dedicated SAR variant.

MIL MI-28 'HAVOC'
Although it lost out to the Kamov Ka-50 'Hokum', this two-crew anti-tank, close-support and air combat helicopter, which flew on 10 November 1982, is still actively marketed.

MILES M.2 HAWK
The two-seat Miles M.2 Hawk was the direct descendant of the M.1 Satyr. First flown in 1933, the Hawk was built in a number of variants and can be viewed as the foundation of the Miles series of light aeroplane designs.

A Messerschmitt Me 262A-1a of Erprobungskommando 262 at Lechfeld in the autumn of 1944. Although a very good design, the Me 262 was troubled by its turbojets, which were not sufficiently developed.

appear in growing numbers, carrying out low-level attacks on Allied targets, mainly moving columns. There were also two reconnaissance versions, the Me 262A-1a/U3 and Me 262A-5a.

A new Me 262 fighter unit, known as Jagdgeschwader JG 7 'Hindenburg', was formed under the command of Major Johannes Steinhoff towards the end of 1944. Later, authority was also given for the formation of a second Me 262 jet fighter unit, which was known as Jagdverband 44 and commanded by Lieutenant-General Adolf Galland. It comprised 45 highly experienced pilots, many of them Germany's top-scoring aces. Its principal operating base was München-Riem, where its main targets were the bombers of the Fifteenth Army Air Force, coming up from the south.

Several variants of the Me 262 were proposed, including the radar-equipped Me 262B-1a/U1 two-seat night-fighter, which saw brief operational service from March 1945.

Specifications apply to the Me 262A-1a interceptor.

MESSERSCHMITT ME 323   GERMANY: 1942

The giant Messerschmitt Me 323 was slow and ponderous, and suffered appalling losses early in 1943 in attempts to keep the Afrika Korps supplied during its last stand in Tunisia.

Crew: 5–7
Powerplant: six 850kW (1140hp) Gnome-Rhone 14N radial engines
Performance: max speed 285km/h (177mph); range 1100km (683 miles); service ceiling 4000m (13,100ft)
Dimensions: wingspan 55.00m (180ft 5.5in); length 28.15m (92ft 4.25in); height 10.15m (33ft 3.5in)
Weight: 43,000kg (94,815lb)
Armament: up to 11 20mm (0.79in) cannon and four 13mm (0.51in) machine guns

THE MESSERSCHMITT ME 323 was a powered version of the Me 321 glider, using six Gnome-Rhone engines. The prototype flew in April 1942, and the type appeared in several versions. The Me 323 had clamshell nose doors and fuselage doors for loading, and featured a 10-wheeled bogie-type undercarriage. The type became operational in Sicily in November 1942. Other Me 323 units operated on the Eastern Front.

MESSERSCHMITT ME 410 HORNISSE   GERMANY: 1942

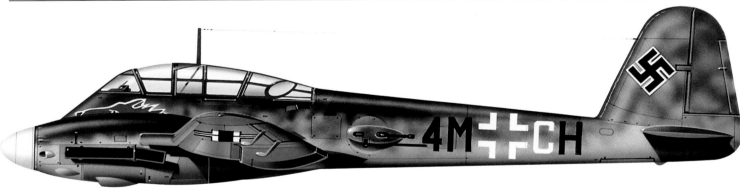

THE MESSERSCHMITT ME 410 Hornisse was a development of the unsuccessful Me 210, with revised aerodynamic and structural features and DB 603A engines. It was flown in prototype form in the autumn of 1942 and production ran to 1913 aircraft. The principal sub-types were the A-1 fighter-bomber, the A-1/U2 and A-2 heavy fighters, and the reconnaissance A-3. The Me 410 played a significant part in the so-called 'Little Blitz' against Britain in the early weeks of 1944.

The heavy fighter version was armed with a 50mm (1.97in) cannon for attacks on American daylight bomber formations, and all variants of the Me 410 featured a 13mm (0.51in) rearward-firing

A Messerschmitt Me 410 Hornisse in the markings of II/ZG 76. The Me 410 carried out fast attack missions against British targets.

machine gun in a remotely controlled barbette on either side of the rear fuselage.

Specifications apply to the Me 410A-2.

Crew: 2
Powerplant: two 1306kW (1750hp) DB 605A 12-cylinder inverted-Vee engines
Performance: max speed 624km/h (388mph); range 1670km (1037 miles); service ceiling 10,000m (32,808ft)
Dimensions: wingspan 16.35m (53ft 7in); length 12.48m (40ft 11in); height 4.28m (14ft)
Weight: 10,650kg (23,478lb) loaded
Armament: one 50mm (1.97in) and two 20mm (0.79in) cannon; two 13mm (0.51in) machine guns

MESSERSCHMITT ME 328

GERMANY: 1944

An artist's impression of how the Me 328 would have looked in flight, under the power of its Argus pulse jets. The Me 328 was simple and was designed for mass production.

THE MESSERSCHMITT ME 328 was conceived in 1942 as a cheap and simple high-speed low-level bomber and emergency fighter. Smaller than the He 162, its construction was to be mainly of wood and power was to be provided by a pair of Argus pulsejet engines, similar to those used by the V-1 flying bomb. Two versions were proposed, the Me 328A fighter and Me 328

bomber; it was estimated that four Me 328s could be built for every Fw 190 or Me 109 fighter. Gliding trials were made, the aircraft being air-launched from a Dornier 217, but powered trials in 1944 proved disappointing. A further version, the Me 328C, was proposed, to be fitted with a Jumo 004 turbojet. This and a proposed piloted glider-bomb version came to nothing.

Crew: 1
Powerplant: two 600kg (1320lb) Argus pulse jets
Performance: max speed 755km/h (470mph); range 770km (480 miles); service ceiling not known
Dimensions: wingspan 6.40m (21ft); length 6.83m (22ft 5in); height 2.10m (6ft 10.5in)
Weight: 2200kg (4840lb) loaded
Armament: two 20mm (0.79in) cannon

MIGNET HM SERIES

FRANCE: 1932

Crew: 1
Powerplant: one adapted two-stroke automobile or motorbike engine, typically 26kW (35hp)
Performance: cruising speed 120km/h (75mph)
Dimensions: wingspan 6.00m (19ft 6in); length 3.60m (11ft 8in); height 1.70m (5ft 6in)
Weight: 227kg (500lb) maximum take-off weight
Payload: one person

THE HM14 'SKY LOUSE', or 'Flying Flea' (Pou-de-Ciel), the father of today's microlights, followed earlier unconventional designs by Henri Mignet. It had two wings, and the larger one in front of the pilot offered variable incidence.

Pictured is a later (HM-19) version of the Mignet series sporting a number of changes including enclosed engine and cabin areas.

Pilot control was via a single stick. During the mid-1930s the aircraft became popular in Europe and beyond, and it was licence- or home-built in the hundreds. The type was grounded by some author-

ities in 1936 after a number of accidents. Modifications eventually overcame this. Despite slipping into post-World War II obscurity, HM14s are still home-built. Specifications apply to HM14.

MIKOYAN-GUREVICH MiG-1/MiG-7

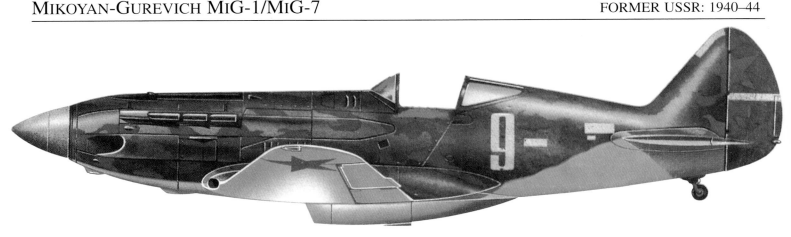

The MiG-1 was one of the few Russian fighters that could truly be classed as modern at the time of the German invasion in June 1941.

THE MiG-1 (I-200) was developed to meet a requirement, issued by the Soviet Air Force in 1938, for a high-altitude fighter. Although unstable and difficult to fly, it was rushed into production because of its high performance. The prototype flew in April 1940. The aircraft

was of composite construction, the forward fuselage up to the rear of the cockpit consisting of a steel frame with fabric covering, while the rear section was all wood. The wing centre section was duralumin, the outer panels wooden. The MiG-1 was redesignated MiG-3 after the 100th machine had been produced, the main improvements being a fully enclosed cockpit and the addition of an auxiliary fuel tank. Increased combat radius

meant MiG-3s were used extensively for fighter reconnaissance. Total production was 3322 aircraft. The next MiG fighter design, the MiG-5, was basically a MiG-3 with a Shvetsov M-82A radial engine and was produced only in small numbers in 1943. The MiG-7, featuring an in-line engine, was developed as a high-altitude interceptor in 1944. Like its predecessor, it appeared only in small numbers. Specifications apply to the MiG-3.

Crew: 1
Powerplant: one 1007kW (1350hp) Mikulin AM-35A 12-cylinder Vee-type engine
Performance: max speed 640km/h (398mph); range 1195km (742 miles); service ceiling 12,000m (39,370ft)
Dimensions: wingspan 10.20m (33ft 5in); length 8.25m (27ft); height 2.65m (8ft 8in)
Weight: 3350kg (7385lb) loaded
Armament: one 12.7mm (0.50in) and two 7.62mm (0.30in) machine guns

MIKOYAN-GUREVICH MiG-9 'FARGO'

Crew: 1
Powerplant: two 800kg (1746lb) thrust RD-20 (BMW 003A) turbojet engines
Performance: max speed 911km/h (566mph); range 1448km (900 miles) with underwing tanks; service ceiling 13,500m (44,290ft)
Dimensions: wingspan 10.00m (32ft 10in); length 9.75m (32ft); height 3.96m (13ft)
Weight: 5070kg (11,177lb) loaded
Armament: one 37mm (1.46in) and two 23mm (0.90in) cannon

DEVELOPMENT OF THE MiG-9, the second Soviet jet fighter, began in February 1945, the aircraft initially known as the I-300. The prototype flew on 24 April 1946, powered by two BMW 003 turbojets. A small series production batch was built; deliveries to the Soviet Air Force began in December 1946. Early in 1947, production MiG-9s were

fitted with the uprated RD-21 engine and redesignated MiG-9F. The last batch of production aircraft had pressurized cockpits and carried the designation MiG-9FR. About 550 aircraft were built, including a two-seat trainer variant, the MiG-9UTI. The MiG-9 was known by the NATO reporting name 'Fargo'. Specifications apply to the MiG-9.

The MiG-9 was much heavier and less manoeuvrable than the first Soviet jet fighter, the Yak-15, and it had an appalling accident rate.

MIKOYAN-GUREVICH MiG-15 'FAGOT'

ONE OF THE MOST famous jet fighters of all time, and certainly one of the most outstanding combat aircraft of the postwar years, the MiG-15 was designed by a Russo-

German team headed by Artem I. Mikoyan and Mikhail I. Gurevich. The type flew for the first time on 30 December 1947 and entered series production in the following

year. The first MiG-15s were powered by a Rolls-Royce Nene copy, designated RD-45. The prototype crashed during testing, killing its pilot, and the second

aircraft was extensively modified, with a strengthened wing featuring slight anhedral and boundary layer fences. Many first-line fighter units of the Soviet Air Force had equipped

The MiG-15 was the first Russian jet fighter to be used by the Soviet Air Force's aerobatic team, in whose colours the type is seen here. Although it had faults, the MiG-15 was an excellent fighter.

with the type by the end of 1948, and a number of improvements were made to the basic design. Airframe design progress, in fact, proceeded in parallel with engine development, and from November 1948 the MiG-15's fuselage was modified to accommodate an uprated version of the Nene designated VK-1. This engine had redesigned turbine blades and larger combustion chambers, and developed 2697kg (5953lb) thrust (3058kg/6750lb with water injection). The uprated aircraft was designated MiG-15B and was serving in large numbers with the Soviet Air Force by the end of 1950. Mig-15 production eventually reached some 18,000 aircraft, this figure including a tandem two-seat trainer version, the MiG-15UTI. The MiG-15 was built under licence in the People's Republic of China as the Shenyang F-2, in Poland as the LIM-1 and in Czechoslovakia as the S-102.

The MiG-15 saw a great deal of action in its heyday, starting with the Korean War, where it fought the US F-86 Sabre in history's first jet-versus-jet air battles. It also took part in the various Arab–Israeli conflicts, serving with the Syrian and Egyptian air forces, and was used operationally over North Vietnam and in the Nigerian civil war. In action over Korea the MiG proved to have a better acceleration, rate of climb and operational ceiling than the F-86 Sabre, but it was a poor gun platform at high speed, being prone to 'snaking', and it could be out-turned by the US fighter. Moreover, its large-calibre cannon armament, designed for bomber interception, placed it at a disadvantage in action against other fighters, the guns having a slow rate of fire and lacking sufficient ammunition capacity. Nevertheless, the MiG-15 was a formidable opponent, and it was later learned that the great majority of MiG sorties flown over North Korea were by Soviet Air Force personnel, whole air regiments being deployed to Chinese bases in Manchuria on a rotational basis.

Compared with its Western contemporaries, the MiG-15 was a robust and rudimentary aircraft. This was reflected in its cockpit layout and equipment. The gunsight was a mechanical type with a maximum range setting of 808m (2650ft), radar-ranging equipment only being included in models built after autumn 1952. The MiG-15's avionics were updated as a result of lessons learned over Korea; standard equipment on the MiG-15B included a RSIU-3M VHF transceiver, ARK-5 radio compass, RV-2 or RV-10 radio altimeter, and an RSO IFF transponder.

Specifications apply to MiG-15B.

Crew: 1
Powerplant: one 2700kg (5952lb) Klimov VK-1 turbojet engine
Performance: max speed 1100km/h (684mph); range 1424km (885 miles); service ceiling 15,545m (51,000ft)
Dimensions: wingspan 10.08m (33ft); length 11.05m (36ft 3in); height 3.40m (11ft 1in)
Weight: 5700kg (12,566lb) loaded
Armament: one 37mm (1.46in) N-37 and two 23mm (0.90in) NS-23 cannon; up to 500kg (1102lb) of underwing stores

This MiG-15UTI two-seat trainer is seen in the markings of the Egyptian Air Force. Egypt received large numbers of MiG-15s in the 1950s, many seeing action in the various Arab–Israeli conflicts.

MIKOYAN-GUREVICH MiG-17 'FRESCO'

FORMER USSR: 1950

Trailing smoke from its underwing canisters, a MiG-17 shows off its aerobatic paces. The MiG-17 was a tough opponent for US pilots over North Vietnam in the 1960s.

WHEN THE MiG-17 FIRST appeared in the early 1950s, at first Western observers believed that it was an improved MiG-15, with new features that reflected the technical lessons learned in the Korean War. In fact, design of the MiG-17 had begun in 1949, the new type incorporating a number of aerodynamic refinements that included a new tail on a longer fuselage and a thinner wing with different section and planform and with three boundary layer fences to improve handling at high speed. The prototype flew in January 1950 and the basic version of the MiG-17, known to NATO as 'Fresco-A', entered service in 1952; this was followed by the MiG-17P all-weather interceptor ('Fresco-B') and then the major production variant, the MiG-17F ('Fresco-C') which had structural refinements and was fitted with an afterburner. The last variant, the MiG-17PFU, was armed with air-to-air missiles. Full-scale production of the MiG-17 in the Soviet Union lasted only five years before the type was superseded by the supersonic MiG-19 and MiG-21, but it has been estimated that around 8800 were built in that time, many of these being exported. MiG-17s saw action in the Congo, in the Nigerian civil war, in the Middle East and over North Vietnam.

Specifications apply to the MiG-17F 'Fresco-C'.

Crew: 1
Powerplant: one 3383kg (7452lb) thrust Klimov VK-1F turbojet engine
Performance: max speed 1145km/h (711mph); range 1470km (913 miles); service ceiling 16,600m (54,460ft)
Dimensions: wingspan 9.45m (31ft); length 11.05m (36ft 3in); height 3.35m (11ft)
Weight: 6215kg (13,701lb) loaded
Armament: one 37mm (1.46in) N-37 and two 23mm (0.90in) NS-23 cannon; up to 500kg (1102lb) of underwing stores

MIKOYAN-GUREVICH MiG-19 'FARMER'

FORMER USSR: 1953

Crew: 1
Powerplant: two 3250kg (7165lb) thrust Klimov RD-9B turbojet engines
Performance: max speed 1480km/h (920mph); range 2200km (1367 miles); service ceiling 17,900m (58,725ft)
Dimensions: wingspan 9.00m (29ft 6in); length 13.58m (44ft 7in); height 4.02m (13ft 2in)
Weight: 9500kg (20,944lb)
Armament: four AA-1 Alkali or AA-2 Atoll air-to-air missiles on underwing pylons

DESIGNED AS A successor to the MiG-17, the MiG-19, which first flew in September 1953, was the first operational Soviet aircraft capable of exceeding Mach 1 in level flight. The initial production model had stability problems, and after modifications a second variant, MiG-19S, went into service in 1956. Both were known to NATO as 'Farmer-A'. In 1958 an all-weather fighter variant appeared, designated MiG-19P ('Farmer-B'), followed by the MiG-19C ('Farmer-F') with more powerful engines. The MiG-19PF was a missile-armed all-weather variant, while the MiG-19PM was a night-fighter. Like its predecessors, the MiG-19 was built under licence in China, Poland and Czechoslovakia. Chinese-built aircraft, designated Shenyang F-6, were exported to Pakistan and Vietnam. Specifications apply to the MiG-19PM.

Seen in the colours of the Pakistan Air Force, two MiG-19s are flanked by a pair of MiG-17 trainers. The MiG-19s, one of which is a trainer version, are actually Chinese license-built Shenyang F-6s.

MIKOYAN-GUREVICH MiG-21 'FISHBED'

FORMER USSR: 1956

A MiG-21MF of the 5th Frontal Aviation Army, Kiev Military District, 1973–74. The MiG-21 was a robust and effective interceptor.

Crew: 1
Powerplant: one 7507kg (16,535lb) thrust Tumanskii R-25 turbojet engine
Performance: maximum speed 2229km/h (1385mph); range 1160km (721 miles) service ceiling 17,500m (57,400ft);
Dimensions: wingspan 7.15m (23ft 5in); length 15.76m (51ft 8in); height 4.10m (13ft 5in)
Weight: 10,400kg (22,925lb) loaded
Armament: one 23mm (0.90in) GSh-23 twin-barrel cannon in pack under fuselage; four underwing pylons with provision for 1500kg (3307lb) of stores, including air-to-air missiles, rocket pods, napalm tanks and drop tanks

KNOWN BY THE NATO reporting name 'Fishbed', the MiG-21 was a child of the Korean War, where Soviet air combat experience had identified a need for a light, single-seat target defence interceptor with high supersonic manoeuvrability. Two prototypes were ordered, both appearing early in 1956; one, code-named 'Faceplate', featured sharply swept wings and was not developed further. The initial production versions ('Fishbed-A' and '-B') were built in only limited numbers, being short-range day fighters with a comparatively light armament of two 30mm (1.18in) NR-30 cannon, but the next variant, the MiG-21F 'Fishbed-C', carried two K-13 Atoll infrared homing air-to-air missiles, and had an uprated Tumansky R-11 turbojet as well as improved avionics. The MiG-21F was the first major production version and entered service in 1960. It was progressively modified and updated. In the early 1970s the MiG-21 was virtually redesigned, re-emerging as the MiG-21B ('Fishbed-L') multi-role air superiority fighter and ground-attack version.

The 'Fishbed-N', which appeared in 1971, introduced new advanced construction techniques, greater fuel capacity and updated avionics for multi-role air combat and ground attack. In its several versions the MiG-21 became the most widely used jet fighter in the world, being licence-built in India, Czechoslovakia and China, where it was designated Shenyang F-8, and equipping some 25 Soviet-aligned air forces. A two-seat version, the MiG-21U, was given the NATO reporting name 'Mongol'.

In Vietnam, the MiG-21 was the Americans' deadliest opponent. The tactics employed by MiG pilots to intercept US aircraft operating over the North involved flying low, then zooming up to attack the heavily laden fighter-bombers, mainly F-105 Thunderchiefs, forcing them to jettison their bomb loads as a matter of survival. To counter this, Phantoms armed with Sidewinder air-to-air missiles flew at lower altitudes than the F-105s, enabling the crew to sight the MiGs at an early stage in their interception attempt, then use the Phantom's superior speed and acceleration to engage the enemy. These were very much in the nature of hit-and-run tactics, the Phantom pilots avoiding turning combat because of the MiG-21's superior turning ability, but they worked; the Phantom crews had a superb early-warning facility in the shape of EC-121 electronic surveillance aircraft, which were able to direct the MiGCAP fighters on to their targets in good time. In 1966, US fighters destroyed 23 MiGs for the loss of nine of their own aircraft.

Several experimental versions of the MiG-21 were built. One was the 'Fishbed-G' experimental V/STOL aircraft, with a modified fuselage housing two vertically mounted jet lift engines. Another 'one-off' MiG-21 was fitted with a scaled-down replica of Tu-144 supersonic transport's wing. At least 15 versions of the MiG-21 have been produced, and have been operated by over 50 countries, including some friendly to the West. Total MiG-21 production is believed to be in excess of 11,000, making it the most prolific modern jet fighter type. One major customer was India, whose MiG-21MFs were equipped to carry a wide range of weaponry. For air-to-air combat, the IAF used the Soviet K-13A Atoll and R-60 Aphid, as well as the French Matra R550 Magic. Most MiG-21 fighters were armed with the GSh-23L cannon, with a pair of 23mm (0.90in) calibre barrels recessed into the bottom of the fuselage.

Specifications apply to the MiG-21MF 'Fishbed-J'.

A MiG-21MF of the Indian Air Force. Indian 'Fishbeds' carried a mixture of Soviet and Western weaponry, depending on the task in hand.

MILES M.77 SPARROWJET
A descendant of the M.2 and M.5, this twin-engined jet was converted from an M.5 model. In the early postwar years, private customers and airports were not ready for this design and there was no military interest either.

MILES M.65 GEMINI
Gemini was developed from the earlier M.38 Messenger, but with newer engines and a retractable undercarriage. First flown in 1945, the Gemini sold 170 examples, plus two M.75 Aries variants.

MILES/HANDLEY-PAGE M.60 (HP.R1 AND HP.R5) MARATHON
The Marathon was designed to a British Air Ministry requirement for a feeder airliner with up to 20 seats. This four-engined high-wing design first flew in 1946 and 43 were built.

MILES M.100 STUDENT
Following the collapse of the Miles Company, F.G. and George Miles separately designed a two-seat (side by side) jet trainer in 1957 to meet an RAF requirement. The project was unsuccessful.

MILITARY AIRCRAFT FACTORY AE MB2
The Military Aircraft Factory Ae MB2 was a rather ugly light bomber monoplane developed in Argentina in the early 1930s. Fifteen examples were built. The type was capable of carrying 400kg (882lb) of bombs.

MILITARY AIRCRAFT FACTORY AEC3
The Military Aircraft factory AeC3 was a two-seat low-wing cantilever monoplane trainer, produced in Argentina in the late 1930s.

MIKOYAN-GUREVICH MiG-25 'FOXBAT'

FORMER USSR: 1964

Crew: 1
Powerplant: two 10,200kg (22,487lb) thrust Tumanskii R-15B-300 turbojet engines
Performance: max speed 2974km/h (1848mph); combat radius 1130km (702 miles); service ceiling 24,383m (80,000ft)
Dimensions: wingspan 14.02m (45ft 11in); length 23.82m (78ft 1in); height 6.10m (20ft)
Weight: 37,425kg (82,508lb) loaded
Armament: four underwing pylons for various combinations of air-to-air missile

THE PROTOTYPE MiG-25 was flown as early as 1964, and it was apparently designed to counter the projected North American B-70 bomber with its Mach 3.0 speed and ceiling of 21,350m (70,000ft). The cancellation of the B-70, however, left the 'Foxbat' in search

of a role; it entered service as an interceptor in 1970 carrying the designation MiG-25P ('Foxbat-A'). The MiG-25R, MiG-25RB and MiG-25BM are all derivatives of the MiG-25P. The MiG-25R is a reconnaissance variant, while the MiG-25RB has a high-level bombing capability against area targets. Variants of the MiG-25 have been supplied to the Ukraine, Kazakhstan, Azerbaijan, India, Iraq, Algeria, Syria and Libya.
Specifications apply to the MiG-29P 'Foxbat-A'.

Intended originally as a high-speed, high-altitude interceptor to counter an anticipated generation of American supersonic bombers, the MiG-25 'Foxbat' found its true role as a reconnaissance aircraft.

MIKOYAN-GUREVICH MiG-23/27 'FLOGGER'

FORMER USSR: 1967

Crew: 1
Powerplant: one 10,000kg (22,046lb) thrust Tumanskii R-27F2M-300 turbojet engine
Performance: max speed 2445km/h (1520mph); combat radius 966km (600 miles); service ceiling 18,290m (60,000ft)
Dimensions: wingspan 13.97m (45ft 10in) spread, 7.78m (25ft 6in) swept; length 16.71m (54ft 10in); height 4.82m (15ft 9in)
Weight: 18,145kg (40,000lb) loaded
Armament: one 23mm (0.90in) GSh-23L cannon; underwing pylons for various combinations of AAM

THE MiG-23, WHICH flew in prototype form in 1967 and which entered service with the Frontal Aviation's attack units of the 16th Air Army in Germany in 1973, was a variable-geometry fighter-bomber with wings sweeping from 23 to 71 degrees, and was the Soviet Air Force's first true multi-role combat aircraft. The MiG-23M 'Flogger-B' was the first series production version, and it equipped all the major Warsaw Pact air forces; a simplified version for export to Libya and other Middle East air forces was given the designation MiG-23MS 'Flogger-E'.
The MiG-23UB 'Flogger-C' was a two-seat trainer, retaining the combat capability of the single-seat variants, while the MiG-23BN/BM 'Flogger-F' and '-H' were fighter-bomber versions for export. The MiG-27, which began to enter

An Indian Air Force MiG-27 'Flogger'. The type equips several squadrons of the Indian Air Force and has seen action in Kashmir against Pakistani forces.

service in the late 1970s, was a dedicated battlefield support variant known to NATO by the reporting name 'Flogger-D'; the MiG-27D and -27K 'Flogger-J' were improved versions, while the MiG-23P was a dedicated air defence variant. About 5000 MiG-23/27s were built, and in the 1990s the type was in service with 20 air forces. Specifications apply to MiG-23M.

MIKOYAN-GUREVICH MiG-31 'FOXHOUND'   FORMER USSR: 1975

THE MIG-25 INTERCEPTOR is gradually being replaced in first-line service by a greatly improved version, the MiG-31. It was first flown on 16 September 1975 as the Ye-155MP. Originally designated MiG-25MP, the MiG-31 (known by the NATO reporting name 'Foxhound') entered production in 1975, and the first units to arm with the type became operational in 1982, replacing MiG-23s and Su-15s. Designed primarily to counter low-flying aircraft and cruise missiles, the 'Foxhound' is equipped with an infrared search and tracking sensor and 'Flash Dance' Pulse-Doppler radar.

Crew: 2
Powerplant: two 15,500kg (34,171lb) thrust Soloviev D-30F6 turbofan engines
Performance: max speed 3000km/h (1865mph); combat radius 1400km (870 miles); service ceiling 20,600m (67,600ft)
Dimensions: wingspan 13.46m (44ft 2in); length 22.68m (74ft 5.25in); height 6.15m (20ft 2.25in)
Weight: 46,200kg (101,850lb) loaded
Armament: one 23mm (0.90in) cannon; eight underwing hardpoints for various combinations of air-to-air missiles

The MiG-31 'Foxhound' was rushed into service. Its radar and weapon systems are capable of engaging multiple targets.

MIKOYAN-GUREVICH MiG-29 'FULCRUM'   FORMER USSR: 1977

THE MiG-29 'FULCRUM' and another Russian fighter, the Sukhoi Su-27 Flanker, were designed in response to the F-15 and its naval counterpart, the Grumman F-14 Tomcat. Both aircraft share a similar configuration, combining a wing swept at 40 degrees with highly swept wing root extensions, under-slung engines with wedge intakes, and twin fins. The 'Fulcrum-A' became operational in 1985. The MiG-29K is a navalized version, the MiG-29M a variant with advanced fly-by-wire systems and the MiG-29UB a two-seat operational trainer. The MiG-29 is the first aircraft in the world to be fitted with dual-mode air intakes. During flight, the open air intakes feed air to the engines in the normal way, but while the aircraft is taxiing the air intakes are closed and air is fed through the louvres on the upper surface of the wing root to prevent ingestion of foreign objects from the runway, particularly important when operating from unprepared airstrips. The MiG-29 has been widely exported. Specifications apply to the MiG-29M.

Crew: 1
Powerplant: two 9409kg (20,725lb) thrust Sarkisov RD-33K turbofan engines
Performance: max speed 2300km/h (1430mph); range 1500km (932 miles); service ceiling 17,000m (55,775ft)
Dimensions: wingspan 11.36m (37ft 3in); length 17.32m (56ft 10in); height 7.78m (25ft 6in)
Weight: 18,500kg (40,785lb) loaded
Armament: one 30mm (1.18in) cannon; eight external hardpoints with provision for up to 4500kg (9921lb) of stores, including six air-to-air missiles, rocket pods, bombs etc.

As well as seeing service with the Soviet air force and its successors, the MiG-29 'Fulcrum' has been widely exported to countries including Iran, Iraq, Malaysia, North Korea, Peru, Poland and Yemen.

MIL MI-6 AND MI-22 'HOOK'

FORMER USSR: 1957

Crew: 5
Powerplant: two PNPP 'Aviadvigatel' (Soloviev) D-25V (TV-2BM) turboshaft engines each rated at 4045kW (5425shp)
Performance: max speed 304km/h (189mph); combat radius 1000km (621 miles); service ceiling 4500m (14,765ft)
Dimensions: main rotor diameter 35.00m (114ft 10in); length 41.74m (136ft 11.5in); height 9.86m (32ft 4in)
Weight: 27,240kg (60,055lb)
Armament/payload: one 12.7mm (0.50in) Afanaseyev machine gun in the nose; hold can carry 12,000kg (26,455lb) of freight; alternative external freight load of 9000kg (19,845lb)

THE WORLD'S LARGEST rotary-wing aircraft, which entered development in 1954 in response to a Soviet air force and Aeroflot requirement for a large transport helicopter, flew for the first time in September 1957. It is also the first turbine-powered helicopter to enter production in the Soviet Union. The Mi-6T 'Hook-A' is capable of carrying 70 people and the Mi-6A civil transport between 65 and 90 passengers. The Mi-6S is a casevac

helicopter with up to 41 litters. Several other passenger versions and the specialized Mil Mi-10 'Harke' flying crane brought the

numbers to about 800 helicopters when production ended in 1980.
Specifications apply to the Mil Mi-6T 'Hook-A'.

An Aeroflot Mi-6P civil transport, which has accommodation for up to 80 passengers or a smaller number of VIP passengers.

MIL MI-24 'HIND'

FORMER USSR/RUSSIA: 1969

THE MI-24 'HIND' was originally conceived as a flying armoured personnel carrier designed around the Mi-8 dynamic system with a new airframe and smaller tail rotor.

The first of 12 V-24 prototype and development examples flew on 19 September 1969; the type entered first-line service in 1974. Other variants appeared, including the

Mi-24U 'Hind-C' training helicopter, and the Mi-24D 'Hind-D' with its totally new nose accommodating tandem arrangement for the pilot and gunner. Among the many other

subvariants are the Mi-24V 'Hind-E' and Mi-25/Mi-35P export versions. The Mi-24RKR 'Hind-G1' is a NBC environment helicopter; the Mi-24K 'Hind-G2' is an artillery fire-correction machine. Mi-24M (export Mi-35M) versions are offered as upgrades, and a number of early CIS machines have been upgraded to Mi-24VM standard with a modernized cockpit with multi-function displays and compatibility with NVG goggles, and more powerful engines.
Specifications apply to the Mil Mi-24D 'Hind-D'.

Crew: 2
Powerplant: two 1434kW (1923shp) Klimov (Isotov) TV3-117MT turboshaft engines
Performance: max speed 310km/h (192mph); combat radius 160km (99 miles); service ceiling 4500m (14,765ft)
Dimensions: main rotor diameter 17.30m (56ft 9in); length 19.79m (64ft 11in); height 6.50m (21ft 4in)
Weight: 8400kg (18,522lb)
Armament/payload: one 12.7mm (0.50in) YakB-12.7 rotary machine gun; up to 2400kg (5291lb) of disposable stores; up to eight troops or two litters, two seated casualties and one medical attendant in the cabin

Mi-24 'Hind-D' with four UB-32 pods with 32 57mm S-5 rockets and two launch rails for the Skorpion (Swatter) anti-tank missile. The missile guidance/illuminator pod and four-barrelled cannon are mounted below the fuselage.

MIL MI-26 'HALO'

FORMER USSR/RUSSIA: 1977

Crew: 4/5
Powerplant: two ZMDB 'Progress' (Lotarev) D-136 turboshaft engines each rated at 8500kW (11,390shp)
Performance: max speed 295km/h (183mph); combat radius 800km (497 miles); service ceiling 4600m (15,090ft)
Dimensions: main rotor diameter 32.00m (105ft); length 40.03m (131ft 3.25in); height 8.15m (26ft 8.25in)
Weight: 28,200kg (62,170lb)
Payload: up to 20,000kg (44,092lb) of freight carried internally or externally or up to 80 fully equipped troops or 60 litters plus four-five attendants

THE WORLD'S MOST powerful helicopter – indeed the largest and the heaviest operational (civil and military) helicopter worldwide – was designed as a replacement for the Mi-6; however, it far outstrips it predecessor with 50–100 per cent greater capability courtesy of its advanced eight-bladed main rotor and two D-136 turboshaft engines, which are more than twice as powerful as the engines which powered the Mi-6. The Mi-26 first flew on 14 December 1977, and service entry began in 1985.

By the end of the twentieth century, 300 Mi-26s and a number of subvariants had been built with sales of civil versions to 18 overseas customers and military variants to India and Peru.
Specifications apply to the Mil Mi-26 'Halo-A'.

The Mil Mi-26 'Halo' is the first helicopter in the world to operate using an eight-blade main rotor. Delivery of the first export versions to the Indian Air Force (pictured) began in June 1986.

MIL MI-34 'HERMIT'

FORMER USSR/RUSSIA: 1987

Crew: 2
Powerplant: one 239kW (320shp) VOKBM M-14-26V 9-cylinder radial piston engine
Performance: max speed 210km/h (130mph); combat radius 356km (221 miles); service ceiling 4000m (13,120ft)
Dimensions: main rotor diameter 10.00m (32ft 9.75in); length 11.42m (37ft 5.5in); height 2.75m (9ft 0.25in)
Weight: 950kg (2094lb)
Payload: three or four seats

THE 'HERMIT' WAS A replacement for the large number of Mi-2 'Hoplites' in Soviet flying clubs and at the same time intended as a sporting/training helicopter capable of flying conventional loops and rolls. Detailed design began in 1984, and the first Mi-34 flew on 17 November 1987. Production

began in 1993 as the Mi-34S (Mi-34C), but a lack of funding has restricted production to only a few examples. Specifications apply to the Mil Mi-34S 'Hermit'.

Thanks to its advanced rotor system the Mi-34 'Hermit' became the first Soviet-designed helicopter capable of flying conventional loops and rolls.

MILES M.14 MAGISTER

UK: 1937

Affectionately known as the 'Maggie', the M.14 Magister was a very docile aircraft, but could still 'bite' if mishandled by an inexperienced pilot.

THE MILES M.14 MAGISTER was the RAF's first monoplane training aircraft and entered production in October 1937. It served with the elementary flying training schools of the RAF and some Commonwealth countries, and remained in full-scale use throughout World War II; many then passed into private ownership as the Hawk Trainer Mk III.

Crew: 2
Powerplant: one 97kW (130hp) de Havilland Gipsy Major 1 in-line engine
Performance: max speed 212km/h (132mph); range 402km (250 miles);
service ceiling 4270m (14,000ft)
Dimensions: wingspan 10.31m (33ft 10in); length 7.50m (24ft 7.5in); height 2.03m (6ft 8in)
Weight: 862kg (1900lb) loaded

MILES MASTER

UK: 1938

Crew: 2
Powerplant: one 533kW (715hp) Rolls-Royce Kestrel XXX 12-cylinder liquid-cooled Vee-type engine
Performance: max speed 364km/h (226mph); range 800km (500 miles); service ceiling 8200m (27,000ft)
Dimensions: wingspan 11.88m (39ft); length 9.27m (30ft 5in); height 3.05m (10ft)
Weight: 2527kg (5573lb) loaded
Armament: one 7.7mm (0.303in) machine gun

THE PROTOTYPE MILES MASTER advanced trainer, first flown in 1938, was a development of an earlier F.G. Miles trainer design, the Kestrel. Early production aircraft were delivered to the RAF in the spring of the following year. The Mks I and IA, of which 900 were built, were powered by the Rolls-Royce Kestrel in-line engine; however, subsequent versions were re-engined with a 649kW (870hp) Bristol Mercury XX powerplant. The first and most numerous of these was the Mk II, production of which reached a total of 1799. The final version (602 built) was the Master III, powered by the 615kW (825hp) Pratt & Whitney Wasp Junior. Specification refers to the Miles Master Mk I.

The Miles Master was a very effective advanced trainer, bridging the gap between basic flying and a fighter aircraft's cockpit. Seen here is the Mercury-engined Mk II.

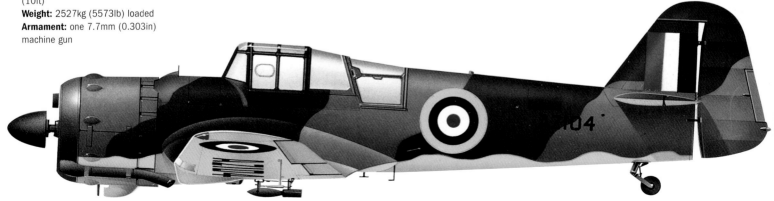

MILES M.52

UK: 1946

THE MILES E.24/43, or M.52, was an extremely advanced project on which Miles Aircraft Ltd worked for three years until a high-level decision suspended further work. It was a decision which may well rank as one of the major tragedies of British aviation.

The Miles company began work on the M.52 in 1943, at a time when knowledge of high-speed aerodynamics was strictly limited. As the project was masked in secrecy, Miles set up its own foundry for the production of the necessary metal components and also built a high-speed wind tunnel. The design that gradually evolved featured a bullet-like fuselage of circular section, 1.5m (5ft) in diameter, constructed of high-tensile steel with an alloy covering. The powerplant, a Power Jets W.2/700, was centrally mounted and fed by an annular air intake, the cockpit forming a centre cone. The whole cockpit cone, in which the pilot sat semi-reclined, could be detached in an emergency by firing small cordite charges; the pilot would then bale out normally when the capsule reached a lower altitude.

The M.52 was fitted with bi-convex section wings, mounted at mid-point on the fuselage. A full-scale wooden mock-up of this unique high-speed wing design was built and tested on a Miles Falcon light aircraft in 1944. As design work progressed, various refinements were incorporated. Split flaps were fitted, together with an all-moving tailplane. The

A mock-up of the British Miles M.52, which would almost certainly have put Britain in the forefront of supersonic flight.

addition of rudimentary afterburners in the form of combustion cans situated at the rear of the engine duct was calculated to produce much greater thrust at supersonic speed. The undercarriage's position presented some headaches; the very thin wing section meant that the wheels had to be positioned to retract into the fuselage, a narrow-track arrangement which might cause landing problems.

Detailed design work on the M.52 was 90 per cent complete by the beginning of 1946, and the jigs were ready for the assembly of three planned prototypes. No snags were envisaged in construction, and it was expected that the first M.52 would fly within six to eight months. Then, in February 1946, quite without warning, F.G. Miles received word from the Director General of Scientific Research at the Ministry of Aircraft Production, Sir Ben Lockspeiser, that all work

on the M.52 project was to cease at once. Secrecy surrounded the cancellation of the M.52, just as it had surrounded its design, and it was not until September 1946 that the British public were made aware that their aircraft industry had been within sight of flying the world's first supersonic aircraft, only to have the chance snatched away.

The stated reason behind the decision to cancel the M.52 was that it had already been decided, early in 1946, to carry out a supersonic research programme with the aid of unmanned models developed by Vickers Ltd. The department responsible was headed by Dr Barnes Wallis, designer of the special mines which had breached the Ruhr dams in 1943. Between May 1947 and October 1948 eight rocket-powered models were launched, only three of which were successful. In each failure (apart from the first attempted launch when the Mosquito launch aircraft got out of control in cloud and the model broke away) it was the rocket motor that failed, not the airframe. The irony was that most of the models were based on the design of the M.52, and the double irony was that, in the light of current knowledge, the full-size M.52 would almost certainly have been a success. Meanwhile, only a year after the M.52's cancellation was made public, Major Charles Yeager, US Air Force, had made history's first supersonic flight in the rocket-powered Bell X-1 research aircraft.

Crew: 1
Powerplant: one 907kg (2000lb) Power Jets W.2/700 turbojet engine with thrust augmentor
Performance (est): max speed 1609km/h (1000mph); range no data; service ceiling 15,250m (50,000ft)
Dimensions: wingspan 8.20m (26ft 10.5in); length 10.20m (33ft 6in)
Weight: 3715kg (8200lb) loaded

This depiction shows how the M.52 would have appeared in flight. Three prototypes were planned; the first could have flown by the end of 1946.

MITSUBISHI KI.1
The Mitsubishi Ki.1, which appeared in 1933, was a twin-engined low-wing monoplane bomber. It was used during the Sino-Japanese war, with 118 examples being built.

MITSUBISHI K-2
The Mitsubishi K-2 twin-engined monoplane bomber of 1933, which was a very successful design, was developed from the Junkers K-37, an example of which had been imported in 1931.

MITSUBISHI F1M
The Mitsubishi F1M biplane was developed in the mid-1930s as a catapult-launched floatplane to be carried on board the Imperial Japanese Navy's capital ships. It was given the Allied code name 'Pete'.

MITSUBISHI B5M1
The Mitsubishi B5M1 light bomber was developed as a rival to the Nakajima B5N, 125 production aircraft entering service as the Type 97 Model 2. The type saw active service in China.

MITSUBISHI KI.30
First flown in 1937, the prototype Ki.30 light bomber was followed by 17 more prototype and service trials aircraft and 686 production machines. Its Allied code name was 'Anne'.

MITSUBISHI KI. 51
First flown in 1939, the Mitsubishi Ki.51 reconnaissance aircraft/dive-bomber was a development of the Ki.30, and the aircraft remained one of the Japanese Army's most important close-support aircraft throughout World War II, being used in every theatre. Its Allied code name was 'Sonia'.

MITSUBISHI A5M 'CLAUDE'

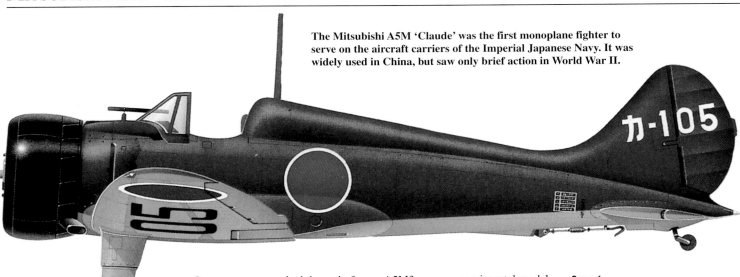

The Mitsubishi A5M 'Claude' was the first monoplane fighter to serve on the aircraft carriers of the Imperial Japanese Navy. It was widely used in China, but saw only brief action in World War II.

KNOWN TO THE Allies as 'Claude', and first flown in January 1935, the Mitsubishi A5M was Japan's first carrier-borne monoplane fighter.

Its appearance marked the end of Japanese dependence on foreign designs. The initial production model was designated A5M1 Type 96 and had an enclosed cockpit, the first to be used by a Japanese fighter. This was not popular with the A5M's pilots, and subsequent variants reverted to an open cockpit. These were the A5M2a, with a more powerful engine, and the A5M2b, with a three-bladed propeller. The

A5M3 was an experimental model with a 20mm (0.79in) cannon firing through the propeller hub, and the last production model was the A5M4, the A5M4-K being a tandem two-seat trainer version. The A5M was widely used in China, but with the exception of one attack on Davao in the Philippines it did not see combat against the Allies. Production totalled 1094 aircraft. Specifications apply to the A5M2b.

Crew: 1
Powerplant: one 586kW (785hp) Nakajima Kotobjuki 41 9-cylinder radial engine
Performance: max speed 435km/h (270mph); range 1400km (870 miles); service ceiling 9800m (32,150ft)
Dimensions: wingspan 11.00m (36ft 1in); length 7.54m (24ft 9in); height 3.27m (10ft 8in)
Weight: 1822kg (4016lb) loaded
Armament: two 7.7mm (0.303in) machine guns

MITSUBISHI G3M 'NELL'

THE IMPERIAL JAPANESE Naval Air Force's Mitsubishi G3M medium bomber was developed by way of a series of experimental designs in the early 1930s, the prototype making its first flight in July 1935. The initial version, the G3M1, went into production in June 1936 as the Navy Type 96 Attack Bomber Model 11, but only 34 examples were built before it was replaced on the production line by the improved G3M2. On 14 August 1937, a week after the second Sino-Japanese conflict had begun, G3M2 bombers of the Kanoya Kokutai based at Taipei, Formosa, attacked targets in the Hangchow and Kwangteh areas of the Chinese mainland. Despite poor weather

conditions, these aircraft made a 2011km (1250-mile) overwater flight to complete the first trans-oceanic raid in the history of aviation, a feat that was repeated the next day by the G3M2s of the Kisarazu Kokutai, operating out of Omura on Kyushu. On both occasions, losses were sustained at the hands of Chinese fighters, revealing the G3M's defensive armament to be inadequate.

Despite these losses, the G3M2 force participating in the conflict was steadily increased, reaching a total of 130 aircraft at its peak. Some G3M1s had been converted

into military transports under the designation L3Y1, and in 1938 about two dozen G3M2s were also converted to the transport role for civil operators. Most of these were used by Nippon Koku K.K (Japan Air Lines) and its successor Dai Nippon Koku K.K. (Greater Japan Air Lines), and in this guise the G3M2 made several notable flights to distant destinations. Beginning on 26 August 1939, and ending on 20 October, one aircraft (J-BACI) made a round-the-world flight, covering a distance of 52,856km (32,850 miles) in 194 flying hours. The aircraft flew from Tokyo via

Nome (Alaska), Seattle and Buenos Aires, crossing the South Atlantic to Dakar in West Africa, then flying on to Rome before returning home via Asia.

Total production of the G3M series, which reached 1048 aircraft, included the Kinsei 42-powered G3M2b, the G3M2d (L3Y2) transport, which received the Allied code name Tina, and the final bomber version, the G3M3, with 970kW (1300hp) Kasei 51 engines. The G3M was widely used in China, and about 250 were still in first-line service when Japan entered World War II. Some

A Mitsubishi G3M2 'Nell' of the Yokosuka Kokutai, March 1944. The aircraft's bright orange colour scheme indicates that it has a training role.

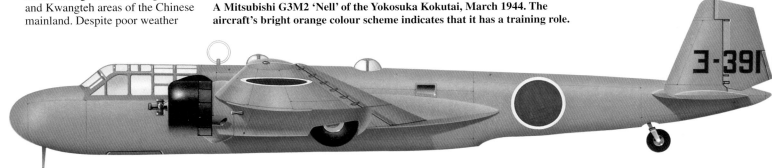

specially converted aircraft were used to photograph American installations in the Pacific in the months before the attack on Pearl Harbor. The G3M saw widespread service during the Pacific War, one of its first successful actions being the sinking of the British warships *Prince of Wales* and *Repulse* off Malaya on 10 December 1941. On

Japan's entry into the war, the Japanese Navy had 204 Mitsubishi G3M2s in first-line service, with another 54 serving with second-line units. The parent company was now turning to the manufacture of the G4M bomber, and the last G3M variant, the G3M3, was produced by Nakajima. Powered by two 970kW (1300hp) Kinsei 51

engines, the G3M3 was the fastest variant of the aircraft. In all, 412 G3M3s were produced by Nakajima. During World War II, the G3M was known by the Allied code name 'Nell'.

Specifications apply to G3M2.

Crew: 7
Powerplant: two 802kW (1075hp) Mitsubishi Kinsei 41/42/45 14-cylinder radial engines
Performance: max speed 373km/h (232mph); range 4380km (2722 miles); service ceiling 9130m (29,950ft)
Dimensions: wingspan 25.00m (82ft); length 16.45m (53ft 11in); height 3.69m (12ft 1in)
Weight: 8000kg (17,637lb) loaded
Armament: one 20mm (0.79in) cannon in dorsal turret and three 7.7mm (0.303in) machine guns, one each in retractable ventral turret and in two beam positions; bomb or torpedo load of 800kg (1764lb)

A Mitsubishi G3M2 pictured on operations over China. The aircraft is carrying an external bomb load on under-fuselage racks.

MITSUBISHI KI.15 'BABS'
JAPAN: 1936

DEVELOPMENT OF THE Mitsubishi Ki.15 long-range reconnaissance aircraft, known to the Allies by the code name of 'Babs', began in July 1935, with the prototype first flying in May 1936. A year later the second prototype, bearing the civil registration J-BAAI and the name Kamikaze (Divine Wind), caused a sensation by flying from Tachikawa to London in a net flying time of 51 hours 17 minutes

and 23 seconds at an average speed of 160km/h (100mph). The Mitsubishi Ki.15 was evaluated in China, and 435 examples were subsequently built for the Japanese Army. The Imperial Japanese Navy also adopted the type, procuring 50 aircraft under the designations C5M1 (20) and C5M2 (30). Both Army and Navy models of the aircraft were relegated to second-line duties in 1943.

Crew: 2
Powerplant: one 671kW (900hp) Mitsubishi Ha-26 14-cylinder radial engine
Performance: max speed 510km/h (317mph); range 1110km (690 miles); service ceiling 9580m (31,430ft)
Dimensions: wingspan 12.00m (39ft 4in); length 3.34m (28ft 6in); height 3.34m (10ft 11in)
Weight: 2481kg (5470lb) loaded
Armament: one 7.7mm (0.303in) machine gun in rear cockpit

MITSUBISHI KI.21 'SALLY'
JAPAN: 1936

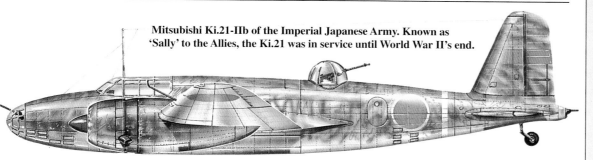

Mitsubishi Ki.21-IIb of the Imperial Japanese Army. Known as 'Sally' to the Allies, the Ki.21 was in service until World War II's end.

THE MITSUBISHI KI.21 (Army Type 97) heavy bomber first flew on 18 December 1936, and when deliveries to the JAAF began in August 1938 it had few equals anywhere in the world. The first production model, the Ki.21-I, was in service from the beginning of the Sino-Japanese conflict of 1939 until the end of the Pacific War, and was at the forefront of the Japanese attacks on Hong Kong,

Thailand, the Philippines, Malaya, the Dutch East Indies and Burma, where it suffered badly in the face of determined fighter opposition because of inadequate defensive armament and lack of armour. Production of the Ki.21-I came to 774 aircraft, followed by 1278 examples of the improved Ki.21-II with a dorsal turret.

Specifications apply to the Mitsubishi Ki.21-11.

Crew: 7
Powerplant: two 1119kW (1500hp) Mitsubishi Ha-101 14-cylinder radial engines
Performance: max speed 486km/h (302mph); range 2700km (1678 miles); service ceiling 10,000m (32,810ft)
Dimensions: wingspan 22.50m (73ft 9in); length 16.00m (52ft 6in); height 4.85m (15ft 11in)
Weight: 10,610kg (23,391lb) loaded
Armament: five 7.7mm (0.303in) machine guns; bomb load of 1000kg (2205lb)

MITSUBISHI KI.57
Codenamed 'Topsy' by the Allies, the Ki.57 was one of Japan's standard military transport types of World War II. The prototype flew in July 1940.

MITSUBISHI J4M1 SENDEN
Of twin-boom design with a Mitsubishi MK9D pusher engine, the J4M1 Senden (Flashing Lightning) was intended as a high-performance interceptor for the Japanese Navy. The type was abandoned in favour of the Kyushu J7W1 Shinden.

MITSUBISHI KI.83
The Mitsubishi Ki.83 was designed as a long-range escort fighter. The prototype flew on 18 November 1944 and displayed a spectacular performance, but the war ended before the type entered production.

MITSUBISHI MU-2
This twin-engined utility and executive light transport first flew in 1963 and achieved nearly 800 orders, many from overseas. With two crew and up to nine passengers the Mu-2 has been produced in a number of versions, including a search-and-rescue version for the Japanese military.

MITSUBISHI T.2
The two-seat Mitsubishi T2, which was first flown in 1971, was Japan's first supersonic aircraft. It bears a strong resemblance to the SEPECAT Jaguar.

MITSUBISHI F.2
First flown in 1995, the Mitsubishi F.2 is a much modified version of the F-16 Falcon. It has a greater wingspan than the Falcon, and more hardpoints, as well as a three-piece canopy.

MITSUBISHI A6M REISEN (ZERO FIGHTER)

ONE OF THE FINEST aircraft of all time, the Mitsubishi A6M Reisen (Zero Fighter) first flew on 1 April 1939, powered by a 582kW (780hp) Zuisei 13 radial engine. After 15 aircraft had been evaluated under combat conditions in China, the type was accepted for service with the Japanese Naval Air Force in July 1940, entering full production in November that year as the A6M2 Model 11. Sixty-four Model 11s were completed, these being powered by the more powerful Sakae 12 engine, and were followed by the Model 21 with folding wingtips. This was the major production version at the time of the attack on Pearl Harbor in December 1941. The A6M2 soon showed itself to be clearly superior to any fighter the Allies could put into the air in the early stages of the Pacific War. Armed with two 20mm (0.79in) Type 99 cannon and two 7.7mm (0.303in) Type 97 machine guns, it was highly manoeuvrable and structurally very strong, despite being lightweight. Instead of being built in several separate units, it was constructed in two pieces. The engine, cockpit and forward fuselage combined with the wings to form one rigid unit, the second unit comprising the rear fuselage and the tail. The two units were joined together by a ring of 80 bolts. Its main drawback was that it had no armour plating for the pilot and no self-sealing fuel tanks, which meant that it could not absorb as much battle damage as Allied fighters.

In 1942 the Americans allocated the code name 'Zeke' to the A6M, but as time went by the name Zero came into general use. During the first months of the Pacific War the Zeros carved out an impressive combat record. In the battle for Java, which ended on 8 March

A Mitsubishi A6M2 Reisen (Zero Fighter) of the 12th Rengo Kokutai (Naval Air Corps) pictured over China shortly after the type's entry into service in 1940.

1942, they destroyed 550 Allied aircraft. These remarkable victories earned enormous prestige for the Japanese Navy pilots and tended to overshadow the achievements of their Army colleagues, who fought no less tenaciously albeit with less spectacular success. Throughout the war, the demands of the Navy were to receive priority. Unlike the Army, the Japanese Navy followed the practice of concentrating its best pilots in elite units. In 1942 Japanese Navy fighter units began to receive the A6M3 Model 32, with a supercharged 970kW (1300hp) Sakae 21 engine. This model had its folding wingtips removed to improve performance, but this impaired the fighter's manoeuvrability and the full-span wing was restored in the A6M3 Model 22. By early 1943 it was

becoming apparent that the A6M3 could no longer retain superiority over the latest Allied fighters, so the A6M5 Model 52 was developed, retaining the Sakae 21 engine but having a shorter-span wing (in essence, a Model 32 wing with rounded tips). Subtypes produced included the A6M5a Model 52A, with strengthened wings and increased ammunition, the A6M5b Model 52B with heavier armament and armour protection, and the A6M5c Model 52C, with more armour, two 20mm (0.79in) and three 13mm (0.51in) guns. The latter subtype had a Sakae 31 engine with methanol injection, bullet-proof fuel tanks and underwing rocket rails. The A6M7 Model 63 was a special Kamikaze version, of which 465 were built; hundreds more Zeros were also expended in

suicide attacks. Other versions were the A6M8c Model 54C, with a 1119kW (1500hp) Mitsubishi Kinsei 62 engine and four wing guns, a twin-float seaplane, the A6M2-N, and the A6M2-K2 two-seat trainer. In all, 10,937 Zeros of all versions were built.

Specifications apply to the Mitsubishi A6M2.

Crew: 1
Powerplant: one 709kW (950hp) Nakajima NK1C Sakae 12 14-cylinder radial engine
Performance: max speed 534km/h (332mph); range 3104km (1929 miles); service ceiling 10,000m (32,810ft)
Dimensions: wingspan 12.00m (39ft 4in); length 9.06m (29ft 8in); height 3.05m (10ft)
Weight: 2796kg (6164lb) loaded
Armament: two 20mm (0.79in) cannon and two fixed 7.7mm (0.303in) machine guns; external bomb load of 120kg (265lb)

A Mitsubishi A6M2 Zero-Sen of the 6th Kokutai, Rabaul, November 1942. The Zero's long range made it ideal for operations over the Pacific.

MITSUBISHI G4M 'BETTY'

JAPAN: 1939

A Mitsubishi G4M1 'Betty' bomber of the 708th Kokutai. Although an excellent fighter in many ways, the type's lack of self-sealing fuel tanks and poor armour protection earned it the nickname 'Flying Lighter'.

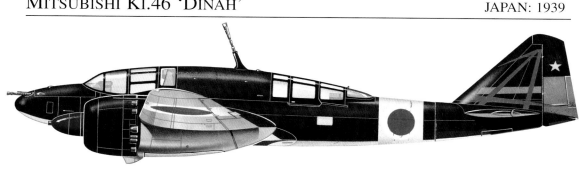

Crew: 7
Powerplant: two 1343kW (1800hp) Mitsubishi MK4P Kasei 21 14-cylinder radial engines
Peformance: max speed 438km/h (272mph); range 6059km (3765 miles); service ceiling 9200m (30,185ft)
Dimensions: wingspan 25.00m (82ft); length 20.00m (65ft 7in); height 6.00m (19ft 8in)
Weight: 12,500kg (27,557lb) loaded
Armament: two 7.7mm (0.303in) machine guns and four 20mm (0.79in) cannon; bomb or torpedo load of 800kg (1764lb)

ALTHOUGH THE G3M had an excellent performance, the Japanese Naval Staff was anxious to make improvements with special regard to speed and range. In the second half of 1937 Mitsubishi developed the G4M, the prototype making its first flight on 23 October 1939 and the initial production G4M1 version coming off the assembly lines from April 1941. About 200 were in service at the time of the attack on Pearl Harbor and were used in the torpedo attack as well as the level-

bombing role. In November 1942 the much improved G4M2 made its appearance, this variant gradually replacing the G4M1, which was assigned to transport, reconnaissance and training duties. The G4M2e was specially modified to carry the Ohka piloted suicide aircraft. One of the drawbacks in the design of the G4M was its lack of protective armour and self-sealing fuel tanks, which made it very easy to shoot down. Specifications apply to the Mitsubishi G4M1.

MITSUBISHI KI.46 'DINAH'

JAPAN: 1939

THE PROTOTYPE KI.46, one of the best reconnaissance aircraft of World War II, first flew in November 1939 and was followed by a small production batch of 34 Ki.46-Is with 671kW (900hp) Mitsubishi Ha.26-I radial engines. Production then switched to the first fully operational model, the Ki.46-II. The Ki.46-IIIa appeared in 1943; this featured a redesigned all-glazed nose section. The Ki.46-III-Kai was an interceptor version with a 'solid'

The Mitsubishi Ki.46-III Kai was an interceptor version, fitted with a 37mm Ho-203 cannon obliquely mounted in the upper fuselage.

nose mounting a 37mm (1.47in) cannon and either two 20mm (0.79in) cannon or two 12.7mm (0.50in) machine guns. The similarly armed Ki.46-IIIb was a ground-attack aircraft. Production of all versions totalled 1783 aircraft. Specifications apply to Ki.46-11.

Crew: 2
Powerplant: two 787kW (1055hp) Mitsubishi Ha.102 14-cylinder radial engines
Performance: max speed 604km/h (375mph); range 2474km (1537 miles); service ceiling 10,720m (35,170ft)
Dimensions: wingspan 14.70m (48ft 2in); length 11.00m (36ft 1in); height 3.88m (12ft 8in)
Weight: 5800kg (12,787lb) loaded
Armament: one 7.7mm (0.303in) machine gun

MITSUBISHI J2M RAIDEN 'JACK'

JAPAN: 1942

THE MITSUBISHI J2M RAIDEN (Thunderbolt), known to the Allies as 'Jack', was the first Japanese naval fighter designed specifically as an interceptor. The first of three

J2M prototypes flew on 20 March 1942, and after some necessary modifications the type was ordered into production in October that year. The tubby, radial-engined

'Jack' was used almost exclusively for home defence, although some were encountered during the Marianas campaign in September 1944. Probably the best variant

MORANE-SAULNIER MS H
The Morane-Saulnier MS H of 1913 stemmed from the family of monoplanes designed by Leon Morane and Raymond Saulnier from 1911 onwards, made famous by the long-distance flights of pioneer aviator Roland Garros.

MORANE-SAULNIER L
Known also by the military designation MS.3, the Morane-Saulnier Type L was the first of the company's parasol monoplane fighters, and was ordered in large numbers at the outbreak of WWI.

MORANE-SAULNIER MS.35
The Morane-Saulnier MS.35 was a two-seat parasol-wing trainer of 1915. More than 400 were built, continuing in service long after World War I.

MORANE-SAULNIER MS.AI
The Morane-Saulnier MS.A1 of 1917 was a high-wing fighter monoplane with a very streamlined fuselage and modern lines. Three versions were developed.

MORANE-SAULNIER MS.130
The Morane-Saulnier MS.130 trainer, which appeared in 1926, was developed from the MS.35. Its parasol wing was slightly swept and braced with substantial struts.

MORANE-SAULNIER MS.180
The Morane-Saulnier MS.180 of 1928 was a fully aerobatic parasol-wing monoplane, powered by a 336kW (450hp) Salmson engine. Only one example was built.

MORANE-SAULNIER MS.230
The Morane-Saulnier MS.230 was a parasol-wing, two-seat advanced trainer of 1929. The aircraft was used by the air forces of France, Belgium and Portugal.

was the J2M5, which had its armament reduced to two 20mm (0.79in) cannon. Its excellent rate of climb made it an ideal high-altitude interceptor, but supply shortages of its Kasei 26a engine resulted in only 35 being built out of a total of about 500.

Specifications apply to J2M3.

A Mitsubishi J2M Raiden seen in rather wretched condition and minus propeller after the end of the Pacific War.

Crew: 1
Powerplant: one 1395kW (1870hp) Mitsubishi MK4R Kasei 23a 14-cylinder radial engine
Performance: max speed 587km/h (365mph); range 1899km (1180 miles); service ceiling 11,700m (38,385ft)
Dimensions: wingspan 10.80m (35ft 5in); length 9.95m (32ft 7.75in); height 3.95m (12ft 11in)
Weight: 3945kg (8697lb) loaded
Armament: four 20mm (0.79in) cannon

MITSUBISHI KI.67 HIRYU 'PEGGY'

THE KI.67 HIRYU (Flying Dragon) was unquestionably the best bomber to see service with the Imperial Japanese Army, combining an excellent performance with good defensive firepower. The prototype flew in December 1942, but deliveries of fully operational

Ki.67-I aircraft did not begin until the summer of 1944. The initial Ki.67-Ia was quickly supplanted by the Ki.67-Ib, which remained in production until the end of the war. Production totalled 698 aircraft, and the Ki.67's code name was 'Peggy'. Specifications apply to Ki.67-Ib.

Crew: 6
Powerplant: two 1417kW (1900hp) Mitsubishi Ha.104 18-cylinder radial engines
Performance: max speed 537km/h (334mph); range 3800km (2361 miles); service ceiling 9470m (31,070ft)

Dimensions: wingspan 22.50m (73ft 9in); length 18.70m (61ft 4in); height 7.70m (25ft 3in)
Weight: 13,765kg (30,347lb) loaded
Armament: one 20mm (0.79in) cannon and five 12.7mm (0.50in) machine guns; bomb or torpedo load of 1070kg (2359lb)

MITSUBISHI A7M REPPU 'SAM'

Crew: 1
Powerplant: one 1171kW (1570hp) Mitsubishi MK9A 18-cylinder radial engine
Performance: max speed 627km/h (390mph); endurance 2 hrs 30 mins; service ceiling 10,900m (35,760ft)
Dimensions: wingspan 14.00m (45ft 11in); length 11.00m (36ft 1in); height 4.28m (14ft)
Weight: 4720kg (10,406lb) loaded
Armament: four wing-mounted 20mm (0.79in) cannon

INTENDED TO REPLACE the Zero as the Imperial Japanese Navy's standard carrier-borne fighter, the A7M Reppu (Hurricane) was ordered into production in 1940, but continual delays meant only nine prototypes and one production aircraft were built. The first prototype, designated A7M2, flew for the first time on 30 October 1944, by which time most of the Japanese carrier force had been destroyed. The Reppu production

schedule was plagued by continual misfortune. In December 1944, a violent earthquake in the Nagoya area, closely followed by a devastating B-29 attack on the factory which was producing the fighter's

engine, combined to disrupt the programme severely, then four of the prototypes were destroyed, one in an accident and the others in air attacks. The Allied code name for the Reppu was 'Sam'.

The Mitsubishi A7M2 Reppu prototype seen in the ruins of its hangar following the Japanese surrender. Production of the Reppu was seriously disrupted by various disasters.

MITSUBISHI J8M SHUSUI

JAPAN: 1945

JAPAN ACQUIRED manufacturing rights to the Messerschmitt Me 163 rocket-powered interceptor and its Walter HWK engine in late 1943. Despite one of the two submarines carrying the necessary technical data sinking en route to Japan, Mitsubishi was given the task of designing and producing the aircraft. After tests with an unpowered glider, the MXY8 Akigusa (Autumn Grass), seven prototypes of the powered J8M1 Shusui (Sword Stroke) were

built under a joint Army/Navy programme, The Army aircraft was designated Ki.200, and one was made ready for testing on 7 July 1945. The only test flight ended in disaster when the rocket motor failed after take-off; the aircraft was destroyed and its pilot killed.

The Mitsubishi J8M Shusui was to have been the licence-built version of Germany's Messerschmitt Me 163 Komet, but arrived too late.

Crew: 1
Powerplant: one 1500kg (3307lb) thrust Toko Ro2 bi-fuel rocket motor
Performance: max speed 900km/h (559mph); powered endurance 5 mins 30 secs; service ceiling 12,000m (39,370ft)
Dimensions: wingspan 9.50m (31ft 2in); length 6.05m (19ft 10in); height 2.70m (8ft 10in)
Weight: 3885kg (8565lb) loaded
Armament: one or two wing-mounted 30mm (1.18in) cannon (J8M1 and Ki.100, respectively)

MITSUBISHI F.1

JAPAN: 1976

Crew: 1
Powerplant: two 3315kg (7308lb) thrust Ishikawajima-Harima TF40 IHI-801A turbojet engines
Performance: max speed 1708km/h (1061mph); combat radius 350km (218 miles); service ceiling 15,240m (50,000ft)
Dimensions: wingspan 7.88m (25ft 10in); length 17.86m (58ft 7in); height 4.39m (14ft 4in)
Weight: 13,700kg (30,203lb) loaded
Armament: one 20mm (0.79in) JM61 Vulcan six-barrel cannon; five hardpoints with provision for up to 2722kg (6000lb) of external stores

DESIGNED TO REPLACE the F-86 Sabre in the Japanese Air Self-Defence Force, the F.1 strike fighter was developed from the T.2 super-sonic trainer. The first of 77 F.1s was

delivered in September 1977, and production lasted until March 1987. The F.1, first flown in November 1976, was the first postwar jet combat aircraft designed in Japan.

A Mitsubishi F.1 strike fighter over Japan. The faired-over space occupied by the rear cockpit in the T.2 trainer, from which the F.1 was developed, was filled with avionics.

MORANE-SAULNIER MS.225
Developed from the earlier MS.121 and MS.224 designs, the MS.225 fighter, which first flew in 1932, retained the parasol-wing configuration of its predecessors. Production totalled 74 aircraft.

MORANE-SAULNIER MS.340–MS.345
The MS.340 was a two-seat, high-wing monoplane design dating from 1933, intended for a touring or training role. Variants up to MS 345 were produced.

MORANE-SAULNIER MS.450
The Morane-Saulnier MS.450 was designed as a successor to the MS.406, the first of three prototypes flying in April 1939. The Dewoitine D.520 was selected in preference.

MORANE-SAULNIER MS.435
The Morane-Saulnier MS.435 was a two-seat advanced trainer development of the MS.405 fighter, the prototype flying in December 1939. Sixty were ordered, but none delivered.

MORANE-SAULNIER MS.760 PARIS
The Morane-Saulnier MS.760 Paris, first flown in 1954, was a four/six-seat military jet communications aircraft, used by France and several Latin American air forces.

MORANE-SAULNIER MS.1500 EPERVIER
The Morane-Saulnier MS.1500 Epervier (Sparrowhawk) was a single-turboprop light attack aircraft, first flown in 1958. It was unsuccessful in attracting customers, the two prototypes being used as test-beds.

MOONEY M20 SERIES

USING EARLY POSTWAR experience with the Mooney M-18 Mite, Al W. Mooney moved into the four-seat monoplane market in the early 1950s with the M20A design, featuring a similar low wing and retractable undercarriage – some subsequent lower specification models were offered with a fixed gear. The M20B had a larger engine and was of all-metal construction. Successive marques of the type (Ranger, Master, Super 21, Chapparal, Executive and Statesman), with its distinctive raked trailing fin edge, have been offered, with over 7500 delivered to date. Specifications apply to the M20M Model 257TLS.

Crew: 1
Powerplant: one 201kW (270hp) Textron Lycoming TIO-540-AFIA turbocharged piston engine
Performance: max speed 413km/h (257mph); range 1983km (1232 miles) with maximum fuel; service ceiling 7620m (25,000ft)
Dimensions: wingspan 11.00m (36ft 1in); length 8.20m (27ft); height 2.50m (8ft 3in)
Weight: 1451kg (3200lb) maximum take-off weight
Payload: four people

The 'squared' corners of the windows on the aircraft pictured are peculiar to the Chapparal and Ranger models of the M20 series.

MORANE-SAULNIER TYPE N

Crew: 1
Powerplant: one 82kW (110hp) Le Rhone 9J rotary engine
Performance: max speed 165km/h (102mph); endurance 1 hr 30 min; service ceiling 4000m (13,123ft)
Dimensions: wingspan 8.30m (27ft 2in); length 6.70m (21ft 11in); height 2.50m (8ft 2in)
Weight: 510kg (1124lb) loaded
Armament: one 7.7mm (0.303in) Vickers machine gun

A superb replica of a Morane-Saulnier Type N presents a major attraction at an air show. The original would have needed an experienced hand to control it.

THE MORANE-SAULNIER Type N was followed into service by two larger, more powerful and better-armed variants, the Type LA and Type P. The latter was the more widely used of the two, being adopted by both the French and British. The Type N was by no means as successful. Of advanced design, with very clean lines, its high landing speed and extremely sensitive controls made it unpopular with all but the most experienced pilots, and only 49 were built. Designated MS.5C.1 in French service, the type was also used by the RFC, in which it was known as the 'Bullet'.

MORANE-SAULNIER MS.405/406

THE MORANE-SAULNIER MS.405 was the first French fighter with a retractable undercarriage and enclosed cockpit. It flew for the first time at Villacoublay on 8 August 1935. Official trials of the MS.405 began at the beginning of 1936, and a second aircraft, the MS.405-02, joined the test programme in February 1937. This aircraft was destroyed on 29 July when its pilot passed out owing to the failure of his oxygen supply. All official trials had been completed by July 1937, the MS.405-01 having emerged the winner of the fighter design contest. The machine was returned to the manufacturer, who used it as a demonstration aircraft until it crashed on the approach to Villa-coublay on 8 December 1937, with

The Morane-Saulnier MS.405, seen here, was the prototype of the production MS.406, which equipped the majority of the French Escadres de Chasse at the outbreak of World War II.

a Lithuanian pilot at the controls. A pre-production batch of 15 machines had been ordered in August 1936, and it was the fourth aircraft of this batch, fitted with an 642kW (860hp) Hispano-Suiza 12-Ycrs engine, that became the prototype MS.406.

In September 1939, the rugged MS.406 was numerically the most important fighter in French service, with 225 aircraft equipping the 2e, 3e, 6e and 7e Escadres de Chasse and a further 1000 on order. The number of MS.406s eventually built reached 1080. The aircraft was very manoeuvrable and could withstand a tremendous amount of battle damage; however, it was outclassed by the Bf 109 and losses were heavy, 150 aircraft being lost in action and 250–300 lost through other causes.

By the time production of the MS.406 began in May 1938, the type had become the subject of foreign orders. The Lithuanian government ordered 12 aircraft, but these were never delivered; 30 were ordered by Finland, being delivered early in 1940, too late to

take part in the Russo-Finnish winter war of 1939–40, although they later saw combat against the Russians in 1941. Forty-five were supplied to Turkey, and 160 were ordered by Poland. Fifty of the latter aircraft were actually embarked for the Polish port of Gdynia in September 1939, but failed to reach their destination before Poland's collapse. Thirteen aircraft were shipped to China, but these were taken over by the French Colonial Administration when they reached the port of Haiphong in Indo-China. Later, a number of captured MS.406s were handed over to Croatia. The MS.406 was also built under licence in Switzerland, where it received the designation D-3800.

Several MS.406 developments were in progress at the time of France's surrender, these including the MS.420 with a completely retractable radiator, a night-fighter variant designated MS.440, and the MS.450, with a metal monocoque fuselage and a more powerful engine. The only Vichy Air Force unit to be equipped with the

MS.406 was GC I/7, based in the Levant, and in July 1941 it saw limited action against British forces during the campaign in Syria. The Morane fighter also equipped the 2e Escadrille of the Free French Air Force in North Africa before this unit converted to Hurricanes in 1941. Several MS.406s were still flying with the French Test Centre at Bretigny as late as 1947, these probably being the last aircraft of the type to be used by the Armée de l'Air.

Specifications apply to MS.406.

Crew: 1
Powerplant: one 642kW (860hp) Hispano-Suiza 12Y-31 12-cylinder Vee-type engine
Performance: max speed 490km/h (304mph); range 1500km (932 miles); service ceiling 9400m (30,850ft)
Dimensions: wingspan 10.62m (34ft 10in); length 8.17m (26ft 9in); height 3.25m (10ft 8in)
Weight: 2722kg (6000lb) loaded
Armament: one 20mm (0.79in) cannon or 7.5mm (0.29in) machine gun in an engine installation, and two 7.5mm (0.29in) machine guns in wing leading edges

MORTIMER AND VAUGHAN SAFETY BIPLANE

UK: 1910

DESIGNED BY TWO AVIATION enthusiasts, Mortimer and Vaughan of Edgware, Middlesex, England, the Safety Biplane was one of history's oddest flying machines. It had two sets of semi-circular

superimposed wings, giving it a ring shape, in the centre of which sat the fuselage. The latter was almost entirely enclosed, rectangular in section, and tapered sharply at the forward end. The

aircraft did become airborne on one occasion, but only when suspended from heavy cables to have its photograph taken.

No detailed specifications are available for this aircraft.

MYASISHCHEV MYA-4 'BISON'

FORMER USSR: 1954

Crew: 6-13, depending on mission
Powerplant: four 13,000kg (28,660lb) thrust Soloviev D15 turbojet engines
Performance: max speed 900km/h (560mph); range 11,000km (6835 miles); service ceiling 15,000m (49,200ft)
Dimensions: wingspan 50.48m (165ft 7in); length 47.20m (154ft 10in); height 14.10m (46ft)
Weight: 170,000kg (375,000lb) loaded
Armament: six 23mm (0.90in) cannon; 4500kg (10,000lb) of ordnance or equipment in internal bay

THE PRODUCTION OF the Soviet Union's first strategic jet bombers was entrusted to the Tupolev and Myasishchev design bureaux; the latter's efforts culminated in the four-engined Mya-4, which first appeared at Tushino in 1954. Although never an outstanding success in the long-range strategic bombing role for which it was

intended, nevertheless the aircraft was still the Soviet Union's first operational four-engined jet bomber, and was roughly comparable with early versions of the Boeing B-52. The Mya-4's main

operational role in later years was maritime and electronic reconnaissance, and some were converted as flight refuelling tankers. Specifications apply to the 'Bison-C' electronic intelligence aircraft.

This Myasishchev Mya-4, part of a static museum exhibit, clearly shows the aircraft's very clean lines. An M-55 Mystic is in the background.

MYASISHCHEV M.50/M.52 'BOUNDER'

FORMER USSR: 1959

Crew: 3
Powerplant: four 13,000kg (28,660lb) thrust Soloviev D-15 turbojet engines
Performance: max speed 1950km/h (1212mph); range 10,000km (6200 miles); service ceiling not known
Dimensions: wingspan 37.00m (121ft 4in); length 57.00m (187ft); height not known
Weight: 90,600kg (200,000lb) loaded
Armament (proposed): one M-61 cruise missile

THE MYASISHCHEV M.50/M.52 was an extremely advanced turbojet-powered bomber with supersonic flight capability. First flight of the M.50 took place in November 1959, and the last of several prototypes, redesignated M.52, took part in the Soviet Aviation Day fly-past in 1961. In configuration the Myasishchev M.50, codenamed 'Bounder' by NATO, had a shoulder-mounted cropped delta-wing, a conventional tail unit with all-swept surfaces, and landing gear comprising retractable tandem main units mounted on the fuselage centreline, each with a four-wheel bogie; while retractable outrigger balancing struts, each with two wheels, were mounted near the wingtips. The programme was terminated in favour of ICBM development.

For a while, the appearance of the mighty 'Bounder' convinced Western observers that the Russians were in possession of a supersonic bomber.

MYASISHCHEV M-55 'MYSTIC'

FORMER USSR/RUSSIA: 1988

CODE-NAMED 'MYSTIC' by NATO, this twin-boom straight-wing jet, currently publicized as a high-altitude research aircraft able to carry around 1500kg (3305lb) of sensors, is now known to exist in two versions. The first of two prototype aircraft, designated M-17 Stratosfera ('Mystic-A'), flew in 1988 and was powered by a single Rybinsk RD-36-51V turbojet developed from the Tu-144 SST powerplant. The second version, the M-55 Geofizika ('Mystic-B'), has two Perm/Soloviev (Aviadvigatel) PS-30-V12 turbojets mounted side by side behind a raised cockpit installed in a longer nose, together with a reduced span wing. The role of the 'Mystic-B' is described as 'environmental sampling missions' or 'high-altitude research'. Production of the aircraft was terminated in 1994 after a small number of M-55s had been built.

Although described as a high-altitude research aircraft, the primary function of the M-55 'Mystic' was reconnaissance.

Crew: 1
Powerplant: two 9988kg (22,050lb) thrust Aviadvigatel PS-30-V1 turbojet engines
Performance: max speed 750km/h (466mph); endurance 6 hrs 30 mins; service ceiling 20,000m (65,600ft)
Dimensions: wingspan 37.40m (122ft 11in); length 22.80m (75ft); height 4.70m (15ft 5in)
Weight: 19,950kg (44,000lb) loaded

NAKAJIMA KI.27 'NATE'

JAPAN: 1936

Crew: 1
Powerplant: one 530kW (710hp)
Nakajima Ha-1b 9-cylinder radial engine
Performance: max speed 470km/h
(292mph); range 1710km (1063 miles);
service ceiling 12,259m (40,190ft)
Dimensions: wingspan 11.31m (37ft 1in);
length 7.53m (24ft 8in); height 3.25m
(10ft 8in)
Weight: 1790kg (3946lb) loaded
Armament: two 7.7mm (0.303in) machine
guns; external bomb load of 100kg
(220lb)

THE NAKAJIMA KI.27 was the
Japanese Army Air Force's first
low-wing monoplane fighter and
the first to have an enclosed cockpit.
The prototype flew in October 1946,
and the Ki.27 was the JAAF's
standard fighter up to the middle of
1942, playing a prominent part in
Japan's campaigns in China and

**Japanese Army pilots did not take kindly to the Ki.27's enclosed cockpit,
claiming that it restricted their all-round vision.**

Southeast Asia. The little fighter
was produced in large numbers:
production totalled 3495 aircraft,
the main variants being the Ki.27a
with an uprated engine and metal-

faired canopy, and the Ki.27b with
a clear-view canopy and underwing
bomb racks. The type was code-
named 'Nate' by the Allies.
Specifications apply to the Ki.27b.

NAKAJIMA B5N 'KATE'

JAPAN: 1937

DESIGNED IN 1936, the prototype
B5N torpedo-bomber was first
flown in January 1937 and became
operational as the B5N1 light
bomber in China. Most B5N-1s
were allocated to the training role
as they were progressively
replaced by the B5N2 in 1939–40.
The B5N2 featured prominently in
the attack on Pearl Harbor, 144
aircraft taking part in the strike,
and in the year that followed
B5N2s delivered fatal blows to the
US aircraft carriers *Lexington*,

Yorktown and *Hornet*, as well as
supporting Japanese amphibious
assaults and taking part in a carrier
strike on Ceylon (Sri Lanka), in
which heavy damage was inflicted
on installations in the port of
Colombo. The B5N2 remained in
production until 1943, by which
time 1149 examples of both
variants had been built. Many
B5Ns were later assigned to anti-
submarine patrol work. The B5N
was known to the Allies as 'Kate'.
Specifications apply to the B5N2.

Crew: 3
Powerplant: one 746kW (1000hp)
Nakajima NK1B Sakae 11 14-cylinder
radial engine
Performance: max speed 378km/h
(235mph); range 2000km (1242 miles);
service ceiling 8260m (27,100ft)
Dimensions: wingspan 15.51m (50ft
11in); length 10.30m (33ft 9in); height
3.70m (12ft)
Weight: 4108kg (9039lb) loaded
Armament: one 7.7mm (0.303in)
machine gun; one 800kg (1764lb)
torpedo

**The Nakajima B5N Kate torpedo-bomber inflicted enormous damage on the US Pacific Fleet at Pearl Harbor,
and took part in several other successful Japanese carrier operations.**

**NAGLER UND
ROLTZ NR.55 AND NR.54**
In 1939 Austrians Bruno Nagler
and Franz Roltz began developing
small single-seat helicopters. The
NR.55 with a single-blade rotor
appeared in 1940, but did not
progress beyond hovering tests.
The NR.54 V1 of 1941 was the
world's first portable helicopter,
weighing just 177kg (390lb) loaded.
Only four machines were built.

**NAGLER (VERTIDYNAMICS)
VERTIGYRO VG-1**
This experimental autogyro first
flew in 1964 and was built using
the fuselage of a Piper Colt and the
rotor system and rotor head controls
from a Sud-Aviation Djinn.

NAKAJIMA A1N
The Nakajima A1N was a version
of the Gloster Gambet biplane
fighter licence-built for the Japanese
Navy. It went into production in
1929 and was built in two versions.

NAKAJIMA A2N
An extremely agile biplane with
stylishly tapered, staggered wings,
the Nakajima A2N entered service
in 1930 as the Navy Type 90 carrier
fighter and was used operationally
in the Sino-Japanese war.

NAKAJIMA E4N
First flown in 1930, the Nakajima
E4N was a single-engined
reconnaissance floatplane. It served
on ships of the Imperial Japanese
Navy, 150 being built.

NAKAJIMA TYPE 91
The Nakajima Type 91, which
entered service in 1931, was a
parasol-wing carrier fighter
powered by a Bristol Jupiter radial
engine. A total of 450 were built.

NAKAJIMA KI.43 HAYABUSA 'OSCAR'

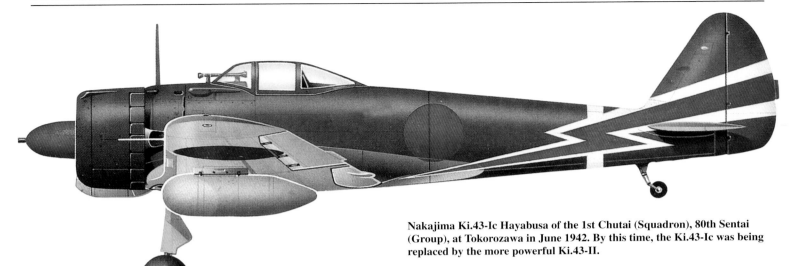

Nakajima Ki.43-Ic Hayabusa of the 1st Chutai (Squadron), 80th Sentai (Group), at Tokorozawa in June 1942. By this time, the Ki.43-Ic was being replaced by the more powerful Ki.43-II.

Crew: 1
Powerplant: one 858kW (1150hp) Nakajima Ha.115 14-cylinder radial engine
Performance: max speed 530km/h (329mph); range 3200km (1988 miles); service ceiling 11,200m (36,750ft)
Dimensions: wingspan 10.84m (35ft 6in); length 8.92m (29ft 3in); height 3.27m (10ft 8in)
Weight: 2925kg (6450lb) loaded
Armament: two 12.7mm (0.50in) machine guns; external bomb load of 500kg (1102lb)

LIKE ITS NAVAL counterpart, the Mitsubishi Zero, the Nakajima Ki.43 Hayabusa (Peregrine Falcon) was in action from the first day of Japan's war until the last, by which time it was woefully outclassed by the latest Allied fighters. Design of the fighter began in December 1937, when the Japanese Army issued a stringent specification for a fighter to supersede the Nakajima Ki.27. Instead of awarding competitive contracts to several Japanese manufacturers, the Army placed the development of the new aircraft entirely in the hands of a Nakajima design team led by Hideo Itokawa. The prototype was completed within a year and flew in early January 1939, 716 early production models being produced. These were the Ki.43-I, Ki.43-Ia, Ki.43-Ib and Ki.43-Ic, the last two having a better armament. They were followed in 1942 by a much improved model, the Ki.43-II; this was to appear in three subvariants, the Ki.43-IIa and -IIb, and the

Ki.43-Kai, which adopted all the refinements incorporated in the earlier models. The final model was the Ki.43-III, the only variant to include cannon in its armament. Production of all versions totalled 5878 aircraft, including 3200 by Nakajima and 2629 by Tachikawa.

The Hayabusa was the Allies principal opponent in Burma and was encountered in large numbers during the battle for Leyte, in the Philippines, and in the defence of the Kurile Islands north of Japan. An excellent and versatile fighter, the Hayabusa's main drawback was its lack of adequate armament.

In the early part of the war there was a great deal of speculation as to the type's identity, and for a time it was known as 'Oscar' in the south-west Pacific theatre and 'Jim' in the China-Burma-India theatre, 'Oscar' being the code name that was finally retained when the Allies realized that they were dealing with the same aircraft.

The Hayabusa was numerically the most important aircraft on the Japanese Army Air Force's inventory in World War II, and it was to fight on every front. Some Ki.43-Is were supplied to Thailand, which was controlled by a Japanese

puppet government, and saw action against aircraft of the US 14th Air Force in southern China. After the war, some salvaged Ki.43s were used by Indonesian rebels against Dutch forces, and some were used very briefly by pilots of the French Groupes de Chasse I/7 and II/7 against communist insurgents in Indo-China before more modern equipment arrived in the shape of Grumman F8F Bearcats. Some of the Royal Thai Air Force Ki.43s remained in service until 1949.

Specifications apply to the Ki.43-IIb.

An early model Nakajima Ki.43 in flight. The Hayabusa was used in large numbers and was an excellent fighter design, although it lacked adequate armament.

NAKAJIMA KI.49 DONRYU 'HELEN'

JAPAN: 1939

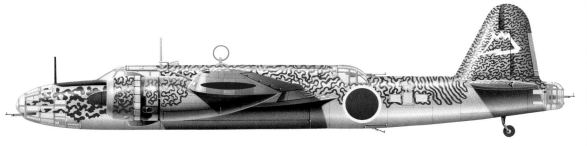

Crew: 8
Powerplant: two 1119kW (1500hp)
Nakajima Ha.109 14-cylinder radial
engines
Performance: max speed 492km/h
(306mph); range 2950km (1833 miles);
service ceiling 9300m (30,510ft)
Dimensions: wingspan 20.42m (67ft);
length 16.50m (54ft 1in); height 4.25m
(13ft 11in)
Armament: one 20mm (0.79in) cannon;
three 12.7mm (0.50in) and two 7.7mm
(0.303in) machine guns; bomb load of
1000kg (2205lb)

THE NAKAJIMA KI.49 Donryu
(Storm Dragon), known as 'Helen'
to the Allies, was designed in 1938
as a replacement for the Mitsubishi
Ki.21, but from the moment of its
first flight in August 1939 it
became apparent that it would have
to supplement, rather than replace,
the older type. Deliveries of the
Donryu to the JAAF began in the
summer of 1941, and the aircraft
was used in attacks on Australia
and in the New Guinea campaign.
Combat experience showed that

**The Nakajima Ki.49 Donryu was a
disappointment to the Japanese
Army Air Force.**

the type was badly underpowered,
with speed and payload suffering
as a consequence. The type was
produced in two main versions, the
Ki.49-I and Ki.49-II, the latter
having uprated engines, more
armour and better defensive
firepower. Total production was
819. Specifications apply to the
Nakajima Ki.49-IIa.

NAKAJIMA KI.44 SHOKI 'TOJO'

JAPAN: 1940

Crew: 1
Powerplant: one 1134kW (1520hp)
Nakajima Ha.109 14-cylinder radial
engine
Performance: max speed 605km/h
(376mph); range 1700km (1056 miles);
service ceiling 11,200m (36,745ft)
Dimensions: wingspan 9.45m (31ft);
length 8.79m (28ft 10in); height 3.25m
(10ft 8in)
Weight: 2993kg (6598lb) loaded
Armament: four 12.7mm (0.50in)
machine guns

THE NAKAJIMA KI.44 SHOKI
(Demon-Queller), which first flew
in August 1944 and which entered
service in the summer of 1942, was
designed specifically as an interceptor. It proved outstanding in
this role, due to its excellent speed

**The Ki.44 took a leading role in
the defense of the Japanese home
islands against B-29 bombers.**

and rate of climb, although its high
take-off and landing speeds made
it unpopular with Japanese pilots.
The most effective version of the
Shoki was the heavily armed
Ki.44-IIc, which was used in the
air defence of Japan and achieved
some noteworthy successes against
B-29 bombers. One Ki.44 unit,
known as the Shinten Seikutai, was

**Its high wing-loading, resulting in
high take-off and landing speeds,
made the Ki.44 Shoki a dangerous
aircraft in the hands of any but the
most experienced pilots.**

formed in November 1944 as an
airborne kamikaze unit, its specific
task being to ram enemy bombers
after the fighters' ammunition had
been expended. Specifications
apply to the Ki.44-II.

NAKAJIMA E8N
A small reconnaissance floatplane,
the Nakajima E8N of 1933 was
designed to be catapult-launched
from the IJN's capital ships and to
operate from coastal bases. Its
Allied code name was 'Dave'.

NAKAJIMA A4N
The A2N's replacement was the
Nakajima A4N1, which entered
service as the Type 95 Carrier
Fighter. It, too, participated in the
Sino-Japanese conflict.

NAKAJIMA AT-2
The Nakajima AT-2, which
appeared in 1936, was a twin-
engined light transport used for
both civil and military purposes,
including paratroop training.

NAKAJIMA KI.19
The Nakajima Ki.19 was a twin-
engined medium bomber,
developed in 1937. The Mitsubishi
Ki.21 was selected in preference,
and only one Ki.19 prototype was
built.

NAKAJIMA G5N1 SHINZAN
Flown in April 1941, the Nakajima
G5N1 Shinzan (Deep Mountain)
was a four-engined heavy bomber
based on the Douglas DC-4
prototype. Only four aircraft were
completed.

NAKAJIMA G10N1 FUGAKA
The Nakajima G10N1 Fugaka
(Mount Fuji) was a projected six-
engined heavy bomber capable of
attacking the US mainland from
Pacific bases. It was never built.

NAKAJIMA J5N1 TENRAI
The Nakajima J5N1 Tenrai
(Heavenly Thunder), which first
flew in July 1944, was a twin-
engined heavy interceptor.
Performance proved disappointing,
and only six prototypes were built.

NAKAJIMA J1N GEKKO 'IRVING'

JAPAN: 1941

A Nakajima J1N1-S Gekko. This was a night-fighter version from the outset, featuring a redesigned upper fuselage eliminating the step between the rear of the observer's cockpit and the base of the tail fin, and armed with an obliquely mounted 20mm (0.79in) cannon.

Crew: 3
Powerplant: two 843kW (1130hp) Nakajima NK1F Sakae 14-cylinder radial engines
Performance: max speed 530km/h (329mph); range 2700km (1678 miles); service ceiling 10,300m (33,795ft)

Dimensions: wingspan 16.98m (55ft 8in); length 12.18m (39ft 11in); height 4.56m (15ft)
Weight: 7542kg (16,594lb) loaded
Armament: one 7.7mm (0.303in) machine gun

CODE-NAMED 'IRVING' by the Allies, the J1N Gekko (Moonlight) first flew in May 1941; the type was used in the reconnaissance, light bomber and night-fighter roles. The reconnaissance variant made

its operational debut as the J1N1-C early in 1943. Some aircraft were converted to emergency night-fighters and designated J1N1-R. The J1N1-S was also a night-fighter. Specifications apply to J1N1-C.

NAKAJIMA B6N TENZAN 'JILL'

JAPAN: 1942

THE NAKAJIMA B6N TENZAN (Heavenly Mountain) torpedo-bomber was developed as an urgent replacement for the B5N 'Kate', the prototype flying in March 1942. The engine selected for the first production model, the B6N1, was the 1395kW (1870hp) Mamoru II radial. Although constant trouble was experienced with this

powerplant, 133 B6N1s were built; the first entered service in 1943. The next version, the B6N2, had the much more reliable Kasei 25; 1135 examples were built, bringing the total to 1268. Known by the Allied code name 'Jill', the B6N suffered from a lack of aircraft carriers and a shortage of trained crews. Specifications apply to B6N2.

Crew: 3
Powerplant: one 1380kW (1850hp) Mitsubishi MK4T Kasei 25 14-cylinder radial engine
Performance: max speed 481km/h (299mph); range 3045km (1892 miles); service ceiling 9040m (29,660ft)

Dimensions: wingspan 14.89m (48ft 10in); length 10.87m (35ft 7in); height 3.80m (12ft 5in)
Weight: 5650kg (12,456lb) loaded
Armament: one or two 7.7mm (0.303in) machine guns; one 800kg (1764lb) torpedo

A Nakajima B6N2 Tenzan of the Imperial Japanese Navy, 1944. A great many surviving Tenzans were expended in kamikaze attacks at Okinawa and Iwo Jima in the latter part of the Pacific War.

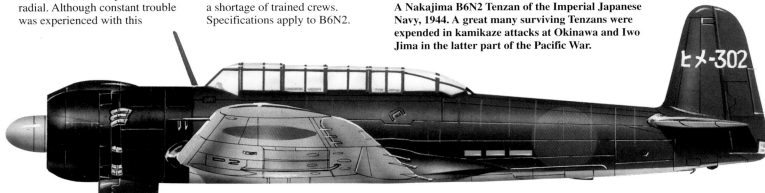

NAKAJIMA A6M2-N 'RUFE'

JAPAN: 1942

Crew: 1
Powerplant: one 709kW (950hp) Nakajima NK1C Sakae 12 14-cylinder radial engine
Performance: max speed 434km/h (270mph); range 1780km (1107 miles); service ceiling 10,000m (32,810ft)
Dimensions: wingspan 12.00m (39ft 4in); length 10.10m (33ft 2in); height 4.30m (14ft 1in)
Weight: 2895kg (6349lb) loaded
Armament: two 20mm (0.79in) cannon; one 12.7mm (0.50in) and one 7.7mm (0.303in) machine guns

INTENDED FOR OPERATIONS from water bases among the scattered Pacific atolls, Nakajima's A6M2-N was a floatplane fighter adaptation of the A6M2 Zero, and 327 aircraft were completed between April 1942 and September 1943. The A6M2-N was used mainly for home defence and reconnaissance, although it was occasionally

encountered in its fighter role at the Aleutian Islands, Guadalcanal and over the Bay of Bengal. Its Allied code name was 'Rufe'.

The A6M2-N, built by Nakajima as a floatplane version of Mitsubishi's A6M2 Zero fighter, was very manoeuvrable despite its floats.

NAKAJIMA C6N SAIUN 'MYRT'

JAPAN: 1943

The distinguishing feature of the Nakajima C6N Saiun was its long 'glasshouse' cockpit. The type, total production of which was 463 aircraft, was very fast and could often outrun pursuing Allied fighters.

Crew: 3
Powerplant: one 1328kW (1780hp) Nakajima NK9B Homare 18-cylinder radial engine
Performance: max speed 648km/h (403mph); range 4595km (2855 miles); service ceiling 10,470m (35,236ft)
Dimensions: wingspan 12.50m (41ft); length 11.12m (36ft 5in); height 3.96m (13ft)
Weights: 5260kg (11,596lb) loaded
Armament: one 7.7mm (0.303in) machine gun in rear cockpit; one torpedo

DESIGNED PRIMARILY FOR the reconnaissance role, the first prototype of the Nakajima C6N Saiun (Painted Cloud), which was known to the Allies as 'Myrt', flew on 15 May 1943 and was followed by no fewer than 23 more prototypes in an effort to shorten development time. Deliveries of the series production C6N1 to the Imperial Japanese Navy began in August 1944 after lengthy delays caused by the problematic Homare engine.

The reconnaissance variant could outpace and outclimb most Allied fighters. The C6N1-B was a three-seat torpedo-bomber variant, and the C6N1-S was a night-fighter conversion with a crew of two and two obliquely mounted 20mm (0.79in) cannon. The last aircraft to be destroyed in World War II was a C6N1, shot down by a US Navy pilot, Lt Cdr Reidy, at 0540 on 15 August 1945. Specifications apply to the C6N-1B.

NAKAJIMA G8N RENZAN
The Nakajima G8N Renzan (Mountain Range), codenamed 'Rita' by the Allies, was a Japanese Navy four-engine heavy bomber. Four prototypes were built, the first flying in October 1944.

NAKAJIMA KI.201 KARYU
The Nakajima Ki.201 Karyu was a twin-engined jet fighter based on the Messerschmitt Me 262, detailed plans of which were shipped to Japan in 1944. It was never built.

NAKAJIMA J8N1 KIKKA
The Nakajima J8N1 Kikka (Orange Blossom) was the only turbojet-powered aircraft built and flown in Japan during World War II, the sole completed prototype flying in August 1945.

NARDI FN.315
An Italian design of 1938, developed from the earlier FN.305. The FN.315 was a single-engined touring/training/aerobatic design, with one or two seats and a retractable undercarriage. Customers included the Italian military and civilian exports.

NARDI FN.333 RIVIERA
Dating from 1952, this Italian single-engine (rear-mounted) flying-boat/amphibian offered a four-seat cabin area. Over 30 production models were built by Savoia-Marchetti, mostly for export to the United States.

NAVAL AIRCRAFT FACTORY N3N-1
First flown in 1935, the Naval Aircraft Factory N3N-1 two-seat primary training biplane served with the US armed forces for 26 years. It could be fitted with either floats or wheels.

NAKAJIMA KI.84 HAYATE 'FRANK'

JAPAN: 1943

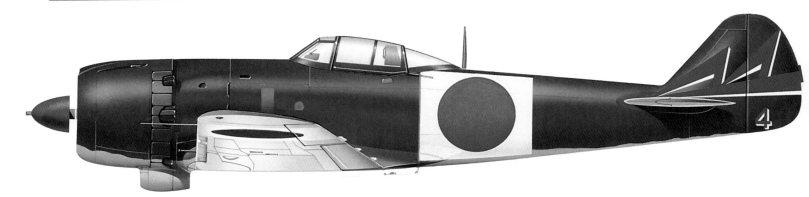

AT THE END OF 1944, production of the Ki.44 Shoki was suspended in favour of another army fighter type, the Nakajima Ki.84 Hayate (Gale). First flown in April 1943, the Hayate was more agile than the Shoki and far easier to handle. Service trials in the autumn of 1943 produced promising results, and the fighter was ordered into mass production, with about 3500 examples being completed in the

18 months before hostilities ended. The Hayate proved to be more manoeuvrable and have a better rate of climb than both the P-47N Thunderbolt and P-51D Mustang. The type was produced in two principal variants, the Ki.84-I and the Ki.84-II, which had a wooden rear fuselage and fittings in an attempt to reduce the drain on Japan's dwindling reserves of strategic light alloys. The last

The Ki.84 Hayate was the best Japanese fighter to be mass-produced in World War II, but its operations were severely restricted due to shortages of aviation fuel.

version produced was the Ki.116, a converted Ki.84-Ia with a lighter engine. The Ki.84 was known as 'Frank' to the Allies.

Specification refers to the Nakajima Ki.84-Ia.

Crew: 1
Powerplant: one 1417kW (1900hp) Nakajima Ha.45 18-cylinder radial engine
Performance: max speed 631km/h (392mph); range 2168km (1347 miles); service ceiling 10,500m (34,450ft)
Dimensions: wingspan 11.24m (36ft 10in); length 9.92m (32ft 6in); height 3.39m (11ft 1in)
Weight: 4170kg (9193lb) loaded
Armament: two 20mm (0.79in) cannon and two 12.7mm (0.50in) machine guns

NAMC YS-11

JAPAN: 1962

Today around 50 YS-11s remain operational – this example, operated by the Japanese Air Self-Defence Force, was delivered in 1965.

SIX JAPANESE aerospace companies were brought together under TADA, which was later changed to NAMC (Nihon Aircraft Manufacturing Company) in 1956, primarily to furnish domestic needs for a short-/medium-haul commuter airliner. The resulting YS-11 went into service

in 1965. In all, 182 YS-11s were produced in a number of variants and subvariants for domestic and export customers until 1974, including Japanese military role training derivatives, and increased weight 500 to 700 series.
Specifications apply to YS-11A-300.

Crew: 2
Powerplant: two 2282ekW (3060hp) Rolls-Royce Dart RDA.10/1 Mk 542-10K turboprop engines
Performance: max cruising speed 469km/h (291mph) at 4570m (15,000ft); range with maximum payload 1090km (677 miles); service ceiling

6980m (22,900ft)
Dimensions: wing span 32.00m (104ft 11.75in); length 26.30m (86ft 3.5in); height 8.98m (29ft 5.5in)
Weight: 24,500kg (54,012lb) maximum take-off weight
Payload: up to 60 passengers or 6170kg (13,602lb) of freight

NANCHANG Q-5 FANTAN

CHINA: 1964

Crew: 1
Powerplant: two 3250kg (7165lb) thrust Shenyang WP-6 turbojet engines
Performance: max speed 1190km/h (739mph); combat radius 400km (249 miles); service ceiling 16,000m (52,500ft)
Dimensions: wingspan 9.68m (31ft 9in); length 15.65m (51ft 4in); height 4.33m (14ft 2in)
Weight: 11,830kg (26,080lb) loaded
Armament: two 23mm (0.90in) cannon; up to 2000kg (4409lb) of external stores

THE NANCHANG Q-5 Fantan was based on the Shenyang F-6, which in turn was a Chinese copy of the MiG-19. The Chinese aircraft retained a similar wing and rear fuselage configuration, but featured a new nose containing an attack radar and air intakes on either side of the forward fuselage. The prototype flew in 1964, and first deliveries to the Chinese People's Air Force were made in

1970. Overseas customers for the Nachang Q-5 Nantang are Bangladesh, Pakistan, North Korea and Myanmar (Burma).

The Nanchang Q-5 Fantan was essentially a MiG-19 with a completely revised nose section, permitting the installation of attack radar. The aircraft's air intakes were repositioned on either side of the fuselage.

NAVAL AIRCRAFT FACTORY P SERIES

USA: 1925–37

MUCH FLYING-BOAT development work was carried out by the Naval Aircraft Factory on behalf of the US Navy in the 1920s, beginning with

The P series of flying boats carried out much invaluable experimental work on behalf of the US Navy in the 1920s.

the PN-7 twin-engined biplane, which represented an effort to improve on the Felixstowe F-5L flying boat of World War I. The

PN-8, PN-11 and PN-12 featured progressive design changes, paving the way for other, more advanced flying-boat designs. The PN flying boats were manufactured by various companies, the function of the Naval Aircraft Factory being purely development, and a number of other designs were based on them. Specifications apply to the PN-7.

Crew: 5
Powerplant: two 392kW (525hp) Wright R-1750D cyclone radial engines
Performance: max speed 183km/h (114mph); range 2091km (1300 miles); service ceiling 3324m (10,900ft)
Dimensions: wingspan 22.23m (72ft 11in); length 15m (49ft 2in); height 5m (16ft 4in)
Weight: 6397lb (14,122lb) loaded
Armament: various small calibre bombs

NAVY-WRIGHT NW-1/NW-2
The Navy-Wright NW-1 was a racing sesquiplane, built for the US Navy to take part in the Pulitzer Trophy race of 1922. Later rebuilt in biplane configuration, and redesignated NW-2, the aircraft sank during a race at Cowes, Isle of Wight, in 1923.

NEIVA 360C (C.42) AND 460L (L.42) REGENTE AND LANCEIRO
A Brazilian high-wing, four-seat, single-engined light training/communications aeroplane dating from 1961, the Regente was acquired by the Brazilian Air Force (the L.42 was an improved version). Some 120 examples were manufactured until 1971 when production ceased. The civil version, the Lanceiro, was only produced to prototype standard.

NHI H-3 KOLIBRIE (HUMMING BIRD)
The Kolibrie was a two-seat helicopter powered by two rotor-tip-mounted 20kg (44lb) thrust TJ-5/5A ramjets and first flown in May 1956. After 10 were completed production passed to Aviolanda in May 1959, but was later abandoned.

NIEUPORT 6M
The Nieuport 6M, which appeared in 1914, was a single-seat unarmed reconnaissance aircraft with a top speed of 112km/h (70mph).

NIEUPORT 24
A further development of the Nieuport 17, the Nieuport 24 appeared in 1916 and was used by all Allied air arms. Some were built by Nakajima in Japan as KO-4s.

NIEUPORT 11

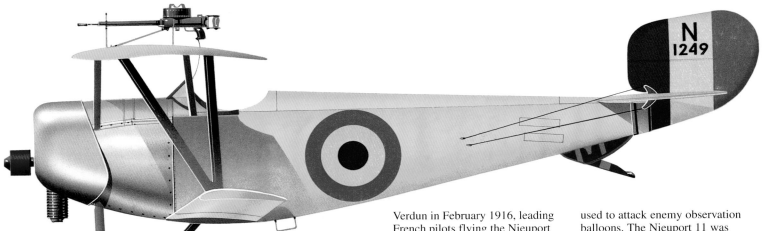

A Nieuport 11 in the markings of the Belgian Aviation Militaire. The type played a huge part in gaining an Allied air advantage in 1916.

THE NIEUPORT 11, nicknamed 'Bébé' by its pilots, was without doubt one of the most effective fighter aircraft of World War I. It made its combat debut over the Western Front in the summer of 1915, and was mainly responsible for restoring the balance of air power during the 'Fokker scourge' of that year. During the Battle of Verdun in February 1916, leading French pilots flying the Nieuport 11 inflicted very heavy casualties on the Germans.

Fast and manoeuvrable, the Nieuport 11 also served with the RFC and RNAS, and one of Britain's leading air aces, Captain Albert Ball (later to be awarded the Victoria Cross), scored the first of his 43 victories while flying the type. The Nieuport 16 was a more powerful version, powered by a 82kW (110hp) engine. Some were armed with Le Prieur rockets on the interplane struts, which were used to attack enemy observation balloons. The Nieuport 11 was also manufactured in Italy, where 646 were built by Macchi.

Crew: 1
Powerplant: one 60kW (80hp) Le Rhone 9C 9-cylinder rotary engine
Performance: max speed 155km/h (97mph); endurance 2 hrs 30 mins; service ceiling 4500m (14,765ft)
Dimensions: wingspan 7.55m (24ft 9in); length 5.80m (19ft); height 2.45m (8ft)
Weight: 480kg (1058lb) loaded
Armament: one 7.7mm (0.303in) machine gun

NIEUPORT 17

THE NIEUPORT 17 was among the finest Allied fighting aircraft of World War I. The prototype flew for the first time in January 1916, and deliveries to frontline units began in May. The type was highly manoeuvrable, with a good all-round performance and an excellent rate of climb. Its lower mainplane was strengthened to overcome the problem of wing-twist experienced by the Nieuport 11 during a high-speed dive. Hundreds were built for France's Aviation Militaire, the British RFC and RNAS, plus Belgium, Russia, Holland, Italy, Finland and the US Army Air Service.

Crew: 1
Powerplant: one 82kW (110hp) Le Rhone 9J rotary engine
Performance: max speed 170km/h (106mph); endurance 2 hrs; service ceiling 5300m (17,388ft)
Dimensions: wingspan 8.20m (26ft 11in); length 5.96m (19ft 7in); height 2.44m (8ft)
Weight: 560kg (1235lb) loaded
Armament: one 7.7mm (0.303in) machine gun

The Nieuport 17 was strong and rugged, and had a better performance than most contemporary German fighters. It was widely used by all the Allied air forces.

NIEUPORT 28

FRANCE: 1917

Crew: 1
Powerplant: one 119kW (160hp) Gnome-Le Rhone 9N rotary engine
Performance: max speed 195km/h (121mph); range 400km (248 miles); service ceiling 5200m (17,060ft)
Dimensions: wingspan 8.00m (26ft 3in); length 6.20m (20ft 4in); height 2.48m (8ft 2in)
Weight: 740kg (1631lb) loaded
Armament: two 7.7mm (0.303in) machine guns

THE NIEUPORT 28, which became operational in the spring of 1918, was one of the company's best designs, although it suffered from an unreliable engine. The V-struts which had been a hallmark of earlier Nieuports were replaced by parallel struts bracing wings of equal proportion. The Nieuport 28 had some unpleasant faults, including a tendency to shed its fabric during violent manoeuvres at high speed, but it was the only fighter available in numbers to equip the American Expeditionary Force when the latter arrived in France. It served well until eventually replaced by Spads.

The Nieuport 28 was a firm favourite with all who flew it. This example is in the colours of the 94th Pursuit Squadron, United States Army Air Service.

NIEUPORT-DELAGE NID 29

FRANCE: 1918

Crew: 1
Powerplant: one 224kW (300hp) Hispano-Suiza 8Fb 8-cylinder Vee-type engine
Performance: max speed 235km/h (146mph); range 580km (360 miles); service ceiling 8500m (27,885ft)
Dimensions: wingspan 9.70m (31ft 10in); length 6.49m (21ft 3in); height 2.56m (8ft 5in)
Weight: 1150kg (2535lb) loaded
Armament: two 7.7mm (0.303in) machine guns

ALTHOUGH THE Nieuport-Delage NiD 29 arrived too late to participate in World War I, it went on to become one of the most widely used fighters of the postwar years. It was the first of Gustave Delage's designs for the Nieuport company to feature a Vee-type engine instead of a rotary. The first NiD 29 failed to meet the altitude requirement of 9129m (29,930ft), but this was achieved by the second prototype in June 1919. This aircraft provided the pattern for the production NiD 29C. Over 250 examples were built for the Aviation Militaire, equipping 25 escadrilles at their peak. The type also formed the main fighter element of the Belgian and Italian air arms in the 1920s.

The NiD 29C1 equipped 25 Escadrilles at the peak of its service career, forming the main fighter element of the French air arm in the early 1920s.

NIEUPORT 27
A progression of the Nieuport 24, the Nieuport 27 had a modified tailplane and tail skid. The American Expeditionary Force ordered 287, but not all were delivered.

NIEUPORT NIGHTHAWK
Designed at the end of World War I, the Nieuport Nighthawk fighter was not a success, mainly because of its unreliable ABC engine. It entered production, but did not see service.

NIEUPORT NI.140
The Nieuport Ni.140, which appeared in 1935, was a two-seat shipboard fighter/dive-bomber. The prototype, redesignated Ni.161, was destroyed during flight trials.

NIEUPORT-DELAGE 1921 SESQUIPLANE
The Nieuport-Delage Sesquiplane of 1921 was a racing aircraft which won the Henry Deutsch de la Meurthe Cup in that year with a speed of 278.408km/h (172.994mph).

NIEUPORT-DELAGE NID 42
The Nieuport-Delage NiD 42 single-seat fighter appeared in 1924, and 25 examples were ordered as NiD 42C-1s. The type established 16 world records between August and October 1924.

NIEUPORT-DELAGE NID 52
The NiD 52 fighter of 1928 was a development of the NiD 41 sesquiplane, and was built under licence in Spain as the NiD 52C-1. It fought in the Spanish Civil War, by which time it was outclassed.

NIEUPORT-DELAGE NiD 62 SERIES

A FURTHER LINE of excellent fighter aircraft from the Nieuport-Delage stable was the biplane 62 series, which emerged victorious from various military aviation competitions of the 1920s. The NiD-62C-1 was the most important variant, 345 examples of which were built and which began to replace the NiD 29 from 1927. By 1932 it equipped some two-thirds of the French Air Force's fighter escadrilles. The follow-on NiD 622 had a more powerful engine, a metal propeller and modified ailerons; it went into service in 1931, 330 being delivered. Fifty examples of the more powerful NiD 629 were also delivered. Specifications apply to the NiD 62C-1.

Crew: 1
Powerplant: one 373kW (500hp) Hispano-Suiza 12Md 12-cylinder liquid-cooled Vee-type engine
Performance: max speed 248km/h (154mph); range 650km (404 miles); service ceiling 7700m (25,260ft)
Dimensions: wingspan 12.00m (39ft 5in); length 7.63m (25ft); height 3.00m (9ft 10in)
Weight: 1838kg (4052lb) loaded
Armament: two 7.7mm (0.303in) machine guns

The Nieuport-Delage NiD 62 series of fighters were the mainstay of France's fighter force during the interwar years. The type was also exported, notably to Japan.

NOORDUYN NORSEMAN

A TOUGH AND ROBUST single-engined monoplane designed for safe operation in the rugged Canadian climate, the Noorduyn Norseman was first flown on 14 November 1935. The main prewar production model was the Norseman IV of 1936, which had a more powerful Pratt & Whitney Wasp engine instead of the 313kW (420hp) Wright Whirlwind of the earlier models. As well as seeing much commercial service, the Norseman was used by the RCAF and USAAF, 904 being built. The final model, produced postwar by the Canadian Car & Foundry Company, was the Norseman V.

Specifications apply to the Norseman IV.

Crew: 1
Powerplant: one 419kW (550hp) Pratt & Whitney S3H-1 or R-1340-AN-1 Wasp 9-cylinder radial engine
Performance: max speed 241km/h (150mph); range 966km (600 miles); service ceiling 6705m (22,000ft)
Dimensions: wingspan 15.70m (51ft 6in); length 9.75m (32ft); height 3.12m (10ft 3in)
Weight: 2928kg (6450lb)
Payload: 8/9 passengers

The rugged Noorduyn Norseman was the workhorse of the Canadian Arctic for many years. It could be fitted with wheels, floats or skis, and it was powered by the extremely dependable Pratt & Whitney Wasp engine.

NORD 262

FRANCE: 1961

Crew: 2
Powerplant: two 735kW (986hp) Turbomeca Bastan IV turboprop engines
Performance: max speed 385km (239mph); range 1590km (988 miles); service ceiling 9750m (31,988ft);
Dimensions: wingspan 21.85m (71ft 8in); length 18.04m (59ft 2.25in); height 7.11m (23ft 4in)
Weight: 9800kg (21,605lb) loaded
Payload: 23 passengers

THE NORD 262 AIRLINER, in the same class as the Fokker F.27 Friendship, started life as the Max Holste MH.250, which first flew in 1949 with twin piston engines. This was followed by a turboprop-powered variant, the MH.260, which flew in July 1960. Due to lack of orders, production ended after only 10 aircraft had been

After a shaky start, the Nord 262 enjoyed considerable success in the commercial feeder-line market, both in France and abroad.

built; however, in 1961 the project was taken over by Nord Aviation, who developed an improved and more powerful version, the Nord

262. The company subsequently produced 100 Nord 262A, B, C and D Models. Specifications apply to the MH.260.

NORTH AMERICAN AT-6 TEXAN

USA: 1940

The North American AT-6 Texan was developed from the fixed-undercarriage BC-1 combat trainer, seen here. The Texan was known as the Harvard in RAF and Commonwealth service.

Crew: 2
Powerplant: one 448kW (600hp) Pratt & Whitney R-1340-49 Wasp 9-cylinder radial engine
Performance: max speed 335km/h (208mph); range 1205km (750 miles); service ceiling 7325m (24,300ft)
Dimensions: wingspan 12.80m (42ft); length 8.84m (29ft); height 3.55m (11ft 9in)
Weight: 2404kg (5300lb) loaded
Armament: two 7.62mm (0.30in) machine guns

THE AT-6 TEXAN WAS designed in the late 1930s as a low-cost advanced trainer with the handling characteristics of a high-speed fighter, and was developed from the fixed-undercarriage BC-1 combat trainer produced for the USAAC in 1937. The first production AT-6 appeared in 1940 and was followed in 1941 by the AT-6A (US Navy SNJ-3), 1549 of which were built. The AT-6B was similar, but intended for gunnery training; the AT-6C (SNJ-4) had

structural modifications to save on aluminium, 2970 being built. The major production version of the type was the AT-6D (SNJ-5), 4388 of which were produced, while the last variant was the more powerful AT-6F (965 built). Around 15,000 Texans were produced in total, some 5000 of which went to the RAF and Commonwealth air forces. The type was also produced under licence in Australia, Canada and Sweden. Specifications apply to the AT-6A.

NORTH AMERICAN B-25 MITCHELL

Crew: 5
Powerplant: two 1268kW (1700hp) Wright R-2600-13 18-cylinder two-row radial engines
Performance: max speed 457km/h (284mph); range 2454km (1525 miles); service ceiling 6460m (21,200ft)
Dimensions: wingspan 20.60m (67ft 7in); length 16.13m (52ft 11in); height 4.82m (15ft 10in)
Weight: 18,960kg (41,800lb) loaded
Armament: six 12.7mm (0.50in) machine guns; internal and external bomb/torpedo load of 1361kg (3000lb)

The North American B-25 Mitchell was one of the most versatile aircraft to see service in World War II. In the Pacific theatre, it was particularly effective in the anti-shipping role.

ONE OF THE MOST important US tactical warplanes of World War II, the North American B-25 Mitchell flew for the first time in January 1939. On 16 April 1942, the Mitchell leapt into the headlines when the aircraft carrier USS *Hornet*, from a position at sea 1075km (668 miles) from Tokyo, launched 16 B-25Bs of the 17th AAF Air Group, led by Lt Col J.H. Doolittle, for the first attack on the Japanese homeland. USAAF Mitchells operated effectively against Japanese forces in New Guinea, carrying out low-level strafing attacks in the wake of Allied bombing operations. The B-25B was followed into service by the virtually identical B-25C and B-25D. The two variants were

used in most theatres of war, and 533 B-25C/D aircraft were delivered to the RAF as Mitchell Mk IIs to supplement an earlier delivery of 23 Mitchell Mk I (B-25B) aircraft.

The dedicated anti-shipping version of the Mitchell was the B-25G, 405 of which were produced. Developed for use in the Pacific theatre, the B-25G had a four-man crew and was fitted with a 75mm

(2.95in) M4 gun in the nose, adding to its already powerful nose armament of four 12.7mm (0.50in) guns. The follow-on variant, the B-25H (1000 built) had a lighter 75mm (2.95in) gun. The 4318 examples of the next variant, the B-25J, featured either a glazed B-25D nose or, in later aircraft, a 'solid' nose with eight 12.7mm (0.50in) machine guns. The RAF

took delivery of 313 B-25Js as the Mitchell III, and 458 B-25Js were transferred to the US Navy from 1943, these aircraft being designated PBJ-1H. The Soviet Union also took delivery of 862 Mitchells under Lend-Lease, and surplus B-25s were widely exported after World War II.

Specifications apply to the North American B-25D Mitchell.

NORTH AMERICAN P-51 MUSTANG

This P-51D Mustang bears the code letters of the 335th Fighter Squadron, 4th Fighter Group, US Army Air Force.

an 821kW (1100hp) Allison V-1710-39 engine. RAF test pilots soon found that with this powerplant the aircraft did not perform well at high altitude, but that its low-level performance was excellent. It was therefore decided to use the type as a high-speed ground-attack and tactical reconnaissance fighter, and it was in this role that it entered service with Army Co-operation Command in July 1942.

The USAAF, somewhat belatedly, realized the fighter's potential and evaluated two early production Mustang Is under the designation P-51. The RAF suggested that the P-51 would perform much better as a high-altitude interceptor if it were re-engined with the Rolls-Royce Merlin, but the suggestion

THE NORTH AMERICAN P-51 Mustang was initially produced in response to a 1940 RAF requirement for a fast, heavily armed fighter

able to operate effectively at altitudes in excess of 6100m (20,000ft). North American built the prototype in 117 days, and the aircraft,

designated NA-73X, flew on 26 October 1940. The first of 320 production Mustang Is for the RAF flew on 1 May 1941, powered by

was initially ignored and the first two USAAF Mustang variants, both optimized for ground-attack and designated A-36A and P-51A, were fitted with Allison engines. Trials with Mustangs fitted with Packard-built Rolls-Royce Merlin 61 engines showed a dramatic improvement in performance, maximum speed being raised from 627km/h (390mph) to 710km/h (441mph). Production of the Merlin-powered P-51B finally got under way in the autumn of 1942. North American's Inglewood factory went on to build 1988 P-51Bs, while the 1750 aircraft built at the new Dallas plant were designated P-51C.

The RAF, which had ordered 1000 P-51Bs under the designation Mustang Mk III, began to receive its first aircraft early in 1944, the first 36 aircraft having been diverted to the US Eighth AAF to alleviate the critical shortage of escort fighters. The RAF was not happy with the very poor visibility from the Mustang's cockpit and replaced the existing canopy with a stream-lined frameless bubble-type hood designed by Malcolm Aircraft Ltd. The canopy was also fitted to

some of the USAAF's P-51Cs. The real solution to the problem, however, was found by North American, which tested two P-51Bs with a one-piece sliding canopy and cut-down rear fuselage. In this guise, the aircraft became the P-51D.

The first production P-51Ds began to arrive in England in the late spring of 1944 and quickly became the standard equipment of the USAAF Eighth Fighter Command. There is no doubt at all that the Mustang won the daylight battle over Germany. Operating from bases in England and Italy, it provided not only fighter escort for the bombers engaged in a two-pronged assault on Hitler's Reich; it also hunted the Luftwaffe on its own airfields. In the Pacific, Mustangs operating from the captured Japanese islands of Iwo Jima and Okinawa adopted similar tactics from April 1945, escorting B-29s to their targets and neutralizing the Japanese air force on the ground. Production totalled 7956 P-51Ds and 1337 basically similar P-51K (which had an Aeroproducts propeller instead of the Hamilton Standard unit); 876

became Mustang IVs with the RAF, and 299 became reconnaissance F-6Ds or F-6Ks. The fastest Mustang version, which saw service in the Pacific towards the end of the war, was the P-51H, with a top speed of 784km/h (487mph). The Mustang continued to serve with some 20 air forces around the world for years after the end of WWII, and gave valiant service during the early months of the Korean War with US, Australian, South African and South Korean air units.

Specifications apply to the North American P-51D Mustang.

Crew: 1
Powerplant: one 1112kW (1490hp) Packard Rolls-Royce Merlin V-1650-7 Vee-type engine
Performance: max speed 704km/h (437mph); range 3347km (2080 miles); service ceiling 12,770m (41,900ft)
Dimensions: wingspan 11.28m (37ft); length 9.85m (32ft 3in); height 3.71m (12ft 2in)
Weight: 5493kg (12,100lb) loaded
Armament: six 12.7mm (0.50in) machine guns; provision for up to two 454kg (1000lb) bombs or six 12.7cm (5in) rockets

NORTH AMERICAN F-82 TWIN MUSTANG

USA: 1945

The F-82 Twin Mustang came too late to see action in World War II, but it scored the US Air Force's first victory in the Korean war, an aircraft of the 68th Fighter Squadron shooting down a North Korean Yak-7 over Kimpo.

THE NORTH AMERICAN F-82 Twin Mustang was conceived in 1943 to meet a requirement for a long-range escort fighter for service in the Pacific theatre. Design was begun in January 1944, the aircraft consisting basically of two F-51H Mustang fuselages joined together by a constant chord wing centre section and a rectangular tailplane. The pilot was housed in the port fuselage, the second pilot/navigator

in the starboard. The end of the Pacific War reduced an original order for 500 Twin Mustangs to 20 aircraft; however, in 1947 orders were placed for a night and all-weather fighter version of the F-82, equipped with AI radar and carrying a radar operator in place of the second pilot. Around 100 Twin Mustangs were completed as F-82Es and Gs. Specifications apply to the F-82G.

Crew: 2
Powerplant: two 1194kW (1600hp) Allison V-1710-145 Vee-type engines
Performance: max speed 741km/h (461mph); range 3600km (2240 miles); service ceiling 11,856m (38,900ft)
Dimensions: wingspan 15.62m (51ft 3in); length 12.92m (42ft 5in); height 4.21m (13ft 10in)
Weight: 11,632kg (25,591lb) loaded
Armament: six 12.7mm (0.50in) machine guns; 1818kg (4000lb) of bombs

NORTH AMERICAN FJ-1 FURY

The North American FJ-1 Fury was the direct ancestor of the F-86 Sabre. It served with Navy Fighter Squadron VF-51.

ON 18 MAY 1945, 100 NA-141s (production developments of the NA-134 naval jet fighter under development by North American) were ordered for the US Navy as FJ-1s. This order was subsequently reduced to 30 aircraft. Known as the Fury, the FJ-1 first flew on 27 November 1946 and remained in service until 1949. The FJ-1 was the first US carrier jet fighter to be deployed in squadron strength.

Crew: 1
Powerplant: one 1816kg (4000lb) thrust Allison J35-A-2 turbojet engine
Performance: max speed 880km/h (547mph); range 2414km (1500 miles); service ceiling 9754m (32,000ft)

Dimensions: wingspan 9.80m (32ft 2in); length 10.50m (34ft 5in); height 4.50m (14ft 10in)
Weight: 7076kg (15,600lb) loaded
Armament: six 12.7mm (0.50in) machine guns

NORTH AMERICAN F-86 SABRE

IN 1944, BEFORE German advanced aeronautical research data became available, the USAAF issued specifications drawn up around four different fighter requirements, the first of which was a medium-range day fighter that could also serve in the ground-attack and bomber-escort roles. This awakened the interest of North American Aviation, the design team of which was then working on the NA-134, a projected carrier-borne jet fighter for the US Navy (which emerged as the FJ-1 Fury). The NA-134 was of conventional straight-wing design and was well advanced, so North American offered a land-based version to the USAAF under the company designation NA-140. On 18 May 1945, North American received a contract for the building of three NA-140 prototypes under the USAAF designation XP-86. A mock-up of the XP-86 was built and, in June 1945, was approved by the USAAF. At this point, material on German research into high-speed flight, in particular swept-wing designs, became available. North American obtained a complete Me 262 wing assembly and, after carrying out over 1000 wind tunnel tests on it, decided that the swept wing was the key to raising the XP-86's performance.

The redesigned XP-86 airframe, featuring sweepback on all flying surfaces, was accepted by the USAAF on 1 November 1945 and received final approval on 28 February 1946. In December 1946 the USAAF placed a contract for an initial batch of 33 P-86A production aircraft, and on 8 August 1947 the first of two flying prototypes was completed, making its first flight under the power of a General Electric J35 turbojet. The second prototype, designated XF-86A, made its first flight on 18 May 1948, fitted with the more powerful General Electric J-47-GE-1 engine; deliveries of production F-86As began 10 days later. The first operational F-86As were delivered to the 1st Fighter Group early in 1949. On 4 March 1949, the North American F-86 was officially named the Sabre. Production of the F-86A ended with the 554th aircraft in December 1950, a date which coincided with the arrival of the first F-86As in Korea with the 4th Fighter Wing. During the next two

and a half years, Sabres were to claim the destruction of 810 enemy aircraft, 792 of them MiG-15s.

The next Sabre variants were the F-86C penetration fighter (redesignated YF-93A and flown only as a prototype) and the F-86D all-weather fighter, which had a complex fire-control system and a ventral rocket pack; 2201 were built, the F-86L being an updated version. The F-86E was basically an F-86A with power-operated controls and an all-flying tail; 396 were built before the variant was replaced by the F-86F, the major production version with 2247 examples delivered. The F-86H was a specialized fighter-bomber armed with four 20mm (0.79in) cannon and capable of carrying a tactical nuclear weapon; the F-86K was essentially a simplified F-86D; and the designation F-86J was applied to the Canadair-built

Sabre Mk 3. Most Sabres built by Canadair were destined for NATO air forces; the RAF, for example, received 427 Sabre Mk 4s. The Sabre Mk 6 was the last variant built by Canadair. The total number of Sabres built by North American, Fiat and Mitsubishi was 6208, with a further 1815 built by Canadair. Specifications apply to the F-86E.

Crew: 1
Powerplant: one 2358kg (5200lb) thrust General Electric J47-GE-13 turbojet engine
Performance: max speed 1086km/h (675mph); range 1260km (783 miles); service ceiling 14,720m (48,300ft)
Dimensions: wingspan 11.30m (37ft 1in); length 11.43m (37ft 6in); height 4.47m (14ft 8in)
Weight: 6675kg (14,720lb) loaded
Armament: six 12.7mm (0.50in) Colt-Browning machine guns; up to 907kg (2000lb) of underwing stores

A North American F-86F Sabre in the colours of the Pakistan Air Force. These aircraft were used during the Indo-Pakistan war of 1965.

NORTH AMERICAN B-45 TORNADO

USA: 1947

FLOWN FOR THE first time on 17 March 1947, the XB-45 Tornado was the first American multi-jet bomber to be ordered into

production. The initial production version was the B-45A, of which 96 examples were built. The B-45C (10 examples built) was an

updated version of the B-45A, while the RB-45C (33 built), which was equipped for in-flight refuelling, was a high-altitude photo-reconnaissance variant with five camera stations. The first unit to equip with the Tornado was the 47th BW, which exchanged its B-26s for the new type in 1948.

Specifications apply to the North American RB-45C Tornado.

Crew: 4
Powerplant: four 2721kg (6000lb) thrust General Electric J47-GE-13 turbojet engines
Performance: max speed 917km/h (570mph); range 4070km (2530 miles); service ceiling 12,270m (40,250ft)
Dimensions: wingspan 29.26m (96ft); length 23.14m (75ft 11in); height 7.67m (25ft 2in)
Weight: 50,223kg (110,721lb) loaded
Armament: two 12.7mm (0.50in) machine guns in tail position

The North American B-45 Tornado was the first multi-jet bomber of US design to be ordered into production. Pictured here is the XB-45 prototype.

NORTH AMERICAN FJ-2/FJ-4 FURY

USA: 1952

THE NORTH AMERICAN FJ-2 Fury was a 'navalized' version of the F-86E Sabre, the XFJ-2 flying on 19 February 1952. Carrier trials aboard the USS *Midway* were completed in August 1952 and the type entered full production for the US Navy as the FJ-2 Fury. The FJ-2 gave way on the production line to the FJ-3, with a Wright J65-W-3 turbojet, and the last variant was the FJ-4, which incorporated so many new design features that it was virtually a new aircraft. The FJ-4B was developed specifically for low-level attack, featuring a good deal of structural strengthening and a low-altitude bombing system for the delivery of a tactical nuclear weapon. Specifications apply to the FJ-3M.

Crew: 1
Powerplant: one 3573kg (7800lb) thrust Wright J65-W-2 turbojet engine
Performance: max speed 1091km/h (678mph); range 1344km (835 miles); service ceiling 16,640m (54,600ft)
Dimensions: wingspan 11.30m (37ft 1in); length 11.43m (37ft 6in); height 4.47m (14ft 8in)
Weight: 9350kg (20,611lb) loaded
Armament: six 12.7mm (0.50in) Colt-Browning M-3 machine guns; up to 907kg (2000lb) of underwing stores

The FJ-4 Fury was the US Navy's counterpart of the US Air Force's F-86H Sabre, and like its land-based counterpart it was able to deliver a tactical nuclear weapon.

NORTH AMERICAN F-100 SUPER SABRE

USA: 1953

THE FIRST PROTOTYPE F-100 flew on 25 May 1953 and exceeded Mach 1 on its maiden flight. The type was grounded in November 1954 after a series of unexplained crashes; however, following various modifications the F-100A began flying operationally again in February 1955 and 22 examples were built. The next series production variant was the F-100C, which was capable of carrying out both ground-attack and interception missions. First deliveries to the USAF were made in July 1955 and total production was 451, of which 260 went to the Turkish Air Force. The F-100D differed from the F-100C in having an automatic pilot, jettisonable underwing pylons and modified vertical tail surfaces; it was supplied to the USAF Tactical Air Command and Denmark, France and Greece. The TF-100C was a two-seat trainer variant and served as the prototype of the TF-100F, which flew in July 1957. Total production of all Super Sabre variants was 2294, many aircraft serving in Vietnam.

Specifications apply to F-100C.

Crew: 1
Powerplant: one 7711kg (17,000lb) thrust Pratt & Whitney J57-P-21A turbojet engine
Performance: max speed 1390km/h (864mph); range 966km (600 miles); service ceiling 14,020m (46,000ft)
Dimensions: wingspan 11.82m (38ft 9in); length 14.36m (47ft 1in); height 4.95m (16ft 3in)
Weight: 15,800kg (34,832lb) loaded
Armament: four 20mm (0.79in) cannon; eight external hardpoints with provision for up to 3402kg (7500lb) of stores

Protecting the United States at the height of the Cold War, these North American F-100 Super Sabres are pictured at George AFB, California.

NORTH AMERICAN A-5/RA-5 VIGILANTE

USA: 1958

FIRST FLOWN AS THE YA-5A on 31 August 1958, the Vigilante completed its carrier trials in July 1960. The aircraft was designed to carry either conventional or nuclear weapons in a linear bomb bay consisting of a tunnel inside the fuselage, the bombs being ejected rearwards between the two jet pipes. Fifty-seven A-5As were built, followed by 20 examples of the A-5B, an interim long-range variant. The Vigilante's career as an attack bomber was relatively short-lived,

the majority of A-5A and A-5B airframes being converted to RA-5C reconnaissance configuration. First service deliveries of the RA-5C were made in January 1964. Of the 10 RA-5C squadrons activated, eight saw service in Vietnam. The RA-5C proved so successful in action over Vietnam that the production line was reopened in 1969 and an additional 48 aircraft built. Eighteen aircraft were lost on operations. Specifications apply to the RA-5 Vigilante.

Crew: 2
Powerplant: two 8101kg (17,860lb) thrust General Electric J79-GE-10 turbojet engines
Performance: max speed 2230km/h (1385mph); range 5150km (3200 miles); service ceiling 20,400m (67,000ft)
Dimensions: wingspan 16.15m (53ft); length 23.11m (75ft 10in); height 5.92m (19ft 5in)
Weight: 36,285lb (80,000lb) loaded
Armament: none

The North American RA-5C Vigilante performed extremely well in the low-level reconnaissance role over Vietnam, although the cost was heavy.

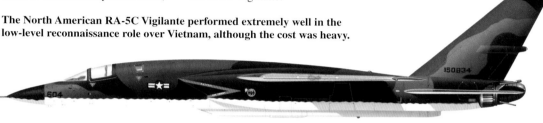

NORTH AMERICAN X-15

USA: 1959

NORTH AMERICAN'S X-15 rocket-powered research aircraft bridged the gap between manned flight within the atmosphere and manned flight beyond the atmosphere into space. After completing initial test flights in 1959, it became the first winged aircraft to attain velocities of Mach 4, 5, and 6. Three X-15s were built, the aircraft being air-launched at altitude from a B-29.

The second X-15A was rebuilt after a landing accident to become the X-15A-2, and was the fastest aircraft ever flown. The third X-15 was destroyed during a test flight. Specifications apply to the X-15A.

The North American X-15A-2 remains the fastest aircraft ever flown, having reached a speed of Mach 6.72 (7297km/h or 4534mph).

Crew: 1
Powerplant: one 31,751kg (70,000lb) thrust Thiokol (Reaction Motors) XLR99-RM-2 rocket unit
Performance: max speed 6693km/h (4159mph); maximum ceiling 107,960m (354,200ft)
Dimensions: wingspan 6.70m (22ft); length 15.24m (50ft); height 4.10m (13ft 6in)
Weight: 14,186kg (31,276lb)

NORTH AMERICAN XB-70A VALKYRIE

USA: 1964

Crew: 2
Powerplant: six 14,060kg (31,000lb) thrust General Electric YN93-GE-3 turbojet engines
Performance: max speed Mach 3; range (est) 12,230km (7600 miles); service ceiling (est) 18,300m (60,000ft)
Dimensions: wingspan 32.00m (105ft); length 59.64m (196ft); height 9.14m (30ft)
Weight: 249,480kg (550,104lb)
Armament: up to 14 nuclear weapons (projected)

PROBABLY THE LARGEST and most complex experimental aircraft ever built, the North American XB-70A was originally planned as a long-range, high- and low-altitude supersonic bomber, but was relegated to a research role in 1961. Two aircraft were built, the first flying in September 1964. The second prototype was lost on 8 June 1966, when an F-104 chase aircraft collided with it. The XB-70A exceeded Mach 3 for the first time in January 1966. Test flying continued until 4 February 1969, when the surviving XB-70A made its last flight.

Originally designed as a supersonic bomber to replace the B-52, the huge delta-wing B-70 was in fact produced only as a research aircraft, the first of two prototypes flying in September 1964.

NORTHROP P-61 BLACK WIDOW

USA: 1942

THE FIRST PROTOTYPE Northrop XP-61 flew on 21 May 1942, but it was another 18 months before the first production P-61A Black Widow aircraft appeared. Early P-61A operations were plagued by unserviceability of the aircraft's Pratt & Whitney R-2800-65 engines, and after 200 P-61As had been built production switched to the P-61B, of which 450 were built. This version was modified for night intruder operations, being capable of carrying up to four 726kg (1600lb) bombs or four 1136-litre (300 US gal) drop tanks under the wings. In the central Pacific, the US Seventh Air Force had three Black Widow squadrons, and there were two in the China-Burma-India (CBI) theatre and two in the European theatre. In Italy, the P-61 was flown by the 414th, 415th, 416th and 417th NFS, assigned to the Twelfth Air Force. The last production version was the P-61C, which had 2089kW (2800hp) R-2800-73 engines; 41 were built. Specifications apply to the P-61B.

The Northrop P-61 Black Widow was the most powerful night-fighter used by the Allies in World War II. It saw action in all theatres, and was replaced by the F-82 Twin Mustang postwar.

Crew: 3
Powerplant: two 1492kW (2000hp) Pratt & Whitney R-2800-65 18-cylinder radial engines
Performance: max speed 589km/h (366mph); range 4506km (2800 miles); service ceiling 10,090m (33,100ft)
Dimensions: wingspan 20.12m (66ft); length 15.11m (49ft 7in); height 4.46m (14ft 8in)
Weight: 13,472kg (29,700lb) loaded
Armament: four 20mm (0.79in) cannon or 12.7mm (0.50in) machine guns

Northrop XB-35/YB-49

USA: 1946

Crew: 6
Powerplant: eight 1812kg (4000lb) thrust Allison J35-A-5 turbojet engines
Performance: max speed 796km/h (495mph); range 6436km (4000 miles); service ceiling 12,810m (42,000ft)
Dimensions: wingspan 52.46m (172ft); length 16.2m (53ft 1in); height 4.63m (15ft 2in)
Weight: 96,715kg (213,500lb) loaded
Armament: up to 7248kg (16,000lb) of bombs

THE NORTHROP XB-35 was the first of the company's flying-wing bombers. Two prototypes were ordered in 1942, the first making its maiden flight on 25 June 1946. Early test flights produced no handling problems, but trouble was experienced with the XB-35's engines, which were four 2425kW (3250hp) Pratt & Whitney R-4360-17/21 Wasp Major radials, driving eight-bladed contra-rotating pusher propellers. Four YB-35s, three YB-35As and six YB-35Bs were ordered for evaluation, the first being delivered in 1947. The earlier teething troubles persisted, and it was decided to abandon further development of the piston-engined machine. Two of the YB-35s were converted as jet-powered YB-49s and the second YB-35B as a YRB-49 jet recon-naissance version. Both YB-49s were destroyed during flight testing, the first exploding in mid-air on 5 June 1949 and the second being destroyed during a high-speed taxi run on 15 March 1950. Further development was abandoned, and the flying-wing bomber concept was only resur-rected with the advent of the B-2 Spirit, 40 years later.

Specifications apply to YB-49.

The Northrop YB-49 proved the theory that a large, jet-powered flying-wing design would present no handling problems.

Northrop F-89 Scorpion

USA: 1948

THE FIRST OF TWO Northrop XF-89 prototypes flew on 16 August 1948, and after USAF evaluation Northrop received an order for an initial 48 production aircraft, the first of these flying late in 1950. The first production model of the Scorpion, the F-89A, carried a nose

The Northrop F-89 Scorpion, seen here in prototype form in 1948, provided the US Air Defense Command with a powerful and effective all-weather interceptor.

NORTHROP XP-56
The Northrop XP-56 (N-2B) was an experimental tailless single-seat fighter, flown in 1943. It was not a true all-wing design, the engine and cockpit being housed in a small central nacelle. It was built entirely of magnesium and nicknamed the 'Black Bullet'.

NORTHROP MX-324
The Northrop MX-324 was a rocket-powered research aircraft of flying-wing design. It underwent limited testing in 1943, being towed to altitude by a P-38 Lightning.

NORTHROP XP-79B
The Northrop XP-79B was the only jet aircraft designed specifically for ramming attack, its wing leading edges being built of heavy magnesium plate. It crashed on its first flight, on 12 September 1945.

NORTHROP F-15A REPORTER
The Northrop F-15A Reporter, flown in 1945, was a reconnaissance development of the P-61 Black Widow. A contract for 175 aircraft was placed, but only 36 had been delivered when this was terminated at the end of WWII.

NORTHROP X-4 BANTAM
First flown in December 1948, the X-4 Bantam was a twin-jet research aircraft built to investigate the flight characteristics of tailless aircraft at high subsonic speeds.

NORTHROP YC-125 RAIDER
The Northrop YC-125 Raider twin-engined transport, first flown in 1949, was intended for operation from rough airstrips in forward areas. It was abandoned in favour of transport helicopters.

armament of six 20mm (0.79in) cannon. The F-89B and F-89C were progressive developments, while the F-89D had its cannon deleted and carried an armament of 104 folding-fin aircraft rockets in wingtip pods. Additional fuel tanks gave an 11 per cent range increase over the F-89C, and the aircraft was fitted with an automatic fire-control system. The F-89H followed, which could carry Falcon missiles as well as the MB-1 Genie nuclear air-to-air missile. Specifications apply to the F-89D.

Crew: 2
Powerplant: two 3266kg (7200lb) thrust Allison J35-A-35 turbojet engines
Performance: max speed 1023km/h (636mph); range 2200km (1370 miles); service ceiling 14,995m (49,200ft)
Dimensions: wingspan 18.18m (59ft 8in); length 16.40m (53ft 10in); height 5.36m (17ft 7in)
Weight: 19,160kg (42,241lb) loaded
Armament: six Hughes GAR-1 Falcon missiles and 42 folding-fin air rockets, or one MB-1 Genie nuclear air-to-air missile (F-89H)

NORTHROP T-38A TALON
USA: 1959

As well as providing US military jet pilots with supersonic experience, the Northrop T-38A Talon was used in the astronaut training programme.

FIRST FLOWN IN April 1959, the Northrop T-38A Talon jet trainer stemmed from the same programme that produced the F-5 Freedom Fighter. Three YF-38 prototypes were ordered; after three years of development flight trials were undertaken to assess performance of different powerplants before the type entered USAF service in 1961. The type was highly successful, with 1139 examples built. Some T-38s were used for astronaut training, while others simulated MiG-21s in various air combat schools.

Crew: 2
Powerplant: two 1746kg (3850lb) General Electric J85-GE-5 turbojet engines
Performance: max speed 1381km/h (858mph); range 1759km (1093 miles) on internal fuel; service ceiling 16,340m (53,600ft)
Dimensions: wingspan 7.70m (25ft 3in); length 14.14m (46ft 4in); height 3.92m (12ft 10in)
Weight: 5361kg (11.820lb) loaded
Armament: none

NORTHROP F-5 TIGER
USA: 1959

Crew: 1
Powerplant: two 1850kg (4080lb) thrust General Electric J85-GE-13 turbojet engines
Performance: max speed 1487km/h (924mph); combat radius 314km (195 miles); service ceiling 15,390m (50,491ft)
Dimensions: wingspan 7.70m (25ft 3in); wing area 15.78m² (170 sq ft); length 14.38m (47ft 2in); height 4.01m (13ft 2in)
Weight: 9374kg (20,667lb) loaded
Armament: two 20mm (0.79in) M39 cannon; up to 1996kg (4400lb) of external stores

AFTER NEARLY THREE years of intensive testing and evaluation, it was announced on 25 April 1962 that the Northrop N156, which had first flown in 1959, had been selected as the new all-purpose fighter for supply to friendly nations under the Mutual Aid Pact, and the aircraft entered production as the F-5A Freedom Fighter, the first example flying in October 1963. The F-5A entered service with USAF Tactical Air Command in April 1964. The first overseas customer was the Imperial Iranian Air Force, followed by the Royal Hellenic and Royal Norwegian Air Forces. Between 1965 and 1970 Canadair built 115 aircraft for the Canadian Armed Forces under the designation CF-5A/D, these using Orenda-built J85-CAN-15 engines. Other nations using the type were Ethiopia, Morocco, South Korea, Republic of Vietnam, Nationalist China, the Philippines, Libya, the Netherlands, Spain, Thailand and Turkey. An improved version, the F-5E Tiger II, was selected in November 1970 as a successor to the F-5A series. It served with a dozen overseas air forces, and also in the 'aggressor' air-combat training role with the US Air Force. The RF-5E TigerEye is a photo-reconnaissance version.

Specifications apply to the Northrop F-5A Tiger.

In 1975, the US Navy Fighter Weapons School at Miramar borrowed 10 F-5Es and three F-5Fs from the US Air Force to provide Navy pilots with dissimilar combat air training. Two of the F-5Es are seen here.

NORTHROP GRUMMAN B-2 SPIRIT

USA: 1989

A Northrop B-2 Spirit about to touch down with 'everything extended'. In designing the B-2, Northrop drew heavily on the experience of its flying-wing designs of 40 years earlier.

Crew: 4
Powerplant: four 8618kg (19,000lb) thrust General Electric F118-GE-110 turbofan engines
Performance: max speed 764km/h (475mph); range 11,675km (7255 miles); service ceiling 15,240m (50,000ft)
Dimensions: wingspan 52.43m (172ft); length 21.03m (69ft); height: 5.18m (17ft)
Weight: 181,437kg (400,000lb) loaded
Armament: 16 AGM-129 Advanced Cruise Missiles, or alternatively 16 B.61 or B.83 free-fall nuclear bombs, 80 Mk 82 227kg (500lb) bombs, 16 Joint Direct Attack Munitions, 16 Mk 84 907kg (2000lb) bombs, 36 M117 340kg (750lb) fire bombs, 36 CBU-87/89/97/98 cluster bombs, 80 Mk 36 254kg (560lb) bombs or Mk 62 sea mines

DEVELOPMENT OF THE B-2 was begun in 1978 and the US Air Force originally wanted 133 examples, but by 1991 successive budget cuts had reduced this to 21 aircraft. The prototype flew on 17 July 1989, and the first production B-2 was delivered to the 393rd Bomb Squadron of the 509th Bomb Wing at Whiteman AFB, Missouri, on 17 December 1993.

In designing the Advanced Technology Bomber (ATB), as the B-2 project was originally known, the Northrop Company decided on an all-wing configuration from the outset. Flying-wing devotees such as Hugo Junkers and Jack Northrop have existed as long as aviation itself, arguing that a flying wing will carry the same payload as a conventional aircraft while weighing less and using less fuel. The weight and drag of the tail surfaces are absent, as is the weight of the structure that supports them. The wing structure

itself is far more efficient because the weight of the aircraft is spread across the wing, rather than concentrated in the centre.

Northrop's experimental piston-engined flying-wing bomber of the 1940s, from which ideas for the B-2 were drawn, was designed to equal the range and carry the same warload as the Convair B-36, but at two-thirds the gross weight and also at two-thirds the power. The company produced a prototype flying-wing jet bomber, the YB-49, in 1947; however, this had little influence on the decision to pursue

an all-wing solution for the B-2; the all-wing approach was selected because it promised to result in an exceptionally clean configuration for minimizing radar cross-section, including the elimination of vertical tail surfaces, with added benefits such as span-loading structural efficiency and high lift/drag ratio for efficient cruise. Outboard wing panels were added for longitudinal balance to increase lift/drag ratio and to provide sufficient span for pitch, roll and yaw control. Leading-edge sweep was selected for balance and trans-sonic

This photograph gives a good impression of the B-2's angular flying surfaces. The outboard wing panels were added to enhance longitudinal stability and to increase the lift/drag ratio.

aerodynamics, while the overall planform was designed for neutral longitudinal (pitch) static stability. Because of its short length, the aircraft had to produce stabilizing pitchdown moments beyond the stall for positive recovery. The original ATB design had elevons on the outboard wing panels only but, as the design progressed, additional

elevons were added inboard, giving the B-2 its distinctive 'double-W' trailing edge. The wing leading edge is so designed that air is channelled into the engine intakes from all directions, allowing the engines to operate at high power and zero airspeed. In trans-sonic cruise, air is slowed from supersonic speed before it enters

the hidden compressor faces of the GE F118 engines.

A stores management processor is in place to hande the B-2's 22,730kg (50,120lb) weapons load. A separate processor controls the Hughes APQ-181 synthetic-aperture radar and its input to the display processor. The Ku-band radar has 21 operational modes,

including high-resolution ground mapping. The B-2 lifts off at 260km/h (160mph), the speed independent of take-off weight. Normal operating speed is in the high subsonic range and maximum altitude around 15,240m (50,000ft). The aircraft is highly manoeuvrable, with fighter-like handling characteristics.

NORTHROP-McDONNELL DOUGLAS YF-23A

USA: 1990

Crew: 1
Powerplant: two 15,890kg (35,000lb) Pratt & Whitney YF119-PW-100 turbofan engines
Performance: max speed Mach 2.0; range 1200km (750 miles); service ceiling 19,812m (65,000ft)
Dimensions: wingspan 13.20m (43ft 7in); length 20.50m (67ft 4in); height 4.20m (13ft 10in)
Weight: 29,030kg (64,000lb) loaded
Armament: one 20mm (0.79in) M61 cannon, various combinations of air-to-air missiles and air-to-surface missiles

THE NORTHROP/McDONNELL DOUGLAS YF-23A was a contender in the bid for an advanced tactical fighter to replace the McDonnell Douglas F-15 Eagle in US Air Force service. The first of two prototypes flew in August 1990, the second aircraft being powered by General Electric YF120-GE-100 turbofan engines. The YF-23A was designed to be ultra-stealthy and incorporated many of the stealth features of the Northrop

Grumann B-2 bomber, and all its planned weaponry was to be housed in an internal bay to reduce the radar signature. The two YF-23s

successfully completed their flight test programme, but the Lockheed YF-22 was selected to meet the USAF requirement.

The YF-23A was intended to replace the F-15 Eagle. Both YF-23A prototypes remain in storage at Edwards Air Force Base.

OEMICHEN HELICOPTERS

FRANCE: 1921–1938

IN 1920 ÉTIENNE OEMICHEN, an engineer working for the Peugeot Motor Company, began experimenting with rotorcraft all powered

by rotary engines. His first machine was fitted with twin rotors, but its 18kW (25hp) Le Rhône was not powerful enough to lift it off the

ground. He therefore derived extra lift from an elongated hydrogen-filled balloon, which was fastened to the framework of the machine. It

Étienne Oemichen at the controls of his most successful design, the No 2, in November 1922.

first flew on 15 January 1921. Other experimental rotorcraft followed, and he vied with Pescara to set the first officially recognized helicopter records. Oemichen's most successful design was No 2, which established the first-ever FAI helicopter records in 1924. On 4 May 1924, Oemichen made the first ever closed-circuit helicopter flight, covering a circular course of 1676m (5550ft) in 14 minutes at a maximum height of 15.24m (50ft). The No 2 went on to set speed and weight-lifting records. After helicopter No 2, all of Oemichen's helicopter designs, which continued until 1938, utilized a single main rotor arrangement and two smaller anti-torque rotors.

PANAVIA TORNADO

INTERNATIONAL: 1974

A German Tornado IDS (Interdictor/Strike) aircraft over the Baltic. Germany also developed a dedicated defence-suppression version of the Tornado, the ECR (Electronic Combat/Reconnaissance).

THE VARIABLE-GEOMETRY Tornado was the result of a 1960s requirement for a strike and reconnaissance aircraft capable of carrying a heavy and varied weapons load and of penetrating foreseeable Warsaw Pact defensive systems by day and night, at low level and in all weathers. A consortium was formed under the name Panavia to build and develop the aircraft, consisting principally of the British Aircraft Corporation (later British Aerospace, or BAe), Messerschmitt-Bølkow-Blohm (MBB) and Aeritalia. Turbo-Union, another consortium, was formed by Rolls-Royce, MTU of Germany and Fiat to build the Tornado's Rolls-Royce RB.199 turbofan engines.

The first of nine Tornado IDS (Interdictor/Strike) prototypes flew in Germany on 14 August 1974. Aircrews of the participating nations had been trained at RAF Cottesmore in the United Kingdom, which received the first Tornado GR.1s in July 1980. The RAF took delivery of 229 GR.1 strike aircraft, the Luftwaffe 212, the German Naval Air Arm 112, and the Italian

Air Force 100. In 1990 deliveries of the Tornado GR.1A variant with a centreline reconnaissance pod began, while the GR.4, armed with Sea Eagle anti-shipping missiles, is an anti-shipping version, the GR.4A being the tactical reconnaissance equivalent. Saudi Arabia received 48 Tornado IDSs.

The UK Ministry of Defence issued Air Staff Target 395 in 1971, calling for a minimum change, minimum cost but effective interceptor to replace the British Aerospace Lightning and the F.4 Phantom in the United Kingdom's air defence. Primary armament was to be the British Aerospace Dynamics XJ521 Sky Flash medium-range air-to-air missile, and the primary sensor a Marconi Avionics pulse-Doppler radar. The result was the Air Defence Variant (ADV) of the Panavia Tornado interdictor/strike (IDS) aircraft. Three prototypes were built. The first ADV squadron, No 29, was formed at RAF Coningsby in May 1987 and was declared operational at the end of November. The aircraft

eventually armed seven squadrons in addition to No 229 OCU (which became No 56 Reserve Squadron on 1 July 1992), 18 F.Mk 2s being followed by 155 F.Mk 3s, with improved radar. The Tornado ADV also serves with the air forces of Italy and Saudi Arabia.

Specifications apply to the Tornado ADV.

Crew: 2
Powerplant: two 38.48kN (8,650 lb) thrust Turbo-Union RB.199-34R Mk 104 turbofan engines
Performance: max speed 2337km/h (1452mph); intercept radius about 1853km (1150 miles); service ceiling 21,335m (70,000ft)
Dimensions: wingspan 13.91m (45ft 7in) spread, 8.60m (28ft 2in) swept; length 18.68m (61ft 3in); height 5.95m (19ft 6in)
Weight: 27,987kg (61,700lb) loaded
Armament: two 27mm (2.53in) IWKA-Mauser cannon; six external hardpoints with provision for up to 5806kg (12,800lb) of stores, including short- and medium-range air-to-air missiles, and drop tanks

The Tornado IDS was known as the GR.Mk.1 in RAF service, the GR.Mk.1A being the reconnaissance version.

PACKARD-LE PÈRE LUSAC-11 AND -21
The Packard-Le Père LUSAC-11 and -21 two-seat fighters were excellent designs, but only 27 were built and only two of these reached the Western Front before the end of World War I.

PANDER S.4 POSTJAGER
The Pander S.4 Postjager was a fast, twin-engined mailplane. In 1933 it inaugurated the first airmail service between the Netherlands and Dutch East Indies.

PARNALL SCOUT
Parnall's first aircraft design, the Scout single-seat biplane fighter of 1916, was intended to intercept airships. It was too heavy and made only two flights.

PARNALL PANTHER
The two-seat Parnall Panther of 1918 was a two-seat shipboard fighter/reconnaissance aircraft designed to replace the Sopwith One-and-a-Half Strutter. It remained in service until 1926, with 150 examples being built.

PARNALL PUFFIN
Flown in 1921, the Parnall Puffin was a large amphibious biplane powered by a 336kW (450hp) Napier Lion engine. Three prototypes only were built.

PARNALL PLOVER
The Parnall Plover of 1923 was an attractive naval biplane fighter with a good performance. Only six were built, the Royal Navy preferring the Fairey Flycatcher.

PARNALL PIXIE
The Pixie dates from 1923 as the Pixie I ultralight monoplane, further developed as the Pixie II. The Pixie III became the Pixie IIIA two-seat biplane.

PARNALL POSSUM
The Parnall Possum, first flown in 1923, was a triplane with twin tractor engines driven by shafts from the fuselage. It was not developed beyond prototype stage.

PARNALL PERCH
Developed in 1925, the Parnall Perch biplane was intended to train naval pilots in deck landing techniques, and could also be fitted with floats. No production order was forthcoming.

PARNALL PETO
The Parnall Peto, flown in 1926, was a small reconnaissance biplane designed to operate from submarines. The concept of submarine-launched aircraft was short-lived, and it was soon abandoned.

PEMBERTON-BILLING PB TYPES

Crew: 1
Powerplant: one 37kW (50hp) Gnome 7-cylinder Gnome rotary engine
Performance: max speed 80.5km/h (50mph); other performance details unknown
Dimensions: wingspan 9.14m (30ft); length 8.23m (27ft); height not known
Weight: 440kg (970lb)

ONE OF THE MOST eccentric aircraft pioneers, Noel Pemberton-Billing, was the founder of the Supermarine Aviation Works at Woolston, Southampton, an enterprise that was to play no small part in shaping aviation history. In 1914, 'PB' built the first of a series of flying boats, the PB.1, a very clean design which aroused much interest when it was displayed at the Olympia Aero Show in London that year. Other pre-World War I flying-boat designs included the PB.2, PB.3 and PB.7, the latter two designed so that their wings and tail units could be removed and the hulls used as cabin cruisers. With the outbreak of World War I, 'PB'

The Pemberton-Billing PB.25. As far as is known, none of the 20 PB.25s produced was used operationally, although the type was certainly flown at operational airfields such as Eastchurch.

designed a series of landplanes for the RNAS, although only one, the PB.25 Scout, went into production, and that did not enter service.

Other designs included the PB.29E 'Zeppelin Destroyer' and the PB.31E Nighthawk, the latter armed with a recoilless gun firing a 0.67kg

(1.5lb) shell. Both were twin-engined designs with four wings. Specifications apply to Pemberton-Billing (Supermarine) PB.1.

PERCIVAL D.3 GULL SIX

THE GULL SIX WAS a development of the racing light aircraft designs begun with Percival's D.1 Gull, retaining a fixed undercarriage and the low folding wings of the Gull Four. The Gull Six dates from Percival's move to its own factory at Gravesend and continued production at Luton in 1936. The Gull Six is famously associated with two pioneering women flyers. Amy Johnson recaptured the solo London–Cape Town (and back) record in a Gull Six (her last major event) and New Zealander Jean Batten was also to create a number of notable records in her Gull Six, and E.W. Percival himself was not averse to demonstrating the type's combination of speed and 3200km (2000-mile) range.

Crew: 1
Powerplant: one 149kW (200hp) Gipsy Six piston engine
Performance: cruising speed 257km/h (160mph); range 1030km (640 miles); service ceiling 4270m (14,000ft)
Dimensions: wingspan 11.03m (36ft 2in); length 7.54m (24ft 9in)
Weight: 1111kg (2450lb) maximum take-off weight
Payload: one person

The Gull Six pictured here remained in Percival ownership for a while after manufacture, during which time E.W. Percival showed the type's speed and range by flying to Oran (Algeria) and back to England in a single day.

PERCIVAL PROCTOR

UK: 1939

Crew: 1 (3/4 in a radio trainer role)
Powerplant: one de Havilland Gipsy Queen in-line piston engine rated at 157kW (210hp)
Performance: max speed 257km/h (160mph); range 805km (500 miles); service ceiling 4265m (14,000ft)
Dimensions: wingspan 12.04m (39ft 6in); length 8.59m (28ft 2in); height 2.21m (7ft 3in)
Weight: 1588kg (3500lb) maximum take-off weight
Payload: four seats in radio trainer mode

THE PROCTOR WAS an important component of the RAF's wartime communications and radio training needs. This low-wing, fixed-tailwheel light aircraft served in large numbers, having been selected against a tender specification, although it was itself developed from the Vega Gull racing aeroplane. The Mk I was produced for communications.

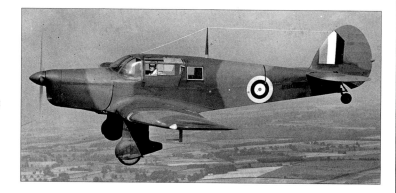

This particular Proctor Mk.1A was one of the earliest to be sold for private civilian use in the United Kingdom soon after World War II.

Subsequent versions were for radio training. and the Proctor Mk IV featured a larger four-seat cabin, and in some cases dual controls. More than 1200 Proctors were produced, many during wartime by F. Hills and Sons of Manchester.

Some continued in service with the RAF until 1955. After the war successful civilian conversions led to new production of 150 Proctor 5 series new civil builds.
Specifications apply to the Percival Proctor Mk IV.

PESCARA HELICOPTERS

SPAIN: 1921–1925

SPANISH MARQUESS Raul Patera Pescara built his first helicopter in Barcelona in 1919–20, but its 33.5kW (45hp) Hispano engine was not powerful enough to lift the 590kg (1300lb) machine. It was fitted with two co-axial rotors, each of which had a diameter of 6.4m (21ft) and consisted of six pairs of blades in the clumsy biplane arrangement, giving a total of 24 lifting surfaces. Early in 1921 the Hispano was replaced by a 127kW (170hp) Le Rhone rotary engine and it was enough to enable a very short flight in May that year. In

1922 Pescara moved to France. With the help of funds from the Service Technique de l'Aeronautique, he built a second helicopter. This made several vertical test flights, but was unimpressive. In 1923 Pescara built a third design, again featuring a co-axial rotor system, but with biplane pairs of blades and a 134kW (180hp) Hispano-Suiza Vee-type engine. The pitch of all 16 blades could be altered in flight and the whole blade assembly could be angled by tilting the rotor head to provide forward thrust and eliminating the need for a conventional propeller to move the

Pescara's third helicopter design appeared in 1923 – the pitch of all 16 blades could be altered in flight.

machine in horizontal flight. Another innovation was the auto-rotation of the main rotors. During 1923–24, Pescara's machine competed with Étienne Oemichen machines in setting up the first helicopter duration and distance records. By early 1925 the Pescara 3F with a 187kW (250hp) engine appeared, but was not successful. Later that year Pescara returned to Spain and entered the automobile industry.

PETLYAKOV PE-8

Crew: 11
Powerplant: four 1007kW (1350hp)
Mikulin AM-35A Vee-type engines
Performance: max speed 438km/h
(272mph); range 5445km (3383 miles);
service ceiling 9750m (31,988ft);
Dimensions: wingspan 39.94m (131ft);
wing area 188.68m² (2031 sq ft); length
22.47m (73ft 8in); height 6.10m (20ft)
Weight: 33,325kg (73,469lb) loaded
Armament: one 20mm (0.79in) ShVAK
cannon in each of the dorsal and tail
turrets; one 12.7mm (0.50in) and two
7.62mm (0.30in) machine guns; bomb
load of up to 4000kg (8818lb)

THE PETLYAKOV PE-8 (military
designation TB-7) was the only
Soviet four-engined strategic heavy
bomber to see service in World
War II. First flown on 27 December
1936, the Pe-8 entered service in
1940, and in the summer of 1941
carried out the first major strategic
attack of World War II when a
small force of bombers raided
Berlin. The Petlyakov Pe-8 was
dogged by engine difficulties
throughout its career and various

A Petlyakov Pe-8 pictured at RAF Leuchars, Scotland, in 1942. The aircraft had flown from Moscow with a VIP passenger: M. Molotov, the Soviet Foreign Minister, who was visiting the United Kingdom.

powerplants were tried, including
M-30B diesel engines. From 1943,
production Pe-8s were fitted with
Mikulin M-82FN fuel-injection
engines. This version incorporated

various aerodynamic improvements;
however, the problems persisted
and production ended in 1944 after
79 examples had been built. Despite
its troubles, the Pe-8 was to make

some notable long-distance flights,
including one of more than
17,700km (11,000 miles) from
Moscow to Washington and back
via Scotland, Iceland and Canada.

PETLYAKOV PE-2

Crew: 3
Powerplant: two 940kW (1260hp) Klimov
VK-105PF 12-cylinder Vee-type engines
Performance: max speed 580km/h
(360mph); range 1315km (817 miles);
service ceiling 8800m (28,870ft)
Dimensions: wingspan 17.11m (56ft 1in);
length 12.78m (41ft 11in); height 3.42m
(11ft 2in)
Weight: 8520kg (18,783lb) loaded
Armament: two 7.62mm (0.30in) or one
7.62mm (0.30in) and one 12.7mm
(0.50in) machine guns in nose; one
7.62mm (0.30in) machine gun in dorsal
turret; one 7.62mm (0.30in) or 12.7mm
(0.50in) machine gun in ventral position,
and one 7.62mm (0.30in) or 12.7mm
(0.50in) lateral-firing machine gun in window
positions; 1600kg (3527lb) of bombs

ORIGINALLY DESIGNATED PB-100,
the Pe-2 prototype flew for the first
time in April 1940. By June 1941,
when the Germans invaded the
Soviet Union, the total number of
Pe-2s delivered had risen to 462,
but comparatively few of these saw
action during the early days
because of a shortage of trained
crews. It was not until late August
that the Pe-2 was committed to the
battle in any numbers, making low-
level attacks on German armoured
columns. In these early actions the
Pe-2's high speed and defensive
armament proved their worth; in
one action, when Pe-2s of the 39th
Bomber Air Regiment were
attacked by 10 Bf 109s, they shot

down three of the German fighters
and fought off the others.
Pe-2 operations received a setback
in the spring of 1942, when the
Messerschmitt Bf 109F appeared
on the Russian front. This aircraft
was some 50km/h (30mph) faster
than the Pe-2 at 3000m (9840ft),
the Russian bomber's preferred
altitude for horizontal bombing.
The Pe-2s were forced to push up
their bombing altitude to
5000–7000m (16,400–22,960ft),
which presented problems to the
109Fs, but at the same time
reduced bombing accuracy.
The solution was to improve the
Pe-2's armament and armour, so
that it could return to medium-

level bombing operations with a
chance of survival, and late in
1942 the Pe-2FT appeared. This
variant had two 940kW (1260hp)
Klimov M-105PF engines and a
12.7mm (0.50in) UBT machine
gun in a dorsal turret replacing the
flexible ShKAS machine gun at
the rear of the cockpit. The FT
suffix denoted Frontovoye
Trebovanie (Front Requirement).
The increase in armour and
armament, however, also meant an
increase in weight and deterioration
in performance, and losses began
to climb when the Messerschmitt
Bf 109G and the Focke-Wulf Fw
190 were deployed to the Eastern
Front. It was only when modern

**This Pe-2 bears the inscription 'Leningrad-
Königsberg' on the side of its fuselage.**

Soviet fighters such as the Lavochkin La-5 became available for escort work in 1943 that the loss rate showed a decline. The leading Soviet Pe-2 dive-bombing exponent was twice Hero of the Soviet Union Colonel Ivan S. Polbin, who commanded the 150th Bomber Air Regiment in 1942 and, in 1943, the 1st Bomber Air Corps, which distinguished itself at the Battle of Kursk in July that year. In 1944 Polbin was given command of the elite 4th Bomber Air Corps, which he led in action during the Soviet advance into Poland.

In the last year of World War II, the Pe-2 played an important part in reducing German strongpoints ahead of the advancing Red Army, particularly in East Prussia, where many towns had been fortified. The type was also used effectively against the Japanese in Manchuria in August 1945. Numerous Pe-2 variants made their appearance during the aircraft's operational career. These included the Pe2-2M, a prototype with VK-105 engines and an enlarged bomb bay to carry

A formation of Petlyakov Pe-2s over the Leningrad Front. The Pe-2, although mostly employed as a dive-bomber, was also used in a number of other roles, including as a night-fighter (Pe-3).

a 500kg (1100lb) bomb; the Pe-2FZ, a variant of the Pe-2FT with better cabin facilities; the Pe-2I, which had a mid- instead of a low-wing configuration; the Pe-2RD, which had an RD-1 auxiliary rocket engine in the tail (and which exploded during trials in 1944);

and the Pe-2UT dual-control trainer. A multi-purpose fighter version armed with cannon, machine guns and underwing rockets, designated Pe-3, was also produced. Total production of the Pe-2/3, all variants, was 11,427 aircraft.

Specifications apply to the Pe-2.

PFALZ D.III

GERMANY: 1917

The D.III was the first design of the Pfalz Flugzeug-Werke GmbH, the designers of which learned from the mistakes of others and made the aircraft structurally much stronger than its contemporaries.

THE PFALZ FLUGZEUG-WERKE GmbH was established at Speyer-am-Rhein, Germany, in 1913 by the Everbusch brothers. The company initially licence built aircraft, such as the Morane-Saulnier Type H and Type L. During the early part of World War I Pfalz Flugzeug-Werke was involved in manufacturing the Moranes (under

the A.I and E.I designations) and later L.F.G. Roland designs.

The D.III, which appeared in the spring of 1917, was the first biplane fighter produced entirely by the Pfalz Flugzeug-Werke. Its design, by Rudolfo Gehringer, owed much to the Roland fighters that Pfalz had been building under licence, but it was slimmer and

generally neater. The Pfalz D.III was robust and well built, with a semi-monocoque ply fuselage, and the wings were of unequal chord to give the pilot a better downward view. Other aircraft using this design technique almost always suffered a structural penalty, which Pfalz avoided by incorporating two spars in the lower wing. As a result,

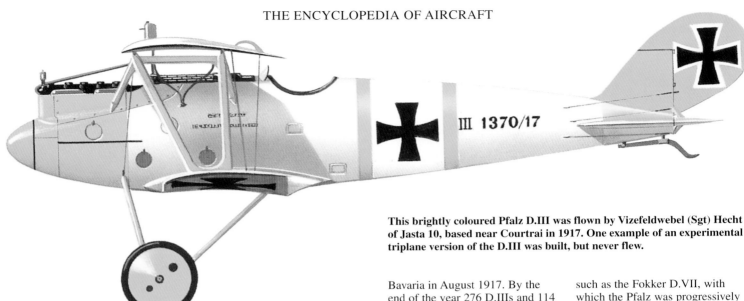

This brightly coloured Pfalz D.III was flown by Vizefeldwebel (Sgt) Hecht of Jasta 10, based near Courtrai in 1917. One example of an experimental triplane version of the D.III was built, but never flew.

the Pfalz could be dived at higher speeds than contemporary German fighter types without the risk of structural failure, an attribute its pilots found very useful when making high-speed diving attacks on enemy observation balloons. The gap between the upper wing and the fuselage was kept to a minimum, giving the pilot a good all-round field of view.

The prototype D.III was evaluated in June 1917. Very few modifications were found necessary, and the type

was quickly cleared for production. To reduce drag, its twin Spandau machine guns were completely buried in the forward fuselage, with only the muzzles protruding. The D.III was followed into production by the D.IIIa, which had an uprated Mercedes engine and guns mounted on top of the fuselage, where they were easier to aim and service. The D.IIIa's wingtips were also more rounded.

The D.III/IIIa was initially issued to home defence units in

Bavaria in August 1917. By the end of the year 276 D.IIIs and 114 D.IIIas were in service, and from then on the former was gradually replaced by the latter, of which 433 were with frontline units in April 1918. Forty-six Jagdstaffeln (Jastas) received some D.III/IIIas, but only about a dozen were fully equipped with the type.

Despite its robustness, the Pfalz does not seem to have been popular with many pilots, although some of Germany's leading air aces flew it. Part of the problem probably lay with its rate of climb, which was poor when compared with that of other German types

such as the Fokker D.VII, with which the Pfalz was progressively replaced in the summer of 1918.

Specifications apply to the Pfalz D.IIIa.

Crew: 1
Powerplant: one 134kW (180hp) Mercedes D.IIIa in-line engine
Performance: max speed 165km/h (103mph); range 350km (217 miles); service ceiling 5180m (17,000ft)
Dimensions: wingspan 9.40m (30ft 10in); length 6.95m (22ft 9in); height 2.67m (8ft 9in)
Weight: 935kg (2061lb) loaded
Armament: two 7.92mm (0.31in) machine guns

PIAGGIO P.108

ITALY: 1939

The Piaggio P.108 was used to attack Gibraltar on several occasions. Bruno Mussolini, son of the Italian dictator, lost his life while flying one.

DESIGNED BY Giovanni Casiraghi, the Piaggio P.108 was the Regia Aeronautica's only four-engined bomber. The prototype was first flown on 24 November 1939 and the first examples were delivered in May 1941, but the type did not

become operational until June 1942. Although only 163 P.108s were built, the bomber was very active in the Mediterranean during the last year of Italy's war; among other missions, it made several attacks on Gibraltar.

Crew: 6
Powerplant: four 1007kW (1350hp) Piaggio P.XII RC35 18-cylinder radial engines
Performance: max speed 420km/h (261mph); range 3520km (2190 miles); service ceiling 8050m (26,410ft)

Dimensions: wingspan 32.00m (105ft); length 22.92m (75ft 2in); height 5.18m (17ft)
Weight: 29,885kg (65,970lb) loaded
Armament: eight 12.7mm (0.50in) Breda-SAFAT machine guns; up to 3500kg (7700lb) of bombs or three torpedoes

PIAGGIO P.166

ITALY: 1957

Crew: 2
Powerplant: two 447kW (599hp) Avco Lycoming LTP 101-600 turboprop engines
Performance: max speed 400km/h (248mph); range with reserves 2035km (1264 miles); service ceiling 8840m (29,000ft)
Dimensions: wingspan with tiptanks 14.69m (48ft 2.5in); length 11.88m (39ft); height 5.00m (16ft 5in)
Weight: 4300kg (9480lb) maximum take-off weight
Payload: up to six passengers (if used in a transport role)

THIS HIGH-WING aircraft had its wing-mounted engines configured in pusher mode, and was initially designed as a civil light transport, and was sold widely in that role.

However, subsequent versions were evaluated and acquired by the Italian and South African militaries, who went on to use the P.166 for battlefield support and coastal patrol duties respectively. Other features of the type included

good STOL performance, a retractable undercarriage and detachable wing-tip fuel tanks.

Specifications apply to the Piaggio P.166-M3.

The P.166 enjoyed orders from several airlines including Alitalia, as illustrated here.

PIAGGIO PD-808

ITALY: 1964

THE PD-808 ORIGINATES in an ultimately unsuccessful attempt by the Douglas Aircraft Corporation to enter the business jet market in the late 1950s. Piaggio approached Douglas in 1961 and took over detailed design and development work on the project, along with some residual advice and assistance from Douglas. Initial versions of this low-wing business jet had 'bought in' (rear fuselage-mounted) Rolls-Royce engines, but

production versions were both more powerful and licence-built. Production from 1966 totalled only 29, including two initial civil orders, followed by 25 from the Italian military – 12 as calibration/navaid types, three as ECM platforms, six as communications/navigation trainers, and four as VIP transports, many of which continue in service.

Specifications apply to the Piaggio PD-808.

Crew: 1/2
Powerplant: two 14.94kN (3361lb st) Piaggio (licence-built) Viper MK 526 turbojet engines
Performance: max speed 850km/h (528mph); range 2100km (1305 miles); service ceiling 13,700m (44,950ft)
Dimensions: wingspan with tip tanks 13.20m (43ft 3.75in); length 12.85m (42ft 2in); height 4.80m (15ft 9in)
Weight: 8165kg (18,001lb) maximum take-off weight
Payload: six-seat cabin in military VIP role

Photographed here is the civilian VIP demonstrator version of the PD-808, versions of which were offered for a number of years. The type did not, however, enjoy commercial success.

PIASECKI PV-1/2/PV-3 RESCUER (HRP-1/-2)

USA: 1945

The first of five PV-17/Navy Designation HRP-2 improved and modernized all-metal rescue versions of the HRP-1 during an early flight at the Morton, Pennsylvania, heliport in November 1949.

THE P-V ENGINEERING FORUM came into being in August 1940. This discussion group of engineers interested in the development of rotary-wing aircraft began work on a small helicopter designated the PV-2. When it first flew on 11 April 1943 powered by a 67kW (90hp) Franklin engine, it was only the second US-built helicopter to be flown in public. On 1 February 1944 P-V Engineering Forum was awarded a contract by the US Navy for development and construction of a large tandem-rotor transport helicopter; the XHRP-1 prototype, known as the 'Flying Banana' because of its unique shape, flew in March 1945. In June 1946 the new Piasecki Helicopter Corporation received an initial service test order for 10 PV-3 transport helicopters; this was followed by a repeat order for 10 more. The HRP-1 was the largest cargo or passenger transport helicopter and the first successful tandem rotorcraft to be put into production, the first being finished on 15 August 1947. HRP-1s operated with the US Navy, US Marine Corps and US Coast Guard. In June 1948 Piasecki received a limited production contract from the Navy Department for all-metal rescue versions of the HRP-1 (PV-17/Navy Designation HRP-2), the first example flying in 1949.

Specifications apply to the Piasecki PV-3 Rescuer.

Crew: 2
Powerplant: one 597kW (800hp) Pratt & Whitney R-1340 wasp air-cooled radial engine
Performance: max speed 167km/h (104mph); range 423km (265 miles); service ceiling 1554m (5100ft)
Dimensions: rotor diameter 12.50m (41ft); length 14.64m (48ft); height 4.27m (14ft)
Weight: 2270kg (5000lb)
Payload: maximum load 908kg (2000lb)

PIEL EMERAUDE

FRANCE: 1951

THE EMERAUDE WAS designed by Claude Piel. It originated in the 1950s with the CP.30. Since then an array of variants (fundamentally different in terms of engine, cabin size and aerobatic properties) have been offered. The general configuration remains a single-engined, low-wing monoplane, of which the CP.301 is perhaps the classic example. The Emeraude has been available as a licence-built product in its variant types in a number of countries. Plans remain available for home-build versions. Variants include the one-seat CP.90 Pinocchio, the three- or four-seat Super Diamante and the aerobatic CP.70/750 Beryl. Specifications apply to the CP.301.

Crew: 1
Powerplant: one Continental C90-14F 67kW (90hp) piston engine
Performance: cruising speed 161km/h (100mph); range 800km (500 miles)
Dimensions: wingspan 8.30m (27ft 3in); length 6.00m (19ft 9in)
Weight: 650kg (1433lb) maximum take-off weight
Payload: two seats total

Known to many by the nickname of 'Little Spitfire' because of its elliptical wing planform, the Piel Emeraude provided hundreds of private pilots across Europe with a great deal of enjoyment.

PILATUS PC-6 PORTER AND TURBO-PORTER

SWITZERLAND: 1959

Crew: 1
Powerplant: one 507kW (680shp) Pratt & Whitney Aircraft of Canada PT6A-27 turboprop engine flat rated to 410kW (550shp)
Performance: max cruising speed 260km/h (161mph); range 1050km (652 miles); service ceiling 8535m (28,000ft)
Dimensions: wingspan 15.13m (49ft 8in); length 10.90m (35ft 9in); height 3.20m (10ft 6in)
Weight: 2770kg (6107lb) maximum take-off weight
Payload: up to 10 persons

DESIGNED AS A high-braced monoplane for STOL operation on land, sea or ice, the initial Pilatus PC-6 Porter benefited from the early introduction of a turboprop engine in 1961, which has been successively uprated in later marques. This ubiquitous design, with a large free space aft of the cockpit, has been used as an air ambulance (often within a winter sports context) and for survey, parachuting or glider-towing roles. Domestic operator Mount Cook

Airline has used ski-equipped examples of the Porter for a number of years to land tourists and skiers onto glaciers in South Island, New Zealand. More than 550 PC-6 examples have been produced. Specifications apply to the PC-6/B2-H2 Turbo-Porter.

More than 250 PC-6s remain active to date, including this Turbo-Porter, which was the last delivered to the Swiss Air Force in 1976. Deliveries began in 1961.

PILATUS PC-9

SWITZERLAND: 1984

Crew: 2
Powerplant: one 783kW (1050hp) Pratt & Whitney Canada PTA-62 turboprop engine
Performance: max speed 593km/h (368mph); range 1642km (1020 miles); service ceiling 11,582m (38,000ft)
Dimensions: wingspan 10.30m (33ft 9in); length 10.20m (33ft 2in); height 3.30m (10ft 8in)
Weight: 3200kg (7055lb)
Armament: none

FIRST FLOWN IN 1984, the Pilatus PC-9 single-engine, two-seat trainer is a development of the PC-7 Turbo Trainer and is fitted with Martin Baker Mk 11A ejection seats. In addition to its use by the Swiss Air Force, the type has been supplied to Angola, Australia, Croatia, Cyprus, Germany, Iraq, Ireland, Myanmar, Oman, Saudi Arabia, Slovenia and Thailand. In

Australia, the PC-9 was licence-built by Hawker de Havilland, and in Omani service it replaced the BAe Strikemaster. By 2003, Pilatus had sold over 300 PC-9s, making the aircraft a leader in its class.

Pilatus PC-9s HB-HQA and HB-HQB on a formation test flight over the Swiss Alps. The type has proved extremely popular.

PILCHER GLIDERS

UK: 1895

PERCY SINCLAIR PILCHER, a Scottish engineer born in 1866, was impressed by Lilienthal's experiments. He visited Germany and bought one of Lilienthal's creations, after which he set about designing his own hang-gliders, the first of which he built in 1895 and named the Bat. Pilcher's next two gliders, the Beetle (1895) and the Gull (1896), were unsuccessful, but in 1897 he set a distance record of 229m (250 yards) in his latest design, the Hawk. Pilcher was killed two years later when the Hawk crashed as a result of structural

failure. At the time he was building a prototype of a powered aircraft which was to have been driven by a small oil engine; this had already been tested and Pilcher may have achieved powered flight before the Wright brothers if not for his early death. No precise details of Pilcher's gliders have survived. All except one were monoplanes, the exception being a triplane design.

A marine engineer, Percy Pilcher flew his first glider, the Bat, on the banks of the River Clyde, Scotland, in 1895.

PIPER J-3 CUB, O-59, L-4 GRASSHOPPER AND J-4 CUB COUPE

USA: 1930

THE ORIGINAL DESIGNER of the Cub series was the Taylor Brothers Aircraft Company, the first Cub flying in 1930. After the company's insolvency in 1937, the Taylor Cub was resurrected under the auspices of the Piper Aircraft Corporation. This simple high-wing monoplane (designated J-3) was then offered in a variety of tailskid, tail-wheel and float configurations with progressively more powerful engine

options, and attracted thousands of orders in pre-World War II America. The US Army realized the Cub's potential in an observer role; it was designated O-59A (later changed to L-4 Grasshopper) and went on to serve in communications, covert personnel-dropping and evacuation roles. Over 5700 were built. It saw widespread service in the US armed forces during World War II and after, and only the helicopter was

more versatile. Piper, however, built the Cub largely for private customers and the total number manufactured exceeds 14,000. In the postwar period the Cub was upgraded and renamed the J-4 Cub Coupe, changes including a larger wingspan, strengthening of the fixed landing gear, and further powerplant changes. A total of 1250 Cub Coupe's were built. Specifications apply to the J-3C-65 Cub.

Crew: 1
Powerplant: one Continental A65 flat-four piston engine rated at 48kW (65hp)
Performance: maximum speed 148km/h (92mph); range 402km (250 miles); service ceiling 3660m (12,000ft)
Dimensions: wingspan 10.73m (35ft 2.5in); length 6.78m (22ft 3in); height 2.03m (6ft 8in)
Weight: 499kg (1100lb) maximum take-off weight
Payload: two seats total

The aircraft pictured was built as an L-4 version and served initially with the US military, but is now privately owned.

PIPER PA-18 SUPER CUB AND L-18/L-21/U-7 SERIES

USA: 1948

Crew: 1
Powerplant: one Avco Lycoming O-320 flat-four piston engine rated at 112kW (150hp)
Performance: max speed 209km/h (130mph); range with maximum payload 740km (460 miles); service ceiling 5790m (19,000ft)
Dimensions: wingspan 10.73m (35ft 2.5in); length 6.88m (22ft 7in); height 2.04m (6ft 8.5in)
Weight: 794kg (1750lb) maximum take-off weight
Payload: two seats

The Continental C90-8F-powered aircraft pictured was built in 1952 as a model L-18C. It remains active as a member of the famous Tiger Club collection based at Headcorn-Lashenden Airfield in Kent.

FOLLOWING ON FROM the enormously successful J-3 Cub series, Piper launched the PA-18 Super Cub in 1949. This new version, although ostensibly similar, featured a slightly larger wing and a small stretch to the fuselage, and it was offered with (progressively) more powerful engines that gave it greater speed, height and range, making it popular with private flyers, as well as for agricultural and glider-towing functions. The PA-18 remained in production until 1981 when WTA Inc. acquired the rights and produced another 250 in addition to the 3500 plus built by Piper. This total includes military L-18 (later re-designated U-7) versions that were used by the US Army and supplied overseas on aid programmes as observers or trainers. Specifications apply to the PA-18-150 Super Cub.

PIPER PA-20 PACER

USA: 1950

The Piper Pa-20 Pacer was widely sold during the 1950s, including this German-registered aeroplane. Active examples are, however, fairly rare today.

Crew: 1
Powerplant: one 93kW (125hp) Lycoming O-290-D piston engine
Performance: cruising speed 180km/h (112mph); range 933km (580 miles)
Dimensions: wingspan 8.93m (29ft 4in); length 6.21m (20ft 5in)
Weight: 816kg (1800lb) loaded
Payload: four persons

THE PA-20 SUPERSEDED the earlier PA-16. Changes included larger tailplane and fuel capacity and improved landing gear and interior, while retaining the braced high-wing monoplane configuration. Several versions of the PA-20 were introduced with differing sizes of powerplant, and the last PA-20-135 version included a variable-speed propeller. The Piper PA-20 Pacer proved popular in the early 1950s and more than 1100 were built until 1955 (in land, float and ski versions), when the PA-20 was superseded by the PA-22 Tri-Pacer.
Specifications apply to the Piper PA-20-125.

PILATUS PC-8 TWIN PORTER
The Twin Porter was a twin-engined, high-wing monoplane design based on experience with the PC-6 Porter. Dating from 1967, only one example was built.

PILATUS PC-7 TURBO-TRAINER
This Swiss single-engined, two-seat trainer first flew in 1978 and has been widely exported to military customers. More than 500 examples have been built.

PILATUS PC-12
First flown in 1993, the Pilatus PC-12 is a single-turboprop short-range executive aircraft, capable of seating nine passengers or being fitted out for light cargo.

PIPER PA.7 SKYCOUPE
An early postwar Piper light aircraft, the Skycoupe was a low-wing design with a bubble cabin and a single pusher engine mounted on its rear. The aircraft was also notable for a twin-boom tailplane arrangement.

PIPER PA-22 TRI-PACER, COLT AND CARIBBEAN
A development from the PA-20 with changes that included a tricycle undercarriage with steerable nose wheel, a higher rated engine and superior flight controls. The four-seat Pa-22 was later varied as the two-seat Colt 108 and smaller engined Caribbean.

PIPER PA-25 PAWNEE
A braced low-wing, single-seat, single-engined monoplane designed for agricultural application. The 1950s design was progressively updated until the early 1980s. Over 5000 were built.

PIPER PA-29 PAPOOSE
This single-engined, two-seat cabin monoplane was an experiment in the use of honeycomb plastics as a base material. Dating from 1958, the Papoose ran into manufacturing difficulties and the programme was cancelled in 1963.

PIPER PA-32 CHEROKEE SIX/SARATOGA
Dating from 1963, the Six is a six-seat development of the PA-28 Cherokee. The Six has been progressively updated and was eventually superseded by the Saratoga, which features a number of further configuration changes including a constant speed propeller.

PIPER PA-23 APACHE AND AZTEC

USA: 1952

Crew: 1
Powerplant: two Avco Lycoming TIO-540-C1A turbocharged flat-six piston engines
Performance: max speed 407km/h (254mph); range with maximum fuel 2120km (1317 miles); service ceiling 7315m (24,000ft)
Dimensions: wingspan 11.37m (37ft 3.75in); length 9.52m (31ft 2.75in); height 3.07m (10ft 1in)
Weight: 2359kg (5200lb) maximum take-off weight
Payload: six people and luggage

THE APACHE WAS the first version of the PA-23, having been revised to a conventional tail-fin arrangement following the twin-finned prototype known as the Twin Stinson. Sales of the both types were generally for private use or air-taxi services, and the Apache was built in several marques until 1965, by which time it had sold more than 2000 examples. With Apache sales dwindling, Piper launched the modernized and more powerful PA23-250 Aztec in 1960. The Aztec was manufactured in five versions, including the US Navy's U-11A, until 1982, when nearly 5000 examples had been produced in total.

Specifications apply to the Piper PA-23T-250 Turbo Aztec F.

Although superseded by later designs, both Aztecs (pictured) and Comanches remain in service in modest numbers to date – often with air taxi firms.

PIPER PA-24 COMANCHE

USA: 1956

DESIGNED AS A light touring, training or club aircraft, the low-wing Comanche offered a retractable tricycle undercarriage.

From the start of production, the PA-24-180 was available in four versions – Basic, Custom, Super Custom and top-range AutoFlite – each with progressively superior levels of equipment. The PA-24-180 was later superseded by the dash 250 and later 260, these designations denoting the engine size as expressed in horse power (hp). The clean design, simple menu of options and minimization of variants contributed to a total of 4708 examples built until 1973.

Specifications apply to the Piper PA-24T-260 Turbo Comanche.

Crew: 1
Powerplant: one 194kW (260hp) Avco Lycoming IO-540 flat-six turbo-charged piston engine
Performance: max speed 389km/h (242mph); range with maximum fuel 2398km (1490 miles); service ceiling 7620m (25,000ft)
Dimensions: wingspan 10.97m (36ft); length 7.62m (25ft); height 2.29m (7ft 6in)
Weight: 1451kg (3200lb) maximum take-off weight
Payload: four people

The PA-24-260C was a stretched variant of the Comanche with 5–6 seats, hence the third side window in the aircraft pictured here.

PIPER PA-28 CHEROKEE SERIES

USA: 1960

SINCE ITS ARRIVAL on the light aircraft market in 1960 (to replace the PA-22 series), the Cherokee has been offered in a vast array of alternatives and derivatives starting with the PA-28-150, powered by a 112kW (150hp) engine. The 1967 Cherokee Arrow PA-28-180R introduced a retractable undercarriage to this low-wing design, while the PA-28-236 Dakota of 1977 is fitted with a 175kW (235hp) engine and has also been licence-built by Embraer. Successive changes have ensured that the Cherokee has remained a popular choice of light aircraft or (dual-control) trainer. It remains in production to date with over 30,000 examples sold. Current versions include the PA-28-161 Warrior III and PA-28-181 Archer III. Specifications apply to the Piper PA-28RT-201T Turbo Arrow IV.

Crew: 1
Powerplant: one Teledyne Continental TSIO-360-FB flat-six turbocharged piston engine rated at 149kW (200hp)
Performance: max speed 330km/h (205mph); range 1665km (1035 miles); operational ceiling 6095m (20,000ft)
Dimensions: wingspan 10.80m (35ft 5in); length 8.33m (27ft 3.75in); height 2.52m (8ft 3.25in)
Weight: 1315kg (2900lb) maximum take-off weight
Payload: four people

Less common versions of the Cherokee include this Pa-28-180, which has been converted to a floated seaplane configuration.

PIPER PA-30 AND PA-39 TWIN COMANCHE

USA: 1962

EFFECTIVELY THE PA-30 is an enlarged development of the PA-24 Comanche, designed to succeed the PA-23 Apache in the twin-engined, four-seat class. Similar to its predecessors, the Twin Comanche has a retractable undercarriage and is a low-wing design. The PA-30 underwent two upgrades involving extra windows, a turbocharged engine option, improved instruments and wing-tip tank options before the PA-39 superseded it in 1970, principally different in having counter-rotating propellers. More than 2100 examples of all types were produced until 1972.

Specifications apply to the Piper PA-39 Twin Comanche C/R.

Crew: 1
Powerplant: two 119kW (160hp) Avco Lycoming IO-320-B1A flat-four piston engines
Performance: max speed 330km/h (205mph); range 1931km (1200 miles); service ceiling 6095m (20,000ft)
Dimensions: wingspan over tiptanks 11.21m (36ft 9.5in); length 7.67m (25ft 2in); height 2.51m (8ft 3in)
Weight: 1690kg (3725lb) maximum take-off weight
Payload: up to four persons

Depicted here is a demonstrator version of the earlier PA-30 Twin Comanche – a turbo-charged engine was optional.

PIPER PA-31 NAVAJO

USA: 1964

The PA-31 in pressurized form remains popular with small or charter airlines and air taxi operators due to its combination of accommodation and operating economics.

THE NAVAJO WAS launched in the mid-1960s to straddle the growing market requirements of corporate transport and small airliner operatives. The type became known colloquially as the Miniliner and offered advantageous economics of operation. Early versions were unpressurized, but introduction of the PA-31P offered this facility from 1970, and the PA-31-350 Chieftain of 1973 offered a 10-seat capacity. A later derivative was the PA-31T Cheyenne, which has turboprop engines, wingtip fuel tanks and in some variants a T tail. The last variant – the PA-31P-350 Mohave – utilizes the Cheyenne I fuselage and the Chieftain powerplant. More than 5000 of all Navajo variants have been built for domestic and export customers, serving with over 1300 different operators. The type remains a favourite with small scheduled airlines and air-taxi firms in lightly populated areas such as Alaska.

Specifications apply to the Piper PA-31-350 Navajo Chieftain.

Crew: 1
Powerplant: two Avco Lycoming TIO-540-J2BD turbocharged flat-six piston engines each rated at 261kW (350hp)
Performance: max speed 428km/h (266mph) at 9144m (30,000ft); range 2388km (1484 miles); certified altitude 7315m (24,000ft)
Dimensions: wingspan 12.40m (40ft 8in); length 10.55m (34ft 7.5in); height 3.96m (13ft)
Weight: 3175kg (7000lb) maximum take-off weight
Payload: up to eight people

PIPER PA-34 SENECA

USA: 1969

Crew: 1
Powerplant: two 164kW (220hp) Continental TSIO-360-KB turbocharged flat-six piston engines
Performance: max speed 364km/h (226mph) at optimum altitude; range 1667km (1036 miles); certified ceiling 7620m (25,000ft)
Dimensions: wingspan 11.86m (38ft 10.75in); wing area 19.39m² (208.70 sq ft); length 8.72m (28ft 7.5in); height 3.02m (9ft 10.75in)
Weight: 1905kg (4200lb) maximum take-off weight
Payload: up to seven persons

THE SENECA CAME onto the market in 1972 positioned as a twin-engined version of the Cherokee Six with a new fuselage structure and a retractable tricycle undercarriage. The initial design has since undergone several upgrades of engine and airframe to improve performance and MTOW. In 1977, PZL Mielec of Poland began licenced construction of the Seneca as the M-20 Mewa. Including these, there are approaching 5000 examples built, which have proved extremely popular with air-charter/air-taxi operators. Specifications apply to PA-34-220T Seneca III.

Similarly to the PA-31 Navajo, the Seneca remains popular in the air taxi and general-purpose light business aircraft market, and for this reason the design has remained in production.

POLIKARPOV PO-2

FORMER USSR: 1928

The Polikarpov Po-2 utility biplane was widely used as a 'nuisance bomber' during World War II and the Korean War, achieving success out of all proportion to the weight of bombs it could carry.

PRODUCED IN MASSIVE quantities, some 33,000 leaving the assembly lines between 1928 and 1952, the Polikarpov Po-2 biplane carried out many duties over and above the training role for which it was intended. One of them was 'nuisance' night bombing, which it carried out in World War II and in Korea. The prototype, known also as the U-2, first flew in 1928 and was heavy and cumbersome, so Polikarpov redesigned the aircraft from scratch. The first production aircraft were delivered to the Red Air Fleet in 1930, and 13,500 had been built by the time Germany invaded the Soviet Union in June 1941. Not all of these were trainers; many diverse variants of the type had appeared, their roles ranging from light bombing to crop spraying. In the latter role the variant was the U-2AP, the suffix denoting Aeroopylitel – literally, 'scatterer from the air'.

Crew: 2
Powerplant: one 75kW (100hp) M-11 5-cylinder radial engine
Performance: max speed 149km/h (93mph); range 530km (329 miles); service ceiling 4000m (13,120ft)
Dimensions: wingspan 11.40m (37ft 5in); length 8.15m (26ft 9in); height 2.92m (9ft 6in)
Weight: 981kg (2167lb) loaded
Armament: one 7.62mm (0.30in) machine gun; up to 250kg (550lb) of bombs

POLIKARPOV R-5 SERIES

FORMER USSR: 1928

DESIGNED OVER A three-year period and first flown in 1928, the Polikarpov R-5 entered service in 1931 as a light reconnaissance bomber. Some 6000 examples were subsequently built, including the R-Z ground-attack aircraft, armed with as many as seven machine guns, and the R-5T of 1935, a single-seat torpedo-bomber. The R-5 was used by the Soviet Union while fighting the Japanese in the Far East, by the Republican Army in the Spanish Civil War, and against Finland in the Winter War. The latter two wars, however, proved its deficiencies against modern monoplane fighters.

The Polikarpov R-Z light reconnaissance bomber was easy to build and fly, but against modern monoplane fighters was practically defenceless.

Crew: 2
Powerplant: one 507kW (680hp) M17 12-cylinder Vee-type engine
Performance: max speed 228km/h (142mph); range 800km (500 miles); service ceiling 6400m (21,000ft)
Dimensions: wingspan 15.50m (50ft 10in); length 10.55m (34ft 8in); height 3.25m (10ft 8in)
Weight: 2955kg (6515lb) loaded
Armament: two 7.62mm (0.30in) machine guns; 240kg (530lb) of bombs

POLIKARPOV TSKB-15
The Polikarpov TsKB-15 was a highly streamlined modern low-wing monoplane fighter prototype which flew in September 1934 – before Britain's Hurricane and Spitfire or Germany's Bf 109.

POLIKARPOV I-17
The Polikarpov I-17 (TsKB-19) was a sleek fighter monoplane with a water-cooled engine, built for comparative trials with the I-16. Only a few prototypes were built.

POLIKARPOV R-10
Tested in 1937–38, the Polikarpov R-10 'Ivanov' was a light attack and reconnaissance monoplane. It was abandoned in favour of a rival design, the Nieman R-10.

POLIKARPOV VIT-1/2
Developed in 1937, the VIT-1 was a twin-engined assault aircraft, the VIT-2 being a re-engined and more streamlined variant. Neither was ordered into production.

POLIKARPOV NB(T)
The Polikarpov NB(T) was a purpose-built, twin-engined night bomber. It began flight testing in 1944, but was abandoned after the designer's death.

POMILIO PE
The Pomilio PE was an effective Italian reconnaissance biplane produced in large numbers in the last years of World War I.

POTEZ XV
The Potez XV two-seat reconnaissance aircraft of the 1920s was widely used by France, Denmark, Poland, Romania, Spain and Yugoslavia; a derivative, the Potez XVIII, was used by Bulgaria.

POTEZ 29
The Potez 29 of 1926 was a five-passenger cabin biplane. It was intended mainly for civil use, but some were used as utility aircraft by the French Air Force.

POTEZ 39
The Potez 39 was a high-wing reconnaissance monoplane which was used by the French Air Force in the early 1930s, alongside the Potez 25 and Breguet 27.

POTEZ 58
The Potez 58 was designed as a three-seat touring aeroplane powered by a single radial engine. Over 200 were produced from 1934 and nearly half of these were converted for air-ambulance use as the Potez 585 with the French Services during World War II.

POLIKARPOV I-5

Crew: 1
Powerplant: one 358kW (480hp) M-22 9-cylinder radial engine
Performance: max speed 278km/h (173mph); range 660km (410 miles); service ceiling 7300m (23,950ft)
Dimensions: wingspan 10.24m (33ft 7in); length 6.78m (22ft 3in); height 2.98m (9ft 9in)
Weight: 1355kg (2767lb) loaded
Armament: four 7.7mm (0.303in) machine guns

IN 1927 ONE OF THE most successful aircraft designers of this period, Nikolai N. Polikarpov, produced a single-seat fighter, the I-3. In 1929 he modified the basic design and produced the DI-2 two-seat fighter,

which had an armament of three machine guns, one in the nose and two on a movable mount in the rear cockpit. In the spring of 1930 Polikarpov, in collaboration with Dmitri Grigorovitch, produced the I-5, a single-seat biplane fighter with exceptional manoeuvrability and an armament of four PV-1 machine guns with a rate of fire of 800–900 rounds per minute. The prototype flew in April 1930, and about 800 Polikarpov I-5s were subsequently built.

The I-5 proved exceptionally manoeuvrable and had an armament twice as powerful as contemporary fighter biplanes.

POLIKARPOV I-15

Crew: 1
Powerplant: one 560kW (750hp) M-25B 9-cylinder radial engine
Performance: max speed 370km/h (230mph); range 530km (329 miles); service ceiling 9000m (29,530ft)
Dimensions: wingspan 10.20m (33ft 5in); length 6.33m (20ft 9in); height 2.19m (7ft 2in)
Weight: 1730kg (3814lb) loaded
Armament: four 7.62mm (0.30in) machine guns

IN 1933 POLIKARPOV designed the I-13 biplane, forerunner of the famous I-15 fighter, which made its first flight in October of that year. The I-15 was a biplane with a fixed undercarriage and the upper wing was gull-shaped, giving an excellent view forwards and upwards. In 1934, the I-15 was followed by the I-15bis, with an improved M-25V engine which

raised its top speed to 370km/h (230mph). I-15s were supplied to China and saw action against Japanese forces in the late 1930s. Specifications apply to the I-15.

This I-15 served as a trainer in Nationalist colours after the end of the Spanish Civil War. Note the 'yoke-and-arrows' emblem of the postwar Nationalist forces.

POLIKARPOV I-16

Crew: 1
Powerplant: one 821kW (1100hp) Shvetsov M-63 9-cylinder radial engine
Performance: max speed 489km/h (304mph); range 700km (435 miles); service ceiling 9000m (29,530ft)
Dimensions: wingspan 9.00m (29ft 6in); length 6.13m (20ft 1in); height 2.57m (8ft 5in)
Weight: 2095kg (4619lb) loaded
Armament: four 7.62mm (0.30in) machine guns or two 7.62mm (0.30in) machine guns and two 20mm (0.79in) cannon; external bomb and rocket load of 500kg (1102lb)

ON 31 DECEMBER 1933, two months after the appearance of the I-15 biplane, a new Polikarpov fighter made its first flight. This was the I-16 or TsKB-12, a low-wing monoplane with a retractable undercarriage, two wing-mounted 7.62mm (0.30in) guns and a large 358kW (480hp) M-22 engine. As the first production monoplane in the world to feature a retractable undercarriage, the I-16 attracted great interest among foreign observers. During the mid-1930s, the basic design was progressively

modified to carry out a variety of different tasks. Among the variants produced was the TsKB-18, an assault version armed with four PV-1 synchronized machine guns, two wing-mounted machine guns and 100kg (225lb) of bombs. The pilot was protected by armour plating in front, below and behind. In 1938 the I-16 Type 17 was tested, armed with two wing-mounted cannon. This version was produced in large numbers. The last fighter version of the I-16 was the Type 24, fitted with a 746kW (1000hp)

M-62R engine which gave it a top speed of 523km/h (325mph). Altogether, 6555 I-16s were built before production ended in 1940.

The I-16 saw considerable action during its career, starting with the Spanish Civil War. The first machines to arrive in Spain went into battle on 15 November 1936, providing air cover for a Republican offensive against Nationalist forces advancing on Valdemoro, Sesena and Equivias. The I-16 – nicknamed Mosca (Fly) by the Republicans and Rata (Rat)

The pilot of a Polikarpov I-16 demonstrates the little aircraft's ability to whip itself smartly off the ground. In combat against more modern fighters, the I-16's biggest asset was its manoeuvrability.

by the Nationalists – proved markedly superior to the Heinkel He 51. It was also faster than its most numerous Nationalist opponent, the Fiat CR.32, although the Italian fighter was slightly more manoeuvrable and provided a better gun platform.

In 1937–39 the I-16 also saw action during the Sino-Japanese conflict and also over the disputed Khalkhin-Gol area on the Soviet-Manchurian border. The air battles over this region produced an interesting and novel incident. On 20 August 1939, five I-16s, led by Lt N.I. Zvonarev and armed with RS-82 air-to-ground rocket projectiles, fired rocket salvoes at

a formation of Japanese aircraft and brought down two of them in what was the world's first aircraft-to-aircraft rocket engagement. I-16s also took part in the Russo-Finnish Winter War of 1939–40, specializing mainly in low-level attacks on Finnish airfields by flights of three or four aircraft. The I-16 still equipped the majority of the Red Air Force's first-line fighter units at the time of the German invasion in June 1941. Outperformed and outflown by their Luftwaffe opponents, the I-16 pilots often resorted to desperate measures. On at least five occasions during the first day of the air war in the east, Soviet I-

16s deliberately rammed their adversaries. Three of the pilots involved were members of the 123rd Fighter Air Regiment. The only asset enjoyed by the I-16 during these desperate air combats was manoeuvrability; if an I-16 pilot found himself in a corner he would throw his aircraft into a tight turn and head for his opponent at full throttle. The I-16 continued to operate as a first-line combat aircraft on the Leningrad front and in the Crimea until 1942, when it began to be replaced by more modern types and was relegated to second-line training duties. Specifications apply to the I-16 Type 17.

Polikarpov I-16 Type 5 of the 4th Escuadrilla de Moscas, Spanish Republican Air Arm, 1938. The first I-16s to arrive in Spain went into action on 15 November 1916.

POLIKARPOV DI-6

A TWO-SEAT FIGHTER BIPLANE, the Polikarpov DI-6 first appeared in 1935 and was subsequently used in fairly large numbers. Of mixed wood and metal construction, it featured a retractable undercarriage.

The DI-6 saw combat during the 1939 Manchurian conflict with the Japanese; its last frontline role was as a close-support aircraft, after which it was relegated to training and communication duties.

Crew: 2
Powerplant: one 537kW (720hp) M-25 radial engine (Wright R-1820 Cyclone copy)
Performance: max speed 372km/h (231mph); range 550km (340 miles); service ceiling 8000m (26,240ft)

Dimensions: wingspan 10.82m (35ft 5in); length 7.80m (25ft 7in); height 3.20m (10ft 5in)
Weight: 1947kg (4299lb)
Armament: three to six 7.62mm (0.30in) machine guns; 40kg (88lb) bomb load

POLIKARPOV I-153

FIRST FLOWN IN 1938, the I-153 was developed from the I-15 fighter biplane. Unlike its predecessor it featured a retractable undercarriage, but the maximum speed of the early I-153s (386km/h / 240mph) was still insufficient when compared with that of the new monoplane fighter aircraft beginning to enter service with the principal European air forces. The M-25V engine was consequently replaced by an M-62R developing 746kW (1000hp), and

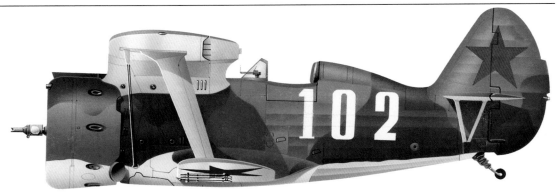

then by a 746kW (1000hp) M-63, which raised the I-153's speed to its ultimate of 426km/h (265mph). The I-153, dubbed Chaika (Seagull) because of its distinctive wing shape, was a first-rate combat aircraft and proved its worth in air fighting, being able to out-turn almost every aircraft that opposed it in action. Specifications apply to the I-153 Chaika.

A rugged aircraft, the I-153 could be fitted with either wheels or skis, the latter essential for operations in Karelia, where the type could operate from frozen lakes.

The I-153 was one of the principal Soviet fighter types used in the 1939–40 Winter War with Finland.

Crew: 1
Powerplant: one 746kW (1000hp) Shvetsov M-62 9-cylinder radial engine
Performance: max speed 444km/h (276mph); range 880km (547 miles); service ceiling 10,700m (35,105ft)
Dimensions: wingspan 10.00m (32ft 9in); length 6.17m (20ft 3in); height 2.80m (9ft 2in)
Weight: 2110kg (4652lb) loaded
Armament: four ShKAS 7.62mm (0.30in) machine guns, plus a light bomb load or six RS-82 air-to-ground rockets

POTEZ 25

Potez 25A2 of the 2do Escadron de Reconocimiento y Bombardio of the Paraguayan Air Force, during operations against Bolivia in 1933.

a formation of 33 Potez 25 TOEs, led by General Vuillemin, made a 'show-the-flag' tour of France's colonies in Africa, a venture that became known as the Croisière Noire (Black Cruise).

Crew: 2
Powerplant: one 336kW (450hp) Lorraine-Dietrich 12-cylinder liquid-cooled Vee-type engine
Performance: max speed 220km/h (137mph); range 660km (410 miles); service ceiling 7200m (23,620ft)
Dimensions: wingspan 14.19m (46ft 7in); length 9.19m (30ft 2in); height 3.65m (11ft 11in)
Weight: 2500kg (5512lb) loaded
Armament: three 7.7mm (0.303in) machine guns; up to 200kg (441lb) of bombs

FLOWN FOR THE first time early in 1925, the Potez 25 army cooperation biplane saw widespread service throughout France's colonial

empire, 1948 examples of the TOE (Colonial) version being produced for that specific purpose. Another 322 were exported to 17 countries. In addition, 150 were built under

licence in Poland, over 200 in Yugoslavia and 27 in Portugal. Total production in France alone exceeded 4000 aircraft. Between November 1933 and January 1934

POTEZ 54

Crew: 5
Powerplant: two 410kW (550hp) Hispano-Suiza 12Xbrs liquid-cooled Vee-type engines
Performance: max speed 331km/h (206mph); range 997km (620 miles); service ceiling 4000m (13,125ft)
Dimensions: wingspan 22.10m (72ft 6in); length 16.20m (53ft 2in); height 3.88m (12ft 9in)
Weight: 5959kg (13,155lb) loaded
Armament: three 7.5mm (0.29in) MAC 34 machine guns at rear, front and ventral turret; 500kg (1102lb) of bombs

A Potez 54 high-wing reconnaissance-bomber of the Armée de l'Air. Note the dihedral on the wingtips, an unusual feature for that time.

THE POTEZ 54 twin-engined, high-wing monoplane reconnaissance-bomber was described by its makers as an 'aerial cruiser'. Its defensive armament was positioned so as to leave no blind spots. It carried one machine gun in the nose, dorsal and ventral positions, the latter in the form of a retractable 'dustbin'. The cabin and nose turret were fully enclosed, but the dorsal gunner's turret was open. The prototype Potez 54.01 flew for the first time on 14 November 1933. The Potez 54 was originally developed as a private venture, the company being anxious to provide an entry in the French Government's competition to find a new bomber type in 1934.

POTEZ 540

Crew: 5
Powerplant: two 515kW (690hp) Hispano-Suiza 12Kirs 12-cylinder liquid-cooled Vee-type engines
Performance: max speed 310km/h (193mph); range 1200km (745 miles); service ceiling 6000m (19,680ft)
Dimensions: wingspan 22.10m (72ft 6in); length 16.20m (53ft 2in); height 3.88m (12ft 9in)
Weight: 5950kg (13,115lb) loaded
Armament: three 7.5mm (0.29in) machine guns; 900kg (1984lb) of bombs

THE POTEZ 540 was the definitive version of the Potez 54 reconnaissance bomber. It was the Potez 540M4 which was accepted by the French Air Force at the end of its evaluation in 1934 and placed in production, the first of 185 aircraft being delivered in November that year. Some aircraft, fitted with high-altitude Hispano-Suiza 12-Y engines, carried out clandestine reconnaissance missions over northern Italy and the Franco-

Close-up of the nose section of the Potez 540, the definitive bomber version of the reconnaissance bomber Potez 54.

German border just prior to the outbreak of World War II. Many Potez 540s were used as transports in North Africa. The type had also seen service on the Republican side in the Spanish Civil War. Total production of the Potez 540 reached 185 examples.

PROGETTI (PROCAER) F.400 COBRA
A single-(Marbore) engined two-seat Italian light jet design dating from 1960. Flown, but no further development.

PUTZER ELSTER-B
A motorized and improved version of the Doppelraab sailplane dating from 1957. Small numbers were produced for German flying clubs.

PWS 10
The PWS 10 parasol-wing fighter was developed as an interim aircraft until the PZL P-7 was ready for service. Deliveries began in 1932 and the aircraft's first-line career was short.

PWS 24
First flown in 1931, the PWS 24 was a small high-wing cabin monoplane with a Wright Whirlwind J5 engine. It seated four passengers.

PWS 14
The PWS 14 was a two-seat biplane basic trainer serving with the Polish Air Force in small numbers in the early 1930s.

PWS 16
The PWS 16 was a biplane trainer produced in small numbers for the Polish Air Force from 1933.

PWS 18
PWS 18 was the Polish designation of the Avro Tutor biplane trainer, which was built under licence in Poland in the early 1930s.

PWS RWD-8
The PWS RWD-8 was a two-seat parasol-wing monoplane trainer. Several hundred were built for the Polish Air Force from 1934. The type was licence-built in Romania.

PWS 26
A development of the PWS 16, the PWS 26 armed training and liaison biplane flew in 1936. The Polish Air Force took delivery of 240, and some saw action against the Germans in September 1939.

PZL P-38 WILK
First flown in 1938, the P-38 Wilk (Wolf) heavy fighter performed disappointingly, due mainly to its inadequate Foka engines. Two prototypes were completed.

PZL P-50 JASTRZAB
The P-50 Jastrzab (Hawk) single-seat, radial-engined fighter was intended to enter service with the Polish Air Force in 1941, but Poland had been overrun long before then. Two prototypes were completed, the first flying in late 1938.

POTEZ 63.11

Crew: 3
Powerplant: two 522kW (700hp)
Gnome-Rhone 14M-4 radial engines
Performance: max speed 425km/h
(264mph); range 1500km
(932 miles); service ceiling 8500m
(27,885ft)
Dimensions: wingspan 16.00m (52ft 6in);
length 10.93m (35ft 10in); height 3.08m
(10ft 1in)
Weight: 4530kg (9987lb) loaded
Armament: three 7.62mm (0.30in)
machine guns; up to 199kg (440lb) of
disposable stores, usually four 50kg
(110lb) bombs

A MODIFIED VERSION of an earlier
reconnaissance aircraft, the Potez
637, the Potez 63.11 flew for the
first time on 31 December 1938. It
featured a completely redesigned
forward fuselage that included an
angular glazed nose section.
Between November 1939 and June
1940, the Armée de l'Air took
delivery of 723 Potez 63.11s. After
the armistice, surviving aircraft saw
extensive service with both Free
French and Vichy forces; in 1942
many were adopted by the Luftwaffe
for training and liaison duties.

Used in large numbers by the Armée de l'Air in early World War II, the Potez 63.11 suffered serious losses during its reconnaissance forays into enemy air space. In all, 225 aircraft were destroyed or abandoned.

PZL P-7

Crew: 1
Powerplant: one 362kW (485hp) Bristol
Jupiter VIIF 9-cylinder radial engine
Performance: max speed 327km/h
(203mph); range 700km/h (430mph);
service ceiling 10,000m (32,800ft)
Dimensions: wingspan 10.31m (33ft 10in);
length 7.46m (24ft 6in); height 2.74m (9ft)
Weight: 1380kg (3050lb) loaded
Armament: two 7.7mm (0.303in)
machine guns

POWERED BY A Bristol Jupiter
radial engine, the gull-winged PZL
P-7a was one of the leading fighter
aircraft of the interwar years.
Deliveries began in the latter half of

The 27th production PZL P-7a, fitted with a Skoda-built 485hp (362kW) Bristol Jupiter VII radial engine.

1932 to the Kosciuszko Squadron,
and by the end of 1933 all first-line
fighter squadrons of the Polish Air
Force's 1st, 2nd, 3rd and 4th Air
Regiments were equipped with it.
Designed by Ing Zygmunt
Pulawski, the P-7 stemmed from
his original P-1 fighter, one of the
first aircraft to emerge from the
Panstwowe Zaklady Lotnicze
(National Aviation Establishments)
when these were founded in
Warsaw in 1928. Two P-1
prototypes were built, both with
Hispano-Suiza Vee-type engines,
and from these were developed the
radial-engined P-6 and P-7.

PZL P-11

Crew: 1
Powerplant: one 418kW (560hp) Bristol
Mercury VS2 radial engine
Performance: max speed 370km/h
(230mph); range 810km (503 miles);
service ceiling 9500m (31,170ft)
Dimensions: wingspan 10.72m (35ft 2in);
length 7.55m (24ft 9in); height 2.85m
(9ft 4in)
Weight: 1590kg (3505lb) loaded
Armament: two 7.7mm (0.303in)
machine guns

THE P-7'S SUCCESSOR, the PZL
P-11, was basically a more
powerful derivative first flown in
September 1931, with deliveries
beginning in 1934. Most P-11s
were powered by Bristol Mercury
engines, built under licence by
Skoda. The definitive version of
the fighter was the P-11c, of which
175 were built. The P-11 was to
have been replaced by a low-wing
fighter monoplane, the P-50
Jastrzeb (Hawk), but military

PZL P-11b in the colours of the Royal Romanian Air Force. Romania, which subsequently became an ally of Germany, continued to use the type as an advanced trainer.

budget cuts resulted in the cancellation of an order for 300 P-50s;
more P-11s were bought instead.
They suffered heavy losses during

the German invasion of Poland in
September 1939, but were effective
against German bombers which
did not have the benefit of a fighter

escort. The P.11b was an export
model for Romania, which also
built a small number of the type
under licence.

PZL P-37 LOS

POLAND: 1936

Crew: 4
Powerplant: two 651kW (873hp) Bristol Pegasus XIIB 9-cylinder radial engines
Performance: max speed 445km/h (276mph); range 1500km (932 miles); service ceiling 6000m (19,680ft)
Dimensions: wingspan 17.93m (58ft 10in); length 12.92m (42ft 5in); height 5.08m (16ft 8in)
Weight: 8560kg (18,872lb) loaded
Armament: three 7.7mm (0.303in) machine guns; 2580kg (5688lb) of bombs

DESIGNED IN 1934, the prototype PZL P-37 Los (Elk) medium bomber flew in 1936 and service deliveries of the P-37A production model began in 1938, these aircraft having a single fin and rudder. The 30 Los-As were followed by 70 P-37Bs, with twin fins, but many of

The PZL P-37 Los bomber was the best in service with the Polish Air Force when Germany invaded. Pictured is a P-37B with twin fins.

these had still to be delivered to operational units at the time of the German attack in 1939. Of the 61 operational Los-B bombers, 50 escaped to Romania, some being

used later against the Russians. The Los was a very effective combat aircraft, but came too late to have a decisive effect. Specifications apply to the PZL P-37B.

PZL P-46 SUM

POLAND: 1938

THE PZL P-46 Sum (Swordfish) was a light reconnaissance bomber developed from 1936. Four prototypes were ordered, one for static and three for flight testing, and the first of these flew in August 1938. Two of the flying prototypes were powered by the Bristol Pegasus engine and the third, designated P-43B, by a Gnome-Rhone 14N21, which was to be installed in 12 aircraft ordered by Bulgaria.

By March 1939 300 P-46s were on order for the Polish Air Force, but none was ready for action when the Germans invaded Poland. On 23 September 1939, test pilot Stanislaw Riess flew the second prototype P-46 Sum into besieged Warsaw with documents concerning future Polish resistance; Riess and his crew then flew to Lithuania, where they took ship for England. The fate of their aircraft is unknown.

Crew: 3
Powerplant: one 709kW (950hp) Bristol Pegasus XX radial engine
Performance: max speed 425km/h (264mph); range 1099km (683 miles); service ceiling 7700m (25,250ft)
Dimensions: wingspan 14.60m (47ft 11in); length 10.50m (34ft 5in); height 3.30m (10ft 10in)
Weight: 3550kg (7828lb)
Armament: eight 7.7mm (0.303in) machine guns; up to 598kg (1320lb) of bombs

The prototype PZL P-46 Sum, which came too late to see action in World War II. The second prototype, after carrying out a secret mission, escaped to Lithuania.

PZL TS-11 ISKRA

Crew: 2
Powerplant: one 1100kg (2425lb) thrust IL SO-3W turbojet engine
Performance: max speed 770km/h (478mph); range 1260km (783 miles); service ceiling 11,000m (36,090ft)
Dimensions: wingspan 10.06m (33ft); length 11.15m (36ft 7in); height 3.50m (11ft 7in)
Weight: 3840kg (8465lb)
Armament: one 23mm (0.90in) cannon; four external hardpoints for stores up to 400kg (882lb)

THE POLISH AIRCRAFT industry produced some very worthwhile training aircraft during the 1950s and 1960s, including the PZL TS-8 Bies (Daredevil) basic trainer, which remained standard equipment from 1957 to 1962, when it was replaced by the TS-11

Iskra (Spark). First flown in 1961, the Iskra was Poland's first indigenous jet aircraft, and more than 600 were built up to the late 1980s, the figure including a combat/reconnaissance version. The Indian Air Force also took delivery of 50 examples.

First flown in 1961, Poland's TS-11 Iskra turned out to be an outstanding success story, with more than 600 being built.

PZL/WSK-MIELEC M-15

The radical configuration of the M-15 is clearly depicted in this picture, but practical application failed to live up to the designer's concept.

THIS JOINT VENTURE by PZL/WSK-Mielec and the Soviet Union's Antonov to produce an agricultural aircraft resulted in the world's first jet-powered biplane. The pod fuselage sits ahead of the unequal-span wings, which are connected by two large chemical tanks and an outer brace. The single jet engine sits above and to the rear of the cabin connecting it to the upper wing. The radical design of the M-15 is completed by a twin boom tail-fin arrangement and a fixed tricycle undercarriage. At the outset there was perceived to be a need for up to 3000 M-15s to replace An-2s (compared to which it could spray a two to three times

Crew: 1/2
Powerplant: one Ivchenko AI-25 turbofan engine rated at 1500kg (3307lb) thrust
Performance: max cruise speed 200km/h (124mph); range 600km (372 miles)
Dimensions: wingspan 22.00m (72ft 2in); length 12.53m (41ft 1in); height 5.20m (17ft)
Weight: 5650kg (12,456lb) maximum take-off weight
Payload: three persons or 2900 litres (638 gallons) of chemicals

wider area) and other agricultural types. However, design problems and high fuel consumption meant only 175 were built.

Specifications apply to the PZL/WSK-Mielec M-15.

PZL I-22 IRYDA

Crew: 2
Powerplant: two 1100kg (2425lb) thrust PZL-Rzeszow SO-3W22 turbojet engines
Performance: max speed 840km/h (522mph); range 420km (261 miles); service ceiling 11,000m (36,090ft)
Dimensions: wingspan 9.60m (31ft 6in); length 13.22m (43ft 4in); height 4.30m (14ft 1in)
Weight: 6900kg (15,211lb) loaded
Armament: one 23mm (0.90in) GSh-23L cannon; four external hardpoints for up to 1200kg (2645lb) of stores

FIRST FLOWN IN March 1985, the PZL I-22 Iryda was designed to replace the TS-11 as the primary jet trainer of the Polish Air Force. In the same class as the Dassault/Dornier Alpha Jet, the aircraft can undertake reconnaissance, ground-attack and air combat tasks.

Deliveries of the I-22 Iryda to the Polish Air Force began in 1993. The early production model of the Iryda proved to be somewhat underpowered, however, and at one stage the Polish Air Force considered abandoning the type because of this problem.

Although a good design, based on the sound engineering principles of the TS-11, the PZL I-22 Iryda suffered from being somewhat underpowered.

RAYTHEON T-6A TEXAN II

The Raytheon T-6A Texan II features a digital cockpit, Martin-Baker ejection seats, cockpit pressurization and an onboard oxygen-generating system.

THE RAYTHEON T-6A TEXAN II is a US development of the Raytheon (Beech/Pilatus) PC-9 turboprop-powered training aircraft. It began development flight testing in 1998,

became operational with the US Air Force in 2001, and is one component of the Joint Primary Aircraft Training System (JPATS). The intention is for the T-6A to replace the US Navy's T-34C and the USAF's T-37B trainers.

Crew: 2
Powerplant: one 821kW (1100hp) Pratt & Whitney Canada PT6A-68 turboprop engine
Performance: max speed 515km/h (320mph); range 1667km (1035 miles); service ceiling 9449m (31,000ft)
Dimensions: wingspan 10.30m (33ft 4in); length 10.20m (33ft 2in); height 3.30m (10ft 8in)
Weight: 3200kg (7055lb)
Armament: none

REGGIANE RE 2000 FALCO I

Crew: 1
Powerplant: one 735kW (985hp) Piaggio P.XI RC40 14-cylinder radial engine
Performance: max speed 530km/h (329mph); range 1400km (870 miles); service ceiling 10,500m (34,450ft)
Dimensions: wingspan 11.00m (36ft 1in); length 7.99m (26ft 2in); height 3.20m (10ft 6in)
Weight: 2880kg (6349lb) loaded
Armament: two 12.7mm (0.50in) machine guns

Some Re 2000 Falcos were 'navalized' for service aboard Italy's aircraft carrier *Aquila*, which remained incomplete at the time of the armistice.

FIRST FLOWN IN MAY 1939, the Re 2000 Falco (Falcon) was the first fighter designed by Reggiane, a subsidiary of Caproni. Although it intially failed to win domestic orders, it went into production as the Re 2000 Series I to meet export orders from Sweden (60 aircraft) and Hungary (70, plus 191 built under

licence). Of the 27 that remained in Italy, 10 were converted as shipborne fighters (Series II) for service aboard the aircraft carrier *Aquila*;

the other 17 were converted to the long-range fighter-bomber role as Series III aircraft. Specifications apply to Re 2000 Falco I Series I.

REGGIANE RE 2001 FALCO II

THE REGGIANE RE 2001 FALCO II was a variant of the Re 2000 fitted with an Italian-built Daimler-Benz DB 601 liquid-cooled engine. The

modified aircraft flew for the first time in 1940 and was issued to first-line units early in 1942. Although the Falco II was one of

Reggiane Re 2001 of the 150a Squadriglia, 2 Gruppo 'Golletto', Regia Aeronautica, based on the island of Pantellaria in 1942.

RAYTHEON BEECHJET 400
Originating as the Mitsubishi MU-300 Diamond in 1978, in the region of 400 examples of this twin-engine business jet have been sold.

RAYTHEON RC-12 GUARDRAIL
The Raytheon RC-12 Guardrail is an adaptation of the Beech Super King Air 200B and is a specialized battlefield surveillance aircraft, providing real-time targeting data for field commanders. Deliveries began in 1983.

RAYTHEON (BAE) HAWKER 800
Originating from the Bae 125 design, the Hawker 800 is a medium-size, twin-turbofan business jet. Over 500 examples of this 14-passenger aircraft have been produced for civil and military applications since it entered service in 1984 as the first business jet with an EFIS cockpit.

RAYTHEON (BAE) HAWKER 1000
A stretched version of the Hawker 800 twin-engine business jet, the 1000 dates from 1989 and more than 50 have been delivered. It has the capacity for 15 passengers.

RAYTHEON PREMIER
The Raytheon Premier is a twin-turbofan, six-seat business jet design, including an all-composite materials fuselage. The aircraft was flown for the first time in 1998 and was certificated in 2001.

Italy's most successful fighters during World War II, production of the type was limited to 252 aircraft because of engine shortages. It did, however, serve in North Africa, Malta, Greece and in the role of air defence. The principal model was

the Re 2001 CN, which was intended primarily for the night-fighting role and which was armed with two 20mm (0.79in) Mauser MG 151 cannon mounted in underwing gondolas. Specifications apply to the Falco II Series II.

Crew: 1
Powerplant: one 877kW (1175hp) Alfa Romeo RA 1000 RC-41-1a Monsonie 12-cylinder inverted-Vee engine
Performance: max speed 545km/h (339mph); range 1100km (684 miles); service ceiling 11,000m (36,090ft)

Dimensions: wingspan 11.00m (36ft 1in); length 8.36m (27ft 5in); height 3.15m (10ft 4in)
Weight: 3280kg (7231lb) loaded
Armament: two 12.7mm (0.50in) and two 7.7mm (0.303in) machine guns

REGGIANE RE 2002 ARIETE

ITALY: 1940

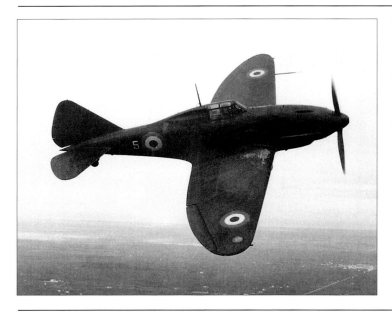

THE RE 2002 ARIETE (Battering Ram) was developed in 1940, using the same wing planform as the Reggiane Re 2001, but with a redesigned forward fuselage to accommodate the radial engine (a radial engine had been used on the Re 2000). The prototype flew in October 1940, but production aircraft were not issued to squadrons until March 1942. The 5th Dive Bomber Group became operational in July 1943 and were used in the defence of Sicily and mainland Italy.

The Reggiane Re 2002 was an effective ground-attack aircraft. It fought on both sides, some being used by the Co-Belligerent Air Force after the Italian armistice of September 1943.

After the armistice in September 1943, 40 Re 2002s fought on the Allied side with the Co-Belligerent Air Force. Others were seized by the Germans and were used by the Luftwaffe as counterinsurgency aircraft against resistance fighters in southern France.

Crew: 1
Powerplant: one 821kW (1100hp) Paiggio P.XIX RC 45 radial engine
Performance: max speed 529km/h (329mph); range 1099km (683 miles); service ceiling 10,507m (34,450ft)
Dimensions: wingspan 11.00m (36ft 1in); length 8.15m (26ft 9in); height 3.15m (10ft 4in)
Weight: 3116kg (6878lb) loaded
Armament: two 12.7mm (0.50in) and two 7.7mm (0.303in) machine guns; one 200kg (440lb) bomb

REGGIANE RE 2005 SAGITTARIO

ITALY: 1942

THE REGGIANE RE 2005 Sagittario (Archer), thought by many to be one of the most beautiful fighters produced by the Axis in World War II, was the ultimate development of the Re 2000 series, but it had little in common with its predecessors.

The first prototype was completed at the end of 1942. After further modification, the Regia Aeronautica ordered 750, but only a few were built, some of which were used by the Luftwaffe. The type was used in the defence of Rome and Naples.

Crew: 1
Powerplant: one 1100kW (1475hp) Daimler-Benz DB.605A 12-cylinder liquid-cooled Vee-type engine
Performance: max speed 678km/h (421mph); range 1250km (780 miles); service ceiling 12,000m

Dimensions: wingspan 11.00m (36ft 1in); length 8.73m (28ft 8in); height 3.15m (10ft 4in)
Weight: 3610kg (7970lb) loaded
Armament: three 20mm (0.79in) cannon; two 12.7mm (0.50in) machine guns

REPUBLIC P-43 LANCER

USA: 1940

Crew: 1
Powerplant: one 895kW (1200hp) Pratt & Whitney R-1830-49 Twin Wasp 14-cylinder radial engine
Performance: max speed 570km/h (356mph); range 1290km (800 miles); service ceiling 11,000m (36,000ft)
Dimensions: wingspan 10.97m (36ft); length 8.68m (28ft 6in); height 4.27m (14ft)
Weight: 3600kg (7935lb) loaded
Armament: four 7.62mm (0.30in) machine guns

THE REPUBLIC P-43 LANCER was a development of the Seversky P-35. Inadequate as a fighter, the aicraft was later converted to the photo-reconnaissance role. Total production of the P-43 was 272 aircraft, of which 103 examples

were sent to China; these were in fact the only Lancers to see action, although six of P-43B fighter-reconnaissance version were supplied to the Royal Australian Air Force in 1942. The P-43C was a slightly modified version of the original P-43A production version, only two examples being completed. The Lancer was never regarded as anything other than an interim aircraft by the US Army Air Corps, and the type's poor performance in China, where it was continually outclassed by contemporary Japanese fighter aircraft, showed that the Air Corps' decision not to order the Lancer in quantity was correct.

Specifications apply to the Republic P-43A Lancer.

The Republic P-43 Lancer did not measure up to expectations as a fighter; however, six examples were used as photo-reconnaissance aircraft by the Royal Australian Air Force.

REPUBLIC P-47 THUNDERBOLT

USA: 1941

Republic P-47 Thunderbolt of the 512th Fighter Squadron, 406th Fighter Group. This unit was based at Ashford, England, from April to August 1944, before moving to France.

THE REPUBLIC THUNDERBOLT, one of the truly great fighters of World War II, was designed around the most powerful engine then available, the new 1492kW (2000hp) Pratt & Whitney Double Wasp radial. The design was submitted to the US Army Air Corps in June 1940 as the XP-47B and was immediately accepted, orders being placed in September for 171 production P-47Bs and 602 P-47Cs. The two were basically similar, except that the P-47C had a slightly longer fuselage to improve stability. The XP-47B flew for the first time on 6 May 1941. Numerous teething troubles manifested themselves, examples being the 'snatching and freezing' of the ailerons at altitudes above 9150m (30,000ft), excessive control loads and the jamming of the cockpit canopy at high altitudes, but these were progressively eradicated, and in March 1942 the first production P-47B came off the assembly line.

In June 1942 the 56th Fighter Group began to rearm with the P-47, and in December 1942–January 1943 it deployed to England, flying its first combat mission – a fighter sweep over St Omer – on 13 April 1943. During the next two years it was to destroy more enemy aircraft than any other fighter group of the Eighth USAAF. From that first operational sortie over Europe until the end of the fighting in the Pacific in August 1945, Thunderbolts flew 546,000 combat sorties, dropped 134,129 tonnes (132,000 tons) of bombs, launched 60,000 rockets and expended more than 135 million rounds of ammunition. In the European Theatre alone, from D-Day (6 June 1944) to VE Day (8 May 1945), the Thunderbolt was credited with destroying 9000 locomotives, 86,000 railway wagons, and 6000 armoured

vehicles. In all theatres of war, its pilots claimed the destruction of 3752 enemy aircraft in the air and a further 3315 on the ground.

By the time the 56th Fighter Wing flew its first operational sortie in the spring of 1943, huge orders had been placed for the P-47D, which was at first externally almost identical to the P-47C. As time went by, however, so many changes were introduced in the P-47D that it differed as much from the original P-47D as did that fighter from the XP-47B prototype. In all, 12,602 P-47Ds were built by Republic in four batches, a further 354 being built by Curtiss-Wright as P-47Gs. The RAF acquired 354 early model P-47Ds as the Thunderbolt I, while a further 590 later model P-47Ds were supplied as the Thunderbolt II. All the RAF's Thunderbolts were assigned to squadrons in South-East Asia Command (India and Burma), where they replaced the Hawker Hurricane in the ground-attack role.

The next production version was the P-47M, 130 being completed with the 2089kW (2800hp) R-2800-57 engine. It was built specifically to help combat the V-1 flying-bomb attacks on Britain. The last variant was the P-47N, a

Crew: 1
Powerplant: one 1716kW (2300hp) Pratt & Whitney R-2800-59 radial engine
Performance: max speed 689km/h (428mph); range 2028km (1260 miles); service ceiling 12,800m (42,000ft)
Dimensions: wingspan 12.43m (40ft 9in); length 11.01m (36ft 1in); height 4.32m (14ft 2in)
Weight: 8800kg (19,400lb) loaded
Armament: six or eight 12.7mm (0.50in) machine guns; two 454kg (1000lb) bombs or 10 RPs

very-long-range escort and fighter bomber, of which Republic built 1816. Overall P-47 production, which ended in December 1945, was 15,660 aircraft. About two-thirds of these, almost all P-47Ds, survived the war and found their way into the air forces of Brazil, Chile, Colombia, Dominica, Ecuador, Mexico, Peru, Turkey and Yugoslavia. France also used the P-47D in its operations against dissidents in Algeria during the 1950s, the Armée de l'Air having found jet aircraft unsuitable for close support in that particular environment. During World War II, the Soviet Union received 195 P-47s out of the 203 allocated, some having been lost en route.

Specifications apply to P-47D.

P-47 Thunderbolt of the 63rd Fighter Squadron, 56th Fighter Group, Boxted, England, 1944. The 56th Fighter Group was one of the USAAF's most active and distinguished fighter groups of World War II.

RAYTHEON HAWKER HORIZON
A twin-engine, medium-size business jet designed for 21 crew and 12 passengers, with a wide stand-up cabin, the Horizon first flew in 2001 and has an order book exceeding 150.

REARWIN CLOUDSTER
Dating from the early 1930s, the Cloudster was an American-designed two- or three-seat light cabin monoplane. It was powered by a single Ken Royce 89.4kW (120hp) engine.

REID AND SIGRIST RS.1 SNARGASHER
The Reid and Sigrist RS.1 Snargasher was a three-seat, twin-engine training monoplane, first flown in 1939. No production was undertaken.

REID AND SIGRIST RS.3 DESFORD
First flown in 1945, the Reid and Sigrist RS.3 Desford was a twin-engine, two-seat pilot trainer. The sole prototype was extensively tested until 1949, when it was renamed Bobsleigh and used for prone-pilot and other experiments.

REIMS F.406 CARAVAN II
A twin-turboprop engine, 12-seat light transport derived (in France) from a Cessna Titan airframe for commercial and military use, and dating from 1985.

REISSNER ENTE
Designed by Hans Jacob Reissner in collaboration with Hugo Junkers, and flown in 1912, the Ente (Duck) was the world's first all-metal tail-first (canard) aircraft. It crashed in 1913.

REPUBLIC F-84 THUNDERJET

USA: 1946

THE REPUBLIC F-84 Thunderjet, which was to provide many of NATO's air forces with their initial jet experience, began life in the summer of 1944, when Republic Aviation's design team investigated the possibility of adapting the airframe of the P-47 Thunderbolt to take an axial-flow turbojet. This proved impractical, and in November 1944 the design of an entirely new airframe was begun around the General Electric J35 engine. The first of three XP-84 prototypes was completed in December 1945 and made its first flight on 28 February 1946.

Three prototypes were followed by 15 YP-84As for the US Air Force. Delivered in the spring of 1947, they were later converted to F-84B standard. The F-84B was the first production model, featuring an ejection seat, six 12.7mm (0.50in) M3 machine guns and underwing rocket racks. Deliveries of the F-84B began in the summer of 1947 to the 14th Fighter Group, and 226 were built. The F-84C, of which 191 were built, was externally similar to the F-84B, but incorporated an improved electrical system and an improved bomb-release mechanism. The next model to appear, in November 1948, was the F-84D, which had a strengthened wing and a modified fuel system. Production totalled 151 aircraft. It was followed, in May 1949, by the F-84E, which in addition to its six 12.7mm (0.50in) machine guns could carry two 453kg (1000lb) bombs, or 32 rockets. The F-84G, which appeared in 1952, was the first Thunderjet variant to be equipped for flight refuelling from the outset. It was also the first US Air Force fighter to have a tactical nuclear capability.

F-84 Thunderjets over Korea. The Thunderjet played an important part in the Korean War, attacking strategic targets such as irrigation dams and hydro-electric plants.

The Thunderjet was widely used during the Korean War. Although completely outclassed as a fighter by the MiG-15, it was very effective in the ground-attack role. The F-84G made its appearance in Korea in 1952, and in the closing months of the war Thunderjets of the 49th and 58th Fighter-Bomber Wings carried out a series of heavy attacks on North Korea's irrigation dams, vital to that country's economy. The first target was the Toksan dam, a 700m (2300ft) earth and stone structure on the Potong river 32km (20 miles) north of Pyongyang. The dam was attacked in the afternoon of 13 May by 59 Thunderjets of the 58th FBW, armed with 454kg (1,000lb) bombs, and the result seemed

disappointing; apart from a slight crumbling of the structure, the dam still stood. The next morning, however, photographs brought back by an RF-80 revealed a scene of total destruction. At some time during the night the pressure of water in the reservoir had caused the dam to collapse, sending a mighty flood down the Potong valley. Five square miles of rice crops had been swept away, together with 700 buildings; Sunan airfield was under water, and 8km (5 miles) of railway line, together with a 3.2km (2-mile) stretch of the adjacent north–south highway, had been destroyed or damaged. In this one attack, the F-84s had inflicted more damage on the enemy's transport system than

they had done in several weeks of interdiction work. The Thunderjet's final missions in Korea were flown on 27 July, the very last day of hostilities, when the 49th and 58th Fighter-Bomber Wings attacked three airfields in the north.

Specifications apply to the F-84G.

Crew: 1
Powerplant: one 2542kg (5600lb) thrust Wright J65-A-29 turbojet engine
Performance: max speed 973km/h (605mph); range 1609km (1000 miles); service ceiling 12,353m (40,500ft)
Weights: 12,701kg (28,000lb) loaded
Dimensions: wingspan 11.05m (36ft 4in); length 11.71m (38ft 5in); height 3.90m (12ft 10in)
Armament: six 12.7mm (0.50in) Browning M3 machine guns; provision for up to 1814kg (4000lb) of external stores

Republic F-84E Thunderjet of the 9th Fighter Bomber Squadron, the 'Iron Knights'. This particular aircraft was named 'Sandy'. The 9th FBS saw combat in Korea.

REPUBLIC F-84F THUNDERSTREAK

The swept-wing Republic XF-84F Thunderstreak, which utilized about 60 per cent of the F-84's components, flew for the first time on 3 June 1950, only 167 days after it was ordered. The first production F-84F flew on 22 November 1952, and the type was officially accepted by the US Air Force in the following month. The first US Air Force unit to arm with the F-84F, in 1954, was the 407th Tactical Fighter Wing. The F-84F replaced the Republic F-84

Thunderjet in several NATO air forces, giving many European pilots their first experience of modern, swept-wing jet aircraft. In French Air Force service, the aircraft saw action during the 1956 Anglo-French operation to secure the Suez Canal, flying from a base in Israel to destroy a number of Egyptian Il-28 jet bombers that had been evacuated to Luxor.

The Republic RF-84F Thunderflash was a low-level tactical reconnaissance variant.

Crew: 1
Powerplant: one 3278kg (7220lb) thrust Wright J65-W-3 turbojet engine
Performance: max speed 1118km/h (695mph); combat radius 1304km (810 miles); service ceiling 14,020m (46,000ft)
Dimensions: wingspan 10.24m (33ft 7in); length 13.23m (43ft 4in); height 4.39m (14ft 4in)
Weight: 12,701kg (28,000lb) loaded
Armament: six 12.7mm (0.50in) Browning M3 machine guns; provision for up to 2722kg (6000lb) of external stores

A Republic F-84F Thunderstreak carrying out a test missile launch. During the Suez crisis of 1956, French Air Force F-84Fs destroyed 20 Egyptian Il-28 jet bombers on the ground using cannon fire.

REPUBLIC F-105 THUNDERCHIEF

Crew: 1
Powerplant: one 11,113kg (24,500lb) thrust Pratt & Whitney J75-19W turbojet engine
Performance: max speed 2382km/h (1480mph); combat radius 370km (230 miles); service ceiling 15,850m (52,000ft)
Dimensions: wingspan 10.65m (34ft 11in); length 19.58m (64ft 3in); height 5.99m (19ft 8in)
Weight: 23,834kg (52,546lb) loaded
Armament: one 20mm (0.79in) M61 cannon; provision for up to 3629kg (8000lb) of bombs internally and 2722kg (6000lb) externally

ALTHOUGH BESET BY continual difficulties and delays during its early development career, the Republic F-105 Thunderchief emerged as the workhorse of the US Air Force's Tactical Air Command during the 1960s. The Thunderchief was conceived as a

successor to the Republic F-84F Thunderstreak at a time when the US Department of Defense was giving top priority to building up the American nuclear deterrent, and consequently the evolution of

a supersonic strike-fighter came low on the list of considerations. Nevertheless, in March 1953 the Department of Defense ordered an initial batch of 37 aircraft for evaluation, this being reduced to

Conceived for the nuclear-strike role, the F-105 Thunderchief was pitched into the Vietnam war and flew missions for which it was never intended.

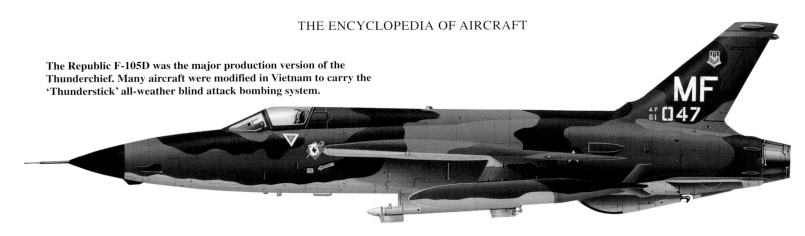

The Republic F-105D was the major production version of the Thunderchief. Many aircraft were modified in Vietnam to carry the 'Thunderstick' all-weather blind attack bombing system.

15 aircraft in February the following year. In September 1954 the number of aircraft ordered was cut to three, and it was not until February 1955 that the order was raised to 15 once more.

The first of two YF-105 prototypes flew on 22 October 1955, powered by a Pratt & Whitney J57-P-25 turbojet, and a third aircraft flew on 26 May 1956. Designated YF-105B-1-RE, this employed the P&W J75-P-3 and was the first of a production batch of 12 machines for test purposes. The F-105B was ordered into production in January 1957, deliveries of operational aircraft beginning in May 1958 to the 4th Tactical Fighter Wing. Only 75 F-

105Bs were built, this variant being replaced on the production line in 1959 by the all-weather ground-attack F-105D version.

The F-105D, which first flew on 9 June 1959 and entered service with Tactical Air Command the following year, embodied what was at the time the most advanced automatic navigation system in the world. Its ASG-19 Thunderstick fire-control system permitted either automatic or manual weapons delivery in modes ranging from over-the-shoulder toss to retarded laydown. Production of the F-105D totalled 610 aircraft, and although the type was initially unpopular, mainly because of early snags with its avionics systems, it proved its

worth over Vietnam, where it flew more than 70 per cent of US Air Force strike missions with an abort rate of less than one per cent. For the largest and heaviest single-seat fighter-bomber in the world, it also showed an astonishing ability to absorb tremendous battle damage and still get back to base. However, the type suffered terrible losses to enemy ground fire and 397 F-105s were lost on operations in Vietnam, an attrition rate that earned the F-105 the nickname of 'Thud', this representing the noise a crashing aircraft makes when it hits the ground.

Several two-seat versions of the F-105 were proposed, the first of which, the F-105C and F-105E,

were both cancelled before completion, the few F-105E examples under construction being finished as F-105Ds. The only other two-seat variant to enter production was the F-105F, which first flew on 11 June 1963. The F-105F, of which 143 were built, had full operational capability and was assigned in small numbers to each F-105D squadron. In Vietnam, F-105Fs frequently led strikes, providing accurate navigation to the target. F-105Fs were the first Thunderchiefs to assume the 'Wild Weasel' defence suppression role. F-105Fs fitted with improved defence suppression equipment were designated F-105G.

Specifications apply to F-105D.

RFB FANTRAINER 400 AND 600

WEST GERMANY: 1973

THIS RADICAL DESIGN by ducted-fan protagonists RFB was designed as a two-seat (tandem) jet trainer, offering low operating costs by use of a ducted-fan engine mounted aft of the cabin and fore of the T tail. A rotary engine was considered initially, but the specified Allison type prevailed. The design proved too radical for many and commercial success was not forthcoming. The Fantrainer only saw service in small numbers with the Luftwaffe and the Royal Thai Air Force. Specifications apply to the 400.

Crew: 1/2
Powerplant: one Allison 250-C30 turboshaft ducted-fan engine rated at 485kW (650hp)
Performance: max speed 463km/h (288mph); range 2316km (1500 miles); service ceiling 7620m (25,000ft)
Dimensions: wingspan 9.70m (31ft 11in); length 9.20m (30ft 2in); height 3.20m (10ft 4in)
Weight: 1600kg (3528lb) maximum take-off weight
Payload: two persons

Only two customers selected the radical Fantrainer design as a basic trainer – the Luftwaffe (example pictured) and the Royal Thai Air Force. Many air forces opted for more traditional basic trainer designs.

ROBIN HR.100 ROYAL, SAFARI AND R.1180 AIGLON   FRANCE: 1969

Crew: 1
Powerplant: one 213kW (285hp) Continental Tiara 6-285B flat-six piston engine
Performance: max speed 325km/h (202mph); range 2130km (1323 miles); service ceiling 5700m (18,700ft)
Dimensions: wingspan 9.08m (29ft 9.5in); wing area 15.20m² (163.62 sq ft); length 7.59m (24ft 10.75in); height 2.71m (8ft 10.75in)
Weight: 1400kg (3086lb) maximum take-off weight
Payload: four adults

THIS FIRST ALL-METAL design from Robin was also the first designed without a gull-wing configuration that had been inherited from Jodel designs, and the prototype was a modified DR.253. The initial HR.100-200 Royal version had a 149kW (200hp) engine, but this was up-rated for the Safari version. The specified HR 100/285 introduced a retractable undercarriage, and late in production life a 186kw (250hp) Tiara engine was offered. Production of the HR.100 ended in 1976 with 174 examples built. Since then modifications to weight, cabin and cabin content have been implemented and re-designated as marques of the R.1180 Aiglon which continued production in modest numbers.

Specifications apply to the HR.100/285.

Depicted is an HR.100/285 version, which features a retractable undercarriage and the Continental Tiara engine.

ROBIN DR.200 SERIES   FRANCE: 1972

Crew: 1
Powerplant: one 86kW (115hp) Avco Lycoming O-235-C2A flat-four piston engine
Performance: max cruising speed 205km/h (127mph); range 910km (565 miles); service ceiling 3900m (12,795ft)
Dimensions: wingspan 8.72m (28ft 7.25in); wing area 13.60m² (146.39 sq ft); length 7.00m (22ft 11.5in); height 1.85m (6ft 0.75in)
Weight: 840kg (1852lb) maximum take-off weight
Payload: three adults

THE DR.200 SERIES WAS developed from the DR.100 series, and continued the familial resemblance to earlier Jodels. CEA succeeded Jodel and was renamed Avions Pierre Robin in 1969. The DR.200 (HR.200) series were progressively updated, then later replaced by R.2000 marques. Development of these touring, training and aerobatic types continues. Specifications apply to the DR.221 Dauphin.

In the foreground of this photograph is the larger and more powerful DR.250 Capitaine, centre is a DR.221, with a DR.220 to the rear.

REPUBLIC XR-12 RAINBOW
The Republic XR-12 Rainbow was a four-engined reconnaissance aircraft flown in 1946. Two prototypes of this beautifully streamlined machine were built; six production aircraft were ordered as F-12As, but cancelled.

REPUBLIC RC3 SEABEE
The Seabee was a single-engined (rearward-mounted), four-seat amphibious light aeroplane design produced in modest numbers during the early post-war years in the United States.

REPUBLIC XF-91
First flown in 1949, the Republic XF-91 was designed as a high-altitude interceptor and used both jet and rocket engines. Only one prototype was built.

REPUBLIC XF-103
The Republic XF-103 was a high-speed delta-wing interceptor project. It was cancelled in 1957 while in the mock-up phase.

REY R-1
A French twin-engined monoplane design, originally built in 1940, the R-1 was resurrected in 1949. This experimental type was flown with differing wing configurations and technology.

RFB (RHEIN) RF-1
Following on from the Multoplane, RFB designed a six-seat STOL transport, the RF-1, which first flew in 1960. This high-wing monoplane had two Lycoming engines mounted centrally in a duct atop the wing, driving a single pusher propeller.

ROBIN DR.400 AND DR.500 SERIES

FRANCE: 1972

Crew: 1
Powerplant: one 134kW (180hp) Avco Lycoming O-360-A flat-four piston engine
Performance: max speed 278km/h (173mph); range 1450km (900 miles); service ceiling 4715m (15,470ft)
Dimensions: wingspan 8.72m (28ft 7.25in); length 6.96m (22ft 10in); height 2.23m (7ft 3.75in)
Weight: 1100kg (2425lb) maximum take-off weight
Payload: four seats

THE INITIAL AIRCRAFT in the DR.400 series was the DR.400/125 Petit Prince, which showed its Jodel lineage by retaining the cranked-wing configuration, while offering a new four-seat cabin and a (fixed) tricycle landing gear. The more powerful Regent followed in 1972 along with the DR.400/160 Major, both replacements for DR.300 series types. Further variants were added in the form of the DR.400/180R Remo and the DR.400/120 Dauphin two-seat, and DR.400/140 four-seat Dauphin version. In 1997 the DR.500 President was derived from an updated DR.400i. This and other versions of this popular light aircraft remain available, with over 1700 sales to date. Specifications apply to the DR.400/180 Regent.

A pre-production model of the DR.400/180 which was used as a demonstrator – performance as per the adjacent specification.

ROBINSON R.22/R.44

USA: 1975

THE ROBINSON R.22 prototype two-seat lightweight helicopter flew for the first time on 28 August 1975. Some 500 R.22 Alpha production helicopters were built Variants include the R.22 Mariner float version, R.22 Police, R.22 IFR trainer and External Load R.22 with additional cargo hook to carry a 181kg (400lb) cargo load. In 1985 the R.22 was superseded in production by the more powerful R.22 Beta. In 1986 Robinson announced that its next logical development would be the four-seat R.44, the prototype of which flew on 31 March 1990. In 1997 the R.44 became the first piston-engined helicopter to fly around the world. By late 2000, 868 R.44s had been delivered and by early 2001 over 3000 R.22s of all versions had been sold. Specifications apply to the R.22 Beta.

Crew: 2
Powerplant: one 119kW (160hp) Textron Lycoming D-320-132C flat-four piston engine
Performance: max speed 180km/h (112mph); range 592km (368 miles); service ceiling 4265m (14,000ft)
Dimensions: main rotor diameter 7.67m (25ft 2in); length 6.30m (20ft 8in); height 2.67m (8ft 9in)
Weight: 379kg (835lb)
Payload: two seats

Starting in the mid-1970s, some 500 R.22 Alpha two-seat lightweight helicopters were produced for the private market at a price comparable to that of two-seat fixed-wing aircraft.

ROCKWELL (NORTH AMERICAN) T-39 SABRELINER

USA: 1958

Crew: 2
Powerplant: two 1360kg (3000lb) Pratt & Whitney J60-P-3 turbojet engines
Performance: max speed 808km/h (502mph); range 3140km (1950 miles); service ceiling 13,715m (45,000ft)
Dimensions: wingspan 13.53m (44ft 5in); length 13.33m (43ft 9in); height 4.88m (16ft)
Weight: 8055kg (17,760lb) loaded
Payload: four–eight passengers

TO MEET THE US Air Force's UTX (Utility Trainer Experimental) requirement for a combat readiness trainer and utility aircraft, North American built the prototype of a small swept-wing twin-jet aircraft, which they named the Sabreliner, as a private venture. Design work began in March 1956 and the prototype, powered by two General Electric J85 turbojet engines, flew for the first time on 16 September 1958. The T-39 Sabreliner was subsequently produced in several versions for the US Air Force and US Navy and was later developed as an executive jet.

Specifications apply to the T-39A.

This example of the Rockwell (North American) T-39 Sabreliner was used for VIP transport and communications duties with the USAF Strategic Air Command.

ROCKWELL (NORTH AMERICAN) OV-10 BRONCO

USA: 1965

FIRST FLOWN IN JULY 1965, the OV-10A battlefield support aircraft entered service with the US Marine Corps and US Air Force in 1968, 270 being built. Fifteen aircraft were modified for night forward air control. The OV-10B was a target-towing version supplied to Federal Germany (24 examples), while the OV-10C was a version for the Royal Thai Air Force (36 delivered), where it is still used in border operations.

Other variants were the OV-10E for Venezuela (16) and the OV-10F for Indonesia (6). In the United States, a number of OV-10s are now used in fire-spotting operations. Specifications apply to the Rockwell (North American) OV-10A.

The Rockwell (North American) OV-10 Bronco was extremely effective in the battlefield support role and was used in the latter stages of the war in Vietnam.

Crew: 2
Powerplant: two 533kW (715hp) AiResearch T76-410/411 turboprop engines
Performance: max speed 452km/h (281mph); range 960km (600 miles); service ceiling 9150m (30,000ft)
Dimensions: wingspan 12.19m (40ft); length 12.67m (41ft 7in); height 4.62m (15ft 2in)
Weight: 6536kg (14,466lb) loaded
Armament: two 7.62mm (0.30in) machine gun in sponsons on lower fuselage; up to 1632kg (3600lb) of bombs and/or rockets

RHEIN (RFB) (RWF) RW-3 MULTOPLANE
The Multoplane was a German design of sailplane, powered by a Porsche engine with the propeller fitted between the fin and rudder. The first production model was produced in 1958.

RHEIN-FLUGZEUBAU GMBH FANLINER
A German design in collaboration with Grumman-American produced this two-seat light aeroplane utilizing a rotary engine. Two prototypes were built.

RIKUGUN KI.93
The twin-engined Ki.93 was the only aircraft designed by the Rikogun Kokugijutsu Kenkyujo (Army Aerotechnical Research Institute). Two prototypes of the aircraft were built, one of which flew in April 1945.

ROBEY-PETERS DAVIS GUN THREE-SEATER
The Robey-Peters Davis Gun Three-Seater of 1917 was a single-engined biplane with two wing-mounted nacelles, each housing a gunner and equipped with a Davis recoilless gun. The aircraft crashed on its first flight.

ROBIN 3000
First flown in 1981, the 3000 series light aeroplane is discernible by its T tailplane and up-turned wingtips. This four-seat touring design has alternative 87kW (116hp) or 104kW (140hp) engines.

ROCKWELL B-1B LANCER

A Rockwell B-1B Lancer, wings fully swept, making a high-speed run over a desert test range in the United States. The B-1 project was rescued by former US President Ronald Reagan.

DESIGNED TO REPLACE the B-52 and FB-111 in the low-level penetration role, the B-1 prototype flew on 23 December 1974; on 2 December 1976 the US Secretary of Defense, Donald H. Rumsfeld, following consultations with President Gerald Ford, authorized the US Air Force to proceed with production of the B-1. In September, however, Congress had restricted funding of the B-1 programme to $87 million per month, slowing the programme and effectively leaving the decision on the B-1's future to President Jimmy Carter, who would take office on 20 January 1977.

The decision hung in the balance until 30 June 1977, when President Carter delivered his bombshell and stated in a nationwide TV address that the B-1 would not be produced.

On 2 October 1981, however, President Ronald Reagan's new administration took the decision to resurrect the Rockwell B-1 programme. Between 1977 and 1981, the US Air Force had used the B-1 prototype in a bomber penetration evaluation. This had resulted in a unique opportunity to rate the combat effectiveness of an advanced bomber already cancelled as a production programme, with no pressure to prove the case one way or the other. The conclusion reached was that, with skilled crews and flexible tactics, the bombers were getting through to their targets more often than the computers had predicted, a fact that was firmly presented in a report which was submitted to the US Congress early in 1981.

The operational designation of the supersonic bomber, 100 of which were to be built for SAC, was to be B-1B, the prototypes already built now being known as B-1As. The first B-1B flew in October 1984 well ahead of schedule, despite the crash several weeks earlier of one of the two B-1A prototypes taking part in the test programme. The first operational B-1B (83-0065) was delivered to the 96th Bomb Wing at Dyess Air Force Base on 7 July 1985, although in fact it was the fleet prototype, 82-0001, which underwent the SAC acceptance ceremony, the other aircraft having suffered engine damage from ingesting nuts and bolts from a faulty air conditioner.

Despite a series of problems with avionics and systems, B-1B

deliveries to SAC reached a tempo of four per month in 1986. In January 1987 the trials aircraft successfully launched a SRAM for the first time; in April an aircraft from the 96th BW completed a 21 hr 40 mins mission that involved five in-flight refuellings to maintain a high all-up weight, the aircraft flying at about 741km/h (460mph) and covering 15,148km (9407 miles). This operation was in connection with development of operational techniques involving carriage of very heavy loads over long distances. Most B-1B missions are flown at high subsonic speeds; the aircraft is fitted with fixed-geometry engine inlets which feed the engines through curved ducts incorporating stream-wise baffles, blocking radar reflections from the fan. These reduce maximum speed to Mach 1.2; the earlier B-1A had external-compression inlets and could reach Mach 2.2, but had about 10 times the B-1B's radar signature. A good deal of so-called 'stealth' technology has been built into the B-1B, greatly enhancing its prospects of penetrating the most advanced enemy defences.

Specifications apply to B-1B.

Crew: 4
Powerplant: four 13,962kg (30,780lb) thrust General Electric F101-GE-102 turbofan engines
Performance: max speed 1328km/h (825mph); range 12,000km (7455 miles); service ceiling 15,240m (50,000ft)
Dimensions: wingspan 41.67m (136ft 8in); length 44.81m (147ft); height 10.36m (34ft)
Weight: 216,634kg (477,000lb) loaded
Armament: up to 38,320kg (84,500lb) of Mk 82 or 10,974kg (24,200lb) of Mk 84 iron bombs in the conventional role; 24 SRAMs; 12 B-28 and B-43 or 24 B-61 and B-83 free-fall nuclear bombs; eight ALCMs on internal rotary launchers and 14 more on underwing launchers; various combinations of other underwing stores. Low-level operations are flown with internal stores only

The B-1B was being delivered to the USAF Strategic Air Command at the rate of four aircraft per month in 1986, the 96th Bomb Wing at Dyess AFB being the first to equip with the type.

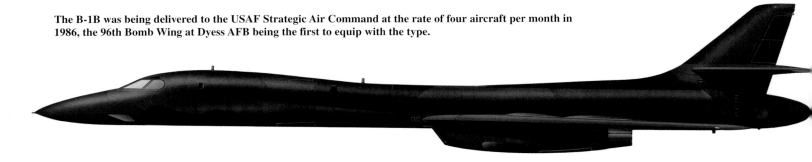

ROE NO 1 TRIPLANE

UK: 1909

Crew: 1
Powerplant: one 6.7kW (9hp) JAP
2-cylinder Vee-type engine
Performance: max speed 40km/h
(25mph)
Dimensions: wingspan 6.10m (20ft);
length 7.01m (23ft); height 3.35m (11ft)
Weight: 204kg (450lb)

ALLIOT VERDON ROE, the founder
of Avro, the firm that was to play
such a huge part in the development
of aviation, embarked on his career

as an aircraft designer in 1907 with
a canard pusher biplane design, the
Roe No 1. He entered the aircraft
in the contest to be the first pilot to
fly round the Brooklands racing
circuit, which carried a £2500
prize, but was unsuccessful.

Undeterred, he embarked on the
design of a triplane and on 23 July
1909, with Roe at the controls, the
resulting Triplane No 1 became
the first British aircraft powered
by a British-designed engine to

**Alliot Verdon Roe's Triplane No 1,
the first British aircraft to make a
successful flight in England under
the power of a British engine.**

make a successful flight in
England. A second aircraft, the
Roe II Triplane, flew successfully
at Brooklands. These early designs
provided invaluable experience
when it came to the development
of A.V. Roe's first true success, the
celebrated Avro 504.

ROHRBACH ROLAND

GERMANY: 1927

Crew: 2
Powerplant: three 239kW (320hp) BMW
Va 6-cylinder in-line engines
Performance: max speed 177km/h
(110mph); range 1300km (807 miles);
service ceiling 5350m (17,550ft)
Dimensions: wingspan 26.30m (86ft
3.5in); length 16.40m (53ft 9.5in); height
4.50m (14ft 9in)
Weight: 7400kg (16,314lb)
Payload: 10 passengers

THE ROHRBACH ROLAND was one
of the first commercial aircraft
produced for Deutsche Luft Hansa,
which was seeking to re-equip with
modern types. The Roland, which
entered service in 1927, was a
successful design, and six examples
were operated by the German
airline. In 1929 it was followed by
the more powerful Roland II. Both
types were high-wing tri-motor

monoplanes and were the brain-
children of Adolf Rohrbach, who
had also designed the massive
Zeppelin-Staaken E.4/20 of 1920,
a very advanced four-engined
airliner whose prototype had been
destroyed on the orders of the
Allied Control Commission.

Specifications apply to the
Rohrbach Roland II.

**Rohrbach Roland 10-passenger airliner in
Deutsche Luft Hansa's livery. The Roland
gave valuable service for many years.**

ROBIN ATL CLUB
The ATL Club is a lightweight,
single-engined, two-seat design
with a Vee tail dating from 1983.
Production continued until 1991.

**ROCKWELL (AERO
COMMANDER) 112/114**
Dating from 1970, this single-
engined four-seat light aircraft was
produced in two main models, the
main difference being the 114 was
more powerful. A total of 1310
were produced until 1979.

ROGOZARSKI SIM-XIV
Flown in 1938, the Rogozarski
SIM-XIV was a twin-engined, low-
wing floatplane with an extensively
glazed nose. Fourteen examples
were delivered to the Yugoslav Air
Force before the German invasion
of 1941.

ROHRBACH RO V ROCCO
The Rohrbach Ro V was a German
commercial flying boat powered by
two Rolls-Royce Condor engines.
Only one example was built, flying
in 1927.

ROLLASON (LUTON) BETA
A single-seat racer based on Luton
Group's design for the 1965
competition, this monoplane was
built and flown with a variety of
engines.

ROSHON MULTIPLANE
Designed in the United States in
1908, the Roshon Multiplane was a
freakish structure which took little
or no account of aerodynamic
principles. Not surprisingly, it
never left the ground.

ROLAND D.II

Crew: 1
Powerplant: one 119kW (160hp)
Mercedes D.III 6-cylinder liquid-cooled
engine
Performance: max speed 169km/h
(105mph); endurance 2 hrs; service
ceiling 5000m (16,400ft)
Dimensions: wingspan 8.91m (29ft 3in);
length 6.91m (22ft 8in); height 2.82m
(9ft 3in)
Weight: 793kg (1794lb)
Armament: two 7.5mm (0.30in)
machine guns

THE ROLAND D.II and the slightly
more powerful D.IIa of 1917 were
good, sturdy designs, but were not
the equal of Germany's Albatros
fighter series. About 300 were
built, these being used mainly on
the Macedonian front. Other
Roland designs were the D.VIb,
which was built in small numbers
in 1918 as an insurance against any
delay in delivery of the excellent
Fokker D.VII, and the D.VIIb,
which saw very limited service in
the closing weeks of World War I.
  Specification refers to the
Roland D.II.

Line-up of Roland D.II fighters of Jagdstaffel (Jasta) 25, which was based at Catnatlarzi, Macedonia, in 1917.
A sturdy design, the Roland was nevertheless inferior to the Albatros fighter types.

ROYAL AIRCRAFT FACTORY BE.2 SERIES

IN 1909, HM BALLOON FACTORY
at Farnborough, which as its name
implies had been involved in the
production of lighter-than-air craft,
began building aeroplanes and
changed its title to Royal Aircraft
Factory. Its first aircraft product,
built in 1911, was the BE.1 (Bleriot
Experimental) tractor biplane; the
BE.2 that followed used the same
basic airframe and was the first
military machine to be built as such
in Britain. By mid 1913 it equipped
13 squadrons of the recently formed
Royal Flying Corps. Production
gave way to the BE.2a with wing
of unequal span, and the BE.2b
with revised decking around the
cockpits and ailerons instead of
wing-warping controls. The BE.2c
introduced the 67kW (90hp) RAF
1a engine and was the first to be
armed with a machine gun. In the
night-fighter role, it was used with
success against German Zeppelin
airships in 1916. The last variant
was the BE.2e. In wartime service
BE.2 variants performed well in
the reconnaissance role, but a great
many were lost during the 'Fokker
Scourge' of 1915–16. Existing
records show that 3535 BE.2s of
all types were built, but the real
figure is certainly much higher.
Specifications apply to the BE.2c.

Crew: 2
Powerplant: one 60kW (80hp) RAF 1a
in-line engine
Performance: max speed 145km/h
(90mph); endurance 4 hrs; service ceiling
2745m (9000ft)
Dimensions: wingspan 12.42m (40ft 9in);
length 8.31m (27ft 3in); height 3.66m (12ft)
Weight: 953kg (2100lb) loaded
Armament: one 7.7mm (0.303in) Vickers
machine gun

A BE.2b built by the Blackburn Aeroplane and Motor Co. of Leeds, Yorkshire. The BE.2b was the first model to
feature ailerons instead of wing-warping controls.

ROYAL AIRCRAFT FACTORY BE.12

UK: 1915

Crew: 1
Powerplant: one 112kW (150hp) RAF 4a 12-cylinder in-line Vee-type engine
Performance: max speed 164km/h (102mph); endurance 3 hrs; service ceiling 3810m (12,500ft)
Dimensions: wingspan 11.28m (37ft); length 8.31m (27ft 3in); height 3.39m (11ft 1in)
Weight: 1067kg (2352lb) loaded
Armament: one or two 7.7mm (0.303in) machine guns

ORIGINALLY DESIGNED AS a fighter to counter the threat of the Fokker Monoplane, the BE.12 first flew in 1915. It proved disappointing in its intended role and after only a few weeks in service was relegated to light bombing in September 1916, serving in Palestine and Macedonia as well as France. BE.12s also served with British Home Defence squadrons, with one shooting down a Zeppelin L.48 in June 1917. Total orders amounted to 600 aircraft.

The prototype BE.12 pictured at Farnborough in 1915. The BE.12's main contribution to the war effort was as a home defence fighter.

ROYAL AIRCRAFT FACTORY FE.2B

UK: 1915

Crew: 2
Powerplant: one 90kW (120hp) Beardmore in-line engine
Performance: max speed 129km/h (80mph); endurance 3 hrs; service ceiling 2745m (9000ft)
Dimensions: wingspan 14.55m (47ft 9in); length 9.83m (32ft 3in); height 3.85m (12ft 7in)
Weight: 1347kg (2970lb)
Armament: one or two 7.7mm (0.303in) Lewis machine guns; up to 159kg (350lb) of bombs

THE NIEUPORT 11 virtually held the line against the Fokker Monoplane until the introduction of two British fighter types, the FE.2b and DH.2. The original FE.2a was completed in August 1913, but it was a year before the initial 12 aircraft were ordered, the first of these flying in January 1915. The first FE.2b flew in March 1915, and in May a few production examples arrived in France for service with No 6 Squadron RFC at Abeele, Belgium; however, it was not until January 1916 that the first squadron to be fully equipped with the FE, No 20, deployed to France. A two-seat 'pusher' type, the FE.2b, was slightly slower than the Fokker E.III, but proved a match for it in manoeuvrability. Later in World War I, the FE was used in the light night-bombing role. The FE.2d was a variant with a longer span. Total production of the FE.2 was 2325 aircraft.

The FE.2b was the RFC's answer to the 'Fokker Scourge' of 1915. Although slower than the German monoplane, it was its equal when it came to manoeuvrability. The 'Fee' was later used as a night-bomber.

ROTORCRAFT GRASSHOPPER

This British two-seat light utility helicopter was designed to sell at a price comparable to that of a luxury car, and first flew in March 1962. Unusually, it had twin engines, the 48kW (65hp) Walter Mikrons being replaced on production models by Rolls-Royce Continental O-200-A engines.

ROTORCRAFT MINICOPTER

This South African single-seat ultra-light autogyro was designed and developed by Llew Strydom, and first flew in September 1962 powered by a McCulloch O-100-1 engine.

ROTORMASTER BOOMERANG

American two-seat light autogyro which first flew in July 1964.

ROTORWAY SCORPION

American single-seat light helicopter, which was originally known as the Rotorway Javelin when it first appeared in 1965.

ROUSSEL R.30

The Roussel R.30 was a French radial-engined monoplane fighter design. Only one prototype was built, flying in 1939.

ROYAL AIRCRAFT FACTORY BE.8

Making its appearance in 1912, the BE.8 was issued in small numbers to various RFC squadrons from May 1914. The BE.8 had a singularly unspectacular career in France and was withdrawn by the spring of 1915.

ROYAL AIRCRAFT FACTORY RE.8

UK: 1916

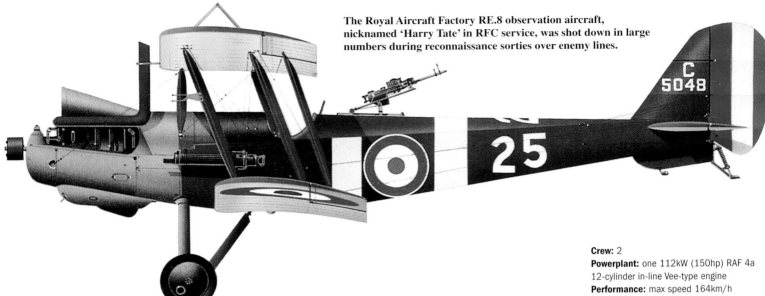

The Royal Aircraft Factory RE.8 observation aircraft, nicknamed 'Harry Tate' in RFC service, was shot down in large numbers during reconnaissance sorties over enemy lines.

Crew: 2
Powerplant: one 112kW (150hp) RAF 4a 12-cylinder in-line Vee-type engine
Performance: max speed 164km/h (102mph); endurance 4 hrs 15 mins; service ceiling 4115m (13,500ft)
Dimensions: wingspan 12.98m (42ft 7in); length 6.38m (20ft 11in); height 2.9m (9ft 6in)
Weight: 1301kg (2869lb)
Armament: two 7.7mm (0.303in) machine guns; up to 102kg (224lb) of bombs

NICKNAMED 'HARRY TATE' after the Cockney comedian, the RE.8 reconnaissance and artillery spotting aircraft resembled a scaled-up BE.2, but it had a much sturdier fuselage and a far better armament.

The prototype flew in June 1916 and the first aircraft were delivered that autumn, but were grounded after a series of accidents that led to the redesign of the tail unit. The RE.8 was subsequently very widely

used, equipping 33 RFC squadrons. Like the BE.2, it was far too stable to be agile in combat and suffered serious losses, usually having to operate under heavy escort. Production totalled 4077 aircraft.

ROYAL AIRCRAFT FACTORY SE.5

UK: 1917

The SE.5 was without doubt one of the best fighter designs to emerge from World War I. It was rugged, and pilots praised its excellent rate of climb, which often gave it an advantage in combat.

149kW (200hp) Hispano-Suiza engine. Deliveries were slowed by an acute shortage of engines, but the pilots of the units that did receive the SE.5a were full of praise for the aircraft's fine flying qualities, physical strength and performance. It is probably no exaggeration to say that, in most respects, the S.E.5a was the Spitfire of the Great War. At the end of World War I some 2700 SE.5as were on RAF charge, the type having served with 24 British, two American and one Australian squadrons. Specifications apply to the Royal Aircraft Factory SE.5a.

Crew: 1
Powerplant: one 149kW (200hp) Wolseley (licence-built Hispano-Suiza 8a eight-cylinder Vee-type engine)
Performance: max speed 222km/h (138mph); range 483km (300 miles); service ceiling 5185m (17,000ft)
Dimensions: wingspan 8.11m (26ft 7in); length 6.38m (20ft 11in); height 2.89m (9ft 6in)
Weight: 902kg (1988lb) loaded
Armament: two 7.7mm (0.303in) machine guns

THE SE.5 SINGLE-SEAT scout entered RFC service in the spring of 1917, being delivered to No 56 Squadron in March. Although less manoeuvrable than the French-built Nieuports or Spads, the SE.5

was faster and had an excellent rate of climb, enabling it to hold its own in combat with the latest German fighter types. The original SE.5 was followed into service in June 1917 by the SE.5a, with a

RUTAN VARIEZE

USA: 1975

Crew: 1
Powerplant: initially one 75kW (100hp) Volkswagen automobile engine
Performance: max speed 290km/h (180mph); range 1127km (700 miles)
Dimensions: wingspan 6.80m (22ft 2in); length 4.30m (14ft 2in); height 1.50m (4ft 11in)
Weight: 263kg (585lb)
Payload: two people

BURT RUTAN SET UP the Rutan Aircraft Factory in 1974 and set about radically altering the format of home-build light aircraft by designing and building the Rutan VariEze. The revolutionary design of the VariEze belied its simplicity. It was initially powered by a pusher Volkswagen engine (but later a larger Avco Lycoming type), and the wing configuration was forward canards with a swept and wingletted main rear wing. The secret of the VariEze's endurance

lay in extensive use of lightweight composite materials. It and the later Rutan LongEZ were built in many thousands and used to break endurance records, as would the later Rutan Voyager.

At first sight the parked demeanour of the VariEze worries many people, due to it not having a nosewheel, but it was designed this way. This example was homebuilt in Switzerland in 1986.

RUTAN VOYAGER

USA: 1984

The unconventional configuration and (in terms of scale) vast wingspan of the Voyager are clearly visible in this photograph.

Crew: 2
Powerplant: one rear-mounted (pusher) 82kW (110hp) Teledyne Continental IOL-200 liquid-cooled engine and one 97kW (130hp) Teledyne Continental O-240 air-cooled engine mounted in tractor mode. Both engines equipped with Hartzell constant-speed variable-pitch aluminium propellers
Performance: cruising speed 186km/h (116mph); distance travelled on record-setting flight 40,252km (24,996 miles)
Dimensions: wingspan 33.80m (110ft 8in); length 8.90m (29ft 2in); height 3.10m (10ft 3in)
Weight: 4397kg (9695lb)
Payload: two persons

BY THE EARLY 1980s there were few aviation records that had not been already set or achieved. The Rutan Voyager which was conceived in 1981 would in one flight become the first aircraft to fly nonstop around the world without refuelling, so breaking the records for the longest timed flight and the longest distance flight. Burt Rutan utilized his experience in the design of ultra-light home-build aircraft such as the VariViggen and the VariEze when he and brother Dick Rutan, along with Jeana Yeager, determined to try to gain the Collier Trophy. Dick Rutan, a former Vietnam fighter pilot, and Yeager had already set a

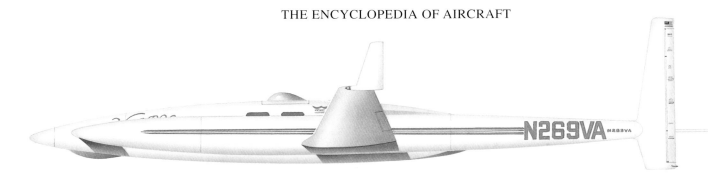

number of lesser records in earlier Burt Rutan designs.

Configuration of the Voyager's design was itself extraordinary. There were two engines mounted at either end of the cockpit, but the forward tractor mode engine was only utilized during take-off and the initial 70 hours of the journey when the Voyager was at its heaviest. Similar to earlier Rutan designs, there was a forward canard wing accompanied by a rear main wing, but the Voyager's design connected these by means of a twin boom fin arrangement. The cockpit and single cabin accommodation were side by side. Composite materials, including graphite fibre, kevlar and paper honeycomb, accounted for 98 per cent of the Voyager's airframe and no metals were used. In fact,

substantial parts of the Voyager's structure were manufactured of this specially treated paper.

Construction of the Voyager began in 1982 at Mohave in California, with the project being funded by private means and donations. Successful completion resulted in a first flight on 22 June 1984. The unladen weight of the Voyager was a mere 425kg (939lb) and the flexibility of the wing caused a deflection of up to 1.5m (4.92ft) in flight. The aircraft was designed to carry a vast amount of fuel for the unrefuelled flight around the Earth and the 3181kg (7011lb) capacity was distributed around 17 tanks aboard the craft, accounting for over 70 per cent of its gross weight. Regular rebalancing of this load between tanks would be an important feature of the in-flight

duties. The accuracy of Rutan's calculations was so critical that only 48kg (106lb) of fuel remained at the end of the Voyager's historic flight.

The Voyager, crewed by Dick Rutan and Jeana Yeager, required the full length of the runway at Edwards Air Force Base, California, in order to lift off at 0801 hours Pacific time on 14 December 1986, and the wobble of the wings caused their tips to scrape the runway. The loosened tips had to be released in flight by airframe manipulation, but there was no critical damage. The routing of the Voyager took into account avoidance of severe weather, including typhoons, and had to negotiate the geo-political realities of that era. Critical failures were limited to a fuel blockage in the rear engine that occasioned

The confined cabin area of the Voyager is shown to good effect in this illustration – two people spent nine days confined within it.

temporary restart of the frontal unit. However, the flight lasted nine days until the Voyager touched down back at Edwards Air Force Base at 0805 hours on 23 December 1986. The physical and mental strain placed upon the crew in this confined space, under constant pressure, was as much a feat of endurance as that of the machine itself. A record for the first unrefuelled flight around the world had been made, and the distance record – previously held by a B-52 – was doubled. The Voyager had earned its place at the Smithsonian Museum, Washington DC, where it resides today.

RYAN NYP 'SPIRIT OF ST LOUIS' USA: 1927

IN 1919 A $25,000 prize was offered by Charles Orteig, a New York-based hotel owner and magnate, for the first crossing of the Atlantic Ocean by an aeroplane. An attempt from North America was always more likely to succeed due to the prevailing winds, but it was to be 1927 before the combination of the right people and technological ability facilitated not one but two successful crossings from the United States.

Charles Lindbergh was a graduate of the University of Wisconsin, which put his theoretical skills to practical use in the Nebraska

Crew: 1
Powerplant: one Wright J-5 Whirlwind radial piston engine rated at 168kW (225hp)
Performance: max speed 209km/h (130mph); range 6730km (4182 miles)
Dimensions: wingspan 14.02m (46ft); length 8.41m (27ft 7in); height 2.99m (9ft 10in)
Weight: 2330kg (5135lb) gross weight
Payload: one person

The NYP was a specifically re-engineered version of the Ryan M-2 mailplane, but the work necessary to tailor it for the Atlantic crossing made it a less commercially attractive option than Bellanca's Columbia.

Aircraft Company in 1922, while he pursued alternative work as a barnstorming pilot. Later he gained a reserve commission as an Army Air Service pilot, but Lindbergh also harboured an ambition to fly across the Atlantic and win the Orteig prize. Lindbergh initially approached designer Giuseppe Bellanca, whose designs were acquiring a great reputation, but the engine makers Wright had recently sold Bellanca's aeroplane manufacture division to businessman Charles Levine, who was making his own plans for involvement in an Orteig prize bid using Bellanca's WB-2 Columbia design. Lindbergh was therefore turned away. Having raised money from a group of St Louis businessmen, Lindbergh then approached Ryan Airlines, which designed and produced the M-2 high-wing, single-engined monoplane mailplane.

Ryan was able to offer a specially adapted version of the M-2 and Lindbergh placed his order with them in early 1927, with the intention of challenging for the Orteig prize in the coming spring. Adaptation of the M-2 involved stretching the wingspan by 3.00m (10ft) and strengthening the structure and superstructure to accommodate the massively increased fuel requirement. To embody the large fuel tank the fuselage needed to be stretched by 0.6m (2ft) and the cockpit was positioned further back, with the engine further forward, in order to recover the centre of gravity.

The NYP was ready by April 1927 – named 'Spirit of St Louis' – and after a series of test flights it was necessary to ferry it to the Atlantic coast. This was achieved in some style by Lindbergh, who flew from San Diego to New York, with a stop at St Louis, Missouri, between 10 and 12 May in a new record time of 21 hours and 40 minutes.

The rival challenge to Lindbergh from Charles Levine's Bellanca Columbia was technically ready, but Levine and other involved parties had descended into litigation which was to delay their attempt. Lindbergh was aware of the Bellanca's capabilities and only waited at New York for a few days to gain better weather for his solo transatlantic attempt. His opportunity came on 20 May when he set off in the NYP for Paris in an aircraft which required a periscope

Charles Lindbergh became a hero to millions around the world after making the first solo transatlantic crossing by air.

to see directly ahead. Some 33 hours 30 minutes and 5810km (3610 miles) later, Lindbergh landed the NYP at Le Bourget airfield near Paris in front of a huge crowd and to world acclaim.

The NYP returned to the United States aboard the USS *Memphis* to a rapturous welcome on 11 June. Some weeks later, the two-seat Bellanca Columbia made it to

Berlin in a time that broke the NYP's record, but the Orteig prize went to Lindbergh. After a tour of Central and South America, which took in several more record journey times, Lindbergh retired the NYP after its last flight from St Louis to Washington DC on 30 April 1928. It remains in the US capital as the centrepiece of the Smithsonian Museum.

RYAN FR-1 FIREBALL

USA: 1944

Crew: 1
Powerplant: one 1007kW (1350hp) Wright R-1820-72W radial engine in the nose, and one 726kg (1600lb) thrust General Electric J31-GE-3 turbojet engine in the tail
Performance: max speed 650km/h (404mph); range 2606km (1620 miles); service ceiling 13,136m (43,100ft)
Dimensions: wingspan 12.19m (40ft); length 9.85m (32ft 4in); height 4.24m (13ft 11in)
Weight: 5296kg (11,652lb) loaded
Armament: four 12.7mm (0.50in) machine guns

Although it saw service only in small numbers, the Ryan FR-1 Fireball was an innovative design with its mixed powerplants.

DESIGN WORK ON THE Ryan Model 28, or FR-1, carrier-borne fighter began in 1943, and the aircraft was in production before the end of the war in the Pacific. It was the first operational aircraft in which a piston engine was combined with a turbojet, using both powerplants for take-off, climb and combat, and had the ability to fly and land with either engine shut down. The prototype flew on 25 June 1944 and the type entered service with Navy Fighter Squadron VF-66 in March 1945. Only 69 aircraft were built, the last delivered to VF-1E in June 1947.

RYAN NAVION (NORTH AMERICAN NA145) AND NAVION RANGEMASTER

USA: 1945

Crew: 1/2
Powerplant: one 195kW (260hp) Lycoming GO435C2 flat-six piston engine
Performance: max speed 280km/h (174mph); range 2560km (1590 miles); service ceiling 6553m (21,500ft)
Dimensions: wingspan 10.19m (33ft 5in); length 8.38m (27ft 6in); height 2.54m (8ft 4in)
Weight: 1293kg (2850lb) maximum take-off weight
Payload: four people

THIS AIRCRAFT ORIGINATES in the North American NA145 design, created to replace cancelled military contracts at the end of World War II

This aircraft, originally designed for military use as the North American NA145, helped to meet post-World War II demand for private flying.

and satisfy the boom in postwar private flying. The NA145 low-wing light aircraft was also procured by the US military as the L-17 observer; rights were passed to Ryan in 1948. Ryan designated the standard type as Navion 205 and developed the uprated Super Navion 260 and Model H. More than 1000 of all Ryan marques were produced until the early 1950s. In 1960 the Navion Aircraft Company was formed, and it updated this design again, producing a five-seat version named the Rangemaster until 1976. Specifications apply to the Super 260 Navion.

RYAN X-13 VERTIJET

USA: 1955

Crew: 1
Powerplant: one 4530kg (10,000lb) thrust Rolls-Royce Avon turbojet engine
Performance: max speed 563km/h (350mph); service ceiling 6100m (20,000ft)
Dimensions: wingspan 6.40m (21ft); length 7.32m (24ft); height 4.57m (15ft)
Weight: 3261kg (7200lb)

IN 1953, THE Ryan Aeronautical Company received a US Air Force contract to built a prototype VTOL jet aircraft, the X-13 Vertijet. This was intended to be launched from its own self-contained servicing trailer, which incorporated an hydraulically operated inclined launch ramp. The X-13 prototype first flew on 10 December 1955, fitted with a temporary undercarriage for normal

take-off and landing trials, and the first vertical take-off was made on 28 May 1956. A second aircraft was built, and this went on to make the full sequence of vertical take-off, transition to horizontal flight and transition back to the vertical for a landing on 11 April 1957. This aircraft is now in the US Air Force Museum at Wright-Patterson Air Force Base, Dayton, Ohio. The XV-13 proved that vertical flight was feasible, provided the engine thrust exceeded the weight of the aircraft by a considerable margin.

The Ryan X-13 Vertijet did much to advance the development of vertical flight by an aircraft other than a helicopter.

SAAB B.18

Although originally intended as a reconnaissance aircraft, the Saab B.18 was eventually used in several different roles, including torpedo-bomber and anti-shipping strike.

Crew: 3
Powerplant: two 794kW (1065hp) Pratt & Whitney Twin Wasp 14-cylinder radial engines
Performance: max speed 465km/h (289mph); range 2200km (1367 miles); service ceiling 8000m (26,250ft)
Dimensions: wingspan 17.00m (55ft 9in); length 13.23m (43ft 5in); height 4.35m (14ft 3in)
Weight: 8140kg (17,946lb) loaded
Armament: two 13.2mm (0.52in) and one 7.92mm (0.31in) machine guns; 1500kg (3307lb) of bombs; rocket projectiles on underwing racks

THE SAAB B.18 originated in a 1930 Swedish Air Force requirement for a reconnaissance aircraft, this being altered later to a dive-bomber. The first prototype flew on 19 June 1942 and was followed by 60 production Saab B.18As. These aircraft entered service in 1944. A few examples were later converted to the reconnaissance role as the S.18A. The B.18A was powered by two Pratt & Whitney Twin Wasp engines; however, the next variant, the Saab B.18B, had Daimler-Benz DB.605s as its powerplant, bringing about a marked improvement in the aircraft's performance. This model entered service in 1946 and 120 examples were built. The final variant, the T.18B, was originally intended as a torpedo-bomber, but the 62 aircraft produced were modified for the attack role with a 57mm (2.24in) Bofors and two 20mm (0.79in) cannon in the nose. The Saab 18 remained in first-line service until 1956.

Specifications apply to the Saab B.18A.

SAAB J-21A/R

ALTHOUGH SWEDEN HAD been mostly reliant on foreign combat types before and during World War II, Swedish aircraft manufacturer SAAB did produce an indigenous fighter aircraft, the J-21A. A twin-boom pusher design, powered by a Daimler-Benz DB605B liquid-cooled engine, the J-21A made its first flight on 13 July 1943. The new aircraft entered service with the Royal Swedish Air Force late in 1945, 298 production aircraft being delivered. By this time SAAB was working on a jet-powered version of the type, the

Based on the piston-engined Saab J-21A, the J-21R was Sweden's first jet-powered combat aircraft.

J-21R. This flew for the first time on 10 March 1947; however, because of the many modifications that were required to be made to the airframe, production deliveries did not take place until 1949, and an original order for 120 aircraft was cut back to 60. After a short career as a pure fighter, the J-21 had become obsolete in this role and was converted to the attack role as the Saab A-21R. The type was the only aircraft ever to see first-line service with both piston and jet power. Specifications apply to the Saab J-21R.

Crew: 1
Powerplant: one 1361kg (3000lb) thrust de Havilland Goblin turbojet engine
Performance: max speed 800km/h (497mph); range 720km (450 miles); service ceiling 12,000m (39,400ft)
Dimensions: wingspan 11.37m (37ft 4in);

length 10.45m (34ft 3in); height 2.90m (9ft 8in)
Weight: 5000kg (11,023lb) loaded
Armament: one 20mm (0.79in) Bofors cannon and four 13.2mm (0.51in) M/39A machine guns; centreline pod housing eight 13.2mm (0.51in) guns; wing racks for rocket projectiles

SAAB J-29   SWEDEN: 1948

Crew: 1
Powerplant: one 2800kg (6170lb) licence-built DH Ghost 50 turbojet engine
Performance: max speed 1060km/h (659mph); range 1700km (1060 miles); service ceiling 15,500m (50,850ft)
Dimensions: wingspan 11.00m (36ft 1in); length 10.10m (33ft 2in); height 3.73m (12ft 3in)
Weight: 8000kg (17,637lb) loaded
Armament: four 20mm (0.79in) Hispano cannon; 500kg (1100lb) of underwing stores

THE SAAB J-29 WAS the first swept-wing fighter of Western European design to enter service after World War II. The first of three prototypes flew on 1 September 1948 and the first production model, the J-29A, entered service in 1951. Other variants of the basic design were the J-29B with increased fuel tankage, the A-29 ground-attack version (identical to the J-29 except for underwing ordnance racks), and the S-29C reconnaissance version. The J-29D was an experimental version with an afterburner, while the J-29E interceptor had a modified 'saw-tooth' wing. The last production variant was the

J-29F, which combined the refinements of the J-29D and E and began to enter service in 1954. The J-29 saw limited action in support of UN forces during the Congo

crisis of 1962–63. It was the first Swedish aircraft to be exported, several being delivered to the small Austrian Air Force. Specifications apply to the Saab J-29F.

A simple but effective design, the J-29 served the Royal Swedish Air Force well for a decade, and the type saw action during UN 'police' operations in the Belgian Congo.

SAAB A/J-32 LANSEN   SWEDEN: 1952

The sleek Saab A/J-32 Lansen was the first Swedish combat aircraft to exceed Mach 1. Although never envisaged as anything more than an interim type, it became a true multi-role combat aircraft.

Crew: 2
Powerplant: one 6890kg (15,190lb) thrust licence-built Rolls-Royce Avon turbojet engine
Performance: max speed 1114km/h (692mph); range 3220km (2000 miles) with external fuel; service ceiling 16,013m (52,500ft)
Dimensions: wingspan 13.00m (42ft 7in); length 14.50m (47ft 6in); height 4.65m (15ft 3in)
Weight: 13,529kg (29,800lb) loaded
Armament: four 30mm (1.18in) Aden cannon; air-to-air missiles or folding-fin aircraft rockets

THE PROTOTYPE SAAB A-32 Lansen (Lance), flew for the first time on 3 November 1952, powered by a Rolls-Royce Avon RA7R turbojet. Three more prototypes were built, and one of these exceeded Mach 1 in a shallow dive on 25 October

1953. The A-32A attack variant was followed by the J-32B all-weather fighter, which first flew in January 1957. A two-seater, the J-32B, was powered by an RM6 (licence-built RA28) turbojet and had improved armament, navigation and fire-control systems. The J-37B was very much an interim aircraft, filling a gap until the advent of a much more potent system, the Saab J-35 Draken. The S-32C was a recon- naissance version. The Lansen equipped seven squadrons at its peak and served in many other roles, including target tug and trials aircraft, well into the 1990s. Specifications apply to the J-32B.

SAAB J-35 DRAKEN

SWEDEN: 1955

Crew: 1
Powerplant: one 7830kg (17,262lb) thrust Svenska Flygmotor RM6C (licence-built Rolls-Royce Avon 300 series) turbojet engine
Performance: max speed 2125km/h (1320mph); range 3250km (2020 miles) with maximum fuel; service ceiling 20,000m (65,000ft)
Dimensions: wingspan 9.40m (30ft 10in); length 15.40m (50ft 4in); height 3.90m (12ft 9in)
Weight: 16,000kg (35,274lb) loaded
Armament: one 30mm (1.18in) Aden cannon; four air-to-air missiles; up to 4082kg (9000lb) of bombs

THE J-35 DRAKEN represented a quantum leap over anything that had gone before and was, at the time of its service debut, a component of the finest fully integrated air defence system in western Europe. The first of three prototypes of this unique 'double delta' fighter flew for the first time on 25 October 1955, and the initial production version, the J-35A, entered service early in 1960. The major production version of the Draken was the J-35F, which was virtually designed around the Hughes HM-55 Falcon radar-guided air-to-air missile. The J-35C was a two-seat operational trainer, while the last new-build variant, the J-35J, was a develop- ment of the J-35D with more capable radar, collision-course fire control and a Hughes infrared sensor to allow carriage of the Hughes Falcon AAM. The Saab RF-35 was a reconnaissance version. The type was also exported to Finland and Denmark. The Draken was the first fully supersonic aircraft in western Europe to be deployed operationally.

Specifications apply to the Saab J-35J Draken.

Seen here in the colours of the Royal Danish Air Force, the Saab J-35 Draken formed a component part of one of the most advanced integrated air defence systems in the world.

SAAB SF-37 VIGGEN

SWEDEN: 1957

Powerplant: one 11,899kg (26,015lb) thrust Volvo Flygmotor RM8 turbofan engine
Performance: max speed 2124km/h (1320mph); combat radius 1000km (621 miles); service ceiling 18,290m (60,000ft)
Dimensions: wingspan 10.60m (34ft 9in); length 16.30m (53ft 5in); height 5.60m (18ft 4in)
Weight: 20,500kg (45,194lb) loaded
Armament: in secondary attack role, seven external hardpoints with provision for 6000kg (13,228lb) of stores, including 30mm (1.18in) Aden cannon pods, 135mm (5.31in) rocket pods, air-to-air missiles and air-to-surface missiles

ONE OF THE MOST potent combat aircraft of the 1970s, the Saab 37 Viggen (Thunderbolt) was designed to carry out the four roles of attack, interception, reconnaissance and training. The first of seven prototypes flew for the first time on 8 February 1967, followed by

SAIMAN 202
A single-engined, two-seat cabin monoplane dating from the mid-1930s designed for touring purposes, but also taken up by Italy's Reggia Aeronautica.

SIAI-MARCHETTI SA.202 BRAVO
See FFA AS.202.

SIAI-MARCHETTI SF.600TP CANGURO
This twin-turboprop-engined, high-wing monoplane was devised in the late 1970s as a nine-seat commuter airliner aimed at the low end of the commuter/air-taxi market. Only a small number were built.

SALMSON 2
The Salmson 2 was the most widely used Allied reconnaissance aircraft in the final year of World War I. The type served with both the French and US air services on the Western Front.

SALMSON D6 CRI-CRI
Salmson of France switched to light aircraft designs in the 1930s and produced the Cri-Cri parasol monoplane with a radial engine. A D7 variant was also produced early after World War II.

SAML S.2
The SAML (Societa Aeronautica Meccanica Lombarda) S.2 reconnaissance biplane entered service in 1917. The type was operated by 16 squadrons in Italy, Albania and Macedonia.

SARO CUTTY SARK
The Cutty Sark flying boat was designed as a passenger-carrying type and produced in small numbers in two versions – single and twin engine. Only one example of the long-range, single-engined version was produced. It was first flown in 1929.

the first production AJ-37 single-seat all-weather attack variant in February 1971. Deliveries of the first of 110 AJ-37s to the Royal Swedish Air Force began in June that year. The JA-37 interceptor version of the Viggen, 149 of which were built, replaced the J35F Draken; the SF-37 (26 examples delivered) was a single-seat armed photo-reconnaissance variant; and the SH-37 (26 delivered) was an all-weather maritime reconnaissance version, replacing the S-32C Lansen.

The SK-37 (18 delivered) was a tandem two-seat trainer, retaining a secondary attack role. Some Viggens were expected to remain in service until 2010.

Specifications apply to the Saab SF-37 Viggen.

The Viggen's wing incorporates hydraulically activated two-section elevons on the trailing edge; the leading edge has compound sweep and is extended forward on the outer sections.

SAAB JAS-39 GRIPEN

SWEDEN: 1988

THE SAAB JAS-39 Gripen (Griffon) lightweight multi-role fighter was conceived as a replacement for the attack, reconnaissance and interceptor versions of the Viggen. The prototype was rolled out on 26 April 1987 and first flew on 9 December 1988. The loss of this aircraft in a landing accident on 2 February 1989 led to a revision of the Gripen's advanced fly-by-wire control

system. Orders totalled 140 aircraft, all for the Royal Swedish Air Force, and the type entered service in 1995. The JAS-39 is a canard delta design with triplex digital fly-by-wire controls, a multi-mode Ericsson pulse-Doppler radar, laser inertial navigation system, wide-angle head-up display and three monochrome head-down displays. On 3 December 1999, the South

African Air Force announced that Saab and British Aerospace would supply 28 Gripens and 24 Hawk 100s, to be delivered between 2005 and 2012. Specifications apply to the JAS-39A Gripen.

Crew: 1
Powerplant: one 8210kg (18,100lb) thrust Volvo Flygmotor RM12 turbofan engine
Performance: max speed Mach 2 plus;

range 3250km (2020 miles); service ceiling classified
Dimensions: wingspan 8.00m (26ft 3in); length 14.10m (46ft 3in); height 4.70m (15ft 5in)
Weight: 12,473kg (27,500lb) loaded
Armament: one 27mm (1.06in) Mauser BK27 cannon; six external hardpoints for air-to-air missiles, air-to-surface missiles, bombs, cluster bombs, reconnaissance pods, drop tanks, ECM pods etc.

Saab's JAS-39 is proving to be an excellent multi-role combat aircraft, competing with the Eurofighter and Rafale in the lucrative export market.

SAAB 2000

Crew: 2
Powerplant: two flat-rated 3096kW (4152shp) Rolls-Royce Allison AE2100A turboprop engines
Performance: max cruising speed 682km/h (423mph); range with max payload 2868km (1782 miles); service ceiling 9450m (31,000ft)
Dimensions: wingspan 24.76m (81ft 2.25in); length 27.28m (89ft 6in); height 7.73m (25ft 4in)
Weight: 22,800kg (50,265lb) maximum take-off weight
Payload: up to 58 passengers

BUILDING ON THE success of its Saab 340, Swedish company Saab proceeded to develop a stretched, 50-seat version to fulfil the growing market for larger capacity regional airliners and offer a product that could compete against jet designs, but with lower costs and greater flexibility. The launch customer was the Swiss airline Crossair, which began operations with the Saab 2000 in September 1994. Despite Saab's reputation for producing innovative civil and

military designs, the arrival of a new generation of regional jets, particularly in the North American market, coupled with customer preference, contributed to slow sales, and Saab ceased the type's manufacture in 1998 with a total of only 63 examples built.

Despite the Saab 2000's superior operating economics and relatively fast speed, sales failed to live up to the product's promise due to strong competition.

SANTOS-DUMONT DEMOISELLE

Crew: 1
Powerplant: one 26kW (35hp) Dutheil-Chalmers 2-cylinder horizontally opposed piston engine
Performance: max speed 90km/h (56mph)
Dimensions: wingspan 5.10m (16ft 8.75in); length 8.00m (26ft 3in); height 2.40m (7ft 10.5in)
Weight: 143kg (315lb) loaded

ALBERTO SANTOS-DUMONT was a Brazilian expatriate who settled in Paris and who played such an important part in making Europe air-minded through his little airship designs at the beginning of the twentieth century. He went on to produce a series of heavier-than-

air craft which may be justifiably described as the world's first true light aircraft. The first of them was the 14bis, which was tested in 1906

The talented and innovative Alberto Santos-Dumont, one of aviation's early pioneers, helped to make Europe air-minded.

suspended under Santos-Dumont's Airship No 14 and which later made a series of short powered 'hops'. Further designs led to a series of little single-seat aircraft known collectively by the name Demoiselle

(Dragonfly), the first of which (Demoiselle No 19) flew in 1907. In September 1909, Demoiselle No 20, a much modified version with a more powerful engine, flew for 16 minutes and covered about 18km

(11 miles). The Demoiselle was the first aircraft to be produced for sporting purposes, between 10 and 15 being built for sale to aspiring aviators. Unfortunately, it was also Santos-Dumont's first and last

really successful design, as the onset of multiple sclerosis in 1910 compelled him to retire from an active life. He committed suicide in 1932. Specifications apply to the Demoiselle No 20.

SARO (SAUNDERS-ROE) LONDON

UK: 1934

This Saro London flying boat carries the BN code letters of No 240 Squadron, RAF Coastal Command. The squadron, later equipped with Catalinas, moved to Madras, India, in 1942.

THE SARO A.27 LONDON coastal patrol flying boat was produced to Air Ministry Specification R.24/31 and was a development of the earlier Saro A.7, the first of 10 London Mk I aircraft being delivered in 1936. The next 20 aircraft, with uprated engines, were

designated London Mk II, and all existing Mk Is were upgraded to Mk II standard.

The London equipped seven Coastal Command squadrons and was operational in the early months of World War II, equipping Nos 201 and 240 Squadrons for

North Sea patrols and No 202 Squadron at Gibraltar. After being withdrawn from first-line duties, some Londons were issued to No 4 (Coastal) Operational Training Unit. Ex-RAF Londons were also transferred to the Royal Canadian Air Force.

Crew: 5
Powerplant: two 787kW (1055hp) Bristol Pegasus X radial engines
Performance: max speed 249km/h (155mph); range 1770km (1100 miles) service ceiling 6065m (19,900ft)
Dimensions: wingspan 24.38m (80ft); length 17.31m (56ft 9in); height 5.72m (18ft 9in)
Weight: 8346kg (18,400lb) loaded
Armament: three 7.7mm (0.303in) machine guns; up to 907kg (2000lb) of bombs or depth charges on underwing racks

SARO (SAUNDERS-ROE) LERWICK

UK: 1938

Crew: 6
Powerplant: two 1026kW (1375hp) Bristol Hercules 11 14-cylinder radial engines
Performance: max speed 347km/h (216mph); service ceiling 4267m (14,000ft)
Dimensions: wingspan 24.63m (80ft 10in); length 19.39m (63ft 7in); height 6.09m (20ft)
Weight: 15,060kg (33,200lb) loaded
Armament: twin 7.7mm (0.303in) Browning machine guns in dorsal turret and four in tail turret; one 7.7mm (0.303in) Vickers gun in nose; four 227kg (500lb) or eight 113kg (250lb) bombs

DESIGNED TO FULFIL Air Ministry Specification R.1/36, the Saro Lerwick flying boat flew for the first time in 1938 and was ordered into production for RAF Coastal Command straight off the drawing board. Despite many shortcomings, the type entered service with No 209 Squadron in December 1939.

The last of 21 aircraft was delivered in May 1941, but the Lerwick was withdrawn from RAF service almost immediately afterwards. In July 1942, however, eight ex-RAF Lerwicks were issued to the newly

formed No 422 Squadron RCAF, based at Lough Erne in Northern Ireland, which used them on Arctic convoy escort duty until September of that year, when they began to be replaced by Catalinas.

Saro Lerwick Mk I of No 209 Squadron, RAF Coastal Command. The Lerwick's career with the RAF was short-lived, the type being replaced by the much more effective Catalina.

SARO (SAUNDERS-ROE) SR/A1   UK: 1947

The Saunders-Roe SR/A1 handled well and would have been a very agile combat aircraft, but the requirement for a high-speed water-based fighter vanished with the end of the Pacific war.

Crew: 1
Powerplant: two 1475kg (3250lb) thrust Metropolitan-Vickers Beryl MVB-1 axial-flow turbojet engines
Performance: max speed 824km/h (512mph); range 893km (554 miles); service ceiling 12,810m (42,000ft)
Dimensions: wingspan 14.02m (46ft); length 15.24m (50ft); height 5.10m (16ft 9in)
Weight: 8872kg (19,560lb)
Armament: four 20mm (1.18in) cannon

THE SAUNDERS-ROE SR/A1 was the world's first jet-fighter flying boat, and was developed in response to Specification E6/44, calling for a high-speed water-based fighter. The first of three prototypes flew for the first time on 16 July 1947, the second and third aircraft following in 1948. The second prototype had Beryl MVB-2 turbojets, while the third had fully rated Beryl Mk 1s of

1746kg (3850lb) thrust. The third aircraft, in the hands of test pilot Geoffrey Tyson, gave a spirited display at the 1948 Farnborough air show in England, leaving an impression of compactness and agility; however, the SR/A1 had been overtaken by progress and no production order was placed. The first prototype is now in the Skyfame Museum at Staverton, Gloucestershire.

SARO SR.45 PRINCESS   UK: 1952

Crew: not defined in a production standard
Powerplant: 10 2819kW (3780ehp) Bristol Proteus 600 turboprop engines – eight in coupled pairs with eight-bladed counter-rotating propellers, plus two (farthest port/starboard, outboard mounted) single Proteus engines with four-bladed propellers
Performance: cruising speed 579km/h (360mph); range 8484km (5272 miles)
Dimensions: wingspan 66.90m (219ft 6in); length 45.11m (148ft); height 17.37m (57ft)
Weight: 156,457kg (345,000lb) maximum take-off weight
Payload: up to 200 passengers

THE PRINCESS WAS THE last of the big flying boats. It was raised as an Air Ministry requirement during World War II in order to service the perceived level of postwar transatlantic traffic. However, landplane technology/reliability and the large number of airfields created during the war rendered the

requirement obsolete. Nevertheless the Princess went into development and production when three were ordered for BOAC in 1946. Still the type was out of date when the prototype flew in 1952. The BOAC

order was cancelled. The RAF were interested in operating the type at one point, but obsolescence and the design problems ensured only the prototype flew and all three examples were scrapped.

The Bristol Brabazon is often referred to as the 'white elephant' of British postwar aerospace endeavour, but the Princess has equal claim to that title.

SARO (SAUNDERS-ROE) SR.53

UK: 1957

Crew: 1
Powerplant: one 744kg (1640lb) thrust Armstrong Siddeley Viper turbojet engine and one 3630kg (8004lb) thrust de Havilland Spectre rocket motor
Performance: max speed 2135km/h (1326mph); service ceiling 18,300m (60,000ft)
Dimensions: wingspan 7.65m (25ft); length 13.72m (45ft); height 3.29m (10ft 9in)
Weight: 8618kg

FIRST FLOWN ON 16 May 1957, the Saunders-Roe SR.53 experimental interceptor employed the mixed-power concept, utilizing an Armstrong Siddeley Viper turbojet and a de Havilland Spectre rocket motor. A second aircraft, which joined the test programme in December 1957, was completely destroyed in a fatal crash on 5 June 1958 when it overran the runway and disintegrated. The accident was to bring the SR.53 programme to an end; the first aircraft was grounded and never flew again. An advanced mixed-powerplant interceptor project, the Saro SR.177, was cancelled.

The Saunders-Roe SR.53 was in effect a technology demonstrator for a more advanced mixed-powerplant interceptor, the SR.177. Both fell victim to the 1957 British defence cuts.

SARO-CIERVA SKEETER AOP.12

UK: 1948

Saro-Cierva Skeeter Mk.6 XK773 powered by a de Havilland 'Gipsy Major' 200 engine. By 1960 when production ceased, some 67 Skeeters had been built for air observation post and dual-control trainer roles.

Crew: 1/2
Powerplant: one 134kW (180hp) Blackburn Cirrus Bombardier engine
Performance: max speed 153km/h (95mph); range 300km (186 miles); service ceiling 4350m (14,250ft)
Dimensions: main rotor diameter 9.75m (32ft); length 8.67m (28ft 5in); height 3.05m (10ft)
Weight: 544kg (1200lb)
Payload: two seats

SAUNDERS-ROE MADE its name manufacturing flying boats, but after World War II the market had deteriorated to such an extent that in 1951 the company purchased the Cierva Company to branch out into the construction of rotary-winged aircraft. Its first production model, the Skeeter 1, had flown on 8 October 1948 as the experimental Cierva W.14.

By 1960 when production ceased, some 67 Skeeters had been built for the British Army, which used them in the air observation post (AOP) and dual-control trainer roles, and the RAF. Another 10 examples were built for the Federal German Army and Navy.

SAVOIA-MARCHETTI S.55

ITALY: 1924

Crew: 2
Powerplant: two 656kW (880hp) Isotta-Fraschini Asso 750-Vee-type engines
Performance: max speed 279km/h (173mph); range 3500km (2175 miles); service ceiling 5000m (16,405ft)
Dimensions: wingspan 24.00m (78ft 9in); length 16.75m (54ft 11in); height 5.00m (16ft 5in)
Weight: 8260kg (18,210lb) loaded
Armament: two 7.7mm (0.303in) machine guns; one torpedo or 2000kg (4409lb) of bombs

FLOWN FOR THE first time in 1924, the Savoia-Marchetti S.55 was, despite its ungainly appearance (an impression created mainly by its twin-catamaran hulls), one of the most advanced flying boats of the interwar years, and in the 1930s it was virtually indispensable to the operations of Italy's Regia Marina. The latter's interest in the type was initially lukewarm, mainly because of the S.55's unconventional layout, but after a civil version (the

This photograph clearly shows the distinctive catamaran hull design of the Savoia-Marchetti S.55.

S.55C) proved successful an initial order was placed in 1926. The Italian Navy took delivery of 170 S.55s. The type was subsequently made famous by the long-distance record flights it made in the 1930s, usually involving large formations of aircraft led by Italo Balbo. Specifications apply to the S.55.

SAVOIA-MARCHETTI SM.79 SPARVIERO

ITALY: 1934

Crew: 5
Powerplant: three 746kW (1000hp) Piaggio P.XI RC 40 radial engines
Performance: max speed 435km/h (270mph); range 1900km (1181 miles); service ceiling 6500m (21,325ft)
Dimensions: wingspan 21.20m (69ft 2in); length 15.62m (51ft 3in); height 4.40m (14ft 5in)
Weight: 11,300kg (24,912lb) loaded
Armament: three 12.7mm (0.50in) and one 7.7mm (0.303in) machine guns; two 450mm (17.7in) torpedoes or 1250kg (2756lb) of bombs

THE PROTOTYPE SM.79 was a fast eight-seater airliner which flew for the first time in October 1934. Production of the military SM.79 Sparviero (Sparrowhawk) began in October 1936 and was to have an uninterrupted run until June 1943, by which time 1217 aircraft had been built. The Regia Aeronautica lost no time in testing the SM.79 operationally in Spain, where it was used with considerable success. When Italy entered World War II in June 1940, SM.79s accounted for

well over half the Italian Air Force's total bomber strength. They saw continual action in the air campaign against Malta and in North Africa, becoming renowned for their high-level precision bombing; the torpedo-bomber version was active against British shipping. The SM.79B, first flown in 1936, was a twin-engined export model, the middle engine being replaced by an extensively glazed nose.

Specifications apply to the SM.79 Sparviero.

Arguably one of the finest torpedo-bombers of World War II, the SM.79 was notable for its three-engined configuration and 'hunchback' fuselage.

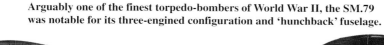

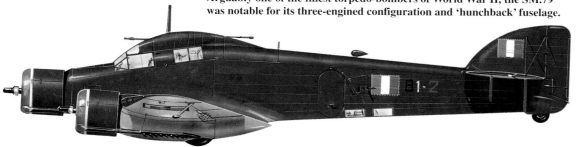

SAVOIA-MARCHETTI SM.83
The Savoia-Marchetti SM.83, which made its appearance in 1937, was a civil transport version of the SM.79, capable of carrying six to ten passengers.

SAVOIA-MARCHETTI SM.85
An all-wood, twin-engined dive-bomber, the SM.85 first flew in 1939. Only 36 examples were built. The type flew one abortive combat mission in World War II before being withdrawn.

SAVOIA-MARCHETTI SM.87
The Savoia-Marchetti SM.87 was a floatplane version of the SM.75, appearing in 1939. Only four examples were built.

SAVOIA-MARCHETTI SM.84
The Savoia-Marchetti SM.84, developed in 1940, was a twin-finned version of the SM.79, but proved to be less successful than its predecessor.

SAVOIA-MARCHETTI SM.93
Tested in 1941, the Savoia-Marchetti SM.93 was intended as a dive-bomber and ground-attack aircraft, the pilot occupying a prone position. Only one example was built.

SAVOIA-MARCHETTI SM.91/92
In 1943 Savoia-Marchetti developed two almost identical twin-boom, two-seat heavy fighters, the SM.91 and SM.92. Both were powered by DB.605A engines.

SCHEIBE SF-23A
Developed from preceding high-wing glider designs, the SF-23A two-seat single-engined design first flew in 1955, and was produced in considerable numbers thereafter.

SAVOIA-MARCHETTI SM.75 MARSUPIALE

ITALY: 1937

Crew: 4/5
Powerplant: three 560kW (750hp) Alfa Romeo AR.126 RC34 radial engines
Performance: max speed 363km/h (225mph); range 1720km (1070 miles); service ceiling 6250m (20,500ft)
Dimensions: wingspan 29.68m (97ft 5in); length 21.60m (70ft 10in); height 5.10m (16ft 9in)
Weight: 13,000kg (28,700lb) loaded
Armament/Payload: one 7.7mm (0.303in) machine gun; 18 passengers

FIRST FLOWN IN 1937, the Savoia-Marchetti SM.75 Marsupiale was a three-engined civil airliner, an enlarged version of the SM.73 transport with main landing-gear units that retracted into the wing-mounted engine nacelles. The 34 (out of a total of 94 built) aircraft in service at the time of Italy's entry into World War II in June 1940 were requisitioned as military transports and were eventually joined by 56 more new-built machines. Ten were later seized by the Germans. Some survivors remained in service until 1949.

Ten SM.75s, seized after Italy's surrender in World War II, were a welcome and much-needed addition to the German fleet.

SAVOIA-MARCHETTI SM.95

ITALY: 1943

THE LOW-WING SM.95's production and deployment were complicated by Italy's shift from the Axis to the Allied side in World War II. Two, for example, were sequestered by the Luftwaffe, but later transferred to the Italian Air Force. This retractable-undercarriage airliner was intended for transatlantic services, and production resumed after the war. The new version featured a stretched fuselage and a choice of Bristol or Pratt & Whitney engines. No more than 23 SM.95s were built, but they served with Alitalia on destinations in Europe and the Americas until 1951. Specifications apply to the SM.95.

Crew: 4
Powerplant: four Alfa Romeo 128RC.18 piston engines each rated at 641kW (860hp); or four Bristol Pegasus 48 9-cylinder radial piston engines each rated at 552kW (740hp); or four Pratt & Whitney R-1830-S1C3-G Twin Wasp 14-cylinder radial engines each rated at 783kW (1050hp)

Performance: max speed 400km/h (248mph); range 2000km (1243 miles); service ceiling 6500m (21,325ft)
Dimensions: wingspan 34.28m (112ft 5.5in); length 24.77m (81ft 3.25in); height 5.70m (18ft 8.5in)
Weight: 24,000kg (52,910lb) maximum take-off weight
Payload: up to 30 passengers

The SM.95 provided Italian national carrier Alitalia with an airliner capable of catering for that country's early postwar civil needs. This example is seen on a service to Northolt in 1948, shortly before the prevalence of Heathrow as London's premier airport.

SCOTTISH AVIATION (PRESTWICK) PIONEER

UK: 1947

Crew: 1
Powerplant: one 388kW (520hp) Alvis Leonides 501/4 9-cylinder radial engine
Performance: max speed 195km/h (121mph); range 690km (430 miles); service ceiling 7010m (23,000ft)
Dimensions: wingspan 15.16m (49ft 9in); length 10.59m (34ft 9in); height 3.12m (10ft 2.5in)
Weight: 2630kg (5800lb) loaded
Payload: four passengers

THE SCOTTISH AVIATION (Prestwick) Pioneer army cooperation and light transport aircraft first flew in 1947; however, it was not until 1950, when a more powerful engine became available, that the RAF decided to order the type. It had an astonishing STOL performance and equipped six RAF squadrons, giving magnificent service in Malaya and Aden, often flying supplies into rough airstrips only 180m (600ft) long. The last Pioneers were withdrawn in 1969, having been used in the forward air-control role in Singapore.

The Scottish Aviation Pioneer demonstrates its phenomenal climbing ability, a distinct advantage when the type had to operate from jungle clearings during the Malayan Emergency.

SEPECAT JAGUAR

INTERNATIONAL: 1968

Crew: 1
Powerplant: two 3313kg (7305lb) thrust Rolls-Royce/Turboméca Adour Mk 102 turbofan engines
Performance: max speed 1593km/h (990mph); combat radius 557km (357 miles); 11,000m (36,090ft); service ceiling 15,250m (50,000ft)
Weight: 15,500kg (34,172lb) loaded
Dimensions: wingspan 8.69m (28ft 6in); length 16.83m (55ft 2in); height 4.89m (16ft)
Armament: two 30mm (1.18in) DEFA cannon; five external hardpoints with provision for 4535kg (10,000lb) of underwing stores; two overwing-mounted AIM-9L Sidewinders for self-defence

DEVELOPED JOINTLY by the British Aircraft Corporation and Breguet (later Dassault-Breguet) under the banner of SEPECAT (Societé Européenne de Production de l'Avion Ecole de Combat et Appui Tactique), the Jaguar emerged from protracted development as a much more powerful and effective aircraft than originally envisaged. The first French version to fly, in September 1968, was the two-seat E model, 40 being ordered by the French Air Force, followed in March 1969 by the single-seat Jaguar A tactical support aircraft. Service deliveries of the E began in May 1972, with the first of 160 Jaguar As following in 1973. The British versions, known as the Jaguar S (strike) and Jaguar B (trainer), flew on 12 October 1969 and 30 August 1971, respectively, being delivered to the RAF as the Jaguar GR.Mk 1(165 examples) and T.Mk 2 (38 examples).

French Air Force Jaguars were fitted with a stand-off bomb release system consisting of two parts, the first of which was the ATLIS (Automatic Tracking Laser Illumination System) fire-control equipment contained in a pod mounted on the aircraft's centreline. The pod held a laser designator and a wide-angle TV camera the field of view of which was centred down the line of the laser beam. The assembly was stabilized and held steady regardless of aircraft movement. The second component of the system comprised a modular laser guidance unit call ARIEL, which was implanted in the nose cones of rockets, missiles or bombs.

The British Jaguars were fitted with two weapon guidance systems: a Laser Ranging and Marked Target Seeker (LRMTS) and a Navigation and Weapon Aiming Subsystem (NAVWASS), both developed by Ferranti (later Marconi-Elliott). At the time of its delivery, the system, with its E3R inertial platform and MSC920M computer, seemed remarkable, offering a single-seat fighter pilot the best possible chance of making a first-pass attack without reference to tactical air navigation (TACAN) equipment or any other external aid, which might be

SCHEUTZOW MODEL B
Two-seat light helicopter in which the blades were carried on rubber bushings, begun by Webb Scheutzow of Ohio in 1964.

SCOTTISH AVIATION TWIN PIONEER
The Scottish Aviation Twin Pioneer twin-engined STOL transport was produced in both civil and military versions, the first flying in 1955 and the second in 1957.

SEDDON BIPLANE
The Seddon biplane of 1910 was an extraordinary contraption, with two sets of biplane wings held together by an intricate maze of metal tubing. It never flew.

SEREMET WS.3/WS.4 MINICOPTER
Danish one-man 'strap-on' helicopters.

SEREMET WS.5 GYRO-GLIDER
Single-seat gyro-glider.

SEREMET WS.6 AUTOGIRO
Single-seat light autogyro with a similar airframe to the WS.5 and a 54kW (72hp) McCulloch engine.

SEVERSKY SEV-3XAR AND SEV-3M-WW
Developed as a three-seat amphibious monoplane, the SEV-3M-WW went on to set world speed records for amphibious aeroplanes in 1933 and 1935 which remain unbeaten. Powered by a Wright R-975-E2 engine, the American SEV-3XAR design sold only a few examples.

Three RAF Jaguars, each wearing a different colour scheme, in formation above the clouds. Jaguars which were deployed to Muharraq for Operation Desert Storm in 1991 were painted in 'desert pink' overall.

unavailable in wartime. Steering commands were generated in the HUD, and aircraft position (which could be updated by observations in flight) was displayed on a moving map. The equipment marked a new level of navigational accuracy for non radar-equipped single-crew aircraft. During the mid-1980s, NAVWASS was replaced in RAF and Omani Jaguars by the even better Ferranti FIN 1064, which also acted as a

weapons delivery computer. Five black boxes were replaced by one, saving 50kg (110lb) in weight, quadrupling memory and saving much space. The pilot aligned his map on the TABS (Total Avionics Briefing System) digitizing map table in the briefing room, using a cursor to plot waypoints and enter them into a tiny portable data store which could be plugged into the cockpit. TABS also supplied a hard copy on paper.

The Jaguar International, first flown in August 1976, was a version developed for the export market. It was purchased by Ecuador (12), Nigeria (18) and Oman (24), and was licence-built in India by HAL (98, including 40 delivered by BAe). A French plan to produce a carrier-borne version of the Jaguar was abandoned, the Dassault Super Etendard being ordered instead.

When Britain and France decided to contribute personnel

and material to Operation Desert Storm in 1991, it was inevitable that the Jaguar, which was capable of rapid deployment with minimal support and could function in relatively primitive conditions, should be included in the Coalition Forces' Order of Battle. The aircraft performed extremely well. It has also participated in peace-keeping operations since then.

Specifications apply to the GR.Mk 1A Jaguar.

SEVERSKY P-35
USA: 1935

Seversky P-35A of the 17th Pursuit Squadron, US Army Air Corps, which was based at Nichols Field in the Philippines in 1941.

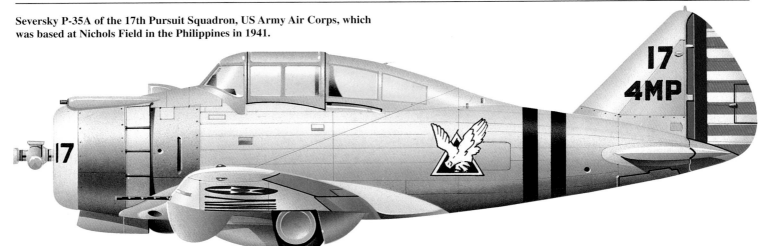

Crew: 1
Powerplant: one 709kW (950hp) Pratt & Whitney R-1830-9 14-cylinder radial engine
Performance: max speed 452km/h (281mph); range 1851km (1150 miles); service ceiling 9325m (30,600ft)

Dimensions: wingspan 10.97m (36ft); length 7.67m (25ft 2in); height 2.77m (9ft 1in)
Weight: 2855kg (6295lb) loaded
Armament: one 12.7mm (0.50in) and one 7.62mm (0.30in) machine gun

THE ARMY AIR CORPS' first modern fighter aircraft was the Seversky P-35, development of which originated in 1935. Designed by Alexander Kartveli, it first flew in August 1935 and an order for 76 production models was placed by

the Air Corps in June 1936, delivery taking place between July 1937 and August 1938. Of the 177 P-35s built, 40 were exported to Sweden and 60 were used in the Philippines at the time of the Japanese attack at the end of 1941.

SEVERSKY SEV-S2

USA: 1937

THE SEVERSKY SEV-S2, a powerful, low-wing racing monoplane, was virtually identical to the Seversky P-35, which was undergoing trials in 1937. It dominated the last three Bendix Trophy air races, beginning in 1937 when Frank Fuller won at an average speed of 415.51km/h (258.2mph), having flown for 7 hrs 54 min 26 sec. On 3 September the following year, the famous aviatrix

Jacqueline Cochran won the race at an average speed of 401.83km/h (249.6mph). The Sev-S2 was an important aircraft, the forerunner of a line that led directly to the Republic P-47 Thunderbolt.

The Seversky Sev-S2 had its origin as a powerful low-wing racing monoplane, dominating US racing circuits in the the late 1930s.

Crew: 1
Powerplant: one 746kW (1000hp) Pratt & Whitney Twin Wasp 14-cylinder radial engine
Performance: max speed 491km/h (305mph); range 1930km (1200 miles); service ceiling 9050m (29,685ft)
Dimensions: wingspan 10.97m (36ft); length 7.77m (25ft 6in); height 2.97m (9ft 9in)
Weight: 2899kg (6390lb) loaded

SHIN MEIWA PS/US-1

JAPAN: 1967

FIRST FLOWN ON 5 October 1967 as the PX-S, this long-range STOL amphibian entered service with the Japanese Maritime Self-Defence Force (JMSDF) in 1973 in its PS-1 anti-submarine form, with 20 examples being built. Procurement of the PS-1 was halted in 1980. Early in PS-1 production, the JMSDF had asked Shin Meiwa to develop an amphibious version for search-and-rescue (SAR) duties to

replace the service's Grumman UF-1 Albatross flying boats; this emerged as the US-1, which flew in prototype form on 15 October 1974. Specifications apply to the Shin Meiwa US-1A.

The Shin Meiwa PS/US-1 continued the Japanese tradition, begun in the 1930s, of building excellent flying boats. It was used for both ASW and ASR work.

Crew: 9
Powerplant: four 2604kW (3490hp) Ishikawajima-built General Electric T64-1H1-10J turboprop engines
Performance: max speed 495km/h (310mph); range 4200km (2610 miles); service ceiling 8200m (27,000ft)
Dimensions: wingspan 33.15m (108ft 9in); length 33.46m (109ft 9in); height 9.82m (32ft 3in)
Weight: 45,000kg (99,200lb) loaded
Armament: none

SHORT BIPLANE NO 1   UK: 1909

Crew: 1
Powerplant: one 22kW (30hp) Bariquand and Marre engine
Performance: figures never released
Dimensions: wingspan 12.20m (40ft); length 7.50m (24ft 7in)
Weight: 545kg (1200lb) loaded

HORACE SHORT BEGAN designing his first aircraft, the Short No 1 Biplane, in 1909; a month later he exhibited the uncovered airframe at the first Aero and Motor Show, Olympia, in London. Superficially similar to the Wright Flyer, the No 1 differed substantially in design detail. In November 1909, pioneer aviator Frank McLean made three attempts to fly it at Leysdown, but the machine stalled and was wrecked. A second biplane, built on behalf of J.T.C. Moore-Brabazon, was flown successfully in 1910.

The Short Biplane No 1 was built at the request of Frank (later Sir Francis) McLean, a noted British pioneer aviator and a leading light in the Aero Club, who became a generous patron.

SHORT MONOPLANES   UK: 1912

HORACE SHORT'S FIRST monoplane design was a 37kW (50hp) Gnome-engined aircraft, which was built in January 1912. It was a Bleriot type and was test flown by a number of naval pilots before being abandoned. The second aircraft was built to an Admiralty order and was fitted with two 52kW (70hp) Gnome engines fitted at either end of the two-man crew nacelle. Rather unfortunately the engines showered the occupants with castor oil, earning the aircraft the nickname of 'Double-Dirty'. This second monoplane was flown on several occasions, but was not accepted for naval service, although the Admiralty issued Short with a list of instructions, including folding wings, to suit it for shipboard stowage. Specifications apply to the Monoplane No 1.

Crew: 1
Powerplant: one 37kW (50hp) Gnome engine
Performance: max speed 88.6km/h (55mph)
Dimensions: wingspan 8.90m (29ft 3in); length 7.60m (25ft)
Weight: not recorded

SHORT S.41   UNITED KINGDOM: 1912

IN 1912 HORACE SHORT received an Admiralty contract to build two tractor biplanes with interchangeable landing gear so that they could be used from either land or water. The larger of the two, the S.41, flew for the first time in April 1912 and was converted into a seaplane. On 3 May, after being ferried to Weymouth for the 1912 Naval Review, it was lowered overboard from the cruiser HMS *Hibernia*

One of Short's early biplanes, the S.38, being winched aboard HMS *Hibernia*, from which Commander Samson RN made the first take-off from a moving ship in May 1912.

and flown to Portland by Commander C.R. Samson, who had piloted it on its first flight. Three days later, the same pilot flew the S.41 19km (12 miles) out to sea to rendezvous with the Fleet and escorted the flagship into Weymouth Bay. The S.41, which made many more successful flights, was the forerunner of a series of successful tractor-engined seaplanes built by Short.

Crew: 1
Powerplant: one 75kW (100hp) Gnome engine
Performance: max speed 96.6km/h (60mph); endurance 5 hrs
Dimensions: wingspan 15.30m (50ft); length 11.90m (39ft)
Weight: 680kg (1500lb) loaded

SHORT FOLDER

UK: 1913

Crew: 1
Powerplant: one 119kW (160hp) Gnome 14-cylinder rotary engine
Performance: max speed 126km/h (78mph); endurance 5 hrs
Dimensions; wingspan 17.07m (56ft); length 12.19m (40ft); height 3.66m (12ft)
Weight: 1406kg (3100lb) loaded
Armament: one 367kg (810lb) torpedo

THE SHORT BROTHERS' long-standing involvement with maritime aviation became firmly established in 1913, when Horace Short developed a mechanism that enabled a seaplane's wings to be folded back to lie alongside the fuselage. This device meant that the aircraft could easily be stored on board a warship. The Short Folder, as the new type was known, was to enter service with the Royal Naval Air Service in 1913, and on 28 July 1914 one of these aircraft, flown by Squadron Commander A.M. Longmore, air-dropped a torpedo for the first time in Britain.

No 119 was one of four Short Folders, powered by 119kW (160hp) engines, which went into service with the Royal Navy at the Isle of Grain and undertook varied technical trials.

SHORT ADMIRALTY TYPES

UK: 1914

THE SHORT ADMIRALTY (Type A) seaplanes were built specifically for operational use aboard the Royal Navy's first seaplane carriers. The first batch of six aircraft embarked on the first of these, HMS *Ark Royal*, in November 1915, and were used at Salonika, spotting for naval gunfire. A smaller class of seaplane, the Type C (the Type B was never built), took part in the famous raid on the Zeppelin sheds at Cuxhaven on Christmas Day, 1914. A development, the Type 827, was powered by a Sunbeam engine and widely used at home and overseas. One of its most famous actions was against the German cruiser *Kønigsberg* in the Rufiji river delta in 1915. Specifications apply to the Type A.

Crew: 2
Powerplant: one 101kW (135hp) Salmson engine
Performance: max speed 104.6km/h (65mph); endurance 4 hrs
Dimensions: wingspan 17.45m (57ft 3in); length 12.40m (40ft 7in)
Weight: 2080kg (4580lb) loaded
Armament: none

A Short Admiralty Type 827 seaplane being prepared for take-off at a station in German East Africa.

SHORT 184

One of three Short 184s attached to the seaplane carrier HMS *Vindex*. Seen here carrying a torpedo, this aircraft dropped bombs on the Zeppelin sheds at Tondern on 25 March 1916, without success.

FIRST FLOWN IN THE spring of 1915, the Short Type 184 was built in response to an Admiralty requirement for a torpedo-carrying and reconnaissance seaplane. It went on to give excellent service in all theatres where the Royal Navy was engaged in World War I, from Arctic waters to the Indian Ocean. The Type 184 had a famous association with the seaplane carrier *Ben-my-Chree*, a converted Isle of Man packet which operated in the Dardanelles. In August 1915, Short 184s torpedoed three enemy vessels, one torpedo being released while the aircraft was taxiing on the water, having been compelled to land with engine trouble. Freed of the weight of the torpedo, it took off and safely regained the *Ben-my-Chree*. The 184s also bombed the Maritza railway bridge on the enemy's main supply route from Germany through Bulgaria. In home waters, Short 184s carried out long-range patrols over the North Sea and English Channel.

Crew: 1
Powerplant: one 194kW (260hp) Sunbeam Maori Vee-type engine
Performance: max speed 142km/h (88mph); endurance 2 hrs 45 mins; service ceiling 2745m (9000ft)
Dimensions: wingspan 19.36m (63ft 6in); length 12.38m (40ft 7in); height 4.11m (13ft 6in)
Weight: 2433kg (5363lb) loaded
Armament: one 7.7mm (0.303in) machine gun; one 355mm (14in) torpedo

SHORT SINGAPORE

Crew: 6
Powerplant: four 417kW (560hp) Rolls-Royce Kestrel VIII 12-cylinder Vee-type engines
Performance: max speed 233km/h (145mph); range 1609km (1000 miles); service ceiling 4570m (15,000ft)
Dimensions: wingspan 27.43m (90ft); length 23.16m (76ft); height 7.19m (23ft 7in)
Weight: 12,474kg (27,500lb) loaded
Armament: three 7.7mm (0.303in) machine guns; up to 907kg (2000lb) of bombs

THE SINGAPORE SERIES of flying boats began with the Singapore I of 1926, which is famous for its circumnavigation of Africa in the hands of Sir Alan Cobham. It was followed in 1930 by the Short Singapore II, which did not go into production, but provided the basis for the Singapore III, ordered into series production for delivery from 1935. The first of four development aircraft flew in July 1934 and these were followed by 37 production Singapore IIIs, all of which had been delivered by mid-1937. Singapores equipped Nos 203, 205, 209, 210, 228, 230 and 240 Squadrons of the RAF at home and overseas. A few were still in service with Nos 203 and 205 Squadrons at the outbreak of World War II, and some were acquired by the Royal New Zealand Air Force. Specifications apply to the Singapore III.

The Short Singapore III served mainly in the Middle and Far East until mid-1941, when it was replaced by the Short Sunderland.

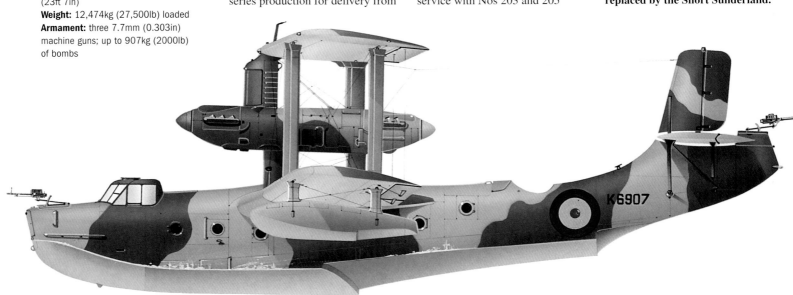

SHORT S.8 CALCUTTA

UK: 1928

Crew: 2

Powerplant: three 403kW (540hp) Bristol Jupiter XIF 9-cylinder radial engines

Performance: max speed 190km/h (118mph); range 1046km (650 miles); service ceiling 4115m (13,500ft)

Dimensions: wingspan 28.35m (93ft); length 20.35m (66ft 9in); height 7.24m (23ft 9in)

Weight: 10,206kg (22,500lb) maximum take-off weight

Payload: 15 passengers

THE CALCUTTA BIPLANE flying boat originated from an Imperial Airways requirement to service the Mediterranean legs of its services from and to India. The Calcutta itself was derived from the Short Singapore military flying boat; however, it is noteworthy for being the first stressed skin, metal-hulled flying boat. Imperial Airways operated five of the seven Calcuttas produced, and a single

The Calcutta flying boats were used on a number of British domestic services. The example pictured was written off in an accident in the Sudan circa 1932.

sale to the French government was followed by the French company Breguet licence-building four Calcuttas as the Bizerte. Further examples were built for the RAF as the S.8/8 Rangoon.

SHORT S.17 KENT AND L.17 SCYLLA

UK: 1931

Crew: 2

Powerplant: four 414kW (555hp) Bristol Jupiter XFBM nine-cylinder radial engines

Performance: max speed 220km/h (137mph); range 724km (450 miles); service ceiling 5335m (17,500ft)

Dimensions: wingspan 34.44m (113ft); length 23.90m (78ft 5in); height 8.53m (28ft)

Weight: 14,515kg (32,000lb) maximum take-off weight

Payload: 16 passengers (up to 39 on the Scylla)

THE CLOSURE OF ITALIAN and Italian colonial seaports to Imperial Airways in the Mediterranean in 1929 brought a need for a longer range flying boat, with mail carriage a priority. The Kent biplane flying boat was Short's response, and three were built. Imperial Airways also persuaded Short to produce a landplane version of the Kent – the Scylla – which was principally different in

The Scylla landplane version pictured here was rebuilt after a serious accident in 1935 and served early into World War II, when it was damaged beyond economic repair by a storm in 1940.

having a rectangular fuselage and a fixed undercarriage. The two Scylla examples stayed in service longer, and had very short RAF

careers in 1939–40. They were the last of Short's biplane designs and the last in service. Specifications apply to the Short S.17 Kent.

SHORT CHAMOIS
The Short Chamois was a much-modified Springbok, intended as a Bristol Fighter replacement. Only one aircraft was built, which flew in 1927.

SHORT STURGEON
First flown in 1927, the Short Sturgeon was a three-seat fleet reconnaissance floatplane, intended as a Fairey IIID replacement. Only two prototypes were built.

SHORT GURNARD
The Short Gurnard biplane fighter of 1929 was intended to replace the Fairey Flycatcher. Two examples were tested in landplane, floatplane and amphibian configurations.

SHORT VALETTA
This three-engined floated monoplane seaplane first flew in 1930, and after an African tour was converted to a landplane. No commercial customers were found, and the sole example was used as an Air Ministry test bed before suffering an accident.

SHORT SARAFAND
The Short Sarafand was a large six-engined biplane flying boat, powered by six engines mounted in tandem pairs. One prototype was built, flying in 1932.

SHORT R.24/31
Unofficially known as the 'Knuckleduster', the Short R.24/31 was a twin-engined maritime reconnaissance flying boat. The only prototype of the type flew in November 1933.

SHORT S.16 SCION AND S.22 SCION SENIOR

UK: 1933

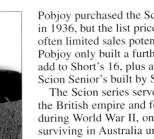

Pobjoy purchased the Scion rights in 1936, but the list price thereon often limited sales potential and Pobjoy only built a further six to add to Short's 16, plus another six Scion Senior's built by Short.

The Scion series served all over the British empire and for the RAF during World War II, one example surviving in Australia until 1965.

Specifications apply to the Short Scion 2.

Crew: 1
Powerplant: two de Havilland 67kW (90hp) Niagara III piston engines
Performance: max speed 206km/h (128mph); range 628km (390 miles); service ceiling 9144m (30,000ft)
Dimensions: wingspan 12.80m (42ft); length 9.60m (31ft 6in); height 3.16m (10ft 4.5in)
Weight: 1451kg (3200lb) maximum take-off weight
Payload: five or six passengers

Pictured is one of several Scions that went on to operate in Australia and New Guinea. One stayed in service after World War II and remained on the Australian register until 1965.

SHORT DECIDED THAT there was a need for an inexpensive light transport landplane and the high-wing Scion was developed using the small but effective Pobjoy engine. It sold in modest numbers, and the Scion was joined by the four-engined Scion Senior (capable of carrying nine passengers) in 1935. Short, however, wanted to turn its resources back to the flying-boat market. Douglas

SHORT S.23, S.30 AND S.33 EMPIRE

UK: 1936

Crew: 3/4
Powerplant: four Bristol Pegasus XC piston engines each rated at 686kW (920hp)
Performance: max speed 322km/h (200mph); range 1223km (760 miles); service ceiling 6095m (20,000ft)
Dimensions: wingspan 34.75m (114ft); length 26.82m (88ft); height 9.70m (31ft 9.75in)
Weight: 18,370kg (40,500lb) maximum take-off weight
Payload: 24 passengers or 16 sleeping berth passengers

ADVANCES IN LANDPLANE technology and the growing mail networks of its rivals spurred Imperial Airways to re-equip with a new all-metal flying-boat design, offering new levels of passenger comfort. This became the Empire series, and 28 were ordered from

the drawing board. Imperial Airways required a flying boat to service its empire trunk routes because they suffered none of the seasonal limitations imposed on landplanes by tropical and subtropical airfields. A total of 31 S.23s were built, followed by nine S.30s, which included an uprated Bristol Perseus

engine (XIIC) and structural improvements to increase gross weights; some were equipped for in-flight refuelling systems. Imperial Airways ordered three more S.33 Empire class flying boats in 1938, an order placed owing to fleet attrition. The S.33 combined the XC Pegasus engine with the S.30's

structural improvements – the engines were later updated; only two S.33s were completed due to wartime priorities. The Empire class boats were involved in a number of notable wartime events and incidents and the last one was removed from service in 1947, truly the end of an era. Specifications apply to the S.23.

Depicted here is S.23 Empire class flying boat *Caledonia*, which was used on transatlantic services as well as empire routes up until 1947.

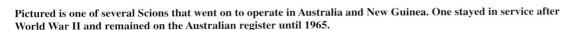

SHORT S.20 AND S.21 MAYO COMPOSITE

UK: 1937

Crew: 2
Powerplant: four 276kW (370hp) Napier Rapier VI 'H' in-line engines
Performance: max speed 333km/h (207mph); range 6112km (3798 miles); cruising speed 280km/h (174mph)
Dimensions: wingspan 22.25m (73ft); length 15.54m (51ft)
Weight: 9435kg (20,800lb) maximum take-off weight
Payload: 454kg (1000lb) of mail

DURING THE 1930s new methods of extending aircraft range were being considered, particularly in relation to the lucrative transatlantic mail-carriage business. In-flight refuelling and catapult/re-catapult launch were two such areas, but Major Robert Mayo, Imperial Airways Technical Director, inspired a third (much cheaper) means – 'pick a back' launch, where the 'carried'

aircraft would be free from the fuel penalties associated with take-off and climb to cruising altitude, enabling long range, while the ferrying aircraft could be used between ferries for other normal duties. An Empire class flying boat (designated S.21) was modified as the means of ferry, while a bespoke floatplane (S.20) was designed as the high-speed mail carrier. The

aircraft first flew independently on 5 September 1937, flew 'pick a back' on 20 January 1938 and achieved air launch/separation on 6 February 1938. Trials were a success and Imperial Airways took delivery of the Composite; however, World War II and technical advances overtook any further exploitation of the idea. Specifications apply to the S.20 Mercury.

SHORT RANGOON
The Rangoon was a military version of the Short Calcutta flying boat operated by No 203 Squadron from Basra (now in Iraq) from 1934, and was armed with bombs as well as machine guns.

SHORT S.32 AIRLINER
The S.32 four-engined, low-wing monoplane was the British Air Ministry's chosen successor to the Armstrong Whitworth Ensign. Prototype development was abandoned in 1940.

SHORT SHETLAND
First flown in 1944, the Short Shetland was a large long-range flying boat. Two prototypes only were built, the type coming too late to see service in World War II.

SHORT STURGEON
The second Short type to bear the name Sturgeon was originally designed as a twin-engine naval attack aircraft, but instead served as a fast multi-purpose gunnery training and target aircraft. It first flew in 1946.

SHORT SEALAND
A two-engined amphibious design for commercial application, the Sealand first flew in 1948, capable of carrying up to eight passengers. It was only produced in small numbers.

SHORT SB.3
The Short SB.3 was an anti-submarine warfare aircraft, powered by two Mamba turboprops and fitted with a large nose radome. It flew in 1949 and proved to be unstable in flight. The Fairey Gannet was selected in preference.

The Short-Mayo Composite Aircraft was a bold attempt to produce a combination of passenger-carrying flying boat and long-range mailplane for service on the British empire air routes.

SHORT SUNDERLAND

UK: 1937

Crew: 10
Powerplant: four 895kW (1200hp) Pratt & Whitney R-1830-90 Twin Wasp 14-cylinder air-cooled radial engines
Performance: max speed 349km/h (213mph); range 4796km (2980 miles); service ceiling 5445m (17,900m)
Dimensions: wingspan 34.36m (112ft 9in); length 26.00m (85ft 3in); height 10.52m (34ft 6in)
Weight: 27,216kg (60,000lb) loaded
Armament: 10 7.7mm (0.303in) machine guns; up to 2250kg (4960lb) of bombs, mines or depth charges on retractable racks in hull sides

THE DESIGN OF the Short Sunderland, which eventually was to become one of the RAF's longest-serving operational aircraft, was based on that of the stately Short C Empire class flying boats, operated by Imperial Airways in the 1930s. The maiden flight of the prototype took place on 16 October 1937, powered by

four 709kW (950hp) Bristol Pegasus X radial engines. The first production Sunderland Mk Is, powered by Pegasus XXII engines and with a revised nose and tail armament, were delivered to No 230 Squadron in Singapore early in June 1938. The Sunderland Mk II was fitted with Pegasus XVIII engines with two-stage super-chargers, a twin-gun dorsal turret, an improved rear turret and ASV Mk II radar. Production of the Sunderland Mk II reached 55 aircraft, these equipping Nos 119, 201, 202, 204, 228 and 230 Squadrons. The fitting of extra equipment meant that the Mk II had a much higher operating weight than the Mk I, and a new planing hull bottom was designed, with a less pronounced forward step that gave better unstick characteristics. The hull was tested on a Mk II, which in effect became the prototype of the next variant, the

Mk III, which was to be the major production model Sunderland.

The first Short-built Sunderland Mk III flew on 15 December 1941, and the parent company eventually produced 286 Mk IIIs, a further 170 being built by Blackburn Aircraft. (The latter company had already built 15 Mk Is and five Mk IIs.) One of the principal exponents of the Sunderland as an anti-submarine weapon was No 10 Squadron RAAF, which was based in Britain and which first experimented with a group of four 7.7mm (0.303in) machine guns mounted on either side of the aircraft's bow, bringing the total armament to 10 guns. The revised forward-firing armament meant that the Sunderland could lay down effective fire on a surfaced U-boat as the aircraft made its run-in, and with 10 guns the flying

A Short Sunderland of No 230 Squadron. This Coastal Command unit operated from various locations in the Mediterranean theatre in 1940–41.

boat presented a dangerous target to enemy fighters, which learned to be wary of it at an early stage of the war. The Germans gave the Sunderland the nickmane of 'Stachelschwein' (porcupine).

The Sunderland III equipped 11 RAF squadrons (including one Polish and one Free French), and was followed by the Sunderland IV, which was a larger and heavier development with 1268kW

(1700hp) Bristol Hercules engines, eight 12.7mm (0.50in) machine guns and two 20mm (0.79in) cannon. In fact, only two prototypes and eight production aircraft were built and given the name Seaford – after evaluation by Coastal and Transport Commands the Sunderland IV/Seaford was abandoned and the aircraft later converted for commercial use as the Short Solent. The last

operational Sunderland, therefore, was the Mk V, 100 of which were built by Short and 50 by Blackburn. The Mk V, which was powered by four 895kW (1200hp) Pratt & Whitney R-1830-90 Twin Wasps and carrying the ASV Mk VIc radar, made its appearance late in 1943 and continued to serve for many years after World War II, the last RAF Sunderland Vs retiring from No 205 Squadron at Changi,

Singapore, in 1959. Nineteen Sunderland Mk Vs were exported to France's Aéronavale, retiring in 1960, and 16 examples went to the Royal New Zealand Air Force, where they served until 1966.

At the end of World War II, Sunderland flying boats equipped no fewer than 28 RAF squadrons at home and overseas.

Specifications apply to the Short Sunderland Mk V.

SHORT STIRLING

UK: 1938

THE FIRST OF THE RAF's trio of four-engined heavy bombers, the other two being the Halifax and Lancaster, the Short Stirling was designed to a 1936 specification

and the aircraft was first flown as a half-scale prototype in 1938. The full-scale prototype flew in May 1939 and was damaged beyond repair on its first flight when its

undercarriage collapsed. Production deliveries of the Stirling Mk I were made to No 7 Squadron in August 1940. The Stirling Mk II, powered by Wright Cyclone engines, did

not progress beyond the prototype stage; the main bomber variant was the Mk III, which had Hercules XVI engines and which introduced the two-gun dorsal turret. Stirlings flew their last bombing mission in September 1944, having equipped 15 squadrons of RAF Bomber Command. By this time the aircraft had found a new role as a transport and glider tug (Stirling Mk IV). The last variant was the Mk V transport, which entered service in January 1945 and was unarmed.

Specifications apply to the Short Stirling Mk I.

A Short Stirling about to be bombed-up. The Stirling's wingspan was restricted because of a requirement that it should be able to fit into existing prewar hangars, and its operational ceiling suffered accordingly.

Crew: 7
Powerplant: four 1231kW (1650hp) Bristol Hercules XVI 14-cylinder radial engines
Performance: max speed 434km/h (270mph); service ceiling 5180m (17,000ft); range 3235km (2010 miles)
Dimensions: wingspan 30.20m (99ft 1in); length 26.59m (87ft 3in); height 6.93m (22ft 9in)
Weight: 31,752kg (70,000lb) loaded
Armament: eight 7.7mm (0.303in) machine guns; internal bomb load of 6350kg (14,000lb)

SHORT S.26 G (GOLDEN HIND) CLASS

UK: 1939

Crew: up to five
Powerplant: four Bristol Hercules IV or XIV 14-cylinder radial piston engines
Performance: max speed 336km/h (209mph); range 5120km (3200 miles)
Dimensions: wingspan 40.90m (134ft 4in); length 31.40m (103ft 2in); height 11.45m (37ft 7in)
Weight: 33,800kg (74,500lb)
Payload: 40 passengers

FOLLOWING ON FROM the Empire class flying boats, Short was keen to explore the limits of the flying-boat design, while also investing in the S.32 land airliner. A number of drag and stability improvements were proved and then embodied in

Only *Golden Hind* herself (pictured) survived World War II, spending a brief period plying Mediterranean services before being scrapped in 1947.

the enlarged version of the Empire boat named the G, or Golden Hind, class and featuring improved power and range. The intention for this design (of which three were ordered by Imperial Airways) was to implement a regular scheduled service across the Atlantic in association with Pan Am. However, World War II intervened and the three G boats were sequestered by the RAF and converted for ASW/reconnaissance use. In late 1941 the two surviving G boats were returned to civil duties, but only one example survived the war. After a brief operational period the aircraft fell into disuse.

SHORT S.25V SANDRINGHAM AND HYTHE, AND S.45 SOLENT   UK: 1945

Crew: up to five
Powerplant: four 1260kW (1690hp)
Bristol Hercules 637 14-cylinder radial
piston engines
Performance: max speed 439km/h
(272mph); range 2897km (1800 miles);
service ceiling 5180m (17,000ft)
Dimensions: wingspan 34.38m (112ft
9.5in); wing area 156.7m² (1687 sq ft);
length 26.72m (87ft 8in); height 10.44m
(34ft 3in)
Weight: 35,381kg (78,000lb) maximum
take-off weight
Payload: up to 44 passengers

THE S.25 SUNDERLAND flying boat
was a candidate for passenger and
freight conversion, even in wartime,
and early conversions date from
1942. In late 1945, with the war
over, civil airliners were quickly
needed, resulting in a comprehensive
conversion, the S.25V Sandringham.
The need for further conversions
by BOAC resulted in a further
improved version, the Hythe.
Short's last flying-boat airliner was
the Solent, itself derived from an
enlarged Sunderland design named

the Seaford. The Solent first flew
in August 1946 and was ordered by
BOAC. A total of 22 Solents were
built in four marques and examples
remained in service until 1960;
Sandringhams remained operational
into the 1970s. Specifications
apply to the S.45 Solent 2.

After BOAC's exit from the flying-boat market in late 1950, this S.45 Solent was taken over by Aquila Airways, which continued to operate flying boats until 1958.

SHORT SPERRIN   UK: 1951

Crew: 5
Powerplant: four 2944kg (6500lb) thrust
Rolls-Royce Avon RA.3 turbojet engines
Performance: max speed 913km/h
(564mph); range 6050km (3760 miles);
service ceiling 13,725m (45,000ft)
Dimensions: wingspan 33.20m (109ft);
length 31.42m (102ft 2.5in); height
8.69m (28ft 6.25in)
Weight: 52,200lb (115,000lb)
Armament: one 4530kg (10,000lb)
MC.Mk 1 special store (Blue Danube)

DESIGNED TO Specification B.14/46,
the Short Sperrin was intended as
an insurance against failure of the
Vickers Valiant, the first of the
RAF's V-bombers. Two prototypes
were built, the first flying on 10
August 1951 and used to test new
high-altitude radar navigation and

The Short Sperrin underwent much development work on behalf of the RAF's V-Force, in the event of failure of the Vickers Valiant.

bombing equipment that was to be
incorporated in the V-bombers.
The second aircraft, which flew in
August 1952, was used to test

aerodynamic bomb shapes in
connection with the development
of Britain's first atomic bomb, the
MC.Mk 1 'Blue Danube'.

SHORT SC.1

Crew: 1
Powerplant: four 965kg (2130lb) thrust Rolls-Royce RB.108 lift engines and one RB.108 cruise engine
Performance: max speed 396km/h (246mph); range 240km (150 miles)
Dimensions: wingspan 7.16m (23ft 6in); length 9.10m (29ft 10in)
Weight: 3650kg (8050lb) loaded

IN 1953, THE Ministry of Supply issued Specification ER.143 for a research aircraft which could take off vertically by jet lift, then accelerate forward into normal cruising flight. The result was the Short SC.1, which was powered by four RB.108 lift engines vertically mounted on gimbals in the centre fuselage and one RB.108 cruise engine in the rear for forward flight. The SC.1 was designed to study hover, transition and low-speed flight, and had a fixed landing gear. Bleeds from the four lift engines powered nose, tail and wing-tip reaction jets for control at low speeds. The first conventional flight was made on 2 April 1957; first tethered vertical flight was on 26 May 1958; first free vertical flight was on 25 October 1958; and the first transition was on 6 April 1960. The SC.1 appeared at the Farnborough air show in 1960 and Paris air show in 1961 (for the latter it flew the English Channel both ways). Two test aircraft were built, the second of which crashed on 2 October 1963 due to a controls malfunction, killing the pilot. It was rebuilt and the two aircraft continued to fly until 1967.

The Short SC.1 was a very important milestone in the development of the Harrier V/STOL aircraft. Two prototypes were built, one of which crashed but was later rebuilt.

SHORT SC.7 SKYVAN/SKYLINER

THE SKYVAN HAD its origins in the Miles Aerovan, the concept of which was taken on by Short in a radically overhauled design. The high aspect ratio SC.7 Skyvan prototype flew with Continental piston engines, but it was decided that turboprop power was required, so the prototype and early production (Series 2) examples were ultimately fitted with Astazou II turboprops. These engines were not ideal for hot-and-high conditions or American customers, however, so the Series 3 was upgraded to the specified Garrett type. In all, 149 Skyvans were built and sold to commercial freight/passenger 'bush' operators and military/paramilitary

operators up until 1986. The Skyliner was a dedicated passenger-carrying version. Specifications apply to the Skyvan Series 3.

Crew: 2
Powerplant: two 533kW (715shp) Garrett TPE331-201 turboprop engines
Performance: max cruising speed 325km/h (202mph); max range with fuel reserves 1033km (642 miles); service ceiling 6860m (22,500ft)
Dimensions: wingspan 19.79m (64ft 11in); length 12.22m (40ft 1in); height 4.60m (15ft 1in)
Weight: 5670kg (12,500lb) maximum take-off weight
Payload: up to 19 passengers or 2086kg (4600lb) of freight

This sole example of the Skyvan sold to the Sharjah Amiri Air Wing was delivered in 1986. It was also the last Skyvan build completed.

SHORT 330

UK: 1974

Crew: 2/3
Powerplant: two 893kW (1198shp) Pratt & Whitney Canada T101-CP-100 (PT6A-45R) turboprop engines
Performance: max cruising speed 352km/h (218mph); range 1239km (770 miles); service ceiling 6095m (20,000ft)
Dimensions: wingspan 22.76m (74ft 8in); length 17.69m (58ft 0.5in); height 4.95m (16ft 3in)
Weight: 11,566kg (25,500lb) maximum take-off weight
Payload: up to 30 troops

THE SHORT 330 WAS developed from the SC.7 Skyvan, with a fuselage stretched to accommodate 30 passengers while retaining the Skyvan's twin tail fin, but including a semi-retractable under-carriage. The Short 330 was aimed at regional, commuter and bush operators that required a simple, unpressurized, reliable aircraft. Like the Skyvan, the 330 attracted a combination of commercial and military/paramilitary customers,

Sales of the Short 330 to the United States (commercial and military) matched those made into the UK domestic market. Commuter airline Golden West was among the American customers.

including the US Air Force/Army, which purchased 34 C-23 Sherpa examples from a total of 141 Short 330s built.

Specifications apply to the Short C-23A Sherpa.

SHORT 360

UK: 1981

Crew: 2
Powerplant: two Pratt & Whitney Canada PT6A-67R turboprop engines each rated at 1062kW (1424shp)
Performance: max cruising speed 400km/h (248mph); range 745km (463 miles)
Dimensions: wingspan 22.80m (74ft 9.5in); wing area 42.2 m² (454.00 sq ft); length 21.58m (70ft 9.5in); height 7.26m (23ft 10in)
Weight: 12,292kg (27,100lb) maximum take-off weight
Payload: up to 36 passengers

THE SHORT 360 WAS designed as an enlarged successor to the Short 330, but embodying a number of design alterations. An extra six seats (in two rows) were accommodated by stretching the cabin and deleting the 330's rear loading ramp, and the tail arrangement was changed

The Short 360 found a niche in a commuter and island/isolated community services role, both as a passenger and freighter aircraft.

to a conventional single fin. Like its predecessors, the 360 was aimed at regional and commuter operators, and it sold a creditable 164 examples in that market up until 1991, although it never

realized its full potential in the American market. Many examples continue in service, some with their original operators.

Specifications apply to the Short 300 Series.

SHORT-BRISTOW CRUSADER

Crew: 1
Powerplant: one air-cooled 604kW
(810hp) Bristol Mercury 9-cylinder radial
engine
Performance: max speed 435km/h
(270mph)
Dimensions: wingspan 8.07m (26ft 6in);
length 7.62m (25ft)
Weight: 1227kg (2712lb) maximum
take-off weight
Payload: one person

PUBLIC PRESSURE RESULTED in the
British government's return to
funding Schneider trophy entries
from the public purse, and the
1927 entries were sponsored
around two different engine types.
The Bristol Mercury engine design
was placed under the guidance of
Colonel W.A. Bristow, who subsequently subcontracted airframe
detail design of this low-wing,
wooden racing floatplane to Short.
The Crusader was not as fast as its
Supermarine S.5 counterparts that
won the race in Italy, but it travelled
to the event as a back-up aircraft.
Unfortunately, it was written off in
an accident. Although not a
landmark aircraft, the Crusader
was important in developing the
Mercury engine, a key component
of 1930s British flying boats.

**The development of racing aircraft
such as the Crusader aided the
technological advancement of both
military and commercial aviaton.**

SIEBEL FH 104 HALLORE

The prototype Siebel Fh 104 Hallore light transport, D-IMCH. One Hallore was used as Feldmarschall Kesselring's personal transport.

IN 1934 HANS KLEMM set up a
new aircraft factory at Halle for the
production of all-metal military
aircraft, including the Klemm Kl
104 five-seat light transport. When
the factory was handed over to the
Siebel concern in 1937, the aircraft
became known as the Siebel Fh
104 Hallore. Production ceased in
1942 after only 46 had been built,
most being used by the Luftwaffe
on communication and liaison duty.

Crew: 2
Powerplant: two 209kW (280hp) Hirth HM
508D inverted-Vee engines
Performance: max speed 350km/h
(217mph); range 920km (570 miles);
service ceiling 6600m (21,648ft)

Dimensions: wingspan 12.06m
(39ft 6.75in); length 9.50m (31ft 2in);
height 2.64m (8ft)
Weight: 5600kg (12,348lb) loaded
Payload: five passengers

SIEBEL SI 204

GERMANY: 1941

USED IN SUBSTANTIAL numbers by the Luftwaffe as a light communications aircraft and crew trainer, the Siebel Si 204 was essentially a scaled-up Fh 104. Two versions were produced, the Si 104A and Si 104D, the first of these flying in 1941. The Si 204A was intended as a feederliner for Lufthansa, but only a few had been produced before production switched to the militarized Si 204D. The majority

This Siebel Si 204D was used by 2 Staffel, Nachtschlachtgruppe 4, which was based at Malacky in Slovakia in November 1944.

of these were built at the Hanriot factory in France and the Aero factory in Czechoslovakia, and production continued in both countries for several years after World War II. Specifications apply to the Siebel Si 204D.

Crew: 2/3
Powerplant: two 269kW (360hp) Argus As 410 engines
Performance: max speed 364 km/h (226mph); range 1800km (1118 miles); service ceiling 7500m (24,600ft)
Dimensions: wingspan 21.33m (69ft 11.75in); length 11.95m (39ft 2.5in); height 4.25m (13ft 11in)
Weight: 5600kg (12,348lb) loaded
Armament: one 7.5mm (0.29in) machine gun

SIEMENS-SCHUCKERT SSW D.III

GERMANY: 1917

Crew: 1
Powerplant: one 149kW (200hp) Siemens-Halske Sh.IIIa rotary engine
Performance: max speed 180km/h (112mph); endurance 2 hrs; service ceiling 8000m (26,245ft)
Dimensions: wingspan 8.43m (27ft 8in); length 5.70m (18ft 8in); height 2.80m (9ft 2in)
Weight: 725kg (1598lb) loaded
Armament: two 7.92mm (0.31in) machine guns

BELIEVED BY SOME German pilots to be the best fighter at the front in the summer of 1918, the Siemens-Schuckert SSW D.III was a stubby, compact little biplane of wooden construction. During flight trials in October 1917, the prototype reached a level speed of 180km/h (112mph) and climbed to 5974m (19,600ft) in less than 20 minutes, a performance which justified its being ordered into immediate

production for use in World War I. The first batch of 30 SSW D.III scouts was delivered for operational trials in January 1918, and a further 30 aircraft were ordered in February. Beginning in late April, 41 examples were allocated to operational units on the Western Front, most of these going to JG 2. Small orders were placed for two further developments, the SSW D.IV and SSW D.V.

A fine fighter aircraft, the SSW D.III might have made a greater impact on the air war in 1918 had it not been for constant trouble with its rotary engine, which led to the type's temporary withdrawal.

SIKORSKY ILYA MUROMETZ

RUSSIA: 1914

The world's first four-engined bomber, the Ilya Murometz carried out a significant bombing campaign against German targets before the Imperial Russian Air Service ceased to exist in 1918.

SIKORSKY USED THE basic Bolshoi Bal'tisky design to build a larger aircraft, the Ilya Murometz, 10 of which were ordered for military use after some very successful proving flights, including one in which the aircraft lifted 16 passengers and a dog to an altitude of 2000m (6560ft) and flew for five hours at 100km/h (62mph) over Moscow. With the outbreak of World War I the order was increased to 80 aircraft. Several variants were produced, the Type V being the first to be conceived from the outset as a bomber. The bombers were concentrated into a special unit named the Eskadra Vozdushnykh Korablei (Squadron of Flying Ships), which became operational in February 1915. Between then and the October Revolution of 1917 the huge machines made over 400 raids on targets in Germany and Lithuania, operating from Vinnitza in Poland. Only one aircraft was lost to enemy action; most of the others were destroyed on the ground to prevent their capture by the Germans in the wake of the armistice concluded with the Bolsheviks in 1918.

Specifications apply to the Ilya Murometz Type V.

Crew: 4–7
Powerplant: four 112kW (150hp) Sunbeam 8-cylinder in-line engines
Performance: max speed 121km/h (75mph); endurance 5 hrs; service ceiling 3000m (9840ft)
Dimensions: wingspan 29.80m (97ft 9in); length 17.10m (56ft 1in); height 4.72m (15ft 6in)
Weight: 4589kg (10,117lb) loaded
Armament: three-seven 7.62mm (0.30in) machine guns; 522kg (1150lb) of bombs

SIKORSKY S-38

USA: 1928

Before Russian-born Igor Sikorsky's name became synonymous with helicopter design, the S-39 biplane of 1928 was his first commercial success.

Crew: 2
Powerplant: two 313kW (420hp) Pratt & Whitney Wasp 9-cylinder radial engines
Performance: max speed 200km/h (124mph); cruising speed 176km/h (109mph); range 958km (595 miles)
Dimensions: wingspan 21.84m (71ft 8in); length 12.27m (40ft 3in); height 4.22m (13ft 10in)
Weight: 4754kg (10,480lb) maximum take-off weight
Payload: 10 passengers

THE WOODEN-FRAMED S-38 was a Duralumin alloy covered biplane with a twin-boom tail arrangement. There were three production versions, the S-38A, the increased fuel/range S-38B and the S-38C, which had a shorter range but could accommodate 12 passengers. Pan American operated 30 S-38s. The type also saw service with the US military as the C-6, XRS-2 and RS-3. Specifications apply to S-38B.

SIKORSKY S-42

USA: 1934

SIKORSKY S-56 (H-37 MOJAVE AND HR2S)
The S-56 was the first Sikorsky twin-engined helicopter, designed to provide the US Marine Corps with a large assault helicopter. Beginning in July 1956, some 60 HR2S and 94 H-37A Mojave examples for the US Army were delivered.

SIKORSKY S-59
Experimental turbine-powered helicopter developed from the YH-18B and first flown on 24 July 1953.

SIKORSKY S-60 SKYCRANE AND S-64 (H-54 TARHE)
The S-60 Skycrane was a 60-seat troop transport development of the S-56 which first flew on 25 March 1959. An enlarged version known as the S-64, with a six-bladed rotor driven by two 3020kW (4050shp) JFTD-12A turboshafts, flew on 9 May 1962. In June 1963 the US Army ordered the first six of 60 S-64A models as the CH-54A Tarhe; 10 re-engined CH-54Bs followed.

SIKORSKY S-62
First flying on 22 May 1958, about 50 amphibious commercial S-62s were built and 99 HH-52A SAR versions were delivered to the US Coast Guard from 1963. Others went to the Indian Air Force, the Thai Police and JASDF.

SIKORSKY S-67
In 1964 the S-66 entry in the Advanced Aerial Fire Support System (AAFSS) competition lost out to the Lockheed AH-56A Cheyenne, but Sikorsky went on to develop the S-67 attack helicopter, capable of carrying up to 3629kg (8000lb) of ordnance.

THE S-42 WAS SIKORSKY'S response to a 1931 Pan American Airways requirement for a long-range flying boat. It was appreciably more modern than its predecessors, with an all-metal construction and four engines mounted on the leading edge of a parasol wing. The S-42 was largely used for services in the Americas and Pacific, but it was also used to inaugurate the joint

Pan American Airlines bought 10 S-42s and was the only customer. The type played a key role in the airline's development of its Pacific network before World War II.

New York–Bermuda service. Ten S-42s were built in the United States, but all examples were scrapped by 1946. Specifications apply to the S-42B.

Crew: 4
Powerplant: four 559kW (750hp) Pratt & Whitney Hornet S1EG radial piston engines
Performance: max speed 302km/h (187.5mph); range 1931km (1200 miles)
Dimensions: wingspan 34.80m (114ft 2in); length 21.08m (69ft 2in); height 5.28m (17ft 4in)
Weight: 19,051kg (42,000lb) maximum take-off weight
Payload: up to 32 passengers

SIKORSKY VS-300, HO2S, R-4, R-5, R-6

USA: 1942

IGOR SIKORSKY BUILT his first rotary-wing aircraft in 1909, but the 18kW (25hp) Anzani-powered machine failed to lift off the ground. Sikorsky's second machine built in 1910 was equally unsuccessful, and he turned his attention to fixed-wing designs. It was not until 1939, when he was engineering manager of Vought Sikorsky in the United States, that he began construction of a new helicopter, the VS-300, which made its first free flight on 13 May 1940. The VS-316A (XR-4) two-seat version made its first flight on 14 January 1942 and became the first helicopter in the world to enter series production. Some 30 pre-production YR-4 models powered by the 134kW (180hp) Warner R-500s were followed by 100 R-4B

Trials with various auxiliary rotors proved unsuccessful, but the VS-300 benefited from an anti-torque rotor and the resulting VS-316A (XR-4).

examples. Some 193 VS-316B/XR-6 versions were built for the US Army Air Force (R-6A), US Navy (HO2S-1) and RAF (Hoverfly Mk II). The VS-337 (XR-5) first flew on 18 August 1943; 64 examples were produced. Specifications apply to the Sikorsky R-4.

Crew: 2
Powerplant: one 149kW (200hp) Warner R-550-3 7-cylinder radial air-cooled engine
Performance: max speed 132km/h (82mph) at sea level; combat radius 370km (230 miles); service ceiling 2440m (8000ft)
Dimensions: main rotor diameter 11.58m (38ft); length 10.80m (35ft 5in); height 3.78m (12ft 5in)
Weight: 912kg (2010lb)
Payload: one passenger

SIKORSKY S-51

USA: 1946

Of 100 R-4B utility helicopters built, the US Navy received 24 HNS-1 versions, the first in 1942, and units of the US Coast Guard used the HNS-1 in the air-sea rescue role.

Crew: 1
Powerplant: one 336kW (450hp) Pratt & Whitney R-985-AN-7 9-cylinder radial air-cooled engine
Performance: max speed 167km/h (104mph); range 451km (280 miles); service ceiling 4115m (13,500ft)
Dimensions: main rotor diameter 14.94m (49ft); length 13.70m (44ft 11.5in); height 3.90m (12ft 11in)
Weight: 2494kg (5500lb) fully loaded
Payload: three passengers

ESSENTIALLY A REDESIGN of the VS-316B (R-6), this four-seat utility helicopter first flew on 16 February 1946. A total of 379 examples were built between 1946 and 1951, including 66 H-5 models for the US Army Air Force Air Rescue Service. Westland built 139 examples under licence in Britain as the Dragonfly. Specifications apply to the Sikorsky S-51.

SIKORSKY S-55 (H-19 CHICKASAW)

USA: 1949

THE S-55 WAS A 12-seat utility helicopter for civil and military use, similar in most respects to the layout of final models of the H-5 series. It was first flown on 7 November 1949, and no fewer than 1026 production examples were built for the US military. The 410–448kW (550–600hp) Wright R-1340/-57 engine was located in the nose so that the long extension shaft could be carried straight up to

the main three-blade rotor-gear drive, thus leaving the main cabin below the flight deck free for occupancy by troops or freight. In 1951 the US Air Force placed its first order for 50 H-19As and a further 270 522kW (700hp) R-1300-3 engined H-19Bs followed.

CH-19D of 357 Squadron of the Royal Hellenic Air Force at Elefsis, Greece, in May 1968.

The US Air Force used its H-19s principally to equip MATS Air Rescue squadrons, for which they were designated SH-19. From 1952 the US Army received 72 H-19Cs and 338 H-19D Chickasaws, equivalent to the H-19A and H-19B models, respectively. From April 1950 the US Navy placed orders for 10 HO4S-1 and 61 HO4S-3 versions. In April 1952 deliveries of 151 HRS-1/2 troop and assault transport examples

were made and 84 HRS-3 models with more powerful R-1300-3 engines followed. The H-19 was used in transport, troop support, engagement and rescue roles, and saw combat in Korea and Vietnam. Westland produced the turbine-powered Whirlwind development (547 examples) in Britain, and SNCA du Sud Est in France also undertook licenced production. Specifications apply to the Sikorsky H-19/HO4S-1/HRS-1.

Crew: 2
Powerplant: one Pratt & Whitney R1340 S1H2 Wasp radial engine rated at 410kW (550hp) at 2440m (8000ft)
Performance: max speed 178km/h (110mph); combat radius 758km (470 miles); service ceiling 2745m (9000ft)
Dimensions: main rotor diameter 16.10m (52ft 9in); length 12.70m (41ft 8.5in); height 4.46m (14ft 8in)
Weight: 1940kg (4267lb)
Payload: 8-10 passengers or up to eight stretchers

SIKORSKY S-58 (HSS-1, HUS-1 AND H-34)   USA: 1954

The HSS-1 Seabat entered anti-submarine squadron service in August 1955; the HSS-1N (SH-34J) was developed later for night operations.

THE S-58 WAS THE result of a US Navy requirement to overcome the range and offensive payload limitations of the Sikorsky ASW HO4S version of the S-55. The prototype, which flew on 8 March 1954, was powered by an 1137kW (1525hp) Wright (Lycoming-built) R-1820 engine. The angled front-fuselage

mounting was retained, but the fuselage was a complete redesign, as were the transmission system and the four-blade main and tail rotors. A tail-wheel replaced the H-19's nose-wheel. On 20 September 1954, production of HSS-1 Seabat (later SH-34G) began, and the first examples entered squadron service

in August 1955. On 15 October 1954, the US Marine Corps ordered the HUS-1 Seahorse (UH-34D); this model entered service in February 1957. The US Army received several hundred H-34A/B and H-34C Choctaws powered by 1063kW (1425hp) R-1820-84 engines. Westland produced the turbine-powered Wessex version and a few S-58B/D civil passenger and cargo transport versions were built. Production ended in January 1970. Specifications apply to the S-58.

Crew: 1
Powerplant: one 1137kW (1525hp) Wright Cyclone R-1820-84 9-cylinder radial engine
Performance: max speed 158km/h (98mph); combat radius 450km (280 miles); service ceiling 2740m (9000ft)
Dimensions: main rotor diameter 17.07m (56ft); length 14.25m (46ft 9in); height 4.36m (14ft 3.5in)
Weight: 3515kg (7750lb)
Payload: 16-18 passengers or up to eight stretchers

SIKORSKY S-61B-1 (SH-3A SEA KING)   USA: 1959

Crew: 2-4
Powerplant: (SH-2A) two 932kW (1250shp) General Electric T58-GE-8/8B turboshaft engines
Performance: max speed 267km/h (166mph); combat radius 1005km (625 miles); service ceiling 4480m (14,700ft)
Dimensions: main rotor diameter 18.90m (62ft); length 22.15m (72ft 8in); height 5.13m (16ft 10in)
Weight: 5601kg (12,350lb)
Payload: up to 381kg (840lb) of disposable stores

EXPERIENCE WITH THE H-34 Seabat exposed its limitations in the ASW role, so on 23 September 1957 Sikorsky was awarded a contract to develop an all-weather amphibious helicopter which could combine the hunter and killer roles

An SH-3A Sea King of HS-6 lifts off from the flight deck of the amphibious assault ship USS *New Orleans* in the Pacific Ocean in July 1975, during an *Apollo* spacecraft recovery mission.

SIKORSKY S-69
This two-seat research helicopter was powered by a 1360kW (1825shp) P&WC PT6T-3 Turbo Twin Pac and two 13.35kN (3000lb st) P&W J60-P-3A turbojets (mounted in pods on the sides of the fuselage) to test the Advancing Blade Concept (ABC) rotor system.

SIKORSKY S-76 SPIRIT/H-76 EAGLE
New twin-turbine general-purpose all-weather commercial and military helicopter with accommodation for 12 passengers, which first flew on 13 March 1977.

SIKORSKY S-92 HELIBUS
Originally conceived as an outgrowth of the S-70 and appearing in 1995, this civil multi-purpose, twin-engined helicopter is partnered in production with Mitsubishi in Japan, AIDC in Taiwan, EMBRAER in Brazil, Gamesa in Spain and Jingdexzhen in China.

SILVERCRAFT SH-4A
Italian light agricultural helicopter developed from the SIAI-Marchetti SH-4.

SIMMERING-GRAZ-PAUKER M.222
In 1964, the Austrian Simmering-Graz-Pauker company produced a prototype four-seat light aircraft, the SGP M.222. Plans for quantity production were abandoned.

SINO SWEARINGEN SJ30
This light, twin-engined business jet has been jointly developed in the USA and Taiwan. The SJ30 has undergone a number of design revisions after first flying in 1991. Orders exceed 170 for this six-passenger corporate jet.

within a single airframe. The machine's design incorporated a five-bladed rotor, rugged fuselage, a two-man cockpit and a cabin for two sensor operators and their ASW equipment, plus provision for dipping sonar, search radar and two torpedoes or depth charges.

The resulting S-61 prototype (YHSS-2) flew on 11 March 1959. Some 245 SH-3As were built. A prototype and 73 production

examples of the SH-3D with 1044kW (1400shp) T58-GE-10 engines and upgraded sonar and radar equipment followed. Some 103 SH-3A and two SH-3D models were progressively converted to SH-3G general-purpose rescue platforms and transports by removing the ASW equipment and installing 15 canvas seats and long-range fuel tanks. In all, 116 SH-3s were converted to SH-3H

standard with the installation of upgraded sonar and radar and MAD equipment to perform not only the inner-zone ASW mission, but also planeguard, surface surveillance and surface targeting missions. The S-61 has also been widely built under licence in Italy by Agusta, in Japan by Mitsubishi, and in Britain by Westland. In Canada, United Aircraft assembled 37 CHSS-2 helicopters after the

supply of four Sikorsky-built aircraft for the CAF, and Argentina, Brazil, Denmark, Malaysia and Spain have also acquired S-61s. The S-61L and S-61N commercial transports are basically similar to the S-61A and S-61B, while the S-61R amphibious transport helicopter is based on the SH-3A.

Specifications apply to the S-61 (SH-3H Sea King).

SIKORSKY S-65 (CH-53A/RH-53A SEA STALLION, HH-53B/C SUPER JOLLY) AND S-80 USA:1964

Some 139 CH-53A Sea Stallion assault transports were built, and the US Air Force received 8 HH-53B Super Jolly SAR versions with refuelling probe and 20 CH-53C Super Jolly aircraft without the probe. Some 11 S-80M-1 Sea Dragon export derivatives of the MH-53E were built for the JMSDF.

Crew: 3
Powerplant: three 3266kW (4380shp) GE T64-GE-416 turboshaft engines
Performance: max speed 315km/h (196mph); combat radius 2076km (1290 miles); service ceiling 5640m (18,500ft)
Dimensions: main rotor diameter 24.08m (79ft); length: 22.35m (73ft 4in); height 7.60m (24ft 11in)
Weight: 33,340kg (73,500lb)
Payload: 55 troops or up to 16,329kg (36,000lb) of freight or vehicles

THE S-65 WAS built to meet a formal HH(X) requirement for a ship-based heavy-lift helicopter in 1962. It utilized the transmission system of the S-64, the six-bladed main rotor and tail rotor of the CH-37, and a scaled-up version of the CH-3 airframe. The first of two YCH-53A prototypes flew on 14 October 1964 and the production assault helicopter was selected for delivery as the CH-53A Sea Stallion to the

US Marine Corps. In all, 139 were built and 15 were converted to RH-53A minesweeper versions for the US Navy, followed by 30 up-engined RH-53Ds. The US Air Force received eight HH-53B Super Jolly SAR versions, 20 CH-53C and 44 HH-53C SAR aircraft, while the Marine Corps received 124 improved assault CH-53D Sea Stallions and 30 up-engined RH-53Ds. Several HH-53H and

MH-53H/HH-53B/Cs have been upgraded to Pave Low III standard and fitted with an in-flight refuelling probe. All surviving frontline helicopters have since been upgraded to MH-53M Pave Low IV standard. Some 177 three-engined CH-53E Super Stallions have been built for the USMC and US Navy, while 56 MH-53E Sea Dragon minesweepers have been received by the US Navy.

SIKORSKY MODEL S-70A (H-60) BLACK HAWK USA: 1974

Designed to carry 11 fully equipped troops and a payload of more than 4536kg (10,000lb), many versions of the UH-60A Black Hawk have been delivered to the American military and overseas customers.

IN 1965 THE US ARMY identified a need to replace the Bell UH-1, but it was not until August 1972 and presentation of the Utility Tactical Transport Aircraft System (UTTAS) that a formal requirement calling for a new helicopter with the same capacity as the UH-1 but better survivability and performance was made known. Sikorsky and Boeing-Vertol were selected to build three prototypes each. Sikorsky's first

YUH-60A flew on 17 October 1974 and, after a fly-off evaluation against the YUH-61A in December 1976, Sikorsky's design was declared the winner. The UH-60A Black Hawk production model first flew in October 1978; deliveries began in June 1979. By early 1986 well in excess of 600 examples of 1107 ordered had been delivered in several versions. Specifications apply to the UH-60A Black Hawk.

Crew: 3
Powerplant: two General Electric T700-GE-700 turboshaft engines each rated at 1164kW (1560shp)
Performance: max speed 296km/h (184mph); combat radius 2220km (1380 miles); service ceiling 5790m (19,000ft)
Dimensions: main rotor diameter 16.36m (53ft 8in); length 15.26m (50ft 0.75in); height 5.13m (16ft 10in)
Weight: 9979kg (22,000lb)
Payload: over 4536kg (10,000lb)

SIKORSKY MODEL S-70B SH-60 SEAHAWK USA: 1979

Crew: 3
Powerplant: two General Electric T700-GE-401 or 401C turboshaft engines each rated at 1260kW (1690shp) or 1417kW (1900shp) respectively
Performance: max speed 234km/h (145mph); range 704km (437 miles); service ceiling 4511m (14,800ft)
Dimensions: main rotor diameter 16.36m (53ft 8in); length 15.26m (50ft 0.75in); height 5.18m (17ft)
Weight: 9182kg (20,244lb)
Armament: two Mk 46 torpedoes or Kongsberg Penguin Mk 2 anti-ship missiles

FIRST FLOWN IN PROTOTYPE form on 12 December 1979, the SH-60B is an advanced LAMPS (Light Airborne Multi-Purpose System) Mk III helicopter. Specifications apply to H-60 Seahawk.

Some 181 SH-60B helicopters were ordered by the US Navy for use as carrier-borne inner zone ASW defence and SAR. The majority of these have been converted to SH-60J standard.

SIPA S.12
First flown in 1951, the SIPA S.12 trainer was derived from the Arado Ar 396, and served with the Armée de l'Air in large numbers. A variant, the SIPA 121, was used in the light attack role in Algeria.

SIPA 300
The SIPA 300 was a tandem two-seat ab initio jet trainer first flown on 4 September 1954. It was powered by a 159kg (350lb st) Turboméca Palas, as the Sipa 200.

SIPA S.1100
First flown in 1958, the SIPA S.1100 was a twin-engined counter-insurgency aircraft, designed for operations in Algeria. The first of two prototypes flew in 1958.

SIPA ANTILOPE
First flown on 7 November 1962, the SIPA Antilope was a low-wing touring monoplane, seating four people. It was powered by a 504kW (675hp) Turboméca Astazou turboprop.

SIPAVIA S.261 ANJOU
First flown in July 1959, the Sipavia S.261 Anjou was a twin-engined, four-seat cabin monoplane, intended to compete with America's light twins.

SIVEL SRL SD-27 AND SD-28
A two-seat, single-engined Italian light training/touring aeroplane dating from 1992.

SKANDINAVSK AERO INDUSTRI KZ VII
A Danish four-seat, high-wing, single-engined light aircraft dating from the late 1940s, powered by a 90kW (125hp) Continental engine.

SIPA 200 MINIJET

FRANCE: 1952

Crew: 2
Powerplant: one 150kg (330lb) thrust
Turboméca Palas turbojet engine
Performance: max speed 400km/h
(248mph); range 500km (310 miles);
service ceiling 8000m (26,240ft)
Dimensions: wingspan 7.20m (23ft 7in);
length 5.12m (16ft 9in); height 1.78m
(5ft 10in)
Weight: 759kg (1673lb) loaded

THE SIPA 200 MINIJET was a
single-engined, turbojet-powered
two-seat training and liaison aircraft.
It was distinctive in its twin-boom
configuration and short, tubby
nacelle housing the engine and
cockpit. The S200 made its first
flight on 14 January 1952. Early
test flights revealed that it was
underpowered and performance
fell short of expectations, and it
was unable to compete with
contemporary types such as the
Fouga Magister. Seven prototypes
were built. The SIPA 200 was built
at the request of the French
government, which was evaluating
new aviation concepts as part of
the progressive build-up of
France's postwar aircraft industry.

Built at the request of the French government, the SIPA 200 Minijet was designed to evaluate new concepts as France strove to build up its post-World War II aviation industry.

SKODA-KAUBA V1 TO V8

AUSTRIA: 1942–44

THE AUSTRIAN AERONAUTICAL
engineer Otto Kauba approached
the Reichsluftministerium (RLM)
with a proposal for a flying-bomb
early in 1942. The ministry was
sufficiently interested in his ideas
to assist in establishing the Skoda-
Kauba design bureau in Prague,
Czechoslovakia. The proposed
flying-bomb layout was tested in a
light monoplane, the SK V1, which
was written off in a crash. Two
modified aircraft, the SK V1A and
SK V2, were tested before the
project was abandoned in 1943.

Other designs in the series were
the SK V3 light sports aircraft, the
SK V4 fighter trainer, the V5
piston-engined fighter, the V6
twin-boom pusher monoplane, the
V7 canard research aircraft and the
V8 primary trainer, none of which
entered production.

Specifications apply to the
SK V4.

The Skoda-Kauba SK 257V-1 prototype, D-EZWA, was designed as an intermediate fighter trainer, a step on the road to flying the tricky Messerschmitt Bf 109.

Crew: 1
Powerplant: one 179kW (240hp) Argus
As 10C-3 engine
Performance: max speed 420km/h
(261mph); range 900km (560 miles);
service ceiling 7500m (24,600ft)
Dimensions: wingspan 7.60m (24ft
11.25in); length 5.60m (18ft 4.5in);
height 2.90m (9ft 6in)
Weight: 1250kg (2750lb) loaded
Armament: none

SLINGSBY T67 FIREFLY

UK/FRANCE: 1981

Crew: 1/2
Powerplant: one Textron Lycoming AEIO-540-D4A4 piston engine
Performance: max speed 361km/h (224mph); range 753km (468 miles); service ceiling 4000m (13,125ft)
Dimensions: wingspan 10.60m (34ft 9in); wing area 13.00m² (139.94 sq ft); length 7.60m (24ft 10in); height 2.40m (7ft 9in)
Weight: 975kg (2150lb) maximum take-off weight
Payload: two people

IN 1980 SLINGSBY Engineering UK acquired rights to licence build the Fournier RF-6 two 'side-by-side' seat basic trainer. The purpose of this move was to furnish the British military with a basic trainer, although the ownership remains civil. Indeed, most T67 sales have been associated with the military, although some have gone to commercial/airline flying schools. More than 260 examples

Military sales of the Slingsby T67 include a substantial batch for the US Air Force – one is pictured here prior to delivery.

of this fixed tricycle undercarriage light aeroplane have been produced with varying powerplants, and later versions are constructed from composite materials. Other military operators of the type include China and Jordan.

SNCASO SO.30P BRETAGNE

FRANCE: 1947

Crew: 2
Powerplant: two 1209kW (1620hp) Pratt & Whitney R-2800-B43 Double Wasp 14-cylinder radial engines
Performance: max speed 416km/h (258mph); range 1500km (932 miles); service ceiling 6500m (21,325ft);
Dimensions: wingspan 26.89m (88ft 3in); length 18.95m (62ft 2in); height 5.89m (19ft 4in)
Weight: 18,900kg (39,881lb) loaded
Payload: 30-37 passengers

THE SO.30 BRETAGNE twin-engined transport was designed in the early part of World War II, in spite of the difficulties facing the project given the German occupation of France. Indeed, the two prototypes were damaged during Allied bombardment of Cannes. It was resurrected once peace had been restored. In its definitive form, the SO.30P, the aircraft first flew on 11 December 1947. The subsequent production run totalled 45 examples, four of which were used for a time by Air

SNCASO SO.30P Bretagne F-BAYK of Air Algeria. The Bretagne was a neat and workmanlike design, but it was produced only in limited numbers for use by French and French colonial airlines.

France. Eight SO.30Ps served with Air Algérie and 12 with Air Maroc. Some were bought by charter companies, continuing in service

for a number of years. Others were operated, sometimes under charter, by units of the French Air Force's Transport Command.

SKODA-KAUBA SK 257
The SK 257 was a more powerful version of the SK V4. It possessed excellent performance and handling qualities; however, only four prototypes and five production aircraft were built.

SKYFOX AVIATION CA22 AND CA25
The CA22 ultra-light, single-engined, two-seat light plane first flew in 1989 as a trainer/leisure/surveillance type. It differs from the later CA25 in having a tail wheel rather than nose wheel.

SKYWAY AC-35
American two-seat 'roadable' autogyro developed from an original 1937 design.

SLINGSBY HENGIST
The Slingsby Hengist was a 15-seat passenger glider, tested in 1941. Four prototypes and 18 production aircraft were built, these being used for equipment transport.

SLINGSBY MOTOR TUTOR
Dating from 1948 the Motor Tutor was effectively a Tutor glider fitted with an engine and landing gear.

SNCAC NC.130
The SNCAC NC.130, flown in 1940, was an experimental twin-engined low-wing monoplane with a pressurized cabin, built to assist high-altitude bomber development.

SNCAC NC.150
The SNCAC NC.150 was a high-altitude bomber project under study at the time of France's collapse in May 1940. A third engine in the fuselage was intended to drive the compressor for the aircraft's pressurized cabin.

SNCASO SO.95 CORSE II

THE SO.95 CORSE II was a light twin-engined transport, the prototype flying on 17 July 1947. The type was originally fitted with a tailwheel undercarriage, which was retained in the civil version, but the military variant featured a tricycle landing gear. The Corse II was used almost exclusively by the light transport units of the French Naval Air Arm; only two saw

This SO.95 Corse II bears the markings of the Aéronavale, which used the type almost exclusively. Only two saw airline service.

regular airline service, operating with Air Services of India between Bombay, Bangalore and Delhi before being withdrawn in 1950.

Crew: 2
Powerplant: two 433kW (580hp) Renault 12S-02-201 12-cylinder Vee-type engines
Performance: max speed 330km/h (205mph); range 1300km (807 miles); service ceiling 7000m (22,960ft)
Dimensions: wingspan 18.00m (59ft 0.75in); length 12.32m (40ft 5in); height 4.30m (14ft 1in)
Weight: 5600kg (12,345lb) loaded
Payload: 10–13 passengers

SNECMA C-450 COLEOPTÈRE

Crew: 1
Powerplant: one 3700kg (8150lb) thrust SNECMA Atar E5V turbojet engine
Performance (est): max speed 800km/h (497mph); initial climb rate 130m/sec (427ft/sec)
Dimensions: diameter (span) 4.51m (13ft 3in); length 8.02m (26ft 3in)
Weight: 3000kg (6615lb) loaded

THE SNECMA C-450 Coleoptère was one of the oddest VTOL aircraft ever devised, and was built to investigate the annular (circular) wing concept. A tail-sitter, it was transported by means of a special cradle-truck which raised the aircraft from the horizontal to the vertical position for take-off, the pilot's seat being mounted on gimbals and tilted forward as the aircraft assumed vertical attitude. Directional control at take-off and landing was maintained by jet deviation, and by four swivelling fins in orthodox flight. The first vertical take-off and landing were on 17 April 1959, but the aircraft was destroyed in a crash shortly afterwards. This happened on 25 July 1959, when test pilot Auguste Morel, making the Coleoptère's third free flight and the first test for transitional horizontal flight, lost control and ejected with no injury only 15m (50ft) from the ground. The C-450's trials programme followed experiments with a VTOL engine test-bed, the 'Atar Volant'.

The C-450 was one of the more radical experimental French aircraft designs of the 1950s, a period when French aircraft designers strived to take innovative strides in aviation technology.

SOCATA RALLYE SERIES   FRANCE: 1959

ORIGINATING IN A Morane
Saulnier/Yves Gardan design, the
Rallye light/private aeroplane
series began deliveries in 1961.
The group was later incorporated
as Socata (a Sud-Aviation
subsidiary), and later still within
Aêrospatiale. In 1979 the Rallye
range of four-seat, low-wing
light/training aircraft underwent a
rebranding exercise, thus changing
the nomenclature. However, the
series has been offered in a wide

**More than 3500 examples of all
the varying types and subtypes of
Socata's Rallye series have been
delivered to date.**

variety of variants and subtypes
including the Rallye Club, Rallye
Commodore, Koliber (licence-built
in Poland) and the militarized R
235 Guerrier, which features
armament points.
    Specifications apply to the
Gabier (Rallye 235GT).

Crew: 1
Powerplant: one 175kW (235hp)
Avco Lycoming 0-540-B4B5 flat-six
piston engine
Performance: max speed 275km/h
(171mph); range 1090km (677 miles);
service ceiling 4500m (14,765ft)
Dimensions: wingspan 9.75m (31ft
11.75in); length 7.25m (23ft 9.5in);
height 2.80m (9ft 2.5in)
Weight: 1200kg (2646lb) maximum take-
off weight
Payload: four people

SOCATA GY 80 HORIZON AND ST 10 DIPLOMATE   FRANCE: 1960

Crew: 1
Powerplant: one 134kW (180hp) Avco
Lycoming 0-360-A flat-four engine
Performance: max speed 250km/h
(155mph); maximum range with maximum
fuel 953km (592 miles)
Dimensions: wingspan 9.70m (31ft 10in);
length 6.60m (21ft 9in); height 2.60m (8ft
6in)
Weight: 11000kg (24,250lb) maximum
take-off weight
Payload: four people

THE HORIZON ORIGINATES in an
independent design by Yves
Gardan built in 1960. Sud-Aviation
procured the manufacturing rights
to the Horizon and began to manufacture the type in 1963. Several
different piston-engined versions
of this low-wing, retractable-
undercarriage monoplane have
been produced, and rearrangement
of the French aerospace industry
led to the Horizon becoming a
Socata product from the mid-

**The ST 10 Diplomate pictured served as a demonstrator for the manufac-
turer during the early 1970s.**

1960s. A slightly larger, improved
version – the ST 10 Diplomate,
first called Super Horizon 200 –
was introduced from 1967. Total
deliveries of all types exceed 310,

and the Horizon remains popular
with European private/club flyers,
although it ceased production in
1969. Specifications apply to the
Socata GY-80.

SOKO G-2A GALEB

Although the Soko Galeb's main customer was the former Yugoslav Air Force, the aircraft also enjoyed limited sales abroad.

FIRST FLOWN IN MAY 1961, the SOKO G-2A Galeb (Seagull) jet trainer was the first Yugoslav-designed jet aircraft to go into production, entering service with the Yugoslav Air Force in 1963. Also used as a light attack aircraft, it was operated mainly by the Yugoslav Air Force Air Academy, but was also exported to Libya and Zambia as the G-2AE. During the Yugoslav civil war, the Galeb was used in action by the 105th Fighter-Bomber Regiment of the Serbian Air Force.

Crew: 2
Powerplant: one 1134kg (2500lb) thrust Rolls-Royce Viper 11 Mk 226 turbojet engine
Performance: max speed 730km/h (454mph); range 1240km (771 miles); service ceiling 12,000m (39,370ft)
Dimensions: wingspan 9.73m (31ft 11in); length 10.34m (33ft 11in); height 3.28m (10ft 9in)
Weight: 4300kg (9480lb) loaded
Armament: two 12.7mm (0.50in) machine guns; underwing racks for bombs, rockets and bomblet containers

SOKO J-1 JASTREB

THE J-1 JASTREB is a single-seat ground-attack development of the Galeb with a more powerful engine, structural strengthening, extra hardpoints for rockets and three 12.7mm (0.50in) guns in the nose. The RJ-1 is a reconnaissance variant, with a fuselage camera and one in each wingtip. About 250 to 300 Jastrebs were built, including 30 or 50 RJ-ls, plus around 30 two-seat JT-1 trainers. In addition 20 J-lEs and RJ-1Es were delivered to the Zambian Air Force in 1971.

Crew: 1
Powerplant: one 1361kg (3000lb) thrust Rolls-Royce Viper Mk 531 turbojet engine
Performance: max speed 820km/h (510mph); range 1520km (944 miles); service ceiling 12,000m (39,370ft)

Dimensions: wingspan 11.68m (38ft 3in); length 11.78m (38ft 8in); height 3.64m (11ft 11in)
Weight: 5100kg (11,244lb) loaded
Armament: three 12.7mm (0.50in) machine guns; up to 500kg (1102lb) of weapons

First flown in 1974, with deliveries from 1975, the Soko Jastreb was a logical single-seat ground-attack variant of the Galeb.

SOKO/Avioane J-22 Orao

THE J-22 Orao (Hawk) was the result of a collaborative effort between SOKO of Yugoslavia and the Intrepinderea De Avione Bucaresti company of Romania. Each country built prototypes, which flew simultaneously in 1974, and production of an initial batch of 20 Romanian aircraft, designated IAR-93A, began in 1979, with SOKO starting production of the similar J-22 in 1980. An improved version with

Development of the J-22 Orao was protracted, and further disrupted by political events in Romania and Yugoslavia in the 1980s and 1990s.

afterburning engines, the J-22M Orao 2 (IAR-93B), went into production in 1984 with orders totalling 165 in both countries. Production was seriously disrupted following the collapse of the communist regime in Romania and the civil war in Yugoslavia.

Crew: 1
Powerplant: two 2268kg (5000lb) thrust Turbomécanica (Rolls-Royce Viper Mk 633-47) turbojet engines
Performance: max speed 1160km/h (721mph); combat radius 530km (329 miles); service ceiling 12,500m (41,010ft)
Dimensions: wingspan 9.62m (31ft 6in); length 14.90m (48ft 10in); height 4.45m (14ft 7in)
Weight: 10,100kg (22,267lb)
Armament: two 23mm (0.90in) cannon; up to 2800kg (6173lb) of external stores

Sopwith One-and-a-Half-Strutter

Crew: 2
Powerplant: one 97kW (130hp) Clerget rotary engine
Performance: max speed 164km/h (102mph); range 565km (350 miles); service ceiling 3960m (13,000ft)
Dimensions: wingspan 10.21m (33ft 6in); length 7.70m (25ft 3in); height 3.12m (10ft 3in)
Weight: 975kg (2149lb) loaded
Armament: one 7.7mm (0.303in) machine gun; up to four 25kg (56lb) bombs

THE SOPWITH One-and-a-Half-Strutter, so called because of its unusual wing bracing, was originally designed as a high-performance two-seat fighter. The type went into production for the RNAS at the beginning of 1916 and was the first British aircraft to feature an efficient synchronized forward-firing armament. It was deployed to France with No 5

This photograph clearly shows why the Sopwith One-and-a-half Strutter acquired its unusual name, courtesy of its 'half-struts'.

Wing RNAS in April 1916. Used initially for bomber escort, it later switched to the bombing role, as did aircraft issued to Nos 43, 45 and 70 Squadrons RFC. The type was a key component of Britain's

home defence squadrons. Others went to sea aboard the Royal Navy's early aircraft carriers and other major warships, flying from specially constructed platforms in the latter case.

SOCATA TBM-700
Designed for business users, this French six-seat, single turboprop design has proved popular in a number of applications. Originally developed in partnership with Mooney, more than 200 TBM-700s have been delivered since first flying in 1988.

SOCIETE AERIENNE BORDELAISE (DYLE AND BACALAN) DB-70
The DB-70 was a French twin-fuselage tri-motor design dating from 1929. A military version of this passenger design, with four engines, was also considered.

SOH SOH-01
Hungarian experimental two-seat helicopter first tested in 1956.

SOKO SUPER GALEB
The G-4 Super Galeb, although based on the earlier aircraft, was in fact a completely new design, with swept flying surfaces and updated systems. It first flew in 1980.

SOPWITH BAT BOAT
The Bat Boat was a single-engined flying-boat design dating from 1913. Along with the Tabloid it provided the basis for Sopwith's famous World War I fighters.

SOPWITH D1/THREE SEATER
The first biplane to bear the Sopwith name was the single-engined Three Seater of 1913.

SOPWITH TABLOID
This British single-engined 1913 design was equipped with floats in order to challenge for and win the 1914 Schneider trophy.

SOPWITH PUP

UK: 1916

Crew: 1
Powerplant: one 60kW (80hp) Le Rhone rotary engine
Performance: max speed 179km/h (112mph); range 500km (310 miles); service ceiling 5334m (17,500ft)
Dimensions: wingspan 8.08m (26ft 6in); length 5.89m (19ft 4in); height 2.87m (9ft 5in)
Weight: 556kg (1225lb) loaded
Armament: two 7.7mm (0.303in) machine guns

A DELIGHTFUL AIRCRAFT to fly, and with an exceptionally good rate of climb, the Sopwith Pup single-seat scout first flew in February 1916, powered by an 60kW (80hp) Le Rhone rotary engine. It was very small, simple and reliable, and its large wing area gave it a good performance at altitude. The Pup was initially ordered for the Royal Naval Air Service, 170 being delivered, and a further 1600 were built for the Royal Flying Corps. The Pup was superior to many German first-line scouts, thanks mainly to its small radius of turn, and it could still hold its own at the time of its withdrawal early in 1918. Many Pups subsequently served on home defence duties, some being armed with eight Le Prieur anti-Zeppelin rockets mounted on the interplane struts, and in various training roles.

The name 'Pup' was an unofficial one, acquired because the aircraft resembled a scaled-down offspring of the One-and-a-Half Strutter.

SOPWITH CAMEL

UK: 1916

The Sopwith Camel destroyed more enemy aircraft than any other type in World War I. The aircraft's rather vicious flying characteristics could be exploited by a skilled pilot.

DESIGNED BY HERBERT SMITH as a successor to the Sopwith Pup and Triplane, the Sopwith Camel was a far from docile aircraft with some vicious tendencies that resulted in the demise of many trainee pilots.

For those who mastered it, turning its idiosyncracies to their advantage in combat, it was a superb fighting machine, and was credited with destroying more enemy aircraft than any other Allied type. The

strong torque from its Clerget rotary engine meant that it could out-turn any German fighter, with the possible exception of the Fokker Dr.I Triplane. The Camel prototype made its appearance in

December 1916. Early production aircraft were powered either by the 97kW (130hp) Clerget 9B or 112kW (150hp) Bentley BR1 rotary engine, but subsequent aircraft were fitted with either the Clerget or the 82kW (110hp) Le Rhone 9J. Armament comprised twin Vickers guns mounted in front of the cockpit, and four 9kg (20lb) Cooper bombs could be carried under the fuselage for ground attack.

The first unit to receive Camel F.1s was No 4 Squadron of the Royal Naval Air service, followed by No 70 Squadron RFC, both in July 1917. By the end of the year 1325 Camels (out of a total of 3450 on order at that time) had been delivered, and were used widely for ground attack during the Battles of Ypres and Cambrai. In March 1917, meanwhile, a shipboard version of the Camel, the 2F.1, had undergone trials. It was designed to operate from platforms on warships, from towed lighters or from the Royal Navy's new aircraft carriers, and differed from the F.1 in having a slightly shorter wingspan, and, instead of the starboard Vickers gun, a Lewis gun angled to fire upwards through a cutout in the upper-wing

centre section. The 2F.1's principal mission was Zeppelin interception; 340 examples were built, but the first of these were not operational until the spring of 1918. By the end of the war, however, 2F.1 Camels were deployed on five aircraft carriers, two battleships and 26 cruisers of the Royal Navy. On 11 August 1918, a 2F.1 Camel flown by Lt Stuart Culley, and launched from a lighter towed behind the destroyer HMS *Redoubt*, intercepted and destroyed Zeppelin L.53 over the Heligoland Bight.

Early in 1918, with an increase in night attacks on southern England by German heavier-than-air bombers, several home-based night-fighter units rearmed with the Sopwith Camel. The cessation of night attacks in May meant that aircraft could be released for service in the night-fighting role on the Western Front, and in June No 151 Squadron, a specialist Camel-equipped night-fighting unit, moved to France and began operations against Gotha night-bombers and their airfields.

At the end of October 1918 the RAF had 2548 Camel F.1s on charge, and 129 2F.1s. By this

time the Camel was already being replaced by the Sopwith Snipe, but it continued to serve for some years after the war with the Belgian Aviation Militaire, the Canadian Air Force, the Royal Hellenic Naval Air Service, the Polish Air Force and the US Navy.

The last RAF squadron to use the Camel in combat was No 47, which deployed to southern Russia in March 1919 to support the Allied Intervention Force, in action against the Bolsheviks. During the same period, Camels operating from the carrier HMS *Vindictive* flew in support of Allied forces resisting Russian advances into the Baltic States.

Specifications apply to the Sopwith Camel F.1.

Crew: 1
Powerplant: one 97kW (130hp) Clerget 9B rotary engine
Performance: max speed 182km/h (113mph); endurance 2 hrs 30 mins; service ceiling 5791m (19,000ft)
Dimensions: wingspan 8.53m (28ft); length 5.72m (18ft 9in); height 2.59m (8ft 6in)
Weight: 659kg (1453lb) loaded
Armament: two 7.7mm (0.303in) machine guns

SOPWITH BABY   UK: 1917

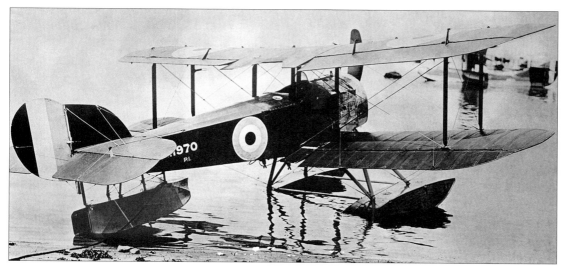

ONE OF THE TRULY successful seaplane designs of World War I, the Sopwith Baby was derived from the Tabloid, which had won the Schneider Trophy in 1914. Production of the Baby totalled 457, these serving at Royal Navy coastal bases and on board a variety of warships. The Baby was used in the reconnaissance and anti-submarine roles in theatres of war

An excellent seaplane design, the Sopwith Baby was widely used in all theatres of war.

as diverse as the North Sea, English Channel, Mediterranean, Egypt, Palestine and Italy. The type also served with the air arms of Canada, the United States, France, Chile, Greece and Norway, and was built under licence by Ansaldo of Italy.

Crew: 1
Powerplant: one 97kW (130hp) Clerget 9-cylinder rotary engine
Performance: max speed 161km/h (100mph); endurance 2 hrs 15 mins; service ceiling 2317m (7600ft)
Dimensions: wingspan 7.82m (25ft 8in); length 7.01m (23ft); height 3.05m (10ft)
Weight: 778kg (1715lb) loaded
Armament: one 7.7mm (0.303in) machine gun; 59kg (130lb) of bombs

SOPWITH TRIPLANE
A delightful and effective fighting scout, the Sopwith Triplane first flew in 1916 and was issued mainly to the RNAS, giving a good account of itself in the air battles of 1917. It bridged the gap between the Pup and the Camel

SOPWITH SALAMANDER
First flown in April 1918, the Sopwith Salamander was an armoured ground-attack derivative of the Snipe. Six prototypes and 102 production aircraft were built before all contracts were cancelled at the end of World War II.

SOPWITH ATLANTIC
Built in 1918 for the *Daily Mail*'s 1919 transatlantic flight competition, the Atlantic was a single-engine biplane with two seats and was capable of 22 hours sustained flight at 160km/h (100mph). The record bid was unsuccessful, but the Atlantic was the first powered aeroplane to operate from Newfoundland.

SOPWITH GRASSHOPPER
Following the armistice of 1918, Sopwith designed and produced the Grasshopper, a two-seat, radial-engined biplane for the commercial touring market. The Grasshopper bore some resemblance to the famous Sopwith Camel fighter of World War I.

SOPWITH DRAGON
The Sopwith Dragon was basically a Snipe re-engined with a 254kW (340hp) ABC Dragonfly engine. The latter proved to be a failure, and although 200 Dragons were built before production was halted, none were issued to squadrons.

SOPWITH DOLPHIN

Crew: 1
Powerplant: one 164kW (220hp)
Hispano-Suiza 8E water-cooled
Vee-type engine
Performance: max speed 192km/h
(119mph); endurance 1 hr 45 mins;
service ceiling 5791m (19,000ft)
Dimensions: wingspan 9.91m (32ft 6in);
length 6.78m (22ft 3in); height 2.59m
(8ft 6in)
Weight: 894kg (1970lb)
Armament: two 7.7mm (0.303in)
machine guns

DESIGNED AS A replacement for the
Camel, the Sopwith 5F.1 Dolphin
flew for the first time in May 1917,
and entered service with No 19
Squadron on the Western Front in
January 1918. The type was also
issued to three other squadrons in
France, Nos 23, 79 and 87. The
Sopwith Dolphin proved unpopular
at first with its pilots. After all, the
engine was virtually in the pilot's
lap; his face was uncomfortably
close to the butts of the twin Lewis

Although possessing a good performance, the Sopwith Dolphin was unpopular with its pilots, mainly because of the cockpit design, which placed the pilot's face too close to the breeches of the twin machine guns.

machine guns; he had a square
steel-tube cockpit frame around his
neck; and the aircraft's fuel tank
was directly behind him. Once

early misgivings had been
overcome, however, pilots found
that the Dolphin was an excellent
fighting machine. One home

defence squadron, No 141, was
armed with Dolphins; however,
they were generally unsuccessful
as night-fighters.

SOPWITH CUCKOO

The Sopwith Cuckoo was an excellent torpedo-bomber design, but it did not become operational until the closing weeks of World War I.

THE SOPWITH T.1 CUCKOO was an
excellent torpedo-bomber design
first flown in June 1917; 350 were
eventually ordered, but it did not
have the chance to prove itself in
action. The first examples were not

delivered until September 1918.
Although 150 Cuckoos had been
built by the time of the Armistice
in November, only 61 had been
taken on charge by the RAF, issued
to Nos 185 and 186 Squadrons.

Crew: 1
Powerplant: one 149kW (200hp)
Hispano-Suiza water-cooled
Vee-type engine
Performance: max speed 166km/h
(103mph); endurance 3 hrs 15 mins;

service ceiling 4755m (15,600ft)
Dimensions: wingspan 14.25m (46ft 9in);
length 8.69m (28ft 6in); height 3.35m
(11ft)
Weight: 1620kg (3572lb) loaded
Armament: one 457mm (18in) torpedo

SOPWITH SNIPE

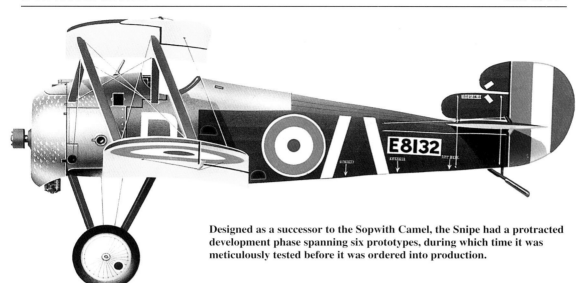

Designed as a successor to the Sopwith Camel, the Snipe had a protracted development phase spanning six prototypes, during which time it was meticulously tested before it was ordered into production.

A MUCH DEVELOPED follow-on to the Sopwith Camel, the Sopwith 7F.1 Snipe was built around the new 172kW (230hp) Bentley BR.2 rotary engine and was considered the best Allied fighter in service at the time of the Armistice. Ordered into production at the start of 1918 after a somewhat protracted development programme, the Snipe was issued to No 43 Squadron in France in September, followed by No 208 Squadron and No 4 (Australian)

Squadron. By 30 September, 161 Snipe Mk Is had been delivered, together with two long-range Mk IAs. Over 4500 examples of this very effective fighter were ordered, but there were heavy cancellations and only 497 were built. The Snipe became the RAF's standard post-war fighter, equipping 21 squadrons, and some remained in service until 1926. The type was replaced in first-line RAF service from 1924 by the Gloster Grebe.

Crew: 1
Powerplant: one 172kW (230hp) Bentley BR.2 rotary engine
Performance: max speed 195km/h (121mph); service ceiling 5945m (19,500ft)
Dimensions: wingspan 9.17m (30ft 1in); length 6.02m (19ft 9in); height 2.67m (8ft 9in)
Weight: 916kg (2020lb) loaded
Armament: two 7.7mm (0.303in) machine guns; up to four 11.3kg (25lb) bombs on external racks

SPAD VII

Many examples of the SPAD VII, like this one, served with the squadrons of the RFC and RNAS, replacing aircraft types which were no match for the latest German models.

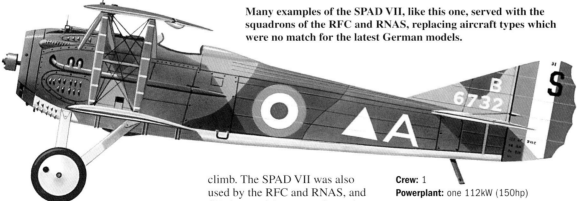

IN THE AUTUMN OF 1916, many Escadrilles of France's Aviation Militaire began to equip with a new fighter type, the SPAD VII. Although less manoeuvrable than the Nieuport types, the SPAD VII was a strong, stable gun platform with a top speed of 191km/h (119mph) and an excellent rate of

climb. The SPAD VII was also used by the RFC and RNAS, and filled a crucial gap at a time when many units were still equipped with ageing and vulnerable aircraft. Others were supplied to Italy, where they equipped five squadrons, and to the United States, equipping seven squadrons of the American Expeditionary Force. Ultimately, 5600 SPAD VIIs were built in France by eight manufacturers.

Crew: 1
Powerplant: one 112kW (150hp) Hispano-Suiza 8Aa water-cooled Vee-type engine
Performance: max speed 191km/h (119mph); endurance 2 hrs 15 mins; service ceiling 5334m (17,500ft)
Dimensions: wingspan 7.82m (25ft 8in); length 6.18m (20ft 3in); height 2.13m (7ft)
Weight: 740kg (1632lb) loaded
Armament: one 7.62mm (0.30in) machine gun

SPAD XI

THE S.XI TWO-SEAT reconnaissance aircraft had a similar but longer fuselage than the SPAD S.VII, from which it was derived via the SPAD VIII (which did not progress beyond the design stage), and staggered wings. Because of stability and engine problems it was unsuitable as a fighter, and was used as a reconnaissance aircraft. One was built as a night-fighter with a searchlight fitted in front of the propellor. The S.XI went into service in 1917 as the SPAD XIA.2, and more than 1000 were built. The XVIA.2 version,

Although it bore a superficial resemblance to the SPAD VII fighter, the two-seat SPAD XI observation aircraft was by no means as successful.

which appeared in January 1918, had a more powerful engine.

Specifications apply to the SPAD XIA.2

Crew: 2
Powerplant: one 175kW (235hp) Hispano-Suiza 8Bc water-cooled Vee-type engine
Performance: max speed 176km/h (109mph); endurance 2 hrs 15 mins; service ceiling 7000m (22,966ft)
Dimensions: wingspan 11.23m (36ft 10in); length 7.75m (25ft 5in); height 2.59m (8ft 6in)
Weight: 1048kg (2310lb) loaded

SPAD XIII

Crew: 1
Powerplant: one 164kW (220hp) Hispano-Suiza 8BEc 8-cylinder Vee-type engine
Performance: max speed 224km/h (140mph); endurance 2 hrs; service ceiling 6710m (22,000ft)
Dimensions: wingspan 8.10m (26ft 7in); length 6.30m (20ft 8in); height 2.35m (7ft 8in)
Weight: 845kg (1863lb) loaded
Armament: two 7.62mm (0.30in) machine guns

IN MAY 1917, the French Escadrilles de Chasse began to standardize on a new type, the SPAD XIII. Like its predecessor, it was an excellent gun platform and was extremely strong, although it was tricky to fly at low speeds. Powered by a Hispano-Suiza 8Ba engine and armed with two forward-firing Vickers guns, it had a top speed of nearly 225km/h (140mph) – quite exceptional for that time – and

The SPAD XIII was the subject of some of the largest production contracts placed for any single aircraft type in WWI, and was the dominant type in terms of both numbers and performance in the last 18 months of hostilities.

could climb to 6710m (22,000ft). The SPAD XIII subsequently equipped more than 80 Escadrilles, and 8472 were built. The type also equipped 16 squadrons of the American Expeditionary Force (893 examples) and was supplied to Italy, which still had 100 in service in 1923. After World War I, surplus French SPAD XIIIs were sold to Belgium (37), Czechoslovakia, Japan and Poland (40).

SPAD TYPES 27, 33, 46, 50 AND 56 SERIES

Crew: 2
Powerplant: one 313kW (420hp) Bristol Jupiter Ac 9-cylinder radial engine
Performance: max speed 160km/h (99mph); range 485km (301 miles); service ceiling 4000m (13,125ft)
Dimensions: wingspan 13.13m (43ft 1in); length 9.00m (29ft 6.25in)
Weight: 2712kg (5979lb) loaded
Payload: four passengers

IMMEDIATELY AFTER World War I, André Herbemont embarked on the design of a series of small passenger-carrying aircraft, starting with the SPAD 27 of 1919. The first major production version was the SPAD

33, which flew in December 1920. Forty production aircraft were built, a few being used for experimental purposes. The series continued with the SPAD 46, a slightly larger version of the Type 33, and the Type 50. Only two prototypes of the latter were built, but its successor, the SPAD 56 of 1923, was produced in six versions. All aircraft were built by Blériot. Specifications apply to the SPAD Type 56-4.

Following World War I, SPAD was quick to turn combat aircraft designs into commercial ventures. One such was the SPAD 56.

SPARTAN CRUISER (SARO-PERCIVAL A-24 MAILPLANE)

UK: 1932

Crew: 2
Powerplant: three 97kW (130hp) de Havilland Gipsy Major III piston engines
Performance: max speed 214km/h (133mph); range 514km (310 miles); service ceiling 4575m (15,000ft)
Dimensions: wingspan 16.40m (54ft); length 12.00m (39ft 2in)
Weight: 2812kg (6200lb) maximum take-off weight
Payload: up to six passengers – 10 in later marques

THIS WOODEN-FRAMED, low-wing tri-motor was originally designed in collaboration by Saro and Percival as the A-24 Mailplane in 1931. The consortium lost interest in the venture as pure mail contracts dissipated, but the design was offered to Spartan Aircraft UK on the Isle of Wight, which marketed the type as a passenger aircraft.

Pictured here is the second of three Mk III Cruisers built, immediately different from earlier versions in having squared cabin windows.

Orders for modest numbers were received, the first from Yugoslavia's Aeroput. Other examples went to Iraq, Egypt and India. Some later versions were built for Spartan Airlines, which was subsumed into British Airways and three were impressed into World War II RAF service. Specifications apply to the Cruiser I.

STAMPE ET VERTONGEN SV.4

BELGIUM: 1933

Crew: 1/2
Powerplant: one de Havilland Gipsy I inverted in-line piston engine rated at 97kW (130hp)
Performance: max speed 200km/h (124mph); range 600km (372 miles); service ceiling 5500m (18,045ft)
Dimensions: wingspan 8.40m (27ft 6.75in); length 6.50m (21ft 4in); height 2.60m (8ft 6.25in)
Weight: 780kg (1720lb) maximum take-off weight
Payload: two seats

HAVING DESIGNED a number of primary training and touring aircraft after World War I, Stampe produced its most notable design, the SV.4, in 1933. This biplane was designed as a trainer or touring aircraft, initially powered by a de Havilland Gipsy Major III engine. However, the first production SV.4A utilized a Renault 4-PO5 engine, which was changed to the Gipsy Major in the improved SV.4B. Pre-World War II production of the SV.4B was not vast, and it was interrupted by the hostilities, and the 65 built after the war amounted to a total of fewer than 110. Yet the SV.4 was much appreciated in Europe, particularly by the French military, and in the region of 1000 examples were licence-built after World War II by SNCAN in France and Atelier in Algeria. Today a number of SV.4s remain operational in private flying clubs. Specifications apply to the SV.4B.

The Stampe became popular with private and aerobatic flyers in the late 1960s and early 1970s, including this British-owned SV.4B, which remains an active aircraft to date.

STINSON DETROITER SERIES

USA: 1927

Crew: 1/2
Powerplant: one 224kW (300hp) Wright J-6 radial piston engine
Performance: max speed 214km/h (132mph); range 1125km (700 miles); service ceiling 4267m (14,000ft)
Dimensions: wingspan 14.22m (46ft 8in); length 10.01m (32ft 10in)
Weight: 1580kg (3485lb) maximum take-off weight
Payload: up to seven seats

THE STINSON DETROITER was the first operational airliner of Northwest Airways (predecessor to Northwest Airlines), and it is notable for having a soundproofed

A ski-equipped Detroiter SB-1 of Northwest Airways. The early SB-1 (as pictured) was built in a biplane configuration.

and heated cabin. In the region of 36 of this braced high-wing monoplane were produced in a number of versions. Later builds had the more powerful J-6 Wright engine, and some earlier builds were later retro-fitted with the type. Detroiters were involved in a number of long-distance and pioneering flight exploits, but one notable first involved a Detroiter acquired by Packard Motor Co. It was fitted with a diesel engine, and on 19 September 1928 it was to become the first diesel-powered aircraft to fly. Specifications apply to the SM1-F.

STINSON L-5 SENTINEL

USA: 1942

Crew: 2
Powerplant: one 138kW (185hp) Lycoming O-435-1 4-cylinder air-cooled engine
Performance: max speed 209km/h (130mph); range 805km (500 miles); service ceiling 6100m (20,000ft)
Dimensions: wingspan 10.36m (34ft); length 7.34m (24ft 1in); height 2.41m (7ft 11in)
Weight: 916kg (2020lb) loaded
Armament: none

THE STINSON L-5 Sentinel was the military version of the commercial Stinson 105 Voyager. Six Voyagers were bought by the USAAF in 1941 as YO-54s for testing, and quantity orders for Sentinels began in 1942, at first as O-62s before the designation was changed to 'L' for liaison in April 1942. Between 1942 and 1945, the USAAF ordered 3590 L-5s. The unarmed L-5 with its short field take-off and landing capability was used for reconnaissance, removing litter patients

from frontline areas, delivering supplies to isolated units, laying communications wire, spotting enemy targets for attack aircraft, transporting personnel, rescuing

Allied personnel in remote areas and even as a light bomber. In Asia and the Pacific, L-5s remained in service with US Air Force units as late as 1955.

The L-5 Sentinel is a fine example of a successful commercial design turned to equally successful military use. Quantity production for the USAAF began in 1942.

STRINGFELLOW AERONAUTICAL DESIGNS

UK: 1848–1886

BORN IN 1799, over time John Stringfellow became interested in the possibilities of manned flight. He went into partnership with William Samuel Henson, designer of the Aerial Steam Carriage, in the mid 19th century, and made an abortive attempt to set up an air freight concern known as the Aerial

John Stringfellow, one of the principal architects of aviation, attempted to form the world's first commercial aviation company in partnership with Samuel Henson.

Steam Transit Company. When Henson became disillusioned and emigrated to the United States, Stringfellow set about improving the little steam engine which his friend had built, and installed it in a new monoplane model which had a wingspan of about 3m (10ft). This was tested in 1848, but the results were disappointing. It was launched from a high cable at Chard, Somerset, but did not achieve sustained flight.

Stringfellow took a break from aeronautical design for the best

part of 20 years, but in 1868 he produced another model, this time involving a triplane. He exhibited his design at the world's first aeronautical exhibition, which was held at London's Crystal Palace in that same year, and the innovative nature of his model triplane won him an award of £100 donated by the Aeronautical Society. The prize was in fact more in recognition of the efficiency of his little steam engine, which was found to have the best power-to-weight ratio of any tested. A contemporary

This steam-powered model aeroplane, fitted with twin propellers, was designed and built by John Stringfellow's son in 1886. It proved that steam engines were too heavy to power an aircraft.

description of this model exists in an Aeronautical Society journal:

'It consisted of three superposed surfaces aggregating 28 square feet and a tail of 8 square feet more. The weight was under 12 pounds and it was driven by a central propeller actuated by a steam engine overestimated at one-third of a horsepower. It ran suspended to a wire on its trials but failed of free flight, in consequence of defective equilibrium.'

According to one eyewitness account, Stringfellow continued to test his model after the Crystal Palace exhibition, following his return to Somerset:

'When freed, it descended an incline with apparent lightness until caught in the canvas; but the impression conveyed was that had there been sufficient fall, it would have recovered itself… It was

intended at the last to set this model free in the open country, when the requirements of the Exhibition were satisfied, but it was found that the engine, which had done much work, required repairs. Many months afterward, in the presence of the author [M. Brearey] an experiment was tried in a field at Chard, by means of a wire stretched across it. The engine was fed with methylated spirits, and during some portion of its run under the wire, the draft occasioned thereby invariably extinguished the flames, and so these interesting trials were rendered abortive.'

With the prize money he had been awarded, Stringfellow: '… erected a building over 70 ft. long, in which to experiment with a view of ultimately constructing a large machine to carry a person to

guide and conduct it, his experience with models having evidently impressed him with the necessity for intelligent control of any aerial apparatus not possessing automatic stability; but he was already 69 years of age, his sight became impaired, and he died in 1883 without having accomplished any advance on his previous achievements.'

John Stringfellow's demise did not mean the end of the family name's involvement with aviation. His son, F.J. Stringfellow, pursued his father's line of research, and in 1886 designed a steam-powered biplane model with twin propellers; however, this also proved a failure. If the reasearch carried out by the senior and junior Stringfellows proved anything, it was that steam was not the answer to the problem of achieving powered flight.

SUD-AVIATION ALOUETTE III SERIES

FRANCE: 1959

Accommodation: pilot and 6 passengers
Powerplant: One 649kW (870shp)Turboméca Artouste IIIB turboshaft derated to 425 kW (570 shp)
Performance: max speed 210km/h (130mph); combat radius 480km (298 miles); service ceiling 3200m (10,500ft)
Dimensions: main rotor diameter 11.02m; (36ft 1.75in); length 12.84m (42ft 1.5in); height 3m (9ft 10in)
Weight: 2200kg (4,850lb)

Austrian Air Force Alouette III at Hörsching in March 1980. In all 1453 Alouette IIIs have been produced, with sales to 190 operators.

THE ALOUETTE III seven-seat general-purpose helicopter was derived from the Alouette II and featured a more powerful 410kW (550shp) Turboméca Artouste IIIB turboshaft engine and an enlarged

cabin. The first of two prototypes flew on 28 February 1959 and was followed by four pre-production machines, the first production

Alouette III flying in July 1961. In 1962 HAL in India began building a modest number of Chetak (SA-316A) versions. All Alouette IIIs delivered up to the end of 1969 were designated SE-3160, and from 1970 these aircraft were redesignated SA-316B, principally with strengthened main and rear transmission and increased payload. The SA-319B Alouette III Astazou version is a direct development of the SA-316B, from which it differs principally in having a 649kW (870hp) Astazou XIV turboshaft engine derated to 447kW (600shp) and other improvements. Licence production in Romania by ICA-Brasov of the IAR-316B totalled 230 examples, and in Switzerland FFA built 60 Alouette IIIs, and HAL also undertook SA-316B licensed production. In 1970 the more powerful SA-316C entered limited production.

In all, Sud and Aérospatiale (which was created in 1970 by the merger of the Sud and Nord companies) produced a total of 1453 Alouette IIIs, with sales to 190 operators (60 of them military) in no fewer than 74 countries.

SUD-AVIATION SA-321 SUPER FRELON (SUPER HORNET)   FRANCE: 1962

Crew: 2-3
Powerplant: three 1216kW (1630hp) Turboméca Turmo IIIE6 turboshaft engines
Performance: max speed 275km/h (171mph); range 815km (506 miles); service ceiling 3150m (10,325ft)
Dimensions: main rotor diameter 18.90m (62ft); length 23m (75ft 7in); height 6.66m (21ft 10in)
Weight: 6626kg (14,607lb)
Armament/payload: two Exocet anti-ship missiles or four torpedoes; or 27-30 troops, or 15 stretchers and two attendants; or 5000kg (11,020lb) of freight

IN JULY 1969, Sikorsky Aircraft signed a technical contract with Sud-Aviation to provide assistance with the design and construction of the rotor system for the Super Frelon. Fiat, meanwhile, would produce the main gearcase and transmission box in Italy. A plan to produce the Super Frelon in West Germany never reached fruition, but development proceeded and the SA-321 prototype flew on 7

SA-321G of the Aéronavale at Caselle in June 1979. By the end of 1982, some 99 Super Frelons had been completed for both the French Navy (321G) and Army (321H) for anti-ship attack.

December 1962. In October 1965, the French government placed an order for 18 Super Frelons for the Aéronavale and, by the end of 1982, some 99 Super Frelons had been completed for both the Navy (321G) and Army (321H) for anti-ship attack. The Chinese Air Force and Navy received the Changhe Zhi-8 derivative of the SA 321Ja utility version and export versions went to Libya, Iraq, Israel, Pakistan, South Africa and Zaire.

Specifications apply to the Sud-Aviation SA-321 Super Frelon.

SUD-AVIATION (AÉROSPATIALE/WESTLAND) SA-330 PUMA   FRANCE: 1965

Originally developed for the French Army, the Puma was chosen for the RAF for tactical transport duties and Westland Helicopters became a partner in the production of 48 examples.

ORIGINALLY DEVELOPED for the French Army as a medium-sized all-weather helicopter for day and night operation, in 1967 the Puma was also chosen for the RAF for tactical transport duties. British-based Westland Helicopters became a partner in production, producing 30 per cent of the helicopter's airframe and some components, and was responsible for final assembly and flight testing of 48 examples. Similarly, Rolls-Royce was involved in the provision of Turboméca Turmo engines for these machines. The first Westland-assembled Puma flew on 25 November 1970. By 1977, sales of the Puma exceeded 500 with most of these examples exported to over 19 countries.

Crew: 2
Powerplant: two 991kW (1328hp) Turboméca Turmo IIIC4 turboshaft engines
Performance: max speed 257km/h (159mph); combat radius 580km (360 miles); service ceiling 4100m (13,450ft)
Dimensions: main rotor diameter 15.00m (49ft 2.5in); length 18.15m (59ft 6.5in); height 5.14m (16ft 10.5in)
Weight: 7000kg (15,430lb)
Armament/payload: many customer options including weapon pylons for gun pods or missiles and various axial- or side-firing cannon or Minigun installations; 20 troops or 3000kg (6600lb) slung load

SUD-AVIATION GAZELLE SERIES

FRANCE: 1967

Crew: 1
Powerplant: one 440kW (590shp) Turboméca Astazou turboshaft engine
Performance: max speed 264km/h (164mph); combat radius 670km (416 miles); service ceiling 4100m (13,450ft)
Dimensions: main rotor diameter 10.50m (34ft 5.5in); length 11.97m (39ft 3.25in); height 3.15m (10ft 2.5in)
Weight: 908kg (2002lb)
Armament/Payload: two pods of 36mm (1.42in) rockets; two forward-firing Miniguns or four AS.11, HOT or TOW missiles; or two AS.12 missiles, side-firing Minigun, GPMG or Emerson TAT; four passengers

THE GAZELLE WAS a natural successor to the Alouette and the first collaborative project between Aêrospatiale and Westland, which jointly produced 628 examples. After development, Westland was responsible for 65 per cent of its structure; by 1984 when production ceased 294 Gazelles, including 282 for the British forces, had been built. Some 212 AH.1 (341B) were delivered to the British Army; the rest are HT.2 (341C) trainers for the Royal Navy and HT.3 trainers and HCC.4 (D and E) VIP transports for the RAF. Some 170 SA-341Fs were delivered to the ALAT (French Army), and about 164 341H export versions were built, with licence production in Yugoslavia of 132 Soko-built SA-341H Partizans and 170 SA-342s before 1991. The more powerful, heavier SA-342 flew on 11 May 1973; by 1 February 1980, over 200 armed with four HOTs and an M397 sight had been delivered to the French Army. Gazelle production ceased in 1996, but existing machines continue to receive regular modifications and upgrades to armament and avionics. Specifications apply to the SA-341.

When Westland ceased production of the Gazelle in 1984 282 examples had been built for the British forces, of which 212 were AH.1 (341B) for the British Army. Gazelles continue to serve with 25 military operators.

SUD-AVIATION (AÊROSPATIALE) SA-315B LAMA

FRANCE: 1969

THIS HELICOPTER DESIGN combined the airframe of a Sud Alouette II with the dynamic components of an Aêrospatiale SA-316B Alouette III. Highly successful trial flights were made in the Himalayas in 1969: one take-off was made from 7500m (24,605ft), and an absolute height record of 12,442m (40,820ft) was recorded on 21 June 1972. The first of 20 Indian-assembled Cheetahs flew on 6 October 1972, and production went on to exceed over 177 examples. In 1978 Helibras in Brazil began assembly of SA-314B Lamas and later entered into full licence production with the HB-315B Gavião for the armed forces of Brazil and Bolivia. French production of the Lama ceased in 1991 after 407 had been delivered. Specifications apply to SA-315B.

Designed originally to meet a 1960s requirement for the Indian armed forces, the Lama has also been produced as the Gavião by Helibras.

Crew: 1
Powerplant: one 723kW (970shp) Turboméca Artouste IIIB turboshaft engine derated to 410kW (550shp)
Performance: max cruising speed 120km/h (75mph); combat radius 515km (320 miles); service ceiling 3000m (9840ft)
Dimensions: main rotor diameter 11.02m (36ft 1in); length 10.26m (33ft 8in); height 3.09m (10ft 1in)
Weight: 1950kg (4300lb)
Payload: four passengers, or two stretchers and a medical attendant; up to 1135kg (2502lb) of freight in a slung load

SUD-EST SE.161 LANGUEDOC

FRANCE: 1939

Crew: 5
Powerplant: four 895kW (1200hp)
Gnome-Rhone 14N 68/69 14-cylinder
radial engines
Performance: max speed 405km/h
(252mph); range 1000km (620 miles);
service ceiling 7200m (23,625ft)
Dimensions: wingspan 29.38m (96ft
4.75ft); length 24.25m (79ft 6.75in);
height 5.57m (18ft 3in)
Weight: 22,940kg (50,576lb) loaded
Payload: 33 passengers

ORIGINALLY DEVELOPED by
Marcel Bloch, the SE.161
Languedoc prototype flew for the
first time in September 1939.

**During its career the Languedoc was put to many different uses. This one
was an engine test-bed. Others tested radio and navigational equipment.**

Further development of the aircraft
was authorized by the Vichy
government after France's collapse
and the German occupation, and
the first production aircraft flew in
September 1945.

Forty Languedocs were acquired
by Air France for its European and
North African services, while other
operators included Air Atlas, Air
Liban, Misrair, LOT and
Tunis Air. Several aircraft were
also supplied to the Armée de
l'Air and the Aéronavale as crew
trainers, and some were used as
carrier aircraft for the Leduc series
of ramjet research aircraft.

SUD-EST SE.2410 GROGNARD

FRANCE: 1950

**This comparatively rare picture
shows the lines of the SE.2410
Grognard to good advantage. The
project was abandoned.**

DESIGNED AS A single-seat ground-
attack aircraft, the Sud-Est SE.2410
Grognard (Grumbler – a nickname
for a soldier of Napoleon's Old
Guard) prototype flew for the first
time on 30 April 1950, powered by
two 2197kg (4850lb) thrust
Hispano-Suiza Nene 101 turbojets
mounted one above the other in the
fuselage. A second prototype, the
SE.2415 Grognard II, flew in
February 1945. A two-seater, it was
damaged in a belly landing. The
definitive production version would
have been the SE.2418, which was

to have been powered by Rolls-
Royce Tay turbojets, but the SO
Vautour was selected to meet the
Armée de l'Air's ground-attack
requirement instead. Specifications
apply to the SE.2410 Grognard.

Crew: 1
Powerplant: two 2197kg (4850lb) thrust
Hispano-Suiza Nene 101 turbojet engines
Performance: max speed 1038km/h
(645mph); range 853km (530 miles);
service ceiling 11,590m (38,000ft)
Dimensions: wingspan 13.57m (44ft
6.5in); length 15.40m (50ft 6in); height
not known
Weight: 14,481kg (31,967lb) loaded
Armament: two 30mm (1.18in) DEFA
cannon; various combinations of bombs
and rocket projectiles

SUD-EST SE.5000 BAROUDEUR

FRANCE: 1953

Crew: 1
Powerplant: one 3395kg (7495lb) thrust
SNECMA Atar 101C turbojet engine
Performance: max speed 1094km/h
(680mph); service ceiling 17,000m
(55,760ft)
Dimensions: wingspan 10.00m (32ft
10in); length 13.66m (44ft 10in); height
3.25m (10ft 7in)
Weight: 7150kg (15,765lb) loaded
Armament: two 30mm (1.18in) cannon; up
to 950kg (2095lb) of underwing ordnance

THE NAME BAROUDEUR is Franco-
Arabic, a term used by troops of
the French Foreign Legion to mean
'brawler'. The strike aircraft to
which it was applied first flew on
1 August 1953, powered by an Atar
101B turbojet. A second prototype,
which differed from the first in

having an uprated Atar 101C engine,
slightly modified tail surfaces and
a three-degree increase in wing
anhedral, flew on 12 May 1954. On
17 July 1954, this aircraft exceeded

Mach 1 in a dive. Although the
Baroudeur concept worked well,
the project was abandoned in
favour of the F-84F Thunderstreak.
Specifications apply to SE.5000-02.

**The SE.5000 Baroudeur was
designed to take off from a trolley
and land on skids, making
operation from rough unprepared
forward airstrips possible.**

SUD-OUEST SO.6020 ESPADON

FRANCE: 1948

Several experimental versions of the SO.6020 Espadon were built, extra power being provided by auxiliary rocket motors in the later models.

FRANCE'S FIRST jet fighter design, the SO.6020 Espadon (Swordfish) flew for the first time on 12 November 1948. It had slightly swept wings and a jet engine in the tail with a ventral intake. The aircraft proved to be underpowered, and auxiliary rocket motors were added to subsequent prototypes, the SO.6025 having one under the fuselage and the SO.6026 one in the tail. The SO.6021 was a much redesigned version, having lateral jet intakes, and, later, wingtip-mounted jet engines. No production of the type was undertaken.

Specifications apply to the Sud-Ouest SO.6020.

Crew: 1
Powerplant: one 2270kg (5005lb) thrust Rolls-Royce Nene turbojet engine
Performance: max speed 967km/h (600mph); endurance 2.5 hrs; service ceiling 15,250m (50,000ft)
Dimensions: wingspan 10.60m (34ft 9in); length 15.00m (49ft 2in); height 4.72m (15ft 6in)
Weight: 4750kg (10,474lb) empty
Armament: six 20mm (0.79in) cannon (proposed)

SUD-OUEST SO.4000

FRANCE: 1951

The Sud-Ouest SO.4000 was France's first jet-bomber design. Its development was beset by serious technical problems, quite apart from the fact that it was underpowered and flew badly.

THE SO.4000 WAS France's first jet-bomber design and was preceded by two scale models, the SO.M-1 and SO.M-2. The first, a glider, was launched from a He 274 parent aircraft; the other was powered by a Rolls-Royce Derwent turbojet. The SO.4000 first flew on 16 March 1951 (it should have flown in 1950, but its complex undercarriage collapsed during taxi trials). Its flying characteristics were bad and it was seriously underpowered. As a consequence, there were no further test flights and the aircraft was abandoned. The SO.4000's twin turbojets were mounted side by side in the centre fuselage, exhausting below the vertical tail surfaces. It was to have had two remotely controlled 20mm (0.79in) cannon, mounted in wingtip barbettes.

Crew: 2
Powerplant: two 2265kg (5000lb) thrust Hispano-Suiza Nene 102 turbojet engines
Performance: max speed 849km/h (528mph) estimated
Dimensions: wingspan 17.87m (58ft 7in); length 16.72m (54ft 10in)
Weight: 21,975kg (48,510lb) loaded
Armament: two 20mm (0.79in) remotely controlled cannon (proposed)

SUD-EST SE.2010 ARMAGNAC
First flown in 1949, the SE.2010 Armagnac was a large four-engined transport aircraft with a capacity for 84 passengers, or 160 in high-density configuration. Eleven examples were built.

SUD-EST SE.22 DURANDAL
An experimental interceptor intended to carry a single air-to-air missile, the SE.22 Durandal flew for the first time in April 1956 powered by an Atar 101G turbojet and a SEPR rocket motor. Durandal was the sword of Roland, the French medieval hero.

SUD-EST SE.116 VOLTIGEUR
The Sud-Est SE.116 Voltigeur was a three-seat, twin-engined counter-insurgency aircraft, first flown in 1958. It did not enter production.

SUD-OUEST SO.6000 TRITON
The Sud-Ouest SO.6000 Triton was France's first jet research aircraft. It first flew in December 1946, powered by a Junkers Jumo 004 engine.

SUD-OUEST SO.8000 NARVAL
On 1 April 1949, Sud-Ouest flew the prototype of a twin-boom, long-range naval strike fighter designated SO.8000 Narval, powered by an Arsenal 12H-02 piston engine. A second prototype flew before the programme was abandoned.

SUD-OUEST SO.1100 ARIEL
The Ariel was an experimental helicopter. The rotor tips were driven by tip jets fed by a Turboméca compressor driven by a 164kW (220hp) Mathis G8 air-cooled engine. It was first flown on 23 March 1949.

SUD-OUEST SO.4050 VAUTOUR

FRANCE: 1952

Crew: 2
Powerplant: two 3500kg (7716lb) thrust SNECMA Atar 101E-3 turbojet engines
Performance: max speed 1102km/h (685mph); range 2575km (1600 miles); service ceiling 15,000m (49,200ft)
Dimensions: wingspan 15.11m (51ft 11in); length 15.84m (49ft 7in); height 4.95m (16ft 2in)
Weight: 20,700kg (45,635lb) loaded
Armament: 2400kg (5300lb) of bombs

DESIGNED FROM THE outset to carry out three tasks – all-weather interception, close support and high-altitude bombing – the Sud-Ouest SO.4050 Vautour (Vulture) first flew on 16 October 1952. Two production versions were ordered, the Vautour IIB light bomber and the IIN all-weather interceptor. The first of 70 Vautour IINs entered service in 1956 with the 6e

Escadre de Chasse, followed by EC 30 in the following year, while the first of 40 Vautour IIBs entered service in December 1957 with 1/92 'Bourgogne' and 2/92 'Aquitaine' at Bordeaux. The final version of the Vautour was the IIBR, a bomber-reconnaissance variant. The close-support version of the Vautour, the IIA, was not used by the French Air Force, but

20 examples were supplied to Israel, together with four IINs, and saw action in the Six-Day War of 1967. Specifications apply to the Vautour IIB.

Prototype 003 was the light bomber variant of the Vautour, designated Vautour IIB. The Vautour was also produced as a night-fighter and a ground-attack aircraft.

SUD-OUEST SO.9000 TRIDENT

FRANCE: 1953

Crew: 1
Powerplant: two 1100kg (2425lb) Turboméca Gabizo turbojet engines, plus one 3000kg (6615lb) thrust SEPR 631 rocket motor
Performance: max speed 1805km/h (1122mph); absolute ceiling 24,217m (79,431ft)
Dimensions: wingspan 6.95m (22ft 10in); length 13.26m (43ft 6in); height 3.20m (10ft 6in)
Weight: 5900kg (13,000lb)

THE SUD-OUEST SO.9000 Trident was an experimental short-range interceptor, with a turbojet mounted at each end of a short, thin unswept wing and an auxiliary rocket motor mounted in the fuselage. The prototype Trident I first flew on 2 March 1953 under turbojet power only; a second prototype crashed on its maiden flight in August that

year. Development continued with the first aircraft, and Sud-Ouest went on to build the SO.9050 Trident II, which was to be the progenitor of

The SO.9000 Trident mixed-powerplant interceptor was intended mainly for short-range, high-altitude target defence.

the definitive fighter version. Two Trident II prototypes were built, the first being destroyed in an accident in December 1955, and in May

1957 the first prototype Trident exploded in flight, killing its pilot. Further development of the Trident was halted soon afterwards.

SUD-OUEST (SUD-AVIATION) ALOUETTE II

FRANCE: 1955

Crew: 1
Powerplant: (SA 313B) one 269kW
(360shp) Artouste II turboshaft engine
Performance: max speed 205km/h
(127mph); combat radius 100km (62 miles)
Dimensions: main rotor diameter 10.20m
(33ft 5in); length 9.75m (31ft 11.75 in);
height 2.75m (9ft)
Weight: 1500kg (3307lb)
Armament/payload: various weapons
such as four Nord SS-11 air-to-air
missiles; up to four passengers

THE ALOUETTE IS ONE of the most
successful helicopters of all time.
By 28 February 1966, some 950
Alouette IIs had been delivered,
including 365 for the French armed
forces. Thirty-five of these were
SA-318Cs with 395kW (530hp)
Turboméca Astazou IIA turboshaft
engines derated to 269kW (360shp),

the first flying on 31 January 1961.
Production of the Alouette 318C
ceased in 1975 after more than 350
had been built. Specifications
apply to the SA.313 Alouette II.

**Sud-Ouest's Alouette (Skylark)
helicopter equipped the French
armed forces and the air arms of
35 other countries. An SE-313
of the Belgian Army is seen here.**

SUKHOI SU-7 'FITTER'

FORMER USSR: 1955

**A Sukhoi Su-7B of the Indian Air Force. The 'Fitter' has seen considerable action in service with foreign air
forces and has proved itself well adapted to the ground-attack role.**

Powerplant: one 9008kg (19,842lb)
thrust Lyulka AL-7F turbojet engine
Performance: max speed 1700km/h
(1065mph); combat radius 320km (199
miles); service ceiling 15,200m (49,865ft)
Dimensions: wingspan 8.93m (29ft
3.5in); length 18.75m (61ft 6in); height
5.00m (16ft 5in)
Weight: 13,500kg (29,750lb) loaded
Armament: two 30mm (1.18in) NR-30
cannon; four external pylons with provision
for two 750kg (1653lb) and two 500kg
(1102lb) bombs

THE SUKHOI SU-7, first seen in 1956
and designed for close air support
with the Frontal Aviation, remained
the Soviet Air Force's standard
tactical fighter-bomber throughout
the 1960s. The Su-7U, codenamed
'Moujik', was a two-seat trainer
version. The Su-7 was the principal
tactical fighter of the Polish and
other Warsaw Pact air forces, and
pilots of Su-7s in service with the
Polish Air Force were trained for
the tactical nuclear role. The Su-7

saw a good deal of action with the
Egyptian Air Force, initially during
the Six-Day War of 1967, while
eight squadrons of Egyptian Air
Force Su-7BMs (backed up by
three Algerian units) were involved
in the 1973 Yom Kippur War. The
Su-7 gained itself a good combat
record during the conflict, proving
remarkably resistant to ground fire.
It was given the NATO reporting
name 'Fitter'. Specifications apply
to Su-7B 'Fitter-A'.

SUD-OUEST SO 1221 DJINN
The Djinn was the world's first tip-
jet helicopter to enter production
and flew in prototype form on 16
December 1953. Of the 178 built,
100 went to the French Army and
47 were built for agricultural roles
in 10 countries.

SUKHOI SU-2
The Sukhoi Su-2, which was
designed in 1936 in competition
with the Ilyushin Il-2 as a close-
support aircraft, never enjoyed
anything like the success of the
Ilyushin. It was relegated to
secondary duties in 1943.

SUKHOI SU-10
The Sukhoi Su-10 was a jet
bomber project of 1949. The
aircraft featured two pairs of
superimposed TR-1A turbojets.
It was never built.

SUKHOI SU-26
First of Sukhoi's line of specifically
aerobatic designs, the single-
engined Su-26 first flew in 1984
and went on to win a number of
aerobatic contests. The Su-26 has
ceased production and is
superseded by the later Su-29 and
Su-31.

SUKHOI SU-35
The Sukhoi Su-35, which is
derived from the 'Flanker-B' and
was originally designated Su-27M,
is a second-generation version with
improved agility and enhanced
operational capability. Its maiden
flight was in 1988.

SUKHOI SU-9/SU-11 'FISHPOT'

FORMER USSR: 1955

The delta-wing Sukhoi Su-9 'Fishpot-A' supersonic interceptor, which entered service in 1956, was one of the fruits of the enormous technological strides made by Soviet military aircraft designers in the 1950s.

KNOWN TO NATO as 'Fishpot', the Su-9 'Fishpot-A' was a single-seat interceptor – to some extent, an Su-7 with a delta wing. In 1961 a new model, the Su-11 'Fishpot-B', was developed from the Su-9, and

was followed into service by the 'Fishpot-C' with uprated engine. A tandem two-seat trainer variant of the Su-9 had the NATO reporting name 'Maiden'. Specifications apply to the Sukhoi Su-9.

Crew: 1
Powerplant: one 10,000kg (22,045lb) thrust Lyulka AL-7F TRD31 turbojet engine
Performance: max speed 1915km/h (1190mph); range 1450km (900 miles); service ceiling 16,765m (55,000ft)

Dimensions: wingspan 8.23m (27ft); length 17.68m (58ft); height 4.88m (16ft)
Weight: 13,610kg (30,000lb) loaded
Armament: four Alkali radar-homing or two Anab infrared homing air-to air missiles

SUKHOI SU-15 'FLAGON'

FORMER USSR: 1965

Crew: 1
Powerplant: two 6205kg (13,668lb) thrust Tumanskii R-11F2S turbojet engines
Performance: max speed 2230km/h (1386mph); combat radius 725km (450 miles); service ceiling 20,000m (65,615ft)
Dimensions: wingspan 8.61m (28ft 3in); length 21.33m (70ft); height 5.10m (16ft 8in)
Weight: 18,000kg (39,680lb) loaded
Armament: four external pylons for medium-range air-to-air missiles

THE FOLLOW-ON TO the Su-11 aircraft was the Su-15, a twin-engined delta-wing interceptor that first flew in 1965 and was in Soviet Air Force service by 1969. Intended to counter low-level penetration by

The Sukhoi Su-15 'Flagon' filled a crucial night and all-weather gap in the Soviet Union's air defences during the Cold War.

US bombers, it was given the NATO reporting name 'Flagon'. Capable of carrying two air-to-air missiles, the 'Flagon' was numerically Russia's most important all-weather interceptor by the mid-1970s, some 1500 being produced in total. The T-5 prototype from which the Su-15 was developed was basically an enlarged version of the Su-11 with the same nose intake, but the T-58 which followed had a 'solid' nose housing AI radar equipment and intakes on the fuselage sides. A number of 'Flagon' variants were produced, culminating in the definitive Su-15TM 'Flagon-F' of 1971. Specifications apply to the Sukhoi Su-15.

SUKHOI SU-17/20

FORMER USSR: 1966

IN 1966, THE SUKHOI bureau redesigned the Su-7, giving it a more powerful engine, variable-geometry wings and increased fuel tankage. In this guise it became the Su-17/20 'Fitter C', which was unique among combat aircraft in

that it was a variable-geometry derivative of a fixed-wing machine.

This aircraft is an excellent example of the remarkable Russian talent for developing existing designs to their fullest extent, enabling them to keep one

basic design of combat aircraft in service for 30 or 40 years, and foster long-term standardization.

The Su-17 entered service in 1971, the Su-20 being the export version. The Su-22 was an updated

version with terrain-avoidance radar and other improved avionics.

Specifications apply to the Sukhoi Su-17M-4 'Fitter-K'.

Following the reunification of Germany in the 1990s, the Federal German Luftwaffe inherited some Sukhoi Su-20 aircraft from the East German Air Force. They were evaluated, then placed in storage.

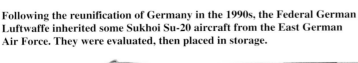

Crew: 1
Powerplant: one 11,250kg (24,802kb) thrust Lyulka AL-21F-3 turbojet engine
Performance: max speed 2220km/h (1380mph); combat radius 675km (419 miles); service ceiling 15,200m (49,865ft)
Dimensions: wingspan 13.80m (45ft 3in); length 18.75m (61ft 6in); height 5.00m (16ft 5in)
Weight: 19,500kg (42,990lb) loaded
Armament: two 30mm (1.18in) cannon; nine external pylons with provision for up to 4250kg (9370lb) of stores

SUKHOI SU-24 'FENCER'

FORMER USSR: 1970

Crew: 2
Powerplant: two 11,250kg (24,802lb) thrust Lyulka AL-21F3A turbojet engines
Performance: max speed 2316km/h (1439mph); combat radius 1050km (650 miles); service ceiling 17,500m (57,415ft)
Dimensions: wingspan 17.63m (57ft 10in) spread, 10.36m (34ft) swept; length 24.53m (80ft 5in); height 4.97m (16ft)
Weight: 39,700kg (87,520lb) loaded
Armament: one 23mm (0.90in) GSh-23-6 six-barrelled cannon; nine external pylons with provision for up to 8000kg (17,635lb) of stores

IN 1965, THE Soviet government instructed the Sukhoi design bureau to begin design studies of a new variable-geometry strike aircraft in the same class as the General Dynamics F-111. One criteria was that the new aircraft must be able to fly at very low level in order to penetrate increasingly effective air defence systems. The resulting aircraft, the Su-24, first flew in 1970, and deliveries of the first

production version, the 'Fencer-A', began in 1974. Several variants were produced, culminating in the Su-24M 'Fencer-D', which entered service in 1986. This variant has in-flight refuelling equipment, upgraded nav/attack systems, and laser/TV designators. The Su-24MR is a tactical reconnaissance version. The Su-24 is known to NATO by the reporting name 'Flanker'.

The Sukhoi Su-24 'Fencer' presented a serious threat to NATO targets in Europe during the dangerous years of the Cold War.

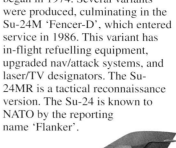

SUKHOI SU-25 'FROGFOOT'

FORMER USSR: 1975

Powerplant: two 4500kg (9921lb) Tumanskii R-195 turbojet engines
Performance: max speed 975km/h (606mph); combat radius 750km (466 miles); service ceiling 7000m (22,965ft)
Dimensions: wingspan 14.36m (47ft 1in); length 15.53m (50ft 11in); height 4.80m (15ft 9in)
Weight: 17,600kg (38,800lb) loaded
Armament: one 30mm (1.18in) GSh-30-2 cannon; eight external pylons with provision for up to 4400kg (9700lb) of stores

A RUSSIAN REQUIREMENT for an attack aircraft in the A-10 Thunderbolt II class materialized in the Sukhoi Su-25, which was selected in preference to a rival design, the Ilyushin Il-102. In fact, it is true to say that the Il-102 was the true equivalent of the A-10, the Su-25 – allocated the NATO reporting name 'Frogfoot' – approximating more closely to the Dassault-Dornier Alpha Jet or the British Aerospace Hawk.

Deployment of the single-seat close-support Su-25K began in

1978, and it saw considerable operational service during the former Soviet Union's involvement in Afghanistan (the first machines to be deployed being pre-production aircraft, designated T-8) and the ruggedness of the design was revealed in dramatic fashion on numerous occasions. One particular aircraft, flown by Colonel Alexander V. Rutskoi, was actually heavily damaged on two occasions, once by anti-aircraft fire, then by Sidewinder air-to-air missiles launched by Pakistani Air Force F-16s. On each occasion the pilot managed to return to his base. The aircraft was repaired, repainted and returned to service. Rutskoi was less lucky – while flying a second Su-25 on a combat mission, his aircraft was hit by anti-aircraft fire and a Blowpipe shoulder-launched missile, which exploded in the starboard engine. The aircraft still flew, but another burst of AA brought it down. Rutskoi ejected and spent some

time as a prisoner of the Pakistani authorities before being repatriated. However, operations in Afghanistan also revealed a number of serious shortcomings. For example, the close positioning of the Su-25's engines meant that if one took a hit and caught fire, the other was likely to catch fire, too. When the 'Frogfoot' first encountered the Stinger shoulder-launched missile, four aircraft were shot down in two days, with the loss of two pilots; it was found that missile fragments shredded the rear fuselage fuel tank, which was situated directly above the jet exhaust.

As a result of lessons learned during the Afghan conflict an upgraded version known as the Su-25T was produced, with improved defensive systems to counter weapons such as the Stinger. The improvements included the insertion of steel plates several

The Sukhoi Su-25 'Frogfoot' received its baptism of fire during the Soviet Union's intervention in Afghanistan in the 1980s, when it was called upon to support ground forces in extremely rugged, mountainous terrain.

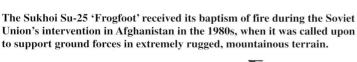

SUPERMARINE NAVYPLANE
The Supermarine Navyplane was a two-seat floatplane with a pusher engine. A biplane, it flew in 1915. Only one prototype was built.

SUPERMARINE N1B BABY
Tested in 1918, the Supermarine N1B Baby biplane was a small shipboard seaplane fighter powered by a 149kW (200hp) Hispano-Suiza engine. Only one was built.

SUPERMARINE CHANNEL TYPES
Following the armistice of 1918, the Channel Types were a number of former military AD flying boats quickly converted for commercial use, often on pleasure flights around the English coastline and carrying three passengers.

SUPERMARINE COMMERCIAL AMPHIBIAN MK I
Built to compete in a 1920 Air Ministry commercial competition, the Mk I was an amphibious biplane with a single pusher engine. Only one example was built.

SUPERMARINE SEAL
The Supermarine Seal of 1921 was a tractor-engined amphibious biplane designed by Reginald Mitchell, later of Spitfire fame. One Seal was exported to Japan.

SUPERMARINE SEA KING (SEA LION II)
Ultimately renamed the Sea Lion II, the Sea King was designed as an amphibious scout.

SUPERMARINE SEA EAGLE
An amphibious biplane type, powered by a single pusher engine. Three Sea Eagles were built and one participated in the 1923 King's Cup air race.

millimetres thick between the engine bays and below the fuel cell. Following this modification no further Su-25s were lost to shoulder-launched missiles. In total, 22 Su-25s and eight pilots were lost in the nine years of the Afghan conflict.

The Su-25UBK is a two-seat export variant, while the Su-25UBT is a navalized version with a strengthened undercarriage and arrester gear. The Su-25UT (Su-28) was a trainer version, lacking the weapons pylons and combat capability of the standard Su-25UBK, but retaining the original aircraft's rough field capability and endurance. It was planned as a replacement for the huge numbers of Aero L-29 and L-39 trainers in service with the former Soviet Air Force, but only one aircraft was flown in August 1985, appearing in the colours of DOSAAF, the Soviet Union's paramilitary 'private flying' organization, which provided students with basic flight training. The aircraft, which actually outperformed the L-39, appeared in many aerobatic displays.

During its service with the Soviet Air Force, the Su-25 gained the nickname of 'Grach' (Rook), and most aircraft deployed to Afghanistan featured a cartoon rook design. Russian infantrymen called the aircraft 'Rascheska' (The Comb) because of its 10 weapon pylons, which gave it a comb-like appearance when it was viewed from below.

Specifications apply to the Sukhoi Su-25 'Frogfoot A'.

SUKHOI SU-27 'FLANKER' FORMER USSR: 1977

A Sukhoi Su-27K, the navalized version of the type, undergoing carrier trials aboard the *Tbilisi* (later the *Kuznetzov*) in 1989.

THE SUKHOI SU-27, like the F-15, is a dual-role aircraft. In addition to its primary air superiority task it was designed to escort Su-24 'Fencer' strike aircraft on deep-penetration missions. The prototype first flew in May 1977, the type being given the code-name 'Flanker' by NATO.

Full-scale production of the Su-27P 'Flanker-B' air defence fighter began in 1980, but the aircraft did not become fully operational until 1984. Like its contemporary, the MiG-29 Fulcrum, the Su-27 combines a wing swept at 40 degrees with highly swept wing root extensions, underslung engines with wedge intakes, and twin fins. The combination of modest wing sweep with highly swept root extensions is designed to enhance manoeuvrability and generate lift, making it possible to achieve quite extraordinary angles of attack. The Su-27UB 'Flanker-C' is a two-seat training version. Specifications apply to the Su-27P.

Crew: 1
Powerplant: two 12,500kg (27,557lb) thrust Lyulka AL-31M turbofan engines
Performance: max speed 2500km (1500mph); combat radius 1500km (930 miles); service ceiling 18,000m (59,055ft)
Dimensions: wingspan 14.70m (48ft 2in); length 21.94m (71ft 11in); height 6.36m (20ft 10in)
Weight: 30,000kg (66,138lb) loaded
Armament: one 30mm (1.18in) GSh-3101 cannon; 10 external hardpoints with provision for various combinations of air-to-air missiles

SUPERMARINE SEA LION SERIES UK: 1919

Crew: 1
Powerplant: one Napier Lion V12 engine rated at 336kW (450hp)
Performance: max speed 233km/h (145mph)
Dimensions: wingspan 9.75m (32ft); length 7.54m (24ft 7in)
Weight: 1425kg (3142lb)

R.J. MITCHELL, WHO later designed the Spitfire, joined Supermarine in 1917. A racing design, the Sea Lion was developed from an earlier aircraft designed to meet an Admiralty experimental requirement to compete in the 1919 Schneider

This is the ill-fated original Sea Lion, slated to compete in the 1919 Schneider Trophy race until damaged by a submerged obstruction.

Trophy race, but was badly damaged by an underwater obstruction. Undeterred, Mitchell went on to redesign the Sea Lion (II) biplane flying boat (itself a derivative of the Sea King fighter), powered by a strut-mounted single pusher engine. The new Sea Lion won the 1922 Schneider race in Naples. The Sea Lion (III) was fitted with an uprated engine for the 1923 event at Cowes, but only managed third place. Mitchell was well aware of the need to decrease drag and moved on to design the S.IV. Specifications apply to Sea Lion II.

SUPERMARINE SEAGULL

UK: 1922

Crew: 3
Powerplant: one 336kW (450hp) Napier Lion pusher engine
Performance: max speed 129km/h (80mph); endurance 3.5 hrs; service ceiling 2743m (9000ft)
Dimensions: wingspan 13.99m (45ft 11in); length 10.51m (34ft 6in); height 4.11m (13ft 6in)
Weight: 2477kg (5462lb) loaded
Armament: one 7.7mm (0.303in) machine gun

THE FIRST SUPERMARINE SEAGULL was a converted Seal fitted with a more powerful Napier Lion II engine. Production began with six wooden Seagull Is for the Fleet Air Arm, these being deployed on board the aircraft carrier HMS *Eagle* from 1923 to 1925. They were subsequently transferred to the Royal Australian Air Force, which used them to continue aerial survey work started by a flight of Fairey IIIDs in 1924. Two more

The Supermarine Seagull, first ordered by the Air Ministry in 1922, literally kept the company afloat until orders for other designs came along.

batches of five and 13 aircraft were ordered for service with the Royal Navy. Two Supermarine Seagulls took part in the King's Cup Air Race of 1924, one being forced to

make an emergency landing on the old racecourse at Blaydon-on-Tyne when the propeller shattered.

Specifications apply to the Supermarine Seagull I.

SUPERMARINE SCYLLA AND SWAN

UK: 1924

Crew: 2
Powerplant: two 266kW (360hp) Rolls-Royce Eagle IX or two 336kW (450hp) Napier Lion IIB engines
Performance: max speed 175km/h (108mph); range 1400km (870 miles); service ceiling 3089m (10,200ft)
Dimensions: wingspan 20.90m (68ft 8in); length 17.06m (56ft); height 7.95m (26ft 1in)
Weight: 5820kg (12,832lb) loaded
Payload: 10 passengers

SHORTLY AFTER World War I, Supermarine received two Air Ministry contracts, one in 1921 for a five-seat military seaplane and the other in 1922 for a commercial seaplane, the former named Scylla and the latter Swan. The Scylla emerged as a monoplane, but was apparently converted to triplane configuration in 1923, when it carried out taxi trials at Felixstowe. There is no evidence that it ever

The sole Supermarine Swan, built as a maritime reconnaissance flying boat, was turned over to civilian use after its flight trials.

flew. The Swan was completed as planned in 1924, but as a maritime reconnaissance flying-boat biplane. After completing its flight trials, it was converted to civilian use. Specifications apply to the Lion-engined Swan variant.

SUPERMARINE SCARAB AND SHELLDRAKE
Dating from 1924, these were early amphibious transport designs from Supermarine, the Scarab being proposed for military applications as a bomber.

SUPERMARINE SPARROW I AND II
An earlier design by R.J. Mitchell, the Sparrow was a high-wing, ultra-light, monoplane with a single 26kW (35hp) engine built to participate in the Lympne trials of 1924. Only one example was built, and it was re-engineered and rebuilt for the same event in 1926 as the Sparrow II.

SUPERMARINE NANOK
The Nanok, flown in 1927, was a three-engined version of the Supermarine Southampton for the Royal Danish Navy. It was found to be nose-heavy, and was cancelled. After modifications, it was renamed Solent and turned over to civil use.

SUPERMARINE SEAMEW
First flown in 1928, the Supermarine Seamew was a small shipborne twin-engined amphibian, powered by two Armstrong Siddeley Lynx IV engines. Two prototypes were built.

SUPERMARINE S.5/S.6
The superbly streamlined Supermarine S.5 and S.6 of 1929 are remembered as the aircraft that captured the Schneider Trophy for Britain – and led to the development of the Spitfire.

SUPERMARINE AIR YACHT
The Air Yacht was a large, all-metal four-engined flying-boat designed by R.J. Mitchell for the millionaire A.E. Guinness, who used the single example to cruise on Irish lakes. The Air Yacht dates from 1929.

SUPERMARINE SOUTHAMPTON

UK: 1925

Crew: 5
Powerplant: two 373kW (500hp) Napier Lion VA W-12 in-line engines
Performance: max speed 174km/h (108mph); range 1497km (930 miles); service ceiling 4265m (14,000ft)
Dimensions: wingspan 22.86m (75ft); length 15.58m (51ft 1in); height 6.82m (22ft 4in)
Weight: 6895kg (15,200lb) loaded
Armament: three 7.7mm (0.303in) machine guns; up to 499kg (1100lb) of bombs

FIRST FLOWN IN March 1925, the elegant Supermarine Southampton flying boat was selected for service with the RAF's coastal reconnaissance flights. The Mk I had a wooden hull, but the Mk II's hull was of Duralumin, representing a considerable weight saving. The Southampton III of 1928 had Bristol Jupiter VIII engines. A further

variant, the Southampton IV, fitted with Rolls-Royce Kestrel engines, was renamed the Scapa, while the Southampton V was named the Stranraer. Most of the 78 aircraft

built were Mk IIs. In 1927–28, four Southamptons made a UK–Singapore–Australia– UK cruise of 43,443km (27,000 miles). Specifications apply to the Mk II.

The Supermarine Southampton, designed by Reginald Mitchell, carried out some notable long-distance flights during its career with the Royal Air Force.

SUPERMARINE STRANRAER

UK: 1935

Originally named the Southampton V, the Supermarine Stranraer was one of the RAF's most important maritime patrol assets in the 1930s.

ORIGINALLY THE Southampton V, the Supermarine Stranraer evolved in response to Air Ministry Specification R.24/31. Much larger than the Scapa, it flew in 1935; 17 aircraft were built in Britain and 40 in Canada. The first RAF deliveries were made to No 228 Squadron in December 1936. The type was also issued to Nos 201, 209 and 240 Squadrons in the United Kingdom. Some RAF Stranraers remained in service until 1941; the Canadian aircraft were withdrawn in 1943, some passing to the civil register.

Crew: 5
Powerplant: two 653kW (875hp) Bristol Pegasus X 9-cylinder radial engines
Performance: max speed 266km/h (165mph); range 1650km (1025 miles); service ceiling 5639m (18,500ft)
Dimensions: wingspan 25.91m (85ft); length 16.71m (54ft 10in); height 6.64m (21ft 9in)
Weight: 8625kg (19,000lb) loaded
Armament: three 7.7mm (0.303in) machine guns; up 525kg (1160lb) of bombs

SUPERMARINE WALRUS

UK: 1936

Crew: 4
Powerplant: one 560kW (750hp) Bristol Pegasus VI radial engine
Performance: max speed 217km/h (135mph); range 966km (600 miles); service ceiling 5210m (17,100ft)
Dimensions: wingspan 13.97m (45ft 10in); length 11.35m (37ft 3in); height 4.65m (15ft 3in)
Weight: 3266kg (7200lb) loaded
Armament: two or three 7.7mm (0.303in) machine guns; up to 272kg (600lb) of bombs or depth charges

THE SUPERMARINE WALRUS began life as the Supermarine Seagull V fleet spotter amphibian, fitted with a Bristol Pegasus engine in a pusher configuration. The type was ordered

for service with the Fleet Air Arm as the Walrus Mk I. Production began in 1936, and 746 aircraft were eventually produced. The Walrus, nicknamed the 'Shagbat', was stressed for catapult launching and saw combat service on capital ships and cruisers. It was also used as an air-sea rescue aircraft by the RAF.

The Supermarine Walrus saw service in almost every theatre of war, both as a fleet spotter and an air-sea rescue aircraft.

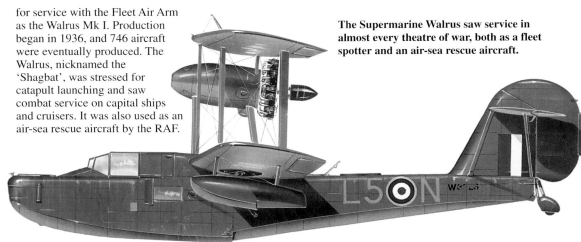

SUPERMARINE SPITFIRE

UK: 1936

Crew: 1
Powerplant: one 1074kW (1440hp) Rolls-Royce Merlin 45/46/50 V-12 engine
Performance: max speed 602km/h (374mph); range 756km (470 miles); service ceiling 11,280m (37,000ft)
Dimensions: wingspan 11.23m (36ft 10in); length 9.11m (29ft 11in); height 3.48m (11ft 5in)
Weight: 3078kg (6785lb) loaded
Armament: two 20mm (0.79in) cannon and four 7.7mm (0.303in) machine guns

Spitfire Mk IX of No 453 Squadron, RAAF, wearing D-Day invasion stripes. No 453, which was based in Hampshire on 6 June 1944, was one of the first Spitfire squadrons to deploy to Normandy.

THE PROTOTYPE SPITFIRE, K5054, first flew on 5 March 1936 and, like the Hawker Hurricane with which it was to share so much fame, was powered by a Rolls-Royce Merlin C engine. The first Spitfire Mk Is were delivered to No 19 Squadron at Duxford in August 1938. Eight other squadrons had equipped with Spitfires by September 1939, and two Auxiliary Air Force units, Nos 603 and 609, were undergoing operational training. Production of the Mk I eventually reached 1566 aircraft. It was this variant that saw the most combat in the Battle of Britain, the Mk II with the 877kW (1175hp) Merlin XII engine being issued to the squadrons of Fighter Command in September 1940.

The Spitfire Mk III was an experimental one-off aircraft, while the Mk IV (229 built) was a photo-reconnaissance version. It was actually produced after the next variant, the Mk V, which began to reach the squadrons in March 1941. Converted from Mk I and II airframes, the Mk V was to be the major Spitfire production version, with 6479 examples built. The Spitfire V's debut came just in time, for in May 1941 Luftwaffe fighter units began to receive the improved Messerschmitt Bf 109F, its service debut having been delayed due to technical problems.

To counter the activities of high-flying German reconnaissance aircraft, the Spitfire Mk VI was produced, with a long, tapered wing and a pressurized cockpit; the aircraft was assigned to one flight of the RAF's home defence squadrons. The Mk VII was powered by a Rolls-Royce Merlin 60 engine, a two-stage, two-speed, inter-cooled powerplant which was to take development of the Merlin to its ultimate. Early in 1942, the Air Staff envisaged production of both the Spitfire VII and, in much larger numbers, the Spitfire VIII, basically an unpressurized version of the Mk VII intended for low-level air superiority operations. But the Mk VIII design needed a lot of refinement, meaning that production would be delayed for an unacceptably long time. Air Staff thoughts consequently turned to an interim aircraft: a Mk V Spitfire airframe combined with a Merlin 61 engine. The resulting combination was the Spitfire Mk IX, which for a stop-gap aircraft was to be a resounding success. Deliveries to the RAF began in June 1942, and 5665 were built.

The Spitfire Mk X and XII were unarmed photo-reconnaissance variants, while the Mk XII, powered by a 1294kW (1735hp) Rolls-Royce Griffon engine, was developed specifically to counter low-level attacks by Focke-Wulf 190s. Only 100 Mk XII Spitfires were built. They were followed by the more numerous Mk XIV, based on the Mk VIII, with an airframe strengthened to take a 1529kW (2050hp) Griffon 65 engine. The Spitfire XVI, a ground-attack version with a Packard-built Merlin 266 engine, entered service in 1944. The Spitfire XVIII was a fighter-reconnaissance variant, just starting to enter service at World War II's end, as was the PR Mk XIX. The last variants, produced until 1947, were the Mks 21, 22 and 24. Total Spitfire production was 20,351. Specifications apply to the Spitfire Mk VB.

The Griffon-engined Spitfire PR Mk 19 was the last of the photo-reconnaissance Spitfires, and continued in this role for some years after World War II.

SUPERMARINE SEAFIRE

UK: 1941

Crew: 1
Powerplant: one 1194kW (1600hp)
Rolls-Royce Merlin 55m 12-cylinder
Vee-type engine
Performance: max speed 560km/h
(348mph); range 890km (553 miles);
service ceiling 7315m (24,000ft)
Dimensions: wingspan 11.23m (36ft
10in); length 9.21m (30ft 2in); height
3.42m (11ft 2in)
Weight: 3465kg (7640lb) loaded
Armament: two 20mm (0.79in) cannon
and four 7.7mm (0.303in) machine
guns; external bomb or rocket load of
227kg (500lb)

IN LATE 1941 it was decided to
adapt the Spitfire for naval use
under the name of Seafire. The
main variants were the Seafire Mk
IB (166 conversions from Spitfire
VB airframes); Mk IIC (372 for
low- and medium-altitude air
combat and air reconnaissance); 30
Mk III (Hybrid) aircraft with fixed

wings, and 1220 examples of the
definitive Seafire Mk III with
folding wings. The Seafire Mks
XV, XVII, 45, 46 and 47 were
Griffon-engined variants. The
Seafire saw much action in the
Mediterranean in 1943 and in the
Pacific in 1945. The Seafire 47,
operating from HMS *Triumph*,

took part in air strikes against
terrorists in Malaya and during the
Korean War. Although far from
suitable for carrier operations due
to its narrow-track undercarriage
and long nose, the Seafire still
performed well. Specifications
apply to the Seafire Mk III.

**The Supermarine Seafire Mk 47 was the last of the Spitfire/Seafire line to
see combat. In 1950, Seafire 47s operating from the light carrier HMS
Triumph carried out air strikes on targets in Korea.**

SUPERMARINE ATTACKER

UK: 1947

THE ATTACKER, the Royal Navy's
first jet fighter, was based on the
Vickers-Supermarine E.10/44, which
had originally been proposed as a
land-based fighter for the RAF, but
had been ousted by the Gloster
Meteor and de Havilland Vampire.
Supermarine therefore offered a
navalized version to the Admiralty,
which wrote Specification E.1/45
around it. The prototype first flew in
its navalized form on 17 June 1947
and as the Vickers-Supermarine
Attacker F.Mk 1 entered service
with the Royal Navy, 60 aircraft
being acquired. A further 36
aircraft were supplied to the
Pakistan Air Force in 1952–53.

**The Attacker was the Royal Navy's
first jet fighter. It also served with
the Pakistan Air Force, where it was
eventually replaced by US types.**

Crew: 1
Powerplant: one 2313kg (5100lb) thrust
Rolls-Royce Nene 3 turbojet engine
Performance: max speed 949km/h
(590mph); range 1915km (1190 miles);
service ceiling 13,715m (45,000ft)
Dimensions: wingspan 11.25m (36ft
11in); length 11.43m (37ft 6in); height
3.02m (9ft 11in)
Weight: 5216kg (11,500lb) loaded
Armament: four 20mm (0.79in) cannon

SUPERMARINE SWIFT

UK: 1951

Crew: 1
Powerplant: one 4287kg (9450lb) thrust Rolls-Royce Avon 114 turbojet engine
Performance: max speed 1100km/h (685mph); range 1014km (630 miles); service ceiling 13,959m (45,800ft)
Dimensions: wingspan 9.85m (32ft 4in); length 12.88m (42ft 3in); height 3.80m (12ft 6in)
Weight: 9706kg (21,400lb) loaded
Armament: two 30mm (1.18in) cannon

WJ960 was one of the development Type 541 Swifts. It was used for engine surge trials and other tests before it was withdrawn from service.

TRACING ITS ANCESTRY back to the Type 510, the Swift first flew on 1 August 1951 and was ordered into 'super-priority' production for RAF Fighter Command. The Swift F.Mks 1 to 4, however, were unsuitable for the primary role of high-level interception, being prone to tightening in turns and suffering high-altitude flameouts as a result of shock waves entering the air intakes when the cannon were fired. It was adapted to the low-level fighter reconnaissance role, and as the Swift FR.5 equipped Nos 2 and 79 Squadrons of the 2nd Allied Tactical Air Force in Germany. Sixty-two Swift FR.Mk 5s were delivered, 35 being converted from Mk 4 airframes.

SUPERMARINE SCIMITAR

UK: 1956

The Supermarine Scimitar was the last operational aircraft produced by the company that had designed and built the famous Spitfire.

THE SUPERMARINE SCIMITAR naval strike fighter was the end product of a lengthy development process that began with the Supermarine Type 505 and evolved via the Types 508, 525 and 529. The first of three Scimitar prototypes flew on 20 January 1956, and the first production Scimitar F.1 flew on 11 January 1957. The type became operational with No 803 Squadron in June 1958 and three other Fleet Air Arm squadrons were later equipped with it, an original order for 100 aircraft having been cut back to 76.

The Supermarine Scimitar had been withdrawn from first-line units by the end of 1966.

Crew: 1
Powerplant: two 5105kg (11,250lb) thrust Rolls-Royce Avon 202 turbojet engines
Performance: max speed 1143km/h (710mph); range 966km (600 miles); service ceiling 15,240m (50,000ft)
Dimensions: wingspan 11.33m (37ft 2in); length 16.87m (55ft 4in); height 4.65m (15ft 3in)
Weight: 15,513kg (34,200lb) loaded
Armament: four 30mm (1.18in) cannon; up to 1816kg (4000lb) of bombs or missiles

SVENSKA J6B JAKTFALK

SWEDEN: 1928

Crew: 1
Powerplant: one 373kW (500hp) Armstrong Siddeley Jaguar radial engine
Performance: max speed 310km/h (193mph); service ceiling 9302m (30,500ft)
Dimensions: wingspan 9.00m (29ft 8in); length 7.10m (23ft 5in); height 3.50m (11ft 4in)
Weight: 1467kg (3240lb) loaded
Armament: two 7.7mm (0.303in) machine guns

THE JAKTFALK (Hawk) single-seat fighter biplane was designed in 1928 by the Svenska Aerobolaget, a prototype being ordered for the Royal Swedish Air Force in 1929 under the designation J5. Two more prototypes were built as J6s.

Production aircraft were fitted with a 373kW (500hp) Armstrong Siddeley Jaguar radial engine. The Jaktfalk was an excellent aircraft for its time, fully up to international standards and considered by many to be one of the finest fighter biplanes of its class. Production was undertaken in 1934-35, and one aircraft, fitted with a 399kW (535hp) Armstrong Siddeley Panther engine, found its way to Finland, where it was used as a fighter trainer during the Russo-Finnish War in the winter of 1939–40. The last Jaktfalk was withdrawn from service in 1941.

TACHIKAWA KI.36 'IDA'

Crew: 2
Powerplant: one 336kW (450hp) Hitachi Ha-13a 9-cylinder radial engine
Performance: max speed 348km/h (216mph); range 1235km (767 miles); service ceiling 8150m (26,740ft)
Dimensions: wingspan 11.80m (38ft 8in); length 8.00m (26ft 3in); height 3.64m (11ft 11in)
Weight: 1660kg (3660lb) loaded
Armament: two 7.7mm (0.303in) machine guns

Many Tachikawa Ki.36 army cooperation aircraft, abandoned by the Japanese in Manchuria, were subsequently used by the Chinese People's Air Force, the insignia of which this example bears.

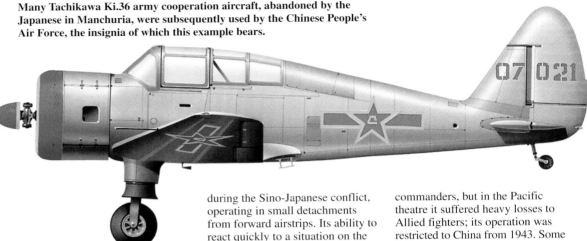

CODENAMED 'IDA' BY the Allies, the Tachikawa Ki.36 was a fast single-engined army cooperation monoplane. The first of two prototypes flew in April 1938, and the type went into production as the Army Type 98. The Ki.36 saw action during the Sino-Japanese conflict, operating in small detachments from forward airstrips. Its ability to react quickly to a situation on the ground made it popular with field commanders, but in the Pacific theatre it suffered heavy losses to Allied fighters; its operation was restricted to China from 1943. Some Ki.36s were supplied to Thailand.

TACHIKAWA KI.54 'HICKORY'

Crew: 2
Powerplant: two 336kW (450hp) Hitachi Ha-13a 9-cylinder radial engines
Performance: max speed 376km/h (234mph); range 960km (597 miles); service ceiling 7180m (23,555ft)
Dimensions: wingspan 17.90m (58ft 9in); length 11.94m (39ft 2in); height 3.58m (11ft 8in)
Weight: 3897kg (8591lb) loaded
Armament: four 7.7mm (0.303in) machine guns

ORIGINALLY DEVELOPED as a multi-purpose trainer and designed to duplicate the handling characteristics of the Japanese Army Air

This particular Tachikawa Ki.54 'Hickory', seen at Hangchow, China, was taken over by the Chinese Nationalist Air Force.

Force's twin-engined monoplane bombers as closely as possible, the Tachikawa Ki.54 flew for the first time in the summer of 1940. The first model, the Ki.54a, was optimized for pilot training only; however, the Ki.54b had provision for training an entire bomber crew. The Ki.54c was a light transport and communications version and was fitted with eight seats, while the Ki.54d was an anti-submarine patrol variant, carrying eight 60kg (132lb) depth charges. A very successful design, the Ki.54 was codenamed 'Hickory' by the Allies. Specification refers to the Ki.54b.

TACHIKAWA KI.77

Crew: 5
Powerplant: two 873kW (1170hp) Nakajima Ha-115 14-cylinder radial engines
Performance: max speed 440km/h (273mph); service ceiling 8700m (28,545ft)
Dimensions: wingspan 29.40m (96ft 6in); length 15.30m (50ft 2in); height 3.85m (12ft 7in)
Weight: 16,725kg (36,872lb) loaded

THE TACHIKAWA KI.77 had its origin in January 1940, when the Japanese newspaper *Asahi Shimbun* approached the Aeronautical Research Institute of the University of Tokyo and asked it to design an aircraft capable of flying at least 15,000km (9321 miles) at a cruising speed of 300km/h (186mph).

The Ki.77 which, in July 1944, set an unofficial closed-circuit distance record by flying 16,435km (10,212 miles) nonstop in 57 hours 12 minutes.

Tachikawa was given the task of building the aircraft, which emerged as a highly streamlined twin-engined design with a high aspect ratio laminar-flow wing, but work had to be shelved in 1941 because of the firm's military commitments and a prototype did not fly until November 1942. In February 1943, it flew non-stop from Japan to Singapore, a distance of 5330km (3312 miles) in 19 hrs 13 mins. A second prototype attempted to fly from Japan to Germany in July 1943, but was lost somewhere over the Indian Ocean, cause unknown. In July 1944 the first prototype flew 19 circuits over Manchuria, a total of 16,435km (10,212 miles) in 57 hrs 12 mins, establishing an unofficial world record.

TCHETVERIKOV MDR-6

FORMER USSR: 1937

Crew: 5
Powerplant: two 821kW (1100hp) M-63 9-cylinder radial engines
Performance: max speed 360km/h (224mph); range 1200km (746 miles); service ceiling 9000m (29,500ft)
Dimensions: wingspan 19.78m (64ft 11in); length 14.70m (48ft 3in)
Weight: 6790kg (14,969lb) loaded
Armament: two 7.62mm (0.30in) machine guns; 600kg (1320lb) of bombs

IGOR V. TCHETVERIKOV followed his ARK-3 with an excellent design, the MDR-6, which flew for the first time in 1937 and entered service with the Soviet Navy in 1939. Larger and more powerful than its predecessor, the original MDR-6 was succeeded by the MDR-6A of 1941 and the MDR-6B of 1944, each with improved engines and payload capacity. The

MDR-6 remained in operational use until 1955. Throughout the aircraft's development career, Tchetverikov strove to improve its overall performance by refining the design, but it grew progressively heavier and performance suffered accordingly. Post–World War II, the MDR-6 received the NATO reporting name 'Mule'.

Specifications apply to MDR-6.

Tchetverikov MDR-6 in the insignia of the Soviet Naval Aviation. The MDR-6 had a lengthy service career which lasted until 1955.

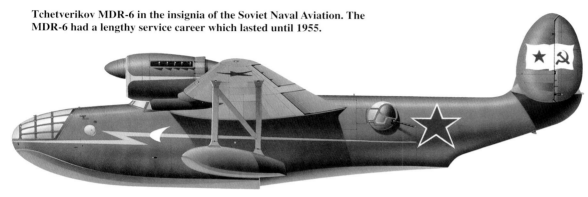

TEMCO TT-1 PINTO

USA: 1956

Crew: 2
Powerplant: one 4.13kN (930lb) thrust Continental J69-T-9 turbojet engine
Performance: max speed 555km/h (345mph); range 724km (450 miles); service ceiling 9821m (32,200ft)
Dimensions: wingspan 9.15m (30ft); length 9.38m (30ft 9.25in); height 3.30m (10ft 10.75in)
Weight: 1959kg (4325lb) loaded

FIRST FLOWN IN 1956, the Temco (Texas Engineering and Manufacturing Company) TT-1 Pinto was designed in response to a US Air Force requirement for a jet-powered primary trainer. Fourteen examples were ordered for evaluation by the US Navy, but no further production was undertaken, the requirement being filled by the Cessna T-37.

Some Pintos passed into civilian hands, a few being fitted with the 1291kg (2850lb) J85 CJ610 engine and dubbed Super Pinto.

A neat and functional design, the Temco TT-1 Pinto was designed to meet the US Air Force requirement for a primary jet trainer, but lost out to the Cessna T-37.

THOMAS-MORSE S-4

USA: 1917

Crew: 1
Powerplant: one 60kW (80hp) Le Rhone 9C rotary engine
Performance: max speed 153km/h (95mph); endurance 2 hrs 30 mins; service ceiling 4572m (15,000ft)
Dimensions: wingspan 8.08m (26ft 6in); length 6.05m (19ft 10in); height 2.46m (8ft 1in)
Weight: 623kg (1373lb)
Armament: one 7.62mm (0.30in) machine gun

THE THOMAS-MORSE Aircraft Corporation was organized in January 1917 through a merger of the Thomas Brothers Aeroplane Company and the Morse Chain Company. It produced its first fighter trainer, the S-4B, in November that year, and obtained an order for the supply of 100 machines to the US Signal Corps for advanced training. The aircraft's handling qualities were generally good, but trouble was experienced with the original 75kW (100hp) Gnome Monosoupape engine, so the type was re-engined with the 60kW (80hp) Le Rhone 9C and emerged as the S-4C. Orders for the S-4C variant totalled 597,

The S-4 was the first fighter trainer produced by the Thomas-Morse Aircraft Corporation. The little aircraft became famous for its participation in the aviation films which became all the rage after World War I.

some having been cancelled with the end of World War I. The final variant was the S-4E, with tapered wings and a higher speed, but only one prototype was built. The S-4 was well represented in post-war aviation films, notably the famous *Hell's Angels*. Many found their way into the hands of private owners, and appeared on the racing circuit in the United States for a number of years. Specifications apply to S-4C.

TIPSY T.66 NIPPER

BELGIUM: 1957

The series III Tipsy Nipper was a heavier and more powerful version of the Mk.II, and usually had a fully-cowled engine, whereas the earlier Mk.I and Mk.II had the cylinderheads sticking out of the fuselage.

Crew: 1
Powerplant: one 33kW (45hp) converted Stamo (VW Beetle) engine
Performance: max speed 160km/h (100mph); standard range 400km (248 miles); service ceiling 3600m (11,800ft)
Dimensions: wingspan 6.00m (19ft 7in); length 4.56m (14ft 8in)
Weight: 330kg (728lb) maximum take-off weight
Payload: one person

THE NIPPER WAS designed by Ernest Tips, an engineer with the Belgian Avions Fairey Company. His design criteria was to build a rugged, easy-to-fly single-seat light aeroplane which could be produced or home built. Avions Fairey produced the Nipper in several marques up until 1962, by which time 78 had been built. Cobelavia (and later Nipper Aircraft) acquired rights to build the type in the United Kingdom and produced a further 30 examples. A number of one-off enhancements (often engine or range improvements) have since been made to operational examples. Specifications apply to the Tipsy T.66 II.

TRANSALL C-160

INTERNATIONAL: 1963

THE TRANSALL C-160 tactical transport was designed and produced as a joint venture between France and Federal Germany. 'Transall' is an abbreviation of the specially formed consortium Transporter Allianz, comprising the companies of MBB, Aérospatiale and VFW-Fokker. The prototype flew for the first time on 25 February 1963, and series production began four years later. The principal variants were the C-160A, consisting of six pre-series aircraft; the C-160D for the Luftwaffe (90 built); the C-160F for France (60 built); the C-160T (20 built for export to Turkey); and the C-160Z (nine built for South Africa). An upgraded Transall C-160 series was produced in limited numbers. Specifications apply to the Transall C-160F.

Crew: 4
Powerplant: two 4551kW (6100hp) Rolls-Royce Tyne RTy.20 Mk 22 turboprop engines
Performance: max speed 536km/h (333mph); range 4558km (2832 miles); service ceiling 8500m (27,900ft)
Dimensions: wingspan 40.00m (131ft 3in); length 32.40m (106ft 3in); height 11.65m (38ft 5in)
Weight: 16,000kg (35,270lb) loaded

A Transall C-160 of the German Luftwaffe. The Transall has proved to be a very effective tactical transport and is a good design with the added benefit of reliable Rolls-Royce Tyne engines.

TSAGI 1-EA TO 11-EA

FORMER USSR: 1930–1941

IN 1928 THE VERTICAL flight section of the Moscow Aviation Institute (TsAGI) was expanded and renamed the 'Special Constructions Section', and a project for a helicopter designated TsAGI 1-EA was initiated under the direction of Boris Yuryev, a pupil of Prof. N. Ye. Zhuikovsky, the 'father' of Soviet aviation.

Completed in 1930 the 1-EA had an open-framework fuselage, a four-blade lifting rotor powered by two 90kW (120hp) M-2 rotary engines and a pair of three-blade control rotors mounted at nose and tail. It established altitude and endurance records in 1932–33 before being lost in a crash. The 3-EA had a new rotor assembly consisting of three rigid blades. Mounted between the main lifting blades were three shorter blades with a diameter of 7.8m (25.5ft) attached to the hub by feathering hinges. Their pitch could be altered to provide directional control. Redesignated TsAGI 5-EA it made its first tethered flights late in 1933. In 1934 the rotor system was used in the tandem two-seat TsAGI 11-EA which was powered by a 470kW (630hp) Curtiss Conqueror water-cooled engine. Small anti-torque rotors were mounted near the tips of a short fixed wing and the machine had a conventional tail unit with fin, rudder, tailplane and elevators. In May 1936 after ground tests the wooden main rotor was replaced with one of all-metal construction. In 1938 the fixed wings were replaced by open steel-tube outriggers with tandem pairs of anti-torque rotors mounted at the end of each. Some forward-thrust was added and the machine was redesignated 11-EA PV (Proplsivinii Variant – propulsion version), flying for the first time in October 1940. In spring 1941 a shortage of spares for the Conqueror engine brought testing to a close.

Specifications apply to the TsAGI 5-EA.

Crew: 1
Powerplant: two 90kW (120hp) M-2 engine
Performance: max speed 20km/h (12.4mph); endurance 8.5 mins; service ceiling not exceeding 40m (131ft)
Dimensions: main rotor diameter 12.00m (39ft 4.5in) with small blades, 7.80m (25ft 7in) with large blades; length 11.00m (36ft 11in); height 3105m (10ft 2in)
Weight: 1047kg (2308lb)

TUPOLEV ANT-5 (I-4)

FORMER USSR: 1927

BY 1927, ANDREI TUPOLEV had established a firm reputation as a pioneer in all-metal aircraft construction, and his ANT-5, also known by the military designation I-4, was the first Russian fighter built in this way. A single-seater with a fixed undercarriage, the I-4 was superior to all other contemporary Russian fighter designs, and quantity production continued for several years after the type's service debut in 1928, about 370 being built. Several different versions of the I-4 were produced, including a twin-cannon variant, a seaplane variant and a version with six solid-fuel rockets for short

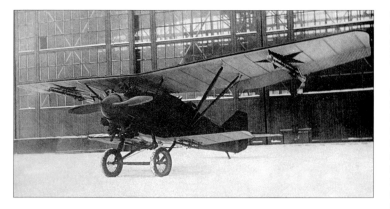

take-off. The I-4 also took part in parasite fighter trials, two being carried on the wings of a TB-1 bomber. Specifications apply to the Tupolev ANT-5.

Crew: 1
Powerplant: one 343kW (460hp) M-22 (Bristol Jupiter) radial engine
Performance: max speed 257km/h (160mph); range 750km (466 miles); service ceiling 7655m (25,100ft)
Dimensions: wingspan 11.42m (37ft 5in); length 7.27m (23ft 10in); height 2.82m (9ft 2in)
Weight: 1359kg (3000lb) loaded
Armament: two 7.62mm (0.30in) machine guns

Tupolev I-4 armed with DRP-76 rocket projectiles. The Russians pioneered the use of rocketry in all fields of aviation, from weapons to take-off.

TUPOLEV TB-3

FORMER USSR: 1930

ONE OF THE MORE antiquated bombers in service with the Soviet Air Force at the time of the German invasion was the TB-3 (ANT-6), a massive four-engined type which had entered service in 1931. The ANT-6 prototype flew for the first time on 22 December 1930, powered by four Curtiss V-1760 Conqueror engines. The aircraft had a troubled development, and did not appear in its definitive form until 1935. It was

rushed into production for reasons of prestige; nine of the giant aircraft, now allocated the military designation TB-3, were built in less than a year, and these took part in a flypast over Red Square, Moscow, on 1 May 1932. For a period of several months in that year, three TB-3s were being delivered to the Red Air Force every two days. Production ended in 1937, by which time 818 had been delivered. The

type saw action against the Japanese in 1939, and against the Finns in the Winter War of 1939–40. In 1941 it was relegated to freight and paratroop transport roles, its designation being changed to G-2. It was withdrawn in 1944.

The TB-3 prototype almost came to grief on its maiden flight in 1930 when the throttle levers slipped back during take-off.

Crew: 8
Powerplant: four 533kW (715hp) M-17F (BMW) 12-cylinder Vee-type engines
Performance: max speed 288km/h (179mph); range 3225km (2004 miles); service ceiling 3800m (12,470ft)
Dimensions: wingspan 40.48m (132ft 10in); length 25.54m (83ft 9in); height 8.47m (27ft 9in)
Weight: 17,400kg (38,360lb) loaded
Armament: six 7.62mm (0.30in) machine guns; 2200kg (4800lb) of bombs

TUPOLEV SB-2

FORMER USSR: 1934

A Tupolev SB-2 captured and used by the Finnish Air Force. The Finns used considerable numbers of Soviet aircraft, forced down more or less intact during the 'Winter War' of 1939–40 and repaired.

THE TUPOLEV SB-2 was almost certainly the most capable light bomber in service anywhere in the world in the mid-1930s. It was the first aircraft of modern stressed-skin construction to be produced in the USSR, and in numerical terms was also the most important bomber of its day. The story of the SB-2 began in the early 1930s, when Andrei N. Tupolev embarked on design studies for a fast tactical bomber. Considering

the official requirement to be inadequate, he built two prototypes according to the Air Force Technical Office specification, and a third according to his own. All three prototypes flew in 1934, and Tupolev's own version, the ANT-40-2, proved the best. The type was ordered into production, entering service in 1936, and 6967 aircraft were built before production ended in 1941.

Specifications apply to SB-2bis.

Crew: 3
Powerplant: two 716kW (960hp) Klimov M-103 12-cylinder Vee-type engines
Performance: max speed 450km/h (280mph); range 2300km (1429 miles); service ceiling 9000m (29,530ft)
Dimensions: wingspan 20.33m (66ft 8in); length 12.57m (41ft 2in); height 3.25m (10ft 8in)
Weight: 7880kg (17,372lb) loaded
Armament: four 7.62mm (0.30in) machine guns; bomb load of 600kg (1323lb)

TUPOLEV TU-2

FORMER USSR: 1941

IN 1938, THE DESIGN bureau led by Andrei N. Tupolev was assigned the task of developing a light bomber that would have a performance equalling that of contemporary fighter aircraft while carrying a substantial internal bomb load. The aircraft also had to have a good combat radius, and be suitable for dive-bombing. The resulting project, known as Aircraft 103 for security reasons, was given the bureau designation ANT-58. An all-metal, mid-wing monoplane

with a crew of three, it was fitted with two 1044kW (1400hp) Mikulin AM-37 V-12 in-line engines.

The prototype flew for the first time on 29 January 1941 and subsequent flight testing showed that the aircraft had an outstanding performance. A second machine, Aircraft 103U (bureau designation ANT-59), flew on 18 May 1941, powered by the same AM-37 engines, but with some changes that included provision for a fourth crew member to man a ventral gun

The Tu-2, an excellent light bomber with outstanding performance, was in use with Soviet bloc countries long after the end of World War II.

position introduced just forward of the tail, protecting an area which had hitherto been vulnerable. Preparations were made for immediate series production, but at this point a crop of problems arose, not least of which was that the AM-37 engine was in short

THK-5A
Produced in small numbers in Turkey at the end of World War II, the THK-5A was a twin-engined light ambulance aircraft. One example was sold to Denmark.

THOMAS-MORSE MB-3
First flown in 1919, the Thomas-Morse MB-3 was the company's second fighter design. Of the 250 examples built, many remained in service until the late 1920s.

THOMAS MORSE O-19
The Thomas-Morse O-19 was a two-seat armed observation biplane, powered by a Pratt & Whitney Wasp engine. Over 170 were built from 1928 for the US Army Air Corps.

THRUXTON GADFLY
British two-seat light autogyro project.

THULIN TYPE K
The Thulin Type K was a Swedish monoplane fighter, first flown in 1917. Two examples were used by Sweden, and 15 by the Royal Netherlands Navy.

TIMM N2T-1
The Timm N2T-1 of 1941 was a two-seat training monoplane, used in small numbers by the US Navy.

TIPSY MODEL B
A two-seat, single-engined, ultra-light aircraft dating from the 1930s, the Model B was previously manufactured by Belgian Fairey subsidiary Avions-Fairey in a number of variants.

TIPSY MODEL BELFAIR
After World War II, the canopied version of the earlier Tipsy Model B single-engined trainer was relaunched and named the Belfair.

TOKYO KI.107
First flown in 1944, the Tokyo Ki.107 was an experimental all-wood primary trainer. Development was suspended after the prototype was destroyed in an accident.

TRAVEL AIR MYSTERY SHIP (MODEL R)
Built quickly and secretly in spare time by two Travel Air engineers, the first Model R (as it was later known) won the 1929 Thompson Trophy in the United States, beating a field of mostly military biplanes and signalling the arrival of the monoplane design as the way of the future.

supply. As a consequence, it was decided to replace the AM-37s with a pair of 992kW (1330hp) Shvetsov Ash-82 radial engines. These powered the third prototype, Aircraft 103V (ANT-60), which flew in December 1941 and carried the same crew and armament as the ANT-59. Limited production at last got under way at the beginning of 1942, the bomber now being designated Tu-2, but deliveries were slow because of the need to relocate many Soviet aircraft factories ahead of the rapid German advance into Russia. In some areas the design of the Tu-2 was too complex, so Tupolev was ordered to simplify the structure of the aircraft in order to make it more suitable for mass production.

The first three production aircraft were delivered to a service evaluation unit near Kalinin, completing their operational trials in September 1942. Pilots were particularly enthusiastic about the bomber, their reports stressing its substantial bomb load and excellent combat radius, good defensive armament, its ability to fly on one engine, and the ease with which crews were able to convert to the new type. Because of the earlier problems, however, series production of the Tu-2 did not start until 1943, and combat units did not begin to rearm with the bomber until the spring of 1944. The Tu-2 first saw action on a large scale in June 1944 on the Karelian (Finnish) front. In its primary bombing role, the Tu-2 carried out some extremely effective missions in the closing months of the war, particularly against fortified enemy towns. The aircraft was also used extensively in the brief Soviet campaign against the Japanese Kwantung Army in Manchuria in August 1945. Total wartime production was 1111 aircraft. In October 1944 a long-range variant, the Tu-2D (ANT-62), made its appearance. A torpedo-bomber variant, the Tu-2T (ANT-62T), was tested between January and March 1945, and issued to units of the Soviet Naval Aviation. The Tu-2R, which was also designated Tu-6, carried a battery of cameras in the bomb bay, while an experimental ground-attack version, the Tu-2Sh, was tested with various armament combinations.

After World War II, the Tu-2 proved to be an ideal test vehicle for various powerplants, including the first generation of Soviet jet engines. Production continued after 1945, some 3000 aircraft eventually being delivered to various Soviet Bloc air forces. Chinese Tu-2s were encountered by UN fighter pilots during the Korean War, proving easy targets for jet fighters such as the F-86 Sabre.

Specification refers to the Tupolev Tu-2S.

Crew: 4
Powerplant: two 1380kW (1850hp) Shvetsov Ash-82FN radial engines
Performance: max speed 547km/h (340mph); range 2000km (1243 miles); service ceiling 9500m (31,170ft)
Dimensions: wingspan 18.86m (61ft 10in); length 13.80m (45ft 3in); height 4.56m (14ft 11in)
Weight: 12,800kg (28,219lb) loaded
Armament: two 20mm (0.79in) cannon and three 12.7mm (0.50in) machine guns

TUPOLEV TU-4 'BULL'
FORMER USSR: 1946

Crew: 10-14
Powerplant: four 1641kW (2200hp) Shvetsov ASh-73TK 18-cylinder air-cooled supercharged radial engines
Performance: max speed 569km/h (354 mph); range 5229km (3250 miles); service ceiling 10,248m (33,600ft)
Dimensions: wingspan 43.08m (141ft 3in); length 30.00m (98ft 5in); height 9.01m (29ft 7in)
Weight: 54,360kg (120,000lb) loaded
Armament: 12 12.7mm (0.50in) machine guns and one 20mm (0.79in) cannon; up to 5436kg (12,000lb) of bombs or maritime stores

THE TUPOLEV TU-4, codenamed 'Bull' by NATO, was a copy of the Boeing B-29 Superfortress, three of which had force-landed in the eastern Soviet Union after attacking targets in Manchuria. A prototype Tu-4 flew in 1946; however, the Russians encountered numerous

The Tupolev Tu-4, a copy of the Boeing B-29 Superfortress, gave the Soviet Air Force its first true strategic bombing capability.

engineering problems in copying the complex American type and the first production aircraft were not issued to the Soviet long-range bomber force until early in 1948, and it was not until the middle of 1949 that the type was declared fully operational.

The Tu-4, although essentially an interim aircraft pending the introduction of strategic jet bombers, nevertheless proved a valuable tool in Russia's nuclear weapons programme, carrying out the first air drop of a Soviet atomic weapon. Some were issued to Soviet Naval Aviation units. About 1200 Tu-4s are thought to have been built, some of which were turned over to China.

TUPOLEV TU-14 'BOSUN'
FORMER USSR: 1949

Crew: 4
Powerplant: two 2700kg (5952lb) thrust Klimov VK-1 turbojet engines
Performance: max speed 845km/h (525mph); range 3010km (1870 miles); service ceiling 11,200m (36,745ft)
Dimensions: wingspan 21.68m (71ft 1in); length 21.95m (72ft); height 6.68m (21ft 11in)
Weight: 23,350kg (51,477lb) loaded
Armament: four 12.7mm (0.50in) machine guns and two 23mm (0.90in) cannon; up to 3000kg (6614lb) of bombs

The Tupolev Tu-14 was an important component of the Soviet Navy's anti-shipping capability in the early 1950s.

LIKE ILYUSHIN'S IL-28, the Tu-14 – known to NATO as 'Bosun' – was designed to meet a Soviet Air Force requirement for a light jet attack bomber to replace the Tu-2. The prototype first flew in 1949 and, although the Ilyushin Il-28 was selected in preference, it was recognized that the Tu-14's greater endurance and its lengthy weapons bay capable of housing torpedoes would make it a very viable land-based naval strike aircraft. The type was subsequently produced in two versions, the Tu-14T torpedo-bomber and the Tu-14R maritime reconnaissance aircraft.

TUPOLEV TU-16 'BADGER'

FORMER USSR: 1952

Egypt's squadron of Tu-16 'Badgers' was destroyed on the ground during the Six-Day War of 1967. They were replaced by 20 'Badger-G's, two of which are seen here.

Crew: 7
Powerplant: two 9500kg (20,944lb) thrust Mikulin RD-3M turbojet engines
Performance: max speed 960km/h (597mph); range 4800km (2983 miles); service ceiling 15,000m (49,200ft)
Dimensions: wingspan 32.99m (108ft 3in); length 34.80m (114ft 2in); height 10.36m (34ft 2in)
Weight: 75,800kg (167,110lb) loaded
Armament: two 23mm (0.90in) cannon in radar-controlled barbettes in upper forward and lower ventral fuselage positions

DEPLOYED IN THE mid 1950s, Tupolev's Tu-16 was the most effective of Russia's trio of new strategic bombers, the others being the Myasishchev Mya-4 Bison and Tupolev Tu-95 Bear. The Tu-16 jet bomber flew for the first time in 1952 under the manufacturer's designation Tu-88, and was destined to become the most important bomber type on the inventories of the Soviet Air Force and Naval Air Arm. Production of the Tu-16, allocated the NATO reporting name 'Badger', began in 1953 and it first entered service with the Soviet Air Force's Long-Range Aviation in 1955. The first production version was the 'Badger-A', which had many elements based on those of the Tu-4, combined with a new swept wing, retractable landing gear of tricycle configuration, and new indigenous AM-3 turbojets designed and developed by the Mikulin Bureau. Later production aircraft were powered by the uprated Mikulin AM-3M, providing better maximum range and speed.

The 'Badger-A' was also supplied to Iraq (9) and Egypt (30).

The principal subvariant of the 'Badger-A' was the Tu-16A, configured to carry the USSR's air-deliverable nuclear weapons. Other subvariants were the Tu-16T torpedo-bomber, Tu-16K airborne lifeboat carrier, Tu-16N wingtip-to-wingtip flight refuelling tanker and an undesignated probe-and-drogue tanker; some converted as Tu-16G (Tu-104G) for training Aeroflot crews and for fast mail services. The next major variant, the Tu-16KS-1 'Badger-B', was similar to 'Badger-A' but was equipped initially to carry the KS 1 Komet III (AS 1 Kennel) anti-shipping missile, with a retractable dustbin radome aft of the bomb bay. Many examples were reconfigured to the free-falling bombing role.

The Tu-16K-10 'Badger-C' was an anti-shipping version armed with the K-10 (AS-2 Kipper) ASM beneath the fuselage, with a Puff Ball radar housed in a broad flat nose radome. Tu-16K-26 'Badger-C' Mod was a conversion of the Tu-16K-10 with provision for the smaller K-26 (AS-6 Kingfish) ASM under the wings instead of, or in addition to, the centreline-mounted K-10. The Tu-16R 'Badger-D' was a conversion of the 'Badger-C' for maritime reconnaissance. The 'Badger-F' was also a maritime reconnaissance version. The 'Badger-E' was basically an '-A' with a battery of cameras in the bomb bay for high-altitude maritime reconnaissance. The 'Badger-G' was a dedicated anti-shipping version, while the 'Badger-J' was equipped for barrage-jamming in the A- to I-bands. The 'Badger-L' was one of the last variants in a long line of electronic intelligence gatherers. The Tu-16, over 2000 examples of which are thought to have been produced, was also licence-built in China as the Xian H-6.

Specifications apply to the Tu-16PM Badger-L.

A Tu-16 'Badger' on a maritime patrol mission from a base on the Kola Peninsula in northern Russia.

TUPOLEV TU-95/TU-142 'BEAR'

Crew: 10
Powerplant: four 11,190kW (15,000hp) Kuznetsov NK-12MV turboprop engines
Performance: Max speed 805km/h (500mph); service ceiling 13,400m (44,000ft); range 12,550km (7800 miles)
Dimensions: Wing span 48.50m (159ft); length 47.50 (155ft 10in); height 11.78m (38ft 8in)
Weight: 154,000kg (340,000lb) loaded
Armament: six 23mm (0.90in) cannon; bomb load of up to 11,340kg (25,000lb)

GIVEN THE NATO reporting name 'Bear', the Tupolev Tu-95 flew for the first time on 12 November 1952. The type entered service with the Soviet Strategic Air Forces (Dal'naya Aviatsiya) in 1957, early examples having played a prominent part in Soviet nuclear weapons trials.

The initial Tu-95M 'Bear-A' freefall nuclear bomber was followed by the Tu-95K-20 'Bear-B' of 1961, this being a maritime attack and reconnaissance version with a large radome under the nose and a Kh-20 (AS-3 Kangaroo) cruise missile. The Tu-95KD was similar, but was fitted with a flight refuelling probe. The Tu-95KM 'Bear-C', thought to be a new-build

Like America's B-52, the Tupolev Tu-95/142 became the Soviet Union's primary airborne cruise missile carrier. Its primary function during the Cold War, however, was to track and if necessary engage enemy naval task forces.

variant, was a specialized maritime reconnaissance version, as was the similar 'Bear-D', while the 'Bear-E' and '-F' were upgraded variants with a new electronics suite. These

and later aircraft were designated Tu-142. Later models include the 'Bear-H', equipped to carry up to four cruise missiles, and the 'Bear-J', a very long frequency (VLF)

communications platform based on the 'Bear-F'. Eight Tu-142s were supplied to the Indian Navy.

Specifications refer to the Tupolev Tu-95 'Bear-A'.

TUPOLEV TU-104 'CAMEL'

IN THE 1950s the Soviet Union realized the necessity to modernize Aeroflot's passenger fleet both to reduce journey times and to compete with developments in the

West. Part of this programme involved the development of a medium-range jet airliner, and the task was placed upon a team led by Andrei N. Tupolev in 1953.

In order to rationalize resources, minimize costs and meet timescales it was decided to utilize significant elements of the Tu-16 bomber design, including the wing, nose,

fin and initially the powerplant, which were all married to a new pressurized fuselage design. The result was the Tu-104 turbojet airliner, which first flew as the Tu-104G (G denoting civil) prototype on 17 June 1955. This made it only the second jet airliner to enter service following the ill-fated de Havilland Comet 1.

The initial production version (simply referred to as the Tu-104) had a capacity for 50 passengers and was powered by two Mikulin AM-3 turbojets each rated at 66.18kN (14,881lb); like the Tu-16 these were mounted either side of the fuselage in the wing root, and the main undercarriage retracted in two large fairings on the trailing edge. The effect of the Tu-104 in service was radical, with some domestic journey times more than halved in comparison with the preceding Ilyushin Il-12 and Il-14. Moscow to Irkutsk, for example, was reduced from nearly 18 hours to six and a half hours. The visit of a prototype to Western Europe in

Czechoslovakian national carrier CSA was the only customer other than Aeroflot for the Tu-104; the Tu-104A pictured here was the first delivered to that airline in 1957.

the spring of 1956 caused a major re-evaluation of Soviet capability.

The Mikulin powerplant was later uprated to 85.29kN (19,180lb thrust). This version was designated AM-3M and it was subsequently used on the first higher capacity variant, the Tu-104A, which had a capacity of 70 passengers and entered service in 1958. Further development of the Mikulin powerplant (to the AM-M500 as specified) resulted in the ability to stretch the Tu-104's fuselage by 1.21m (3ft 11 0.5in); the resulting variant was designated Tu-104B and this version would eventually be capable of accommodating up to 100 passengers.

The Tu-104B entered service in 1959 as the final production development of the Tu-104, and it became the most commonly used aircraft on Aeroflot's international service network. Production of the Tupolev Tu-104 ended in 1960 with over 200 examples built, although the Tu-104 was the subject of a retrospective conversion programme that raised capacity to 100 persons in the Tu-104D (Tu-104B) or alternatively 85 persons in the Tu-104V (Tu-104A).

The only export customer for the Tu-104 was to be CSA of Czechoslovakia, which purchased six variants of the Tu-104A fitted

The Tu-104 in this picture is the prototype, which first flew on 17 June 1955. It was also the first to visit the West, in March 1956.

in an 81-seat layout. Other examples saw service with the Soviet space programme as research or transport aircraft. However, the Tu-104s of Aeroflot and CSA became a relatively common sight in the West on scheduled flights in the 1960s, although progressively replaced by the Tu-154 during the 1970s. During the late 1960s and early 1970s, the Soviet Union made a great attempt to sell its Black Sea resorts to Western tourists in order to improve foreign exchange relations, and the Tu-104 was the type generally utilized for these charters, which involved up to five flights a day from Western destinations on summer weekends. After this service discontinued, the number of Tu-104s remaining in

service steadily diminished, and the aircraft were largely used for internal flights, the last example being retired in 1981.

Specifications apply to the Tupolev Tu-104B.

Crew: 3
Powerplant: two 95.10kN (21,397lb) thrust Mikulin AM-M500 turbojet engines
Performance: max speed 950km/h (590mph) at 10,000m (32,810ft); range with maximum payload 2650km (1647 miles); service ceiling 11,500m (37,730ft)
Dimensions: wingspan 34.54m (113ft 4in); length 40.05m (131ft 4.75in); height 11.90m (39ft 0.5in)
Weight: 76,000kg (167,551lb) maximum take-off weight
Payload: 100 passengers in a high-density layout

TUPOLEV TU-128 'FIDDLER'   FORMER USSR: 1957

Crew: 2
Powerplant: two 11,000kg (24,690lb) thrust Lyulka AL-21F turbojet engines
Performance: max speed 1850km/h (1150mph); range 5000km (3105 miles); service ceiling 20,000m (65,615ft)
Dimensions: wingspan 18.10m (59ft 4in); length 27.20m (89ft 3in); height 7.00m (23ft)
Weight: 40,000kg (88,185lb) loaded
Armament: four AA-5 Ash long-range AAMs

THE TU-128 LONG-RANGE interceptor was derived from the Tu-98, a supersonic low-level strike aircraft which did not go into production. First flown in 1957, the Tu-128 was rushed into service to meet an urgent Soviet Air Force requirement for an aircraft capable of intercepting B-52 bombers armed with stand-off missiles such as the Hound Dog while the latter aircraft

The Tupolev Tu-28 pictured here is now a museum piece at Monino, near Moscow.

were still outside missile launch range. The Tu-128 received the NATO codename 'Fiddler', the major production version being the Tu-128 'Fiddler-B'. The type was first publicly revealed at the 1961 Tushino air display.

TUPOLEV TU-114 ROSSIYA 'CLEAT'

TO FULFIL AEROFLOT'S growing long-range domestic and international requirements, Tupolev provided an adaptation of the TU-95 'Bear' bomber. Initially several TU-95 conversions were trialled under designations Tu-116 and Tu-114D. These were superseded by the designated Tu-114, which had a redesigned circular fuselage tailored to passenger-carrying needs. The Tu-114 went into service in 1960 as the world's fastest propeller-driven aircraft (each engine drove two eight-bladed contra-rotating propellers). It was also the heaviest airliner of its time and the only non-jet with swept wings. In the region of 30 Tu-114s were built solely for

A derivative of the civil Tu-114 shown here was designated Tu-126 and developed as an AWACS (airborne warning and control) aeroplane.

Aeroflot and these served into the early 1970s when they were superseded by Ilyushin's Il-62. Specifications apply to the Tu-114.

Crew: 5
Powerplant: four 11,033ekW (14,795eshp) Kuznetsov NK-12MV turboprop engines
Performance: cruising speed 770km/h (478mph); range with maximum payload 6200km (3853 miles); service ceiling 12,000m (39,370ft)
Dimensions: wingspan 51.10m (167ft 7.75in); length 54.10m (177ft 6in); height 15.50m (50ft 10.25in)
Weight: 171,000kg (376,990lb) maximum take-off weight
Payload: maximum 220 passengers, but typically 120–170 in two or three classes

TUPOLEV TU-22 'BLINDER'

First seen at Tushino Air Display in 1961, the Tupolev Tu-22 'Blinder' supersonic bomber and reconnaissance aircraft had a limited range.

Crew: 4
Powerplant: two 16,000kg (35,273lb) thrust Koliesov VD-7M turbojet engines
Performance: max speed 1487km/h (924mph); range 3100km (1926 miles); service ceiling 18,300m (60,040m)
Dimensions: wingspan 23.75m (77ft 11in); length 40.53m (132ft 11in); height 10.67m (35ft)
Weight: 84,000kg (185,188lb) loaded
Armament: one 23mm (0.90in) NR-23 cannon in tail position; bomber variants: up to 12,000kg (26,455lb) of bombs, or one AS-4 Kitchen air-to-surface missile semi-recessed under fuselage

THE TUPOLEV TU-22 'Blinder', designed as a supersonic successor to the 'Badger', was first seen publicly at the Tushino air display

in 1961. The Tu-22s seen at Tushino were pre-series trials aircraft, and first deliveries of the type to the Dalnaya Aviatsiya (Soviet Strategic Air Force) were not made until the following year. The first operational version, code-named 'Blinder-A', was produced in limited numbers only. the Tu-22K 'Blinder-B', was equipped with a flight refuelling probe; 12 aircraft were supplied to Iraq and 24 to Libya. The Tu-22R 'Blinder-C' was a maritime reconnaissance variant, about 60 of which were built, and the Tu-22P 'Blinder-E' was an ECM aircraft. Total Tu-22 production was 250 aircraft.
    Specification refers to the Tupolev Tu-22P 'Blinder E'.

TUPOLEV TU-134 'CRUSTY'

THE TU-134 WAS designed as a long-term replacement for the stop-gap Tu-124 short-range jet airliner and involved two firsts for Tupolev – rear fuselage-mounted engines and a T-tail arrangement, while retaining some fuselage synergy with the Tu-124.
    Early versions were built with glazed noses, but the prevalent Tu-134A replaced this with a nose cone covering a Weather Radar scanner. The Tu-134 was exported widely in the Eastern Bloc and over 700 were built until 1978, and many examples remain in service.
    Specifications apply to the Tupolev Tu-134A.

Over 300 Tu-134s remain in service, supported by upgrades and overhaul packages.

Crew: 3
Powerplant: two 66.68kN (14,991lb) Aviadvigatel (Soloviev) D-30 II turbofan engines
Performance: max cruising speed 900km/h (559mph); range 3500km (2175 miles); service ceiling 11,900m (39,040ft)
Dimensions: wingspan 29.00m (95ft 1.25in); length 37.10m (121ft 8.75in); height 9.14m (30ft)
Weight: 47,000kg (103,616lb) maximum take-off weight
Payload: up to 96 passengers

TUPOLEV TU-144 'CHARGER'

FORMER USSR: 1968

Crew: 3
Powerplant: four Kuznetsov NK-144 turbofan engines each rated at 127.5kN (28,687lb st) dry and 196.1kN (44,122lb) with afterburning
Performance: max speed 2500km/h (1550mph) or Mach 2.35: max range with 140 passengers at an average speed of 2000km/h (1243mph) or Mach 1.9, 3500km (2173 miles); cruising altitude 16,000–18,000m (52,492 to 59,054ft)
Dimensions: wingspan 28.80m (94ft 6in); length 65.70m (215ft 6.5in); height 12.85m (42ft 2in)
Weight: 180,000kg (396,830lb) maximum take-off weight
Payload: up to 140 passengers

Pictured here is the prototype Tu-144 which first flew on 31 December 1968, several months ahead of Concorde.

DURING AN INTENSE period of rivalry between the West and the Soviet Union, the Tu-144 project directly rivalled the Aérospatiale/BAC Concorde and picked up some notable records. The Tu-144 was the world's first supersonic transport to fly (1968), the first to exceed Mach 1 and Mach 2 in level flight, and the first to enter service, in 1975. Superficially the Tu-144

resembled the Concorde, but it had a wider (five seats abreast) fuselage and utilized four turbofan rather than turbojet engines. Distinctive but retractable canards were progressively added immediately to the rear of the cockpit. The Tu-144, however, did not enjoy the long service life of Concorde. It was dogged by design problems and poor economics. Early fatal

accidents rooted in the rush to be first were never fully surmounted, and its superior capacity was compromised by its inferior range. Seventeen Tu-144s were built, but after a fatal accident in 1978 the type was quietly relegated to freight and secondary duties. One example found a second life in the 1990s as a NASA experimental aircraft. Specifications apply to Tu-144.

TUPOLEV TU-154 'CLASSIC'

FORMER USSR: 1968

Crew: 3/4
Powerplant: three 103.95kN (23,388lb) PNPP Aviadvigatel (Soloviev) D-30KU-154-II turbofan engines
Performance: cruising speed 950km/h (590mph) at 11,900m (39,040ft); range 6600km (4100 miles); service ceiling 12,500m (41,000ft)
Dimensions: wingspan 37.55m (123ft 2.5in); length 47.90m (157ft 1.75in); height 11.40m (37ft 4.75in)
Weight: 100,000kg (220,459lb) maximum take-off weight
Payload: up to 180 passengers

THE TU-154 TRI-JET was designed as a replacement for the Tu-104 and Il-18 types on the Soviet Union's demanding medium-range domestic and international service network, requiring good hot, high and short airfield performance. The Tu-154A went into service in 1972 with Kuznetsov NK-8 engines, but these and the avionics were replaced in the Tu-154B. The later Tu-154M incorporates many additional improvements and has been widely exported to countries including

The Tu-154 remains predominant within the CIS, but numbers used on services outside that arena are plummeting, in part because only the Tu-154M version is currently EU Stage 3 noise compliant.

China, Cuba and Poland. Over 1000 Tu-154s have been built, and many hundreds remain in service, mostly in the CIS with the myriad of successor airlines that followed dissolution of the Soviet Union. Specifications apply to Tu-154M.

TUPOLEV TU-22M 'BACKFIRE'

FORMER USSR: 1971

The Tupolev Tu-22M 'Backfire' was conceived from the outset as a counter to NATO's powerful carrier task forces. Its flight refuelling capability enabled it to range far out into the North Atlantic and Pacific.

The original design ('Backfire-A') underwent major modifications and re-emerged as the Tu-22M2 'Backfire-B'. About 400 Tu-22Ms were produced, 240 of them M-2s/3s. The M3 ('Backfire-C') variant had reduced defensive armament and the flight refuelling probe was deleted; a reconnaissance version, the Tu-22MR, entered service in 1985, and the Tu-22ME is the latest of the attack variants.

Specification refers to the Tupolev Tu-22M3 'Backfire-C'.

Crew: 4
Powerplant: two 20,000kg (44,100lb) thrust Kuznetsov NK-144 turbofan engines
Performance: max speed 2125km/h (1321mph); range 4000km (2485 miles); service ceiling 18,000m (59,055ft)
Dimensions: wingspan 34.30m (112ft 6in) spread; 23.40m (76ft 9in) swept; length 36.90m (121ft 1in); height 10.80m (35ft 5in)
Weight: 130,000kg (286,596lb) loaded
Armament: one 23mm (0.90in) GSh-23 twin-barrel cannon in radar-controlled tail barbette; up to 12,000kg (26,455lb) of stores in weapons bay, or one S-4 missile, or three AS-16 missiles

ALLOCATED THE NATO reporting name 'Backfire', the Tupolev Tu-22M first flew in 1971, reached initial operational capability (IOC) in 1973 and, during the years that followed, replaced the Tu-16 'Badger' in Soviet service. The ostensible mission of the new bomber – peripheral attack or inter-continental attack – became one of the most fiercely contested intelligence debates of the Cold War, and it was a long time before the true nature of the threat it posed (anti-shipping attack) became known.

TUPOLEV TU-160 'BLACKJACK'

FORMER USSR: 1981

Crew: 4
Powerplant: four 25,000kg (55,115lb) thrust Kutnetsov NK-321 turbofan engines
Performance: max speed 2000km/h (1243mph); range 14,000km (8694 miles); service ceiling 18,300m (60,040ft)
Dimensions: wingspan 55.70m (182ft 9in) spread, 35.60m (116ft 9in) swept; length 54.10m (177ft 6in); height 13.10m (43ft)
Weight: 275,000kg (606,261lb) loaded
Armament: provision for up to 16,500kg (36,376lb) of stores in two internal weapons bays and on underwing hardpoints

The Tupolev Tu-160 'Blackjack' supersonic variable-geometry bomber was the ultimate in Soviet Cold War military aircraft technology. It was in the same class as America's Rockwell B-1, but much larger.

THE TUPOLEV TU-160 supersonic bomber flew for the first time on 19 December 1981, but one of the two prototypes was lost in an accident. Comparable to but much larger than the Rockwell B-1B, the type entered series production in 1984, and the first examples were deployed in May 1987, becoming operational in 1989. Thirty-six aircraft (out of a planned total of 100, the figure reduced following the collapse of the Soviet Union) were in service with the Soviet Air Force, these being divided between the 184th Air Regiment in the Ukraine and the 121st Air Regiment at Engels Air Base. The Ukraine-based aircraft, which had become Ukrainian property after the Soviet break-up, were eventually returned to Russia, along with 600 air-launched missiles, as part of a deal involving payment of energy debts. The type was given the NATO reporting name 'Blackjack'.

VEB (BAADE-BONIN) 152

FORMER EAST GERMANY: 1958

A single 152 fuselage survived the Cold War era in use as a tool store at an East German airbase – it is now on display at Dresden Airport, Germany.

THE POLITICAL AMBITION of the East German politburo and the cancellation of the Alekseyev 150 Soviet bomber project led to the return to East Germany in 1953 of a group of German engineers and scientists deported to Russia in 1945. They were sponsored to proceed with one of the many commercial designs that they had formulated while in Russia. One of these was the 152 airliner, which was based on their experience with the Alekseyev 150 and would be powered by a development of the Junkers Jumo turbojet engine named Pirna 014. The prototype had a glazed nose and an unusual undercarriage arrangement featuring a single central gear assisted by wingtip pod-mounted outriggers. Late availability of the Pirna engines meant the prototype first flew with Tumansky Rd-9b engines. On its second flight, while rehearsing for the Leipzig trade fair, the prototype 152 crashed due to pressure equalization problems between the multifarious tanks and the inadequate engines. The second heavily modified (152A) model (with modified tanks, conventional undercarriage and a glazed nose) flew twice more before the project was cancelled in 1961 due to national economic crises which were exacerbated by the defection of key design team members.

Specifications apply to the 152.

Crew: 4/5
Powerplant: four VDL Pirna 014A-1 turbojet engines each rated at 30.89kN (6970lb st) wing-mounted in pod pairs
Performance: (estimated) max speed 920km/h (572mph); range 2500km (1553 miles)
Dimensions: wingspan 26.40m (86ft 7.3in); length 31.30m (102ft 8in); height 9.70m (31ft 9in)
Weight: 46,500kg (102,515lb) maximum take-off weight
Payload: up to 58 passengers

VICKERS FB.5

UK: 1915

Crew: 2
Powerplant: one 75kW (100hp) Gnome Monosoupape 9-cylinder rotary engine
Performance: max speed 113km/h (70mph); endurance 4 hrs 30 mins; service ceiling 2743m (9000ft)
Dimensions: wingspan 11.13m (36ft 6in); length 8.28m (27ft 2in); height 3.51m (11ft 6in)
Weight: 930kg (2050lb) loaded
Armament: one or two 7.7mm (0.303in) machine guns

AT THE 1913 Aero Show, London, Vickers Ltd exhibited its Type 18 'Destroyer', a two-seat biplane with a water-cooled Wolseley pusher engine and a free-firing, belt-fed Maxim gun mounted in the nose. No 11 Squadron, the first to be fully armed with the type, was the first specialized fighter squadron ever to form. It deployed to Villers-Bretonneux, France, in July 1915 and for several months carried out

Although a good workhorse, the Vickers FB.5, popularly known as the 'Gunbus', was no match in air combat for its German opponents.

offensive patrols and ground-attack work. No 18 Squadron, also armed with FB.5s, arrived in France in November 1915. The FB.9 was an improved version with rounded wingtips, rounded tailplane and a more streamlined nacelle.

VALMET LEKO-70
The Valmet Leko-70 is a three-seat basic trainer. The prototype flew in 1975 and deliveries to the Finnish Air Force began in 1980.

VANCE VIKING
The Vance Viking of 1932 was a high-speed mail carrier. A single-engined monoplane, it featured twin booms. Only one was built.

VERVILLE VCP-R
Originally designated VCP-1, the Verville VCP-R was a racing biplane. It won the 1920 Pulitzer Trophy and went on to take part in several more races, being redesignated R-1 in 1922.

VERVILLE-SPERRY R-3
The Verville-Sperry R-3 of 1923 was a fast, single-engined, low-wing monoplane with a retractable undercarriage, a most unusual feature for that time.

VFW WFG-H2
This late 1960s West German single-seat experimental autogyro was similar to the Bensen Gyro-Copter. The WFG-H2 was powered by a 54kW (72hp) McCulloch engine with tiny tip blade burners for hovering capability.

VFW-FOKKER H3S SPRINTER
This West German three-seat light compound helicopter first flew in 1970.

VFW-FOKKER VFW-614
Seen by many as the godfather to today's regional jet designs, the twin-jet-engined VFW-614 first flew in 1971. Only 19 were built and few examples remain today.

VICKERS FB.7
The Vickers FB.7 was a large twin-engined fighter biplane in which the gunner in the front cockpit, well ahead of the wings, aimed a 0.45kg (1lb) quick-firing cannon. Only two were built, in 1915.

VICKERS FB.16
Tested in 1916, the Vickers FB.16 single-seat scout had a good performance and was fitted with a stationary radial engine, rather than a rotary. It did not enter production.

VICKERS FB.26 VAMPIRE
The Vickers FB.26 Vampire, flown in May 1917, was a single-seat 'pusher' fighter biplane. Six prototypes were ordered and three completed.

VICKERS VIMY

UK: 1918

Designed to attack Berlin, the Vickers Vimy came too late to see operational service in World War I, only three being on RAF charge at the time of the Armistice in 1918.

IN THE CLOSING STAGES of World War I, Vickers produced a large biplane bomber, the FB.27 Vimy, with the object of attacking Berlin. Ordered into large-scale production for the newly formed Independent

Force (the RAF's strategic bombing force), the Vimy showed exceptional handling qualities and proved capable of lifting a greater load than the Handley Page O/400 on half the power. Production of the

Vimy Mk I, which really got under way after the end of World War I, totalled 158 aircraft, deliveries to RAF bomber squadrons beginning in July 1919. The type began to be withdrawn from the bomber role in

1924, but many served on with various training establishments and parachute schools, the last military Vimy being retired from No 4 Flying Training School at Abu Sueir, Egypt, in 1933. Many different variants of the basic Vimy were produced, both military and civil; the last two were the Vimy Ambulance and the Vernon bomber/transport. The aircraft is best remembered for its long-range pioneering flights, including the crossing of the Atlantic by Alcock and Brown in 1919.

Specification refers to the Vickers Vimy Mk II.

Crew: 3
Powerplant: two 270kW (360hp) Rolls-Royce Eagle VIII 12-cylinder Vee-type engines
Performance: max speed 166km/h (103mph); range 1464km (910 miles); service ceiling 2135m (7000ft)
Dimensions: wingspan 20.75m (68ft 1in); length 13.27m (43ft 6in); height 4.76m (15ft 7in)
Weight: 5670kg (12,500lb) loaded
Armament: three 7.7mm (0.303in) machine guns; up to 2179kg (4804lb) of bombs

VICKERS VILDEBEEST

UK: 1928

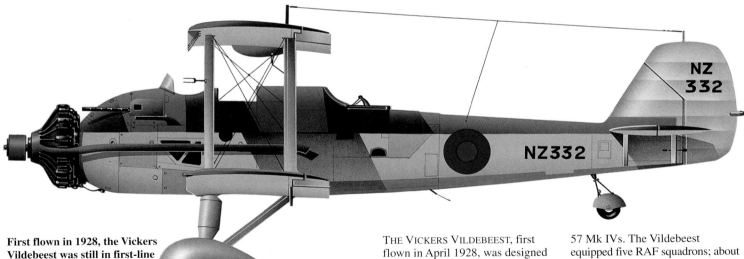

First flown in 1928, the Vickers Vildebeest was still in first-line operational service in the Far East in December 1941.

Crew: 3
Powerplant: one 492kW (660hp) Bristol Pegasus IIM3 sleeve-valve radial engine
Performance: max speed 230km/h (142mph); range 2500km (1553 miles); service ceiling 5182m (17,000ft)
Dimensions: wingspan 14.94m (49ft);

length 11.17m (36ft 8in); height 5.42m (17ft 9in)
Weight: 3673kg 8100lb) loaded
Armament: two 7.7mm (0.303in) machine guns; one 457mm (18in) torpedo or 499kg (1100lb) of bombs under fuselage

THE VICKERS VILDEBEEST, first flown in April 1928, was designed to replace the Hawker Horsley in the day-/torpedo-bomber role. The Vildebeest Mks I and II had different variants of the Bristol Pegasus engine, while the Mk III featured a revised cockpit to accommodate a third crew member. The production run for the first three series amounted to 152 aircraft, these being followed by

57 Mk IVs. The Vildebeest equipped five RAF squadrons; about 100 aircraft were still operational in the Far East at the outbreak of World War II. In December 1941, Nos 36 and 100 Squadrons, which were based on Singapore Island, suffered nearly 100 per cent casualties in attempting to attack Japanese invasion shipping.

Specifications apply to the Vickers Vildebeest Mk III.

VICKERS WELLESLEY
UK: 1935

DESIGNED IN 1933 as a private venture in response to a requirement for a general-purpose aircraft and torpedo-bomber, the Wellesley featured the novel geodetic construction devised by Barnes Wallis. The prototype of this high aspect ratio, cantilever monoplane first flew in June 1935. The design showed such promise that the Air Ministry placed an order for 96 Wellesley Mk I aircraft, the first of these entering service in April 1937.

An early model Vickers Wellesley Mk I, featuring two separate cockpits. Later aircraft had a long, continuous 'glasshouse' cockpit.

Production up to May 1938 came to 176 aircraft. The type equipped 12 RAF squadrons, giving useful service in East and North Africa in the early campaigns against the Italians, and was also notable for several very long-range flights before the war.

Crew: 3
Powerplant: one 623kW (835hp) Bristol Pegasus XX 9-cylinder radial engine
Performance: max speed 367km/h (228mph); range 4635km (2880 miles); service ceiling 7770m (25,500ft)
Dimensions: wingspan 22.73m (74ft 7in); length 11.66m (39ft 3in); height 4.67m (15ft 3in)
Weight: 5670kg (12,500lb) loaded
Armament: two 7.7mm (0.303in) machine guns; bomb load of 907kg (2000lb) in underwing panniers

VICKERS WELLINGTON
UK: 1936

THE VICKERS WELLINGTON was designed by Barnes Wallis, who was later to conceive the mines that destroyed the Ruhr dams, to Specification B.9/32. Like its predecessor the Vickers Wellesley, the aircraft featured geodetic construction, a system that enabled the aircraft to absorb a tremendous amount of battle damage and still survive. In December 1933 Vickers was awarded a contract for the construction of a single prototype under the designation Type 271, this aircraft (K4049) flying on 15 June 1936. This aircraft was lost on 19 April 1937 when it broke up during an involuntary high-speed dive, the cause being determined as elevator imbalance. As a result, the production prototype Wellington Mk I and subsequent aircraft were fitted with a revised fin, rudder and elevator adapted from a parallel

Vickers Wellington III of No 419 (RCAF) Squadron, which operated the type from January to November 1942. It subsequently rearmed with Halifaxes at RAF Middleton St George, County Durham.

VICKERS VIRGINIA
Designed to replace the Vimy, the Vickers Virginia was the standard heavy bomber of the Royal Air Force between 1924 and 1937. The aircraft was to appear in many different variations.

VICKERS VENTURE
The Vickers Venture of 1923 was a two-seat reconnaissance fighter, the prototype of which appeared in 1924. Only five production aircraft were ordered for evaluation.

VICKERS VIXEN
The Vickers Vixen was an armed general-purpose biplane of 1924. Eighteen examples were purchased by the Chilean Air Force.

VICKERS VALPARAISO
The Vickers Valparaiso was a two-seat fighter-reconnaissance biplane of 1924, developed from the Vixen. Nineteen examples were sold to Chile, and at least 27 to Portugal.

VICKERS VEDETTE
The Vedette of 1923, built by Canadian Vickers, was a three-seat biplane flying boat powered by an Armstrong Siddeley Lynx pusher engine. It was used to map vast areas of northern Canada.

VICKERS VARUNA
The Vickers Varuna of 1926 was designed to an RCAF requirement for a seaplane capable of transporting men and equipment to forest-fire locations. One Mk I and seven Mk IIs were built.

VICKERS VICTORIA
A transport variant of the Vickers Virginia was known as the Victoria, with 97 being built, and a Pegasus-engined development (28 built and 54 converted from Victorias) was named the Valentia.

VICKERS SCOUT
The Vickers Scout parasol monoplane fighter of 1926 was developed from the Wibault W1B. Twenty-six examples were built for Chile.

VICKERS VENDACE
The Vickers Vendace of 1928 was designed to have an interchangeable float and wheel undercarriage. Three were delivered to Bolivia.

VICKERS VESPA
The Vickers Vespa of 1929 was designed as an army cooperation aircraft for the RAF, but was not adopted. Six examples were purchased by Bolivia and eight supplied to the Irish Air Corps.

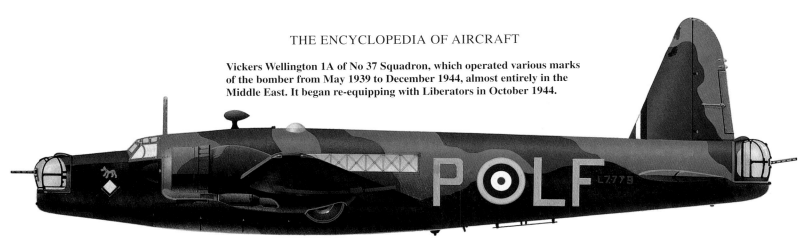

Vickers Wellington 1A of No 37 Squadron, which operated various marks of the bomber from May 1939 to December 1944, almost entirely in the Middle East. It began re-equipping with Liberators in October 1944.

project, the Vickers B.1/35, which would enter service later as the Warwick. The fuselage was also to undergo considerable modification, so that production Wellingtons, ordered to Specification 29/36, bore little resemblance to the ill-fated prototype. The first Mk I, L4212, flew on 23 December 1937, powered by two Pegasus XX engines; the first Bomber Command squadron to rearm, No 9, began receiving its aircraft in December 1938.

The most numerous of the early models was the Mk IC, which had Pegasus XVIII engines and self-sealing fuel tanks, adopted after two disastrous daylight raids in the Heligoland Bight area on 14 and 18 December 1939, when 17 out of a total of 34 Wellingtons sent out were shot down by flak or fighters. In all, 2685 Wellington Mk 1C aircraft were built. By early 1942 the principal version in

service with Bomber Command was the Mk III (1519 built), with two 1119kW (1500hp) Bristol Hercules engines replacing the much less reliable Pegasus, although four squadrons (Nos 142, 300, 301 and 305, the last three being Polish units) used the Mk IV, powered by American Pratt & Whitney Twin Wasps. The Wellington III entered service with the experienced No 9 Squadron on 22 June 1941, and was to be the backbone of Bomber Command's night offensive against Germany until such time as the Command's four-engined heavy bombers became available in numbers.

Coastal Command also found its uses for the versatile Wellington. The first general reconnaissance version of the aircraft, which made its appearance in the spring of 1942, was the GR.III, 271 being converted from standard Mk IC

airframes. The aircraft were fitted with ASV Mk II radar and adapted to carry torpedoes. Fifty-eight more GR.IIIs were equipped as anti-submarine aircraft, being fitted with a powerful Leigh Light searchlight to illuminate U-boats travelling on the surface, which they often did at night in transit to and from their Biscay bases. The last bomber version of the Wellington was the Mk X, of which 3803 were built, accounting for more than 30 per cent of all Wellington production. Its career with Bomber Command was brief, but it was used in the Far East until the end of the war. Coastal Command's next version was the GR.Mk XI, which was the first of four purpose-built variants; the GR.XI and GR.XIII were specifically intended for the torpedo-bomber role, while the GR.XII and GR.XIV were dedicated anti-submarine aircraft.

Other Wellingtons were converted as transports and trainers, and a special variant designated DWI was fitted with a large electro-magnetic ring to trigger off enemy magnetic mines. A pressurized high-altitude variant, the Wellington Mk V, was flown in prototype form only.

Specification refers to the Vickers Wellington Mk III.

Crew: 6
Powerplant: two 1119kW (1500hp) Bristol Hercules XI radial engines
Performance: max speed 411km/h (255mph); range 2478km (1540 miles); service ceiling 5790m (19,000ft)
Dimensions: wingspan 26.26m (86ft 2in); length 19.68m (64ft 7in); height 5.00m (16ft 5in)
Weight: 15,422kg (34,000lb) loaded
Armament: eight 7.7mm (0.303in) machine guns; up to 2041kg (4500lb) of bombs

VICKERS VC1 VIKING

UK: 1945

Crew: 3
Powerplant: two 1260kW (1690hp) Bristol Hercules 634 sleeve radial piston engines
Performance: max cruising speed 338km/h (210mph) at 1830m (6000ft); range with maximum payload 837km (520 miles); service ceiling 7240m (23,753ft)
Dimensions: wingspan 27.20m (89ft 3in); length 19.86m (65ft 2in); height 5.94m (19ft 6in)
Weight: 15,354kg (34,000lb) maximum take-off weight
Payload: up to 36 passengers (originally 27)

BEFORE THE ARRIVAL of the new postwar designs reached fruition, Britain had an urgent and immediate need for stopgap types. Consequently, the Vickers Viking was developed from the Wellington bomber (retaining its tail-wheel undercarriage), and it plugged an important gap in BEA's postwar domestic and European operations

from 1946 prior to arrival of the Viscount. A total of 163 commercial Vikings were produced, and these aircraft were widely exported to countries with similar needs; however, a larger number (251) of military Valetta versions with a strengthened floor were also built. In the 1950s and 1960s the Viking became a popular choice of British

independent start-up airlines, and both military and civil cast-offs of the type were to remain in service until the early 1970s.

Specifications apply to the Vickers Viking IB.

Over 60 Vikings were sold new to overseas airlines. Although a number of Vikings were operated in West Germany (including the example depicted, which was leased by Lufthansa), most were acquired second-hand.

VICKERS VC2 VISCOUNT

Crew: 3
Powerplant: four Rolls-Royce Dart Rda.7/1 Mk 525 turboprop engines each rated at 1566ekW (2100ehp)
Performance: max cruising speed 563km/h (350mph) at 6095m (20,000ft); range 2776km (1725 miles) with maximum payload and no reserves; service ceiling 7620m (25,000ft)
Dimensions: wingspan 28.56m (93ft 8.5in); wing area 89.46m² (963sq ft); length 26.11m (85ft 8in); height 8.15m (26ft 9in)
Weight: 32,885kg (72,500lb) maximum take-off weight
Payload: up to 71 passengers

The last operational Viscount in Europe (an 800 series built in 1958), which had a long career with BEA and British Air Ferries/British World.

THE VISCOUNT WAS the first turbine-powered aircraft to carry paying passengers and also the most successful airliner manufactured in post-World War II Britain, an accolade ensured by the cessation of commercial airliner design and production in the United Kingdom circa 2001. The Viscount originates in the specification of a 24-seat airliner issued by the wartime Brabazon Committee, projected as a DC-3 replacement with a very modest range and speed. Initially the Vickers project was named as Type 609 and was to be powered by four Armstrong Siddeley Mamba engines, and it was this design that prevailed over the rival Armstrong Whitworth AW.55 Apollo for Air Ministry approval. It was also agreed that the accommodation should be revised from a 24-seat to a 32-seat pressurized cabin, resulting in the new designation of V.630.

Availability of the superior Dart Rda.1 Mk 502 738ekW (990ehp) turboprop engine persuaded Vickers and the Air Ministry to change to this powerplant. The early name of Viceroy was changed to Viscount ahead of the first flight on 16 July 1948, marking the first flight of a civil turboprop-powered aircraft. But a changing design format and uncertainty about use of a turbine-powered engine contributed to

BEA's decision (under government pressure) to purchase the piston-powered Airspeed Ambassador for its short-haul operations. There was therefore still no guarantee of commercial orders for the Viscount.

During the summer of 1948 the V.630 attracted a great deal of interest, but perhaps more vitally for the Viscount's future Rolls-Royce announced availability of the Dart Rda.3 engine, offering a 40 per cent increase in power over the original Dart engine and the prospect of higher weight and capacity versions. These events culminated in launch and development of the stretched Viscount 700, a 40- to 53-seat airliner powered by four Rolls-Royce Dart Mk 505 turboprops each fitted with a four-bladed paddle-shaped propeller, producing a cruising speed of 522km/h (324mph) and a range of up to 1932km (1200 miles). The V.700 first flew on 28 August 1950, accompanied by an order for 20 examples from BEA, the first of which flew in August 1952, and entered service in April 1953.

The BEA order was followed by orders from Air France, Aer Lingus, Trans-Australia Airlines and Air Canada. The Viscount was effectively in a class of its own with regard to speed, customer appreciation/comfort and economics

for short- and medium-haul services. This led to the launch of the 700D series with regulatory improvements to meet US FAA requirements, and modest expansion in the operational envelope which resulted in a large order from Capital Airlines along with several other overseas orders.

Vickers proceeded to launch the stretched Viscount 800 in 1952, designed to carry 52–65 (later 71) passengers. First flown in 1956, it was placed in passenger service by BEA in 1957. The 800 series went on to attract further export sales. A total of 444 examples (of all Viscount types) were produced until 1964. The Viscount served into the early 1980s with BEA successor British Airways, and other regional/scheduled operators. In the 1980s British Air Ferries (later British World) acquired a number of examples for use on diverse charter operations; some were later converted to freighters for a Parcel Force contract, retiring in 1998. At Tucson, Arizona, Jadepoint, Go-Air and later Viscount services operated the type for executive/charter work – often rock group tours. By 2003 only a very small number of Viscounts remained operational in Southern and West Africa. Specifications apply to the Viscount 810 series.

Air France was the first overseas customer to receive the Viscount (700 series) (in 1953) and continued to operate the type until 1974.

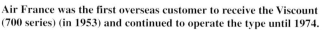

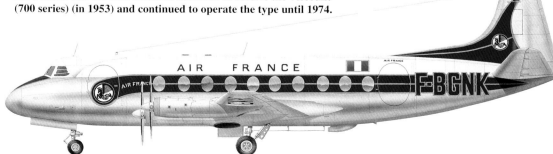

VICKERS VALIANT

The Vickers Valiant B.Mk.1 was a very clean design, as this photograph shows to good advantage. It was an extremely capable aircraft, pioneering most of the V-Force's operational techniques, and saw additional service as a flight refuelling tanker.

DESIGNED TO MEET the requirements of Specification B.9/48, the Vickers Valiant was the first of the RAF's trio of 'V-Bombers', and played a vital part in building up Britain's strategic nuclear deterrent. The first Vickers Type 660 Valiant flew on 18 May 1951 and production Valiant B.Mk Is were delivered to No 232 OCU at Gaydon, Warwick-shire, in January 1955. The Valiant subsequently armed Nos 7, 18 (ECM), 49, 90, 138, 148, 199, 207, 214 and 543 Squadrons, the latter being equipped with the B.(PR)I strategic reconnaissance variant. No 138 Squadron was the first to equip with the type, and No 49 Squadron was the nuclear weapons trials unit, its aircraft participating in nuclear weapons tests in Australia (1956) and Christmas Island (1957–58). Valiants saw action in the Anglo-French Suez operation of October–November 1956, attacking Egyptian airfields with conventional bombs. In 1963 the Valiant force was assigned to SACEUR in the tactical bombing role; however, it was withdrawn prematurely because of fatigue cracks in the main spar. The Valiant BK.I was a flight refuelling tanker conversion, and the Valiant B.Mk II was a one-off prototype stressed for low-level, high-speed

An aerodynamically simple design allowed the Valiant to enter service earlier than the other two V-bombers. This No. 7 Squadron aircraft, with flaps deployed, is about to land. The squadron relinquished its Valiants in July 1960.

penetration. Valiant production amounted to 108 aircraft, plus two prototypes and the solitary B.Mk II. Of this total, 14 were B.(PR)K.Is and 45 were BK.Is, most of them conversions.

During their career, Valiants made several notable long-distance flights. In October 1953 the second prototype aircraft, WB215, took part in the London–New Zealand air race, being specially fitted with underwing fuel tanks. On 9 July 1959 a Valiant of No 214 Squadron made the first nonstop flight from the United Kingdom to Cape Town in South Africa, being refuelled in the air twice, and on 2–3 March 1960 a Valiant of the same unit made the longest nonstop flight by an RAF aircraft up to that time, 13,676km (8500 miles) around the United Kingdom. In May that year

another 214 Squadron aircraft flew nonstop from the United Kingdom to Singapore.

The Valiant tended to be overshadowed by the RAF's later V-bombers, the Vulcan and Victor; however, the contribution it made to the development of Bomber Command's nuclear alert force was immeasurably important. Not only did it pioneer the introduction of free-fall nuclear weapons into operational service, but it also acted as trials aircraft for the Avro Blue Steel stand-off bomb, the weapon that would have given the V-bombers a chance of survival in the 1960s. In addition, the Valiant pioneered the techniques that would have ensured the V-force's viability in the event of a war alert; dispersal techniques, overseas deployments and so on. And, if the Air Staff had seen fit to develop

the strengthened low-level version, it is likely that the Valiant would have continued to be a viable weapons system for many years.

Specifications apply to the Vickers Valiant B.Mk I.

Crew: 5
Powerplant: four 4559kg (10,050lb) Rolls-Royce Avon 204 turbojet engines
Performance: max speed 912km/h (567mph); range 7424km (4500 miles); service ceiling 16,460m (54,000ft)
Dimensions: wingspan 34.85m (114ft 4in); length 33.00m (108ft 3in); height 9.80m (32ft 2in)
Weight: 79,378kg (175,000lb) loaded
Armament: one 4530kg (10,000lb) MC Mk 1 Blue Danube nuclear bomb; four 906kg (2000lb) Red Beard tactical nuclear bombs; one 2721kg (6000lb) Mk 5 (US) nuclear bomb; four Mk 28 or Mk 43 (US) thermonuclear bombs; or 21 x 453kg (1000lb) conventional bombs

VL Myrsky

FINLAND: 1940

Finland's indigenous Myrsky fighter was not a success, all four prototypes being destroyed in accidents. The few that were used fought on both sides, first against the Russians and then against the Germans.

Crew: 1
Powerplant: one 794kW (1065hp) Pratt & Whitney R-1830 Twin Wasp radial engine
Performance: max speed 519km/h (323mph); range 499km (310 miles); service ceiling 8997m (29,500ft)
Dimensions: wingspan 11.00m (36ft 1in); length 8.35m (27ft 5in); height 2.98m (9ft 10in)
Weight: 3207kg (7080lb) loaded
Armament: four 12.7mm (0.50in) machine guns

DESIGNED BY Dipl Ing E. Wegeluis and built by the Finnish State Aircraft Factory in Tannerfors, Finland, the first prototype Myrsky (Storm) fighter flew in 1940 and was followed by three more prototypes, known as the Myrsky I. The prototypes suffered numerous teething troubles, however, and were all destroyed in crashes. After considerable modification, this indigenous Finnish fighter entered

production in 1942 as the Myrsky II, the first of 47 production aircraft being delivered in 1944. The Myrsky III was an improved version, but only 10 examples were built. Overall, the Myrsky was not a success and was used on a very limited scale during World War II, initially against the Russians, then against the Germans.

Specifications apply to the VL Myrsky II.

VOUGHT F4U CORSAIR

Crew: 1
Powerplant: one 1492kW (2000hp) Pratt & Whitney R-2800-8 radial engine
Performance: max speed 671km/h (417mph); range 1633km (1015 miles); service ceiling 11,247m (36,900ft)
Dimensions: wingspan 12.50m (41ft); length 10.17m (33ft 4in) height 4.90m (16ft 1in)
Weight: 6350kg (14,000lb) loaded
Armament: six 12.7mm (0.50in) machine guns in wings

IN FEBRUARY 1936, the US Navy invited the Chance Vought Division of United Aircraft to take part in a design contest for a new single-seat, single-engined carrier-borne fighter. Under the leadership of Rex B. Beisel, the Vought design team presented two proposals: the V-166A, designed around the most powerful production engine then available, the Pratt & Whitney R-1830 Twin Wasp, and the V-166B, powered by the still experimental Pratt & Whitney XR-2800-2 Double Wasp. Two months after proposals had been submitted, the US Navy placed a contract for one prototype of the V-166B under the designation XF4U-1. The Double Wasp engine was fitted with a two-stage two-speed supercharger and developed 1343kW (1800hp). To make the maximum use of this power, Hamilton Standard designed what was at the time the largest propeller ever used by a fighter. This in itself caused some problems because if it were fitted to a low-wing design a very long undercarriage would be needed to provide the required 45cm (18in) ground clearance. Vought solved the problem by adopting the inverted gull-wing planform that was

Chance Vought F4U-5 Corsairs. This model did not fly in production form until 1947, but was widely used during the war in Korea, where it did excellent work in the close-support role.

to be the F4U's main recognition feature. This permitted the use of an undercarriage of normal dimensions and also improved visibility for the pilot, which was restricted forward by the huge engine. The rearward-retracting main undercarriage members rotated through 90 degrees to lie flush with the wing surfaces.

The prototype XF4U-1 first flew on 29 May 1940. On 2 April 1941, Vought received a contract for 584 aircraft, the type to be named Corsair in US Navy service. Many necessary modifications, however, meant that the first production aircraft did not fly until 25 June 1942, by which time the Brewster and Goodyear companies had been designated associated Corsair constructors. The former built 735 aircraft under the designation

F3A-1 (its contract was cancelled in 1944 because of shoddy work practices and other misdemeanours) and the latter 3808, designated FG-1. The first Vought-built F4U-1 was delivered to the US Navy on 31 July 1944. Carrier trials began in September 1942; the first Corsair unit, Marine Fighting Squadron VMF-214, was declared combat ready in December, deploying to Guadalcanal in February 1943. After trials with VF-12, the Corsair became operational with Navy Fighting Squadron VF-17 in April 1943, deploying to a land base in New Georgia in September. Despite a rather inauspicious start, as pilots became experienced in flying their powerful new fighter-bombers they became formidable opponents.

Of the 12,681 Corsairs built during World War II, 2012 were

supplied to the Royal Navy, equipping 19 squadrons of the Fleet Air Arm; some of these were diverted to three squadrons of the Royal New Zealand Air Force, operating in the Solomons. Corsair variants used by the Royal Navy were the Corsair I (F4U-1A), Corsair III (F3A-1) and Corsair IV (FG-1). Variants included the F4U-1C cannon-armed fighter, F4U-1D fighter-bomber, F4U-2 night-fighter, F4U-3 high-altitude research version, and F4U-4 fighter. Post-war developments included the F4U-5 fighter-bomber, F4U-5N night-fighter and F4U-5P photo-reconnaissance aircraft (which all served during the Korean War of 1950–53), the F4U-6 (later A-1) attack aircraft and the F4U-7, also supplied to the French Navy. Specifications apply to the F4U-1.

F4U-1 Corsair flown by US Navy ace Ira Kepford of Navy Fighter Squadron VF-17, the 'Jolly Rogers'. Kepford ended the war with 16 confirmed victories. He retired as a lieutenant commander in 1956.

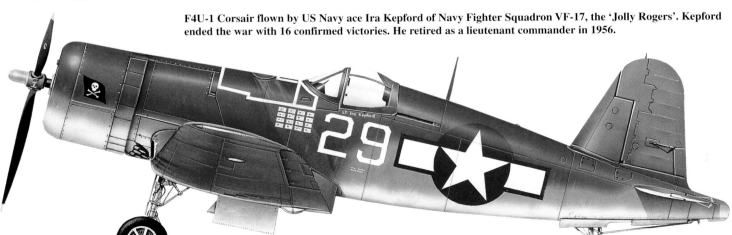

VOUGHT F7U CUTLASS

USA: 1948

The F7U-3M Cutlass, seen here, was armed with four Sparrow air-to-air missiles. Much work had to be done on the design of the Cutlass before the aircraft was accepted for service by the US Navy.

THE RADICAL Chance Vought F7U Cutlass, first flown as the XF7U-1 prototype on 29 September 1948, had several claims to fame. It was the first production naval aircraft to achieve supersonic flight; the first to release bombs at supersonic speed; and, in its day, it was the heaviest single-seat carrier fighter in service. Its unorthodox design was very advanced for the time, but the performance of the F7U-1 fell short of US Navy require-

ments and production was halted after 14 aircraft so that major modifications could be made. The much-redesigned aircraft emerged as the F7U-3, which entered service in April 1954. The F7U-3M was armed with four Sparrow air-to-air missiles, while the F7U-3P was a photo-reconnaissance version. Production totalled 307 F7U-3s, 98 F7U-3Ms, and 12 F7U-3Ps. Specifications apply to the Vought F7U-1 Cutlass.

Crew: 1
Powerplant: two 1905kg (4200lb) Westinghouse J34-32 turbojet engines
Performance: max speed 1070km/h (665mph); combat radius 966km (600 miles); service ceiling 12,500m (41,000ft)
Dimensions: wingspan 11.78m (38ft 8in); length 12.07m (39ft 7in); height 3.00m (9ft 10in)
Weight: 7604kg (16,840lb) loaded
Armament: four 20mm (0.79in) M-2 cannon

VOUGHT F-8 CRUSADER

USA: 1955

Crew: 1
Powerplant: one 8165kg (18,000lb) thrust Pratt & Whitney J57 P-20 turbojet engine
Performance: max speed 1800km/h (1120mph); combat radius 966km (600 miles); service ceiling 12,192m (40,000ft)
Dimensions: wingspan 10.72m (35ft 2in); length 16.61m (54ft 6in); height 4.80m (15ft 9in)
Weight: 15,422kg (34,000lb) loaded
Armament: four 20mm (0.79in) cannon; various underwing combinations of rockets, bombs and air-to-surface missiles

THE FIRST CARRIER-BORNE fighter capable of supersonic speed in level flight, the Vought F-8 Crusader was the winner of a May 1953 US Navy competition for a new day-fighter. The prototype XF8U-1 flew on 25 March 1955 and exceeded Mach 1 on its maiden flight, powered by a Pratt

& Whitney J57 engine. The first production F8U-1 flew on 30 September 1955, and completed carrier trials in April 1956. The type was accepted into service as the F8U-1 in the following December, only 21 months after the prototype flew. Production of the F8U-1 (later F-8A) ended in 1958, by which time 218 had been built. The F8U-1 was followed in September 1958 by the F8U-1E (F-8B). This version, of which 130 were built, had a larger nose radome and limited all-weather capability. Meanwhile, a reconnaissance version, the F8U-1P (RF-8A), had flown in December 1956. This variant was capable of both day and night reconnaissance and was used extensively for surveillance during the Cuban crisis of 1962 and its aftermath. Of the 144 built, 53 were modernized

in 1965–66 and redesignated RF-8G; these were used for fast low-level reconnaissance over Vietnam. The F8U-2N (F-8D) Crusader, which first flew in February 1960, had an all-weather capability and was powered by a J57-P20 turbojet with reheat, giving it a maximum speed approaching Mach 2.0. Unlike earlier crusaders, this variant had no HVAR rocket belly pack, but retained its 20mm (0.79in) gun armament and four Sidewinders. Deliveries to the US Navy and Marine Corps were completed in January 1962 after 152 had been built; 89 were later refurbished, given an attack capability and designated F-8H. The last Crusader variant to carry the old US Service nomenclature was the F8U-2NE (F-8E), which was basically similar to the F-8D, but with more

VOISIN 8
Although basically a good design, the Voisin 8 bomber, which made its appearance in 1916, was plagued by problems with its Peugeot engine. About 1100 examples were built.

VOISIN-FARMAN I
The Voisin-Farman I biplane of 1907 was Henry Farman's first aircraft. It took 225 attempts before he made his first short flight, little more than a hop of 80m (262ft).

VON ASBOTH AH-4
In 1930 Oscar von Asboth, an Austrian engineer, built the AH-4 helicopter which was powered by an 82kW (110hp) Clerget rotary engine driving co-axial rotors. It is unofficially reported to have reached an altitude of 30m (100ft) and covered a distance of 3.22km (2 miles) at 19km/h (12mph).

VON BAUMHAUER HELICOPTER
In 1924, Dutch designer A.G. von Baumhauer began development of a helicopter with a small anti-torque rotor at the tail. However, a second engine was fitted to drive this, undoing the advantage of the tail rotor through extra weight. The machine never rose to a height of more than 1.5m (5ft) and never flew horizontally.

VOS SPRINGBOK
The VOS Springbok is a two-seat light helicopter designed by Marquand Vos which began trials in South Africa early in 1964.

VOUGHT VE-7
The Vought VE-7 (or more correctly Lewis-Vought, as it was a product of the then Lewis & Vought Company) was a biplane advanced trainer produced in 1921, 129 being built as both land- and floatplanes. The VE-9 was a slightly improved version.

VOUGHT FU-1
The Vought FU-1, which appeared in 1927, was a single-seat land- or floatplane fighter trainer. Twenty were built, operating mainly from the USS *Langley*.

VOUGHT V-141/143
The Vought V-143 was a modified version of the V-141 (formerly designated Northrop 3-A). The sole prototype was sold to Japan in 1937, its retractable undercarriage serving as a pattern for that of the Mitsubishi Zero.

advanced search and fire-control radar equipment. The F-8E was the first Crusader to be developed for the strike role, being fitted with underwing pylons to carry a wide variety of offensive loads. More than 250 F-8Es were built, and 136 of them were refurbished under the designation F-8J. The F-8E(FN) was a version for the French Navy; 42 were ordered in August 1963 and the last aircraft was delivered in January 1965, this being the final new Crusader to be built. Specifications apply to the F-8E.

F-8J Crusader of Navy Fighter Squadron VF211, the 'Checkmates'. VF211 flew the F-8J, the US Navy's last all-gun fighter, until 1975, when it was replaced by the Grumman F-14 Tomcat.

VOUGHT A-7 CORSAIR II

USA: 1965

Crew: 1
Powerplant: one 6465kg (14,250lb) thrust Allison TF41-1 (Rolls-Royce Spey) turbofan engine
Performance: max speed 1123km/h (698mph); range 1127km (700 miles); service ceiling 15,545m (51,000ft)
Dimensions: wingspan 11.80m (38ft 9in); length 14.06m (46ft 1in); height 4.90m (16ft)
Weight: 19,050kg (42,000lb) loaded
Armament: one 20mm (0.79in) M61 Vulcan cannon; provision for up to 6804kg (15,000lb) of external stores

THE PROTOTYPE OF THE A-7 Corsair II was flown for the first time on 27 September 1965, and several versions were subsequently produced for the US Navy and US Air Force by the Vought Corporation, a subsidiary of Ling-Temco-Vought.

The first attack variant was the A-7A, which made its combat debut in the Gulf of Tonkin on 4 December 1966 with Attack Squadron VA-147, operating from the USS *Ranger*. In all, 199 A-7As

were delivered before production switched to the A-7B, which had an uprated engine. The first production model flew on 6 February 1968, the US Navy taking delivery of 198 examples.

The next variant was the A-7D tactical fighter for the US Air Force, which went into action in Vietnam in October 1972; 459 were built, many being allocated to Air National Guard units. The final major Corsair variant, the two-seat A-7K, served only with

the Air National Guard. Corsair IIs were also operated by the Hellenic, Portuguese and Thai air forces.

Specifications apply to the Vought A-7E Corsair II.

The A-7 Corsair II was one of the most successful ground-attack aircraft ever designed. The type made its combat debut in Vietnam in October 1972. Many examples, one of which is seen here, were subsequently used by the US Air National Guard.

VOUGHT-SIKORSKY SB2U VINDICATOR

USA: 1936

ORDERED IN October 1934, the SB2U was the US Navy's first monoplane scout and dive-bomber. The XSB2U-1 prototype flew for the first time in January 1936, and deliveries of SB2U-1 Vindicator production aircraft began in 1937. The SB2U-2 had updated equipment, while the SB2U-3 had heavier armament and fuel tankage. France purchased 39 SB2U-2s under the designation V-156F, while 50 went to the Royal Navy as the Chesapeake Mk I,

these being used for training and target towing. The French aircraft were operational during the Battle of France of World War II, where they suffered heavy losses.

Specifications apply to the Vought-Sikorsky SB2U-3.

Vought-Sikorsky V-156F of Escadrille AB1, Aéronavale, 1940. This French version of the SB2U saw combat during the later stages of the Battle of France, suffering heavy losses to enemy ground fire.

Crew: 2
Powerplant: one 615kW (825hp) Pratt & Whitney R-1535-2 Twin Wasp 14-cylinder radial engine
Performance: max speed 391km/h (243mph); range 1802km (1120 miles); service ceiling 7195m (23,600ft)
Dimensions: wingspan 12.77m (41ft 11in); length 10.36m (33ft 11in); height 4.34m (14ft 3in)
Weight: 4273kg (9421lb) loaded
Armament: two 12.7mm (0.50in) machine guns; external bomb load of up to 454kg (1000lb)

VULTEE A-35 VENGEANCE

USA: 1941

THE VULTEE VENGEANCE had its origin in a French order for a dive-bomber, the V-72, 300 of which were to be delivered by September 1941. After the fall of France, the programme was revived by the British, who placed orders for 700 V-72s with the designations Vengeance Mks I and II. The United States also purchased 200

Vultee A-35 Vengeance of the USAAF. The type did not match up to expectations – almost all were soon relegated to target-towing and other training duties. The Vengeance was also used by the RAF and Indian Air Force.

aircraft as Vengeance Mk IIIs (A-31s) for Lend-Lease transfer to the UK, then provided funds for 100 A-35s and 99 A-35A conversions. Further improvements resulted in the Vengeance Mk IV (563 built). The Vengeance was mostly used as a target tug by the RAF, but some were used operationally as dive-bombers by the RAF and Indian Air Force in the Burma campaign, by the Royal Australian Air Force in the south-west Pacific and by the Free French in North Africa. Specifications apply to the Mk IV.

Crew: 2
Powerplant: one 1268kW (1700hp) Wright R-2600-13 14-cylinder radial engine
Performance: max speed 449km/h (279mph); range 2253km (1400 miles); service ceiling 6795m (22,300ft)
Dimensions: wingspan 14.63m (48ft); length 12.12m (39ft 9in); height 4.67m (15ft 4in)
Weight: 7439kg (16,400lb) loaded
Armament: seven 12.7mm (0.50in) machine guns; up to 907kg (2000lb) of bombs

VOUGHT-SIKORSKY OS2U KINGFISHER
Designed in 1937, the prototype OS2U Kingfisher catapult seaplane flew in July 1938 and entered service with the US Navy as the OS2U-1 in August 1940. The major variant was the OS2U-3, more than 1000 of which were built out of a total of 1519 aircraft.

VOUGHT-SIKORSKY VS-44A EXCALIBUR
A four-engined, long-range flying-boat design dating from 1940. Three examples were built for American Export Airlines and were operated for largely civilian purposes during WWII. The 4990km (3100-mile) range of these flying boats allowed them to traverse the Atlantic non-stop.

VUIA NO 1
Designed by a Romanian lawyer living in France, the Vuia No 1 monoplane made several attempts at flight in 1906. The best it could manage, however, was a hop of about 24m (80ft).

VULCANAIR VF600W MISSION
This Italian 10-seat, single-engined high-wing monoplane was displayed at the 2003 Paris Air Show. It is powered by a Walter M601F-11 turbine.

VULTEE V-1
The Vultee V-1 of 1932 was a single-engined monoplane feeder-liner with a capacity for eight passengers. The V-1A was a slightly larger version.

VULTEE V-11
The Vultee V-11 was a military attack version of the V-1A, 129 being delivered to the US Navy. It was evaluated by the USAAC as the YA-19.

VULTEE BT-13 VALIANT
The Vultee BT-13 Valiant, which appeared in 1939, was one of the outstanding training aircraft of World War II. The final variant was the BT-15, by which time 11,537 had been built.

VULTEE XP-54
The XP-54 was an experimental interceptor with twin tail booms and a Pratt & Whitney X-1800-4AG pusher engine. The first of two aircraft flew in January 1943.

VULTEE XA-41
The Vultee XA-41, first flown in April 1944, was a prototype naval attack aircraft. The Douglas AD Skyraider was selected instead.

WALLIS AUTOGYROS

Crew: 1 (WA-116-T pillion two-seater)
Powerplant: one 54kW (72hp)
Wallis-McCulloch 4318A 4-cylinder
air-cooled engine
Performance: max speed 185km/h
(115mph); range 225km (140 miles)
Dimensions: rotor diameter 6.20m (20ft
4in); length 3.38m (11ft 1in); height
1.85m (6ft 1in)
Weight: 116kg (255lb)

WING COMMANDER Ken Wallis designed and built a range of autogyros. The first was the WA-116 Agile which first flew on 2 August 1961. He followed this with five Beagle-built WA-116s for British Army evaluation in 1962 and five WA-116 Agile aircraft. Variants include a WA-116-T pillion two-seat version, three WA-117s, two WA-118 Meteorites with 90kW (120hp) Meteor Alfa engines and a WA-119 with a 990cc Hillman Imp. The WA-120 is a high-performance, long-range, 97kW (130hp) single-seat autogyro with fully enclosed cockpit and bubble canopy and the small, streamlined WA-121 is powered by a 67kW (90hp) Wallis McCulloch for high-speed, high-altitude research. Specifications apply to the Wallis WA-116 Agile.

World-famous aircraft pioneer Wing Commander Ken Wallis at the controls of the 75kW (100hp) Rolls-Royce Continental O-200-B powered WA-117 making a low pass at his house at Reymerston Hall, Norfolk.

WESTLAND WAPITI

THE WESTLAND WAPITI two-seat general-purpose biplane was designed to replace the DH.9A, the prototype flying in March 1927. As first flown, it had DH.9A wings and tail assembly, but the Wapiti I had an enlarged tailplane and a 313kW (420hp) Bristol Jupiter VI engine. Ten Wapiti IIs with uprated Jupiter VI engines were followed by the Wapiti IIA with the 410kW (550hp) Jupiter VIII, this variant appearing in 1931. In all, Westland built 565 Wapitis, including eight Mk Is and 20 Mk IIs for the RAF. Specifications apply to the Mk III.

Crew: 2
Powerplant: one 366kW (490hp) Armstrong Siddeley Jaguar VI 14-cylinder radial engine
Performance: max speed 225km/h (140mph); range 1062km (660 miles); service ceiling 6280m (20,600ft)
Dimensions: wingspan 14.15m (46ft 5in); length 9.91m (32ft 6in); height 3.61m (11ft 10in)
Weight: 2449kg (5400lb) loaded
Armament: two 7.7mm (0.303in) machine guns; external bomb load of 263kg (580lb)

Westland Wapiti J9237 was sent to Canada in 1930 for cold-weather trials, being experimentally fitted with skis. The Wapiti, an excellent general-purpose biplane, was used by the RAF on India's rugged Northwest Frontier.

WESTLAND LYSANDER
UK: 1936

The Westland Lysander was a splendid army cooperation aircraft, but it will be forever associated with its clandestine activities involving delivery and collection of agents to and from occupied Europe.

Crew: 2
Powerplant: one 664kW (890hp) Bristol Mercury XII 9-cylinder radial engine
Performance: max speed 369km/h (229mph); range 966km (600 miles); service ceiling 7925m (26,000ft)
Dimensions: wingspan 15.24m (50ft); length 9.30m (30ft 6in); height 3.35m (11ft)
Weight: 3402kg (7500lb) loaded
Armament: three 7.7mm (0.303in) machine guns; external bomb load of 227kg (500lb)

ORIGINATING IN A 1934 requirement for a battlefield army cooperation and reconnaissance aircraft, the Westland Lysander prototype first flew in June 1936, the Lysander Mk I entering service in June 1938. The Lysander Mk II had a 675kW (905hp) Bristol Perseus engine, while the Mk III was fitted with the Mercury XX. The type was in widespread use in its intended role in the early years of World War II, particularly in France and North Africa, but was progressively replaced by the Curtiss Tomahawk from 1941. Seventy Mk IIIs were converted to Mk IIIA standard for target towing and air-sea rescue duties, 100 new aircraft also being built. The type was used to infiltrate Allied agents into enemy-occupied territory and bring them out again. Total production was 1593 aircraft, comprising 131 Mk Is, 433 Mk IIs and 804 Mk IIIs built in Great Britain, and 225 built in Canada.

Specifications apply to the Westland Lysander Mk I.

WESTLAND WHIRLWIND
UK: 1938

Crew: 1
Powerplant: two 571kW (765hp) Rolls-Royce Peregrine 12-cylinder Vee-type engines
Performance: max speed 579km/h (360mph); range 1287km (800 miles); service ceiling 9150m (30,000ft)
Dimensions: wingspan 13.72m (45ft); length 9.83m (32ft 3in); height 3.20m (10ft 6in)
Weight: 5166kg (11,388lb) loaded
Armament: four 20mm (0.79in) cannon; external bomb load of 454kg (1000lb)

DESIGNED ORIGINALLY as a long-range escort fighter, the Westland Whirlwind first flew on 11 October 1938, but did not enter RAF service until June 1940. Its intended powerplant was the Rolls-Royce Merlin, but as this was earmarked for the Spitfire and Hurricane the Rolls-Royce Peregrine – an upgraded version of the Kestrel – was chosen instead. The Whirlwind was highly manoeuvrable, faster than a Spitfire at low altitude, and its armament of four 20mm (0.79in) cannon in the nose made it a match for any German fighter of the day. Continual problems with the engine, however, delayed its service debut; only two squadrons (Nos 137 and 263) were equipped with it. It was later converted to the fighter-bomber role as the Whirlwind Mk IA. Specifications apply to Whirlwind Mk 1A.

Westland Whirlwind P6989 of No 263 Squadron, RAF.

WESTLAND WYVERN

THE WESTLAND WYVERN was unique in that it was the world's first turboprop-powered combat aircraft and also the only turboprop-powered strike-fighter ever to reach squadron service. Originally fitted with a Rolls-Royce Eagle piston engine, the first Python-engined aircraft flew on 22 March 1949; the type was fully operational by September 1953. It was withdrawn from first-line service by mid-1958. Total production was 127 aircraft.

Crew: 1
Powerplant: one Armstrong Siddeley Python ASP.3 turboprop engine
Performance: max speed 616km/h (383mph); range 1455km (904 miles); service ceiling 8535m (28,000ft)
Dimensions: wingspan 13.41m (44ft); length 12.87m (42ft 3in); height 4.80m (15ft 9in)
Weight: 11,113kg (24,500lb) loaded
Armament: four 20mm (0.79in) cannon; 1360kg (3000lb) of bombs, 16 rocket pods or one torpedo

The Westland Wyvern had the distinction of being the world's first turboprop-powered combat aircraft. Large and very heavy, it was not well suited to aircraft carrier operations. It saw action in the 1956 Suez crisis.

WESTLAND WESSEX

THIS LICENCE-BUILT version of the Sikorsky S-58 differed from the American Wright R-1820 piston-engined version in having British engines. The first Wessex was an S-58 re-engined with an 820kW (1100shp) Napier Gazelle 161 free-turbine turboshaft. It first flew on 17 May 1957 and became the company demonstrator. A Westland-built prototype and two pre-production examples followed before manufacture began of 128 Wessex HAS.Mk 1s for the Royal Navy as 'hunter-killer' pairs in the ASW role and as Royal Marine transports. Two coupled Gnome turboshaft engines powered the RAF's 74 HC.Mk 2s and these operated in the ambulance, transport and utility roles. The Wessex HAS.Mk 3 for the Royal Navy, the majority of which were produced by converting 43 HAS.1 airframes to the new standard, differed in having more powerful Gazelle Nga.22 engines and the ability to carry a formidable array of weapons. Most importantly, a new duplex AFCS enabled a complete ASW search or strike mission to be performed automatically, from take-off to positioning for landing.

This system operated in conjunction with the Ecko lightweight search radar, and the Marconi Doppler navigation system enabled the HAS.3 to operate autonomously at night or in bad weather. Two HC.Mk 4 VIP transports for the Queen's flight and 100 Commando HU.Mk 5 assault examples for the Royal Marines (both similar to the HC.Mk 2) were built. Twenty Wessex Mk 60 civil versions were exported and 27 HAS.Mk 31s (later redesignated HAS.Mk 31B) were completed for the Royal Australian Navy. All told, 382 Wessexes were produced.

Crew: 2
Powerplant: (HAS.1) one 1081kW (1450shp) Gazelle Mk 161; (HAS.2) two coupled Bristol Siddeley Gnome turboshafts each rated at 1007kW (1350shp)
Performance: max speed 214km/h (133mph); combat radius 630km (390 miles); service ceiling 3048-4300m (10,000-14,000ft)
Dimensions: main rotor diameter 17.07m (56ft); length 20.03m (65ft 9in); height 4.93m (16ft 2in)
Weight: 3447kg (7600lb)
Armament: one or two homing torpedoes and provision for guns or a wide range of missiles and rockets; provision for up to 16 fully equipped troops

Some 74 Wessex HC.Mk 2s were acquired by the RAF for operation in the ambulance, transport and utility roles. Two coupled Gnome turboshaft engines were installed for double redundancy.

WESTLAND SCOUT/WASP

UK: 1959

Crew: 1
Powerplant: one 511kW (685shp) Rolls-Royce Nimbus 102 free-turbine turboshaft engine
Performance: max speed 211km/h (131mph); combat radius 510km (315 miles); service ceiling 4085m (13,400ft)
Dimensions: main rotor diameter 9.83m (32ft 3in); length 12.29m (40ft 4in); height 3.56m (11ft 9in)
Weight: 1465kg (3232lb)
Armament/payload: 20mm (0.79in) guns; fixed 7.62mm (0.30in) GPMG; rocket pods or guided missiles (Wasp); two Mk 44 torpedoes; five passengers

THE WESTLAND SCOUT/WASP began life as the Saunders-Roe P.531 that first flew on 9 August 1959. All development from the second prototype onwards was carried out by Westland, which built eight AH.Mk 1 development aircraft and 141 AH.Mk 1 production aircraft.

First deliveries of the machine to the British Army began in March 1963, quantity production ending in 1970. Two Wasp pre-production HAS.Mk 1 and 96 Wasp HAS.Mk 1 production aircraft

were built for the Royal Navy, which operated them for 25 years from June 1963 to April 1988. The Royal New Zealand Air Force, South African Air Force, Brazil and Indonesia purchased a few refurbished and new-built Wasps.

Westland Scout of 658 Squadron of the Army Air Corps. A total of 141 AH.Mk 1 production aircraft were acquired for the British Army beginning in March 1963. Quantity production of the type ended in 1970.

WESTLAND SEA KING AND COMMANDO

UK: 1966

THE RESULT OF a 1968 agreement between Westland and Sikorsky for licensed production of the S-61, the Sea King was a navalized SH-3D that first flew on 11 October 1966. The first of 56 Sea King HAS Mk 1s for the Royal Navy flew on 7 May 1969. Some 13 HAS Mk 2s with uprated Gnome H.1400 engines and 15 HAR Mk

3s for the RAF's SAR role followed. Deliveries of 30 new-build HAS Mk 5 ASW examples to the Royal Navy were made between October 1980 and July 1986; all surviving 50 HAS.2s were converted to HAS.5 standard. Six improved HAS.Mk 6 new-build examples have been supplemented by the conversion of existing Sea Kings to

this standard. The non-amphibious Commando assault, tactical and general transport was developed in 1971 from the Sea King, and led to export orders from Egypt and Qatar and orders from the Royal Navy for 41 HC.Mk 4 helicopters combining the Commando's fixed landing gear with the Sea King's folding rotor. By 1990 a total of

321 Westland Sea King and Commando helicopters had been built, with 147 being exported to at least eight countries.

Specifications apply to the Sea King ASW.

One of the 15 HAR Mk 3s built for the RAF from September 1977 to operate in the search and rescue (SAR) role. These were followed by eight HAS Mk 2 aircraft.

Crew: 2
Powerplant: two Rolls-Royce Gnome (derived from GE T58) free-turbine turboshaft engines
Performance: max speed 230km/h (143mph); combat radius 563km (350 miles); service ceiling 3048m (10,000ft)
Dimensions: main rotor diameter 18.90m (62ft); length 22.15m (72ft 8in); height 5.13m (16ft 10in)
Weight: 7019kg (15,474lb)
Payload: (Commando) up to 28 troops or equivalent cargo payload; or 3630kg (8000lb) slung externally

WESTLAND LYNX

UK/FRANCE: 1971

IN JUNE 1966, Westland was developing its WG.13 design when a Joint Service Requirement detailed the specific needs of the British Army and Royal Navy, the latter having a requirement for a second-generation helicopter capable of operating from small ships such as frigates and

destroyers. France's parallel need for an armed reconnaissance and tactical medium support helicopter resulted in a February 1967 Anglo-French agreement whereby production of the WG.13/W.13 would be shared in the ratio of 70:30 between Westland and Aêrospatiale (now Eurocopter

France). The prototype first flew on 21 March 1971 and the first Royal Navy HAS.Mk 2 DB aircraft flew on 25 May 1972. In May 1974 Westland received orders for 100 Lynx; 22 AH.Mk 1 battlefield helicopters for the Army Air Corps (AAC), 60 HAS.2s for the RN and 18 Mk 2 (FN)s for the

Aéronavale (French Navy). Some 113 AH.1s were delivered between 1977 and 1984 and the Royal Navy received 86 HAS.2 examples. The Aéronavale received 28 Mk 2/4 examples. Thirty new-build HAS.Mk 3s and conversions of existing aircraft fitted with more powerful Gem engines were built,

G-LYNX, the company demonstrator, which set a new Absolute World Helicopter Speed record of 400.87km/h (249.10mph) on 11 August 1986, beating the previous records held by the MiL-A10 and the Sikorsky S-76A.

and 103 AH.Mk 1s were later brought up to Mk 7 standard. The Lynx HAS.Mk 8, which introduced an improved composite tail rotor, British Experimental Rotor Programme (BERP) main-rotor blades and a central tactical system, became the principal model in Royal Navy service. By 1990 a total of 382 Lynx had been built. Specifications apply to the Westland Lynx AH Mk 1.

Crew: 2
Powerplant: two 671kW (900shp) Rolls-Royce Gem 10001 three-shaft turbine engines
Performance: max speed 333km/h (207mph); combat radius 761km (473 miles); service ceiling 7600m (24,934ft)
Dimensions: main rotor diameter 12.80m (42ft); length 15.16m (49ft 9in); height 3.66m (12ft)
Weight: 2370kg (5225lb)

Armament/payload: two torpedoes of Sting Ray or Mk 44/46 type; or two depth charges, or four Sea Skua or similar anti-ship missiles; or four wire-guided air-to-surface missiles. Army Lynx can carry cabin- or external-mounted 7.62mm (0.30in) machine guns, or 20mm (0.79in) or 25mm (0.98in) cannon; up to eight TOW, HOT or Hellfire anti-armour missiles; or two rocket pods; 10 service personnel (13 people in civil versions)

WRIGHT FLYER SERIES

USA: 1903

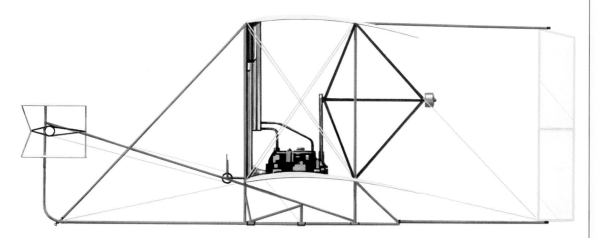

Side view of the Wright Flyer, showing the position of the engine and arrangement of the crankshafts for driving the propellers. The Wright brothers' design showed a great deal of ingenuity.

ON 17 DECEMBER 1903, at Kill Devil Hills, Kitty Hawk, North Carolina, the Wright Flyer became the first powered, heavier-than-air machine to achieve controlled, sustained flight with a pilot aboard. It flew forward without losing speed and landed at a point as high as that from which it started. With Orville Wright as pilot, the aircraft took off from a launching rail and flew for 12 seconds, covering a distance of 37m (120ft). The aircraft was flown three more times that day, with Orville and his brother Wilbur alternating as pilot. The longest flight, with Wilbur at the controls, was 260m (852ft) and lasted 59 seconds. It was to be nearly four years before Henry Farman, in the Voisin-Farman I, made a better flight than this in Europe, and by that time the Wright aeroplane could stay aloft for about three quarters of an hour.

The Flyer, designed and built by the Wright brothers, was one step in a broad experimental programme that had begun in 1899 with their first kite and concluded in 1905, when they built the first truly practical aircraft. The basic problems of mechanical flight, lift, propulsion and control were solved in the Wright design.

The Flyer was constructed of spruce and ash covered with muslin. The framework 'floated' within fabric pockets sewn inside, making the muslin covering an integral part of the structure. This ingenious feature made the aircraft light, strong and flexible.

The 1903 Flyer was powered by a simple four-cylinder engine of the Wrights' own design. To fly the aircraft, the pilot lay prone with his head forward, his left hand operating the elevator control. Lateral control was achieved by warping the wing tips in opposite directions via wires attached to a hip cradle mounted on the lower wing. The pilot shifted his hips from side to side to operate the mechanism, which also moved the rudder.

The Wrights flew their first glider in October 1900. It was followed by two more, and it was

on the third aircraft, the No 3 glider, that the Flyer of 1903 was based. The second biplane, or Flyer II, was flown for the first time on 23 May 1904, the flying site having now moved from Kill Devil Hills to the Huffmann Prairie. Hitherto the Flyer had been launched from a rail, the aircraft being tethered while the engine was run up and then released; however, at Huffmann Prairie the aircraft's take-off was assisted by a weight-and-derrick apparatus that was to be used successfully in hundreds of subsequent take-offs.

On 9 November 1904, after completing its first circuit flight, the Flyer II, powered by a 12kW (16hp) Wright engine, covered 4.5km (2.75 miles) in a flight lasting over five minutes. In 1905, after being offered to – and rejected by – the US and British War Departments, it was broken up and various components used in the construction of the greatly improved Flyer III. This was the Wrights' first fully practical

WESTLAND DRAGONFLY
Westland undertook licence production of 149 Alvis Leonides and Wasp Junior-powered Dragonfly and S-51 helicopters in 1949–54.

WESTLAND WIDGEON
The Westland Widgeon was a five-seat conversion of the WS-51 Dragonfly, although 12 were built as new in 1955–59.

WESTLAND WHIRLWIND
The Whirlwind was based on the Sikorsky S-55. Westland undertook licence production of 364 examples and 11 different marks were built mainly for the Royal Navy and Royal Air Force in 1953–56.

WESTLAND 30 SERIES 100/200/300
These 13-seat versions of the Lynx, the first flying on 27 September 1981, had limited export success in the civil market before production ceased in January 1988.

WIBAULT 72C-1
Designed for high-altitude interception, the Wibault 72 of 1923 was a metal-framed aircraft with fabric-covered surfaces. Sixty production Wibault 72s were ordered by the Aviation Militaire, the first entering service in 1926.

WIBAULT-PENHOET 280T-283T
A series of triple-engined, low-wing airliners with an enclosed cabin and space for up to 10 passengers, the 283 series were regularly used on the London (Croydon)–Paris services in the period 1934–1938.

WSK SM-IW
In 1955 the WSK (Equipment Manufacturing Centre) at Swidnik, Poland, began licence production of the Mi-1 utility helicopter under the designation SM-1, the first Polish-built model flying in 1956.

WSK M-4 TARPAN
The WSK M-4 Tarpan was a two-seat, low-wing monoplane trainer, first flown in 1961. The M-4A was a fully aerobatic variant.

WSK M-15 BELPHEGOR
The prototype of the WSK M-15, a jet-powered development of the Antonov An-2 built in Poland, flew in 1973. Production ended in 1981 after only 175 (out of an anticipated 3000) examples had been built.

XAC Y7/MA60
Xian Aircraft Company continue to develop the Y7 from its origins as the An-24. The MA60 is the latest version, including Western engines, avionics and winglets.

The historic moment at Kill Devil Hills, Kitty Hawk, North Carolina, when Orville Wright became the first man to make a controlled, powered, sustained flight in a heavier-than-air flying machine.

aircraft, and it made some 50 flights by mid-October.

After a lull of about two and a half years, during which time they undertook no flying at all, the Wrights produced the Flyer A, which Wilbur Wright took on a demonstration tour of France in 1908. Meanwhile, the US Army had at last awarded the Wrights a contract for an evaluation aircraft. Called the Military Flyer, it crashed on 17 September 1908 after its tenth flight, but was rebuilt and purchased by the US Army as the Signal Corps No 1. Together with the original Flyer, it is now in the National Air and Space Museum, Washington DC.

Specification refers to the Wright Flyer No III.

Crew: 1
Powerplant: one 12kW (16hp) Wright 4-cylinder water-cooled in-line engine
Performance: max speed 56km/h (35mph)
Dimensions: wingspan 12.34m (40ft 6in); length 8.53m (28ft); height 2.44m (8ft)
Weight: 388kg (855lb)

WRIGHT-BELLANCA WB-2, CAC COLUMBIA AND BELLANCA CH-300   USA: 1926

Crew: 2
Powerplant: one Pratt & Whitney R-985 Wasp Jr 337kW (450hp) cylinder radial engine
Performance: max speed 225km/h (140mph); range 1368km (850 miles); service ceiling 5486m (18,000ft)
Dimensions: wingspan 14.10m (46ft 4in); length 8.50m (27ft 9in); height 2.50m (8ft 2.5in)
Weight: 1847kg (4072lb) fully loaded
Payload: two people

FOLLOWING EARLIER aviation exploits, Giuseppe Bellanca joined forces with the Wright Aero Corporation in 1924 as a consultant. Wright required an airframe to best demonstrate its new J-2 Whirlwind engine, and the WB-2, which went on to win many events in the 1926 air race calendar, was the result. Despite the aircraft's success, Wright decided to concentrate on engine manufacture and sold the airframe business to Charles Levine, whom Bellanca went into partnership with under the name of Columbia Aircraft Company. Consequently, the WB-2 was renamed Columbia.

Charles Lindbergh approached the company to use the Columbia for his planned Atlantic crossing, but was refused by Levine, who was preparing to use the Columbia

in his own bid for the title in 1927 (Levine was to be a passenger). Levine became involved in a legal wrangle with his team of aviators and Lindbergh's Ryan-designed machine succeeded in crossing the

Atlantic first. Weeks later the Columbia made the transatlantic journey to Berlin in a record time, and the Columbia was hailed as a great design, not least in having a passenger seat and windshield.

Consequently Bellanca, who parted with Levine, went on to achieve great commercial success, first with the CH-300 derived from the high-wing monoplane WB-1 and WB-2. Specifications apply to CH-300.

Only days after Lindbergh made his solo trans-Atlantic flight, a Bellanca WB.2 monoplane called Columbia flew non-stop from New York to Esleben, near Berlin, crewed by Clarence D. Chamberlin and Charles A. Levine.

YAKOVLEV YAK-1

FORMER USSR: 1940

IT WAS NOT until 1939–40 that the prototypes of three Soviet fighters that could really be classed as modern made their appearance. The first was the LaGG-3, the second was the MiG-1, and the third was the Yak-1 Krasavyets (Little Beauty), which made its first public appearance during an air display on 7 November 1940. It earned Aleksandr S. Yakovlev the Order of Lenin, the gift of a Zis car and a prize of 100,000 roubles. The Yak-1

The Yak-1 was a delightful aircraft to fly and was the first of a line of modern monoplane fighters designed by Aleksandr Yakovlev.

was of mixed construction, fabric and plywood covered; it was simple to build and service, and a delight to fly. Production of the Yak-1 was accelerated following the German invasion of Russia in June 1941, and in the second half of the year 1019 aircraft were turned out.

Crew: 1
Powerplant: one 821kW (1100hp) Klimov M-105P 12-cylinder Vee-type engine
Performance: max speed 600km/h (373mph); range 700km (435 miles); service ceiling 10,000m (32,810ft)
Dimensions: wingspan 10.00m (32ft 9.7in); length 8.48m (27ft 10in); height 2.64m (8ft 8in)
Weight: 2847kg (6276lb) loaded
Armament: one 20mm (0.79in) cannon; two 7.62mm (0.30in) machine guns; up to 200kg (441lb) of bombs or rockets

YAKOVLEV YAK-9 'FRANK'

FORMER USSR: 1942

Crew: 1
Powerplant: one 1230kW (1650hp) Klimov VK-107A Vee-type engine
Performance: max speed 700km/h (435mph); range 870km (540 miles); service ceiling 11,900m (39,040ft)
Dimensions: wingspan 9.77m (32ft); length 8.55m (28ft); height 2.44m (8ft)
Weight: 3068kg (6760lb) loaded
Armament: one 23mm (0.90in) cannon and two 12.7mm (0.50in) machine guns

THE YAK-1 SUFFERED a slow production rate in some areas following the wartime relocation of factories, particularly in Siberia, with a consequent reduction in deliveries to frontline units. Therefore, it was decided to convert a trainer variant of the Yak-1, the Yak-7V, into a single-seat fighter by covering the second cockpit with metal sheeting and

Developed from the trainer version of the Yak-1, the Yak-9, seen here in Polish markings, at last gave the Soviet Air Force an aircraft that could meet Germany's latest fighters on equal terms.

arming the aircraft with one ShVAK cannon and two ShKAS machine guns. In this new guise the aircraft was designated the

YAKOVLEV YA-6 (AIR-6)
The Yakovlev Ya-6 (AIR-6) was a high-wing cabin monoplane with a capacity for two passengers in addition to the pilot. The aircraft appeared in 1931.

YAKOVLEV OKO-1
The Yakovlev OKO-1 of 1937 was a low-wing, single-engined, six-passenger monoplane with a 'trousered' undercarriage. It was not a success.

YAKOVLEV YAK-4
The Yakovlev Yak-4, first flown in 1941, was an elegant twin-engined light bomber. The aircraft proved vulnerable to ground fire, and the few examples built were used for high-altitude reconnaissance.

YAKOVLEV YAK-11
The Yakovlev Yak-11 was an advanced trainer produced in 1946. Its existence remained unknown to the West until 1948, when one made an emergency landing in Turkey. Its NATO reporting name was 'Moose'.

YAKOVLEV YAK-18
Developed from the Yakovlev UT-2 trainer, the Yak-18 entered production in 1947 and was the forerunner of a long line of aerobatic training aircraft developed by the bureau. It was known as 'Max' to NATO.

YAKOVLEV YAK-19
The Yakovlev Yak-19, flown in 1947, was a jet-fighter prototype with a straight laminar flow wing. It was the first Soviet fighter to be equipped with an afterburner. Two prototypes only were built.

YAKOVLEV YAK-23
First flown in 1947, the Yak-23 was a development of the Yak-15/17 series and was produced as an insurance against the failure of the more advanced MiG-15. Known as 'Flora' to NATO, it was issued to the air forces of Bulgaria, Czechoslovakia and Poland.

Yakovlev Yak-7A. A robust aircraft, yet with a performance identical to that of the Yak-1, its development proceeded through a line of variants with heavier armament and longer range.

It culminated in the Yak-9, a superb fighter aircraft that did much to win air superiority over the eastern battlefront. The type was initially built in two versions, the Yak-9D with a 20mm (0.79in) cannon and a 12.7mm (0.50in) machine gun, and the Yak-9T, which was armed with the 37mm (1.45in) cannon, used for anti-shipping attack. The Yak-9L, -9M,

-9U and -9P were later variants, with the latter being used by three Soviet and satellite air arms for some years after World War II. Yak-9s also saw combat over Korea, and received the NATO code name of 'Frank'.

Specification refers to the Yakovlev Yak-9U.

Yak-9Ds of a Guards Fighter regiment operating in the Crimea. The nearest aircraft is the mount of Colonel Andreyev and bears the Order of the Red banner. The photograph was taken over Sevastopol in the summer of 1944.

YAKOVLEV YAK-3 FORMER USSR: 1942

Crew: 1
Powerplant: one 912kW (1222hp) VK-105PF-2 or 1208kW (1620hp) VK-107 engine
Performance: (with VK-105PF) max speed 658km/h (409mph); range 900km (560 miles); service ceiling 10,800m (35,475ft)
Dimensions: wingspan 9.20m (30ft 2in); length 8.55m (28ft); height 3.00m (9ft 10in)
Weight: 2660kg (5863lb) loaded
Armament: one 20mm (0.79in) cannon and two 12.7mm (0.50in) machine guns

IN 1942 THE basic Yak-1 design evolved into the Yak-1M, which had a smaller wing area, a revised rear fuselage and a three-piece sliding cockpit hood; it was also slightly faster than the Yak-1. Further refinements to the Yak-1M were introduced before the aircraft entered quantity production in the spring of 1943, these including suppression of the radio mast (although it was reintroduced at a later date) and the transfer of the

oil-cooler intake from beneath the nose to the port wing root. The production fighter was redesignated Yak-3. The structure was basically similar to that of the Yak-1, the one-piece two-spar wing being entirely of wooden construction with plywood skinning, and the fuselage being of welded steel tube, the forward portion of which was covered by detachable metal panels and the aft portion by plywood and, finally, doped fabric. The aircraft was powered by a 912kW (1222hp) VK-105PF engine, and armament comprised one 20mm (0.79in) ShVAK cannon with 120 rounds firing through the propeller shaft, and two 12.7mm (0.50in) Beresin BS machine guns in the forward fuselage decking.

The first Yak-3s reached the front line during the early summer months of 1943, in time to take part in the battle of Kursk, but it was not until the spring of 1944 that the fighter was available in

really substantial numbers. The Yak-3 quickly proved itself in combat; it rarely operated above 3500m (11,500ft), below which it was markedly more manoeuvrable than either the Fw 190A or Bf 109G. In fact, it was probably the most manoeuvrable fighter aircraft to see service during World War II. As well as performing the role of interceptor, the Yak-3 was extensively employed in close support of the ground forces, and for the escort of Pe-2 and Il-2 assault aircraft, one formation of Yak-3s preceding the bombers and attacking German fighter airfields while another provided closer escort. At a relatively early stage in the production life of the Yak-3 the wooden wing spars were replaced by spars of light alloy, first introduced in the Yak-9, and the VK-105 engine was replaced by the more powerful 1208kW (1620hp) VK-107. During State

Acceptance Trials with the new engine early in 1944, the aircraft reached a speed of 720km/h (447mph) at 5750m (18,865ft). At 5000m (16,400ft) the Yak-3 was 95–110km/h (60–70mph) faster than either the Fw 190A-4 or Me 109G-2. The Soviet Air Force received a total of 4848 Yak-3s.

One famous unit to fly the Yak-3 was the Regiment Normandie, composed of Free French pilots and ground crews who had arrived in Russia from the Middle East in 1942. They entered combat with the 303rd Fighter Division of the 1st Air Army in the Smolensk region in March 1943, flying Yak-1s and Yak-9s before receiving Yak-3s, which they flew until April 1945. In that time the French pilots flew 5240 missions, fought 869 air combats and were credited with 273 victories. They lost 42 pilots killed or missing, and four of their number were made Heroes of the Soviet Union. The air regiment was given the title 'Normandie-Niemen' in honour of its exploits.

By late 1944, the extremely agile Yak-3 was being replaced by aircraft such as the Lavochkin La-5, but senior officers such as Major General G.N. Zakharov of the 303rd Fighter Aviation Division preferred to retain the Yak-3 as a personal aircraft.

YAKOVLEV YAK-15 'FEATHER' FORMER USSR: 1946

IN 1945, ALEKSANDR S. Yakovlev set about adapting a standard Yak-3 airframe to accommodate a Junkers Jumo 004B turbojet. The engine was one of a large quantity

seized by the Russians during their advance into Germany and which had been distributed among the various Soviet aircraft designers for experimental use while the engine

manufacturers made arrangements to produce them in series. The resulting aircraft, designated Yak-15, flew for the first time on 24 April 1946. Deliveries to Soviet

Air Force fighter squadrons began early in 1947, production aircraft retaining a tailwheel undercarriage and being powered by the RD-10 engine, as the Jumo 004B copy was known. About 280 examples were constructed. At the time of its introduction the Yak-15 was the lightest jet fighter in the world, the lightweight structure of the Yak-3's airframe compensating for the relatively low power of the engine. The Yak-15's NATO reporting name was 'Feather'.

Crew: 1
Powerplant: one 900kg (1984lb) thrust RD-10 (Jumo 004) turbojet engine
Performance: max speed 785km/h (488 mph); range 740km (460 miles); service ceiling 13,350m (43,800ft)
Dimensions: wingspan 9.20m (30ft 2in); length 8.78m (28ft 10in); height 2.20m (7ft 3in)
Weight: 2742kg (6045lb) loaded
Armament: two 23mm (0.90in) cannon

The Yak-15 was basically a Yak-3 airframe modified to take a captured German Junkers Jumo 004B turbojet engine.

YAKOVLEV YAK-24 'HORSE'

FORMER USSR: 1952

Crew: 3
Powerplant: two 1267kW (1700hp) Shvetsov ASh-82V radial piston engines
Performance: max speed 175km/h (109mph); combat radius 265km (165 miles); service ceiling 4200m (13,779ft)
Dimensions: main rotor diameter 21.00m (68ft 10.75in); length 21.29m (69ft 11in); height 6.50m (21ft 4in)
Weight: 10,607kg (23,384lb)
Payload: up to 30 armed troops or stretcher cases or 3000kg (6614lb) of freight/vehicles

THE YAK-24 WAS a large and powerful tandem-rotor transport helicopter originating from a direct order by Stalin in late 1951, who insisted that the first of four of these machines (two for static and resonance test and two for flight) must fly within a year. The first flight article was not readied until spring 1952, but problems with vibration on full-power flights grounded the project for five months until the problem was solved by cutting 0.5m (19.7in) off each main rotor blade. In October 1953, the fourth aircraft was delivered for testing, but was destroyed when its tethers broke during ground running. Finally, in mid-1955, the Yak-24 flew untethered for the first time and it entered production at GAZ in Leningrad. Known by the NATO code name 'Horse', the Yak-24 was first seen in public at the Aviation Day at Tushino in August 1955. About 100 Yak-24s operated with the Soviet Air Force. By 1960 at least one Yak-24A (Aerolinyi, or airline) example with provision for 30 seats was built, but it never saw commercial operation.

A Yak-24 being used to hoist 30 metal trusses during restoration of Katherine's Palace in Leningrad, where about 100 of these 'Flying Wagon' helicopters, as they were known, were produced by GAZ.

YAKOVLEV YAK-16
Making its appearance in 1948, the Yak-16 was a small twin-engined civil transport. Some were used by the military as crew trainers and liaison aircraft.

YAKOVLEV YAK-17
In 1948 the Yak-15 was replaced on the production line by the Yak-17, which had a tricycle undercarriage, an RD-10A turbojet and redesigned vertical tail surfaces. Like the Yak-15, it was known as 'Feather' to NATO.

YAKOVLEV YAK-30
First flown in September 1948, the Yak-30 fighter prototype was built to the same specification as the MiG-15, but during comparative trials the MiG fighter emerged as the better all-round design. The designation Yak-30 was later applied to an unsuccessful jet trainer design.

YAKOVLEV YAK-100
This general-purpose helicopter looked not unlike the Sikorsky S-51, and was completed late in 1947 and first flown in 1949. Two prototypes were built but it lost out to the Mi-1, which had already been adopted.

YAKOVLEV YAK-42
Designed as a replacement for the Tu-134 jet and other turbo-powered Soviet types, the tri-jet Yak-42 first flew in 1975. Capable of carrying 120 passengers, the Yak-42 has sold more than 200 examples.

YAKOVLEV YAK-141
The end product of an experimental programme that began with the Yak-36 Freehand of 1963, the Yak-141 supersonic STOVL aircraft, named 'Freestyle' by NATO, flew for the first time in 1987. Two prototypes only were built.

YAKOVLEV YAK-130
First flown in 1994, the Yak-130 is a two-seat advanced jet trainer and light attack aircraft, developed jointly with Aermacchi of Italy. In 2002 it was selected to replace the L-39 in the Russian Air Force.

YAKOVLEV YAK-25 'FLASHLIGHT'

Crew: 2
Powerplant: two 2600kg (5730lb) thrust Mikulin AM-5 turbojet engines
Performance: max speed 1015km/h (630mph); range 2000km (1250 miles); service ceiling 14,000m (46,000ft)
Dimensions: wingspan 11.00m (36ft 1in); length 15.67m (51ft 5in); height 3.80m (12ft 6in)
Weight: 9900kg (21,826lb) loaded
Armament: two 37mm (1.46in) cannon; 50 x 50mm (2in) air-to-air rockets

KNOWN TO NATO as 'Flashlight', the prototype Yak-25 all-weather interceptor flew for the first time in 1952. The type entered service with a Soviet Air Force development unit in 1955 and became fully operational in the following year. It was fitted with a PD6 AI radar in a bulbous nose. The 'Flashlight-B'

(MiG-25R) was a reconnaissance variant with a radome under the nose, while the Yak-27 ('Flashlight-C') had longer engine nacelles, housing VK-9 afterburning turbojets, a pointed nose radome and extended wing root chord. A further development, the Yak-26 ('Mangrove') reconnais-

sance aircraft was basically a Yak-27 with a glazed nose, while the Yak-25RV ('Mandrake') was a high-altitude reconnaissance aircraft with an extended wingspan.

The Yak-25 'Flashlight' twin-jet night and all-weather fighter filled a critical gap in the air defences of the Soviet Union.

YAKOVLEV YAK-28 'BREWER'

Deployment of the two-seat tactical version of the Yak-28, the 'Brewer-A', in Eastern Europe caused a few headaches for NATO at the height of the Cold War.

ALTHOUGH BEARING A strong resemblance to the Yak-25 series of aircraft, the Yak-28, first revealed at Tushino in 1961, was a totally new design. The two-seat tactical

version, known to NATO as 'Brewer-A', entered service with the Soviet Frontal Aviation in 1961, replacing the Il-28 Beagle. The 'Brewer-B' and '-C' differed from the early production version in minor detail, while the Yak-28R 'Brewer-D' was a reconnaissance verion. The 'Brewer-E' was an ECM version, with an active ECM pack partially recessed in the bomb bay, while the Yak-28P ('Firebar') was a two-seat all-weather fighter variant, replacing the Yak-25 'Flashlight'. A two-seat trainer version was code-named 'Maestro'. Some Yak-28s were converted to the role of electronic warfare aircraft. In the tactical role, the

Yak-28 presented a serious threat to NATO's European defences during the most dangerous period of the Cold War. Specifications apply to the Yakovlev Yak-28P.

Crew: 2
Powerplant: two 6206kg (13,681lb) thrust Tumanskii R-11 turbojet engines
Performance: max speed 1180km/h (733mph); combat radius 925km (575 miles); service ceiling 16,000m (52,495ft)
Dimensions: wingspan 12.95m (42ft 6in); length 23.00m (75ft 7in); height 3.95m (12ft 11in)
Weight: 19,000kg (41,890lb) loaded
Armament: four underwing pylons for air-to-air missiles

YAKOVLEV YAK-40

Crew: 2
Powerplant: three 14.71kN (3307lb) Ivchenko AI-25 turbofan engines
Performance: max cruising speed 550km/h (342mph); range with maximum payload 1450km (901 miles); service ceiling 11,800m (38,715ft)
Dimensions: wingspan 25.00m (82ft); length 20.36m (66ft 9in); height 6.50m (21ft 3in)
Weight: 16,500kg (36,375lb) maximum take-off weight
Payload: up to 32 passengers

IN THE EARLY 1960s, Aeroflot realized a requirement to replace its large fleet of Lisunov Li-2s (licence-built DC-3s). Operational

criterion for the Li-2 replacement was a demanding one, and one unparalleled in any Western jet designs. The Yak-40 had to operate from remote areas with unpaved runways with few local facilities.

Consequently the Yak-40 was fitted with three engines to ensure good short-field performance and engine failure survival. An APU was also fitted as standard. More than 1000 Yak-40s were built until 1976, including ambulance and freight versions. A few were exported to the West, many other examples survive today and some have found a new role carrying out executive jet work.

The Yak-40 pictured here was one of six operated by the Yugoslav Government/Air Force as a military/state executive transport.

YAKOVLEV YAK-38 'FORGER'

FORMER USSR: 1971

Crew: 1
Powerplant: two 3050kg (6724lb) thrust Rybinsk RD-36-35VFR turbojet engines and one 6950kg (15,322lb) thrust Tumanskii R-27V-300 vectored-thrust turbojet engine
Performance: max speed 1009km/h (627mph); combat radius 370km (230 miles); service ceiling 12,000m (39,370ft)
Dimensions: wingspan 7.32m (24ft); length 15.43m (50ft 8in); height 4.37m (14ft 4in)
Weight: 11,700kg (25,795lb) loaded
Armament: four external hardpoints with provision for up to 2000kg (4409lb) of stores

THE FIRST PROTOTYPE of the USSR's first and so far only STOVL carrier-borne fighter-bomber, named 'Forger' by NATO, flew in 1971. The Yak-38 (originally designated Yak-36M) first appeared to the West in July 1976 when the Kiev deployed with a development squadron of 'Forger-A's and passed through the Mediterranean en route to join the Northern Fleet. The normal complement for the Kiev-class aircraft carrier was a dozen

single-seat Forger-As and one or two twin-seat trainer Yak-38U 'Forger-B's. The primary roles were fleet defence (particularly against shadowing maritime surveillance aircraft), reconnaissance and anti-ship strike. The 'Forger' was retired from frontline service in 1992–93, although a few remained in the inventory for another year as limited proficiency training aircraft. A total of 231 aircraft had been built when production ended in 1988.

This Yakovlev Yak-38 'Forger' naval strike-fighter carries the insignia of the Soviet Northern Fleet. The Yak-38 was deployed on Russia's Kiev-class carriers.

YERMOLAYEV YER-2

FORMER USSR: 1940

THE YERMOLAYEV YER-2 (DB-240) twin-engined heavy bomber first flew in June 1940, 128 examples being delivered by July 1941. In the autumn of that year the type saw action with two air regiments, making long-range bombing attacks on Berlin and Kønigsberg. During the months that followed the type underwent several modifications, all designed to increase its already respectable range. Despite

this, most of its missions were flown against targets in the vicinity of the combat area. Total Yer-2 production was 300 aircraft. The Yer-4 was a slightly bigger version with diesel engines.

The Yer-2 (DB-240) bomber was developed from the STAL-7 transport by Yermolayev. Only 300 were built before the Voronezh factory had to be evacuated.

Crew: 4
Powerplant: two 783kW (1050hp) Klimov M-105 Vee-type engines
Performance: max speed 491km/h (305mph); range 4000km (2485 miles); service ceiling 7000m (22,965ft)
Dimensions: wingspan 23.00m (75ft 5in); length 16.34m (53ft 7in)
Weight: 11,920kg (26,279lb) loaded
Armament: one 12.7mm (0.50in) and two 7.7mm (0.303in) machine guns; up to 1000kg (2204lb) of bombs

YOKOSUKA K2Y
A development of the Avro 504, the Yokosuka K2Y (Navy Type 3 Primary Trainer) flew for the first time in 1928. In total, 360 aircraft were produced.

YOKOSUKA K4Y-1
The Yokosuka K4Y-1 biplane was a single-engined floatplane primary trainer. Production continued until 1940, by which time 211 examples had been built.

YOKOSUKA K5Y1
Code-named 'Willow' by the Allies, the Yokosuka K5Y1 first flew in 1933. The K5Y1 was a landplane, but a floatplane version, the K5Y2, was also produced. Production totalled 5589 aircraft.

YOKOSUKA B4Y
The Yokosuka B4Y carrier-based attack bomber biplane, first flown in 1935, saw action in the war with China. It received the Allied code name 'Jean', and 205 were built.

YOKOSUKA E14Y1
Known to the Allies as 'Glen', the Yokosuka E14Y1 floatplane was a small monoplane designed to be carried as a spotter aircraft on ocean-going submarines. In June 1942 an aircraft of this type dropped several small bombs in woodland on the state of Oregon, United States.

YOKOSUKA R2Y KEIUN
The Yokosuka R2Y Keiun (Beautiful Cloud) was a fast land-based reconnaissance aircraft powered by two coupled 1268kW (1700hp) Atsuta engines. It made one flight, in May 1945, before being destroyed by American bombs.

YOKOSUKA D3Y MYOJO
The Yokosuka D3Y Myojo (Venus) was an all-wood bomber trainer, only a few examples of which were built. A special attack (suicide) version was proposed, but the project was abandoned.

YOKOSUKA D4Y1 SUSEI 'JUDY'

JAPAN: 1940

Crew: 2
Powerplant: one 884kW (1185hp) Aichi Atsuta 21 12-cylinder Vee-type engine
Performance: max speed 552km/h (343mph); range 1575km (978 miles); service ceiling 9900m (32,480ft)
Dimensions: wingspan 11.50m (37ft 9in); length 10.22m (33ft 6in); height 3.67m (12ft 1in)
Weight: 4260kg (9390lb) loaded
Armament: three 7.7mm (0.303in) machine guns; 310kg (683lb) of bombs

FIRST FLOWN IN December 1940, the Yokosuka D4Y Susei (Comet) was widely used by the Imperial Japanese Navy and, in its D4Y2 version, was the fastest carrier-borne

dive-bomber in service during World War II. The Susei was developed as a replacement for the Aichi D3A1 'Val' – it was the Aichi company which built most of the 2319 aircraft completed. The Susei went into service in March 1943, and in June the following year the type suffered savage losses while attempting to attack US carrier task forces in the battle for the Marianas islands, most of the 170 aircraft committed being destroyed by the US fighter screen before reaching their targets in what became known as the 'Marianas Turkey Shoot'. The Susei was produced in three versions, culminating in the D4Y3

model, which had a Mitsubishi Insei radial engine in place of the earlier Atsuta.
Specifications apply to the D4Y1.

A photograph of a Yokosuka D4Y Susei taken during service trials. The aircraft's performance exceeded all expectations.

YOKOSUKA P1Y1 GINGA 'FRANCIS'

JAPAN: 1943

Crew: 3
Powerplant: two 1231kW (1650hp) Nakajima NK9B Homare 11 18-cylinder radial engines
Performance: max speed 547km/h (340mph); range 2574km (1600 miles); service ceiling 9400m (30,840ft)
Dimensions: wingspan 20.00m (65ft 7in); length 4.32m (14ft 2in); height 4.29m (14ft 1in)
Weight: 10,500kg (23,149lb) loaded
Armament: two 20mm (0.79in) cannon; one 800kg (1764lb) torpedo or up to 1000kg (2205lb) of bombs

THE YOKOSUKA P1Y GINGA (Milky Way), undoubtedly one of the best and most versatile Japanese aircraft of World War II,

The P1Y was a good design, but serviceability and reliability left much to be desired, and it was some time before the type was accepted.

was roughly the Japanese equivalent of the de Havilland Mosquito and the Junkers Ju 88. It was also the Japanese Navy's first fast twin-

engined medium bomber. The type first entered service in 1942 as a fast bomber, 1002 examples of the initial P1Y1 version being built. Later in the war, with increasing priority being given to the defence of the Japanese homeland, a night-fighter version, the P1Y2-S Kyokko (Aurora), was produced by Nagasaki. Only 97 examples were built, powered by 1380kW (1850hp) Kasei 25 engines, fitted with rudimentary radar and an armament of three 20mm (0.79in) cannon. Their performance at altitude fell short of expectations, so most of these aircraft operated as bombers. Specifications apply to the Yokosuka P1Y1.

YOKOSUKA MXY7 OHKA

JAPAN: 1944

Crew: 1
Powerplant: three solid-fuel Tpe 4 Mk 1 Model 20 rockets with total thrust of 800kg (1764lb)
Performance: max speed 927km/h (576mph) in terminal dive; range 37km (23 miles)
Dimensions: wingspan 5.12m (16ft 9in); length 6.07m (19ft 10in); height 1.16m (3ft 9in)
Weight: 2140kg (4718lb) loaded
Armament: one 1200kg (2646lb) warhead

THE MXY7 OHKA (Cherry Blossom) suicide aircraft was one of the more sinister weapons to emerge from World War II. The unpowered prototype flew in October 1944 and was followed by 45 examples of the Ohka K-1

training model, which was also unpowered. The production model was the Ohka Model 11, of which 755 were built between September 1944 and March 1945. The Ohka went into action for the first time on 21 March 1945, but the 16 Mitsubishi G4M2e parent aircraft (which carried the Ohkas shackled under the open bomb bay) were intercepted and forced to release their bombs short of the target. The first success came on 1 April 1945, when Ohkas damaged the battleship USS *West Virginia* and three transport vessels. The first ship to be sunk by an Ohka was the destroyer *Mannert L. Abele*, lost off Okinawa on 12 April.
Specifications apply to the MXY7 Ohka Model 11.

This Yokosuka Ohka suicide bomber was discovered by US Marines on Okinawa after the island's capture in 1945. The war ended before the Ohka could be used in significant quantities.

ZEPPELIN STAAKEN R.VI

GERMANY: 1917

The Zeppelin-Staaken R.VI, showing the four engines arranged in tandem pairs. The Zeppelin 'Giants' posed a serious threat to Britain's air defences in the early months of 1918.

Crew: 7
Powerplant: four 183kW (245hp) Maybach Mb.IV 6-cylinder in-line engines
Performance: max speed 130km/h (81mph); range 800km (500 miles); service ceiling 3800m (12,467ft)
Dimensions: wingspan 42.20m (138ft 6in); length 22.10m (72ft 6in); height 6.30m (20ft 8in)
Weight: 11,460kg (25,265lb) loaded
Armament: up to five 7.92mm (0.31in) machine guns; maximum bomb load of 2000kg (4409lb)

THE LARGEST AIRCRAFT used in World War I were the sluggish but effective Riesenflugzeuge (giant aircraft) series designed by the Zeppelin Werke Staaken. Prior to its move to Staaken in mid-1916, the design team responsible for these aircraft was based at the Versuchsbau Gotha-Ost (East Gotha Experimental Works), the first design being the VGO.I of 1915. The first aircraft in the series to have an R designation from the

outset was the four-engined R.IV, which entered service on the Western Front. After several 'one-off' bombers had been built, production standardized on the R.VI. One was built by the Staaken works, six by Aviatik, four by OAW and seven by Schütte-Lanz. All the bombers were used in attacks on England or on the Eastern Front. During their combat career two R.VIs were lost in action and eight were destroyed in accidents.

ZLIN Z.26 TO Z.726

CZECHOSLOVAKIA: 1948

The Zlin trainer series was selected and used by many countries outside the Western sphere of influence in the 1950s, including those of Egypt (pictured) and Iraq.

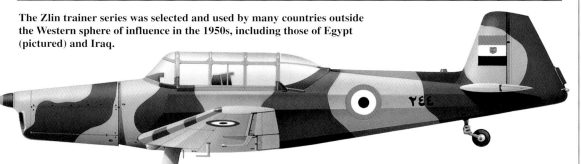

ZLIN SPECIALIZED in postwar aerobatic trainers and the early Z.26 was a response to a Czech Air Force requirement. The Z.126 and Z.226 followed (the latter with a larger engine) and the Z.326 was similar to the Z.226 Trener, but with

a retractable main undercarriage retaining the former's tail wheel. The Z.526 design moved the pilot to the rear position and introduced a constant-speed propeller. The Z.726 of 1973 introduced a more powerful Walter M337 157kW (210hp) engine. Over 1400 of this series of trainer/aerobatic low-wing light aircraft were produced until 1977. Specifications apply to the Z.326 Trener-master.

Crew: 1/2
Powerplant: one 109kW (147hp) Walter Minor 6-III in-line piston engine
Performance: max speed 245km/h (152mph); range 580km (360 miles); service ceiling 4800m (15,750ft)
Dimensions: wingspan 10.60m (34ft 8in); length 7.82m (25ft 6in); height 2.06m (6ft 9in)
Weight: 900kg (1984lb) maximum take-off weight
Payload: two persons

GLOSSARY

AAM: Air-to-Air Missile

ADP: Automatic Data Processing

ADV: Air Defence Variant (of the Tornado)

Aeronautics: the science of travel through the Earth's atmosphere

Aeroplane (Airplane): powered heavier-than-air craft supported in flight by fixed wings

AEW: Airborne Early Warning

Afterburning (reheat): method of increasing the thrust of a gas turbine aircraft engine by injecting additional fuel into the hot exhaust duct between the engine and the tailpipe, where it ignites to provide a short-term increase of power

Aileron: an aerofoil used for causing an aircraft to roll around its longitudinal axis, usually fitted near the wingtips. Ailerons are controlled by use of the pilot's control column

ALARM: Air-Launched Anti-Radiation Missile

All-Up Weight: the total weight of an aircraft in operating condition. Normal maximum AUW is the maximum at which an aircraft is permitted to fly

The Luftwaffe took delivery of 750 examples of the Lockheed F-104G Starfighter, some of which were manufactured in Europe. Here a German Starfighter is pictured in formation with its US Air Force counterpart.

A Boeing-Vertol Model 107 twin-rotor helicopter in service with the Japanese Self-Defence forces. The Model 107 was one of the big success stories of the American helicopter industry.

within normal design restrictions, while overload weight is the maximum AUW at which an aircraft is permitted to fly subject to ultimate flying restrictions

Altimeter: instrument that measures altitude, or height above sea level

AMRAAM: Advanced Medium-Range Air-to-Air Missile

Angle of Attack: the angle between the wing (airfoil) and the airflow relative to it

Aspect Ratio: the ratio of wing span to chord

ASV: Air to Surface Vessel – airborne detection radar for locating ships and submarines

ASW: Anti-Submarine Warfare

ATF: Advanced Tactical Fighter

Autogiro: heavier-than-air craft which supports itself in the air by means of a rotary wing (rotor), forward propulsion being provided by a conventional engine

Automatic Pilot (Autopilot): automatic device that keeps an aircraft

flying on a set course at a set speed and altitude

AWACS: Airborne Warning and Control System

Basic Weight: the tare weight of an aircraft plus the specified operational load

Bf: abbreviation for Bayerische Flugzeugwerke (Bavariant Aircraft Factories)

CAP: Combat Air Patrol

Centre of Gravity: point in a body through which the sum of the weights of all its parts passes. A body

suspended from this point is said to be in a state of equilibrium

Centre of Pressure: point through which the lifting force of a wing acts

Charged Particle Beam: a stream of charged atomic particles of intense energy, focused on a target

Chord: cross-section of a wing from leading edge to trailing edge

Circular Error Probable (CEP): A measure of the accuracy attributable to ballistic missiles, bombs and

One of the greatest fighters of all time, the North American F-86 Sabre owed much to captured German aerodynamic research information. It established a ten-to-one kill ratio in combat with the Russian MiG-15 over Korea.

shells. It is the radius of a circle into which 50 per cent of the missiles aimed at the centre of the circle are expected to fall.

Clutter: a term used in radar parlance to describe reflected echoes on a cathode ray tube caused by the ground, sea or bad weather

Convertiplane: vertical take-off and landing craft with wing-mounted rotors that act as helicopter rotors for take-off, then tilt to act as conventional propellers for forward flight

Delta Wing: aircraft shaped like the Greek letter delta

Disposable Load: the weight of crew and consumable load (fuel, missiles etc.)

Electronic Combat Reconnaissance (ECR): a variant of the Panavia Tornado optimized for electronic warfare

Electronic Countermeasures (ECM): systems designed to confuse and disrupt enemy radar equipment

Electronic Counter-Countermeasures (ECCM): measures taken to reduce the effectiveness of ECM by improving the resistance of radar equipment to jamming

Elevator: a horizontal control surface used to control the upward or downward inclination of an aircraft in flight. Elevators are usually hinged to the trailing edge of the tailplane

ELF: Extremely Low Frequency. A radio frequency used for

communication with submarines

ELINT: Electronic Intelligence. Information gathered through monitoring enemy electronic transmissions by specially equipped aircraft, ships or satellites

Empty Equipped (also known as Tare Weight): the weight of an aircraft equipped to a minimum scale, i.e. with all equipment plus the weight of coolant in the engines, radiators and associated systems, and residual fuel in tanks, engines and associated systems

EW: Electronic Warfare

FAC: Forward Air Controller. A battlefront observer who directs strike aircraft on to their targets near the front line

FAE: Fuel-Air Explosive. A weapon that disperses fuel into the atmosphere in the form of an aerosol cloud. The cloud is ignited to produce intense heat and heat effects

FGA: Fighter Ground Attack

FLIR: Forward-Looking Infra-Red. Heat-sensing equipment fitted in an aircraft that scans the path ahead to detect heat from objects such as vehicle engines

FRS: Fighter Reconnaissance Strike

Gas turbine: engine in which burning fuel supplies hot gas to spin a turbine

Geodetic construction: a 'basket weave' system of aircraft construction

producing a self-stabilizing framework in which loads in any direction are automatically equalized by forces in the intersecting set of frames, producing high strength for low weight

GPS: Global Positioning System. A system of navigational satellites

GR: General Reconnaissance

Helicopter: powered aircraft that achieves both lift and propulsion by means of a rotary wing (rotor)

HOTAS: Hands on Throttle and Stick. A system whereby the pilot exercises full control over his aircraft in combat without the need to remove his hands from the throttle and control column to operate weapons selection switches or other controls

HUD: Head-Up Display. A system in which essential information is projected on to a cockpit windscreen so that the pilot has no need to look down at his instrument panel

IFF: Identification Friend or Foe. An electronic pulse emitted by an aircraft to

Already obsolescent by the outbreak of World War II, the Fairey Swordfish nevertheless achieved some spectacular successes, including the crippling of the Italian fleet at Taranto in November 1940.

Although it experienced some early technical problems, the variable-geometry F-111 went on to become one of the most important weapons in NATO's strike aircraft arsenal, with its ability to penetrate enemy territory at low level.

identify it as friendly on a radar screen

INS: Inertial Navigation System. An on-board guidance system that steers an aircraft or missile over a pre-determined course by measuring factors such as the distance travelled and reference to 'waypoints' (landmarks) en route

Interdiction: Deep air strikes into enemy areas to sever communications with the battlefield

IR: Infra-Red

Jet propulsion: method of propulsion in which an

object is propelled in one direction by a jet, or stream of gases, moving in the other

JSTARS: Joint Surveillance and Target Attack Radar System. An airborne command and control system that directs air and ground forces in battle

Jumo: abbreviation for Junkers Motorenwerke (Junkers Engine Works)

Kiloton: Nuclear weapon yield, one kiloton (kT) being roughly equivalent to 1000 tons of TNT

Laminar Flow: airflow passes over an aircraft's

wing in layers, the first of which, the boundary layer, remains stationary while successive layers progressively accelerate; this is known as laminar flow. The smoother the wing surface, and the more efficient its design, the smoother the airflow

LAMPS: Light Airborne Multi-Purpose System. Anti- submarine helicopter equipment, comprising search radar, sonobuoys and other detection equipment

Landing Weight: the AUW of an aircraft at the moment of landing

Lantirn: Low-Altitude Navigation and Targeting Infra-Red for Night. An infra-red system fitted to the F-15E Strike Eagle that combines heat sensing with terrain-following radar to enable the pilot to view the ground ahead of the aircraft during low-level night operations. The information is projected on the pilot's head-up display

LWR: Laser Warning Radar. Equipment fitted to an aircraft that warns the pilot if he is being tracked by a missile-guiding radar beam

Mach: named after the Austrian Professor Ernst

The huge turboprop-powered Tupolev Tu-114 Rossiya civil airliner, the largest in the world when it entered service, was based on the Tu-95 Bear strategic bomber. It was very noisy, which restricted its commercial operations.

The massive Antonov An-124 was designed to transport very heavy loads, primarily strategic missiles, from their centres of production to sites in Siberia. It found important commercial applications after the Cold War ended.

Mach, a Mach number is the ratio of the speed of an aircraft or missile to the local speed of sound. At sea level, Mach One (1.0M) is approximately 1226 km/h (762mph), decreasing to about 1062 km/h (660mph) at 30,000 feet. An aircraft or missile travelling faster than Mach One is said to be supersonic. Mach numbers are dependent on variations in atmospheric temperature and pressure and are registered on a Machmeter in the aircraft's cockpit

MAD: Magnetic Anomaly Detection. The passage of a large body of metal, such as a submarine, through the earth's magnetic field, causes disturbances which can be detected by special equipment, usually housed in an extended tail boom, in an anti-submarine warfare aircraft

Maximum Landing Weight: the maximum AUW, due to design or operational limitations, at which an aircraft is permitted to land

Maximum Take-Off Weight: the maximum AUW, due to design or operational limitations, at which an aircraft is permitted to take off

Megaton: Thermonuclear weapon yield, one megaton (mT) being roughly equal to 1,000,000 tons of TNT

MG: Machine gun (*Maschinengewehr* in German, hence MG 15)

Microlight: very light aircraft with a small engine; a powered hang-glider

Mk: mark (of aircraft)

MK: *Maschinenkanone* (automatic cannon, e.g. MK.108)

Muzzle Velocity: the speed at which a bullet or shell leaves a gun barrel

NATO: North Atlantic Treaty Organization

NBC: Nuclear, Chemical and Biological (warfare)

NVG: Night Vision Goggles. Specially designed goggles that enhance a pilot's ability to see at night

OBOGS: On-Board Oxygen Generating System. A system that generates oxygen, avoiding the need to rely on pre-charged oxygen bottles and extending the time a pilot can stay airborne during long transit flights over the ocean, for example

Operational Load: The weight of equipment necessarily carried by an aircraft for a particular role

Payload: the weight of passengers and/or cargo

Phased-Array Radar: A warning radar system using many small aerials spread over a large flat area, rather than a rotating scanner. The advantage of this system is that it can track hundreds of targets simultaneously, electronically directing its beam from target to target in microseconds (millionths of a second)

PLSS: Precision Location Strike System. A battlefield surveillance system installed in the Lockheed TR-1 that detects the movement of enemy forces and directs air and ground attacks against them

Pulse-Doppler Radar: a type of airborne interception radar that picks out fast-moving targets from background clutter by measuring the change in frequency of a series of pulses bounced off the

The Caproni-Campini CC-2 was Italy's attempt to produce a prototype jet-propelled aircraft using ducted-fan technology. It was tested briefly during World War II, but its performance did not meet expectations.

targets. This is based on the well-known Doppler Effect, an apparent change in the frequency of waves when the source emitting them has a relative velocity towards or away from an observer. The MiG-29's noted tail-slide manoeuvre is a tactical move designed to break the lock of a pulse-Dopper radar

Ramjet: simple form of jet engine which is accelerated to high speed causing air to be forced into the combustion chamber, into which fuel is sprayed and then ignited. The Pulse Jet engine, used in the V-1 flying bomb, is a form of ramjet

Rudder: movable vertical surface or surfaces forming

part of the tail unit, by which the yawing of an aircraft is controlled

RWR: Radar Warning Receiver. A device mounted on an aircraft that warns the pilot if he is being tracked by an enemy missile guidance or intercept radar

SAM: Surface-to-Air Missile

SHF: Super High Frequency (radio waves)

SIGINT: Signals Intelligence. Information on enemy intentions gathered by monitoring electronic transmissions from his command, control and communications network

SLAM: Stand-off Land Attack Missile – a missile

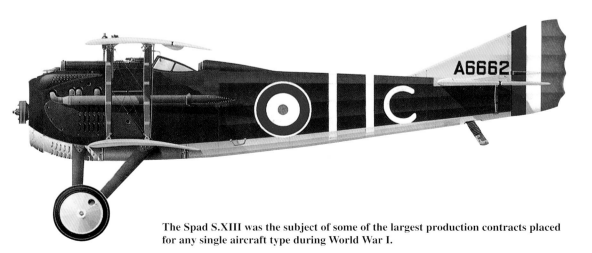

The Spad S.XIII was the subject of some of the largest production contracts placed for any single aircraft type during World War I.

that can be air-launched many miles from its target

SLAR: Side-Looking Airborne Radar. A type of radar that provides a continuous radar map of the ground on either side of the aircraft carrying the equipment

Sound Barrier: popular name for the concept that the speed of sound (see Mach) constitutes a limit to to flight through the atmosphere to all aircraft except those specially designed to penetrate it. The cone-shaped shock wave

created by an aircraft breaking the 'barrier' produces a 'sonic boom' when it passes over the ground

Spin: a spin is the result of yawing or rolling an aeroplane at the point of a stall

SRAM: Short-range Attack Missile

Stall: condition that occurs when the smooth flow of the air over an aircraft's wing changes to a turbulent flow and the lift decreases to the point where control is lost

Stealth Technology: technology applied to aircraft or fighting vehicles to reduce their radar signatures. Examples of stealth aircraft are the Lockheed F-117 and the Northrop B-2

STOVL: Short Take-off, Vertical Landing

Stuka: abbreviation of *Sturzkampfflugzeug* (literally Diving Battle Aircraft)

TADS: Target Acquisition/Designation System. A laser sighting system fitted to the AH-64 Apache attack helicopter

Take-Off Weight: the AUW of an aircraft at the moment of take-off

Thermal Imager: Equipment fitted to an aircraft or fighting vehicle which typically comprises a telescope to collect and focus infra-red energy emitted by objects on a battlefield, a mechanism to scan the scene across an array of heat-sensitive detectors, and a processor to turn the signals from these detectors into a 'thermal image' displayed on a TV screen

Fitted with the Packard-built Rolls-Royce Merlin engine, the North American P-51D Mustang, seen here in the markings of the 357th Fighter Squadron, established air superiority in European skies in 1944.

The awesome Lockheed SR-71A Blackbird, unsurpassed by any other manned reconnaissance system, first flew in 1964. The aircraft was so effective that it was brought out of retirement to undertake further missions in the 1990s.

TIALD: Thermal Imaging/Airborne Laser Designator. Equipment fitted to the Panavia Tornado IDS enabling it to locate and attack precision targets at night

Turbofan engine: type of jet engine fitted with a very large front fan that not only sends air into the engine for combustion but also around the engine to produce additional thrust. This results in faster and more fuel-efficient propulsion

Turbojet engine: jet engine that derives its thrust from a stream of hot exhaust gases

Turboprop engine: jet engine that derives its thrust partly from a jet of exhaust gases, but mainly from a propeller powered by a turbine in the jet exhaust

Variable-Geometry Wing: a type of wing whose angle of sweep can be altered to suit a particular flight profile. Popularly called a Swing Wing

VHF: Very High Frequency

VLF: Very Low Frequency

V/STOL: Vertical/Short Take-off and Landing

Wild Weasel: code name applied to specialized combat aircraft tasked with defence suppression

Window: strips of tinfoil cut to the wavelengths of enemy radars and scattered from attacking aircraft to confuse enemy defences. Also known as 'chaff'

Yaw: the action of turning an aircraft in the air around its normal (vertical) axis by use of the rudder. An aircraft is said to yaw when the fore-and-aft axis turns to port or starboard, out of the line of flight

INDEX

Page numbers in *italics* refer to illustrations. Model names are indexed where there is significant information given in the text.

536

PICTURE CREDITS